CW00350214

INTRODUCTION

This tome is a comprehensive compilation of over 2,250 cocktails collected during ten years of visiting and writing about the world's best bars. It is the seventh edition of what one could comfortably call an ongoing project.

I'd like to thank the many cocktail aficionados and professional bartenders who have shared their recipes and insights with me. In the course of testing, refining and standardising recipes, I've 'tweaked' many drinks to what I consider the best balance. Some may have originally been created using brands other than the ones I recommend. Others may have originally been made in different proportions.

I have also adapted a few recipes to make them simpler, avoiding ingredients that are obscure or obsolete, or taking advantage of new ingredients that improve the original while staying true to its essence. Throughout, I have endeavoured to credit drink inventors, while making it clear that my adaptation varies slightly from their original creation.

I'd be the first to admit that some of the recipes are better than others (most definitely including my own). So I've graded cocktails on a scale of one to five and discreetly indicated this score by dots above each drink's name.

Anyone looking to treat themselves to their very own home cocktail cabinet should begin with the fourteen 'Key Ingredients' featured in the opening pages. These are the most frequently used cocktail ingredients and by combining them with such easy-to-find ingredients as fruits and juices you will be able to make literally hundreds of drinks. I have marked these key cocktails with the key symbol throughout this guide.

This book is intended not only to encourage more people to make and enjoy cocktails at home but to help them appreciate them when drinking out. A great cocktail is as luxuriously satisfying as a fine wine, a vintage champagne or a family reserve cognac. However, while many have had the opportunity to taste a great wine, fairly few have ever experienced a truly great cocktail.

Cocktail recipes are a very personal thing, and I would love to hear what you think of the recipes in this book. Do you have a better version of a classic cocktail? Is one of your own creations worth inclusion? Drop me a line at simon@diffordsguide.com.

I also write email newsletters with drinks, bar reviews and new cocktail recipes from all around the world. If you'd like to receive these, please email me direct, or sign up at our website, diffordsguide.com.

Cheers

Simon Difford
simon@diffordsguide.com

diffordsguide are:

Publisher & Author Simon Difford, **Design, Art Direction & Photography** Dan Malpass, **PR & Marketing** Hannah Sharman-Cox **Cocktail Photography** Rob Lawson
Published by Sauce Guides Limited, diffordsguide, 1 Futura House, 169 Grange Road, London, SE1 3BN. **diffordsguide.com digital.diffordsguide.com**

Don't blame us:

This guide is intended for adults of legal drinking age. • Please enjoy alcohol and cocktails in a responsible manner. • Consumption of alcohol in excess can be harmful to your health. • The high sugar levels in some cocktails may mask their alcohol content. • Please do not consume cocktails and drive or operate machinery. • Great care should be exercised when combining flames and alcohol. • Consumption of raw and unpasteurised eggs may be harmful to health. • Please follow the alcohol content guidelines included in this guide where a shot is equal to 25ml or 1 US fluid ounce (29.6ml) at most. A 25ml measure of spirit at 40% alc./vol. is equal to 1 unit of alcohol. Most men can drink up to three to four units of alcohol a day and most women can drink up to two to three units of alcohol a day without significant risks to their health. • Women who are trying to conceive or who are pregnant should avoid getting drunk and are advised to consume no more than one to two units of alcohol once or twice a week.

ISBN: 978-0-9556276-0-6

A BRIEF HISTORY OF COCKTAILS

FROM EARLY CHINA TO LASER COCKTAILS VIA THE SALOONS OF THE WILD WEST, MIXED DRINKS HAVE A SURPRISINGLY LONG HISTORY. HERE'S OUR TAKE ON IT ALL.

Mixing Drinks

For almost as long as people have been drinking alcohol (and most believe that wine is at least 10,000 years old and beer and mead rather older), they have been mixing their drinks. 3000 years ago the Minoan Cretans were blending a proto-cocktail of beer, mead and wine; in Homer's Iliad, slave-girls prepared concoctions of wine, cheese, honey and raw onions.

Adding a hint of spice was nothing new, either. The Greeks flavoured their wine with everything from honey to seawater; in pagan England, wassail, an aromatic blend based on cider, was served in communal cups and bowls to celebrate the harvest. From beer spiked with intoxicants such as henbane through to wine infused with thyme, it's fair to say that the desire both to increase the mood-altering effects of booze and to improve the taste of an indifferent raw product have been with the human race for millennia.

But the arrival of sugar opened up a new era in producing mixed drinks. By medieval times, the rich were flavouring their ales, their meads and metheglin with the new luxury goods – spices and sugars, brought all the way from the East by land and sea. And it is this combination of spice, sugar and booze that we find in the first cocktails.

Distillation added a new layer of possibilities. Although probably known to the Chinese as early as 1000 BC, the technique reached Europe via the Arabs and then, most probably, the monks, more than two millennia later. In medieval times, both the monks and the aristocracy began to produce their own liqueurs in house (for medicinal reasons, naturally), steeping herbs and spices in home-distilled alcohol, and sweetening to help the medicine go down.

By Shakespeare's time, with palates sweeter, mixing drinks was big news. Sherry, then called 'sack', was the drink du jour, and folk would settle down to watch the bear-baiting with tankards of 'sugar sack' (sweetened sherry) or sack-possets (a blend of ale, sherry, eggs, cream, sugar, mace and nutmeg, served warm).

A tate of India

Probably the world's most enduring cocktail, punch, has its origins in India, of all places. Here folk had been distilling for rather longer than in Europe, and were blessed with local resources such as sugar, citrus fruit and spices. Punch, which takes its name from the Hindi word for five – 'panch' – was based on five ingredients: a spirit (originally arrack), sugar, spices, water and citrus fruit, and had a heritage in its home country which stretched back, some suggest, for almost 1500 years.

As Europeans began to discover, then colonise India during the 17th century, punch made its way to Europe, where it was adopted and localised rather more rapidly than curries, which had to wait another three centuries or so.

Rum, a new exotic spirit, became the chosen spirit of high society. Rum punches were served hot and warming against the European climate. Enriched with the phenomenally expensive new citrus fruits, they were drunk cool in summer as a refreshing alternative to wine. (Admiral Edward Russell is reported to have held a party for thousands of people and converted his garden fountain into a punch bowl so large that a cabin boy rowed around the drink in a dinghy with a ladle.)

This very social drink took off rapidly, also, in America, where clubs and taverns would concoct their own secret recipes. The Fish House Punch, created by a club named the State in Schuylkill, Philadelphia, gave George Washington a most monstrous hangover. (The drink survives today, as does the club, and is featured in this guide.)

With 'punch', the balance of sweet, sour and spirit which is at the heart of many of the most popular cocktails had arrived, although the flavouring element, spice, remained key.

Taverns and Pioneers

The drinks writer David Wondrich has described the cocktail as America's first culinary tradition, and mixed drinks thrived in the democratic world of its18th century taverns.

These drinks, many of which were served warm, most often featured a flavour profile that majored on sweetness, perhaps with some spice – a taste that to today's palates is more dessert than drink. In fact, some drinks, like syllabub, would evolve into desserts.

The flip, for example, which appeared in American taverns around 1690, was beer sweetened with sugar, molasses or dried pumpkin, empowered by rum and enriched with eggs and spices. Intriguingly, it was heated in its tankard with a red-hot piece of iron from which it took its name. In Britain, the Negus, a combination of claret and sugar, arrived at around the same time: it takes its name from the eponymous colonel, who died in 1732.

Some popular drinks that made their appearance during the 1700s were Sherry Cobblers (sherry with sugar – and possibly a twist of lemon or a liqueur), Slings (a spirit – generally rum - with sugar and water, served hot or room temperature), Toddies (sweetened, heated, watered, spiced spirits), and Sangarees (like the Spanish Sangria from which they were derived, generally spiced and sweetened wine). In the Southern US, folk would start their day with a mint-flavoured whisky, clearly a prototype of the mint julep: the British blend of rum, sugar and water known as 'grog' made its first known print appearance in 1718.

Ice, Ice baby

Around the turn of the nineteenth century, just as the word 'cocktail' was making its print debut, four significant developments occurred. In 1767, artificial carbonation was achieved; by 1800 ice was for sale in America (in the form of slabs hacked from frozen lakes); in 1803 refrigeration arrived on the scene; and in 1826 Robert Stein invented continuous distillation, marking the way for Aeneas Coffey to develop his still so that good quality spirits could reliably be mass-produced.

While it is probably no coincidence that bartending began to flourish as a profession in the decades after decent quality spirits arrived, probably the most important element in the development of the modern cocktail was the availability of ice. As anyone who has consumed a room temperature cocktail can confirm, ice is absolutely critical to a contemporary drink. It doesn't just chill the blend, but dilutes it, melds flavours and smoothes rough edges in a way that water alone cannot.

Spirits were lighter, easier to transport and less perishable than beer, so it was these, rather than softer alcohols, that fuelled the development of the American West. Like the British, working Americans drank all day, every day (booze was a useful antibacterial agent in days of bad water). And the quality of the early American spirits was such that it required disguising with whatever came to hand.

By the 1820s, saloons were featuring their own in-house speciality drinks, giving them quirky titles such as Sweet Ruination, or even naming them for celebrities of the time.

When Captain Marryatt visited America during the 1830s, the Mint Julep had attained its classical form: a blend of spirit, sugar and mint laboriously hand-made by slaves with hand-crushed ice in two separate glasses and served absolutely frosted.

The development of bitters was also very significant. This packaged the flavours of spices, which had previously been infused into a drink by warming, or using hot water, into a form that was soluble cold. And the craze for bitters led to cocktails with a flavour profile much more recognisable than the original callow blends of sugar and alcohol, or sugar, alcohol and water. In fact, the earliest known definition of the cocktail as a 'bittered sling' makes reference to this balance of bitter and sweet.

The Creole immigrant and apothecary Antoine Peychaud created his bitters in New Orleans during the 1830s. The Sazerac, which is made with his bitters and almost certainly descends from a drink he created, hit the scene most likely thanks to Sewell Taylor during the 1850s, and is probably the earliest known example of a producer using a cocktail to market their spirit. (Angostura bitters, another enduring brand, were created in 1824.) Joseph Santina, who opened the Jewel of the South on Gravier Street, New Orleans, in 1852, invented the Crusta, most likely during the 1850s.

But it appears that it was the Gold Rush of 1849 that really drove development of the cocktail. California miners would down a 'gin cocktail' for breakfast, slamming it back for a quick sugar and alcohol hit, as one might chug a strong and sweet espresso to get one going in the morning.

News from elsewhere

Food history has a relatively lengthy heritage, yet cocktail history is something very new, and there is room for much research into the mixed drinks tradition in countries outside the US.

James Pimm, the man who lent his name to Pimm's No. 1 Cup, was not the only English restaurateur during the first half of the nineteenth century to have created his own blends of fruits, herbs and spices, topped it with some fizz, and served it to his guests as a 'cup'. In fact, the British tradition of mixed drinks was strong enough by 1863 for H. Porter to write an entire book on 'Cups and Their Customs', and cups, some topped with luxurious ingredients such as champagne,

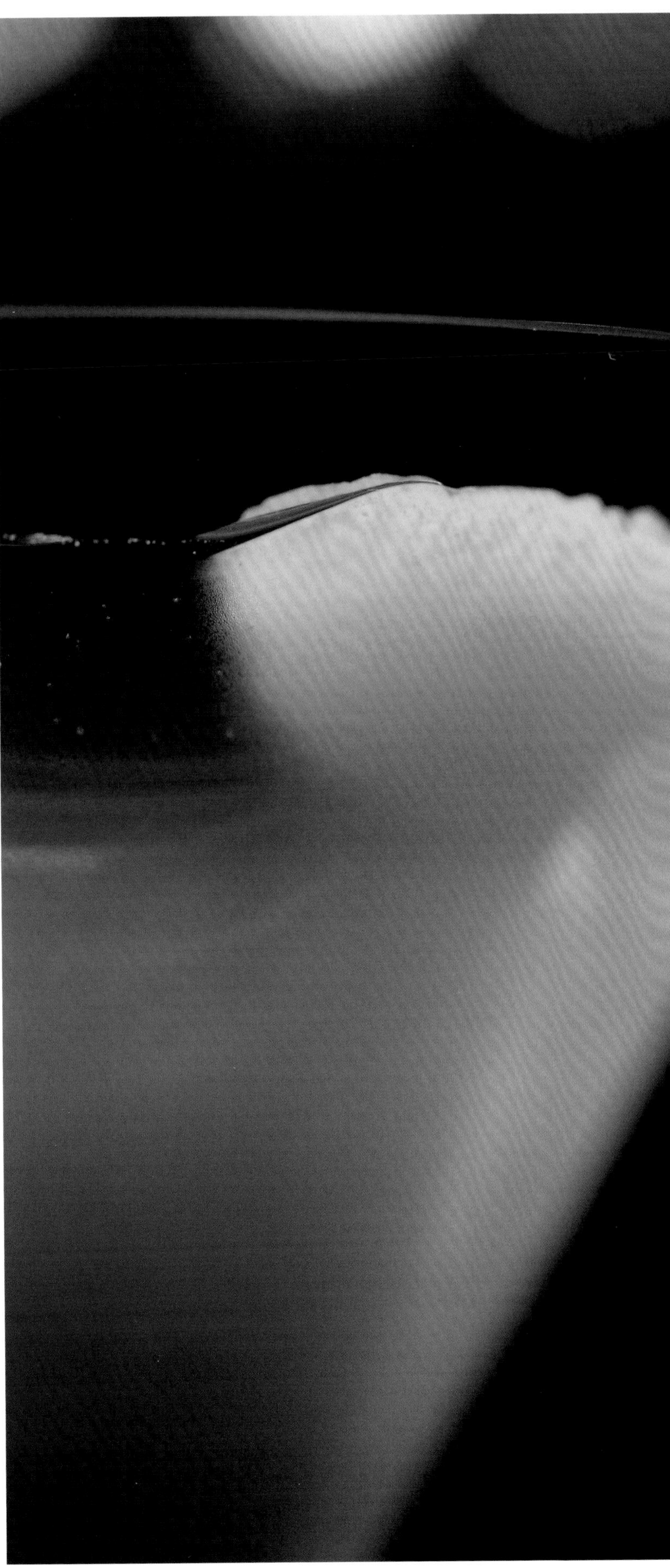

WHAT'S IN A NAME?

The word cocktail is first known to have entered the world of print through the pages of the Farmer's Cabinet, an early American newspaper, in 1803. But its birthday is celebrated on 13th May, thanks to a reader who wrote to another early paper, The Balance and Columbian Repository, in 1806, enquiring what was meant by a 'cocktail'. The editor's first known definition of the word states that 'Cocktail is a stimulating liquor composed of spirits of any kind, sugar, water, and bitters--it is vulgarly called a bittered sling.'

Nobody knows where the word comes from: the Oxford English Dictionary confirms that its derivation is lost. And, although it originally referred to only one type of mixed drink, it is now a catchall term for mixed drinks in general. The following theories about its origins are ranked in order of implausibility.

An Aztec noble once ordered his daughter, Princess Xochitl (or various spellings), to serve a mixed drink to a guest. Her name entered the language and became corrupted as 'cocktail'.

Betsy Flanagan, an innkeeper during the American Revolution, stole a neighbour's chickens to serve to some French soldiers who were fighting on the American side. She used feathers from their tails to garnish their drinks, whereupon the military shouted in Franglais, 'Vive le cock-tail.'

The word comes from the West African kaketal, meaning 'scorpion', which, like a cocktail, has a sting in its tail.

Cock-ale was an old English ale, spiced, with a ground-up red cockerel mixed in – the word became applied to other drinks (containing neither beer nor cockerel) and gained a t.

In a Mexican tavern, English sailors noticed that mixed drinks were stirred with the root of a plant known as cola de gallo, or in English 'cock's tail': the sailors brought the name to England, and thence to the US.

Coquetel was a term for a mixed drink in Bordeaux, which rapidly became 'cocktail' in America.

Coquetier is French for an egg cup, the vessel in which Antoine-Amedée Peychaud of bitters fame prepared his mixes. Anglo-American pronunciation rapidly turned it into 'cocktail'.

In English 'cocktail' meant a horse which was not a thoroughbred racehorse but raced all the same – such horses' tails were docked as a sign of their mixed blood. Hence a cocktail meant not just a mixed horse but a mixed drink.

In some old taverns, the last dregs of booze from the barrels of spirits, known as the cock-tailings, were chucked together and sold off cheap to drinkers, who would then call for 'cocktailings', later shortened to cocktails. This is Gary Regan's etymology of choice and, sadly, ours too.

THIS WAY TO
SPEAKEASY

seemed to have spread as far as Russia. By 1869, William Terrington's Cooling Cups and Dainty Drinks included mixed drinks based on ale, spirits and spices, as well as bittered sherry or Madeira.

The British Navy brought the world a number of medicinal blends, noticeably the pink gin, a blend of gin and angostura that was supposed to ward off upset tummies. Naval types benefited from the classic combination of citrus, sugar, spirit and water as the daily rum ration was diluted with limes to ward off scurvy, then sugared for palatability. And England is one of several countries which claims ownership of the classic Collins cocktail, attributing it to a John Collins of Limmer's Hotel in Conduit Street.

The French, with their lengthy tradition of aperitifs and digestifs, were combining liqueurs certainly during the 1850s, and probably earlier. Pousse-café seems to have been a general term for a mixture of liqueurs and/or spirits served after dinner, and most probably originated in France. (Although the term pousse-café today describes a layered drink, that was not originally the case.)

The Italians, too, had a long tradition of making aromatised wines (vermouths) and liqueurs. Gaspare Campari invented his namesake bitters blend around 1860, and soon it was being combined with vermouth into a Milano-Torino (or Torino-Milano, depending where you came from), and topped with soda for an Americano.

The Australians, who had a number of their own Gold Rushes in the middle of the century, invented some truly terrifying macho concoctions.

Thefirst celebrity bartenders

But it was an American, Jerry Thomas, born in 1830 and dead before his last book came out, who revolutionised the bartending profession when he published the first known bartender's guide in 1862. A character whose career stretched from Gold Rush San Francisco to New York via London and New Orleans, and encompassed stints as a showman, gold miner and sailor, Thomas' book, How to Mix Drinks or The Bon-Vivant's Companion, brought a new professionalism to the industry.

His book featured a range of different styles of drinks – the cocktail was then a subset of mixed drinks, rather than the general catchall term for mixed drinks it has become. Besides Cups, Sangarees, Flips and Pousse-Cafés, there were Cobblers, Crustas, Cocktails, Fixes, Toddies, Sours, Slings, Smashes and even a section of Temperance Drinks. He also includes a recipe for the Martinez, which most consider the original ancestor of the Martini.

Arguably the first ever flair bartender, Thomas' pièce de résistance was the Blue Blazer, with which, according to his biographer Herbert Asbury, he once toured Europe, showing off his bartending skills with a set of solid silver bar tools. This spectacular drink, which only a handful of people can actually make, is based on whiskey and boiling water, flambéed, and poured in a stream of roaring blue flame between two silver cups.

A rival, Harry Johnson, would continue the work. The practical tips on bar management and good business practice in Johnson's book seem very much sharper when one reads Thomas' complaint in print that someone named Johnson had taken over a lapsed lease on a thriving venue.

The great saloons of the guilded age

Thomas, who reportedly started his career at the El Dorado in San Francisco in 1849 (and certainly jumped ship there as a sailor during that year), and worked in Virginia City, Nevada, as well as the Rockies, was very much a creature of the wild west saloon. But these saloons weren't all the swing-door and sawdust emporia seen in Westerns. Some, like the El Dorado, were elaborate, fantastical places, decked out in expensive art, antiques, opulent fabrics and mirrors. They offered everything from gambling to live music to ladies of the night (some, just like in the westerns, had a brothel upstairs) – essentially, anything that could most easily separate a tired and emotional miner from his bag of gold dust.

Over the second half of the nineteenth century, the US surfed a wave of phenomenal wealth, transformed by gold booms, oil booms and the coming of the railroad. The new rich sought places to mingle and spend their money, so grand hotels and clubs sprang up to accommodate them, places like the Astor House, the Hoffman House, the Manhattan Club, the Jockey Club and the Metropolitan Hotel. Their décor, from the gilt to the murals to the elaborate bars, owed much to the saloons of the west.

American bartenders, and their skill at combining drinks, managing orders and sliding completed mixes down the bar, were famous: even when the theatrical method of mixing drinks by throwing gave way to the more efficient shaker, their shaking attracted awe-struck comments from overseas visitors.

The Manhattan is a product of this period, most likely created at some point during the 1870s (although, sadly, the story which attributes it to a banquet attended by Winston Churchill's mother in 1874 is not correct: others credit it, less excitingly, to a man named Black). During this era, too, one finds luxurious drinks like the champagne cocktail becoming popular, while bourbon distiller James E. Pepper brought the Old-Fashioned cocktail from the Pendennis Club in Louisville, Kentucky, to the Waldorf-Astoria Hotel in New York. Towards the end of the century, American-style grand hotels and clubs, complete with American bars, began to open in London, Paris, Rome and summer resorts such as the South of France. American bartenders arrived to run many of their bars, although the bar at London's Savoy was staffed for some time by a British woman, Ada Coleman.

The Bronx cocktail, probably created by either a Joseph S. Sormani who owned a restaurant called the Bronx or by Johnnie Solon, bartender at the Manhattan hotel, was a product of this era. Its innovation? Whereas previously drinks had tended to look for orange flavour in bitters or curaçao, The Bronx used fresh orange juice.

In the USA, cocktails were so established that Heublein (an ancestor of Diageo), was producing Club Cocktails – among them Martinis and Manhattans – and selling them by the case as early as 1907.

Even the First World War did not dent the thirst for cocktails. With gallows humour, someone named the French 75 cocktail for a large artillery gun used in the trenches of the war. The Sidecar, too is a product of this era and, like the Buck's Fizz, a creation of Pat MacGarry, head bartender of Buck's Club in London.

Prohibition and Cuba

Yet clouds were gathering. The combination of a spirits-based drinking culture where men often worked away from home for months at a time with America's puritan heritage was not generating pretty results. Dives like those where – according to Herbert Asbury – bartender Gallus Mag kept pickled ears behind the bar, or punters were entertained by 45-minute long headbutting sessions, damaged the image of the drinks industry, and alcohol undoubtedly caused huge harm to individuals and the families they supported.

Saloons offered free lunches, which could lure in the unsuspecting worker to spend his wages on booze rather than feeding the family, and functioned as a mecca for violence and prostitution. All the kinds of tales which were being told about absinthe in France at the time were attached to spirits by the campaigning Women's Christian Temperance Union, and in an attempt to cure the nation's drink problem, American senators signed the Volstead Act, prohibiting recreational consumption of alcohol.

In 1919, America embarked on 'the noble experiment', and those distilleries which could not switch over to production of 'medicinal' alcohols shut down. Most skilled bartenders left the country – Harry Craddock came to the Savoy bar this way – and many headed to Cuba, to which luxuriously outfitted ferries would transport American citizens for weekends of drinking and debauchery.

At the beginning of the century, Cuba had given the world the Daiquiri, the iconic blend of rum, sugar and citrus which reached America via Admiral Lucius W. Johnson around 1909. Although a combination which had probably existed, like the Brazilian caipirinha, since time immemorial, it was almost certainly named, codified and brought to a wider public by an American mining engineer, Jennings Cox. (It was originally served tall, over cracked ice.) The Mojito adds mint and (later in its evolution) soda to the classic sour trinity and may in fact predate the daiquiri. At the original Floridita, bartender Constante Ribailagua Vert would later create the Hemingway Daiquiri for the heavy-drinking writer.

Trained by some of the best the US had to offer, Cuban bartenders took their craft so seriously that by 1924 they had set up the Club de Cantineros (Barmen's Association).

Feds and Speakeasies

Those who chose not to ship out of the USA altogether and set up residence in Europe turned for booze and entertainment to the wonderful world of the speakeasy, beautifully designed venues which combined bar, restaurant and club in one. Although firmly illegal – and often shut down – these places drew women as well as men, unlike the old saloons which had been, but for the odd hooker, all male spaces.

These underground venues were often decorated more luxuriously by far than their legal predecessors, and featured elaborate systems to conceal all signs of boozing within seconds of the alarm being raised. The Stork Club offered silver leather, torch singers and chanteuses; Jack and Charlie's Puncheon Club (later the 21 Club) had a secret wine cellar concealed behind a wall, located under the house next door and opened only by inserting a skewer into a tiny hole in the bricks.

The Prohibition era, however, was not kind to cocktails. It made economic sense to smuggle in good quality Scotch, yet Capone and his ilk were not really interested in boot-legging volumes of vermouth or bitters. Long, fully stocked back bars would take time to clear away if a venue was raided. So most decent places served drinks by the bottle.

Although the better speakeasies used smuggled spirits, there was plenty of toxic home-made hooch around. 'Bathtub gin', so called because flavourings could be mixed with raw spirit in a bath, had a raw taste that benefited from covering with fruits, juices or cream. The taste of alcohol, which had been central to mixed drinks, understandably receded from centre stage and drinks such as the Alexander, which was possibly created for the birthday party of a Phoebe Snow, began their ascent.

When Prohibition was repealed in 1933, cocktails embarked on their long and distinguished career on the silver screen. Humphrey Bogart fixed Ingrid Bergman a Champagne Cocktail in Casablanca; Marilyn Monroe's husband breakfasted on Whiskey Sours in The Seven Year Itch; William Powell explained to a bartender how to shake in The Thin Man; and, of course, James Bond would request his martini 'shaken, not stirred'.

Cocktails performed a helpful cinematic function (of giving the characters something to do with their hands while they talked), but this did not diminish their impact. In a world mired in first Depression then world war, they became synonymous with glamour.

The Tiki Thing

In 1934 Ernest Raymond Beaumont Gantt, a Louisiana native who had made some money boot-legging rum during Prohibition, opened a bar called Don's Beachcomber in Hollywood, decorated it in a tropical vein and began to offer up rum based cocktails. Fairly soon after, Victor 'Trader Vic' Bergeron transformed his restaurant Hinky Dinks into a very similar style.

Between them, the two were the founding fathers of Tiki, the wonderfully escapist style of eating, drinking and carousing that invented a Polynesian way of life and translated it (eventually) to every city in the United States. The cocktails served in the Trader's venues, in Donn Beach's, and, later, in huge venues such as the Mai Kai were based on rum, liqueurs and (generally) tropical fruits, often packing a lethal alcoholic punch that was advertised in the name. Though Donn Beach and Trader Vic argue over who created the Mai Tai, the most famous tiki drink of all, most attribute it to Bergeron: the Zombie undeniably belongs to Donn Beach.

Tiki bars reached peak popularity during the 50s and 60s, the era of the Cold War, Vietnam and the A-bomb, when their escapism, and the friendly pictures it created of a world outside America, were ever more important. Other loosely tropical drinks such as the Piña Colada and the Margarita are also products of the 1950s.

When properly made, with fine rums, good liqueurs and fresh ingredients, the great tiki drinks and tropical drinks are fantastic. But when tiki goes bad it goes very, very bad, and when tiki meets premixes it is horrid.

Soda Guns and Premixes

After the Depression, Europe had segued, with barely a pause, into the largest war the world has so far known: America joined in 1941. Distilleries from Finland to London were turned over to the production of industrial alcohol for use in the war effort, leaving a long-term deficit of aged spirits such as bourbon, Scotch and cognac.

It is therefore no coincidence that vodka's rise to global recognition, courtesy of Heublein's Jack Martin, began after World War II with the Moscow Mule. In cocktails, vodka tastes of almost nothing. The Moscow Mule was designed to sell ginger beer and Smirnoff, which it did perfectly. It also launched a generation of mixed drinks in which the taste of alcohol was not the dominant flavour, not a flavouring element, but something to be actively avoided: in the 1990s, Absolut would pull a similar trick with the Sea Breeze.

The wartime and post-war period saw the birth of convenience foods: highly processed ingredients such as powdered mash potato or jello mixes that were easy to store, quick to prepare and, apparently, the modern way forwards. In 1937 an enterprising American invented the first cocktail premix, a powder that could deliver the sought-after balance of sweet and sour without the need to painstakingly juice fresh citrus and balance it with sugar. Soda guns arrived, and the syrup dispensers were duly stocked not only with cola, soda and lemonade but with tonic, ginger ale and even "fruit juices". Finally, ice making machines arrived, that could produce lots of ice extremely quickly but in very small cubes. These tiny, fast-melting things replaced the chunkier cubes and slabs of ice from earlier days, leaving drinks watery.

In America, faced with these trends, the vast majority of bar owners opted for mechanical solutions to the bartending skills deficit. Rather than train their staff to make a balanced, fresh drink, they chose to teach them to produce a chemically balanced, mediocre drink, using premixes. The standard of drink-making dropped hugely, and drinks such as the grenadine-infused Tequila Sunrise, the Harvey Wallbanger and the Blue Lagoon did little to further the cause of good bartending. In London, by the early 1980s cocktails were so prevalent and so badly made that Del Boy, an icon of working class aspiration and bad taste, chose the Piña Colada as his drink of choice.

By the mid-1980s, the Long Island Iced Tea - a bunch of white spirits with a cola top, most likely created in the 1970s, although multiple theories abound – was taking America by storm. Low bartender skilling levels and consumer expectations which seem to have extended not much further than getting wasted meant that the balance and precision of a well-made drink was a vanishing art.

The Rival Begins

Yet, independently and simultaneously, in London and New York, Dale DeGroff and Dick Bradsell were reinventing the craft of bartending, and bringing cocktails to a wider audience, DeGroff at New York's Rainbow Room, Bradsell at the Atlantic Bar.

DeGroff took the Cosmopolitan recipe (probably descended from a drink of the 1930s), and made it his own; Bradsell created drinks such as the Bramble, the Russian Spring Punch and the Wibble. They returned to basics, using fresh fruit and freshly squeezed juices, just as the first bartenders had.

The new-style fruit 'martinis' appeared on the scene. Drinks such as the Watermelon Martini provided a new kind of balance for a drink, one based on subtle but carefully balanced fruit. And fresh fruit drinks were the flavour of the 90s.

Between them, Bradsell and DeGroff trained a huge number of influential bartenders, who picked up on their enthusiasm and skills base and ran with it. Liquor companies rose to the challenge, providing ever more exotic flavouring ingredients as bartenders experimented with ingredients from cardamom to rose petals. Some bartenders also began a slow and studied return to the classics, and others experimented with vigour.

A Global Word

The internet has transformed global society, and bartenders are very much a part of that transition. To discover what peers or leaders in other countries are doing, they need only to go on the internet: bartenders in less restrictive alcohol regimes than the United States can also track down almost any product they want online.

Research into the origins of older drinks is becoming much easier. Material such as old newspapers that would, ten years ago, have been available only on microfilm in a library in a single country, are now online and digitally searchable. More and more rare books are being posted on the net.

And new ideas can be shared and communicated. Audrey Saunders' research into the best treatment of ice for different drinks travelled across the Atlantic in seconds.

Many of the world's best bartenders, in fact, do stints in one or more of the world's great cities before returning home to start their own business, spreading expertise from city to city around the world. They are helped by supportive spirits companies, who are once again flinging bags of cash at cocktail creators.

Molecular Mixology

One of the most interesting current trends in bartending is the loosely aligned group of people who are sometimes called molecular mixologists, sometimes bar chefs. They use techniques derived from cookery, from science and from molecular chefs such as Ferran Adria and Heston Blumenthal to play with the taste and texture of their drinks.

These folk have broken down a Manhattan into a jelly with a chilled foam, reversed a Mai Tai into citrus topped with a butane-flamed "meringue", transformed a dirty Martini into what looks like an olive, served a mojito in an atomiser, warmed pine wood with lasers to extract its scented oils, dyed tomato juice yellow, set into a yolk then served it in an oyster shell, and much, much more.

It's too early to tell how many of these techniques or drinks will last the distance, and how many will go the way of nouvelle cuisine, yet some of these cocktails are truly phenomenal. But Jerry Thomas, the showman who created the Blue Blazer, would get the point.

BARTENDING BASICS

By definition any drink which is described as a cocktail contains more than one ingredient. So if you are going to make cocktails you have to know how to combine these various liquids. Firstly, as in cooking, there is a correct order in which to prepare things and with few exceptions, that runs as follows:

1. Select glass and chill or pre-heat (if required).
2. Prepare garnish (if required).
3. Pour ingredients.
4. Add ice (if required - add last to minimise melt).
5. Combine ingredients.
6. Add garnish (if required).
7. Consume or serve to guest.

Essentially, there are four different ways to mix a cocktail: shake, stir, blend and build. (Building a drink means combining the ingredients in the glass in which the cocktail will be served.)

A fifth construction method, 'layering', isn't strictly mixing. The idea here is to float each ingredient on its predecessor without the ingredients merging at all. At the heart of every cocktail lies at least one of these five methods. So understanding these terms is fundamental.

Shake

When you see the phrase "shake with ice and strain" or similar in a method, you should place all the necessary ingredients with cubed ice in a cocktail shaker and shake briskly for fifteen seconds. Then you should strain the liquid into the glass, leaving the ice behind in the shaker.

Shaking not only mixes a drink, it also chills and dilutes it. This dilution is just as important to the resulting cocktail as using the right proportions of each ingredient. If you use too little ice it will quickly melt in the shaker, producing an over-diluted drink - so always fill your shaker at least two-thirds full with fresh ice.

Losing your grip while shaking is likely to make a mess and could result in injury, so always hold the shaker firmly with two hands and never shake fizzy ingredients (unless in a minute proportion to rest of drink).

Although shakers come in many shapes and sizes there are two basic types.

Standard Shaker

A standard shaker consists of three parts and hence is sometimes referred to as a three-piece shaker. The three pieces are 1/ a flat-bottomed, conical base or 'can', 2/ a top with a built-in strainer and 3/ a cap.

I strongly recommend this style of shaker for amateurs due to its ease of use. Be sure to purchase a shaker with a capacity of at least one pint as this will allow the ice room to travel and so mix more effectively.

To use:

1/ Combine all ingredients in the base of the shaker and fill two-thirds full with ice.
2/ Place the top and cap firmly on the base.
3/ Pick up the closed shaker with one hand on the top and the other gripping the bottom and shake vigorously. The cap should always be on the top when shaking and should point away from guests.
4/ After shaking briskly for a count of around 15 seconds, lift off the cap, hold the shaker by its base with one finger securing the top and pour the drink through the built-in strainer.

1

2.

3.

4.

Boston Shaker

A Boston shaker comprises two flat-bottomed cones, one larger than the other. The large cone, or 'can', is made of stainless steel while the smaller cone can be either glass or stainless steel. I prefer glass as this allows both mixer and guest to see the drink being made.

Avoid Boston shakers that rely on a rubber ring to seal. I use Alessi Boston tins as I find these seal without a thump and open with the lightest tap. However good your Boston shaker, these devices demand an element of skill and practice is usually required for a new user to become proficient.

To use:

1/ Combine ingredients in the glass, or smaller of the two cans.
2/ Fill the large can with ice and briskly upend over the smaller can (or glass), quickly enough to avoid spilling any ice. Lightly tap the top with the heel of your hand to create a seal between the two parts.
3/ Lift shaker with one hand on the top and the other gripping the base and shake vigorously. The smaller can (or glass) should always be on the top when shaking and should point away from guests.
4/ After shaking for around 15 seconds, hold the larger (base) can in one hand and break the seal between the two halves of the shaker by tapping the base can with the heel of your other hand at the point where it meets the upper can (or glass).
5/ Before pouring place a strainer with a coiled rim (also known as a Hawthorne strainer) over the top of the can and strain the mixture into the glass, leaving the ice cubes behind.

5

1.

2.

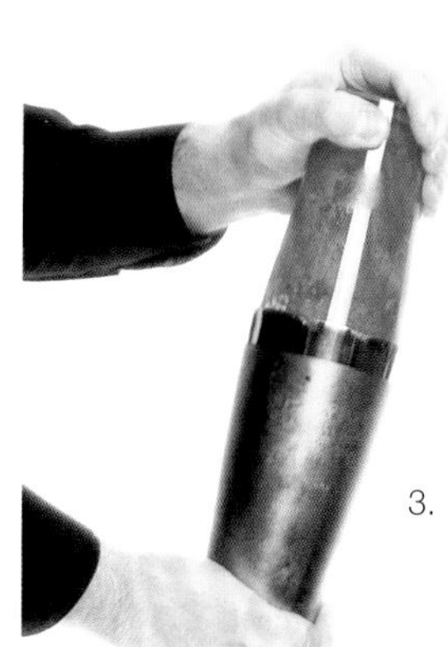

3.

4.

Fine Strain

Most cocktails that are served 'straight up' without ice benefit from an additional finer strain, over and above the standard strain which keeps ice cubes out of the drink. This 'fine strain' removes small fragments of fruit and fine flecks of ice which can spoil the appearance of a drink. Fine straining is achieved by simply holding a fine sieve, like a tea strainer, between the shaker and the glass. Another popular term for this method is 'double strain'.

Stir

If a cocktail recipe calls for you to 'stir with ice and strain', stir in a mixing glass using a bar spoon with a long, spiralling stem. If a lipped mixing glass is not available, one half of a Boston shaker, or the base of a standard shaker, will suffice.

Combine the ingredients in the mixing glass, adding the ice last. Slide the back of the spoon down the inside of the mixing glass and stir the drink. You should stir a drink for at least 20 seconds, then strain into a glass using a strainer (or the top of a standard shaker if you are using a standard shaker base in place of a mixing glass).

Blend

When a cocktail recipe calls for you to 'blend with ice', place ingredients and ice into a blender and blend until a smooth, even consistency is achieved. Ideally you should use crushed ice, as this lessens wear on the blender's blades. Place liquid ingredients in the blender first, adding the ice last, as always. If you have a variable speed blender, always start slowly and build up speed.

Layer

As the name would suggest, layered drinks include layers of different ingredients, often with contrasting colours. This effect is achieved by carefully pouring each ingredient into the glass so that it floats on its predecessor.

The success of this technique is dependent on the density (specific gravity) of the liquids used. As a rule of thumb, the less alcohol and the more sugar an ingredient contains, the heavier it is. The heaviest ingredients should be poured first and the lightest last. Syrups are non-alcoholic and contain a lot of sugar so are usually the heaviest ingredient. Liqueurs, which are high in sugar and lower in alcohol than spirits, are generally the next heaviest ingredient. The exception to this rule is cream and cream liqueurs, which can float.

One brand of a particular liqueur may be heavier or lighter than another. The relative temperatures of ingredients may also affect their ability to float or sink. Hence a degree of experimentation is inevitable when creating layered drinks.

Layering can be achieved in one of two ways. The first involves pouring down the spiral handle of a bar spoon, keeping the flat, disc-shaped end of the spoon over the surface of the drink. Alternatively you can hold the bowl end of a bar spoon (or a soup spoon) in contact with the side of the glass and over the surface of the drink and pour slowly over it.

The term 'float' refers to layering the final ingredient on top of a cocktail.

Muddle

Muddling means pummelling fruits, herbs and/or spices with a muddler (a blunt tool similar to a pestle) so as to crush them and release their flavour. (You can also use a rolling pin.) As when using a pestle and mortar, push down on the muddler with a twisting action.

Only attempt to muddle in the base of a shaker or a suitably sturdy glass. Never attempt to muddle hard, unripe fruits in a glass as the pressure required could break the glass. I've witnessed a bartender slash his hand open on a broken glass while muddling and can't over-emphasize how careful you should be.

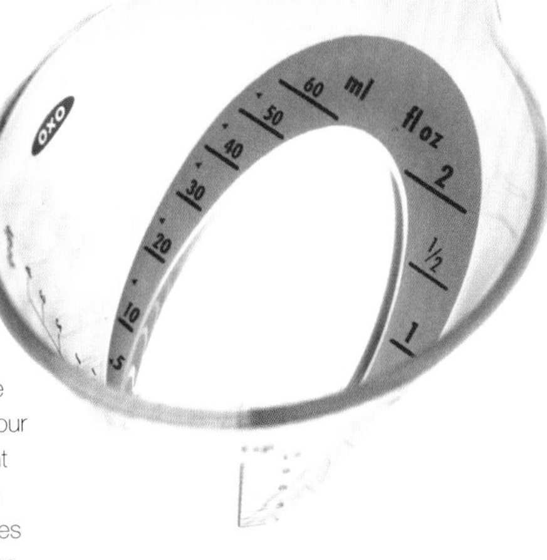

Measuring (Shots & Spoons)

Balancing each ingredient within a cocktail is key to making a great drink. Therefore the accuracy with which ingredients are measured is critical to the finished cocktail.

In this guide I've expressed the measures of each ingredient in 'shots'. Ideally a shot is 25ml or one US fluid ounce (29.6ml), measured in a standard jigger. (You can also use a clean medicine measure or even a small shot glass.) Whatever your chosen measure, it should have straight sides to enable you to accurately judge fractions of a shot. Look out for measures which are graduated in ounces and marked with quarter and half ounces.

The measure 'spoon' refers to a bar spoon, which is slightly larger than a standard teaspoon. Personally, I measure in ounces and count a flat bar spoon as an 1/8 of an ounce.

Some bartenders attempt to measure shots by counting time and estimating the amount of liquid flowing through a bottle's spout. This is known as 'free-pouring' and in unskilled hands can be terribly inaccurate. I strongly recommend the use of a physical measure and a great deal of care.

Ice

A plentiful supply of fresh ice is essential to making good cocktails. When buying bagged ice avoid the hollow, tubular kind and the thin wafers. Instead look for large, solid cubes of ice. I have a Hoshizaki ice machine which produces large (inch square) solid cubes, and thoroughly recommend it.

When filling ice cube trays, use bottled or filtered water to avoid the taste of chlorine often apparent in municipal water supplies. Your ice should be dry, almost sticky to the touch. Avoid 'wet' ice that has started to thaw.

Whenever serving a drink over ice, always fill the glass with ice, rather than just adding a few cubes. This not only makes the drink much colder, but the ice lasts longer and so does not dilute into the drink.

Never use ice in a cocktail shaker twice, even if it's to mix the same drink as last time. You should always throw away ice after straining the drink and use fresh ice to fill the glass if so required. Not straining shaken ice and pouring it straight into the glass with the liquid is one of the worst crimes a bartender can commit.

Unless otherwise stated, all references to ice in this guide mean cubed ice. If crushed ice is required for a particular recipe, the recipe will state 'crushed ice'. This is available commercially. Alternatively you can crush cubed ice in an ice-crusher or simply bash a bag or tea towel of cubed ice with a rolling pin.

If a glass is broken near your ice stocks, melt the ice with warm water, clean the container and re-stock with fresh ice. If this occurs in a busy bar and you are not immediately able to clean the ice chest, mark it as being contaminated with a liberal coating of red grenadine syrup and draw ice from another station.

How to make sugar syrup

To make your own sugar syrup, gradually pour TWO cups of granulated sugar into a saucepan containing ONE cup of hot water. Stir as you pour and carry on stirring and simmering until the sugar is dissolved. Do not let the water even come close to boiling and only simmer for as long as it takes to dissolve the sugar. Allow syrup to cool and pour into an empty bottle. Ideally, you should finely strain your syrup into the bottle to remove any undissolved crystals which could otherwise encourage crystallisation. If kept in a refrigerator this mixture will last for a couple of months.

Flame

The term ignite, flame or flambé means that the drink should be set alight. Please exercise extreme care when setting fire to drinks. Be particularly careful not to knock over a lit drink and never attempt to carry a drink which is still alight. Before drinking, cover the glass so as to suffocate the flame and be aware that the rim of the glass may be hot.

Garnishes

Garnishes are used to decorate cocktails and are often anchored to the rim of the glass. Strictly speaking, garnishes should be edible, so please forget about paper parasols. Anything from banana chunks, strawberries or redcurrants to coffee beans, confectionery, basil leaves and slices of fresh ginger can be used as a garnish. The correct garnish will often enhance the aroma and flavour as well as the look of a drink.

Fruit should be unblemished and washed prior to use. Olives, in particular, should be washed thoroughly to prevent oil from spoiling the appearance of a drink. Cut citrus fruits have a maximum shelf life of 24 hours when refrigerated. Cherries and olives should be stored refrigerated and left in their own juices.

Olives, cherries, pickled onions and fresh berries are sometimes served on cocktail sticks. A whole slice of citrus fruit served on a cocktail stick 'mast' is known as a 'sail': this is often accompanied by a cherry.

Celery sticks may be placed in drinks as stirring rods while cinnamon sticks are often placed in hot drinks and toddies.

To sprinkle chocolate on the surface of a drink you can either shave chocolate using a vegetable peeler or crumble a Cadbury's Flake bar. The instruction 'dust with chocolate' refers to a fine coating of cocoa powder on the surface of a drink. (When dusting with nutmeg it is always best to grate fresh nutmeg as the powdered kind lacks flavour.)

Citrus peels are often used as a garnish. Besides the variations listed under 'zest twist', thin, narrow lengths of citrus peel may be tied in a 'knot'. A 'Horse's Neck' is the entire peel of either an orange, a lemon or a lime, cut in a continuous spiral and placed so as to overhang the rim of the glass.

Wedges of lemons and limes are often squeezed into drinks or fixed to the glass as a garnish. A wedge is an eighth segment of the fruit. Cut the 'knobs' from the top and bottom of the fruit, slice the fruit in half lengthwise, then cut each half into four equal wedges lengthwise.

Mint sprigs are often used to garnish cups and juleps.

Zest Twist

This term refers to flavouring a drink by releasing the aromatic oils from a strip of citrus zest. Using a knife or peeler, cut a half inch (12mm) wide length of zest from an unwaxed, cleaned fruit so as to leave just a little of the white pith. Hold it over the glass with the thumb and forefinger of each hand, coloured side down. Turn one end clockwise and the other anticlockwise so as to twist the peel and force some of its oils over the surface of the drink. Deposit any flavoursome oils left on the surface of the peel by wiping the coloured side around the rim of the glass. Finally, drop the peel onto the surface of the drink. (Some prefer to dispose of the spent twist.)

A flamed zest twist is a dramatic variation on this theme which involves burning the aromatic oils emitted from citrus fruit zest over the surface of a drink. Lemons and limes are sometimes treated in this way but oranges are most popular. Firm, thick-skinned navel oranges, like Washington Navels, are best.

You will need to cut as wide a strip of zest as you can, wider than you would for a standard twist. Hold the cut zest, peel side down, between the thumb and forefinger about four inches above the drink and gently warm it with a lighter flame. Then pinch the peel by its edges so that its oils squirt through the flame towards the surface of the drink - there should be a flash as the oils ignite. Finally, wipe the zest around the rim of the glass.

Salt/Sugar Rim

Some recipes call for the rim of the glass to be coated with salt, sugar or other ingredients such as desiccated coconut or chocolate: you will need to moisten the rim first before the ingredient will hold. When using salt, wipe a cut wedge of lime around the outside edge of the rim, then roll the outside edge through a saucer of salt. (Use sea salt rather than iodised salt as the flavour is less biting.) For sweet ingredients like sugar and chocolate, either use an orange slice as you would a lime wedge or moisten a sponge or paper towel with a suitable liqueur and run it around the outside edge of the glass.

Whatever you are using to rim the glass should cling to the outside edge only. Remember, garnishes are not a cocktail ingredient but an optional extra to be consumed by choice. They should not contaminate your cocktail. If some of your garnish should become stuck to the inside edge of the glass, remove it using a fresh fruit wedge or a paper towel.

It is good practice to salt or sugar only two-thirds of the rim of a glass. This allows the drinker the option of avoiding the salt or sugar. If you rim glasses some hours prior to use, the lime juice or liqueur will dry, leaving a crust of salt or sugar crystals around the rim. The glasses can then be placed in a refrigerator to chill ready for use.

A professional piece of equipment with the unfortunate title of a 'rimmer' has three sections, one with a sponge for water or lime juice, one containing sugar and another containing salt. Beware, as this encourages dipping the glass onto a moist sponge and then into the garnish, and so contaminating the inside of the glass.

GLASSWARE

Cocktails are something of a luxury. You don't just ping a cap and pour. These drinks take time and skill to mix so deserve a decent glass.

Before you start, check your glassware is clean and free from chips and marks such as lipstick. Always handle glasses by the base or the stem to avoid leaving finger marks and never put your fingers inside a glass.

Ideally glassware should be chilled in a freezer prior to use. This is particularly important for martini and flute glasses, in which drinks are usually served without ice. It takes about half an hour to sufficiently chill a glass in the freezer.

If time is short, you can chill a glass by filling it with ice (ideally crushed, not cubed) and topping it up with water. Leave the glass to cool while you prepare the drink, then discard the ice and water once you are ready to pour. This method is quicker than chilling in the freezer but not nearly so effective.

To warm a glass ready for a hot cocktail, place a bar spoon in the glass and fill it with hot water. Then discard the water and pour in the drink. Only then should you remove the spoon, which is there to help disperse the shock of the heat.

There are thousands of differently shaped glasses, but if you own those mentioned here you have a glass to suit practically every drink and occasion. Failing that, a set of Collins, Martini and Old-fashioned or Rocks glasses, and possibly flutes if you fancy champagne cocktails, will allow you to serve the majority of drinks in this guide. Use a Martini in place of a Coupette and a Collins as a substitute for Hurricane and Sling glasses.

1. Martini

Those in the old guard of bartending insist on calling this a 'cocktail glass'. It may once have been, but to most of us today a V-shaped glass is a Martini glass. The recent resurgence in vintage cocktails has also led to a vogue for using a champagne saucer (AKA Coup) to serve straight-up drinks. Whatever your glassware preference, when choosing either a Martini or a Coup it should be no bigger than 7oz, as a true Martini warms up too much in the time it takes to drink such a large one. I'd suggest keeping your glasses in the refrigerator or even the freezer so they are chilled before use.

Capacity to brim: 7oz / 20cl

2. Sling

This elegant glass has recently become fashionable again – partly due to the popularity of long drinks such as the Russian Spring Punch.

Capacity to brim: 11oz / 32cl

3. Shot

Shot glasses come in all shapes and sizes. You'll need small ones if you're sensible and big ones if you're not!

Capacity to brim (pictured glass): 2oz / 6cl

4. Flute

Flutes are perfect for serving champagne cocktails as their tall, slim design helps maintain the wine's fizz. Chill before use.

Capacity to brim: 6oz / 17cl

5. Collins

In this guide I refer to a tall glass as a 'Collins'. A hi-ball is slightly squatter than a Collins but has the same capacity. A 12oz Collins glass will suffice for cocktails and is ideal for a standard 330ml bottle of beer. However, I favour 14oz glasses with the occasional 8oz for drinks such as Fizzes which are served tall but not very long.

Capacity to brim: 14oz / 40cl or 8oz / 24cl

6. Coupette

This is commonly referred to as a 'Margarita glass' since it is used to serve the hugely popular cocktail of the same name. Its rim cries out for salt.

Capacity to brim: 8oz / 24cl

7. Goblet

Not often used for cocktails, but worth having, if for no other reason than to enjoy your wine. An 11oz glass is big enough to be luxurious.

Capacity to brim: 11oz / 32cl

8. Boston

A tall, heavy conical glass with a thick rim, designed to be combined with a Boston tin to form a shaker. It can also be used as a mixing glass for stirred drinks.

Capacity to brim: 17oz / 48cl

9. Hurricane

Sometimes referred to as a 'poco grande' or 'Piña Colada' glass, this big-bowled glass is commonly used for frozen drinks. It screams out for a pineapple wedge, a cherry and possibly a paper parasol as well. Very Del Boy.

Capacity to brim: 15oz / 43cl

10. Old-fashioned

Another glass whose name refers to the best-known drink served in it. It is also great for enjoying spirits such as whiskey. Choose a luxuriously large glass with a thick, heavy base. Alternatively, the similarly shaped 'Rocks' glass has a thick rim and is usually made from toughened glass so better suited to drinks that require muddling in the glass.

Capacity to brim: 11oz / 32cl

11. Snifter

Sometimes referred to as a 'brandy balloon'. The bigger the bowl, the more luxurious the glass appears. Use to enjoy cocktails and deluxe aged spirits such as Cognac.

Capacity to brim: 12oz / 35cl

12. Toddy

Frequently referred to as a 'liqueur coffee glass', which is indeed its main use, this glass was popularised by the Irish Coffee. Toddy glasses have a handle on the side, allowing you to comfortably hold hot drinks.

Capacity to brim: 8.5oz / 25cl

13. Sour

This small glass is narrow at the stem and tapers out to a wider lip. As the name would suggest, it is used for serving Sours straight-up. I favour serving Sours over ice in an Old-fashioned but any of the recipes in this guide can be strained and served 'up' in this glass.

Capacity to brim: 4oz / 12cl

14. Rocks

Like an Old-fashioned with a thick rim, this is usually made from toughened glass - perfect for drinks that require muddling in the glass. A hardy glass, if there is such a thing.

Capacity to brim: 9oz / 27cl

KETEL ONE VODKA

PLYMOUTH GIN

LIGHT WHITE RUM

PARTIDA TEQUILA

BUFFALO TRACE BOURBON

BLENDED SCOTCH WHISKY

REMY MARTIN V.S.O.P COGNAC

COINTREAU LIQUEUR

COFFEE LIQUEUR

GRAND MARNIER LIQUEUR

GIFFARD APRICOT BRANDY

RICH BERRY LIQUEUR

DRY VERMOUTH

CHAMPAGNE

THE 14 KEY INGREDIENTS

MAKE MORE THAN 450 COCKTAILS IN THIS GUIDE WITH JUST THE 14 KEY ALCOHOLIC INGREDIENTS. LOOK FOR THE

You don't need a fully stocked bar to start mixing cocktails. After all, many of the greatest cocktails require few ingredients: a Martini is made with just two and a Margarita three ingredients.

With just the fourteen Key Ingredients opposite, a few mixers, some fresh fruit, copious amounts of ice and a handful of kitchen basics you will be able to make more than a hundred cocktails (listed overleaf).

Add your favourite spirits and liqueurs to these fourteen and then refer to our full ingredients index on page 374 to find yet more fantastic drinks.

ESSENTIAL JUICES & MIXERS

CRANBERRY JUICE

ORANGE JUICE

PRESSED APPLE JUICE

PINK GRAPEFRUIT JUICE

PINEAPPLE JUICE

SODA WATER

COLA

GINGER ALE & GINGER BEER

TONIC WATER

FRIDGE & LARDER ESSENTIALS

SUGAR (GOMME) SYRUP

GRENADINE SYRUP

LIME CORDIAL

ANGOSTURA AROMATIC BITTERS

FRESH LEMONS

FRESH LIMES

FRESH MINT

STRAWBERRIES

RASPBERRIES

MARASCHINO CHERRIES

VANILLA PODS

DOUBLE CREAM

MILK

EGGS

SUGAR CUBES

RUNNY HONEY

FILTER & ESPRESSO COFFEE

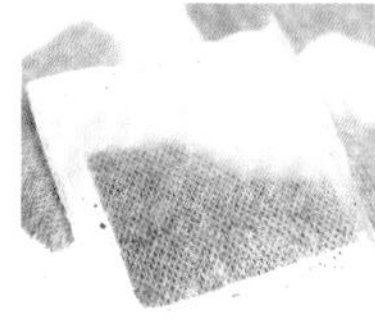

EARL GREY TEA

NOT FORGETTING... ICE - THE MOST IMPORTANT COCKTAIL INGREDIENT

IF YOU HAVE THE 14 KEY ALCOHOLIC INGREDIENTS LISTED ON THE PREVIOUS PAGE ALONG WITH THE FRIDGE AND LARDER ESSENTIALS FEATURED OPPOSITE THEN YOU HAVE ALL YOU NEED TO MAKE THE FOLLOWING COCKTAILS.

WE MARK ALL COCKTAILS WHICH CAN BE MADE USING THESE BASIC INGREDIENTS WITH OUR KEY ALCOHOLIC INGREDIENT LOGO

Absolutely Fabulous
Acupulco Daiquiri
Adios
Adios Amigo Cocktail
Agent Orange
Aggravation
Alan's Apple Breeze
Alice From Dallas
Alice In Wonderland
Americana
Anita's Attitude Adjuster
Apple Daiquiri
Apple Martini # 1
Apple Virgin Mojito
Appily Married
Apricot Fizz
Apricot Lady Sour
Apricot Martini
Arizona Breeze
Arnaud Martini
Arnold Palmer
Attitude Adjuster
Bacardi Cocktail
Balalaika
Bald Eagle
Ballet Russe
Barnum (Was Right)
Batanga
Bay Breeze
Beach Iced Tea
Bebbo
Bee's Knees # 2
Bee's Knees # 3
Bermuda Rose Cocktail
Between Decks
Between The Sheets # 1 (Classic Formula)
Between The Sheets # 2 (Difford's Formula)
Beverly Hills Iced Tea
Biarritz
Bingo
Bitter Sweet Symphony
Black Cherry Martini
Black Feather
Black Russian
Blinker
Blue Blazer
Boston
Boulevard
Bourbon Smash
Bradford
Brandy Buck
Brandy Fizz
Brandy Flip
Brandy Smash
Brandy Sour
Breakfast Martini
The Buck
Buck's Fizz
Buena Vida
Bulldog
Bull's Blood
C C Kazi
Cactus Banger
Caipirissima
Caipirovska
Cajun Martini
Californian Martini
Call Me Old-Fashioned
Canchanchara
Cape Codder
Carrol Cocktail
Cassini
Celtic Margarita
Champagne Cocktail
Champagne Cup
Charlie Chaplin
Chelsea Sidecar
Chimayo
Chin Chin
Cinderella
Claridge Cocktail
Clipper Cocktail
Clockwork Orange
Clover Leaf Cocktail # 1 (Classic Formula)
Clover Leaf Cocktail # 2 (Modern Formula)
Coffee & Vanilla Daiquiri
Colonel Collins
Colonel T
Colonel's Big Opu
Colorado Bulldog
Cordless Screwdriver
Cosmopolitan # 4 (1934 Recipe)
Country Breeze
Cowboy Martini
Cranberry Delicious (Mocktail)
Cranberry & Mint Martini
Creamsicle
The Crow Cocktail
Cuba Libre
Cuba Pintada
Cuban Island
Cuban Master
Cuban Special
Daiquiri No. 1 # 1 (Classic Formula)
Daiquiri No. 1 # 2 (Modern Formula)
Daiquiri No. 2
Daiquiri On The Rocks
Daisy Duke
Derby Daiquiri
Derby Fizz
Detroit Martini
Detropolitan
Diable Rouge
El Diablo
Diamond Fizz
Dickens' Martini
Dorian Gray
Dorothy parker
Dowa
Dreamsicle
Dry Martini # 1 (Traditional)
Dry Martini # 2 (Naked)
Dulchin
Dyevitchka
Earl Grey Mar-Tea-Ni
East India # 2
Eggnog # 1 (Cold)
Eggnog # 2 (Hot)
El Burro
El Presidente No. 1 (Daiquiri) # 1
El Presidente # 2
El Presidente # 3
El Presidente # 4
El Torado
Elegante Margarita
Embassy Cocktail
The Estribo
Fairbanks Cocktail No. 1
Fancy Brandy
Fancy Drink
Fantasia (Mocktail)
Fifty-Fifty Martini
Fine & Dandy
Fizz
Flip
The Flirt
Flirtini # 1
Flirtini # 2
The Flo Ziegfeld
Florida Cocktail (Mocktail)
Floridita Margarita
Flutter
Flying Tigre Coctel
Fog Horn
Frank Sullivan Cocktail
The Frankenjack Cocktail
Franklin Martini
French 75
French 76
French Daiquiri
French Martini
French Mojito
French Mule
French Sherbet
Fresca Nova
Froth Blower Cocktail
Frozen Daiquiri
Frozen Margarita
Fruit Sour
Fruit Tree Daiquiri
Gentle Breeze (Mocktail)
Gibson
Gimlet # 1
Gimlet # 2 (Schumann's Recipe)
Gin & Sin
Gin & Tonic
Gin & Berry
Gin Berry
Gin Cocktail
Gin Fix
Gin Fixed
Gin Fizz
Gin Punch
Gin Sour
Gina
Gloom Chaser Cocktail # 1
Gloria
Golden Fizz # 1
Golden Fizz # 2
Golden Screw
Golf Cocktail
Grand Margarita
Grand Mimosa
Grand Sidecar
Grande Champagne Cosmo
Grapefruit Julep
Greyhound
Havanatheone
Hobson's Choice (Mocktail)
Honey & Marmalade Dram'tini
Honey Bee
Honey Daiquiri
Honey Limeaid (Mocktail)
Honeysuckle Daiquiri
Honolulu
Honolulu Cocktail No. 1
Hoopla
Hop Toad # 1
Hop Toad # 3
Horse's Neck With A Kick
Hot Toddy # 3
Hot Tub
Houla-Houla Cocktail
Huapala Cocktail
Iced Tea Martini
Icy Pink Lemonade
Iguana
Icognito
Jack Dempsey
Jalisco Espresso
Ja-Mora
John Collins
Jose Collins
Judy (Mocktail)
Julep
Julep Martini
Jungle Juice
Kamikaze
Katinka
Kentucky Jewel
Kentucky Tea
Kir Royale
Klondike
Larchmont
Lazarus
Lemon Drop
Lemon Lime & Bitters
LIFE (Life In the Future Ecstasy)
Limeade (Mocktail)
Livingstone
Lolita Margarita
Lonely Bull
Long Island Iced Tea
Loved Up
Lucky Lindy
Lush
Lutkins Special Martini
Madras
Madroska
Maiden's Blush
Maiden's Prayer
Mainbrace
Major Bailey # 1
Major Bailey # 2
Magic Bus
Manhattan Dry
Margarita # 1 (Straight Up)
Margarita # 2 (On The Rocks)
Margarita # 3 (Frozen)
Margarita # 4 (Salt Foam Float)
Maria Theresa Margarita
Marmarita
Marny Cocktail
Marquee
Matador
Mayan
Mayan Whore
Mesa Fresca
Mexican
Mexican 55
Mexican Coffee (Hot)
Mexican Martini
Mexican Mule
Mexican Surfer
Mexican Tea (Hot)
Mexicano (Hot)
Mexico City
Miami Beach
Million Dollar Margarita
Millionaire
Mimosa
Mint & Honey Daiquiri
Mint Collins
Mint Daiquiri
Mint Julep
Mint Limeade (Mocktail)
Miss Martini
Mississippi Punch
Mojito
Mojito De Casa
Momo Special
Moscow Mule
Nacional Daiquiri # 1
Nacional Daiquiri # 2
Nantucket
Naranja Daiquiri
Natural Daiquiri
Nautilus
New Orleans Mule
Niagara Falls
Nicky's Fizz
Not So Cosmo (Mocktail)
November Seabreeze (Mocktail)
Oh Gosh!
Old Fashioned # 1 (Classic Version)
Olympic
Opal
Orange Blossom
Paisley Martini
Paradise # 1
Paradise # 2
Parisian Martini # 1
Park Lane
Pavlova Shot
Pedro Collins
Pegu Club # 1
Pegu Club # 2
Periodista Daiquiri
Pharmaceutical Stimulant
Picador
Pierre Collins
Piña Martini
Pineapple Blossom
Pineapple Daiquiri # 1 (On The Rocks)
Pineapple Daiquiri # 2 (Frozen)
Pineapple Margarita
Pink Gin # 1 (Traditional)
Pink Gin # 2 (Modern)
Pink Gin & Tonic
Pink Grapefruit Margarita
Pink Hound
Pink Lady
Pink Lemonade (Mocktail)
Pink Palace
Pino Pepe
Planter's Punchless (Mocktail)
Playa Del Mar
Playmate Martini
Pogo Stick
Poinsettia
Polly's Special
Pompanski Martini
President
President Vincent
Presidente
Prince of Wales
Princeton Martini
Purple Haze
Purple Hooter
Pussyfoot (Mocktail)
Raspberry Margarita
Raspberry Martini # 1
Raspberry Watkins
Rat Pack Manhattan
Ray's Hard Lemonade
Real Lemonade (Mocktail)
Red Lion # 1 (Modern Formula)
Red Lion # 2 (Embury's Formula)
Red Marauder
Remsen Cooler
Resolute Rickey (Gin Rickey)
Rosarita Margarita
Roselyn Martini
Royal Mojito
Rude Cosmopolitan
Rum Sour
Russian Spring Punch
Saigon Cooler
St Kitts (Mocktail)
Santiago Daiquiri
Scofflaw
Scotch Milk Punch
Screwdriver
Seabreeze # 1 (Simple)
Seabreeze # 2 (Layered)
Seelbach
Serendipity # 2
Shady Grove Cooler
Shirley Temple (Mocktail)
Showbiz
Sidecar # 1 (Classic Formula)
Sidecar # 2 (Difford's Formula)
Sidecar # 3 (Embury's Formula)
Silent Third
Silver Fizz
Sleepy Hollow
Sling
Sloppy Joe
Smoky Martini # 1
Snood Murdekin
Snow White Daiquiri
Snyder Martini
Sour
South Of The Border
Southside Royale
Spencer Cocktail
Sputnik # 2
Stanley Cocktail
Stork Club
Strawberry Margarita
Strawberry Martini
Summer Time Martini
Sundowner # 1
Sunshine Cocktail # 1
Sunshine Cocktail # 2
Sunstroke
Swizzle
Tequila Fizz
Tequila Slammer
Tequila Sour
Tequila Sunrise
Tequila Sunset
Tequila'tini
Teresa
Tex Collins
Texas Iced Tea
Texsun
Thai Lady
Three Miler
Tipperary # 2
Tom Arnold
Tomahawk
Tre Martini
Tres Compadres Margarita
Union Club
Valencia
Vavavoom
Venus Martini
The Vesper Martini
Victorian Lemonade
Vodka Collins
Vodka Espresso
Vodka Gimlet
Vodka Sour
Vodkatini
Wanton Abandon
Ward Eight
Webster Martini
Wet Martini
What The Hell
Whiskey Cobbler
Whiskey Collins
Whiskey Daisy
Whiskey Sour # 1 (Classic)
Whiskey Sour # 2 (Difford's)
Whisky Fizz
White Lady
White Lion
White Russian
Zoom

COCKTAILS A-Z

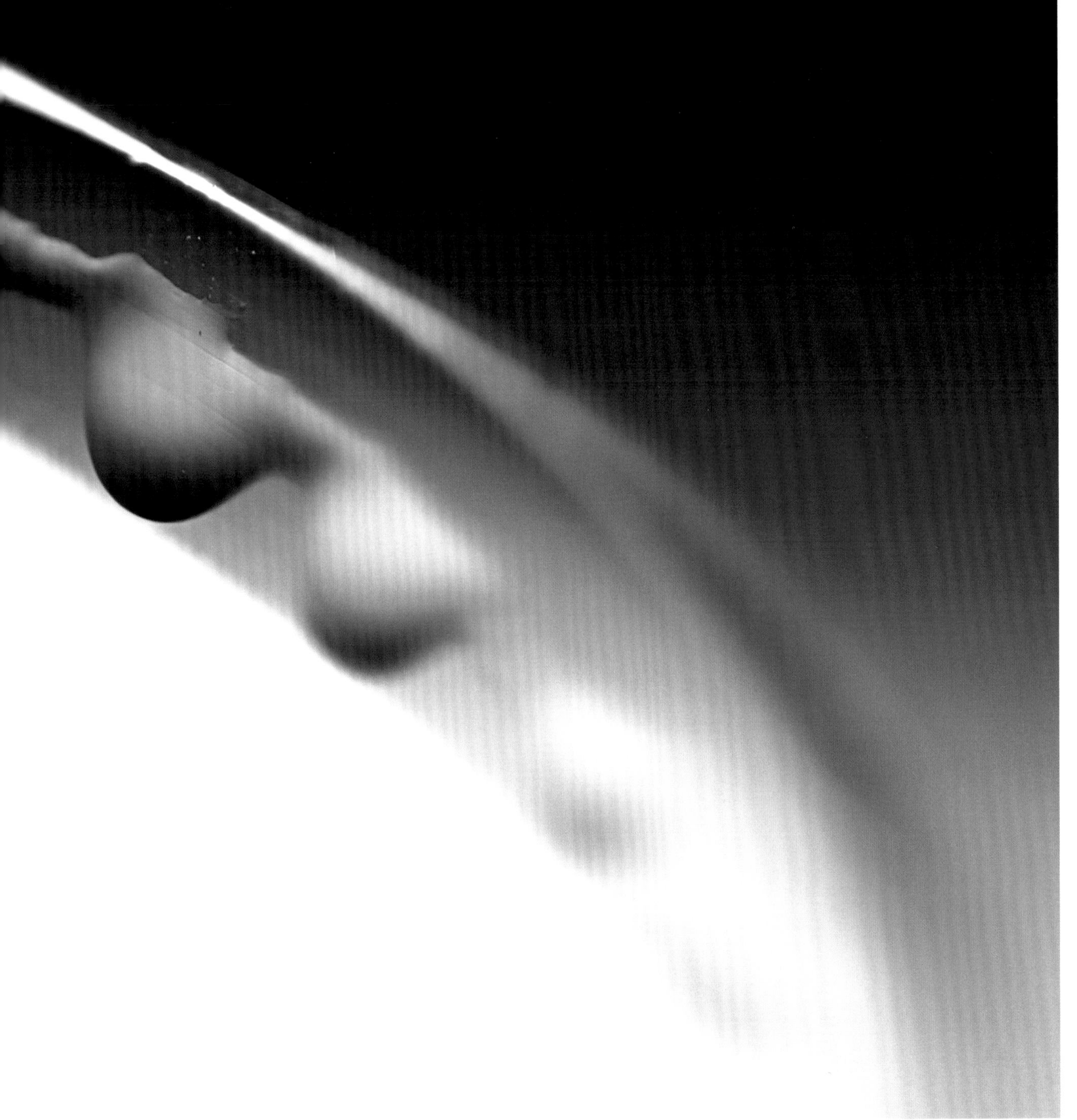

A

ABACAXI RICAÇO [UPDATED #7]

Glass: Pineapple shell (frozen)
Garnish: Cut a straw sized hole in the top of the pineapple and replace it as a lid.
Method: Cut the top off a small pineapple and carefully scoop out the flesh from the base to leave a shell with 12mm (1/2") thick walls. Place the shell in a freezer to chill. Remove the hard core from the pineapple flesh and discard; roughly chop the remaining flesh, add other ingredients and **BLEND** with one 12oz scoop of crushed ice. Pour into the pineapple shell and serve with straws. (The flesh of one pineapple blended with the following ingredients will fill at least two shells.)

1	fresh	**Pineapple**
3	shot(s)	**Golden rum**
3/4	shot(s)	**Freshly squeezed lime juice**
1/2	shot(s)	**Sugar syrup (2 sugar to 1 water)**

Origin: Adapted from David A. Embury's 1948 'Fine Art of Mixing Drinks'. Pronounced 'Ah-bah-Kah-shee Rich-kah-SO', the Portuguese name of this Brazilian drink literally translates as 'Extra Delicious Pineapple'.
Comment: Looks and tastes great but a load of hassle to make.

A.B.C.

Glass: Shot
Method: Refrigerate ingredients then **LAYER** in chilled glass by carefully pouring in the following order.

1/2	shot(s)	**Luxardo Amaretto di Saschira**
1/2	shot(s)	**Irish cream liqueur**
1/2	shot(s)	**Rémy Martin cognac**

Comment: A stripy shooter with almond, whiskey, cream and cognac.

'GOT TIGHT LAST NIGHT ON ABSINTHE AND DID KNIFE TRICKS. GREAT SUCCESS SHOOTING THE KNIFE UNDERHAND INTO THE PIANO.'
ERNEST HEMINGWAY

ABACI BATIDA

Glass: Collins
Garnish: Pineapple wedge on rim
Method: **SHAKE** all ingredients with ice and strain into glass filled with crushed ice.

2 1/2	shot(s)	**Leblon cachaça**
3	shot(s)	**Freshly extracted pineapple juice**
1/2	shot(s)	**Sugar syrup (2 sugar to 1 water)**
1/2	shot(s)	**Freshly squeezed lemon juice**

Origin: The Batida is a traditional Brazilian drink and 'Abaci' means pineapple in Portuguese, the official language of Brazil.
Comment: Unfortunately, this excellent drink has not transferred as quickly from its homeland as the Caipirinha.

ABSINTHE COCKTAIL #1

Glass: Martini
Garnish: Mint leaf
Method: **SHAKE** all ingredients with ice and fine strain into chilled glass.

1	shot(s)	**La Fée Parisienne (68%) absinthe**
1	shot(s)	**Chilled mineral water**
1/4	shot(s)	**Sugar syrup (2 sugar to 1 water)**

Variant: If grenadine (pomegranate syrup) is substituted for the sugar syrup this becomes a Tomate.
Origin: Dr. Ordinaire perfected his recipe for absinthe in 1792 and from day one it required the addition of water and sugar to make it palatable.
Comment: Absinthe tamed and served up.

ABBEY MARTINI

Glass: Martini
Garnish: Orange zest twist
Method: **SHAKE** all ingredients with ice and fine strain into chilled glass.

2	shot(s)	**Plymouth gin**
1	shot(s)	**Sweet vermouth**
1	shot(s)	**Freshly squeezed orange juice**
3	dashes	**Angostura aromatic bitters**

Origin: This 1930s classic cocktail is closely related to the better known Bronx.
Comment: A dry, orangey, herbal, gin laced concoction.

ABSINTHE COCKTAIL #2 [UPDATED #7]

Glass: Martini
Garnish: Lemon zest twist
Method: **SHAKE** all ingredients with ice and fine strain into chilled glass.

1	shot(s)	**La Feé Parisienne (68%) absinthe**
1/4	shot(s)	**Almond (orgeat) syrup**
1/4	shot(s)	**Anisette liqueur**
1	dash	**Angostura aromatic bitters**
3/4	shot(s)	**Chilled mineral water** (reduce if wet ice)

Variant: Absinthe Frappé - served over crushed ice.
Origin: My adaptation of a classic recipe.
Comment: This aniseed flavoured mix tastes surprisingly tame but includes a shot of the notorious green fairy.

ABSINTHE DRIP COCKTAIL #1 [NEW #7]
(FRENCH METHOD)

Glass: Old-fashioned or absinthe glass
Method: POUR absinthe into glass. **PLACE** cube of sugar on a slotted absinthe spoon resting across the top of the glass. Using a bottle of chilled mineral water with a small hole in the cap, **DRIP** water over the sugar so it dissolves and drips into the glass. Traditionally the same amount of sugar is added as water but I find full strength absinthe requires more dilution. Add ice, stir and serve.

1½	shot(s)	**La Feé Parisienne (68%) absinthe**
1	large	**Sugar cube**
2	shot(s)	**Chilled mineral water**

Origin: This is the traditional method of serving absinthe. It was common until shortly before the First World War, when the drink was banned in most countries.
Comment: Patience is a virtue. Slow dripping of the water is essential to dissolve the entire sugar cube and give the drink enough sweetness to balance the absinthe.

ABSINTHE DRIP COCKTAIL #2 [NEW #7]
(CZECH METHOD)

Glass: Old-fashioned or absinthe glass
Method: PLACE sugar cube on a slotted absinthe spoon resting across the top of the glass. **POUR** absinthe over the sugar cube into the glass. **LIGHT** the absinthe soaked cube and leave to burn and caramelise. Using a bottle of chilled mineral water with a small hole in the cap, **DRIP** water over what's left of the sugar so it dissolves and drips into the glass. Add ice, stir and serve.

1½	shot(s)	**La Feé Parisienne (68%) absinthe**
1	large	**Sugar cube**
2	shot(s)	**Chilled mineral water**

Origin: This supposedly bohemian method of serving absinthe came back in to being in 1998 with the UK launch of Hill's Absinth.
Comment: More about the theatrics involved in its making than the taste of the finished drink.

ABSINTHE FRAPPÉ [UPDATED #7]

Glass: Old-fashioned
Garnish: Mint sprig
Method: SHAKE all ingredients with ice and fine strain into glass filled with crushed ice. **CHURN** (stir) and serve with straws.

1½	shot(s)	**La Fée Parisienne (68%) absinthe**
½	shot(s)	**Marie Brizard anisette liqueur**
1½	shot(s)	**Chilled mineral water**
¼	shot(s)	**Sugar syrup (2 sugar to 1 water)**

Origin: Created in 1874 by Cayetano Ferrer at Aleix's Coffee House, New Orleans, which consequently became known as The Absinthe Room. Today the establishment is fittingly known as the Old Absinthe House but sadly US law prevents it from actually serving absinthe.
Comment: Aniseed and the fire of absinthe are moderated by sugar and ice but still a dangerous combination.

ABSINTHE ITALIANO COCKTAIL [NEW #7]

Glass: Martini
Garnish: Lemon zest twist
Method: SHAKE all ingredients with ice and fine strain into chilled glass.

1	shot(s)	**La Fée Parisienne (68%) absinthe**
½	shot(s)	**Marie Brizard anisette liqueur**
¼	shot(s)	**Luxardo maraschino liqueur**
1½	shot(s)	**Chilled mineral water** (reduce if wet ice)

Origin: A long lost classic.
Comment: Liqueurs sweeten and tame the absinthe burn in this milky green concoction.

ABSINTHE SOUR

Glass: Old-fashioned
Garnish: Lemon zest twist
Method: SHAKE all ingredients with ice and strain into ice-filled glass.

1	shot(s)	**La Fée Parisienne (68%) absinthe**
1	shot(s)	**Sugar syrup (2 sugar to 1 water)**
1	shot(s)	**Freshly squeezed lemon juice**
½	fresh	**Egg white**

Variant: Served 'up' in sour glass.
Comment: A touch of the sours for absinthe lovers.

ABSINTHE SPECIAL COCKTAIL [NEW #7]

Glass: Martini
Garnish: Lemon zest twist
Method: SHAKE all ingredients with ice and fine strain into chilled glass.

1	shot(s)	**La Fée Parisienne (68%) absinthe**
¼	shot(s)	**Plymouth gin**
¼	shot(s)	**Marie Brizard anisette liqueur**
1	dash	**Fee Brothers orange bitters**
2	dashes	**Angostura aromatic bitters**
1½	shot(s)	**Chilled mineral water** (reduce if wet ice)

Origin: A long lost classic.
Comment: Tongue numbingly strong in flavour and alcohol.

ABSINTHE SUISESSE

Glass: Old-fashioned
Garnish: Mint sprig
Method: SHAKE all ingredients with ice and strain into glass filled with crushed ice.

1½	shot(s)	**La Fée Parisienne (68%) absinthe**
½	shot(s)	**Orgeat (almond) sugar syrup**
1	fresh	**Egg white**
½	shot(s)	**Double (heavy) cream**
½	shot(s)	**Milk**

Origin: New Orleans 1930s.
Variant: Also spelt 'Suissesse' and sometimes made with absinthe, vermouth, sugar, crème de menthe and egg white shaken and topped with sparkling water.
Comment: Absinthe smoothed with cream and sweet almond.

A

ABSINTHE WITHOUT LEAVE

Glass: Shot
Method: Refrigerate ingredients then **LAYER** in chilled glass by carefully pouring in the following order.

3/4	shot(s)	**Pisang Ambon liqueur**
3/4	shot(s)	**Irish cream liqueur**
1/2	shot(s)	**La Fée Parisienne (68%) absinthe**

Origin: Discovered in 2003 at Hush, London, England.
Comment: This green and brown stripy shot is easy to layer but not so easy to drink.

ACE

Glass: Martini
Garnish: Maraschino cherry on rim
Method: SHAKE all ingredients with ice and fine strain into chilled glass.

2	shot(s)	**Plymouth gin**
1/2	shot(s)	**Pomegranate (grenadine) syrup**
1/2	shot(s)	**Double (heavy) cream**
1/2	shot(s)	**Milk**
1/2	fresh	**Egg white**

Comment: Pleasant, creamy, sweetened gin. Add more pomegranate syrup to taste.

ABSOLUTELY FABULOUS [UPDATED #7]

Glass: Flute
Garnish: Strawberry on rim
Method: SHAKE first two ingredients with ice and strain into glass. **TOP** with champagne.

1	shot(s)	**Ketel One vodka**
2	shot(s)	**Ocean Spray cranberry juice**
Top up with		**Brut champagne**

Origin: Created in 1999 at Monte's Club, London, England, and named after the Absolutely Fabulous television series where Patsy consumed copious quantities of Stoli and Bolly – darlings.
Comment: Easy to quaff – Patsy would love it.

ACE OF CLUBS DAIQUIRI

Glass: Martini
Garnish: Dust with cocoa powder
Method: SHAKE all ingredients with ice and fine strain into chilled glass.

2	shot(s)	**Golden rum**
1/2	shot(s)	**Giffard white crème de cacao**
1/2	shot(s)	**Freshly squeezed lime juice**
1/8	shot(s)	**Sugar syrup (2 sugar to 1 water)**

Origin: A long lost classic thought to have heralded from the Bermudian nightclub of the same name.
Comment: A Daiquiri with a hint of chocolate.

ACAPULCO

Glass: Collins
Garnish: Pineapple wedge on rim
Method: SHAKE all ingredients with ice and strain into ice-filled glass.

1	shot(s)	**Partida tequila**
1	shot(s)	**Golden rum**
1	shot(s)	**Freshly squeezed grapefruit juice**
2 1/2	shot(s)	**Pressed pineapple juice**
1/2	shot(s)	**Sugar syrup (2 sugar to 1 water)**

Comment: An innocuous, fruity mixture laced with tequila and rum.

ACHILLES HEEL

Glass: Collins
Garnish: Apple slice
Method: SHAKE all ingredients with ice and strain into ice-filled glass.

2	shot(s)	**Zubrówka bison vodka**
1/4	shot(s)	**Chambord black raspberry liqueur**
1/4	shot(s)	**Teichenné Peach Schnapps Liqueur**
1	shot(s)	**Pressed apple juice**
1/2	shot(s)	**Freshly squeezed lemon juice**

Origin: Created in 2005 at Koba, Brighton, England.
Comment: If you like French Martinis you'll love this semi-sweet Tatanka with knobs on.

ACAPULCO DAIQUIRI

Glass: Martini
Garnish: Lime wedge on rim
Method: SHAKE all ingredients with ice and fine strain into chilled glass.

1 1/2	shot(s)	**Light white rum**
1/2	shot(s)	**Cointreau triple sec**
3/4	shot(s)	**Freshly squeezed lemon juice**
3/4	shot(s)	**Rose's lime cordial**
1/2	fresh	**Egg white**

Comment: A smooth, yet citrus-rich Daiquiri.

ADAM & EVE

Glass: Old-fashioned
Garnish: Lemon zest twist
Method: SHAKE all ingredients with ice and strain into ice-filled glass.

2	shot(s)	**Buffalo Trace bourbon whiskey**
1/2	shot(s)	**Galliano liqueur**
1/4	shot(s)	**Sugar syrup (2 sugar to 1 water)**
3	dashes	**Angostura aromatic bitters**

Comment: Lovers of the Sazerac will appreciate this herbal, bourbon-laced concoction.

ADELAIDE SWIZZLE [NEW #7]

Glass: Collins
Garnish: Lime slice
Method: POUR all ingredients into glass filled with crushed ice and SWIZZLE.

2	shot(s)	**Light white rum**
1/2	shot(s)	**Freshly squeezed lime juice**
3/4	shot(s)	**Velvet Falernum liqueur**
2	dashes	**Peychaud's aromatic bitters**

Origin: This is the signature cocktail at Café Adelaide's Swizzle Stick Bar, New Orleans, USA. There it is made with a liquid poured from a plain bottle marked 'top secret' but, having tried a drop, I think it is Falernum.
Comment: A slightly pink, dry, spicy long drink with rum and a hint of cloves and lime.

ADIOS

Glass: Shot
Method: Refrigerate ingredients then **LAYER** in chilled glass by carefully pouring in the following order.

3/4	shot(s)	**Kahlúa coffee liqueur**
3/4	shot(s)	**Partida tequila**

Comment: Surprisingly tasty with a potent agave reminder of what you've just knocked back.

ADIOS AMIGOS COCKTAIL [NEW #7]

Glass: Martini
Garnish: Lemon zest twist
Method: SHAKE all ingredients with ice and fine strain into chilled glass.

1	shot(s)	**Light white rum**
1/2	shot(s)	**Dry vermouth**
1/2	shot(s)	**Rémy Martin cognac**
1/2	shot(s)	**Plymouth gin**
1/4	shot(s)	**Freshly squeezed lime juice**
1/4	shot(s)	**Sugar syrup (2 sugar to 1 water)**
1/2	shot(s)	**Chilled mineral water** (omit if wet ice)

Origin: Adapted from Victor Bergeron's 'Trader Vic's Bartender's Guide' (1972 revised edition).
Comment: To quote Vic, "You know that adios means good-bye. You drink two or three of these, and it's adios, believe me, it's adios."

ADONIS

Glass: Martini
Garnish: Orange zest twist
Method: STIR all ingredients with ice and strain into chilled glass.

2	shot(s)	**Tio Pepe fino sherry**
1	shot(s)	**Sweet vermouth**
2	dashes	**Fee Brothers orange bitters**

Origin: Thought to have been created in 1886 to celebrate the success of a Broadway musical.
Comment: Surprisingly delicate, dry, aromatic oldie.

AFFINITY

Glass: Martini
Garnish: Lemon zest twist
Method: STIR all ingredients with ice and strain into chilled glass.

2	shot(s)	**Scotch whisky**
1	shot(s)	**Sweet vermouth**
1	shot(s)	**Dry vermouth**
3	dashes	**Angostura aromatic bitters**

AKA: Scotch Manhattan
Variant: Rob Roy & Violet Affinity
Comment: This classic cocktail may be something of an acquired taste for many modern drinkers.

AFTER EIGHT

Glass: Shot
Method: SHAKE all ingredients with ice and fine strain into chilled glass.

1/2	shot(s)	**Ketel One vodka**
1/2	shot(s)	**Giffard white crème de cacao**
1/2	shot(s)	**Giffard Giffard green crème de menthe**

Comment: Looks like mouthwash but tastes like liquid After Eight chocolates.

AFTER SIX SHOT

Glass: Shot
Method: Refrigerate ingredients then **LAYER** in chilled glass by carefully pouring in the following order.

1/2	shot(s)	**Kahlúa coffee liqueur**
1/2	shot(s)	**Giffard white crème de Menthe Pastille**
1/2	shot(s)	**Irish cream liqueur**

Comment: A layered, creamy, coffee and mint shot.

AFTERBURNER

Glass: Snifter
Method: POUR all ingredients into glass, swirl to mix, **FLAMBÉ** and then extinguish flame. Please take care and beware of hot glass rim.

1	shot(s)	**Giffard white crème de Menthe Pastille**
1	shot(s)	**Kahlúa coffee liqueur**
1/2	shot(s)	**Wray & Nephew overproof rum**

Comment: A surprisingly smooth and moreish peppermint-laced drink.

DRINKS ARE GRADED AS FOLLOWS:

● DISGUSTING ●◐ PRETTY AWFUL ●● BEST AVOIDED
●●◐ DISAPPOINTING ●●● ACCEPTABLE ●●●◐ GOOD
●●●● RECOMMENDED ●●●●◐ HIGHLY RECOMMENDED
●●●●● OUTSTANDING / EXCEPTIONAL

AGED HONEY DAIQUIRI

Glass: Martini
Garnish: Lime wedge on rim
Method: **STIR** honey with rum in base of shaker until honey dissolves. Add lime juice and water, **SHAKE** with ice and fine strain into chilled glass.

2	shot(s)	**Aged rum**
1½	spoons	**Runny honey**
½	shot(s)	**Freshly squeezed lime juice**
½	shot(s)	**Chilled mineral water** (omit if wet ice)

Comment: Sweet honey replaces sugar syrup in this natural Daiquiri. Try experimenting with different honeys. I favour orange blossom honey.

'IT IS FUNNY THE TWO THINGS MOST MEN ARE PROUDEST OF IS THE THING THAT ANY MAN CAN DO AND DOING DOES IN THE SAME WAY, THAT IS BEING DRUNK AND BEING THE FATHER OF THEIR SON.'

GERTRUDE STEIN

AGENT ORANGE

Glass: Old-fashioned
Garnish: Orange zest twist
Method: **SHAKE** all ingredients with ice and strain into ice-filled glass.

1	shot(s)	**Ketel One vodka**
½	shot(s)	**Grand Marnier liqueur**
½	shot(s)	**Cointreau triple sec**
2	shot(s)	**Freshly squeezed orange juice**

Comment: Fresh orange is good for you. This has all of the flavour but few of the health benefits.

AGGRAVATION

Glass: Old-fashioned
Garnish: Dust with freshly grated nutmeg
Method: **SHAKE** all ingredients with ice and strain into ice-filled glass.

2	shot(s)	**Scotch whisky**
¾	shot(s)	**Kahlúa coffee liqueur**
¾	shot(s)	**Double (heavy) cream**
¾	shot(s)	**Milk**
¼	shot(s)	**Sugar syrup (2 sugar to 1 water)**

Comment: If you like Scotch and enjoy creamy drinks, you'll love this.

AIR MAIL

Glass: Martini
Garnish: Mint leaf
Method: **STIR** honey with rum in base of shaker until honey dissolves. Add lemon and orange juice, **SHAKE** with ice and fine strain into chilled glass. **TOP** with champagne.

1	shot(s)	**Golden rum**
2	spoons	**Runny honey**
½	shot(s)	**Freshly squeezed lime juice**
½	shot(s)	**Freshly squeezed orange juice**
Top up with		**Brut champagne**

Origin: This old classic is basically a Honeysuckle topped up with champagne.
Comment: Rum, honey and a touch of citrus freshness make this one of the better champagne cocktails.

A.J.

Glass: Martini
Garnish: Dust with cinnamon powder
Method: **SHAKE** all ingredients with ice and fine strain into chilled glass.

2	shot(s)	**Boulard Grand Solage Calvados**
2	shot(s)	**Freshly squeezed grapefruit juice**
½	shot(s)	**Sugar syrup (2 sugar to 1 water)**

Comment: Amazingly simple and beautifully balanced. I hope you like apple brandy as much as I do.

AKU AKU [NEW #7]

Glass: Large Martini (10oz)
Garnish: Pineapple wedge & cherry on rim
Method: **BLEND** all ingredients with 12oz scoop crushed ice. Serve with short straws.

1	shot(s)	**Light white rum**
½	shot(s)	**Teichenné Peach Schnapps Liqueur**
1½	shot(s)	**Pressed pineapple juice**
½	shot(s)	**Sugar syrup (2 sugar to 1 water)**
¾	shot(s)	**Freshly squeezed lime juice**
10	fresh	**Mint leaves**

Origin: Adapted from Victor Bergeron's 'Trader Vic's Bartender's Guide' (1972 revised edition).
Comment: This Tiki classic looks a little like frozen stagnant pond water but tastes minty fresh and rather good.

ALABAMA SLAMMER #1 [UPDATED #7]

Glass: Martini
Garnish: Orange zest twist
Method: **SHAKE** all ingredients with ice and fine strain into chilled glass.

1½	shot(s)	**Ketel One vodka**
¾	shot(s)	**Southern Comfort liqueur**
1	shot(s)	**Freshly squeezed orange juice**
¼	shot(s)	**Pomegranate (grenadine) syrup**

Comment: None of the ingredients come from Alabama and the drink is served too long to slam. However, it's a good, rhythmic, rhyming name, if a little naff these days.

ALABAMA SLAMMER #2 [UPDATED #7]

Glass: Old-fashioned
Garnish: Peach wedge on rim
Method: SHAKE all ingredients with ice and strain into ice-filled glass.

1½	shot(s)	**Southern Comfort liqueur**
½	shot(s)	**Plymouth sloe gin liqueur**
½	shot(s)	**Luxardo Amaretto di Saschira**
2	shot(s)	**Freshly squeezed orange juice**
¾	shot(s)	**Freshly squeezed lemon juice**

Comment: Rich in flavour and quite sweet with a citrus bite. Surprisingly peachy!

THE ALAMAGOOZLUM COCKTAIL [UPDATED #7]

Glass: Martini
Garnish: Pineapple wedge on rim
Method: SHAKE all ingredients with ice and fine strain into chilled glass.

1	shot(s)	**Bokma jonge genever**
¾	shot(s)	**Yellow Chartreuse liqueur**
¾	shot(s)	**Wray & Nephew overproof white rum**
¼	shot(s)	**Grand Marnier liqueur***
¾	shot(s)	**Sugar syrup (2 sugar to 1 water)**
1	shot(s)	**Chilled mineral water**
¼	shot(s)	**Angostura aromatic bitters**
¼	fresh	**Egg white**

Origin: Adapted from David A. Embury's 1948 'Fine Art of Mixing Drinks', where he writes, "This cocktail is supposed to have been a speciality of the elder Morgan of the House of Morgan, which goes to prove as a bartender he was an excellent banker."
Comment: Even Mr Embury would approve of this version. Overproof Jamaican rum and copious amounts of bitters make this drink.

ALAN'S APPLE BREEZE

Glass: Collins
Garnish: Apple wedge on rim
Method: SHAKE all ingredients with ice and strain into ice-filled glass.

2	shot(s)	**Light white rum**
¾	shot(s)	**Giffard apricot brandy du Roussillon**
2	shot(s)	**Pressed apple juice**
2	shot(s)	**Ocean Spray cranberry juice**
½	shot(s)	**Freshly squeezed lime juice**
½	shot(s)	**Sugar syrup (2 sugar to 1 water)**

Origin: Created in 2002 by Alan Johnston at Metropolitan, Glasgow, Scotland.
Comment: A sweet, tangy version of the Apple Breeze.

DRINKS ARE GRADED AS FOLLOWS:

● DISGUSTING ●◐ PRETTY AWFUL ●● BEST AVOIDED
●●◐ DISAPPOINTING ●●● ACCEPTABLE ●●●◐ GOOD
●●●● RECOMMENDED ●●●●◐ HIGHLY RECOMMENDED
●●●●● OUTSTANDING / EXCEPTIONAL

ALASKA MARTINI [UPDATED #7]

Glass: Martini
Garnish: Orange zest twist
Method: SHAKE all ingredients with ice and fine strain into chilled glass.

2½	shot(s)	**Plymouth gin**
¾	shot(s)	**Yellow Chartreuse liqueur**
1	shot(s)	**Tio Pepe fino sherry**
3	dashes	**Fee Brothers orange bitters**

AKA: Nome
Origin: In his 1930 'The Savoy Cocktail Book', Harry Craddock writes, "So far as can be ascertained this delectable potion is NOT the staple diet of the Esquimaux. It was probably first thought of in South Carolina – hence its name." The addition of dry sherry is recommended in David Embury's 1948 'Fine Art of Mixing Drinks'.
Comment: If you like gin and Chartreuse, you'll love this strong and complex Martini.

ALASKAN MARTINI [NEW #7]

Glass: Martini
Garnish: Lime zest twist discarded & mint leaf
Method: STIR all ingredients with ice and strain into chilled glass.

2½	shot(s)	**Plymouth gin**
¾	shot(s)	**Yellow Chartreuse liqueur**

Origin: Modern version of the Alaska.
Comment: Stir long and well – this needs dilution. The result will appeal to gin and Chartreuse fans.

ALESSANDRO [UPDATED #7]

Glass: Martini
Garnish: Lemon zest twist
Method: SHAKE all ingredients with ice and fine strain into chilled glass.

1½	shot(s)	**Opal Nera black sambuca**
¾	shot(s)	**Plymouth gin**
¾	shot(s)	**Double (heavy) cream**
¾	shot(s)	**Milk**

Comment: Hints of aniseed, elderflower and gin emerge from this grey, creamy drink.

ALEXANDER

Glass: Martini
Garnish: Dust with freshly grated nutmeg
Method: SHAKE all ingredients with ice and fine strain into chilled glass.

1½	shot(s)	**Plymouth gin**
1	shot(s)	**Giffard white crème de cacao**
¾	shot(s)	**Double (heavy) cream**
¾	shot(s)	**Milk**

AKA: Gin Alexander or Princess Mary
Comment: A Prohibition favourite – white, smooth and better than you'd imagine.

ALEXANDER

The original Alexander, a mix of gin, crème de cacao and cream, came into existence early in the twentieth century, certainly before 1917. It became a Prohibition favourite as the cream and nutmeg garnish disguised the rough taste of homemade 'bathtub' gin. While the original, gin based Alexander has slipped from popularity, its successors, particularly the Brandy Alexander, have an enduring place on the world's cocktail lists.

Alexander variations include
Alessandro
Alexander the Great
Alexander's Big Brother
Alexander's Sister
Alexandra
Bird of Paradise
Brandy Alexander
Cherry Alexander
Irish Alexander

ALEXANDER THE GREAT [UPDATED #7]

Glass: Martini
Garnish: Dust with freshly grated nutmeg
Method: SHAKE all ingredients with ice and fine strain into chilled glass.

1½ shot(s) **Ketel One vodka**
½ shot(s) **Kahlúa coffee liqueur**
½ shot(s) **Giffard white crème de cacao**
¾ shot(s) **Double (heavy) cream**
¾ shot(s) **Milk**

Comment: A tasty combination of coffee, chocolate and cream, laced with vodka.

ALEXANDER'S BIG BROTHER

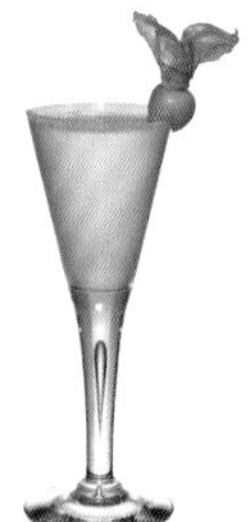

Glass: Martini
Garnish: Physalis (Cape gooseberry) on rim
Method: SHAKE all ingredients with ice and fine strain into chilled glass.

1½ shot(s) **Plymouth gin**
¼ shot(s) **Cointreau triple sec**
¾ shot(s) **Bols Blue curaçao liqueur**
¾ shot(s) **Double (heavy) cream**
¾ shot(s) **Milk**

Comment: Orangey in taste and creamy blue in colour - mildly better than pink for the macho out there.

ALEXANDER'S SISTER

Glass: Martini
Garnish: Mint leaf
Method: SHAKE all ingredients with ice and fine strain into chilled glass.

1½ shot(s) **Plymouth gin**
¾ shot(s) **Giffard white crème de Menthe Pastille**
¾ shot(s) **Double (heavy) cream**
¾ shot(s) **Milk**

Comment: A green minty thing for dairy lovers.

ALEXANDRA

Glass: Martini
Garnish: Dust with freshly grated nutmeg
Method: SHAKE all ingredients with ice and fine strain into chilled glass.

1½ shot(s) **Pusser's navy rum**
1 shot(s) **Kahlúa coffee liqueur**
¾ shot(s) **Double (heavy) cream**
¾ shot(s) **Milk**

Comment: Surprisingly potent and spicy, despite the ladylike name.

ALFONSO

Glass: Flute
Garnish: Twist of lemon
Method: Coat sugar cube with bitters and drop into glass. **POUR** Dubonnet and then champagne into chilled glass.

1	cube	**Sugar**
4	dashes	**Angostura aromatic bitters**
1/2	shot(s)	**Dubonnet Red**
Top up with		**Brut champagne**

Origin: Named after the deposed Spanish king Alfonso XIII, who first tasted this drink while exiled in France.
Comment: Herbal variation on the classic Champagne Cocktail.

ALFONSO MARTINI [NEW #7]

Glass: Martini
Garnish: Orange zest twist
Method: SHAKE all ingredients with ice and fine strain into chilled glass.

1/2	shot(s)	**Plymouth gin**
1	shot(s)	**Grand Marnier liqueur**
1/2	shot(s)	**Dry vermouth**
1/4	shot(s)	**Sweet vermouth**
2	dashes	**Angostura aromatic bitters**
1/2	shot(s)	**Chilled mineral water** (omit if wet ice)

Origin: Adapted from Victor Bergeron's 'Trader Vic's Bartender's Guide' (1972 revised edition).
Comment: Dry yet slightly sweet with hints of orange, gin and warm spice.

ALGERIA [NEW #7]

Glass: Martini
Garnish: Orange zest twist
Method: SHAKE all ingredients with ice and fine strain into chilled glass.

2	shot(s)	**Pisco**
1/2	shot(s)	**Cointreau triple sec**
1/2	shot(s)	**Giffard apricot brandy du Roussillon**
3/4	shot(s)	**Chilled mineral water** (reduce if wet ice)

Origin: Modern adaptation of a classic.
Comment: Pisco, apricot and orange combine wonderfully in this medium dry, balanced cocktail with a tangy bite.

ALGONQUIN

Glass: Old-fashioned
Garnish: Cherry on stick
Method: SHAKE all ingredients with ice and strain into ice-filled glass.

2	shot(s)	**Rye whiskey**
1 1/4	shot(s)	**Dry vermouth**
1 1/4	shot(s)	**Pressed pineapple juice**
2	dashes	**Peychaud's aromatic bitters**

Origin: One of several classic cocktails accredited to New York City's Algonquin Hotel in the 1930s. Its true origins are lost in time.
Comment: Pineapple juice adds fruit and froth, while Peychaud's bitters combine subtly with the whiskey in this dry, aromatic drink.

ALICE FROM DALLAS

Glass: Shot
Method: Refrigerate ingredients then **LAYER** in chilled glass by carefully pouring in the following order.

1/2	shot(s)	**Kahlúa coffee liqueur**
1/2	shot(s)	**Grand Marnier liqueur**
1/2	shot(s)	**Partida tequila**

Comment: Coffee and orange spiked with tequila.

ALICE IN WONDERLAND

Glass: Shot
Garnish: Lime wedge
Method: Refrigerate ingredients then **LAYER** in chilled glass by carefully pouring in the following order.

1	shot(s)	**Grand Marnier liqueur**
1/2	shot(s)	**Partida tequila**

Comment: Brings a whole new dimension to tequila and orange.

ALIEN SECRETION [NEW #7]

Glass: Collins
Garnish: Pineapple wedge & cherry
Method: SHAKE all ingredients with ice and strain into ice-filled glass.

2	shot(s)	**Ketel One vodka**
1/2	shot(s)	**Midori melon liqueur**
1/2	shot(s)	**Malibu coconut rum liqueur**
3	shot(s)	**Pressed pineapple juice**

Origin: One of many 80s cocktails with a dodgy name.
Comment: Lime green and fruity but all too drinkable, with a distinct bite despite its mild sweetness.

ALL FALL DOWN

Glass: Shot
Method: Refrigerate ingredients then **LAYER** in chilled glass by carefully pouring in the following order.

1/2	shot(s)	**Kahlúa coffee liqueur**
1/2	shot(s)	**Partida tequila**
1/2	shot(s)	**Pusser's Navy (54.5%) rum**

Comment: Too many of these and you will.

'RUM, N. GENERICALLY, FIERY LIQUORS THAT PRODUCE MADNESS IN TOTAL ABSTAINERS.'

AMBROSE BIERCE

A

ALL WHITE FRAPPÉ

Glass: Old-fashioned
Garnish: Lemon zest
Method: BLEND ingredients with 6oz scoop of crushed ice. Pour into glass and serve with short straws.

1	shot(s)	**Luxardo Sambuca dei Cesari**
1	shot(s)	**White crème de cacao liqueur**
1	shot(s)	**Giffard white creme de menthe pastille**
1	shot(s)	**Freshly squeezed lemon juice**

Comment: Aniseed, chocolate, peppermint and lemon juice are an unlikely but tasty combination for summer afternoons.

ALLEGROTTINI [NEW #7]

Glass: Martini
Garnish: Orange zest twist
Method: SHAKE all ingredients with ice and fine strain into chilled glass.

1½	shot(s)	**Ketel One Citroen vodka**
¾	shot(s)	**Cointreau triple sec**
¼	shot(s)	**Dry vermouth**
¾	shot(s)	**Freshly squeezed orange juice**
¼	shot(s)	**Freshly squeezed lime juice**

Origin: Discovered in 2005 at the Four Seasons Hotel, Prague, Czech Republic.
Comment: Strongly citrus but dry rather than bitter.

ALMOND MARTINI #1

Glass: Martini
Garnish: Sink three roasted almonds
Method: SHAKE all ingredients with ice and fine strain into chilled glass.

2	shot(s)	**Ketel One vodka**
½	shot(s)	**Freshly squeezed lemon juice**
½	shot(s)	**Almond (orgeat) sugar syrup**
1	shot(s)	**Pressed apple juice**
2	dashes	**Fee Brothers peach bitters (optional)**

Origin: Created in 2004 by Matt Pomeroy at Baltic, London, England.
Comment: Almond inspired with hints of apple and lemon juice.

ALMOND MARTINI #2 [UPDATED #7]

Glass: Martini
Garnish: Sink three almonds
Method: SHAKE all ingredients with ice and fine strain into chilled glass.

2	shot(s)	**Almond flavoured vodka**
¾	shot(s)	**Luxardo Amaretto di Saschira**
¼	shot(s)	**Dry vermouth**
¾	shot(s)	**Chilled mineral water** (omit if wet ice)

Origin: Created in 2005 by yours truly.
Comment: A delicate, almond flavoured Vodka Martini.

ALMOND OLD FASHIONED

Glass: Old-fashioned
Garnish: Orange zest twist
Method: STIR one shot of tequila with two ice cubes in a glass. Add amaretto, agave syrup, bitters and two more ice cubes. Stir some more then add another two ice cubes and the remaining tequila. Stir lots more so as to melt ice then add more ice. The melting and stirring in of ice cubes is essential to the dilution and taste of the drink.

2	shot(s)	**Partida tequila**
¼	shot(s)	**Luxardo Amaretto di Saschira**
¼	shot(s)	**Agave syrup**
3	dashes	**Fee Brothers orange bitters**

Origin: Created in 2005 by Mark Pratt at Maze, London, England.
Comment: One to please fans of both tequila and the Old Fashioned drinks genre.

AMARETTO SOUR

Glass: Old-fashioned
Garnish: lemon & cherry on stick (sail)
Method: SHAKE all ingredients with ice and strain into ice-filled glass.

2	shot(s)	**Luxardo Amaretto di Saschira**
1¼	shot(s)	**Freshly squeezed lemon juice**
½	fresh	**Egg white**
2	dashes	**Angostura aromatic bitters**

Comment: Sweet 'n' sour – frothy with an almond buzz

AMBER

Glass: Collins
Garnish: Apple wedge & nutmeg dust
Method: MUDDLE ginger in base of shaker. Add other ingredients, **SHAKE** with ice and strain into glass filled with crushed ice.

4	slices	**Fresh root ginger (thumbnail sized)**
1½	shot(s)	**Zubrówka bison vodka**
4	shot(s)	**Pressed apple juice**
½	shot(s)	**Sugar syrup (2 sugar to 1 water)**
½	shot(s)	**Apple schnapps liqueur**

Origin: Created in 2001 by Douglas Ankrah for Akbar at the Red Fort, Soho, London, England.
Comment: A fantastic combination of adult flavours in a long, thirst-quenching drink. Also great served up.

AMBROSIA

Glass: Flute
Method: SHAKE first four ingredients with ice and strain into glass. **TOP** with champagne.

1	shot(s)	**Rémy Martin cognac**
1	shot(s)	**Boulard Grand Solage Calvados**
¼	shot(s)	**Freshly squeezed lemon juice**
¼	shot(s)	**Cointreau triple sec**
Top up with		**Brut champagne**

Comment: Dry, fortified champers with a hint of apple.

AMBROSIA COCKTAIL

Glass: Martini
Garnish: Dust with freshly grated nutmeg
Method: SHAKE all ingredients with ice and fine strain into chilled glass.

$^3/_4$ shot(s) **Rémy Martin cognac**
2 shot(s) **Bols Advocaat liqueur**
1 shot(s) **Cuarenta Y Tres (Licor 43) liqueur**
$^1/_2$ shot(s) **Yellow Chartreuse liqueur**

Origin: I created this drink and named it after the Greek for 'elixir of life, the food of the gods'. In Britain Ambrosia is a brand of custard, so advocaat seemed appropriate, while, if there is a God, he/she/it surely drinks Chartreuse.
Comment: Easy-drinking but complex with a herbal edge.

AMERICAN BEAUTY #1 [UPDATED #7]

Glass: Large (10oz) Martini
Garnish: Float rose petal
Method: SHAKE first six ingredients with ice and fine strain into chilled glass.
Use the back of a spoon to **FLOAT** red wine over drink.

$2^1/_2$ shot(s) **Rémy Martin cognac**
$^1/_2$ shot(s) **Dry vermouth**
$^1/_2$ shot(s) **Giffard white crème de Menthe Pastille**
$^1/_2$ shot(s) **Freshly squeezed orange juice**
$^1/_2$ shot(s) **Pomegranate (grenadine) syrup**
$^3/_4$ shot(s) **Chilled mineral water** (reduce if wet ice)
$^1/_4$ shot(s) **Red wine**

Origin: Adapted from David A. Embury's 1948 'Fine Art of Mixing Drinks'.
Variant: When served in a tall glass with crushed ice this is called an American Beauty Punch.
Comment: Both fresh and refreshing - a subtle hint of peppermint gives zing to this cognac cocktail.

AMERICAN BEAUTY #2 [NEW #7]

Glass: Martini
Garnish: Mint leaf
Method: SHAKE first five ingredients with ice and fine strain into chilled glass. Use the back of a soup spoon to **FLOAT** port over drink.

1 shot(s) **Rémy Martin cognac**
1 shot(s) **Dry vermouth**
$^1/_4$ shot(s) **White crème de menthe**
1 shot(s) **Freshly squeezed orange juice**
$^1/_2$ shot(s) **Pomegranate (grenadine) syrup**
$^1/_2$ shot(s) **Tawny port**

Origin: Adapted from Victor Bergeron's 'Trader Vic's Bartender's Guide' (1972 revised edition).
Comment: Invigorating and peppermint fresh yet sophisticated and complex.

AMERICAN PIE MARTINI

Glass: Martini
Garnish: Apple wedge on rim
Method: SHAKE all ingredients with ice and fine strain into chilled glass.

$1^1/_2$ shot(s) **Buffalo Trace bourbon whiskey**
$^1/_2$ shot(s) **Apple schnapps liqueur**
$^1/_2$ shot(s) **Giffard crème de myrtille**
$^3/_4$ shot(s) **Ocean Spray cranberry juice**
$^1/_2$ shot(s) **Pressed apple juice**
$^1/_4$ shot(s) **Freshly squeezed lime juice**

Origin: Adapted from a recipe discovered at Oxo Tower Restaurant & Bar, London, England.
Comment: This berry and apple pie has a tangy bite.

AMERICANA

Glass: Flute
Garnish: Peach slice
Method: Coat sugar cube with bitters and drop into glass. **POUR** bourbon and then champagne into chilled glass.

1 cube **Sugar**
4 dashes **Angostura aromatic bitters**
$^1/_2$ shot(s) **Buffalo Trace bourbon whiskey**
Top up with **Brut sparkling champagne**

Comment: The Wild West take on the classic Champagne Cocktail.

AMERICANO

Glass: Collins
Garnish: Orange slice
Method: POUR Campari and vermouth into ice-filled glass and **TOP** with soda. Stir and serve with straws.

2 shot(s) **Campari**
2 shot(s) **Sweet vermouth**
Top up with **Soda water (club soda)**

Origin: First served in the 1860s in Gaspare Campari's bar in Milan, this was originally known as the 'Milano-Torino' as Campari came from Milano (Milan) and Cinzano from Torino (Turin). It was not until Prohibition that the Italians noticed an influx of Americans who enjoyed the drink and so dubbed it Americano.
Comment: A bitter, fizzy, long refreshing drink, which you'll love if you like Campari.

AMSTERDAM COCKTAIL [NEW #7]

Glass: Martini
Garnish: Orange zest twist
Method: SHAKE all ingredients with ice and fine strain into chilled glass.

2 shot(s) **Bokma Oude Genever**
1 shot(s) **Cointreau triple sec**
1 shot(s) **Freshly squeezed orange juice**
3 dashes **Fee Brothers orange bitters**

Origin: Adapted from Victor Bergeron's 'Trader Vic's Bartender's Guide' (1972 revised edition).
Comment: Very orange, dry but wonderfully smooth.

ANGEL FACE [NEW #7]

Glass: Martini
Garnish: Apple wedge on rim
Method: SHAKE all ingredients with ice and fine strain into chilled glass.

1	shot(s)	**Plymouth gin**
1	shot(s)	**Boulard Grand Solage Calvados**
1	shot(s)	**Giffard apricot brandy du Roussillon**

Origin: Adapted from Harry Craddock's 1930 'The Savoy Cocktail Book'.
Comment: Rich apricot and apple with a backbone of botanical gin. Balanced rather than dry or sweet.

ANGEL'S SHARE #1 [NEW #7]

Glass: Martini
Garnish: Orange zest twist
Method: STIR heaped spoon of orange marmalade with cognac in base of shaker until marmalade dissolves. Add other ingredients, **SHAKE** with ice and fine strain into chilled glass.

1	spoon	**Orange marmalade**
2	shot(s)	**Rémy Martin cognac**
$^{1}/_{4}$	shot(s)	**Cuarenta Y Tres (Licor 43) liqueur**
$^{1}/_{2}$	shot(s)	**Freshly squeezed lemon juice**
$^{1}/_{4}$	shot(s)	**Sugar syrup (2 sugar to 1 water)**

Origin: Created in 2005 by Milo Rodriguez, London.
Comment: Tangy citrus fruit and cognac smoothed with a sweet hint of vanilla.

ANGEL'S SHARE #2 [NEW #7]

Glass: Snifter
Method: POUR the Chartreuse into glass and coat the inside of the glass with the liqueur by tilting and rotating it. **DISCARD** excess liqueur. Carefully set the liqueur on the interior of the glass alight and allow it to **BURN** for a few seconds. Extinguish flame by placing a saucer over the glass, add other ingredients and **SWIRL** to mix. Beware of hot glass rim.

$^{1}/_{4}$	shot(s)	**Green Chartreuse liqueur**
$1^{1}/_{2}$	shot(s)	**Rémy Martin cognac**
$^{3}/_{4}$	shot(s)	**Nocello walnut liqueur**
$^{1}/_{2}$	shot(s)	**Tawny port**

Origin: Adapted from a recipe created in 2005 by Jacques Bezuidenhout at Harry Denton's Starlight Room, San Francisco, USA.
Comment: A fabulous drink, especially when VEP Chartreuse, family reserve cognac and 20 year old tawny port are used as per the original Starlight Room recipe.

DRINKS ARE GRADED AS FOLLOWS:

ANIS'TINI

Glass: Martini
Garnish: Star anise
Method: MUDDLE star anise in base of shaker. Add other ingredients, **SHAKE** with ice and fine strain into chilled glass.

2	dried	**Star anise**
1	shot(s)	**Ketel One vodka**
$^{3}/_{4}$	shot(s)	**Luxardo Sambuca dei Cesari**
$^{1}/_{2}$	shot(s)	**Pernod anis**
$1^{1}/_{2}$	shot(s)	**Chilled mineral water** (reduce if wet ice)

Origin: Discovered in 2002 at Lot 61, New York City, USA.
Comment: Specks of star anise are evident in this aniseedy Martini.

ANITA'S ATTITUDE ADJUSTER

Glass: Sling
Garnish: Lemon and cherry on stick (sail)
Method: SHAKE first seven ingredients with ice and strain into ice-filled glass. **TOP** with champagne and gently stir.

$^{1}/_{2}$	shot(s)	**Cointreau triple sec**
$^{1}/_{2}$	shot(s)	**Partida tequila**
$^{1}/_{2}$	shot(s)	**Light white rum**
$^{1}/_{2}$	shot(s)	**Plymouth gin**
$^{1}/_{2}$	shot(s)	**Ketel One vodka**
$^{1}/_{2}$	shot(s)	**Freshly squeezed lime juice**
$^{1}/_{2}$	shot(s)	**Sugar syrup (2 sugar to 1 water)**
Top up with		**Brut champagne**

Comment: Anita has a problem – she's indecisive when it comes to choosing base spirits.

ANTE [NEW #7]

Glass: Martini
Garnish: Orange zest twist
Method: STIR all ingredients with ice and strain into chilled glass.

2	shot(s)	**Boulard Grand Solage Calvados**
1	shot(s)	**Dubonnet Red**
$^{1}/_{2}$	shot(s)	**Cointreau triple sec**
2	dashes	**Angostura aromatic bitters**

Origin: Recipe adapted from one discovered in 2006 on drinkboy.com.
Comment: Medium dry, complex spiced apple with hints of orange.

APACHE

Glass: Shot
Method: Refrigerate ingredients then **LAYER** in chilled glass by carefully pouring in the following order.

$^{3}/_{4}$	shot(s)	**Kahlúa coffee liqueur**
$^{1}/_{2}$	shot(s)	**Midori melon liqueur**
$^{1}/_{2}$	shot(s)	**Irish cream liqueur**

AKA: Quick F.U.
Comment: A coffee, melon and whiskey cream layered shot.

APHRODISIAC

Glass: Collins
Garnish: Apple slice on rim
Method: MUDDLE ginger in base of shaker. Add other ingredients, **SHAKE** with ice and fine strain into ice-filled glass.

2	slices	**Fresh root ginger (thumbnail sized)**
2	shot(s)	**Vanilla-infused Ketel One vodka**
$\frac{1}{2}$	shot(s)	**Green Chartreuse liqueur**
$2\frac{1}{2}$	shot(s)	**Pressed apple juice**
$1\frac{1}{2}$	shot(s)	**Sauvignon Blanc wine**

Origin: Created in 2002 by Yannick Miseriaux at The Fifth Floor Bar, London, England.
Comment: As strong in flavour as it is high in alcohol.

'A MEDIUM VODKA DRY MARTINI—WITH A SLICE OF LEMON PEEL. SHAKEN AND NOT STIRRED.'

APPLE & BLACKBERRY PIE [UPDATED #7]

Glass: Martini
Garnish: Cinnamon dust & blackberry
Method: MUDDLE blackberries in base of shaker. Add vodka and apple juice, **SHAKE** with ice and fine strain into chilled glass. **FLOAT** cream on the surface of the drink by pouring over the back of a spoon and swirl to form a thin layer. Depending on the sweetness of your blackberries, you may need to add a touch of sugar syrup.

7	fresh	**Blackberries**
2	shot(s)	**Ketel One vodka**
1	shot(s)	**Pressed apple juice**
Float		**Double (heavy) cream**

Origin: Created in 2005 by yours truly.
Comment: A dessert in a glass, but not too sweet.

APPLE & CRANBERRY PIE [UPDATED #7]

Glass: Martini
Garnish: Dust with cinnamon powder
Method: SHAKE first three ingredients with ice and fine strain into chilled glass. **FLOAT** cream on surface of drink by pouring over the back of aspoon and swirl to form a thin layer.

$1\frac{1}{2}$	shot(s)	**Ketel One vodka**
$\frac{3}{4}$	shot(s)	**Apple schnapps liqueur**
1	shot(s)	**Ocean Spray cranberry juice**
Float		**Double (heavy) cream**

Origin: Created in 2003 by yours truly.
Comment: Sip apple and cranberry through a creamy cinnamon layer.

APPLE & CUSTARD COCKTAIL

Glass: Martini
Garnish: Apple wedge on rim
Method: SHAKE all ingredients with ice and fine strain into chilled glass.

2	shot(s)	**Bols advocaat liqueur**
$1\frac{1}{2}$	shot(s)	**Boulard Grand Solage Calvados**
$\frac{1}{2}$	shot(s)	**Apple schnapps liqueur**
$\frac{1}{4}$	shot(s)	**Vanilla sugar syrup**

Origin: I created this in 2002 after rediscovering advocaat on a trip to Amsterdam.
Comment: Smooth and creamy, this tastes like its name.

APPLE & ELDERFLOWER COLLINS [UPDATED #7]

Glass: Collins
Garnish: Lemon slice
Method: SHAKE first fouringredients with ice and strain into ice-filled glass. **TOP** with soda, stir and serve with straws.

$1\frac{1}{2}$	shot(s)	**Plymouth gin**
1	shot(s)	**St-Germain elderflower liqueur**
1	shot(s)	**Apple schnapps liqueur**
1	shot(s)	**Freshly squeezed lime juice**
Top up with		**Soda water (club soda)**

Origin: Formula by yours truly in 2004.
Comment: A John Collins with lime in place of lemon and sweetened with apple and elderflower liqueurs.

APPLE & ELDERFLOWER MARTINI (FRESH FRUIT) [NEW #7]

Glass: Martini
Garnish: Float wafer thin apple slice
Method: SHAKE all ingredients with ice and fine strain into chilled glass.

$1\frac{3}{4}$	shot(s)	**Ketel One vodka**
1	shot(s)	**St-Germain elderflower liqueur**
$1\frac{1}{4}$	shot(s)	**Pressed apple juice**

Origin: Created in 2006 by yours truly.
Comment: Light and easy - apple and elderflower laced with vodka.

APPLE & MELON MARTINI

Glass: Martini
Garnish: Apple wedge on rim
Method: SHAKE all ingredients with ice and fine strain into chilled glass.

2	shot(s)	**Ketel One vodka**
1	shot(s)	**Sour apple liqueur**
$\frac{1}{2}$	shot(s)	**Midori melon liqueur**
$\frac{1}{2}$	shot(s)	**Freshly squeezed lime juice**

Comment: The ubiquitous Green Apple Martini with extra colour and flavour thanks to a dash of melon liqueur.

A

APPLE & SPICE

Glass: Shot
Garnish: Dust with cinnamon powder
Method: Refrigerate ingredients then **LAYER** in chilled glass by carefully pouring in the following order.

3/4	shot(s)	**Boulard Grand Solage Calvados**
3/4	shot(s)	**Double (heavy) cream**

Comment: Creamy apple shot.

APPLE BUCK

Glass: Collins
Garnish: Apple wedge
Method: SHAKE first four ingredients with ice and strain into ice-filled glass. **TOP** with ginger ale.

1 1/2	shot(s)	**Boulard Grand Solage Calvados**
1/2	shot(s)	**Sour apple liqueur**
1	shot(s)	**Pressed apple juice**
1/2	shot(s)	**Freshly squeezed lime juice**
Top up with		**Ginger ale**

Origin: Adapted from a drink created in 2004 by Wayne Collins.
Comment: A refreshing long number with a taste reminiscent of cider.

APPLE BLOSSOM COCKTAIL [NEW #7]

Glass: Martini
Garnish: Apple wedge on rim
Method: SHAKE all ingredients with ice and fine strain into chilled glass.

2	shot(s)	**Boulard Grand Solage Calvados**
2	shot(s)	**Sweet vermouth**

Origin: Adapted from Victor Bergeron's 'Trader Vic's Bartender's Guide' (1972 revised edition).
Comment: Stupidly simple to mix but complex to taste – spiced and concentrated apple juice.

APPLE CART [UPDATED #7]

Glass: Martini
Garnish: Apple wedge on rim
Method: SHAKE all ingredients with ice and fine strain into chilled glass.

1 1/2	shot(s)	**Boulard Grand Solage Calvados**
1	shot(s)	**Cointreau triple sec**
1	shot(s)	**Freshly squeezed lemon juice**
1/2	shot(s)	**Chilled mineral water** (omit if wet ice)

AKA: Calvados Sidecar
Variant: Deauville
Origin: This classic cocktail is an adaptation of the even older Sidecar.
Comment: A serious combination of apple with orange and sweet with sour.

APPLE BRANDY SOUR [UPDATED #7]

Glass: Old-fashioned
Garnish: Lemon slice & cherry on stick (sail)
Method: SHAKE all ingredients with ice and strain into ice-filled glass.

2	shot(s)	**Boulard Grand Solage Calvados**
1	shot(s)	**Freshly squeezed lemon juice**
3/4	shot(s)	**Sugar syrup (2 sugar to 1 water)**
3	dashes	**Angostura aromatic bitters**
1/2	fresh	**Egg white**

Comment: Sour by name - balanced sweet and sour apple by nature.

APPLE CRUMBLE MARTINI #1

Glass: Martini
Garnish: Apple wedge on rim
Method: SHAKE all ingredients with ice and fine strain into chilled glass.

2	shot(s)	**Scotch whisky**
1/4	shot(s)	**Teichenné butterscotch Schnapps**
1	shot(s)	**Pressed apple juice**
1/2	shot(s)	**Freshly squeezed lemon juice**
1/4	shot(s)	**Sugar syrup (2 sugar to 1 water)**

Comment: That's the way the apple crumbles - in this case enhancing the flavour of the Scotch.

APPLE BREEZE [UPDATED #7]

Glass: Collins
Garnish: Apple wedge on rim
Method: SHAKE all ingredients with ice and strain into ice-filled glass.

2	shot(s)	**Zubrówka bison vodka**
2 1/2	shot(s)	**Pressed apple juice**
1 1/2	shot(s)	**Ocean Spray cranberry juice**

Variant: Substitute vodka for Zubrówka bison vodka.
Comment: A lot more interesting than the better known Sea Breeze.

APPLE CRUMBLE MARTINI #2

Glass: Martini
Garnish: Dust with cinnamon powder
Method: SHAKE all ingredients with ice and fine strain into chilled glass.

2	shot(s)	**Tuaca Italian liqueur**
1/2	shot(s)	**Freshly squeezed lemon juice**
2	shot(s)	**Pressed apple juice**

Origin: Created in 2002 by Eion Richards at Bond's Bar, London, England.
Comment: Easy to make and equally easy to drink.

APPLE DAIQUIRI 

Glass: Martini
Garnish: Apple wedge on rim
Method: SHAKE all ingredients with ice and fine strain into chilled glass.

2	shot(s)	**Light white rum**
1½	shot(s)	**Pressed apple juice**
½	shot(s)	**Freshly squeezed lime juice**
¼	shot(s)	**Sugar syrup (2 sugar to 1 water)**

Origin: Formula by yours truly in 2004.
Comment: A classic Daiquiri with a very subtle hint of apple.

APPLE MAC

Glass: Martini
Garnish: Float apple slice
Method: SHAKE all ingredients with ice and strain into ice-filled glass.

2	shot(s)	**Scotch whisky**
1½	shot(s)	**Pressed apple juice**
½	shot(s)	**Stone's Original green ginger wine**

Variant: Also suits being served over ice in an old-fashioned glass.
Origin: I created this twist on the classic Whisky Mac in 2004.
Comment: Scotch, ginger and apple are a threesome made in heaven.

APPLE MANHATTAN #1 [UPDATED #7]

Glass: Martini
Garnish: Apple slice on rim
Method: SHAKE all ingredients with ice and fine strain into chilled glass.

2	shot(s)	**Buffalo Trace bourbon whiskey**
1½	shot(s)	**Apple schnapps liqueur**
½	shot(s)	**Sweet vermouth**

Origin: My take on a drink created by David Marsden at First on First in New York City and latterly popularised by Dale DeGroff. Traditionalists may want to stir it.
Comment: Rusty gold in colour, this is a flavoursome number for bourbon lovers.

APPLE MANHATTAN #2 [NEW #7]

Glass: Martini
Garnish: Apple wedge on rim
Method: STIR all ingredients with ice and strain into chilled glass.

2	shot(s)	**Buffalo Trace bourbon whiskey**
¾	shot(s)	**Apple schnapps liqueur**
¼	shot(s)	**Cointreau triple sec**
½	shot(s)	**Sweet vermouth**

Origin: Created in 2005 by Åsa Nevestveit and Robert Sörman at Grill, Stockholm, Sweden.
Comment: Exactly as billed – a Manhattan with a hint of apple.

APPLE MARTINI #1 (SIMPLE VERSION) 

Glass: Martini
Garnish: Cherry in base of glass
Method: SHAKE all ingredients with ice and fine strain into chilled glass.

2½	shot(s)	**Ketel One vodka**
2	shot(s)	**Pressed apple juice**
¼	shot(s)	**Sugar syrup (2 sugar to 1 water)**

Variant: Sour Apple Martini, Caramelised Apple Martini
Origin: Formula by yours truly in 2004.
Comment: This is subtitled the simple version for good reason but, if freshly pressed juice is used, it's as good if not better than other Apple Martini recipes.

'FRANKLY, I WAS HORRIFIED BY LIFE, AT WHAT A MAN HAD TO DO SIMPLY IN ORDER TO EAT, SLEEP AND KEEP HIMSELF CLOTHED. SO I STAYED IN BED AND DRANK.'

APPLE MARTINI #2

Glass: Martini
Garnish: Apple wedge on rim
Method: SHAKE all ingredients with ice and fine strain into chilled glass.

2	shot(s)	**Ketel One vodka**
¾	shot(s)	**Apple schnapps liqueur**
2	shot(s)	**Pressed apple juice**

Comment: There are as many different recipes for this drink as there are varieties of apple and brands of apple liqueur: this is one of the more popular.

APPLE MOJITO [UPDATED #7]

Glass: Collins
Garnish: Mint sprig
Method: Lightly **MUDDLE** (just to bruise) mint in base of glass. Add other ingredients, half fill glass with crushed ice and **CHURN** (stir) with bar spoon. Fill glass to brim with more crushed ice and churn some more. Serve with straws.

12	fresh	**Mint leaves**
2	shot(s)	**Light white rum**
1	shot(s)	**Freshly squeezed lime juice**
1	shot(s)	**Apple schnapps liqueur**

Origin: Recipe by yours truly in 2005.
Comment: An enduring classic given a touch of apple. Those with a sweet tooth may want to add more apple liqueur or even a dash of sugar syrup.

A

APPLE OF ONE'S EYE

Glass: Collins
Garnish: Apple wedge on rim
Method: **SHAKE** first three ingredients with ice and strain into ice-filled glass. **TOP** with ginger beer.

2	shot(s)	**Rémy Martin cognac**
1/2	shot(s)	**Freshly squeezed lime juice**
1 1/2	shot(s)	**Pressed apple juice**
Top up with		**Ginger beer**

Comment: This spicy concoction is long and refreshing.

APPLE PIE MARTINI

Glass: Martini
Garnish: Apple wedge on rim
Method: **SHAKE** all ingredients with ice and fine strain into chilled glass.

1 1/2	shot(s)	**Zubrówka bison vodka**
1/2	shot(s)	**Cinnamon schnapps liqueur**
2	shot(s)	**Pressed apple juice**
1	shot(s)	**Ocean Spray cranberry juice**

Origin: Created in 2000 by Alexia Pau Barrera at Sand Bar, Clapham, England.
Comment: There's a good hit of cinnamon in this apple pie.

APPLE PIE SHOT

Glass: Shot
Garnish: Dust with cinnamon powder
Method: **SHAKE** first two ingredients with ice and strain into chilled glass. **FLOAT** cream on drink by carefully pouring over the back of a spoon.

1	shot(s)	**Apple schnapps liqueur**
1/2	shot(s)	**Frangelico hazelnut liqueur**
1/4	shot(s)	**Double cream**

Comment: Nuts, apple, cinnamon and cream – pudding, anyone?

APPLEISSIMO

Glass: Collins
Garnish: Apple slice on rim
Method: **SHAKE** first three ingredients with ice and strain into ice-filled glass. **TOP** with anis and serve with straws.

1 1/2	shot(s)	**Apple schnapps liqueur**
2	shot(s)	**Pressed apple juice**
1 1/2	shot(s)	**Ocean Spray cranberry juice**
1 1/2	shot(s)	**Pernod anis**

Comment: Stir the anis in with straws before drinking. Anis is best added last as it reacts on contact with ice.

APPLE SPRITZ

Glass: Flute
Garnish: Peach or apple slice on rim
Method: **POUR** first two ingredients into glass and top with champagne.

3/4	shot(s)	**Apple schnapps liqueur**
1/4	shot(s)	**Teichenné Peach Schnapps Liqueur**
Top up with		**Brut champagne**

Origin: Discovered in 2003 at Paramount Hotel, New York City, USA.
Comment: Sweet, fruity champagne – oh yeah, baby.

APPLE STRUDEL #1

Glass: Martini
Garnish: Dust with cinnamon powder
Method: **SHAKE** first five ingredients with ice and fine strain into chilled glass. Carefully **FLOAT** cream by pouring over the back of a spoon.

1	shot(s)	**Apple schnapps liqueur**
1/2	shot(s)	**Cinnamon schnapps liqueur**
1/2	shot(s)	**Giffard white crème de cacao**
1/2	shot(s)	**Giffard brown crème de cacao**
1	shot(s)	**Pressed apple juice**
3/4	shot(s)	**Double (heavy) cream**

Variant: May also be served as a shot.
Origin: Created in 1999 by Alex Kammerling, London, England.
Comment: This sweet dessert cocktail tastes just like mum's home-made apple pie with cream.

APPLE STRUDEL #2 [UPDATED #7]

Glass: Martini
Garnish: Coat half rim with cinnamon and sugar
Method: **SHAKE** all ingredients with ice and fine strain into chilled glass.

1 1/2	shot(s)	**Vanilla-infused Ketel One vodka**
1/2	shot(s)	**Scotch whisky**
1/2	shot(s)	**Apple schnapps liqueur**
1/2	shot(s)	**Dry vermouth**
1	shot(s)	**Pressed apple juice**

Origin: Recipe by yours truly in 2006.
Comment: Apple, vanilla and a hint of Scotch – reminiscent of the dessert but a good deal drier.

APPLE SUNRISE

Glass: Collins
Garnish: Apple slice
Method: **SHAKE** all ingredients with ice and strain into ice-filled glass.

2	shot(s)	**Boulard Grand Solage Calvados**
1/2	shot(s)	**Giffard Cassis Noir de Bourgogne**
3 1/2	shot(s)	**Freshly squeezed orange juice**

Origin: Created in 1980 by Charles Schumann, Munich, Germany.
Comment: A pleasing blend of fruits with the apple punch of Calvados.

APPLE VIRGIN MOJITO (MOCKTAIL)

Glass: Collins
Garnish: Mint sprig
Method: MUDDLE mint in base of glass. Add apple juice, sugar and lime juice. Half fill glass with crushed ice and **CHURN** (stir) with bar spoon. Fill glass to brim with more crushed ice and churn some more. Continue adding crushed ice and churning until glass is filled. Serve with straws.

12	fresh	**Mint leaves**
2	shot(s)	**Pressed apple juice**
1	shot(s)	**Freshly squeezed lime juice**
1/4	shot(s)	**Sugar syrup (2 sugar to 1 water)**

Variant: Add three dashes of Angostura aromatic bitters.
Comment: As non-alcoholic cocktails go this is one of the best.

APPLESINTH

Glass: Old-fashioned
Garnish: Apple wedge on rim
Method: SHAKE all ingredients with ice and strain into glass filled with crushed ice.

1	shot(s)	**La Fée Parisienne (68%) absinthe**
1	shot(s)	**Apple schnapps liqueur**
2	shot(s)	**Pressed apple juice**
3/4	shot(s)	**Freshly squeezed lime juice**
1/2	shot(s)	**Passion fruit sugar syrup**

Origin: Created in 1999 by Alex Kammerling, London, England.
Comment: Hints of apple and liquorice combine to make a very moreish cocktail.

APPLES 'N' PEARS

Glass: Martini
Garnish: Apple or pear slice on rim
Method: SHAKE all ingredients with ice and fine strain into chilled glass.

1	shot(s)	**Pear flavoured vodka**
1	shot(s)	**Boulard Grand Solage Calvados**
3/4	shot(s)	**Xanté pear brandy liqueur**
1 1/2	shot(s)	**Pressed apple juice**

Origin: Created in 2005 by yours truly.
Comment: 'Apples and pears' means stairs. Well worth climbing.

APPILY MARRIED [UPDATED #7]

Glass: Martini
Garnish: Coat half rim with cinnamon and sugar
Method: STIR honey with vodka in base of shaker until honey dissolves. Add apple juice, **SHAKE** with ice and fine strain into chilled glass.

2	spoons	**Runny honey**
2 1/2	shot(s)	**Ketel One vodka**
1/2	shot(s)	**Pressed apple juice**

Origin: Created in 2005 by yours truly.
Comment: Apple and honey are indeed a marriage made in heaven, especially when laced with grainy vodka notes.

APRICOT COSMO

Glass: Martini
Garnish: Apricot slice
Method: STIR apricot preserve with vodka until preserve dissolves. Add other ingredients, **SHAKE** with ice and fine strain into chilled glass.

2	shot(s)	**Ketel One vodka**
1	spoon	**Apricot preserve (St. Dalfour)**
1	shot(s)	**Ocean Spray cranberry juice**
1/4	shot(s)	**Passion fruit sugar syrup**
1/2	shot(s)	**Freshly squeezed lime juice**
2	dashes	**Fee Brothers orange bitters**

Origin: Created in 2004 at Aura Kitchen & Bar, London, England.
Comment: The apricot preserve adds a flavoursome tang to the contemporary classic.

APRICOT FIZZ [UPDATED #7]

Glass: Collins (8oz max)
Garnish: Lemon wedge
Method: SHAKE first three ingredients with ice and strain into ice-filled glass. **TOP** with soda water.

2	shot(s)	**Giffard apricot brandy du Roussillon**
1	shot(s)	**Freshly squeezed orange juice**
1/2	shot(s)	**Freshly squeezed lime juice**
Top up with		**Soda water (from siphon)**

Comment: This low-alcohol, refreshing cocktail is perfect for a summer afternoon.

APRICOT LADY SOUR

Glass: Old-fashioned
Garnish: Lemon sail (lemon slice & cherry)
Method: SHAKE all ingredients with ice and strain into ice-filled glass.

1 1/2	shot(s)	**Light white rum**
1	shot(s)	**Giffard apricot brandy du Roussillon**
1	shot(s)	**Freshly squeezed lemon juice**
1/4	shot(s)	**Sugar syrup (2 sugar to 1 water)**
1/2	fresh	**Egg white**

Comment: This seemingly soft and fluffy, apricot flavoured drink hides a most unladylike rum bite.

APRICOT MANGO MARTINI

Glass: Martini
Garnish: Mango slice
Method: MUDDLE mango in base of shaker. Add other ingredients, **SHAKE** with ice and fine strain into glass.

1	cupful	**Fresh diced mango**
2	shot(s)	**Plymouth gin**
1/2	shot(s)	**Giffard apricot brandy du Roussillon**
3/4	shot(s)	**Freshly squeezed lemon juice**
1/2	shot(s)	**Sugar syrup (2 sugar to 1 water)**

Variant: Use one-and-a-half shots of mango purée in place of fresh mango and halve amount of sugar syrup.
Comment: A simple, great tasting variation on the fresh fruit Martini.

A

APRICOT MARTINI

Glass: Martini
Garnish: Lemon zest twist
Method: SHAKE all ingredients with ice and fine strain into chilled glass.

1 1/2	shot(s)	**Plymouth gin**
1	shot(s)	**Giffard apricot brandy du Roussillon**
1/4	shot(s)	**Freshly squeezed lemon juice**
1/8	shot(s)	**Pomegranate (grenadine) syrup**
3	dashes	**Angostura aromatic bitters**
3/4	shot(s)	**Chilled mineral water** (omit if wet ice)

Comment: This scarlet cocktail combines gin, apricot and lemon juice.

APRIL SHOWER [UPDATED #7]

Glass: Martini
Garnish: Orange zest twist
Method: SHAKE all ingredients with ice and fine strain into chilled glass.

2	shot(s)	**Rémy Martin cognac**
1/2	shot(s)	**Bénédictine D.O.M. liqueur**
1 1/2	shot(s)	**Freshly squeezed orange juice**

Comment: This mustard coloured, medium dry, cognac-based drink harnesses the uniquely herbal edge of Bénédictine.

APRICOT SOUR

Glass: Old-fashioned
Garnish: Lemon zest twist
Method: STIR apricot jam (preserve) with bourbon until it dissolves. Add other ingredients, **SHAKE** with ice and fine strain into ice-filled glass.

2	spoons	**Apricot jam (preserve)**
1 1/2	shot(s)	**Buffalo Trace bourbon whiskey**
1/2	shot(s)	**Giffard apricot brandy du Roussillon**
1	shot(s)	**Pressed apple juice**
1/2	shot(s)	**Freshly squeezed lemon juice**

Origin: Created in 2005 by Wayne Collins for Maxxium UK.
Comment: Short and fruity.

AQUARIUS

Glass: Old-fashioned
Method: SHAKE all ingredients with ice and strain into ice-filled glass.

2	shot(s)	**Scotch whisky**
1	shot(s)	**Cherry (brandy) liqueur**
1 1/2	shot(s)	**Ocean Spray cranberry juice**

Comment: A sweet cherry edge is balanced by the dryness of cranberry and Scotch.

THE ARGYLL [NEW #7]

Glass: Martini
Garnish: Orange zest twist
Method: STIR all ingredients with ice and strain into chilled glass.

2	shot(s)	**Southern Comfort liqueur**
1	shot(s)	**Sweet vermouth**
1	dash	**Fee Brothers orange bitters**

Comment: Southern Comfort lovers only need apply.

ARIZONA BREEZE

Glass: Collins
Garnish: Grapefruit wedge on rim
Method: SHAKE all ingredients with ice and strain into ice-filled glass.

2 1/2	shot(s)	**Plymouth gin**
3	shot(s)	**Ocean Spray cranberry juice**
2	shot(s)	**Freshly squeezed grapefruit juice**

Comment: A tart variation on the Sea Breeze – as dry as Arizona.

ARMILLITA CHICO [NEW #7]

Glass: Martini (large 10oz)
Garnish: Lime wedge on rim
Method: BLEND all ingredients with 12oz scoop crushed ice.

2	shot(s)	**Partida tequila**
1	shot(s)	**Freshly squeezed lime juice**
1/2	shot(s)	**Pomegranate (grenadine) syrup**
2	dashes	**Orange flower water**

Comment: Similar to a frozen Margarita but more subtle and dry.

ARMY & NAVY [NEW #7]

Glass: Martini
Garnish: Lemon zest twist
Method: SHAKE all ingredients with ice and fine strain into chilled glass.

2	shot(s)	**Plymouth gin**
1/2	shot(s)	**Freshly squeezed lemon juice**
1/4	shot(s)	**Almond (orgeat) syrup**
1/2	shot(s)	**Chilled mineral water** (omit if wet ice)

Origin: This old classic was originally made to an 8:4:4 formula but I have borrowed this 8:2:1 formula from David A. Embury's 1948 'Fine Art of Mixing Drinks' (he describes the original formulation as "horrible"). The addition of water is a Difford touch.
Comment: Almond and lemon flavoured gin. Subtle, citrusy and dry.

ARNAUD MARTINI [UPDATED #7]

Glass: Martini
Garnish: Blackberry on rim
Method: STIR all ingredients with ice and strain into chilled glass.

1	shot(s)	**Plymouth gin**
1	shot(s)	**Dry vermouth**
1	shot(s)	**Giffard Cassis (or Chambord)**

Origin: A classic cocktail named after the pre-war stage actress Yvonne Arnaud.
Comment: An interesting balance of blackcurrant, vermouth and gin. Sweet palate and dry finish.

ARNOLD PALMER (MOCKTAIL) [NEW #7]

Glass: Collins
Garnish: Lemon slice
Method: SHAKE all ingredients with ice and strain into ice-filled glass.

2	shot(s)	**Freshly squeezed lemon juice**
1	shot(s)	**Sugar syrup (2 sugar to 1 water)**
3	shot(s)	**Cold breakfast tea**

Variants: Tom Arnold, John Daly
Origin: A popular drink throughout the United States. Named after and said to be a favourite of the legendary golfer.
Comment: Real lemon iced tea. Balanced and wonderfully refreshing.

ARTLANTIC

Glass: Collins
Garnish: Orange wedge
Method: SHAKE all ingredients with ice and strain into ice-filled glass.

1	shot(s)	**Spiced rum**
1/2	shot(s)	**Luxardo Amaretto di Saschira**
1/2	shot(s)	**Bols Blue curaçao liqueur**
1/2	shot(s)	**Freshly squeezed lime juice**
3	shot(s)	**Pressed apple juice**

Origin: Atlantic Bar & Grill, London, England.
Comment: This sea green cocktail tastes much better than it looks.

ASIAN GINGER MARTINI

Glass: Martini
Garnish: Ginger slice on rim
Method: MUDDLE ginger in base of shaker. Add other ingredients, **SHAKE** with ice and fine strain into chilled glass.

2	slices	**Fresh root ginger (thumbnail sized)**
1 1/2	shot(s)	**Ketel One vodka**
2 1/4	shot(s)	**Sake**
1/4	shot(s)	**Sugar syrup (2 sugar to 1 water)**

Origin: Adapted from a recipe created in 2004 by Chris Langan of Barnomadics.
Comment: Lightly spiced with ginger, distinctly oriental in character.

ASIAN MARY

Glass: Collins
Garnish: Lemongrass
Method: MUDDLE ginger in base of shaker and add vodka. Squeeze wasabi paste onto bar spoon and **STIR** with vodka and ginger until dissolved. Add other ingredients, **SHAKE** with ice and fine strain into ice-filled glass.

3	slices	**Fresh root ginger (thumbnail sized)**
3	peas	**Wasabi paste**
2	shot(s)	**Ketel One Citroen vodka**
1	spoon	**Soy sauce**
4	shot(s)	**Tomato sauce**
1/2	shot(s)	**Freshly squeezed lemon juice**

Comment: An aptly named Bloody Mary with plenty of Asian spice.

ASIAN PEAR MARTINI

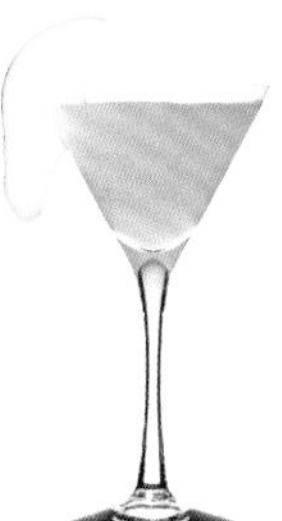

Glass: Martini
Garnish: Pear slice on rim
Method: SHAKE all ingredients with ice and fine strain into chilled glass.

2	shot(s)	**Sake**
1/4	shot(s)	**Xanté pear brandy liqueur**
1/2	shot(s)	**Poire William eau de vie**
1 1/2	shot(s)	**Freshly extracted pear juice**
1/4	shot(s)	**Freshly squeezed lemon juice**

Origin: Created in 2002 by yours truly.
Comment: Sake and pear juice with a kick.

ASSISTED SUICIDE

Glass: Shot
Method: SHAKE first two ingredients with ice and strain into chilled glass. **TOP** with cola.

1	shot(s)	**Wray & Nephew overproof rum**
1/2	shot(s)	**Jägermeister**
Top up with		**Cola**

Comment: Not for the faint-hearted.

ASYLUM COCKTAIL [NEW #7]

Glass: Old-fashioned
Method: POUR ingredients into glass without ice and **STIR**. Gently add ice and do NOT stir again. Consume once drink has turned cloudy.

1 1/2	shot(s)	**Plymouth gin**
1 1/2	shot(s)	**Pernod anis**
1/4	shot(s)	**Pomegranate (grenadine) syrup**

Origin: Created by William Seabrook, famous for his account of eating human flesh, and first published in a 1935 book, 'So Red the Nose, or Breath in the Afternoon'.
Comment: Seabrook said of this drink, "look like rosy dawn, taste like the milk of Paradise, and make you plenty crazy." He must have been a Pernod lover!

A

ATHOLL BROSE

Glass: Martini
Garnish: Dust with freshly grated nutmeg
Method: Prepare oatmeal water by soaking three heaped tablespoons of oatmeal in half a mug of warm water. Stir and leave to stand for fifteen minutes. Then strain to extract the creamy liquid and discard what's left of the oatmeal.

To make the drink, **STIR** honey with Scotch until honey dissolves. Add other ingredients, **SHAKE** with ice and fine strain into chilled glass.

2 spoons **Runny heather honey**
2 shot(s) **Scotch whisky**
$1^1/_2$ shot(s) **Oatmeal water**
$^1/_4$ shot(s) **Drambuie liqueur**
$^1/_4$ shot(s) **Luxardo Amaretto di Saschira**
$^1/_2$ shot(s) **Double (heavy) cream**

Origin: My adaptation of a Scottish classic. Legend has it that Atholl Brose was created by the Earl of Atholl in 1475 when he was trying to capture Iain MacDonald, Lord of the Isles and leader of a rebellion against the king. Hearing rumours that MacDonald was drawing his drinking water from a small well, the Earl ordered it to be filled with honey, whisky and oatmeal. MacDonald lingered at the well enjoying the concoction and was captured.
Comment: Forget the porridge and kick start your day with a Atholl Brose.

ATLANTIC BREEZE

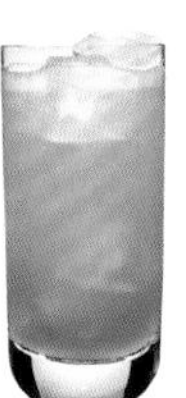

Glass: Collins
Garnish: Orange slice
Method: SHAKE all ingredients with ice and strain into ice-filled glass.

$1^1/_2$ shot(s) **Light white rum**
$^1/_2$ shot(s) **Giffard apricot brandy du Roussillon**
$^1/_4$ shot(s) **Galliano liqueur**
$2^1/_2$ shot(s) **Pressed pineapple juice**
$^1/_2$ shot(s) **Freshly squeezed lemon juice**

Comment: A fruity, tropical cocktail finished with herbal and citrus notes.

ATOMIC COCKTAIL

Glass: Martini
Garnish: Orange zest twist
Method: SHAKE first three ingredients with ice and fine strain into chilled glass. **TOP** with champagne.

$1^1/_4$ shot(s) **Ketel One vodka**
$1^1/_4$ shot(s) **Rémy Martin cognac**
$^1/_2$ shot(s) **Amontillado sherry**
Top up with **Brut champagne**

Origin: Created in the early 50s in Las Vegas. A-bomb tests were being conducted in Nevada at the time.
Comment: Golden and flavoursome – handle with care.

ATOMIC DOG

Glass: Collins
Garnish: Pineapple wedge and cherry
Method: SHAKE all ingredients with ice and strain into ice-filled glass.

$1^1/_2$ shot(s) **Light white rum**
$^3/_4$ shot(s) **Midori melon liqueur**
$^3/_4$ shot(s) **Malibu coconut rum liqueur**
$2^1/_2$ shot(s) **Pressed pineapple juice**
$^3/_4$ shot(s) **Freshly squeezed lemon juice**

Comment: A long, refreshing tropical drink with melon, coconut and pineapple juice.

ATTITUDE ADJUSTER

Glass: Hurricane
Garnish: Orange slice& cherry on stick (sail)
Method: SHAKE first three ingredients with ice and strain into ice-filled glass. **TOP** with cola then **DRIZZLE** orange and coffee liqueurs.

2 shot(s) **Plymouth gin**
1 shot(s) **Cointreau triple sec**
$^3/_4$ shot(s) **Freshly squeezed lime juice**
Top up with **Cola**
$^1/_4$ shot(s) **Grand Marnier**
$^1/_4$ shot(s) **Kahlúa coffee liqueur**

Comment: I've simplified and tried to improve this somewhat dodgy but popular cocktail – sorry, I failed!

THE ATTY COCKTAIL [NEW #7]

Glass: Martini
Garnish: Lemon zest twist
Method: SHAKE all ingredients with ice and fine strain into chilled glass.

$2^1/_4$ shot(s) **Plymouth gin**
$^3/_4$ shot(s) **Dry vermouth**
$^1/_4$ shot(s) **La Feé Parisienne (68%) absinthe**
$^1/_4$ shot(s) **Benoit Serres violet liqueur**

Origin: Adapted from Harry Craddock's 1930 'The Savoy Cocktail Book'.
Comment: Dry and aromatic with floral hints and aniseed notes.

AUNT AGATHA

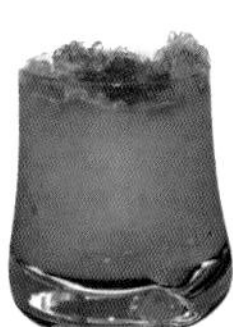

Glass: Old-fashioned
Garnish: Orange zest twist
Method: SHAKE first three ingredients with ice and strain into glass filled with crushed ice. **DRIP** bitters over surface.

$1^1/_2$ shot(s) **Pusser's navy rum**
2 shot(s) **Freshly squeezed orange juice**
1 shot(s) **Pressed pineapple juice**
3 dashes **Angostura aromatic bitters**

Origin: Aunt Hagatha was one of Samantha's aunts in the 1960s TV series 'Bewitched'; Aunt Agatha was Bertie Wooster's terrifying aunt in P.G. Wodehouse's books.
Comment: A most unusual looking, tropical tasting concoction.

AUNT EMILY

Glass: Martini
Garnish: Apricot wedge on rim
Method: SHAKE all ingredients with ice and fine strain into chilled glass.

$1\frac{1}{2}$	shot(s)	**Plymouth gin**
$1\frac{1}{2}$	shot(s)	**Boulard Grand Solage Calvados**
$\frac{3}{4}$	shot(s)	**Giffard apricot brandy du Roussillon**
$\frac{3}{4}$	shot(s)	**Freshly squeezed orange juice**
$\frac{1}{8}$	shot(s)	**Pomegranate (grenadine) syrup**

Origin: A forgotten classic.
Comment: Aunt Emily is onto something as these ingredients combine to make a stylish fruity Martini.

AUNTIE'S HOT XMAS PUNCH

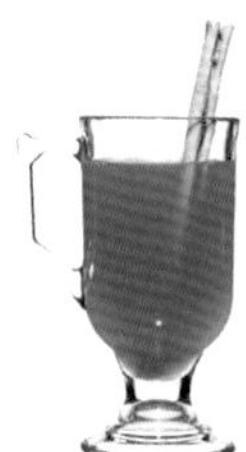

Glass: Toddy
Garnish: Cinnamon stick in glass
Method: POUR all ingredients into glass and stir. **MICROWAVE** for a minute (vary time depending on your microwave oven), stir again and serve.

$\frac{3}{4}$	shot(s)	**Freshly squeezed lemon juice**
$1\frac{1}{2}$	shot(s)	**Pedro Ximénez sherry**
$2\frac{1}{4}$	shot(s)	**Rémy Martin cognac**
3	shot(s)	**Pressed apple juice**
4	dashes	**Peychaud's aromatic bitters**

Origin: I created this drink to serve live on Christmas Eve 2002 during a broadcast on BBC radio. 'Auntie' is a nickname for the BBC and the drink uses the traditional punch proportions of 1 sour, 2 sweet, 3 strong and 4 weak.
Comment: A fruity seasonal warmer.

'IT'S BEEN SO LONG SINCE I'VE HAD CHAMPAGNE.'
LAST WORDS OF ANTON CHEKHOV

AUTUMN MARTINI

Glass: Martini
Garnish: Orange zest twist
Method: Cut passion fruit in half and scoop out flesh into shaker. Add other ingredients, **SHAKE** with ice and fine strain into chilled glass.

1	fresh	**Passion fruit**
2	shot(s)	**Zubrówka bison vodka**
1	shot(s)	**Pressed apple juice**
$\frac{1}{2}$	shot(s)	**Passion fruit sugar syrup**
$\frac{1}{2}$	fresh	**Egg white**

Origin: Created in 2004 by yours truly, inspired by Max Warner's excellent Autumn Punch.
Comment: An easy drinking, smooth, fruity cocktail with grassy hints courtesy of bison vodka.

A

AUTUMN PUNCH

Glass: Sling
Garnish: Physalis (Cape gooseberry) on rim
Method: Cut passion fruit in half and scoop out flesh into shaker. Add vodka, passion fruit sugar syrup, pear and lemon juice, **SHAKE** with ice and strain into ice-filled glass. **TOP** with champagne.

1	fresh	**Passion fruit**
2	shot(s)	**Zubrówka bison vodka**
$\frac{1}{4}$	shot(s)	**Passion fruit sugar syrup**
1	shot(s)	**Freshly extracted pear juice**
$\frac{1}{2}$	shot(s)	**Freshly squeezed lemon juice**
Top up with		**Brut champagne**

Origin: Created in 2001 by Max Warner at Baltic Bar, London, England.
Comment: Autumnal in colour with a wonderful meld of complementary flavours.

AVALANCHE

Glass: Collins
Garnish: Banana slice on rim
Method: BLEND ingredients with 12oz scoop of crushed ice. Pour into glass and serve with straws.

2	shot(s)	**Giffard crème de banane du Brésil**
1	shot(s)	**Bols White crème de cacao**
$\frac{1}{2}$	shot(s)	**Luxardo Amaretto di Saschira**
1	shot(s)	**Double (heavy) cream**
1	shot(s)	**Milk**
$\frac{1}{2}$	fresh	**Peeled banana**

Origin: Created in 1979 at Maudes Bar, New York City, USA.
Comment: Creamy, rich and smooth. Fluffy but lovely.

AVALANCHE SHOT

Glass: Shot
Method: Refrigerate ingredients then **LAYER** in chilled glass by carefully pouring in the following order.

$\frac{1}{2}$	shot(s)	**Kahlúa coffee liqueur**
$\frac{1}{2}$	shot(s)	**Giffard white crème de cacao**
$\frac{1}{2}$	shot(s)	**Southern Comfort liqueur**

Comment: Rich, smooth and sticky – peculiarly, this has an almost nutty taste.

AVENUE

Glass: Martini
Garnish: Orange zest twist
Method: Cut passion fruit in half and scoop flesh into shaker. Add other ingredients, **SHAKE** with ice and fine strain into chilled glass.

1	fresh	**Passion fruit**
1	shot(s)	**Buffalo Trace bourbon whiskey**
1	shot(s)	**Boulard Grand Solage Calvados**
$\frac{1}{4}$	shot(s)	**Pomegranate (grenadine) syrup**
$\frac{1}{8}$	shot(s)	**Orange flower water**
$\frac{3}{4}$	shot(s)	**Chilled mineral water** (omit if wet ice)

Origin: A modern adaptation of a classic.
Comment: Fruity and floral.

A

AVIATION #1 (SIMPLE FORMULA) [UPDATED #7]

Glass: Martini
Garnish: Lemon zest twist
Method: SHAKE all ingredients with ice and fine strain into chilled glass.

2 shot(s) **Plymouth gin**
1/2 shot(s) **Luxardo maraschino liqueur**
1/2 shot(s) **Freshly squeezed lemon juice**
1/2 shot(s) **Chilled mineral water** (omit if wet ice)

Variant: Bee's Knees, Blue Moon
Origin: A classic cocktail thought to have originated in 1916.
Comment: This is a fantastic, tangy cocktail and dangerously easy to drink – too many of these and you really will be flying.

'I'M FOR ANYTHING THAT GETS YOU THROUGH THE NIGHT, BE IT PRAYER, TRANQUILIZERS, OR A BOTTLE OF JACK DANIEL'S.'

FRANK SINATRA

AVIATION #2 (CLASSIC FORMULA) [NEW #7]

Glass: Martini
Garnish: Lemon zest twist
Method: SHAKE all ingredients with ice and fine strain into chilled glass.

2 shot(s) **Plymouth gin**
1/2 shot(s) **Benoit Serres violet liqueur**
1/4 shot(s) **Luxardo maraschino liqueur**
1/2 shot(s) **Freshly squeezed lemon juice**
1/2 shot(s) **Chilled mineral water** (omit if wet ice)

Variant: Blue Moon
Origin: The original 1916 Aviation recipe used crème de violette (violet liqueur), which is sadly almost always omitted in modern day bars.
Comment: This floral Aviation still retains its dry sourness and punch.

AVIATOR [UPDATED #7]

Glass: Martini
Garnish: Lemon zest twist
Method: STIR all ingredients with ice and strain into chilled glass.

1 shot(s) **Plymouth gin**
1 shot(s) **Dry vermouth**
1 shot(s) **Sweet vermouth**
1 shot(s) **Dubonnet Red**

Origin: A classic cocktail of unknown origins.
Comment: On the bitter side of bittersweet.

AWOL

Glass: Shot
Method: LAYER in chilled glass by carefully pouring ingredients in the following order. Then **FLAME** drink and allow to burn for no more than ten seconds before extinguishing flame and consuming. Take extreme care and beware of hot glass.

1/2 shot(s) **Midori melon liqueur**
1/2 shot(s) **Pressed pineapple juice**
1/2 shot(s) **Ketel One vodka**
1/2 shot(s) **Wray & Nephew overproof rum**

Origin: Created in 1993 by Lane Zellman at Louis XVI Restaurant, St. Louis Hotel, New Orleans, USA.
Comment: A strong but surprisingly palatable shot.

AZURE MARTINI

Glass: Martini
Garnish: Apple slice on rim
Method: SHAKE all ingredients with ice and fine strain into chilled glass.

2 shot(s) **Leblon cachaça**
1/4 shot(s) **Cinnamon schnapps liqueur**
1 shot(s) **Pressed apple juice**
1/2 shot(s) **Freshly squeezed lime juice**
1/4 shot(s) **Sugar syrup (2 sugar to 1 water)**

Origin: Created in 1998 by Ben Reed at the Met Bar, London, England, and originally made with muddled fresh apple.
Comment: A tangy cocktail – reminiscent of a cinnamon laced apple pie. Shame it's not blue.

B2C2

Glass: Martini
Garnish: Orange zest twist
Method: SHAKE first three ingredients with ice and strain into ice-filled glass. **TOP** with champagne.

1 shot(s) **Rémy Martin cognac**
1 shot(s) **Bénédictine D.O.M. liqueur**
1 shot(s) **Cointreau triple sec**
Top up with **Brut champagne**

Origin: Named after the four ingredients and created in France during World War II by American soldiers using ingredients liberated from retreating Germans.
Comment: Strong and sweet. This wartime drink can still be deadly if not handled with care.

B5200

Glass: Shot
Method: Refrigerate ingredients then **LAYER** in chilled glass by carefully pouring in the following order.

1/2 shot(s) **Kahlúa coffee liqueur**
1/2 shot(s) **Irish cream liqueur**
1/2 shot(s) **Wood's 100 rum**

Origin: Discovered in 2003 at Circus Bar, London,.
Origin: Layering this drink is as easy as inflating a lifejacket – drink a few and you'll need one.

B-52 SHOT

Glass: Shot
Method: Refrigerate ingredients then **LAYER** in chilled glass by carefully pouring in the following order.

1/2 shot(s) **Kahlúa coffee liqueur**
1/2 shot(s) **Irish cream liqueur**
1/2 shot(s) **Grand Marnier liqueur**

Origin: Named after B-52 bombers in Vietnam.
Comment: Probably the best-known and most popular shot.

B-53 SHOT

Glass: Shot
Method: Refrigerate ingredients then **LAYER** in chilled glass by carefully pouring in the following order.

1/2 shot(s) **Kahlúa coffee liqueur**
1/2 shot(s) **Irish cream liqueur**
1/2 shot(s) **Ketel One vodka**

Comment: Why settle for a 52 when you can have a 53?

B-54 SHOT

Glass: Shot
Method: Refrigerate ingredients then **LAYER** in chilled glass by carefully pouring in the following order.

1/2 shot(s) **Luxardo Amaretto di Saschira**
1/2 shot(s) **Kahlúa coffee liqueur**
1/2 shot(s) **Irish cream liqueur**

Comment: Layered and sticky – but nice.

B-55 SHOT

Glass: Shot
Method: Refrigerate ingredients then **LAYER** in chilled glass by carefully pouring in the following order.

1/2 shot(s) **Kahlúa coffee liqueur**
1/2 shot(s) **Irish cream liqueur**
1/2 shot(s) **La Fée Parisienne (68%) absinthe**

Comment: The latest and scariest of the B-something range of layered shots.

B-52 FROZEN

Glass: Old-fashioned
Garnish: Crumbled Cadbury's Flake bar
Method: BLEND ingredients with 6oz scoop of crushed ice. Pour into glass and serve with straws.

1 shot(s) **Irish cream liqueur**
1 shot(s) **Grand Marnier liqueur**
1 shot(s) **Kahlúa coffee liqueur**

Comment: The classic shot blended with ice.

B & B

Glass: Old-fashioned
Garnish: Lemon zest twist
Method: STIR ingredients with ice and strain into ice-filled glass.

2 shot(s) **Bénédictine D.O.M. liqueur**
2 shot(s) **Rémy Martin cognac**

Origin: Created in 1937 by a bartender at New York's famous 21 Club.
Comment: Honeyed and spiced cognac.

B. J. SHOT

Glass: Shot
Garnish: Thin layer of single cream
Method: Refrigerate ingredients then **LAYER** in chilled glass by carefully pouring in the following order.

1/2 shot(s) **Grand Marnier liqueur**
1/2 shot(s) **Irish cream liqueur**

Comment: You know what the letters stand for – tastes better!

BABY BLUE MARTINI

Glass: Martini
Garnish: Orange zest twist
Method: SHAKE all ingredients with ice and fine strain into chilled glass.

2 shot(s) **Plymouth gin**
3/4 shot(s) **Bols Blue curaçao liqueur**
3/4 shot(s) **Squeezed pink grapefruit juice**
3/4 shot(s) **Pressed pineapple juice**

Comment: Turquoise blue, easy drinking, fruity gin.

BABY GUINNESS

Glass: Shot
Method: Refrigerate ingredients then **LAYER** in chilled glass by carefully pouring in the following order.

1 shot(s) **Kahlúa coffee liqueur**
1/2 shot(s) **Irish cream liqueur**

Comment: Looks like a miniature pint of Guinness stout.

BABY WOO WOO

Glass: Shot
Garnish: Lime wedge
Method: SHAKE all ingredients with ice and fine strain into chilled glass.

1/2 shot(s) **Ketel One vodka**
1/2 shot(s) **Teichenné Peach Schnapps Liqueur**
1/2 shot(s) **Ocean Spray cranberry juice**

Comment: Pink, sweet and all too easy to shoot.

BACARDI COCKTAIL [UPDATED #7]

Glass: Martini
Garnish: Maraschino cherry
Method: **SHAKE** all ingredients with ice and fine strain into chilled glass.

- $2\frac{1}{2}$ shot(s) **Bacardi light rum**
- 1 shot(s) **Freshly squeezed lime juice**
- $\frac{1}{2}$ shot(s) **Pomegranate (grenadine) syrup**
- $\frac{1}{4}$ shot(s) **Chilled mineral water** (omit if wet ice)

Origin: In 1936, a bar in New York was found to be selling the Bacardi Cocktail – without including Bacardi rum. To protect their brand, Bacardi sued. A premise of their case was that Bacardi was a unique rum: although the president of the company refused to reveal any details of production, the court found that it was indeed unique and ruled that a Bacardi
Cocktail must be made with Bacardi.
Comment: This classic pinky drink is a perfectly balanced combination of the flavour of rum, the sourness of lime juice and the sweetness of pomegranate syrup.

> 'THE RELATIONSHIP BETWEEN A RUSSIAN AND A BOTTLE OF VODKA IS ALMOST MYSTICAL.'
> RICHARD OWEN

BAHAMA MAMA

Glass: Collins
Garnish: Pineapple wedge & cherry
Method: **SHAKE** all ingredients with ice and strain into ice-filled glass.

- $\frac{3}{4}$ shot(s) **Pusser's navy rum**
- $\frac{3}{4}$ shot(s) **Aged rum**
- 1 shot(s) **Malibu coconut rum liqueur**
- $1\frac{3}{4}$ shot(s) **Freshly squeezed orange juice**
- $2\frac{1}{2}$ shot(s) **Pressed pineapple juice**
- 3 dashes **Angostura aromatic bitters**

Comment: A tropical, fruity number laced with flavoursome rum.

BAHAMAS DAIQUIRI

Glass: Martini
Garnish: Pineapple wedge on rim
Method: **SHAKE** all ingredients with ice and fine strain into chilled glass.

- $1\frac{1}{2}$ shot(s) **Myers's Planter's Punch rum**
- $\frac{3}{4}$ shot(s) **Malibu coconut rum liqueur**
- $\frac{1}{4}$ shot(s) **Kahlúa coffee liqueur**
- $1\frac{1}{2}$ shot(s) **Freshly extracted pineapple juice**
- $\frac{1}{2}$ shot(s) **Freshly squeezed lime juice**

Origin: Adapted from the Bahamas Martini created in 2002 by Yannick Miseriaux at the Fifth Floor Bar, London, England.
Comment: Totally tropical with a sweet tangy edge.

BAHIA [NEW #7]

Glass: Collins
Garnish: Mint sprig, pineapple wedge & cherry
Method: **BLEND** all ingredients with 12oz scoop crushed ice and serve with straws.

- $2\frac{1}{2}$ shot(s) **Light white rum**
- 3 shot(s) **Pressed pineapple juice**
- $\frac{1}{2}$ shot(s) **Coco López cream of coconut**

Origin: Bahia is one of the 26 states of Brazil. It is also a pre-Prohibition drink containing dry vermouth, sherry, absinthe and bitters. This more recent Piña Colada style offering has more mass market appeal.
Comment: If you like Piña Coladas but are too embarrassed to order one then this drink is for you.

BAJAN DAIQUIRI [NEW #7]

Glass: Martini
Garnish: Lime wedge
Method: **SHAKE** all ingredients with ice and fine strain into chilled glass.

- 2 shot(s) **Golden rum**
- $\frac{1}{2}$ shot(s) **Velvet Falernum liqueur**
- $\frac{3}{4}$ shot(s) **Freshly squeezed lime juice**
- $\frac{1}{2}$ shot(s) **Chilled mineral water** (omit if wet ice)

Origin: Created in 2006 by yours truly.
Comment: A full-flavoured Daiquiri with clove spice.

BAJAN MOJITO [UPDATED #7]

Glass: Collins
Garnish: Passion fruit slice / mint sprig
Method: Cut passion fruit in half and scoop flesh into glass. Add mint and gently **MUDDLE** (just to bruise mint). Add Gold Rum, lime juice and crushed ice. Churn drink in glass to mix. **DRIZZLE** passion fruit liqueur.

- 1 fresh **Passion fruit**
- 8 fresh **Mint leaves**
- 2 shot(s) **Golden rum**
- $\frac{1}{2}$ shot(s) **Freshly squeezed lime juice**
- $\frac{1}{2}$ shot(s) **Sugar syrup (2 sugar to 1 water)**

Origin: Adapted from a recipe by Wayne Collins, London, England
Comment: A laid-back fruity Mojito.

BAJAN PASSION

Glass: Martini
Garnish: Float passion fruit slice
Method: Cut passion fruit in half and scoop flesh into shaker. Add other ingredients, **SHAKE** with ice and fine strain into chilled glass.

- 1 fresh **Passion fruit**
- $1\frac{1}{2}$ shot(s) **Golden rum**
- $\frac{1}{2}$ shot(s) **Giffard apricot brandy du Roussillon**
- 1 shot(s) **Freshly squeezed lime juice**
- $\frac{1}{4}$ shot(s) **Sugar syrup (2 sugar to 1 water)**
- $\frac{1}{4}$ shot(s) **Vanilla sugar syrup**

Origin: Created in 2004 by Wayne Collins for Maxxium UK.
Comment: A Daiquiri laced with fruit and spice.

BAJITO

Glass: Collins
Garnish: Mint sprig
Method: Lightly **MUDDLE** mint and basil in glass just enough to bruise. Add rum, sugar and lime juice. Half fill glass with crushed ice and **CHURN** (stir) with bar spoon. Add more crushed ice and churn some more. Continue adding crushed ice and churning until glass is full.

6 fresh **Basil leaves**
6 fresh **Mint leaves**
2 shot(s) **Light white rum**
1 shot(s) **Freshly squeezed lime juice**
¼ shot(s) **Sugar syrup (2 sugar to 1 water)**

Origin: Discovered in 2004 at Excelsior Bar, Boston, USA.
Comment: Basically a Mojito with basil as well as mint.

BALALAIKA 

Glass: Martini
Garnish: Orange zest twist
Method: SHAKE all ingredients with ice and fine strain into chilled glass.

1¼ shot(s) **Ketel One vodka**
1¼ shot(s) **Cointreau triple sec**
1¼ shot(s) **Freshly squeezed lemon juice**

Comment: Richly flavoured with orange and lemon.

BALD EAGLE SHOT

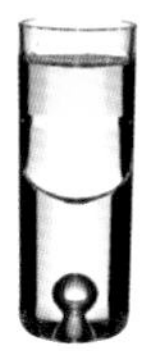

Glass: Shot
Method: Refrigerate ingredients then **LAYER** in chilled glass by carefully pouring in the following order.

½ shot(s) **Giffard white crème de Menthe Pastille**
¾ shot(s) **Partida tequila**

Comment: Minty tequila – fresh breath tastic.

BALD EAGLE [UPDATED #7]

Glass: Martini
Garnish: Salt rim
Method: SHAKE all ingredients with ice and fine strain into chilled glass.

2 shot(s) **Partida tequila**
¾ shot(s) **Freshly squeezed pink grapefruit juice**
½ shot(s) **Ocean Spray cranberry juice**
¼ shot(s) **Freshly squeezed lime juice**
¼ shot(s) **Freshly squeezed lemon juice**
¼ shot(s) **Sugar syrup (2 sugar to 1 water)**

Origin: Created for me in 2001 by Salvatore Calabrese at The Lanesborough Library Bar, London, England.
Comment: If you like Tequila and you like your drinks on the sour side, this is for you.

BALI TRADER

Glass: Martini
Garnish: Banana chunk on rim
Method: SHAKE all ingredients with ice and fine strain into chilled glass.

2 shot(s) **Ketel One vodka**
1 shot(s) **Pisang Ambon green banana liqueur**
1 shot(s) **Pressed pineapple juice**

Comment: A tasty Caribbean combination of banana and pineapple.

BALLET RUSSE

Glass: Martini
Garnish: Lime wedge on rim
Method: SHAKE all ingredients with ice and fine strain into chilled glass.

2 shot(s) **Ketel One vodka**
¾ shot(s) **Giffard Cassis Noir de Bourgogne**
1 shot(s) **Freshly squeezed lime juice**
¼ shot(s) **Sugar syrup (2 sugar to 1 water)**

Comment: Intense sweet blackcurrant balanced by lime sourness.

BALTIC SPRING PUNCH

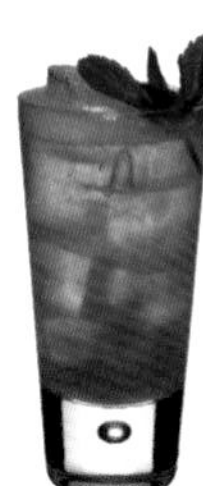

Glass: Collins
Garnish: Mint sprig
Method: MUDDLE peach in base of shaker. Add other ingredients, **SHAKE** with ice and fine strain into ice-filled glass.

1 ripe **Peach skinned and diced**
1½ shot(s) **Rose petal liqueur**
½ shot(s) **Freshly squeezed lemon juice**
¼ shot(s) **Sugar syrup (2 sugar to 1 water)**
Top up with **Brut champagne**

Variant: If using peach purée omit the sugar.
Origin: Created in 2002 at Baltic, London, England.
Comment: Just peachy, baby.

BALTIMORE EGG NOG

Glass: Collins
Garnish: Dust with freshly grated nutmeg
Method: SHAKE all ingredients with ice and fine strain into ice-filled glass.

1½ shot(s) **Rémy Martin cognac**
1½ shot(s) **Madeira**
1 shot(s) **Pusser's Navy rum**
1 shot(s) **Double (heavy) cream**
1 shot(s) **Milk**
1 shot(s) **Sugar syrup (2 sugar to 1 water)**
1 fresh **Beaten egg**

Comment: A flavoursome liquid meal.

B

BAMBOO [UPDATED #7]

Glass: Martini
Garnish: Orange zest twist
Method: STIR all ingredients with ice and strain into chilled glass.

2	shot(s)	**Tio Pepe fino sherry**
2	shot(s)	**Dry vermouth**
1/4	shot(s)	**Cointreau triple sec**
3	dashes	**Fee Brothers orange bitters**

Variants: Add two dashes of Angostura aromatic bitters in place of triple sec. Also see East Indian.
Origin: A classic and all but forgotten cocktail from the 1940s.
Comment: Dry, refined and subtle - for sophisticated palates only.

BANANA BATIDA

Glass: Collins
Garnish: Banana chunk on rim
Method: BLEND ingredients with 12oz scoop of crushed ice. Pour into glass and serve with straws.

2 1/2	shot(s)	**Leblon cachaça**
1	shot(s)	**Giffard crème de banane du Brésil**
3/4	shot(s)	**Freshly squeezed lemon juice**
1	fresh	**Peeled banana**

Origin: The Batida is a traditional Brazilian drink.
Comment: A wonderfully tangy drink for a summer's afternoon.

BANANA BLISS [UPDATED #7]

Glass: Martini
Garnish: Orange zest twist
Method: STIR all ingredients with ice and strain into chilled glass.

2	shot(s)	**Rémy Martin cognac**
1	shot(s)	**Giffard crème de banane du Brésil**
1/2	shot(s)	**Chilled mineral water** (omit if wet ice)
2	dashes	**Fee Brothers orange bitters**

AKA: Golden Brown
Comment: Crème de bananes and cognac go shockingly well together.

BANANA BOOMER

Glass: Martini
Garnish: Banana chunk on rim
Method: SHAKE all ingredients with ice and strain into chilled glass.

1	shot(s)	**Ketel One vodka**
1	shot(s)	**Giffard crème de banane du Brésil**
1/2	shot(s)	**Giffard apricot brandy du Roussillon**
1/2	shot(s)	**Cherry (brandy) liqueur**
3/4	shot(s)	**Freshly squeezed orange juice**
3/4	shot(s)	**Pressed pineapple juice**

Comment: Fortified bubble gum for the young at heart.

BANANA COLADA

Glass: Hurricane
Garnish: Banana chunk on rim
Method: BLEND ingredients with 12oz scoop of crushed ice. Pour into glass and serve with straws.

2	shot(s)	**Golden rum**
1/2	shot(s)	**Giffard crème de banane du Brésil**
4	shot(s)	**Pressed pineapple juice**
1	fresh	**Peeled banana**
1	shot(s)	**Coco López cream of coconut**

Comment: Don't skimp, use a whole banana per drink for real flavour.

BANANA COW [NEW #7]

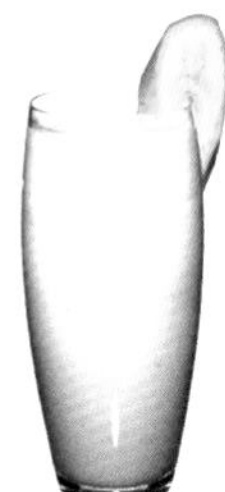

Glass: Collins
Garnish: Banana chunk on rim
Method: BLEND all ingredients with 12oz scoop crushed ice and serve with straws.

1	shot(s)	**Light white rum**
3	shot(s)	**Fresh milk**
1	dash	**Vanilla extract**
1/4	shot(s)	**Sugar syrup (2 sugar to 1 water)**
1	fresh	**Peeled banana**
1	dash	**Angostura aromatic bitters**

Origin: Created by Victor J. Bergeron. This recipe is adapted from his 'Trader Vic's Bartender's Guide' (1972 revised edition).
Comment: The Trader writes of his drink, "The world's finest, greatest, oh-so good peachy hangover special. This'll do it when nothing else will." I think Vic is somewhat overselling this malty banana meal of a drink.

BANANA DAIQUIRI [UPDATED #7]

Glass: Hurricane
Garnish: Banana chunk on rim
Method: BLEND all ingredients with 12oz scoop of crushed ice. Pour into glass and serve with straws.

2	shot(s)	**Light white rum**
1	shot(s)	**Giffard crème de banane du Brésil**
1/2	shot(s)	**Freshly squeezed lime juice**
1	fresh	**Peeled banana**

Variant: Add a dash of maraschino liqueur.
Comment: A tangy banana disco drink that's not too sweet.

DRINKS ARE GRADED AS FOLLOWS:

● DISGUSTING ●◐ PRETTY AWFUL ●● BEST AVOIDED
●●◐ DISAPPOINTING ●●● ACCEPTABLE ●●●◐ GOOD
●●●● RECOMMENDED ●●●●◐ HIGHLY RECOMMENDED
●●●●● OUTSTANDING / EXCEPTIONAL

BANANA SMOOTHIE (MOCKTAIL)

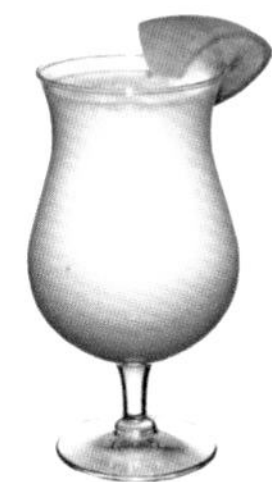

Glass: Hurricane
Garnish: Banana chunk on rim
Method: BLEND ingredients with 12oz scoop of crushed ice. Pour into glass and serve immediately with straws.

3	shot(s)	**Pressed apple juice**
7	spoons	**Natural yoghurt**
3	spoons	**Runny honey**
1	fresh	**Banana**

Origin: Created in 2005 by Lisa Ball, London, England.
Comment: Serve with breakfast cereal and you'll be set up for the day. The high fresh banana content means this drink will quickly turn brown if left. This can be countered by adding fresh lemon juice and balancing with more honey but this detracts from the fresh banana flavour.

BANANAS & CREAM

Glass: Collins
Garnish: Banana chunk on rim
Method: BLEND ingredients with 12oz scoop of crushed ice. Pour into glass and serve with straws.

2	shot(s)	**Giffard crème de banane du Brésil**
1	shot(s)	**Luxardo Amaretto di Saschira**
1	shot(s)	**Irish cream liqueur**
1	shot(s)	**Double (heavy) cream**
2	shot(s)	**Milk**

Comment: Banana and cream frappé with hints of almond – one for a summer afternoon.

BANOFFEE MARTINI

Glass: Martini
Garnish: Dust with cocoa powder
Method: MUDDLE banana in base of shaker. Add other ingredients, **SHAKE** with ice and fine strain into chilled glass.

1/4	fresh	**Banana**
1 1/2	shot(s)	**Vanilla flavoured vodka**
3/4	shot(s)	**Teichenné butterscotch Schnapps**
3/4	shot(s)	**Giffard crème de banane du Brésil**
1	spoon	**Maple syrup**
1/2	shot(s)	**Double (heavy) cream**
1/2	shot(s)	**Milk**

Origin: Adapted from a recipe created in 2002 by Barry Wilson, Zinc Bar & Grill, Edinburgh, Scotland.
Comment: Thick and rich, one for after the cheese course.

BANSHEE

Glass: Shot
Method: SHAKE all ingredients with ice and fine strain into chilled glass.

1/2	shot(s)	**Giffard crème de banane du Brésil**
1/2	shot(s)	**Giffard white crème de cacao**
1/2	shot(s)	**Double (heavy) cream**

Comment: Creamy chocolate banana.

BARBARA

Glass: Martini
Garnish: Dust with freshly grated nutmeg
Method: SHAKE all ingredients with ice and fine strain into chilled glass.

1 1/2	shot(s)	**Ketel One vodka**
3/4	shot(s)	**Giffard white crème de cacao**
3/4	shot(s)	**Double (heavy) cream**
3/4	shot(s)	**Milk**

Comment: Quite neutral and subtle – the nutmeg garnish is as important to the flavour as cacao.

BARBARA WEST

Glass: Martini
Garnish: Lemon twist
Method: SHAKE all ingredients with ice and fine strain into chilled glass.

2	shot(s)	**Plymouth gin**
1	shot(s)	**Amontillado sherry**
1/2	shot(s)	**Freshly squeezed lemon juice**
1/4	shot(s)	**Sugar syrup (2 sugar to 1 water)**
2	dashes	**Angostura aromatic bitters**

Origin: A classic from the 1930s.
Comment: Well balanced but for serious gin and sherry drinkers only.

BARBARY COAST HIGHBALL

Glass: Collins
Method: SHAKE all but soda with ice and strain into ice-filled glass. **TOP** with soda and stir.

1	shot(s)	**Buffalo Trace bourbon whiskey**
1	shot(s)	**Plymouth gin**
1	shot(s)	**Giffard brown crème de cacao**
1/2	shot(s)	**Double (heavy) cream**
1/2	shot(s)	**Milk**
Top up with		**Soda water (club soda)**

Variant: Omit soda and serve straight-up in a Martini glass.
Comment: Looks like a glass of frothy weak tea - bourbon and chocolate predominate.

BARBARY COAST [UPDATED #7]

Glass: Martini
Garnish: Dust with cinnamon powder
Method: SHAKE all ingredients with ice and fine strain into chilled glass.

1	shot(s)	**Scotch whisky**
1	shot(s)	**Plymouth gin**
1	shot(s)	**Giffard white crème de cacao**
1	shot(s)	**Double (heavy) cream**

Origin: Adapted from Victor Bergeron's 'Trader Vic's Bartender's Guide' (1972 revised edition).
Comment: It may be creamy, but this is a serious drink.

B

BARNACLE BILL [UPDATED #7]

Glass: Old-fashioned
Garnish: Mint sprig
Method: SHAKE all ingredients with ice and strain into glass filled with crushed ice.

1/2	shot(s)	**Yellow Chartreuse liqueur**
1/2	shot(s)	**Parfait Amour liqueur**
1/2	shot(s)	**Pernod anis**
1/2	shot(s)	**Chilled mineral water** (omit if wet ice)

Origin: Adapted from Victor Bergeron's 'Trader Vic's Bartender's Guide' (1972 revised edition).
Comment: This sweetie is great after a meal on a warm night.

BARNAMINT

Glass: Hurricane
Garnish: Oreo cookie
Method: BLEND ingredients with 12oz scoop of crushed ice. Pour into glass and serve with straws.

2	shot(s)	**Irish cream liqueur**
1 1/2	shot(s)	**Giffard green crème de menthe**
1	shot(s)	**Double (heavy) cream**
1	shot(s)	**Milk**
2	scoops	**Vanilla ice cream**
3	whole	**Oreo cookies**

Origin: This original TGI Friday's cocktail is named after the Barnum & Bailey Circus, which also inspired the red and white awnings outside Friday's restaurants.
Comment: If you're after a drinkable dessert, then this TGI classic may be the cocktail for you.

BARNUM (WAS RIGHT) [UPDATED #7] 

Glass: Martini
Garnish: Lemon zest twist
Method: SHAKE all ingredients with ice and fine strain into chilled glass.

2	shot(s)	**Plymouth gin**
1	shot(s)	**Giffard apricot brandy du Roussillon**
1/2	shot(s)	**Freshly squeezed lemon juice**
2	dashes	**Angostura aromatic bitters**
1/2	shot(s)	**Chilled mineral water** (omit if wet ice)

Origin: 1930s classic resurrected by Ted Haigh in his 2004 book 'Vintage Spirits & Forgotten Cocktails'.
Comment: A classic cocktail flavour combination that still pleases.

BARRANQUILLA GREEN JADE [NEW #7]

Glass: Martini
Garnish: Green cherry & mint sprig
Method: SHAKE all ingredients with ice and fine strain into chilled glass.

2	shot(s)	**Plymouth gin**
1	shot(s)	**Giffard green crème de menthe**
1/2	shot(s)	**Double (heavy) cream**
1/2	shot(s)	**Milk**
1/4	fresh	**Egg white**

Comment: Lime green in colour, a tad minty and creamy smooth.

BARTENDER'S MARTINI

Glass: Martini
Garnish: Orange zest twist
Method: SHAKE all ingredients with ice and fine strain into chilled glass.

1	shot(s)	**Plymouth gin**
1	shot(s)	**Tio Pepe fino sherry**
1	shot(s)	**Dubonnet Red**
1	shot(s)	**Dry vermouth**
1/2	shot(s)	**Grand Marnier liqueur**

Comment: This classic cocktail resembles an aromatic Martini. Hints of sherry and orange are followed by a dry finish.

BARTENDER'S ROOT BEER

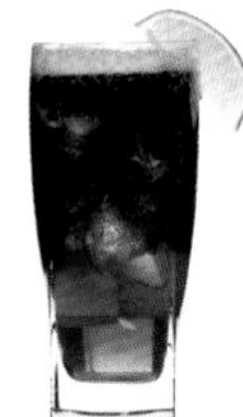

Glass: Collins
Garnish: Lime wedge on rim
Method: POUR first three ingredients into ice-filled glass and top up with cola.

1	shot(s)	**Galliano liqueur**
1	shot(s)	**Kahlúa coffee liqueur**
1/4	shot(s)	**Freshly squeezed lime juice**
Top up with		**Cola**

Comment: Not quite the root of all evil, but tasty all the same.

BASIL & HONEY DAIQUIRI [UPDATED #7]

Glass: Martini
Garnish: Float basil leaf
Method: STIR honey and rum in base of shaker until honey dissolves. Add other ingredients, **SHAKE** with ice and fine strain into chilled glass.

2	spoons	**Runny honey**
2 1/2	shot(s)	**Havana Club light rum**
3	torn	**Fresh basil leaves**
1/2	shot(s)	**Freshly squeezed lime juice**

Origin: Formula by yours truly in 2005.
Comment: Basil adds dry vegetable notes to this outstanding classic drink.

BASIL GIMLET [NEW #7]

Glass: Martini
Garnish: Lime wedge or cherry
Method: SHAKE all ingredients with ice and fine strain into chilled glass.

2 1/2	shot(s)	**Plymouth gin**
1/4	shot(s)	**Freshly squeezed lime juice**
1 1/2	shot(s)	**Rose's lime cordial**
3	torn	**Fresh basil leaves**

Origin: Adapted from a drink discovered in 2006 at Stella, Boston, USA.
Comment: Tangy, citrus fresh and balanced.

BASIL BEAUTY [UPDATED #7]

Glass: Martini
Garnish: Pineapple wedge on rim
Method: Cut passion fruit in half and scoop flesh into shaker. Add other ingredients, **SHAKE** with ice and fine strain into chilled glass.

1	whole	**Passion fruit**
3	torn	**Basil leaves**
2	shot(s)	**Ketel One Citroen vodka**
2	shot(s)	**Pressed pineapple juice**
1/4	shot(s)	**Freshly squeezed lime juice**
1/2	shot(s)	**Coconut syrup (or sugar syrup)**

Origin: Created in 1999 by Wayne Collins, London, England.
Comment: Pineapple and passion fruit laced with citrus vodka and infused with hints of lime, basil and coconut.

BASIL MARY [UPDATED #7]

Glass: Collins
Garnish: Basil leaf
Method: SHAKE all ingredients with ice and fine strain into ice-filled glass.

7	fresh	**Torn basil leaves**
2	shot(s)	**Pepper-infused Ketel One vodka**
4	shot(s)	**Pressed tomato juice**
1/2	shot(s)	**Freshly squeezed lemon juice**
8	drops	**Tabasco pepper sauce**
4	dashes	**Lea & Perrins Worcestershire sauce**
1/2	spoon	**Horseradish sauce**
1/2	shot(s)	**Tawny port**
2	pinch	**Celery salt**
2	pinch	**Black pepper**

Origin: Discovered in 2004 at Indigo Yard, Edinburgh, Scotland.
Comment: A Mary with a herbal twist.

'FRANKLY, I WAS HORRIFIED BY LIFE, AT WHAT A MAN HAD TO DO SIMPLY IN ORDER TO EAT, SLEEP AND KEEP HIMSELF CLOTHED. SO I STAYED IN BED AND DRANK.'

BASIL BRAMBLE SLING

Glass: Sling
Garnish: Mint sprig
Method: MUDDLE basil in base of shaker. Add rest of ingredients, **SHAKE** with ice and strain into ice-filled glass. Serve with straws.

7	fresh	**Basil leaves**
2	shot(s)	**Plymouth gin**
1 1/2	shot(s)	**Freshly squeezed lemon juice**
1/2	shot(s)	**Sugar syrup (2 sugar to 1 water)**
1/2	shot(s)	**Giffard mûre (blackberry)**

Origin: Created in 2003 by Alexandra Fiot at Lonsdale House, London, UK.
Comment: Wonderfully refreshing and balanced.

BASIL GRANDE

Glass: Martini
Garnish: Strawberry and dust with black pepper.
Method: MUDDLE strawberries and basil in base of shaker. Add other ingredients, **SHAKE** with ice and fine strain into glass.

4	fresh	**Hulled strawberries**
5	fresh	**Basil leaves**
3/4	shot(s)	**Ketel One vodka**
3/4	shot(s)	**Chambord black raspberry liqueur**
3/4	shot(s)	**Grand Marnier liqueur**
2	shot(s)	**Ocean Spray cranberry juice**

Origin: Created in 2001 by Jamie Wilkinson at Living Room, Manchester, England.
Comment: Fruity, with interest courtesy of the basil and grind of pepper.

BASILIAN [NEW #7]

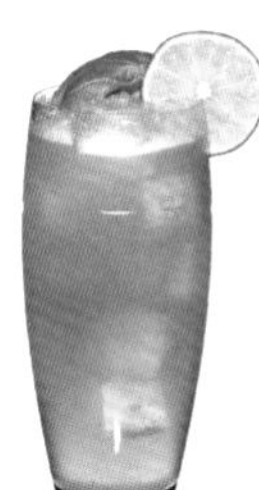

Glass: Collins
Garnish: Lime slice & basil leaf
Method: MUDDLE cucumber and basil in base of shaker. Add next four ingredients, **SHAKE** with ice and fine strain into ice-filled glass. **TOP** with ginger ale.

1	inch	**Fresh cucumber peeled and chopped**
5	fresh	**Basil leaves**
2	shot(s)	**Leblon cachaça**
3/4	shot(s)	**Grand Marnier liqueur**
1/2	shot(s)	**Freshly squeezed lime juice**
1/4	shot(s)	**Sugar syrup (2 sugar to 1 water)**
Top up with		**Ginger ale**

Origin: Created in 2005 by Duncan McRae at Dragonfly, Edinburgh, Scotland.
Comment: Vegetable notes with hints of orange and ginger. Healthy tasting!

BASILICO

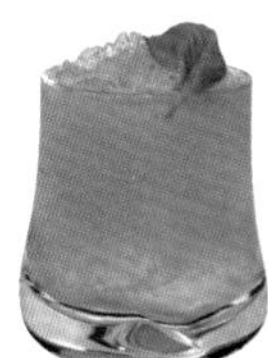

Glass: Old-fashioned
Garnish: Basil leaf
Method: MUDDLE basil in base of shaker. Add other ingredients, **SHAKE** with ice and strain into glass filled with crushed ice.

7	fresh	**Basil leaves**
2	shot(s)	**Ketel One vodka**
1/2	shot(s)	**Luxardo limoncello**
1/2	shot(s)	**Freshly squeezed lemon juice**
1/2	shot(s)	**Sugar syrup (2 sugar to 1 water)**

Origin: Discovered in 2004 at Atlantic Bar & Grill, London, England.
Comment: A lemon Caipirovska with basil.

B

BATANGA [NEW #7] 

Glass: Collins
Garnish: Salt rim
Method: POUR ingredients into ice-filled glass, stir and serve with straws.

2 shot(s) **Partida tequila**
$^1/_2$ shot(s) **Freshly squeezed lime juice**
Top up with **Cola**

Origin: The signature drink of the now legendary Don Javier Delgado Corona, the owner/bartender of La Capilla (The Chapel) in Tequila, Mexico. Still mixing, even in his eighties, Corona is noted for ritualistically stirring this drink with a huge knife.
Comment: Basically a Cuba Libre made with tequila in place of rum – an improvement.

BATIDA DE COCO

Glass: Collins
Garnish: Pineapple wedge and cherry
Method: BLEND ingredients with 12oz scoop of crushed ice. **POUR** into glass and serve with straws.

$2^1/_2$ shot(s) **Leblon cachaça**
$1^1/_2$ shot(s) **Coco López cream of coconut**
1 shot(s) **Coconut milk**

Origin: Traditional Brazilian drink.
Comment: Sweet, almost creamy coconut with a hint of cachaça.

BAY BREEZE [UPDATED #7]

Glass: Collins
Garnish: Pineapple wedge on rim
Method: SHAKE all ingredients with ice and strain into ice-filled glass.

2 shot(s) **Ketel One vodka**
$1^1/_2$ shot(s) **Ocean Spray cranberry juice**
$2^1/_2$ shot(s) **Pressed pineapple juice**

Comment: Pink, fluffy, sweet and easy to drink.

BAZOOKA

Glass: Shot
Method: SHAKE all ingredients with ice and fine strain into chilled glass.

$^3/_4$ shot(s) **Southern Comfort liqueur**
$^1/_2$ shot(s) **Giffard crème de banane du Brésil**
$^1/_8$ shot(s) **Pomegranate (grenadine) syrup**
$^1/_4$ shot(s) **Double (heavy) cream**

Comment: A sticky, pink shot.

BAZOOKA JOE

Glass: Shot
Method: Refrigerate ingredients then **LAYER** in chilled glass by carefully pouring in the following order.

$^1/_2$ shot(s) **Bols Blue curaçao liqueur**
$^1/_2$ shot(s) **Giffard crème de banane du Brésil**
$^1/_2$ shot(s) **Irish cream liqueur**

Comment: Banana and orange topped with whiskey cream.

BBC

Glass: Martini
Garnish: Dust with freshly grated nutmeg
Method: SHAKE all ingredients with ice and fine strain into chilled glass.

$1^1/_4$ shot(s) **Rémy Martin cognac**
1 shot(s) **Bénédictine D.O.M. liqueur**
$^3/_4$ shot(s) **Double (heavy) cream**
$^3/_4$ shot(s) **Milk**

Origin: Thought to have originated in the UK in the late 1970s and named, not after the British Broadcasting Company, but brandy, Bénédictine and cream.
Comment: Brandy and Bénédictine (a classic combo) smoothed with cream. Drier than you might expect.

BE-TON

Glass: Collins
Garnish: Squeezed lime wedge in glass
Method: POUR Becherovka into ice-filled glass, then top up with tonic water and stir.

2 shot(s) **Becherovka (Carlsbad Becher)**
Top up with **Tonic water**

Origin: Becherovka (or Carlsbad Becher as it's sometimes known) is the Czech national liqueur. Matured in oak, it contains cinnamon, cloves, nutmeg and other herbs.
Comment: This spicy drink is the Czech Republic's answer to the Gin 'n' Tonic.

BEACH BLONDE

Glass: Collins
Garnish: Banana slice on rim
Method: BLEND ingredients with 12oz scoop of crushed ice. Pour into glass and serve with straws.

$^1/_2$ fresh **Peeled banana**
1 shot(s) **Wray & Nephew overproof white rum**
3 shot(s) **Bols advocaat liqueur**
3 shot(s) **Freshly squeezed orange juice**

Origin: Created in 2002 by Alex Kammerling, London, England.
Comment: Fruity, creamy holiday drinking.

BATIDA

Like the Caipirinha, the Batida is a traditional Brazilian drink based on cachaça. The name literally translates as 'cocktail' and is a broad term for a drink usually containing fresh fruit, sugar and/or sweetened condensed milk (leite condensado).

They are often blended with crushed ice or shaken and served over crushed ice.

In Brazil the most popular Batidas are made with passion fruit (batida de maracujá) and coconut milk (batida de coco). Unfortunately, this excellent drink has not transferred as quickly from its homeland as the Caipirinha.

Batida variations include
Abaci (pineapple) Batida
Banana Batida
Batida de Coco (with coconut milk)
Carneval (mango) Batida
Goiaba (guava) Batida
Mango Batida
Maracujá (passion fruit) Batida
Milho Verde (sweetcorn) Batida
Morango (strawberry) Batida

BEACH ICED TEA

B

Glass: Sling
Garnish: Lemon slice
Method: SHAKE all ingredients with ice and strain into ice-filled glass.

1/2	shot(s)	**Light white rum**
1/2	shot(s)	**Plymouth gin**
1/2	shot(s)	**Ketel One vodka**
1/2	shot(s)	**Partida tequila**
1/2	shot(s)	**Cointreau triple sec**
1	shot(s)	**Freshly squeezed lemon juice**
1/2	shot(s)	**Sugar syrup (2 sugar to 1 water)**
3	shot(s)	**Ocean Spray cranberry juice**

Comment: A Long Island Iced Tea with cranberry juice instead of cola.

BEACHCOMBER

Glass: Martini
Garnish: Lime wedge on rim
Method: SHAKE all ingredients with ice and fine strain into chilled glass.

2	shot(s)	**Light white rum**
1/2	shot(s)	**Cointreau triple sec**
3/4	shot(s)	**Freshly squeezed lime juice**
1/4	shot(s)	**Luxardo maraschino liqueur**
1/2	shot(s)	**Chilled mineral water** (omit if wet ice)

Comment: A Daiquiri with the addition of a dash of triple sec and maraschino.

BEAM-ME-UP SCOTTY SHOT [NEW #7]

Glass: Shot
Method: Refrigerate ingredients then **LAYER** in chilled glass by carefully pouring in the following order.

1/2	shot(s)	**Kahlúa coffee liqueur**
1/2	shot(s)	**Giffard crème de banane du Brésil**
1/2	shot(s)	**Irish cream liqueur**

Comment: Coffee, banana and creamy whiskey. Very sweet but not too offensive and easy to layer.

BEBBO [UPDATED #7]

Glass: Martini
Garnish: Lemon zest twist
Method: STIR honey with gin in base of shaker until honey dissolves. Add other ingredients, **SHAKE** with ice and fine strain into chilled glass.

2	spoons	**Runny honey**
1 1/2	shot(s)	**Plymouth gin**
1	shot(s)	**Freshly squeezed lemon juice**
1/2	shot(s)	**Freshly squeezed orange juice**
1/4	shot(s)	**Chilled mineral water** (omit if wet ice)

Origin: A long lost relation of the Bee's Knees below. This recipe is based on one from Ted Haigh's 2004 book 'Vintage Spirits & Forgotten Cocktails'.
Comment: Fresh, clean and citrusy with honeyed notes. Choose your honey wisely.

BEE STING

Glass: Collins
Garnish: Apple slice
Method: STIR honey with whiskey in base of shaker until honey dissolves. Add tequila and apple juice, **SHAKE** with ice and strain into ice-filled glass. **TOP** with a splash of ginger ale.

1	spoon	**Runny honey**
1	shot(s)	**Jack Daniel's Tennessee whiskey**
1	shot(s)	**Partida tequila**
2	shot(s)	**Pressed apple juice**
Top up with		**Ginger ale**

Origin: Discovered in 2005 at The Royal Exchange Grand Café & Bar, London, England.
Comment: A delicately spiced, long, refreshing drink.

BEE'S KNEES #1

Glass: Martini
Garnish: Orange zest twist
Method: STIR honey with rum until honey dissolves. Add other ingredients, **SHAKE** with ice and fine strain into chilled glass.

1 1/4	shot(s)	**Light white rum**
1 1/4	shot(s)	**Pusser's navy rum**
2	spoons	**Runny honey**
1	shot(s)	**Freshly squeezed orange juice**
1/2	shot(s)	**Double (heavy) cream**
1/2	shot(s)	**Milk**

Comment: Smooth and orangey to start, with a rum and honey finish.

BEE'S KNEES #2 [UPDATED #7]

Glass: Martini
Garnish: Orange zest twist
Method: In base of shaker **STIR** honey with gin until honey dissolves. Add lemon and orange juice, **SHAKE** with ice and fine strain into chilled glass.

2	shot(s)	**Plymouth gin**
3	spoons	**Runny honey**
1	shot(s)	**Freshly squeezed lemon juice**
1	shot(s)	**Freshly squeezed orange juice**

Variant: Made with light rum in place of gin this drink becomes a Honeysuckle Martini.
Origin: Adapted from David A. Embury's 1948 'The Fine Art of Mixing Drinks'.
Comment: This concoction really is the bee's knees.

BEE'S KNEES #3 [NEW #7]

Glass: Martini
Garnish: Lemon zest twist
Method: In base of shaker **STIR** honey with gin until honey dissolves. Add lemon juice, **SHAKE** with ice and fine strain into chilled glass.

2	shot(s)	**Plymouth gin**
3	spoons	**Runny honey**
3/4	shot(s)	**Freshly squeezed lemon juice**

Comment: The combination of honey and lemon suggests flu relief but don't wait for an ailment before trying this soothing concoction.

BELLINI

It has long been traditional in Italy to marinade fresh peaches in wine and the Bellini draws on this tradition, combining prosecco wine with puréed white peaches (with added sugar and lemon juice).

Giuseppe Cipriani created this drink at Harry's Bar, Venice, in 1945, fourteen years after he opened his tiny place on the edge of the Grand Canal, not far from St. Mark's Square. Cipriani named his cocktail after the 15th-century Venetian painter Giovanni Bellini due to the drink's pink hue and the painter's penchant for using rich pinks on his canvases.

Like many other legendary bars around the world, Harry's owes some of its notoriety to being patronised by probably the world's greatest drinker, Ernest Hemingway. It was also the haunt of Sinclair Lewis, Orson Welles, F. Scott Fitzgerald and Dorothy Parker, and continues to attract celebrities to this day. But you don't have to be a celebrity to go to Harry's Bar. Cocktail aficionados from around the world make pilgrimages to the birthplace of the Bellini to sample the original recipe.

Prosecco is a sparkling wine which must come from a specific region in Northern Italy. White peaches are in season in Italy from May to September, so in Venice the best bars only sell the drink between May and October. Bars which serve the drink year round use frozen purée.

Bellini variations include
Bellini (original)
Bellini (Difford's formula)
Bellini-Tini
Kiwi Bellini
Puccini (tangerine/mandarin) Bellini
Raspberry Bellini
Rhubarb & Honey Bellini
Rossini (strawberry)
Tintoretto (pomegranate) Bellini
Tiziano (Fragola grape) Bellini

B

BEETLE JEUSE

Glass: Collins
Garnish: Mint sprig
Method: Lightly **MUDDLE** mint in base of shaker just enough to bruise. Add other ingredients, **SHAKE** with ice and strain into ice-filled glass.

7	fresh	**Mint leaves**
1	shot(s)	**Green Chartreuse liqueur**
1	shot(s)	**Zubrówka bison vodka**
3½	shot(s)	**Pressed apple juice**
¼	shot(s)	**Passion fruit sugar syrup**

Origin: Created in 2003 by Milo Rodriguez at Raoul's Bar, Oxford, and named after Beetlejuice, the Tim Burton black comedy about a young couple whose premature death leads them to a series of bizarre afterlife exploits.
Comment: Long and refreshing with a flavour reminiscent of caramelised apple.

BEHEMOTH

Glass: Martini
Garnish: Lemon zest twist
Method: SHAKE all ingredients with ice and fine strain into chilled glass.

1½	shot(s)	**Buffalo Trace bourbon whiskey**
1	shot(s)	**Sweet vermouth**
¾	shot(s)	**Giffard white crème de cacao**
¾	shot(s)	**Freshly squeezed lemon juice**
½	shot(s)	**Sugar syrup (2 sugar to 1 water)**
½	fresh	**Egg white (optional)**
2	dashes	**Peychaud's aromatic bitters (optional)**

Origin: This monstrous beast was created in 2004 by yours truly.
Comment: Tangy, citrus bourbon with a hint of chocolate.

BEJA FLOR

Glass: Martini
Garnish: Banana chunk on rim
Method: SHAKE all ingredients with ice and fine strain into chilled glass.

2	shot(s)	**Leblon cachaça**
1	shot(s)	**Cointreau triple sec**
1	shot(s)	**Giffard crème de banane du Brésil**
½	shot(s)	**Freshly squeezed lemon juice**

Comment: Sharp and quite dry but with a sweet banana twang.

'WHY DOES MAN KILL? HE KILLS FOR FOOD. AND NOT ONLY FOR FOOD: FREQUENTLY THERE MUST BE A BEVERAGE.'
WOODY ALLEN

BELLA DONNA DAIQUIRI

Glass: Martini
Garnish: Wipe rim with lemon & dust with cinnamon powder
Method: SHAKE all ingredients with ice and fine strain into chilled glass.

1½	shot(s)	**Gosling's Black Seal rum**
1½	shot(s)	**Luxardo Amaretto di Saschira**
½	shot(s)	**Freshly squeezed lemon juice**
¼	shot(s)	**Sugar syrup (2 sugar to 1 water)**
½	shot(s)	**Chilled mineral water** (omit if wet ice)

Origin: Adapted from a drink discovered in 2003 at Bellagio, Las Vegas, USA.
Comment: This was the hit cocktail for diffordsguide staff at the Bellagio, Las Vegas, after working at the Nightclub & Bar Beverage Convention. Try one and see why.

BELLINI #1 (ORIGINAL) [UPDATED #7]

Glass: Flute
Garnish: Peach slice on rim
Method: STIR all ingredients with ice and strain into chilled glass.

1	shot(s)	**Puréed white peaches** (10% added sugar)
⅛	shot(s)	**Freshly squeezed lemon juice**
2	shot(s)	**Prosecco sparkling wine (chilled)**

Origin: Created in 1934 by Giuseppe Cipriani at Harry's Bar, Venice, Italy.
Comment: It's hard not to like this blend of peaches and sparkling wine.

BELLINI #2 (DIFFORD'S FORMULA) [UPDATED #7]

Glass: Flute
Garnish: Peach slice on rim
Method: SHAKE first four ingredients with ice and fine strain into chilled glass. Add Prosecco and gently stir. (Alternatively, refrigerate all ingredients, blend briefly without ice and serve in chilled glass.)

2	shot(s)	**Puréed white peaches** (10% added sugar)
¼	shot(s)	**Teichenné Peach Schnapps Liqueur**
¼	shot(s)	**Peach eau de vie (de pêche)**
⅛	shot(s)	**Freshly squeezed lemon juice**
Top up with		**Prosecco sparkling wine**

Origin: Created in 2003 by yours truly.
Comment: My version is more alcoholic and drier than the classic Bellini.

BELLINI-TINI

Glass: Martini
Garnish: Peach wedge
Method: SHAKE all ingredients with ice and fine strain into chilled glass.

2	shot(s)	**Ketel One vodka**
½	shot(s)	**Teichenné Peach Schnapps Liqueur**
2	shot(s)	**Fresh white peach purée**
3	dashes	**Peach bitters (optional)**

Comment: Peachy, peachy, peachy! Based on the Bellini, funnily enough.

BELLISSIMO

Glass: Old-fashioned
Garnish: Orange slice
Method: SHAKE all ingredients with ice and fine strain into ice-filled glass.

1	shot(s)	**Frangelico hazelnut liqueur**
1	shot(s)	**Campari**
1	shot(s)	**Luxardo limoncello liqueur**
1/2	shot(s)	**Freshly squeezed lemon juice**

Origin: Adapted from a drink created in 2003 by Ben Davidson at Posh Lounge, Sydney, Australia.
Comment: An unusual meld of flavours, but Campari lovers should give this a try.

BENSONHURST [NEW #7]

Glass: Martini
Garnish: Maraschino cherry
Method: STIR all ingredients with ice and strain into chilled glass.

2	shot(s)	**Buffalo Trace bourbon whiskey**
1	shot(s)	**Dry vermouth**
1/2	shot(s)	**Luxardo maraschino liqueur**
1/4	shot(s)	**Cynar artichoke liqueur**

Origin: Adapted from a drink created in 2006 by Chad Solomon and named after a neighbourhood close to his home in Brooklyn, New York City, USA
Comment: A refined and balanced Manhattan-style drink.

BENTLEY [UPDATED #7]

Glass: Old-fashioned
Garnish: Orange zest twist
Method: STIR all ingredients with ice and strain into ice-filled glass.

1 1/2	shot(s)	**Boulard Grand Solage Calvados**
1 1/2	shot(s)	**Dubonnet Red**
2	dashes	**Peychaud's aromatic bitters (optional)**

Variant: Served straight-up.
Origin: Adapted from Harry Craddock's 1930 'The Savoy Cocktail Book'.
Comment: Dry, spiced wine impregnated with apple – pretty damn good.

BERMUDA COCKTAIL [NEW #7]

Glass: Martini
Garnish: Orange zest twist
Method: SHAKE all ingredients with ice and fine strain into chilled glass.

2	shot(s)	**Plymouth gin**
1/2	shot(s)	**Teichenné Peach Schnapps Liqueur**
1/2	shot(s)	**Freshly squeezed orange juice**
1/4	shot(s)	**Pomegranate (grenadine) syrup**

Origin: Adapted from Victor Bergeron's 'Trader Vic's Bartender's Guide' (1972 revised edition).
Comment: Gin with a sweetening touch of peach, orange and pomegranate.

BERMUDA ROSE COCKTAIL [NEW #7]

Glass: Martini
Garnish: Apricot slice (dried or fresh) on rim
Method: SHAKE all ingredients with ice and fine strain into chilled glass.

2	shot(s)	**Plymouth gin**
1/2	shot(s)	**Giffard apricot brandy du Roussillon**
1/4	shot(s)	**Pomegranate (grenadine) syrup**
1/2	shot(s)	**Chilled mineral water** (omit if wet ice)

Origin: Adapted from Victor Bergeron's 'Trader Vic's Bartender's Guide' (1972 revised edition).
Comment: Delicate, floral and aromatic. A hint of sweetness but not so as to offend.

BERMUDA RUM SWIZZLE [NEW #7]

Glass: Collins
Garnish: Orange & cherry on stick (sail)
Method: POUR all ingredients into glass, add crushed ice and SWIZZLE. Serve with straws.

2	shot(s)	**Goslings Black Seal dark rum**
1	shot(s)	**Freshly squeezed lime juice**
1	shot(s)	**Pressed pineapple juice**
1	shot(s)	**Freshly squeezed orange juice**
1/4	shot(s)	**Velvet Falernum liqueur**

Origin: Recipe adapted from drinkboy.com.
Comment: Tangy fruit for the poolside.

BERRY CAIPIRINHA

Glass: Old-fashioned
Method: MUDDLE lime and berries in base of glass. Add other ingredients and fill glass with crushed ice. **CHURN** drink with bar spoon and serve with short straws.

3/4	fresh	**Lime cut into wedges**
3	fresh	**Raspberries**
3	fresh	**Blackberries**
2	shot(s)	**Leblon cachaça**
3/4	shot(s)	**Sugar syrup (2 sugar to 1 water)**

Variant: Black 'N' Blue Caipirovska
Comment: A fruity version of the popular Brazilian drink.

BERRY NICE [UPDATED #7]

Glass: Collins
Garnish: Blackberries
Method: MUDDLE blackberries in base of shaker. Add next three ingredients, **SHAKE** with ice and strain into ice-filled glass. **TOP** with ginger beer and serve with straws.

9	fresh	**Blackberries**
2	shot(s)	**Ketel One vodka**
1/4	shot(s)	**Chambord black raspberry liqueur**
1/2	shot(s)	**Freshly squeezed lemon juice**
Top up with		**Jamaican ginger beer**

Origin: Adapted from a drink created in 2001 in the UK's The Living Room chain of bars.
Comment: Rich blackberry flavour with a ginger finish.

BESSIE & JESSIE

Glass: Collins
Garnish: Orange slice
Method: SHAKE all ingredients with ice and strain into ice-filled glass.

2	shot(s)	**Scotch whisky**
2	shot(s)	**Bols advocaat liqueur**
3½	shot(s)	**Milk**

Comment: Malty, creamy and eggy, but tasty.

BETWEEN DECKS [NEW #7]

Glass: Collins
Garnish: Pineapple wedge, mint & cherry
Method: SHAKE all ingredients with ice and strain into ice-filled glass.

2½	shot(s)	**Plymouth gin**
1	shot(s)	**Freshly squeezed orange juice**
1	shot(s)	**Ocean Spray cranberry juice**
½	shot(s)	**Freshly squeezed lime juice**
¼	shot(s)	**Sugar syrup**
½	shot(s)	**Chilled mineral water** (omit if wet ice)

Origin: Adapted from Victor Bergeron's 'Trader Vic's Bartender's Guide' (1972 revised edition).
Comment: I've upped the ante on this drink with more gin and less fruit than the original - so beware.

BETWEEN THE SHEETS #1 [NEW #7]
(CLASSIC FORMULA)

Glass: Martini
Garnish: Lemon zest twist
Method: SHAKE all ingredients with ice and fine strain into chilled glass.

1	shot(s)	**Light White rum**
1	shot(s)	**Rémy Martin cognac**
1	shot(s)	**Cointreau triple sec**
¼	shot(s)	**Freshly squeezed lemon juice**

Origin: Created in the 1930s by Harry MacElhone, of Harry's New York Bar in Paris, and derived from the Sidecar.
Comment: Three shots of 40% alcohol and a splash of lemon juice make for a tart drink which should not be undertaken lightly.

BETWEEN THE SHEETS #2 [UPDATED #7]
(DIFFORD'S FORMULA)

Glass: Martini
Garnish: Lemon zest twist
Method: SHAKE all ingredients with ice and fine strain into chilled glass.

¾	shot(s)	**Light White rum**
¾	shot(s)	**Rémy Martin cognac**
¾	shot(s)	**Cointreau triple sec**
¼	shot(s)	**Freshly squeezed lemon juice**
½	shot(s)	**Chilled mineral water** (omit if wet ice)

Comment: Maintains the essential flavour and ingredients of the classic formula but is a little more approachable.

BEVERLY HILLS ICED TEA

Glass: Sling
Garnish: Lime zest spiral
Method: SHAKE first five ingredients with ice and strain into ice-filled glass. **TOP** with champagne and gently stir.

¾	shot(s)	**Plymouth gin**
¾	shot(s)	**Ketel One vodka**
1	shot(s)	**Cointreau triple sec**
½	shot(s)	**Freshly squeezed lime juice**
½	shot(s)	**Sugar syrup (2 sugar to 1 water)**
Top up with		**Brut champagne**

Comment: Very strong and refreshing.

BIARRITZ

Glass: Old-fashioned
Garnish: Orange & cherry on stick (sail)
Method: SHAKE all ingredients with ice and strain into ice-filled glass.

2	shot(s)	**Rémy Martin cognac**
1	shot(s)	**Grand Marnier liqueur**
¾	shot(s)	**Freshly squeezed lemon juice**
½	fresh	**Egg white**
3	dashes	**Angostura aromatic bitters**

Comment: Basically a brandy sour with a little something extra from the orange liqueur.

BIG APPLE MARTINI

Glass: Martini
Garnish: Apple wedge on rim
Method: SHAKE all ingredients with ice and fine strain into chilled glass.

2½	shot(s)	**Ketel One vodka**
1	shot(s)	**Sour apple liqueur**
1	shot(s)	**Apple schnapps liqueur**

AKA: Apple Martini, Sour Apple Martini
Comment: There's no apple juice in this Martini, but it has an appealing light minty green hue.

THE BIG EASY

Glass: Collins
Garnish: Half orange slice
Method: SHAKE first three ingredients with ice and strain into ice-filled glass. **TOP** with ginger ale.

1¾	shot(s)	**Southern Comfort liqueur**
¾	shot(s)	**Cointreau triple sec**
2	shot(s)	**Freshly squeezed orange juice**
Top up with		**Ginger ale**

Comment: Fruity and refreshing with a hint of spice.

BIJOU [NEW #7]

Glass: Martini
Garnish: Cherry & discarded lemon zest twist
Method: SHAKE all ingredients with ice and fine strain into chilled glass.

1 1/2	shot(s)	**Plymouth gin**
1/2	shot(s)	**Green Chartreuse liqueur**
1/2	shot(s)	**Sweet vermouth**
2	dashes	**Fee Brothers orange bitters**
1/2	shot(s)	**Chilled mineral water** (omit if wet ice)

AKA: Amber Dream, Golden Glow
Origin: A forgotten Classic
Comment: Serious and packed with bold flavours. Fellow Chartreuse fans will approve.

BIKINI MARTINI [UPDATED #7]

Glass: Martini
Garnish: Orange zest twist
Method: SHAKE all ingredients with ice and fine strain into chilled glass.

2	shot(s)	**Plymouth gin**
3/4	shot(s)	**Bols Blue curaçao liqueur**
1/4	shot(s)	**Teichenné Peach Schnapps Liqueur**
1/4	shot(s)	**Freshly squeezed lemon juice**
1/2	shot(s)	**Chilled mineral water** (omit if wet ice)

Origin: Adapted from a cocktail created in 1999 by Dick Bradsell for an Agent Provocateur swimwear launch. The bikini swimsuit was named after Bikini Atoll, where A-bombs were tested after World War II, on the basis that such a revealing garment would cause as much shock as a thermonuclear device.
Comment: A vivid blue combination of lemon, orange and peach laced with gin.

BINGO

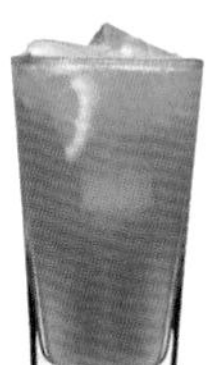

Glass: Collins
Garnish: Lemon wheel
Method: SHAKE first four ingredients with ice and strain into ice filled glass. Top with soda water.

1	shot(s)	**Ketel One vodka**
1	shot(s)	**Grand Marnier liqueur**
1	shot(s)	**Giffard apricot brandy du Roussillon**
1/2	shot(s)	**Freshly squeezed lemon juice**
Top up with		**Soda water (club soda)**

Comment: Refreshing, fruity long drink.

BIRD OF PARADISE

Glass: Martini
Garnish: Dust with freshly grated nutmeg
Method: SHAKE all ingredients with ice and fine strain into chilled glass.

1 1/4	shot(s)	**Partida tequila**
3/4	shot(s)	**Giffard white crème de cacao**
1/2	shot(s)	**Luxardo Amaretto di Saschira**
1	shot(s)	**Double (heavy) cream**
3/4	shot(s)	**Milk**

Comment: If you like tequila and creamy drinks, the two don't mix much better than this.

BISHOP [UPDATED #7]

Glass: Toddy
Garnish: Dust with freshly grated nutmeg
Method: MUDDLE cloves in the base of shaker. Add boiling water and **STIR** in honey and other ingredients. Fine strain into glass and **MICROWAVE** for twenty seconds to boost temperature. **STIR**, garnish and serve.

7	whole	**Cloves**
3	shot(s)	**Boiling water**
2	spoons	**Runny honey**
2 1/2	shot(s)	**Tawny port**
1	shot(s)	**Freshly squeezed orange juice**

Origin: My quick 'n' easy take on this variation of the 18th century Negus - reputedly a favourite of the writer Dr. Johnson. The traditional recipe begins with studding an orange with cloves and roasting it in the oven.
Comment: A flavoursome and warming variation on mulled wine.

'I HAD TO STOP DRINKING BECAUSE I GOT TIRED OF WAKING UP IN MY CAR GOING 90.'

THE BISTRO SIDECAR [NEW #7]

Glass: Martini
Garnish: Lemon zest twist
Method: SHAKE all ingredients with ice and fine strain into chilled glass.

1 1/2	shot(s)	**Rémy Martin cognac**
1/2	shot(s)	**Tuaca liqueur**
1/2	shot(s)	**Frangelico liqueur**
1/4	shot(s)	**Freshly squeezed lemon juice**
1/4	shot(s)	**Freshly squeezed orange juice**

Origin: Adapted from a recipe by chef Kathy Casey of Kathy Casey Food Studios, Seattle, USA. Kathy's original recipe called for a sugar rim and tangerine juice.
Comment: Although significantly twisted from the classic, this is still recognisably a Sidecar in style.

BIT-O-HONEY

Glass: Shot
Method: Refrigerate ingredients then **LAYER** in chilled glass by carefully pouring in the following order.

3/4	shot(s)	**Teichenné butterscotch Schnapps**
3/4	shot(s)	**Irish cream liqueur**

Variant: Layered with butterscotch, then honey liqueur and an Irish cream float.
Comment: A sweet but pleasant tasting shot.

B

BITTER ELDER [UPDATED #7]

Glass: Collins
Garnish: Lemon wedge
Method: SHAKE all ingredients with ice and strain into ice-filled glass.

2	shot(s)	**Plymouth gin**
1	shot(s)	**St-Germain elderflower liqueur**
2	shot(s)	**Pressed apple juice**
3/4	shot(s)	**Freshly squeezed lemon juice**
3	dashes	**Angostura aromatic bitters**

Origin: Adapted from a short drink created in 2005 by Tonin Kacaj at Maze, London, England.
Comment: The eponymous elderflower is well balanced with the other ingredients to make a dry refreshing long drink.

BITTER SWEET SYMPHONY

Glass: Martini
Garnish: Apricot slice
Method: SHAKE all ingredients with ice and fine strain into chilled glass.

1/2	shot(s)	**Ketel One vodka**
1	shot(s)	**Cointreau triple sec**
1	shot(s)	**Giffard apricot brandy du Roussillon**
1/2	shot(s)	**Freshly squeezed lime juice**
1 1/2	shot(s)	**Freshly squeezed grapefruit juice**

Origin: Adapted from a drink created in 2003 by Wayne Collins for Maxxium UK.
Comment: This roller coaster ride of bitter and sweet mainly features apricot and grapefruit.

BITTEREST PILL

Glass: Shot
Method: Refrigerate ingredients then **LAYER** in chilled glass by carefully pouring in the following order.

1/2	shot(s)	**Passion fruit sugar syrup**
1/2	shot(s)	**Campari**
1/2	shot(s)	**Ketel One vodka**

Created by: Alex Kammerling, London, England
Comment: The bitterness of Campari, toned down by passion fruit sugar syrup.

BLACK & TAN

Glass: Boston
Method: POUR lager into chilled glass then **FLOAT** Guinness on top.

1/2	pint	**Lager**
1/2	pint	**Guinness stout**

Comment: Lager downstairs, Guinness upstairs.

BLACK & VELVET [NEW #7]

Glass: Boston
Method: POUR cider into chilled glass then **FLOAT** Guinness on top.

1/2	pint	**Cider**
1/2	pint	**Guinness stout**

Comment: Cider downstairs, Guinness upstairs.

BLACK & WHITE DAIQUIRI

Glass: Martini
Garnish: Blackberry in drink
Method: MUDDLE berries in base of shaker. Add other ingredients, **SHAKE** with ice and fine strain into chilled glass.

12	fresh	**Blackberries**
2	shot(s)	**Malibu coconut rum liqueur**
1	shot(s)	**Light white rum**
3/4	shot(s)	**Giffard mûre (blackberry)**
1/2	shot(s)	**Freshly squeezed lime juice**
1/2	shot(s)	**Chilled mineral water** (omit if wet ice)

Origin: I named this drink after the black berries and the white Malibu bottle.
Comment: Blackberries and coconut add depth to the classic Daiquiri.

BLACK BEARD

Glass: Boston
Method: POUR ingredients into glass and serve.

2	shot(s)	**Spiced rum**
1/2	pint	**Guinness** (chilled)
Top up with		**Cola** (chilled)

Origin: Thought to have originated in Stirling, Scotland, during the late 1990s.
Comment: Something of a student drink, this tastes better than it sounds.

BLACK BISON MARTINI

Glass: Martini
Garnish: Apple wedge
Method: SHAKE all ingredients with ice and fine strain into chilled glass.

2	shot(s)	**Plymouth gin**
1/2	shot(s)	**Apple schnapps liqueur**
1 1/2	shot(s)	**Pressed apple juice**
1/4	shot(s)	**Dry vermouth**

Origin: Adapted from a drink discovered in 2001 at Oxo Tower Bar, London, England.
Comment: A fragrant cocktail with a dry finish. As the name suggests, also works well with Zubrówka bison vodka in place of gin.

BLACK CHERRY MARTINI [NEW #7]

Glass: Martini
Garnish: Fresh or maraschino cherry
Method: SHAKE all ingredients with ice and fine strain into chilled glass.

2½	shot(s)	**Ketel One vodka**
1	shot(s)	**Chambord liqueur**

Comment: Subtle berry fruit tames vodka's sting.

BLACK DREAM

Glass: Shot
Method: Refrigerate ingredients then **LAYER** in chilled glass by carefully pouring in the following order.

½	shot(s)	**Opal Nera black sambuca**
½	shot(s)	**Irish cream liqueur**

Comment: Slippery Nipple with black sambuca.

BLACK FEATHER [NEW #7]

Glass: Martini
Garnish: Lemon zest twist
Method: STIR all ingredients with ice and strain into chilled glass.

2	shot(s)	**Rémy Martin cognac**
1	shot(s)	**Dry vermouth**
½	shot(s)	**Cointreau triple sec**
1	dash	**Angostura aromatic bitters**

Origin: Adapted from a drink created in 2000 by Robert Hess and published on drinkboy.com.
Comment: Rounded cognac notes with a hint of orange. For dry, adult palates.

BLACK FOREST GATEAU MARTINI

Glass: Martini
Garnish: Dust with cocoa powder
Method: SHAKE first four ingredients with ice and strain into chilled glass. **FLOAT** cream on drink.

2	shot(s)	**Ketel One vodka**
¾	shot(s)	**Chambord black raspberry liqueur**
¾	shot(s)	**Giffard crème de fraise de bois**
¼	shot(s)	**Giffard Cassis Noir de Bourgogne**
1	shot(s)	**Double (heavy) cream**

Origin: Created in 2002 at Hush, London, England.
Comment: Dessert by name and dessert by nature. Wonderfully moreish, naughty but very nice.

BLACK IRISH

Glass: Hurricane
Garnish: Dust with cocoa powder
Method: BLEND ingredients with 12oz scoop of crushed ice. Pour into glass and serve with straws.

1	shot(s)	**Ketel One vodka**
1	shot(s)	**Irish cream liqueur**
1	shot(s)	**Kahlúa coffee liqueur**
2	scoops	**Vanilla ice cream**

AKA: Frozen Black Irish
Comment: Like a very sweet, alcoholic, frozen caffè latte.

BLACK JACK SHOT

Glass: Shot
Method: Refrigerate ingredients then **LAYER** in chilled glass by carefully pouring in the following order.

¾	shot(s)	**Opal Nera black sambuca**
¾	shot(s)	**Jack Daniel's Tennessee whiskey**

Comment: Whiskey sweetened with sambuca.

BLACK JACK COCKTAIL [NEW #7]

Glass: Martini
Garnish: Lemon peel twist
Method: STIR all ingredients with ice and strain into chilled glass.

1½	shot(s)	**Plymouth gin**
½	shot(s)	**Kirschwasser eau de vie**
½	shot(s)	**Giffard Cassis Noir de Bourgogne**
¾	shot(s)	**Chilled mineral water** (reduce if wet ice)

Origin: The name Black Jack traditionally refers to a water bottle made from air dried leather. When the leather was dried it tended to turn black.
Comment: More burgundy than black but dark fruits of the forest dominate this medium dry cocktail.

BLACK JAPAN [NEW #7]

Glass: Collins
Method: POUR melon liqueur into chilled glass then **FLOAT** Guinness on top.

1½	shot(s)	**Midori green melon liqueur**
Float & Top		**Guinness Original stout**

Origin: Black Japan' is the name of a protective lacquer applied to metal.
Comment: This student-style drink will appeal to those with youthful exuberance and a sweet tooth.

B

BLACK MAGIC [UPDATED #7]

Glass: Flute
Garnish: Black grape on rim
Method: **MUDDLE** grapes in base of shaker. Add liqueur, **SHAKE** with ice and fine strain into chilled glass. **TOP** with champagne.

12	fresh	**Red grapes**
1/2	shot(s)	**Grand Marnier liqueur**
Top up with		**Brut champagne**

Comment: More peachy in colour than black but balanced and tasty. Not sweet.

BLACK MARTINI

Glass: Martini
Garnish: Float grated white chocolate
Method: **SHAKE** all ingredients with ice and fine strain into chilled glass.

1 1/2	shot(s)	**Light white rum**
1 1/2	shot(s)	**Giffard brown crème de cacao**
1 1/2	shot(s)	**Cold espresso coffee**

Origin: Created in March 2004 by yours truly.
Comment: This flavoursome mix of coffee and chocolate is further enhanced if vanilla-infused rum is used.

BLACK MUSSEL

Glass: Flute
Garnish: Orange zest twist discarded
Method: **POUR** first two ingredients into glass and top up with champagne.

1/2	shot(s)	**Blue curaçao liqueur**
1/4	shot(s)	**Giffard Cassis Noir de Bourgogne**
Top up with		**Brut champagne**

Comment: Blue curaçao adds a hint of orange to a Kir Royale.

BLACK 'N' BLUE CAIPIROVSKA

Glass: Old-fashioned
Method: **MUDDLE** berries in base of glass. Add other ingredients. Fill glass with crushed ice, **CHURN** (stir) with bar spoon and serve with straws.

6	fresh	**Blackberries**
10	fresh	**Blueberries**
2	shot(s)	**Ketel One vodka**
1/2	shot(s)	**Freshly squeezed lime juice**
3/4	shot(s)	**Sugar syrup (2 sugar to 1 water)**

Comment: A great fruity twist on the regular Caipirovska.

BLACK NUTS

Glass: Shot
Method: **LAYER** in chilled glass by carefully pouring ingredients in the following order.

3/4	shot(s)	**Opal Nera black sambuca**
3/4	shot(s)	**Frangelico hazelnut liqueur**

Comment: It's something of a challenge to get the Hazelnut liqueur to float on the black sambuca. If you store the Opal Nera in a freezer and the hazelnut liqueur at room temperature, this helps.

BLACK RUSSIAN 

Glass: Old-fashioned
Garnish: Lemon slice & cherry (sail)
Method: **STIR** all ingredients with ice and strain into ice-filled glass.

2	shot(s)	**Ketel One vodka**
1/2	shot(s)	**Kahlúa coffee liqueur**

Variants: 1/ Served straight-up in a Martini glass. 2/ Topped with cola and served over ice in a Collins glass. 3/ Made into a White Russian.
Comment: Most popularly served with cola. With or without, this drink is not that interesting.

BLACK VELVET

Glass: Flute
Garnish: Shamrock or mint leaf
Method: **POUR** ingredients into chilled glass.

2 1/2	shot(s)	**Guinness stout**
Top up with		**Brut champagne**

Origin: Thought to have originated in 1861 at Brook's Club, London, after the death of Prince Albert. Some credit it to the Shelbourne Hotel, Dublin, Ireland.
Comment: A fitting tipple for Saint Patrick's Day in honour of Ireland's patron saint, who's credited with banishing snakes from the island back in 441 AD.

BLACK WIDOW

Glass: Martini
Garnish: Liquorice
Method: **SHAKE** all ingredients with ice and fine strain into chilled glass.

1	shot(s)	**Opal Nera black sambuca**
1	shot(s)	**Giffard crème de fraise de bois**
1	shot(s)	**Malibu coconut rum liqueur**
1/2	shot(s)	**Double (heavy) cream**
1/2	shot(s)	**Milk**

Comment: This sticky, fruity, liquorice cocktail tastes a little like an Allsort sweet.

BLACKTHORN COCKTAIL [NEW #7]

Glass: Martini
Garnish: Lemon zest twist
Method: STIR all ingredients with ice and strain into chilled glass.

1 1/2	shot(s)	**Plymouth gin**
3/4	shot(s)	**Dubonnet Red**
3/4	shot(s)	**Kirschwasser eau de vie**

Comment: This drink benefits from a long, chilling and diluting stir. The result is Martini-style, fruity but dry.

BLACKTHORN ENGLISH

Glass: Martini
Garnish: Flamed orange zest twist
Method: SHAKE all ingredients with ice and fine strain into chilled glass.

1 1/2	shot(s)	**Plymouth sloe gin liqueur**
3/4	shot(s)	**Plymouth gin**
3/4	shot(s)	**Sweet vermouth**
3	dashes	**Fee Brothers orange bitters**
1/2	shot(s)	**Chilled mineral water** (omit if wet ice)

Origin: A classic cocktail whose origins are unknown.
Comment: A dry, subtle rust-coloured Martini.

BLACKTHORN IRISH

Glass: Martini
Garnish: Flamed lemon zest twist
Method: SHAKE all ingredients with ice and fine strain into chilled glass.

1 1/2	shot(s)	**Irish whiskey**
1	shot(s)	**Dry vermouth**
1/4	shot(s)	**Pernod anis**
4	dashes	**Angostura aromatic bitters**
1/2	shot(s)	**Chilled mineral water** (omit if wet ice)

Origin: A classic cocktail whose origins are unknown.
Comment: A dry and aromatic Martini with hints of anis. Some may prefer to add a dash of sugar syrup.

BLADE RUNNER [NEW #7]

Glass: Collins
Garnish: Pineapple wedge & cherry
Method: SHAKE all ingredients with ice and strain into ice-filled glass.

2	shot(s)	**Light white rum**
1/2	shot(s)	**Myers's dark rum**
2 1/2	shot(s)	**Pressed pineapple juice**
1/4	shot(s)	**Sugar syrup (2 sugar to 1 water)**
2	shot(s)	**Angostura aromatic bitters**
1/2	shot(s)	**Freshly squeezed lime juice**

Origin: Discovered in 2005 at Zoulou Bar, Berlin, Germany.
Comment: Tangy and fruity but not too sweet.

BLIMEY [UPDATED #7]

Glass: Old-fashioned
Garnish: Lime wedge
Method: MUDDLE blackberries in base of shaker. Add other ingredients, **SHAKE** with ice and fine strain into glass filled with crushed ice. Serve with straws.

7	fresh	**Blackberries**
2	shot(s)	**Ketel One vodka**
3/4	shot(s)	**Giffard Cassis Noir de Bourgogne**
1	shot(s)	**Freshly squeezed lime juice**
1/8	shot(s)	**Sugar syrup (2 sugar to 1 water)**

Origin: Created in 2002 by yours truly.
Comment: This blackberry and lime blend is both fruity and aptly named.

'SO LONG AS ANY MAN DRINKS WHEN HE WANTS TO AND STOPS WHEN HE WANTS TO, HE ISN'T A DRUNKARD, NO MATTER HOW MUCH HE DRINKS OR HOW OFTEN HE FALLS UNDER THE TABLE.'

BLING! BLING!

Glass: Shot
Method: MUDDLE raspberries in base of shaker. Add vodka, lime and sugar, **SHAKE** with ice and fine strain into glass. **TOP** with champagne.

8	fresh	**Raspberries**
1/2	shot(s)	**Ketel One vodka**
1/2	shot(s)	**Freshly squeezed lime juice**
1/2	shot(s)	**Sugar syrup (2 sugar to 1 water)**
Top up with		**Brut champagne**

Origin: Created in 2001 by Phillip Jeffrey at the GE Club, London, England.
Comment: An ostentatious little number.

BLINKER [UPDATED #7]

Glass: Martini
Garnish: Lemon twist
Method: SHAKE all ingredients with ice and fine strain into chilled glass.

2	shot(s)	**Buffalo Trace bourbon whiskey**
1	shot(s)	**Freshly squeezed pink grapefruit juice**
1/4	shot(s)	**Pomegranate (grenadine) syrup**

Origin: A 1930s classic revisited.
Comment: Back in the 1930s David Embury wrote of this drink, "One of a few cocktails using grapefruit juice. Not particularly good but not too bad." How times have changed!

BLOODY MARY

The creation of The Bloody Mary is a matter of some dispute, but is generally credited to Fernand Petiot. Whether this was in 1920 (or 1921), when Petiot was a young bartender at Harry's New York Bar in Paris, or in America, during the 1940s, after the comedian George Jessel had first popularised the unspiced combination of vodka and tomato juice, is not clear.

If you believe that Petiot first created it around 1920, then you will believe that the name is borrowed not from the English Queen Mary the First, whose persecution of Protestants gave her that name, or for the silent movie actress Mary Pickford, but from one of Petiot's customers, apparently the entertainer Roy Barton. He had worked at a nightclub (or knew a bar) called the Bucket of Blood in Chicago, where there was a waitress known as 'Bloody Mary', and he said the drink reminded him of her.

If you believe Petiot invented it in New York, where he worked at the St. Regis Hotel certainly from the end of Prohibition, then he may have had assistance in its creation from Serge Obolansky, the manager of the hotel, who asked him to spice up his 50-50 blend of vodka and tomato juice. According to this version, he attempted to rename the drink Red Snapper, after Vincent Astor, who owned the hotel, found the name too crude for his clientele.

The celery stick garnish apparently dates back to 1960 when a bartender at the Ambassador Hotel in Chicago noticed a lady stirring her drink with a celery stick. Whatever the precise story behind this fantastic drink, Bloody Mary recipes are as personal as Martinis. Purists will only use Tabasco, Worcestershire sauce, salt and lemon to spice up tomato and vodka but everything from oysters to V8 can be added.

The Bloody Mary's many variations include
Asian Mary (with wasabi, ginger & soy sauce)
Bloody Bull (with beef consommé)
Bloody Caesar (with clam juice)
Bloody Joseph (with Scotch whisky)
Bloody Maria (with tequila)
Bloody Maru (with sake)
Bloody Mary (original)
Bloody Mary (modern)
Bloody Shame (mocktail)
Bullshot (with beef bouillon)
Cubanita (with rum)
Peppered Mary (with pepper vodka)
Red Snapper (with gin)

BLOOD & SAND #1 (CLASSIC FORMULA) [UPDATED #7]

Glass: Martini
Garnish: Orange zest twist
Method: SHAKE all ingredients with ice and fine strain into chilled glass.

3/4	shot(s)	**Scotch whisky**
3/4	shot(s)	**Cherry brandy liqueur**
3/4	shot(s)	**Sweet vermouth**
3/4	shot(s)	**Freshly squeezed orange juice**

Origin: Created for the premiere of the 1922 Rudolph Valentino movie, Blood and Sand. This equal parts formula comes from the 1930 edition of 'The Savoy Cocktail Book'.
Comment: One of the best classic Scotch cocktails but a little sweet.

BLOOD & SAND #2 (DIFFORD'S FORMULA) [NEW #7]

Glass: Martini
Garnish: Orange zest twist
Method: SHAKE all ingredients with ice and fine strain into chilled glass.

1 1/2	shot(s)	**Scotch whisky**
3/4	shot(s)	**Cherry brandy liqueur**
3/4	shot(s)	**Sweet vermouth**
3/4	shot(s)	**Freshly squeezed orange juice**

Origin: Formula by yours truly in 2006.
Comment: A dry, more spirited Blood & Sand for those who like Scotch.

BLOODHOUND

Glass: Collins
Garnish: Lime wedge
Method: SHAKE all ingredients with ice and strain into ice-filled glass.

2	shot(s)	**Campari**
1	shot(s)	**Ketel One vodka**
3 1/2	shot(s)	**Freshly squeezed grapefruit juice**

Comment: A dry, tart, refreshing long drink.

BLOOD ORANGE [UPDATED #7]

Glass: Collins
Garnish: Raspberries
Method: MUDDLE raspberries in base of shaker. Add other ingredients, **SHAKE** with ice and fine strain into ice-filled glass.

7	fresh	**Raspberries**
2	shot(s)	**Orange zest infused Ketel One vodka**
1/2	shot(s)	**Raspberry (framboise) liqueur**
1 1/2	shot(s)	**Freshly squeezed orange juice**
1 1/4	shot(s)	**Ocean Spray cranberry juice**
1/2	shot(s)	**Freshly squeezed lime juice**

Origin: Adapted from a drink created in 2005 by Mark Pratt at Maze, London, England.
Comment: Long, refreshing and very fruity. Appropriately named given its colour and taste.

BLOODY CAESAR [NEW #7]

Glass: Collins
Garnish: Pickled bean
Method: SHAKE all ingredients with ice and strain into ice-filled glass.

2	shot(s)	**Ketel One vodka**
4	shot(s)	**Mott's Clamato juice**
1/2	shot(s)	**Freshly squeezed lime juice**
7	drops	**Tabasco pepper sauce**
3	dashes	**Lea & Perrins Worcestershire sauce**
2	pinch	**Celery salt**
2	pinch	**Black pepper**

Origin: Created by Walter Chell in 1969 to celebrate the opening of Marco's Italian restaurant at the Calgary Inn, Canada. Walter was inspired by the flavours of Spaghetti Vongole (spaghetti with clams) and named the drink after the Roman emperor.
Comment: A peculiarly Canadian fishy twist on the classic Bloody Mary.

BLOODY JOSEPH

Glass: Collins
Garnish: Stick of celery
Method: SHAKE all ingredients with ice and strain into ice-filled glass.

2	shot(s)	**Scotch whisky**
4	shot(s)	**Pressed tomato juice**
1/2	shot(s)	**Freshly squeezed lemon juice**
8	drops	**Tabasco pepper sauce**
4	dashes	**Lea & Perrins Worcestershire sauce**
1/2	spoon	**Horseradish sauce**
1/2	shot(s)	**Tawny port**
2	pinch	**Celery salt**
2	pinch	**Black pepper**

Comment: A Bloody Mary with whisky.

BLOODY MARU

Glass: Collins
Garnish: Lemongrass stick
Method: SHAKE all ingredients with ice and strain into ice-filled glass.

3	shot(s)	**Sake**
3	shot(s)	**Pressed tomato juice**
1/2	shot(s)	**Freshly squeezed lemon juice**
8	drops	**Tabasco pepper sauce**
4	dashes	**Lea & Perrins Worcestershire sauce**
2	pinch	**Celery salt**
2	pinch	**Black pepper**

Origin: A Bloody Mary based on sake.

BLOODY MARY (1930S RECIPE)

Glass: Old-fashioned
Garnish: Salt & pepper rim
Method: SHAKE all ingredients with ice and strain into empty glass.

2	shot(s)	**100-proof (50% alc./vol.) vodka**
2	shot(s)	**Thick pressed tomato juice**
1/4	shot(s)	**Freshly squeezed lemon juice**
5	dashes	**Lea & Perrins Worcestershire sauce**
4	pinch	**Salt**
2	pinch	**Black pepper**
2	pinch	**Cayenne pepper**

Variant: Red Snapper
Origin: A 1933 version of the classic created in 1920 by Fernand Petiot at Harry's New York Bar, Paris, France.
Comment: Fiery stuff. The modern version is more user friendly.

'IN NEVADA... THE CHEAPEST AND EASIEST WAY TO BECOME AN INFLUENTIAL MAN... WAS TO STAND BEHIND A BAR, WEAR A DIAMOND CLUSTER-PIN, AND SELL WHISKY.'

BLOODY MARIA

Glass: Collins
Garnish: Salt & pepper rim plus celery stick
Method: SHAKE all ingredients with ice and strain into ice-filled glass.

2	shot(s)	**Partida tequila**
4	shot(s)	**Pressed tomato juice**
1/2	shot(s)	**Freshly squeezed lemon juice**
8	drops	**Tabasco pepper sauce**
4	dashes	**Lea & Perrins Worcestershire sauce**
1/2	spoon	**Horseradish sauce**
1/2	shot(s)	**Tawny port**
2	pinch	**Celery salt**
2	pinch	**Black pepper**

Comment: Tequila adds a very interesting kick to the classic Bloody Mary.

BLOODY MARY (MODERN RECIPE)

Glass: Collins
Garnish: Salt & pepper rim plus celery stick
Method: SHAKE all ingredients with ice and strain into ice-filled glass.

2	shot(s)	**Ketel One vodka**
4	shot(s)	**Pressed tomato juice**
1/2	shot(s)	**Freshly squeezed lemon juice**
8	drops	**Tabasco pepper sauce**
4	dashes	**Lea & Perrins Worcestershire sauce**
1/2	spoon	**Horseradish sauce**
1/2	shot(s)	**Tawny port**
2	pinch	**Celery salt**
2	pinch	**Black pepper**

Comment: A fiery Mary with the heat fuelled by horseradish. If you like to fight a hangover with spice, this is for you.

B

BLOODY SHAME (MOCKTAIL)

Glass: Collins
Garnish: Celery stick
Method: SHAKE all ingredients with ice and strain into ice-filled glass.

5	shot(s)	**Pressed tomato juice**
1/2	shot(s)	**Freshly squeezed lemon juice**
8	drops	**Tabasco pepper sauce**
4	dashes	**Lea & Perrins Worcestershire sauce**
1/2	spoon	**Horseradish sauce**
2	pinch	**Celery salt**
2	pinch	**Black pepper**

AKA: Virgin Mary
Comment: Somehow missing something.

BLOOMSBURY MARTINI [NEW #7]

Glass: Martini
Garnish: Lemon zest twist
Method: STIR all ingredients with ice and strain into chilled glass.

2	shot(s)	**Plymouth gin**
1/2	shot(s)	**Cuarenta Y Tres (Licor 43) liqueur**
1/2	shot(s)	**Dry vermouth**
2	dashes	**Peychaud's aromatic bitters**

Origin: Adapted from a drink created in 2003 by Robert Hess and published on drinkboy.com.
Comment: This pinky/rusty drink benefits from a good long stir but the result is an aromatic, medium dry, spicy vanilla Martini.

BLOW JOB

Glass: Shot
Garnish: Drop cherry into glass then float cream
Method: SHAKE all ingredients with ice and fine strain into chilled glass.

1/2	shot(s)	**Grand Marnier liqueur**
1/2	shot(s)	**Giffard crème de banane du Brésil**
1/2	shot(s)	**Kahlúa coffee liqueur**

Comment: A juvenile but pleasant tasting sweet shot.

BLUE ANGEL

Glass: Martini
Garnish: Orange zest twist
Method: SHAKE all ingredients with ice and fine strain into chilled glass.

3/4	shot(s)	**Bols Blue curaçao liqueur**
3/4	shot(s)	**Parfait Amour liqueur**
3/4	shot(s)	**Rémy Martin cognac**
3/4	shot(s)	**Freshly squeezed lemon juice**
3/4	shot(s)	**Double (heavy) cream**

Comment: This baby blue cocktail is sweet, creamy and floral.

BLUE BIRD

Glass: Martini
Garnish: Orange zest twist
Method: SHAKE all ingredients with ice and fine strain into chilled glass.

2	shot(s)	**Plymouth gin**
1	shot(s)	**Bols Blue curaçao liqueur**
3/4	shot(s)	**Freshly squeezed lemon juice**
1/4	shot(s)	**Almond (orgeat) syrup**

Origin: Thought to have been created in the late 1950s in Montmartre, Paris, France.
Comment: A blue rinsed, orange washed, gin based 'tini' that benefits from being sweetened with almond rather than plain syrup.

● DISGUSTING ●◐ PRETTY AWFUL ●● BEST AVOIDED
●●◐ DISAPPOINTING ●●● ACCEPTABLE ●●●◐ GOOD
●●●● RECOMMENDED ●●●●◐ HIGHLY RECOMMENDED
●●●●● OUTSTANDING / EXCEPTIONAL

BLUE BLAZER

Glass: Two old-fashioned glasses
Method: STIR honey with boiling water until honey dissolves. Add Scotch and peel. **FLAME** the mixture and stir with a long handled bar spoon. If still alight, extinguish flame and strain into second glass.

2	spoons	**Runny honey**
3/4	shot(s)	**Boiling water**
3	shot(s)	**Scotch whisky**
6	twists	**Lemon peel**

Variant: This drink was originally mixed by pouring the ingredients from one metal mug to another while ignited.
Origin: Created by 'Professor' Jerry Thomas, inventor of many famous cocktails in the 19th century. Thomas toured the world like a travelling showman, displaying this and other drinks.
Comment: Only attempt to make this the original way if you're very experienced or very stupid.

BLUE CHAMPAGNE

Glass: Flute
Method: SHAKE first four ingredients with ice and strain into glass. **TOP** with champagne.

3/4	shot(s)	**Ketel One vodka**
1/8	shot(s)	**Cointreau triple sec**
1/4	shot(s)	**Bols Blue curaçao liqueur**
1/4	shot(s)	**Freshly squeezed lemon juice**
Top up with		**Brut champagne**

Variant: With gin in place of vodka.
Comment: Fortified, citrussy champagne.

BLUE COSMO

Glass: Martini
Garnish: Orange zest twist
Method: SHAKE all ingredients with ice and fine strain into chilled glass.

2	shot(s)	**Ketel One Citroen vodka**
3/4	shot(s)	**Bols Blue curaçao liqueur**
1 1/2	shot(s)	**Ocean Spray white cranberry**
1/4	shot(s)	**Freshly squeezed lime juice**

Variant: Purple Cosmo
Comment: This blue rinsed drink may have sales appeal but sadly is not quite as good as a traditional red Cosmo.

BLUE FIN

Glass: Martini
Garnish: Gummy fish
Method: SHAKE all ingredients with ice and fine strain into chilled glass.

2	shot(s)	**Ketel One Citroen vodka**
1	shot(s)	**Hpnotiq tropical liqueur**
1 1/2	shot(s)	**Ocean Spray white cranberry**

Origin: Created in 2003 at The Blue Fin, W Hotel, Times Square, New York, USA.
Comment: Citrussy, reminiscent of a blue Cosmo.

BLUE HAWAIIAN

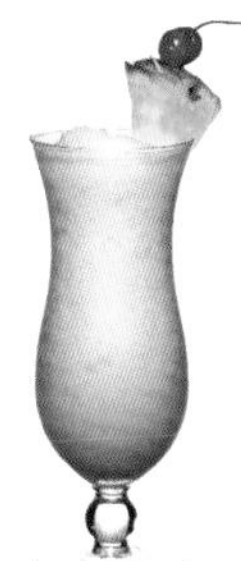

Glass: Hurricane
Garnish: Pineapple wedge & cherry on rim
Method: BLEND ingredients with 12oz scoop of crushed ice. Pour into glass and serve with straws.

2	shot(s)	**Light white rum**
1	shot(s)	**Bols Blue curaçao liqueur**
1 1/2	shot(s)	**Coco López cream of coconut**
3	shot(s)	**Pressed pineapple juice**
1/4	shot(s)	**Freshly squeezed lemon juice**

Origin: Probably created by Don the Beachcomber in Los Angeles, USA.
Comment: A blue rinsed Piña Colada.

BLUE HEAVEN

Glass: Collins
Garnish: Pineapple wedge & cherry sail
Method: SHAKE all ingredients with ice and strain into ice-filled glass.

2	shot(s)	**Light white rum**
1	shot(s)	**Bols Blue curaçao liqueur**
1/2	shot(s)	**Luxardo Amaretto di Saschira**
1/2	shot(s)	**Rose's lime cordial**
4	shot(s)	**Pressed pineapple juice**

Comment: Actually more aqua than blue, this sweet concoction includes orange, almond, lime cordial and pineapple.

BLUE KAMIKAZE

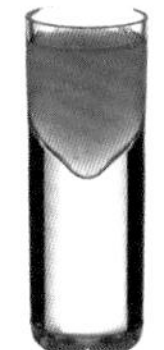

Glass: Shot
Method: SHAKE all ingredients with ice and fine strain into chilled glass.

1/2	shot(s)	**Ketel One vodka**
1/2	shot(s)	**Bols Blue curaçao liqueur**
1/2	shot(s)	**Freshly squeezed lime juice**

Comment: Tangy orange - but it's blue.

BLUE LADY

Glass: Martini
Garnish: Orange zest twist
Method: SHAKE all ingredients with ice and fine strain into chilled glass.

1	shot(s)	**Plymouth gin**
2	shot(s)	**Bols Blue curaçao liqueur**
1	shot(s)	**Freshly squeezed lemon juice**
1/2	fresh	**Egg white**

Comment: Quite sweet with an orange, citrus finish.

BLUE LAGOON

Glass: Collins
Garnish: Orange slice
Method: BLEND ingredients with 18oz scoop of crushed ice. Pour into glass and serve with straws.

1	shot(s)	**Plymouth gin**
1	shot(s)	**Ketel One vodka**
1	shot(s)	**Bols Blue curaçao liqueur**
1	shot(s)	**Freshly squeezed lime juice**
1	shot(s)	**Sugar syrup (2 sugar to 1 water)**

Variant: Vodka, blue curaçao and lemonade on the rocks.
Origin: Created in 1972 by Andy MacElhone (son of Harry) at Harry's New York Bar, Paris, France.
Comment: Better than the film – not hard!

BLUE MARGARITA [UPDATED #7]

Glass: Coupette
Garnish: Lime slice on rim
Method: BLEND all ingredients with one 12oz scoop crushed ice. Serve with straws.

2	shot(s)	**Partida tequila**
1	shot(s)	**Bols blue curaçao liqueur**
1	shot(s)	**Freshly squeezed lime juice**
1/2	shot(s)	**Sugar syrup**

Comment: As the name suggests, a Margarita, only blue. This 'Disco Drink' looks scary but tastes pretty good.

BLUE MONDAY [UPDATED #7]

Glass: Old-fashioned
Garnish: Orange zest twist
Method: SHAKE all ingredients with ice and fine strain into ice filled glass.

1½	shot(s)	**Ketel One Citroen vodka**
¾	shot(s)	**Bols blue curaçao liqueur**
½	shot(s)	**Cointreau triple sec**
½	shot(s)	**Dry vermouth**
2	dashes	**Fee Brothers orange bitters**

Origin: Created in 2003 by yours truly.
Comment: Disco blue but medium dry with a bittersweet orange taste.

'BACK IN MY RUMMY DAYS, I WOULD TREMBLE AND SHAKE FOR HOURS UPON ARISING. IT WAS THE ONLY EXERCISE I GOT.'
W.C. FIELDS

BLUE MOON [UPDATED #7]

Glass: Martini
Garnish: Orange zest twist
Method: SHAKE all ingredients with ice and fine strain into chilled glass.

2	shot(s)	**Plymouth gin**
¾	shot(s)	**Benoit Serres violet liqueur (or Parfait Amour)**
½	shot(s)	**Freshly squeezed lemon juice**
½	fresh	**Egg white**

AKA: Blue Devil
Variant: Aviation
Origin: Adapted from David A. Embury's 1948 'The Fine Art of Mixing Drinks'. This long lost drink was originally made with the now extinct Crème Yvette liqueur. 'Blue Moon' is an astronomical term for the second of two full moons to occur in the same calendar month.
Comment: More dirty grey than blue but a must for Aviation lovers, whatever the colour.

BLUE PASSION

Glass: Old-fashioned
Garnish: Orange zest twist
Method: SHAKE all ingredients with ice and strain into glass filled with crushed ice.

1	shot(s)	**Light white rum**
1	shot(s)	**Bols Blue curaçao liqueur**
1¾	shot(s)	**Freshly squeezed lime juice**
1	shot(s)	**Sugar syrup (2 sugar to 1 water)**

Comment: This sweet and sour tangy drink is surprisingly good.

BLUE RIBAND

Glass: Martini
Garnish: Cherry dropped into glass
Method: STIR all ingredients with ice and strain into chilled glass.

2	shot(s)	**Plymouth gin**
1	shot(s)	**Cointreau triple sec**
1	shot(s)	**Bols Blue curaçao liqueur**

Origin: The 'Blue Riband' was awarded to the liner that made the fastest Atlantic crossing. This cocktail is thought to have been created on one of these ships.
Comment: A sweetened, blue rinsed, orange and gin Martini.

BLUE STAR

Glass: Martini
Garnish: Orange zest twist
Method: SHAKE all ingredients with ice and fine strain into chilled glass.

1½	shot(s)	**Plymouth gin**
¾	shot(s)	**Dry vermouth**
¾	shot(s)	**Freshly squeezed orange juice**
¾	shot(s)	**Bols Blue curaçao liqueur**

Comment: Gin, orange and a kick.

BLUE VELVET MARGARITA

Glass: Coupette
Garnish: Lime wedge on rim
Method: SHAKE all ingredients with ice and fine strain into chilled glass.

2	shot(s)	**Partida tequila**
½	shot(s)	**Cointreau triple sec**
½	shot(s)	**Bols Blue curaçao liqueur**
1	shot(s)	**Freshly squeezed lime juice**

Origin: Discovered in 2005 at Velvet Margarita Cantina, Los Angeles, USA.
Comment: May look lurid but is a surprisingly tasty Margarita.

BLUE WAVE

Glass: Hurricane
Garnish: Pineapple wedge on rim
Method: SHAKE ingredients with ice and strain into ice-filled glass.

1	shot(s)	**Plymouth gin**
1	shot(s)	**Light white rum**
½	shot(s)	**Bols Blue curaçao liqueur**
3	shot(s)	**Pressed pineapple juice**
1¾	shot(s)	**Freshly squeezed lime juice**
¾	shot(s)	**Sugar syrup (2 sugar to 1 water)**

Comment: A fruity holiday drink.

BLUEBERRY DAIQUIRI [UPDATED #7]

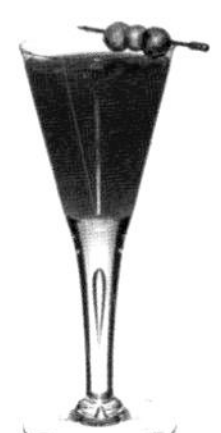

Glass: Martini
Garnish: Blueberries on stick
Method: MUDDLE blueberries in base of shaker. Add other ingredients, **SHAKE** with ice and fine strain into chilled glass.

20	fresh	**Blueberries**
2	shot(s)	**light white rum**
1/2	shot(s)	**Giffard Blueberry liqueur (crème de myrtille)**
1/2	shot(s)	**Freshly squeezed lime juice**

Origin: Created in December 2002 by yours truly.
Comment: Blueberry juice and liqueur lengthens and sweetens an otherwise classic Daiquiri.

BLUEBERRY MARTINI #1 [UPDATED #7]

Glass: Martini
Garnish: Lemon zest twist (discarded) & blueberries on stick
Method: MUDDLE blueberries in base of shaker. Add other ingredients, **SHAKE** with ice and fine strain into chilled glass.

20	fresh	**Blueberries**
2	shot(s)	**Ketel One vodka**
1/4	shot(s)	**Giffard Blueberry liqueur (crème de myrtilles)**
1/8	**shot(s)**	**Sugar syrup (2 sugar to 1 water)**

Comment: Rich blueberry fruit fortified with grainy vodka. Not too sweet.

BLUEBERRY MARTINI #2

Glass: Martini
Garnish: Blueberries on stick.
Method: MUDDLE blueberries in base of shaker. Add other ingredients, **SHAKE** with ice and fine strain into chilled glass.

30	fresh	**Blueberries**
2	shot(s)	**Ketel One vodka**
1/4	shot(s)	**Sugar syrup (2 sugar to 1 water)**
3/4	shot(s)	**Sauvignon Blanc wine**

Comment: Rich blueberry fruit fortified with vodka – much more interesting with the additional splash of wine.

BLUEBERRY TEA

Glass: Toddy
Garnish: Lemon slice & cinnamon stick
Method: POUR first two ingredients into glass, top up with tea and stir.

3/4	shot(s)	**Luxardo Amaretto di Saschira**
3/4	shot(s)	**Grand Marnier liqueur**
Top up with		**Hot black breakfast tea**

Comment: This does indeed taste just as described on the tin.

BLUSH MARTINI

Glass: Martini
Garnish: Dust with cinnamon powder
Method: SHAKE all ingredients with ice and fine strain into chilled glass.

1	shot(s)	**Ketel One vodka**
3/4	shot(s)	**Vanilla schnapps liqueur**
1/2	shot(s)	**Luxardo Amaretto di Saschira**
3/4	shot(s)	**Milk**
3/4	shot(s)	**Double (heavy) cream**
1/4	shot(s)	**Ocean Spray cranberry juice**

Origin: Created by Colin William Crowden, Mashed Bar, Leicester, England.
Comment: Drier than it looks, but still one to follow the dessert trolley.

BLUSHIN' RUSSIAN

Glass: Martini
Garnish: Float three coffee beans
Method: SHAKE all ingredients with ice and fine strain into chilled glass.

1	shot(s)	**Ketel One vodka**
1	shot(s)	**Kahlúa coffee liqueur**
1/2	shot(s)	**Luxardo Amaretto di Saschira**
3/4	shot(s)	**Double (heavy) cream**
3/4	shot(s)	**Milk**

Comment: White Russian with a hint of almond.

BOBBY BURNS

Glass: Martini
Garnish: Maraschino cherry in drink
Method: SHAKE all ingredients with ice and fine strain into chilled glass.

1 1/2	shot(s)	**Scotch whisky**
1 1/2	shot(s)	**Sweet vermouth**
1/4	shot(s)	**Bénédictine D.O.M. liqueur**

Comment: Strictly speaking this drink should be stirred, but I prefer mine shaken so that's how it appears here.

BOHEMIAN ICED TEA

Glass: Old-fashioned
Garnish: Lemon zest twist
Method: STIR all ingredients with ice and strain into ice-filled glass.

1 1/2	shot(s)	**Becherovka liqueur**
1/2	shot(s)	**Ketel One Citroen vodka**
1/2	shot(s)	**Krupnik honey liqueur**
1/2	shot(s)	**Teichenné Peach Schnapps Liqueur**
2 1/2	shot(s)	**Chilled Earl Grey lemon tea**

Origin: Created by Alex Kammerling at Detroit, London, England. Originally stirred in a tea pot and served in tea cups.
Comment: A fruity and refreshing drink with surprising flavours.

B

BOILERMAKER [UPDATED #7]

Glass: Boston & shot
Method: POUR whiskey to brim of shot glass and then manoeuvre shot glass so it is held tight up against the inside base of an upturned Boston glass. Then quickly flip the Boston glass over so that the bourbon is trapped in the now upside-down shot glass. Now pour beer into Boston glass over the whiskey filled shot glass.

1 shot(s) **Buffalo Trace bourbon whiskey**
1 pint **Beer (well chilled)**

Origin: Unknown but in his book The Joy of Mixology Gary Regan credits steelworkers in western Pennsylvania.
Comment: When you get to the end of the beer the shot glass lifts and the whiskey is released as a chaser.

BOLERO

Glass: Martini
Garnish: Float apple slice
Method: STIR all ingredients with ice and strain into chilled glass.

1½ shot(s) **Light white rum**
¾ shot(s) **Boulard Grand Solage Calvados**
¼ shot(s) **Sweet vermouth**

Origin: A classic of unknown origins.
Comment: A dry, challenging drink for modern palates. Be sure to stir well as dilution is key.

BOLERO SOUR [UPDATED #7]

Glass: Old-fashioned
Garnish: Orange & lime zest twists (discarded)
Method: SHAKE all ingredients with ice and strain into ice-filled glass.

1 shot(s) **Aged rum**
1 shot(s) **Rémy Martin cognac**
½ shot(s) **Freshly squeezed orange juice**
1 shot(s) **Freshly squeezed lime juice**
½ shot(s) **Sugar syrup (2 sugar to 1 water)**
½ fresh **Egg white**

Origin: Adapted from David A. Embury's 1948 'The Fine Art of Mixing Drinks'.
Comment: A beautifully balanced, flavoursome medley of sweet and sour.

BOLSHOI PUNCH

Glass: Old-fashioned
Method: SHAKE all ingredients with ice and strain into glass filled with crushed ice.

1½ shot(s) **Wray & Nephew white overproof rum**
1 shot(s) **Giffard Cassis Noir de Bourgogne**
¾ shot(s) **Freshly squeezed lime juice**
½ shot(s) **Sugar syrup (2 sugar to 1 water)**

Comment: Innocuous-seeming pink classic – richly flavoured and easy to drink.

BOMBAY NO. 2 [UPDATED #7]

Glass: Martini
Garnish: Orange zest twist
Method: SHAKE all ingredients with ice and fine strain into chilled glass.

1½ shot(s) **Rémy Martin cognac**
¾ shot(s) **Dry vermouth**
¾ shot(s) **Sweet vermouth**
¼ shot(s) **Cointreau triple sec**
⅛ shot(s) **La Fée Parisienne (68%) absinthe**

Origin: My 2006 adaptation of a recipe from Harry Craddock's 1930 'The Savoy Cocktail Book'.
Comment: A smooth, complex, Sazerac-style Martini.

"IT HAD NEVER OCCURRED TO US THAT THE KREMLIN'S NEW ANTI-BOOZE CAMPAIGN WOULD APPLY TO JOURNALISTS. NOW, THAT'S A HUMAN-RIGHTS VIOLATION.'

BOMBER

Glass: Collins
Garnish: Lime squeeze
Method: SHAKE first three ingredients with ice and strain into ice-filled glass. **TOP** with ginger beer, stir and serve with straws.

1 shot(s) **Light white rum**
1 shot(s) **Spiced rum**
1 shot(s) **Freshly squeezed lime juice**
Top up with **Ginger beer**

Origin: Created in 1998 by the B. Bar crew at The Reading Festival, England.
Comment: Cross between a Moscow Mule and a Cuba Libre.

BON BON [UPDATED #7]

Glass: Martini
Garnish: Lemon zest twist (or a Bon Bon)
Method: SHAKE all ingredients with ice and fine strain into chilled glass.

1 shot(s) **Vanilla-infused Ketel One vodka**
½ shot(s) **Teichenné butterscotch Schnapps**
¾ shot(s) **Luxardo limoncello liqueur**
¾ shot(s) **Freshly squeezed lemon juice**
¼ shot(s) **Sugar syrup (2 sugar to 1 water)**
½ shot(s) **Chilled mineral water** (omit if wet ice)

Origin: Adapted from a drink discovered in 2001 at Lab Bar, London, England.
Comment: Relive your youth and the taste of those big round sweets in this bitter-sweet, lemony cocktail.

BONNIE PRINCE CHARLES [NEW #7]

Glass: Martini
Garnish: Lime wedge on rim
Method: SHAKE all ingredients with ice and fine strain into chilled glass.

$2^1/_4$ shot(s) **Rémy Martin cognac**
$^3/_4$ shot(s) **Drambuie liqueur**
$^3/_4$ shot(s) **Freshly squeezed lime juice**

Origin: Recipe to proportions found in Victor Bergeron's 'Trader Vic's Bartender's Guide' (1972 revised edition).
Comment: Honeyed, spiced cognac with a touch of citrus. But is it fit for a Prince?

BOOMERANG [UPDATED #7]

Glass: Martini
Garnish: Maraschino cherry
Method: SHAKE all ingredients with ice and fine strain into chilled glass.

$1^1/_2$ shot(s) **Buffalo Trace bourbon whiskey**
$^3/_4$ shot(s) **Dry vermouth**
$^3/_4$ shot (s) **Sweet vermouth**
$^1/_4$ shot(s) **Luxardo maraschino liqueur**
$^1/_2$ shot(s) **Freshly squeezed lemon juice**
$^1/_2$ shot(s) **Sugar syrup (2 sugar to 1 water)**
2 dashes **Angostura aromatic bitters**

Comment: A very Sweet Manhattan with lemon juice.

BORA BORA BREW MOCKTAIL

Glass: Collins
Garnish: Pineapple wedge
Method: SHAKE first two ingredients with ice and strain into ice-filled glass.

3 shot(s) **Pressed pineapple juice**
$^1/_8$ shot(s) **Pomegranate (grenadine) syrup**
Top up with **Ginger ale**

Comment: Fruity and frothy ginger beer.

BORDERLINE

Glass: Martini
Garnish: Orange twist
Method: SHAKE all ingredients with ice and fine strain into chilled glass.

2 shot(s) **Buffalo Trace bourbon whiskey**
$^1/_2$ shot(s) **Maple syrup**
$^1/_2$ shot(s) **Freshly squeezed lemon juice**
$^3/_4$ shot(s) **Punt E Mes**

Origin: Created in 2004 by James Mellor at Mint Leaf, London, England.
Comment: Bourbon sweetened with maple syrup, soured by lemon and made more complex by vermouth.

BOSOM CARESSER

Glass: Martini
Garnish: Orange peel twist (discarded)
Method: SHAKE all ingredients with ice and fine strain into chilled glass.

2 shot(s) **Rémy Martin cognac**
$^1/_2$ shot(s) **Grand Marnier liqueur**
$^1/_2$ shot(s) **Malmsey Madeira**
$^1/_4$ shot(s) **Pomegranate (grenadine) syrup**
1 fresh **Egg yolk**

Comment: No bosoms to hand? Then caress your throat.

BOSSA NOVA #1 [UPDATED #7]

Glass: Collins
Garnish: Lime wheel
Method: SHAKE all ingredients with ice and strain into ice-filled glass.

2 shot(s) **Golden rum**
$^3/_4$ shot(s) **Galliano liqueur**
$^3/_4$ shot(s) **Giffard apricot brandy du Roussillon**
2 shot(s) **Pressed apple juice**
$^3/_4$ shot(s) **Freshly squeezed lime juice**

Origin: Named after the Brazilian dance which in turn comes from the Portuguese 'bossa', meaning 'tendency', and 'nova', meaning 'new'.
Comment: Apple with the added zing of rum, Galliano, apricot and lime juice.

BOSSA NOVA #2 [UPDATED #7]

Glass: Collins
Garnish: Pineapple wedge
Method: SHAKE all ingredients with ice and strain into ice-filled glass.

2 shot(s) **Golden rum**
$^1/_2$ shot(s) **Galliano liqueur**
$^1/_2$ shot(s) **Giffard apricot brandy du Roussillon**
2 shot(s) **Pressed pineapple juice**
$^1/_2$ shot(s) **Freshly squeezed lemon juice**

Comment: Long and frothy with fruity rum and subtle anis notes. Not too sweet.

BOSTON

Glass: Martini
Garnish: Apricot slice on rim
Method: SHAKE all ingredients with ice and fine strain into chilled glass.

$1^3/_4$ shot(s) **Plymouth gin**
1 shot(s) **Giffard apricot brandy du Roussillon**
1 shot(s) **Freshly squeezed lemon juice**
$^1/_4$ shot(s) **Sugar syrup (2 sugar to 1 water)**
$^1/_8$ shot(s) **Pomegranate (grenadine) syrup**

Comment: Gin laced tangy fruit.

B

BOSTON FLIP

Glass: Wine goblet
Garnish: Dust with freshly grated nutmeg
Method: SHAKE all ingredients with ice and fine strain into chilled glass.

2	shot(s)	**Buffalo Trace bourbon whiskey**
2	shot(s)	**Blandy's Alvada Madeira**
1	fresh	**Egg**
1/4	shot(s)	**Sugar syrup (2 sugar to 1 water)**

Comment: A good dusting of freshly grated nutmeg makes this old school drink.

BOSTON TEA PARTY

Glass: Collins
Garnish: Orange slice
Method: SHAKE first ten ingredients with ice and strain into ice-filled glass. **TOP** with cola and serve with straws.

1/2	shot(s)	**Ketel One vodka**
1/2	shot(s)	**Scotch whisky**
1/2	shot(s)	**Dry vermouth**
1/2	shot(s)	**Cointreau triple sec**
1/2	shot(s)	**Pusser's navy rum**
1/2	shot(s)	**Plymouth gin**
1/2	shot(s)	**Partida tequila**
1/2	shot(s)	**Freshly squeezed orange juice**
1	shot(s)	**Freshly squeezed lime juice**
1/2	shot(s)	**Sugar syrup (2 sugar to 1 water)**
Top up with		**Cola**

Origin: Named after the revolt by early US settlers against the imposition of tax by the British Crown, which became the War of Independence.
Comment: Just about every spirit from the speedrail plus a splash of orange, lime and coke.

'IT'S NOT EVERY ONE THAT CAN SAY THAT HE HAS HAD CHOLERA THREE TIMES, AND CURED HIMSELF BY LIVING ON RED PEPPER AND BRANDY.'
SIR ARTHUR CONAN DOYLE

BOULEVARD [NEW #7]

Glass: Martini
Garnish: Twist of orange (discarded) & two maraschino cherries
Method: STIR all ingredients with ice and strain into chilled glass.

2 1/2	shot(s)	**Buffalo Trace bourbon whiskey**
1	shot(s)	**Dry vermouth**
1/2	shot(s)	**Grand Marnier liqueur**
2	dashes	**Fee Brothers orange bitters**

Origin: A classic of unknown origins.
Comment: A Manhattan-style cocktail which takes no prisoners.

BOURBON BLUSH

Glass: Martini
Garnish: Strawberry on rim
Method: MUDDLE strawberries in base of shaker. Add other ingredients, **SHAKE** with ice and fine strain into chilled glass.

3	fresh	**Strawberries**
2	shot(s)	**Buffalo Trace bourbon whiskey**
3/4	shot(s)	**Giffard crème de framboise**
1/4	shot(s)	**Maple syrup**

Origin: Created in 2003 by Simon King at MJU @ Millennium Hotel, London, England.
Comment: Strawberry and maple syrup combine brilliantly with bourbon in this drink.

BOURBON COOKIE

Glass: Old-fashioned
Garnish: Dust with cinnamon powder
Method: SHAKE all ingredients with ice and strain into ice-filled glass.

2	shot(s)	**Buffalo Trace bourbon whiskey**
1/2	shot(s)	**Double (heavy) cream**
1/2	shot(s)	**Milk**
1/2	shot(s)	**Mango or passion fruit sugar syrup**
1/2	shot(s)	**Teichenné butterscotch Schnapps**

Origin: Created in 2002 by Andres Masso, London, England.
Comment: Looks tame but packs a flavoursome punch.

BOURBON CRUSTA [NEW #7]

Glass: Small wine goblet or flute
Garnish: See 'Crusta' for instructions
Method: SHAKE all ingredients with ice and fine strain into pre-prepared glass.

2	shot(s)	**Buffalo Trace bourbon whiskey**
1/4	shot(s)	**Cointreau triple sec**
1/8	shot(s)	**Luxardo maraschino liqueur**
1/2	shot(s)	**Freshly squeezed lemon juice**
1/4	shot(s)	**Sugar syrup (2 sugar to 1 water)**
2	dashes	**Fee Brothers orange bitters**
1/2	shot(s)	**Chilled mineral water** (omit if wet ice)

Variant: Brandy Crusta
Comment: Beautifully balanced bourbon and fresh lemon.

BOURBON MILK PUNCH

Glass: Martini
Garnish: Dust with freshly grated nutmeg
Method: SHAKE all ingredients with ice and fine strain into chilled glass.

1 1/2	shot(s)	**Buffalo Trace bourbon whiskey**
1/2	shot(s)	**Galliano liqueur**
1	shot(s)	**Double (heavy) cream**
1	shot(s)	**Milk**
1/4	shot(s)	**Sugar syrup (2 sugar to 1 water)**

Comment: The character of bourbon shines through in this creamy number.

BOURBON SMASH 

Glass: Collins
Garnish: Lime wheel
Method: MUDDLE raspberries in base of shaker. Add other ingredients, **SHAKE** with ice and fine strain into ice-filled glass.

12	fresh	**Raspberries**
4	fresh	**Torn mint leaves**
2½	shot(s)	**Buffalo Trace bourbon whiskey**
3	shot(s)	**Ocean Spray cranberry juice**
1	shot(s)	**Freshly squeezed lime juice**
½	shot(s)	**Sugar syrup (2 sugar to 1 water)**
2	dashes	**Angostura aromatic bitters**

Comment: This refreshing long drink has a sharp edge that adds to its appeal.

BOURBONELLA

Glass: Martini
Garnish: Stemmed cherry on rim
Method: STIR all ingredients with ice and fine strain into chilled glass.

1¾	shot(s)	**Buffalo Trace bourbon whiskey**
¾	shot(s)	**Dry vermouth**
¾	shot(s)	**Cointreau triple sec**
¼	shot(s)	**Pomegranate (grenadine) syrup**
3	dashes	**Peychaud's aromatic bitters**

Comment: If you like bourbon, you'll love this fruity Manhattan.

BRADFORD 

Glass: Martini
Garnish: Olive on stick or lemon zest twist
Method: SHAKE all ingredients with ice and fine strain into chilled glass.

2½	shot(s)	**Plymouth gin**
½	shot(s)	**Dry vermouth**
3	dashes	**Fee Brothers orange bitters (optional)**

Origin: A Bradford is a Martini which is shaken rather than stirred. Like the Martini itself, the origin of the Bradford is lost in time.
Comment: More approachable than a stirred Traditional Dry Martini and downright soft compared to a Naked Martini.

BRAINSTORM

Glass: Martini
Garnish: Orange zest twist
Method: STIR all ingredients with ice and strain into chilled glass.

1½	shot(s)	**Buffalo Trace bourbon whiskey**
1	shot(s)	**Dry vermouth**
¾	shot(s)	**Bénédictine D.O.M. liqueur**
½	shot(s)	**Chilled mineral water** (omit if wet ice)

Origin: Another long lost classic.
Comment: Spiced and slightly sweetened bourbon.

BRAKE TAG [NEW #7]

Glass: Old-fashioned
Garnish: Orange zest twist
Method: SHAKE all ingredients with ice and strain into ice-filled glass.

1½	shot(s)	**Southern Comfort liqueur**
½	shot(s)	**Luxardo Amaretto di Saschira**
1	shot(s)	**Freshly squeezed orange juice**
1	shot(s)	**Ocean Spray cranberry juice**
3	dashes	**Peychaud's aromatic bitters**

Origin: Discovered in 2005 at Café Adelaide's Swizzle Stick Bar, New Orleans, USA.

BRAMBLE

Glass: Old-fashioned
Garnish: Blackberry & lemon slice
Method: SHAKE first three ingredients with ice and strain into glass filled with crushed ice. **DRIZZLE** liqueur over drink to create a 'bleeding' effect in the glass. Serve with short straws.

2	shot(s)	**Plymouth gin**
1½	shot(s)	**Freshly squeezed lemon juice**
½	shot(s)	**Sugar syrup (2 sugar to 1 water)**
½	shot(s)	**Giffard mûre (blackberry)**

Origin: Created in the mid-80s by Dick Bradsell at Fred's Club, Soho, London, England.
Comment: One of the best and most popular drinks created in the 1980s.

BRAMBLETTE

Glass: Martini
Garnish: Orange zest twist
Method: SHAKE all ingredients with ice and fine strain into chilled glass.

2	shot(s)	**Plymouth gin**
1	shot(s)	**Serres liqueur de violette**
¾	shot(s)	**Freshly squeezed lemon juice**
¼	shot(s)	**Sugar syrup (2 sugar to 1 water)**

Comment: A martini style drink with a floral, gin laced palate.

BRANDY ALEXANDER

Glass: Martini
Garnish: Dust with freshly grated nutmeg
Method: SHAKE all ingredients with ice and fine strain into chilled glass.

2	shot(s)	**Rémy Martin cognac**
½	shot(s)	**Giffard brown crème de cacao**
½	shot(s)	**Giffard white crème de cacao**
½	shot(s)	**Double (heavy) cream**
½	shot(s)	**Milk**

AKA: The Panama
Origin: Created prior to 1930, this classic blend of brandy and chocolate smoothed with cream is based on the original Alexander which calls for gin as its base.
Comment: This after dinner classic is rich, creamy and spicy.

BRANDY BLAZER

Glass: Snifter & old-fashioned
Garnish: Lemon & orange zest twists
Method: POUR cognac into a warmed glass and rest the bowl of the glass on an old-fashioned glass so it lies on its side supported by the rim. **FLAME** the cognac and carefully move the glass back to an upright position sitting normally on your work surface. **POUR** in hot water (this will extinguish any remaining flame) and sugar. Stir, garnish and serve.

2	shot(s)	**Rémy Martin cognac**
2	shot(s)	**Hot water**
1/4	shot(s)	**Sugar syrup (2 sugar to 1 water)**

Origin: A variation on 'Professor' Jerry Thomas' Blue Blazer which involved theatrically pouring ignited brandy between two mugs. Please don't try this at home, kids.
Comment: One way to warm your winter nights.

BRANDY BUCK

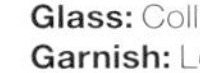

Glass: Collins
Garnish: Lemon wedge
Method: SHAKE first three ingredients with ice and strain into ice-filled glass. **TOP** with ginger ale and serve with straws.

2 1/2	shot(s)	**Rémy Martin cognac**
1/4	shot(s)	**Grand Marnier liqueur**
1/4	shot(s)	**Freshly squeezed lemon juice**
Top up with		**Ginger ale**

Comment: Lemon juice adds balance to the sweet ginger ale. Cognac provides the backbone.

BRANDY CRUSTA [UPDATED #7]

Glass: Small wine goblet or flute
Garnish: See 'Crusta' for instructions
Method: SHAKE all ingredients with ice and fine strain into pre-prepared glass.

2	shot(s)	**Rémy Martin cognac**
1/4	shot(s)	**Cointreau triple sec**
1/8	shot(s)	**Luxardo maraschino liqueur**
1/2	shot(s)	**Freshly squeezed lemon juice**
1/4	shot(s)	**Sugar syrup (2 sugar to 1 water)**
2	dashes	**Angostura aromatic bitters**
3/4	shot(s)	**Chilled mineral water** (reduce if wet ice)

Variant: Bourbon Crusta
Origin: Created in the 1840s-50s by Joseph Santina at Jewel of the South, Gravier Street, New Orleans, USA. The name refers to the crust of sugar around the rim. This recipe is adapted from David A. Embury's 1948 'The Fine Art of Mixing Drinks'.
Comment: This old classic zings with fresh lemon and is beautifully balanced by the cognac base.

● DISGUSTING ●◐ PRETTY AWFUL ●● BEST AVOIDED
●●◐ DISAPPOINTING ●●● ACCEPTABLE ●●●◐ GOOD
●●●● RECOMMENDED ●●●●◐ HIGHLY RECOMMENDED
●●●●● OUTSTANDING / EXCEPTIONAL

BRANDY FIX

Glass: Old-fashioned
Garnish: Lemon zest twist
Method: SHAKE all ingredients with ice and strain into ice-filled glass.

2	shot(s)	**Rémy Martin cognac**
1/2	shot(s)	**Pressed pineapple juice**
1/2	shot(s)	**Freshly squeezed lemon juice**
1/4	shot(s)	**Sugar syrup (2 sugar to 1 water)**
1/8	shot(s)	**Yellow Chartreuse liqueur**

Comment: This wonderful classic is on the tart side of well balanced.

BRANDY FIZZ [UPDATED #7]

Glass: Collins (8oz max)
Garnish: Lemon wheel
Method: SHAKE first three ingredients with ice and fine strain into chilled glass (without ice). **TOP** with soda.

2	shot(s)	**Rémy Martin cognac**
1/2	shot(s)	**Freshly squeezed lemon juice**
1/4	shot(s)	**Sugar syrup (2 sugar to 1 water)**
Top up with		**Soda water (from siphon)**

Comment: A refreshing and tasty dry drink: cognac and lemon balanced with a little sugar and lengthened with soda.

BRANDY FLIP [UPDATED #7]

Glass: Wine goblet or Martini
Garnish: Dust with freshly ground nutmeg
Method: SHAKE all ingredients with ice and fine strain into chilled glass.

1 1/2	shot(s)	**Rémy Martin cognac**
1/4	shot(s)	**Sugar syrup (2 sugar to 1 water)**
1/4	shot(s)	**Double (heavy) cream**
1	fresh	**Egg**

Origin: A forgotten classic.
Comment: A serious alternative to advocaat for those without raw egg inhibitions.

BRANDY MILK PUNCH

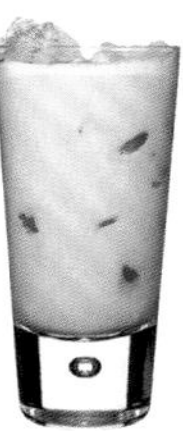

Glass: Collins
Garnish: Dust with freshly grated nutmeg
Method: SHAKE all ingredients with ice and strain into glass filled with crushed ice.

2	shot(s)	**Rémy Martin cognac**
3	shot(s)	**Milk**
1	shot(s)	**Double (heavy) cream**
1/4	shot(s)	**Sugar syrup (2 sugar to 1 water)**
1/8	shot(s)	**Vanilla extract**

Origin: A New Orleans variant of the drink that enjoyed nationwide popularity during Prohibition.
Comment: This traditional New Orleans hangover cure beats your bog-standard vanilla milkshake.

BRANDY SMASH 

Glass: Old-fashioned
Garnish: Mint sprig
Method: Lightly **MUDDLE** mint in base of shaker just enough to bruise. Add other ingredients, **SHAKE** with ice and fine strain into ice-filled glass.

7	fresh	**Mint leaves**
2	shot(s)	**Rémy Martin cognac**
¼	shot(s)	**Sugar syrup (2 sugar to 1 water)**

Origin: A classic from the 1850s.
Comment: Sweetened cognac flavoured with mint. Simple but beautiful.

BRANDY SOUR 

Glass: Old-fashioned
Garnish: Lemon slice & cherry (sail)
Method: SHAKE all ingredients with ice and strain into ice-filled glass.

2	shot(s)	**Rémy Martin cognac**
1	shot(s)	**Freshly squeezed lemon juice**
½	shot(s)	**Sugar syrup (2 sugar to 1 water)**
½	fresh	**Egg white**
3	dashes	**Angostura aromatic bitters**

Comment: After the Whiskey Sour, this is the most requested sour. Try it and you'll see why – but don't omit the egg white.

BRASS MONKEY [NEW #7]

Glass: Collins
Garnish: Lemon slice
Method: SHAKE all ingredients with ice and strain into ice-filled glass.

1	shot(s)	**Light white rum**
1	shot(s)	**Ketel One Citroen vodka**
2½	shot(s)	**Freshly squeezed lemon juice**
1	shot(s)	**Sugar syrup (2 sugar to 1 water)**

Comment: Tangy, alcoholic, almost sherbety lemonade. Packed with Vitamin C.

BRASS RAIL [NEW #7]

Glass: Martini
Garnish: Cape gooseberry
Method: SHAKE all ingredients with ice and fine strain into chilled glass.

1½	shot(s)	**Aged rum**
½	shot(s)	**Bénédictine D.O.M. liqueur**
½	shot(s)	**Freshly squeezed lemon juice**
½	shot(s)	**Sugar syrup (2 sugar to 1 water)**
½	fresh	**Egg white**
2	dashes	**Fee Brothers orange bitters**
½	shot(s)	**Chilled mineral water** (omit if wet ice)

Origin: Adapted from a recipe by Tony Abou Ganim. He was apparently inspired by his cousin Helen's penchant for a nightcap after a special occasion; her favourite was Bénédictine.
Comment: Rather like a Daiquiri, yet subtly sweetened and spiced.

BRAZEN MARTINI

Glass: Martini
Garnish: Frozen blueberries
Method: STIR all ingredients with ice and strain into chilled glass.

2½	shot(s)	**Zubrówka bison vodka**
¼	shot(s)	**Parfait Amour**

Comment: Not for the faint hearted – a great combination of strawy bison vodka with violet Parfait Amour.

BRAZILIAN BERRY

Glass: Old-fashioned
Garnish: Mint sprig
Method: MUDDLE fruit in base of shaker. Add other ingredients, **SHAKE** with ice and fine strain into glass filled with crushed ice. Serve with straws.

4	fresh	**Blackcurrants**
3	fresh	**Raspberries**
1½	shot(s)	**Sauvignon Blanc wine**
1	shot(s)	**Leblon cachaça**
1	shot(s)	**Giffard Cassis Noir de Bourgogne**

Origin: Created in 2002 by Dan Spink at Browns, St Martin's Lane, London, England.
Comment: This drink combines wine, cachaça and rich berry fruits.

BRAZILIAN COFFEE

Glass: Toddy
Garnish: Float 3 coffee beans
Method: BLEND ingredients with 6oz scoop of crushed ice. Pour into glass and serve with straws.

1	shot(s)	**Leblon cachaça**
1	shot(s)	**Double (heavy) cream**
¾	shot(s)	**Sugar syrup (2 sugar to 1 water)**
2	shot(s)	**Espresso coffee (cold)**

Comment: Strong coffee and plenty of sugar are essential in this Brazilian number.

BRAZILIAN COSMOPOLITAN [NEW #7]

Glass: Martini
Garnish: Orange zest twist
Method: SHAKE all ingredients with ice and fine strain into chilled glass.

1	shot(s)	**Leblon cachaça**
1	shot(s)	**Cointreau triple sec**
1½	shot(s)	**Ocean Spray cranberry juice**
½	shot(s)	**Freshly squeezed lime juice**

Comment: The distinctive character of cachaça bursts through the fruit in this twist on the contemporary classic.

BRAZILIAN MONK

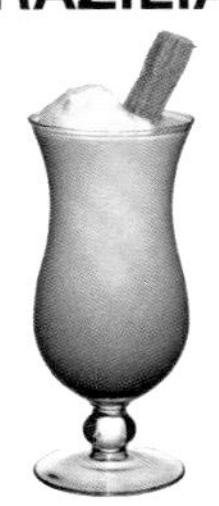

Glass: Hurricane
Garnish: Cadbury's Flake in drink
Method: BLEND ingredients with two 12oz scoops of crushed ice. Pour into glass and serve with straws.

1	shot(s)	**Frangelico hazelnut liqueur**
1	shot(s)	**Kahlúa coffee liqueur**
1	shot(s)	**Giffard brown crème de cacao**
3	scoops	**Vanilla ice cream**

Comment: Nutty and rich dessert in a glass.

'ALWAYS DO SOBER WHAT YOU SAID YOU'D DO WHEN YOU WERE DRUNK. THAT WILL TEACH YOU TO KEEP YOUR MOUTH SHUT!'
CHARLES SCRIBNER, JR.

BREAKFAST AT TERRELL'S

Glass: Flute
Garnish: Kumquat half
Method: SHAKE first four ingredients with ice and strain into chilled glass. **TOP** with champagne.

3/4	shot(s)	**Mandarine Napoléon liqueur**
3/4	shot(s)	**Freshly squeezed orange juice**
3/4	shot(s)	**Double (heavy) cream**
1/8	shot(s)	**Sugar syrup (2 sugar to 1 water)**
Top up with		**Brut champagne**

Origin: Created by Jamie Terrell for Philip Holzberg at Vinexpo, Bordeaux, France, 1999.
Comment: This creamy orange champagne cocktail is almost as smooth as a Sgroppino.

BREAKFAST MARTINI [UPDATED #7]

Glass: Martini
Garnish: Orange zest twist, slice of toast on rim
Method: STIR marmalade with gin in base of shaker until it dissolves. Add other ingredients, **SHAKE** with ice and fine strain into chilled glass.

1	spoon	**Orange marmalade**
2	shot(s)	**Plymouth gin**
3/4	shot(s)	**Cointreau triple sec**
3/4	shot(s)	**Freshly squeezed lemon juice**

Origin: Created in the late 1990s by Salvatore Calabrese at the Library Bar, London, England. It is very similar to the 'Marmalade Cocktail' created in the 1920s by Harry Craddock and published in his 1930 'The Savoy Cocktail Book'.
Comment: The success or failure of this tangy drink is partly reliant on the quality of marmalade used. Basically a White Lady with Marmalade.

BRIGHTON PUNCH

Glass: Collins
Garnish: Pineapple wedge & cherry
Method: SHAKE all ingredients with ice and strain into ice-filled glass.

1½	shot(s)	**Rémy Martin cognac**
1½	shot(s)	**Buffalo Trace bourbon whiskey**
1½	shot(s)	**Bénédictine D.O.M. liqueur**
2½	shot(s)	**Pressed pineapple juice**
2	shot(s)	**Freshly squeezed lemon juice**

Variant: With orange juice in place of pineapple juice.
Origin: Popular in the bars of Berlin, Germany.
Comment: Don't bother trying the version with orange juice but do try halving the quantities and serving up. Served long or short this is beautifully balanced.

THE BROADMOOR [UPDATED #7]

Glass: Martini
Garnish: Flamed orange zest twist
Method: SHAKE all ingredients with ice and fine strain into chilled glass.

2	shot(s)	**Scotch whisky**
1/2	shot(s)	**Green Chartreuse liqueur**
1/2	shot(s)	**Sugar syrup (2 sugar to 1 water)**
4	dashes	**Fee Brothers orange bitters**

Origin: Created in 2001 by Swedish bartender Andreas Norén at The Player, London, and popularised at Milk & Honey, London, England. Named after the infamous British mental institution.
Comment: Beautifully simple and seriously complex.

BRONX [UPDATED #7]

Glass: Martini
Garnish: Maraschino cherry
Method: SHAKE all ingredients with ice and fine strain into chilled glass.

1½	shot(s)	**Plymouth gin**
3/4	shot(s)	**Dry vermouth**
3/4	shot(s)	**Sweet vermouth**
1	shot(s)	**Freshly squeezed orange juice**

Variants: 1/ Bloody Bronx – made with the juice of a blood orange. 2/ Golden Bronx – with the addition of an egg yolk. 3/ Silver Bronx - with the addition of egg white. 4/ Income Tax Cocktail – with two dashes Angostura bitters. Also see the Abbey Martini.
Origin: Created in 1906 by Johnny Solon, a bartender at New York's Waldorf-Astoria Hotel (the Empire State Building occupies the site today), and named after the newly opened Bronx Zoo. Reputedly the first cocktail to use fruit juice.
Comment: A serious, dry, complex cocktail – less bitter than many of its era, but still quite challenging to modern palates.

BROOKLYN #1

Glass: Martini
Garnish: Maraschino cherry
Method: STIR all ingredients with ice and strain into chilled glass.

2½	shot(s)	**Buffalo Trace bourbon whiskey**
½	shot(s)	**Dry vermouth**
½	shot(s)	**Sweet vermouth**
¼	shot(s)	**Luxardo maraschino liqueur**
3	dashes	**Angostura aromatic bitters**

Origin: Though to have originated at the St George Hotel, Brooklyn, New York City, USA.
Comment: A Perfect Manhattan with maraschino liqueur.

BROOKLYN #2

Glass: Martini
Garnish: Maraschino cherry
Method: STIR all ingredients with ice and strain into chilled glass.

2	shot(s)	**Buffalo Trace bourbon whiskey**
¾	shot(s)	**Dry vermouth**
½	shot(s)	**Luxardo Amaretto di Saschira**

Comment: A simple, very approachable Manhattan.

BRUBAKER OLD-FASHIONED

Glass: Old-fashioned
Garnish: Two lemon zest twists
Method: STIR malt extract in glass with Scotch until malt extract dissolves. Add ice and one shot of Scotch and stir. Add remaining Scotch, sugar and Angostura and stir some more. Add more ice and keep stirring so that ice dilutes the drink.

2	spoons	**Malt Extract (available in health-food shops)**
2	shot(s)	**Scotch whisky**
¼	shot(s)	**Sugar syrup (2 sugar to 1 water)**
3	dashes	**Angostura aromatic bitters**

Origin: Created in 2003 by Shelim Islam at the GE Club, London, England. Shelim named this drink after a horse in the sports section of a paper (also a film made in the seventies starring Robert Redford).
Comment: If you like Scotch you should try this extra malty dram. After all that stirring you'll deserve one.

BUBBLEGUM SHOT

Glass: Shot
Method: SHAKE all ingredients with ice and fine strain into chilled glass.

½	shot(s)	**Midori melon liqueur**
½	shot(s)	**Luxardo Amaretto di Saschira**
¼	shot(s)	**Double (heavy) cream**

Comment: As the name suggests, this tastes a little like bubble gum.

THE BUCK

The Buck originated during the Prohibition era in the form of the Gin Buck. Like the Ricky, the Collins and the Fizz it is a tall drink served with citrus juice and a carbonate. (A Highball is also tall but never contains citrus juice.)

Originally a Buck was made by cutting a large lemon into quarters and squeezing the juice of one quarter into the drink using a hand squeezer. The squeezed shell was also dropped into the glass with the juice. Unlike the other drinks above, no sugar is added – sufficient sweetness to balance the lemon is provided by the sweet carbonate.

THE BUCK 

Glass: Collins
Garnish: Lemon wedge
Method: POUR first two ingredients into ice-filled glass and top up with ginger ale. Stir and serve with straws.

2 1/2	shot(s)	**Plymouth gin** (or other spirit)
1/2	shot(s)	**Freshly squeezed lemon juice**
Top up with		**Ginger ale**

Variant: The recipe above is for a Gin Buck, but this drink can also be based on brandy, calvados, rum, whiskey, vodka etc.
Comment: The Buck can be improved by adding a dash of liqueur appropriate to the spirit base. E.g. add a dash of Grand Marnier to a Brandy Buck.

BUCK'S FIZZ 

Glass: Flute
Method: POUR ingredients into chilled glass and gently stir.

2	shot(s)	**Freshly squeezed orange juice**
Top up with		**Brut champagne**

AKA: Mimosa
Origin: Created in 1921 by Mr McGarry, first bartender at the Buck's Club, London.
Comment: Not really a cocktail and not that challenging, but great for brunch.

BUENA VIDA 

Glass: Old-fashioned
Garnish: Pineapple wedge on rim
Method: SHAKE all ingredients with ice and strain into glass filled with crushed ice.

2	shot(s)	**Partida tequila**
1 3/4	shot(s)	**Squeezed pink grapefruit juice**
3/4	shot(s)	**Pressed pineapple juice**
1/2	shot(s)	**Vanilla sugar syrup**
3	dashes	**Angostura aromatic bitters**

Comment: The fruits combine brilliantly with the tequila and spice comes courtesy of Angostura.

BULLDOG 

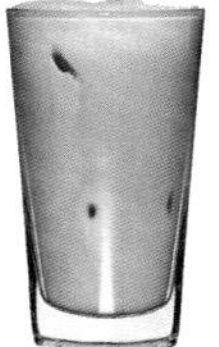

Glass: Collins
Method: SHAKE first four ingredients with ice and strain into ice-filled glass. **TOP** with cola, stir and serve with straws.

1	shot(s)	**Light white rum**
1	shot(s)	**Kahlúa coffee liqueur**
1 1/2	shot(s)	**Double (heavy) cream**
1 1/2	shot(s)	**Milk**
Top up with		**Cola**

Comment: Surprisingly nice – cola cuts through the cream.

BULLFROG

Glass: Old-fashioned
Garnish: Maraschino cherry
Method: SHAKE all ingredients with ice and strain into glass filled with crushed ice.

1 1/2	shot(s)	**Ketel One vodka**
3/4	shot(s)	**Giffard white crème de Menthe Pastille**
1	shot(s)	**Double (heavy) cream**
1	shot(s)	**Milk**

Comment: Mint ice cream.

BULL'S BLOOD 

Glass: Martini
Garnish: Orange zest twist
Method: SHAKE all ingredients with ice and fine strain into chilled glass.

1/2	shot(s)	**Light white rum**
1	shot(s)	**Rémy Martin cognac**
1	shot(s)	**Grand Marnier liqueur**
1 1/2	shot(s)	**Freshly squeezed orange juice**

Comment: This beautifully balanced fruity cocktail has a dry finish.

BULL'S MILK

Glass: Collins
Method: SHAKE all ingredients with ice and strain into ice-filled glass.

1	shot(s)	**Gosling's Black Seal rum**
1 1/2	shot(s)	**Rémy Martin cognac**
4	shot(s)	**Milk**
1/2	shot(s)	**Maple syrup**

Comment: Dark spirits tamed by thick maple syrup and milk.

BUMBLE BEE

Glass: Shot
Method: Refrigerate ingredients then **LAYER** in chilled glass by carefully pouring in the following order.

1/2	shot(s)	**Kahlúa coffee liqueur**
1/2	shot(s)	**Luxardo Sambuca dei Cesari**
1/2	shot(s)	**Irish cream liqueur**

Comment: A B-52 with a liquorice kick.

BUONA SERA SHOT

Glass: Shot
Method: SHAKE all ingredients with ice and fine strain into chilled glass.

1/2	shot(s)	**Kahlúa coffee liqueur**
1/2	shot(s)	**Luxardo Amaretto di Saschira**
1/2	shot(s)	**Vanilla-infused light white rum**

Comment: As sweet shots go this is one of my favourites.

BURNING BUSH SHOT

Glass: Shot
Method: POUR ingredients into chilled glass.

1 shot(s) **Partida tequila**
6 drops **Tabasco pepper sauce**

AKA: Prairie Dog, Prairie Fire
Comment: Hold onto your bowels!

BURNT TOASTED ALMOND

Glass: Martini
Garnish: Dust with freshly grated nutmeg
Method: SHAKE all ingredients with ice and fine strain into chilled glass.

1 shot(s) **Ketel One vodka**
1/2 shot(s) **Irish cream liqueur**
1/2 shot(s) **Kahlúa coffee liqueur**
1 shot(s) **Luxardo Amaretto di Saschira**
1 shot(s) **Double (heavy) cream**
1 shot(s) **Milk**

Variant: Toasted Almond
Comment: There's more than just almond to this sweety.

BUTTERFLY'S KISS

Glass: Martini
Garnish: Cinnamon stick
Method: STIR all ingredients with ice and strain into chilled glass.

2 shot(s) **Vanilla-infused Ketel One vodka**
1 shot(s) **Frangelico hazelnut liqueur**
1/2 shot(s) **Cinnamon schnapps liqueur**
1/2 shot(s) **Sugar syrup (2 sugar to 1 water)**
1/2 shot(s) **Chilled mineral water** (omit if wet ice)

Origin: Adapted from a drink I discovered in 2003 at Bar Marmont, Los Angeles, USA.
Comment: Golden coloured Martini style drink complete with the odd gold flake and a hazelnut cinnamon twang.

BUTTERSCOTCH DAIQUIRI

Glass: Martini
Garnish: Butterscotch sweet in drink
Method: SHAKE all ingredients with ice and fine strain into chilled glass.

2 shot(s) **Light white rum**
1 shot(s) **Teichenné butterscotch Schnapps**
1/2 shot(s) **Freshly squeezed lime juice**
1/2 shot(s) **Chilled mineral water** (omit if wet ice)

Comment: A candified Daiquiri.

BUTTERSCOTCH DELIGHT

Glass: Shot
Method: Refrigerate ingredients then **LAYER** in chilled glass by carefully pouring in the following order.

3/4 shot(s) **Teichenné butterscotch Schnapps**
3/4 shot(s) **Irish cream liqueur**

Origin: The origin of this drink is unknown but it is very popular in the bars in and around Seattle, USA.
Comment: Sweet connotations!

BUTTERSCOTCH MARTINI

Glass: Martini
Garnish: Butterscotch sweet
Method: SHAKE all ingredients with ice and fine strain into chilled glass.

2 shot(s) **Golden rum**
3/4 shot(s) **Teichenné butterscotch Schnapps**
3/4 shot(s) **Giffard white crème de cacao**
1/8 shot(s) **Sugar syrup (2 sugar to 1 water)**
1/2 shot(s) **Chilled mineral water** (omit if wet ice)

Comment: Sweet and suckable.

BUZZARD'S BREATH

Glass: Hurricane
Garnish: Pineapple wedge on rim
Method: BLEND ingredients with 12oz scoop of crushed ice. Pour into glass and serve with straws.

2 1/2 shot(s) **Leblon cachaça**
1 shot(s) **Coco López cream of coconut**
2 shot(s) **Pressed pineapple juice**
1/4 shot(s) **Double (heavy) cream**

Comment: A Piña Colada made with cachaça.

BYZANTINE

Glass: Collins
Garnish: Basil leaf
Method: MUDDLE basil in base of shaker. Add other ingredients apart from tonic water, **SHAKE** with ice and strain into ice-filled glass. **TOP** with tonic water.

6 fresh **Basil leaves**
1 1/2 shot(s) **Plymouth gin**
1/2 shot(s) **Passion fruit sugar syrup**
2 shot(s) **Pressed pineapple juice**
1/2 shot(s) **Lime & lemongrass cordial**
Top up with **Tonic water**

Origin: Created in 2001 by Douglas Ankrah for Akbar, Soho, London, England.
Comment: This fruity, herbal drink is even better made the way Douglas originally intended, with basil infused gin instead of muddled leaves.

C C KAZI

Glass: Martini
Garnish: Lime wedge on rim
Method: **SHAKE** all ingredients with ice and fine strain into chilled glass.

$1\frac{3}{4}$	shot(s)	**Partida tequila**
$1\frac{3}{4}$	shot(s)	**Ocean Spray cranberry juice**
$\frac{1}{2}$	shot(s)	**Freshly squeezed lime juice**
$\frac{1}{4}$	shot(s)	**Sugar syrup (2 sugar to 1 water)**

Comment: A Rude Cosmo without the liqueur.

CABLE CAR [UPDATED #7]

Glass: Martini
Garnish: Half cinnamon & sugar rim
Method: **SHAKE** all ingredients with ice and fine strain into chilled glass.

2	shot(s)	**Spiced rum**
1	shot(s)	**Cointreau triple sec**
$\frac{1}{2}$	shot(s)	**Freshly squeezed lemon juice**
$\frac{1}{4}$	shot(s)	**Sugar syrup (2 sugar to 1 water)**
$\frac{1}{2}$	fresh	**Egg white**

Origin: Created in 1996 by Cory Reistad at the Starlight Room, atop San Francisco's Sir Francis Drake Hotel. The Nob Hill cable cars pass by the bar, hence its catchphrase 'Between the stars and the cable cars'.
Comment: Vanilla and spice from the rum interact with the orange liqueur in this balanced, Daiquiri style drink.

CACHAÇA DAIQUIRI

Glass: Martini
Garnish: Lime wedge on rim
Method: **SHAKE** all ingredients with ice and fine strain into chilled glass.

2	shot(s)	**Leblon cachaça**
$\frac{1}{2}$	shot(s)	**Freshly squeezed lime juice**
$\frac{1}{4}$	shot(s)	**Sugar syrup (2 sugar to 1 water)**
$\frac{1}{2}$	shot(s)	**Chilled mineral water**

Comment: Might be in a Martini glass but it tastes like a Caipirinha.

CACTUS BANGER 

Glass: Martini
Garnish: Lime wedge on rim
Method: **SHAKE** all ingredients with ice and fine strain into chilled glass.

1	shot(s)	**Partida tequila**
1	shot(s)	**Grand Marnier liqueur**
2	shot(s)	**Freshly squeezed orange juice**
$\frac{1}{2}$	shot(s)	**Freshly squeezed lime juice**

Comment: A golden, sunny looking and sunny tasting drink.

CACTUS JACK

Glass: Martini
Garnish: Pineapple leaf
Method: **SHAKE** all ingredients with ice and fine strain into chilled glass.

1	shot(s)	**Partida tequila**
$\frac{3}{4}$	shot(s)	**Bols Blue curaçao liqueur**
$1\frac{1}{4}$	shot(s)	**Freshly squeezed orange juice**
1	shot(s)	**Pressed pineapple juice**
$\frac{1}{2}$	shot(s)	**Freshly squeezed lemon juice**

Comment: Vivid in colour, this orange led, tequila based drink has a balanced sweet and sourness.

CAFÉ GATES

Glass: Toddy
Garnish: Three coffee beans
Method: Place bar spoon in glass, **POUR** first three ingredients and top up with coffee, then **FLOAT** cream by pouring over the back of a spoon.

$\frac{3}{4}$	shot(s)	**Grand Marnier liqueur**
$\frac{3}{4}$	shot(s)	**Kahlúa coffee liqueur**
$\frac{3}{4}$	shot(s)	**Giffard brown crème de cacao**
Top up with		**Filter coffee (hot)**
$\frac{3}{4}$	shot(s)	**Double (heavy) cream**

Comment: Chocolate orange with coffee and cream.

CAIPIGINGER [NEW #7]

Glass: Old-fashioned
Garnish: Lime zest twist (discarded) & lime wedge
Method: **MUDDLE** ginger in base of shaker. Add other ingredients, **SHAKE** with ice and strain into glass filled with crushed ice. Serve with straws.

2	slices	**Fresh root ginger (thumbnail sized)**
2	shot(s)	**Leblon cachaça**
1	shot(s)	**Freshly squeezed lime juice**
$\frac{3}{4}$	shot(s)	**Sugar syrup (2 sugar to 1 water)**

Comment: A ginger spiced take on the Caipirinha.

CAIPIRINHA (CLASSIC SERVE) [UPDATED #7]

Glass: Old-fashioned
Method: **MUDDLE** lime in base of glass to release the juices and oils in its skin. Pour cachaça and sugar into glass, add crushed ice and **CHURN** (stir) with bar spoon. Serve with straws.

$\frac{3}{4}$	fresh	**Lime cut into wedges**
2	shot(s)	**Leblon cachaça**
$\frac{3}{4}$	shot(s)	**Sugar syrup (2 sugar to 1 water)**

Origin: A traditional Brazilian drink
Comment: Those who enjoy chewing on undissolved sugar should use granulated sugar in place of syrup.

CAIPIRINHA (DIFFORD'S SERVE) [NEW #7]

Glass: Old-fashioned
Garnish: Lime zest twist (squeezed & discarded) & lime wedge
Method: SHAKE all ingredients with ice and strain into ice-filled glass. Serve with straws.

2	shot(s)	**Leblon cachaça**
1	shot(s)	**Freshly squeezed lime juice**
1/2	shot(s)	**Sugar syrup (2 sugar to 1 water)**

Origin: My adaptation of the traditional Brazilian drink.
Variant: Strained over crushed ice, with a quarter shot more sugar syrup.
Comment: Using measures of freshly squeezed lime juice and sugar syrup ensures a perfect balance of sweet and sour. I'm not a fan of crushed ice, hence this is served on the rocks.

CAIPIRISSIMA 

Glass: Old-fashioned
Method: MUDDLE lime in base of glass. Add other ingredients and fill glass with crushed ice. **CHURN** (stir) drink with bar spoon and serve with straws.

3/4	fresh	**Lime cut into wedges**
2	shot(s)	**Light white rum**
3/4	shot(s)	**Sugar syrup (2 sugar to 1 water)**

Comment: A Daiquiri style drink made like a Caipirinha to give that rustic edge.

CAIPIROVSKA 

Glass: Old-fashioned
Method: MUDDLE lime in base of glass. Add other ingredients and fill glass with crushed ice. **CHURN** (stir) drink with bar spoon and serve with straws.

3/4	fresh	**Lime cut into wedges**
2	shot(s)	**Ketel One vodka**
3/4	shot(s)	**Sugar syrup (2 sugar to 1 water)**

Comment: Lacks the character of a cachaça-based Caipirinha.

CAIPIRUVA

Glass: Old-fashioned
Method: MUDDLE grapes in base of shaker. Add other ingredients, **SHAKE** with ice and fine strain into glass filled with crushed ice.

10	fresh	**Seedless grapes**
2	shot(s)	**Leblon cachaça**
3/4	shot(s)	**Freshly squeezed lime juice**
3/4	shot(s)	**Sugar syrup (2 sugar to 1 water)**

Comment: A grape juice laced twist on the Caipirinha.

CAIPIRINHA

Pronounced 'Kie-Pur-Reen-Yah', the name of this traditional Brazilian cocktail means 'little countryside drink'. It is made by muddling green lemons known as 'limon subtil', which are native to Brazil (limes are the best substitute when these are not available), and mixing with sugar and cachaça. Be sure to muddle in a sturdy, non-breakable glass.

There is much debate among bartenders as to whether granulated sugar or syrup should be used to make this drink. Those who favour granulated sugar argue that muddling with the abrasive crystals helps extract the oils from the lime's skin. Personally, I hate the crunch of sugar as inevitably not all the granulated sugar dissolves. Whether you should use brown or white sugar to make your syrup is another question! Either way, this is a refreshing drink.

Cachaça, a spirit distilled from fermented sugar cane juice, is the national spirit of Brazil and Brazilians consume it in huge quantities. Capirinhas and variations on the theme are staples in cachaçerias, down home Brazilian bars which specialise in cachaça.

Caipirinha variations include
Berry Caipirinha
Black 'N' Blue Caipirovska
Caipirissima
Caipirovska
Caipiruva
Citrus Caipirovska
Grapefruit & Ginger Caipirinha
Passionate Caipirinha
Pineapple & Basil Caipirinha

CAJUN MARTINI [UPDATED #7] 

Glass: Martini
Garnish: Chilli pepper
Method: STIR vermouth with ice. Strain, discarding vermouth to leave only a coating on the ice. Pour pepper vodka into mixing glass, stir with coated ice and strain into chilled glass.

1/2	shot(s)	**Dry vermouth**
2 1/2	shot(s)	**Ketel One pepper infused vodka**

Comment: A very hot vodka Martini. I dare you!

CALIFORNIAN MARTINI [NEW #7] 

Glass: Martini
Garnish: Orange zest twist
Method: STIR all ingredients with ice and strain into chilled glass.

2	shot(s)	**Ketel One vodka**
1	shot(s)	**Grand Marnier liqueur**
1/2	shot(s)	**Dry vermouth**
2	dashes	**Fee Brothers orange bitters (optional)**

Comment: A medium dry, fragrant orange Martini.

CALIFORNIA ROOT BEER

Glass: Sling
Garnish: Lime wedge
Method: SHAKE first three ingredients with ice and strain into ice-filled glass. **TOP** with soda.

1	shot(s)	**Ketel One vodka**
1/2	shot(s)	**Kahlúa coffee liqueur**
3/4	shot(s)	**Galliano liqueur**
Top up with		**Soda water (club soda)**

Variant: Bartender's Root Beer
Comment: Does indeed taste like root beer.

CALL ME OLD-FASHIONED 

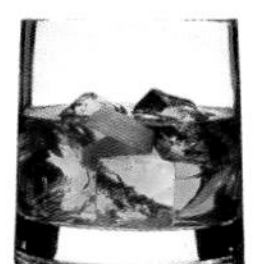

Glass: Old-fashioned
Garnish: Orange peel twist
Method: STIR sugar syrup and bitters with two ice cubes in a glass. Add one shot of cognac and two more ice cubes. Stir some more and add another two ice cubes and another shot of cognac. Stir lots more and add more ice.

2	shot(s)	**Rémy Martin cognac**
1/4	shot(s)	**Sugar syrup (2 sugar to 1 water)**
2	dashes	**Angostura aromatic bitters**

Origin: Created in 2001 by yours truly.
Comment: An Old-Fashioned made with cognac instead of whiskey – works well.

CALVADOS COCKTAIL [UPDATED #7]

Glass: Martini
Garnish: Orange zest twist
Method: SHAKE all ingredients with ice and fine strain into chilled glass.

1 1/2	shot(s)	**Boulard Grand Solage Calvados**
3/4	shot(s)	**Cointreau triple sec**
1 1/2	shot(s)	**Freshly squeezed orange juice**
2	dashes	**Fee Brothers orange bitters**

Origin: Adapted from Harry Craddock's 1930 'The Savoy Cocktail Book'.
Comment: Tangy orange with an alcoholic apple bite.

CAMERON'S KICK [UPDATED #7]

Glass: Martini
Garnish: Lemon zest twist
Method: SHAKE all ingredients with ice and fine strain into chilled glass.

1 1/2	shot(s)	**Scotch whisky**
1 1/2	shot(s)	**Irish whiskey**
3/4	shot(s)	**Freshly squeezed lemon juice**
1/2	shot(s)	**Almond (orgeat) syrup**

Origin: Adapted from Harry Craddock's 1930 'The Savoy Cocktail Book'.
Comment: Peaty, honeyed whiskey with a cleansing hint of lemon rounded by almond.

CAMOMILE & BLACKFRUIT BREEZE [UPDATED #7]

Glass: Collins
Garnish: Lemon slice
Method: SHAKE all ingredients with ice and strain into ice-filled glass.

2	shot(s)	**Ketel One Citroen vodka**
1	shot(s)	**Chambord black raspberry liqueur**
3	shot(s)	**Cold camomile tea**

Origin: Created in 2002 by yours truly.
Comment: Adult, clean and subtle in flavour with a twang of fruit.

CANADIAN APPLE (MOCKTAIL) [NEW #7]

Glass: Collins
Garnish: Apple slice
Method: SHAKE all ingredients with ice and fine strain into ice-filled glass.

3 1/2	shot(s)	**Pressed apple juice**
1 1/2	shot(s)	**Freshly squeezed lemon juice**
3/4	shot(s)	**Maple syrup**

Origin: Adapted from a drink discovered in 2005 at the Four Seasons Hotel, Prague, Czech Republic.
Comment: Refreshing and balanced with just the right amount of citrus acidity.

CANARIE

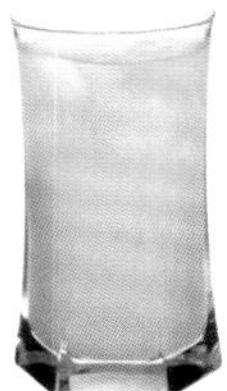

Glass: Collins (10oz/290ml max)
Method: POUR pastis and lemon syrup into glass. Serve iced water separately in a small jug (known in France as a 'broc') so the customer can dilute to their own taste (I recommend five shots). Lastly, add ice to fill glass.

1 shot(s) **Ricard pastis**
1/2 shot(s) **Lemon (citron) sugar syrup**
Top up with **Chilled mineral water**

Origin: Very popular throughout France, this drink is fittingly named after the bird, which is typically bred for its bright yellow plumage.
Comment: The traditional French café drink with a twist of lemon sweetness.

CANARIES

Glass: Hurricane
Garnish: Pineapple wedge on rim
Method: SHAKE ingredients with ice and strain into ice-filled glass.

3/4 shot(s) **Light white rum**
3/4 shot(s) **Cointreau triple sec**
3/4 shot(s) **Giffard crème de banane du Brésil**
3/4 shot(s) **Cherry (brandy) liqueur**
2 shot(s) **Pressed pineapple juice**
2 shot(s) **Freshly squeezed orange juice**

Comment: A long, fruity sweet drink that's only fit for consumption on a tropical beach.

CANARY FLIP

Glass: Martini
Garnish: Lemon zest twist
Method: SHAKE all ingredients with ice and fine strain into chilled glass.

2 shot(s) **Bols advocaat liqueur**
2 shot(s) **Sauvignon Blanc wine**
3/4 shot(s) **Freshly squeezed lemon juice**

Origin: Created in 2002 by Alex Kammerling, London, England.
Comment: A delightful balance of egg, brandy and wine.

CANCHANCHARA [NEW #7]

Glass: Old-fashioned
Garnish: Lemon slice
Method: STIR honey with rum in the glass drink is to be served in. ADD lemon juice and ice. **STIR** and serve.

3 spoons **Runny honey**
2 shot(s) **Light white rum**
1 1/2 shot(s) **Freshly squeezed lemon juice**

Origin: The Cuban forerunner of the Daiquiri, as drunk by Cuban revolutionaries fighting off the Spanish at the end of the nineteenth century. To be really authentic omit the ice. Origin and this recipe from Christine Sismondo's 2005 'Mondo Cocktail'.
Comment: Achieve the perfect balance between sweet honey and sour lemon and this is a great drink.

CANTEEN MARTINI

Glass: Martini
Garnish: Cherry in drink
Method: SHAKE all ingredients with ice and fine strain into chilled glass.

1 1/2 shot(s) **Light white rum**
1 1/2 shot(s) **Southern Comfort liqueur**
1/2 shot(s) **Luxardo Amaretto di Saschira**
1/2 shot(s) **Freshly squeezed lime juice**

Origin: Originally created by Joey Guerra at Canteen, New York City, and adapted by author and columnist Gary Regan.
Comment: Tangy, sweet and sour – Southern Comfort drinkers will love this.

CAPE CODDER

Glass: Old-fashioned
Garnish: Lime wedge
Method: SHAKE all ingredients with ice and strain into ice-filled glass.

2 shot(s) **Ketel One vodka**
3 shot(s) **Ocean Spray cranberry juice**
1/4 shot(s) **Freshly squeezed lime juice**

Variant: Without lime juice this is a Cape Cod. Lengthened with soda becomes the Cape Cod Cooler.
Origin: Named after the resort on the Massachusetts coast. This fish shaped piece of land is where some of the first Europeans settled in the US. Here they found cranberries, the indigenous North American berry on which this drink is based.
Comment: Dry and refreshing but not particularly interesting.

CAPPERCAILLE

Glass: Martini
Garnish: Pineapple wedge on rim
Method: STIR honey with whisky until honey dissolves. Add other ingredients, **SHAKE** with ice and fine strain into chilled glass.

2 spoons **Runny honey**
2 shot(s) **Scotch whisky**
1/2 shot(s) **Cointreau triple sec**
1/2 shot(s) **Giffard apricot brandy du Roussillon**
1 shot(s) **Pressed pineapple juice**
1/2 shot(s) **Freshly squeezed lemon juice**

Origin: Created by Wayne Collins for Maxxium UK.
Comment: Wonderfully tangy, fruity Scotch.

CAPRICE [NEW #7]

Glass: Martini
Garnish: Orange zest twist
Method: STIR all ingredients with ice and strain into chilled glass.

1 1/2 shot(s) **Plymouth gin**
1/2 shot(s) **Dry vermouth**
1/2 shot(s) **Bénédictine D.O.M. liqueur**
1 dash **Fee Brothers orange bitters**

Comment: A long stir delivers the dilution necessary for this aromatic, spiced Wet Martini.

CAPTAIN COLLINS

Glass: Collins
Garnish: Orange slice & cherry on stick (sail)
Method: SHAKE first three ingredients with ice and strain into ice-filled glass. **TOP** with soda, stir and serve with straws.

2	shot(s)	**Canadian whiskey**
1	shot(s)	**Freshly squeezed lemon juice**
1/2	shot(s)	**Sugar syrup (2 sugar to 1 water)**
Top up with		**Soda water (club soda)**

Origin: Classic Collins variation.
Comment: Sweetened, soured and diluted whiskey.

CARAMEL MANHATTAN

Glass: Martini
Garnish: Lemon twist (discarded) & pineapple wedge on rim
Method: SHAKE all ingredients with ice and fine strain into chilled glass.

1 1/2	shot(s)	**Buffalo Trace bourbon whiskey**
3/4	shot(s)	**Cartron Caramel liqueur**
1/2	shot(s)	**Sweet vermouth**
1	shot(s)	**Pressed pineapple juice**
2	dashes	**Peychaud's aromatic bitters**

Origin: Adapted from a drink created in 2002 by Nick Strangeway, London, England.
Comment: Flavours combine harmoniously with the character of the bourbon still evident.

CARAVAN

Glass: Collins
Garnish: Cherries
Method: POUR ingredients into ice-filled glass. Stir and serve with straws.

3	shot(s)	**Red wine**
1/2	shot(s)	**Grand Marnier liqueur**
Top up with		**Cola**

Origin: Popular in the French Alpine ski resorts.
Comment: A punch-like long drink.

CARDINAL PUNCH

Glass: Old-fashioned
Method: POUR cassis into ice-filled glass and top up with wine. Stir and serve with straws.

1	shot(s)	**Giffard Cassis Noir de Bourgogne**
Top up with		**Red wine**

Comment: A particularly fruity red.

CARDINALE [NEW #7]

Glass: Old-fashioned
Garnish: Orange slice
Method: SHAKE all ingredients with ice and fine strain into chilled glass.

2	shot(s)	**Plymouth gin**
1 1/2	shot(s)	**Campari**
1	shot(s)	**Dry vermouth**

Origin: A varaition on the classic equal parts Negroni.
Comment: An extra dry Negroni for hardcore fans. I have to admit to being one.

CARIBBEAN BREEZE

Glass: Collins
Garnish: Pineapple wedge on rim
Method: SHAKE all ingredients with ice and strain into ice-filled glass.

1 1/4	shot(s)	**Pusser's navy rum**
1/2	shot(s)	**Giffard crème de banane du Brésil**
2 1/2	shot(s)	**Pressed pineapple juice**
2	shot(s)	**Ocean Spray cranberry juice**
1/2	shot(s)	**Rose's lime cordial**

Comment: A long drink with bags of tangy fruit flavours.

CARIBBEAN CRUISE

Glass: Collins
Garnish: Pineapple wedge on rim
Method: SHAKE all ingredients with ice and strain into ice-filled glass.

1 1/2	shot(s)	**Light white rum**
1 1/2	shot(s)	**Malibu coconut rum liqueur**
4	shot(s)	**Pressed pineapple juice**
1	spoon	**Pomegranate (grenadine) syrup**

Comment: Long, frothy and fruity - one for the beach bar.

CARIBBEAN PIÑA COLADA

Glass: Hurricane
Garnish: Pineapple wedge & cherry
Method: BLEND ingredients with 12oz scoop of crushed ice. Pour into glass and serve with straws.

2	shot(s)	**Light white rum**
3	shot(s)	**Pressed pineapple juice**
1/2	shot(s)	**Coco López cream of coconut**
4	dashes	**Angostura aromatic bitters**
1	pinch	**Salt**

Comment: Angostura and salt make this a less sticky Colada.

CARIBBEAN PUNCH

Glass: Collins
Method: SHAKE all ingredients with ice and strain into glass filled with crushed ice.

2 1/4	shot(s)	**Wray & Nephew overproof rum**
1/2	shot(s)	**Luxardo Amaretto di Saschira**
1/2	shot(s)	**Malibu coconut rum liqueur**
1/4	shot(s)	**Galliano liqueur**
1/4	shot(s)	**Pomegranate (grenadine) syrup**
3/4	shot(s)	**Freshly squeezed lemon juice**
3	shot(s)	**Pressed pineapple juice**

Comment: Red in colour and innocent looking, this flavoursome drink sure packs a punch.

CARIBE DAIQUIRI [NEW #7]

Glass: Martini
Garnish: Lemon zest wedge
Method: SHAKE all ingredients with ice and fine strain into chilled glass.

2	shot(s)	**Light white rum**
1	shot(s)	**Pressed pineapple juice**
1/2	shot(s)	**Freshly squeezed lemon juice**
1/4	shot(s)	**Velvet Falernum liqueur**

Comment: A dry, fruity spicy Daiquiri.

CARNEVAL BATIDA

Glass: Collins
Garnish: Mango slice on rim
Method: SHAKE all ingredients with ice and strain into glass filled with crushed ice.

2 1/2	shot(s)	**Leblon cachaça**
1 1/2	shot(s)	**Mango purée**
1 1/2	shot(s)	**Freshly squeezed orange juice**
1/2	shot(s)	**Freshly squeezed lime juice**
1/2	shot(s)	**Sugar syrup (2 sugar to 1 water)**

Origin: The Batida is a traditional Brazilian drink.
Comment: Long, rich, refreshing and strangely filling.

CAROL CHANNING

Glass: Flute
Garnish: Raspberries
Method: SHAKE first three ingredients with ice and strain into chilled glass. **TOP** with champagne.

1/4	shot(s)	**Giffard Crème de framboise**
1/4	shot(s)	**Framboise eau de vie**
1/8	shot(s)	**Sugar syrup (2 sugar to 1 water)**
Top up with		**Brut champagne**

Origin: Created by Dick Bradsell in 1984 with the milliner Stephen Jones. Named after the famously large mouthed American comedienne Carol Channing because of her appearance in the film 'Thoroughly Modern Milly', where, for some unknown reason, she spends much of the time running around shouting 'raspberries'.
Comment: Fortified raspberry and champagne.

CARROL COCKTAIL [NEW #7]

Glass: Martini
Garnish: Pickled walnut or onion
Method: STIR all ingredients with ice and strain into chilled glass.

2	shot(s)	**Rémy Martin cognac**
1	shot(s)	**Sweet vermouth**

Origin: Adapted from Victor Bergeron's 'Trader Vic's Bartender's Guide' (1972 revised edition).
Comment: Aromatic wine and cognac – dry yet easy.

CARROT CAKE

Glass: Martini
Garnish: Dust with cinnamon powder
Method: SHAKE all ingredients with ice and fine strain into chilled glass.

2	shot(s)	**Irish cream liqueur**
3/4	shot(s)	**Cinnamon schnapps liqueur**
1 1/2	shot(s)	**Kahlúa coffee liqueur**

Comment: Tastes nothing like carrot cake - surely that's a good thing.

CARUSO MARTINI [NEW #7]

Glass: Martini
Garnish: Mint leaf
Method: SHAKE all ingredients with ice and fine strain into chilled glass.

1	shot(s)	**Plymouth gin**
1	shot(s)	**Dry vermouth**
1	shot(s)	**Giffard green crème de menthe**

Origin: The recipe is adapted from Harry Craddock's 1930 'The Savoy Cocktail Book'. The drink was created at The Savoy for the tenor Enrico Caruso in the early 20th century.
Comment: Emerald green with full-on mint. Good as a digestif after a tenor-sized meal.

CASABLANCA #1 [NEW #7]

Glass: Martini
Garnish: Orange zest twist
Method: SHAKE all ingredients with ice and fine strain into chilled glass.

2	shot(s)	**Light white rum**
3/4	shot(s)	**Cointreau triple sec**
3/4	shot(s)	**Freshly squeezed lime juice**
1/2	shot(s)	**Luxardo maraschino liqueur**
1/2	fresh	**Egg white**

Origin: Named after Michael Curtiz's 1942 classic starring Bogie and Ingrid Bergman.
Comment: A rum based variation on the White Lady, with zingy citrus and sweet maraschino.

CASABLANCA #2 [UPDATED #7]

Glass: Martini
Garnish: Dust with freshly grated nutmeg
Method: SHAKE all ingredients with ice and fine strain into chilled glass.

1	shot(s)	**Ketel One vodka**
1/4	shot(s)	**Galliano liqueur**
1	shot(s)	Bols advocaat liqueur
1/4	shot(s)	**Freshly squeezed lemon juice**
1	shot(s)	**Freshly squeezed orange juice**
1/2	shot(s)	**Double (heavy) cream**

Comment: Creamy, fruity, alcoholic custard. Different!

CASANOVA

Glass: Martini
Garnish: Crumble Cadbury's Flake bar over drink
Method: SHAKE all ingredients with ice and fine strain into chilled glass.

1 1/2	shot(s)	**Buffalo Trace bourbon whiskey**
3/4	shot(s)	**Blandy's Alvada madeira**
3/4	shot(s)	**Kahlúa coffee liqueur**
3/4	shot(s)	**Double (heavy) cream**
3/4	shot(s)	**Milk**
1/8	shot(s)	**Sugar syrup (2 sugar to 1 water)**

Comment: Rich, medium-sweet and creamy with a mocha coffee finish.

CASCADE MARTINI [UPDATED #7]

Glass: Martini
Garnish: Raspberries on stick
Method: SHAKE all ingredients with ice and fine strain into chilled glass.

8	fresh	**Raspberries**
2	shot(s)	**Ketel One vodka**
1	shot(s)	**Ocean Spray cranberry juice**
3/4	shot(s)	**Freshly squeezed lemon juice**
1/4	shot(s)	**Chambord black raspberry liqueur**
1/4	shot(s)	**Vanilla sugar syrup**

Comment: Rich raspberry with hints of citrus and vanilla.

CASINO

Glass: Martini
Garnish: Maraschino cherry
Method: SHAKE all ingredients with ice and fine strain into chilled glass.

2 1/2	shot(s)	**Plymouth gin**
1/2	shot(s)	**Luxardo maraschino liqueur**
1/2	shot(s)	**Freshly squeezed lemon juice**
1/2	shot(s)	**Chilled mineral water** (omit if wet ice)
3	dashes	**Fee Brothers orange bitters**

Variant: Bee's Knees, Blue Moon
Comment: Basically an Aviation dried with orange bitters.

CASSINI [UPDATED #7]

Glass: Martini
Garnish: Three blackberries
Method: SHAKE all ingredients with ice and fine strain into chilled glass.

2	shot(s)	**Ketel One vodka**
1 1/2	shot(s)	**Ocean Spray cranberry juice**
1/4	shot(s)	**Giffard Cassis (or Chambord)**

Origin: Created in 1998 by yours truly.
Comment: A simple but pleasant berry drink.

CASTRO

Glass: Martini
Garnish: Lime wedge on rim
Method: SHAKE all ingredients with ice and fine strain into chilled glass.

1 1/2	shot(s)	**Aged rum**
3/4	shot(s)	**Boulard Grand Solage Calvados**
1/4	shot(s)	**Freshly squeezed orange juice**
1/2	shot(s)	**Freshly squeezed lime juice**
1/4	shot(s)	**Rose's lime cordial**
1/4	shot(s)	**Sugar syrup (2 sugar to 1 water)**

Origin: Named after the Cuban.
Comment: Tangy and fruity.

CAUSEWAY

Glass: Collins
Method: SHAKE first five ingredients with ice and strain into ice-filled glass, **TOP** with ginger ale.

2	shot(s)	**Black Bush Irish whiskey**
1	shot(s)	**Drambuie liqueur**
4	dashes	**Angostura aromatic bitters**
2	dashes	**Fee Brothers orange bitters**
1/4	shot(s)	**Freshly squeezed lemon juice**
Top up with		**Ginger ale**

Origin: Created by David Myers at Titanic, London, England.
Comment: Dry aromatic long whiskey drink.

CELERY MARTINI

Glass: Martini
Garnish: Salt rim & celery
Method: SHAKE all ingredients with ice and fine strain into chilled glass.

1 3/4	shot(s)	**Freshly extracted celery juice**
2	shot(s)	**Ketel One vodka**
1/4	shot(s)	**Sugar syrup (2 sugar to 1 water)**

Origin: Created by Andreas Tsanos at Momos, London, England in 2001.
Comment: I only usually like celery when loaded with blue cheese - but I love this Martini.

CHAMPAGNE COCKTAILS

In most bars cocktails and champagne are the two most expensive things available by the glass so a champagne cocktail makes a very bling bar call. Yet put all thoughts of Donald Trump aside - champagne cocktails don't have to be a crying waste of decent bubbly and can even be superb.

Champagne cocktails have been around for as long as the cocktail: one of the earliest references appears in Mark Twain's 1869 novel, Innocents Abroad. One of the earliest champagne cocktails is also by far the best known: 'The Champagne Cocktail', which is referenced in Jerry Thomas's 1862 book 'How To Mix Drinks'.

Sadly this is a very overrated drink.

Be aware that sugar makes champagne fizz profusely. Try sprinkling a few grains over a glass of champagne and watch the effect. Champagne cocktails often include a sweet liqueur or even sugar, so when adding the champagne pour even more slowly and carefully than you would normally. Also consider pouring down the handle of a barspoon.

For a complete list of champagne cocktails, please see 'Champagne' in the ingredients index.

CELTIC MARGARITA

Glass: Coupette
Garnish: Salt rim & lemon wedge
Method: SHAKE all ingredients with ice and fine strain into chilled glass.

2	shot(s)	**Scotch whisky**
1	shot(s)	**Cointreau triple sec**
1	shot(s)	**Freshly squeezed lemon juice**

Origin: Discovered in 2004 at Milk & Honey, London, England.
Comment: A Scotch Margarita – try it, it works.

CHAM 69 #1

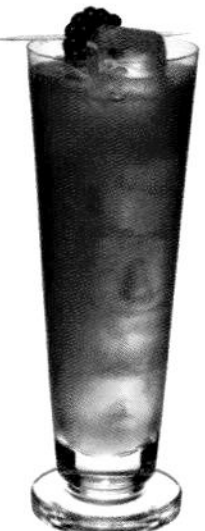

Glass: Sling
Garnish: Berries
Method: SHAKE first four ingredients with ice and strain into ice-filled glass. **TOP** with 7-Up, stir and serve with straws.

2	shot(s)	**Ketel One vodka**
3/4	shot(s)	**Chambord black raspberry liqueur**
3/4	shot(s)	**Luxardo Amaretto di Saschira**
3/4	shot(s)	**Freshly squeezed lime juice**
Top up with		**7-Up (or lemonade)**

Origin: I created this drink back in 1998 and I've noticed it on cocktail menus across Europe. I was something of a beginner with a sweet tooth at the time but this new formulation is better balanced.
Comment: Medium sweet, long and fruity.

CHAM 69 #2

Glass: Sling
Garnish: Berries
Method: SHAKE first four ingredients with ice and strain into ice-filled glass. **TOP** with champagne, stir and serve with straws.

1	shot(s)	**Ketel One vodka**
1/2	shot(s)	**Chambord black raspberry liqueur**
1/2	shot(s)	**Luxardo Amaretto di Saschira**
1/4	shot(s)	**Freshly squeezed lime juice**
Top up with		**Brut champagne**

Origin: While re-examining my old creation in 2005 I decided champagne would be more appropriate considering the name.
Comment: Long, fruity and refreshing.

CHAM CHAM

Glass: Flute
Garnish: Berries
Method: POUR liqueur into chilled glass and top with champagne.

1/2	shot(s)	**Chambord black raspberry liqueur**
Top up with		**Brut champagne**

Comment: A pleasing blend of fruit and champagne to rival the Kir Royale.

CHAMPAGNE COCKTAIL

Glass: Flute
Garnish: Lemon peel twist
Method: Rub sugar cube with lemon peel, coat with bitters and drop into glass. Cover soaked cube with cognac, then **POUR** champagne.

1	cube	**Brown sugar**
3	dashes	**Angostura aromatic bitters**
1	shot(s)	**Rémy Martin cognac**
Top up with		**Brut champagne**

Origin: First recorded in Jerry Thomas's 1862 book 'How To Mix Drinks', or 'The Bon Vivant's Companion', where he almost certainly mistakenly specifies this as a shaken drink. That would be explosive. It's thought the drink found popularity after a bartender named John Dougherty won an 1899 New York cocktail competition with a similar drink named Business Brace.
Comment: An over hyped classic cocktail that gets sweeter as you reach the dissolving cube at the bottom.

'I DRINK TO MAKE OTHER PEOPLE INTERESTING.'
GEORGE JEAN NATHAN

CHAMPAGNE CUP

Glass: Flute
Garnish: Maraschino cherry
Method: STIR first three ingredients with ice and strain into chilled glass. **TOP** with champagne and gently stir.

3/4	shot(s)	**Rémy Martin cognac**
1/2	shot(s)	**Grand Marnier liqueur**
1/4	shot(s)	**Maraschino syrup (from cherry jar)**
Top up with		**Brut champagne**

Comment: Sweet maraschino helps balance this dry drink.

CHAMPAGNE DAISY

Glass: Flute
Garnish: Pomegranate wedge
Method: SHAKE first three ingredients with ice and fine strain into chilled glass, **TOP** with champagne.

1	shot(s)	**Yellow Chartreuse liqueur**
1/8	shot(s)	**Pomegranate (grenadine) syrup**
1	shot(s)	**Freshly squeezed lemon juice**
Top up with		**Brut champagne**

Comment: You'll need to like Chartreuse and citrus champagne to appreciate this drink.

CHAMPS-ELYSÉES

Glass: Martini
Garnish: Lemon zest twist
Method: SHAKE all ingredients with ice and fine strain into chilled glass.

1¾	shot(s)	**Rémy Martin cognac**
¼	shot(s)	**Green Chartreuse liqueur**
½	shot(s)	**Freshly squeezed lemon juice**
½	shot(s)	**Sugar syrup (2 sugar to 1 water)**
3	dashes	**Angostura aromatic bitters**
¾	shot(s)	**Chilled mineral water** (omit if wet ice)
½	fresh	**Egg white (optional)**

Origin: Named after the touristy Parisienne boulevard where (coincidentally) Rémy Cointreau have their offices.
Comment: A great after dinner drink for lovers of cognac and Chartreuse.

CHANCELLOR [NEW #7]

Glass: Martini
Garnish: Orange zest twist
Method: SHAKE all ingredients with ice and fine strain into chilled glass.

2	shot(s)	**Scotch whisky**
1	shot(s)	**Tawny port**
½	shot(s)	**Dry vermouth**
¼	shot(s)	**Sugar syrup (2 sugar to 1 water)**
2	dashes	**Fee Brothers orange bitters**

Origin: A classic of unknown origins.
Comment: Complex and sophisticated Scotch with fruity notes.

CHARENTE COLLINS [NEW #7]

Glass: Collins
Garnish: Mint sprig & orange zest twist
Method: Lightly **MUDDLE** mint in base of shaker (just to bruise). Add other ingredients, **SHAKE** with ice and strain into glass filled with crushed ice. Serve with straws.

5	fresh	**Mint leaves**
2	shot(s)	**Grand Marnier liqueur**
1	shot(s)	**Freshly squeezed lemon juice**
1	shot(s)	**St-Germain elderflower liqueur**

Origin: Created in 2005 by Kieran Bailey, The Light Bar, London, England.
Comment: Refreshing orange and lemon with a hint of elderflower.

DRINKS ARE GRADED AS FOLLOWS:

● DISGUSTING ●◐ PRETTY AWFUL ●● BEST AVOIDED
●●◐ DISAPPOINTING ●●● ACCEPTABLE ●●●◐ GOOD
●●●● RECOMMENDED ●●●●◐ HIGHLY RECOMMENDED
●●●●● OUTSTANDING / EXCEPTIONAL

CHARLES DAIQUIRI

Glass: Martini
Garnish: Lime wedge on rim
Method: SHAKE all ingredients with ice and fine strain into chilled glass.

1	shot(s)	**Light white rum**
1	shot(s)	**Pusser's navy rum**
½	shot(s)	**Cointreau triple sec**
½	shot(s)	**Freshly squeezed lime juice**
⅛	shot(s)	**Sugar syrup (2 sugar to 1 water)**
½	shot(s)	**Chilled mineral water** (omit if wet ice)

Comment: Navy rum and triple sec add special interest to this Daiquiri.

CHARLIE CHAPLIN

Glass: Old-fashioned
Garnish: Lemon zest twist
Method: SHAKE all ingredients with ice and strain into ice-filled glass.

1½	shot(s)	**Plymouth sloe gin liqueur**
1½	shot(s)	**Giffard apricot brandy du Roussillon**
1	shot(s)	**Freshly squeezed lemon juice**

Comment: This fruity number was originally served 'up' but is better over ice.

'GIVING MONEY AND POWER TO GOVERNMENT IS LIKE GIVING WHISKEY AND CAR KEYS TO TEENAGE BOYS.'
P.J. O'ROURKE

CHAS

Glass: Martini
Garnish: Orange zest twist
Method: SHAKE all ingredients with ice and fine strain into chilled glass.

1¾	shot(s)	**Buffalo Trace bourbon whiskey**
½	shot(s)	**Bénédictine D.O.M. liqueur**
½	shot(s)	**Luxardo Amaretto di Saschira**
½	shot(s)	**Cointreau triple sec**
½	shot(s)	**Grand Marnier liqueur**

Origin: Created in 2003 by Murray Stenson at Zig Zag Café, Seattle, USA.
Comment: A wonderfully tangy cocktail with great bourbon personality and hints of almond and orange.

C

CHATHAM HOTEL SPECIAL [NEW #7]

Glass: Martini
Garnish: Nutmeg dust
Method: SHAKE all ingredients with ice and fine strain into chilled glass.

2	shot(s)	**Rémy Martin cognac**
3/4	shot(s)	**Tawny port**
1/2	shot(s)	**Giffard brown crème de cacao**
1/4	shot(s)	**Double (heavy) cream**
1/4	shot(s)	**Milk**

Origin: This mid-1900s classic from New York's Chatham Hotel was resurrected by Ted Haigh in his 2004 book 'Vintage Spirits & Forgotten Cocktails'.
Comment: I've slightly changed the proportions and replaced the original lemon zest garnish with a little extra spice.

CHEEKY MONKEY [UPDATED #7]

Glass: Martini
Garnish: Orange zest twist
Method: SHAKE all ingredients with ice and fine strain into chilled glass.

1	shot(s)	**Ketel One Citroen vodka**
1	shot(s)	**Yellow Chartreuse liqueur**
1 1/2	shot(s)	**Freshly squeezed orange juice**
1/4	shot(s)	**Sugar syrup (2 sugar to 1 water)**
3	dashes	**Fee Brothers orange bitters**

Origin: Adapted from a recipe created by Tony Conigliaro in 2001 at Isola, Knightsbridge, London, England.
Comment: Fire yellow in colour, this drink features the distinctive flavour of Chartreuse with a citrus supporting cast.

CHELSEA SIDECAR

Glass: Martini
Garnish: Lemon zest twist
Method: SHAKE all ingredients with ice and fine strain into chilled glass.

1 1/2	shot(s)	**Plymouth gin**
1	shot(s)	**Cointreau triple sec**
1	shot(s)	**Freshly squeezed lemon juice**
1/4	shot(s)	**Sugar syrup (2 sugar to 1 water)**

Comment: Gin replaces cognac in this variation on the classic Sidecar.

CHERRUTE

Glass: Martini
Garnish: Maraschino cherry in drink
Method: SHAKE all ingredients with ice and fine strain into chilled glass.

2	shot(s)	**Ketel One vodka**
3/4	shot(s)	**Cherry (brandy) liqueur**
1 1/2	shot(s)	**Freshly squeezed golden grapefruit juice**

Comment: Sweet cherry brandy balanced by the fruity acidity of grapefruit, laced with vodka.

CHERRY ALEXANDER

Glass: Martini
Garnish: Maraschino cherry
Method: SHAKE all ingredients with ice and fine strain into chilled glass.

1	shot(s)	**Vanilla flavoured vodka**
1/2	shot(s)	**Cherry (brandy) liqueur**
1/2	shot(s)	**Giffard white crème de cacao**
1	shot(s)	**Double (heavy) cream**
1	shot(s)	**Milk**

Origin: Created by Wayne Collins for Maxxium UK.
Comment: A fruity twist on the creamy classic.

CHERRY & HAZELNUT DAIQUIRI

Glass: Martini
Garnish: Cherry on rim
Method: SHAKE all ingredients with ice and fine strain into chilled glass.

2	shot(s)	**Light white rum**
3/4	shot(s)	**Luxardo maraschino liqueur**
1 1/2	shot(s)	**Frangelico hazelnut liqueur**
1/2	shot(s)	**Freshly squeezed lime juice**
1/2	shot(s)	**Chilled mineral water**

Origin: Adam Wyartt and I created this in 2003.
Comment: Nutty and surprisingly tangy.

CHERRY BLOSSOM

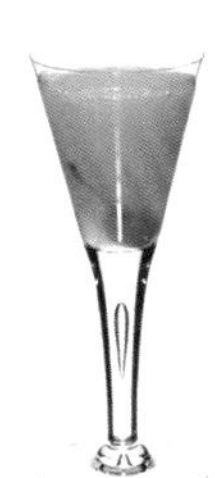

Glass: Martini
Garnish: Maraschino cherry in drink
Method: SHAKE all ingredients with ice and fine strain into chilled glass.

3/4	shot(s)	**Cherry (brandy) liqueur**
3/4	shot(s)	**Kirsch eau de vie**
1/2	shot(s)	**Cointreau triple sec**
1 1/4	shot(s)	**Freshly squeezed lemon juice**
1/4	shot(s)	**Maraschino syrup (from cherry jar)**

Comment: Bundles of flavour – tangy and moreish.

CHERRY DAIQUIRI

Glass: Martini
Garnish: Cherry on rim
Method: MUDDLE cherries in base of shaker. Add other ingredients, **SHAKE** with ice and fine strain into chilled glass.

8	fresh	**Stoned cherries**
2	shot(s)	**Vanilla-infused light white rum**
1	shot(s)	**Cherry (brandy) liqueur**
1/8	shot(s)	**Maraschino syrup (from cherry jar)**
1/2	shot(s)	**Freshly squeezed lime juice**
1/2	shot(s)	**Chilled mineral water**

Origin: Created in 2003 by yours truly.
Comment: Cherry sweetness paired with Daiquiri sharpness.

CHERRY MARTINI [UPDATED #7]

Glass: Martini
Garnish: Lemon zest twist
Method: SHAKE all ingredients with ice and fine strain into chilled glass.

2	shot(s)	**Ketel One Citroen vodka**
3/4	shot(s)	**Cherry brandy liqueur**
1/2	shot(s)	**Dry vermouth**
1/2	shot(s)	**Chilled mineral water** (omit if wet ice)

Origin: Created in 2005 by yours truly.
Comment: A hint of cherry is balanced by citrus freshness, and dried and deepened by vermouth.

'CANDY IS DANDY, BUT LIQUOR IS QUICKER.'

CHERRY MASH SOUR

Glass: Old-fashioned
Garnish: Lemon twist & cherry
Method: SHAKE all ingredients with ice and strain into ice-filled glass.

2	shot(s)	**Jack Daniel's Tennessee whiskey**
1/2	shot(s)	**Cherry (brandy) liqueur**
3/4	shot(s)	**Freshly squeezed lemon juice**
1/2	shot(s)	**Sugar syrup (2 sugar to 1 water)**

Origin: Created by Dale DeGroff when Beverage Manager at the Rainbow Room Promenade Bar, New York City, USA.
Comment: The rich flavour of Tennessee whiskey soured with lemon and sweetened with cherry liqueur.

CHE'S REVOLUTION

Glass: Martini
Garnish: Pineapple wedge on rim
Method: MUDDLE mint with rum in base of shaker. Add other ingredients, **SHAKE** with ice and fine strain into chilled glass.

4	fresh	**Mint leaves**
2	shot(s)	**Light white rum**
1/4	shot(s)	**Maple syrup**
2	shot(s)	**Pressed pineapple juice**

Origin: Created in 2003 by Ben Reed for the launch party of MJU Bar @ Millennium Hotel, London, England.
Comment: Complex and smooth with hints of maple syrup and mint amongst the pineapple and rum.

CHICLET DAIQUIRI

Glass: Martini
Garnish: Banana slice on rim
Method: BLEND ingredients with a 12oz scoop of crushed ice and serve in large chilled glass.

2 1/2	shot(s)	**Light white rum**
1/2	shot(s)	**Giffard crème de banane du Brésil**
1/8	shot(s)	**Giffard white crème de Menthe Pastille**
1/2	shot(s)	**Freshly squeezed lime juice**
1/4	shot(s)	**Sugar syrup (2 sugar to 1 water)**

Origin: Often found on Cuban bar menus, this was created at La Floridita, Havana.
Comment: A wonderfully refreshing drink on a summer's day with surprisingly subtle flavours.

CHIHUAHUA MAGARITA

Glass: Martini
Method: SHAKE all ingredients with ice and fine strain into chilled glass.

2	shot(s)	**Partida tequila**
2	shot(s)	**Freshly squeezed golden grapefruit juice**
1/8	shot(s)	**Agave syrup** (from health food shop)
3	dashes	**Angostura aromatic bitters**

Comment: Tequila and grapefruit juice pepped up with Angostura.

CHILL-OUT MARTINI

Glass: Martini
Garnish: Pineapple wedge on rim
Method: SHAKE all ingredients with ice and fine strain into chilled glass.

1	shot(s)	**Orange zest infused Ketel One vodka**
1	shot(s)	**Malibu coconut rum**
1	shot(s)	**Irish cream liqueur**
1	shot(s)	**Freshly squeezed orange juice**

Comment: Smooth, creamy sweet orange and surprisingly strong.

CHIMAYO [UPDATED #7]

Glass: Martini
Garnish: Float apple slice
Method: SHAKE all ingredients with ice and fine strain into chilled glass.

2	shot(s)	**Partida tequila**
1/2	shot(s)	**Giffard Cassis (or Chambord)**
3/4	shot(s)	**Pressed apple juice**
1/4	shot(s)	**Freshly squeezed lemon juice**

Origin: Named after El Potrero de Chimayó in northern New Mexico, USA.
Comment: Apple juice and cassis take the sting off tequila.

C

CHIN CHIN [UPDATED #7]

Glass: Flute
Method: STIR honey with Scotch in base of shaker. Add apple juice, **SHAKE** with ice and strain into chilled glass**TOP** with champagne.

1	spoon	**Runny honey**
2	shot(s)	**Scotch whisky**
1	shot(s)	**Pressed apple juice**
Top up with		**Brut champagne**

Origin: Created by Tony Conigliaro at Isola, Knightsbridge, London, England.
Comment: Golden honey in colour and also in flavour. An unusual and great tasting Champagne cocktail.

CHINA BEACH

Glass: Martini
Garnish: Ginger slice on rim
Method: SHAKE all ingredients with ice and fine strain into chilled glass.

1	shot(s)	**Ketel One vodka**
1	shot(s)	**Giffard Ginger of the Indies**
2	shot(s)	**Ocean Spray cranberry juice**

Comment: Dry and lightly spiced.

CHINA BLUE

Glass: Collins
Garnish: Orange slice in drink
Method: SHAKE all ingredients with ice and strain into ice-filled glass.

1	shot(s)	**Bols Blue curaçao liqueur**
1	shot(s)	**Soho lychee liqueur**
4	shot(s)	**Freshly squeezed grapefruit juice**

Origin: Emerged in Japan in the late 1990s and still popular along the Pacific Rim.
Comment: Looks sweet, but due to a generous splash of grapefruit is actually balanced and refreshing.

CHINA BLUE MARTINI

Glass: Martini
Garnish: Peeled lychee in drink
Method: SHAKE all ingredients with ice and fine strain into chilled glass.

1	shot(s)	**Blue curaçao liqueur**
1	shot(s)	**Soho lychee liqueur**
2	shot(s)	**Freshly squeezed grapefruit juice**
1/4	shot(s)	**Freshly squeezed lemon juice**

Origin: An almost inevitable short adaptation of the original long drink above.
Comment: This simple cocktail with its turquoise colour tastes more adult and interesting than its colour might suggest.

CHINA MARTINI

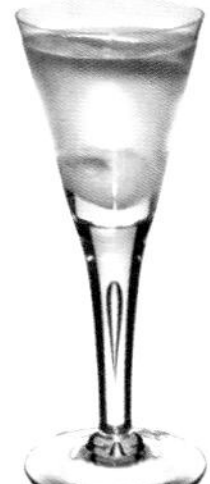

Glass: Martini
Garnish: Orange zest twist & lychee in glass
Method: STIR all ingredients with ice and fine strain into chilled glass.

1 1/2	shot(s)	**Plymouth gin**
1/2	shot(s)	**Soho lychee liqueur**
1/4	shot(s)	**Cointreau triple sec**
1/2	shot(s)	**Dry vermouth**

Origin: Created in 2004 by Wayne Collins for Maxxium UK.
Comment: A complex, not too sweet lychee Martini.

CHINESE COSMOPOLITAN

Glass: Martini
Garnish: Flamed orange zest twist
Method: SHAKE all ingredients with ice and fine strain into chilled glass.

2	shot(s)	**Krupnik honey liqueur**
3/4	shot(s)	**Soho lychee liqueur**
1/2	shot(s)	**Freshly squeezed lime juice**
1	shot(s)	**Ocean Spray cranberry juice**

Origin: Discovered in 2003 at Raoul's Bar, Oxford, England.
Comment: Oriental in name and style – perhaps a tad sweeter than your standard Cosmo.

CHINESE WHISPER MARTINI

Glass: Martini
Garnish: Lemon zest twist
Method: MUDDLE ginger in base of shaker. Add other ingredients, **SHAKE** with ice and fine strain into chilled glass.

2	slices	**Fresh root ginger (thumbnail sized)**
2	shot(s)	**Ketel One Citroen vodka**
1	shot(s)	**Soho lychee liqueur**
1/2	shot(s)	**Freshly squeezed lime juice**
1/4	shot(s)	**Ginger syrup**

Origin: Adapted from a recipe discovered in 2003 at Oxo Tower Bar, London, England.
Comment: There's more than a whisper of ginger in this spicy Martini.

CHOC & NUT MARTINI

Glass: Martini
Garnish: Wipe rim with orange and dust with cocoa powder.
Method: SHAKE all ingredients with ice and fine strain into chilled glass.

2	shot(s)	**Ketel One vodka**
1	shot(s)	**Frangelico hazelnut liqueur**
1	shot(s)	**Giffard white crème de cacao**
1/4	shot(s)	**Chilled mineral water** (omit if wet ice)

Comment: Surprise, surprise - it's sweet chocolate and hazelnut.

CHOCOLARITA [NEW #7]

Glass: Coupette
Garnish: Chocolate rim
Method: SHAKE all ingredients with ice and fine strain into chilled glass.

2	shot(s)	**Partida tequila**
1/4	shot(s)	**Giffard brown crème de cacao**
1/4	shot(s)	**Kahlúa liqueur**
1	shot(s)	**Freshly squeezed lime juice**
1/4	shot(s)	**Sugar syrup (2 sugar to 1 water)**

Origin: Adapted from a recipe discovered in 2005 at Agave, Hong Kong, China.
Comment: As the name suggests – a Margarita with chocolate and coffee.

CHOCOLATE & CRANBERRY MARTINI

Glass: Martini
Garnish: Wipe rim with cacao liqueur & dust with cocoa powder
Method: SHAKE all ingredients with ice and fine strain into chilled, rimmed glass.

2	shot(s)	**Ketel One vanilla infused vodka**
1/2	shot(s)	**Giffard white crème de cacao**
1/2	shot(s)	**Dry vermouth**
1	shot(s)	**Ocean Spray cranberry juice**

Origin: Created in 2003 by yours truly.
Comment: The chocolate rim sounds naff but makes this drink. Surprisingly dry.

CHOCOLATE BISCUIT

Glass: Martini
Garnish: Bourbon cream biscuit on rim
Method: SHAKE all ingredients with ice and fine strain into chilled glass.

2	shot(s)	**Rémy Martin cognac**
1	shot(s)	**Kahlúa coffee liqueur**
1	shot(s)	**Giffard brown crème de cacao**

Origin: Created in 1999 by Gillian Stanfield at The Atlantic Bar & Grill, London, England.
Comment: Sweet and rich, with coffee and chocolate – one to chase dessert.

CHOCOLATE MARTINI

Glass: Martini
Garnish: Wipe rim with cacao liqueur & dust with cocoa powder
Method: SHAKE all ingredients with ice and fine strain into chilled glass.

2	shot(s)	**Ketel One vodka**
1	shot(s)	**Giffard white crème de cacao**
1	shot(s)	**Dry vermouth**

Comment: Vodka and chocolate made more interesting with a hint of vermouth.

CHOCOLATE MINT MARTINI

Glass: Martini
Garnish: Wipe rim with cacao liqueur & dust with cocoa powder
Method: STIR all ingredients with ice and strain into chilled glass.

2	shot(s)	**Ketel One vodka**
1/2	shot(s)	**Giffard white crème de Menthe Pastille**
1/2	shot(s)	**Giffard white crème de cacao**
1/2	shot(s)	**Dry vermouth**

Comment: An after dinner sweety that tastes of chocolate mints.

CHOCOLATE PUFF

Glass: Old-fashioned
Garnish: Crumbled Cadbury's Flake bar
Method: SHAKE all ingredients with ice and fine strain into chilled glass.

1	shot(s)	**Golden rum**
1	shot(s)	**Giffard brown crème de cacao**
6	spoons	**Natural yoghurt**
2	zests	**Fresh orange**
1/4	shot(s)	**Sugar syrup (2 sugar to 1 water)**

Origin: Created by Wayne Collins for Maxxium UK.
Comment: Smooth as you like. The orange is surprisingly evident.

CHOCOLATE SAZERAC

Glass: Old-fashioned
Garnish: Lemon twist (discarded) & apple wedge
Method: Fill glass with ice, **POUR** in absinthe, top up with water and leave the mixture to stand in the glass. Separately **SHAKE** bourbon, cacao, sugar and bitters with ice. Finally discard contents of glass (absinthe, water and ice) and strain contents of shaker into empty absinthe-coated glass.

1/2	shot(s)	**La Fée Parisienne (68%) absinthe**
2	shot(s)	**Buffalo Trace bourbon whiskey**
1/2	shot(s)	**Giffard white crème de cacao**
1/4	shot(s)	**Sugar syrup (2 sugar to 1 water)**
2	dashes	**Peychaud's aromatic bitters**

Origin: Created in 2005 by Tonin Kacaj at Maze, London, England.
Comment: This twist on the classic Sazerac pairs absinthe, bourbon and chocolate to great effect.

CHOCOLATE SIDECAR

Glass: Martini
Garnish: Wipe rim with cacao liqueur & dust with cocoa powder
Method: SHAKE all ingredients with ice and fine strain into chilled glass.

1	shot(s)	**Rémy Martin cognac**
1	shot(s)	**Giffard brown crème de cacao**
1	shot(s)	**Ruby port**
1	shot(s)	**Freshly squeezed lime juice**
1/2	shot(s)	**Sugar syrup (2 sugar to 1 water)**

Origin: Created in 2005 by Wayne Collins for Maxxium UK.

CICADA COCKTAIL

Glass: Martini
Garnish: Dust with freshly grated nutmeg
Method: SHAKE all ingredients with ice and fine strain into chilled glass.

2	shot(s)	**Jack Daniel's Tennessee whiskey**
1	shot(s)	**Luxardo Amaretto di Saschira**
$^1/_2$	shot(s)	**Double (heavy) cream**
$^3/_4$	shot(s)	**Sugar syrup (2 sugar to 1 water)**

Origin: Those familiar with the Grasshopper cocktail (named for its green colour) will understand why this one is called the Cicada (they're a bit browner).
Comment: Smoothed whiskey with more than a hint of almond.

CINNAMON DAIQUIRI

Glass: Martini
Garnish: Dust with cinnamon powder
Method: SHAKE all ingredients with ice and fine strain into chilled glass.

2	shot(s)	**Light white rum**
$^1/_2$	shot(s)	**Cinnamon schnapps liqueur**
$^1/_2$	shot(s)	**Freshly squeezed lime juice**

Origin: Created in 1999 by Porik at Che, London, England.
Comment: A subtle spicy cinnamon taste with tangy length.

CIDER APPLE COOLER

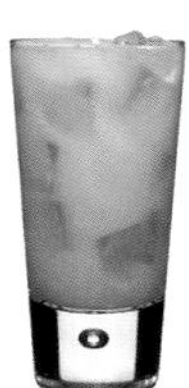

Glass: Collins
Method: SHAKE all ingredients with ice and strain into ice-filled glass.

2	shot(s)	**Boulard Grand Solage Calvados**
1	shot(s)	**Apple schnapps liqueur**
$4^1/_2$	shot(s)	**Pressed apple juice**

Comment: Not unlike the taste of strong dry cider.

CITRUS CAIPIROVSKA

Glass: Old-fashioned
Method: MUDDLE lemon in base of glass. Add other ingredients and fill glass with crushed ice. **CHURN** drink with bar spoon and serve with short straws.

$^3/_4$	fresh	**Lemon cut into wedges**
2	shot(s)	**Ketel One Citroen vodka**
$^3/_4$	shot(s)	**Sugar syrup (2 sugar to 1 water)**

Comment: Superbly refreshing balance of sweet and citrus sourness.

CIDER APPLE MARTINI

Glass: Martini
Garnish: Apple wedge
Method: SHAKE all ingredients with ice and fine strain into chilled glass.

$1^1/_2$	shot(s)	**Boulard Grand Solage Calvados**
$^3/_4$	shot(s)	**Apple schnapps liqueur**
$^3/_4$	shot(s)	**Freshly squeezed lemon juice**
1	shot(s)	**Pressed apple juice**
$^1/_4$	shot(s)	**Sugar syrup (2 sugar to 1 water)**

Origin: Created in 1998 by Jamie Terrell at Lab, London, England.
Comment: As the name suggests, rich cider flavours with a sharp finish.

CITRUS MARTINI

Glass: Martini
Garnish: Orange zest twist
Method: SHAKE all ingredients with ice and fine strain into chilled glass.

$1^1/_2$	shot(s)	**Ketel One Citroen vodka**
1	shot(s)	**Freshly squeezed lemon juice**
$^1/_4$	shot(s)	**Sugar syrup (2 sugar to 1 water)**
$^1/_4$	shot(s)	**Cointreau triple sec**
3	dashes	**Fee Brothers orange bitters**

AKA: Lemon Martini
Origin: Created by Dick Bradsell at Fred's, London, England, in the late 80s.
Comment: Orange undertones add citrus depth to the lemon explosion.

CINDERELLA

Glass: Collins
Garnish: Lemon wheel
Method: SHAKE first five ingredients with ice and strain into ice-filled glass. **TOP** with soda water.

2	shot(s)	**Freshly squeezed orange juice**
$1^1/_2$	shot(s)	**Pressed pineapple juice**
$^3/_4$	shot(s)	**Freshly squeezed lemon juice**
$^1/_8$	shot(s)	**Pomegranate (grenadine) syrup**
3	dashes	**Angostura aromatic bitters**
Top up with		**Soda water (club soda)**

Comment: Long, fresh and fruity.

CLARET COBBLER

Glass: Goblet
Garnish: Mint sprig
Method: SHAKE all ingredients with ice and fine strain into glass filled with crushed ice. Serve with straws.

$1^1/_2$	shot(s)	**Rémy Martin cognac**
1	shot(s)	**Grand Marnier liqueur**
$2^1/_2$	shot(s)	**Red wine**

Origin: My version of an old classic.
Comment: Fortified and slightly sweetened wine cooled and lengthened by ice.

CLARIDGE COCKTAIL [UPDATED #7]

Glass: Martini
Garnish: Lemon zest twist
Method: SHAKE all ingredients with ice and fine strain into chilled glass.

$1\frac{1}{2}$	shot(s)	**Plymouth gin**
$1\frac{1}{2}$	shot(s)	**Dry vermouth**
$\frac{1}{2}$	shot(s)	**Cointreau triple sec**
$\frac{1}{2}$	shot(s)	**Giffard apricot brandy du Roussillon**

Origin: Adapted from Harry Craddock's 1930 'The Savoy Cocktail Book'.
Comment: Gin for strength, vermouth for dryness and liqueur to sweeten – an interesting combination.

CLASSIC COCKTAIL [UPDATED #7]

Glass: Martini
Garnish: Lemon zest twist (optional sugar rim)
Method: SHAKE all ingredients with ice and fine strain into chilled glass.

2	shot(s)	**Rémy Martin cognac**
$\frac{1}{2}$	shot(s)	**Freshly squeezed lemon juice**
$\frac{1}{2}$	shot(s)	**Grand Marnier liqueur**
$\frac{1}{2}$	shot(s)	**Luxardo maraschino liqueur**
$\frac{1}{2}$	shot(s)	**Chilled mineral water** (omit if wet ice)

Origin: Adapted from Harry Craddock's 1930 'The Savoy Cocktail Book'.
Comment: Reminiscent of a Sidecar with maraschino.

CLEMENTINE

Glass: Shot
Garnish: Sugar coated orange wedge
Method: Refrigerate ingredients then **LAYER** in chilled glass by carefully pouring in the following order. Instruct drinker to down in one and bite into the wedge.

$\frac{1}{2}$	shot(s)	**Luxardo limoncello liqueur**
$\frac{1}{2}$	shot(s)	**Mandarine Napoléon liqueur**

Comment: Short, sweet and very fruity.

CLIPPER COCKTAIL

Glass: Martini
Garnish: Lemon peel knot
Method: SHAKE all ingredients and fine strain into glass filled with crushed ice.

2	shot(s)	**Light white rum**
2	shot(s)	**Dry vermouth**
$\frac{1}{2}$	shot(s)	**Pomegranate (grenadine) syrup**

Origin: Peggy Guggenheim's biography mentions that this cocktail was served during the 1940s on the Boeing flying boats known as Clippers.
Comment: Light, easy drinking and very refreshing.

CLOCKWORK ORANGE [UPDATED #7]

Glass: Collins
Garnish: Orange wheel in glass
Method: SHAKE all ingredients with ice and strain into ice-filled glass.

$1\frac{1}{2}$	shot(s)	**Rémy Martin cognac**
$1\frac{1}{2}$	shot(s)	**Grand Marnier liqueur**
3	shot(s)	**Freshly squeezed orange juice**

Comment: Neither as memorable nor as controversial as the film but a pleasant orange drink all the same.

CLOVER LEAF COCKTAIL #1 [NEW #7] (CLASSIC FORMULA)

Glass: Martini
Garnish: Float mint leaf
Method: SHAKE all ingredients with ice and fine strain into chilled glass.

2	shot(s)	**Plymouth gin**
$\frac{3}{4}$	shot(s)	**Freshly squeezed lemon juice**
$\frac{3}{4}$	shot(s)	**Pomegranate (grenadine) syrup**
$\frac{1}{2}$	fresh	**Egg white**

Variant: With raspberry syrup in place of pomegranate syrup.
AKA: Without the mint garnish this drink called a 'Clover Club'.
Origin: This classic cocktail is thought to have been created at the Bellevue-Stratford Hotel in Philadelphia.
Comment: Smooth, aromatic, fruity and medium sweet.

'I HAVE DRUNK SINCE I WAS FIFTEEN AND FEW THINGS HAVE GIVEN ME MORE PLEASURE... THE ONLY TIME IT ISN'T GOOD FOR YOU IS WHEN YOU WRITE OR WHEN YOU FIGHT. YOU HAVE TO DO THAT COLD. BUT IT ALWAYS HELPS MY SHOOTING.'

ERNEST HEMINGWAY

CLOVER LEAF COCKTAIL #2 [UPDATED #7] (MODERN FORMULA)

Glass: Martini
Garnish: Clover/mint leaf
Method: MUDDLE raspberries in base of shaker. Add other ingredients, **SHAKE** with ice and fine strain into chilled glass.

7	fresh	**Raspberries**
3	fresh	**Mint leaves (torn)**
2	shot(s)	**Plymouth gin**
3/4	shot(s)	**Freshly squeezed lemon juice**
1/2	shot(s)	**Pomegranate (grenadine) syrup**
1/2	fresh	**Egg white**

Comment: Carpet scaring red, this fruity adaptation perhaps has a wider appeal than the original Clover Leaf.

'I COULD NEVER QUITE ACCUSTOM MYSELF TO ABSINTHE, BUT IT SUITS MY STYLE SO WELL.'
OSCAR WILDE

CLUB COCKTAIL #1 [NEW #7]

Glass: Martini
Garnish: Orange zest twist
Method: STIR all ingredients with ice and strain into chilled glass.

1 1/2	shot(s)	**Fino sherry**
1 1/2	shot(s)	**Tawny port**
1	dash	**Fee Brothers orange bitters**

Origin: In his 1948 'The Fine Art of Mixing Drinks', David A. Embury writes, "Perhaps it would not be too much of an exaggeration to say there are as many Club Cocktails as there are clubs." This example is adapted from the same book.
Comment: Dry and incredibly aromatic. A perfect aperitif.

CLUB COCKTAIL #2 [NEW #7]

Glass: Martini
Garnish: Stuffed olive
Method: SHAKE all ingredients with ice and strain into chilled glass.

2	shot(s)	**Plymouth gin**
1	shot(s)	**Sweet vermouth**
1/8	shot(s)	**Yellow Chartreuse liqueur**

Origin: Adapted from Harry Craddock's 1930 'The Savoy Cocktail Book'.
Comment: A sweet Martini with a hint of Chartreuse.

CLUB COCKTAIL #3 [UPDATED #7]

Glass: Martini
Garnish: Maraschino cherry in drink
Method: STIR all ingredients with ice and fine strain into chilled glass.

2	shot(s)	**Golden rum**
1/2	shot(s)	**Sweet vermouth**
1/2	shot(s)	**Dry vermouth**
1/2	shot(s)	**Maraschino syrup (from cherry jar)**
3	dashes	**Angostura aromatic bitters**
3/4	shot(s)	**Chilled mineral water** (reduce if wet ice)

Origin: Adapted from a drink created in 2002 by Michael Butt at Milk & Honey, London, England.
Comment: An aromatic, spirited, classical cocktail.

COBBLED RASPBERRY MARTINI [UPDATED #7]

Glass: Martini
Garnish: Mint leaf/raspberries on stick
Method: MUDDLE raspberries in base of shaker. Add other ingredients, **SHAKE** with ice and fine strain into chilled glass.

12	fresh	**Raspberries**
2	shot(s)	**Ketel One vodka**
1	shot(s)	**Red wine**
1/4	shot(s)	**Sugar syrup (2 sugar to 1 water)**

Origin: Created by yours truly in 2004.
Comment: The addition of a splash of wine to a simple Raspberry Martini adds another level of complexity.

COCO CABANA

Glass: Martini
Garnish: Pineapple wedge on rim
Method: SHAKE all ingredients with ice and fine strain into chilled glass.

1 1/2	shot(s)	**Malibu coconut rum liqueur**
1/2	shot(s)	**Midori melon liqueur**
2	shot(s)	**Pressed pineapple juice**
3/4	shot(s)	**Double (heavy) cream**
3/4	shot(s)	**Milk**

Comment: A sweet, creamy tropical number for Barry Manilow fans.

COCO NAUT

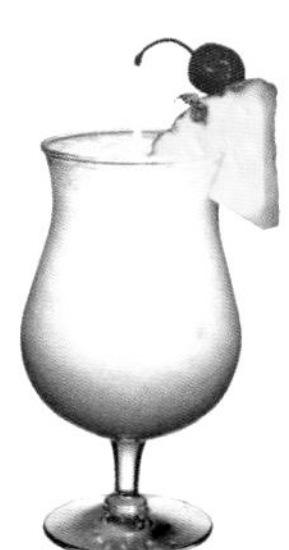

Glass: Hurricane
Garnish: Pineapple wedge & cherry on rim
Method: BLEND ingredients with 12oz scoop of crushed ice. Pour into glass and serve with straws.

2	shot(s)	**Wray & Nephew overproof rum**
1 1/2	shot(s)	**Coco López cream of coconut**
1	shot(s)	**Freshly squeezed lime juice**

Comment: This snow-white drink is hardly innocent with a double shot of overproof rum masked by the sweet coconut.

COCONUT DAIQUIRI

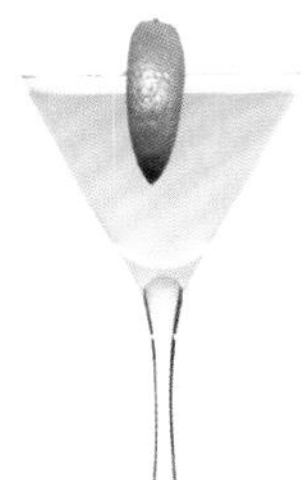

Glass: Martini
Garnish: Lime wedge
Method: SHAKE all ingredients with ice and fine strain into chilled glass.

2	shot(s)	**Light white rum**
1	shot(s)	**Malibu coconut rum liqueur**
1/2	shot(s)	**Freshly squeezed lime juice**
1/2	shot(s)	**Coconut syrup**
3/4	shot(s)	**Chilled mineral water** (omit if wet ice)

Variant: Blend with a 12oz scoop of crushed ice and a tad more coconut syrup.
Comment: That special Daiquiri flavour with a pleasing tropical touch.

COCONUT WATER

Glass: Martini
Method: STIR all ingredients with ice and fine strain into chilled glass.

2 1/4	shot(s)	**Malibu coconut rum liqueur**
1	shot(s)	**Ketel One vodka**
1/8	shot(s)	**Coconut syrup**
1 1/4	shot(s)	**Chilled mineral water** (reduce if wet ice)

Origin: Created in 2003 by yours truly.

Comment: Have you ever drunk from a fresh coconut in the Caribbean? Well, this is the alcoholic equivalent.

COFFEE BATIDA [NEW #7]

Glass: Old-fashioned
Garnish: Float three coffee beans
Method: BLEND all ingredients with crushed ice and serve with straws.

2	shot(s)	**Leblon cachaça**
1	shot(s)	**Espresso coffee**
1	shot(s)	**Coffee liqueur**
1/2	shot(s)	**Sugar syrup (2 sugar to 1 water)**

Comment: Looks like frozen mud with a frothy head but fortunately this caffeine and cachaça laced cocktail tastes a good deal better than it looks.

COFFEE & VANILLA DAIQUIRI 

Glass: Martini
Garnish: Float three coffee beans
Method: SHAKE all ingredients with ice and fine strain into chilled glass.

2	shot(s)	**Vanilla-infused Havana Club rum**
1	shot(s)	**Kahlúa coffee liqueur**
1/2	shot(s)	**Freshly squeezed lime juice**
1/8	shot(s)	**Sugar syrup (2 sugar to 1 water)**
3/4	shot(s)	**Chilled mineral water** (omit if wet ice)

Origin: Created in 2002 by yours truly.
Comment: Coffee, vanilla, sweetness and sourness all in harmony.

COBBLERS

Cobblers emerged in the mid 1800s and circa 1880 the bartender Harry Johnson said of the Sherry Cobbler, "This drink is without doubt the most popular beverage in this country, with ladies as well as with gentlemen. It is a very refreshing drink for old and young."

Cobblers are served with straws in a goblet filled with crushed ice and decorated with fruit and a sprig or two of mint. They are based on spirits and/or wine sweetened with sugar syrup or sweet liqueur. Classically Cobblers contain little or no citrus but modern variations often call for citrus and other fruits to be muddled. Personally I believe it's the lack of citrus that sets Cobblers apart. The best examples of these use the tannin and acidity in the wine to bitter and so balance.

Cobblers are also classically built in the glass. I prefer to shake mine to properly cool and mix them before straining over fresh crushed ice and stirring (see my recipe for the Claret Cobbler). I've also recently taken to calling neo-Martinis which use wine in place of citrus 'Cobbled Martinis' (see Cobbled Raspberry Martini).

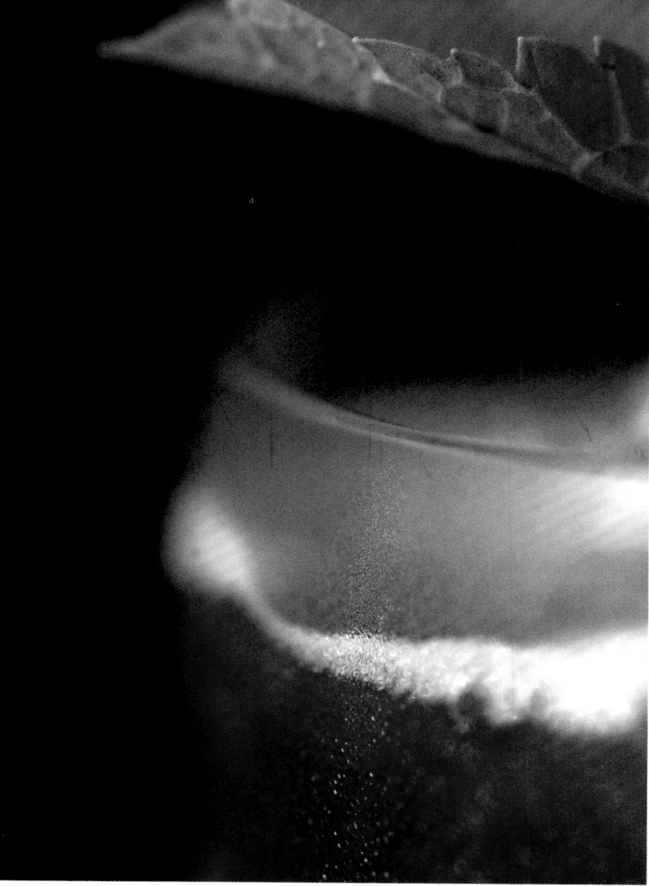

COLLINS

The Collins is thought to have been created by John Collins, a bartender at Limmer's Hotel, Conduit Street, London, during the nineteenth century. However, others claim that the drink was invented around the same time in New Jersey, or San Francisco, USA.
The original Collins was based on gin, but there is a debate as to whether it was Old Tom or London Dry. See also Gin Punch, John Collins and Tom Collins.

Collins variations include
Captain Collins (with Canadian whiskey)
Colonel Collins (with bourbon)
Jack Collins (with applejack)
Joe Collins (with vodka)
John Collins (with London Dry gin or jenever)
José or Pepito Collins (with tequila)
Mike Collins (with Irish whiskey)
Pedro Collins (with rum)
Pierre Collins (with cognac/brandy)
Raspberry Collins
Sandy or Jock Collins (with Scotch whisky)
Tom Collins (with Old Tom gin)
Vodka Collins (AKA Joe Collins)

COLA DE MONO

Glass: Martini
Garnish: Dust with cinnamon powder
Method: MUDDLE cinnamon stick and pisco in base of shaker. Add other ingredients, **SHAKE** with ice and fine strain into a chilled glass.

1	inch	**Cinnamon stick**
2	shot(s)	**Pisco**
1	shot(s)	**Cold espresso coffee**
1	shot(s)	**Kahlúa coffee liqueur**

Origin: I based this on a Chilean drink traditionally consumed at Christmas, the name of which translates as 'Tail of Monkey'. The original uses milk and sugar instead of coffee liqueur.
Comment: Coffee and cinnamon – a drink to be savoured.

COLD COMFORT

Glass: Old-fashioned
Method: SHAKE all ingredients with ice and strain into ice-filled glass.

2	shot(s)	**Wray & Nephew overproof rum**
6	spoons	**Runny honey**
1	shot(s)	**Freshly squeezed lime juice**

Origin: I discovered this while in Jamaica in 2001.
Comment: Take at the first sign of a cold, and then retreat under your bedcovers. Repeat dose regularly while symptoms persist. Warning – do not consume with other forms of medication.

THE COLD WINTER WARMER SOUR [NEW #7]

Glass: Old-fashioned
Garnish: Orange slice & cherry on stick (sail)
Method: STIR honey with vodka in base of shaker until honey dissolves. Add other ingredients, **SHAKE** with ice and strain into ice-filled glass.

1	spoon	**Runny honey**
1	shot(s)	**Ketel One Citroen vodka**
1/2	shot(s)	**Bénédictine D.O.M. liqueur**
1	shot(s)	**Freshly squeezed lemon juice**
1/2	fresh	**Egg white**

Origin: Created in 2006 by yours truly.
Comment: Flavours reminiscent of a hot toddy but served in a cold sour.

COLLAR & CUFF [UPDATED #7]

Glass: Toddy
Garnish: Orange slice
Method: PLACE bar spoon in glass, add ingredients and **STIR**.

2	spoons	**Runny honey**
1	shot(s)	**Scotch whisky**
1	shot(s)	**Giffard Ginger of the Indies**
1	shot(s)	**Freshly squeezed lemon juice**
Top up with		**Boiling water**

Origin: Created in 2003 by yours truly.
Comment: This blonde drink is warmed with ginger. But do they match?

COLLECTION MARTINI

Glass: Martini
Garnish: Lime wedge
Method: SHAKE all ingredients with ice and fine strain into chilled glass.

3/4	shot(s)	**Ketel One vodka**
3/4	shot(s)	**Ketel One Citroen vodka**
3/4	shot(s)	**Bénédictine D.O.M liqueur**
3/4	shot(s)	**Giffard mûre (blackberry)**
1/2	shot(s)	**Freshly squeezed lime juice**

Origin: Originally created by Matthew Randall whilst at The Collection, London, England.
Comment: Honey, spice and vodka enhanced by blackberries, with a very alcoholic edge.

COLLINS

Glass: Collins
Garnish: Orange slice & cherry on stick (sail)
Method: SHAKE first three ingredients with ice and strain into ice-filled glass. **TOP** with soda, stir and serve with straws.

2	shot(s)	**Bokma Jonge Genever**
1	shot(s)	**Freshly squeezed lemon juice**
1/2	shot(s)	**Sugar syrup (2 sugar to 1 water)**
Top up with		**Soda water (club soda)**

Comment: A refreshing combination of spirit, lemon and sugar.

COLONEL COLLINS

Glass: Collins
Garnish: Orange slice & cherry on stick (sail)
Method: SHAKE first three ingredients with ice and strain into ice-filled glass. **TOP** with soda, stir and serve with straws.

2	shot(s)	**Buffalo Trace bourbon whiskey**
1	shot(s)	**Freshly squeezed lemon juice**
1/2	shot(s)	**Sugar syrup (2 sugar to 1 water)**
Top up with		**Soda water (club soda)**

Origin: Classic Collins variation.
Comment: Sweetened, soured and diluted bourbon.

COLONEL T

Glass: Sling
Garnish: Pineapple wedge
Method: SHAKE all ingredients with ice and strain into ice-filled glass.

2	shot(s)	**Buffalo Trace bourbon whiskey**
1	shot(s)	**Giffard apricot brandy du Roussillon**
2 1/2	shot(s)	**Pressed pineapple juice**

Comment: Mellow and long with pineapple, apricot and bourbon.

COLONEL'S BIG OPU [NEW #7] 

Glass: Collins
Garnish: Orange slice & cherry (sail)
Method: SHAKE first three ingredients with ice and strain into ice-filled glass. **TOP** with champagne and serve with straws.

1	shot(s)	**Plymouth gin**
1	shot(s)	**Cointreau triple sec**
$\frac{1}{2}$	shot(s)	**Freshly squeezed lime juice**
Top up with		**Brut Champagne**
1	dash	**Fee Brothers orange bitters (optional)**

Origin: Adapted from a recipe created by Victor J. Bergeron and taken from his 'Trader Vic's Bartender's Guide' (1972 revised edition), where he writes "This is one of our old drinks. The colonel's big opu: the colonel's big belly."
Comment: A long, fruity yet dry drink charged with champagne.

COLONIAL ROT

Glass: Collins
Garnish: Mint sprig
Method: Lightly **MUDDLE** mint in base of shaker just enough to bruise. Add next four ingredients, **SHAKE** with ice and fine strain into ice-filled glass. **TOP** up with half soda and half lemonade.

7	fresh	**Mint leaves**
$\frac{1}{2}$	shot(s)	**La Fée Parisienne (68%) absinthe**
1	shot(s)	**Ketel One Citroen vodka**
$\frac{1}{2}$	shot(s)	**Sugar syrup (2 sugar to 1 water)**
$\frac{1}{2}$	shot(s)	**Freshly squeezed lime juice**
Top up with		**Half soda and half lemonade**

Comment: Long and green with more than a touch of the green fairy.

COLORADO BULLDOG

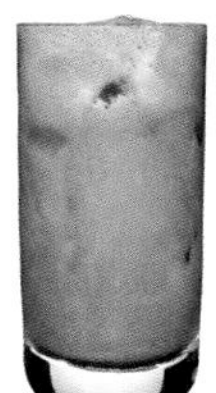

Glass: Collins
Method: SHAKE first four ingredients with ice and strain into ice-filled glass. **TOP** with cola.

$1\frac{1}{2}$	shot(s)	**Ketel One vodka**
1	shot(s)	**Kahlúa coffee liqueur**
1	shot(s)	**Double (heavy) cream**
1	shot(s)	**Milk**
Top up with		**Cola**

Variant: Colorado Mother (with tequila in place of vodka).
Comment: This dog's bite is hidden by cream.

COLUMBUS DAIQUIRI [NEW #7]

Glass: Martini
Garnish: Lime wedge on rim
Method: SHAKE all ingredients with ice and fine strain into chilled glass.

1	shot(s)	**Golden rum**
1	shot(s)	**Giffard Apricot brandy**
1	shot(s)	**Freshly squeezed lime juice**
$\frac{1}{2}$	shot(s)	**Chilled mineral water** (omit if wet ice)

Comment: A tangy, apricot flavoured Daiquiri.

THE COMET [NEW #7]

Glass: Martini
Garnish: Lemon zest twist
Method: MUDDLE grapes in base of shaker. Add other ingredients, **SHAKE** with ice and fine strain into chilled glass.

7	fresh	**White grapes**
2	shot(s)	**Rémy Martin cognac**
$\frac{3}{4}$	shot(s)	**Grand Marnier liqueur**
1	dash	**Angostura aromatic bitters**

Origin: Created by Eddie Clark at the Albany Club, Albermarle Street, London, to celebrate the launch of the Comet jetliner in 1952.
Comment: Cognac with freshly extracted grape juice and a splash of orange liqueur.

'I AM ONLY A BEER TEETOTALLER, NOT A CHAMPAGNE TEETOTALLER.'
GEORGE BERNARD SHAW

COMMODORE #1 [NEW #7]

Glass: Martini
Garnish: Maraschino cherry
Method: SHAKE all ingredients with ice and fine strain into chilled glass.

2	shot(s)	**Golden rum**
$\frac{1}{2}$	shot(s)	**Freshly squeezed lemon juice**
$\frac{1}{4}$	shot(s)	**Sugar syrup (2 sugar to 1 water)**
$\frac{1}{8}$	shot(s)	**Pomegranate (grenadine) syrup**
$\frac{1}{2}$	fresh	**Egg white**

Origin: Adapted from David A. Embury's 1948 'The Fine Art of Mixing Drinks', where he writes, "Another version of the Commodore calls for whisky instead of rum, omits the egg white, and uses orange bitters in place of the grenadine. Obviously, the two Commodores command two different fleets."
Comment: A smooth, sweet Daiquiri with flavoursome rum.

COMMODORE #2 [NEW #7]

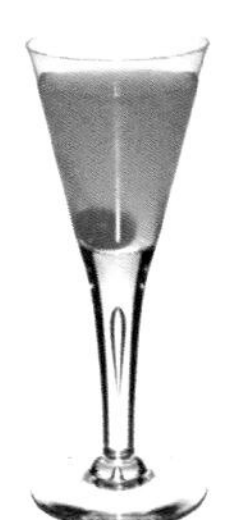

Glass: Martini
Garnish: Maraschino cherry
Method: SHAKE all ingredients with ice and fine strain into chilled glass.

2	shot(s)	**Buffalo Trace bourbon whiskey**
$\frac{3}{4}$	shot(s)	**Giffard white crème de cacao**
$\frac{1}{2}$	shot(s)	**Freshly squeezed lemon juice**
$\frac{1}{4}$	shot(s)	**Pomegranate (grenadine) syrup**
2	dashes	**Fee Brothers orange bitters (optional)**

Comment: Fruity, tangy Bourbon - surprisingly dry.

CONCEALED WEAPON [NEW #7]

●●●○○

Glass: Old-fashioned
Garnish: Lemon zest twist
Method: SHAKE all ingredients with ice and strain into ice-filled glass.

1	shot(s)	**La Feé Parisienne (68%) absinthe**
1	shot(s)	**Chambord black raspberry liqueur**
3/4	shot(s)	**Freshly squeezed lemon juice**
1/2	shot(s)	**Sugar syrup (2 sugar to 1 water)**
1	dash	**Peychaud's aromatic bitters**
1	dash	**Angostura aromatic bitters**
1/2	fresh	**Egg white**

Origin: Created in 2000 by Danny Smith at Che, London, England.
Comment: Absinthe is the 'weapon' that's 'concealed' in this full-on short berry drink.

CONGO BLUE

Glass: Martini
Garnish: Lemon zest twist
Method: SHAKE all ingredients with ice and fine strain into chilled glass.

1 1/4	shot(s)	**Zubrówka bison vodka**
1/2	shot(s)	**Midori melon liqueur**
1	shot(s)	**Pressed apple juice**
1/2	shot(s)	**Giffard mûre (blackberry) liqueur**
1/4	shot(s)	**Freshly squeezed lemon juice**

Origin: Created in 1999 by Marc Dietrich at Atlantic Bar & Grill, London and apparently named after the beauty of the Congo sunset.
Comment: Flavoursome and sweet.

COOL MARTINI

Glass: Martini
Garnish: Apple slice chevron
Method: SHAKE all ingredients with ice and fine strain into chilled glass.

1 1/2	shot(s)	**Midori melon liqueur**
1	shot(s)	**Partida tequila**
1 1/2	shot(s)	**Ocean Spray cranberry juice**

Comment: Tastes nothing like the ingredients - which include melon, tequila and cranberry juice. Try it and see if you taste toffee.

DRINKS ARE GRADED AS FOLLOWS:

● DISGUSTING ●◐ PRETTY AWFUL ●● BEST AVOIDED
●●◐ DISAPPOINTING ●●● ACCEPTABLE ●●●◐ GOOD
●●●● RECOMMENDED ●●●●◐ HIGHLY RECOMMENDED
●●●●● OUTSTANDING / EXCEPTIONAL

COOL ORCHARD

Glass: Old-fashioned
Garnish: Pineapple wedge & cherry
Method: MUDDLE ginger in base of shaker. Add other ingredients, **SHAKE** with ice and fine strain into ice-filled glass.

2	slices	**Fresh root ginger (thumbnail sized)**
1 1/2	shot(s)	**Aged rum**
1/2	shot(s)	**Ginger sugar syrup**
1/4	shot(s)	**Almond (orgeat) sugar syrup**
1	shot(s)	**Pressed pineapple juice**
1/2	shot(s)	**Vanilla schnapps liqueur**
1/4	shot(s)	**Freshly squeezed lime juice**

Origin: Created in 2001 by Douglas Ankrah for Akbar, Soho, London, England.
Comment: An unusual line up of cocktail ingredients combine to make a great drink.

COOLMAN MARTINI

Glass: Martini
Garnish: Orange zest twist
Method: SHAKE all ingredients with ice and fine strain into chilled glass.

1 3/4	shot(s)	**Zubrówka bison vodka**
1/2	shot(s)	**Cointreau triple sec**
2	shot(s)	**Pressed apple juice**
1/4	shot(s)	**Freshly squeezed lemon juice**

Origin: Created in 2001 by Jack Coleman at The Library Bar, Lanesborough Hotel, London, England.
Comment: Fragrant and complex. Integrated hints of apple and orange are laced with grassy vodka.

COPPER ILLUSION

Glass: Old-fashioned
Garnish: Orange zest twist
Method: STIR all ingredients with ice and strain into ice-filled glass.

1 1/2	shot(s)	**Plymouth gin**
3/4	shot(s)	**Campari**
3/4	shot(s)	**Cointreau triple sec**

Variant: Negroni
Origin: Unknown but brought to my attention in 2005 courtesy of Angus Winchester andalconomics.com.
Comment: Basically a Negroni with liqueur replacing sweet vermouth. Like the Italian classic this is both bitter and sweet.

COQUETAIL AU VANILLA [NEW #7]

●●●●◐

Glass: Old-fashioned
Garnish: Maraschino cherry
Method: SHAKE all ingredients with ice and strain into glass filled with crushed ice. Serve with straws.

2	shot(s)	**Vanilla infused light white rum**
1/4	shot(s)	**Velvet Falernum liqueur**

Origin: My adaptation of a classic.
Comment: This drink may look fluffy and sweet but it's dry and lightly spiced. Perfect for a sunny afternoon.

C

CORDLESS SCREWDRIVER [UPDATED #7]

Glass: Shot
Garnish: Sugar coated half orange slice
Method: POUR vodka and champagne into chilled glass and serve. Instruct drinker to down in one and then bite into the orange wedge.

1	shot(s)	Orange zest infused **Ketel One vodka**
Top up with		**Brut champagne**

Comment: A slammer style drink for those looking for a fruity alternative to tequila.

CORONATION

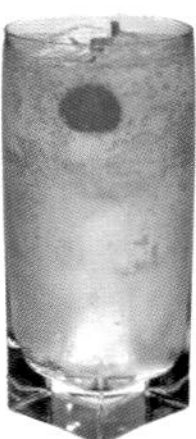

Glass: Collins
Garnish: Maraschino cherry
Method: STIR first five ingredients with ice and strain into ice-filled glass. **TOP** with soda, stir and serve with straws.

1	shot(s)	**Tio Pepe fino sherry**
1	shot(s)	**Dry vermouth**
2	shot(s)	**Sauvignon Blanc / unoaked Chardonnay wine**
1/4	shot(s)	**Luxardo maraschino liqueur**
2	dashes	**Angostura aromatic bitters**
Top up with		**Soda water (club soda)**

Comment: Light and aromatic.

CORONATION COCKTAIL NO. 1 [UPDATED #7]

Glass: Martini
Garnish: Orange zest twist
Method: STIR all ingredients with ice and strain into chilled glass.

1 1/2	shot(s)	**Tio Pepe fino sherry**
1 1/2	shot(s)	**Dry vermouth**
1/4	shot(s)	**Luxardo maraschino liqueur**
2	dashes	**Fee Brothers orange bitters**

Origin: Adapted from Harry Craddock's 1930 'The Savoy Cocktail Book'.
Comment: Medium dry and wonderfully aromatic.

CORPSE REVIVER NO. 1 #1 [UPDATED #7]

Glass: Martini
Garnish: Orange zest twist
Method: STIR ingredients with ice and strain into chilled glass.

1 1/2	shot(s)	**Rémy Martin cognac**
3/4	shot(s)	**Boulard Grand Solage Calvados**
3/4	shot(s)	**Sweet vermouth**
1/2	shot(s)	**Chilled mineral water** (omit if wet ice)

Origin: Created by Frank Meier, Ritz Bar, Paris, France. This recipe is adapted from Harry Craddock's 1930 'The Savoy Cocktail Book', where he writes, "To be taken before 11am, or whenever steam and energy are needed."
Comment: Dry and potent. A 'pick-me-up' hangover cure – or possibly put-you-right-back-down-again!

CORPSE REVIVER #2 [NEW #7]

Glass: Martini
Garnish: Lemon zest twist
Method: SHAKE all ingredients with ice and fine strain into chilled glass.

3/4	shot(s)	**Plymouth gin**
3/4	shot(s)	**Carlshamns Flaggpunsch Torr Swedish punch**
3/4	shot(s)	**Cointreau triple sec**
1/8	shot(s)	**La Feé Parisienne (68%) absinthe**
3/4	shot(s)	**Freshly squeezed lemon juice**

Origin: Adapted from Victor Bergeron's 'Trader Vic's Bartender's Guide' (1972 revised edition).
Comment: Perhaps a tad sweet but the kill or cure alcohol is well masked. Steady!

COSMOPOLITAN #1 (SIMPLE VERSION) [UPDATED #7]

Glass: Martini
Garnish: Flamed orange zest twist
Method: SHAKE all ingredients with ice and fine strain into chilled glass.

1	shot(s)	**Ketel One Citroen vodka**
1	shot(s)	**Cointreau triple sec**
1 1/2	shot(s)	**Ocean Spray cranberry juice**
1/2	shot(s)	**Freshly squeezed lime juice**

Origin: Formula by yours truly in 2005.
Comment: When a quality juice with at least 24% cranberry is used, the balance of citrus, berry fruit and sweetness is perfect.

COSMOPOLITAN #2 (COMPLEX)

Glass: Martini
Garnish: Flamed orange zest twist
Method: SHAKE all ingredients with ice and fine strain into chilled glass.

1	shot(s)	**Ketel One Citroen vodka**
1	shot(s)	**Cointreau triple sec**
1 1/2	shot(s)	**Ocean Spray cranberry juice**
1/2	shot(s)	**Freshly squeezed lime juice**
1/4	shot(s)	**Rose's lime cordial**
4	dashes	**Fee Brothers orange bitters**

Origin: Formula by yours truly in 2005.
Comment: For those who are not content with simplicity..

COSMOPOLITAN #3 (POPULAR VERSION) [NEW #7]

Glass: Martini
Garnish: Orange zest twist
Method: SHAKE all ingredients with ice and fine strain into chilled glass.

1 1/2	shot(s)	**Ketel One Citroen vodka**
1/2	shot(s)	**Cointreau triple sec**
1	shot(s)	**Ocean Spray cranberry juice**
1/4	shot(s)	**Freshly squeezed lime juice**

Origin: The most widely used Cosmopolitan recipe.
Comment: Every bar has a different Cosmo recipe but this seems to be the most popular.

COSMOPOLITAN

The Cosmopolitan is one of those drinks that has had various incarnations through the ages – some of them, quite probably, independent of one another. And during the 1990s, the familiar blend of cranberry, citrus and vodka was one of the most popular cocktails in London and New York.

Most people agree a Cosmopolitan appeared on the West Coast of America at some point during the 1980s, and travelled from there to New York and beyond. Cheryl Cook has a claim to have invented the drink during the latter half of the 1980s while head bartender at The Strand on Washington Avenue, South Beach, Miami. She apparently based her drink on the newly available Absolut Citron vodka and added a splash of triple sec, a dash of Rose's lime and, in her own words, "just enough cranberry to make it oh so pretty in pink".

Her version is believed to have travelled by way of San Francisco to Manhattan where Toby Cecchini is credited with first using fresh lime juice in place of Rose's at his Passerby bar.

A likely early ancestor of the Cosmopolitan is the Harpoon, a drink promoted by Ocean Spray during the 1960s which consisted of vodka, cranberry juice and a squeeze of fresh lime. And a long-forgotten 1934 book of gin recipes, 'Pioneers of Mixing Gin at Elite Bars', contains a recipe for a Cosmopolitan that is very similar to today's drink, only with lemon in place of lime, gin in place of vodka, and raspberry in place of cranberry.

Whatever the origin, however, it was Sex And The City's Carrie Bradshaw who popularised the drink when she swapped Martinis for Cosmos. And Dale DeGroff played a large part in refining today's popular recipe.

This bears an uncanny resemblance to the modern day, vodka based Cosmopolitan so casting yet more questions over the drink's origin.

Cosmopolitan variations include
Apricot Cosmo
Blue Cosmo
Blue Fin
Chinese Cosmopolitan
Cosmopolitan #1 (simple version)
Cosmopolitan # 2 (complex version)
Cosmopolitan #3 (popular version)
Cosmopolitan #4 (1934 version)
Creole Cosmo
Detropolitan
Ginger Cosmo
Grand Cosmopolitan
Hawaiian Cosmopolitan
Limey Cosmo
Metropolitan
Raspberry Cosmo
Royal Cosmopolitan
Rude Cosmopolitan
Rude Ginger Cosmopolitan
Sake'politan
Strawberry Cosmo
Watermelon Cosmo
White Cosmo
The Windsor Rose

C

COSMOPOLITAN #4 (1934 RECIPE) [NEW #7]

Glass: Martini
Garnish: Orange zest twist
Method: SHAKE all ingredients with ice and fine strain into chilled glass.

2 shot(s) **Plymouth gin**
1/2 shot(s) **Cointreau triple sec**
3/4 shot(s) **Freshly squeezed lemon juice**
1/4 shot(s) **Raspberry syrup (or Pomegranate syrup)**

Origin: Recipe adapted from 1934 'Pioneers of Mixing Gin at Elite Bars'.
Comment: Reminiscent of a Sidecar and, dependent on your syrup, well balanced. Thanks to drinkboy.com forum for first bringing this drink to my attention.

COSMOPOLITAN DELIGHT

Glass: Martini
Garnish: Flamed orange zest twist
Method: SHAKE all ingredients with ice and fine strain into chilled glass.

1 1/2 shot(s) **Rémy Martin cognac**
1/2 shot(s) **Grand Marnier liqueur**
1 1/4 shot(s) **Shiraz red wine**
3/4 shot(s) **Freshly squeezed lemon juice**
1/4 shot(s) **Almond (orgeat) syrup**
1/4 shot(s) **Sugar syrup (2 sugar to 1 water)**

Origin: Adapted from Dale DeGroff's book, 'The Craft of the Cocktail'. He credits the original recipe to a 1902 book by Charlie Paul.
Comment: No relation to the modern Cosmopolitan, this is a mellow, balanced blend of citrus, brandy and red wine.

COUNTRY BREEZE

Glass: Collins
Garnish: Berries
Method: SHAKE all ingredients with ice and strain into ice-filled glass.

2 shot(s) **Plymouth gin**
1/2 shot(s) **Giffard Cassis Noir de Bourgogne**
3 1/2 shot(s) **Pressed apple juice**

Comment: Not too sweet. The gin character shines through the fruit.

COVADONGA [NEW #7]

Glass: Martini
Garnish: Orange slice
Method: SHAKE all ingredients with ice and fine strain into chilled glass.

1 1/2 shot(s) **Campari**
1 shot(s) **Sweet vermouth**
1 shot(s) **Freshly squeezed orange juice**
1/2 shot(s) **Pomegranate (grenadine) syrup**
5 dashes **Angostura aromatic bitters**

Origin: Adapted from Victor Bergeron's 'Trader Vic's Bartender's Guide' (1972 revised edition).
Comment: Sweet, tart and fruity. My kinda girl!

COWBOY MARTINI

Glass: Martini
Garnish: Orange zest twist
Method: Lightly **MUDDLE** mint in base of shaker just enough to bruise. Add other ingredients, **SHAKE** with ice and fine strain into chilled glass.

7 fresh **Mint leaves**
3 shot(s) **Plymouth gin**
1/2 shot(s) **Sugar syrup (2 sugar to 1 water)**
3 dashes **Fee Brothers orange bitters (optional)**

AKA: The Cooperstown Cocktail
Origin: Created in the early 90s by Dick Bradsell at Detroit, London, England.
Comment: Sweetened gin shaken with fresh mint.

COX'S DAIQUIRI

Glass: Martini
Garnish: Cox's apple ring (in memory of Jennings Cox)
Method: SHAKE all ingredients with ice and fine strain into chilled glass.

2 1/2 shot(s) **Vanilla-infused Havana Club rum**
1/2 shot(s) **Freshly squeezed lime juice**
1/4 shot(s) **Vanilla sugar syrup**
1 shot(s) **Freshly pressed pineapple juice**

Origin: One of two cocktails with which I won 'The Best Daiquiri in London Competition' in 2002. It is named after Jennings Cox, the American mining engineer credited with first creating the Daiquiri.
Comment: Vanilla and pineapple bring out the sweetness of the rum against a citrus background.

CRANAPPLE BREEZE

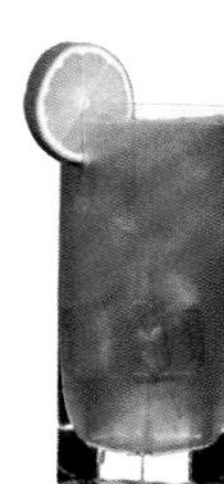

Glass: Collins
Garnish: Lime wheel on rim
Method: SHAKE first five ingredients with ice and strain into ice-filled glass. **TOP** with ginger ale and stir.

1 shot(s) **Ketel One Citroen vodka**
1 shot(s) **Cointreau triple sec**
1 shot(s) **Ocean Spray cranberry juice**
1 shot(s) **Pressed apple juice**
1/2 shot(s) **Freshly squeezed lime juice**
Top up with **Ginger ale**

Origin: Created in 2002 by Wayne Collins.
Comment: A refreshing cooler for a hot day by the pool.

CRANBERRY COOLER

Glass: Collins
Garnish: Orange slice
Method: SHAKE all ingredients with ice and strain into ice-filled glass.

2 shot(s) **Luxardo Amaretto di Saschira**
2 shot(s) **Ocean Spray cranberry juice**
2 shot(s) **Freshly squeezed orange juice**

Comment: Easy drinking for those with a sweet tooth.

CRANBERRY DELICIOUS (MOCKTAIL) [NEW #7]

Glass: Collins
Garnish: Mint sprig
Method: MUDDLE mint in base of shaker. Add other ingredients, **SHAKE** with ice and strain into ice-filled glass.

12	fresh	**Mint leaves**
1	shot(s)	**Freshly squeezed lime juice**
1/2	shot(s)	**Sugar syrup (2 sugar to 1 water)**
4	shot(s)	**Ocean Spray cranberry juice**
3	dashes	**Angostura aromatic bitters**

Origin: Adapted from a drink created in 2006 by Damian Windsor at Bin 8945 Wine Bar & Bistro, West Hollywood, USA.
Comment: Cranberry juice given more interest with mint, lime and bitters. This drink contains trace amounts of alcohol but remains an effective driver's option.

'IT'S BEEN SO LONG SINCE I'VE HAD CHAMPAGNE.'
LAST WORDS OF ANTON CHEKHOV

CRANBERRY & MINT MARTINI [UPDATED #7]

Glass: Martini
Garnish: Dried cranberries in base of glass & float mint leaf.
Method: Lightly **MUDDLE** mint in base of shaker, just enough to bruise. Add other ingredients, **SHAKE** with ice and fine strain into chilled glass.

9	fresh	**Mint leaves**
2	shot(s)	**Ketel One vodka**
1 1/2	shot(s)	**Ocean Spray cranberry juice**
1/4	shot(s)	**Pomegranate (grenadine) syrup**

Origin: Created in 2003 by yours truly.
Comment: This little red number combines the dryness of cranberry, the sweetness of grenadine and the fragrance of mint.

CRANBERRY SAUCE [UPDATED #7]

Glass: Martini
Garnish: Lime wedge
Method: SHAKE all ingredients with ice and fine strain into chilled glass.

2	shot(s)	**Ketel One vodka**
3/4	shot(s)	**Lapponia cranberry liqueur**
2 1/2	shot(s)	**Ocean Spray cranberry juice**
1/4	shot(s)	**Freshly squeezed lime juice**

Origin: Created in 2003 by yours truly.
Comment: Rich and fruity with that customary dry cranberry finish.

CREAMSICLE [UPDATED #7]

Glass: Martini
Garnish: Orange zest twist
Method: SHAKE all ingredients with ice and fine strain into chilled glass.

1 1/2	shot(s)	**Orange zest infused Ketel One vodka**
1	shot(s)	**Grand Marnier liqueur**
1/2	shot(s)	**Double cream**
1/2	shot(s)	**Milk**
1/8	shot(s)	**Sugar syrup (2 sugar to 1 water)**

Comment: A milky orange number with a surprisingly pleasant taste.

CREAMY BEE

Glass: Martini
Garnish: Cinnamon rim & raspberry
Method: SHAKE all ingredients with ice and fine strain into chilled glass.

1 1/2	shot(s)	**Krupnik honey liqueur**
1/2	shot(s)	**Irish cream liqueur**
1/2	shot(s)	**Chambord black raspberry liqueur**
1/2	shot(s)	**Frangelico hazelnut liqueur**
1/4	shot(s)	**Cinnamon schnapps liqueur**

Origin: Created in 2002 at Hush, London, England and originally made with cinnamon syrup in place of Goldschläger.
Comment: Creamy cinnamon with hints of honey, nuts and berries.

CREAMY CREAMSICLE [UPDATED #7]

Glass: Martini
Method: SHAKE all ingredients with ice and fine strain into chilled glass.

1/2	shot(s)	**Orange zest infused Ketel One vodka**
1 1/4	shot(s)	**Luxardo Amaretto di Saschira**
1	shot(s)	**Freshly squeezed orange juice**
3/4	shot(s)	**Double (heavy) cream**
3/4	shot(s)	**Milk**

Comment: Ultra smooth and creamy. Dessert, anyone?

CREAM CAKE

Glass: Martini
Garnish: Crumbled Cadbury's Flake bar
Method: SHAKE all ingredients with ice and fine strain into chilled glass.

1 1/4	shot(s)	**Irish cream liqueur**
1 1/4	shot(s)	**Teichenné Peach Schnapps Liqueur**
1 1/4	shot(s)	**Luxardo Amaretto di Saschira**
1	shot(s)	**Double (heavy) cream**

Comment: Creamy pleasure for the sweet of tooth.

CRUSTAS

The invention of the Crusta is credited to a Joseph Santina at the Jewel of the South or a Joseph Santini at the City Exchange in New Orleans sometime during the 1840s or 1850s. It first appeared in print as 'The Brandy Crusta' in Jerry Thomas' 1862 bartender's guide.

Crustas always contain a spirit, lemon juice and sugar – sometimes in the form of a liqueur or liqueurs. They are so named due to their sugar rim, which should be applied hours before the drink is made so that it is dried hard, or indeed crusty, when the drink is served. Crustas are also distinguished by being garnished with a band of orange or lemon zest, and are drunk from the rim of the fruit, rather than the rim of the glass.

As David A. Embury writes in his 1948 'The Fine Art of Mixing Drinks', "The distinguishing feature of the Crusta is that the entire inside of the glass is lined with lemon or orange peel. The drink may be served in either a wineglass or an Old-Fashioned glass, although it is much harder to make the peel fit in the Old-Fashioned glass. Take a large lemon or a small orange of a size approximating that of the glass to be used. Cut off both ends and peel the remainder in spiral fashion so as to keep the peel all in one place. Line the inside of the glass with this peel, wet the edge of the glass, and dip in powdered sugar to frost the edge of both peel and glass."

The trick is to find a fruit. I favour lemon, which fits into a small wineglass tightly enough to act as a watertight extension to the glass. The fact that wineglasses tend to curve in on themselves helps retain the fruit. You have little or no chance of successfully making a Crusta using a classically shaped old-fashioned glass.

Embury goes on to say, "While the 'Brandy Crusta' is the most common form of this drink, it is, after all, merely a Sour-type drink served in fancy style. Substitution of a different liquor as a base will give a Gin Crusta, a Rum Crusta, an Applejack Crusta, A Whisky Crusta, and so on." Please see my Bourbon Crusta and Brandy Crusta recipe in this guide and Jerry Thomas' below.

Some cocktail historians, Ted Haigh included, consider the Crusta the forerunner of the Sidecar and in turn the Margarita. It's a very logical argument.

THE BRANDY CRUSTA (JERRY THOMAS' RECIPE)

Sadly, I don't have a copy of Jerry Thomas' 1862 bartender's guide so I've taken this recipe from Ted Haigh's 'Vintage Spirits & Forgotten Cocktails'. "Cut a lemon in half. Pare the full peel off half, and squeeze the juice from the lemon. Moisten glass rim with lemon juice, and dip it in bar or table sugar. Insert a lemon peel into the glass. Mix in a cocktail shaker of crushed ice:"

2 ounces Cognac
1 teaspoon Orange curaçao
½ teaspoon Freshly squeezed lemon juice
1 dash Broker's bitters (substitute Angostura)

CRÈME ANGLAISE MARTINI

Glass: Martini
Garnish: Dust with cocoa powder
Method: SHAKE all ingredients with ice and fine strain into chilled glass.

1	shot(s)	**Vanilla infused Ketel One vodka**
2	shot(s)	**Bols advocaat liqueur**
1	shot(s)	**Milk**

Origin: Created in 2004 by yours truly.
Comment: Very reminiscent of alcoholic crème anglaise.

CRÈME BRÛLÉE MARTINI [UPDATED #7]

Glass: Martini
Garnish: Dust with cinnamon powder
Method: SHAKE all ingredients with ice and fine strain into chilled glass.

2	shot(s)	**Vanilla infused Ketel One vodka**
1/2	shot(s)	**Cartron caramel liqueur**
3/4	shot(s)	**Licor 43 (Cuarenta Y Tres) liqueur**
1	shot(s)	**Double (heavy) cream**
1/2	fresh	**Egg yolk**

Origin: Adapted from a drink created in 2002 by Yannick Miseriaux at the Fifth Floor Bar, London, England.
Comment: OK, so there's no crust, but this does contain egg yolk, caramel, vanilla, sugar and cream. Due to the cinnamon, it even has a brown top.

CRÈME DE CAFÉ

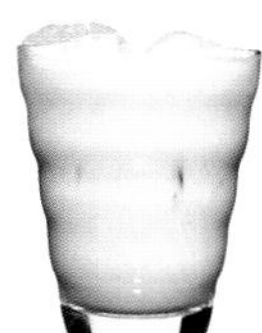

Glass: Old-fashioned
Method: SHAKE ingredients with ice and strain into ice-filled glass.

1	shot(s)	**Kahlúa coffee liqueur**
3/4	shot(s)	**Golden rum**
3/4	shot(s)	**Luxardo Sambuca dei Cesari**
1	shot(s)	**Double (heavy) cream**
1	shot(s)	**Milk**

Comment: Coffee predominates over the creaminess with hints of aniseed and rum.

CREOLE COSMO [NEW #7]

Glass: Martini
Garnish: Lime zest twist
Method: SHAKE all ingredients with ice and fine strain into chilled glass.

1	shot(s)	**Martinique agricole white rum (50% abv)**
1	shot(s)	**Clément Creole Shrubb**
1	shot(s)	**Ocean Spray cranberry juice**
1/2	shot(s)	**Freshly squeezed lime juice**

Comment: Dry, tangy and more sophisticated than your bog-standard Cosmo.

CRIMEA [NEW #7]

Glass: Martini
Garnish: Float coriander leaf
Method: MUDDLE coriander in base of shaker. Add other ingredients, **SHAKE** with ice and fine strain into chilled glass.

5	fresh	**Coriander leaves (not stems)**
2	shot(s)	**Plymouth gin**
1	shot(s)	**Pressed apple juice**
1/4	shot(s)	**Freshly squeezed lemon juice**
1/8	shot(s)	**Sugar syrup (2 sugar to 1 water)**
1/2	shot(s)	**Chilled mineral water** (omit if wet ice)

Origin: Adapted from a drink discovered in 2006 at the Ballroom, London, England.
Comment: Fragrant, herbal gin with a hint of citrus.

CRIMSON BLUSH

Glass: Martini
Garnish: Berries
Method: SHAKE all ingredients with ice and fine strain into chilled glass.

2	shot(s)	**Ketel One Citroen vodka**
1/2	shot(s)	**Chambord black raspberry liqueur**
2	shot(s)	**Squeezed golden grapefruit juice**
1/4	shot(s)	**Sugar syrup (2 sugar to 1 water)**

Origin: Created in 2004 by Jonathan Lamm at The Admirable Crichton, London, England.
Comment: Well balanced, fruity sweet and sour.

CROSSBOW [NEW #7]

Glass: Martini
Garnish: Orange zest twist
Method: SHAKE all ingredients with ice and fine strain into chilled glass.

2	shot(s)	**Plymouth gin**
1/2	shot(s)	**Cointreau triple sec**
1/4	shot(s)	**Giffard white crème de cacao**
1/2	shot(s)	**Chilled mineral water** (omit if wet ice)

Origin: Adapted from a drink discovered in 2005 at Bar Opiume, Singapore.
Comment: Surprisingly dry orange and chocolate laced with gin.

CROUCHING TIGER

Glass: Shot
Method: SHAKE all ingredients with ice and fine strain into chilled glass.

3/4	shot(s)	**Partida tequila**
1/2	shot(s)	**Soho lychee liqueur**

Comment: Tequila and lychee combine harmoniously in this semi –sweet shot.

C

●●●○○

THE CROW COCKTAIL [NEW #7]

Glass: Martini
Garnish: Lemon zest twist
Method: SHAKE all ingredients with ice and fine strain into chilled glass.

2	shot(s)	**Scotch whisky**
1	shot(s)	**Freshly squeezed lemon juice**
½	shot(s)	**Pomegranate (grenadine) syrup**

Origin: Adapted from Harry Craddock's 1930 'The Savoy Cocktail Book'.
Comment: If you use great syrup and have a penchant for Scotch then you could be pleasantly surprised by this drink.

●●●◐○

CROWN STAG

Glass: Old-fashioned
Garnish: Slice of lemon
Method: SHAKE ingredients with ice and strain into ice-filled glass.

1½	shot(s)	**Ketel One vodka**
1½	shot(s)	**Jägermeister liqueur**
1	shot(s)	**Chambord black raspberry liqueur**

Comment: A surprisingly workable combination.

●●●◐○

CRUEL INTENTION [NEW #7]

Glass: Martini
Garnish: Lime slice on rim
Method: SHAKE all ingredients with ice and fine strain into chilled glass.

2	shot(s)	**Buffalo Trace bourbon whiskey**
¼	shot(s)	**Giffard apricot brandy du Roussillon**
¼	shot(s)	**Luxardo Amaretto di Saschira**
1	shot(s)	**Pressed pineapple juice**
½	shot(s)	**Freshly squeezed lime juice**

Origin: Discovered in 2005 at The Mansion, Amsterdam, The Netherlands.
Comment: Bourbon with a hint of apricot, almond, pineapple and lime. Hardly cruel!

●●●◐○

CRUX [NEW #7]

Glass: Martini
Garnish: Orange zest twist
Method: SHAKE all ingredients with ice and fine strain into chilled glass.

1	shot(s)	**Rémy Martin cognac**
1	shot(s)	**Dubonnet Red**
1	shot(s)	**Cointreau triple sec**
1	shot(s)	**Freshly squeezed lemon juice**

Comment: The 'crux' of the matter is rarely as tasty as this fruity and none too sweet cognac.

●●●◐○

CUBA LIBRE [UPDATED #7]

Glass: Collins
Garnish: Lime wedge
Method: POUR ingredients into ice-filled glass, stir and serve with straws.

2	shot(s)	**Light rum**
½	shot(s)	**Freshly squeezed lime juice**
Top up with		**Cola**

Variants: Cuba Pintada & Cuba Campechana
Origin: Said to have been created in Cuba by American soldiers fighting the Spanish-American War of 1898.
Comment: Basically a rum and cola with a squeeze of lime – Cuba Libre sounds better though!

●●●◐○

CUBA PINTADA [NEW #7]

Glass: Collins
Garnish: Lime wedge
Method: POUR ingredients into ice-filled glass, stir and serve with straws.

2	shot(s)	**Havana Club light rum**
1	shot(s)	**Cola**
Top up with		**Soda water**

Variant: Cuba Campechana – rum with half soda and half cola; Cuba Libre – rum, cola and a dash of lime juice.
Origin: The name of this popular Cuban drink literally means 'stained Cuba' and there is just enough cola in this rum and soda to stain the drink brown.

●●●◐○

CUBAN COCKTAIL NO. 2 #1 [NEW #7]

Glass: Martini
Garnish: Lemon peel twist
Method: SHAKE all ingredients with ice and fine strain into chilled glass.

1½	shot(s)	**Light white rum**
⅛	shot(s)	**Luxardo maraschino liqueur**
⅛	shot(s)	**Pomegranate (grenadine) syrup**
¼	shot(s)	**Freshly squeezed lemon juice**
1	dash	**Fee Brothers orange bitters**
½	shot(s)	**Chilled mineral water** (omit if wet ice)

Origin: Adapted from Victor Bergeron's 'Trader Vic's Bartender's Guide' (1972 revised edition).
Comment: Perfumed yet not sweetened rum.

DRINKS ARE GRADED AS FOLLOWS:

● DISGUSTING ●◐ PRETTY AWFUL ●● BEST AVOIDED
●●◐ DISAPPOINTING ●●● ACCEPTABLE ●●●◐ GOOD
●●●● RECOMMENDED ●●●●◐ HIGHLY RECOMMENDED
●●●●● OUTSTANDING / EXCEPTIONAL

CUBA LIBRE

The Cuba Libre (Spanish for 'Free Cuba') was allegedly so named in August 1900 when some off-duty members of Teddy Roosevelt's Rough Rider soldiers were celebrating a victory during the Spanish-American war to free Cuba. They gathered in a bar in Havana when John Doe, a captain in the U.S. Signal Corp, entered the bar and ordered a rum and Coca Cola. The Captain raised his glass and sang out the battle cry that had inspired Cuba's victorious soldiers at war, 'Cuba Libre'.

This touching story, however, is unlikely to be true. The Spanish-American war was in 1898; Coca-Cola was bottled in America for the first time in 1899 and did not begin international exports for a decade or more; and John Doe is US slang for an unknown individual.

The Cuba Libre peaked in popularity during the 1940s, partly aided by the Andrews Sisters who in 1945 had a hit with 'Rum and Coca-Cola', named after the drink's ingredients. During the war, all spirits production went over to industrial alcohol - in the absence of whiskey and gin, Americans turned to imported rum.

CUBAN COCKTAIL NO. 3 #2 [NEW #7]

Glass: Martini
Garnish: Lemon peel twist
Method: SHAKE all ingredients with ice and fine strain into chilled glass.

1½	shot(s)	**Golden rum**
¼	shot(s)	**Rémy Martin cognac**
½	shot(s)	**Giffard apricot brandy du Roussillon**
½	shot(s)	**Freshly squeezed lime juice**
1	dash	**Fee Brothers orange bitters**
½	shot(s)	**Chilled mineral water** (omit if wet ice)

Origin: Adapted from Victor Bergeron's 'Trader Vic's Bartender's Guide' (1972 revised edition).
Comment: Like much of the Caribbean, this drink has French influences. Thank goodness for Admiral Rodney.

'NO WOMAN SHOULD MARRY A TEETOTALLER, OR A MAN WHO DOES NOT SMOKE.'
ROBERT LOUIS STEVENSON

CUBAN ISLAND [NEW #7]

Glass: Martini
Garnish: Orange zest twist
Method: SHAKE all ingredients with ice and fine strain into chilled glass.

2	shot(s)	**Light white rum**
½	shot(s)	**Dry vermouth**
½	shot(s)	**Freshly squeezed lemon juice**
¼	shot(s)	**Sugar syrup (2 sugar to 1 water)**

Origin: Adapted from a drink discovered in 2005 at DiVino's, Hong Kong, China.
Comment: The Daiquiri meets the Wet Martini. Interesting!

CUBAN MASTER

Glass: Collins
Garnish: Pineapple wedge
Method: SHAKE all ingredients with ice and strain into ice-filled glass.

1½	shot(s)	**Light white rum**
1	shot(s)	**Rémy Martin cognac**
1½	shot(s)	**Freshly squeezed orange juice**
1½	shot(s)	**Pressed pineapple juice**
½	shot(s)	**Freshly squeezed lemon juice**
¼	shot(s)	**Sugar syrup (2 sugar to 1 water)**

Origin: A classic cocktail I discovered in 1999 during a trip to Cuba.
Comment: Well balanced, wonderfully fruity.

CUBAN SPECIAL

Glass: Old-fashioned
Garnish: Orange zest twist
Method: SHAKE ingredients with ice and strain into ice-filled glass.

1½	shot(s)	**Light white rum**
¾	shot(s)	**Cointreau triple sec**
2	shot(s)	**Pressed pineapple juice**
¼	shot(s)	**Freshly squeezed lime juice**

Comment: Not that special, but certainly OK.

CUBANITA

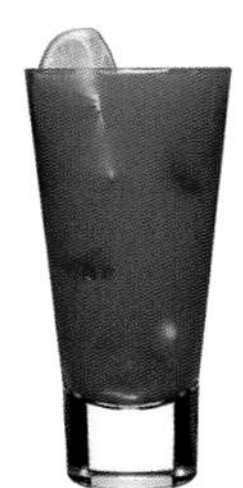

Glass: Collins
Garnish: Lime wedge
Method: SHAKE all ingredients with ice and strain into ice-filled glass.

2	shot(s)	**Light white rum**
4	shot(s)	**Pressed tomato juice**
½	shot(s)	**Freshly squeezed lemon juice**
8	drops	**Tabasco pepper sauce**
4	dashes	**Lea & Perrins Worcestershire sauce**
½	spoon	**Horseradish sauce**
2	pinch	**Celery salt**
2	pinch	**Black pepper**

Comment: The Bloody Mary returns - this time with rum.

CUCUMBER MARTINI

Glass: Martini
Garnish: Strip of cucumber
Method: MUDDLE cucumber in base of shaker. Add other ingredients, **SHAKE** with ice and strain into glass.

2	inches	**Peeled chopped cucumber**
1	shot(s)	**Zubrówka bison vodka**
1	shot(s)	**Ketel One vodka**
½	shot(s)	**Sugar syrup (2 sugar to 1 water)**

Origin: There are many different Cucumber Martini recipes; this is mine.
Comment: Cucumber has never tasted so good.

CUCUMBER & MINT MARTINI

Glass: Martini
Garnish: Cucumber wheel
Method: MUDDLE cucumber and mint in base of shaker. Add other ingredients, **SHAKE** with ice and fine strain into chilled glass.

2	inches	**Peeled diced cucumber**
7	fresh	**Mint leaves**
2	shot(s)	**Ketel One vodka**
1	shot(s)	**Pressed apple juice**
¼	shot(s)	**Sugar syrup (2 sugar to 1 water)**

Origin: Created in 2004 by David Ramos in the Netherlands.
Comment: A well balanced fortified salad in a glass – almost healthy.

CUCUMBER SAKE-TINI

Glass: Martini
Garnish: Three cucumber slices
Method: MUDDLE cucumber in base of shaker. Add other ingredients, **SHAKE** with ice and fine strain into chilled glass.

1 1/2	inch	**Peeled diced cucumber**
1 1/2	shot(s)	**Ketel One vodka**
1 1/2	shot(s)	**Sake**
1/4	shot(s)	**Sugar syrup (2 sugar to 1 water)**

Origin: Created in 2004 by Lisa Ball, London, England.
Comment: Subtle and dry. Cucumber and sake are made for each other.

CUMBERSOME

Glass: Martini
Garnish: Physalis (Cape gooseberry) on rim
Method: MUDDLE cucumber in base of shaker. Add other ingredients, **SHAKE** with ice and strain into a chilled Martini glass.

4	inch	**Fresh chopped peeled cucumber**
2	shot(s)	**Plymouth gin**
1/2	shot(s)	**Campari**
1	shot(s)	**Freshly squeezed orange juice**
1/2	shot(s)	**Sugar syrup (2 sugar to 1 water)**

Origin: Created in 2002 by Shelim Islam at the GE Club, London, England.
Comment: Interesting and fresh as you like with a pleasant bitterness.

CUPPA JOE

Glass: Martini
Garnish: Lemon zest twist
Method: SHAKE all ingredients with ice and fine strain into chilled glass.

1 1/2	shot(s)	**Ketel One vodka**
1 1/2	shot(s)	**Frangelico hazelnut liqueur**
1 1/2	shot(s)	**Espresso coffee (cold)**

Origin: Created in 2003 at Cellar Bar, New York City, USA.
Comment: Nutty coffee fortified with vodka – well balanced.

CURDISH MARTINI [UPDATED #7]

Glass: Martini
Garnish: Lemon zest twist
Method: STIR lemon curd with gin in base of shaker until curd dissolves. Add other ingredients, **SHAKE** with ice and fine strain into chilled glass.

2	spoons	**Lemon curd**
2	shot(s)	**Plymouth gin**
1/2	shot(s)	**Sourz Sour apple liqueur**
1/2	shot(s)	**Freshly squeezed lemon juice**

Origin: Created in 2001 by Tadgh Ryan at West Street, London, England.
Comment: Beautifully balanced with the tang of lemon curd.

THE CURRIER [NEW #7]

Glass: Martini
Garnish: Float mint leaf
Method: SHAKE all ingredients with ice and fine strain into chilled glass.

1 1/2	shot(s)	**Buffalo Trace bourbon whiskey**
1/2	shot(s)	**Kümmel liqueur**
1/4	shot(s)	**Freshly squeezed lime juice**
1/4	shot(s)	**Rose's lime cordial**

Origin: Recipe submitted in July 2006 by Murray Stenson at ZigZag Café, Seattle, USA.
Comment: A wonderfully cleansing after dinner cocktail with bourbon and lime plus hints of caraway and fennel courtesy of the Kümmel.

CUSTARD TART

Glass: Shot
Garnish: Physalis (Cape gooseberry) on rim
Method: MUDDLE physalis fruits in base of shaker can. Add other ingredients, **SHAKE** with ice and strain.

3	fresh	**Physalis fruits**
3/4	shot(s)	**Light white rum**
1/2	shot(s)	**Teichenné Peach Schnapps Liqueur**
1/4	shot(s)	**Freshly squeezed lime juice**
1/2	shot(s)	**Bols advocaat liqueur**

Origin: Created by Alex Kammerling in 2001.
Comment: Custardy, strangely enough.

CVO FIREVAULT [NEW #7]

Glass: Martini
Garnish: Orange zest twist
Method: SHAKE all ingredients with ice and fine strain into chilled glass.

1 1/2	shot(s)	**Orange zest infused Ketel One vodka**
3/4	shot(s)	**Campari**
3/4	shot(s)	**Freshly squeezed orange juice**
3/4	shot(s)	**Pressed pineapple juice**

Origin: Discovered in 2005 at CVO Firevault, London, England.
Comment: Fruity yet slightly bitter. Orange predominates with strong bursts of Campari.

CYDER PRESS [NEW #7]

Glass: Martini
Garnish: Float wafer thin apple slice
Method: SHAKE all ingredients with ice and fine strain into chilled glass.

2	shot(s)	**Boulard Grand Solage Calvados**
1/2	shot(s)	**St-Germain elderflower liqueur**
1	shot(s)	**Apple cider**
3/4	shot(s)	**Pressed apple juice**

Origin: Created in 2006 by yours truly.
Comment: Fresh, fermented and distilled apple juice with a hint of elderflower.

DAIQUIRI

Pronounced 'Dye-Ker-Ree', this drink is thought to have been created by Jennings Cox, an American engineer who was working at a copper mine near Santiago, Cuba, in 1896. It also bears a close relationship to the Canchanchara, a 19th century Cuban blend of rum, lemon, honey and water: some people believe that the Daiquiri itself was originally made with lemon in place of lime and extra water.

The popular version of the drink's origin states that another engineer called Pagliuchi was viewing mines in the region and met with Cox. During their meeting they set about making a drink from the ingredients Cox had to hand: rum, limes and sugar. The concoction was exquisite and Cox named the drink Daiquiri after the nearby port. According to Cox's granddaughter, however, Cox ran out of gin when entertaining American guests. Wary of serving them straight rum, he added lime and sugar.

The Daiquiri seems to have come to America with US Admiral Lucius Johnson, who fought in the Spanish-American war of 1898. He introduced the drink to the Army & Navy Club in Washington DC and a plaque in their Daiquiri Lounge records his place in cocktail history.

The classic proportions of a Daiquiri are 8 parts rum to 2 parts lime juice to 1 part sugar syrup. (This translates as two shots of rum, half a shot of lime juice and quarter of a shot of sugar syrup.) Most of the Daiquiri recipes in this guide are based on these proportions.

Daiquiris are classically shaken and served straight-up or on the rocks. The frozen, blended version is said to have first been produced by Emilio Gonzalez at the Plaza Hotel in Cuba. However, Constantino (Constante) Ribalaigua Vert of Havana's Floridita bar made the drink famous and today the Floridita is known as 'the cradle of the Daiquiri'.

Ernest Hemingway, the hard-drinking, Nobel prize-winning author, lived in Cuba for years, indulging his passions for fishing, shooting and boozing. In the 30s and the 40s he would often work his way through twelve of the Floridita's frozen Daiquiris - often doubles, called Papa Dobles in his honour. The Hemingway Special Daiquiri, which includes grapefruit, was created for him and continues to bear his name.

In his book 'Islands in the Stream', Hemingway's hero stares deep into his frozen Daiquiri, and Hemingway observes, "It reminded him of the sea. The frappéd part of the drink was like the wake of a ship and the clear part was the way the water looked when the bow cut it when you were in shallow water over marl bottom. That was almost the exact colour." The great man's bar stool can still be seen at the Floridita today.

DAIQUIRI VARIANTS

Acapulco Daiquiri
Ace Of Clubs Daiquiri
Aged Honey Daiquiri
Apple Daiquiri
Bahamas Daiquiri
Banana Daiquiri
Basil & Honey Daiquiri
Bella Donna Daiquiri
Black & White Daiquiri
Blueberry Daiquiri
Blueberry Pie Daiquiri
Butterscotch Daiquiri
Cachaça Daiquiri
Charles Daiquiri
Cherry & Hazelnut Daiquiri
Cherry Daiquiri
Chiclet Daiquiri
Cinnamon Daiquiri
Classic Daiquiri
Coconut Daiquiri
Coffee & Vanilla Daiquiri
Cox's Daiquiri
Daiquiri De Luxe
Dark Daiquiri
Derby Daiquiri
Difford's Daiquiri
El Presidente Daiquiri
Epestone Daiquiri
Floridita Daiquiri
Four W Daiquiri
French Daiquiri
Fruit Tree Daiquiri
Fu Manchu Daiquiri
Grapefruit Daiquiri
Greta Garbo
Havanatheone
Hemingway Special Daiquiri
Honey Daiquiri
Honeysuckle Daiquiri
Lisa B's Daiquiri
Lux Daiquiri
Mango Daiquiri
Melon Daiquiri
Miami Daiquiri
Millionaire's Daiquiri
Mulata Daiquiri
Naranja Daiquiri
Natural Daiquiri
Nevada Daiquiri
Orange Daiquiri
Passion Fruit Daiquiri
Peach Daiquiri
Peach Daiquiri Frozen
Pineapple & Cardamom Daiquiri
Pirate Daiquiri
Plum Daiquiri
Snow White Daiquiri
Spiced Apple Daiquiri
Strawberry Daiquiri
Strawberry Frozen Daiquiri
Turquoise Daiquiri
Vanilla Daiquiri

DAIQUIRI NO.1 #1 (CLASSIC FORMULA)

Glass: Martini
Garnish: Lime wedge on rim
Method: SHAKE all ingredients with ice and fine strain into chilled glass.

2	shot(s)	**Light or aged rum**
1/2	shot(s)	**Freshly squeezed lime juice**
1/4	shot(s)	**Sugar syrup (2 sugar to 1 water)**
1/2	shot(s)	**Chilled mineral water** (omit if wet ice)

Origin: The creation of this drink is attributed to Mr Jennings Cox, an American engineer who was working at a mine near Santiago, Cuba in 1896.
Comment: Sometimes called a classic Daiquiri or a natural Daiquiri, both terms are generally recognised as denoting that the drink should be shaken and served 'up' rather than blended with crushed ice.

'MR EDITOR. I LEAVE WHEN THE PUB CLOSES.'
WINSTON [illegible]

DAIQUIRI NO.1 #2 [NEW #7] (MODERN FORMULA)

Glass: Martini
Garnish: Lime wedge on rim
Method: SHAKE all ingredients with ice and fine strain into chilled glass.

2	shot(s)	**Light or aged rum**
1/4	shot(s)	**Freshly squeezed lime juice**
1/8	shot(s)	**Sugar syrup (2 sugar to 1 water)**
1/2	shot(s)	**Chilled mineral water** (omit if wet ice)

Origin: Throughout 2006 I kept encountering bartenders who favour this Daiquiri formula, particularly in London.
Comment: This modern style of Daiquiri emphasises the character of the rum. The influences of lime and sugar are very subtle.

DAIQUIRI NO.1 #3 (DIFFORD'S LUXE FORMULA) [NEW #7]

Glass: Old-fashioned
Garnish: Lime wedge
Method: SHAKE all ingredients with ice and strain into ice-filled glass.

2 1/2	shot(s)	**Light or aged rum**
1/2	shot(s)	**Freshly squeezed lime juice**
1/4	shot(s)	**Martinique cane juice syrup**
1/8	shot(s)	**Maraschino syrup (from cherry jar)**
1/2	shot(s)	**Chilled mineral water** (omit if wet ice)

Origin: A luxurious twist on the classic Daiquiri by yours truly.
Comment: This Daiquiri benefits from a splash more rum than the classical proportions. Martinique syrup made from freshly pressed sugar cane and maraschino syrup deliver sweetness.

DAIQUIRI NO.2 [NEW #7]

Glass: Martini
Garnish: Lime wedge on rim
Method: SHAKE all ingredients with ice and fine strain into chilled glass.

2	shot(s)	**Light white rum**
1/8	shot(s)	**Cointreau triple sec**
1/4	shot(s)	**Freshly squeezed orange juice**
1/2	shot(s)	**Freshly squeezed lime juice**
1/4	shot(s)	**Sugar syrup (2 sugar to 1 water)**
1/2	shot(s)	**Chilled mineral water** (omit if wet ice)

Origin: Created circa 1915 by Constantino (Constante) Ribalaigua Vert at the Floridita bar in Havana, Cuba.
Comment: Best described as a Daiquiri with subtle orange notes.

DAIQUIRI NO.3 [NEW #7]

Glass: Martini
Garnish: Lime wedge on rim
Method: SHAKE all ingredients with ice and fine strain into chilled glass.

2	shot(s)	**Light white rum**
1/2	shot(s)	**Freshly squeezed lime juice**
1/4	shot(s)	**Sugar syrup (2 sugar to 1 water)**
1/4	shot(s)	**Squeezed pink grapefruit juice**
1/8	shot(s)	**Luxardo maraschino liqueur**
1/2	shot(s)	**Chilled mineral water** (omit if wet ice)

Origin: Thought to have been created by Constantino (Constante) Ribalaigua Vert at the Floridita bar in Havana, Cuba, circa 1915.
If this was invented as early as 1915, then this was the predecessor of the Hemingway Daiquiri, since Hemingway did not arrive in Cuba until 1928.
Comment: A classic Daiquiri with a hint of grapefruit and maraschino liqueur (add more maraschino to taste). Essentially a Hemingway Special Daiquiri (Papa Doble Daiquiri) for folk without the great author's constitution or love of the sours.

DAIQUIRI NO.5 [NEW #7]

Glass: Martini
Garnish: Lime wedge on rim
Method: SHAKE all ingredients with ice and fine strain into chilled glass.

2	shot(s)	**Light white rum**
1/2	shot(s)	**Freshly squeezed lime juice**
1/2	shot(s)	**Pomegranate (grenadine) syrup**
1/4	shot(s)	**Luxardo maraschino liqueur**
3	dashes	**Angostura aromatic bitters**
1/2	shot(s)	**Chilled mineral water** (omit if wet ice)

AKA: Pink Daiquiri
Comment: This classically tangy Daiquiri is sweetened with pomegranate syrup and a splash of maraschino.

DAISY (& FIX)

There is little difference, if any, between a Daisy and a Fix. Both are very old drinks dating back to Victorian times and both terms are used fairly loosely. Both are of the Sour genre and consist of a citrus juice, sweetened with a syrup or liqueur, and fortified with a base spirit. However, Fixes tend to call for pineapple or sugar syrup while Daisies usually call for raspberry syrup or grenadine.

Daisies and Fixes are most commonly served in a goblet filled with crushed ice but Daisies can also be served straight-up or in a Collins glass.

Both drinks are traditionally garnished with seasonal fruit but modern tastes dictate simplicity.

DAIQUIRI ELIXIR [NEW #7]

Glass: Martini
Garnish: Lime wedge on rim
Method: SHAKE all ingredients with ice and fine strain into chilled glass.

2 shot(s) **Light or aged rum**
1/2 shot(s) **Freshly squeezed lime juice**
1/4 shot(s) **Martinique cane juice syrup**
1/8 shot(s) **Green Chartreuse liqueur**
1/2 shot(s) **Chilled mineral water**

Origin: Another Daiquiri variation from yours truly.
Comment: Freshly pressed sugar cane syrup and the French elixir Chartreuse add complexity to the classic Daiquiri.

DAIQUIRI DE LUXE

Glass: Martini
Garnish: Lime wedge on rim
Method: SHAKE all ingredients with ice and fine strain into chilled glass.

2 shot(s) **Light white rum**
1/4 shot(s) **Rose's lime cordial**
1/2 shot(s) **Freshly squeezed lime juice**
1/4 shot(s) **Almond (orgeat) syrup**
1/4 shot(s) **Chilled mineral water** (omit if wet ice)

Comment: A classic Daiquiri but with lime cordial and almond syrup replacing sugar as the sweetener.

DAIQUIRI ON THE ROCKS

Glass: Old-fashioned
Garnish: Lime wedge & maraschino cherry
Method: SHAKE all ingredients with ice and strain into ice-filled glass.

2 shot(s) **Light white rum (or aged rum)**
1/2 shot(s) **Freshly squeezed lime juice**
1/4 shot(s) **Sugar syrup (2 sugar to 1 water)**

Comment: Some hardened Daiquiri-philes prefer their tipple served over ice in an old-fashioned glass, arguing that a Martini glass is too dainty.

DAISY CUTTER MARTINI [NEW #7]

Glass: Martini
Garnish: Float mint leaf
Method: Lightly MUDDLE mint in base of shaker (just to bruise). Add other ingredients, **SHAKE** with ice and fine strain into chilled glass.

3 fresh **Mint leaves**
1 1/2 shot(s) **Ketel One vodka**
1 shot(s) **St-Germain liqueur**
1 shot(s) **Dry vermouth**
1/4 shot(s) **Yellow Chartreuse liqueur**

Origin: Created in 2006 by yours truly. I named it not for the bomb but after the cricketing term for a ball bowled so incompetently that it skims along the ground.
Comment: Floral, minty and herbal with a dry finish.

DAISY DUKE

Glass: Old-fashioned
Garnish: Berries
Method: SHAKE all ingredients with ice and strain into glass filled with crushed ice. Serve with straws.

2	shot(s)	**Buffalo Trace bourbon whiskey**
1	shot(s)	**Freshly squeezed lemon juice**
1/2	shot(s)	**Pomegranate (grenadine) syrup**

Origin: Created in 2002 by Jake Burger at Townhouse, Leeds, England.
Comment: This bright red drink tastes more adult than it looks.

DAMN-THE-WEATHER

Glass: Martini
Method: SHAKE all ingredients with ice and fine strain into chilled glass.

1	shot(s)	**Plymouth gin**
1	shot(s)	**Sweet vermouth**
1/2	shot(s)	**Cointreau triple sec**
1 1/2	shot(s)	**Freshly squeezed orange juice**

Comment: Gin and herbal notes emerge in this predominantly orange drink.

DAMSON IN DISTRESS

Glass: Shot
Method: SHAKE all ingredients with ice and fine strain into chilled glass.

1 1/2	shot(s)	**Plymouth damson gin liqueur**
1/2	shot(s)	**Luxardo Amaretto di Saschira**
1/4	shot(s)	**Freshly squeezed lemon juice**

Origin: Discovered in 2003 at Hush, London, England.
Comment: Damson and amaretto sharpened by lemon juice.

DANDY COCKTAIL [UPDATED #7]

Glass: Martini
Garnish: Lemon and orange zest twists
Method: SHAKE all ingredients with ice and fine strain into chilled glass.

1 1/2	shot(s)	**Buffalo Trace bourbon whiskey**
1 1/2	shot(s)	**Dubonnet Red**
1/2	shot(s)	**Cointreau triple sec**
1	dash	**Angostura aromatic bitters**

Origin: Adapted from Harry Craddock's 1930 'The Savoy Cocktail Book'.
Comment: This complex Manhattan variant is a well balanced combo of spirit, liqueur and aromatic wine.

DARK DAIQUIRI

Glass: Martini
Garnish: Lime wedge
Method: SHAKE all ingredients with ice and fine strain into chilled glass.

1 1/2	shot(s)	**Aged rum**
1/2	shot(s)	**Pusser's Navy rum**
1/2	shot(s)	**Freshly squeezed lime juice**
1/2	shot(s)	**Sugar syrup (2 sugar to 1 water)**
3/4	shot(s)	**Chilled mineral water** (omit if wet ice)

Comment: The fine sweet and sour balance of a great Daiquiri with hints of molasses.

D

DARK 'N' STORMY

Glass: Collins
Garnish: Lime wedge
Method: SHAKE first three ingredients with ice and strain into ice-filled glass. **TOP** with ginger beer, stir and serve with straws.

2	shot(s)	**Gosling's Black Seal rum**
1	shot(s)	**Freshly squeezed lime juice**
1/2	shot(s)	**Sugar syrup (2 sugar to 1 water)**
Top up with		**Ginger beer**

Origin: The national drink of Bermuda, where ginger beer and Gosling's rum are produced.
Comment: This deliciously spicy drink is part of the Mule family - but is distinctive due to the strong flavour of the rum.

D'ARTAGNAN [NEW #7]

Glass: Martini
Garnish: Lemon zest twist
Method: SHAKE first four ingredients with ice and fine strain into chilled glass. **TOP** with champagne.

1/2	shot(s)	**Armagnac**
1/2	shot(s)	**Grand Marnier liqueur**
2	shot(s)	**Freshly squeezed orange juice**
1/4	shot(s)	**Sugar syrup (2 sugar to 1 water)**
Top up with		**Brut champagne**

Comment: Use genuine freshly pressed juice and you'll have a tasty Mimosa-style drink.

DC MARTINI

Glass: Martini
Method: STIR all ingredients with ice and strain into chilled glass.

2	shot(s)	**Vanilla infused aged rum**
1/4	shot(s)	**Frangelico hazelnut liqueur**
1/4	shot(s)	**Giffard white crème de cacao**
1/4	shot(s)	**Sugar syrup (2 sugar to 1 water)**
1/2	shot(s)	**Chilled mineral water** (omit if wet ice)

Origin: Discovered in 2000 at Teatro, London, England.
Comment: Vanilla, chocolate and a hint of nut. Add more sugar to taste.

DE LA LOUISIANE #1 [NEW #7]

Glass: Martini
Garnish: Lemon zest twist
Method: STIR all ingredients with ice and strain into chilled glass.

2	shot(s)	**Buffalo Trace bourbon whiskey**
1/4	shot(s)	**Bénédictine D.O.M. liqueur**
1	dash	**Angostura aromatic bitters**
1/2	shot(s)	**Chilled mineral water** (omit if wet ice)

Origin: The signature cocktail of the Restaurant de la Louisiane in New Orleans which opened in 1881.
Comment: Whiskey with hints of honey and spice.

DE LA LOUISIANE #2 [NEW #7]

Glass: Martini
Garnish: Maraschino cherry
Method: STIR all ingredients with ice and strain into chilled glass.

1	shot(s)	**Buffalo Trace bourbon whiskey**
1	shot(s)	**Bénédictine D.O.M. liqueur**
1	shot(s)	**Sweet vermouth**
1/8	shot(s)	**La Fée Parisienne (68%) absinthe**
3	dashes	**Peychaud's aromatic bitters**

Origin: Recipe adapted from Stanley Clisby Arthur's 1938 'Famous New Orleans Drinks and How to Mix 'Em'.
Comment: Full flavoured and complex, yet fairly sweet, with herbal notes and a touch of absinthe.

DE LA LOUISIANE #3 [NEW #7]

Glass: Martini
Garnish: Orange zest twist
Method: STIR all ingredients with ice and strain into chilled glass.

1 1/2	shot(s)	**Buffalo Trace bourbon whiskey**
1	shot(s)	**Dubonnet Red**
1/4	shot(s)	**Cointreau triple sec**
2	dashes	**Peychaud's aromatic bitters**
1/2	shot(s)	**Chilled mineral water** (omit if wet ice)

Origin: Another variation on this New Orleans classic.
Comment: Beautifully balanced. This fruity whiskey drink manages to be both approachable and serious.

DEAD MAN'S MULE

Glass: Collins
Garnish: Lime wedge on rim
Method: SHAKE first four ingredients with ice and strain into ice-filled glass. **TOP** with ginger beer.

3/4	shot(s)	**La Fée Parisienne (68%) absinthe**
3/4	shot(s)	**Cinnamon schnapps liqueur**
3/4	shot(s)	**Almond (orgeat) syrup**
1/2	shot(s)	**Freshly squeezed lime juice**
Top up with		**Ginger beer**

Origin: Discovered in 2003 at the Met Bar, London, England.
Comment: Strong in every respect. Big, full-on flavours of aniseed, cinnamon and ginger.

DEAN'S GATE MARTINI

Glass: Martini
Garnish: Orange zest twist
Method: SHAKE all ingredients with ice and fine strain into chilled glass.

2	shot(s)	**Light white rum**
1	shot(s)	**Drambuie liqueur**
1	shot(s)	**Rose's lime cordial**
3/4	shot(s)	**Chilled mineral water** (omit if wet ice)

Comment: Rich and strong with a warm, honeyed citrus flavour.

DEATH BY CHOCOLATE

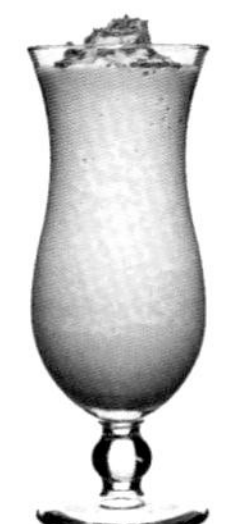

Glass: Hurricane
Garnish: Chocolate shavings (crumbled Cadbury's Flake bar)
Method: BLEND all ingredients with two 12oz scoops of crushed ice and serve with straws.

1	shot(s)	**Ketel One vodka**
1 1/2	shot(s)	**Irish cream liqueur**
1	shot(s)	**Giffard brown crème de cacao**
3	scoops	**Chocolate ice cream**

Comment: Unsophisticated but delicious. Don't be cheap – use deluxe ice cream

DEATH IN THE AFTERNOON [UPDATED #7]

Glass: Flute
Garnish: Float rose petal
Method: SHAKE first three ingredients with ice and fine strain into chilled glass. **TOP** with champagne.

1/4	shot(s)	**La Fée Parisienne (68%) absinthe**
1/2	shot(s)	**Freshly squeezed lemon juice**
1/4	shot(s)	**Sugar syrup (2 sugar to 1 water)**
Top up with		**Brut champagne**

Origin: Created by Ernest Hemingway (not just named after his book), this recipe was the author's contribution to a 1935 cocktail book titled, 'So Red the Nose, or Breath in the Afternoon'.
Comment: Bravado (absinthe) dominates this drink, alongside hints of citrus and biscuity champagne.

DEAUVILLE #1

Glass: Martini
Garnish: Lemon zest twist
Method: SHAKE all ingredients with ice and fine strain into chilled glass.

1	shot(s)	**Boulard Grand Solage Calvados**
1	shot(s)	**Rémy Martin cognac**
3/4	shot(s)	**Cointreau triple sec**
1/2	shot(s)	**Freshly squeezed lemon juice**
1/8	shot(s)	**Sugar syrup (2 sugar to 1 water)**
1/2	shot(s)	**Chilled mineral water** (omit if wet ice)

Variant: Apple Cart, Calvados Sidecar
Origin: A classic drink of unknown origin.
Comment: A well-balanced appley twist on the classic Sidecar.

DEAUVILLE #2 [NEW #7]

Glass: Martini
Garnish: Lemon zest twist
Method: SHAKE all ingredients with ice and fine strain into chilled glass.

1	shot(s)	**Boulard Grand Solage Calvados**
1	shot(s)	**Rémy Martin cognac**
1	shot(s)	**Cointreau triple sec**
1	shot(s)	**Freshly squeezed lemon juice**
1/4	shot(s)	**Sugar syrup (2 sugar to 1 water)**

Origin: A classic drink of unknown origin.
Comment: The classic recipe omits the sugar syrup, which makes this drink too sour for my taste. Duly sweetened, it is very much in the Sidecar vein.

DEEP SOUTH

Glass: Old-fashioned
Garnish: Lime wedge
Method: MUDDLE ginger in base of shaker. Add other ingredients, **SHAKE** with ice and fine strain into glass filled with crushed ice.

2	slices	**Fresh root ginger (thumbnail sized)**
1 1/2	shot(s)	**Clément Creole Shrubb liqueur**
1 1/2	shot(s)	**Freshly squeezed orange juice**
3/4	shot(s)	**Freshly squeezed lime juice**

Origin: Discovered in 1999 at AKA Bar, London, England.
Comment: Citrussy with delicate orange and ginger flavours.

THE DELICIOUS SOUR

Glass: Old-fashioned
Garnish: Cherry & lemon slice (sail)
Method: SHAKE all ingredients with ice and strain into ice-filled glass.

2	shot(s)	**Boulard Grand Solage Calvados**
1	shot(s)	**Teichenné Peach Schnapps Liqueur**
3/4	shot(s)	**Freshly squeezed lemon juice**
1/4	shot(s)	**Sugar syrup (2 sugar to 1 water)**
1/2	fresh	**Egg white**

Origin: Adapted from a drink in Ted Haigh's book 'Vintage Spirits & Forgotten Cocktails'. Ted in turn credits an 1892 book, 'The Flowing Bowl' by William Schmidt.
Comment: Aptly named, this sour is tasty to say the least.

DELMARVA COCKTAIL NO.1 [NEW #7]

Glass: Martini
Garnish: Float mint sprig
Method: SHAKE all ingredients with ice and fine strain into chilled glass.

2	shot(s)	**Buffalo Trace bourbon whiskey**
1/2	shot(s)	**Dry vermouth**
1/2	shot(s)	**Giffard white crème de Menthe Pastille**
1/2	shot(s)	**Freshly squeezed lemon juice**

Origin: Created by Ted 'Dr. Cocktail' Haigh, who hails from America's Delmarva Peninsula.
Comment: A minty fresh, dry, whiskey-based palate cleanser.

DELMARVA COCKTAIL NO.2 [NEW #7]

Glass: Martini
Garnish: Lemon zest twist
Method: SHAKE all ingredients with ice and fine strain into chilled glass.

2	shot(s)	**Buffalo Trace bourbon whiskey**
1/2	shot(s)	**Dry vermouth**
1/2	shot(s)	**Giffard white crème de cacao**
1/2	shot(s)	**Freshly squeezed lemon juice**

Origin: Gary Regan adapted Ted Haigh's original Delmarva Cocktail and published this version in his 'Joy of Mixology'.
Comment: Whiskey's distinctive character shines through but is softened and flavoured by chocolate and a hint of citrus.

DELMONICO

Glass: Martini
Garnish: Orange zest twist
Method: STIR all ingredients with ice and strain into chilled glass.

1 1/4	shot(s)	**Rémy Martin cognac**
1 1/2	shot(s)	**Sweet vermouth**
1 1/4	shot(s)	**Dry vermouth**
3	dashes	**Angostura aromatic bitters**

Variant: If orange bitters are used in place of Angostura this becomes a Harvard.
Origin: A classic from the 1930s.
Comment: A Perfect Manhattan with cognac substituted for the whiskey.

DELMONICO SPECIAL [NEW #7]

Glass: Martini
Garnish: Orange zest twist
Method: STIR all ingredients with ice and strain into chilled glass.

2 1/4	shot(s)	**Plymouth gin**
1/4	shot(s)	**Rémy Martin cognac**
3/4	shot(s)	**Dry vermouth**
3	dashes	**Angostura aromatic bitters**

Origin: A classic from the 1930s.
Comment: A Wet Martini dried with a splash of cognac.

DEMPSEY

Glass: Martini
Garnish: Maraschino cherry
Method: SHAKE all ingredients with ice and fine strain into chilled glass.

1 1/2	shot(s)	**Plymouth gin**
1 1/2	shot(s)	**Boulard Grand Solage Calvados**
1/4	shot(s)	**Ricard pastis**
1/2	shot(s)	**Pomegranate (grenadine) syrup**

Origin: Forgotten classic.
Comment: Not sweet, not sour and not too strong. The pastis is well integrated.

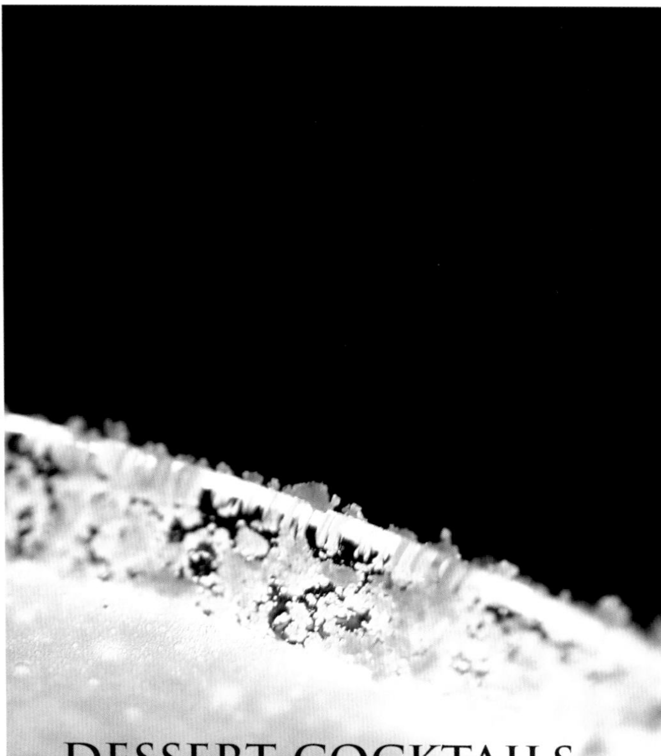

DESSERT COCKTAILS

Dessert cocktails are a great way to end a meal, often even better than traditional desserts. They tend to fall into two camps. Either they are cocktails named after and tasting like actual desserts or they are simply sweet cocktails that befit the occasion. You might also consider a coffee-based cocktail in place of that after dinner coffee.

Examples of dessert cocktails:
Banoffee Martini
Caramel Sutra Martini
Casanova
Chocolate Martini
Crème Anglaise Martini
Crème Brûlée Martini
Death By Chocolate
Dreamsicle
Friar Tuck
Fruit & Nut Martini
Jaffa Martini
Jelly Belly Beany
Key Lime Pie
Lemon Chiffon Pie
Lemon Meringue Martini
Lemon Meringue Pie'tini
Lemon Sorbet
Mocha Martini
Russian Bride
Upside-down Raspberry Cheesecake
Zabaglione Martini

DEPTH BOMB [UPDATED #7]

Glass: Old-fashioned
Garnish: Lime wedge
Method: **SHAKE** all ingredients with ice and strain into ice-filled glass.

1	shot(s)	**Boulard Grand Solage Calvados**
1	shot(s)	**Rémy Martin cognac**
1/2	shot(s)	**Freshly squeezed lemon juice**
1/4	shot(s)	**Pomegranate (grenadine) syrup**
1/8	shot(s)	**Sugar syrup (2 sugar to 1 water)**

Comment: Brandy and apple brandy benefit from a sour hint of lemon, balanced by grenadine.

DEPTH CHARGE

Glass: Boston & shot
Method: **POUR** lager into Boston glass. **POUR** vodka into shot glass. **DROP** shot glass into lager and consume.

1	glass	**Pilsner lager**
1 1/2	shot(s)	**Ketel One vodka**

Variant: Boilermaker
Comment: One way to ruin good beer.

DERBY DAIQUIRI

Glass: Martini
Garnish: Orange zest twist
Method: **SHAKE** all ingredients with ice and fine strain into chilled glass.

2	shot(s)	**Light white rum**
3/4	shot(s)	**Freshly squeezed orange juice**
1/2	shot(s)	**Freshly squeezed lime juice**
1/4	shot(s)	**Sugar syrup (2 sugar to 1 water)**

Comment: A fruity twist on the Classic Daiquiri.

DERBY FIZZ 

Glass: Collins (8oz max)
Garnish: Lemon slice
Method: **SHAKE** first six ingredients with ice and strain into chilled glass. **TOP** with soda.

1 3/4	shot(s)	**Buffalo Trace bourbon whiskey**
1/2	shot(s)	**Light white rum**
1/4	shot(s)	**Grand Marnier liqueur**
1	shot(s)	**Freshly squeezed lemon juice**
1/2	shot(s)	**Sugar syrup (2 sugar to 1 water)**
1/2		**Egg white (optional)**
Top up with		**Soda water (from siphon)**

Comment: An elongated sour with perfectly balanced strength, sweetness and sourness.

DESERT COOLER

Glass: Collins
Garnish: Orange slice
Method: **SHAKE** first three ingredients with ice and strain into ice-filled glass. **TOP** with ginger beer.

2	shot(s)	**Plymouth gin**
3/4	shot(s)	**Cherry (brandy) liqueur**
1 1/2	shot(s)	**Freshly squeezed orange juice**
Top up with		**Ginger beer**

Comment: Sandy in colour - as its name suggests - with a refreshing bite.

DEVIL'S COCKTAIL

Glass: Martini
Garnish: Lemon zest twist
Method: **SHAKE** all ingredients with ice and fine strain into chilled glass.

2	shot(s)	**Tawny port**
1 1/2	shot(s)	**Dry vermouth**
1/4	shot(s)	**Freshly squeezed lemon juice**

Comment: A devil to get out of your carpet but quite dry and aromatic on the palate.

DETOX

Glass: Shot
Garnish: Lime wedge on drink
Method: Refrigerate ingredients then **LAYER** in chilled glass by carefully pouring in the following order.

1/2	shot(s)	**Teichenné Peach Schnapps Liqueur**
1/2	shot(s)	**Ocean Spray cranberry juice**
1/2	shot(s)	**Ketel One vodka**

Comment: Hardly a detox but tasty all the same.

DEVIL'S MANHATTAN

Glass: Martini
Garnish: Lemon zest twist
Method: **STIR** all ingredients with ice and strain into chilled glass.

2	shot(s)	**Buffalo Trace bourbon whiskey**
1	shot(s)	**Southern Comfort liqueur**
1/2	shot(s)	**Sweet vermouth**
3	dashes	**Peychaud's aromatic bitters**

Comment: A Sweet Manhattan with a hint of the south.

DETROIT MARTINI

Glass: Martini
Garnish: Mint sprig
Method: Lightly **MUDDLE** mint in base of shaker (just to bruise). Add other ingredients, **SHAKE** with ice and fine strain into chilled glass.

7	fresh	**Mint leaves**
2 1/2	shot(s)	**Ketel One vodka**
1/2	shot(s)	**Sugar syrup (2 sugar to 1 water)**
3/4	shot(s)	**Chilled mineral water** (reduce if wet ice)

Origin: Created by Dick Bradsell and based on the Cowboy Martini.
Comment: You can also add a splash of lime juice to this minty Martini.

DIABLE ROUGE

Glass: Martini
Garnish: Berries on stick
Method: **SHAKE** all ingredients with ice and fine strain into chilled glass.

2	shot(s)	**Ketel One vodka**
2	shot(s)	**Pressed pineapple juice**
1/4	shot(s)	**Giffard crème de cassis**

Comment: Not quite as rouge as the name would suggest. Hard to hate.

DETROPOLITAN

Glass: Martini
Garnish: Flamed orange zest
Method: **SHAKE** all ingredients with ice and fine strain into chilled glass.

1	shot(s)	**Ketel One vodka**
1/2	shot(s)	**Cointreau triple sec**
1/4	shot(s)	**Giffard crème de cassis**
1 1/2	shot(s)	**Ocean Spray cranberry juice**
1/2	shot(s)	**Freshly squeezed lime juice**

Origin: Created at Detroit, London, England.
Comment: Yet another twist on the Cosmopolitan.

EL DIABLO [UPDATED #7]

Glass: Collins
Garnish: Lime wedge
Method: **SHAKE** first three ingredients with ice and strain into ice-filled glass. **TOP** with ginger beer.

2	shot(s)	**Partida tequila**
3/4	shot(s)	**Giffard crème de cassis**
1	shot(s)	**Freshly squeezed lime juice**
Top up with		**Ginger beer**

Origin: Thought to have originated in California during the 1940s. The name translates as 'The Devil'.
Comment: The tequila, red fruit and ginger aren't exactly subtle, but there's a time and place for everything.

D

DIAMOND DOG

Glass: Old-fashioned
Garnish: Orange slice
Method: SHAKE all ingredients with ice and strain into ice-filled glass.

1	shot(s)	**Campari**
1	shot(s)	**Dry vermouth**
1	shot(s)	**Rose's lime cordial**
1	shot(s)	**Freshly squeezed orange juice**

Origin: Discovered in 2005 at Four Seasons George V, Paris, France.
Comment: Bittersweet and refreshingly different.

ONE UNIT OF ALCOHOL CONTAINS MORE THAN 100 TRILLION BILLION (100,000,000,000,000,000,000,000) MOLECULES OF ALCOHOL.

DIAMOND FIZZ

Glass: Collins (8oz max)
Garnish: Lemon slice
Method: SHAKE first three ingredients with ice and strain into chilled glass. **TOP** with champagne.

2	shot(s)	**Plymouth gin**
1	shot(s)	**Freshly squeezed lemon juice**
1/2	shot(s)	**Sugar syrup (2 sugar to 1 water)**
Top up with		**Brut champagne**

Origin: A long lost classic.
Comment: Why top a Fizz with soda when you can use champagne?

DIANA'S BITTER

Glass: Martini
Garnish: Split lime wedge
Method: SHAKE all ingredients with ice and fine strain into chilled glass.

2	shot(s)	**Plymouth gin**
1	shot(s)	**Campari**
1	shot(s)	**Freshly squeezed lime juice**
1/2	shot(s)	**Sugar syrup (2 sugar to 1 water)**

Comment: A drink for the Campari aficionado: bittersweet and strong.

DICKENS' MARTINI

Glass: Martini
Method: STIR vermouth with ice and strain to **DISCARD** excess, leaving the mixing glass and ice coated with vermouth. **POUR** gin over vermouth coated ice, **STIR** and strain into chilled glass.

3/4	shot(s)	**Dry vermouth**
2 1/2	shot(s)	**Plymouth gin**

Comment: A Dry Martini served without a twist.

DIFFORD'S DAIQUIRI [UPDATED #7]

Glass: Old-fashioned
Garnish: Lime zest twist
Method: SHAKE all ingredients with ice and strain into ice-filled glass.

2 1/2	shot(s)	**Aged rum**
1/2	shot(s)	**Freshly squeezed lime juice**
1	shot(s)	**Difford's Daiquiri Water**

Origin: Created in 2005 by yours truly and served exclusively at the Cabinet Room Bar, London, England.
Comment: The better the rum, the better the Daiquiri. However, this recipe can make a light white rum Daiquiri taste like it has been well aged.

DIFFORD'S OLD-FASHIONED [UPDATED #7]

Glass: Old-fashioned
Garnish: Orange zest twist
Method: STIR all ingredients with ice and strain into ice-filled glass.

2 1/2	shot(s)	**Buffalo Trace bourbon whiskey**
1	shot(s)	**Difford's Daiquiri Water**

Origin: Created in 2005 by yours truly and served exclusively at the Cabinet Room Bar, London, England.
Comment: Due to the use of Daiquiri Water, this tasty Old-Fashioned doesn't require the arduous stirring and dilution traditionally associated with the drink.

DIKI-DIKI [NEW #7]

Glass: Martini
Garnish: Half sugar rim
Method: SHAKE all ingredients with ice and fine strain into chilled glass.

2	shot(s)	**Boulard Grand Solage Calvados**
1/2	shot(s)	**Carlshamns Torr Swedish Flaggpunsch**
1/2	shot(s)	**Squeezed pink grapefruit juice**

Origin: Adapted from Harry Craddock's 1930 'The Savoy Cocktail Book'.
Comment: Fruity yet tart. The sourness is a challenge initially but very rewarding.

DINGO [NEW #7]

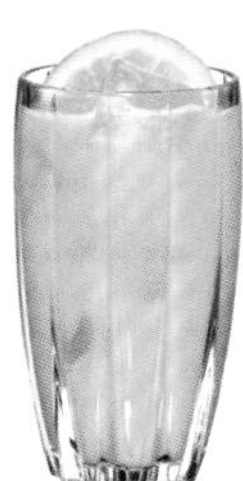

Glass: Collins
Garnish: Orange slice
Method: SHAKE all ingredients with ice and strain into ice-filled glass.

1	shot(s)	**Light white rum**
1	shot(s)	**Jack Daniel's Tennessee whiskey**
½	shot(s)	**Luxardo Amaretto di Saschira**
2	shot(s)	**Freshly squeezed orange juice**
1	shot(s)	**Freshly squeezed lemon juice**
¼	shot(s)	**Pomegranate (grenadine) syrup**
¼	shot(s)	**Sugar syrup (2 sugar to 1 water)**

Comment: Very fruity but with a rum and whiskey kick.

DINO SOUR

Glass: Old-fashioned
Garnish: Lemon slice & cherry (sail)
Method: SHAKE all ingredients with ice and fine strain into chilled glass.

1	shot(s)	**Light white rum**
1	shot(s)	**Gosling's Black Seal rum**
1	shot(s)	**Freshly squeezed lemon juice**
½	shot(s)	**Sugar syrup (2 sugar to 1 water)**
½	fresh	**Egg white**

Comment: Two diverse rums combine brilliantly in this classic sour.

DIPLOMAT [UPDATED #7]

Glass: Old-fashioned
Garnish: Orange zest twist
Method: STIR all ingredients with ice and strain into ice-filled glass.

2	shot(s)	**Dry vermouth**
1	shot(s)	**Sweet vermouth (or Punt E Mes)**
⅛	shot(s)	**Luxardo maraschino liqueur**
2	dashes	**Fee Brothers orange bitters**

Origin: Adapted from Harry Craddock's 1930 'The Savoy Cocktail Book'.
Comment: Wonderfully aromatic and dry. Too good to waste on diplomats.

DIRTY BANANA

Glass: Collins
Garnish: Banana slice on rim
Method: BLEND all ingredients with 12oz scoop crushed ice. Serve with straws.

1½	shot(s)	**Aged rum**
1	shot(s)	**Kahlúa coffee liqueur**
1	shot(s)	**Giffard crème de banane du Brésil**
1	fresh	**Peeled banana**
1	shot(s)	**Double (heavy) cream**
1	shot(s)	**Milk**

Origin: A popular cocktail in Jamaica.
Comment: Long, creamy and filling banana drink with a 'dirty' flavour and colour courtesy of coffee liqueur.

DIRTY MARTINI [UPDATED #7]

Glass: Martini
Garnish: Olive on stick
Method: STIR all ingredients with ice and strain into a chilled glass.

2½	shot(s)	**Plymouth gin**
¼	shot(s)	**Brine from cocktail olives**
¼	shot(s)	**Dry vermouth**

AKA: F.D.R. Martini after the American president Franklin Delano Roosevelt.
Variant: Substitute vodka for gin.
Origin: Some attribute the creation of this drink to Roosevelt: the 32nd president was a keen home bartender, although his cocktails were reportedly 'horrendous', and there is no evidence that he used olive brine in his Martinis.
Comment: This drink varies from delicious to disgusting, depending on the liquid in your jar of olives. Oil will produce a revolting emulsion: make sure that your olives are packed in brine.

DIRTY SANCHEZ

Glass: Collins
Garnish: Lime wheel on rim
Method: SHAKE first four ingredients with ice and strain into ice-filled glass. **TOP** with ginger beer.

2	shot(s)	**Partida tequila**
¾	shot(s)	**Agavero tequila liqueur**
½	shot(s)	**Chambord black raspberry liqueur**
½	shot(s)	**Freshly squeezed lime juice**
Top up with		**Jamaican ginger beer**

Origin: Created in 2001 by Phillip Jeffrey and Ian Baldwin at the GE Club, London, England.
Comment: A wonderfully refreshing and complex long summer drink.

DIVINO'S

Glass: Martini
Garnish: Chocolate shavings
Method: SHAKE all ingredients with ice and fine strain into chilled glass.

½	shot(s)	**Ketel One vodka**
2½	shot(s)	**Barolo wine**
1	shot(s)	**Giffard brown crème de cacao**

Origin: Discovered in 2005 at DiVino, Hong Kong.
Comment: The chocolate liqueur takes the acidity off the wine without masking its flavour.

DIXIE DEW

Glass: Martini
Garnish: Orange zest twist
Method: SHAKE all ingredients with ice and fine strain into chilled glass.

2	shot(s)	**Buffalo Trace bourbon whiskey**
½	shot(s)	**Giffard white crème de Menthe Pastille**
½	shot(s)	**Cointreau triple sec**
¾	shot(s)	**Chilled mineral water** (omit if wet ice)

Comment: A peppermint fresh, bourbon laced drink.

DNA #1 [UPDATED #7]

Glass: Martini
Garnish: Orange zest twist
Method: SHAKE all ingredients with ice and fine strain into chilled glass.

$1\frac{1}{2}$	shot(s)	**Plymouth gin**
$\frac{3}{4}$	shot(s)	**Giffard apricot brandy du Roussillon**
1	shot(s)	**Freshly squeezed lemon juice**
$\frac{1}{4}$	shot(s)	**Sugar syrup (2 sugar to 1 water)**
2	dashes	**Fee Brothers orange bitters (optional)**

Origin: Created by Emmanuel Audermatte at The Atlantic Bar & Grill, London, England, in 1999.
Comment: Slightly sharp and very fruity, but pleasantly so.

DOCTOR FUNK

Glass: Sling
Garnish: Lime wedge
Method: SHAKE first six ingredients with ice and strain into glass filled with crushed ice. **TOP** with soda and serve with straws.

$2\frac{1}{2}$	shot(s)	**Gosling's Black Seal rum**
$\frac{1}{4}$	shot(s)	**Pernod anis**
$\frac{1}{2}$	shot(s)	**Freshly squeezed lemon juice**
$\frac{1}{4}$	shot(s)	**Freshly squeezed lime juice**
$\frac{1}{4}$	shot(s)	**Pomegranate (grenadine) syrup**
$\frac{1}{4}$	shot(s)	**Sugar syrup (2 sugar to 1 water)**
Top up with		**Soda water (club soda)**

Origin: A Tiki drink adapted from one created circa 1937 by Don The Beachcomber.
Comment: Too many and you'll need your very own doctor.

THE USSR'S MIG-25 FIGHTER-BOMBER CARRIED HALF A TON OF ALCOHOL FOR BRAKE FLUID. IT WAS NICKNAMED THE 'FLYING RESTAURANT' BY ITS SOVIET CREWS.

DOLCE-AMARO

Glass: Martini
Garnish: Orange zest twist
Method: STIR all ingredients with ice and strain into chilled glass.

$1\frac{1}{2}$	shot(s)	**Campari**
$1\frac{1}{2}$	shot(s)	**Bianco vermouth**
$\frac{3}{4}$	shot(s)	**Luxardo Amaretto di Saschira**

Comment: The very apt name translates as 'bittersweet'.

DNA #2

Glass: Martini
Garnish: Lemon zest twist
Method: SHAKE all ingredients with ice and fine strain into chilled glass.

1	shot(s)	**Plymouth gin**
1	shot(s)	**Plymouth damson gin liqueur**
$\frac{3}{4}$	shot(s)	**Giffard apricot brandy du Roussillon**
$\frac{1}{2}$	shot(s)	**Freshly squeezed lime juice**
2	dashes	**Angostura aromatic bitters**
$\frac{1}{2}$	shot(s)	**Chilled mineral water** (omit if wet ice)

Origin: Created in 2005 by Tonin Kacaj at Maze, London, England.
Comment: Tangy, fruity and gin laced.

DOLCE HAVANA

Glass: Martini
Method: SHAKE all ingredients with ice and fine strain into chilled glass.

$1\frac{1}{4}$	shot(s)	**Light white rum**
$\frac{1}{2}$	shot(s)	**Campari**
$\frac{1}{2}$	shot(s)	**Cointreau triple sec**
$1\frac{1}{4}$	shot(s)	**Freshly squeezed orange juice**
$1\frac{1}{4}$	shot(s)	**Freshly squeezed lime juice**
$\frac{1}{8}$	shot(s)	**Sugar syrup (2 sugar to 1 water)**

Origin: Created by Fabrizio Musorella in 2000 at the Library Bar, Lanesborough Hotel, London, England.
Comment: A melange of Mediterranean fruit.

DOCTOR

Glass: Martini
Garnish: Lime zest twist
Method: SHAKE all ingredients with ice and fine strain into chilled glass.

$1\frac{1}{2}$	shot(s)	**Aged rum**
$1\frac{1}{2}$	shot(s)	**Carlshamns Swedish Torr Flagg Punsch**
$\frac{3}{4}$	shot(s)	**Freshly squeezed lime juice**

Origin: In David Embury's classic, 'The Fine Art of Mixing Drinks', my hero lists four wildly different drinks using Swedish Punch. Trader Vic's 'Bartender's Guide' lists two variations of a single drink, for which the above is my own recipe.
Comment: Retitled 'Swedish Daiquiri', this could be a hit.

DOLORES #1

Glass: Martini
Garnish: Lemon zest twist
Method: SHAKE all ingredients with ice and fine strain into chilled glass.

2	shot(s)	**Aged rum**
2	shot(s)	**Dubonnet Red**
1	shot(s)	**Tio Pepe fino sherry**

Origin: A classic. Some recipes include a splash of orange juice.
Comment: Aromatic and well balanced, provided you use French-made Dubonnet.

DOLORES #2 [NEW #7]

Glass: Martini
Garnish: Dust with grated nutmeg
Method: SHAKE all ingredients with ice and fine strain into chilled glass.

1½	shot(s)	**Rémy Martin cognac**
¾	shot(s)	**Marnier cherry liqueur**
¾	shot(s)	**Giffard white crème de cacao**
1	fresh	**Egg white**

Comment: A chocolaty after dinner libation.

DONEGAL

Glass: Martini
Garnish: Orange zest twist
Method: SHAKE all ingredients with ice and fine strain into chilled glass.

1½	shot(s)	**Irish whiskey**
1¼	shot(s)	**Dry vermouth**
½	shot(s)	**Luxardo maraschino liqueur**
½	shot(s)	**Mandarine Napoléon liqueur**

Comment: Aromatised Irish whiskey with cherry and orange.

DON JUAN

Glass: Martini
Garnish: Orange zest twist
Method: SHAKE all ingredients with ice and fine strain into chilled glass.

1¾	shot(s)	**Rémy Martin cognac**
1	shot(s)	**Licor 43 (Cuarenta Y Tres) liqueur**
1	shot(s)	**Freshly squeezed orange juice**
½	shot(s)	**Double (heavy) cream**
½	shot(s)	**Milk**

Comment: A lightly creamy orange affair with vanilla spice.

DONNA'S CREAMY'TINI

Glass: Martini
Garnish: Cherry on rim
Method: SHAKE all ingredients with ice and fine strain into chilled glass.

1	shot(s)	**Luxardo Amaretto di Saschira**
1	shot(s)	**Cherry (brandy) liqueur**
1	shot(s)	**Giffard brown crème de cacao**
1	shot(s)	**Double (heavy) cream**

Origin: Adapted from a drink created in 2002 by Yannick Miseriaux at the Fifth Floor Bar, London, England.
Comment: A fine example of an alcoholic liquid pudding.

DORIAN GRAY

Glass: Martini
Garnish: Orange zest twist
Method: SHAKE all ingredients with ice and fine strain into chilled glass.

1½	shot(s)	**Light white rum**
¾	shot(s)	**Grand Marnier liqueur**
1	shot(s)	**Freshly squeezed orange juice**
¾	shot(s)	**Ocean Spray cranberry juice**

Origin: Discovered in 1999 at One Aldwych, London, England. This cocktail takes its name from Oscar Wilde's novel, in which a socialite's wish to remain as young and charming as his own portrait is granted. Allured by his depraved friend Lord Henry Wotton, Dorian Gray assumes a life of perversion and sin. But every time he sins the painting ages, while Gray stays young and healthy.
Comment: Fruity and rum laced, not overly sweet.

DOROTHY PARKER [NEW #7]

Glass: Martini
Garnish: Sugar rim
Method: SHAKE first four ingredients with ice and fine strain into chilled glass. **TOP** with champagne.

1½	shot(s)	**Ketel One Citroen vodka**
½	shot(s)	**Cointreau triple sec**
¼	shot(s)	**Chambord liqueur**
½	shot(s)	**Freshly squeezed lemon juice**
Top up with		**Brut champagne**

Origin: Discovered in 2007 at Town Hall, San Francisco, USA, and named for the wit and drinker.
Comment: Light, fruity and easy to drink.

DOUBLE GRAPE MARTINI

Glass: Martini
Garnish: Grapes on stick
Method: MUDDLE grapes in base of shaker. Add other ingredients, **SHAKE** with ice and fine strain into chilled glass.

12	fresh	**Seedless white grapes**
2	shot(s)	**Ketel One vodka**
¾	shot(s)	**Sauvignon Blanc wine**
½	shot(s)	**Sugar syrup (2 sugar to 1 water)**

Origin: Created by yours truly in 2004.
Comment: The wine adds complexity to a simple Grape Martini.

DOUBLE VISION

Glass: Martini
Garnish: Blackcurrants on stick
Method: SHAKE all ingredients with ice and fine strain into chilled glass.

1	shot(s)	**Ketel One Citroen vodka**
1	shot(s)	**Raspberry flavoured vodka**
1	shot(s)	**Pressed apple juice**
½	shot(s)	**Freshly squeezed lime juice**
¼	shot(s)	**Sugar syrup (2 sugar to 1 water)**
3	dashes	**Angostura aromatic bitters**

Comment: Citrus fresh with strong hints of apple and red berries.

DOUGHNUT MARTINI

Glass: Martini
Garnish: Segment of doughnut
Method: SHAKE all ingredients with ice and fine strain into chilled glass.

1½	shot(s)	**Light white rum**
¾	shot(s)	**Buffalo Trace bourbon whiskey**
½	shot(s)	**Vanilla schnapps liqueur**
½	shot(s)	**Licor 43 (Cuarenta Y Tres) liqueur**
⅛	shot(s)	**Teichenné butterscotch Schnapps**
¾	shot(s)	**Chilled mineral water** (omit if wet ice)

Origin: Created in 2003 by yours truly.
Comment: My attempt at mimicking the taste of a Krispy Kreme Original Glazed doughnut without ending up with an overly sweet cocktail.

DOWA

Glass: Old-fashioned
Garnish: Lime wedge
Method: STIR honey and vodka in base of shaker until honey dissolves. Add lime juice, **SHAKE** with ice and strain into glass filled with crushed ice. Serve with straws.

4	spoons	**Runny honey**
2½	shot(s)	**Ketel One vodka**
¼	shot(s)	**Freshly squeezed lime juice**

Origin: This cocktail is particularly popular in upscale hotel bars in Kenya where it is enjoyed by the safari set. The name translates as 'medicine'.
Comment: Very similar to the Caipirovska in its use of vodka, lime and crushed ice: the honey makes the difference.

DOWNHILL RACER

Glass: Martini
Garnish: Pineapple wedge on rim
Method: SHAKE all ingredients with ice and fine strain into chilled glass.

1¾	shot(s)	**Aged rum**
¾	shot(s)	**Luxardo Amaretto di Saschira**
1¾	shot(s)	**Pressed pineap\ple juice**

Comment: Aged rum sweetened, softened and flavoured with pineapple and amaretto.

'ALCOHOL IS LIKE LOVE. THE FIRST KISS IS MAGIC, THE SECOND IS INTIMATE, THE THIRD IS ROUTINE. AFTER THAT YOU TAKE THE GIRL'S CLOTHES OFF.'
RAYMOND CHANDLER

DR ZEUS

Glass: Old-fashioned
Method: POUR Fernet Branca into ice-filled glass, **TOP** with chilled mineral water and leave to stand. Separately **MUDDLE** raisins in base of shaker, add other ingredients and **SHAKE** with ice. Finally **DISCARD** contents of glass and strain contents of shaker into the Fernet Branca coated glass.

1	shot(s)	**Fernet Branca**
20		**Raisins**
2	shot(s)	**Rémy Martin cognac**
¼	shot(s)	**Sugar syrup (2 sugar to 1 water)**
⅛	shot(s)	**Kahlúa coffee liqueur**
1	dash	**Fee Brothers orange bitters**

Origin: Created by Adam Ennis in 2001 at Isola, Knightsbridge, London, England.
Comment: Not that far removed from a Sazerac cocktail, this is innovative and great tasting.

DRAGON BLOSSOM

Glass: Martini
Garnish: Maraschino cherry in drink
Method: SHAKE all ingredients with ice and fine strain into chilled glass.

1¾	shot(s)	**Rose petal vodka**
¼	shot(s)	**Soho lychee liqueur**
¼	shot(s)	**Maraschino syrup**
1¾	shot(s)	**Ocean Spray cranberry juice**

Comment: Light, aromatic, semi-sweet and distinctly oriental in style.

DRAMATIC MARTINI

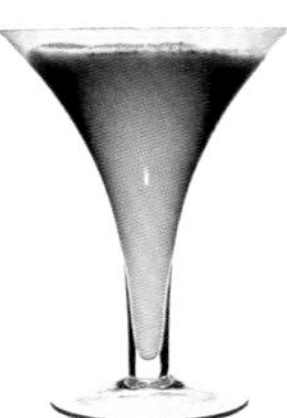

Glass: Martini
Garnish: Grate nutmeg over drink
Method: SHAKE all ingredients with ice and fine strain into chilled glass.

1	shot(s)	**Tuaca Italian liqueur**
1	shot(s)	**Grand Marnier liqueur**
1	shot(s)	**Irish cream liqueur**
1	shot(s)	**Milk**

Comment: Creamy and sweet with orangey, herbal notes.

DREAM COCKTAIL [NEW #7]

Glass: Martini
Garnish: Orange zest twist
Method: SHAKE all ingredients with ice and fine strain into chilled glass.

1½	shot(s)	**Rémy Martin cognac**
¾	shot(s)	**Cointreau triple sec**
¼	shot(s)	**Anisette liqueur**
½	shot(s)	**Chilled mineral water** (omit if wet ice)

Comment: An after dinner drink with brandy, orange liqueur and a refreshing burst of aniseed.

DREAMSICLE 

Glass: Martini
Method: SHAKE first three ingredients with ice and fine strain into chilled glass. **FLOAT** cream.

1 1/2	shot(s)	**Kahlúa coffee liqueur**
3/4	shot(s)	**Cointreau triple sec**
1	shot(s)	**Freshly squeezed orange juice**
3/4	shot(s)	**Double (heavy) cream**

Comment: Sweet coffee and orange smoothed by a creamy top. A veritable dessert in a glass.

DROWNED OUT

Glass: Collins
Garnish: Lime wedge
Method: POUR ingredients into ice-filled glass, stir and serve with straws.

2	shot(s)	**Pernod anis**
1	shot(s)	**Freshly squeezed lime juice**
Top up with		**Ginger ale**

Comment: Ginger combines with aniseed rather than drowning it.

DRY ICE MARTINI

Glass: Martini
Garnish: Orange zest twist
Method: STIR all ingredients with ice and strain into chilled glass.

2	shot(s)	**Ketel One vodka**
1/2	shot(s)	**Dry vermouth**
3/4	shot(s)	**Icewine**

Origin: Created by yours truly in 2004.
Comment: Despite the name, this is slightly honeyed rather than dry.

DRY MARTINI #1 (TRADITIONAL) 

Glass: Martini
Garnish: Chilled olive on stick or lemon zest twist
Method: STIR vermouth with ice and strain to discard excess, leaving the glass and ice coated with vermouth. **POUR** gin over vermouth coated ice, **STIR** and strain into a chilled glass.

3/4	shot(s)	**Dry vermouth**
2 1/2	shot(s)	**Plymouth gin**
2	dashes	**Fee Brothers orange bitters (optional)**

Variant: The proportion of gin to vermouth is a matter of taste, some say 7 to 1, others that one drop is sufficient. I recommend you ask the drinker how they would like their Martini, in the same manner that you might ask how they have their steak. If the drinker orders a 'Sweet Martini', use sweet red vermouth rather than dry and use a cherry as garnish instead of an olive.
Comment: This drink is an acquired taste, but all too easy to acquire.

DRY MARTINI

The Martini and its origins is a topic that can raise temperatures among drinks aficionados and, as so often, no one really knows.

Today the drink is a blend of dry gin or vodka with a hint of dry vermouth. Yet it seems to have evolved from the Manhattan via the Martinez, a rather sweet drink based on Old Tom gin with the addition of sweet vermouth, curaçao and orange bitters. The Martini, like the Martinez, was initially sweet, not dry (hence the need to specify that its descendant was a 'Dry' Martini), and very heavy on the vermouth by modern standards.

Martinis were known in the late 1880s but the Dry Martini most likely appeared with the emergence of the London Dry gin style. In 1906 Louis Muckenstrum wrote up a Dry Martini Cocktail which, like the Martinez, benefited from curaçao and bitters as well as vermouth. Yet, unlike earlier versions, both the gin and the vermouth were dry. According to Gary Regan, the marketeers at Martini & Rossi vermouth were advertising a Dry Martini cocktail heavily at that time.

One myth attributes the creation of the Dry Martini to one Martini di Arma di Taggia, head bartender at New York's Knickerbocker Hotel, in 1911, although this is clearly too late. It is also no longer believed that the name relates to Martini & Henry rifles, the first of which was launched in 1871.

The Dry Martini seems to have got drier and drier over the years. Curaçao rapidly left the drink, but orange bitters remained a usual ingredient until the 1940s (interestingly, these are now coming back into vogue in some bars).

After the second world war, vermouth proportions dropped rapidly, and the Naked Martini began to appear. Traditionally both vermouth and gin had been stirred with ice. In a Naken Martini they are mixed by merely dosing a well chilled glass with a hint of vermouth and then pouring frozen gin into the vermouth coated glass. There is some debate as to whether a Martini should be shaken or stirred. It should be stirred. If shaken, it becomes a 'Bradford'. Shaking the drink increases the dilution and introduces air bubbles into the drink, making it taste fresher and colder but making the drink appear cloudy due to the introduction of tiny air bubbles.

DRY MARTINI #2 (NAKED) [UPDATED #7]

Glass: Martini (ice-coated)
Garnish: Chilled olive on stick or lemon zest twist
Method: POUR water into glass, swirl around to coat and place in freezer for at least two hours, alongside gin, until the inside of the glass is covered in a thin layer of ice and the gin is frozen. **POUR** vermouth into icy glass and swirl to coat the ice with vermouth. **POUR** frozen gin into glass and serve immediately.

1/4	shot(s)	**Chilled mineral water**
1/8	shot(s)	**Dry vermouth**
2 1/2	shot(s)	**Plymouth gin (frozen)**

Variant: Use an atomiser to coat glass with vermouth. Based on vodka.
Origin: Recipe courtesy of Salvatore Calabrese and originally from Duke's Hotel, London, England.
Comment: Dilution is achieved as the water you have frozen in the glass begins to melt. Both glass and gin must be freezing cold so that the temperature masks the strength of the alcohol. You have been warned!

'WORK IS THE CURSE OF THE DRINKING CLASSES.'
OSCAR WILDE

DRY ORANGE MARTINI

Glass: Martini
Garnish: Grapefruit twist
Method: STIR all ingredients with ice and strain into chilled glass.

2	shot(s)	**Plymouth gin**
3/4	shot(s)	**Dry vermouth**
1/4	shot(s)	**Cointreau triple sec**
2	dashes	**Fee Brothers orange bitters**

Origin: Created in 2003 by Wayne Collins for Maxxium UK.
Comment: Bone dry, orangey, aptly named Martini.

DUBLINER [NEW #7]

Glass: Martini
Garnish: Green cherry
Method: STIR all ingredients with ice and strain into chilled glass.

2	shot(s)	**Irish whiskey**
1/2	shot(s)	**Grand Marnier liqueur**
1/2	shot(s)	**Sweet vermouth**
1	dash	**Fee Brothers orange bitters**

Origin: Adapted from a recipe by Gary Regan and discovered in 2007 at Death & Company, New York City, USA.
Comment: Irish whiskey shines through the spicy orange.

THE DUBONNET COCKTAIL [NEW #7]

Glass: Martini
Garnish: Lemon zest twist
Method: STIR all ingredients with ice and strain into chilled glass.

1 1/2	shot(s)	**Plymouth gin**
1 1/2	shot(s)	**Dubonnet Red (French made)**
2	dashes	**Angostura aromatic bitters**

Origin: A classic which was popular in Britain during the 1920s.
Comment: Simple yet complex. Dry and aromatic.

DULCHIN

Glass: Martini
Garnish: Orange zest twist
Method: SHAKE all ingredients with ice and fine strain into chilled glass.

2	shot(s)	**Pisco**
1/2	shot(s)	**Grand Marnier liqueur**
1/2	shot(s)	**Giffard apricot brandy du Roussillon**
1/4	shot(s)	**Rose's lime cordial**
1/4	shot(s)	**Pomegranate (grenadine) syrup**
3/4	shot(s)	**Chilled mineral water** (omit if wet ice)

Comment: This dry, amber coloured, fruity cocktail carries a pisco punch.

DURANGO

Glass: Collins
Garnish: Orange wheel
Method: SHAKE first three ingredients with ice and strain into ice filled glass. **TOP** with soda.

2	shot(s)	**Partida tequila**
3/4	shot(s)	**Luxardo Amaretto di Saschira**
1	shot(s)	**Freshly squeezed grapefruit juice**
Top up with		**Soda water (club soda)**

Comment: This sandy coloured drink makes tequila, amaretto and grapefruit juice into unlikely but harmonious bedfellows.

DUTCH BREAKFAST MARTINI

Glass: Martini
Garnish: Orange zest twist
Method: SHAKE all ingredients with ice and fine strain into chilled glass.

1 1/2	shot(s)	**Plymouth gin**
1 1/2	shot(s)	**Bols advocaat liqueur**
1	shot(s)	**Freshly squeezed lemon juice**
1/4	shot(s)	**Sugar syrup (2 sugar to 1 water)**
1/8	shot(s)	**Galliano liqueur**

Origin: Created in 2002 by Alex Kammerling, London, England.
Comment: A tasty, aromatic, almost creamy alternative to a fry-up.

DUTCH COURAGE

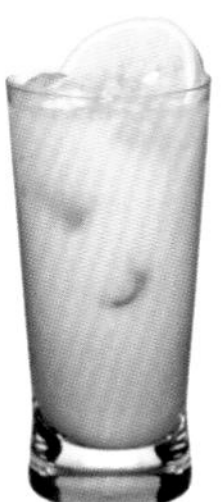

Glass: Collins
Garnish: Lemon slice
Method: SHAKE all ingredients with ice and strain into ice-filled glass.

1	shot(s)	**Plymouth gin**
1	shot(s)	**Bols advocaat liqueur**
$\frac{3}{4}$	shot(s)	**Freshly squeezed lemon juice**
3	shot(s)	**Pressed apple juice**

Origin: Created in 2002 by Alex Kammerling, London, England.
Comment: A refreshing alternative to a traditional English lemonade.

DYEVITCHKA 

Glass: Martini
Garnish: Orange zest twist
Method: SHAKE all ingredients with ice and fine strain into chilled glass.

1	shot(s)	**Ketel One vodka**
1	shot(s)	**Cointreau triple sec**
$\frac{1}{2}$	shot(s)	**Freshly squeezed lime juice**
$\frac{1}{4}$	shot(s)	**Sugar syrup (2 sugar to 1 water)**
$1\frac{1}{2}$	shot(s)	**Pressed pineapple juice**

Comment: Pineapple replaces cranberry in this Cosmo-like cocktail.

EARL GREY FIZZ

Glass: Flute
Garnish: Lemon knot
Method: SHAKE first three ingredients with ice and strain into chilled glass. **TOP** with champagne.

1	shot(s)	**Zubrówka bison vodka**
$\frac{1}{2}$	shot(s)	**Strong cold Earl Grey tea**
$\frac{1}{4}$	shot(s)	**Sugar syrup (2 sugar to 1 water)**
Top up with		**Brut champagne**

Origin: Created in 2002 by Henry Besant at Lonsdale House, London, England.
Comment: Looks like a glass of champagne but has a well judged little extra something.

EARL GREY MAR-TEA-NI

Glass: Martini
Garnish: Lemon zest twist
Method: SHAKE all ingredients with ice and fine strain into chilled glass.

2	shot(s)	**Plymouth gin**
$1\frac{1}{4}$	shot(s)	**Strong cold Earl Grey tea**
$\frac{3}{4}$	shot(s)	**Freshly squeezed lemon juice**
$\frac{1}{2}$	shot(s)	**Sugar syrup (2 sugar to 1 water)**
$\frac{1}{2}$	fresh	**Egg white**

Origin: Adapted from a drink created in 2000 by Audrey Saunders at Bemelmans Bar at The Carlyle, New York City.
Comment: A fantastic and very English drink created by a New Yorker. The botanicals of gin combine wonderfully with the flavours and tannins of the tea.

EAST INDIA #1

Glass: Martini
Garnish: Orange zest twist
Method: SHAKE all ingredients with ice and fine strain into chilled glass.

$2\frac{1}{2}$	shot(s)	**Rémy Martin cognac**
$\frac{1}{8}$	shot(s)	**Grand Marnier liqueur**
$\frac{1}{8}$	shot(s)	**Luxardo maraschino liqueur**
$\frac{1}{4}$	shot(s)	**Pomegranate (grenadine) or raspberry syrup**
1	dash	**Angostura aromatic bitters**

Origin: An old classic. This recipe is adapted from one in Ted Haigh's book 'Vintage Spirits & Forgotten Cocktails'.
Comment: Cognac tamed and given an additional hint of fruit.

EAST INDIA #2

Glass: Martini
Garnish: Orange zest twist & nutmeg dust
Method: SHAKE all ingredients with ice and fine strain into chilled glass.

$1\frac{1}{2}$	shot(s)	**Rémy Martin cognac**
1	shot(s)	**Grand Marnier liqueur**
2	shot(s)	**Pressed pineapple juice**
2	dashes	**Angostura aromatic bitters**

Origin: Another version of the East India classic, thought to originate with Frank Meier at the Ritz Bar, Paris.
Comment: A rich but bitter short drink based on cognac.

'A MAN WHO EXPOSES HIMSELF WHEN HE IS INTOXICATED, HAS NOT THE ART OF GETTING DRUNK.'
SAMUEL JOHNSON

EAST INDIA HOUSE [NEW #7]

Glass: Martini
Garnish: Lemon zest twist
Method: SHAKE all ingredients with ice and fine strain into chilled glass.

2	shot(s)	**Rémy Martin cognac**
$\frac{1}{2}$	shot(s)	**Aged rum**
$\frac{1}{2}$	shot(s)	**Cointreau triple sec**
$\frac{1}{2}$	shot(s)	**Pressed pineapple juice**
2	dashes	**Fee Brothers orange bitters**

Origin: I've adapted this recipe from a classic cocktail which is thought to have been created in the 19th century by Harry Johnson: I've doubled the quantities of everything but cognac.
Comment: Dry and challenging – rewarding for some.

EAST INDIAN

Glass: Martini
Garnish: Olive on stick
Method: STIR all ingredients with ice and strain into chilled glass.

2	shot(s)	**Tio Pepe fino sherry**
2	shot(s)	**Dry vermouth**
1/4	shot(s)	**Sugar syrup (2 sugar to 1 water)**
3	dashes	**Fee Brothers orange bitters**

Variant: Bamboo
Comment: Dry and pretty flat (like much of India) but perfectly balanced with subtle hints of orange zest.

EASTER MARTINI

Glass: Martini
Garnish: Grated chocolate (crumbled Cadbury's Flake bar)
Method: MUDDLE cardamom pods in base of shaker. Add other ingredients, **SHAKE** with ice and fine strain into chilled glass.

4	pods	**Green cardamom**
2	shot(s)	**Vanilla infused Ketel One vodka**
1	shot(s)	**Giffard white crème de cacao**
1/4	shot(s)	**Sugar syrup (2 sugar to 1 water)**
1/2	shot(s)	**Chilled mineral water** (omit if wet ice)
1/2	fresh	**Egg white**

Origin: Created in 2003 by Simon King at MJU Bar, Millennium Hotel, London, England.
Comment: A standard Chocolate Martini with extra interest thanks to the clever use of vanilla and cardamom. The egg white was my own addition. It seemed appropriate given the Easter in the title.

EASTERN MARTINI

Glass: Martini
Garnish: Japanese ume plum in drink
Method: SHAKE all ingredients with ice and fine strain into chilled glass.

2	shot(s)	**Ketel One vodka**
1 1/2	shot(s)	**Choya Umeshu plum liqueur**
1	shot(s)	**Pressed apple juice**

Origin: Created in 2003 by Chris Langan, Barnomadics, Scotland.
Comment: Light, fragrant and fruity – distinctly oriental.

EASTERN PROMISE

Glass: Martini
Garnish: Lemon zest twist
Method: SHAKE all ingredients with ice and fine strain into chilled glass.

2	shot(s)	**Orange zest infused Ketel One vodka**
1/4	shot(s)	**Giffard apricot brandy du Roussillon**
1/2	shot(s)	**Rose syrup**
1/2	shot(s)	**Freshly squeezed lemon juice**
1/2	shot(s)	**Chilled mineral water** (omit if wet ice)

Origin: Adapted from a drink discovered in 2004 at Oxo Tower Bar, London, England.
Comment: Citrus dominates this drink but the result is floral rather than tart.

EASY TIGER

Glass: Martini
Garnish: Orange zest twist
Comment: MUDDLE ginger in base of shaker. Add honey and tequila, and **STIR** until honey is dissolved. Add other ingredients, **SHAKE** with ice and fine strain into chilled glass.

2	slices	**Fresh ginger (thumb nail sized)**
2	spoons	**Runny honey**
2	shot(s)	**Partida tequila**
1	shot(s)	**Freshly squeezed lime juice**
3/4	shot(s)	**Chilled mineral water** (omit if wet ice)

Origin: Created in 1999 by Alex Kammerling.
Comment: Tangy and zesty with rich honey and ginger.

ECLIPSE

Glass: Collins
Garnish: Mint leaf & raspberry
Method: MUDDLE raspberries in base of shaker. Add other ingredients, **SHAKE** with ice and strain into glass filled with crushed ice. Serve with straws.

12	fresh	**Raspberries**
2	shot(s)	**Jack Daniel's Tennessee whiskey**
1	shot(s)	**Chambord black raspberry liqueur**
1/2	shot(s)	**Freshly squeezed lime juice**
2	shot(s)	**Ocean Spray cranberry juice**

Origin: Signature cocktail at the chain of Eclipse Bars, London, England.
Comment: A fruity summer cooler which I challenge anyone not to like.

EDEN [UPDATED #7]

Glass: Collins
Garnish: Orange zest string
Method: SHAKE first three ingredients with ice and strain into ice-filled glass. **TOP** with tonic water.

2	shot(s)	**Orange peel infused Ketel One vodka**
1/2	shot(s)	**St-Germain elderflower liqueur**
1 1/2	shot(s)	**Pressed apple juice**
Top up with		**Tonic water**

Origin: Adapted from a drink created in 2003 by Sylvain Solignac at Circus, London, England.
Comment: Orange zest predominates in a long, refreshing drink that's perfect for warm days.

EDEN MARTINI

Glass: Martini
Garnish: Orange zest twist
Method: SHAKE all ingredients with ice and fine strain into chilled glass.

2 1/2	shot(s)	**Plymouth gin**
1/2	shot(s)	**Parfait amour liqueur**
1/4	shot(s)	**Rose water**
1/4	shot(s)	**Freshly squeezed lemon juice**
1/4	shot(s)	**Chilled mineral water** (omit if wet ice)

Origin: Adapted from a recipe discovered in 2003 at Oxo Tower Bar, London, England.
Comment: Rich purple in colour with rose, vanilla, almond, citrus and gin.

EGG CUSTARD MARTINI

Glass: Martini
Garnish: Dust with freshly ground nutmeg
Method: SHAKE all ingredients with ice and fine strain into chilled glass.

$1^1/_2$	shot(s)	**Ketel One vodka**
1	shot(s)	**Bols advocaat liqueur**
$^1/_2$	shot(s)	**Vanilla infused Ketel One vodka**
$^1/_2$	shot(s)	**Buffalo Trace bourbon whiskey**
$^1/_4$	shot(s)	**Sugar syrup (2 sugar to 1 water)**

Origin: Created in 2002 by Alex Kammerling, London, England.
Comment: As custardy as the name would suggest but surprisingly potent.

EGGNOG #1 (COLD)

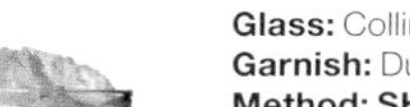

Glass: Collins
Garnish: Dust with freshly grated nutmeg
Method: SHAKE all ingredients with ice and strain into ice-filled glass.

$2^1/_2$	shot(s)	**Rémy Martin cognac**
$^1/_2$	shot(s)	**Sugar syrup (2 sugar to 1 water)**
$^1/_2$	shot(s)	**Double (heavy) cream**
1	fresh	**Egg**
2	shot(s)	**Milk**

Comment: Lightly flavoured alcoholic egg custard. Also try swapping dark rum for the cognac.

EGGNOG #2 (HOT)

Glass: Toddy
Garnish: Dust with freshly grated nutmeg
Method: POUR ingredients into heatproof glass and **STIR** thoroughly. **HEAT** in microwave oven for a minute (adjust time as appropriate to your oven) and **STIR** again. Alternatively, mix and warm in pan over heat – do not boil.

$2^1/_2$	shot(s)	**Rémy Martin cognac**
$^1/_2$	shot(s)	**Sugar syrup (2 sugar to 1 water)**
$^1/_2$	shot(s)	**Double (heavy) cream**
1	fresh	**Egg (white & yolk)**
2	shot(s)	**Milk**

Comment: A warming, spicy and filling meal in a glass.

EL BURRO

Glass: Collins
Garnish: Lime slice
Method: SHAKE first four ingredients with ice and strain into ice-filled glass. **TOP** with ginger beer.

2	shot(s)	**Partida tequila**
$^1/_2$	shot(s)	**Freshly squeezed lime juice**
$^1/_4$	shot(s)	**Sugar syrup (2 sugar to 1 water)**
3	dashes	**Angostura aromatic bitters**
Top up with		**Ginger beer**

AKA: Mexican Mule
Origin: Created by Henry Besant and Andres Masso, London, England. The name of this Mexican version of the Moscow Mule translates from Spanish as 'The Donkey'.
Comment: Ginger spice and tequila soured with lime.

EGGNOGS

Drunk in America around Christmas and New Year, these festive, custardy comfort drinks are one of the oldest mixed drinks around. They make their first known print appearance in America in 1825, although they were already well-known at that time, and a combination of eggs, milk or cream and beer, served hot, is traditional in Germany and Iceland.

While the 'egg' bit of the name is clear enough, there is debate over where the 'nog' (or 'nogg') element comes from. Some say it derives from the term 'nog', which was originally a type of strong ale brewed in East Anglia. Others think they might first have been served in a small cup or ladle called a noggin, which makes sense as eggnogs are generally made in a communal bowl.

It is perhaps more likely that eggnogs take their name from the Scots word 'nugg', for ale warmed with a poker. This would suggest that they began as close relatives of flips: a blend of ale, eggs, spices and spirits served after heating with a poker. (Eggnogs would appear to differ from flips in that milk and/or cream are included, although the OED does not mention milk or cream in its definition.)

It seems likely that eggnogs evolved into their current form, a blend of eggs, cream, sugar, spices and generally a spirit or wine served cold, as better heating made it both practicable and pleasant to serve a cold drink in winter and ale and cider were less commonly drunk at home.

Eggnog Variants:
Eggnog #1
Eggnog #2
Tom and Jerry

EL PRESIDENTE NO. 1 (DAIQUIRI) #1

Glass: Martini
Garnish: Lime wedge on rim
Method: SHAKE all ingredients with ice and fine strain into chilled glass.

2	shot(s)	**Light white rum**
3/4	shot(s)	**Pressed pineapple juice**
1/2	shot(s)	**Freshly squeezed lime juice**
1/4	shot(s)	**Pomegranate (grenadine) syrup**

Origin: Classic variation on the Daiquiri, of unknown origin.
Comment: Rum and pineapple combine wonderfully and the Daiquiri is the king of cocktails.

EL PRESIDENTE #2 [NEW #7]

Glass: Martini
Garnish: Lime zest twist
Method: SHAKE all ingredients with ice and fine strain into chilled glass.

2	shot(s)	**Light white rum**
1	shot(s)	**Dry vermouth**
1	dash	**Angostura aromatic bitters**

Comment: Bone dry. Rather like a rum based, old school Martini.

EL PRESIDENTE #3 [NEW #7]

Glass: Martini
Garnish: Orange zest twist
Method: SHAKE all ingredients with ice and fine strain into chilled glass.

2	shot(s)	**Light white rum**
1	shot(s)	**Dry vermouth**
1/2	shot(s)	**Cointreau triple sec**
1/4	shot(s)	**Pomegranate (grenadine) syrup**

Origin: Adapted from Victor Bergeron's 'Trader Vic's Bartender's Guide' (1972 revised edition). Vic writes of this drink, "This is the real recipe".
Comment: A sweeter version of #2 above.

EL PRESIDENTE #4 [NEW #7] 

Glass: Martini
Garnish: Orange zest twist
Method: STIR all ingredients with ice and strain into chilled glass.

1 1/2	shot(s)	**Light white rum**
3/4	shot(s)	**Dry vermouth**
1/2	shot(s)	**Cointreau triple sec**

Comment: Dry but not bone dry, with balanced fruit from the triple sec and vermouth.

EL TORADO

Glass: Martini
Garnish: Float thin apple slice
Method: SHAKE all ingredients with ice and fine strain into chilled glass.

2	shot(s)	**Partida tequila**
1/2	shot(s)	**Dry vermouth**
1 1/2	shot(s)	**Pressed apple juice**

Origin: Popular throughout Mexico.
Comment: Dry, sophisticated and fruity, with tequila body.

ELDER & WISER [NEW #7]

Glass: Old-fashioned
Garnish: Lemon zest twist
Method: SHAKE all ingredients with ice and fine strain into ice-filled glass.

2	shot(s)	**Buffalo Trace bourbon whiskey**
1	shot(s)	**St-Germain elderflower liqueur**
1	shot(s)	**Pressed apple juice**

Origin: Created in 2006 by yours truly and named for its original base, Wiser's Canadian whisky.
Comment: Apple and elderflower combine wonderfully with bourbon.

THE ELDER AVIATOR [NEW #7]

Glass: Martini
Garnish: Lemon zest twist
Method: SHAKE all ingredients with ice and fine strain into chilled glass.

2	shot(s)	**Plymouth gin**
1/2	shot(s)	**St-Germain elderflower liqueur**
1/4	shot(s)	**Luxardo maraschino liqueur**
1/2	shot(s)	**Freshly squeezed lemon juice**
1/2	shot(s)	**Chilled mineral water** (omit if wet ice)

Origin: Created in 2006 by yours truly.
Comment: Fans of the classic Aviation may appreciate this floral twist.

ELDER FASHIONED [NEW #7]

Glass: Old-fashioned
Garnish: Orange zest twist
Method: STIR one shot of bourbon with two ice cubes in a glass. **ADD** elderflower liqueur, orange bitters and two more ice cubes. **STIR** some more and add another two ice cubes and the rest of the bourbon. **STIR** lots more and add more ice.

2	shot(s)	**Buffalo Trace bourbon whiskey**
3/4	shot(s)	**St-Germain elderflower liqueur**
1	dash	**Fee Brothers orange bitters**

Origin: Created in 2006 by yours truly.
Comment: Whiskey and elderflower served in the Old-Fashioned style. The elderflower liqueur smoothes the bourbon.

ELDER SOUR [NEW #7]

Glass: Old-fashioned
Garnish: Lemon slice & cherry
Method: SHAKE all ingredients with ice and strain into ice-filled glass.

2	shot(s)	**St-Germain elderflower liqueur**
1	shot(s)	**Freshly squeezed lime juice**
1/2	fresh	**Egg white**
1	dash	**Fee Brothers orange bitters (optional)**

Variation: Served 'up' in a sour glass.
Origin: Created in 2006 by yours truly.
Comment: So smooth it's almost fluffy. A great after-dinner drink.

ELDERFLOWER COLLINS #1 [UPDATED #7]

Glass: Collins
Garnish: Lemon slice
Method: SHAKE first four ingredients with ice and strain into ice-filled glass. **TOP** with soda.

2	shot(s)	**Plymouth gin**
1 1/2	shot(s)	**St-Germain elderflower liqueur**
1	shot(s)	**Freshly squeezed lemon juice**
1/8	shot(s)	**Sugar syrup (2 sugar to 1 water)**
Top up with		**Soda water (club soda)**

Comment: A hint of elderflower adds interest to the classic Collins cocktail – long, balanced and refreshing.

ELDERFLOWER COLLINS #2

Glass: Collins
Garnish: Lemon slice
Method: SHAKE first four ingredients with ice and strain into ice-filled glass. **TOP** with soda.

2	shot(s)	**Ketel One Citroen vodka**
1/8	shot(s)	**Luxardo maraschino liqueur**
1/4	shot(s)	**St Germain Elderflower liqueur**
3/4	shot(s)	**Freshly squeezed lemon juice**
Top up with		**Soda water (club soda)**

Comment: Long and refreshing with a floral, cherry and citrus flavour.

ELDERFLOWER COSMO [NEW #7]

Glass: Martini
Garnish: Lime zest twist
Method: SHAKE all ingredients with ice and fine strain into chilled glass.

1 1/2	shot(s)	**Ketel One vodka**
1	shot(s)	**St-Germain elderflower liqueur**
1/2	shot(s)	**Pressed pineapple juice**
1/4	shot(s)	**Freshly squeezed lime juice**

Origin: Created in 2006 by yours truly.
Comment: Despite the absence of citrus vodka, orange liqueur and cranberry, this delicate blend is still Cosmopolitan in style.

ELDERFLOWER DAIQUIRI [NEW #7]

Glass: Martini
Garnish: Lime wedge on rim
Method: SHAKE all ingredients with ice and fine strain into chilled glass.

2	shot(s)	**Light white rum**
1	shot(s)	**St-Germain elderflower liqueur**
1/2	shot(s)	**Freshly squeezed lime juice**

Origin: Created in 2006 by yours truly.
Comment: Elderflower liqueur adds floral interest to the classic Daiquiri.

ELDERFLOWER MANHATTAN [NEW #7]

Glass: Martini
Garnish: Maraschino cherry in drink
Method: SHAKE all ingredients with ice and fine strain into chilled glass.

2	shot(s)	**Buffalo Trace bourbon whiskey**
1	shot(s)	**St-Germain elderflower liqueur**
1/2	shot(s)	**Dry vermouth**
2	dashes	**Angostura aromatic bitters**

Origin: Created in 2006 by yours truly.
Comment: Elderflower replaces sweet vermouth in this 'perfect' and aromatic Manhattan.

ELDERFLOWER MARTINI #1 [UPDATED #7]

Glass: Martini
Garnish: Lime zest twist
Method: SHAKE all ingredients with ice and fine strain into chilled glass.

2	shot(s)	**Zubrówka bison vodka**
1	shot(s)	**St-Germain elderflower liqueur**
1/2	shot(s)	**Dry vermouth**

Comment: This veritable shrubbery is floral and grassy with dry borders.

ELDERFLOWER MARTINI #2 [NEW #7]

Glass: Martini
Garnish: Lemon zest twist
Method: SHAKE all ingredients with ice and fine strain into chilled glass.

1	shot(s)	**Ketel One vodka**
1	shot(s)	**Zubrówka bison vodka**
1	shot(s)	**St-Germain elderflower liqueur**
1/2	shot(s)	**Dry vermouth**

Comment: Dry but not bone dry with aromatic hints of grass and elderflower.

ELDERFLOWER MOJITO [NEW #7]

Glass: Collins
Garnish: Mint sprig
Method: Lightly MUDDLE (just to bruise) mint in base of glass. Add other ingredients, half fill glass with crushed ice and **CHURN** (stir) with bar spoon. Fill glass to brim with more crushed ice and churn some more. Serve with straws.

12 fresh **Mint leaves**
2 shot(s) **Light white rum**
1 shot(s) **St-Germain elderflower liqueur**
1 shot(s) **Freshly squeezed lime juice**

Comment: The enduring classic benefits from a touch of elderflower.

ELDERFLOWER PISCO PUNCH [NEW #7]

Glass: Collins
Garnish: Pineapple wedge dusted with ground cloves
Method: MUDDLE clove in base of shaker. Add next three ingredients, **SHAKE** with ice and fine strain into ice-filled glass. **TOP** with champagne.

1 dried **Clove**
1½ shot(s) **Pisco**
1 shot(s) **St-Germain elderflower liqueur**
¾ shot(s) **Pressed pineapple juice**
Top up with **Brut champagne**

Origin: Created in 2006 by yours truly.
Comment: Tangy and fruity. Clove spice, fragrant pisco and floral elderflower with a hint of pineapple and biscuity champagne.

ELIXIR

Glass: Collins
Garnish: Mint sprig
Method: Lightly **MUDDLE** mint in base of shaker. Add next three ingredients, **SHAKE** with ice and strain into ice-filled glass. **TOP** with soda, stir and serve with straws.

7 fresh **Mint leaves**
1½ shot(s) **Green Chartreuse liqueur**
1 shot(s) **Sugar syrup (2 sugar to 1 water)**
¾ shot(s) **Freshly squeezed lime juice**
Top up with **Soda water (club soda)**

Origin: Created in 2003 by Gian Franco Pola for Capannina in Cremona and Coconuts in Rimini, Italy.
Comment: A minty, herbal, refreshing summer drink.

ELK MARTINI [NEW #7]

Glass: Martini
Garnish: Lemon zest twist
Method: STIR all ingredients with ice and fine strain into chilled glass.

1 shot(s) **Plymouth gin**
1 shot(s) **La Vieille Prune plum brandy**
¼ shot(s) **Dry vermouth**

Origin: Adapted from Harry Craddock's 1930 'The Savoy Cocktail Book'.
Comment: Craddock calls for this drink to be shaken, but in this instance stirring seems more in order.

> 'THE SWAY OF ALCOHOL OVER MANKIND IS UNQUESTIONABLY DUE TO ITS POWER TO STIMULATE THE MYSTICAL FACULTIES OF HUMAN NATURE, USUALLY CRUSHED TO EARTH BY THE COLD FACTS AND DRY CRITICISMS OF THE SOBER HOUR.'
>
> JAMES

ELEGANTE MARGARITA

Glass: Coupette
Garnish: Lime wedge & salted rim (optional)
Method: SHAKE all ingredients with ice and fine strain into chilled glass.

1½ shot(s) **Partida tequila**
½ shot(s) **Cointreau triple sec**
½ shot(s) **Rose's lime cordial**
¾ shot(s) **Freshly squeezed lime juice**
½ shot(s) **Sugar syrup (2 sugar to 1 water)**

Origin: Created in 1999 by Robert Plotkin and Raymon Flores of BarMedia, USA.
Comment: One of the best Margarita recipes around. Richly endowed with flavour.

ELLE FOR LEATHER

Glass: Collins
Garnish: Vanilla pod
Method: SHAKE first four ingredients with ice and strain into glass filled with crushed ice. **TOP** with champagne.

1½ shot(s) **Scotch whisky**
1 shot(s) **Vanilla schnapps liqueur**
¼ shot(s) **Freshly squeezed lemon juice**
⅛ shot(s) **Sugar syrup (2 sugar to 1 water)**
Top up with **Brut champagne**

Origin: Created in 2001 by Reece Clark at Hush Up, London, England.
Comment: A long, cool champagne cocktail pepped up with Scotch whisky and vanilla schnapps. Easy drinking - yet adult.

ELYSIAN [UPDATED #7]

Glass: Martini
Garnish: Float apple slice
Method: STIR all ingredients with ice and strain into chilled glass.

2	shot(s)	**Boulard Grand Solage Calvados**
1/2	shot(s)	**Sweet vermouth**
1/2	shot(s)	**Dry vermouth**
1/4	shot(s)	**Maple syrup**
3	dashes	**Angostura aromatic bitters**
3	dashes	**Peychaud's aromatic bitters**

Origin: Created in 2004 by Mickael Perror at Millbank Lounge Bar, London, England.
Comment: Dry and aromatic, although not for all tastes.

EMBASSY COCKTAIL [NEW #7] 

Glass: Martini
Garnish: Orange zest twist
Method: SHAKE all ingredients with ice and fine strain into chilled glass.

1	shot(s)	**Rémy Martin cognac**
1	shot(s)	**Light white rum**
1	shot(s)	**Cointreau triple sec**
3/4	shot(s)	**Freshly squeezed lime juice**
1	dash	**Angostura aromatic bitters**

Origin: Created in 1930 at the famous Embassy Club speakeasy in Hollywood, USA.
Comment: Bone dry – one for hardened palates.

EMBASSY ROYAL

Glass: Martini
Garnish: Orange zest twist
Method: SHAKE all ingredients with ice and fine strain into chilled glass.

1 3/4	shot(s)	**Buffalo Trace bourbon whiskey**
1	shot(s)	**Drambuie liqueur**
1	shot(s)	**Sweet vermouth**
1	shot(s)	**Freshly squeezed orange juice**

Comment: An aromatic, herbal and altogether pleasant concoction.

EMERALD MARTINI

Glass: Martini
Garnish: Sprayed and discarded lemon & lime zest twists plus mint leaf
Method: STIR all ingredients with ice and strain into chilled glass.

2	shot(s)	**Lime flavoured vodka**
1	shot(s)	**Green Chartreuse liqueur**
1	shot(s)	**Chilled mineral water**

Origin: Discovered in 2005 at Bugsy's, Prague, Czech Republic.
Comment: A serious drink that's rammed with alcohol and flavour.

EMPEROR'S MEMOIRS

Glass: Collins
Garnish: Orange & lemon zest twists
Method: SHAKE first four ingredients with ice and strain into ice-filled glass. **TOP** with ginger beer.

1	shot(s)	**Plymouth gin**
1/2	shot(s)	**Punt E Mes**
1/4	shot(s)	**Ginger cordial (non-alcoholic)**
1/4	shot(s)	**Freshly squeezed lemon juice**
Top up with		**Ginger beer**

Origin: Created in 2001 by Douglas Ankrah for Akbar, Soho, London, England.
Comment: Not particularly alcoholic, but strong in a gingery, spicy way.

EMPIRE COCKTAIL [NEW #7]

Glass: Martini
Garnish: Apricot slice on rim
Method: SHAKE all ingredients with ice and fine strain into chilled glass.

1 1/2	shot(s)	**Plymouth gin**
3/4	shot(s)	**Boulard Grand Solage Calvados**
3/4	shot(s)	**Giffard apricot brandy du Roussillon**

Origin: Adapted from Harry Craddock's 1930 'The Savoy Cocktail Book'.
Comment: Apricot dried by gin and apple brandy.

ENCANTADO [NEW #7]

Glass: Martini
Garnish: Mint sprig
Method: SHAKE all ingredients with ice and fine strain into chilled glass.

1 1/2	shot(s)	**Partida tequila**
1/2	shot(s)	**Rémy Martin cognac**
1/2	shot(s)	**Teichenné Peach Schnapps Liqueur**
1/2	shot(s)	**Chambord raspberry liqueur**
1/2	shot(s)	**Freshly squeezed lime juice**

Comment: Essentially a Margarita with a hint of peach and raspberry. Not too sweet.

ENCHANTED

Glass: Collins
Garnish: Lychee/mint sprig
Method: MUDDLE grapes in base of shaker. Add next three ingredients, **SHAKE** with ice and fine strain into ice-filled glass. **TOP** with ginger ale.

7	fresh	**White seedless grapes**
1 1/2	shot(s)	**Rémy Martin cognac**
1/2	shot(s)	**Soho lychee liqueur**
1/2	shot(s)	**Freshly squeezed lime juice**
Top up with		**Ginger ale**

Origin: Created by Wayne Collins, UK.
Comment: Light, fruity and easy drinking with lychee and ginger dominating.

E

ENGLISH BREAKFAST MARTINI [NEW #7]

Glass: Martini
Garnish: Orange zest twist
Method: SHAKE all ingredients with ice and fine strain into chilled glass.

1	shot(s)	**Plymouth gin**
1	shot(s)	**St-Germain elderflower liqueur**
1	shot(s)	**Cold English Breakfast tea**
1/2	shot(s)	**Freshly squeezed lemon juice**

Origin: Created in 2006 by yours truly.
Comment: Light and fragrant, thanks to tea, elderflower and the botanicals in the gin.

ENGLISH CHANNEL [NEW #7]

Glass: Martini
Garnish: Lemon zest twist
Method: SHAKE all ingredients with ice and fine strain into chilled glass.

3/4	shot(s)	**Grand Marnier liqueur**
3/4	shot(s)	**Bénédictine D.O.M. liqueur**
2	shot(s)	**Cold Earl Grey tea**

Origin: Adapted from a drink discovered in 2005 at Bellini, Auckland, New Zealand.
Comment: The Earl Grey tannins balance the spice and orange in the liqueurs to make a harmonious aperitif.

ENGLISH GARDEN [UPDATED #7]

Glass: Collins
Garnish: Three slices of cucumber
Method: SHAKE all ingredients with ice and strain into ice-filled glass.

2	shot(s)	**Plymouth gin**
2 1/2	shot(s)	**Pressed apple juice**
1	shot(s)	**St-Germain elderflower liqueur**
1/2	shot(s)	**Freshly squeezed lime juice**

Comment: Quintessentially English in flavour – anyone for tennis?

ENGLISH MARTINI [UPDATED #7]

Glass: Martini
Garnish: Rosemary
Method: Strip rosemary leaves from stem and MUDDLE in base of shaker. Add other ingredients, **SHAKE** with ice and strain into chilled glass.

1	sprig	**Rosemary**
2 1/2	shot(s)	**Plymouth gin**
1	shot(s)	**St-Germain elderflower liqueur**

Origin: Adapted from a drink created in 2003 at MJU, Millennium Hotel, London, England.
Comment: Rosemary and sweet elderflower combine wonderfully with the gin botanicals to make an interesting and approachable Martini.

ENGLISH ROSE

Glass: Martini
Garnish: Maraschino cherry
Method: STIR all ingredients with ice and strain into chilled glass.

1 3/4	shot(s)	**Plymouth gin**
3/4	shot(s)	**Dry vermouth**
1/2	shot(s)	**Parfait Amour liqueur**
1/4	shot(s)	**Freshly squeezed lemon juice**
1/8	shot(s)	**Pomegranate (grenadine) syrup**

Comment: A dry, complex, gin laced drink. Stir well.

ENVY

Glass: Martini
Garnish: Star fruit on rim
Method: SHAKE all ingredients with ice and fine strain into chilled glass.

1/2	shot(s)	**Ketel One vodka**
2	shot(s)	**Midori melon liqueur**
1	shot(s)	**Teichenné Peach Schnapps Liqueur**
3/4	shot(s)	**Frangelico hazelnut liqueur**
1/4	shot(s)	**Freshly squeezed lime juice**

Comment: Green with … melon, oh, and a hint of hazelnut. A tad on the sweet side.

EPESTONE DAIQUIRI

Glass: Martini
Garnish: Lime wedge
Method: SHAKE all ingredients with ice and fine strain into chilled glass.

2	shot(s)	**Light white rum**
1/2	shot(s)	**Giffard crème de cassis**
1/2	shot(s)	**Freshly squeezed lime juice**
1/2	shot(s)	**Chilled mineral water** (omit if wet ice)

Comment: A pleasant, maroon coloured, black-currant flavoured Daiquiri.

EPIPHANY

Glass: Martini
Garnish: Berries on stick
Method: SHAKE all ingredients with ice and fine strain into chilled glass.

1 3/4	shot(s)	**Buffalo Trace bourbon whiskey**
1/2	shot(s)	**Giffard mûre (blackberry)**
2	shot(s)	**Pressed apple juice**

Origin: Created in 2004 by Naomi Young at Match, London, England.
Comment: Not sure what a fruity bourbon drink has to do with the manifestation of Christ.

EPISCOPAL

Glass: Old-fashioned
Method: STIR ingredients with ice and fine strain into chilled glass.

1½	shot(s)	**Green Chartreuse liqueur**
¾	shot(s)	**Yellow Chartreuse liqueur**

Origin: A well-established drink promoted by the marketeers at Chartreuse and named after the devotees in the purple dresses.
Comment: My favourite way to enjoy Chartreuse. Especially good when made with V.E.P. Chartreuse.

ESCALATOR MARTINI

Glass: Martini
Garnish: Pear slice on rim
Method: SHAKE all ingredients with ice and fine strain into chilled glass.

1	shot(s)	**Poire William eau de vie**
½	shot(s)	**Zubrówka bison vodka**
2	shot(s)	**Pressed apple juice**
⅛	shot(s)	**Sugar syrup (2 sugar to 1 water)**

Origin: Created in 2002 by Kevin Connelly, England. It's called an escalator because the 'apples and pears', rhyming slang for 'stairs', are shaken.
Comment: This orchard-fresh concoction was originally made with Korte Palinka (Hungarian pear schnapps) - if using that or Poire William liqueur in place of Poire William eau de vie, little or no sugar is necessary.

ESPECIAL DAY

Glass: Martini
Garnish: Blackberry & discarded lemon zest twist
Method: MUDDLE blackberries in base of shaker. Add other ingredients, **SHAKE** with ice and fine strain into chilled glass.

3	fresh	**Blackberries**
2	shot(s)	**Light white rum**
½	shot(s)	**Sweet vermouth**
¾	shot(s)	**Giffard mûre (blackberry)**
½	shot(s)	**Pressed pineapple juice**
3	dashes	**Peychaud's aromatic bitters**

Origin: Created in 2005 by Tonin Kacaj at Maze, London, England.
Comment: Beautifully balanced, aromatic, rum laced and fruity.

ESPRESSO DAIQUIRI

Glass: Martini
Garnish: Float 3 coffee beans
Method: SHAKE all ingredients with ice and fine strain into chilled glass.

2	shot(s)	**Light white rum**
1¾	shot(s)	**Cold espresso coffee**
½	shot(s)	**Sugar syrup (2 sugar to 1 water)**

Variant: Espresso Martini
Comment: Rum based twist on the ubiquitous Espresso Martini.

ESPRESSO MARTINI

Glass: Martini
Garnish: Float 3 coffee beans
Method: SHAKE all ingredients with ice and fine strain into chilled glass.

2	shot(s)	**Ketel One vodka**
1¾	shot(s)	**Cold espresso coffee**
½	shot(s)	**Sugar syrup (2 sugar to 1 water)**

Variants: Espresso Daiquiri, Insomniac, Irish Coffee Martini, Jalisco Espresso, Jolt'ini.
Comment: Forget the vodka Red Bull, this is the connoisseur's way of combining caffeine and vodka.

ESQUIRE #1

Glass: Martini
Garnish: Orange zest twist
Method: SHAKE all ingredients with ice and fine strain into chilled glass.

2	shot(s)	**Buffalo Trace bourbon whiskey**
¾	shot(s)	**Grand Marnier liqueur**
¾	shot(s)	**Freshly squeezed orange juice**
1	dash	**Angostura aromatic bitters**
½	shot(s)	**Chilled mineral water** (omit if wet ice)

Comment: Spicy bourbon laden with orange fruit.

ESQUIRE #2

Glass: Martini
Garnish: Blackberry
Method: STIR all ingredients with ice and strain into chilled glass.

1½	shot(s)	**Ketel One vodka**
¾	shot(s)	**Raspberry flavoured vodka**
¾	shot(s)	**Parfait amour liqueur**

Origin: Created in the 1990s by Dick Bradsell for Esquire Magazine.
Comment: One for hardened Martini drinkers.

ESTES

Glass: Collins
Garnish: Raspberry & thin strips of lime zest
Method: MUDDLE raspberries in base of shaker. Add other ingredients, **SHAKE** with ice and fine strain into glass filled with crushed ice.

7	fresh	**Raspberries**
1¾	shot(s)	**Partida tequila**
½	shot(s)	**Chambord black raspberry liqueur**
1¾	shot(s)	**Ocean Spray cranberry juice**
½	shot(s)	**Agave syrup (from health food shop)**
¾	shot(s)	**Freshly squeezed lime juice**

Origin: Created in 2005 by Henry Besant and Andres Masso, London, England, and named in honour of Tomas Estes, the official Tequila Ambassador in Europe.
Comment: This rich, fruity long drink is a real crowd pleaser.

ESTILO VIEJO

Glass: Old-fashioned
Garnish: Lime zest twist
Method: **STIR** half of the tequila with two ice cubes in a glass. Add agave syrup and Angostura and two more ice cubes. Stir some more and add another two ice cubes and the rest of the tequila. Stir lots more and add more ice. The melting and stirring of the ice is essential to the dilution and taste of the drink.

$2^1/_2$	shot(s)	**Partida tequila**
$^1/_2$	shot(s)	**Agave syrup (from health food store)**
3	dashes	**Angostura aromatic bitters**

Origin: The name of this drink literally translates from Spanish as 'Old Style'. It is basically a Tequila Old-fashioned.
Comment: Even better when made with añejo tequila.

THE ESTRIBO

Glass: Martini
Garnish: Berries on stick
Method: **SHAKE** all ingredients with ice and fine strain into chilled glass.

2	shot(s)	**Partida tequila**
$^1/_4$	shot(s)	**Giffard crème de cassis**
1	shot(s)	**Pressed pineapple juice**
$^1/_2$	shot(s)	**Double (heavy) cream**
$^1/_2$	shot	**Milk**

Origin: The signature drink at El Estribo, Mexico City, which sadly closed in 2005. The drink and this once legendary tequila bar's name translate as 'The Stirrup'.
Comment: Pink and creamy but with a tequila kick.

E.T.

Glass: Shot
Method: Refrigerate ingredients and **LAYER** in chilled glass by carefully pouring in the following order.

$^1/_2$	shot(s)	**Midori melon liqueur**
$^1/_2$	shot(s)	**Irish cream liqueur**
$^1/_2$	shot(s)	**Ketel One vodka**

Comment: Fortified creamy melon.

EVERY-BODY'S IRISH COCKTAIL [NEW #7]

Glass: Martini
Garnish: Green cherry on stick
Method: **SHAKE** all ingredients with ice and fine strain into chilled glass.

2	shot(s)	**Irish whiskey**
$^1/_2$	shot(s)	**Green Chartreuse liqueur**
$^1/_4$	shot(s)	**Giffard green crème de menthe**

Origin: In his 1930 'The Savoy Cocktail Book', Harry Craddock writes of this drink, "Created to mark, and now in great demand on, St. Patrick's Day."
Comment: Like the Incredible Hulk, this drink packs a dangerous green punch.

EVITA

Glass: Martini
Garnish: Orange zest twist
Method: **SHAKE** all ingredients with ice and fine strain into chilled glass.

2	shot(s)	**Ketel One vodka**
$^1/_2$	shot(s)	**Midori melon liqueur**
1	shot(s)	**Freshly squeezed orange juice**
$^1/_2$	shot(s)	**Freshly squeezed lime juice**

Comment: A tangy, lime green, medium-sweet combination of melon, orange and lime.

EXOTIC PASSION

Glass: Collins
Garnish: Pineapple wedge & strawberry
Method: **SHAKE** all ingredients with ice and strain into ice-filled glass.

$1^1/_2$	shot(s)	**Ketel One vodka**
$^3/_4$	shot(s)	**Passoã passion fruit liqueur**
$^3/_4$	shot(s)	**Giffard crème de fraise de bois**
$1^1/_2$	shot(s)	**Pressed pineapple juice**
$1^1/_2$	shot(s)	**Freshly squeezed golden grapefruit juice**

Comment: Bittersweet and floral - one for the poolside.

EXTRADITION

Glass: Old-fashioned
Garnish: Strawberry on rim
Method: **MUDDLE** strawberries in base of shaker. Add other ingredients, **SHAKE** with ice and fine strain into ice-filled glass.

3	fresh	**Hulled strawberries**
2	shot(s)	**Pisco**
2	shot(s)	**Pressed apple juice**
$^3/_4$	shot(s)	**Passion fruit sugar syrup**

Origin: Created in 2001 by Francis Timmons at Detroit, London, England.
Comment: A light, fruity drink for a summer afternoon.

F-16 SHOT

Glass: Shot
Garnish: Split stemmed cherry on rim
Method: Refrigerate ingredients then **LAYER** in chilled glass by carefully pouring in the following order.

$^1/_2$	shot(s)	**Kahlúa coffee liqueur**
$^1/_2$	shot(s)	**Irish cream liqueur**
$^1/_2$	shot(s)	**Light white rum**

Origin: Named for the F-16 jet and closely related to the B-52.
Comment: May not break the sound barrier but at least it layers well.

F. WILLY SHOT

Glass: Shot
Method: SHAKE all ingredients with ice and fine strain into chilled glass.

1/2 shot(s) **Ketel One vodka**
1/2 shot(s) **Light white rum**
1/2 shot(s) **Luxardo Amaretto di Saschira**
1/2 shot(s) **Cointreau triple sec**
1/4 shot(s) **Rose's lime cordial**

Comment: Not as bad as it looks or sounds.

FAIR & WARMER COCKTAIL [NEW #7]

Glass: Martini
Garnish: Orange zest twist
Method: SHAKE all ingredients with ice and fine strain into chilled glass.

2 shot(s) **Light white rum**
1 shot(s) **Sweet vermouth**
1/2 shot(s) **Cointreau triple sec**

Origin: Adapted from Harry Craddock's 1930 'The Savoy Cocktail Book'.
Comment: While sure to warm, this is only fairly good.

FAIRBANKS COCKTAIL NO.1 [NEW #7] 

Glass: Martini
Garnish: Maraschino cherry
Method: SHAKE all ingredients with ice and fine strain into chilled glass.

1 shot(s) **Plymouth gin**
1 shot(s) **Dry vermouth**
1 shot(s) **Giffard apricot brandy du Roussillon**
1/4 shot(s) **Freshly squeezed lemon juice**
1/4 shot(s) **Pomegranate (grenadine) syrup**
1/2 shot(s) **Chilled mineral water** (omit if wet ice)

Origin: Adapted from Harry Craddock's 1930 'The Savoy Cocktail Book'.
Comment: Apricot liqueur dominates this cocktail but the dry vermouth and dilution save it from excessive sweetness.

FALLEN LEAVES [NEW #7]

Glass: Martini
Garnish: Lemon peel zest
Method: STIR all ingredients with ice and strain into chilled glass.

1 1/2 shot(s) **Boulard Grand Solage Calvados**
1 1/2 shot(s) **Sweet vermouth**
1/2 shot(s) **Dry vermouth**
1/4 shot(s) **Rémy Martin cognac**

Origin: Created in 1982 by Charles Schumann in Munich, Germany, and first published in his book 'American Bar'.
Comment: Suitably autumnal in colour. The vermouths and brandies are in harmony.

FANCY BRANDY [NEW #7] 

Glass: Martini
Garnish: Lemon peel zest
Method: SHAKE all ingredients with ice and fine strain into chilled glass.

2 shot(s) **Rémy Martin cognac**
1/4 shot(s) **Cointreau triple sec**
1/8 shot(s) **Sugar syrup (2 sugar to 1 water)**
1 dash **Angostura aromatic bitters**
1/2 shot(s) **Chilled mineral water** (omit if wet ice)

Origin: Adapted from a recipe by Charles Schumann, Munich, Germany, and published in his 'American Bar'. Very similar to Jerry Thomas' Fancy Brandy Cocktail, published in his 1862 edition.
Comment: This appropriately named brandy based drink benefits from dilution, hence my addition of a splash of water.

FANCY DRINK

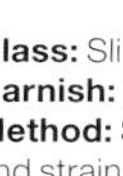

Glass: Sling
Garnish: Lemon slice & kumquat
Method: SHAKE first three ingredients with ice and strain into ice-filled glass. **TOP** with bitter lemon.

1 shot(s) **Grand Marnier liqueur**
1 shot(s) **Light white rum**
2 shot(s) **Freshly squeezed grapefruit juice**
Top up with **Bitter lemon**

Comment: Tasty tart! Refreshingly sour.

FANCY FREE

Glass: Martini
Garnish: Maraschino cherry
Method: SHAKE all ingredients with ice and fine strain into chilled glass.

2 shot(s) **Buffalo Trace bourbon whiskey**
1/2 shot(s) **Luxardo maraschino liqueur**
2 dashes **Angostura aromatic bitters**
2 dashes **Fee Brothers orange bitters**
1/2 shot(s) **Chilled mineral water** (omit if wet ice)

Comment: Aromatised, tamed bourbon.

FANTASIA (MOCKTAIL) 

Glass: Collins
Garnish: Lime wedge
Method: SHAKE first four ingredients with ice and strain into ice-filled glass. **TOP** with 7-Up, stir and serve with straws.

1/4 shot(s) **Freshly squeezed lime juice**
1/4 shot(s) **Freshly squeezed lemon juice**
1/4 shot(s) **Sugar syrup (2 sugar to 1 water)**
5 dashes **Angostura aromatic bitters**
Top up with **7-Up / lemonade**

Origin: Discovered in 2004 at Claris Hotel, Barcelona, Spain.
Comment: A Spanish twist on the popular Australian LLB.

FAT SAILOR

Glass: Old-fashioned
Garnish: Lime wedge
Method: SHAKE all ingredients with ice and strain into glass filled with crushed ice.

1 1/2	shot(s)	**Golden rum**
3/4	shot(s)	**Pusser's Navy rum (54.5% alc./vol.)**
1/4	shot(s)	**Kahlúa coffee liqueur**
1	shot(s)	**Rose's lime cordial**
1/2	shot(s)	**Freshly squeezed lime juice**

Origin: Tiki style drink of unknown origin.
Comment: A tasty, suitably calorie laden, rum concoction.

'ALCOHOL IS A VERY NECESSARY ARTICLE... IT ENABLES PARLIAMENT TO DO THINGS AT ELEVEN AT NIGHT THAT NO SANE PERSON WOULD DO AT ELEVEN IN THE MORNING.'

FAT TIRE [NEW #7]

Glass: Collins
Glass: Old-fashioned
Garnish: Orange zest twist
Method: SHAKE all ingredients with ice and fine strain into ice-filled glass.

1 1/2	shot(s)	**Aged rum**
1	shot(s)	**Averna Amaro Siciliano**
1/2	shot(s)	**Freshly squeezed orange juice**
1/2	shot(s)	**Pressed pineapple juice**

Origin: Discovered in San Francisco in 2006, hence the American spelling of 'Tyre'.
Comment: This flavourful, bittersweet aperitif won't be to everyone's taste.

FBI

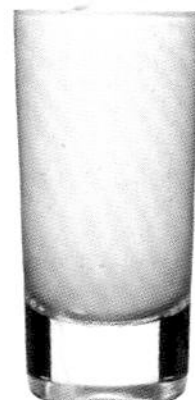

Glass: Collins
Garnish: Crumbled Cadbury's Flake bar
Method: BLEND all ingredients with 18oz scoop of crushed ice and serve with straws.

2	shot(s)	**Ketel One vodka**
1	shot(s)	**Irish cream liqueur**
1	shot(s)	**Kahlúa coffee liqueur**
3	scoops	**Vanilla ice cream**

Comment: Yummy alcoholic milkshake with coffee and whiskey cream.

FEATHER DUSTA CRUSTA [NEW #7]

Glass: Martini
Garnish: Lemon zest twist & optional sugar rim
Method: SHAKE all ingredients with ice and fine strain into chilled glass.

1 1/2	shot(s)	**Boulard Grand Solage Calvados**
1/2	shot(s)	**Luxardo maraschino liqueur**
3/4	shot(s)	**Squeezed pink grapefruit juice**
1/2	shot(s)	**Freshly squeezed lemon juice**
1/4	shot(s)	**Passion fruit syrup**
1/4	shot(s)	**Pomegranate (grenadine) syrup**
2	dashes	**Peychaud's aromatic bitters**

Origin: Created in 2006 by Gregor de Gruyther at Ronnie Scott's, London, England. It is "quite a light Crusta", hence the name.
Comment: In Gregor's own words, "Based on the father of the Sidecar, the granddad of the Margarita, Laydeez an' Gennulmen! The Brandy Crusta."

LA FEUILLE MORTE

Glass: Collins (10oz/290ml max)
Method: POUR first three ingredients into glass. Serve iced water separately in a small jug (known in France as a 'broc') so the customer can dilute to their own taste. (I recommend five shots.) Lastly, add ice to fill glass.

1	shot(s)	**Ricard pastis**
1/2	shot(s)	**Pomegranate (grenadine) syrup**
1/2	shot(s)	**Mint (menthe) syrup**
Top up with		**Chilled mineral water**

Origin: Pronounced 'Fueel-Mort', the name literally means 'The dead leaf', a reference to its colour.
Comment: A traditional French way to serve pastis.

FIESTA

Glass: Martini
Garnish: Pomegranate seeds in drink
Method: SHAKE all ingredients with ice and fine strain into chilled glass.

1	shot(s)	**Light white rum**
1	shot(s)	**Boulard Grand Solage Calvados**
1	shot(s)	**Dry vermouth**
1/8	shot(s)	**Freshly squeezed lime juice**
1/8	shot(s)	**Pomegranate (grenadine) syrup**

Comment: With the right amount of quality pomegranate syrup, this is a great drink.

FIFTH AVENUE SHOT

Glass: Shot
Method: Refrigerate ingredients then **LAYER** in chilled glass by carefully pouring in the following order.

1/2	shot(s)	**Giffard brown crème de cacao**
1/2	shot(s)	**Giffard apricot brandy du Roussillon**
1/2	shot(s)	**Double (heavy) cream**

Comment: A sweet, apricot and chocolate creamy shot.

FIFTY-FIFTY MARTINI [NEW #7]

Glass: Martini
Garnish: Olive on stick
Method: SHAKE all ingredients with ice and fine strain into chilled glass.

1½	shot(s)	**Plymouth gin**
1½	shot(s)	**Dry vermouth**

Origin: Adapted from Harry Craddock's 1930 'The Savoy Cocktail Book'.
Comment: A very 'wet' but wonderfully dry Martini which demands an olive, not a twist. Before you start – Craddock calls for it to be shaken.

57 T-BIRD SHOT

Glass: Shot
Method: SHAKE all ingredients with ice and fine strain into chilled glass.

½	shot(s)	**Ketel One vodka**
½	shot(s)	**Grand Marnier liqueur**
½	shot(s)	**Luxardo Amaretto di Saschira**

Variants: With California Plates add ½ shot orange juice; with Cape Cod Plates add ½ shot cranberry juice; with Florida Plates add ½ shot grapefruit juice; with Hawaiian Plates add ½ shot pineapple juice.
Comment: A '57 T-bird, or 1957 Ford Thunderbird to give it its full title, immortalised in the Beach Boys' song 'Fun Fun Fun', was the classic car for any 1950s teenager. Top down, radio up, girl next to you...

FINE & DANDY

Glass: Martini
Garnish: Lemon zest twist
Method: SHAKE all ingredients with ice and fine strain into chilled glass.

1¾	shot(s)	**Plymouth gin**
¾	shot(s)	**Cointreau triple sec**
½	shot(s)	**Freshly squeezed lemon juice**
⅛	shot(s)	**Sugar syrup (2 sugar to 1 water)**
½	shot(s)	**Chilled mineral water** (omit if wet ice)
2	dashes	**Angostura aromatic bitters**

Comment: A challenging, gin based drink that's soured with lemon and sweetened with orange liqueur.

FINITALY

Glass: Martini
Garnish: Blueberries or raspberries.
Method: SHAKE all ingredients with ice and fine strain into chilled glass.

1½	shot(s)	**Cranberry flavoured vodka**
½	shot(s)	**Sweet vermouth**
½	shot(s)	**Chambord black raspberry liqueur**
¾	shot(s)	**Chilled mineral water** (omit if wet ice)

Origin: Created by Michael Mahe at Hush, London, England.
Comment: A simple, berry led Martini.

FINN ROUGE

Glass: Martini
Garnish: Lemon zest twist
Method: MUDDLE raspberries in base of shaker. Add other ingredients, **SHAKE** with ice and fine strain into chilled glass.

5	fresh	**Raspberries**
1¾	shot(s)	**Cranberry flavoured vodka**
½	shot(s)	**Giffard crème de framboise**
¾	shot(s)	**Ocean Spray cranberry juice**
¼	shot(s)	**Freshly squeezed lemon juice**
⅛	shot(s)	**Sugar syrup (2 sugar to 1 water)**
1	pinch	**Black pepper**

Origin: Adapted from a drink created in 2005 by Jamie Stephenson, Manchester, England.
Comment: A rather red, rasping, berry rich drink.

FINNBERRY MARTINI

Glass: Martini
Garnish: Cranberries
Method: SHAKE all ingredients with ice and fine strain into chilled glass.

2	shot(s)	**Cranberry flavoured vodka**
2	shot(s)	**Lingonberry or cranberry juice**
1	shot(s)	**Lapponia cloudberry liqueur**

Origin: I created this in 2002 after a trip to Finland with Finlandia vodka.
Comment: This rich berry Martini can be varied by using other berry liqueurs in the Lapponia range – try using two with a half shot of each.

FIREBALL

Glass: Shot
Method: SHAKE all ingredients with ice and fine strain into chilled glass.

1	shot(s)	**Cinnamon schnapps liqueur**
3	drops	**Tabasco sauce**

Comment: Down this in one and be prepared for a sweet cinnamon palate quickly followed by a hot, spicy finish.

FIRST OF JULY

Glass: Martini
Garnish: Apple slice & blackberry on stick
Method: MUDDLE blackberries in base of shaker. Add other ingredients, **SHAKE** with ice and fine strain into chilled glass.

4	fresh	**Blackberries**
2	shot(s)	**Boulard Grand Solage Calvados**
1	shot(s)	**Chambord black raspberry liqueur**
2	shot(s)	**Freshly squeezed pink grapefruit juice**

Origin: Created on 1st of July 2004 by David Guidi at Morton's, London, England.
Comment: Rich blackberry fruit with a hint of grapefruit acidity.

FIZZES

Like the Collins, this mid-19th century classic is basically a sour lengthened with charged water and at first glance there is little difference between a Fizz and a Collins. However, there are several distinguishing features. A Collins should be served in a fourteen ounce tall glass while that used for a Fizz should be no bigger than eight ounces. A Collins should be served in an ice-filled glass, while a Fizz should be served in a chilled glass without ice.

Ideally a Fizz should also be made using charged water from a siphon in preference to soda from bottles or cans. The burst of pressure from the siphon bulb generates tiny bubbles which give off carbonic acid, benefiting the flavour and the mouthfeel of the drink.

For the correct proportions I have once again turned to David Embury's seminal 'The Fine Art Of Mixing Drinks'. He recommends "1 - or a little less – sweet (sugar, fruit syrup, or liqueur), 2 sour (lime or lemon juice), 3 - or a little more - strong (spirituous liquor), and 4 weak (charged water and ice). I interpret this as follows: 2 shots spirit (gin, whiskey, vodka, brandy), 1 shot lemon or lime juice, 1/2 shot sugar syrup, topped up with soda. I also like to add half a fresh egg white, which technically makes the drink a 'Silver Fizz'.

FISH HOUSE PUNCH #1

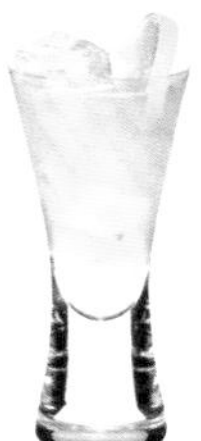

Glass: Collins
Garnish: Lemon wheel
Method: SHAKE all ingredients with ice and strain into ice-filled glass.

1	shot(s)	**Rémy Martin cognac**
1	shot(s)	**Golden rum**
3/4	shot(s)	**Teichenné Peach Schnapps Liqueur**
3/4	shot(s)	**Freshly squeezed lemon juice**
1/4	shot(s)	**Sugar syrup (2 sugar to 1 water)**
2	shot(s)	**Chilled mineral water**

Origin: Probably the most famous of all punch recipes, this originated in 1732 at a Philadelphia fishing and social club called the 'State in Schuylkill'. As a punch the original was mixed in larger quantities and served from a punch bowl.

Many modern variations use soda water (club soda) in place of mineral water. The inclusion of peach liqueur is a modern substitute for the traditional peach brandy. However, it's believed the Schuylkill original omitted peach entirely.
Comment: This fruit laced mix is neither too sweet, nor too strong.

'ABSINTHE MAKES THE TART GROW FONDER.'
ERNEST DOWSON

FISH HOUSE PUNCH #2

Glass: Collins
Garnish: Lemon wheel
Method: SHAKE all ingredients with ice and strain into ice-filled glass.

1	shot(s)	**Rémy Martin cognac**
1	shot(s)	**Light white rum**
1	shot(s)	**Teichenné Peach Schnapps Liqueur**
2	shot(s)	**Strong cold tea (English Breakfast)**
1 1/2	shot(s)	**Freshly squeezed lemon juice**
1/4	shot(s)	**Sugar syrup (2 sugar to 1 water)**

Comment: Over the decades this recipe has constantly morphed. The inclusion of cold tea is the latest adaptation.

FIZZ 

Glass: Collins (8oz max)
Garnish: Lemon slice
Method: SHAKE first four ingredients with ice and strain into chilled glass. **TOP** with soda.

2	shot(s)	**Spirit (gin, whiskey, vodka, brandy)**
1	shot(s)	**Freshly squeezed lemon or lime juice**
1/2	shot(s)	**Sugar syrup (2 sugar to 1 water)**
1/2	fresh	**Egg white (optional)**
Top up with		**Soda water (from siphon)**

Origin: A mid-19th century classic.
Comment: I recommend the Derby Fizz with its combination of liqueur and spirits over these more traditional versions.

FLAMING DR PEPPER

Glass: Shot & Boston
Method: POUR beer into Boston glass. **LAYER** amaretto and rum in chilled shot glass by carefully pouring amaretto and then rum. **IGNITE** the rum and carefully lift shot glass then drop (bottom first) into Boston glass.

1	bottle	**Lager beer**
1/2	shot(s)	**Luxardo Amaretto di Saschira**
1/2	shot(s)	**151° overproof rum**

Origin: So named as the end result resembles the taste of the proprietary Dr Pepper soft drink. This drink inspired an episode of The Simpsons featuring a similar drink titled the 'Flaming Homer' and later the 'Flaming Moe' (after the programme's bartender).
Comment: Please consider the likelihood of burning yourself while attempting to lift the flaming shot into the beer.

FLAMING FERRARI

This flaming drink (to be downed in one) requires an assistant to help the drinker consume the concoction.
Step 1.
Glass: Martini
Method: LAYER ingredients by carefully pouring in the following order.

1/2	shot(s)	**Pomegranate (grenadine) syrup**
1	shot(s)	**Galliano liqueur**
1	shot(s)	**Opal Nera black sambuca**
1	shot(s)	**Green Chartreuse liqueur**

Step 2.
Glass: Two shot glasses.
Method: POUR each ingredient into its own shot glass.

1	shot(s)	**Grand Marnier liqueur**
1	shot(s)	**Pusser's Navy rum**

Step 3.
Method: IGNITE the contents of the Martini glass. Give two long straws to the drinker and instruct them to drink the contents of the Martini glass in one go. As they do so, slowly **POUR** the contents of the two shot glasses into the flaming Martini glass.
Variant: Flaming Lamborghini with coffee liqueur and blue curaçao in the shot glasses.
Comment: Not recommended if you want to remember the rest of the evening and please be careful – alcohol and fire is a risky combination.

FLAMING HENRY

Glass: Shot
Method: LAYER by carefully pouring ingredients in the order below. Finally **IGNITE** bourbon. Extinguish flame prior to drinking and beware of hot glass rim.

1/2	shot(s)	**Luxardo Amaretto di Saschira**
1/2	shot(s)	**Irish cream liqueur**
1/2	shot(s)	**Buffalo Trace bourbon whiskey**

Origin: Created by Henry Smiff and friends in the South of France and popularised by one of their number, John Coe, the successful London drinks wholesaler.
Comment: Flaming good shot.

FLAMINGO #1

Glass: Martini
Garnish: Banana chunk on rim
Method: SHAKE all ingredients with ice and fine strain into chilled glass.

1	shot(s)	**Buffalo Trace bourbon whiskey**
3/4	shot(s)	**Giffard crème de banane du Brésil**
1 1/2	shot(s)	**Freshly squeezed orange juice**
3/4	shot(s)	**Freshly squeezed lemon juice**
1/2	fresh	**Egg white**

Comment: It's not pink but it has bourbon, banana, orange and lemon smoothed with egg white.

FLAMINGO #2

Glass: Martini
Garnish: Star fruit
Method: SHAKE all ingredients with ice and fine strain into chilled glass.

2	shot(s)	**Aged rum**
1 1/2	shot(s)	**Pressed pineapple juice**
1/2	shot(s)	**Freshly squeezed lime juice**
1/8	shot(s)	**Pomegranate (grenadine) syrup**

Origin: Classic of unknown origins.
Comment: A tasty, pink drink with a frothy top.

FLATLINER

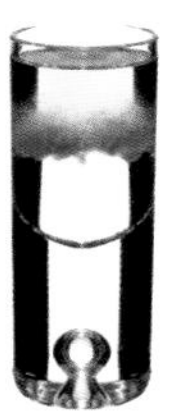

Glass: Shot
Method: POUR sambuca into chilled glass. **LAYER** tequila by carefully pouring over sambuca. Lastly **DRIP** pepper sauce onto drink. This will sink through the tequila to form an orange line on top of the sambuca.

3/4	shot(s)	**Luxardo Sambuca dei Cesari**
3/4	shot(s)	**Partida tequila**
8	drops	**Tabasco pepper sauce**

Comment: A serious combination of sweetness, strength and heat. Looks great but tastes…

FLIP

Glass: Sour or Martini
Garnish: Dust with freshly grated nutmeg
Method: SHAKE all ingredients with ice and fine strain into chilled glass.

2	shot(s)	**Spirit (brandy, gin, whiskey etc.)**
1	shot(s)	**Sugar syrup (2 sugar to 1 water)**
1	fresh	**Egg (white & yolk)**
1/2	shot(s)	**Double (heavy) cream**

Variant: Served hot in a toddy glass. Heat in a microwave oven or mix in a pan over heat.
Comment: I favour creamy, spicy, bourbon based Flips.

FLIPS

The very first Flips, which emerged as early as the late 1600s, were made of ale mixed with sugar, eggs, spices and spirits and heated with a red-hot iron bar. Later they came to mean any fortified wine or liquor shaken with a whole egg and sweetened with sugar. Flips sometimes contain cream and were, in their day, often served hot.

THE FLIRT

Glass: Martini
Garnish: Lipstick on rim
Method: SHAKE all ingredients with ice and fine strain into chilled glass.

2	shot(s)	**Partida tequila**
3/4	shot(s)	**Giffard apricot brandy du Roussillon**
3/4	shot(s)	**Freshly squeezed lime juice**
1	shot(s)	**Ocean Spray cranberry juice**

Origin: Created in 2002 by Dick Bradsell at Lonsdale House, London, England.
Comment: A fruity drink to upset glass washers throughout the land.

FLIRTINI #1

Glass: Martini
Garnish: Pineapple wedge on rim
Method: SHAKE all ingredients with ice and fine strain into chilled glass.

2	shot(s)	**Ketel One vodka**
1 1/2	shot(s)	**Pressed pineapple juice**
1/4	shot(s)	**Chambord black raspberry liqueur**

AKA: French Martini
Origin: Made famous on television's Sex And The City. Said to have been created in 2003 for Sarah Jessica Parker at Guastavinos, New York City, USA.
Comment: It's a French Martini! Hard not to like.

FLIRTINI #2

Glass: Martini
Garnish: Cherry on rim
Method: SHAKE first three ingredients with ice and fine strain into chilled glass. **TOP** with champagne.

3/4	shot(s)	**Ketel One vodka**
3/4	shot(s)	**Cointreau triple sec**
2	shot(s)	**Pressed pineapple juice**
Top up with		**Brut champagne**

Origin: Adapted from a recipe by the New York bartender Dale DeGroff.
Comment: A flirtatious little number that slips down easily.

THE FLO ZIEGFELD [NEW #7]

Glass: Martini
Garnish: Pineapple wedge on rim
Method: SHAKE all ingredients with ice and fine strain into chilled glass.

2	shot(s)	**Plymouth gin**
1	shot(s)	**Pressed pineapple juice**
1/4	shot(s)	**Sugar syrup (2 sugar to 1 water)**

Origin: Named after Florenz Ziegfeld, the Broadway impresario, whose widow recalled the recipe for the 1946 'Stork Club Bar Book'.
Comment: The original recipe omits sugar but was probably made with sweetened pineapple juice.

FLORAL MARTINI [UPDATED #7]

Glass: Martini
Garnish: Edible flower petal
Method: STIR all ingredients with ice and fine strain into chilled glass.

2 shot(s) **Plymouth gin**
1/2 shot(s) **St-Germain elderflower liqueur**
1/4 shot(s) **Dry vermouth**
1/4 shot(s) **Rosewater**
1/2 shot(s) **Chilled mineral water** (omit if wet ice)

Origin: Adapted from a drink created in 2003 at Zander Bar, London, England.
Comment: This aptly named gin Martini is soft but dry.

FLORIDA COCKTAIL (MOCKTAIL) 

Glass: Collins
Garnish: Orange wheel & cherry on stick (sail)
Method: SHAKE first four ingredients with ice and strain into ice-filled glass, **TOP** with soda.

1 shot(s) **Squeezed pink grapefruit juice**
2 shot(s) **Freshly squeezed orange juice**
1/2 shot(s) **Freshly squeezed lemon juice**
1/4 shot(s) **Sugar syrup (2 sugar to 1 water)**
Top up with **Soda water (club soda)**

Comment: The Florida sun shines through this fruity, refreshing drink.

FLORIDA DAIQUIRI

Glass: Martini
Garnish: Maraschino cherry
Method: SHAKE all ingredients with ice and fine strain into chilled glass.

2 shot(s) **Light white rum**
1/2 shot(s) **Freshly squeezed lime juice**
1/4 shot(s) **Sugar syrup (2 sugar to 1 water)**
1/2 shot(s) **Freshly squeezed grapefruit juice**
1/8 shot(s) **Maraschino liqueur**
3/4 shot(s) **Chilled mineral water** (omit if wet ice)

Comment: The classic blend of rum, lime and sugar, but with a hint of freshly squeezed grapefruit juice and maraschino. A user-friendly version of a Hemingway Special.

FLORIDA SLING

Glass: Sling
Garnish: Redcurrants/berries
Method: SHAKE all ingredients with ice and strain into ice-filled glass.

2 shot(s) **Plymouth gin**
1/4 shot(s) **Cherry (brandy) liqueur**
2 shot(s) **Pressed pineapple juice**
3/4 shot(s) **Freshly squeezed lemon juice**
1/4 shot(s) **Pomegranate (grenadine) syrup**

Comment: A tall, pink, dumbed down Singapore Sling.

EL FLORIDITA DAIQUIRI NO.1 [UPDATED #7]

Glass: Martini
Garnish: Maraschino cherry
Method: BLEND all ingredients with 6oz scoop of crushed ice. Pour into glass and serve.

1 1/2 shot(s) **Light white rum**
1/8 shot(s) **Luxardo maraschino liqueur**
1/4 shot(s) **Grapefruit juice**
1/2 shot(s) **Freshly squeezed lime juice**
1/2 shot(s) **Sugar syrup (2 sugar to 1 water)**

Variant: Hemingway Daiquiri
Origin: Emilio Gonzalez is said to have first adapted the Natural Daiquiri into a frozen version at the Plaza Hotel in Cuba. However, Constantino Ribalaigua Vert of Havana's Floridita bar made the frozen daiquiri famous with a recipe that included grapefruit.
Comment: Great on a hot day, but the coldness masks much of the flavour evident when this drink is served straight-up.

'TEQUILA LOVES ME EVEN IF YOU DON'T.'
KENNY CHESNEY

EL FLORIDITA DAIQUIRI NO.2 [NEW #7]

Glass: Martini
Garnish: Lime wedge on rim
Method: SHAKE all ingredients with ice and fine strain into chilled glass.

2 shot(s) **Light white rum**
1/2 shot(s) **Sweet vermouth**
1/2 shot(s) **Freshly squeezed lime juice**
1/4 shot(s) **Giffard white crème de cacao**
1/8 shot(s) **Pomegranate (grenadine) syrup**

Variant: With fruit.
Comment: Like other Daiquiris, this complex version benefits from dilution so consider adding a dash of water.

FLORIDITA MARGARITA

Glass: Coupette
Garnish: Lime wedge & salted rim (optional)
Method: SHAKE all ingredients with ice and fine strain into chilled glass.

1 1/2 shot(s) **Partida tequila**
1/2 shot(s) **Cointreau triple sec**
1/2 shot(s) **Ocean Spray cranberry juice**
1/4 shot(s) **Rose's lime cordial**
1 1/2 shot(s) **Freshly squeezed grapefruit juice**
3/4 shot(s) **Freshly squeezed lime juice**
1/2 shot(s) **Sugar syrup (2 sugar to 1 water)**

Origin: Created in 1999 by Robert Plotkin and Raymon Flores of BarMedia, USA.
Comment: A blush coloured, Margarita-style drink with a well-matched amalgamation of flavours.

FLOWER POWER MARTINI [NEW #7]

Glass: Martini
Garnish: Orange zest twist
Method: SHAKE all ingredients with ice and fine strain into chilled glass.

2	shot(s)	**Plymouth gin**
1/2	shot(s)	**St-Germain elderflower liqueur**
1/2	shot(s)	**Dry vermouth**
1/4	shot(s)	**Benoit Serres violet liqueur**

Origin: Created in 2007 by yours truly.
Comment: A Dry Martini served dripping wet with more flower power than Austin Powers.

FLYING DUTCHMAN MARTINI

Glass: Martini
Garnish: Orange zest twist
Method: STIR all ingredients with ice and strain into chilled glass.

2 1/2	shot(s)	**Bokma Oude genever**
1/4	shot(s)	**Cointreau triple sec**
2	dashes	**Fee Brothers orange bitters**
3/4	shot(s)	**Chilled mineral water**

Comment: A Martini with more than a hint of orange.

FLUFFY DUCK

Glass: Collins
Garnish: Orange slice
Method: SHAKE first four ingredients with ice and strain into ice-filled glass. **TOP** with soda.

1 1/2	shot(s)	**Plymouth gin**
1	shot(s)	**Bols advocaat liqueur**
1/2	shot(s)	**Cointreau triple sec**
1	shot(s)	**Freshly squeezed orange juice**
Top up with		**Soda water (club soda)**

Comment: Light, creamy and easy drinking. The gin's character prevents it from being too fluffy.

FLYING GRASSHOPPER

Glass: Martini
Garnish: Chocolate powder rim & mint leaf
Method: SHAKE all ingredients with ice and fine strain into chilled glass.

1	shot(s)	**Ketel One vodka**
3/4	shot(s)	**Giffard white crème de cacao**
1/2	shot(s)	**Giffard white crème de Menthe Pastille**
3/4	shot(s)	**Double (heavy) cream**
3/4	shot(s)	**Milk**

Comment: A Grasshopper with vodka – tastes like a choc mint ice cream.

FLUTTER

Glass: Martini
Garnish: Orange zest twist
Method: SHAKE all ingredients with ice and fine strain into chilled glass.

2	shot(s)	**Partida tequila**
1	shot(s)	**Kahlúa coffee liqueur**
1 1/4	shot(s)	**Pressed pineapple juice**

Origin: Created in 2003 by Tony Conigliaro at Lonsdale House, London, England.
Comment: The three ingredients combine brilliantly.

FLYING SCOTSMAN

Glass: Old-fashioned
Method: STIR all ingredients with ice and strain into ice-filled glass.

2	shot(s)	**Scotch whisky**
2	shot(s)	**Sweet vermouth**
1/4	shot(s)	**Sugar syrup (2 sugar to 1 water)**
3	dashes	**Angostura aromatic bitters**

Comment: Sweetened Scotch with plenty of spice: like a homemade whisky liqueur.

FLY LIKE A BUTTERFLY

Glass: Martini
Garnish: Orange zest twist
Method: SHAKE all ingredients with ice and fine strain into chilled glass.

1 1/2	shot(s)	**Dry vermouth**
1 1/2	shot(s)	**Sweet vermouth**
3/4	shot(s)	**Dubonnet Red**
3/4	shot(s)	**Freshly squeezed orange juice**

Origin: My take on a classic called a 'Lovely Butterfly'.
Comment: This light, aromatic, sweet and sour beauty has a grown-up, quinine-rich flavour but lacks the 'sting like a bee' finish.

FLYING TIGRE COCTEL

Glass: Martini
Garnish: Orange zest twist
Method: SHAKE all ingredients with ice and fine strain into chilled glass.

1 3/4	shot(s)	**Light white rum**
3/4	shot(s)	**Plymouth gin**
1/4	shot(s)	**Sugar syrup (2 sugar to 1 water)**
1/8	shot(s)	**Pomegranate (grenadine) syrup**
3	dashes	**Angostura aromatic bitters**
3/4	shot(s)	**Chilled mineral water** (omit if wet ice)

Origin: Adapted from a recipe in the 1949 edition of Esquire's 'Handbook For Hosts'. The drink is credited to an unnamed Captain serving in the US Marines, Amphibious Group Seven, at Santiago de Cuba in 1942.
Comment: Light, aromatic and complex – one to sip.

FOG CUTTER #1 [UPDATED #7]

Glass: Collins or tiki mug
Garnish: Orange slice
Method: SHAKE first six ingredients with ice and strain into ice-filled glass. FLOAT sherry on top of drink and serve without straws.

1½	shot(s)	**Light white rum**
¾	shot(s)	**Rémy Martin cognac**
½	shot(s)	**Plymouth gin**
1½	shot(s)	**Freshly squeezed orange juice**
½	shot(s)	**Freshly squeezed lemon juice**
½	shot(s)	**Orgeat (almond) sugar syrup**
½	shot(s)	**Amontillado sherry**

Origin: A version of what became a Tiki classic, sometimes credited to Trader Vic and/or Don the Beachcomber. In his 'Bartender's Guide' (1972 revised edition) Vic remarks, "Fog Cutter, hell. After two of these, you won't even see the stuff."
Comment: Don't be fooled by the innocuous colour. This long, fruity drink packs a serious kick.

FOG CUTTER #2

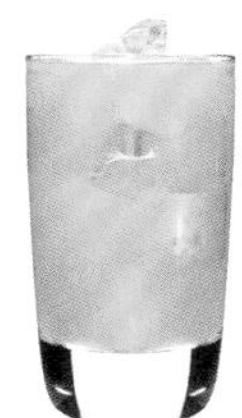

Glass: Old-fashioned
Garnish: Orange slice
Method: SHAKE first five ingredients with ice and strain into glass filled with crushed ice. **DRIZZLE** cherry brandy over drink and serve with straws.

1	shot(s)	**Light white rum**
½	shot(s)	**Rémy Martin cognac**
½	shot(s)	**Plymouth gin**
½	shot(s)	**Freshly squeezed lime juice**
¼	shot(s)	**Sugar syrup (2 sugar to 1 water)**
¼	shot(s)	**Cherry brandy**

Comment: A well balanced (neither too strong nor too sweet), short, fruity drink.

FOG HORN 

Glass: Old-fashioned
Garnish: Lime wedge
Method: POUR ingredients into ice-filled glass and stir.

2	shot(s)	**Plymouth gin**
½	shot(s)	**Rose's lime cordial**
Top up with		**Ginger ale**

Comment: Different! Almost flowery in taste with the spice of ginger beer.

FONTAINEBLEAU SPECIAL [NEW #7]

Glass: Martini
Garnish: Star anise
Method: SHAKE all ingredients with ice and fine strain into chilled glass.

1½	shot(s)	**Rémy Martin cognac**
1½	shot(s)	**Anisette liqueur**
¾	shot(s)	**Dry vermouth**

Comment: Cognac, aniseed and vermouth combine in this pleasant after dinner drink which has a taste reminiscent of liquorice.

FOAMED DRINKS

These cocktails are served with a foam float, the aroma and flavour of which usually contrasts with that of the drink beneath, so adding complexity.

This foam is usually dispensed from a cream whipping siphon. Gelatin or egg white is added to the flavoured mixture so when the siphon is charged with nitrous oxide foam is produced.

Popular base ingredients include cold tea and fruit juice but the foam can be made using pretty much any liquid provided that it is not oily. Both the ingredients and the charged siphon should be stored in a refrigerator as the colder the foam, the thicker it will be when discharged and the longer it will last on the drink.

Nitrous oxide (N2O), the key to these foams, is commonly known as laughing gas and is a colourless non-flammable gas with a pleasant, slightly sweet smell. Its nickname refers to the stimulating effects of inhaling it, which include spontaneous laughter, slight hallucinations and an analgesic effect. It is used in motorsport to boost power (nitrous oxide kit), and in surgery and dentistry as an analgesic. A 50/50 mixture of nitrous oxide and oxygen ('gas and air') is commonly used during childbirth. Nitrous oxide is a powerful greenhouse gas and you add to its global warming effect when opening a bag of potato chips as the gas is used to displace staleness-inducing oxygen in snack food packaging.

WARNING

Inhaling nitrous oxide directly from a whipped cream charger or tank poses very serious health risks. These include potential lung collapse due to the high pressure and frostbite since the gas is very cold when released. I'm not suggesting you try this, but most recreational nitrous oxide users discharge the gas into a balloon before inhaling. Nitrous oxide can also cause mild nausea or dizziness and is unsafe to inhale while standing as you are likely to fall over. I should also add that the possession of and recreational use of nitrous oxide is a criminal offence in much of the US and other areas of the world.

FORBIDDEN FRUITS

Glass: Collins
Garnish: Berries on stick
Method: MUDDLE berries in base of shaker. Add next three ingredients, **SHAKE** with ice and strain into glass filled with crushed ice. **TOP** with ginger beer.

4	fresh	**Blackberries**
4	fresh	**Blueberries**
4	fresh	**Strawberries**
4	fresh	**Raspberries**
2	shot(s)	**Plymouth gin**
1	shot(s)	**Freshly squeezed lime juice**
½	shot(s)	**Sugar syrup (2 sugar to 1 water)**
Top up with		**Ginger beer**

Origin: Created in 2001 by Andres Masso at Lab Bar, London, England.
Comment: Long and fruity with something of a bite.

FORT LAUDERDALE [NEW #7]

Glass: Martini
Garnish: Orange zest twist
Method: SHAKE all ingredients with ice and fine strain into chilled glass.

1½	shot(s)	**Light white rum**
½	shot(s)	**Sweet vermouth**
1	shot(s)	**Freshly squeezed orange juice**
¼	shot(s)	**Freshly squeezed lime juice**

Comment: Rum, vermouth, lime and orange form a challenging combination in this golden drink.

FOSBURY FLIP [UPDATED #7]

Glass: Collins
Garnish: Apricot slice on rim
Method: SHAKE all ingredients with ice and strain into ice-filled glass.

2	shot(s)	**Aged rum**
1	shot(s)	**Frangelico hazelnut liqueur**
1	shot(s)	**Giffard apricot brandy du Roussillon**
2½	shot(s)	**Freshly squeezed orange juice**
¾	shot(s)	**Freshly squeezed lime juice**
⅛	shot(s)	**Pomegranate (grenadine) syrup**
1	fresh	**Egg yolk**

Origin: Created in 2002 by Salvatore Calabrese at the Library Bar, Lanesborough Hotel, London, England, for Kirsten Fosbury. The Fosbury Flop is the style of high jump used by almost all successful high jumpers today and introduced by the American Dick Fosbury, who won the Gold Medal at the 1968 Olympic Games.
Comment: This richly flavoured, yellow, velvety drink is almost custardy in consistency.

FOUR W DAIQUIRI

Glass: Martini
Garnish: Grapefruit wedge on rim
Method: SHAKE all ingredients with ice and fine strain into chilled glass.

2	shot(s)	**Golden rum**
1½	shot(s)	**Freshly squeezed grapefruit juice**
¾	shot(s)	**Maple syrup**
2	dashes	**Angostura aromatic bitters**
½	shot(s)	**Chilled mineral water** (omit if wet ice)

Origin: My version of an old drink created by Herb Smith and popularised by his friend Oscar at the Waldorf, New York City. The drink was named in honour of the Duke of Windsor and his bride, formerly Wallis Warfield Simpson. The four 'W's stand for Wallis Warfield Windsor Wallop.
Comment: The oomph of rum, the sourness of grapefruit and the richness of maple syrup, all aromatised by bitters.

'A MAN YOU DON'T LIKE WHO DRINKS AS MUCH AS YOU DO.'

FOURTH OF JULY COCKTAIL

Glass: Martini
Garnish: Cinnamon dust
Method: POUR bourbon and Galliano into warm glass, **IGNITE** and sprinkle cinnamon while flaming. **SHAKE** last three ingredients with ice and strain into glass over extinguished bourbon and Galliano base.

---base---

1	shot(s)	**Buffalo Trace bourbon whiskey**
1	shot(s)	**Galliano liqueur**
	dust	**Cinnamon over flame**

---top---

1	shot(s)	**Kahlúa coffee liqueur**
1	shot(s)	**Freshly squeezed orange juice**
1	shot(s)	**Double (heavy) cream**

Comment: More a stage show than a cocktail but rich and tasty all the same.

FOURTH OF JULY SHOT

Glass: Shot
Method: Refrigerate ingredients then **LAYER** in chilled glass by carefully pouring in the following order.

¼	shot(s)	**Pomegranate (grenadine) syrup**
½	shot(s)	**Bols Blue curaçao liqueur**
½	shot(s)	**Ketel One vodka**

Comment: Looks cool... tastes less so!

FRANK SULLIVAN COCKTAIL [NEW #7]

Glass: Martini
Garnish: Sugar rim & lemon zest twist
Method: SHAKE all ingredients with ice and fine strain into chilled glass.

1	shot(s)	**Rémy Martin cognac**
1	shot(s)	**Cointreau triple sec**
1	shot(s)	**Dry vermouth**
1	shot(s)	**Freshly squeezed lemon juice**

Origin: Adapted from Harry Craddock's 1930 'The Savoy Cocktail Book'.
Comment: A Sidecar made dry with vermouth: it needs the sweet rim.

THE FRANKENJACK COCKTAIL [UPDATED #7]

Glass: Martini
Garnish: Orange zest twist
Method: SHAKE all ingredients with ice and fine strain into chilled glass.

1½	shot(s)	**Plymouth gin**
1½	shot(s)	**Dry vermouth**
½	shot(s)	**Giffard apricot brandy du Roussillon**
½	shot(s)	**Cointreau triple sec**

Origin: Adapted from Harry Craddock's 1930 'The Savoy Cocktail Book'.
Comment: Dry, sophisticated orange and apricot.

FRANKLIN MARTINI

Glass: Martini
Garnish: Two olives
Method: STIR vermouth with ice and strain to **DISCARD** excess, leaving the glass and ice coated with vermouth. **POUR** gin over vermouth coated ice, **STIR** and strain into chilled glass.

¾	shot(s)	**Dry vermouth**
2½	shot(s)	**Plymouth gin**

Comment: A Dry Martini garnished with two olives.

FREDDY FUDPUCKER

Glass: Collins
Garnish: Orange slice
Method: SHAKE all ingredients with ice and strain into ice-filled glass.

2	shot(s)	**Partida tequila**
3½	shot(s)	**Freshly squeezed orange juice**
½	shot(s)	**Galliano liqueur**

Variant: Harvey Wallbanger
Comment: A Harvey Wallbanger made with tequila in place of vodka. It's usual to build this drink and 'float' Galliano over the top. However, as the Galliano sinks anyway it is better shaken.

FRAPPÉS

To frappé is simply to chill with crushed ice and the term usually applies to a short drink where a spirit, a liqueur, or a combination of the two is simply poured over crushed ice.
Any spirit or liqueur may be served Frappé but absinthe
and crème de menthe are particularly identified with this serving style.

The Stinger, which calls for two shots of cognac to be poured over crushed ice with one shot of white crème de menthe, is probably the best known mixed Frappé.

FREE TOWN

Glass: Martini
Garnish: Maraschino cherry
Method: SHAKE all ingredients with ice and fine strain into chilled glass.

2	shot(s)	**Light white rum**
1	shot(s)	**Tawny port**
1/2	shot(s)	**Sugar syrup (2 sugar to 1 water)**
2	dashes	**Peychaud's aromatic bitters**

Origin: Created in 2004 by Alexandra Fiot at Lonsdale, London, England.
Comment: Great for sipping after dinner.

FRENCH 75

Glass: Flute
Garnish: Maraschino cherry
Method: SHAKE first three ingredients with ice and strain into chilled glass. **TOP** with champagne.

1	shot(s)	**Plymouth gin**
1/2	shot(s)	**Freshly squeezed lemon juice**
1/4	shot(s)	**Sugar syrup (2 sugar to 1 water)**
Top up with		**Brut champagne**

Origin: Legend has it that the drink was created by Harry MacElhone at his Harry's American Bar, Paris, and named after the 75mm field gun used by the French army during the First World War. However, he does not claim credit for the drink in his 1922 book.
Comment: Fresh, clean, sophisticated - very drinkable and hasn't dated.

FRENCH 76

Glass: Flute
Garnish: Maraschino cherry
Method: SHAKE first three ingredients with ice and strain into chilled glass. **TOP** with champagne.

1	shot(s)	**Ketel One vodka**
1/2	shot(s)	**Freshly squeezed lemon juice**
1/4	shot(s)	**Sugar syrup (2 sugar to 1 water)**
Top up with		**Brut champagne**

Variant: Diamond Fizz
Comment: A Vodka Sour topped with champagne. Works well.

FRENCH 77 [NEW #7]

Glass: Flute
Garnish: Lemon zest twist
Method: POUR first two ingredients into chilled glass, and top with champagne.

1	shot(s)	**St-Germain elderflower liqueur**
1/4	shot(s)	**Freshly squeezed lemon juice**
Top up with		**Brut champagne**

Origin: I created this twist on the classic French 75 in 2006.
Comment: Elderflower liqueur adds flavour to champagne while a splash of lemon juice balances the sweetness.

FRENCH APPLE MARTINI [NEW #7]

Glass: Martini
Garnish: Float wafer thin apple slice
Method: SHAKE all ingredients with ice and fine strain into chilled glass.

3/4	shot(s)	**Ketel One vodka**
3/4	shot(s)	**Apple flavoured vodka**
1	shot(s)	**St-Germain elderflower liqueur**
1/4	shot(s)	**Dry vermouth**

Origin: Created in 2006 by yours truly.
Comment: Dry, subtle apple with a delicate hint of elderflower.

FRENCH BISON-TINI

Glass: Martini
Garnish: Raspberries on stick
Method: SHAKE all ingredients with ice and fine strain into chilled glass.

2	shot(s)	**Zubrówka bison vodka**
2	shot(s)	**Pressed pineapple juice**
1/4	shot(s)	**Chambord black raspberry liqueur**

Comment: A French Martini with the distinctive taste of Zubrówka.

FRENCH DAIQUIRI

Glass: Martini
Garnish: Lime wedge on rim
Method: SHAKE all ingredients with ice and fine strain into chilled glass.

2	shot(s)	**Light white rum**
1	shot(s)	**Chambord black raspberry liqueur**
1/2	shot(s)	**Freshly squeezed lime juice**
3/4	shot(s)	**Chilled mineral water** (omit if wet ice)

Comment: A classic Daiquiri with a hint of berry fruit.

FRENCH DAISY [UPDATED #7]

Glass: Martini (champagne saucer)
Garnish: Lemon zest twist
Method: SHAKE first four ingredients with ice and fine strain into chilled glass. **TOP** with champagne.

1	shot(s)	**Rémy Martin cognac**
1/2	shot(s)	**Giffard Cassis Noir de Bourgogne**
1/2	shot(s)	**St-Germain elderflower liqueur**
1	shot(s)	**Freshly squeezed lemon juice**
Top up with		**Brut champagne**

Origin: Adapted from a drink created by Wayne Collins, London, England.
Comment: Rich blackcurrant with hints of elderflower, citrus and champagne. Slightly sweet.
Comment: A classic Mojito with a hint of berry fruit.

FRENCH KISS #1

Glass: Martini
Garnish: Star anise
Method: **SHAKE** first three ingredients with ice and fine strain into chilled glass. **POUR** grenadine into centre of drink. (It should sink.)

1	shot(s)	**Ketel One vodka**
3/4	shot(s)	**Pernod anis**
2	shot(s)	**Freshly squeezed orange juice**
1/8	shot(s)	**Pomegranate (grenadine) syrup**

Comment: Looks like a Tequila Sunrise but tastes of anis and orange.

FRENCH KISS #2

Glass: Martini
Garnish: Raspberries on stick
Method: **SHAKE** all ingredients with ice and fine strain into chilled glass.

1 1/2	shot(s)	**Ketel One vodka**
1/2	shot(s)	**Chambord black raspberry liqueur**
1/2	shot(s)	**Giffard white crème de cacao**
1/2	shot(s)	**Milk**
1/2	shot(s)	**Double (heavy) cream**

Comment: Smooth creamy chocolate and raspberry.

FRENCH LEAVE

Glass: Collins
Garnish: Orange slice
Method: **SHAKE** all ingredients with ice and strain into ice-filled glass.

1 1/2	shot(s)	**Ketel One vodka**
1/2	shot(s)	**Pernod anis**
3 1/2	shot(s)	**Freshly squeezed orange juice**

Comment: An easy drinking blend of vodka, anis and orange juice.

FRENCH MARTINI

Glass: Martini
Garnish: Pineapple wedge on rim
Method: **SHAKE** all ingredients with ice and fine strain into chilled glass.

2	shot(s)	**Ketel One vodka**
1 3/4	shot(s)	**Pressed pineapple juice**
1/4	shot(s)	**Chambord black raspberry liqueur**

AKA: Flirtini
Comment: Raspberry and pineapple laced with vodka. Easy drinking and very fruity.

FRENCH MOJITO

Glass: Collins
Garnish: Raspberry & mint sprig
Method: Lightly **MUDDLE** mint in base of glass (just to bruise). Add rum, liqueur and lime juice. Half fill glass with crushed ice and **CHURN** (stir) with bar spoon. Continue to add crushed ice and churn until drink is level with glass rim.

12	fresh	**Mint leaves**
2	shot(s)	**Light white rum**
1/2	shot(s)	**Chambord black raspberry liqueur**
1	shot(s)	**Freshly squeezed lime juice**
1/4	shot(s)	**Sugar syrup (2 sugar to 1 water)**

Comment: A classic Mojito with a hint of berry fruit.

FRENCH MONKEY [NEW #7]

Glass: Old-fashioned
Garnish: Lemon zest twist
Method: **SHAKE** first three ingredients with ice and strain into ice-filled glass. **TOP** with just a splash of soda.

2	shot(s)	**Scotch whisky**
1/2	shot(s)	**St-Germain elderflower liqueur**
1/2	shot(s)	**Pressed apple juice**
1	shot(s)	**Soda water (club soda)**

Origin: Created in 2006 for my French friend, Xavier Padovani.
Comment: Apple, Scotch and elderflower, honeyed and floral.

FRENCH MULE

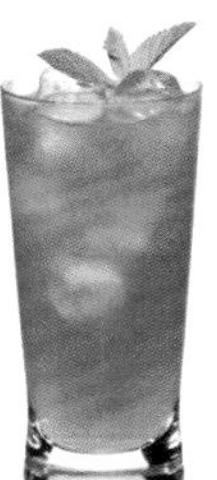

Glass: Collins
Garnish: Sprig of mint
Method: **SHAKE** first four ingredients with ice and strain into ice-filled glass. **TOP** with ginger beer, stir and serve with straws.

2	shot(s)	**Rémy Martin cognac**
1	shot(s)	**Freshly squeezed lime juice**
1	shot(s)	**Sugar syrup (2 sugar to 1 water)**
3	dashes	**Angostura aromatic bitters**
Top up with		**Ginger beer**

Comment: This French answer to the vodka based Moscow Mule uses cognac to make a more flavoursome, long, refreshing drink.

FRENCH SHERBET [NEW #7]

Glass: Martini
Garnish: Orange zest twist
Method: **SHAKE** all ingredients with ice and fine strain into chilled glass.

1	shot(s)	**Plymouth gin**
1	shot(s)	**Cointreau triple sec**
1	shot(s)	**Freshly squeezed orange juice**
1	shot(s)	**Freshly squeezed lime juice**

Comment: Not particularly French or sherbety – just a fresh orange wake-up call.

FRENCH SPRING PUNCH

Glass: Sling
Garnish: Strawberry
Method: SHAKE first four ingredients with ice and strain into ice-filled glass. **TOP** with champagne and serve with straws.

Qty	Measure	Ingredient
1	shot(s)	**Rémy Martin cognac**
1/4	shot(s)	**Giffard crème de fraise de bois**
1/4	shot(s)	**Freshly squeezed lemon juice**
1/4	shot(s)	**Sugar syrup (2 sugar to 1 water)**
Top up with		**Brut champagne**

Origin: Created by Dick Bradsell and Rodolphe Sorel at Match EC1, London, England, during the late 1990s.
Comment: Not as popular as the Russian Spring Punch but still a modern day London classic.

FRENCH TEAR #1

Glass: Martini
Garnish: Pineapple wedge on rim
Method: SHAKE all ingredients with ice and fine strain into chilled glass.

Qty	Measure	Ingredient
1 3/4	shot(s)	**Spiced rum**
3/4	shot(s)	**Grand Marnier liqueur**
2	shot(s)	**Pressed pineapple juice**

Origin: Discovered in 2000 at Quo Vadis, London, England.
Comment: Light, flavoursome, easy drinking. Altogether very gluggable.

FRESA BATIDA [UPDATED #7]

Glass: Collins (8oz)
Garnish: Strawberry
Method: MUDDLE strawberries in base of shaker. Add other ingredients, **SHAKE** with ice and strain into glass filled with crushed ice.

Qty	Measure	Ingredient
7	fresh	**Strawberries**
2 1/2	shot(s)	**Leblon cachaça**
1/2	shot(s)	**Freshly squeezed lemon juice**
1/2	shot(s)	**Sugar syrup (2 sugar to 1 water)**

Origin: The Batida is a traditional Brazilian style of drink and 'Fresa' means strawberry in Portuguese, the official language of Brazil.
Comment: A long, very refreshing strawberry drink laced with cachaça.

FRESCA

Glass: Martini
Garnish: Lemon zest twist
Method: SHAKE first four ingredients with ice and fine strain into chilled glass. **TOP** with 7-Up.

Qty	Measure	Ingredient
1 1/2	shot(s)	**Ketel One Citroen vodka**
1/2	shot(s)	**Chambord black raspberry liqueur**
1	shot(s)	**Squeezed pink grapefruit juice**
1/2	shot(s)	**Freshly squeezed lemon juice**
Top up with		**7-Up or lemonade**

Comment: The sweet, fizzy topping is essential to lengthen and balance this drink.

FRESCA NOVA

Glass: Flute
Method: SHAKE first four ingredients with ice and fine strain into chilled glass. **TOP** with champagne.

Qty	Measure	Ingredient
1 1/2	shot(s)	**Grand Marnier liqueur**
3/4	shot(s)	**Freshly squeezed orange juice**
1/4	shot(s)	**Sugar syrup (2 sugar to 1 water)**
1	shot(s)	**Double (heavy) cream**
Top up with		**Brut champagne**

Origin: Created by Jamie Terrell for Philip Holzberg at Vinexpo 1999.
Comment: Cream, orange and champagne work surprisingly well. Be sure to add the champagne slowly.

FRIAR TUCK

Glass: Martini
Garnish: Dust with freshly ground nutmeg
Method: SHAKE all ingredients with ice and fine strain into chilled glass.

Qty	Measure	Ingredient
1	shot(s)	**Frangelico hazelnut liqueur**
1	shot(s)	**Giffard brown crème de cacao**
1	shot(s)	**Double (heavy) cream**
1	shot(s)	**Milk**

Variant: With amaretto and ice cream.
Comment: Round, jolly and creamy with chocolate and hazelnut.

FRIDA'S BROW

Glass: Martini
Garnish: Dust with cinnamon powder
Method: SHAKE all ingredients with ice and fine strain into chilled glass.

Qty	Measure	Ingredient
2	shot(s)	**Partida tequila**
1/2	shot(s)	**Giffard white crème de cacao**
1/4	shot(s)	**Pomegranate (grenadine) syrup**
1/2	shot(s)	**Double (heavy) cream**
1/2	shot(s)	**Milk**

Origin: Discovered in 2005 at Velvet Margarita Cantina, Los Angeles, USA.
Comment: Creamy, sweetened tequila with hints of chocolate.

FRISKY BISON

Glass: Martini
Garnish: Float apple slice
Method: Lightly **MUDDLE** mint in base of shaker (just to bruise). Add other ingredients, **SHAKE** with ice and fine strain into chilled glass.

Qty	Measure	Ingredient
7	fresh	**Mint leaves**
2	shot(s)	**Zubrówka bison vodka**
1	shot(s)	**Apple schnapps liqueur**
1	shot(s)	**Pressed apple juice**
1/2	shot(s)	**Freshly squeezed lime juice**
1/4	shot(s)	**Sugar syrup (2 sugar to 1 water)**

Origin: Created by Tony Kerr in 1999 at Mash & Air in Manchester.
Comment: Sweet 'n' sour, fruity, minty and fresh.

FRISKY LEMONADE

Glass: Collins
Garnish: Lime wedge
Method: POUR ingredients into ice-filled glass and stir.

2	shot(s)	**Lime flavoured vodka**
1/2	shot(s)	**Dry vermouth**
Top up with		**7-Up or lemonade**

Origin: Created by Aaron Rudd in 2002 at Home, London, England.
Comment: Reminiscent of alcoholic lemon barley water.

FROTH BLOWER COCKTAIL [NEW #7]

Glass: Martini
Garnish: Lemon zest twist (spray & discard)
Method: SHAKE all ingredients well with ice and fine strain into chilled glass.

2	shot(s)	**Plymouth gin**
1/4	shot(s)	**Pomegranate (grenadine) syrup**
1	fresh	**Egg white**

Origin: Adapted from Harry Craddock's 1930 'The Savoy Cocktail Book'.
Comment: Salmon-pink and very frothy but surprisingly complex and tasty.

FROUPE COCKTAIL [NEW #7]

Glass: Martini
Garnish: Orange zest twist
Method: STIR all ingredients with ice and strain into chilled glass.

1 1/2	shot(s)	**Rémy Martin cognac**
1 1/2	shot(s)	**Sweet vermouth**
1/4	shot(s)	**Bénédictine D.O.M. liqueur**

Origin: Adapted from Harry Craddock's 1930 'The Savoy Cocktail Book'.
Comment: A bittersweet, herbal old-school drink that's in line for rediscovery.

FROZEN DAIQUIRI

Glass: Martini
Garnish: Maraschino cherry
Method: BLEND all ingredients with 12oz scoop of crushed ice. Serve heaped in the glass with straws.

2	shot(s)	**Light white rum**
1/2	shot(s)	**Freshly squeezed lime juice**
3/4	shot(s)	**Sugar syrup (2 sugar to 1 water)**

Variant: Floridita Daiquiri or with fruit and/or fruit **liqueur**s.
Origin: Emilio Gonzalez is said to have first adapted the Natural Daiquiri into this frozen version at the Plaza Hotel in Cuba.
Comment: A superbly refreshing drink on a hot day.

FROZEN COCKTAILS

These are cocktails blended with crushed ice. The ingredients are poured into an electric blender with an appropriate amount of crushed ice and then blended until a smooth, almost slushy consistency is achieved.

Frozen drinks are usually served heaped in large Martini glasses and should always be served with straws.

Practically any sour type drink can be adapted to be served frozen but the Frozen Daiquiri and Frozen Margarita are by far the best known examples. When adapting recipes be aware that drinks served frozen usually require more sugar than when served straight-up or on-the-rocks. Cocktails containing egg or cream do not usually make good frozen drinks.

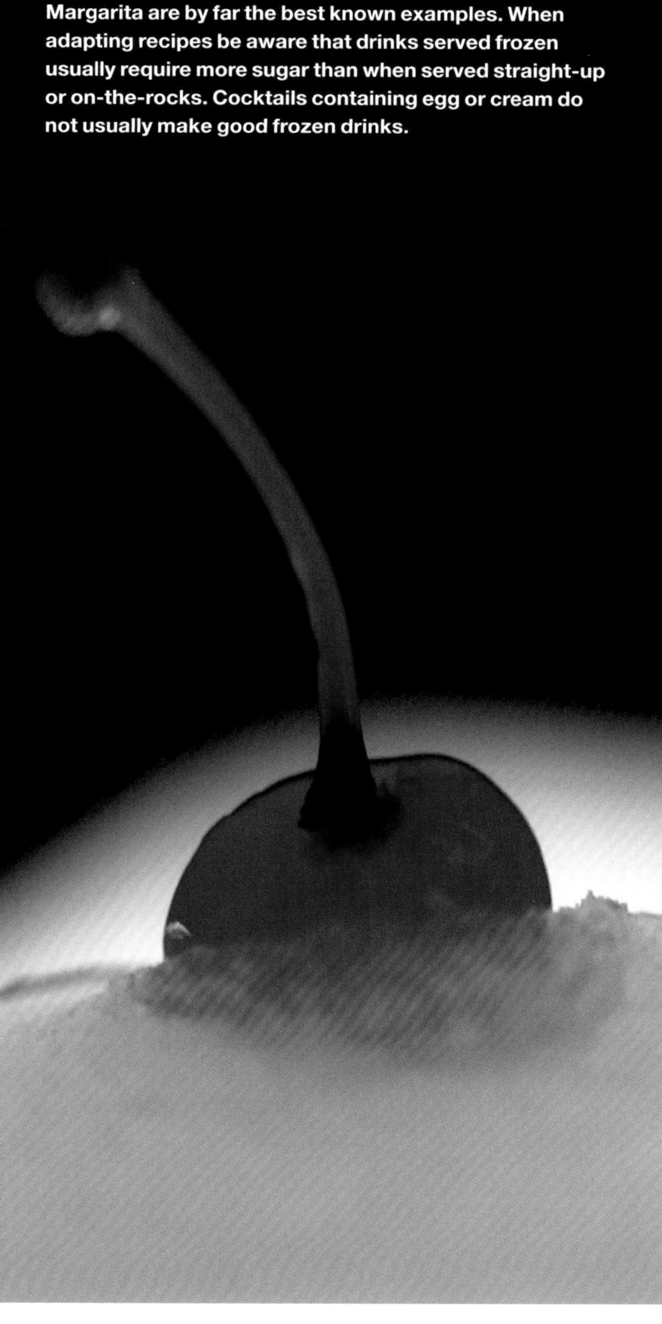

FROZEN MARGARITA

Glass: Martini
Garnish: Maraschino cherry
Method: BLEND all ingredients with 12oz scoop of crushed ice. Serve heaped in the glass and with straws.

1½	shot(s)	**Partida tequila**
¾	shot(s)	**Cointreau triple sec**
¾	shot(s)	**Freshly squeezed lime juice**
½	shot(s)	**Sugar syrup (2 sugar to 1 water)**

Variant: With fruit and/or fruit liqueurs.
Comment: Citrus freshness with the subtle agave of tequila served frozen.

FRU FRU

Glass: Flute
Garnish: Split strawberry
Method: SHAKE first three ingredients with ice and strain into glass. **TOP** with champagne.

¾	shot(s)	**Passoã passion fruit liqueur**
¾	shot(s)	**Giffard crème de fraise de bois**
¾	shot(s)	**Squeezed golden grapefruit juice**
Top up with		**Brut champagne**

Comment: Dry, bitter grapefruit complimented by passion fruit and strawberry.

FRUIT & NUT CHOCOLATE MARTINI

Glass: Martini
Garnish: Crumbled Cadbury's Flake bar
Method: SHAKE all ingredients with ice and fine strain into chilled glass.

1	shot(s)	**Raspberry flavoured vodka**
½	shot(s)	**Frangelico hazelnut liqueur**
½	shot(s)	**Giffard white crème de cacao**
½	shot(s)	**Chambord black raspberry liqueur**
½	shot(s)	**Irish cream liqueur**
¾	shot(s)	**Double (heavy) cream**
¾	shot(s)	**Milk**

Comment: Naughty but nice – one for confectionery lovers.

FRUIT & NUT MARTINI

Glass: Martini
Garnish: Orange zest twist & almond flakes
Method: SHAKE all ingredients with ice and fine strain into chilled glass.

1	shot(s)	**Vanilla infused Ketel One vodka**
1	shot(s)	**Frangelico hazelnut liqueur**
½	shot(s)	**Pedro Ximénez sherry**
1	shot(s)	**Ocean Spray cranberry juice**
½	shot(s)	**Freshly squeezed orange juice**

Origin: Created by yours truly in 2004.
Comment: A rich Christmas pudding of a Martini.

FRUIT PASTEL [NEW #7]

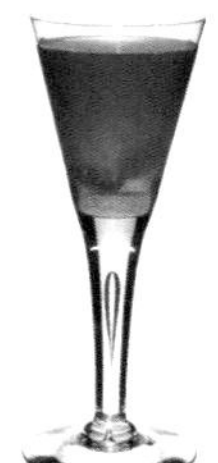

Glass: Martini
Garnish: Fruit Pastille sweets
Method: SHAKE all ingredients with ice and fine strain into chilled glass.

1½	shot(s)	**Ketel One Citroen vodka**
½	shot(s)	**Parfait Amour liqueur**
½	shot(s)	**Apple schnapps liqueur**
¼	shot(s)	**Freshly squeezed lime juice**

Comment: Tastes distinctly like a Fruit Pastille sweet.

FRUIT SALAD

Glass: Sling
Garnish: Fruit Salad chewy sweet / banana slice
Method: SHAKE all ingredients with ice and strain into ice-filled glass.

2	shot(s)	**Ketel One vodka**
½	shot(s)	**Crème de bananes**
2½	shot(s)	**Freshly squeezed orange juice**
½	shot(s)	**Galliano liqueur**
¼	shot(s)	**Pomegranate (grenadine) syrup**

Comment: This variation on the Harvey Wallbanger tastes like Fruit Salad 'penny chew' sweets.

FRUIT SOUR

Glass: Old-fashioned
Garnish: Lemon zest twist
Method: SHAKE all ingredients with ice and strain into ice-filled glass.

1	shot(s)	**Buffalo Trace bourbon whiskey**
1	shot(s)	**Cointreau triple sec**
1	shot(s)	**Freshly squeezed lemon juice**
½	fresh	**Egg white**

Comment: An orange influenced, sweet and sour whiskey cocktail.

FRUITS OF THE FOREST [NEW #7]

Glass: Martini
Garnish: Rasberries on stick
Method: SHAKE first five ingredients with ice and fine strain into chilled glass. **POUR** Chambord into the centre of the drink: it should sink to the bottom.

2	shot(s)	**Zubrówka bison vodka**
½	shot(s)	**St-Germain elderflower liqueur**
1	shot(s)	**Freshly squeezed orange juice**
½	shot(s)	**Freshly squeezed lime juice**
½	fresh	**Egg white**
¼	shot(s)	**Chambord black raspberry liqueur**

Origin: Adapted from a drink created in 2004 by Stuart Barnett at TGI Friday's, Reading, England.
Comment: Grassy, floral, citrus and smooth, but look out for the fruity bottom.

FRUIT TREE DAIQUIRI

Glass: Martini
Garnish: Grapefruit or apricot wedge on rim
Method: SHAKE all ingredients with ice and fine strain into chilled glass.

2	shot(s)	**Light white rum**
3/4	shot(s)	**Giffard apricot brandy du Roussillon**
3/4	shot(s)	**Squeezed pink grapefruit juice**
3/4	shot(s)	**Freshly squeezed lime juice**
1/4	shot(s)	**Maraschino syrup (from cherry jar)**
1/2	shot(s)	**Chilled mineral water** (omit if wet ice)

Comment: A restrained Papa Doble with apricot liqueur.

FU MANCHU DAIQUIRI

Glass: Martini
Garnish: Pineapple wedge on rim
Method: SHAKE all ingredients with ice and fine strain into chilled glass.

2	shot(s)	**Light white rum**
1	shot(s)	**Freshly squeezed lime juice**
1/2	shot(s)	**Sugar syrup (2 sugar to 1 water)**
1/4	shot(s)	**Cointreau triple sec**
1/4	shot(s)	**Giffard white crème de Menthe Pastille**
3/4	shot(s)	**Chilled mineral water** (omit if wet ice)

Origin: Adapted from a recipe by David Embury.
Comment: A natural Daiquiri with a refreshing, clean, citrussy, minty edge.

F

FUEGO MANZANA NO.2 [NEW #7]

Glass: Martini
Garnish: Small red chilli on rim
Method: MUDDLE chilli in base of shaker. Add other ingredients, **SHAKE** with ice and fine strain into chilled glass.

1	inch	**(25mm) Fresh red chilli (deseeded & chopped)**
2	shot(s)	**Partida tequila**
1/2	shot(s)	**Apple schnapps liqueur**
1	shot(s)	**Pressed apple juice**
1/2	shot(s)	**Freshly squeezed lime juice**
1/8	shot(s)	**Sugar syrup (2 sugar to 1 water)**

Origin: Created by Danny Smith at Che, London, England, initially using rum instead of tequila. 'Fuego Manzana' is Spanish for 'Fire Apple'.
Comment: A hint of chilli heat adds interest to an Apple Margarita, creating a full flavoured contemporary classic.

FUNKY MONKEY

Glass: Goblet (or coconut shell)
Garnish: Toasted coconut strips
Method: BLEND all ingredients with 12oz scoop of crushed ice and serve with straws.

1	shot(s)	**Golden rum**
3/4	shot(s)	**Giffard crème de banane du Brésil**
3/4	shot(s)	**Giffard white crème de cacao**
1	shot(s)	**Cream of coconut**
1	shot(s)	**Double (heavy) cream**
1	shot(s)	**Milk**
1	small	**Ripe banana (peeled)**

Origin: Created in 1998 by Tony Abou-Ganim, Las Vegas, USA.
Comment: Be sure to use a ripe or even over-ripe banana in this tropical style drink.

FULL CIRCLE

Glass: Collins
Garnish: Pineapple wedge on rim
Method: Cut pomegranate in half and juice with a spinning citrus juicer. **SHAKE** all ingredients with ice and strain into ice-filled glass.

3	shot(s)	**Freshly extracted pomegranate juice**
2	shot(s)	**Plymouth gin**
3/4	shot(s)	**Pressed pineapple juice**

Origin: Adapted from a drink discovered in 2004 at Mandarin Oriental, New York City, USA. The name is a reference to the bar's location - Columbus Circle, where the world's first one-way rotary system (roundabout) was implemented in 1904.
Comment: Fruity and easy drinking, yet with complexity from the gin.

FUZZY NAVEL

Glass: Collins
Garnish: Lemon wheel in glass
Method: SHAKE all ingredients with ice and strain into ice-filled glass.

2	shot(s)	**Teichenné Peach Schnapps Liqueur**
4	shot(s)	**Freshly squeezed orange juice**

Variant: Hairy Navel with the addition of a shot of vodka.
Origin: A not very well regarded but extremely well-known cocktail whose origins are lost.
Comment: The hairy version is a slightly more interesting, drier, less fluffy concoction. So why have a fluffy navel when you can have a hairy one?

How to make sugar syrup

To make your own sugar syrup, gradually pour TWO cups of granulated sugar into a saucepan containing ONE cup of hot water. Stir as you pour and carry on stirring and simmering until the sugar is dissolved. Do not let the water even come close to boiling and only simmer for as long as it takes to dissolve the sugar. Allow syrup to cool and pour into an empty bottle. Ideally, you should finely strain your syrup into the bottle to remove any undissolved crystals which could otherwise encourage crystallisation. If kept in a refrigerator this mixture will last for a couple of months.

G & TEA [NEW #7]

Glass: Collins
Garnish: Lemon slice
Method: SHAKE first three ingredients with ice and strain into ice-filled glass. **TOP** with tonic water.

1½	shot(s)	**Plymouth gin**
1	shot(s)	**St-Germain elderflower liqueur**
1	shot(s)	**Cold English Breakfast tea**
Top up with		**Tonic water**

Origin: Created in 2006 by yours truly.
Comment: Dry, floral, long and refreshing.

G

GALVANISED NAIL [UPDATED #7]

Glass: Old-fashioned
Garnish: Lemon zest twist
Method: STIR all ingredients with ice and strain into ice-filled glass.

2	shot(s)	**Scotch whisky**
½	shot(s)	**Drambuie liqueur**
¼	shot(s)	**St-Germain elderflower liqueur**
½	shot(s)	**Pressed apple juice**
½	shot(s)	**Freshly squeezed lemon juice**

Origin: Created in 2003 by yours truly, taking inspiration from the Rusty Nail.
Comment: A blend of Scotch and honeyed spice with lemon freshness plus hints of apple and elderflower.

GANSEVOORT FIZZ [NEW #7]

Glass: Collins
Garnish: Lemon slice
Method: SHAKE first four ingredients with ice and strain into ice-filled glass. **TOP** with soda.

2	shot(s)	**Aged rum**
1	shot(s)	**Drambuie liqueur**
1	shot(s)	**Freshly squeezed lemon juice**
2	dashes	**Peychaud's aromatic bitters**
Top up with		**Soda water (club soda)**

Origin: Created for 5 Ninth in Manhattan and originally published in David Wondrich's 2005 'Killer Cocktails'.
Comment: A potent, flavoursome herbal cooler based on aged rum.

GARIBALDI

Glass: Collins
Garnish: Orange slice
Method: POUR Campari into ice-filled glass. **TOP** with orange juice, stir and serve with straws.

2	shot(s)	**Campari**
Top up with		**Freshly squeezed orange juice**

Origin: Appears on cocktail lists throughout Italy. Named after the famous revolutionary general who helped liberate and reunify Italy.
Comment: Reminiscent of red grapefruit juice.

GATOR BITE

Glass: Coupette
Garnish: Salt rim
Method: SHAKE all ingredients with ice and fine strain into chilled glass.

1	shot(s)	**Green Chartreuse liqueur**
1½	shot(s)	**Cointreau triple sec**
1	shot(s)	**Freshly squeezed lime juice**
¾	shot(s)	**Sugar syrup (2 sugar to 1 water)**

Comment: Looks like a Margarita, but instead of tequila features the unique taste of Chartreuse. Yup, it bites.

GAUGUIN [NEW #7]

Glass: Old-fashioned
Garnish: Maraschino cherry
Method: BLEND all ingredients with 6oz crushed ice and serve with straws.

2	shot(s)	**Light white rum**
½	shot(s)	**Freshly squeezed lime juice**
½	shot(s)	**Freshly squeezed lemon juice**
½	shot(s)	**Passion fruit syrup**

Comment: The passion fruit shines through in this drink, which is very much a frozen Daiquiri in style.

GE BLONDE

Glass: Martini
Garnish: Apple wedge
Method: SHAKE all ingredients with ice and fine strain into chilled glass.

1¾	shot(s)	**Scotch whisky**
1¼	shot(s)	**Sauvignon Blanc wine**
1	shot(s)	**Pressed apple juice**
½	shot(s)	**Sugar syrup (2 sugar to 1 water)**
¼	shot(s)	**Freshly squeezed lemon juice**

Origin: A combined effort by the staff of London's GE Club in January 2002, this was named by Linda, a waitress at the club who happens to be blonde. She claimed the name was inspired by the cocktail's straw colour.
Comment: This delicate drink demands freshly pressed apple juice and a flavoursome Scotch with subtle peat.

GEISHA MAR-TEA-KNEE [NEW #7]

Glass: Martini
Garnish: Open tea pearl
Method: SHAKE all ingredients with ice and fine strain into chilled glass.

1½	shot(s)	**Plymouth gin**
¾	shot(s)	**Zen green tea liqueur**
1	shot(s)	**Cold jasmine tea**

Origin: Created in the USA in 2006.
Comment: Surprisingly fresh and light, this starts slightly sweet but finishes with refreshing bitter tannins. Tea pearls - hand-rolled balls of tea leaves - make a wonderful garnish.

GENTLE BREEZE (MOCKTAIL) 

Glass: Collins
Garnish: Lime wedge
Method: POUR ingredients into ice-filled glass, stir and serve with straws.

4	shot(s)	**Ocean Spray cranberry juice**
2	shot(s)	**Freshy squeezed pink grapefruit juice**

Comment: A Seabreeze without the hard stuff.

'A MEDIUM VODKA DRY MARTINI—WITH A SLICE OF LEMON PEEL. SHAKEN AND NOT STIRRED, PLEASE. I WOULD PREFER RUSSIAN OR POLISH VODKA.'

GEORGETOWN PUNCH

Glass: Collins
Garnish: Pineapple wedge
Method: SHAKE all ingredients with ice and fine strain into ice-filled glass.

1	shot(s)	**Light white rum**
3/4	shot(s)	**Gosling's Black Seal rum**
1 1/2	shot(s)	**Malibu coconut rum liqueur**
1	shot(s)	**Ocean Spray cranberry juice**
1	shot(s)	**Pressed pineapple juice**
3/4	shot(s)	**Freshly squeezed lime juice**

Origin: Adapted from a drink discovered in 2005 at Degrees, Washington DC, USA.
Comment: A Tiki-style, fruity rum punch.

GEORGIA JULEP

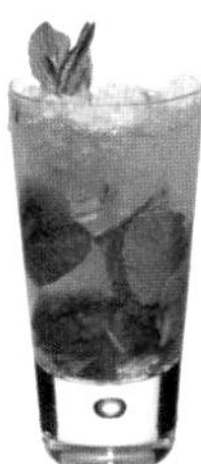

Glass: Metal mug or Collins glass
Garnish: Mint sprig and slice of lemon
Method: Lightly MUDDLE (only to bruise) mint in base of shaker. Add other ingredients, **SHAKE** with ice and strain into chilled glass half filled with crushed ice. **CHURN** (stir) the drink using a bar spoon. Top up the glass with more crushed ice and churn again. Continue adding crushed ice and churning until the drink meets the rim of the glass then serve with long straws.

12	fresh	**Mint leaves**
2 1/2	shot(s)	**Buffalo Trace bourbon whiskey**
1	shot(s)	**Teichenné Peach Schnapps Liqueur**
1/8	shot(s)	**Sugar syrup (2 sugar to 1 water)**
3	dashes	**Angostura aromatic bitters**

Origin: This classic was originally made with peach brandy in place of peach liqueur. It is also sometimes made with apricot brandy.
Comment: Bourbon, peach and mint are flavours that combine harmoniously.

GIMLET

In 1747, James Lind, a Scottish surgeon, discovered that consumption of citrus fruits helped prevent scurvy, one of the most common illnesses on board ship. (We now understand that scurvy is caused by a Vitamin C deficiency and that it is the vitamins in citrus fruit which help ward off the condition.) In 1867, the Merchant Shipping Act made it mandatory for all British ships to carry rations of lime juice for the crew.

Lauchlin Rose, the owner of a shipyard in Leith, Scotland, had been working to solve the problem of how to keep citrus juice fresh for months on board ship. In 1867 he patented a process for preserving fruit juice without alcohol. To give his product wider appeal he sweetened the mixture, packaged it in an attractive bottle and named it 'Rose's Lime Cordial'.

Once the benefits of drinking lime juice became more broadly known, British sailors consumed so much of the stuff, often mixed with their daily ration of rum and water ('grog'), that they became affectionately known as 'Limeys'. Naval officers mixed Rose's lime cordial with gin to make Gimlets.

A 'gimlet' was originally the name of a small tool used to tap the barrels of spirits which were carried on British Navy ships: this could be the origin of the drink's name. Another story cites a naval doctor, Rear-Admiral Sir Thomas Desmond Gimlette (1857-1943), who is said to have mixed gin with lime 'to help the medicine go down'. Although this is a credible story it is not substantiated in his obituary in The Times, 6 October 1943.

GIBSON

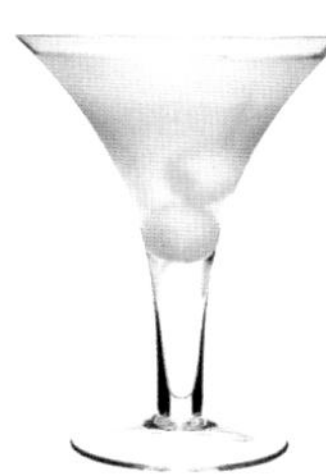

Glass: Martini
Garnish: Two chilled cocktail onions on stick
Method: STIR vermouth with ice in a mixing glass. Strain and discard excess vermouth to leave only a coating on the ice. **POUR** gin into mixing glass containing coated ice and **STIR**. Finally strain into chilled glass.

- 1/2 shot(s) **Dry vermouth**
- 2 1/2 shot(s) **Plymouth gin**

Origin: This twist on the Dry Martini seems to have come into being early in the 20th century. During the 1890s and the first two decades of the 20th century the pen-and-ink drawings of Charles Dana Gibson were published in the glamour magazines of the day. His illustrations of girls were as iconic as the supermodels of today. It is said this drink was named after the well-endowed Gibson Girls - hence the two onions. However, cocktail books published at the time include a Martini-like drink named Gibson but without the onions. Gibson was a member of New York's The Players' club and a bartender there by the name of Charley Connolly is credited for at least adding the garnish, if not actually creating the drink.
Comment: A classic Dry Martini with cocktail onions in place of an olive or twist.

G

GIMLET #1

Glass: Martini
Garnish: Lime wedge or cherry
Method: STIR all ingredients with ice and strain into chilled glass.

- 2 1/2 shot(s) **Plymouth gin**
- 1 1/4 shot(s) **Rose's lime cordial**

Variant: Other spirits, particularly vodka, may be substituted for gin.
Origin: Almost certainly originated in the British Navy.
Comment: A simple blend of gin and sweet lime.

GIMLET #2 (SCHUMANN'S RECIPE)

Glass: Martini
Garnish: Lime wedge or cherry
Method: SHAKE all ingredients with ice and fine strain into chilled glass.

- 2 1/2 shot(s) **Plymouth gin**
- 1/4 shot(s) **Freshly squeezed lime juice**
- 1 1/4 shot(s) **Rose's lime cordial**

Origin: A shaken twist on an already established drink by the famous bartender and cocktail author Charles Schumann of Munich, Germany.
Comment: Generously laced with gin and wonderfully tart.

GIN & IT

Glass: Old-fashioned
Garnish: Orange slice
Method: STIR all ingredients with ice and strain into ice-filled glass.

- 2 shot(s) **Plymouth gin**
- 1 shot(s) **Sweet vermouth**

Origin: The name is short for 'Gin and Italian', a reference to the sweet vermouth, which was traditionally Italian while French vermouth was dry.
Comment: An old school version of the classic Martini. Simple but great.

GIN & SIN

Glass: Martini
Garnish: Orange zest twist
Method: SHAKE all ingredients with ice and fine strain into chilled glass.

- 2 shot(s) **Plymouth gin**
- 1 shot(s) **Freshly squeezed lemon juice**
- 3/4 shot(s) **Freshly squeezed orange juice**
- 1/8 shot(s) **Pomegranate (grenadine) syrup**

Comment: Pleasant and fruity but lacking real personality.

GIN & TONIC

Glass: Collins
Garnish: Run lime wedge around rim of glass. Squeeze and drop into drink.
Method: POUR ingredients into ice-filled glass, stir and serve without straws.

- 2 shot(s) **Plymouth gin**
- Top up with **Tonic water**

Origin: The precise origin of the G&T is lost in the mists of time. Gin (or at least a grain based juniper spirit) was drunk for medicinal reasons from the 1600s onwards. Quinine, the pungent bark extract which gives tonic its distinctive bitterness, had been used against malaria for even longer. The first known quinine-based tonics were marketed during the 1850s.

The popularity of tonic in the British colonies, especially India, is clear. Schweppes launched their first carbonated quinine tonic in 1870, branding it Indian Tonic Water. The ladies and gentlemen of the Raj also drank phenomenal quantities of gin. It is therefore accepted that gin and tonic emerged in India during the second half of the nineteenth century and was drunk partly to ward off malaria.
Comment: This might not be considered a cocktail by most, but it is actually classified as a Highball. Whatever, it's one of the simplest and best drinks ever devised, hence its lasting popularity.

GIN ATOMIC [NEW #7]

Glass: Collins
Garnish: Lemon zest twist
Method: Lightly MUDDLE (just to bruise) basil in base of shaker. Add other ingredients apart from tonic, **SHAKE** with ice and strain into ice-filled glass. **TOP** with tonic water and serve with straws.

3	fresh	**Basil leaves**
2	shot(s)	**Plymouth gin**
1	shot(s)	**St-Germain elderflower liqueur**
$\frac{1}{2}$	shot(s)	**Freshly squeezed lemon juice**
2	dashes	**Fee Brothers lemon bitters (optional)**
Top up with		**Tonic water**

Origin: Created in 2007 by Brendan Mainini at The Ambassador Bar, San Francisco, USA.
Comment: A nuclear gin and tonic – or at least, one that simply radiates flavour.

GIN BERRY

Glass: Martini
Garnish: Lime zest twist
Method: SHAKE all ingredients with ice and fine strain into chilled glass.

$1\frac{1}{2}$	shot(s)	**Plymouth gin**
$\frac{1}{2}$	shot(s)	**Chambord black raspberry liqueur**
$\frac{1}{2}$	shot(s)	**Freshly squeezed lime juice**
$1\frac{1}{2}$	shot(s)	**Ocean Spray cranberry juice**

Origin: Adapted from a drink created in 2004 by Chris Lacey, UK.
Comment: Berry flavours combine harmoniously with gin – what an appropriate name.

GIN COCKTAIL [NEW #7]

Glass: Martini
Garnish: Lemon peel twist
Method: STIR all ingredients with ice and strain into chilled glass.

$2\frac{1}{2}$	shot(s)	**Plymouth gin**
$\frac{1}{8}$	shot(s)	**Cointreau triple sec**
$\frac{1}{8}$	shot(s)	**Sugar syrup (2 sugar to 1 water)**
2	dashes	**Angostura aromatic bitters**

Origin: A classic that was already well-established when Jerry Thomas recorded his version of the recipe in 1862.
Comment: A pink gin made more approachable by a splash of triple sec and sugar syrup.

GIN DAISY

Glass: Goblet
Garnish: Maraschino cherry
Method: SHAKE all ingredients with ice and strain into glass filled with crushed ice. **CHURN** (stir) drink with ice and serve with straws.

$2\frac{1}{2}$	shot(s)	**Plymouth gin**
$\frac{1}{4}$	shot(s)	**Yellow Chartreuse liqueur**
$\frac{1}{4}$	shot(s)	**Pomegranate (grenadine) syrup**
$\frac{1}{4}$	shot(s)	**Freshly squeezed lemon juice**

Origin: A classic Daisy variation.
Comment: If correctly made this serious, gin dominated cocktail should be blush, not pink.

GIN FIX

Glass: Goblet
Garnish: Lemon slice
Method: SHAKE all ingredients with ice and strain into glass filled with crushed ice. **CHURN** (stir) drink with ice and serve with straws.

2	shot(s)	**Plymouth gin**
1	shot(s)	**Freshly squeezed lemon juice**
$\frac{1}{2}$	shot(s)	**Sugar syrup (2 sugar to 1 water)**

Origin: The Fix is an old classic that's very similar to the Daisy.
Comment: A Gin Sour served over crushed ice in a goblet.

GIN FIXED

Glass: Martini
Garnish: Lemon slice
Method: SHAKE all ingredients with ice and strain into glass filled with crushed ice. **CHURN** (stir) drink with ice and serve with straws.

2	shot(s)	**Plymouth gin**
$\frac{1}{4}$	shot(s)	**Cointreau triple sec**
1	shot(s)	**Pressed pineapple juice**
$\frac{1}{2}$	shot(s)	**Freshly squeezed lemon juice**
$\frac{1}{4}$	shot(s)	**Sugar syrup (2 sugar to 1 water)**

Comment: Sweet and sour with a spirity pineapple twang.

'LIKE OTHER PARTIES OF THE KIND, IT WAS FIRST SILENT, THEN TALKY, THEN ARGUMENTATIVE, THEN DISPUTATIOUS, THEN UNINTELLIGIBLE, THEN ALTOGETHERY, THEN INARTICULATE, AND THEN DRUNK.'

LORD BYRON

GIN FIZZ

Glass: Collins (8oz max)
Garnish: Slice of lemon & mint
Method: SHAKE first three ingredients with ice and strain into chilled glass. **TOP** with soda.

2	shot(s)	**Plymouth gin**
1	shot(s)	**Freshly squeezed lemon juice**
½	shot(s)	**Sugar syrup (2 sugar to 1 water)**
Top up with		**Soda water (from siphon)**

Variants: With the addition of egg white this drink becomes a 'Silver Fizz'; with egg yolk it becomes a 'Golden Fizz'. A Royal Fizz includes one whole egg, a Diamond Fizz uses champagne instead of charged water, a Green Fizz has a dash of green crème de menthe and a Purple Fizz uses equal parts of sloe gin and grapefruit juice in place of gin and lemon juice.
Origin: A mid-19th century classic.
Comment: Everyone has heard of this clean, refreshing, long drink but few have actually tried it

GIN GARDEN [UPDATED #7]

Glass: Martini
Garnish: Float cucumber slice
Method: MUDDLE cucumber in base of shaker. Add other ingredients, **SHAKE** with ice and fine strain into chilled glass.

1	inch	**Chopped peeled cucumber**
2	shot(s)	**Plymouth gin**
1	shot(s)	**St-Germain elderflower liqueur**
1	shot(s)	**Pressed apple juice**

Origin: Adapted from a drink that Daniel Warner at Zander and Tobias Blazquez Garcia at Steam collaborated on in London, England, in 2001.
Comment: A veritable English shrubbery with flowers, fruit and vegetables flourishing in harmony.

GIN GENIE

Glass: Collins
Garnish: Mint sprig
Method: Lightly **MUDDLE** mint in base of shaker (just to bruise). Add other ingredients, **SHAKE** with ice and strain into glass filled with crushed ice.

8	fresh	**Mint leaves**
1½	shot(s)	**Plymouth gin**
1	shot(s)	**Plymouth sloe gin liqueur**
1	shot(s)	**Freshly squeezed lemon juice**
½	shot(s)	**Sugar syrup (2 sugar to 1 water)**

Origin: Adapted from a drink created in 2002 by Wayne Collins, UK.
Comment: A fruit-led long drink for gin-loving Bowie fans.

GIN GIN MULE [UPDATED #7]

Glass: Collins
Garnish: Lime wedge
Method: MUDDLE ginger in base of shaker. Add next four ingredients, **SHAKE** with ice and fine strain into ice-filled glass. **TOP** with ginger beer.

2	slices	**Fresh root ginger (thumbnail sized)**
2	shot(s)	**Plymouth gin**
½	shot(s)	**Freshly squeezed lime juice**
¼	shot(s)	**Sugar syrup (2 sugar to 1 water)**
3	dashes	**Angostura aromatic bitters**
Top up with		**Ginger beer**

Origin: Adapted from a drink created in 2004 by Audrey Saunders, New York City, USA.
Comment: Fresh ginger and the herbal notes from gin make this much more than another take on the Moscow Mule.

GIN PUNCH [NEW #7]

Glass: Collins
Garnish: Lemon slice
Method: SHAKE all ingredients with ice and fine strain into chilled glass.

2	shot(s)	**Plymouth gin**
¾	shot(s)	**Freshly squeezed lemon juice**
¾	shot(s)	**Sugar syrup (2 sugar to 1 water)**
2	shot(s)	**Chilled mineral water**
1	dash	**Angostura aromatic bitters**

Origin: This is a version of the drink for which Limmer's Hotel in London was most famed: a Captain Gronow recalled it in his 1860s memoirs as one of the top, if filthy and seedy, sporting hangouts of 1814, thanks in part to its 'famous gin-punch'. A bartender named John Collins worked there later in the 19th century, and was famous enough to inspire a limerick, so many believe he created the Collins, which is similar to gin punch, although the drink is not named in the rhyme.
Comment: Light and refreshing – akin to alcoholic real lemonade.

GIN SLING

Glass: Sling
Garnish: Lemon slice & cherry on stick (sail)
Method: SHAKE first three ingredients with ice and strain into ice-filled glass. **TOP** with soda water.

1½	shot(s)	**Plymouth gin**
1½	shot(s)	**Cherry (brandy) liqueur**
1	shot(s)	**Freshly squeezed lemon juice**
Top up with		**Soda water (club soda)**

Comment: Tangy cherry and gin.

'...ALL MY LIFE I'VE BEEN TERRIBLE AT REMEMBERING PEOPLE'S NAMES. I ONCE INTRODUCED A FRIEND OF MINE AS MARTINI. HER NAME WAS ACTUALLY OLIVE.'

TALLULAH BANKHEAD

GIN SOUR 

Glass: Old-fashioned
Garnish: Cherry & lemon slice on stick (sail)
Method: SHAKE all ingredients with ice and strain into ice-filled glass.

2	shot(s)	**Plymouth gin**
1	shot(s)	**Freshly squeezed lemon juice**
1/2	shot(s)	**Sugar syrup (2 sugar to 1 water)**
1/2	fresh	**Egg white**
3	dashes	**Angostura aromatic bitters**

Comment: The juniper flavours in gin work well in this classic sour.

GINA

Glass: Sling
Garnish: Berries on stick
Method: SHAKE first three ingredients with ice and strain into ice-filled glass. **TOP** with soda.

2	shot(s)	**Plymouth gin**
1/2	shot(s)	**Giffard crème de cassis**
1/2	shot(s)	**Freshly squeezed lemon juice**
Top up with		**Soda water (club soda)**

AKA: Cassis Collins
Comment: The lemon and blackcurrant mask the character of the gin.

GINGER & LEMONGRASS MARTINI

Glass: Martini
Garnish: Float thinly cut apple slice
Method: MUDDLE ginger and lemongrass in base of shaker. Add other ingredients and **STIR** until honey dissolves. **SHAKE** with ice and fine strain into chilled glass.

1	slice	**Fresh root ginger (thumbnail sized)**
1/2	stem	**Lemongrass (chopped)**
2	spoons	**Runny honey**
2	shot(s)	**Plymouth gin**
1/4	shot(s)	**Dry vermouth**
1/4	shot(s)	**Pressed apple juice**
3/4	shot(s)	**Chilled mineral water** (omit if wet ice)

Origin: Created in 2005 by yours truly.
Comment: Consider infusing the lemongrass in gin instead of muddling.

GIN-GER & TONIC

Glass: Collins
Garnish: Lime wedge
Method: MUDDLE ginger in base of shaker, add gin and sugar, **SHAKE** with ice and strain into ice-filled glass. **TOP** with tonic water.

2	slices	**Fresh root ginger (thumbnail sized)**
2	shot(s)	**Plymouth gin**
1/4	shot(s)	**Sugar syrup (2 sugar to 1 water)**
Top up with		**Tonic water**

Comment: A dry, refreshing long drink for those that like their G&Ts gingered.

GINGER COSMO

Glass: Martini
Garnish: Slice of ginger on rim
Method: SHAKE all ingredients with ice and fine strain into chilled glass.

2	shot(s)	**Ketel One Citroen vodka**
3/4	shot(s)	**Giffard Ginger of the Indies**
1 1/4	shot(s)	**Ocean Spray cranberry juice**
1/4	shot(s)	**Freshly squeezed lime juice**
1/8	shot(s)	**Sugar syrup (2 sugar to 1 water)**

Origin: Emerged during 2002 in New York City.
Comment: Just what it says on the tin – your everyday Cosmo given extra vitality courtesy of a hint of ginger spice.

GINGER COSMOS

Glass: Collins
Garnish: Basil leaf
Method: MUDDLE ginger and basil in base of shaker. Add other ingredients, **SHAKE** with ice and fine strain into glass filled with crushed ice. Stir and serve with straws.

2	slices	**Fresh root ginger (thumbnail sized)**
5	fresh	**Basil leaves**
2	shot(s)	**Plymouth gin**
1 1/2	shot(s)	**Pressed pineapple juice**
1 1/2	shot(s)	**Pressed apple juice**
1/4	shot(s)	**Freshly squeezed lime juice**
1/4	shot(s)	**Sugar syrup (2 sugar to 1 water)**

Origin: Created in 2003 by Massimiliano Greco at Zander, London, England. 'Cosmos' is a reference to the botanical name for pineapple, Ananas comosus.
Comment: Warming ginger spice in a very cooling, fruity drink.

GINGER MARGARITA

Glass: Coupette
Garnish: Lime wedge on rim
Method: SHAKE all ingredients with ice and fine strain into chilled glass.

2	shot(s)	**Partida tequila**
1	shot(s)	**Giffard Ginger of the Indies**
1	shot(s)	**Freshly squeezed lime juice**

Comment: A Margarita spiced with ginger.

GINGER MARTINI

Glass: Martini
Garnish: Brandy snap biscuit
Method: MUDDLE ginger in base of shaker. Add other ingredients, **SHAKE** with ice and fine strain into chilled glass.

2	slices	**Fresh root ginger (thumbnail sized)**
2	shot(s)	**Ketel One vodka**
3/4	shot(s)	**Stone's green ginger wine**
3/4	shot(s)	**Pressed apple juice**
1/2	shot(s)	**Freshly squeezed lime juice**
1/4	shot(s)	**Sugar syrup (2 sugar to 1 water)**

Origin: Discovered in 2003 at Hurricane Bar and Grill, Edinburgh, Scotland.
Comment: This Martini may be served chilled but its flavour is distinctly warming.

GINGER MOJITO

Glass: Collins
Garnish: Mint sprig
Method: MUDDLE ginger in base of shaker. Add mint and lightly **MUDDLE** (just to bruise). Add next three ingredients, **SHAKE** with ice and fine strain into glass filled with crushed ice. **TOP** with ginger ale.

- 3 slices **Fresh root ginger (thumbnail sized)**
- 12 fresh **Mint leaves**
- 2 shot(s) **Light white rum**
- $\frac{1}{2}$ shot(s) **Freshly squeezed lime juice**
- $\frac{1}{2}$ shot(s) **Sugar syrup (2 sugar to 1 water)**
- Top up with **Ginger ale**

Comment: A spiced variation on the classic Mojito.

GINGER NUT

Glass: Collins
Garnish: Lemon wedge
Method: POUR ingredients into ice-filled glass and stir.

- $1\frac{1}{2}$ shot(s) **Frangelico hazelnut liqueur**
- $1\frac{1}{2}$ shot(s) **Ketel One Citroen vodka**
- Top up with **Ginger beer**

Comment: A long, refreshing meld of strong flavours.

GINGER PUNCH

Glass: Collins
Garnish: Lime wedge
Method: MUDDLE ginger in base of shaker. Add honey and rum and **STIR** until honey is dissolved. Add lime juice and sugar, **SHAKE** with ice and fine strain into ice-filled glass. **TOP** with ginger ale.

- 2 slices **Fresh root ginger (thumbnail sized)**
- 2 spoons **Runny honey**
- $2\frac{1}{2}$ shot(s) **Golden rum**
- $\frac{3}{4}$ shot(s) **Freshly squeezed lime juice**
- $\frac{1}{4}$ shot(s) **Sugar syrup (2 sugar to 1 water)**
- Top up with **Ginger ale**

Comment: A ginger spiced rum punch.

GIN-GER TOM

Glass: Collins
Garnish: Lime squeeze & mint sprig
Method: MUDDLE ginger in base of shaker. Add other ingredients, **SHAKE** with ice and fine strain into ice-filled glass.

- 2 slices **Fresh root ginger (thumbnail sized)**
- 2 shot(s) **Plymouth gin**
- 1 shot(s) **Freshly squeezed lime juice**
- $\frac{1}{2}$ shot(s) **Sugar syrup (2 sugar to 1 water)**
- Top up with **Soda water (club soda)**

Origin: Adapted from a drink created in 2003 by Jamie Terrell at Lab, London, England.
Comment: A Tom Collins with lime and ginger – very refreshing.

GINGERBREAD MARTINI

Glass: Martini
Garnish: Slice of root ginger
Method: SHAKE all ingredients with ice and fine strain into chilled glass.

- $1\frac{1}{2}$ shot(s) **Buffalo Trace bourbon whiskey**
- $\frac{3}{4}$ shot(s) **Teichenné butterscotch Schnapps**
- $\frac{3}{4}$ shot(s) **Stone's green ginger wine**
- 2 shot(s) **Pressed apple juice**

Origin: Created by yours truly in 2004.
Comment: Sticky, warming and spicy.

GINGERTINI

Glass: Martini
Garnish: Orange zest twist
Method: SHAKE all ingredients with ice and fine strain into chilled glass.

- 2 shot(s) **Plymouth gin**
- $\frac{1}{2}$ shot(s) **Giffard Ginger of the Indies**
- $\frac{1}{4}$ shot(s) **Dry vermouth**
- $\frac{1}{4}$ shot(s) **Sugar syrup (2 sugar to 1 water)**
- $\frac{1}{2}$ shot(s) **Chilled mineral water** (omit if wet ice)

Origin: Created by yours truly in 2002.
Comment: A delicate Martini with a warming hint of ginger.

GIUSEPPE'S HABIT

Glass: Martini
Garnish: Star anise
Method: Spray the oils from two lemon zest twists into the cocktail shaker, wipe them around the rim of the glass and drop them into the shaker. Pour other ingredients into shaker. **SHAKE** with ice and fine strain into chilled glass.

- 2 twists **Lemon zest**
- $1\frac{1}{2}$ shot(s) **Galliano liqueur**
- $\frac{3}{4}$ shot(s) **Frangelico hazelnut liqueur**
- $\frac{3}{4}$ shot(s) **Cointreau triple sec**
- $1\frac{1}{4}$ shot(s) **Pressed apple juice**

Origin: Created in 2002 by Leon Stokes at Zinc Bar & Grill, Birmingham, England.
Comment: An intriguing drink that combines hazelnut, orange, apple, aniseed and peppermint.

GIVE ME A DIME

Glass: Martini
Garnish: Crumbled Cadbury's Flake bar
Method: SHAKE all ingredients with ice and fine strain into chilled glass.

- $1\frac{1}{2}$ shot(s) **Giffard white crème de cacao**
- $1\frac{1}{2}$ shot(s) **Teichenné butterscotch Schnapps**
- $1\frac{1}{2}$ shot(s) **Double (heavy) cream**

Comment: Creamy, sweet and tasty.

GLAD EYE COCKTAIL [NEW #7]

Glass: Martini
Garnish: Star anise
Method: SHAKE all ingredients with ice and fine strain into chilled glass.

1 1/2	shot(s)	**La Feé Parisienne (68%) absinthe**
1	shot(s)	**Giffard white crème de Menthe Pastille**
1	shot(s)	**Chilled mineral water (reduce if wet ice)**

Origin: Adapted from Harry Craddock's 1930 'The Savoy Cocktail Book'.
Comment: This minty aniseed cocktail takes more than its colour from the green fairy.

GLASS TOWER

Glass: Collins
Method: SHAKE first five ingredients with ice and strain into ice-filled glass. **TOP** with 7-Up and stir.

1	shot(s)	**Ketel One vodka**
1	shot(s)	**Light white rum**
1/2	shot(s)	**Cointreau triple sec**
1/2	shot(s)	**Teichenné Peach Schnapps Liqueur**
1/4	shot(s)	**Luxardo Sambuca dei Cesari**
Top up with		**7-Up or lemonade**

Comment: A heady, slightly sweet combination of spirits and liqueurs.

GLENN'S BRIDE [NEW #7]

Glass: Martini
Garnish: Orange zest twist
Method: SHAKE all ingredients with ice and fine strain into chilled glass.

2	shot(s)	**Buffalo Trace bourbon whiskey**
1	shot(s)	**St-Germain elderflower liqueur**
2	dashes	**Angostura aromatic bitters**
1/4	shot(s)	**Rosewater**

Origin: Adapted from a drink created in 2005 by Julian Gibbs, England.
Comment: This serious, bourbon based cocktail ranks alongside the Sazerac in its aromatic complexity.

GLOOM CHASER COCKTAIL #1 [UPDATED #7]

Glass: Martini
Garnish: Orange zest twist
Method: SHAKE all ingredients with ice and fine strain into chilled glass.

3/4	shot(s)	**Grand Marnier liqueur**
3/4	shot(s)	**Cointreau triple sec**
1	shot(s)	**Freshly squeezed lemon juice**
1/4	shot(s)	**Pomegranate (grenadine) syrup**
1	shot(s)	**Chilled mineral water** (reduce if wet ice)

Origin: Adapted from Harry Craddock's 1930 'The Savoy Cocktail Book'.
Comment: A sunny coloured drink for happy souls. And sweet orange and pomegranate soured with lemon would make anyone happy.

GLOOM CHASER COCKTAIL #2 [NEW #7]

Glass: Martini
Garnish: Berries on stick
Method: SHAKE all ingredients with ice and fine strain into chilled glass.

2	shot(s)	**Plymouth gin**
1	shot(s)	**Dry vermouth**
1/2	shot(s)	**La Feé Parisienne (68%) absinthe**
1/4	shot(s)	**Pomegranate (grenadine) syrup**
1/2	shot(s)	**Chilled mineral water** (omit if wet ice)

Origin: Adapted from David A. Embury's 1948 'Fine Art of Mixing Drinks'.
Comment: A little absinthe goes a long way and may even chase your gloom away.

GLOOM LIFTER

Glass: Martini
Garnish: Lime wedge
Method: SHAKE all ingredients with ice and fine strain into chilled glass.

1 1/2	shot(s)	**Irish whiskey**
1/2	shot(s)	**Rémy Martin cognac**
1	shot(s)	**Freshly squeezed lime juice**
1/4	shot(s)	**Pomegranate (grenadine) syrup**
1/4	shot(s)	**Sugar syrup (2 sugar to 1 water)**
1/2	fresh	**Egg white**

Comment: A whiskey and cognac sour with lime juice served straight-up.

GLORIA [NEW #7]

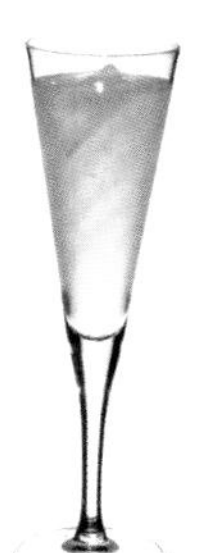

Glass: Flute
Garnish: Lemon zest twist
Method: SHAKE first three ingredients with ice and fine strain into chilled glass. **TOP** with champagne.

1	shot(s)	**Partida tequila**
1/2	shot(s)	**Freshly squeezed lemon juice**
1/2	shot(s)	**Sugar syrup (2 sugar to 1 water)**

Top up with Brut champagne
Comment: A tequila sour topped with champagne or a tequila French 75.

GODFATHER

Glass: Old-fashioned
Method: STIR all ingredients with ice and strain into ice-filled glass.

2	shot(s)	**Scotch whisky**
1	shot(s)	**Luxardo Amaretto di Saschira**

Variant: Based on vodka, this drink becomes a Godmother and when made with cognac it's known as a Godchild.
Comment: Scotch diluted and sweetened with almond – simple but good.

GODFREY

Glass: Old-fashioned
Garnish: Three blackberries on drink
Method: MUDDLE blackberries in base of shaker. Add other ingredients, **SHAKE** with ice and fine strain into glass filled with crushed ice.

6	fresh	**Blackberries**
1½	shot(s)	**Rémy Martin cognac**
½	shot(s)	**Grand Marnier liqueur**
¼	shot(s)	**Giffard mûre (blackberry)**
¼	shot(s)	**Freshly squeezed lemon juice**
¼	shot(s)	**Sugar syrup (2 sugar to 1 water)**

Origin: Created by Salvatore Calabrese at the Library Bar, Lanesborough Hotel, London, England.
Comment: Well balanced with a rich blackberry flavour.

'A REAL HANGOVER IS NOTHING TO TRY OUT FAMILY REMEDIES ON. THE ONLY CURE FOR A REAL HANGOVER IS DEATH.'
ROBERT BENCHLEY

GOLD

Glass: Martini
Garnish: Orange zest twist
Method: SHAKE all ingredients with ice and fine strain into chilled glass.

1½	shot(s)	**Scotch whisky**
1	shot(s)	**Cointreau triple sec**
1	shot(s)	**Crème de bananes**
¾	shot(s)	**Chilled mineral water** (omit if wet ice)

Comment: Sweet, ripe banana, Scotch and a hint of orange.

GOLD MEDALLION

Glass: Martini
Garnish: Flamed orange zest
Method: SHAKE all ingredients with ice and fine strain into chilled glass.

1½	shot(s)	**Rémy Martin cognac**
1	shot(s)	**Galliano liqueur**
1½	shot(s)	**Freshly squeezed orange juice**
¼	shot(s)	**Freshly squeezed lime juice**
½	fresh	**Egg white (optional)**

Comment: Gold by name and golden in colour. Frothy, orange fresh and cognac based.

GOLD MEMBER

Glass: Martini
Garnish: Apple slice
Method: SHAKE all ingredients with ice and fine strain into chilled glass.

¾	shot(s)	**Cinnamon schnapps liqueur**
¾	shot(s)	**Teichenné butterscotch Schnapps**
¾	shot(s)	**Apple schnapps liqueur**
2¼	shot(s)	**Pressed apple juice**

Comment: Hints of cinnamon and apple – an interesting tipple, if a tad sweet.

GOLD RUSH SLAMMER

Glass: Shot
Method: SHAKE first two ingredients with ice and fine strain into chilled glass. **TOP** with champagne.

½	shot(s)	**Cinnamon schnapps liqueur**
½	shot(s)	**Partida tequila**
Top up with		**Brut champagne**

Origin: Discovered in 2003 at Oxo Tower Bar, London, England.
Comment: Flakes of gold dance with the champagne's bubbles.

GOLDEN BIRD

Glass: Martini
Garnish: Orange beak on rim
Method: SHAKE all ingredients with ice and fine strain into chilled glass.

1	shot(s)	**Light white rum**
1	shot(s)	**Grand Marnier liqueur**
½	shot(s)	**Crème de bananes**
1½	shot(s)	**Freshly squeezed orange juice**
1	shot(s)	**Pressed pineapple juice**

Comment: Fruity and sweet – an after dinner cocktail.

GOLDEN CADILLAC

Glass: Martini
Garnish: Dust with freshly ground nutmeg
Method: SHAKE all ingredients with ice and fine strain into chilled glass.

1	shot(s)	**Giffard white crème de cacao**
½	shot(s)	**Galliano liqueur**
1½	shot(s)	**Freshly squeezed orange juice**
½	shot(s)	**Double (heavy) cream**
½	shot(s)	**Milk**
2	dashes	**Fee Brothers orange bitters**

Origin: Adapted from a drink reputedly created in the late sixties at Poor Red's, a barbecue joint favoured by 'sportbike pilots' in El Dorado, California.
Comment: A silky smooth but not very potent cocktail.

GOLDEN DAWN [UPDATED #7]

Glass: Martini
Garnish: Orange zest twist
Method: SHAKE first five ingredients with ice and fine strain into chilled glass. Carefully **POUR** grenadine into centre of drink so that it sinks to create a sunrise effect.

3/4	shot(s)	**Plymouth gin**
1	shot(s)	**Boulard Grand Solage Calvados**
1	shot(s)	**Giffard apricot brandy du Roussillon**
1	shot(s)	**Freshly squeezed orange juice**
2	dashes	**Angostura aromatic bitters**
1/8	shot(s)	**Pomegranate (grenadine) syrup**

Origin: Created in September 1930 by Tom Buttery at the Berkeley Hotel, London, England. There are now many versions of this classic drink (David Embury's 'The Fine Art of Mixing Drinks' lists three) but this is my favourite.
Comment: Although it spoils the sunrise effect, this drink is less tart if the syrup lying on the bottom is stirred into the drink (or, better, included when shaking).

GOLDEN DRAGON

Glass: Collins
Garnish: Green apple wedge
Method: SHAKE all ingredients with ice and strain into ice-filled glass.

2	shot(s)	**Partida tequila**
3/4	shot(s)	**Pisang Ambon liqueur**
2	shot(s)	**Pressed apple juice**
1	shot(s)	**Freshly squeezed lime juice**
1/2	shot(s)	**Passion fruit sugar syrup**

Comment: Bright green, tangy and tropical.

GOLDEN DREAM

Glass: Martini
Garnish: Sponge biscuit on rim
Method: SHAKE all ingredients with ice and fine strain into chilled glass.

1	shot(s)	**Cointreau triple sec**
1	shot(s)	**Galliano liqueur**
2	shot(s)	**Freshly squeezed orange juice**
1	shot(s)	**Double (heavy) cream**

Comment: Tastes remarkably like syllabub.

GOLDEN FIZZ #1

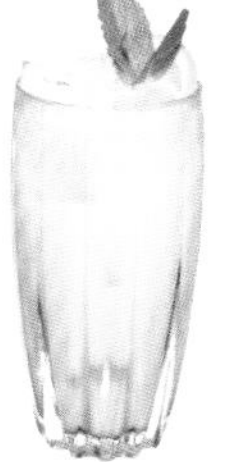

Glass: Collins (8oz max)
Garnish: Lemon slice & mint
Method: SHAKE first four ingredients with ice and fine strain into chilled glass. **TOP** with soda.

2	shot(s)	**Plymouth gin**
1	shot(s)	**Freshly squeezed lemon juice**
1/2	shot(s)	**Sugar syrup (2 sugar to 1 water)**
1	fresh	**Egg yolk**
Top up with		**Soda water (from siphon)**

Variant: Gin Fizz
Origin: Mid-19th century classic.
Comment: You may have some raw egg inhibitions to conquer before you can enjoy this drink.

GOLDEN FIZZ #2

Glass: Collins
Garnish: Orange slice/mint sprig
Method: STIR honey with gin in base of shaker until honey dissolves. Add next three ingredients, **SHAKE** with ice and strain into ice-filled glass. **TOP** with 7-Up.

2	spoons	**Runny honey**
1 1/2	shot(s)	**Plymouth gin**
1	shot(s)	**Cointreau triple sec**
1	shot(s)	**Freshly squeezed golden grapefruit juice**
1/4	shot(s)	**Freshly squeezed lemon juice**
Top up with		**7-Up / lemonade**

Origin: Adapted from a drink created by Wayne Collins, UK.
Comment: More cloudy white than golden but a pleasant, refreshing long drink all the same.

GOLDEN GIRL

Glass: Martini
Garnish: Grated orange zest
Method: SHAKE all ingredients with ice and fine strain into chilled glass.

1 1/4	shot(s)	**Aged rum**
1	shot(s)	**Pressed pineapple juice**
1	shot(s)	**Tawny port**
1/4	shot(s)	**Sugar syrup (2 sugar to 1 water)**
1	fresh	**Egg**

Origin: Created by Dale DeGroff, New York City, USA. I've slightly increased the proportions of rum and port from Dale's original recipe.
Comment: This appropriately named velvety drink is a refined dessert in a glass.

How to make sugar syrup

To make your own sugar syrup, gradually pour TWO cups of granulated sugar into a saucepan containing ONE cup of hot water. Stir as you pour and carry on stirring and simmering until the sugar is dissolved. Do not let the water even come close to boiling and only simmer for as long as it takes to dissolve the sugar. Allow syrup to cool and pour into an empty bottle. Ideally, you should finely strain your syrup into the bottle to remove any undissolved crystals which could otherwise encourage crystallisation. If kept in a refrigerator this mixture will last for a couple of months.

GOLDEN MAC

Glass: Old-fashioned
Garnish: Orange zest twist
Method: MUDDLE ginger in base of shaker. Add honey and Scotch and **STIR** until honey dissolves. Add other ingredients, **SHAKE** with ice and fine strain into ice-filled glass.

2	slices	**Fresh root ginger (thumbnail sized)**
2	spoons	**Runny honey**
2	shot(s)	**Scotch whisky**
1/4	shot(s)	**Teichenné butterscotch Schnapps**
1/4	shot(s)	**Frangelico hazelnut liqueur**

Origin: Adapted from a drink discovered in 2003 at Golden Mac, Glasgow, Scotland.
Comment: Looks, and even tastes golden.

GOLDEN NAIL

Glass: Old-fashioned
Garnish: Orange zest twist
Method: STIR all ingredients with ice and strain into ice-filled glass.

1 1/2	shot(s)	**Buffalo Trace bourbon whiskey**
3/4	shot(s)	**Southern Comfort liqueur**
2	dashes	**Peychaud's aromatic bitters**

Comment: A warming taste of southern hospitality.

GOLDEN RETRIEVER

Glass: Martini
Garnish: Orange zest twist
Method: STIR all ingredients with ice and strain into chilled glass.

1	shot(s)	**Light white rum**
1	shot(s)	**Green Chartreuse liqueur**
1	shot(s)	**Licor 43 (Cuarenta Y Tres) liqueur**
1	shot(s)	**Chilled mineral water** (omit if wet ice)

Origin: Created in 2002 by Dick Bradsell at Alfred's, London, England.
Comment: The simple drinks are the best and this straw yellow cocktail subtly offers a myriad of flavours.

GOLDEN SCREW

Glass: Flute
Garnish: Physalis fruit
Method: POUR all ingredients into chilled glass and lightly stir.

1/2	shot(s)	**Rémy Martin cognac**
1/2	shot(s)	**Giffard apricot brandy du Roussillon**
1	shot(s)	**Freshly squeezed orange juice**
Top up with		**Brut champagne**

Variant: With gin in place of brandy.
Comment: A favourite with Midas and others whose budgets extend beyond a Buck's Fizz or a Mimosa.

GOLDEN SHOT

Glass: Shot
Method: Refrigerate ingredients then **LAYER** in chilled glass by carefully pouring in the following order.

1/2	shot(s)	**Drambuie liqueur**
1/2	shot(s)	**Irish cream liqueur**
1/2	shot(s)	**Scotch whisky**

Comment: A whiskey based layered shot with plenty of character.

GOLDEN SLIPPER

Glass: Martini
Garnish: Apricot slice on rim
Method: SHAKE all ingredients with ice and fine strain into chilled glass.

1 1/2	shot(s)	**Yellow Chartreuse liqueur**
1 1/2	shot(s)	**Giffard apricot brandy du Roussillon**
1	fresh	**Egg yolk**

Comment: Rich in colour and equally rich in flavour. A dessert with a punch.

GOLDEN WAVE [UPDATED #7]

Glass: Old-fashioned
Garnish: Pineapple wedge
Method: BLEND all ingredients with a 6oz scoop of crushed ice and serve with straws.

1	shot(s)	**Light white rum**
1/2	shot(s)	**Cointreau triple sec**
1/2	shot(s)	**Velvet Falernum**
1	shot(s)	**Pressed pineapple juice**
3/4	shot(s)	**Freshly squeezed lemon juice**

Origin: A Tiki drink created in 1969 by Jose 'Joe' Yatco at China Trader, California, USA.
Comment: Rum laced fruit served frozen.

GOLF COCKTAIL

Glass: Martini
Garnish: Orange zest twist
Method: STIR all ingredients with ice and strain into chilled glass.

2	shot(s)	**Plymouth gin**
1	shot(s)	**Dry vermouth**
1	dash	**Angostura aromatic bitters**

Comment: A 'wet' Martini with bitters.

GOOMBAY SMASH [UPDATED #7]

Glass: Collins
Garnish: Lime wedge
Method: **SHAKE** all ingredients with ice and strain into ice filled glass.

2	shot(s)	**Pusser's Navy rum**
3/4	shot(s)	**Malibu coconut rum liqueur**
3	shot(s)	**Pressed pineapple juice**
1/4	shot(s)	**Freshly squeezed lime juice**
1/2	shot(s)	**Cointreau triple sec**

Origin: The Goombay Smash is a speciality of Miss Emily's Blue Bee Bar in the Bahamas. Mrs Emily Cooper is now deceased but her daughter, Violet Smith, presides over her secret recipe.
Comment: Smashes are usually short drinks that include muddled mint, but this potent Tiki-style drink features rum, coconut and fruit.

GRAND COSMOPOLITAN

Glass: Martini
Garnish: Flamed orange zest twist
Method: **SHAKE** all ingredients with ice and fine strain into chilled glass.

1	shot(s)	**Ketel One Citroen vodka**
1	shot(s)	**Grand Marnier liqueur**
1 1/2	shot(s)	**Ocean Spray cranberry juice**
3/4	shot(s)	**Freshly squeezed lime juice**
2	dashes	**Fee Brothers orange bitters (optional)**

Comment: A 'grand' Cosmo indeed.

LE GRAND FEU [NEW #7]

Glass: Martini
Garnish: Mint sprig
Method: **SHAKE** all ingredients with ice and fine strain into chilled glass.

1 1/2	shot(s)	**Rémy Martin cognac**
1 1/2	shot(s)	**Vanilla liqueur**
1/2	shot(s)	**Irish Cream liqueur**
3/4	shot(s)	**Cold chai tea**

Origin: Adapted from a recipe by Tony Venci, La Femme Bar, MGM Grand Hotel, Las Vegas, USA.
Comment: Cognac smoothed with vanilla and cream, spiced with chai tea.

GRAND MARGARITA

Glass: Coupette
Garnish: Salt rim & lime wedge
Method: **SHAKE** all ingredients with ice and fine strain into chilled glass.

2	shot(s)	**Partida tequila**
1	shot(s)	**Grand Marnier liqueur**
1	shot(s)	**Freshly squeezed lime juice**

Comment: A wonderfully balanced and flavoursome Margarita that's far removed from those sweet disco drinks often peddled as Margaritas.

GRAND MIMOSA

Glass: Flute
Garnish: Strawberry on rim
Method: **SHAKE** first two ingredients with ice and strain into chilled glass. **TOP** with champagne.

1	shot(s)	**Grand Marnier liqueur**
2	shot(s)	**Freshly squeezed orange juice**
Top up with		**Brut champagne**

Origin: The Mimosa was created in 1925 at the Ritz Hotel, Paris, and named after the Mimosa plant - probably because of its trembling leaves, rather like the gentle fizz of this mixture. The Grand Mimosa as shown here benefits from the addition of Grand Marnier liqueur.
Comment: As the name suggests, the orange of Grand Marnier heavily influences this drink. Basically a Buck's Fizz with more oomph.

GRAND PASSION [UPDATED #7]

Glass: Martini
Garnish: Float half passion fruit
Method: Cut passion fruits in half and scoop flesh into shaker. Add other ingredients, **SHAKE** with ice and fine strain into chilled glass.

1	fresh	**Passion fruit**
2	shot(s)	**Light white rum**
1	shot(s)	**Pressed apple juice**
1/2	shot(s)	**Sugar syrup (2 sugar to 1 water)**
3	dashes	**Angostura aromatic bitters**
1/2	fresh	**Egg white**

Comment: Are you lacking passion in your life? There's plenty in this fruity little number.

'VODKA IS OUR ENEMY, SO LET'S FINISH IT OFF.'

GRAND SAZERAC

Glass: Old-fashioned
Method: **POUR** absinthe into ice-filled glass and **TOP** with water. Leave the mixture to stand in the glass. Separately, **SHAKE** liqueur, bourbon and bitters with ice. Finally discard contents of absinthe-coated glass and fine strain contents of shaker into absinthe washed glass. (Note that there is no ice in the finished drink.)

1/2	shot(s)	**La Fée Parisienne (68%) absinthe**
Top up with		**Chilled mineral water**
1 1/2	shot(s)	**Grand Marnier liqueur**
1 1/2	shot(s)	**Buffalo Trace bourbon whiskey**
2	dashes	**Angostura aromatic bitters**
3	dashes	**Peychaud's aromatic bitters**

Origin: Created in 2004 by yours truly.
Comment: An orange twist on the classic Sazerac.

GRAND SIDECAR

Glass: Martini
Garnish: Orange zest twist
Method: SHAKE all ingredients with ice and fine strain into chilled glass.

2 1/2	shot(s)	**Grand Marnier liqueur**
1	shot(s)	**Freshly squeezed lemon juice**
1/2	shot(s)	**Chilled mineral water** (omit if wet ice)

Origin: Created by yours truly in June 2005.
Comment: A twist on the classic, simple but very tasty. Also works well shaken and strained into an ice-filled old-fashioned glass.

GRAPE DELIGHT

Glass: Martini
Garnish: Grapes on stick
Method: MUDDLE grapes in base of shaker. Add rest of ingredients, **SHAKE** with ice and fine strain into chilled glass.

12	fresh	**Seedless red grapes**
2	shot(s)	**Plymouth gin**
1/2	shot(s)	**Plymouth sloe gin**
1/2	shot(s)	**Pressed apple juice**
1/4	shot(s)	**Sugar syrup (2 sugar to 1 water)**
1/4	shot(s)	**Freshly squeezed lime juice**
1	dash	**Angostura aromatic bitters**

Comment: This rust coloured drink is fruity and delicate.

G

GRANDE CHAMPAGNE COSMO

Glass: Martini
Garnish: Flamed orange zest twist
Method: SHAKE all ingredients with ice and fine strain into chilled glass.

1 1/2	shot(s)	**Rémy Martin cognac**
3/4	shot(s)	**Grand Marnier liqueur**
1/2	shot(s)	**Freshly squeezed lemon juice**
1	shot(s)	**Ocean Spray cranberry juice**
1/2	fresh	**Egg white**

Comment: 'Grande Champagne' refers to the top cru of the Cognac region: this drink is suitably elite.

GRAPE EFFECT [UPDATED #7]

Glass: Martini
Garnish: Grapes on stick
Method: MUDDLE grapes in base of shaker. Add other ingredients, **SHAKE** with ice and fine strain into chilled glass.

12	fresh	**Seedless white grapes**
2	shot(s)	**Light white rum**
1	shot(s)	**St-Germain liqueur**

Comment: Delicately flavoured but heavily laced with rum.

GRANNY'S

Glass: Martini
Garnish: Apple wedge on rim
Method: SHAKE all ingredients with ice and fine strain into chilled glass.

1 3/4	shot(s)	**Light white rum**
1/4	shot(s)	**Cinnamon schnapps liqueur**
1/2	shot(s)	**Apple schnapps liqueur**
1 1/2	shot(s)	**Pressed apple juice**

Comment: Apple, rum and cinnamon were made for each other.

GRAPE ESCAPE

Glass: Collins
Garnish: Mint sprig
Method: MUDDLE grapes and mint in base of shaker. Add cognac and sugar, **SHAKE** with ice and strain into glass filled with crushed ice. **TOP** with champagne, stir and serve with straws.

8	fresh	**Seedless white grapes**
5	fresh	**Mint leaves**
2	shot(s)	**Rémy Martin cognac**
1/2	shot(s)	**Sugar syrup (2 sugar to 1 water)**
Top up with		**Brut champagne**

Origin: Created in 2000 by Brian Lucas and Max Warner at Long Bar @ Sanderson, London, England.
Comment: A cracking drink – subtle and refreshing.

GRANNY'S MARTINI

Glass: Martini
Garnish: Dust with ground nutmeg
Method: SHAKE all ingredients with ice and fine strain into chilled glass.

1	shot(s)	**Plymouth gin**
1/2	shot(s)	**Tio Pepe fino sherry**
2	shot(s)	**Bols advocaat liqueur**

Origin: I have to own up to creating and naming this drink after three drink categories often identified with a stereotypical English granny. Sorry, mum.
Comment: Creamy, Christmassy drink just for nana.

GRAPE MARTINI

Glass: Martini
Garnish: Grapes on stick
Method: MUDDLE grapes in base of shaker. Add other ingredients, **SHAKE** with ice and fine strain into chilled glass.

12	fresh	**Seedless white grapes**
2	shot(s)	**Ketel One vodka**
1/2	shot(s)	**Sugar syrup (2 sugar to 1 water)**

Origin: Formula by yours truly in 2004.
Comment: Simple but remarkably tasty.

GRAPEFRUIT DAIQUIRI

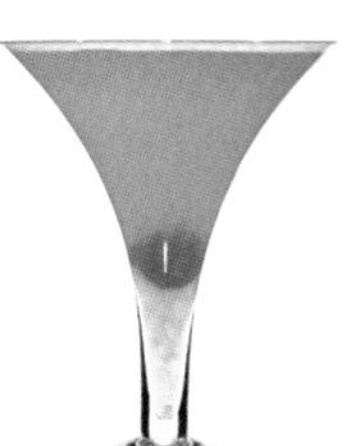

Glass: Martini
Garnish: Cherry
Method: **SHAKE** all ingredients with ice and fine strain into chilled glass.

2	shot(s)	**Aged rum**
1½	shot(s)	**Freshly squeezed grapefruit juice**
¾	shot(s)	**Sugar syrup (2 sugar to 1 water)**

Comment: The flavours of rum and grapefruit combine perfectly – clean and fresh.

GRAPEFRUIT JULEP

Glass: Collins
Garnish: Mint sprig
Method: **STIR** honey with vodka in base of shaker until honey dissolves. Add other ingredients, **SHAKE** with ice and strain into glass filled with crushed ice.

1	spoon	**Runny honey**
2	shot(s)	**Ketel One vodka**
4	fresh	**Mint leaves**
½	shot(s)	**Freshly squeezed lime juice**
½	shot(s)	**Pomegranate (grenadine) syrup**
¾	shot(s)	**Squeezed pink grapefruit juice**

Origin: Created by Dale DeGroff, New York City, USA.
Comment: Wonderfully refreshing. Bring on the sun.

GRAPPA MANHATTAN [UPDATED #7]

Glass: Martini
Garnish: Stemmed maraschino cherry
Method: **STIR** all ingredients with ice and strain into chilled glass.

2	shot(s)	**Grappa**
1	shot(s)	**Sweet vermouth**
¼	shot(s)	**Maraschino syrup (from jar)**
2	dashes	**Angostura aromatic bitters**

Comment: A great drink in which to appreciate modern style grappas, this remains very much a Manhattan.

GRAPPACCINO [NEW #7]

Glass: Martini
Garnish: Float 3 coffee beans
Method: **SHAKE** all ingredients with ice and fine strain into chilled glass.

2	shot(s)	**Grappa**
½	shot(s)	**Luxardo Amaretto di Saschira**
½	shot(s)	**Sugar syrup (2 sugar to 1 water)**
1	shot(s)	**Cold espresso coffee**

Origin: Adapted from a drink created in 2006 by George Sinclair.
Comment: The character of the grappa shines through and is complimented by the amaretto and coffee.

GRAPPARITA

Glass: Coupette
Garnish: Lime wedge on rim
Method: **SHAKE** all ingredients with ice and fine strain into chilled glass.

2	shot(s)	**Grappa**
1	shot(s)	**Luxardo Limoncello liqueur**
1	shot(s)	**Freshly squeezed lemon juice**
½	fresh	**Egg white**

Origin: Adapted from a drink discovered in 2005 at Alfredo's of Rome, New York City, USA. The original called for sour mix.
Comment: Grappa replaces tequila and lemon liqueur triple sec in this Italian twist on the classic Margarita.

'LET US DRINK FOR THE REPLENISHMENT OF OUR STRENGTH, NOT FOR OUR SORROW.'

GRAPPLE MARTINI

Glass: Martini
Garnish: Grapes on stick
Method: **MUDDLE** grapes in base of shaker. Add other ingredients, **SHAKE** with ice and fine strain into chilled glass.

7	fresh	**Seedless white grapes**
2	shot(s)	**Ketel One vodka**
¾	shot(s)	**Sauvignon Blanc or unoaked Chardonnay wine**
1	shot(s)	**Pressed apple juice**
¼	shot(s)	**Sugar syrup (2 sugar to 1 water)**

Origin: Adapted from a recipe created in 2003 by Chris Setchell at Las Iguanas, UK.
Comment: A rounded, fruity Martini-style drink.

GRASSHOPPER [NEW #7]

Glass: Martini
Garnish: Mint leaf
Method: **SHAKE** all ingredients with ice and fine strain into chilled glass.

1	shot(s)	**Giffard green crème de menthe**
1	shot(s)	**Giffard white crème de cacao**
1	shot(s)	**Double (heavy) cream**
1	shot(s)	**Milk**

Origin: Created at Tujague's, the second oldest restaurant in New Orleans, which was opened in 1856 by Guillaume Tujague. Some time before he died in 1912, Guillaume sold the restaurant to Philibert Guichet, who won second prize in a prestigious New York cocktail competition for this drink.
Comment: It's hard not to like this creamy, minty after dinner treat.

GRASSY FINNISH

Glass: Martini
Garnish: Lemongrass
Method: MUDDLE lemongrass in base of shaker. Add other ingredients, **SHAKE** with ice and fine strain into chilled glass.

1	stem	**Fresh lemongrass (chopped)**
2	shot(s)	**Lime flavoured vodka**
1	shot(s)	**Krupnik honey liqueur**
1/4	shot(s)	**Sugar syrup (2 sugar to 1 water)**

Origin: Created in 2003 by Gerard McCurry at Revolution, UK.
Comment: Like Finland, this drink is clean, green, wooded and safe, but deep down there's plenty of spice.

GRATEFUL DEAD

Glass: Sling
Garnish: Lime wedge
Method: SHAKE first seven ingredients with ice and strain into ice-filled glass. **TOP** with soda and serve with straws.

1/2	shot(s)	**Ketel One vodka**
1/2	shot(s)	**Plymouth gin**
1/2	shot(s)	**Light white rum**
1/2	shot(s)	**Cointreau triple sec**
1/2	shot(s)	**Midori melon liqueur**
1	shot(s)	**Freshly squeezed lime juice**
1/2	shot(s)	**Sugar syrup (2 sugar to 1 water)**
Top up with		**Soda water (club soda)**

Origin: LA Iced Tea with Midori in place of Chambord liqueur.
Comment: Don't be put off by the lime green colour. This fruity, sweet 'n' sour drink is actually quite pleasant.

GREAT MUGHAL MARTINI

Glass: Martini
Garnish: Lemon zest twist
Method: MUDDLE raisins in base of shaker. Add other ingredients, **SHAKE** with ice and fine strain into chilled glass.

20		**Raisins**
1 1/2	shot(s)	**Buffalo Trace bourbon whiskey**
1/4	shot(s)	**Sugar syrup (2 sugar to 1 water)**
3/4	shot(s)	**Passion fruit sugar syrup**
1/4	shot(s)	**Freshly squeezed lime juice**
3	drops	**Rosewater**
1	shot(s)	**Lime & lemongrass cordial**

Origin: Created in 2001 by Douglas Ankrah for Red Fort, Soho, London, England.
Comment: Douglas' original recipe called for raisin infused bourbon and I'd recommend you make this drink that way if time permits.

GREEN APPLE & CUCUMBER MARTINI

Glass: Martini
Garnish: Float three cucumber slices
Method: MUDDLE cucumber in base of shaker. Add other ingredients, **SHAKE** with ice and fine strain into chilled glass.

1	inch	**Chopped peeled cucumber**
2	shot(s)	**Cucumber flavoured vodka**
1/2	shot(s)	**Sour apple liqueur**
1/2	shot(s)	**Pressed apple juice**
1/8	shot(s)	**Sugar syrup (2 sugar to 1 water)**

Origin: Adapted from a recipe discovered in 2003 at Oxo Tower Bar, London, England.
Comment: Archetypal English flavours. Clean, green and refreshing.

GREEN DESTINY

Glass: Old-fashioned
Garnish: Kiwi slice
Method: MUDDLE cucumber and kiwi in base of shaker. Add other ingredients, **SHAKE** with ice and fine strain into glass filled with crushed ice.

1	inch	**Chopped peeled cucumber**
1/2	fresh	**Kiwi fruit**
2	shot(s)	**Zubrówka bison vodka**
1 1/2	shot(s)	**Pressed apple juice**
1/4	shot(s)	**Sugar syrup (2 sugar to 1 water)**

Origin: Created in 2001 by Andrew Tounos @ Hakk, Warsaw, Poland.
Comment: Looks green and even tastes green, but pleasantly so.

GREEN DRAGON [NEW #7]

Glass: Martini
Garnish: Mint sprig
Method: SHAKE all ingredients with ice and fine strain into chilled glass.

2	shot(s)	**Plymouth gin**
1/2	shot(s)	**Giffard green crème de menthe**
1/4	shot(s)	**Kümmel liqueur**
1/4	shot(s)	**Freshly squeezed lemon juice**
3	dashes	**Fee Brothers peach bitters**
1/2	shot(s)	**Chilled mineral water** (omit if wet ice)

Origin: Adapted from Harry Craddock's 1930 'The Savoy Cocktail Book'.
Comment: Mint, juniper, caraway and fennel make for an unusual cocktail that's conducive to fresh breath.

GREEN EYES

Glass: Martini
Garnish: Lime wedge on rim
Method: SHAKE all ingredients with ice and fine strain into chilled glass.

2	shot(s)	**Ketel One Citroen vodka**
1/2	shot(s)	**Bols Blue curaçao liqueur**
1	shot(s)	**Freshly squeezed orange juice**
1/2	shot(s)	**Freshly squeezed lemon juice**
1/4	shot(s)	**Almond (orgeat) syrup**

Comment: A cross between a Blue Cosmo and a short Screwdriver.

GREEN FAIRY

Glass: Martini
Method: SHAKE all ingredients with ice and fine strain into chilled glass.

1 shot(s) **La Fée Parisienne (68%) absinthe**
1 shot(s) **Freshly squeezed lemon juice**
3/4 shot(s) **Sugar syrup (2 sugar to 1 water)**
1 shot(s) **Chilled mineral water** (reduce if wet ice)
1 dash **Angostura aromatic bitters**
1/2 fresh **Egg white**

Origin: Created by Dick Bradsell.
Comment: An Absinthe Sour style drink served straight-up.

GREEN FIZZ

Glass: Collins (8oz max)
Garnish: Slice of lemon & mint
Method: SHAKE first four ingredients with ice and strain into chilled glass. **TOP** with soda.

2 shot(s) **Plymouth gin**
1/2 shot(s) **Giffard white crème de Menthe Pastille**
1 shot(s) **Freshly squeezed lemon juice**
1/4 shot(s) **Sugar syrup (2 sugar to 1 water)**
Top up with **Soda water (from siphon)**

Variant: Gin Fizz
Origin: A mid-19th century classic.
Comment: Fresh, cleansing and refreshing - as only a minty Fizz can be.

GREEN FLY

Glass: Shot
Method: Refrigerate ingredients then **LAYER** in chilled glass by carefully pouring in the following order.

1/2 shot(s) **Midori melon liqueur**
1/2 shot(s) **Giffard white crème de Menthe Pastille**
1/2 shot(s) **Green Chartreuse liqueur**

Origin: Created by Alex Turner at Circus, London, England.
Comment: A strong shot comprising three layers of different green liqueurs.

GREEN HORN [NEW #7]

Glass: Martini
Garnish: Pineapple wedge & cherry
Method: SHAKE all ingredients with ice and fine strain into chilled glass.

1 1/2 shot(s) **Aged rum**
1 shot(s) **Pressed pineapple juice**
1 shot(s) **Midori melon liqueur**
1/2 fresh **Egg white**

Comment: Far more interesting and serious than the green hue from the melon liqueur would suggest.

GREEN HORNET

Glass: Shot
Method: SHAKE all ingredients with ice and fine strain into chilled glass.

3/4 shot(s) **Ketel One vodka**
1/8 shot(s) **La Fée Parisienne (68%) absinthe**
3/4 shot(s) **Pisang Ambon liqueur**
1/2 shot(s) **Rose's lime cordial**

Comment: A surprisingly palatable and balanced shot.

GREEN SWIZZLE

Glass: Old-fashioned
Method: POUR all ingredients into glass. Fill glass with crushed ice and **SWIZZLE** (stir) with bar spoon or swizzle stick to mix. Serve with straws.

2 shot(s) **Light white rum**
1/2 shot(s) **Freshly squeezed lime juice**
1/4 shot(s) **Giffard white crème de Menthe Pastille**
1/4 shot(s) **Sugar syrup (2 sugar to 1 water)**
1 dash **Angostura aromatic bitters**

Variant: With gin in place of rum
Origin: This 1940s classic features in 'The Rummy Affair Of Old Biffy' by P.G. Wodehouse. Bertie Wooster sings its praises after enjoying a few at the Panters' Bar of the West Indian stand at the 1924 Empire Exhibition.
Comment: A Daiquiri-like drink with a hint of peppermint.

GREEN TEA MARTINI #1

Glass: Martini
Garnish: Banana slice on rim
Method: SHAKE all ingredients with ice and fine strain into chilled glass.

2 shot(s) **Zubrówka bison vodka**
1/4 shot(s) **Pisang Ambon liqueur**
1/8 shot(s) **Giffard white crème de Menthe Pastille**
2 shot(s) **Pressed apple juice**

Comment: It's green and, although it doesn't actually contain any tea, has something of the flavour of alcoholic peppermint tea.

GREEN TEA MARTINI #2 [NEW #7]

Glass: Martini
Garnish: Shiso (or mint) leaf
Method: SHAKE all ingredients with ice and strain into chilled glass.

2 shot(s) **Plymouth gin**
1 shot(s) **Zen green tea liqueur**
1/4 shot(s) **Dry vermouth**
3/4 shot(s) **Strong cold green tea**

Origin: Created in 2006 by yours truly.
Comment: Exactly what it says on the tin: as subtle and delicate as green tea itself.

GREENBELT [NEW #7]

Glass: Collins
Garnish: Grapes on stick
Method: MUDDLE grapes in base of shaker. Add other ingredients, **SHAKE** with ice and fine strain into ice-filled glass.

12	fresh	**Seedless white grapes**
2	shot(s)	**Pisco**
1	shot(s)	**St-Germain elderflower liqueur**
Top up with		**Brut champagne**

Origin: Created in 2007 by yours truly.
Comment: This tastes as green as it looks - aromatic and refreshing.

GRETA GARBO

Glass: Martini
Garnish: Star anise
Method: SHAKE all ingredients with ice and fine strain into chilled glass.

2	shot(s)	**Light white rum**
1/4	shot(s)	**Luxardo Maraschino liqueur**
1/2	shot(s)	**Sugar syrup (2 sugar to 1 water)**
1	shot(s)	**Freshly squeezed lime juice**
1/8	shot(s)	**Pernod anis**

Comment: A most unusual Daiquiri.

'HELL IS FULL OF MUSICAL AMATEURS: MUSIC IS THE BRANDY OF THE DAMNED.'
GEORGE BERNARD SHAW

GREY MOUSE

Glass: Shot
Method: SHAKE all ingredients with ice and fine strain into chilled glass.

1	shot(s)	**Irish cream liqueur**
1/2	shot(s)	**Opal Nera black sambuca**

Comment: Aniseed and whiskey cream.

GREYHOUND

Glass: Collins
Garnish: Orange slice
Method: POUR ingredients into ice-filled glass and stir.

2	shot(s)	**Ketel One vodka**
Top up with		**Squeezed pink grapefruit juice**

Comment: A sour Screwdriver.

GROG [UPDATED #7]

Glass: Old-fashioned
Garnish: Lime wedge
Method: STIR honey with rum in base of shaker until honey dissolves. Add other ingredients, **SHAKE** with ice and strain into ice-filled glass.

2	spoons	**Runny honey**
1 1/2	shot(s)	**Pusser's Navy rum (54.4%)**
1/4	shot(s)	**Freshly squeezed lime juice**
2 1/2	shot(s)	**Chilled mineral water**
3	dashes	**Angostura aromatic bitters**

Variant: Hot Grog
Origin: A drink which originated from the British Navy tradition of issuing a daily 'tot' of rum.
Comment: Strong, flavoursome Navy rum with a splash of scurvy-inhibiting lime. Too many and you'll be groggy in the morning.

THE GTO COCKTAIL

Glass: Collins
Garnish: Pineapple wedge on rim
Method: SHAKE all ingredients with ice and strain into ice-filled glass.

2	shot(s)	**Jack Daniel's Tennessee whiskey**
1/2	shot(s)	**Luxardo Amaretto di Saschira**
1/2	shot(s)	**Freshly squeezed lemon juice**
3	shot(s)	**Pressed pineapple juice**

Origin: Adapted from a recipe discovered in 2004 at Jones, Los Angeles, USA.
Comment: A fruity, punch-like drink.

GUILLOTINE

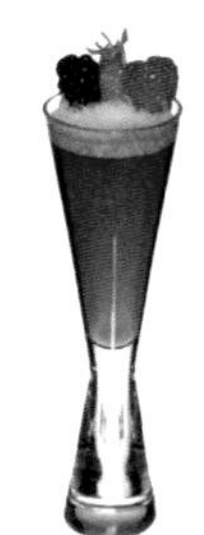

Glass: Flute
Garnish: Berries on rim
Method: POUR first two ingredients into glass and **TOP** with champagne.

1/2	shot(s)	**Giffard crème de cassis**
1/2	shot(s)	**Poire William eau de vie**
Top up with		**Brut champagne**

Comment: Add some life to your bubbly.

GULF COAST SEX ON THE BEACH

Glass: Collins
Method: SHAKE all ingredients with ice and strain into ice-filled glass.

1 1/2	shot(s)	**Light white rum**
3/4	shot(s)	**Midori melon liqueur**
3/4	shot(s)	**Crème de bananes**
1 1/2	shot(s)	**Pressed pineapple juice**
1 1/2	shot(s)	**Ocean Spray cranberry juice**
1/4	shot(s)	**Freshly squeezed lime juice**

Origin: Created in 1997 by Roberto Canino and Wayne Collins at Navajo Joe, London, England.
Comment: Golden tan in colour and tropical in flavour, complete with frothy top.

GUN CLUB PUNCH NO.1 [NEW #7]

Glass: Cartridge mug or Collins
Garnish: Pineapple cube & cherry on stick plus mint sprig
Method: BLEND all ingredients with 12oz scoop crushed ice. Serve with straws.

1	shot(s)	**Light white rum**
1	shot(s)	**Jamaican dark rum (or Pusser's Navy)**
1	shot(s)	**Freshly squeezed lime juice**
1½	shot(s)	**Pressed pineapple juice**
¼	shot(s)	**Cointreau triple sec**
¼	shot(s)	**Pomegranate (grenadine) syrup**

Origin: Victor Bergeron specified that this drink should be served in one of his bespoke green cartridge mugs (pictured here). This recipe comes from 'Trader Vic's Bartender's Guide' (1972 revised edition).
Comment: This Trader Vic classic is balanced rather than sweet. Fruit juice and ice tone down rum's powerful blast.

GUSTO

Glass: Collins
Garnish: Apple slice
Method: MUDDLE grapes in base of shaker. Add other ingredients, **SHAKE** with ice and fine strain into ice-filled glass.

7	fresh	**Seedless green grapes**
2	shot(s)	**Partida tequila**
¾	shot(s)	**Agavero tequila liqueur**
2	shot(s)	**Pressed apple juice**

Origin: Created in 2003 by Thomas Gillgren at The Kingly Club, London, England.
Comment: A pleasing long drink flavoured with apple, grape and tequila.

GYPSY MARTINI

Glass: Martini
Garnish: Rosemary
Method: MUDDLE rosemary and raisins in base of shaker. Add other ingredients, **SHAKE** with ice and fine strain into chilled glass.

1	sprig	**Fresh rosemary (remove stalk)**
10		**Raisins**
2	shot(s)	**Plymouth gin**
½	shot(s)	**Sugar syrup (2 sugar to 1 water)**
1	shot(s)	**Chilled mineral water** (reduce if wet ice)

Origin: Adapted from a recipe created by Jason Fendick in 2002 for Steam, London, England.

Comment: Jason's original recipe called for raisin infused gin and I'd recommend you make this drink that way if time permits.

GROG

For over 300 years the British Navy issued a daily 'tot' of rum, sometimes with double issues before battle. In 1740, as an attempt to combat drunkenness, Admiral Vernon gave orders that the standard daily issue of half a pint of neat, high-proof rum be replaced with two servings of a quarter of a pint, diluted 4:1 with water. The Admiral was nicknamed 'Old Grogram' due to the waterproof grogram cloak he wore, so the mixture he introduced became known as 'grog'. Lime juice was often added to the grog in an attempt to prevent scurvy, lending British sailors their 'limey' nickname.

The 'tot' tradition, which started in Jamaica in 1665, was finally broken on 31st July 1970, a day now known as 'Black Tot Day' – although by then the 'tot' had been reduced to a meagre two ounces.

This sounds plausible to me but drinks historians now say that grog is earlier than Old Grogram.

GYPSY [NEW #7]

Glass: Martini
Garnish: Lime zest twist
Method: SHAKE all ingredients with ice and fine strain into chilled glass.

1 1/2	shot(s)	**Plymouth gin**
3/4	shot(s)	**St-Germain elderflower liqueur**
1/4	shot(s)	**Green Chartreuse liqueur**
1/2	shot(s)	**Freshly squeezed lime juice**

Origin: Created in 2007 by Dominic Venegas at Bourbon & Branch, San Francisco, USA.
Comment: Dominic describes this drink as "a little homage to the 'Last Word' cocktail".

G

GYPSY QUEEN

Glass: Martini
Garnish: Orange zest twist
Method: STIR all ingredients with ice and strain into chilled glass.

1 1/2	shot(s)	**Ketel One vodka**
3/4	shot(s)	**Bénédictine D.O.M. liqueur**
3/4	shot(s)	**Freshly squeezed orange juice**
1/4	shot(s)	**Freshly squeezed lemon juice**

Origin: A long lost classic.
Comment: Tangy, herbal, predominantly orange and not overly sweet.

HAIR OF THE DOG

Glass: Martini
Garnish: Grate fresh nutmeg
Method: STIR honey with Scotch until honey dissolves. Add other ingredients, **SHAKE** with ice and fine strain into chilled glass.

3	spoons	**Runny honey**
2	shot(s)	**Scotch whisky**
1	shot(s)	**Double (heavy) cream**
1	shot(s)	**Milk**

Origin: Traditionally drunk as a pick-me-up hangover cure.
Comment: This drink's name and reputation as a hangover cure may lead you to assume it tastes unpleasant. In fact, honey, whisky and cream combine wonderfully.

HAKKATINI

Glass: Martini
Garnish: Orange zest twist
Method: SHAKE all ingredients with ice and fine strain into chilled glass.

1	shot(s)	**Orange zest infused Ketel One vodka**
1	shot(s)	**Grand Marnier**
1/4	shot(s)	**Campari**
3/4	shot(s)	**Pressed apple juice**

Origin: Adapted from a drink discovered in 2003 at Hakkasan, London, England.
Comment: Balanced bitter sweet orange and apple.

HAMMER OF THE GODS

Glass: Shot & pint glass
Method: LAYER ingredients by carefully pouring into shot glass in the following order. **IGNITE** and hold pint glass upside down a few inches above the flame. Allow the drink to burn for thirty seconds or so before killing the flame, being sure to keep the pint glass in place. Instruct your subject to suck the alcohol vapour from the inverted pint glass using a bendy straw. Finally, remove the pint glass and let your subject consume the drink through the straw.

1	shot(s)	**Tuaca Italian liqueur**
1/2	shot(s)	**La Fée Parisienne (68%) absinthe**

Origin: Created by Dick Bradsell at The Player, London, UK.
Comment: Killjoys would point out the dangers of fire and alcohol and observe that this is hardly 'responsible drinking'.

'I'VE HAD EIGHTEEN STRAIGHT WHISKIES. I THINK THAT'S THE RECORD.'

HANKY-PANKY MARTINI

Glass: Martini
Garnish: Orange zest twist
Method: STIR all ingredients with ice and strain into chilled glass.

1 3/4	shot(s)	**Plymouth gin**
1 3/4	shot(s)	**Sweet vermouth**
1/8	shot(s)	**Fernet Branca**

Origin: Created in the early 1900s by Ada 'Coley' Coleman at The Savoy's American Bar, London, for actor Charles Hawtrey. He often said to Coley, "I am tired. Give me something with a bit of punch in it." This drink was her answer. After finishing his first one, Charles told Coley, "By Jove! That is the real hanky-panky!" And so it has since been named.
Comment: A Sweet Martini made bitter and aromatic by Fernet Branca.

HAPPY NEW YEAR

Glass: Flute
Garnish: Orange slice on rim
Method: SHAKE first three ingredients with ice and fine strain into chilled glass. **TOP** with champagne.

1/4	shot(s)	**Rémy Martin cognac**
3/4	shot(s)	**Tawny port**
3/4	shot(s)	**Freshly squeezed orange juice**
Top up with		**Brut champagne**

Origin: Created in 1981 by Charles Schumann, Munich, Germany.
Comment: Reminiscent of fizzy, fruity claret.

HARD LEMONADE

Glass: Collins
Garnish: Lemon wheel in glass
Method: **SHAKE** first three ingredients with ice and strain into ice-filled glass. **TOP** with soda and serve with straws.

2	shot(s)	**Ketel One vodka**
2	shot(s)	**Freshly squeezed lemon juice**
1	shot(s)	**Sugar syrup (2 sugar to 1 water)**
Top up with		**Soda water (club soda)**

Variants: Vodka Collins, Ray's Hard Lemonade
Origin: Discovered in 2004 at Spring Street Natural Restaurant, New York City, USA.
Comment: Refreshing lemonade with a kick. Great for a hot afternoon.

THE HARLEM

Glass: Martini
Garnish: Cherry in drink
Method: **SHAKE** all ingredients with ice and fine strain into chilled glass.

2	shot(s)	**Plymouth gin**
1/4	shot(s)	**Luxardo Maraschino liqueur**
2	shot(s)	**Pressed pineapple juice**

Origin: Thought to date back to the Prohibition era and the Cotton Club in Harlem.
Comment: Soft and fruity. Careful, it's harder than you think.

HARVARD

Glass: Martini
Garnish: Lemon zest twist
Method: **STIR** all ingredients with ice and strain into chilled glass.

1 1/4	shot(s)	**Rémy Martin cognac**
1 1/2	shot(s)	**Sweet vermouth**
1 1/4	shot(s)	**Dry vermouth**
3	dashes	**Fee Brothers orange bitters**

Origin: A classic from the 1930s.
Comment: A Delmonico with orange bitters in place of Angostura. Rather like a Brandy Manhattan.

HARVARD COOLER

Glass: Collins
Garnish: Lime wedge
Method: **SHAKE** first three ingredients with ice and strain into ice-filled glass. **TOP** with soda, stir and serve with straws.

2	shot(s)	**Boulard Grand Solage Calvados**
1	shot(s)	**Freshly squeezed lime juice**
1/2	shot(s)	**Sugar syrup (2 sugar to 1 water)**
Top up with		**Soda water (club soda)**

Comment: Refreshing and not too sweet. Lime and sugar enhance the appley spirit.

HARVEY WALLBANGER

Glass: Collins
Garnish: Orange slice
Method: **SHAKE** all ingredients with ice and strain into ice-filled glass.

2	shot(s)	**Ketel One vodka**
3 1/2	shot(s)	**Freshly squeezed orange juice**
1/2	shot(s)	**Galliano liqueur**

Variant: Freddie Fudpucker
Origin: Legend has it that 'Harvey' was a surfer at Manhattan Beach, California. His favourite drink was a Screwdriver with added Galliano. One day in the late sixties, while celebrating winning a surfing competition, he staggered from bar to bar, banging his surfboard on the walls, and so a contemporary classic gained its name.

However, an article in Bartender Magazine credits the creation to Bill Doner, the host of a house party held in the mid-sixties in Newport Beach, California. One of the guests, Harvey, was found banging his head the next morning, complaining of the hangover this drink induced.
Comment: It's usual to build this drink and 'float' Galliano over the built drink. However, as the Galliano sinks anyway it is better shaken.

HAVANA COBBLER

Glass: Old-fashioned
Garnish: Lime zest twist
Method: **SHAKE** all ingredients with ice and strain into glass filled with crushed ice.

2	shot(s)	**Light white rum**
1	shot(s)	**Tawny port**
1/2	shot(s)	**Stone's green ginger wine**
1/4	shot(s)	**Sugar syrup (2 sugar to 1 water)**

Comment: An unusual, spiced, Daiquiri-like drink.

'OH NO, DARLING, YOU DIDN'T LISTEN. JULIAN SAID SHE'D GIVEN UP GIN - FOR BRANDY. SHE SAYS SHE CAN DRINK MORE BRANDY.'

HAVANA SPECIAL

Glass: Old-fashioned
Garnish: Lime zest twist
Method: **SHAKE** all ingredients with ice and strain into glass filled with crushed ice.

2	shot(s)	**Light white rum**
1 3/4	shot(s)	**Pressed pineapple juice**
1/2	shot(s)	**Luxardo maraschino liqueur**

Comment: Daiquiri-like without the sourness. Fragrant and all too easy to drink.

HAVANATHEONE

Glass: Martini
Garnish: Mint leaf
Method: Lightly **MUDDLE** mint (just to bruise) in base of shaker. Add rum and honey and **STIR** until honey dissolves. Add other ingredients, **SHAKE** with ice and fine strain into chilled glass.

10	fresh	**Mint leaves**
2	spoons	**Runny honey**
2	shot(s)	**Light white rum**
1/2	shot(s)	**Freshly squeezed lime juice**
1	shot(s)	**Pressed apple juice**

Origin: Discovered in 2003 at Hush, London, England.
Comment: A flavoursome Daiquiri featuring honey, apple and mint.

HAWAIIAN EYE

Glass: Collins
Garnish: Pineapple wedge & cherry
Method: **BLEND** all ingredients with two 12oz scoops of crushed ice. Serve with straws.

1	shot(s)	**Light white rum**
1	shot(s)	**Golden rum**
1/2	shot(s)	**Velvet Falernum**
1/2	shot(s)	**Freshly squeezed lime juice**
1/2	shot(s)	**Sugar syrup (2 sugar to 1 water)**

Origin: A Tiki drink created in 1963 by Tony Ramos at China Trader, California, USA, for the cast of the TV series of the same name.
Comment: Tropical, rum laced cooler.

HAWAIIAN

Glass: Hurricane
Garnish: Pineapple wedge & cherry
Method: **BLEND** all ingredients with two 12oz scoops crushed ice and serve with straws.

2	shot(s)	**Malibu coconut rum liqueur**
1/2	shot(s)	**Cointreau triple sec**
1/2	shot(s)	**Light white rum**
1 1/2	shot(s)	**Freshly squeezed orange juice**
1 1/2	shot(s)	**Pressed pineapple juice**
1	shot(s)	**Freshly squeezed lime juice**
1/2	shot(s)	**Sugar syrup (2 sugar to 1 water)**
1	shot(s)	**Coco López cream of coconut**

Comment: Coconut, rum and fruit juice. Aloha.

HAWAIIAN MARTINI

Glass: Martini
Garnish: Pineapple wedge & cherry
Method: **SHAKE** all ingredients with ice and fine strain into chilled glass.

1 1/2	shot(s)	**Plymouth gin**
1/2	shot(s)	**Dry vermouth**
1/2	shot(s)	**Sweet vermouth**
1 1/2	shot(s)	**Pressed pineapple juice**

Origin: Adapted from a drink discovered in 2005 at the Four Seasons, Milan, Italy.
Comment: An aptly named fruity twist on the classic Martini.

HAWAIIAN COCKTAIL

Glass: Martini
Garnish: Pineapple wedge & cherry on rim
Method: **SHAKE** all ingredients with ice and fine strain into chilled glass.

1 1/2	shot(s)	**Light white rum**
1/2	shot(s)	**Southern Comfort liqueur**
1/2	shot(s)	**Luxardo Amaretto di Saschira**
3/4	shot(s)	**Freshly squeezed orange juice**
1 1/2	shot(s)	**Pressed pineapple juice**

Origin: Discovered in Las Vegas in 2004.
Comment: Sweet, tangy and fruity.

HAWAIIAN SEABREEZE

Glass: Collins
Garnish: Pineapple wedge on rim
Method: **SHAKE** all ingredients with ice and strain into ice-filled glass.

2	shot(s)	**Mango flavoured vodka**
2 1/2	shot(s)	**Ocean Spray cranberry juice**
1 1/2	shot(s)	**Pressed pineapple juice**

Variant: Bay Breeze
Comment: Easygoing, foam topped relative of the Seabreeze.

HAWAIIAN COSMOPOLITAN

Glass: Martini
Garnish: Pineapple wedge on rim
Method: **SHAKE** all ingredients with ice and fine strain into chilled glass.

2	shot(s)	**Ketel One Citroen vodka**
1	shot(s)	**Sour pineapple liqueur**
1	shot(s)	**Pressed apple juice**
1/2	shot(s)	**Freshly squeezed lime juice**

Origin: Created in 2002 by Wayne Collins, UK.
Comment: Fresh, tangy and distinctly tropical.

HAYDENISTIC [NEW #7]

Glass: Martini
Garnish: Lime zest twist
Method: **STIR** all ingredients with ice and strain into chilled glass.

2	shot(s)	**Ketel One vodka**
1/8	shot(s)	**St-Germain elderflower liqueur**
1/8	shot(s)	**Velvet Falernum**

Origin: Created in 2007 by Hayden Lambert at The Merchant Hotel, Belfast, Northern Ireland.
Comment: Extremely subtle, like a very complex Wet Vodkatini.

HAZEL'ITO

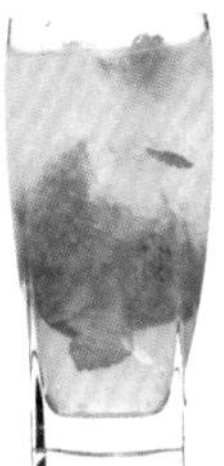

Glass: Collins
Method: Lightly **MUDDLE** mint in base of glass (just to bruise). Add other ingredients, fill glass with crushed ice and **CHURN** (stir) with bar spoon to mix.

12	fresh	**Mint leaves**
2	shot(s)	**Light white rum**
2	shot(s)	**Frangelico hazelnut liqueur**
1	shot(s)	**Freshly squeezed lime juice**
1/2	shot(s)	**Sugar syrup (2 sugar to 1 water)**

Origin: Created in January 2002 by Adam Wyartt, London, England.
Comment: Looks like a Mojito but has a nutty twang courtesy of the hazelnut liqueur.

HAZELNUT ALEXANDER

Glass: Martini
Garnish: Dust with cacao powder
Method: SHAKE all ingredients with ice and fine strain into chilled glass.

1 3/4	shot(s)	**Rémy Martin cognac**
3/4	shot(s)	**Frangelico hazelnut liqueur**
1/2	shot(s)	**Giffard brown crème de cacao**
1/2	shot(s)	**Double (heavy) cream**
1/2	shot(s)	**Milk**
2	dashes	**Angostura aromatic bitters**

Origin: Created in 2005 by James Mellnor at Maze, London, England.
Comment: Great twist on a classic – the use of bitters is inspired.

HAZELNUT MARTINI

Glass: Martini
Garnish: Hazelnut in drink
Method: STIR all ingredients with ice and strain into chilled glass.

2	shot(s)	**Ketel One vodka**
1/2	shot(s)	**Frangelico hazelnut liqueur**
1/2	shot(s)	**Giffard white crème de cacao**
3/4	shot(s)	**Chilled mineral water** (omit if wet ice)

Comment: A hazelnut Vodkatini with a hint of chocolate.

HEAD SHOT [NEW #7]

Glass: Shot
Method: Refrigerate ingredients then **LAYER** in chilled glass by carefully pouring in the following order.

3/4	shot(s)	**Opal Nera black sambuca**
3/4	shot(s)	**Green Chartreuse liqueur**

Comment: Please ask permission from the person who pays the telephone bill before calling... Sorry. Please drink responsibly.

HEARST MARTINI [NEW #7]

Glass: Martini
Garnish: Orange zest twist
Method: STIR all ingredients with ice and strain into chilled glass.

2	shot(s)	**Plymouth gin**
1	shot(s)	**Sweet vermouth**
1	dash	**Fee Brothers orange bitters**
1	dash	**Angostura aromatic bitters**

Origin: This was supposedly a favourite of hacks who worked for the American newspaper magnate, William Randolph Hearst, and is believed to have been created at New York's Waldorf-Astoria. It is nicknamed 'The Disgruntled Journalist' and indeed, is not dissimilar to a Journalist with extra bitters.
Comment: A fantastically wet, sweet and aromatic Martini.

'LOVE MAKES THE WORLD GO ROUND? NOT AT ALL. WHISKY MAKES IT GO ROUND TWICE AS FAST.'

HEATHER JULEP

Glass: Collins
Garnish: Mint sprig
Method: Lightly **MUDDLE** mint in base of shaker (just to bruise). Add other ingredients, **SHAKE** with ice and strain into glass filled with crushed ice. **CHURN** (stir) the drink using a bar spoon. Top the glass with more crushed ice so as to fill it and churn again. Serve with straws.

12	fresh	**Mint leaves**
2 1/2	shot(s)	**Scotch whisky**
1/2	shot(s)	**Drambuie liqueur**
3/4	shot(s)	**Sugar syrup (2 sugar to 1 water)**

Origin: Adapted from a drink discovered in 2001 at Teatro, London, England.
Comment: A Scottish twist on the classic bourbon based Mint Julep.

HEAVEN SCENT

Glass: Martini
Garnish: Orange zest twist
Method: SHAKE all ingredients with ice and fine strain into chilled glass.

1 1/2	shot(s)	**Vanilla infused Ketel One vodka**
1 1/2	shot(s)	**Krupnik honey liqueur**
1/2	shot(s)	**Freshly squeezed lemon juice**
3/4	shot(s)	**Chilled mineral water** (omit if wet ice)

Origin: Discovered in 2003 at Oxo Tower Bar, London, England.
Comment: Honey, vanilla and lemon – reminiscent of a chilled, straight-up toddy.

HEAVENS ABOVE

Glass: Collins
Garnish: Pineapple wedge on rim
Method: SHAKE all ingredients with ice and strain into glass filled with crushed ice.

2	shot(s)	**Golden rum**
1/4	shot(s)	**Coffee liqueur**
1/4	shot(s)	**Giffard brown crème de cacao**
3	shot(s)	**Pressed pineapple juice**

Origin: A Tiki style drink adapted from a drink featured in Jeff Berry's 'Intoxica' and originally created circa 1970 at Top of Toronto, CN Tower, Toronto, Canada.
Comment: Slightly sweet, fruity rum – hard not to like

HEDGEROW SLING

Glass: Sling
Garnish: Seasonal berries & lemon slice
Method: SHAKE first three ingredients with ice and strain into ice-filled glass. **TOP** with soda, stir and serve with straws.

2	shot(s)	**Plymouth sloe gin**
1	shot(s)	**Freshly squeezed lemon juice**
1/2	shot(s)	**Giffard mûre (blackberry)**
Top up with		**Soda water (club soda)**

Origin: Created by Brian Duell at Detroit, London, England.
Comment: Rich, long, berry drink.

HEMINGWAY

Glass: Flute
Garnish: Star anise on rim
Method: POUR anis into chilled glass. Top with champagne.

1	shot(s)	**Pernod anis**
Top up with		**Brut champagne**

AKA: Corpse Reviver #2
Origin: Created at Cantineros' Club, the famous Cuban bar school.
Comment: Why dilute your anis with water when you can use champagne?

HEMINGWAY MARTINI [NEW #7]

Glass: Martini
Garnish: Maraschino cherry
Method: SHAKE all ingredients with ice and fine strain into chilled glass.

2	shot(s)	**Orange zest infused Ketel One vodka**
1/2	shot(s)	**Vanilla liqueur**
1	shot(s)	**Freshly squeezed grapefruit juice**
1/8	shot(s)	**Dry vermouth**
1/8	shot(s)	**Maraschino syrup (from cherry jar)**

Origin: Created in 2005 by Claire Smith, London, England.
Comment: Fresh and refreshing in flavour, traditional yet modern in style.

HEMINGWAY SPECIAL DAIQUIRI

Glass: 10oz Martini (huge)
Garnish: Lime wedge on rim
Method: SHAKE all ingredients with ice and fine strain into chilled glass.

3 1/2	shot(s)	**Light white rum**
1	shot(s)	**Freshly squeezed grapefruit juice**
3/4	shot(s)	**Luxardo Maraschino liqueur**
1	shot(s)	**Freshly squeezed lime juice**
1/2	shot(s)	**Sugar syrup (2 sugar to 1 water)**

AKA: Papa Doble Daiquiri
Origin: Created by Constantino (Constante) Ribailagua Vert, the legendary owner of La Floridita, Havana, Cuba for Ernest Hemingway, after the great man wandered into the bar to use the toilet. When Hemingway tried the Floridita's standard frozen Daiquiri, he is quoted as saying, "That's good but I prefer it without sugar and with double rum," – so the Hemingway Special was born.
Comment: A true Hemingway Special (also known as a Papa Doble) should be served without the addition of sugar. However, Hemingway had a hardened palate and an aversion to sugar - more delicate drinkers may prefer the recipe above.

HENRY VIII

Glass: Flute
Garnish: Orange zest twist
Method: Soak sugar cube with absinthe and drop into chilled glass. **POUR** other ingredients over sugar cube and serve.

1	cube	**Sugar**
1/8	shot(s)	**La Fée Parisienne (68%) absinthe**
1/2	shot(s)	**Ketel One Citroen vodka**
1/2	shot(s)	**Pepper flavoured vodka**
Top up with		**Brut champagne**

Origin: Created in 2004 by Henry Besant, London, England.
Comment: A contemporary twist on the classic Champagne Cocktail.

HIGHLAND SLING

Glass: Sling
Garnish: Apple wedge
Method: SHAKE all ingredients with ice and strain into ice-filled glass.

1 1/2	shot(s)	**Scotch whisky**
1/2	shot(s)	**Galliano liqueur**
1	shot(s)	**Ocean Spray cranberry juice**
1/2	shot(s)	**Giffard apricot brandy du Roussillon**
2	shot(s)	**Pressed apple juice**

Comment: A surprisingly good combination of diverse flavours.

THE HIVE

Glass: Martini
Garnish: Orange zest twist
Method: STIR honey with vodka until honey dissolves. Add other ingredients, **SHAKE** with ice and fine strain into chilled glass.

2	spoons	**Runny honey**
1	shot(s)	**Ketel One vodka**
1	shot(s)	**Krupnik honey liqueur**
2	shot(s)	**Freshly squeezed golden grapefruit juice**

Origin: Discovered in 2004 at Circus, London, England.
Comment: Sour grapefruit balanced by sweet honey.

HOA SUA

Glass: Martini
Garnish: Pineapple wedge on rim
Method: Cut pomegranate in half and juice using a spinning citrus juicer. **SHAKE** all ingredients with ice and fine strain into chilled glass.

$1^1/_2$	shot(s)	**Freshly squeezed pomegranate juice**
$1^1/_2$	shot(s)	**Light white rum**
$^3/_4$	shot(s)	**Sake**
$^1/_8$	shot(s)	**Sugar syrup (2 sugar to 1 water)**
1	dash	**Angostura aromatic bitters**

Origin: Created in 2005 by yours truly for Hoa Sua catering school in Vietnam using locally available products.
Comment: Light and easy drinking – the rum flavour shines through.

HOBSON'S CHOICE (MOCKTAIL)

Glass: Collins
Garnish: Lime wedge on rim
Method: SHAKE all ingredients with ice and strain into ice-filled glass.

$2^1/_2$	shot(s)	**Freshly squeezed orange juice**
$2^1/_2$	shot(s)	**Pressed apple juice**
1	shot(s)	**Freshly squeezed lime juice**
$^1/_4$	shot(s)	**Pomegranate (grenadine) syrup**

Comment: A fruity, non-alcoholic cocktail.

HOFFMAN HOUSE [NEW #7]

Glass: Martini
Garnish: Lemon zest twist
Method: SHAKE all ingredients with ice and fine strain into chilled glass.

2	shot(s)	**Plymouth gin**
1	shot(s)	**Dry vermouth**
2	dashes	**Fee Brothers orange bitters**

Origin: Apparently the house cocktail at Manhattan's Hoffman House in the 1880s.
Comment: A shaken Wet Martini with orange bitters.

HIGHBALL

A 'Scotch & Soda', 'Gin & Tonic', 'Whiskey & Ginger', 'Vodka & Tonic' and 'Rum & Coke' are all examples of Highball cocktails.

Highballs are a type of simple cocktail with only two ingredients, normally a spirit and a carbonate, served in a tall ice-filled glass (often referred to as a highball glass). Unlike Rickeys, Collinses and Fizzes, Highballs do not contain citrus fruit juice.

To make: pour two shots of your chosen spirit (Scotch, bourbon, cognac etc.) into a tall, ice-filled glass. Top up with a carbonated soft drink (ginger ale, soda or tonic water) and stir gently so as not to kill the fizz. Garnish with a slice of orange, lime or lemon as appropriate to the spirit and the carbonate.

H

THE HOLLAND HOUSE COCKTAIL [NEW #7]

Glass: Martini
Garnish: Lemon zest twist
Method: SHAKE all ingredients with ice and fine strain into chilled glass.

- 1 3/4 shot(s) **Bols Zeer Oude Genever**
- 3/4 shot(s) **Dry vermouth**
- 1/2 shot(s) **Freshly squeezed lemon juice**
- 1/4 shot(s) **Luxardo maraschino liqueur**

Origin: A forgotten classic which is rightly being championed by the House of Bols, Amsterdam, The Netherlands.
Comment: Dry and reminiscent of an Aviation but with jenever personality.

HONEY & MARMALADE DRAM'TINI

Glass: Martini
Garnish: Strips of orange peel
Method: STIR honey with Scotch in base of shaker until honey dissolves. Add other ingredients, **SHAKE** with ice and fine strain into chilled glass.

- 2 shot(s) **Scotch whisky**
- 4 spoons **Runny honey**
- 1 shot(s) **Freshly squeezed lemon juice**
- 1 shot(s) **Freshly squeezed orange juice**

Origin: I adapted this recipe from the Honeysuckle Daiquiri.
Comment: This citrussy drink seems to enrich and enhance the flavour of Scotch.

HONEY APPLE MARTINI

Glass: Martini
Garnish: Lemon zest twist
Method: SHAKE all ingredients with ice and fine strain into chilled glass.

- 1 1/2 shot(s) **Zubrówka bison vodka**
- 3/4 shot(s) **Krupnik honey liqueur**
- 1 1/4 shot(s) **Pressed apple juice**
- 1/4 shot(s) **Freshly squeezed lemon juice**

Variant: Polish Martini
Comment: A classically Polish blend of flavours.

HONEY BEE

Glass: Martini
Garnish: Lemon zest twist
Method: STIR honey with vodka in base of shaker until honey dissolves. Add other ingredients, **SHAKE** with ice and fine strain into chilled glass.

- 2 shot(s) **Light white rum**
- 2 spoons **Runny honey**
- 1/2 shot(s) **Freshly squeezed lemon juice**
- 3/4 shot(s) **Chilled mineral water** (omit if wet ice)

Origin: Adapted from a recipe in my 1949 copy of Esquire's 'Handbook For Hosts'.
Comment: Basically a honey Daiquiri – nice, though.

HONEY BERRY SOUR

Glass: Old-fashioned
Garnish: Lemon wedge
Method: SHAKE all ingredients with ice and strain into ice-filled glass.

- 1 1/2 shot(s) **Krupnik honey vodka**
- 3/4 shot(s) **Chambord black raspberry liqueur**
- 1 shot(s) **Freshly squeezed lemon juice**
- 1/4 shot(s) **Sugar syrup (2 sugar to 1 water)**
- 1/2 fresh **Egg white**

Origin: Created by Tim Hallilaj.
Comment: More sweet than sour but berry nice.

HONEY BLOSSOM

Glass: Old-fashioned
Garnish: Pineapple wedge on rim
Method: SHAKE all ingredients with ice and fine strain into ice-filled glass.

- 3 shot(s) **Pressed pineapple juice**
- 1 shot(s) **Freshly squeezed lemon juice**
- 1/4 shot(s) **Vanilla syrup**
- 1/2 fresh **Egg white**
- 3 dashes **Angostura aromatic bitters**

Origin: Created in 2003 by Tim Phillips at the GE Club, London, England.
Comment: Soft, fruity, yet adult. Note: contains trace amounts of alcohol.

HONEY DAIQUIRI

Glass: Martini
Garnish: Lime wedge on rim
Method: STIR honey with rum in base of shaker until honey dissolves. Add other ingredients, **SHAKE** with ice and fine strain into chilled glass.

- 2 spoons **Runny honey**
- 2 shot(s) **Light white rum**
- 1/2 shot(s) **Freshly squeezed lime juice**
- 1/2 shot(s) **Chilled mineral water** (omit if wet ice)

Comment: Sweet honey replaces sugar syrup in this natural Daiquiri. Try experimenting with different honeys. I favour orange blossom honey.

HONEY LIMEAID (MOCKTAIL)

Glass: Collins
Garnish: Lime wedge
Method: STIR honey with lime juice in base of shaker until honey dissolves. **SHAKE** with ice and strain into ice-filled glass. **TOP** with soda.

- 1 1/2 shot(s) **Freshly squeezed lime juice**
- 7 spoons **Runny honey**
- Top up with **Soda water (club soda)**

Origin: Discovered in 2005 at Hotel Quinta Real, Guadalajara, Mexico.
Comment: A refreshing Mexican variation on Real Lemonade.

HONEY VODKA SOUR

Glass: Old-fashioned
Garnish: Lemon wedge
Method: SHAKE all ingredients with ice and strain into ice-filled glass.

2	shot(s)	**Krupnik honey vodka**
$1^1/_2$	shot(s)	**Freshly squeezed lemon juice**
$^1/_2$	shot(s)	**Sugar syrup (2 sugar to 1 water)**
$^1/_2$	fresh	**Egg white**
3	dashes	**Angostura aromatic bitters**

Comment: A vodka sour with true honey character.

HONEY WALL

Glass: Martini
Garnish: Flamed orange zest twist
Method: STIR all ingredients with ice and strain into chilled glass.

$1^1/_4$	shot(s)	**Aged rum**
$1^1/_4$	shot(s)	**Tuaca Italian liqueur**
$1^1/_4$	shot(s)	**Kikor (or dark crème de cacao) liqueur**

Origin: Adapted from a drink created in 2002 by Dick Bradsell at Downstairs at Alfred's, London, England.
Comment: Strong, rich and chocolatey.

HONEYMOON [UPDATED #7]

Glass: Martini
Garnish: Lemon zest twist
Method: SHAKE all ingredients with ice and fine strain into chilled glass.

$1^1/_2$	shot(s)	**Boulard Grand Solage Calvados**
1	shot(s)	**Bénédictine D.O.M. liqueur**
$^1/_4$	shot(s)	**Cointreau triple sec**
$^1/_2$	shot(s)	**Freshly squeezed lemon juice**
$^1/_2$	fresh	**Egg white**

AKA: Farmer's Daughter
Origin: A 1930s classic created in a long since departed New York bar called Brown Derby.
Comment: A romantic combination of apple, orange, lemon and herbs.

HONEYSUCKLE DAIQUIRI 

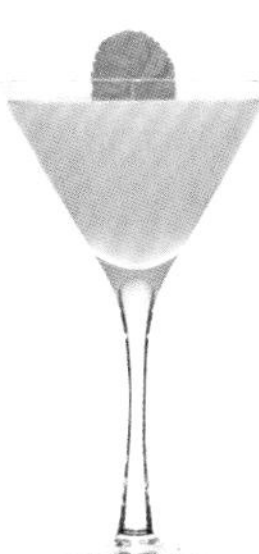

Glass: Martini
Garnish: Mint leaf
Method: STIR honey with rum in base of shaker until honey dissolves. Add lemon and orange juice, **SHAKE** with ice and fine strain into chilled glass.

2	shot(s)	**Light white rum**
4	spoons	**Runny honey**
1	shot(s)	**Freshly squeezed lemon juice**
1	shot(s)	**Freshly squeezed orange juice**

Variant: Made with gin in place of rum this drink becomes the 'Bee's Knees Martini'.
Origin: Adapted from a recipe in David Embury's 'The Fine Art Of Mixing Drinks'.
Comment: Honey – I love it!

HOT COCKTAILS

On a cold winter's night there is nothing that warms the cockles more than a piping hot, spirit laced drink. Such winter warmers transcend the ubiquitous Irish Coffee. In the 1930s cocktail heyday there were a number of recognised categories of popular hot drinks. These include:

Possets - Sweetened and spiced milk mixed with hot ale or wine. If eggs are substituted for the milk, the mixture becomes an Egg Posset.

Mull – A Mull or 'Mulled Wine' is simply spiced and sweetened wine served hot. Traditionally these drinks were heated by dipping a white-hot poker from the fire into the drink. Today the kitchen hob or microwave oven are less spectacular but equally effective.

Negus – A sweetened, spiced wine (usually port) served with hot water. While similar to a Mull, the Negus differs in that it is warmed by the addition of hot water rather than by being heated. The Negus is thought to have been invented by Colonel Francis Negus during the reign of Queen Anne (1702-1714).

Wassail Bowl – An old English hot drink traditionally served on Christmas Eve. It may be made from wine, cider, beer or any combination of the three. Mixed in bulk over a slow heat, flavourings include baked apples, nutmeg, cloves and cinnamon, and it is often thickened with eggs. The Swedes have a similar drink served at Christmas called Glogg, while the Danes call theirs Øgge.

Bishops – Similar to the Wassail Bowl above, except that beer is never used and baked oranges are used instead of apples.

Many other cocktails including the Grog and Punch are more familiarly mixed with ice and served cold but also have hot variations. Other famous hot cocktails include the Blue Blazer, Hot Buttered Rum and Hot Toddy.

International Coffees - The most popular hot, alcohol-laced drink, Irish Coffee was created more recently in 1942. It has since spawned a number of variations, loosely categorised as 'International Coffees'. These include: American Coffee (with bourbon or Southern Comfort), Caribbean Coffee (with rum), French Coffee (with cognac &/or liqueur such as Grand Marnier), Gaelic Coffee (with Scotch &/or Drambuie) and the Italian Coffee (with amaretto). Café noir is a simpler after-dinner coffee drink, where spirits or liqueurs are served to accompany a coffee or simply poured into the coffee.

When serving hot drinks in glassware be sure to use heatproof glasses, pre-warm each glass and place a bar spoon in the glass to help absorb the shock of the heat when the drink is poured.

THE HONEYSUCKLE ORCHARD

Glass: Martini
Garnish: Lemon wedge on rim
Method: STIR honey with vodka in base of shaker until honey dissolves. Add other ingredients, **SHAKE** with ice and fine strain into chilled glass.

1	spoon	**Runny honey**
2	shot(s)	**Zubrówka bison vodka**
1½	shot(s)	**Pressed apple juice**
¼	shot(s)	**Freshly squeezed lemon juice**

Origin: Discovered in 2005 at The Stanton Social, New York City, USA.
Comment: A back to nature Polish Martini - all the better for it.

'I HAVE TAKEN MORE OUT OF ALCOHOL THAN ALCOHOL HAS TAKEN OUT OF ME.'

HONG KONG FUEY

Glass: Collins
Garnish: Orange slice & lime slice
Method: SHAKE first eight ingredients with ice and strain into ice-filled glass. **TOP** with 7-Up, stir and serve with straws.

½	shot(s)	**Ketel One vodka**
½	shot(s)	**Plymouth gin**
½	shot(s)	**Light white rum**
½	shot(s)	**Partida tequila**
½	shot(s)	**Midori melon liqueur**
¼	shot(s)	**Freshly squeezed lemon juice**
¼	shot(s)	**Rose's lime cordial**
½	shot(s)	**Green Chartreuse liqueur**
Top up with		**7-Up / lemonade**

Comment: Readers may recall Hong Kong Phooey, the children's TV series featuring the mild-mannered janitor Penry and his superhero alter ego. This drink is no better than Penry's kung fu but deadly all the same.

HONOLULU [NEW #7]

Glass: Old-fashioned (or Tiki glass)
Garnish: Pineapple wedge and cherry
Method: BLEND all ingredients with 12oz scoop crushed ice and serve with straws.

1½	shot(s)	**Light white rum**
1	shot(s)	**Pressed pineapple juice**
½	shot(s)	**Freshly squeezed lemon juice**
¼	shot(s)	**Pomegranate (grenadine) syrup**
¼	shot(s)	**Sugar syrup (2 sugar to 1 water)**

Origin: Adapted from Victor Bergeron's 'Trader Vic's Bartender's Guide' (1972 revised edition).
Comment: Cooling, fruity and pretty light on alcohol – perfect for a hot afternoon in Honolulu.

HONOLULU COCKTAIL NO.1 [UPDATED #7]

Glass: Martini
Garnish: Pineapple wedge & cherry on rim
Method: SHAKE all ingredients with ice and fine strain into chilled glass.

2	shot(s)	**Plymouth gin**
¼	shot(s)	**Freshly squeezed orange juice**
¼	shot(s)	**Pressed pineapple juice**
¼	shot(s)	**Freshly squeezed lemon juice**
¼	shot(s)	**Sugar syrup (2 sugar to 1 water)**

Origin: Adapted from Harry Craddock's 1930 'The Savoy Cocktail Book'.
Comment: Gin is hardly Hawaiian, but its bite works well in this tropically fruity cocktail.

HONOLULU COCKTAIL NO.2 [NEW #7]

Glass: Martini
Garnish: Maraschino cherry
Method: STIR all ingredients with ice and strain into chilled glass.

¾	shot(s)	**Plymouth gin**
¾	shot(s)	**Bénédictine D.O.M. liqueur**
¾	shot(s)	**Luxardo maraschino liqueur**
¾	shot(s)	**Chilled mineral water** (omit if wet ice)

Origin: Adapted from Harry Craddock's 1930 'The Savoy Cocktail Book'.
Comment: Spicy maraschino dominates this old-school after dinner cocktail.

HONOLULU JUICER

Glass: Collins
Garnish: Pineapple wedge & cherry
Method: SHAKE all ingredients with ice and strain into glass filled with crushed ice.

1	shot(s)	**Gosling's Black Seal rum**
1½	shot(s)	**Southern Comfort liqueur**
2	shot(s)	**Pressed pineapple juice**
¾	shot(s)	**Rose's lime cordial**
¾	shot(s)	**Freshly squeezed lemon juice**
¼	shot(s)	**Sugar syrup (2 sugar to 1 water)**

Origin: A classic Tiki drink.
Comment: A practically tropical, rum laced, fruity number.

HOOPLA

Glass: Martini
Garnish: Orange zest twist
Method: SHAKE all ingredients with ice and fine strain into chilled glass.

1	shot(s)	**Rémy Martin cognac**
1	shot(s)	**Cointreau triple sec**
¾	shot(s)	**Dry vermouth**
¾	shot(s)	**Freshly squeezed lemon juice**
½	fresh	**Egg white**

Comment: Not far removed from a Sidecar.

HOP TOAD #1 

Glass: Martini
Garnish: Apricot wedge on rim
Method: **SHAKE** all ingredients with ice and fine strain into chilled glass.

1¼	shot(s)	**Light white rum**
1¼	shot(s)	**Giffard apricot brandy du Roussillon**
1¼	shot(s)	**Freshly squeezed lime juice**
½	shot(s)	**Chilled mineral water** (omit if wet ice)

Variant: Made with brandy this is sometimes known as a Bullfrog.
Origin: First published in Tom Bullock's 'Ideal Bartender', circa 1917.
Comment: Resembles an apricot Daiquiri that's heavy on the lime yet balanced.

HOP TOAD #2

Glass: Martini
Garnish: Apricot wedge on rim
Method: **SHAKE** all ingredients with ice and fine strain into chilled glass.

1¾	shot(s)	**Aged rum**
1	shot(s)	**Giffard apricot brandy du Roussillon**
¾	shot(s)	**Freshly squeezed lime juice**
½	shot(s)	**Chilled mineral water** (omit if wet ice)

Comment: Alcoholic apricot jam with a lovely twang of aged rum.

HOP TOAD #3 [NEW #7] 

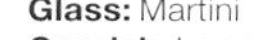

Glass: Martini
Garnish: Lemon zest twist
Method: **SHAKE** all ingredients with ice and fine strain into chilled glass.

1½	shot(s)	**Giffard apricot brandy du Roussillon**
¾	shot(s)	**Freshly squeezed lemon juice**
¾	shot(s)	**Chilled mineral water** (omit if wet ice)

Origin: Adapted from Harry Craddock's 1930 'The Savoy Cocktail Book'.
Comment: Fresh apricot dessert – all it lacks is a dollop of whipped cream.

HORNITOS LAU

Glass: Collins
Garnish: Mint sprig
Method: Lightly **MUDDLE** mint (just to bruise) in base of shaker. Add other ingredients, **SHAKE** with ice and strain into glass filled with crushed ice. **CHURN** (stir) drink and add more crushed ice so drink meets rim of glass.

12	fresh	**Mint leaves**
2	shot(s)	**Partida tequila**
1½	shot(s)	**Licor 43 (Cuarenta Y Tres) liqueur**
½	shot(s)	**Freshly squeezed lime juice**

Origin: Created in 2005 by Jaspar Eyears at Bar Tiki, Mexico City, Mexico.
Comment: Jaspar recommends making a batch in their glasses and refreezing them with the straws already in the glass, like the old colonels and their julep freezers in Kentucky.

HORSE'S NECK WITH A KICK

Glass: Collins
Garnish: Peel rind of a large lemon in a spiral and place in glass with end hanging over rim.
Method: **POUR** ingredients into ice-filled glass and stir.

2	shot(s)	**Buffalo Trace bourbon whiskey**
3	dashes	**Angostura aromatic bitters**
Top up with		**Ginger ale**

Variant: A Horse's Neck without a kick is simply ginger ale and bitters.
Comment: Whiskey and ginger with added shrubbery.

THE HORSESHOE SLING [NEW #7]

Glass: Collins
Garnish: Fresh seasonal fruit
Method: **SHAKE** first five ingredients with ice and strain into ice-filled glass. **TOP** with champagne.

2	shot(s)	**Partida tequila**
¾	shot(s)	**Freshly squeezed lime juice**
½	shot(s)	**Bénédictine D.O.M. liqueur**
½	shot(s)	**Marnier cherry liqueur**
1½	shot(s)	**Pressed pineapple juice**
Top up with		**Brut champagne**

Origin: Adapted from a drink created by Gary Regan, New York, USA.
Comment: Like its creator, this is upfront and refreshingly different.

HOT BUTTERED JACK

Glass: Toddy
Garnish: Grate nutmeg over drink
Method: Place bar spoon in warmed glass. Add ingredients and **STIR** until butter dissolves.

1	large	**Knob (pat) unsalted butter**
2	shot(s)	**Jack Daniel's Tennessee whiskey**
¾	shot(s)	**Sugar syrup (2 sugar to 1 water)**
Top up with		**Boiling water**

Comment: Warming and smooth – great on a cold day or whenever you fancy a warming treat.

HOT BUTTERED RUM

Glass: Toddy
Garnish: Cinnamon stick and slice of lemon studded with cloves
Method: Place bar spoon loaded with honey in warmed glass. Add other ingredients and **STIR** until honey and butter are dissolved.

2	spoons	**Runny honey**
1	large	**Knob (pat) unsalted butter**
2	shot(s)	**Golden rum**
¼	spoon	**Freshly grated nutmeg**
Top up with		**Boiling water (or hot cider)**

Comment: In 'The Fine Art of Mixing Drinks', David Embury says, "The Hot Spiced Rum is bad enough, but the lump of butter is the final insult. It blends with the hot rum just about as satisfactorily as warm olive oil blends with champagne!" It's rare for me to question Embury but I rather like this slightly oily, warming, spicy toddy.

HOT GROG

Glass: Toddy
Garnish: Lemon peel twist
Method: Place bar spoon loaded with honey in warmed glass. Add other ingredients and **STIR** until honey dissolves.

3	spoons	**Runny honey**
1	shot(s)	**Pusser's Navy rum (54.5% alc./vol.)**
1/4	shot(s)	**Freshly squeezed lime juice**
2 1/2	shot(s)	**Boiling water**

Variant: Black Stripe, with molasses replacing the honey.
Comment: Warming, honeyed, pungent rum with a hint of lime.

HOT PASSION

Glass: Collins
Garnish: Maraschino cherry
Method: SHAKE all ingredients with ice and strain into ice-filled glass.

1	shot(s)	**Passoã passion fruit liqueur**
1	shot(s)	**Ketel One vodka**
2	shot(s)	**Ocean Spray cranberry juice**
2	shot(s)	**Freshly squeezed orange juice**

Comment: A fruity, slightly sweet twist on a Madras.

HOT RED BLOODED FRENCHMAN

Glass: Toddy
Garnish: Orange zest twists
Method: Place bar spoon in warmed glass. Add other ingredients and **STIR.**

1	shot(s)	**Grand Marnier liqueur**
2	shot(s)	**Red wine (Claret)**
1/2	shot(s)	**Freshly squeezed orange juice**
1/2	shot(s)	**Freshly squeezed lemon juice**
1/4	shot(s)	**Sugar syrup (2 sugar to 1 water)**
Top up with		**Boiling water**

Comment: Warm, fruity red wine – great on a cold night.

HOT RUM PUNCH

Glass: Toddy
Garnish: Ground nutmeg
Method: Place bar spoon in warmed glass. Add ingredients and **STIR.**

1	shot(s)	**Golden rum**
1	shot(s)	**Rémy Martin cognac**
1/2	shot(s)	**Tio Pepe fino sherry**
1/4	shot(s)	**Sugar syrup (2 sugar to 1 water)**
1	shot(s)	**Freshly squeezed lime juice**
Top up with		**Boiling water**

Origin: Punch originated in India, where it was most probably made with arrack. Rum punches were popular during the 1700s. This version is said to have been a favourite drink of Mozart the composer.
Comment: A great winter warmer.

HOT SHOT

Glass: Shot
Method: LAYER by carefully pouring ingredients in the following order.

3/4	shot(s)	**Galliano liqueur**
3/4	shot(s)	**Hot espresso coffee**
1/2	shot(s)	**Double (heavy) cream**

Origin: A huge drink in Scandinavia during the early nineties.
Comment: The Scandinavian answer to Irish coffee.

HOT TODDY #1

Glass: Toddy
Garnish: Cinnamon stick
Method: Place bar spoon loaded with honey in warmed glass. Add other ingredients and **STIR** until honey dissolves.

1	spoon	**Runny honey**
2	shot(s)	**Scotch whisky**
1/2	shot(s)	**Freshly squeezed lemon juice**
1/2	shot(s)	**Sugar syrup (2 sugar to 1 water)**
3	dried	**Cloves**
Top up with		**Boiling water**

Origin: Lost in time but Dickens refers to a "Whisky Toddy" in 'The Pickwick Papers'.
Comment: The smoky flavours in the Scotch add spice to this warming drink that's great when you're feeling down with a cold or the flu.

HOT TODDY #2

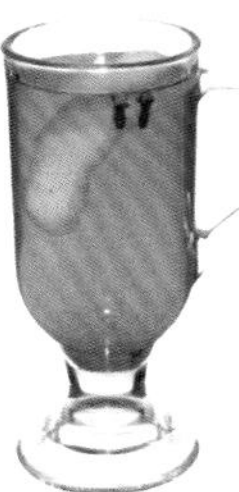

Glass: Toddy
Garnish: Lemon zest twist
Method: Place bar spoon loaded with honey in warmed glass. Add other ingredients and **STIR** until honey dissolves.

1	spoon	**Runny honey**
2	shot(s)	**Scotch whisky**
3	dried	**Cloves**
1/4	spoon	**Freshly grated nutmeg**
Top up with		**Hot black English breakfast tea**

Comment: Tea and Scotch combine wonderfully in this hot and spicy winter warmer.

HOT TODDY #3 [NEW #7]

Glass: Toddy
Garnish: Lemon slice & cinnamon stick
Method: Place bar spoon in warmed glass. Add ingredients and **STIR**.

2	shot(s)	**Rémy Martin cognac**
1/2	shot(s)	**Freshly squeezed lemon juice**
1/4	shot(s)	**Sugar syrup (2 sugar to 1 water)**
Top up with		**Boiling water**

Comment: Warms the cockles with cognac and a good dose of citrus.

HOT TUB

Glass: Martini
Garnish: Pineapple wedge on rim
Method: SHAKE first three ingredients with ice and fine strain into chilled glass. **TOP** with Prosecco.

1½ shot(s)	**Ketel One vodka**
¼ shot(s)	**Chambord black raspberry liqueur**
1 shot(s)	**Pressed pineapple juice**
Top up with	**Prosecco sparkling wine or Champagne**

Origin: Adapted from a drink discovered in 2004 at Teatro, Boston, USA.
Comment: Basically a French Martini with bubbles.

HOULA-HOULA COCKTAIL [NEW #7]

Glass: Martini
Garnish: Orange zest twist
Method: SHAKE all ingredients with ice and fine strain into chilled glass.

2 shot(s)	**Plymouth gin**
1 shot(s)	**Freshly squeezed orange juice**
½ shot(s)	**Cointreau triple sec**
½ shot(s)	**Chilled mineral water** (omit if wet ice)

Origin: Adapted from Harry Craddock's 1930 'The Savoy Cocktail Book'.
Comment: Orange generously laced with gin.

HUAPALA COCKTAIL [NEW #7]

Glass: Martini
Garnish: Lemon wedge on rim
Method: SHAKE all ingredients with ice and fine strain into chilled glass.

1 shot(s)	**Light white rum**
1 shot(s)	**Plymouth gin**
½ shot(s)	**Freshly squeezed lemon juice**
¼ shot(s)	**Pomegranate (grenadine) syrup**
½ shot(s)	**Chilled mineral water** (omit if wet ice)

Origin: Adapted from Victor Bergeron's 'Trader Vic's Bartender's Guide' (1972 revised edition).
Comment: In his book Vic prefaces this cocktail with the comment, "Nice, easy drink". It's basically a lemon Daiquiri with gin and grenadine.

HULK

Glass: Old-fashioned
Method: LAYER ingredients in ice-filled glass by carefully pouring in the following order.

2 shot(s)	**Hpnotiq liqueur**
1 shot(s)	**Rémy Martin cognac**

Comment: Turns green when mixed. A crying waste of good cognac.

HUMMINGBIRD [NEW #7]

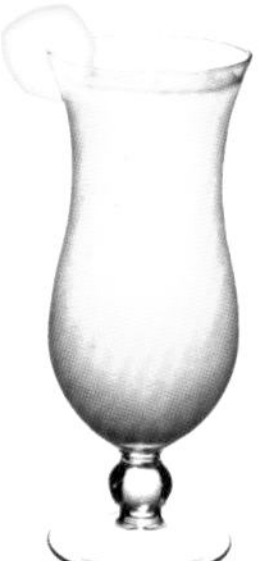

Glass: Hurricane
Garnish: Banana slice
Method: BLEND all ingredients with 12oz scoop crushed ice and serve with straws.

1½ shot(s)	**Light white rum**
½ shot(s)	**Kahlúa coffee liqueur**
1 shot(s)	**Giffard crème de banane du Brésil**
1 shot(s)	**Coco López cream of coconut**
1 fresh	**Banana (peeled & chopped)**

Origin: The house cocktail at the Hummingbird Beach Resort, Soufriere, St. Lucia.
Comment: With flavours of rum, coconut, banana and coffee, this tall, frozen drink tastes rather like dessert.

HUNK MARTINI

Glass: Martini
Garnish: Maraschino cherry in drink
Method: SHAKE all ingredients with ice and fine strain into chilled glass.

2 shot(s)	**Vanilla infused Ketel One vodka**
1¾ shot(s)	**Pressed pineapple juice**
½ shot(s)	**Freshly squeezed lime juice**
¼ shot(s)	**Sugar syrup (2 sugar to 1 water)**

Origin: The drink Carrie and co discovered in the summer of 2003. In this series the Sex And The City stars dropped Cosmopolitans in favour of Hunks – no change there then!
Comment: Pineapple and vanilla combine wonderfully. American readers may notice more than a passing resemblance to a Key Lime Pie served without the Graham Cracker rim.

HURRICANE #1

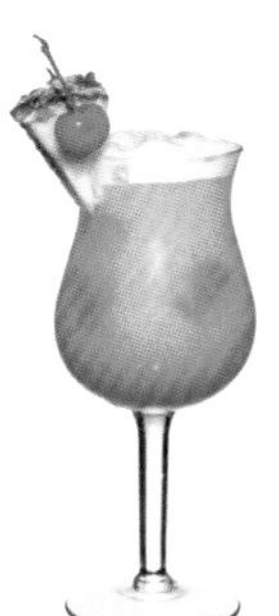

Glass: Hurricane
Garnish: Pineapple wedge & cherry on rim
Method: SHAKE all ingredients with ice and strain into ice-filled glass.

1½ shot(s)	**Light white rum**
1 shot(s)	**Pusser's Navy rum**
1 shot(s)	**Freshly squeezed orange juice**
1 shot(s)	**Pressed pineapple juice**
¾ shot(s)	**Rose's lime cordial**
½ shot(s)	**Freshly squeezed lime juice**
¼ shot(s)	**Passion fruit sugar syrup**

Origin: Named after the shape of a hurricane lamp and served in the tall, shapely glass of the same name. Thought to have originated in 1939 at The Hurricane Bar, New York City, but made famous at Pat O'Brien's in New Orleans. Some old cocktail books list a much earlier Hurricane made with cognac, absinthe and vodka.
Comment: A strong, tangy, refreshing drink packed with fruit and laced with rum.

HURRICANE #2

Glass: Hurricane
Garnish: Orange slice & cherry on stick (sail)
Method: Cut passion fruit in half and scoop flesh into shaker. Add other ingredients, **SHAKE** with ice and strain into ice-filled glass.

1	fresh	**Passion fruit**
1½	shot(s)	**Gosling's Black Seal rum**
1½	shot(s)	**Light white rum**
1	shot(s)	**Freshly squeezed orange juice**
1	shot(s)	**Pressed pineapple juice**
½	shot(s)	**Freshly squeezed lime juice**
¼	shot(s)	**Passion fruit sugar syrup**
¼	shot(s)	**Pomegranate (grenadine) syrup**

Comment: Sweet, tangy and potentially dangerous.

'WHEN I PLAYED DRUNKS I HAD TO REMAIN SOBER BECAUSE I DIDN'T KNOW HOW TO PLAY THEM WHEN I WAS DRUNK.'

HURRICANE #3 [NEW #7]

Glass: Hurricane
Garnish: Pineapple wedge & cherry
Method: SHAKE all ingredients with ice and fine strain into ice-filled glass.

1	shot(s)	**Light white rum**
1	shot(s)	**Goslings Black Seal dark rum**
½	shot(s)	**Galliano liqueur**
2	shot(s)	**Pressed pineapple juice**
2	shot(s)	**Freshly squeezed orange juice**
¾	shot(s)	**Freshly squeezed lime juice**
¾	shot(s)	**Passion fruit sugar syrup**
2	dashes	**Angostura aromatic bitters**

Origin: Adapted from a 2006 recipe by Chris McMillian, New Orleans, USA.
Comment: A veritable tropical fruit salad laced with rum.

THE HYPNOTIC MARGARITA [NEW #7]

Glass: Coupette
Garnish: Lime wedge on rim
Method: SHAKE all ingredients with ice and fine strain into chilled glass.

1½	shot(s)	**Partida blanco tequila**
½	shot(s)	**Cointreau triple sec**
½	shot(s)	**Hpnotiq liqueur**
½	shot(s)	**Freshly squeezed lime juice**

Origin: Created in 2005 by Gary Regan at Painter's, Cornwall-on-Hudson, New York, USA.
Comment: Liqueurs combine harmoniously with lime and tequila in this tangy, fruity Margarita. However, I remain unconvinced by Hpnotiq.

I B DAMM'D [UPDATED #7]

Glass: Martini
Garnish: Peach wedge
Method: SHAKE all ingredients with ice and fine strain into chilled glass.

2	shot(s)	**Bokma Oude Genever**
½	shot(s)	**St-Germain elderflower liqueur**
¼	shot(s)	**Teichenné Peach Schnapps Liqueur**
1	shot(s)	**Pressed apple juice**

Origin: Adapted from a drink discovered in 2003 at Oxo Tower Bar, London, England.
Comment: A subtle combination of fruit and floral flavours.

ICE MAIDEN MARTINI

Glass: Martini
Garnish: Orange zest twist
Method: STIR all ingredients with ice and strain into chilled glass.

1½	shot(s)	**Plymouth gin**
1	shot(s)	**Icewine**
¾	shot(s)	**Sauvignon Blanc or unoaked Chardonnay wine**
¾	shot(s)	**Chilled mineral water** (reduce if wet ice)

Origin: Created in 2004 by yours truly.
Comment: A subtle Martini with the honeyed flavours of icewine melding with botanicals in the gin and balanced by the acidity of the white wine.

ICE 'T' KNEE

Glass: Martini
Garnish: Lemon zest twist
Method: STIR all ingredients with ice and strain into chilled glass.

2	shot(s)	**Ketel One vodka**
1½	shot(s)	**Cold strong jasmine tea**
¾	shot(s)	**Icewine**

Origin: Created by yours truly in 2004.
Comment: Honeyed palate topped off with tannin and jasmine.

ICE WHITE COSMO

Glass: Martini
Garnish: Flamed orange zest twist
Method: SHAKE all ingredients with ice and fine strain into chilled glass.

2	shot(s)	**Ketel One vodka**
¾	shot(s)	**Icewine**
1¼	shot(s)	**Ocean Spray white cranberry**
¼	shot(s)	**Freshly squeezed lime juice**

Origin: Created by yours truly in 2004.
Comment: Recognisably from the Cosmo family but wonderfully different.

ICED SAKE MARTINI

Glass: Martini
Garnish: Float 3 slices cucumber
Method: STIR all ingredients with ice and strain into chilled glass.

2	shot(s)	**Ketel One vodka**
2	shot(s)	**Sake**
1/4	shot(s)	**Icewine**

Origin: Created in 2004 by yours truly.
Comment: The icewine adds interest and wonderfully honeyed notes to this Sake Martini.

ICED TEA

Glass: Collins
Garnish: Lime wedge
Method: SHAKE first six ingredients with ice and strain into glass filled with crushed ice. **TOP** with cola.

1/2	shot(s)	**Rémy Martin cognac**
1/2	shot(s)	**Gosling's Black Seal rum**
1/2	shot(s)	**Cointreau triple sec**
1/2	shot(s)	**Freshly squeezed orange juice**
1/2	shot(s)	**Freshly squeezed lime juice**
2	shot(s)	**Cold breakfast tea**
Top up with		**Cola**

Origin: Created in 1990 by Charles Schumann, Munich, Germany.
Comment: Sweetened and fortified fruity cola.

ICED TEA MARTINI [NEW #7]

Glass: Martini
Garnish: Lemon zest twist
Method: SHAKE all ingredients with ice and strain into chilled glass.

2	shot(s)	**Plymouth gin**
1/2	shot(s)	**Dry vermouth**
1	shot(s)	**Cold Earl Grey tea**
1/2	shot(s)	**Sugar syrup (2 sugar to 1 water)**

Origin: Created in 2006 by yours truly.
Comment: Tannic and bittersweet - a very refreshing after dinner drink.

ICEWINE MARTINI

Glass: Martini
Garnish: Orange zest twist
Method: STIR all ingredients with ice and strain into chilled glass.

1 1/2	shot(s)	**Ketel One vodka**
1 1/2	shot(s)	**Icewine**
1 1/2	shot(s)	**Pressed apple juice**

Origin: Created in 2004 by yours truly.
Comment: Delicate with subtle flavours.

ICY PINK LEMONADE

Glass: Collins
Garnish: Lemon wheel
Method: SHAKE first four ingredients with ice and strain into ice-filled glass. **TOP** with soda.

2	shot(s)	**Ketel One vodka**
1/2	shot(s)	**Chambord black raspberry liqueur**
2	shot(s)	**Freshly squeezed lemon juice**
1/2	shot(s)	**Sugar syrup (2 sugar to 1 water)**
Top up with		**Soda water (club soda)**

Comment: Tangy, citrussy, fruity and refreshing - just not that butch.

IGNORANCE IS BLISS

Glass: Collins
Garnish: Half passion fruit
Method: SHAKE all ingredients with ice and strain into ice-filled glass.

2	shot(s)	**Ketel One Citroen vodka**
1/2	shot(s)	**Campari**
3	shot(s)	**Pressed apple juice**
1/4	shot(s)	**Passion fruit sugar syrup**

Comment: This long drink has a bitter bite.

IGUANA

Glass: Shot
Method: SHAKE all ingredients with ice and fine strain into chilled glass.

1/2	shot(s)	**Ketel One vodka**
1/2	shot(s)	**Partida tequila**
1/2	shot(s)	**Kahlúa coffee liqueur**

Comment: Coffee and tequila's successful relationship is enhanced by the introduction of vodka.

IGUANA WANA

Glass: Old-fashioned
Garnish: Orange slice
Method: SHAKE all ingredients with ice and strain into ice-filled glass.

1	shot(s)	**Ketel One vodka**
3/4	shot(s)	**Teichenné Peach Schnapps Liqueur**
2 1/2	shot(s)	**Freshly squeezed orange juice**

Comment: Orange juice and peach schnapps, laced with vodka.

I'LL TAKE MANHATTAN

Glass: Martini
Garnish: Maraschino cherry
Method: STIR all ingredients with ice and strain into chilled glass.

2 shot(s) **Buffalo Trace bourbon whiskey**
1 shot(s) **Sweet vermouth**
1/2 shot(s) **Cherry (brandy) liqueur**
2 dashes **Angostura aromatic bitters**

Origin: Adapted from a drink discovered in 2005 at The Stanton Social, New York City, USA.
Comment: Cherry is more than a garnish in this twist on the classic Manhattan.

ILLICIT AFFAIR

Glass: Old-fashioned
Garnish: Orange slice
Method: SHAKE all ingredients with ice and strain into ice-filled glass.

2 shot(s) **Raspberry flavoured vodka**
1 3/4 shot(s) **Freshly squeezed orange juice**
1 3/4 shot(s) **Ocean Spray cranberry juice**

Comment: Fruity, easy drinking.

ILLUSION

Glass: Collins
Garnish: Watermelon wedge on rim
Method: SHAKE all ingredients with ice and strain into ice-filled glass.

2 shot(s) **Ketel One vodka**
3/4 shot(s) **Cointreau triple sec**
3/4 shot(s) **Midori melon liqueur**
2 1/2 shot(s) **Freshly pressed pineapple juice**

Comment: This medium-sweet, lime green drink is one for a summer's day by the pool.

IMPERIAL MARTINI

Glass: Martini
Garnish: Maraschino cherry
Method: STIR all ingredients with ice and strain into chilled glass.

1 1/2 shot(s) **Plymouth gin**
1 1/2 shot(s) **Dry vermouth**
3 dashes **Angostura aromatic bitters**
1/8 shot(s) **Luxardo Maraschino liqueur**

Comment: This rust coloured Martini is very dry despite the inclusion of maraschino liqueur – not for everyone.

IN-SEINE [NEW #7]

Glass: Old-fashioned
Garnish: Lemon zest twist (discard) & 3 grapes on stick
Method: POUR absinthe into ice-filled glass, **TOP** with water and leave to stand. Separately **SHAKE** other ingredients with ice. **DISCARD** contents of glass (absinthe, water and ice) and fine strain contents of shaker into absinthe-rinsed glass.

1/2 shot(s) **La Fée Parisienne (68%) absinthe**
2 shot(s) **Rémy Martin cognac**
1 1/2 shot(s) **St-Germain elderflower liqueur**
1/2 fresh **Egg white**

Origin: Created in 2006 by yours truly.
Comment: An insanely good accompaniment to an after dinner cigar.

INCOGNITO 

Glass: Martini
Garnish: Apricot slice on rim
Method: SHAKE all ingredients with ice and fine strain into chilled glass.

1 1/2 shot(s) **Rémy Martin cognac**
1 1/2 shot(s) **Dry vermouth**
1 shot(s) **Giffard apricot brandy du Roussillon**
3 dashes **Angostura aromatic bitters**

Comment: Dry with hints of sweet apricot – most unusual.

INCOME TAX COCKTAIL

Glass: Martini
Garnish: Orange zest twist
Method: SHAKE all ingredients with ice and fine strain into chilled glass.

1 shot(s) **Plymouth gin**
1 shot(s) **Dry vermouth**
1 shot(s) **Sweet vermouth**
1 shot(s) **Freshly squeezed orange juice**
1 dash **Angostura aromatic bitters**

Origin: Classic of unknown origin.
Comment: Income tax should be scrapped in favour of purchase tax but the cocktail is rather good. Dry and aromatic.

INDIAN ROSE

Glass: Martini
Garnish: Edible rose petal
Method: SHAKE all ingredients with ice and fine strain into chilled glass.

2 1/2 shot(s) **Plymouth gin**
1/4 shot(s) **Giffard apricot brandy du Roussillon**
1/4 shot(s) **Rosewater**
1/4 shot(s) **Rose syrup**
1/2 shot(s) **Chilled mineral water** (omit if wet ice)

Origin: Adapted from a drink discovered in 2005 at Mie N Yu, Washington DC, USA.
Comment: Subtle rose hue and flavour.

INGA FROM SWEDEN

Glass: Collins
Garnish: Strawberry
Method: **MUDDLE** strawberries in base of shaker. Add other ingredients, **SHAKE** with ice and fine strain into ice-filled glass.

2	fresh	**Strawberries**
1½	shot(s)	**Xanté pear liqueur**
½	shot(s)	**Campari**
2	shot(s)	**Ocean Spray cranberry juice**
¼	shot(s)	**Sugar syrup (2 sugar to 1 water)**
¼	shot(s)	**Freshly squeezed lime juice**

Comment: Inga must like a touch of bitter Italian with her fruit.

INK MARTINI #1

Glass: Martini
Garnish: Orange zest twist
Method: **SHAKE** all ingredients with ice and fine strain into chilled glass.

1¼	shot(s)	**Plymouth gin**
½	shot(s)	**Bols Blue curaçao liqueur**
½	shot(s)	**Teichenné Peach Schnapps Liqueur**
2	shot(s)	**Ocean Spray cranberry juice**

Origin: Created in 2002 by Gentian Naci at Bar Epernay, Birmingham, England.
Comment: This simple, appropriately named drink is surprisingly quaffable.

INK MARTINI #2

Glass: Martini
Garnish: Orange zest twist
Method: **SHAKE** all ingredients with ice and fine strain into chilled glass.

2	shot(s)	**Ketel One vodka**
½	shot(s)	**Bols Blue curaçao liqueur**
1½	shot(s)	**Ocean Spray cranberry juice**

Origin: Discovered in 2005 at Halo, Atlanta, USA.
Comment: Surprisingly subtle and pleasant in flavour.

INSOMNIAC

Glass: Martini
Garnish: Float three coffee beans
Method: **SHAKE** all ingredients with ice and fine strain into chilled glass.

¾	shot(s)	**Ketel One vodka**
¾	shot(s)	**Frangelico hazelnut liqueur**
¾	shot(s)	**Kahlúa coffee liqueur**
1	shot(s)	**Cold espresso coffee**
½	shot(s)	**Double (heavy) cream**
½	shot(s)	**Milk**

Variant: Espresso Martini
Comment: Wonderfully balanced, creamy and caffeine laced.

INTERNATIONAL INCIDENT

Glass: Martini
Garnish: Dust with freshly grated nutmeg
Method: **SHAKE** all ingredients with ice and fine strain into chilled glass.

¾	shot(s)	**Ketel One vodka**
¾	shot(s)	**Kahlúa coffee liqueur**
¾	shot(s)	**Luxardo Amaretto di Saschira**
¾	shot(s)	**Frangelico hazelnut liqueur**
1½	shot(s)	**Irish cream liqueur**

Comment: Rich and creamy.

INTIMATE MARTINI

Glass: Martini
Garnish: Orange zest twist
Method: **STIR** all ingredients with ice and strain into chilled glass.

2	shot(s)	**Ketel One vodka**
½	shot(s)	**Dry vermouth**
1	shot(s)	**Giffard apricot brandy du Roussillon**
3	dashes	**Fee Brothers orange bitters**

Comment: Sweet apricot dried and balanced by vermouth and bitters. Surprisingly complex and pleasant.

IRISH ALEXANDER

Glass: Martini
Garnish: Crumbled Cadbury's Flake bar
Method: **SHAKE** all ingredients with ice and fine strain into chilled glass.

1½	shot(s)	**Irish cream liqueur**
1½	shot(s)	**Rémy Martin cognac**
1	shot(s)	**Double (heavy) cream**

Comment: Rich, thick, creamy and yummy.

IRISH CHARLIE

Glass: Shot
Method: **SHAKE** all ingredients with ice and fine strain into chilled glass.

¾	shot(s)	**Irish cream liqueur**
¾	shot(s)	**Giffard white crème de Menthe Pastille**

Variant: Float Baileys on crème de menthe
Comment: The ingredients go surprisingly well together.

IRISH CHOCOLATE ORANJ'TINI

Glass: Martini
Garnish: Crumbled Cadbury's Flake bar
Method: SHAKE all ingredients with ice and fine strain into chilled glass.

1 1/2	shot(s)	**Irish cream liqueur**
1 1/2	shot(s)	**Kahlúa coffee liqueur**
1 1/2	shot(s)	**Grand Marnier liqueur**

Comment: A B-52 served 'up'.

IRISH COFFEE [UPDATED #7]

Glass: Toddy
Garnish: Three coffee beans
Method: Place bar spoon in glass. **POUR** whiskey into glass, top with coffee and stir. FLOAT a thin layer of cream.

1	shot(s)	**Irish whiskey**
Top up with		**Hot filter coffee**
Float		**Lightly whipped double (heavy) cream**

Variant: Sweeten with sugar syrup or liqueur to taste before floating cream.
AKA: Gaelic Coffee
Tip: To ensure a good float, lightly whip or simply shake cream in container before pouring over the bowl of a spoon. It also helps if the cream is gently warmed.
Origin: Created in 1942 by Joe Sheridan, a bartender at Foynes airport, Ireland.
Comment: Like most great ideas, this one is very simple. Coffee with a whiskey kick.

IRISH COFFEE MARTINI

Glass: Martini
Garnish: Float three coffee beans
Method: SHAKE all ingredients with ice and fine strain into chilled glass.

1 1/2	shot(s)	**Irish whiskey**
2	shot(s)	**Cold espresso coffee**
1/2	shot(s)	**Sugar syrup (2 sugar to 1 water)**
1	shot(s)	**Double (heavy) cream**

Origin: Created in 2003 by yours truly.
Comment: Forget sipping warm java through a cold head of cream. This Martini version of the classic Irish Coffee offers all the flavour without the moustache.

IRISH ESPRESSO'TINI

Glass: Martini
Garnish: Float three coffee beans
Method: SHAKE all ingredients with ice and fine strain into chilled glass.

2	shot(s)	**Irish cream liqueur**
1 1/4	shot(s)	**Vanilla-infused Ketel One vodka**
1 1/4	shot(s)	**Cold espresso coffee**

Comment: Richly flavoured with a pleasingly bitter finish.

IRISH FLAG

Glass: Shot
Method: Refrigerate ingredients and **LAYER** in chilled glass by carefully pouring in the following order.

1/2	shot(s)	**Giffard white crème de Menthe Pastille**
1/2	shot(s)	**Irish Cream liqueur**
1/2	shot(s)	**Grand Marnier liqueur**

Origin: The Irish tricolour is the national flag of the Republic of Ireland. Its three equal stripes represent the political landscape. Orange stands for the Protestants because of William of Orange, the Protestant king of England who defeated the Roman Catholic James II in 1690. Green stands for the Catholic nationalists of the south and white for the hope for peace between Catholics and Protestants.
Comment: Tricoloured orange and mint smoothed with cream liqueur.

IRISH FRAPPÉ

Glass: Hurricane
Garnish: Float three coffee beans
Method: BLEND all ingredients with two 12oz scoops of crushed ice and serve with straws.

3	shot(s)	**Irish cream liqueur**
2	shot(s)	**Cold espresso coffee**
2	scoops	**Coffee ice cream**

Comment: A tasty frappé with coffee, cream and a hint of whiskey.

IRISH LATTE

Glass: Toddy
Method: POUR ingredients into warmed glass in the following order.

1	shot(s)	**Hot espresso coffee**
1 1/2	shot(s)	**Irish cream liqueur**
Top up with		**Steamed semi-skimmed foaming milk**

Comment: A latte with extra interest and flavour courtesy of Irish cream liqueur.

IRISH MANHATTAN

Glass: Martini
Garnish: Shamrock
Method: STIR all ingredients with ice and strain into chilled glass.

1 1/2	shot(s)	**Buffalo Trace bourbon whiskey**
1	shot(s)	**Tuaca Italian liqueur**
1/2	shot(s)	**Grand Marnier liqueur**
1/4	shot(s)	**Vanilla sugar syrup**

Origin: Adapted from a drink discovered in 2001 at Detroit, London, England.
Comment: There's nothing Irish about this drink, but it's good all the same.

IRISH COFFEE

This now ubiquitous cocktail was created in 1942 by Joe Sheridan, a bartender at Foynes airport (near the present-day Shannon airport). The majority of transatlantic flights used to stop to refuel in Ireland and in 1947 an American journalist, Stan Delaphane, found himself at Joe Sheridan's bar and tried his Irish Coffee. Delaphane was so impressed that on returning home he passed the recipe on to the bartender at his local bar, the Buena Vista Café in San Francisco. The recipe spread and the drink became a classic.

IRRESISTIBLE [NEW #7]

Glass: Martini
Garnish: Lemon zest twist
Method: SHAKE all ingredients with ice and fine strain into chilled glass.

1½ shot(s) **Light white rum**
½ shot(s) **Sweet vermouth**
¼ shot(s) **Bénédictine D.O.M. liqueur**
¼ shot(s) **Freshly squeezed lemon juice**
¾ shot(s) **Chilled mineral water** (omit if wet ice)

Comment: Herbal yet delicate with hints of citrus.

ISLAND BREEZE

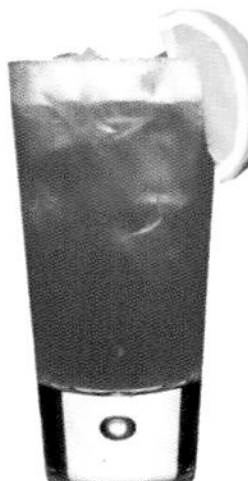

Glass: Collins
Garnish: Grapefruit wedge on rim
Method: SHAKE all ingredients with ice and strain into ice-filled glass.

2 shot(s) **Malibu coconut rum liqueur**
2½ shot(s) **Ocean Spray cranberry juice**
1½ shot(s) **Freshly squeezed grapefruit juice**

Origin: Named after the Twelve Islands Shipping Company, the Caribbean producers of Malibu.
Comment: Great balance of sweet and sour flavours.

ITALIAN JOB # 1

Glass: Collins
Garnish: Orange slice
Method: SHAKE first six ingredients with ice and strain into ice-filled glass. **TOP** with tonic water, stir and serve with straws.

¾ shot(s) **Monasterium liqueur**
¾ shot(s) **Campari**
¾ shot(s) **Mandarine Napoléon liqueur**
1½ shot(s) **Freshly squeezed golden grapefruit juice**
½ shot(s) **Freshly squeezed lemon juice**
¼ shot(s) **Sugar syrup (2 sugar to 1 water)**
Top up with **Tonic water**

Origin: Created by Tony Conigliaro in 2001 at Isola, Knightsbridge, London, England.
Comment: This orange coloured drink combines sweet and sour flavours in a most interesting and grown up way.

ITALIAN JOB #2

Glass: Sling
Garnish: Orange peel twist
Method: SHAKE first three ingredients with ice and strain into glass filled with crushed ice. **TOP** with wine and serve with straws.

1 shot(s) **Tuaca Italian liqueur**
1 shot(s) **Luxardo Amaretto di Saschira**
1 shot(s) **Ocean Spray cranberry juice**
Top up with **Red wine (Shiraz)**

Origin: Discovered in 2002 at Rapscallion, London, England.
Comment: Mix layers with straw prior to drinking for vanillaed, almond, fruity wine.

ITALIAN MARGARITA [NEW #7]

Glass: Martini
Garnish: Lime wedge on rim
Method: SHAKE all ingredients with ice and fine strain into chilled glass.

2 shot(s) **Partida tequila**
½ shot(s) **Cointreau triple sec**
½ shot(s) **Luxardo Amaretto di Saschira**
1 shot(s) **Freshly squeezed lime juice**

Origin: Discovered in 2005 at the Club Bar, The Peninsula Beverly Hills, USA.
Comment: A liberal dash of amaretto adds very Italian subtexts of apricot and almond to your classic Margarita.

ITALIAN SUN

Glass: Martini
Garnish: Lemon zest twist
Method: SHAKE all ingredients with ice and fine strain into chilled glass.

2 shot(s) **Sauvignon Blanc wine**
1½ shot(s) **Luxardo Limoncello liqueur**
¾ shot(s) **Frangelico hazelnut liqueur**
½ shot(s) **Freshly squeezed lemon juice**

Origin: Created in 2002 by Dan Spink at Browns, St Martin's Lane, London, England.
Comment: Tastes rather like a bon bon (a round, sugar coated, lemon flavoured sweet).

ITALIAN SURFER WITH A RUSSIAN ATTITUDE

Glass: Martini
Method: SHAKE all ingredients with ice and fine strain into chilled glass.

1½ shot(s) **Ketel One vodka**
½ shot(s) **Luxardo Amaretto di Saschira**
½ shot(s) **Malibu coconut rum liqueur**
¾ shot(s) **Pressed pineapple juice**
¾ shot(s) **Ocean Spray cranberry juice**

Variant: Served as a long drink, over ice in a Collins glass.
Comment: Fruity and easy drinking but a tad sweet.

I.V.F. MARTINI

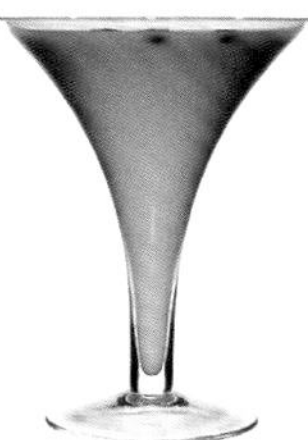

Glass: Martini
Garnish: Float three coffee beans
Method: SHAKE first four ingredients with ice and strain into glass. **FLOAT** cream on drink.

1 shot(s) **La Fée Parisienne (68%) absinthe**
½ shot(s) **Kahlúa coffee liqueur**
½ shot(s) **Tuaca Italian liqueur**
2 shot(s) **Cold espresso coffee**
1 shot(s) **Double (heavy) cream**

Origin: Created by Giovanni Burdi, London, England. In this case I.V.F. stands for 'Italy v France' not 'in vitro fertilisation'.
Comment: Creamy, sweetened absinthe and coffee – hardcore but tasty.

JACK COLLINS

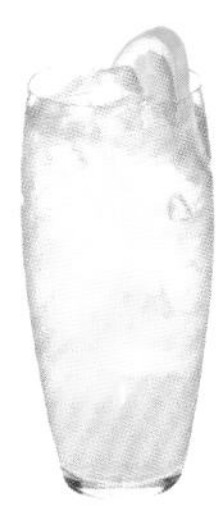

Glass: Collins
Garnish: Lemon slice
Method: SHAKE first three ingredients with ice and strain into ice-filled glass. **TOP** with soda, stir and serve with straws.

2	shot(s)	**Boulard Grand Solage Calvados**
1	shot(s)	**Freshly squeezed lemon juice**
1/2	shot(s)	**Sugar syrup (2 sugar to 1 water)**
Top up with		**Soda water (club soda)**

Origin: A Collins named after its applejack (apple brandy) base.
Comment: Apple brandy makes a great base spirit in this refreshing classic.

JACK DEMPSEY

Glass: Martini
Garnish: Maraschino cherry
Method: SHAKE all ingredients with ice and fine strain into chilled glass.

1 1/2	shot(s)	**Light white rum**
1 1/2	shot(s)	**Plymouth gin**
1/4	shot(s)	**Freshly squeezed lemon juice**
1/4	shot(s)	**Sugar syrup (2 sugar to 1 water)**
3/4	shot(s)	**Chilled mineral water** (omit if wet ice)

Comment: Dilution makes or breaks this subtle, gin laced drink.

JACK FROST

Glass: Old-fashioned
Garnish: Orange zest twist
Method: SHAKE all ingredients with ice and strain into ice-filled glass.

2	shot(s)	**Jack Daniel's Tennessee whiskey**
1/2	shot(s)	**Drambuie liqueur**
3/4	shot(s)	**Freshly squeezed orange juice**
1/2	shot(s)	**Freshly squeezed lemon juice**
1/4	shot(s)	**Pomegranate (grenadine) syrup**

Comment: Tangy and fruity with the whiskey base dominating.

JACK-IN-THE-BOX [UPDATED #7]

Glass: Martini
Garnish: Pineapple wedge on rim
Method: SHAKE all ingredients with ice and fine strain into chilled glass.

2	shot(s)	**Boulard Grand Solage Calvados**
2	shot(s)	**Pressed pineapple juice**
2	dashes	**Angostura aromatic bitters**

AKA: Jersey City
Variant: Pineapple Blossom
Origin: A classic cocktail of unknown origin.
Comment: Smooth 'n' easy apple and pineapple with spirity spice.

JACK MAPLES [NEW #7]

Glass: Martini
Garnish: Dust with ground cinnamon
Method: SHAKE all ingredients with ice and fine strain into chilled glass.

2	shot(s)	**Boulard Grand Solage Calvados**
1/4	shot(s)	**Maple syrup**
1	dash	**Fee Brothers orange bitters**

Comment: Maple syrup smoothes apple brandy, even as it enhances its character.

JACK PUNCH

Glass: Collins
Garnish: Pineapple wedge on rim
Method: Cut passion fruit in half and scoop flesh into shaker. Add other ingredients, **SHAKE** with ice and strain into ice-filled glass.

1	fresh	**Passion fruit**
2	shot(s)	**Jack Daniel's Tennessee whiskey**
1/2	shot(s)	**Licor 43 (Cuarenta Y Tres) liqueur**
3	shot(s)	**Pressed pineapple juice**
1/8	shot(s)	**Sugar syrup (2 sugar to 1 water)**
3	dashes	**Angostura aromatic bitters**

Origin: Adapted from a recipe created in 2002 at Townhouse, London, England.
Comment: Vanilla hints in the whiskey and liqueur combine to dominate this fruity long drink.

JACK ROSE [UPDATED #7]

Glass: Martini
Garnish: Lemon wedge on rim
Method: SHAKE all ingredients with ice and fine strain into chilled glass.

2	shot(s)	**Boulard Grand Solage Calvados**
1/2	shot(s)	**Freshly squeezed lemon juice**
1/2	shot(s)	**Pomegranate (grenadine) syrup**
2	dashes	**Peychaud's aromatic bitters (optional)**
1/2	shot(s)	**Chilled mineral water** (omit if wet ice)

Origin: This drink shares its name with the Jacqueminot rose, which takes its own name from the French general, Jean-François Jacqueminot. According to Albert S. Crockett's 'The Old Waldorf-Astoria Bar Book', it should share the flower's dark red hue. Jack Rose was an early 20th century brand of cigars, and the informant in a notorious 1912 murder case: 'jack' could also be short for 'applejack' and 'rose' a reference to the colour.

According to the Police Gazette of 1905, Frank J. May, better known as Jack Rose, a wrestling bartender who practised in New York and New Jersey, created this drink. Some, however, claim it originated with a late 19th century New York gangster called Jack Rose, whose favourite beverage was applejack brandy with lemon and grenadine, while others credit it to an inn, the Colt's Neck.
Comment: An apple brandy sour sweetened with grenadine. Rose-coloured, tart and appley, this is better with a dash of egg white in place of water.

JACKIE O'S ROSE

Glass: Martini
Garnish: Lime wedge on rim
Method: SHAKE all ingredients with ice and fine strain into chilled glass.

2	shot(s)	**Light white rum**
1	shot(s)	**Freshly squeezed lime juice**
1/2	shot(s)	**Cointreau triple sec**
1/2	shot(s)	**Sugar syrup (2 sugar to 1 water)**
1/2	spoon	**Rosewater (optional)**

Comment: In its simplest form this is a Daiquiri with added liqueur - or a Margarita with rum. Whatever, it's a good balance of sweet and sour.

JACKTINI

Glass: Martini
Method: SHAKE all ingredients with ice and fine strain into chilled glass.

1	shot(s)	**Jack Daniel's Tennessee whiskey**
1	shot(s)	**Mandarine Napoléon liqueur**
1 3/4	shot(s)	**Freshly squeezed lemon juice**
1/2	shot(s)	**Sugar syrup (2 sugar to 1 water)**

Comment: A citrus bite and a smooth Tennessee whiskey draw enhanced with rich mandarin liqueur.

JACUZZI

Glass: Flute
Garnish: Orange slice on rim
Method: SHAKE first three ingredients with ice and fine strain into chilled glass. **TOP** with champagne.

1	shot(s)	**Teichenné Peach Schnapps Liqueur**
1/2	shot(s)	**Plymouth gin**
1	shot(s)	**Freshly squeezed orange juice**
Top up with		**Brut champagne**

Comment: A sweet, peachy champagne cocktail.

JADE DAIQUIRI

Glass: Martini
Garnish: Mint leaf
Method: SHAKE all ingredients with ice and fine strain into chilled glass.

2	shot(s)	**Light white rum**
1/4	shot(s)	**Cointreau triple sec**
1/4	shot(s)	**Giffard white crème de Menthe Pastille**
1/2	shot(s)	**Freshly squeezed lime juice**
1/4	shot(s)	**Sugar syrup (2 sugar to 1 water)**

Comment: A Daiquiri with a splash of orange and mint liqueurs. Fresh breath enhancing.

JADE GARDEN [UPDATED #7]

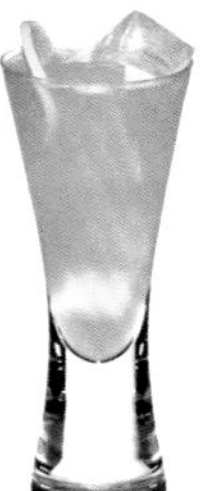

Glass: Collins
Garnish: Lemon slice
Method: SHAKE all ingredients with ice and strain into ice-filled glass.

2	shot(s)	**Ketel One vodka**
1	shot(s)	**St-Germain elderflower liqueur**
1	shot(s)	**Cold jasmine tea**
1 1/2	shot(s)	**Pressed apple juice**
1/2	shot(s)	**Freshly squeezed lemon juice**

Origin: Adapted from a drink created in 2004 by Michael Butt and Giles Looker of Soulshakers, England.
Comment: Not too dry (it has a hint of floral sweetness), nor too sweet (it offers notes of bitter tea and citrus) - just tasty, balanced and refreshing.

JADED LADY [UPDATED #7]

Glass: Martini
Garnish: Grated nutmeg
Method: SHAKE first four ingredients with ice and fine strain into chilled glass. Carefully **POUR** blue curaçao through centre of drink (it should sink to the bottom).

1 1/2	shot(s)	**Plymouth gin**
1 1/2	shot(s)	**Bols advocaat liqueur**
1/2	shot(s)	**Freshly squeezed orange juice**
1	dash	**Fee Brothers orange bitters**
1/8	shot(s)	**Bols Blue curaçao liqueur**

Origin: First created by yours truly in 1996 but reinvented ten years on.
Comment: Distinctly Dutch in style, this thick, creamy drink delivers orange, vanilla and more than a hint of gin.

JAFFA MARTINI

Glass: Martini
Garnish: Float mini Jaffa Cake
Method: SHAKE all ingredients with ice and fine strain into chilled glass.

1	shot(s)	**Cointreau triple sec**
1	shot(s)	**Giffard brown crème de cacao**
1/2	shot(s)	**Orange zest infused Ketel One vodka**
1/2	shot(s)	**Freshly squeezed lemon juice**
1	shot(s)	**Freshly squeezed orange juice**
3	dashes	**Fee Brothers orange bitters (optional)**
1	whole	**Egg**

Origin: Created by yours truly in 2004. McVitie's Jaffa Cakes have a tangy orange jelly centre on a hardish sponge base, covered in dark chocolate. Back in 1991 these tasty little snacks beat off UK Customs & Excise who sought to reclassify them as chocolate biscuits, which, unlike cakes, are categorised as luxuries and so subjected to Value Added Tax.
Comment: Sweet, dessert-style cocktail.

JALISCO

Glass: Martini
Garnish: Grapes on stick
Method: MUDDLE grapes in base of shaker. Add other ingredients, **SHAKE** with ice and fine strain into chilled glass.

12 fresh **Seedless white grapes**
$2^1/_2$ shot(s) **Partida tequila**
$^1/_2$ shot(s) **Sugar syrup (2 sugar to 1 water)**
3 dashes **Fee Brothers orange bitters**

Origin: Created in 2003 by Shelim Islam at GE Club, London, England. Pronounced 'Hal-is-co', this cocktail takes its name from the Mexican state that is home to the town of Tequila and the spirit of the same name.
Comment: It's amazing how well grapes combine with tequila.

JALISCO ESPRESSO

Glass: Martini
Garnish: Float 3 coffee beans
Method: SHAKE all ingredients with ice and fine strain into chilled glass.

2 shot(s) **Partida tequila**
1 shot(s) **Cold espresso coffee**
1 shot(s) **Kahlúa coffee liqueur**

Origin: Adapted from a drink created in 2005 by Henry Besant & Andres Masso, London, England, and named after the Mexican state where the tequila industry is centred.
Comment: A tequila laced wake up call.

JAM ROLL

Glass: Shot
Method: Refrigerate ingredients then **LAYER** in chilled glass by carefully pouring in the following order.

$^1/_2$ shot(s) **Chambord black raspberry liqueur**
$^1/_2$ shot(s) **Frangelico hazelnut liqueur**
$^1/_2$ shot(s) **Irish cream liqueur**

Origin: Created in 2003 at Liquid Lounge, Marbella, Spain.
Comment: A very sweet jam roll laced with alcohol.

JAMAICAN MULE

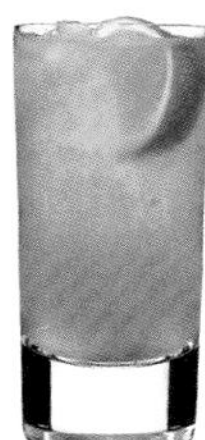

Glass: Collins
Garnish: Lime wedge
Method: POUR ingredients into ice-filled glass and lightly stir.

2 shot(s) **Spiced rum**
$^1/_2$ shot(s) **Freshly squeezed lime juice**
$^1/_2$ shot(s) **Sugar syrup (2 sugar to 1 water)**
Top up with **Ginger beer**

Comment: A long, rum based drink with a spicy ginger taste.

JAMAICAN SUNSET

Glass: Collins
Garnish: Orange slice
Method: SHAKE all ingredients with ice and strain into ice-filled glass.

$1^1/_2$ shot(s) **Wray & Nephew overproof rum**
$1^1/_2$ shot(s) **Ocean Spray cranberry juice**
3 shot(s) **Freshly squeezed orange juice**

Comment: Made with vodka as a base this drink would be called a Madras. Overproof rum adds both strength and flavour.

JAMBALAYA [NEW #7]

Glass: Collins
Garnish: Orange slice & peach wedge
Method: SHAKE all ingredients with ice and strain into glass filled with crushed ice.

2 shot(s) **Partida tequila**
1 shot(s) **Teichenné Peach Schnapps Liqueur**
2 shot(s) **Freshly squeezed orange juice**
$^1/_2$ shot(s) **Freshly squeezed lime juice**
$^1/_4$ shot(s) **Pomegranate (grenadine) syrup**

Comment: Peachy tropical fruit laced with tequila.

JAMBOUREE

Glass: Martini
Garnish: Orange zest twist
Method: STIR preserve with bourbon in base of shaker until mostly dissolved. Add other ingredients, **SHAKE** with ice and fine strain into chilled glass.

2 spoons **Apricot preserve (jam)**
2 shot(s) **Buffalo Trace bourbon whiskey**
$^1/_2$ shot(s) **Grand Marnier liqueur**
$^1/_2$ shot(s) **Freshly squeezed lemon juice**
$^3/_4$ shot(s) **Chilled mineral water** (omit if wet ice)

Comment: Rich and jammy flavours balanced by bourbon and lemon juice.

JAMES JOYCE

Glass: Martini
Garnish: Maraschino cherry
Method: SHAKE all ingredients with ice and fine strain into chilled glass.

$1^1/_2$ shot(s) **Irish whiskey**
$^3/_4$ shot(s) **Sweet vermouth**
$^3/_4$ shot(s) **Cointreau triple sec**
$^1/_2$ shot(s) **Freshly squeezed lime juice**

Origin: Created in 2001 by the American drinks author Gary Regan. This recipe is taken from his book, 'The Joy of Mixology'.
Comment: A balanced adult sour blend.

JA-MORA 

Glass: Flute
Garnish: Float single raspberry
Method: SHAKE first four ingredients with ice and fine strain into chilled glass. **TOP** with champagne.

1	shot(s)	**Ketel One vodka**
1/2	shot(s)	**Chambord black raspberry liqueur**
1/2	shot(s)	**Freshly squeezed orange juice**
1/2	shot(s)	**Pressed apple juice**
Top up with		**Brut champagne**

Origin: Created by Jamie Terrell and Andres Masso in 1998. Named after 'mora', the Spanish for blackberry. The 'j' and 'a' stand for the names of its two creators.
Comment: Ja-more of this fruity champagne cocktail you drink, ja-more you'll like it.

JAPANESE COCKTAIL [UPDATED #7]

Glass: Martini
Garnish: Lemon zest twist
Method: SHAKE all ingredients with ice and fine strain into chilled glass.

2	shot(s)	**Rémy Martin cognac**
1/2	shot(s)	**Almond (orgeat) sugar syrup**
2	dashes	**Angostura aromatic bitters**
3/4	shot(s)	**Chilled mineral water** (reduce if wet ice)

Variant: Stirred rather than shaken.
Origin: Adapted from a recipe first published in Jerry Thomas' 1862 'Bar-Tender's Guide or How To Mix Drinks'.
Comment: Lightly sweetened and diluted cognac flavoured with almond and a hint of spice.

JAPANESE PEAR

Glass: Martini
Garnish: Pear slice on rim
Method: SHAKE all ingredients with ice and fine strain into chilled glass.

1 1/2	shot(s)	**Ketel One vodka**
1	shot(s)	**Sake**
1/2	shot(s)	**Poire William eau de vie**
1/4	shot(s)	**Sugar syrup (2 sugar to 1 water)**

Origin: Adapted in 2002 from a recipe from Grand Pacific Blue Room, Sydney, Australia.
Comment: Originally made with Poire William liqueur, hence this version calls for a little sugar.

JAPANESE SLIPPER

Glass: Martini
Garnish: Salt rim
Method: SHAKE all ingredients with ice and fine strain into chilled glass.

2	shot(s)	**Partida tequila**
1	shot(s)	**Midori melon liqueur**
1	shot(s)	**Freshly squeezed lime juice**

Comment: A Melon Margarita.

JASMINE [UPDATED #7]

Glass: Martini
Garnish: Lemon zest twist
Method: SHAKE all ingredients with ice and fine strain into chilled glass.

1 1/2	shot(s)	**Plymouth gin**
3/4	shot(s)	**Campari**
1	shot(s)	**Cointreau triple sec**
1/2	shot(s)	**Freshly squeezed lemon juice**

Origin: Created in 1999 by Paul Harrington, Berkeley, California, USA.
Comment: This bittersweet cocktail will only appeal to drinkers who have acquired the taste for Campari.

JASMINE & ELDERFLOWER MARTINI [NEW #7]

Glass: Martini
Garnish: Mint leaf
Method: SHAKE all ingredients with ice and fine strain into chilled glass.

2	shot(s)	**Ketel One vodka**
1	shot(s)	**St-Germain elderflower liqueur**
1/4	shot(s)	**Cold jasmine tea**
1/8	shot(s)	**Dry vermouth**

Origin: Created in 2006 by yours truly.
Comment: Delicate and floral yet dry and serious. The tannins in the tea compliment and balance the drink.

JAYNE MANSFIELD

Glass: Flute
Garnish: Strawberry on rim
Method: MUDDLE strawberries in base of shaker. Add next three ingredients, **SHAKE** with ice and fine strain into glass. **TOP** with champagne.

4	fresh	**Hulled strawberries**
1	shot(s)	**Light white rum**
1	shot(s)	**Giffard crème de fraise de bois**
1/4	shot(s)	**Sugar syrup (2 sugar to 1 water)**
Top up with		**Brut champagne**

Origin: Named after the Hollywood actress.
Comment: Champagne is made to go with strawberries.

JEAN GABIN

Glass: Toddy
Garnish: Dust with freshly grated nutmeg
Method: POUR first three ingredients into glass. Add maple syrup and **STIR** until maple syrup dissolves.

1 1/2	shot(s)	**Gosling's Black Seal rum**
3/4	shot(s)	**Boulard Grand Solage Calvados**
5	shot(s)	**Hot milk**
1	spoon	**Maple syrup**

Origin: Created in 1986 by Charles Schumann, Munich, Germany.
Comment: Beats hot chocolate as a nightcap.

JEAN LAFITTE COCKTAIL [NEW #7]

Glass: Martini
Garnish: Orange zest twist
Method: SHAKE all ingredients with ice and fine strain into chilled glass.

2	shot(s)	**Aged rum**
1/4	shot(s)	**La Fée Parisienne (68%) absinthe**
1/4	shot(s)	**Cointreau triple sec**
1/8	shot(s)	**Sugar syrup (2 sugar to 1 water)**
1	fresh	**Egg yolk**
1	dash	**Peychaud's aromatic bitters**

Origin: My adaptation of the New Orleans classic named after the infamous privateer and hero of the Battle of New Orleans.
Comment: Not dissimilar to spicy, fortified advocaat.

JEAN MARC

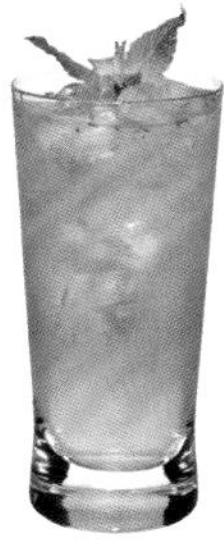

Glass: Collins
Garnish: Mint sprig
Method: MUDDLE mint and ginger in base of shaker. Add next two ingredients, **SHAKE** with ice and fine strain into ice-filled glass. **TOP** with Appletiser, stir and serve with straws.

2	slices	**Fresh root ginger (thumbnail sized)**
4	fresh	**Mint leaves**
1 1/2	shot(s)	**Green Chartreuse liqueur**
1/4	shot(s)	**Apple schnapps liqueur**
Top up with		**Appletiser**

Origin: Created in 2003 by yours truly after judging a Chartreuse cocktail competition in London and realising which flavours best combine with Chartreuse. Named after my friend the President Directeur General of Chartreuse.
Comment: Chartreuse combines well with apple, ginger and mint – they're all in this long, refreshing, summertime drink.

'I'D RATHER HAVE A BOTTLE IN FRONT OF ME THAN A FRONTAL LOBOTOMY.

JELLY BELLY BEANY

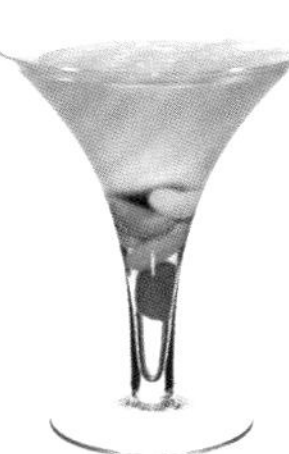

Glass: Martini
Garnish: Jelly beans
Method: SHAKE all ingredients with ice and fine strain into chilled glass.

1 1/2	shot(s)	**Light white rum**
1	shot(s)	**Teichenné Peach Schnapps Liqueur**
1	shot(s)	**Malibu coconut rum liqueur**
2	dashes	**Fee Brothers orange bitters**
1/2	shot(s)	**Chilled mineral water**

Origin: Created in 2002 at Hush, London, England.
Comment: It's a sweetie but you're going to enjoy chewing on it.

JENEVER SOUR

Glass: Old-fashioned
Garnish: Maraschino cherry
Method: SHAKE all ingredients with ice and strain into ice-filled glass.

2	shot(s)	**Bokma Oude Genever**
1	shot(s)	**Freshly squeezed lemon juice**
1/2	shot(s)	**Sugar syrup (2 sugar to 1 water)**
1/2	fresh	**Egg white**

Comment: One of the more delicately flavoured sours.

JEREZ

Glass: Old-fashioned
Method: STIR all ingredients with ice and strain into ice-filled glass.

1/2	shot(s)	**Tio Pepe Fino sherry**
1/2	shot(s)	**Pedro Ximénez sherry**
1	shot(s)	**Teichenné Peach Schnapps Liqueur**
1	shot(s)	**Sauvignon Blanc wine**
1	shot(s)	**La Vieille Prune (prunelle)**
1	dash	**Angostura aromatic bitters**

Origin: This drink heralds from one of the noble houses of Spain – well that's what the sherry PR told me, anyway. I've changed the recipe slightly.
Comment: Sherry depth and stoned fruit flavours.

JERSEY SOUR

Glass: Old-fashioned
Garnish: Lemon zest twist
Method: SHAKE all ingredients with ice and fine strain into chilled glass.

2	shot(s)	**Boulard Grand Solage Calvados**
1	shot(s)	**Freshly squeezed lemon juice**
1/2	shot(s)	**Sugar syrup (2 sugar to 1 water)**
1/2	fresh	**Egg white**

Origin: The classic name for an Applejack sour.
Comment: Apple brandy is possibly the best spirit on which to base a sour.

JEWEL COCKTAIL [NEW #7]

Glass: Martini
Garnish: Maraschino cherry
Method: STIR all ingredients with ice and strain into chilled glass.

1	shot(s)	**Plymouth gin**
1	shot(s)	**Green Chartreuse liqueur**
1	shot(s)	**Sweet vermouth**
1	dash	**Fee Brothers orange bitters**
1/2	shot(s)	**Chilled mineral water** (omit if wet ice)

Comment: Powerful in both alcohol and flavour. An old-school drink to challenge modern palates.

JOAN BENNETT

Glass: Collins
Garnish: Pineapple wedge on rim
Method: SHAKE all ingredients with ice and strain into glass filled with crushed ice.

2	shot(s)	**Light white rum**
1	shot(s)	**Parfait amour**
$2\frac{1}{2}$	shot(s)	**Pressed pineapple juice**

Origin: Adapted from a Tiki drink featured in Jeff Berry's 'Intoxica' and originally created in 1932 at Sloppy Joe's Bar, Havana, Cuba. Named after Hollywood ingénue, Joan Bennett, who in the same year starred in Fox's Careless Lady. Years later she hit the news when her husband, producer Walter Wanger, shot her agent in the crotch after catching them in bed together. Ooerr!
Comment: Fruity and floral, but an unfortunate colour.

'THERE'S NOTHING WRONG WITH SOBRIETY IN MODERATION.'
JOHN CIARDI

JOCKEY CLUB

Glass: Martini
Garnish: Orange zest twist
Method: SHAKE all ingredients with ice and fine strain into chilled glass.

2	shot(s)	**Plymouth gin**
$\frac{1}{2}$	shot(s)	**Luxardo Amaretto di Saschira**
$\frac{1}{2}$	shot(s)	**Freshly squeezed lemon juice**
$\frac{3}{4}$	shot(s)	**Chilled mineral water** (omit if wet ice)
1	dash	**Fee Brothers orange bitters**
1	dash	**Angostura aromatic bitters**

Variant: Some old books, including 'The Fine Art of Mixing Drinks', describe the Jockey Club as a Manhattan with maraschino.
Origin: This classic drink from the 1930s originally called for crème de noyaux, a liqueur similar in flavour to amaretto.
Comment: Peachy almond and gin with citrus overtones.

JODI MAY

Glass: Collins
Garnish: Orange wheel
Method: SHAKE all ingredients with ice and fine strain into chilled glass.

$1\frac{1}{2}$	shot(s)	**Jack Daniel's Tennessee whiskey**
$\frac{1}{2}$	shot(s)	**Cointreau triple sec**
$2\frac{1}{2}$	shot(s)	**Freshly squeezed orange juice**
$1\frac{1}{2}$	shot(s)	**Ocean Spray cranberry juice**
$\frac{1}{4}$	shot(s)	**Freshly squeezed lime juice**

Origin: Adapted from a drink discovered in 2003 at World Service, Nottingham, England.
Comment: Long, fruity and laced with whiskey.

JOHN COLLINS [UPDATED #7]

Glass: Collins
Garnish: Orange slice & cherry on stick (sail)
Method: SHAKE first three ingredients with ice and strain into ice-filled glass. **TOP** with soda, stir and serve with straws.

2	shot(s)	**Plymouth gin**
1	shot(s)	**Freshly squeezed lemon juice**
$\frac{1}{2}$	shot(s)	**Sugar syrup (2 sugar to 1 water)**
Top up with		**Soda water (club soda)**

Origin: The creation of this drink is sometimes credited to John Collins, a bartender at Limmer's Hotel, Conduit Street, London, during the 19th century. It is also attributed to two separate American gentlemen named Tom Collins.
Comment: A refreshing balance of sour lemon and sugar, laced with gin and lengthened with soda.

JOHN DALY [NEW #7]

Glass: Collins
Garnish: Lemon slice
Method: SHAKE all ingredients with ice and strain into ice-filled glass.

$1\frac{1}{2}$	shot(s)	**Ketel One Citroen vodka**
$\frac{1}{4}$	shot(s)	**Cointreau triple sec**
$1\frac{1}{2}$	shot(s)	**Freshly squeezed lemon juice**
$\frac{3}{4}$	shot(s)	**Sugar syrup (2 sugar to 1 water)**
2	shot(s)	**Cold English Breakfast tea**

Variants: Arnold Palmer, Tom Palmer.
Origin: Named after the American professional golfer noted for his victory in the 1991 PGA Championship and colourful personal life.
Comment: Essentially an alcoholic iced tea, this is bittersweet and refreshing - perfect for a hot afternoon.

JOLT'INI

Glass: Martini
Garnish: Float 3 coffee beans
Method: SHAKE all ingredients with ice and fine strain into chilled glass.

2	shot(s)	**Vanilla infused Ketel One vodka**
$\frac{1}{2}$	shot(s)	**Kahlúa coffee liqueur**
1	shot(s)	**Cold espresso coffee**

Origin: Discovered in 2005 at Degrees, Washington DC, USA.
Comment: A flavoursome wake up call of espresso coffee laced with vanilla vodka.

'IT WAS MY UNCLE GEORGE WHO DISCOVERED THAT ALCOHOL WAS A FOOD WELL IN ADVANCE OF MEDICAL THOUGHT.'
P.G. WODEHOUSE

JULEPS

Juleps are tall drinks generally served in Collins glasses but originally served in julep cups and based on a spirit, liqueur or fortified wine. They are most often served with fresh mint over crushed ice.

The name ultimately derives from the Arabic word 'julab', meaning rosewater. Although this had been used to describe any sweetened drink, up to and including medicines, it has attached itself to the Julep's purest incarnation: the Mint Julep, or definitive Deep South American cocktail.

The first known written reference to a cocktail-style Julep was by a Virginian gentleman in 1787, and oddly, contrary to popular belief, the Julep is thought to have originated in Virginia, not Kentucky. Although originally based on brandy not bourbon, by 1803, a julep could be made with rum, brandy or whiskey. By 1900 whiskey had become the normal base.

The Mint Julep reached Britain in 1837, thanks to the novelist Captain Frederick Marryat, who complained of being woken at 7am by a slave brandishing a Julep and popularised it through his descriptions of Fourth of July celebrations. The key to this drink is serving it ice cold and giving the flavours in the mint time to marry with the spirit. Hence, Juleps are ideally prepared hours in advance of serving.

Julep Variations
Georgia Mint Julep
Grapefruit Julep
Heather Julep
Jumbled Fruit Julep
Mint Julep

JOSE COLLINS

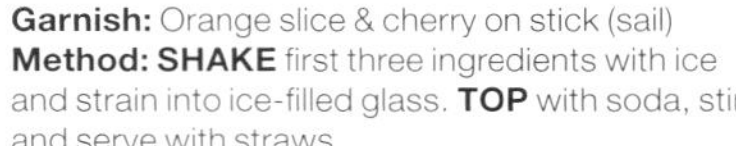
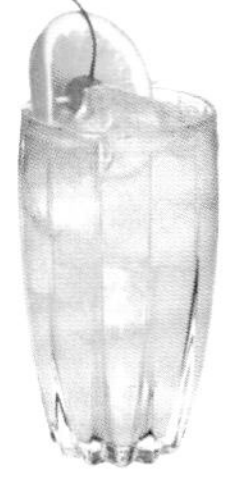

Glass: Collins
Garnish: Orange slice & cherry on stick (sail)
Method: **SHAKE** first three ingredients with ice and strain into ice-filled glass. **TOP** with soda, stir and serve with straws.

2	shot(s)	**Partida tequila**
1	shot(s)	**Freshly squeezed lemon juice**
1/2	shot(s)	**Sugar syrup (2 sugar to 1 water)**
Top up with		**Soda water (club soda)**

AKA: Juan Collins
Comment: The classic long balance of sweet and sour with tequila adding Mexican spirit.

THE JOURNALIST [UPDATED #7]

Glass: Martini
Garnish: Maraschino cherry in drink
Method: **SHAKE** all ingredients with ice and fine strain into chilled glass.

2	shot(s)	**Plymouth gin**
1/2	shot(s)	**Dry vermouth**
1/2	shot(s)	**Sweet vermouth**
1/4	shot(s)	**Cointreau triple sec**
1/4	shot(s)	**Freshly squeezed lemon juice**
2	dashes	**Angostura aromatic bitters**

AKA: Periodista ('journalist' in Spanish).
Comment: Like some journalists I've met, this is bitter and sour.

JUBILANT

Glass: Martini
Garnish: Orange slice on rim
Method: **SHAKE** all ingredients with ice and fine strain into chilled glass.

1 1/2	shot(s)	**Plymouth gin**
3/4	shot(s)	**Bénédictine D.O.M. liqueur**
1/2	shot(s)	**Freshly squeezed lemon juice**
1/2	shot(s)	**Freshly squeezed orange juice**
1/2	fresh	**Egg white**

Origin: A long lost classic.
Comment: Wonderfully balanced, aromatic, herbal and fruity.

JUDY (MOCKTAIL)

Glass: Collins
Garnish: Lime wedge
Method: **SHAKE** all ingredients with ice and strain into ice-filled glass.

2	shot(s)	**Freshly squeezed golden grapefruit juice**
3	shot(s)	**Pressed pineapple juice**
1/2	shot(s)	**Freshly squeezed lemon juice**
1/2	shot(s)	**Rose's lime cordial**

Comment: A refreshing, not sweet, driver's option. Consider adding a couple of dashes of Angostura aromatic bitters, although be aware that these contain some alcohol.

JULEP

Glass: Collins
Garnish: Mint sprig
Method: Lightly **MUDDLE** mint leaves with spirit in base of shaker (just enough to bruise). (At this stage, if time allows, you should refrigerate the shaker, mint and spirit, and the glass in which the drink is to be served, for at least two hours.) Add other ingredients to shaker, **SHAKE** with ice and strain into glass filled with crushed ice. **CHURN** (stir) the drink with the crushed ice using a bar spoon. Top with more crushed ice to fill glass and churn again. Serve with straws.

12	fresh	**Mint leaves**
2 1/2	shot(s)	**Spirit (bourbon, rye, rum, gin, brandy or calvados/applejack)**
3/4	shot(s)	**Sugar syrup (2 sugar to 1 water)**
3	dashes	**Angostura aromatic bitters**

Comment: Adjust sugar to balance if using a fortified wine in place of a spirit.

JULEP MARTINI

Glass: Martini
Garnish: Mint leaf
Method: Lightly **MUDDLE** mint in base of shaker (just to bruise). Add other ingredients, **SHAKE** with ice and fine strain into chilled glass.

8	fresh	**Mint leaves**
2 1/2	shot(s)	**Buffalo Trace bourbon whiskey**
1/2	shot(s)	**Sugar syrup (2 sugar to 1 water)**
3/4	shot(s)	**Chilled mineral water** (omit if wet ice)

Origin: Adapted from a recipe created in the mid 1990s by Dick Bradsell.
Comment: A short variation on the classic Julep: sweetened bourbon and mint.

JULES DELIGHT

Glass: Martini
Garnish: Strawberry
Method: **MUDDLE** strawberries in base of shaker. Add other ingredients, **SHAKE** with ice and fine strain into chilled glass.

3	fresh	**Strawberries**
2	shot(s)	**Ketel One vodka**
1/4	shot(s)	**White balsamic vinegar**
3/4	shot(s)	**Pressed apple juice**
1/4	shot(s)	**Freshly squeezed lemon juice**
1/2	shot(s)	**Sugar syrup (2 sugar to 1 water)**

Origin: Created in 2005 by Julian Gualdonie at Trailer Happiness, London, England.
Comment: Sweet fortified strawberries with a cleansing balsamic vinegar bite.

JULIETTE

Glass: Collins
Garnish: Pineapple wedge & cherry
Method: SHAKE all ingredients with ice and strain into ice-filled glass.

1	shot(s)	**Rémy Martin cognac**
1	shot(s)	**Xanté pear liqueur**
¼	shot(s)	**Chambord black raspberry liqueur**
2½	shot(s)	**Ocean Spray cranberry juice**
1	shot(s)	**Pressed pineapple juice**

Comment: Fruity, medium sweet, cognac laced cooler.

JUMBLED FRUIT JULEP

Glass: Collins
Garnish: Strawberry & mint sprig
Method: MUDDLE strawberries and then mint in base of shaker (just to bruise mint). Add other ingredients, **SHAKE** with ice and strain into glass filled with crushed ice.

4	fresh	**Mint leaves**
3	fresh	**Strawberries (hulled)**
2	shot(s)	**Mango flavoured vodka**
1	shot(s)	**Pressed apple juice**
½	shot(s)	**Passion fruit sugar syrup**
½	shot(s)	**Freshly squeezed lime juice**

Origin: Created in 2005 by Michael Butt and Giles Looker of Soulshakers, England.
Comment: A fruity twist on the classic Julep.

JUMPING JACK FLASH

Glass: Martini
Glass: Pineapple wedge on rim
Method: SHAKE all ingredients with ice and fine strain into chilled glass.

1½	shot(s)	**Jack Daniel's Tennessee whiskey**
½	shot(s)	**Giffard crème de banane du Brésil**
½	shot(s)	**Galliano liqueur**
¾	shot(s)	**Freshly squeezed orange juice**
¾	shot(s)	**Pressed pineapple juice**

Comment: Whiskey further mellowed and sweetened by a tasty combo of liqueurs and juices.

JUNE BUG

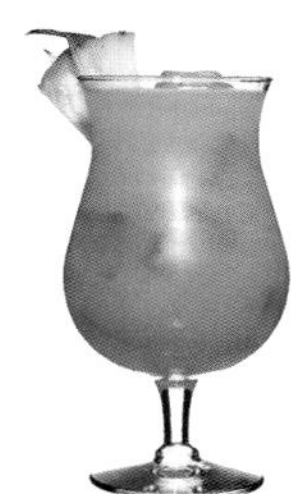

Glass: Hurricane
Garnish: Pineapple wedge & cherry on rim
Method: SHAKE all ingredients with ice and strain into glass filled with crushed ice. Serve with straws.

1	shot(s)	**Midori melon liqueur**
1	shot(s)	**Malibu coconut rum liqueur**
1	shot(s)	**Giffard crème de banane du Brésil**
4	shot(s)	**Pressed pineapple juice**
1	shot(s)	**Freshly squeezed lime juice**

Comment: Sweet & fruity.

JUNGLE BIRD

Glass: Old-fashioned (or Tiki mug)
Garnish: Orange slice & cherry on stick (flag)
Method: SHAKE all ingredients with ice and strain into glass filled with crushed ice.

1½	shot(s)	**Gosling's Black Seal rum**
½	shot(s)	**Campari**
½	shot(s)	**Freshly squeezed lime juice**
½	shot(s)	**Sugar syrup (2 sugar to 1 water)**
2	shot(s)	**Pressed pineapple juice**

Origin: Adapted from a drink featured in Jeff Berry's 'Intoxica' and originally created circa 1978 at the Aviary Bar, Kuala Lumpur, Malaysia.
Comment: Bittersweet and fruity with good rum notes.

'GOT TIGHT LAST NIGHT ON ABSINTHE AND DID KNIFE TRICKS. GREAT SUCCESS SHOOTING THE KNIFE UNDERHAND INTO THE PIANO.'
ERNEST HEMINGWAY

JUNGLE FIRE SLING

Glass: Sling
Garnish: Orange slice & cherry on stick (sail)
Method: SHAKE first four ingredients with ice and strain into ice-filled glass. **TOP** with ginger ale, stir and serve with straws.

1	shot(s)	**Rémy Martin cognac**
1	shot(s)	**Cherry (brandy) liqueur**
½	shot(s)	**Parfait amour liqueur**
½	shot(s)	**Bénédictine D.O.M. liqueur**
Top up with		**Ginger ale**

Comment: Hardly the most refined of drinks, but it does have the refreshing zing of ginger with a soupcon of sticky fruit, herbs and cognac in the background.

JUNGLE JUICE

Glass: Collins
Garnish: Orange slice
Method: SHAKE all ingredients with ice and strain into ice-filled glass.

1	shot(s)	**Ketel One vodka**
1	shot(s)	**Light white rum**
½	shot(s)	**Cointreau triple sec**
1	shot(s)	**Ocean Spray cranberry juice**
1	shot(s)	**Freshly squeezed orange juice**
1	shot(s)	**Pressed pineapple juice**
¾	shot(s)	**Freshly squeezed lime juice**
¼	shot(s)	**Sugar syrup (2 sugar to 1 water)**

Comment: If this is the juice of the jungle, I'm a monkey's uncle. That said, as fruity long drinks go this is not bad at all.

JUPITER MARTINI [UPDATED #7]

Glass: Martini
Garnish: Orange zest twist
Method: SHAKE all ingredients with ice and fine strain into chilled glass.

2	shot(s)	**Plymouth gin**
3/4	shot(s)	**Dry vermouth**
1/8	shot(s)	**Parfait amour liqueur**
1/8	shot(s)	**Freshly squeezed orange juice**
1/2	shot(s)	**Chilled mineral water** (omit if wet ice)

Origin: A classic which is thought to have originated some time in the 1920s.
Comment: Bone dry and aromatic, this drink's colour is the grey hue of an overcast sky.

THE JUXTAPOSITION

Glass: Martini
Garnish: Two pineapple wedges on rim
Method: STIR honey with vodka in base of shaker until honey dissolves. Add other ingredients, **SHAKE** with ice and fine strain into chilled glass.

2	spoons	**Runny honey**
2	shot(s)	**Cranberry flavoured vodka**
1	shot(s)	**Pressed pineapple juice**
3/4	shot(s)	**Freshly squeezed lime juice**
3	dashes	**Angostura aromatic bitters**

Origin: Adapted from a long drink created in 2003 by Michael Butt and Giles Looker of Soulshakers, England.
Comment: Tangy, complex and smoothed by foaming pineapple.

KAMANIWANALAYA

Glass: Collins
Garnish: Pineapple wedge & cherry
Method: SHAKE all ingredients with ice and strain into ice-filled glass.

1 1/2	shot(s)	**Light white rum**
1/2	shot(s)	**Pusser's Navy rum**
1	shot(s)	**Luxardo Amaretto di Saschira**
3	shot(s)	**Pressed pineapple juice**

Comment: Try saying the name after a few of these rum laced, tropical pineapple concoctions.

KAMIKAZE

Glass: Shot
Method: SHAKE all ingredients with ice and fine strain into chilled glass.

1	shot(s)	**Partida tequila**
1/2	shot(s)	**Cointreau triple sec**
1/2	shot(s)	**Freshly squeezed lime juice**

Variant: With vodka in place of tequila.
Comment: A bite-sized Margarita.

KARAMEL SUTRA MARTINI

Glass: Martini
Garnish: Fudge on rim
Method: SHAKE all ingredients with ice and fine strain into chilled glass.

1 1/2	shot(s)	**Vanilla infused Ketel One vodka**
1 1/2	shot(s)	**Tuaca Italian liqueur**
1	shot(s)	**Toffee liqueur**

Origin: Adapted from a drink discovered in 2003 at the Bellagio, Las Vegas, USA.
Comment: Liquid confectionery that bites back.

KATINKA

Glass: Martini
Garnish: Split lime wedge
Method: SHAKE all ingredients with ice and fine strain into chilled glass.

1 1/2	shot(s)	**Ketel One vodka**
1	shot(s)	**Giffard apricot brandy du Roussillon**
1	shot(s)	**Freshly squeezed lime juice**
1/2	shot(s)	**Sugar syrup (2 sugar to 1 water)**

Comment: Medium sweet, yet also tart and tangy.

KATRINA COCKTAIL [NEW #7]

Glass: Old-fashioned
Garnish: Dust with nutmeg
Method: SHAKE all ingredients with ice and fine strain into chilled glass. No ice!

2	shot(s)	**Partida tequila**
1/4	shot(s)	**Kahlúa coffee liqueur**
1/8	shot(s)	**La Fée Parisienne (68%) absinthe**
1/4	shot(s)	**Chambord black raspberry liqueur**
1	shot(s)	**Pressed apple juice**

Origin: Adapted from a drink created in 2005 at Pirates Alley Café, New Orleans, and named after the hurricane which devastated the city in 2005. The name is an acronym of its original ingredients: Kahlúa, Absinthe, Tequila, Raspberry, Ice, Nutmeg and Apple juice.
Comment: Spicy, fruity tequila served in a style synonymous with the Crescent City – full on!

KAVA

Glass: Collins
Garnish: Pineapple wedge & cherry
Method: SHAKE all ingredients with ice and strain into glass filled with crushed ice.

1 1/2	shot(s)	**Light white rum**
1/2	shot(s)	**Golden rum**
1	shot(s)	**Pressed pineapple juice**
1	shot(s)	**Freshly squeezed lemon juice**
1/4	shot(s)	**Pomegranate (grenadine) syrup**
1/4	shot(s)	**Sugar syrup (2 sugar to 1 water)**

Variant: Multiply ingredients by a factor of four to make a Kava Bowl and serve in an ice-filled Tiki bowl.
Origin: Adapted from a drink featured in Jeff Berry's 'Intoxica' and originally created circa 1942 by Trader Vic.
Comment: A wonderfully fruity, fluffy and kitsch Tiki drink.

KEE-WEE MARTINI

Glass: Martini
Garnish: Kiwi slice on rim
Method: Cut kiwi fruit in half, scoop out flesh into base of shaker and **MUDDLE**. Add other ingredients, **SHAKE** with ice and fine strain into chilled glass.

1	fresh	**Kiwi fruit**
2	shot(s)	**Plymouth gin**
1/4	shot(s)	**Freshly squeezed lemon juice**
1/2	shot(s)	**Sugar syrup (2 sugar to 1 water)**

Origin: My version of this ubiquitous drink.
Comment: The citrus hints in the kiwi combine brilliantly with those in the gin and fresh lemon juice.

KENTUCKY JEWEL

Glass: Martini
Garnish: Berries on stick
Method: SHAKE all ingredients with ice and fine strain into chilled glass.

1 1/2	shot(s)	**Buffalo Trace bourbon whiskey**
1/4	shot(s)	**Chambord black raspberry liqueur**
1/4	shot(s)	**Cointreau triple sec**
2	shot(s)	**Ocean Spray cranberry juice**

Origin: Adapted from a drink created in 2004 by Jonathan Lamm, The Admirable Crichton, London, England.
Comment: Easy sipping, fruity bourbon.

YOU CAN'T BE A REAL COUNTRY UNLESS YOU HAVE A BEER AND AN AIRLINE - IT HELPS IF YOU HAVE SOME KIND OF A FOOTBALL TEAM, OR SOME NUCLEAR WEAPONS, BUT AT THE VERY LEAST YOU NEED A BEER.
FRANK ZAPPA

KENTUCKY COLONEL [UPDATED #7]

Glass: Old-fashioned
Garnish: Peach slice & mint sprig
Method: SHAKE all ingredients with ice and strain into glass filled with crushed ice.

1 1/2	shot(s)	**Buffalo Trace bourbon whiskey**
1/4	shot(s)	**Southern Comfort liqueur**
1/4	shot(s)	**Cointreau triple sec**
1	shot(s)	**Peach puree**
1/2	shot(s)	**Freshly squeezed lemon juice**
1/4	shot(s)	**Sugar syrup (2 sugar to 1 water)**

Origin: Created in 2001 by Morgan Watson of Apartment, Belfast, Northern Ireland.
Comment: Peach and bourbon with hints of orange and spice.

KENTUCKY MAC

Glass: Old-fashioned
Garnish: Mint sprig
Method: MUDDLE ginger and mint in base of shaker. Add other ingredients, **SHAKE** with ice and strain into glass filled with crushed ice.

2	slices	**Fresh root ginger (thumbnail sized)**
2	fresh	**Mint leaves**
1 1/2	shot(s)	**Buffalo Trace bourbon whiskey**
1	shot(s)	**Stone's green ginger wine**
2	shot(s)	**Pressed apple juice**

Origin: Created in 1999 by Jamie Terrell, London, England.
Comment: Spicy, yet smooth and easy to sip.

KENTUCKY DREAM

Glass: Old-fashioned
Garnish: Lemon zest twist
Method: STIR vanilla liqueur and bitters with two ice cubes in a glass. Add half the bourbon and two more ice cubes. Stir some more and add another two ice cubes and the rest of the bourbon. Add the last two ingredients and more ice cubes, and stir lots more. The melting and stirring in of ice cubes is essential to the dilution and taste of the drink.

1/2	shot(s)	**Vanilla schnapps liqueur**
2	dashes	**Angostura aromatic bitters**
2	shot(s)	**Buffalo Trace bourbon whiskey**
1/2	shot(s)	**Giffard apricot brandy du Roussillon**
1	shot(s)	**Pressed apple juice**

Origin: Created in 2002 by Wayne Collins for Maxxium UK.
Comment: Tames bourbon and adds hints of apricot, vanilla and apple.

KENTUCKY MUFFIN

Glass: Old-fashioned
Garnish: Blueberries
Method: MUDDLE blueberries in base of shaker. Add other ingredients, **SHAKE** with ice and strain into glass filled with crushed ice. Stir and serve with straws.

12	fresh	**Blueberries**
2	shot(s)	**Buffalo Trace bourbon whiskey**
1	shot(s)	**Pressed apple juice**
1/2	shot(s)	**Freshly squeezed lime juice**
1/2	shot(s)	**Sugar syrup (2 sugar to 1 water)**

Origin: Created in 2000 at Mash, London, England.
Comment: Blueberries, lime and apple combine with and are fortified by bourbon.

KENTUCKY PEAR

Glass: Martini
Garnish: Pear slice on rim
Method: SHAKE all ingredients with ice and fine strain into chilled glass.

1	shot(s)	**Buffalo Trace bourbon whiskey**
1	shot(s)	**Xanté pear liqueur**
1	shot(s)	**Freshly extracted pear juice**
1	shot(s)	**Pressed apple juice**

Origin: Created in 2003 by Jes at The Cinnamon Club, London, England.
Comment: Pear, apple, vanilla and whiskey are partners in this richly flavoured drink.

KENTUCKY TEA

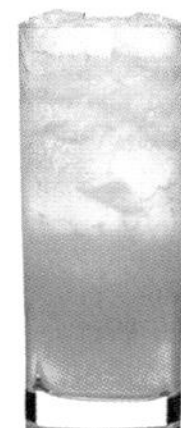

Glass: Collins
Garnish: Lime wedge
Method: SHAKE first four ingredients with ice and strain into ice-filled glass. **TOP** with ginger ale.

2	shot(s)	**Buffalo Trace bourbon whiskey**
1	shot(s)	**Cointreau triple sec**
1	shot(s)	**Freshly squeezed lime juice**
1/2	shot(s)	**Sugar syrup (2 sugar to 1 water)**
Top up with		**Ginger ale**

Comment: Spicy whiskey and ginger.

KEY LIME

Glass: Coupette
Garnish: Lime wedge on rim
Method: BLEND all ingredients without ice and serve.

1 1/2	shot(s)	**Vanilla infused Ketel One vodka**
1 1/2	shot(s)	**Lime flavoured vodka**
1/2	shot(s)	**Sugar syrup (2 sugar to 1 water)**
1/2	shot(s)	**Rose's lime cordial**
3	scoops	**Vanilla ice cream**

Comment: Tangy, smooth and rich! Alcoholic ice cream for the grown-up palate.

KEY LIME PIE #1

Glass: Martini
Garnish: Pie rim (wipe with cream mix and dip into crushed Graham Crackers or digestive biscuits)
Method: SHAKE first three ingredients with ice and fine strain into chilled, rimmed glass. **SHAKE** cream and Licor 43 without ice so as to mix and whip. **FLOAT** cream mix on surface of drink.

2	shot(s)	**Malibu coconut rum liqueur**
1	shot(s)	**Cointreau triple sec**
1	shot(s)	**Freshly squeezed lime juice**
2	shot(s)	**Double (heavy) cream**
1/2	shot(s)	**Licor 43 (Cuarenta Y Tres) liqueur**

Origin: Created by Michael Waterhouse, owner of Dylan Prime, New York City, USA.
Comment: This extremely rich drink is great when served as a dessert alternative.

KEY LIME PIE #2

Glass: Martini
Garnish: Pie rim (wipe with cream mix and dip into crushed Graham Crackers or digestive biscuits)
Method: SHAKE all ingredients with ice and fine strain into chilled, rimmed glass.

2	shot(s)	**Vanilla infused Ketel One vodka**
1 3/4	shot(s)	**Pressed pineapple juice**
1/2	shot(s)	**Freshly squeezed lime juice**
1/4	shot(s)	**Rose's lime cordial**

Comment: Beautiful balance of pineapple, vanilla, sweet and sour.

KEY LIME PIE #3

Glass: Martini
Garnish: Pie rim (wipe with cream mix and dip into crushed Graham Crackers or digestive biscuits)
Method: SHAKE all ingredients with ice and fine strain into chilled, rimmed glass.

2	shot(s)	**Ketel One Citroen vodka**
1/2	shot(s)	**Vanilla schnapps liqueur**
1 1/2	shot(s)	**Pressed pineapple juice**
1/2	shot(s)	**Freshly squeezed lime juice**
1/4	shot(s)	**Rose's lime cordial**

Origin: Recipe adapted from one by Claire Smith in 2005, London, England.
Comment: My favourite rendition of this dessert-in-a-glass cocktail.

KEY WEST COOLER [UPDATED #7]

Glass: Collins
Garnish: Lime wedge on rim
Method: SHAKE all ingredients with ice and strain into ice-filled glass.

2	shot(s)	**Ketel One vodka**
1	shot(s)	**Malibu coconut rum liqueur**
1 1/2	shot(s)	**Ocean Spray cranberry juice**
1 1/2	shot(s)	**Freshly squeezed orange juice**

Origin: Named after the island near the southern-most tip of the Florida Keys in Florida, USA.
Comment: A coconut laced Breeze that's suited to the poolside.

K.G.B.

Glass: Shot
Method: LAYER in glass by pouring carefully in the following order.

1/2	shot(s)	**Kahlúa coffee liqueur**
1/2	shot(s)	**Galliano liqueur**
1/2	shot(s)	**Rémy Martin cognac**

Comment: The initials of this simple peppermint and coffee shooter stand for Kahlúa, Galliano and brandy.

KILLER PUNCH

Glass: Collins
Garnish: Lime wedge
Method: SHAKE all ingredients with ice and strain into ice-filled glass.

1 shot(s) **Ketel One vodka**
1/2 shot(s) **Midori melon liqueur**
1/2 shot(s) **Luxardo Amaretto di Saschira**
1/2 shot(s) **Freshly squeezed lime juice**
3 1/2 shot(s) **Ocean Spray cranberry juice**

Comment: Pretty soft, sweet and fruity as killers go.

KING COLE COCKTAIL [NEW #7]

Glass: Martini
Garnish: Orange & pineapple slices
Method: STIR all ingredients with ice and strain into chilled glass.

2 shot(s) **Buffalo Trace bourbon whiskey**
1/4 shot(s) **Fernet Branca**
1/2 shot(s) **Sugar syrup (2 sugar to 1 water)**
1/2 shot(s) **Chilled water** (omit if wet ice)

Origin: Adapted from Harry Craddock's 1930 'The Savoy Cocktail Book'.
Comment: My Fernet loving friends in San Francisco will appreciate this herbal number.

KIR

Glass: Goblet
Method: POUR cassis into glass and top with chilled wine.

1/2 shot(s) **Giffard crème de cassis**
Top up with **Dry white wine**

Variant: Kir Royale
Origin: This drink takes its name from a colourful politician and WWII resistance hero by the name of Canon Felix Kir, who served as the Mayor of Dijon, France, between 1945 and 1965. In order to promote local products, at receptions he served an aperitif made with crème de cassis and Bourgogne Aligoté white wine. The concoction quickly became known as Canon Kir's aperitif, then Father Kir's aperitif and finally as the 'Kir' aperitif.
Comment: Blackcurrant wine - clean, crisp and not too sweet.

KIR MARTINI

Glass: Martini
Garnish: Berries on stick
Method: STIR all ingredients with ice and strain into chilled glass.

2 shot(s) **Ketel One vodka**
1 shot(s) **Sauvignon Blanc wine**
1 shot(s) **Giffard crème de cassis**

Origin: Created by yours truly in 2004.
Comment: The Canon's traditional white wine and cassis aperitif with added oomph.

KIR ROYALE

Glass: Flute
Method: POUR cassis into glass and **TOP** with champagne.

1/2 shot(s) **Giffard crème de cassis**
Top up with **Brut champagne**

Variant: Kir
Comment: Easy to make, easy to drink.

KISS OF DEATH

Glass: Shot
Method: Take sambuca from freezer and Galliano from refrigerator then **LAYER** in chilled glass by carefully pouring in the following order.

3/4 shot(s) **Luxardo Sambuca dei Cesari**
3/4 shot(s) **Galliano liqueur**

Comment: Will give you fresh breath with which to apply that kiss.

KIWI BATIDA

Glass: Collins
Garnish: Kiwi slice
Method: Cut kiwi in half and scoop flesh into blender. Add other ingredients and **BLEND** with 18oz scoop crushed ice until smooth. Serve with straws.

1 fresh **Kiwi**
2 1/2 shot(s) **Leblon cachaça**
1 shot(s) **Sugar syrup (2 sugar to 1 water)**

Comment: The kiwi fruit flavour is a little lacking so this drink is improved by using kiwi-flavoured sugar syrup.

KIWI BELLINI

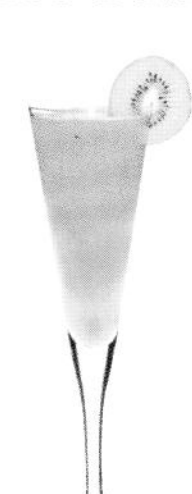

Glass: Flute
Garnish: Kiwi slice on rim
Method: Cut kiwi fruit in half, scoop out flesh into base of shaker and **MUDDLE**. Add next three ingredients, **SHAKE** with ice and fine strain into chilled glass. **TOP** with Prosecco.

1 fresh **Kiwi fruit**
1 1/4 shot(s) **Ketel One vodka**
1/4 shot(s) **Freshly squeezed lemon juice**
1/4 shot(s) **Sugar syrup (2 sugar to 1 water)**
Top up with **Prosecco**

Origin: Adapted from a drink discovered at Zuma, London, England, in 2004.
Comment: Lemon fresh kiwi, fortified with vodka and charged with Prosecco.

KIWI COLLINS

Glass: Collins
Garnish: Kiwi slice
Method: Cut kiwi fruit in half, scoop out flesh into base of shaker and **MUDDLE**. Add next three ingredients, **SHAKE** with ice and fine strain into ice-filled glass. **TOP** with soda water.

1	fresh	**Kiwi fruit**
2	shot(s)	**Ketel One vodka**
1 1/2	shot(s)	**Freshly squeezed lemon juice**
1/2	shot(s)	**Sugar syrup (2 sugar to 1 water)**
Top up with		**Soda water (club soda)**

Origin: Formula by yours truly.
Comment: A fruity adaptation of a Vodka Collins.

KIWI CRUSH

Glass: Martini
Garnish: Kiwi slice
Method: Cut kiwi fruit in half, scoop out flesh into base of shaker and **MUDDLE**. Add other ingredients, **SHAKE** with ice and fine strain into chilled glass.

1	fresh	**Kiwi fruit**
2	shot(s)	**Ketel One Citroen vodka**
1	shot(s)	**Pressed apple juice**
1/2	shot(s)	**Freshly squeezed lemon juice**
1/4	shot(s)	**Almond (orgeat) sugar syrup**

Origin: Recipe adapted from one by Claire Smith in 2005, London, England.
Comment: Spirit laced kiwi, citrus and almond.

KIWI MARTINI (SIMPLE)

Glass: Martini
Garnish: Kiwi slice on rim
Method: Cut kiwi fruit in half, scoop out flesh into base of shaker and **MUDDLE**. Add other ingredients, **SHAKE** with ice and fine strain into chilled glass.

1	fresh	**Kiwi fruit**
2	shot(s)	**Ketel One vodka**
1/2	shot(s)	**Sugar syrup (2 sugar to 1 water)**

Origin: Formula by yours truly in 2004.
Comment: You may need to adjust the sugar depending on the ripeness of your fruit.

KLONDIKE

Glass: Collins
Garnish: Orange slice
Method: **POUR** ingredients into ice-filled glass and stir.

2	shot(s)	**Buffalo Trace bourbon whiskey**
2	shot(s)	**Freshly squeezed orange juice**
Top up with		**Ginger ale**

Comment: A simple drink but the three ingredients combine well.

KNICKERBOCKER MARTINI

Glass: Martini
Garnish: Orange zest twist
Method: **STIR** all ingredients with ice and strain into chilled glass.

1 3/4	shot(s)	**Plymouth gin**
3/4	shot(s)	**Dry vermouth**
1/2	shot(s)	**Sweet vermouth**

Origin: Thought to have been created at the Knickerbocker Hotel, New York City, USA.
Comment: Aromatic vermouth dominates this flavoursome Martini variant.

KNICKERBOCKER SPECIAL

Glass: Martini
Garnish: Pineapple wedge & cherry on rim
Method: **SHAKE** all ingredients with ice and fine strain into chilled glass.

2	shot(s)	**Light white rum**
1/2	shot(s)	**Grand Marnier liqueur**
1/2	shot(s)	**Pressed pineapple juice**
1/2	shot(s)	**Freshly squeezed orange juice**
1/2	shot(s)	**Freshly squeezed lemon juice**
1/4	shot(s)	**Raspberry or strawberry sugar syrup**

Comment: A bit fluffy but fans of French Martinis will love it.

KNICKER DROPPER GLORY

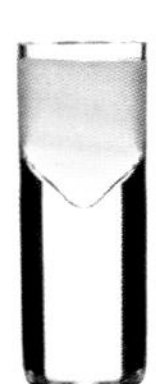

Glass: Shot
Method: **SHAKE** all ingredients with ice and fine strain into chilled glass.

1	shot(s)	**Frangelico hazelnut liqueur**
1/2	shot(s)	**Freshly squeezed lemon juice**

Origin: Created circa 2000 by Jason Fendick, London, England.
Comment: Nutty sweetness sharpened with lemon.

KNOCKOUT MARTINI [UPDATED #7]

Glass: Martini
Garnish: Star anise on rim
Method: **STIR** all ingredients with ice and strain into chilled glass.

1	shot(s)	**Plymouth gin**
1	shot(s)	**Dry vermouth**
1/4	shot(s)	**La Feé Parisienne(68%) absinthe**
1/4	shot(s)	**Giffard white crème de Menthe Pastille**

Comment: A Wet Martini with aniseed and mint. Stir well as it benefits from a little extra dilution.

KOI YELLOW

Glass: Martini
Garnish: Float rose petal
Method: **SHAKE** all ingredients with ice and fine strain into chilled glass.

2	shot(s)	**Raspberry flavoured vodka**
1/2	shot(s)	**Cointreau triple sec**
1	shot(s)	**Freshly squeezed lemon juice**
1/2	shot(s)	**Sugar syrup (2 sugar to 1 water)**

Origin: The signature drink at Koi Restaurant, Los Angeles, USA.
Comment: Sherbet / raspberry Martini with a sweet and citrus sour finish.

KRAKOW TEA

Glass: Collins
Garnish: Mint sprig & lime wedge
Method: Lightly **MUDDLE** mint in base of shaker (just to bruise). **SHAKE** all ingredients with ice and fine strain into ice-filled glass.

12	fresh	**Mint leaves**
2	shot(s)	**Zubrówka bison vodka**
1	shot(s)	**Strong cold camomile tea**
3 1/2	shot(s)	**Pressed apple juice**
1/4	shot(s)	**Freshly squeezed lime juice**
1/4	shot(s)	**Sugar syrup (2 sugar to 1 water)**

Origin: Created in 2002 by Domhnall Carlin at Apartment, Belfast, Northern Ireland.
Comment: Refreshing with a dry, citrus finish.

'I MUST POINT OUT THAT MY RULE OF LIFE PRESCRIBED AS AN ABSOLUTELY SACRED RITE SMOKING CIGARS AND ALSO THE DRINKING OF ALCOHOL BEFORE, AFTER, AND IF NEED BE DURING ALL MEALS AND IN THE INTERVALS BETWEEN THEM.'
WINSTON CHURCHILL

KOOL HAND LUKE

Glass: Rocks
Method: **MUDDLE** lime in base of glass to release its juices. Pour rum and sugar syrup into glass, add crushed ice and **CHURN**. Serve with straws.

1	fresh	**Lime cut into eighths**
2	shot(s)	**Myers's Planters' Punch rum**
1	shot(s)	**Sugar syrup (2 sugar to 1 water)**
2	dashes	**Angostura aromatic bitters**

Comment: This looks like a Caipirinha and has a similar balance of sweet, sour and spirit. The bitters bring out the spice in the rum, which is every bit as pungent as cachaça.

KRETCHMA

Glass: Martini
Garnish: Dust with cocoa powder
Method: **SHAKE** all ingredients with ice and fine strain into chilled glass.

2	shot(s)	**Ketel One vodka**
3/4	shot(s)	**Giffard white crème de cacao**
1/2	shot(s)	**Freshly squeezed lemon juice**
1/8	shot(s)	**Pomegranate (grenadine) syrup**

Variant: Without grenadine this is a 'Ninitchka'.
Origin: Adapted from a recipe in David Embury's 'The Fine Art Of Mixing Drinks'.
Comment: Fortified Turkish Delight.

KOOLAID

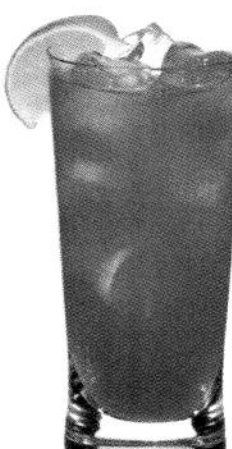

Glass: Collins
Garnish: Lime wedge
Method: **SHAKE** all ingredients with ice and strain into ice-filled glass.

1 1/2	shot(s)	**Ketel One vodka**
3/4	shot(s)	**Midori melon liqueur**
3/4	shot(s)	**Luxardo Amaretto di Saschira**
1/2	shot(s)	**Freshly squeezed lime juice**
2	shot(s)	**Ocean Spray cranberry juice**
1	shot(s)	**Freshly squeezed orange juice**

Origin: A drink with unknown origins that emerged and morphed during the 1990s.
Comment: Tangy liquid marzipan with hints of melon, cranberry and orange juice.

KURRENT AFFAIR [UPDATED #7]

Glass: Collins
Garnish: Lemon wheel
Method: **SHAKE** all ingredients with ice and strain into ice-filled glass.

1 1/2	shot(s)	**Ketel One Citroen vodka**
3/4	shot(s)	**Berry flavoured vodka**
3	shot(s)	**Pressed apple juice**

Comment: Berry and citrus vodka combine with apple in this tall, refreshing summer drink.

L.A. ICED TEA

Glass: Sling
Garnish: Split lime wedge
Method: SHAKE first seven ingredients with ice and strain into ice-filled glass. **TOP** with soda.

1/2	shot(s)	**Ketel One vodka**
1/2	shot(s)	**Plymouth gin**
1/2	shot(s)	**Light white rum**
1/2	shot(s)	**Cointreau triple sec**
1/2	shot(s)	**Midori melon liqueur**
1	shot(s)	**Freshly squeezed lime juice**
1/2	shot(s)	**Sugar syrup (2 sugar to 1 water)**
Top up with		**Soda water (club soda)**

Comment: Long and lime green with subtle notes of melon and fresh lime.

LAGO COSMO

Glass: Martini
Garnish: Orange zest twist
Method: SHAKE all ingredients with ice and fine strain into chilled glass.

1 1/2	shot(s)	**Cranberry flavoured vodka**
3/4	shot(s)	**Cointreau triple sec**
1 3/4	shot(s)	**Freshly squeezed orange juice**
1/4	shot(s)	**Freshly squeezed lime juice**
1/2	shot(s)	**Sugar syrup (2 sugar to 1 water)**

Origin: Discovered in 2003 at Nectar @ Bellagio, Las Vegas, USA.
Comment: A Cosmo with cranberry vodka in place of citrus vodka and orange juice in place of cranberry juice.

L'AMOUR EN FUITE [NEW #7]

Glass: Old-fashioned
Garnish: Orange zest twist
Method: POUR absinthe into ice-filled glass, **TOP** with water and leave to stand. Separately **STIR** gin, vermouth and elderflower liqueur with ice. **DISCARD** contents of glass (absinthe, water and ice) and STRAIN contents of mixing glass into absinthe-coated glass. No ice!

1/2	shot(s)	**La Fée Parisienne (68%) absinthe**
1 1/2	shot(s)	**Plymouth gin**
3/4	shot(s)	**Dry vermouth**
1/4	shot(s)	**St-Germain elderflower liqueur**

Origin: Created in 2007 by Jamie Boudreau, Seattle, USA, originally using Lillet. The name comes from a 1979 French film.
Comment: Serious yet approachably subtle with hints of vermouth and elderflower dominated by absinthe and gin.

LANDSLIDE

Glass: Shot
Method: Refrigerate ingredients then **LAYER** in chilled glass by carefully **pour**ing in the following order.

1/2	shot(s)	**Luxardo Amaretto di Saschira liqueur**
1/2	shot(s)	**Giffard crème de banane du Brésil**
1/2	shot(s)	**Irish cream liqueur**

Comment: A sweet but pleasant combination of banana, almond and Irish cream liqueur.

LARCHMONT [NEW #7]

Glass: Martini
Garnish: Orange zest twist
Method: SHAKE all ingredients with ice and fine strain into chilled glass.

1 1/2	shot(s)	**Light white rum**
1/2	shot(s)	**Grand Marnier liqueur**
1/2	shot(s)	**Freshly squeezed lime juice**
1/4	shot(s)	**Sugar syrup (2 sugar to 1 water)**
1/2	shot(s)	**Chilled mineral water** (omit if wet ice)

Origin: Created by David A. Embury, who in his 1948 'Fine Art of Mixing Drinks' writes of this drink: "As a grand finale to cocktails based on the Rum Sour, I give you one of my favorites which I have named after my favorite community."
Comment: I share Embury's appreciation of this fine drink, although I think of it more as a type of Orange Daiquiri.

'WHAT'S WRONG, A LITTLE PAVEMENT SICKNESS?'
RUSSIAN SAYING

THE LAST STRAW [NEW #7]

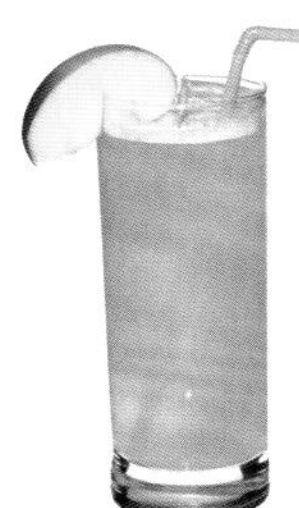

Glass: Collins
Garnish: Apple wedge
Method: SHAKE all ingredients with ice and strain into ice-filled glass.

1 1/2	shot(s)	**Boulard Grand Solage Calvados**
1 1/2	shot(s)	**St-Germain elderflower liqueur**
1 1/2	shot(s)	**Dry cider**
1 1/2	shot(s)	**Pressed apple juice**

Origin: Created in 2006 by yours truly. We used the last straw we had left to sample the first one.
Comment: Three stages of the apple's alcoholic journey - juice, cider and brandy - are sweetened and aromatised by elderflower liqueur.

THE LAST WORD

Glass: Martini
Garnish: Lime wedge on rim
Method: SHAKE all ingredients with ice and fine strain into chilled glass.

3/4	shot(s)	**Plymouth gin**
3/4	shot(s)	**Green Chartreuse liqueur**
3/4	shot(s)	**Luxardo maraschino liqueur**
3/4	shot(s)	**Freshly squeezed lime juice**
1/2	shot(s)	**Chilled mineral water** (omit if wet ice)

Origin: An old classic championed in 2005 by the team at Pegu Club, New York City, USA.
Comment: Chartreuse devotees will love this balanced, tangy drink. I'm one.

LAVENDER & BLACK PEPPER MARTINI

Glass: Martini
Method: Pour the syrup into an ice filled mixing glass. Add the vodka and black pepper. **STIR** and super-fine strain into chilled glass.

$2^1/_2$	shot(s)	**Ketel One vodka**
$^1/_4$	shot(s)	**Sonoma Lavender sugar syrup**
2	grinds	**Freshly ground black pepper**

Origin: Adapted from a recipe created in 2006 by Richard Gillam at The Kenilworth Hotel, Warwickshire, England.
Comment: Subtly sweetened and lavender flavoured vodka with a bump and grind of spicy pepper.

LAVENDER MARGARITA

Glass: Coupette
Garnish: Lime wedge
Method: SHAKE all ingredients with ice and fine strain into chilled glass.

2	shot(s)	**Partida tequila**
1	shot(s)	**Freshly squeezed lime juice**
$^1/_2$	shot(s)	**Sonoma lavender infused sugar syrup**

Origin: Created in 2006 by yours truly.
Comment: Lavender lime and tequila combine harmoniously.

LAVENDER MARTINI

Glass: Martini
Garnish: Lemon zest twist
Method: STIR all ingredients with ice and strain into chilled glass.

$2^1/_2$	shot(s)	**Lavender infused Ketel One vodka**
$^3/_4$	shot(s)	**Parfait amour liqueur**
$^1/_4$	shot(s)	**Dry vermouth**

Origin: Created in 2006 by yours truly.
Comment: Infusing lavender in vodka tends to make it bitter but the parfait amour adds sweetness as well as flavour and colour.

LAZARUS

Glass: Martini
Garnish: Float three coffee beans
Method: SHAKE all ingredients with ice and fine strain into chilled glass.

1	shot(s)	**Ketel One vodka**
1	shot(s)	**Kahlúa coffee liqueur**
$^1/_2$	shot(s)	**Rémy Martin cognac**
1	shot(s)	**Cold espresso coffee**

Origin: Created in 2000 by David Whitehead at Atrium, Leeds, England.
Comment: A flavoursome combination of spirit and coffee.

LCB MARTINI [UPDATED #7]

Glass: Martini
Garnish: Lemon zest twist
Method: SHAKE all ingredients with ice and fine strain into chilled glass.

2	shot(s)	**Ketel One vodka**
$^3/_4$	shot(s)	**Sauvignon Blanc wine**
2	shot(s)	**Squeezed pink grapefruit juice**
$^1/_4$	shot(s)	**Sugar syrup (2 sugar to 1 water)**

Origin: Created by yours truly in 2004 and named after Lisa Clare Ball, who loves both Sauvignon Blanc and pink grapefruit juice. **Comment:** A sweet and sour, citrus fresh Martini.

LEAP YEAR MARTINI

Glass: Martini
Garnish: Lemon peel twist
Method: SHAKE all ingredients with ice and fine strain into chilled glass.

2	shot(s)	**Plymouth gin**
$^1/_2$	shot(s)	**Grand Marnier liqueur**
$^1/_2$	shot(s)	**Sweet vermouth**
$^1/_4$	shot(s)	**Freshly squeezed lemon juice**

Origin: Harry Craddock created this drink for the Leap Year celebrations at the Savoy Hotel, London, on 29th February 1928 and recorded it in his 1930 Savoy Cocktail Book.
Comment: This drink, which is on the dry side, needs to be served ice-cold.

LEAVE IT TO ME MARTINI

Glass: Martini
Garnish: Lemon zest twist
Method: SHAKE all ingredients with ice and fine strain into chilled glass.

$1^1/_2$	shot(s)	**Plymouth gin**
$^1/_2$	shot(s)	**Giffard apricot brandy du Roussillon**
$^3/_4$	shot(s)	**Sweet vermouth**
$^1/_2$	shot(s)	**Freshly squeezed lemon juice**
$^1/_4$	shot(s)	**Pomegranate (grenadine) syrup**

Origin: Adapted from a recipe in Harry Craddock's 1930 Savoy Cocktail Book.
Comment: Gin, apricot, vermouth and lemon create an old fashioned but well balanced drink.

LEFT BANK [NEW #7]

Glass: Martini
Garnish: Lime zest twist
Method: SHAKE all ingredients with ice and fine strain into chilled glass.

$1^1/_2$	shot(s)	**Plymouth gin**
1	shot(s)	**St-Germain elderflower liqueur**
1	shot(s)	**Sauvignon Blanc wine**

Origin: Created in 2006 by yours truly.
Comment: An aromatic, dry blend. For a sweet version, use equal parts of all three ingredients, for a dry one use two shots of gin.

THE LEGEND

Glass: Martini
Garnish: Lime wedge on rim
Method: SHAKE all ingredients with ice and fine strain into chilled glass.

2	shot(s)	**Ketel One vodka**
1	shot(s)	**Freshly squeezed lime juice**
1/4	shot(s)	**Giffard mûre (blackberry)**
1/4	shot(s)	**Sugar syrup (2 sugar to 1 water)**
4	dashes	**Fee Brothers orange bitters**

Origin: Created in the late 1990s by Dick Bradsell for Karen Hampsen at Legends, London, England.
Comment: The quality of orange bitters and blackberry liqueur used dramatically affect the flavour of this blush coloured cocktail.

LEMON BEAT

Glass: Rocks
Garnish: Lemon slice
Method: STIR honey with cachaça in the base of shaker to dissolve honey. Add other ingredients, **SHAKE** with ice and strain into ice-filled glass.

2	spoons	**Clear runny honey**
2	shot(s)	**Leblon cachaça**
1	shot(s)	**Freshly squeezed lemon juice**

Comment: Simple but effective. Use quality cachaça and honey and you'll have a great drink.

LEMON BUTTER COOKIE

Glass: Old-fashioned
Garnish: Lemon zest twist
Method: SHAKE all ingredients with ice and strain into glass filled with crushed ice.

3/4	shot(s)	**Zubrówka bison vodka**
3/4	shot(s)	**Ketel One vodka**
3/4	shot(s)	**Krupnik honey liqueur**
2	shot(s)	**Pressed apple juice**
1/2	shot(s)	**Almond (orgeat) syrup**
1/8	shot(s)	**Freshly squeezed lemon juice**

Origin: Created in 2002 by Mark 'Q-Ball' Linnie and Martin Oliver at The Mixing Tin, Leeds, England.
Comment: An appropriate name for a most unusually flavoured drink modelled on the Polish Martini.

LEMON CHIFFON PIE

Glass: Coupette
Garnish: Grated lemon zest
Method: BLEND all ingredients with crushed ice and serve with straws.

1	shot(s)	**Light white rum**
1	shot(s)	**Giffard white crème de cacao**
1	shot(s)	**Freshly squeezed lemon juice**
2	scoops	**Vanilla ice cream**

Comment: Creamy and tangy – like a lemon pie. Consume in place of dessert.

LEMON CURD MARTINI

Glass: Martini
Garnish: Lemon wedge on rim
Method: SHAKE all ingredients with ice and fine strain into chilled glass.

3	spoons	**Lemon curd**
2	shot(s)	**Ketel One Citroen vodka**
1/2	shot(s)	**Freshly squeezed lemon juice**

Origin: Created by yours truly.
Comment: This almost creamy cocktail is named after and tastes like its primary ingredient. Martini purists may justifiably baulk at the absence of vermouth and the presence of fruit.

LEMON DROP

Glass: Shot
Garnish: Sugar coated slice of lemon
Method: SHAKE all ingredients with ice and fine strain into chilled glass.

1/2	shot(s)	**Ketel One vodka**
1/2	shot(s)	**Cointreau triple sec**
1/2	shot(s)	**Freshly squeezed lemon juice**

Comment: Lemon and orange combine to make a fresh tasting citrus shot.

LEMON DROP MARTINI

Glass: Martini
Garnish: Lemon zest twist
Method: SHAKE all ingredients with ice and fine strain into chilled glass.

2	shot(s)	**Ketel One Citroen vodka**
1	shot(s)	**Cointreau triple sec**
3/4	shot(s)	**Freshly squeezed lemon juice**
1/2	shot(s)	**Sugar syrup (2 sugar to 1 water)**

Comment: Sherbety lemon.

LEMON LIME & BITTERS

Glass: Collins
Garnish: Lime wedge
Method: Squeeze lime wedges and drop into glass. **ADD** Angostura bitters and fill glass with ice. **TOP** with lemonade, stir and serve with straws.

4	fresh	**Lime wedges**
5	dashes	**Angostura aromatic bitters**
Top up with		**7-Up**

AKA: LLB
Origin: Very popular in its homeland, Australia.
Comment: If you're unlucky enough to be the driver, this refreshing long drink is a good low alcohol option.

LEMON MARTINI

Glass: Martini
Garnish: Lemon zest twist
Method: MUDDLE lemongrass in base of shaker. Add other ingredients, **SHAKE** with ice and fine strain into chilled glass.

1	inch	**Lemongrass chopped**
2	shot(s)	**Ketel One vodka**
1/4	shot(s)	**Dry vermouth**
1	shot(s)	**Freshly squeezed lemon juice**
1/2	shot(s)	**Sugar syrup (2 sugar to 1 water)**

Origin: Created in 2006 by yours truly.
Comment: A complex, delicately lemon Vodkatini.

'CLARET IS THE LIQUOR FOR BOYS; PORT FOR MEN; BUT HE WHO ASPIRES TO BE A HERO MUST DRINK BRANDY.'

LEMON MERINGUE MARTINI [UPDATED]

Glass: Martini
Garnish: Lemon zest twist
Method: SHAKE all ingredients with ice and fine strain into chilled glass.

2	shot(s)	**Ketel One Citroen vodka**
1	shot(s)	**Irish cream liqueur**
1	shot(s)	**Freshly squeezed lemon juice**
1/4	shot(s)	**Sugar syrup (2 sugar to 1 water)**

Origin: Adapted from a drink created in 2000 by Ben Reed, London, England.
Comment: Slightly creamy in consistency, this tangy lemon drink is indeed reminiscent of the eponymous dessert.

LEMON MERINGUE PIE'TINI

Glass: Martini
Garnish: Pie rim (wipe outside edge of rim with cream mix and dip into crunched up Graham Cracker or digestive biscuits)
Method: SHAKE first three ingredients with ice and fine strain into chilled and rimmed glass. **SHAKE** cream and Licor 43 without ice so as to mix and whip. **FLOAT** cream mix by pouring over back of a spoon.

1	shot(s)	**Luxardo limoncello liqueur**
1	shot(s)	**Sugar syrup (2 sugar to 1 water)**
1	shot(s)	**Freshly squeezed lemon juice**
2	shot(s)	**Double (heavy) cream**
1/2	shot(s)	**Cuarenta Y Tres (Licor 43) liqueur**

Origin: Created by Michael Waterhouse at Dylan Prime, New York City.
Comment: Rich and syrupy base sipped through a vanilla cream topping.

LEMON SORBET

Glass: Martini (saucer)
Garnish: Strips of lemon rind
Method: Heat water in pan and add sugar. Simmer and stir until sugar dissolves, add lemon juice and grated lemon rind and continue to simmer and stir for a few minutes. Take off the heat and allow to cool. Fine strain into a shallow container and stir in liqueur and orange bitters. Beat egg whites and fold into mix. Place in freezer and store for up to 3-4 days before use.

3/4	cup(s)	**Mineral water**
1	cup(s)	**Granulated white sugar**
1/2	cup(s)	**Freshly squeezed lemon juice**
5	rinds	**Fresh lemon (avoid the pith when grating)**
1/4	cup(s)	**Luxardo limoncello liqueur**
2	spoons	**Fee Brothers orange bitters**
2	fresh	**Egg whites**

Variant: To make any other citrus flavour sorbet, simply substitute the juice and peel of another fruit such as grapefruit, lime or orange.
Comment: My favourite recipe for this dessert and occasional cocktail ingredient.

LEMONGRAD [UPDATED #7]

Glass: Collins
Garnish: Lemon wedge squeezed over drink
Method: SHAKE first four ingredients with ice and strain into ice-filled glass. **TOP** with tonic and lightly stir.

1	shot(s)	**Ketel One vodka**
1/2	shot(s)	**Ketel One Citroen vodka**
1/2	shot(s)	**St-Germain elderflower liqueur**
1/2	shot(s)	**Freshly squeezed lemon juice**
Top up with		**Tonic water**

Origin: Adapted from a drink created in 2002 by Alex Kammerling, London, England.
Comment: A great summer afternoon drink. Fresh lemon with elderflower and quinine.

LEMONGRASS COSMO

Glass: Martini
Garnish: Lemon zest twist
Method: MUDDLE lemongrass in base of shaker. **ADD** other ingredients, **SHAKE** with ice and fine strain into chilled glass.

1/4	stem	**Fresh lemongrass (finely chopped)**
1	shot(s)	**Ketel One Citroen vodka**
1	shot(s)	**Cointreau triple sec**
1 1/2	shot(s)	**Ocean Spray cranberry juice**
1/2	shot(s)	**Freshly squeezed lemon juice**

Origin: Adapted from a drink discovered in 2005 at Opia, Hong Kong, China
Comment: Lemongrass adds complexity to this balanced Cosmo.

LEMONY

Glass: Martini
Garnish: Maraschino cherry
Method: SHAKE all ingredients with ice and fine strain into chilled glass.

2	shot(s)	**Plymouth gin**
1/2	shot(s)	**Yellow Chartreuse liqueur**
1/2	shot(s)	**Luxardo limoncello liqueur**
1/2	shot(s)	**Freshly squeezed lemon juice**
1/2	shot(s)	**Chilled mineral water** (omit if wet ice)

Comment: Lemon subtly dominates this complex, herbal drink.

LENINADE

Glass: Martini
Garnish: Orange zest twist
Method: SHAKE all ingredients with ice and fine strain into chilled glass.

1 1/2	shot(s)	**Ketel One Citroen vodka**
1	shot(s)	**Freshly squeezed lemon juice**
1/4	shot(s)	**Sugar syrup (2 sugar to 1 water)**
1/4	shot(s)	**Cointreau triple sec**
3	dashes	**Fee Brothers orange bitters**

Origin: Created by Dick Bradsell at Fred's, London, England, in the late 80s.
Comment: Orange undertones add citrus depth to the lemon explosion.

LIFE (LOVE IN THE FUTURE ECSTASY)

Glass: Old-fashioned
Garnish: Mint leaf
Method: MUDDLE mint in base of shaker. Add next three ingredients, **SHAKE** with ice and fine strain into glass filled with crushed ice. **DRIZZLE** tea liqueur over drink.

7	fresh	**Mint leaves**
1 1/2	shot(s)	**Ketel One vodka**
1	shot(s)	**Freshly squeezed lime juice**
1/2	shot(s)	**Sugar syrup (2 sugar to 1 water)**
1	shot(s)	**Tea liqueur**

Origin: Adapted from a drink created in 1999 by Nick Strangeway at Ché, London, England, for Martin Sexton (writer and artistic entrepreneur).
Comment: Refreshing tea and mint.

LIGHT BREEZE

Glass: Collins
Garnish: Lemon slice
Method: POUR all ingredients into ice-filled glass. Stir and serve with straws.

3	shot(s)	**Ocean Spray cranberry juice**
2	shot(s)	**Freshly squeezed golden grapefruit juice**
2	shot(s)	**Pernod anis**

Origin: Created in 2000 by yours truly at the Light Bar, London, England (hence the name).
Comment: A Seabreeze based on anis rather than vodka, with aniseed depth and sweetness.

LIGHTER BREEZE

Glass: Collins
Garnish: Apple wedge on rim
Method: POUR all ingredients into ice-filled glass. Stir and serve with straws.

2	shot(s)	**Pressed apple juice**
1/2	shot(s)	**Ocean Spray cranberry juice**
1	shot(s)	**St Germain Elderflower liqueur**
1/2	shot(s)	**Pernod anis**

Comment: Long, fragrant and refreshing.

LIMA SOUR

Glass: Old-fashioned
Garnish: Lemon zest string
Method: BLEND all ingredients with one 12oz scoop of crushed ice. Serve with straws.

2	shot(s)	**Pisco**
1/2	shot(s)	**Luxardo maraschino liqueur**
3/4	shot(s)	**Freshly squeezed golden grapefruit juice**
3/4	shot(s)	**Freshly squeezed lime juice**
3/4	shot(s)	**Sugar syrup (2 sugar to 1 water)**

Origin: Created before 1947 by Jerry Hooker.
Comment: A refreshing blend of pisco, maraschino and citrus.

LIME BLUSH (MOCKTAIL)

Glass: Old-fashioned
Garnish: Lime wedge
Method: SHAKE all ingredients with ice and strain into glass filled with crushed ice.

2	shot(s)	**Freshly squeezed lime juice**
1/2	shot(s)	**Rose's lime cordial**
1/2	shot(s)	**Pomegranate (grenadine) syrup**
1/2	shot(s)	**Sugar syrup (2 sugar to 1 water)**

Origin: Adapted from a drink discovered in 2005 at Blue Bar, Four Seasons Hotel, Hong Kong, China.
Comment: Refreshingly sweet and sour.

LIME BREEZE

Glass: Collins
Garnish: Lime wedge
Method: SHAKE all ingredients with ice and fine strain into ice-filled glass.

2	shot(s)	**Lime flavoured vodka**
3	shot(s)	**Ocean Spray cranberry juice**
1 1/2	shot(s)	**Freshly squeezed golden grapefruit juice**

Comment: A lime driven Sea Breeze.

L

LIME SOUR

Glass: Old-fashioned
Garnish: Lime wedge on rim
Method: SHAKE all ingredients with ice and strain into ice-filled glass.

2	shot(s)	**Lime flavoured vodka**
1¼	shot(s)	**Freshly squeezed lime juice**
¼	shot(s)	**Sugar syrup (2 sugar to 1 water)**
½	fresh	**Egg white**

Comment: Fresh egg white gives this drink a wonderfully frothy top and smoothes the alcohol and lime juice.

LIMEADE (MOCKTAIL)

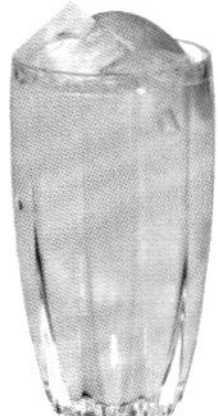

Glass: Collins
Garnish: Lime wedge
Method: SHAKE all ingredients with ice and fine strain into ice filled glass.

2	shot(s)	**Freshly squeezed lime juice**
1	shot(s)	**Sugar syrup (2 sugar to 1 water)**
3	shot(s)	**Chilled mineral water**

Variant: Shake first two ingredients & top with sparkling water.
Comment: A superbly refreshing alternative to lemonade.

LIMELITE

Glass: Collins
Garnish: Lime wedge
Method: SHAKE first four ingredients with ice and strain into ice-filled glass. **TOP** with 7-Up.

2	shot(s)	**Lime flavoured vodka**
½	shot(s)	**Cointreau triple sec**
½	shot(s)	**Freshly squeezed lime juice**
¼	shot(s)	**Sugar syrup (2 sugar to 1 water)**
Top up with		**7-Up**

Comment: Long and citrussy.

LIMEOSA

Glass: Flute
Method: SHAKE first two ingredients with ice and fine strain into chilled glass. **TOP** with champagne and gently stir.

1	shot(s)	**Lime flavoured vodka**
2	shot(s)	**Freshly squeezed orange juice**
Top up with		**Brut champagne**

Comment: Why settle for a plain old Buck's Fizz when you could add a shot of lime-flavoured vodka?

LIMERICK

Glass: Collins
Garnish: Lime wedge squeezed over drink
Method: SHAKE first three ingredients with ice and strain into ice-filled glass. **TOP** with soda water and lightly stir.

2	shot(s)	**Lime flavoured vodka**
1	shot(s)	**Freshly squeezed lime juice**
½	shot(s)	**Sugar syrup (2 sugar to 1 water)**
Top up with		**Soda water (club soda)**

Origin: I created this twist on the classic Vodka Rickey in 2002.
Comment: A refreshing lime cooler.

LIMEY

Glass: Martini
Garnish: Lime zest twist
Method: SHAKE all ingredients with ice and fine strain into chilled glass.

2	shot(s)	**Lime flavoured vodka**
½	shot(s)	**Freshly squeezed lime juice**
½	shot(s)	**Sugar syrup (2 sugar to 1 water)**
⅛	shot(s)	**Rose's lime cordial**
3	dashes	**Angostura aromatic bitters**
½	shot(s)	**Chilled mineral water** (omit if wet ice)

Origin: I created and named this drink after the British naval tradition of mixing lime juice with spirits in an attempt to prevent scurvy. This practice gained British sailors the nickname 'limeys'.
Comment: A rust coloured drink with a delicately sour flavour.

LIMEY COSMO

Glass: Martini
Garnish: Lime wedge on rim
Method: SHAKE all ingredients with ice and fine strain into chilled glass.

1½	shot(s)	**Lime flavoured vodka**
1	shot(s)	**Cointreau triple sec**
1¼	shot(s)	**Ocean Spray cranberry juice**
¼	shot(s)	**Freshly squeezed lime juice**
½	shot(s)	**Rose's lime cordial**

Comment: If you like Cosmopolitans, you'll love this zesty alternative.

LIMEY MULE

Glass: Collins
Garnish: Lime wedge
Method: SHAKE first three ingredients with ice and strain into ice-filled glass. **TOP** with ginger ale, lightly stir and serve with straws.

2	shot(s)	**Lime flavoured vodka**
1	shot(s)	**Freshly squeezed lime juice**
½	shot(s)	**Sugar syrup (2 sugar to 1 water)**
Top up with		**Ginger ale**

Comment: Made with plain vodka this drink is a Moscow Mule. This variant uses lime flavoured vodka.

LIMINAL SHOT

Glass: Shot
Method: Refrigerate ingredients then **LAYER** in chilled glass by carefully pouring in the following order.

1/2 shot(s) **Pomegranate (grenadine) syrup**
1/2 shot(s) **Bols Blue curaçao liqueur**
3/4 shot(s) **Lime flavoured vodka**

Comment: The name means transitional, marginal, a boundary or a threshold. Appropriate since the layers border each other.

LIMITED LIABILITY

Glass: Old-fashioned
Method: SHAKE all ingredients with ice and strain into ice-filled glass.

2 shot(s) **Lime flavoured vodka**
3/4 shot(s) **Freshly squeezed lime juice**
1 shot(s) **Honey liqueur**

Origin: Created in 2002 by yours truly.
Comment: A sour and flavoursome short - honey and lime work well together.

L

LIMNOLOGY

Glass: Martini
Garnish: Lime zest twist
Method: STIR all ingredients with ice and fine strain into chilled glass.

2 shot(s) **Lime flavoured vodka**
1 shot(s) **Rose's lime cordial**
3/4 shot(s) **Chilled water** (reduceif wet ice)

Origin: The name means the study of the physical phenomena of lakes and other fresh waters – appropriate for this fresh green drink.
Comment: A vodka Gimlet made with lime flavoured vodka.

LIMONCELLO MARTINI

Glass: Martini
Garnish: Lemon zest twist
Method: SHAKE all ingredients with ice and fine strain into chilled glass.

1 1/2 shot(s) **Ketel One vodka**
1 1/2 shot(s) **Luxardo limoncello liqueur**
1 shot(s) **Freshly squeezed lemon juice**

Origin: Adapted from a drink created in 2005 by Francesco at Mix, New York City, USA.
Comment: If you like the liqueur you'll love the cocktail.

LIMOUSINE

Glass: Old-fashioned
Method: Place bar spoon in glass. **POUR** ingredients into glass and stir.

2 shot(s) **Lime flavoured vodka**
1 shot(s) **Honey liqueur**
4 shot(s) **Hot camomile tea**

Origin: Created in 2002 by yours truly.
Comment: In winter this hot drink is a warming treat. In summer serve cold over ice, as pictured.

LINSTEAD

Glass: Martini
Garnish: Lemon zest twist
Method: SHAKE all ingredients with ice and fine strain into chilled glass.

2 shot(s) **Scotch whisky**
2 shot(s) **Pressed pineapple juice**
1/4 shot(s) **Sugar syrup (2 sugar to 1 water)**
1/8 shot(s) **La Fée Parisienne (68%) absinthe**

Comment: Absinthe and pineapple come through first, with Scotch last. A great medley of flavours.

LIQUORICE ALL SORT

Glass: Collins
Garnish: Liquorice Allsort sweet
Method: SHAKE first four ingredients with ice and strain into ice-filled glass. **TOP** with lemonade.

1 shot(s) **Opal Nera black sambuca**
1 shot(s) **Giffard crème de banane du Brésil**
1 shot(s) **Giffard crème de fraise de bois**
1 shot(s) **Bols Blue curaçao liqueur**
Top up with **7-Up / lemonade**

Origin: George Bassett (1818-1886), a manufacturer of liquorice sweets, did not invent the Liquorice Allsort that carries his name. That happened 15 years after George died when a salesman accidentally dropped a tray of sweets, they fell in a muddle and the famous sweet was born.
Comment: This aptly named, semi-sweet drink has a strong liquorice flavour with hints of fruit.

LIQUORICE MARTINI

Glass: Martini
Garnish: Piece of liquorice
Method: STIR all ingredients with ice and strain into chilled glass.

2 shot(s) **Plymouth gin**
1/4 shot(s) **Opal Nera black sambuca**
1/8 shot(s) **Sugar syrup (2 sugar to 1 water)**

Origin: Created in 2003 by Jason Fendick, London, England.
Comment: Gin tinted violet, flavoured with liquorice and slightly sweetened.

LIQUORICE SHOT

Glass: Shot
Method: SHAKE all ingredients with ice and fine strain into chilled glass.

1/2	shot(s)	**Ketel One vodka**
1/2	shot(s)	**Luxardo white sambuca**
1/2	shot(s)	**Giffard crème de cassis**

Comment: For liquorice fans.

LIQUORICE WHISKY SOUR

Glass: Old-fashioned
Garnish: Cherry & lemon slice (sail)
Method: SHAKE all ingredients with ice and strain into ice-filled glass.

2	shot(s)	**Scotch whisky**
1/2	shot(s)	**Ricard pastis**
1	shot(s)	**Freshly squeezed lemon juice**
1/2	shot(s)	**Sugar syrup (2 sugar to 1 water)**
1/2	fresh	**Egg white**
3	dashes	**Angostura aromatic bitters**

Origin: Created in 2006 by yours truly.
Comment: Pastis adds a pleasing hint of liquorice to the classic Whisky Sour.

LISA B'S DAIQUIRI

Glass: Martini
Garnish: Grapefruit zest twist
Method: SHAKE all ingredients with ice and fine strain into chilled glass.

2 1/2	shot(s)	**Vanilla infused Light rum**
1/2	shot(s)	**Freshly squeezed lime juice**
1/2	shot(s)	**Sonoma vanilla bean sugar syrup**
1	shot(s)	**Squeezed pink grapefruit juice**

Origin: Created in 2003 by yours truly for a gorgeous fan of both Daiquiris and pink grapefruit juice.
Comment: Reminiscent of a Hemingway Special, this flavoursome, vanilla laced Daiquiri has a wonderfully tangy bitter-sweet finish.

LITTLE ITALY

Glass: Martini
Garnish: Orange zest twist
Method: STIR all ingredients with ice and fine strain into chilled glass.

2	shot(s)	**Buffalo Trace bourbon whiskey**
1	shot(s)	**Sweet vermouth**
1/2	shot(s)	**Cynar liqueur**

Origin: Adapted from a drink discovered in 2006 at Pegu Club, New York City, USA.
Comment: A sweet, Manhattan-style drink, bittered with Cynar.

LIVINGSTONE

Glass: Martini
Garnish: Lemon peel twist
Method: SHAKE all ingredients with ice and fine strain into chilled glass.

2	shot(s)	**Plymouth gin**
1	shot(s)	**Dry vermouth**
1/4	shot(s)	**Sugar syrup (2 sugar to 1 water)**

Variant: Use pomegranate syrup in place of sugar and you have a Red Livingstone, named after London's 'lefty' mayor, Ken.
Origin: This 1930s classic was named after Doctor Livingstone, the famous African missionary.
Comment: The classic gin and vermouth Martini made more approachable with a dash of sugar.

LOCH ALMOND

Glass: Collins
Garnish: Float amaretti biscuit
Method: POUR all ingredients into ice-filled glass, stir and serve with straws.

1 1/2	shot(s)	**Scotch whisky**
1 1/2	shot(s)	**Luxardo Amaretto di Saschira liqueur**
Top up with		**Ginger ale**

Comment: If you haven't got to grips with Scotch but like amaretto, try this spicy almond combination.

LOLA

Glass: Martini
Garnish: Orange zest twist
Method: SHAKE all ingredients with ice and fine strain into chilled glass.

1 1/2	shot(s)	**Golden rum**
1/2	shot(s)	**Mandarine Napoléon liqueur**
1/2	shot(s)	**Giffard white crème de cacao**
1	shot(s)	**Freshly squeezed orange juice**
1/2	shot(s)	**Double (heavy) cream**

Origin: Created in 1999 by Jamie Terrell, London, England.
Comment: Strong, creamy orange.

LOLITA MARGARITA

Glass: Coupette
Garnish: Lime wedge on rim
Method: STIR honey with tequila in base of shaker to dissolve honey. Add other ingredients, **SHAKE** with ice and fine strain into chilled glass.

2	spoons	**Runny honey**
2	shot(s)	**Partida tequila**
1	shot(s)	**Freshly squeezed lime juice**
2	dashes	**Angostura aromatic bitters**

Origin: Named after the novel by Vladimir Nabokov which chronicles a middle-aged man's infatuation with a 12 year old girl. Nabokov invented the word 'nymphet' to describe her seductive qualities.
Comment: A fittingly seductive Margarita.

LONDON CALLING

Glass: Martini
Garnish: Orange zest twist
Method: STIR all ingredients with ice and strain into chilled glass.

2	shot(s)	**Plymouth gin**
1¼	shot(s)	**Plymouth sloe gin liqueur**
½	shot(s)	**Sweet vermouth**
2	dashes	**Fee Brothers orange bitters**

Origin: Discovered in 2003 at Oxo Tower Bar & Brasserie, London, England.
Comment: A traditionally styled sweet Martini with a dry, fruity finish.

LONDON COCKTAIL

Glass: Martini
Garnish: Orange zest twist
Method: SHAKE all ingredients with ice and fine strain into chilled glass.

2½	shot(s)	**Plymouth gin**
⅛	shot(s)	**La Fée Parisienne (68%) absinthe**
⅛	shot(s)	**Sugar syrup (2 sugar to 1 water)**
2	dashes	**Fee Brothers orange bitters**
½	shot(s)	**Chilled mineral water** (omit if wet ice)

Origin: Adapted from a recipe in Harry Craddock's 1930 Savoy Cocktail Book.
Comment: Chilled, diluted and sweetened gin invigorated by a hint of absinthe.

LONDON FOG

Glass: Old-fashioned
Garnish: Orange zest twist
Method: Fill glass with ice. Add ingredients in the following order and **STIR**. Add more ice to fill.

1	shot(s)	**Plymouth gin**
2	shot(s)	**Chilled mineral water**
1	shot(s)	**Pernod anis**

Comment: Dry liquorice and aniseed.

LONELY BULL

Glass: Old-fashioned
Garnish: Dust with freshly grated nutmeg
Method: SHAKE all ingredients with ice and strain into ice-filled glass.

1½	shot(s)	**Partida tequila**
1½	shot(s)	**Kahlúa coffee liqueur**
¾	shot(s)	**Double (heavy) cream**
¾	shot(s)	**Milk**

Comment: Like a creamy iced coffee – yum.

LONG BEACH ICED TEA

Glass: Sling
Garnish: Lemon slice
Method: SHAKE all ingredients with ice and strain into ice-filled glass. Serve with straws.

½	shot(s)	**Kahlúa coffee liqueur**
½	shot(s)	**Partida tequila**
½	shot(s)	**Light white rum**
½	shot(s)	**Plymouth gin**
½	shot(s)	**Ketel One vodka**
1	shot(s)	**Freshly squeezed lime juice**
½	shot(s)	**Sugar syrup (2 sugar to 1 water)**
2	shot(s)	**Ocean Spray cranberry juice**

Comment: One of the more grown-up 'Iced Tea' cocktails

LONG FLIGHT OF STAIRS

Glass: Collins
Garnish: Apple or pear slice
Method: SHAKE all ingredients with ice and strain into ice-filled glass. Serve with straws.

1	shot(s)	**Pear flavoured vodka**
1	shot(s)	**Boulard Grand Solage Calvados**
1	shot(s)	**Pear & cognac liqueur**
2½	shot(s)	**Pressed apple juice**

Origin: Created in 2005 by yours truly as a homage to the G.E. Club's 'Stairs Martini'.
Comment: A seriously tasty, strong, long drink. The name is a reversal of the London rhyming slang 'apples and pears' (stairs).

'HE WAS WHITE AND SHAKEN, LIKE A DRY MARTINI.'
P.G. WODEHOUSE

LONG ISLAND ICED TEA

Glass: Sling
Garnish: Lemon slice
Method: SHAKE first seven ingredients with ice and strain into ice-filled glass. **TOP** with cola, stir and serve with straws.

½	shot(s)	**Light white rum**
½	shot(s)	**Plymouth gin**
½	shot(s)	**Ketel One vodka**
½	shot(s)	**Partida tequila**
½	shot(s)	**Cointreau triple sec**
1	shot(s)	**Freshly squeezed lime juice**
½	shot(s)	**Sugar syrup (2 sugar to 1 water)**
Top up with		**Cola**

Origin: This infamous drink reached the height of its popularity in the early 1980s. It looks like iced tea disguising its contents - hence the name.
Comment: A cooling combination of five different spirits with a hint of lime and a splash of cola.

LONG ISLAND SPICED TEA

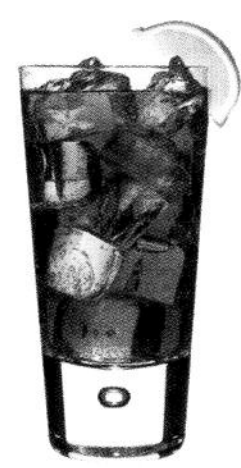

Glass: Collins
Garnish: Lime wedge on rim
Method: **SHAKE** first seven ingredients with ice and strain into ice-filled glass. **TOP** with cola, lightly stir and serve with straws.

1/2 shot(s) **Spiced rum**
1/2 shot(s) **Ketel One vodka**
1/2 shot(s) **Plymouth gin**
1/2 shot(s) **Partida tequila**
1/2 shot(s) **Cointreau triple sec**
1 shot(s) **Freshly squeezed lime juice**
1/2 shot(s) **Sugar syrup (2 sugar to 1 water)**
Top up with **Cola**

Comment: A contemporary spicy twist on an American classic.

'[GRANT] STOOD BY ME WHEN I WAS CRAZY, AND I STOOD BY HIM WHEN HE WAS DRUNK; AND NOW WE STAND BY EACH OTHER ALWAYS.'
GENERAL WILLIAM SHERMAN

LOTUS ESPRESSO

Glass: Martini
Garnish: Float three coffee beans
Method: **SHAKE** all ingredients with ice and fine strain into chilled glass.

2 shot(s) **Ketel One vodka**
1/2 shot(s) **Kahlúa coffee liqueur**
1/2 shot(s) **Maple syrup**
1 shot(s) **Cold espresso coffee**

Origin: Adapted from a drink discovered in 2005 at Lotus Bar, Sydney, Australia.
Comment: Coffee to the fore but with complex, earthy bitter-sweet notes.

LOTUS MARTINI

Glass: Martini
Garnish: Mint leaf
Method: Lightly **MUDDLE** mint (just to bruise) in base of shaker. Add other ingredients, **SHAKE** with ice and fine strain into chilled glass.

7 fresh **Mint leaves**
2 shot(s) **Plymouth gin**
1/4 shot(s) **Bols Blue curaçao liqueur**
1 1/2 shot(s) **Lychee syrup from tinned fruit**
1/4 shot(s) **Pomegranate (grenadine) syrup**

Origin: Created in 2001 by Martin Walander at Match Bar, London, England.
Comment: This violet coloured drink may have an unlikely list of ingredients, but – boy! - does it look and taste good.

LOUD SPEAKER MARTINI

Glass: Martini
Garnish: Lemon peel twist
Method: **SHAKE** all ingredients with ice and fine strain into chilled glass.

1 1/2 shot(s) **Plymouth gin**
1 1/2 shot(s) **Rémy Martin cognac**
1/2 shot(s) **Sweet vermouth**
1/4 shot(s) **Freshly squeezed lemon juice**
1/4 shot(s) **Sugar syrup (2 sugar to 1 water)**

Origin: Adapted from a recipe in the 1930 Savoy Cocktail Book by Harry Craddock.
Comment: I've added a dash of sugar to the original recipe which I found too dry.

LOUISIANA TRADE

Glass: Old-fashioned
Garnish: Lime wedge
Method: **SHAKE** all ingredients with ice and strain into glass filled with crushed ice.

2 shot(s) **Southern Comfort liqueur**
1/2 shot(s) **Maple syrup**
1 shot(s) **Freshly squeezed lime juice**
1/4 shot(s) **Sugar syrup (2 sugar to 1 water)**

Origin: Created in 2001 by Mehdi Otmann at Zeta, London, England.
Comment: Peach and apricot with the freshness of lime and the dense sweetness of maple syrup.

LOVE JUNK

Glass: Old-fashioned
Garnish: Apple wedge
Method: **SHAKE** all ingredients with ice and strain into ice-filled glass.

2 shot(s) **Ketel One vodka**
1/2 shot(s) **Midori melon liqueur**
1/2 shot(s) **Teichenné Peach Schnapps Liqueur**
1 1/2 shot(s) **Pressed apple juice**

Comment: A light, crisp, refreshing blend of peach, melon and apple juice, laced with vodka.

LOVED UP

Glass: Martini
Garnish: Berries on stick
Method: **SHAKE** all ingredients with ice and fine strain into chilled glass.

1 1/2 shot(s) **Partida tequila**
1/2 shot(s) **Cointreau triple sec**
1/2 shot(s) **Chambord black raspberry liqueur**
1/2 shot(s) **Freshly squeezed lime juice**
1 shot(s) **Freshly squeezed orange juice**
1/4 shot(s) **Sugar syrup (2 sugar to 1 water)**

Origin: Adapted from a cocktail discovered in 2002 at the Merc Bar, New York City, where the original name was listed as simply 'Love'.
Comment: Tequila predominates in this rusty coloured drink, which also features orange and berry fruit.

LUCIEN GAUDIN [NEW #7]

Glass: Martini
Garnish: Orange zest twist
Method: **STIR** all ingredients with ice and strain into chilled glass.

1½	shot(s)	**Plymouth gin**
¾	shot(s)	**Cointreau triple sec**
¾	shot(s)	**Campari**
¾	shot(s)	**Dry vermouth**

Origin: Recipe from 'Vintage Spirits and Forgotten Cocktails' by Ted Haigh (Dr. Cocktail). Lucien Gaudin was a French fencer who achieved gold medals with two different weapons at the 1928 Olympics in Amsterdam.
Comment: A must try for anyone who loves Negronis.

LUCKY LILY MARGARITA

Glass: Coupette
Garnish: Pineapple wedge dusted with pepper on rim
Method: **STIR** honey with tequila in base of shaker to dissolve honey. **ADD** other ingredients, **SHAKE** with ice and fine strain into chilled glass.

2	spoons	**Runny honey**
2	shot(s)	**Partida tequila**
1	shot(s)	**Pressed pineapple juice**
¾	shot(s)	**Freshly squeezed lime juice**
5	grinds	**Black pepper**

Origin: Adapted from a drink discovered in 2006 at All Star Lanes, London, England.
Comment: Spicy tequila and pineapple tingle with balance and flavour.

'THEN HASTEN TO BE DRUNK, THE BUSINESS OF THE DAY.'
JOHN DRYDEN

LUCKY LINDY

Glass: Collins
Garnish: Lemon wheel
Method: **STIR** honey with bourbon in base of shaker so as to dissolve honey. Add lemon juice, **SHAKE** with ice and strain into ice-filled glass. **TOP** with 7-Up, lightly stir and serve with straws.

3	spoon(s)	**Runny honey**
2	shot(s)	**Buffalo Trace bourbon whiskey**
½	shot(s)	**Freshly squeezed lemon juice**
Top up with		**7-Up**

Origin: Adapted from a drink discovered in 2003 at The Grange Hall, New York City, USA.
Comment: A long refreshing drink that combines whisky, citrus and honey – a long chilled toddy without the spice.

LUSH

Glass: Flute
Garnish: Raspberry in glass
Method: **POUR** vodka and liqueur into chilled glass, top with champagne and lightly stir.

1	shot(s)	**Ketel One vodka**
½	shot(s)	**Chambord black raspberry liqueur**
Top up with		**Brut champagne**

Origin: Created in 1999 by Spike Marchant at Alphabet, London, England.
Comment: It is, are you?

LUTKINS SPECIAL MARTINI

Glass: Martini
Garnish: Orange zest twist
Method: **SHAKE** all ingredients with ice and fine strain into chilled glass.

1½	shot(s)	**Plymouth gin**
1	shot(s)	**Dry vermouth**
½	shot(s)	**Giffard apricot brandy du Roussillon**
¾	shot(s)	**Freshly squeezed orange juice**

Origin: Adapted from a recipe in Harry Craddock's 1930 Savoy Cocktail Book.
Comment: I've tried many variations on the above formula and none are that special.

LUX DAIQUIRI

Glass: Martini (large)
Garnish: Maraschino cherry
Method: **BLEND** all ingredients with one 12oz scoop of crushed ice and serve in chilled glass.

3	shot(s)	**Light white rum**
¾	shot(s)	**Freshly squeezed lime juice**
½	shot(s)	**Luxardo maraschino liqueur**
¼	shot(s)	**Sugar syrup (2 sugar to 1 water)**
¼	shot(s)	**Maraschino syrup (from cherry jar)**

Origin: This was one of two cocktails with which I won a Havana Club Daiquiri competition in 2002. I named it after Girolamo Luxardo, creator of the now famous liqueur, 'Luxardo Maraschino'. My educated sub also informs me Lux is Latin for light.
Comment: A classic frozen Daiquiri heavily laced with maraschino cherry.

LUXURY COCKTAIL

Glass: Martini
Method: **SHAKE** all ingredients with ice and fine strain into chilled glass.

2	shot(s)	**Plymouth gin**
¾	shot(s)	**Pimm's No.1 Cup**
½	shot(s)	**Giffard crème de banane du Brésil**
¾	shot(s)	**Sweet vermouth**
¼	shot(s)	**Rose's lime cordial**
3	dashes	**Angostura aromatic bitters**

Comment: Sticky banana followed by a bitter, refined aftertaste.

LUXURY MOJITO

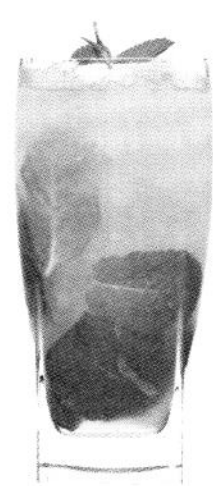

Glass: Collins
Garnish: Mint sprig
Method: MUDDLE mint in glass with sugar and lime juice. Fill glass with crushed ice, add rum, Angostura and champagne , then stir.

12	fresh	**Mint leaves**
1/4	shot(s)	**Sugar syrup (2 sugar to 1 water)**
1	shot(s)	**Freshly squeezed lime juice**
2	shot(s)	**Aged rum**
3	dashes	**Angostura aromatic bitters**
Top up with		**Brut champagne**

Comment: A Mojito made with aged rum and topped with champagne instead of soda water: more complex than the original.

LYCHEE & BLACKCURRANT MARTINI

Glass: Martini
Garnish: Peeled lychee in glass
Method: SHAKE all ingredients with ice and fine strain into chilled glass.

2	shot(s)	**Plymouth gin**
1/2	shot(s)	**Soho lychee liqueur**
1/4	shot(s)	**Giffard crème de cassis**
1/4	shot(s)	**Rose's lime cordial**
3/4	shot(s)	**Chilled mineral water** (omit if wet ice)

Origin: Created by yours truly in 2004.
Comment: Light, fragrant and laced with gin.

LYCHEE & ROSE PETAL MARTINI

Glass: Martini
Garnish: Float rose petal
Method: STIR all ingredients with ice and strain into chilled glass.

2	shot(s)	**Plymouth gin**
1	shot(s)	**Rose petal vodka liqueur**
1	shot(s)	**Lychee syrup from tinned fruit**
2	dashes	**Peychaud's aromatic bitters**

Origin: Created in 2002 by Dick Bradsell for Opium, London, England.
Comment: Light pink in colour and subtle in flavour.

LYCHEE & SAKE MARTINI

Glass: Martini
Garnish: Peeled lychee in glass
Method: STIR all ingredients with ice and strain into chilled glass.

1 1/2	shot(s)	**Plymouth gin**
2	shot(s)	**Sake**
3/4	shot(s)	**Soho lychee liqueur**

Origin: Created in 2004 by yours truly.
Comment: A soft, Martini styled drink with subtle hints of sake and lychee.

LYCHEE MAC

Glass: Old-fashioned
Garnish: Peeled lychee in drink
Method: SHAKE all ingredients with ice and strain into ice-filled glass.

2 1/4	shot(s)	**Scotch whisky**
1	shot(s)	**Soho lychee liqueur**
3/4	shot(s)	**Stone's green ginger wine**

Origin: Created by yours truly in 2004.
Comment: Peaty Scotch with sweet lychee and hot ginger.

LYCHEE MARTINI

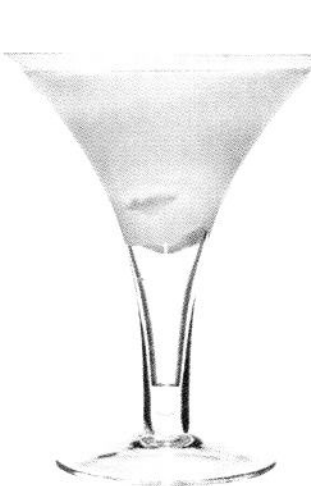

Glass: Martini
Garnish: Whole lychee from tin
Method: STIR all ingredients with ice and fine strain into chilled glass.

2	shot(s)	**Ketel One vodka**
1/2	shot(s)	**Soho lychee liqueur**
1/2	shot(s)	**Dry vermouth**
1	shot(s)	**Lychee syrup from tinned fruit**

Origin: Thought to have been first made in 2001 at Clay, a Korean restaurant in New York City, USA.
Comment: If you like lychee you'll love this delicate Martini.

LYCHEE RICKEY

Glass: Collins (small 8oz)
Garnish: Immerse length of lime peel in drink.
Method: SHAKE first three ingredients with ice and strain into ice-filled glass. **TOP** with soda water.

2	shot(s)	**Plymouth gin**
1	shot(s)	**Soho lychee liqueur**
1/2	shot(s)	**Freshly squeezed lime juice**
Top up with		**Soda water (club soda)**

Origin: Adapted from a drink discovered in 2005 at Club 97, Hong Kong, China.
Comment: The lychee liqueur dominates this surprisingly dry Rickey.

LYNCHBURG LEMONADE

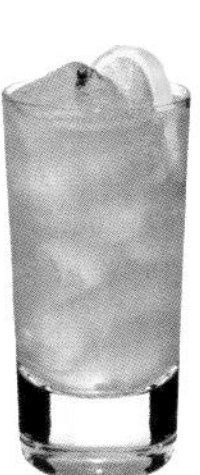

Glass: Collins
Garnish: Lemon slice
Method: SHAKE first three ingredients with ice and strain into ice-filled glass. **TOP** with 7-Up.

1 1/2	shot(s)	**Jack Daniel's Tennessee whiskey**
1	shot(s)	**Cointreau triple sec**
1	shot(s)	**Freshly squeezed lemon juice**
Top up with		**7-Up**

Variant: With three dashes Angostura aromatic bitters.
Origin: Created for the Jack Daniel's distillery in - yep, you guessed it - Lynchburg, Tennessee.
Comment: Tangy, light and very easy to drink.

M.G.F.

Glass: Martini
Garnish: Orange zest twist
Method: SHAKE all ingredients with ice and fine strain into chilled glass.

1	shot(s)	**Orange zest infused Ketel One vodka**
1	shot(s)	**Ketel One Citroen vodka**
1	shot(s)	**Pressed pink grapefruit juice**
1	shot(s)	**Freshly squeezed lemon juice**
1/2	shot(s)	**Sugar syrup (2 sugar to 1 water)**

Origin: Discovered in 2003 at Claridge's Bar, London, England.
Comment: Short and sharp.

MAC ORANGE

Glass: Old-fashioned
Garnish: Orange zest twist
Method: SHAKE all ingredients with ice and fine strain into chilled glass.

2	shot(s)	**Scotch whisky**
1	shot(s)	**Stone's ginger wine**
1	shot(s)	**Freshly squeezed orange juice**
1/4	shot(s)	**Sugar syrup (2 sugar to 1 water)**
3	dashes	**Fee Brothers orange bitters**

Comment: A Whisky Mac with orange topping off the ginger.

MACKA

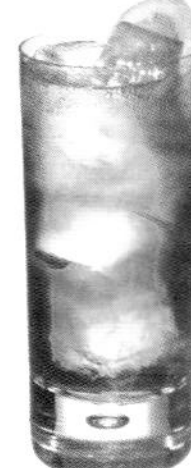

Glass: Collins
Garnish: Lemon slice
Method: SHAKE first four ingredients with ice and strain into ice-filled glass. **TOP** with soda.

2	shot(s)	**Plymouth gin**
1/2	shot(s)	**Dry vermouth**
1/2	shot(s)	**Sweet vermouth**
1/2	shot(s)	**Giffard crème de cassis**
Top up with		**Soda water (club soda)**

Comment: A long fruity drink for parched palates.

THE MACKINNON [NEW #7]

Glass: Martini
Garnish: Lemon zest twist
Method: SHAKE all ingredients with ice and fine strain into chilled glass.

2	shot(s)	**Golden rum**
1	shot(s)	**Drambuie liqueur**
1/2	shot(s)	**Freshly squeezed lemon juice**

Variant: Serve long over ice with soda.
Origin: Named after the MacKinnon family, the makers of Drambuie.
Comment: Honeyed rum with herbal and citrus nuances.

MAD MONK MILKSHAKE

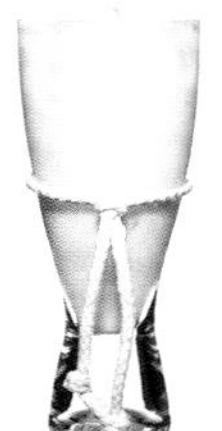

Glass: Collins
Garnish: Tie cord around glass
Method: SHAKE all ingredients with ice and strain into ice-filled glass.

2	shot(s)	**Frangelico hazelnut liqueur**
1	shot(s)	**Irish cream liqueur**
1/4	shot(s)	**Kahlúa coffee liqueur**
1	shot(s)	**Double (heavy) cream**
2	shot(s)	**Milk**

Variant: Blend instead of shaking and serve frozen.
Comment: Long, creamy and slightly sweet with hazelnut and coffee.

MADRAS

Glass: Collins
Garnish: Orange slice
Method: SHAKE all ingredients with ice and strain into ice-filled glass.

2	shot(s)	**Ketel One vodka**
3	shot(s)	**Ocean Spray cranberry juice**
2	shot(s)	**Freshly squeezed orange juice**

Comment: A Seabreeze with orange juice in place of grapefruit juice, making it slightly sweeter.

MADROSKA

Glass: Collins
Garnish: Orange slice
Method: SHAKE all ingredients with ice and strain into ice-filled glass.

2	shot(s)	**Ketel One vodka**
2 1/2	shot(s)	**Pressed apple juice**
1 1/2	shot(s)	**Ocean Spray cranberry juice**
1	shot(s)	**Freshly squeezed orange juice**

Origin: Created in 1998 by Jamie Terrell, London, England.
Comment: A Madras with more than a hint of apple juice.

MAE WEST MARTINI

Glass: Martini
Garnish: Melon wedge on rim
Method: SHAKE all ingredients with ice and fine strain into chilled glass.

2	shot(s)	**Ketel One vodka**
1/2	shot(s)	**Luxardo Amaretto di Saschira liqueur**
1/4	shot(s)	**Midori melon liqueur**
1 1/2	shot(s)	**Ocean Spray cranberry juice**

Comment: A rosé coloured, semi-sweet concoction with a cherry-chocolate flavour.

MAI TAI

In 1934, Victor Jules Bergeron, or Trader Vic as he became known, opened his first restaurant in Oakland, San Francisco. He served Polynesian food with a mix of Chinese, French and American dishes cooked in wood-fired ovens. But he is best known for the rum based cocktails he created.

One evening in 1944 he tested a new drink on two friends from Tahiti, Ham and Carrie Guild. After the first sip, Carrie exclaimed,"Mai Tai-Roa Aé", which in Tahitian means 'Out of this world - the best!'.

So Bergeron named his drink the Mai Tai. The original was based on 17 year old Jamaican J.Wray & Nephew rum which Vic in his own guide describes as being "surprisingly golden in colour, medium bodied, but with the rich pungent flavour particular to the Jamaican blends". Vic states he used "rock candy" syrup. This is an old term for the type of strong sugar syrup I prescribe in this guide. You could dangle a piece of string in it to encourage crystallisation and make rock candy.

When supplies of the Jamaican 17-year-old rum dwindled, Vic started using a combination of dark Jamaican rum and Martinique rum to achieve the desired flavour. Sheer demand in his chain of restaurants later necessitated the introduction of a Mai Tai pre-mix (still available from www.tradervics.com).

Others, particularly Ernest Raymond Beaumont-Gantt, then owner of a Hollywood bar called Don the Beachcomber's, have also laid claim to the creation of this drink. But as Vic says in his own Bartender's Guide, "Anybody who says I didn't create this drink is a dirty stinker."

VIC'S ORIGINAL 1944 MAI TAI

Glass: Mai Tai (16oz old-fashioned)
Garnish: Half spent lime shell, mint sprig, pineapple cube & cherry on stick
Method: "Cut lime in half; squeeze juice over shaved ice in a Mai Tai (double old-fashioned) glass; save one spent shell. Add remaining ingredients and enough shaved ice to fill glass. Hand shake. Decorate with spent lime shell, fresh mint, and a fruit stick."

1	fresh	**Lime**
2	shot(s)	**17 yo Wray & Nephew Jamaican rum**
1/2	shot(s)	**Dutch orange curaçao liqueur**
1/4	shot(s)	**Orgeat (almond) sugar syrup**
1/4	shot(s)	**Rock candy syrup**

Comment: In the words of the master, from his Bartender's Guide.

MAI TAI #2 (BEAUMONT-GANTT'S FORMULA)

Glass: Old-fashioned
Garnish: Mint sprig
Method: Lightly muddle mint in base of shaker (just to bruise). Add other ingredients, **SHAKE** with ice and strain glass filled with crushed ice.

12	fresh	**Mint leaves**
1 1/2	shot(s)	**Myers's Planters' Punch rum**
1	shot(s)	**Light white rum**
3/4	shot(s)	**Cointreau triple sec**
1/2	shot(s)	**Velvet Falernum syrup**
1	shot(s)	**Freshly squeezed lime juice**
1	shot(s)	**Squeezed pink grapefruit juice**
2	dashes	**Angostura aromatic bitters**

Origin: It is claimed that Ernest Raymond Beaumont-Gantt first served this drink in 1933 at his Don The Beachcomber's bar in Hollywood, California. This is some ten years earlier than Bergeron's Mai Tai-Roa Aé moment in cocktail history.
Comment: Whichever of the two created the drink; it is Trader Vic that made it famous and it is his recipe that endures.

MAI TAI #3 (DIFFORD'S FORMULA)

Glass: Old-fashioned
Garnish: Mint sprig & lime wedge
Method: SHAKE all ingredients with ice and strain into glass filled with crushed ice.

2	shot(s)	**Aged rum**
1/2	shot(s)	**Cointreau triple sec**
3/4	shot(s)	**Freshly squeezed lime juice**
1/2	shot(s)	**Orgeat (almond) syrup**
1/4	shot(s)	**Sugar syrup (2 sugar to 1 water)**

Origin: My adaptation of Victor Bergeron's (Trader Vic's) 1944 classic.
Comment: I love Daiquiris and this is basically a classic Daiquiri with a few bells and whistles.

MAIDEN'S BLUSH

Glass: Martini
Garnish: Lemon peel twist
Method: SHAKE all ingredients with ice and fine strain into chilled glass.

2	shot(s)	**Plymouth gin**
1/2	shot(s)	**Cointreau triple sec**
1/2	shot(s)	**Pomegranate (grenadine) syrup**
1/4	shot(s)	**Freshly squeezed lemon juice**
1/2	shot(s)	**Chilled mineral water** (omit if wet ice)

Origin: Adapted from a recipe in Harry Craddock's 1930 Savoy Cocktail Book.
Comment: Pale pink, subtle and light.

MAIDEN'S PRAYER

Glass: Martini
Garnish: Orange zest twist
Method: SHAKE all ingredients with ice and fine strain into chilled glass.

1 1/2	shot(s)	**Plymouth gin**
1	shot(s)	**Cointreau triple sec**
1	shot(s)	**Freshly squeezed orange juice**
1/2	shot(s)	**Freshly squeezed lemon juice**

Origin: Adapted from a recipe in Harry Craddock's 1930 Savoy Cocktail Book.
Comment: Fresh, zesty orange with a pleasing twang of alcohol.

MAINBRACE

Glass: Martini
Garnish: Orange zest twist
Method: SHAKE all ingredients with ice and fine strain into chilled glass.

1 1/2	shot(s)	**Plymouth gin**
1 1/2	shot(s)	**Cointreau triple sec**
1 1/2	shot(s)	**Freshly squeezed golden grapefruit juice**

Comment: Full-on grapefruit laced with gin and a hint of orange. Tart finish.

MAJOR BAILEY #1

Glass: Sling
Garnish: Mint sprig
Method: Lightly **MUDDLE** (only bruise) mint with gin in base of shaker. Add other ingredients, **SHAKE** with ice and fine strain into glass half filled with crushed ice. **CHURN** (stir) drink with the ice using a barspoon. Top the glass to the brim with more crushed ice and churn again. Serve with straws.

12	fresh	**Mint leaves**
2	shot(s)	**Plymouth gin**
1/4	shot(s)	**Freshly squeezed lime juice**
1/4	shot(s)	**Freshly squeezed lemon juice**
1/2	shot(s)	**Sugar syrup (2 sugar to 1 water)**

Origin: Adapted from a recipe in the 1947 Trader Vic's Bartender's Guide by Victor Bergeron.
Comment: As Victor says of this gin based Julep, "This is a hell of a drink."

MAJOR BAILEY #2

Glass: Sling
Garnish: Mint sprig
Method: BLEND all ingredients with one 12oz scoop of crushed ice and serve with straws.

2	shot(s)	**Light white rum**
1	shot(s)	**Cointreau triple sec**
1	shot(s)	**Pressed pineapple juice**
1/2	shot(s)	**Freshly squeezed lemon juice**
1/4	shot(s)	**Sugar syrup (2 sugar to 1 water)**

Origin: Adapted from a drink created by Victor Bergeron.
Comment: Made well, this is a long, fruity, brilliant frozen Daiquiri.

MAGIC BUS

Garnish: Lime wedge on rim
Method: SHAKE all ingredients with ice and fine strain into chilled glass.

1	shot(s)	**Partida tequila**
1	shot(s)	**Cointreau triple sec**
1	shot(s)	**Ocean Spray cranberry juice**
1	shot(s)	**Freshly squeezed orange juice**

Comment: Orange and cranberry laced with tequila.

MALCOLM LOWRY

Glass: Old-fashioned
Garnish: Lime wedge
Method: SHAKE all ingredients with ice and strain into ice-filled glass.

1	shot(s)	**Partida tequila**
1/2	shot(s)	**Wray & Nephew overproof white rum**
1/4	shot(s)	**Cointreau triple sec**
1/2	shot(s)	**Freshly squeezed lime juice**
1/4	shot(s)	**Sugar syrup (2 sugar to 1 water)**

Origin: Created by drinks author David Broom. Named after Malcolm Lowry's 1947 novel 'Under the Volcano' which explores a man's battle with alcoholism in Mexico.
Comment: A suitably 'hard' and flavoursome Daiquiri-like drink.

MAMBO

Glass: Collins
Garnish: Orange slice
Method: SHAKE all ingredients with ice and strain into ice-filled glass.

1	shot(s)	**Ketel One vodka**
1	shot(s)	**Cointreau triple sec**
1	shot(s)	**Giffard apricot brandy du Roussillon**
1/4	shot(s)	**Campari**
3	shot(s)	**Freshly squeezed orange juice**

Origin: Created by Nichole Colella.
Comment: A slightly bitter, tangy, orange, cooling drink.

MAN-BOUR-TINI

Glass: Martini
Garnish: Orange zest twist
Method: SHAKE all ingredients with ice and fine strain into chilled glass.

1	shot(s)	**Mandarine Napoléon liqueur**
3/4	shot(s)	**Buffalo Trace bourbon whiskey**
1/2	shot(s)	**Freshly squeezed lime juice**
2	shot(s)	**Ocean Spray cranberry juice**
1/4	shot(s)	**Sugar syrup (2 sugar to 1 water)**

Origin: Created in 1999 by yours truly.
Comment: A rounded, fruity, bourbon based drink with mandarin and lime sourness.

MANDARINE COLLINS

Glass: Collins
Garnish: Half orange slice
Method: SHAKE first three ingredients with ice and strain into ice-filled glass. **TOP** with soda.

1 1/2	shot(s)	**Plymouth gin**
1	shot(s)	**Mandarine Napoléon liqueur**
1	shot(s)	**Freshly squeezed lemon juice**
Top up with		**Soda water (club soda)**

Comment: A tangy, long refreshing drink with an intense mandarin flavour.

MANDARINE SIDECAR

Glass: Martini
Garnish: Sugar rim (optional) & lemon zest twist
Method: SHAKE all ingredients with ice and fine strain into chilled glass.

1 1/2	shot(s)	**Rémy Martin cognac**
1	shot(s)	**Mandarine Napoléon liqueur**
1	shot(s)	**Freshly squeezed lemon juice**
3/4	shot(s)	**Chilled mineral water** (omit if wet ice)
1/8	shot(s)	**Sugar syrup (2 sugar to 1 water)**

Comment: Wonderfully tart and strong in flavour.

MANDARINE SONGBIRD

Glass: Collins
Garnish: Orange slice
Method: SHAKE first three ingredients with ice and fine strain into ice-filled glass. **TOP** with ginger beer.

2	shot(s)	**Mandarine Napoléon liqueur**
1/2	shot(s)	**Freshly squeezed lemon juice**
3/4	shot(s)	**Freshly squeezed orange juice**
Top up with		**Ginger beer**

Comment: Long, spicy orange.

MANDARINE SOUR

Glass: Old-fashioned
Garnish: Lemon slice
Method: SHAKE all ingredients with ice and strain into ice-filled glass.

2	shot(s)	**Mandarine Napoléon liqueur**
1	shot(s)	**Freshly squeezed lemon juice**
1/4	shot(s)	**Sugar syrup (2 sugar to 1 water)**
1/2	fresh	**Egg white**

Comment: Sour, but with a strong mandarin sweetness.

MANDARINTINI

Glass: Martini
Garnish: Orange slice on rim
Method: SHAKE all ingredients with ice and fine strain into chilled glass.

1 1/2	shot(s)	**Orange zest infused Ketel One vodka**
1/2	shot(s)	**Campari**
1/2	shot(s)	**Grand Marnier liqueur**
1 1/2	shot(s)	**Pressed apple juice**

Origin: Adapted from a drink discovered in 2005 at Aqua Spirit, Hong Kong, China.
Comment: This bittersweet palate cleanser looks like pink grapefruit juice.

MANDARITO [UPDATED]

Glass: Collins
Garnish: Mint sprig
Method: Lightly **MUDDLE** mint (just to bruise) in base of glass. Add next four ingredients, half fill glass with crushed ice and **CHURN** (stir). Fill glass to brim with more crushed ice and churn some more. **TOP** with soda, stir and serve with straws.

12	fresh	**Mint leaves**
1 1/2	shot(s)	**Mandarine Napoléon liqueur**
1	shot(s)	**Ketel One vodka**
1	shot(s)	**Freshly squeezed lime juice**
1/8	shot(s)	**Sugar syrup (2 sugar to 1 water)**
Top up with		**Soda water (club soda)**

Comment: A vodka Mojito with mandarin accents.

MANGO BATIDA

Glass: Collins
Garnish: Mango slice
Method: SHAKE all ingredients with ice and strain into ice-filled glass.

2 1/2	shot(s)	**Leblon cachaça**
2	shot(s)	**Sweetened mango purée**
1	shot(s)	**Freshly squeezed lemon juice**

Origin: Formula by yours truly in 2004.
Comment: Depending on the sweetness of the mango purée, this drink may benefit from the addition of a dash of sugar syrup.

MANGO COLLINS

Glass: Collins
Garnish: Lemon slice
Method: SHAKE first three ingredients with ice and strain into ice-filled glass. **TOP** with soda, stir and serve with straws.

2	shot(s)	**Plymouth gin**
2	shot(s)	**Sweetened mango purée**
1 1/2	shot(s)	**Freshly squeezed lemon juice**
Top up with		**Soda water (club soda)**

Origin: Formula by yours truly in 2004.
Comment: Lemon juice and gin combine with mango in this refreshing tall drink.

MANGO DAIQUIRI

Glass: Martini
Garnish: Lime wedge on rim
Method: SHAKE all ingredients with ice and fine strain into chilled glass.

2	shot(s)	**Light white rum**
2	shot(s)	**Sweetened mango purée**
1/2	shot(s)	**Freshly squeezed lime juice**

Origin: Formula by yours truly in 2004.
Variant: Blended with 12oz scoop crushed ice and an additional half shot of sugar syrup.
Comment: Tropical yet potent and refreshing.

MANGO MARGARITA #1 (SERVED 'UP')

Glass: Coupette
Garnish: Lime wedge on rim
Method: SHAKE all ingredients with ice and fine strain into chilled glass.

2	shot(s)	**Partida tequila**
1	shot(s)	**Sweetened mango purée**
1	shot(s)	**Cointreau triple sec**
1	shot(s)	**Freshly squeezed lime juice**

Origin: Formula by yours truly in 2004.
Comment: The character of the tequila is not overwhelmed by the fruit.

MANGO MARGARITA #2 (FROZEN)

Glass: Coupette
Garnish: Mango slice on rim
Method: BLEND all ingredients with 12oz scoop crushed ice. Serve with straws.

2	shot(s)	**Partida tequila**
3/4	shot(s)	**Sweetened mango purée**
1	shot(s)	**Cointreau triple sec**
1/2	shot(s)	**Freshly squeezed lime juice**
1/4	shot(s)	**Sugar syrup (2 sugar to 1 water)**

Origin: Formula by yours truly in 2006.
Comment: Mango first and Margarita second.

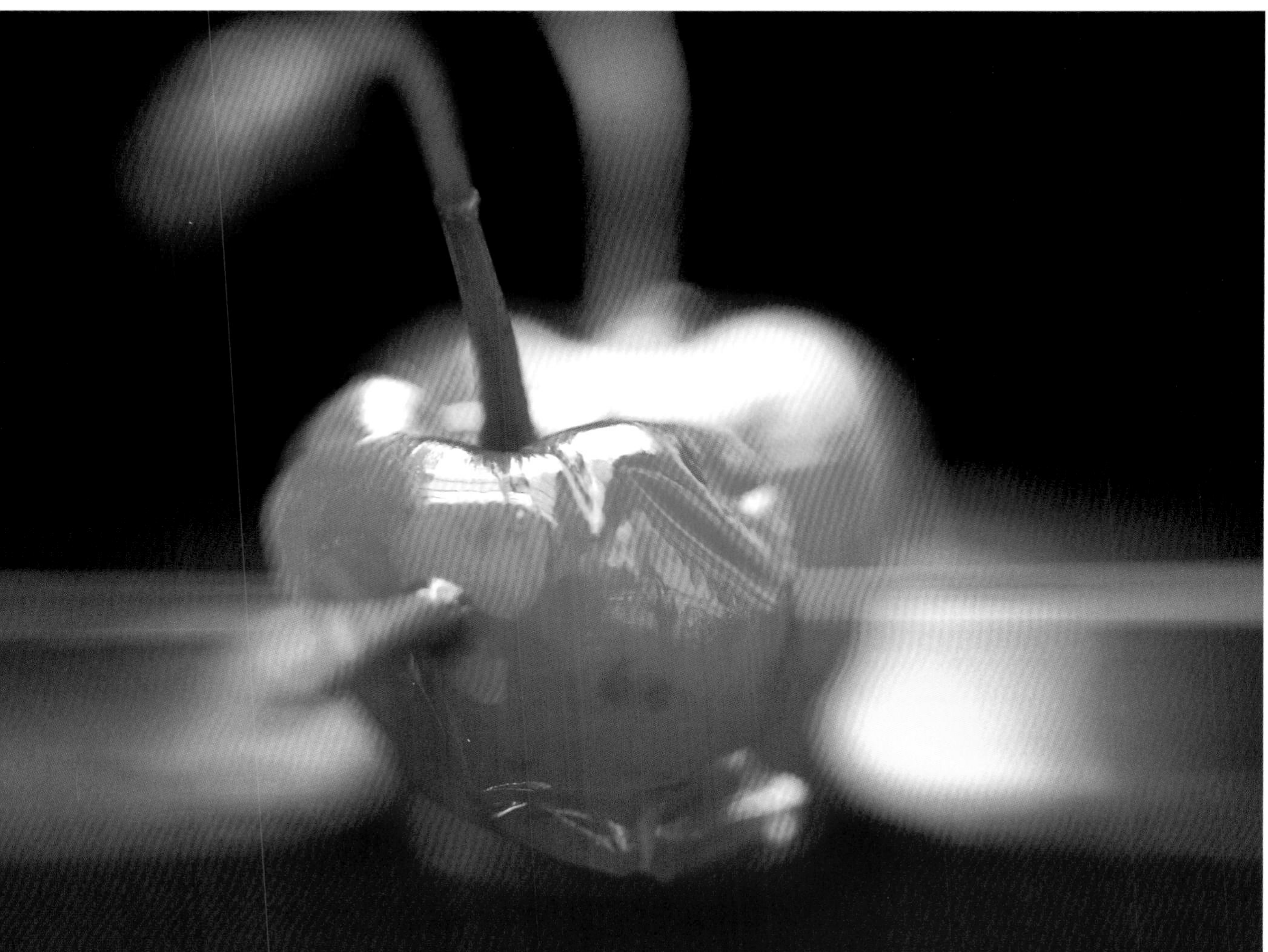

THE MANHATTAN

Like so many cocktails, the origins of the Manhattan are lost in time. And, as neither the name nor the ingredients are so unusual as to prevent inadvertent duplication, the mystery is likely to remain unsolved. The Democrat newspaper remarked in 1882 that, 'It is but a short time ago that a mixture of whiskey, vermouth and bitters came into vogue' and observed that it had been known as a Turf Club cocktail, a Jockey Club cocktail and a Manhattan cocktail.

Until fairly recently, the most popular story was that the drink was created in November 1874 at New York City's Manhattan Club for Lady Randolph Churchill (née Jenny Jerome), while she was celebrating the successful gubernatorial campaign of Samuel Jones Tilden. (The Manhattan Club was opposite the site which now houses the Empire State Building.) However, David Wondrich has pointed out that the banquet in question was held in November 1874, when Lady C was otherwise engaged, in England, giving birth to Winston, and was most likely a men-only affair.

A 1945 article claims that a drink under the name of the Manhattan appeared in an 1860 bar guide; it certainly appears in Harry Johnson's book of 1884. William F. Mulhall claimed in 1923 that "the Manhattan cocktail was invented by a man named Black who kept a place ten doors below Houston Street on Broadway in the sixties".

Whatever the truth of its invention, the Manhattan was probably originally made with rye whiskey, rather than bourbon, as New York was a rye-drinking city, although early bar books just state 'whiskey'. Today it is common to use bourbon, although purists are beginning to revive rye.

When Scotch is substituted for bourbon the Manhattan becomes a Rob Roy, with brandy (cognac) it becomes a Harvard and with applejack it is a Star Cocktail when made with applejack.

Some time in 2005 it became conventional in some bars to garnish a Manhattan with two cherries as a 9/11 tribute.

MANGO MARTINI

Glass: Martini
Garnish: Mango slice on rim
Method: SHAKE all ingredients with ice and fine strain into chilled glass.

$2^1/_2$	shot(s)	**Ketel One Citroen vodka**
2	shot(s)	**Sweetened mango purée**

Origin: Formula by yours truly in 2004.
Comment: This drink doesn't work nearly so well with plain vodka – if citrus vodka is not available, try using gin.

MANGO PUNCH

Glass: Collins
Garnish: Mango slice (dried or fresh)
Method: SHAKE all ingredients with ice and fine strain into glass filled with crushed ice.

2	shot(s)	**Wray & Nephew overproof rum**
3	shot(s)	**Sweetened mango purée**
$^3/_4$	shot(s)	**Freshly squeezed lime juice**
$^3/_4$	shot(s)	**Sugar syrup (2 sugar to 1 water)**

Origin: Created in 2004 by yours truly.
Comment: A distinctly tropical cocktail flavoured with mango.

MANGO RUM COOLER

Glass: Collins
Garnish: Mango slice (dried or fresh)
Method: SHAKE all ingredients with ice and strain into ice-filled glass.

$2^1/_2$	shot(s)	**Light white rum**
$1^1/_2$	shot(s)	**Sweetened mango purée**
1	shot(s)	**Pressed apple juice**
$1^1/_2$	shot(s)	**Freshly squeezed lemon juice**

Origin: Created in 2004 by yours truly.
Comment: Long, fruity and cooling.

MANHATTAN DRY

Glass: Martini
Garnish: Twist of orange (discarded) & two maraschino cherries
Method: STIR all ingredients with ice and strain into chilled glass.

$2^1/_2$	shot(s)	**Buffalo Trace bourbon whiskey**
1	shot(s)	**Dry vermouth**
3	dashes	**Angostura aromatic bitters**

Variant: Served over ice in an old-fashioned glass.
Comment: A bone dry Manhattan for those with dry palates.

MANHATTAN PERFECT

Glass: Martini
Garnish: Twist of orange (discarded) & two maraschino cherries
Method: STIR all ingredients with ice and strain into chilled glass.

$2^1/_2$	shot(s)	**Buffalo Trace bourbon whiskey**
$^1/_2$	shot(s)	**Sweet vermouth**
$^1/_2$	shot(s)	**Dry vermouth**
3	dashes	**Angostura aromatic bitters**

Variant: Served over ice in an old-fashioned glass.
Comment: The Manhattan version most popularly served – medium dry.

MANHATTAN SWEET

Glass: Martini
Garnish: Twist of orange (discarded) & two maraschino cherries
Method: STIR all ingredients with ice and strain into chilled glass.

$2^1/_2$	shot(s)	**Buffalo Trace bourbon whiskey**
1	shot(s)	**Sweet vermouth**
$^1/_8$	shot(s)	**Syrup from jar of maraschino cherries**
3	dashes	**Angostura aromatic bitters**

Variant: Served over ice in an old-fashioned glass.
Comment: I must confess to preferring my Manhattans served sweet, or perfect at a push. The Manhattan is complex, challenging and moreish. Best of all, it's available in a style to suit every palate.

MANHATTAN ISLAND

Glass: Martini
Garnish: Maraschino cherry
Method: STIR all ingredients with ice and fine strain into chilled glass.

2	shot(s)	**Rémy Martin cognac**
1	shot(s)	**Sweet vermouth**
3	dashes	**Angostura aromatic bitters**
$^1/_8$	shot(s)	**Luxardo maraschino liqueur**

Comment: A twist on the classic Harvard, or brandy based Manhattan.

MAPLE OLD-FASHIONED

Glass: Martini
Garnish: Orange zest twist
Method: STIR one shot of the bourbon with two ice cubes in a glass. Add maple syrup and Angostura and two more ice cubes. Stir some more and add another two ice cubes and the rest of the bourbon. Stir lots more so as to melt the ice, then add fresh ice to complete the drink. The melting and stirring in of ice cubes is essential to the dilution and taste of this drink.

2	shot(s)	**Buffalo Trace bourbon whiskey**
$^1/_2$	shot(s)	**Maple syrup**
2	dashes	**Angostura aromatic bitters**

Origin: Discovered in 2004 at Indigo Yard, Edinburgh, Scotland.
Comment: Maple syrup replaces sugar in this reworking of the classic Old-fashioned.

M

MAPLE LEAF

Glass: Old-fashioned
Garnish: Lemon zest twist
Method: SHAKE all ingredients with ice and strain into ice-filled glass.

2	shot(s)	**Buffalo Trace bourbon whiskey**
1/2	shot(s)	**Freshly squeezed lemon juice**
1/4	shot(s)	**Maple syrup**

Comment: This trio combine wonderfully with maple to the fore.

MAPLE POMME

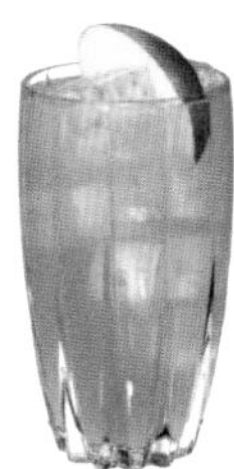

Glass: Collins
Garnish: Apple wedge
Method: SHAKE first four ingredients with ice and strain into ice-filled glass. **TOP** with ginger ale, lightly stir and serve with straws.

2	shot(s)	**Scotch whisky**
1/2	shot(s)	**Freshly squeezed lemon juice**
1	shot(s)	**Pressed apple juice**
1/2	shot(s)	**Maple syrup**
Top up with		**Ginger ale**

Origin: Adapted from a short drink created in 2005 by Tonin Kacaj at Maze, London, England.
Comment: Scotch based drink for warm weather.

MARACUJA BATIDA

Glass: Collins
Garnish: Lemon slice
Method: Cut passion fruit in half and scoop out flesh into shaker. Add other ingredients, **SHAKE** with ice and fine strain into ice-filled glass.

2	fresh	**Passion fruit**
2	shot(s)	**Leblon cachaça**
3/4	shot(s)	**Freshly squeezed lemon juice**
3/4	shot(s)	**Sugar syrup (2 sugar to 1 water)**

Variant: Serve blended with crushed ice (add half a shot of passion fruit syrup to the above recipe).
Origin: The Batida is a traditional Brazilian drink and 'maracuja' means passion fruit in Portuguese.
Comment: Cachaça combines with passion fruit.

MARAMA RUM PUNCH

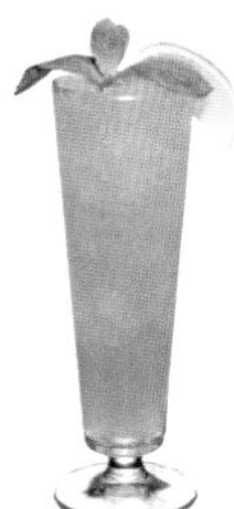

Glass: Sling
Garnish: Mint sprig & lime wedge
Method: Lightly **MUDDLE** mint (just to bruise). Add next five ingredients, **SHAKE** with ice and strain into ice-filled glass. **TOP** with 7-Up, lightly stir and serve with straws.

12	fresh	**Mint leaves**
1 1/2	shot(s)	**Wray & Nephew overproof rum**
1/2	shot(s)	**Cointreau triple sec**
1/2	shot(s)	**Freshly squeezed lime juice**
1/2	shot(s)	**Almond (orgeat) syrup**
3	dashes	**Angostura aromatic bitters**
Top up with		**7-Up**

Comment: A tangy, well-balanced punch.

MARGARITA #1 (STRAIGHT-UP)

Glass: Coupette
Garnish: Salt rim & lime wedge
Method: SHAKE all ingredients with ice and fine strain into chilled glass.

2	shot(s)	**Partida tequila**
1	shot(s)	**Cointreau triple sec**
1	shot(s)	**Freshly squeezed lime juice**

Variant: Margaritas made with premium tequilas are sometimes referred to as 'Deluxe' or 'Cadillac' Margaritas.
Tip: For the perfect salt rim, liquidise sea salt to make it finer, then run a lime wedge around the outside edge of the glass before dipping the rim in salt. Rimming only half the glass with salt gives the drinker the option of enjoying the cocktail with or without salt.
Comment: One of the great classics.

MARGARITA #2 (ON THE ROCKS)

Glass: Old-fashioned
Garnish: Salt rim & lime wedge
Method: SHAKE all ingredients with ice and strain into ice-filled glass.

2	shot(s)	**Partida tequila**
1	shot(s)	**Cointreau triple sec**
1	shot(s)	**Freshly squeezed lime juice**

Comment: Tangy citrus, tequila and salt.

MARGARITA #3 (FROZEN) [UPDATED]

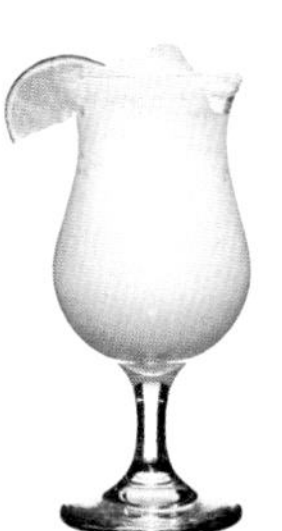

Glass: Martini
Garnish: Maraschino cherry
Method: BLEND all ingredients with 12oz scoop of crushed ice. Serve heaped in the glass and with straws.

1 1/2	shot(s)	**Partida tequila**
3/4	shot(s)	**Cointreau triple sec**
3/4	shot(s)	**Freshly squeezed lime juice**
1/2	shot(s)	**Sugar syrup (2 sugar to 1 water)**

Variant: With fruit and/or fruit liqueurs.
Comment: Citrus freshness with the subtle agave of tequila served frozen.

MARGARITA #4 (SALT FOAM FLOAT)

Glass: Coupette
Garnish: Lime wedge on rim
Method: Combine first three ingredients, **POUR** into cream whipping siphon and **CHARGE** with nitrous oxide. Shake and place siphon in a refrigerator for one hour prior to making drink. **SHAKE** next three ingredients with ice and fine strain into chilled glass. **SQUIRT** salt foam over surface of drink from siphon.

4	spoons	**Sea salt**
1	pint	**Chilled mineral water**
2	fresh	**Egg whites**
2	shot(s)	**Partida tequila**
1	shot(s)	**Cointreau triple sec**
1	shot(s)	**Freshly squeezed lime juice**

Comment: Classic Margarita with a salty foam topping.

MARGUERITE MARTINI

Glass: Martini
Garnish: Orange zest twist
Method: SHAKE all ingredients with ice and fine strain into chilled glass.

2	shot(s)	**Plymouth gin**
1/2	shot(s)	**Dry vermouth**
1	dash	**Fee Brothers orange bitters**

Origin: Adapted from a recipe in Harry Craddock's 1930 Savoy Cocktail Book.
Comment: A slightly wet yet bone dry classic Martini with a hint of orange.

'I'VE BEEN DRUNK FOR ABOUT A WEEK NOW, AND I THOUGHT IT MIGHT SOBER ME UP TO SIT IN A LIBRARY.'

F. SCOTT FITZGERALD

MARIA THERESA MARGARITA

Glass: Martini
Garnish: Lime wedge on rim
Method: STIR honey with tequila in base of shaker to dissolve honey. **ADD** other ingredients, **SHAKE** with ice and fine strain into chilled glass.

2	spoons	**Runny honey**
2	shot(s)	**Partida tequila**
1	shot(s)	**Ocean Spray cranberry juice**
1/2	shot(s)	**Freshly squeezed lime juice**

Origin: Adapted from a Tiki drink created by Victor Bergeron (Trader Vic).
Comment: Originally sweetened with sugar syrup, this is better smoothed with honey.

MARIE ROSE [NEW #7]

Glass: Martini
Garnish: Rosemary sprig
Method: Strip leaves from rosemary and **MUDDLE** with grapes in base of shaker. Add other ingredients, **SHAKE** with ice and fine strain into chilled glass.

1/2	sprig	**Rosemary**
8	fresh	**Green grapes**
2	shot(s)	**Plymouth gin**
3/4	shot(s)	**St-Germain elderflower liqueur**
1/4	shot(s)	**Freshly squeezed lime juice**

Origin: Created in 2007 by Renan Lejeune at Zeta Bar, London, England.
Comment: Rosemary spiced gin with grape juice and elderflower: very aromatic.

MARMALADE COCKTAIL [UPDATED #7]

Glass: Martini
Garnish: Orange zest twist
Method: STIR marmalade with gin until the marmalade dissolves. **SHAKE** other ingredients with ice and fine strain into chilled glass.

4	spoons	**Orange marmalade**
2	shot(s)	**Plymouth gin**
1/2	shot(s)	**Freshly squeezed lemon juice**

Origin: Adapted from a recipe in the 1930 'Savoy Cocktail Book' by Harry Craddock (the original recipe serves six people).
Comment: Harry wrote of his own drink, "By its bitter-sweet taste this cocktail is especially suited to be a luncheon aperitif."

MARMARITA

Glass: Coupette
Garnish: Wipe Marmite (yeast extract) around rim
Method: SHAKE all ingredients with ice and fine strain into chilled glass.

2	shot(s)	**Partida tequila**
1	shot(s)	**Cointreau triple sec**
1	shot(s)	**Freshly squeezed lime juice**

Origin: Created in 2005 by Simon (Ginger) at Blanch House, Brighton, England.
Comment: A Margarita with a Marmite rim. After all, yeast extract is slightly salty.

MARNY COCKTAIL

Glass: Martini
Garnish: Orange zest twist
Method: SHAKE all ingredients with ice and fine strain into chilled glass.

2	shot(s)	**Plymouth gin**
1	shot(s)	**Grand Marnier liqueur**
2	dashes	**Fee Brothers orange bitters (optional)**

Origin: Adapted from a recipe in Harry Craddock's 1930 Savoy Cocktail Book.
Comment: Spirit and liqueur in harmony.

MARQUEE [UPDATED]

Glass: Martini
Garnish: Raspberries on stick
Method: SHAKE all ingredients with ice and fine strain into chilled glass.

1 1/2	shot(s)	**Buffalo Trace bourbon whiskey**
1 1/2	shot(s)	**Ocean Spray cranberry juice**
1/2	shot(s)	**Chambord black raspberry liqueur**
1/2	shot(s)	**Freshly squeezed lemon juice**
1/4	shot(s)	**Sugar syrup (2 sugar to 1 water)**

Origin: Created in 1998 by Giovanni Burdi at Match EC1, London, England.
Comment: Raspberry and bourbon combine perfectly in this short, slightly sweet, fruity drink.

MARGARITA

The Margarita can be considered a Tequila Sour, or a Tequila Sidecar, and two variations of this classic cocktail date back to the 1930s: the Tequila Daisy and the Picador. Both, however, lack the distinctive salt rim.

There are many people who claim to have invented the Margarita, which, as Spanish for 'daisy' and a popular woman's name, would have been a very common name for a drink. A brief summary of the top claimants:

Francisco 'Pancho' Morales, while working in a bar called Tommy's Place in Ciudad Juarez, Mexico, was asked to make a 'Magnolia' on the 4th July 1942, but couldn't remember it so created this drink. The customer's name may even have been Margarita.

Carlos 'Danny' Herrera created the cocktail either in 1947 or 1948 at his Rancho La Gloria bar in Rosarito, Mexico, for an actress called Marjorie King who drank no spirit but tequila. He added Cointreau and lime, and the unique salt rim which caught people's attention at the bar, then named his creation Margarita, the Spanish for Marjorie.

Daniel (Danny) Negrete created the drink in 1936 when he was the manager of Garci Crespo Hotel in Puebla, Mexico. His girlfriend, Margarita, apparently liked salt in her drinks and he is said to have created the drink for her as a present. In 1944 Danny moved to Tijuana, Mexico, and became a bartender at the Agua Caliente Racetrack, a place which has some claim to be the birthplace of the Margarita in the early 1930s.

Vernon Underwood was president of Young's Market Company, who in the 1930s had started distributing Cuervo tequila. He went to Johnny Durlesser, head bartender of the Tail O' The Cock in LA, and asked him to create something using his spirit, then named it after his wife Margaret (Margarita).

Sara Morales, an expert in Mexican folklore, claimed the Margarita was created in 1930 by Doña Bertha, owner of Bertha's Bar in Taxco, Mexico.

The socialite Margaret Sames held a Christmas party in Acapulco, Mexico, in 1948, and created the first Margarita. She thought nothing of it until, when flying home to San Antonio from Acapulco airport, she saw a bar advertising 'Margarita's Drink', a cocktail with exactly the same ingredients as her own.

So... Plenty of Margarets and even Margaritas: there is also a popular holiday destination called Margarita Island, located in the Caribbean north of Venezuela, two-and-a-half hours from Miami. But what about the English, Picador connection?

THE MARTINI

The origin of the classic Martini is disputed and shrouded in mystery. Many books have been written on the subject, and it's a topic which can raise temperatures among drinks aficionados. Most agree that it was created some time around the turn of the last century.

When or wherever the Martini was actually invented, and however it acquired its name, for several decades the name was only applied to a drink containing gin and vermouth in varying proportions. Then came the Vodkatini which extended the meaning of the name. But even then, if a drink didn't contain gin and/or vodka and vermouth it simply wasn't a Martini. Purists hold to this definition today.

Language and the meaning of words are changing faster than ever, and today pretty much any drink served in a V-shaped glass is popularly termed a 'Martini' regardless of its contents. These contemporary, non-traditional Martinis are sometimes referred to as Neo-martinis or Alternatinis and the pages of this guide are filled with such drinks.

I believe a drink should at least be based on gin or vodka to properly be termed a Martini, and ideally should also include vermouth. However, you'll find plenty of drinks in my guides called 'Something' Martini containing all manner of fruits and liqueurs and not a single drop of vermouth – their only claim to the name is the V-shaped glass they are served in.

Even the name of the iconic glass has changed. The old guard of bartending still insist on referring to it as a 'Cocktail Glass'. To my understanding that's now a generic term for glasses designed to hold cocktails, a term which also encompasses the likes of Hurricanes, Slings and Coupettes. Today a V-shaped glass is commonly known as a Martini glass.

For those seeking traditional Martinis based on gin and/or vodka with vermouth and without muddled fruit and suchlike, here are a few classic variations.

Dickens Martini – without a twist.
Dirty Martini – with the brine from an olive jar.
Dry Martini (Traditional) – stirred with gin/vodka.
Dry Martini (Naked) – frozen gin/vodka poured into a frozen glass coated with vermouth.
Franklin Martini - named after Franklin Roosevelt and served with two olives.
Gibson Martini – with two onions instead of an olive or a twist.
Martinez – said to be the original Martini.
Medium Martini – A wet Martini with dry sweet vermouth.
Vesper Martini – James Bond's Martini, with gin and vodka.
Vodkatini – very dry, vodka based Martini.
Wet Martini – heavy on the vermouth.

Please see relevant entries in this guide and my account of the Dry Martini.

MARTINEZ [UPDATED]

Glass: Martini
Garnish: Lemon zest twist
Method: **STIR** all ingredients with ice and strain into chilled glass.

1 1/2	shot(s)	**Plymouth gin**
1 1/2	shot(s)	**Sweet vermouth**
1/4	shot(s)	**Cointreau triple sec**
2	dashes	**Fee Brothers orange bitters (optional)**

Variant: Use maraschino liqueur in place of orange liqueur.
Origin: Supposedly the forerunner of the modern Dry Martini, this was created in 1870 by 'Professor' Jerry Thomas using a sweet style of gin known as 'Old Tom'.
Comment: This medium dry Martini is somewhat more approachable than a Dry Martini.

MARTINI THYME

Glass: Martini
Garnish: Thread three green olives onto thyme sprig
Method: **MUDDLE** thyme in base of shaker. **ADD** other ingredients, **SHAKE** with ice and fine strain into chilled glass.

2	sprigs	**Lemon thyme (remove stalks)**
1	shot(s)	**Plymouth gin**
3/4	shot(s)	**Green Chartreuse liqueur**
1/4	shot(s)	**Sugar syrup (2 sugar to 1 water)**

Origin: A combination of two very similar drinks, that both originally called for thyme infused gin. The first I discovered at The Lobby Bar (One Aldwych, London) and the other came from Tony Conigliaro at Isola, London, England.
Comment: A wonderfully fresh herbal Martini with the distinctive taste of Chartreuse. You'll either love it or hate it.

'I SAW A WEREWOLF DRINKING A PINA COLADA AT TRADER VIC'S, AND HIS HAIR WAS PERFECT.'
WARREN ZEVON

MARTINI ROYALE

Glass: Martini
Garnish: Lemon zest twist
Method: **STIR** vodka and crème de cassis with ice and strain into chilled glass. **TOP** with chilled champagne.

1 1/2	shot(s)	**Ketel One vodka**
1/2	shot(s)	**Giffard crème de cassis liqueur**
Top up with		**Brut champagne**

Origin: Created in 2001 by Dick Bradsell at Monte's, London, England.
Comment: The Kir Royale meets the vodkatini in this pink but powerful drink.

MARTINI SPECIAL

Glass: Martini
Garnish: Orange zest twist
Method: Fill glass with ice and **POUR** absinthe and Angostura over ice. Top with chilled mineral water and leave to stand. **SHAKE** gin, vermouth and orange water with ice. **DISCARD** contents of standing glass and fine strain shaken drink into washed glass.

1/4	shot(s)	**La Fée Parisienne (68%) absinthe**
4	dashes	**Angostura aromatic bitters**
Top up with		**Chilled mineral water**
2	shot(s)	**Plymouth gin**
3/4	shot(s)	**Sweet vermouth**
1/8	shot(s)	**Orange flower water**

Origin: Adapted from a recipe in Harry Craddock's 1930 Savoy Cocktail Book.
Comment: Aromatic, very dry and very serious – yet it has a frothy head.

MARY PICKFORD

Glass: Martini
Garnish: Maraschino cherry
Method: **SHAKE** all ingredients with ice and fine strain into chilled glass.

2	shot(s)	**Light white rum**
1 1/2	shot(s)	**Pressed pineapple juice**
1/4	shot(s)	**Pomegranate (grenadine) syrup**
1/8	shot(s)	**Luxardo maraschino liqueur**

Origin: Created in the 1920s (during prohibition) by Fred Kaufman at the Hotel Nacíonal de Cuba, Havana, for the silent movie star. She was in Cuba filming a movie with her husband Douglas Fairbanks and Charlie Chaplin.
Comment: When made correctly, this pale pink cocktail has a perfect balance between the fruit flavours and the spirit of the rum.

MARY QUEEN OF SCOTS

Glass: Martini
Garnish: Sugar rim & maraschino cherry
Method: **SHAKE** all ingredients with ice and fine strain into chilled glass.

1 1/2	shot(s)	**Scotch whisky**
3/4	shot(s)	**Drambuie liqueur**
3/4	shot(s)	**Green Chartreuse liqueur**

Origin: Discovered in 2006 on Kyle Branch's Cocktail Hotel blog cocktailhotel.blogspot.com). Mary Stuart, Mary Queen of Scots, was born on December 8th 1542 at Linlithgow Palace in West Lothian. On February 8th 1587, she was executed in the Great Hall of Fotheringhay.
Comment: Slightly sweet but herbal, serious and strong.

MARY ROSE

Glass: Martini
Garnish: Lime twist (discard) & rosemary sprig
Method: MUDDLE rosemary in base of shaker. Add other ingredients, **SHAKE** with ice and fine strain into chilled glass.

1	sprig	**Fresh rosemary**
2	shot(s)	**Plymouth gin**
1	shot(s)	**Green Chartreuse liqueur**
1/2	shot(s)	**Sugar syrup (2 sugar to 1 water)**
1/2	shot(s)	**Chilled mineral water** (omit if wet ice)

Origin: Created in 1999 by Philip Jeffrey at the Great Eastern Hotel, London, England. Named after King Henry VIII's warship, sunk during an engagement with the French fleet in 1545 and now on display in Portsmouth.
Comment: Herbal, herbal and herbal with a hint of spice.

'TO ALCOHOL! THE CAUSE OF, AND SOLUTION TO, ALL OF LIFE'S PROBLEMS!'

HOMER SIMPSON

MAT THE RAT

Glass: Collins
Garnish: Lime wedge
Method: SHAKE first four ingredients with ice and strain into ice-filled glass. **TOP** with 7-Up, lightly stir and serve with straws.

2	shot(s)	**Spiced rum**
1/2	shot(s)	**Cointreau triple sec**
1 1/2	shot(s)	**Freshly squeezed orange juice**
1/2	shot(s)	**Freshly squeezed lime juice**
Top up with		**7-Up**

Origin: A popular drink in UK branches of TGI Friday's, where it was created.
Comment: Whether or not Mat was a rat, we shall never know. However, the drink that's named after him is long and thirst-quenching.

MATADOR

Glass: Collins
Garnish: Pineapple wedge on rim
Method: SHAKE all ingredients with ice and strain into ice-filled glass.

2	shot(s)	**Partida tequila**
1	shot(s)	**Cointreau triple sec**
1	shot(s)	**Freshly squeezed lime juice**
2	shot(s)	**Pressed pineapple juice**

Comment: A long Margarita with pineapple juice. The lime and tequila work wonders with the sweet pineapple.

MAURESQUE [UPDATED #7]

Glass: Collins (10oz max)
Method: POUR absinthe and almond syrup into glass. Serve iced water separately in a small jug (known in France as a 'broc') so the customer can dilute to their own taste (I recommend five shots). Lastly, add ice to fill glass.

1 1/2	shot(s)	**La Fée Parisienne (68%) absinthe**
1	shot(s)	**Almond (orgeat) sugar syrup**
Top up with		**Chilled mineral water**

AKA: Bureau Arabe
Origin: Pronounced 'Mor-Esk', this classic drink is very popular in the South of France, where it is now commonly made with pastis in place of absinthe. It was originally created by French soldiers serving in the Bataillon d'Afrique during the Algerian campaign of the 1830s and 40s, and was alternatively known as Bureau Arabe after the military department which dealt with local affairs and was said to act like "an iron fist in a velvet glove".
Comment: Long, refreshing aniseed, liquorice and almond.

MAURICE MARTINI

Glass: Martini
Garnish: Orange zest twist
Method: SHAKE all ingredients with ice and fine strain into chilled glass.

1 1/2	shot(s)	**Plymouth gin**
3/4	shot(s)	**Dry vermouth**
3/4	shot(s)	**Sweet vermouth**
1/4	shot(s)	**La Fée Parisienne (68%) absinthe**
3/4	shot(s)	**Freshly squeezed orange juice**

Origin: Adapted from a recipe in Harry Craddock's 1930 Savoy Cocktail Book.
Comment: A perfect Martini with an aromatic burst of absinthe and a hint of orange.

MAYAN

Glass: Old-fashioned
Garnish: Float 3 coffee beans
Method: SHAKE all ingredients with ice and strain into ice-filled glass.

1 1/2	shot(s)	**Partida tequila**
1/2	shot(s)	**Kahlúa coffee liqueur**
2 1/2	shot(s)	**Pressed pineapple juice**

Comment: Tequila, coffee and pineapple juice combine in this medium dry short drink.

MAYAN WHORE

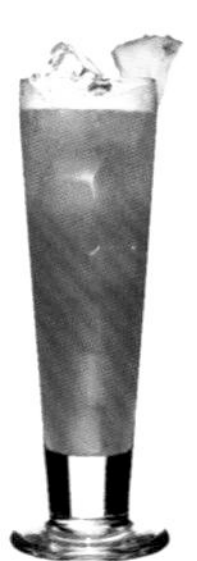

Glass: Sling
Garnish: Split pineapple wedge
Method: SHAKE first three ingredients with ice and strain into ice-filled glass. **TOP** with soda, **DO NOT STIR** and serve with straws.

2	shot(s)	**Partida tequila**
1 1/2	shot(s)	**Pressed pineapple juice**
3/4	shot(s)	**Kahlúa coffee liqueur**
Top up with		**Soda water (club soda)**

Comment: An implausible ménage à trois: coffee, tequila and pineapple, served long.

MAYFAIR COCKTAIL

Glass: Martini
Garnish: Orange zest twist
Method: MUDDLE cloves in base of shaker. Add other ingredients, **SHAKE** with ice and fine strain into chilled glass.

2	dried	**Cloves**
2	shot(s)	**Plymouth gin**
1	shot(s)	**Giffard apricot brandy du Roussillon**
1	shot(s)	**Freshly squeezed orange juice**
$\frac{1}{4}$	shot(s)	**Sugar syrup (2 sugar to 1 water)**

Variant: With World's End Pimento Dram liqueur in place of sugar.
Origin: Adapted from a recipe in Harry Craddock's 1930 Savoy Cocktail Book.
Comment: The kind of spiced drink you'd usually expect to be served hot.

MEDICINAL SOLUTION

Glass: Collins
Garnish: Lime wedge
Method: SHAKE first five ingredients with ice and strain into ice-filled glass. **TOP** with tonic water, lightly stir and serve with straws.

$1\frac{1}{2}$	shot(s)	**Bokma Oude Genever**
$\frac{1}{2}$	shot(s)	**Green Chartreuse liqueur**
$\frac{1}{2}$	shot(s)	**Freshly squeezed lime juice**
$\frac{1}{4}$	shot(s)	**Sugar syrup (2 sugar to 1 water)**
3	dashes	**Angostura aromatic bitters**
Top up with		**Tonic water**

Origin: Created in 2006 by yours truly.
Comment: Every ingredient, apart from the sugar, has at some time been consumed for its medicinal qualities. Even the sugar is still used to make bitter tasting medicine more palatable. Some might say that's just what I've done here.

THE MAYFLOWER MARTINI [UPDATED #7]

Glass: Martini
Garnish: Lemon zest twist
Method: SHAKE all ingredients with ice and fine strain into chilled glass.

$1\frac{1}{2}$	shot(s)	**Plymouth gin**
$\frac{1}{2}$	shot(s)	**St-Germain elderflower liqueur**
$\frac{1}{2}$	shot(s)	**Giffard apricot brandy du Roussillon**
1	shot(s)	**Pressed apple juice**
$\frac{1}{2}$	shot(s)	**Freshly squeezed lemon juice**

Origin: Adapted from a drink created in 2002 by Wayne Collins, London, England.
Comment: Fragrant balance of English fruits and flowers.

MEDIUM MARTINI

Glass: Martini
Garnish: Orange zest twist
Method: STIR all ingredients with ice and strain into chilled glass.

$1\frac{1}{2}$	shot(s)	**Plymouth gin**
$\frac{3}{4}$	shot(s)	**Dry vermouth**
$\frac{3}{4}$	shot(s)	**Sweet vermouth**

Origin: Adapted from a recipe in Harry Craddock's 1930 Savoy Cocktail Book.
Comment: A classic Martini served perfect and very wet. I prefer mine shaken which is the method Harry specifies in his guide.

MAXIM'S COFFEE (HOT)

Glass: Toddy
Garnish: Float 3 coffee beans
Method: POUR all ingredients into warmed glass and **STIR**.

1	shot(s)	**Rémy Martin cognac**
$\frac{1}{2}$	shot(s)	**Bénédictine D.O.M. liqueur**
$\frac{1}{4}$	shot(s)	**Galliano liqueur**
Top up with		**Hot filter coffee**

Comment: An interesting herbal cognac laced coffee.

MELLOW MARTINI

Glass: Martini
Garnish: Fresh lychee on a stick
Method: SHAKE all ingredients with ice and fine strain into chilled glass.

$1\frac{1}{2}$	shot(s)	**Ketel One vodka**
$\frac{1}{2}$	shot(s)	**Soho lychee liqueur**
$\frac{1}{2}$	shot(s)	**Giffard crème de banane du Brésil**
$1\frac{1}{2}$	shot(s)	**Pressed pineapple juice**

Comment: A fruity, tropical drink with a frothy head. Too fluffy to be a Martini.

FOR MORE INFORMATION SEE OUR

MELON BALL

Glass: Shot
Method: SHAKE all ingredients with ice and fine strain into chilled glass.

$\frac{1}{2}$	shot(s)	**Ketel One vodka**
$\frac{1}{2}$	shot(s)	**Midori melon liqueur**
$\frac{3}{4}$	shot(s)	**Freshly squeezed orange juice**

Comment: A vivid green combination of vodka, melon and orange.

MELON COLLIE MARTINI

Glass: Martini
Garnish: Crumbled Cadbury's Flake bar
Method: **SHAKE** all ingredients with ice and fine strain into chilled glass.

1	shot(s)	**Light white rum**
1/2	shot(s)	**Malibu coconut rum**
3/4	shot(s)	**Midori melon liqueur**
1/4	shot(s)	**Giffard white crème de cacao**
3/4	shot(s)	**Double (heavy) cream**
3/4	shot(s)	**Milk**

Origin: Created in 2003 by Simon King at MJU, Millennium Hotel, London, England.
Comment: Something of a holiday disco drink but tasty all the same.

MELON DAIQUIRI #1 (SERVED 'UP')

Glass: Martini
Garnish: Melon slice or melon balls
Method: Cut melon into 8 segments and deseed. Cut cubes of flesh from skin of one segment and **MUDDLE** in base of shaker. Add other ingredients, **SHAKE** with ice and fine strain into chilled glass.

1/8	fresh	**Cantaloupe / Galia melon**
2	shot(s)	**Light white rum**
1/2	shot(s)	**Midori melon liqueur**
1/2	shot(s)	**Freshly squeezed lime juice**
1/8	shot(s)	**Sugar syrup (2 sugar to 1 water)**

Comment: A classic Daiquiri with the gentle touch of melon.

'A MAN SHOULDN'T FOOL WITH BOOZE UNTIL HE'S FIFTY; THEN HE'S A DAMN FOOL IF HE DOESN'T.'
WILLIAM FAULKNER

MELON DAIQUIRI #2 (SERVED FROZEN)

Glass: Martini (large 10oz)
Garnish: Melon slice or melon balls
Method: Cut melon into 8 segments and deseed. Cut cubes of flesh from skin of one segment and place in blender. Add other ingredients and **BLEND** with half scoop crushed ice. Serve with straws.

1/8	fresh	**Cantaloupe / Galia melon**
2	shot(s)	**Light white rum**
1/2	shot(s)	**Midori melon liqueur**
1/2	shot(s)	**Freshly squeezed lime juice**
1/4	shot(s)	**Sugar syrup (2 sugar to 1 water)**

Comment: A cooling, fruity Daiquiri.

MELON MARGARITA #1 (SERVED 'UP')

Glass: Coupette
Garnish: Melon slice or melon balls
Method: Cut melon into 8 segments and deseed. Cut cubes of flesh from skin of one segment and **MUDDLE** in base of shaker. Add other ingredients, **SHAKE** with ice and fine strain into chilled glass.

1/8	fresh	**Cantaloupe / Galia melon**
2	shot(s)	**Partida tequila**
1	shot(s)	**Midori melon liqueur**
1	shot(s)	**Freshly squeezed lime juice**

Comment: Looks like stagnant pond water but tastes fantastic.

MELON MARGARITA #2 (SERVED FROZEN)

Glass: Coupette
Garnish: Melon slice or melon balls
Method: Cut melon into 8 segments and deseed. Cut cubes of flesh from skin of one segment and place in blender. Add other ingredients and **BLEND** with 6oz scoop crushed ice. Serve with straws.

1/8	fresh	**Cantaloupe / Galia melon**
2	shot(s)	**Partida tequila**
1	shot(s)	**Midori melon liqueur**
1/2	shot(s)	**Freshly squeezed lime juice**

Comment: Melon and tequila always combine well - here in a frozen Margarita.

MELON MARTINI #1

Glass: Martini
Garnish: Split lime wedge
Method: **SHAKE** all ingredients with ice and fine strain into chilled glass.

2 1/4	shot(s)	**Ketel One vodka**
1	shot(s)	**Midori melon liqueur**
1/2	shot(s)	**Freshly squeezed lime juice**
1/4	shot(s)	**Sugar syrup (2 sugar to 1 water)**

Comment: Bright green, lime and melon with more than a hint of vodka. Do it properly - have a fresh one.

MELON MARTINI #2 (FRESH FRUIT)

Glass: Martini
Garnish: Melon wedge on rim
Method: Cut melon into 8 segments and deseed. Cut cubes of flesh from skinof one segment and **MUDDLE** in base of shaker. Add other ingredients, **SHAKE** with ice and fine strain into chilled glass.

1/8	fresh	**Cantaloupe / Galia melon**
2	shot(s)	**Ketel One vodka**
1/4	shot(s)	**Sugar syrup (2 sugar to 1 water)**

Variant: Substitute Midori melon liqueur for sugar syrup.
Comment: Probably the most popular of all the fresh fruit martinis.

MELONCHOLY MARTINI

Glass: Martini
Garnish: Mint sprig
Method: **SHAKE** all ingredients with ice and fine strain into chilled glass.

1	shot(s)	**Ketel One vodka**
1	shot(s)	**Midori melon liqueur**
1/2	shot(s)	**Cointreau triple sec**
1/2	shot(s)	**Malibu coconut rum liqueur**
1	shot(s)	**Pressed pineapple juice**
3/4	shot(s)	**Double (heavy) cream**
1/4	shot(s)	**Freshly squeezed lime juice**

Origin: Created in 2002 by Daniel O'Brien at Ocean Bar, Edinburgh, Scotland.
Comment: Sweet, but the flavours in this smooth, tangy, lime-green drink combine surprisingly well.

MENEHUNE JUICE

Glass: Old-fashioned
Garnish: Lime wedge, mint & Menehune
Method: **SHAKE** all ingredients with ice and strain into glass filled with crushed ice. Serve with straws.

2	shot(s)	**Light white rum**
1/2	shot(s)	**Cointreau triple sec**
3/4	shot(s)	**Freshly squeezed lime juice**
1/4	shot(s)	**Almond (orgeat) sugar syrup**
1/4	shot(s)	**Sugar syrup (2 sugar to 1 water)**

Origin: Adapted from a recipe in the 1947-72 Trader Vic's Bartender's Guide by Victor Bergeron.
Comment: Slightly sweet and strong. According to Vic, "One sip and you may see a Menehune."

MERRY WIDOW #1

Glass: Martini
Garnish: Lemon zest twist
Method: **STIR** all ingredients with ice and strain into chilled glass.

1 1/2	shot(s)	**Plymouth gin**
1 1/2	shot(s)	**Dry vermouth**
1/4	shot(s)	**La Fée Parisienne (68%) absinthe**
1/4	shot(s)	**Bénédictine D.O.M. liqueur**
3	dashes	**Angostura aromatic bitters**
1/2	shot(s)	**Chilled minera water** (omit if wet ice)

Origin: Adapted from a recipe in Harry Craddock's 1930 Savoy Cocktail Book.
Comment: Aromatic, complex, strong and bitter.

MERRY WIDOW #2

Glass: Martini
Garnish: Orange zest twist
Method: **STIR** all ingredients with ice and strain into chilled glass.

1 1/4	shot(s)	**Ketel One vodka**
1 1/4	shot(s)	**Dubonnet Red**
1 1/4	shot(s)	**Dry vermouth**
1	dash	**Fee Brothers orange bitters**

Comment: Aromatic and complex - for toughened palates.

MESA FRESCA

Glass: Collins
Garnish: Lime wheel
Method: **SHAKE** all ingredients with ice and strain into ice-filled glass.

2	shot(s)	**Partida tequila**
3	shot(s)	**Squeezed pink grapefruit juice**
1	shot(s)	**Freshly squeeezed lime juice**
1/2	shot(s)	**Sugar syrup (2 sugar to 1 water)**

Origin: Discovered in 2005 at Mesa Grill, New York City, USA.
Comment: Sweet and sour tequila and grapefruit.

MET MANHATTAN

Glass: Martini
Garnish: Orange zest twist
Method: **SHAKE** all ingredients with ice and fine strain into chilled glass.

2	shot(s)	**Buffalo Trace bourbon whiskey**
1	shot(s)	**Grand Marnier liqueur**
1/2	shot(s)	**Teichenné butterscotch Schnapps**
2	dashes	**Fee Brothers orange bitters**

Origin: The Met Bar, Metropolitan Hotel, London, England.
Comment: Smooth and rounded bourbon with a hint of orange toffee.

METROPOLE [NEW #7]

Glass: Martini
Garnish: Maraschino cherry
Method: **STIR** all ingredients with ice and strain into chilled glass.

1 1/2	shot(s)	**Rémy Martin cognac**
1 1/2	shot(s)	**Dry vermouth**
1/8	shot(s)	**Maraschino cherry syrup (from jar)**
1	dash	**Angostura aromatic bitters**
1	dash	**Fee Brothers orange bitters**

Comment: I've added a spoon of cherry syrup to the otherwise bone dry classic recipe.

METROPOLITAN

Glass: Martini
Garnish: Flamed orange twist
Method: **SHAKE** all ingredients with ice and fine strain into chilled glass.

2	shot(s)	**Raspberry flavoured vodka**
1/2	shot(s)	**Cointreau triple sec**
1	shot(s)	**Ocean Spray cranberry juice**
1/2	shot(s)	**Freshly squeezed lime juice**
1/4	shot(s)	**Rose's lime cordial**

Origin: Created in 1993 by Chuck Coggins at Marion's Continental Restaurant & Lounge, New York City. Marion's was originally opened in 1950 by fashion model Marion Nagy, who came to the States after seeking asylum while swimming for Hungary in the Paris Peace Games after WWII.
Comment: A Cosmo with more than a hint of blackcurrant.

MERRY-GO-ROUND MARTINI

Glass: Martini
Garnish: Olive & lemon zest twist
Method: **STIR** all ingredients with ice and fine strain into chilled glass.

2	shot(s)	**Plymouth gin**
$\frac{1}{2}$	shot(s)	**Dry vermouth**
$\frac{1}{2}$	shot(s)	**Sweet vermouth**

Origin: Long lost classic variation on the Dry Martini.
Comment: Stir this 'perfect' Martini around and then get merry.

MEXICAN

Glass: Martini
Garnish: Pineapple wedge on rim
Method: **SHAKE** all ingredients with ice and fine strain into chilled glass.

2	shot(s)	**Partida tequila**
$1\frac{1}{2}$	shot(s)	**Pressed pineapple juice**
$\frac{1}{4}$	shot(s)	**Pomegranate (grenadine) syrup**

Variant: Substitute sugar syrup for pomegranate syrup.
Comment: Fresh pineapple makes this drink.

MEXICAN 55

Glass: Collins
Garnish: Lime wedge
Method: **SHAKE** first four ingredients with ice and strain into ice-filled glass. **TOP** with champagne.

$1\frac{1}{2}$	shot(s)	**Partida tequila**
1	shot(s)	**Freshly squeezed lemon juice**
$\frac{1}{2}$	shot(s)	**Sugar syrup (2 sugar to 1 water)**
2	dashes	**Angostura aromatic bitters**
Top up with		**Brut champagne**

Origin: An adaptation of the classic French '75 created in 1988 at La Perla, Paris, France. The name comes from Fidel Castro's statement that bullets, like wine, came in vintages and Mexican '55 was a good year [for bullets].
Comment: Suitably hard, yet surprisingly refreshing and sophisticated.

MEXICAN COFFEE (HOT)

Glass: Toddy
Garnish: Three coffee beans
Method: Place bar spoon in glass. **POUR** first three ingredients into glass and stir. **FLOAT** cream.

1	shot(s)	**Partida tequila**
$\frac{1}{4}$	shot(s)	**Sugar syrup (2 sugar to 1 water)**
Top up with		**Hot filter coffee**
Float		**Double (heavy) cream**

Tip: Lightly whip or simply shake cream in container before pouring over the bowl of a spoon. It also helps if the cream is gently warmed.
Comment: Tequila's answer to the Irish Coffee.

MEXICAN MANHATTAN

Glass: Martini
Garnish: Maraschino cherry
Method: **STIR** all ingredients with ice and strain into chilled glass.

2	shot(s)	**Partida tequila**
1	shot(s)	**Sweet vermouth**
3	dashes	**Angostura aromatic bitters**

Comment: You've tried this with bourbon, now surprise yourself with an aged tequila.

MEXICAN MARTINI

Glass: Martini
Garnish: Pineapple leaf on rim
Method: **SHAKE** all ingredients with ice and fine strain into chilled glass.

2	shot(s)	**Partida tequila**
$\frac{1}{4}$	shot(s)	**Giffard crème de cassis**
2	shot(s)	**Pressed pineapple juice**

Origin: Discovered in 2004 at Indigo Yard, Edinburgh, Scotland.
Comment: Tequila, pineapple and blackcurrant combine in this medium dry cocktail.

MEXICAN MELON BALL

Glass: Collins
Garnish: Melon balls on stick
Method: Cut melon into 8 segments and deseed. Cut cubes of flesh from skin of one segment and **MUDDLE** in base of shaker. Add other ingredients, **SHAKE** with ice and fine strain into ice-filled glass.

$\frac{1}{8}$	fresh	**Cantaloupe / Galia melon**
2	shot(s)	**Partida tequila**
2	shot(s)	**Freshly squeezed orange juice**
$\frac{1}{4}$	shot(s)	**Sugar syrup (2 sugar to 1 water)**

Origin: Adapted from a drink discovered at the Flying V Bar & Grill, Tucson, Arizona, USA.
Comment: Orange and melon laced with tequila.

MEXICAN MULE

Glass: Collins
Garnish: Lime wedge
Method: **SHAKE** first three ingredients with ice and strain into ice-filled glass. **TOP** with ginger beer, lightly stir and serve with straws.

$1\frac{1}{2}$	shot(s)	**Partida tequila**
$\frac{3}{4}$	shot(s)	**Freshly squeezed lime juice**
$\frac{1}{4}$	shot(s)	**Sugar syrup (2 sugar to 1 water)**
Top up with		**Ginger beer**

AKA: El Burro
Comment: A tequila based version of the Moscow Mule.

MEXICAN SURFER

Glass: Martini
Garnish: Lime wedge on rim
Method: SHAKE all ingredients with ice and fine strain into chilled glass.

2	shot(s)	**Partida tequila**
1½	shot(s)	**Pressed pineapple juice**
½	shot(s)	**Rose's lime cordial**

Comment: Frothy topped, easy to make, and all too easy to drink.

MEXICAN TEA (HOT)

Glass: Toddy
Garnish: Lime slice
Method: Place bar spoon in warmed glass. **POUR** all ingredients into glass and stir.

2	shot(s)	**Partida tequila**
½	shot(s)	**Sugar syrup (2 sugar to 1 water)**
Top up with		**Hot black breakfast tea**

Comment: Tiffin will never be the same again.

MEXICANO (HOT)

Glass: Toddy
Garnish: Dust with nutmeg & cinnamon
Method: POUR tequila and liqueur into warmed glass and top with coffee. **FLOAT** cream over drink.

1	shot(s)	**Partida tequila**
½	shot(s)	**Grand Marnier liqueur**
Top up with		**Hot filter coffee**
Float		**Double (heavy) cream**

Tip: Lightly whip or simply shake cream in container before pouring over the bowl of a spoon. It also helps if the cream is gently warmed.
Comment: A spicy, flavour-packed hot coffee.

MEXICO CITY

Glass: Coupette
Garnish: Lime wedge on rim
Method: SHAKE all ingredients with ice and fine strain into chilled glass.

1½	shot(s)	**Partida tequila**
¾	shot(s)	**Grand Marnier liqueur**
½	shot(s)	**Freshly squeezed lime juice**
½	shot(s)	**Ocean Spray cranberry juice**
¼	shot(s)	**Sugar syrup (2 sugar to 1 water)**

Origin: Adapted from a cocktail discovered in 2002 at the Merc Bar, New York City.
Comment: This pinky-red Margarita benefits from a hint of cranberry.

MIAMI BEACH

Glass: Martini
Garnish: Pineapple wedge & cherry
Method: SHAKE all ingredients with ice and fine strain into chilled glass.

2	shot(s)	**Plymouth gin**
1½	shot(s)	**Pressed pineapple juice**
¼	shot(s)	**Sugar syrup (2 sugar to 1 water)**

Comment: Fruity and well proportioned – like the babes on Miami Beach. Sorry.

MIAMI DAIQUIRI

Glass: Martini
Garnish: Mint leaf
Method: SHAKE all ingredients with ice and fine strain into chilled glass.

2	shot(s)	**Light white rum**
¼	shot(s)	**Giffard white crème de menthe**
½	shot(s)	**Freshly squeezed lime juice**
⅛	shot(s)	**Sugar syrup (2 sugar to 1 water)**
¾	shot(s)	**Chilled mineral water** (omit if wet ice)

Origin: My adaptation of a classic.
Comment: The merest hint of mint in a refreshing Daiquiri with a dry finish.

MICHELADA

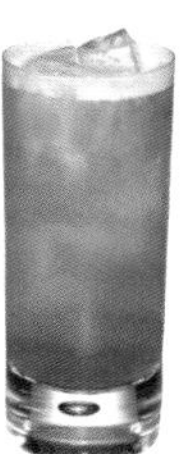

Glass: Collins
Garnish: Lime wedge
Method: STIR first six ingredients in bottom of glass. Fill glass with ice and **TOP** with beer.

¾	shot(s)	**Freshly squeezed lime juice**
⅛	shot(s)	**Soy sauce**
3	drops	**Tabasco pepper sauce**
2	dashes	**Worcestershire sauce**
1	pinch	**Celery salt**
1	pinch	**Black pepper**
Top up with		**Beer**

Origin: A Mexican classic.
Comment: Made with lager this spicy drink is sometimes called a White Mary. It's best made with a dark, flavoursome beer.

MIDNIGHT OVER TENNESSEE [NEW #7]

Glass: Martini
Garnish: Chocolate powder dust
Method: SHAKE first three ingredients with ice and fine strain into chilled glass. Separately **SHAKE** cream and crème de menthe and carefully strain over drink to layer.

2	shot(s)	**Jack Daniel's Tennessee whiskey**
½	shot(s)	**Kahlúa coffee liqueur**
½	shot(s)	**Giffard brown crème de cacao**
½	shot(s)	**Giffard green crème de menthe**
½	shot(s)	**Double (heavy) cream**

Origin: Discovered in 2006 at Restaurant Bar & Grill, Manchester, England.
Comment: One of the best dessert cocktails I've tried. Whiskey, coffee and chocolate sipped through a layer of minty cream.

MILANO

Glass: Old-fashioned
Garnish: Orange slice
Method: STIR all ingredients with ice and strain into ice-filled glass.

1	shot(s)	**Ketel One vodka**
1	shot(s)	**Campari**
1	shot(s)	**Sweet vermouth**

AKA: Negrosky
Comment: A Negroni with vodka in place of gin.

MILANO SOUR

Glass: Old-fashioned
Garnish: Lemon slice & maraschino cherry (sail)
Method: SHAKE all ingredients with ice and fine strain into ice-filled glass.

1½	shot(s)	**Plymouth gin**
1	shot(s)	**Galliano liqueur**
1	shot(s)	**Freshly squeezed lemon juice**
½	fresh	**Egg white**

Origin: Created in 2006 by your truly.
Comment: Delicate anise and peppermint with citrus freshness.

MILHO VERDE BATIDA

Glass: Collins
Garnish: Cinnamon dust
Method: BLEND all ingredients with 12oz scoop crushed ice. Serve with straws.

2½	shot(s)	**Leblon cachaça**
70	grams	**Sweetcorn (canned)**
1½	shot(s)	**Sweetened condensed milk**

Origin: A classic Brazilian drink.
Comment: Quite possibly your first sweetcorn cocktail.

MILK & HONEY

Glass: Martini
Garnish: Grate fresh nutmeg over drink
Method: STIR Scotch with honey in base of shaker to dissolve honey. Add other ingredients, **SHAKE** with ice and fine strain into chilled glass.

2	shot(s)	**Scotch whisky**
3	spoons	**Runny honey**
½	shot(s)	**Honey liqueur**
¾	shot(s)	**Double (heavy) cream**
¾	shot(s)	**Milk**

Origin: Created in 2002 by yours truly.
Comment: The rich flavour of Scotch is tamed by honey and cream.

MILK PUNCH

Glass: Collins
Garnish: Dust with freshly grated nutmeg
Method: SHAKE all ingredients with ice and strain into glass filled with crushed ice.

1	shot(s)	**Rémy Martin cognac**
½	shot(s)	**Goslings Black Seal rum**
½	shot(s)	**Sonoma vanilla bean sugar syrup**
2	shot(s)	**Milk**
1	shot(s)	**Double (heavy) cream**

Comment: The cream, vanilla and sugar tame the cognac and rum.

MILKY MOJITO

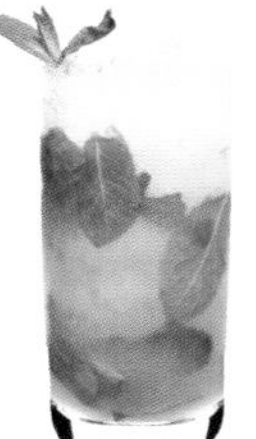

Glass: Collins
Garnish: Mint spring
Method: Lightly **MUDDLE** (just to bruise) mint in glass. Fill glass with crushed ice, add other ingredients. **TOP** with soda, stir and serve with straws.

12	fresh	**Mint leaves**
1	shot(s)	**Freshly squeezed lime juice**
¾	shot(s)	**Sugar syrup (2 sugar to 1 water)**
2	shot(s)	**Pernod anis**
Top up with		**Soda water (club soda)**

Comment: An anise laced alternative to a Mojito. The name refers to the opaque white colour of the drink after soda is added to the anis.

THE MILLION DOLLAR COCKTAIL

Glass: Martini
Garnish: Lemon zest twist (round like an egg yolk in the foam)
Method: SHAKE all ingredients with ice and fine strain into chilled glass.

2	shot(s)	**Plymouth gin**
1	shot(s)	**Sweet vermouth**
½	shot(s)	**Pressed pineapple juice**
¼	shot(s)	**Pomegranate (grenadine) syrup**
½	fresh	**Egg white**

Origin: This classic cocktail is thought to have been created around 1910 by Ngiam Tong Boon at The Long Bar, Raffles Hotel, Singapore. Boon is more famous for the Singapore Sling.
Comment: Serious, yet superbly smooth and a bit fluffy.

MILLION DOLLAR MARGARITA

Glass: Old-fashioned
Garnish: Lime wedge
Method: SHAKE all ingredients with ice and strain into ice-filled glass.

1½	shot(s)	**Partida tequila**
1½	shot(s)	**Grand Marnier (Cuvée du Centenaire)**
½	shot(s)	**Freshly squeezed lime juice**

Origin: Discovered in 2006 at Maison 140 Hotel, Los Angeles, USA where I paid a mere $41.14 plus tip for the drink.
Comment: The proportions of this Margarita accentuate the liqueur.

M

MILLIONAIRE

Glass: Martini
Garnish: Quarter orange slice on rim
Method: **SHAKE** all ingredients with ice and fine strain into chilled glass.

2	shot(s)	**Buffalo Trace bourbon whiskey**
1/2	shot(s)	**Cointreau/ triple sec**
1/2	shot(s)	**Freshly squeezed lemon juice**
1/4	shot(s)	**Pomegranate (grenadine) syrup**
1/2	fresh	**Egg white**

Comment: Rust coloured tangy citrus smoothed and served straight-up.

'I SPENT A LOT OF MONEY ON BOOZE, BIRDS AND FAST CARS. THE REST I JUST SQUANDERED.'

GEORGE BEST

MILLIONAIRE'S DAIQUIRI

Glass: Martini
Garnish: Star fruit
Method: **SHAKE** all ingredients with ice and fine strain into chilled glass.

1 3/4	shot(s)	**Light white rum**
3/4	shot(s)	**Plymouth sloe gin**
3/4	shot(s)	**Giffard apricot brandy du Roussillon**
3/4	shot(s)	**Freshly squeezed lime juice**
1/4	shot(s)	**Pomegranate (grenadine) syrup**

Origin: This heralds from a classic cocktail known simply as the Millionaire. Originally sloe gin was the main base ingredient, but David Embury once wrote, "Since the sloe gin, which is a liqueur, predominates in this drink, I do not regard it as a true cocktail." Thus above is my modern adaptation.
Comment: The colour of this cocktail, due to sloe liqueur and grenadine, belies a surprisingly dry finish.

MILLY MARTINI

Glass: Martini
Garnish: Pineapple wedge on rim
Method: Lightly **MUDDLE** basil (just to bruise) in base of shaker. Add other ingredients, **SHAKE** with ice and fine strain into chilled glass.

5	fresh	**Basil leaves**
2	shot(s)	**Plymouth gin**
2	shot(s)	**Pressed pineapple juice**
1/2	shot(s)	**Sugar syrup (2 sugar to 1 water)**
2	dashes	**Fee Brothers orange bitters**

Origin: Created in 2003 by Shelim Islam at the GE Club, London, England.
Comment: Gin and pineapple with a pleasing hint of basil.

MIMOSA

Glass: Flute
Garnish: Orange zest twist
Method: **POUR** ingredients into chilled glass and gently stir.

1/2	shot(s)	**Grand Marnier liqueur**
1 3/4	shot(s)	**Freshly squeezed orange juice**
Top up with		**Brut champagne**

Variant: When made with mandarin juice this becomes a Puccini.
Origin: Created in 1925 at the Ritz Hotel in Paris and named after the tropical flowering shrub.
Comment: A liqueur-infused take on the Buck's Fizz.

MINT & HONEY DAIQUIRI [UPDATED #7]

Glass: Martini
Garnish: Mint sprig
Method: **STIR** honey and rum in base of shaker until honey dissolves. Add other ingredients, **SHAKE** with ice and fine strain into chilled glass.

2	spoons	**Runny honey**
2	shot(s)	**Light white rum**
3	torn	**Mint leaves**
1/2	shot(s)	**Freshly squeezed lime juice**
1/2	shot(s)	**Chilled mineral water** (omit if wet ice)

Origin: Created in 2006 by yours truly.
Comment: A fresh-breath-tastic twist on the Daiquiri.

MINT COCKTAIL

Glass: Martini
Garnish: Mint leaf
Method: Lightly **MUDDLE** (just to bruise) mint in base of shaker. Add other ingredients, **SHAKE** with ice and fine strain into chilled glass.

12	fresh	**Mint leaves**
2	shot(s)	**Plymouth gin**
1	shot(s)	**Sauvignon Blanc wine**
1/4	shot(s)	**Giffard white crème de Menthe Pastille**
1/4	shot(s)	**Sugar syrup (2 sugar to 1 water)**

Origin: Adapted from a recipe in Harry Craddock's 1930 Savoy Cocktail Book.
Comment: A great grassy, minty digestif with a good balance between acidity and sweetness.

MINT COLLINS

Glass: Collins
Garnish: Mint sprig
Method: Lightly **MUDDLE** (just to bruise) mint in base of shaker. Add next three ingredients, **SHAKE** with ice and fine strain into chilled glass. **TOP** with soda, lightly stir and serve with straws.

12	fresh	**Mint leaves**
2	shot(s)	**Plymouth gin**
1	shot(s)	**Freshly squeezed lemon juice**
1/2	shot(s)	**Sugar syrup (2 sugar to 1 water)**
Top up with		**Soda water (club soda)**

Origin: Adapted from a recipe in the 1947-72 Trader Vic's Bartender's Guide by Victor Bergeron.
Comment: Exactly what the name promises.

MINT DAIQUIRI

Glass: Martini
Garnish: Mint leaf
Method: Lightly **MUDDLE** (just to bruise) mint in base of shaker. Add other ingredients, **SHAKE** with ice and fine strain into chilled glass.

12	fresh	**Mint leaves**
2	shot(s)	**Light white rum**
1/2	shot(s)	**Freshly squeezed lime juice**
1/4	shot(s)	**Sugar syrup (2 sugar to 1 water)**
1/2	shot(s)	**Chilled mineral water** (omit if wet ice)

Origin: Created in 2006 by yours truly.
Comment: A short, concentrated Mojito.

MINT LIMEADE (MOCKTAIL)

Glass: Collins
Garnish: Mint sprig
Method: Lightly **MUDDLE** (just to bruise) mint in base of shaker. Add next three ingredients, **SHAKE** with ice and fine strain into ice-filled glass. **TOP** with 7-Up, lightly stir and serve with straws.

12	fresh	**Mint leaves**
1 1/2	shot(s)	**Freshly squeezed lime juice**
1	shot(s)	**Pressed apple juice**
3/4	shot(s)	**Sugar syrup (2 sugar to 1 water)**
Top up with		**7-Up**

Origin: Created in 2006 by yours truly.
Comment: Superbly refreshing - mint and lime served long.

MINT FIZZ

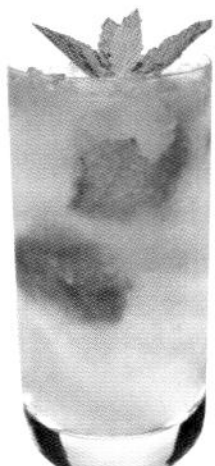

Glass: Collins
Garnish: Mint sprig
Method: Lightly **MUDDLE** mint (just to bruise) in base of shaker. Add other ingredients apart from soda, **SHAKE** with ice and fine strain into ice-filled glass. **TOP** with soda, lightly stir and serve with straws.

7	fresh	**Mint leaves**
2	shot(s)	**Plymouth gin**
1	shot(s)	**Freshly squeezed lime juice**
1/4	shot(s)	**White crème de menthe**
1/2	shot(s)	**Sugar syrup** (2 sugar to 1 water)
Top up with		**Soda (from siphon)**

Comment: Long, refreshing citrus and mint fizz.

MINT MARTINI [UPDATED #7]

Glass: Martini
Garnish: Mint leaf
Method: Lightly **MUDDLE** (just to bruise) mint in base of shaker. Add other ingredients, **SHAKE** with ice and fine strain into chilled glass.

12	fresh	**Mint leaves**
1 1/2	shot(s)	**Ketel One vodka**
1/2	shot(s)	**Dry vermouth**
1/4	shot(s)	**Giffard green crème de menthe**
1 1/2	shot(s)	**Sauvignon Blanc wine**
1/4	shot(s)	**Sugar syrup (2 sugar to 1 water)**

Origin: Created in 2005 by yours truly.
Comment: An after dinner palate cleanser.

'BRANDY, N. A CORDIAL COMPOSED OF ONE PART THUNDER-AND-LIGHTNING, ONE PART REMORSE, TWO PARTS BLOODY MURDER, ONE PART DEATH-HELL-AND-THE-GRAVE AND FOUR PARTS CLARIFIED SATAN.'
AMBROSE BIERCE

MINT JULEP [UPDATED #7]

Glass: Collins
Garnish: Mint sprig and slice of lemon
Method: Lightly **MUDDLE** (only bruise) mint in base of shaker. Add other ingredients, **SHAKE** with ice and strain into glass half filled with crushed ice. **CHURN** (stir) the drink with the crushed ice using a bar spoon. Top up the glass with more crushed ice and **CHURN** again. Repeat this process until the drink fills the glass and serve.

12	fresh	**Mint leaves**
2 1/2	shot(s)	**Buffalo Trace bourbon whiskey**
3/4	shot(s)	**Sugar syrup (2 sugar to 1 water)**
3	dashes	**Angostura aromatic bitters**

Comment: This superb drink is better if the shaker and its contents are placed in the refrigerator for several hours prior to mixing with ice. This allows the mint flavours to infuse in the bourbon.

MISS MARTINI

Glass: Martini
Garnish: Raspberries on stick
Method: **MUDDLE** raspberries in base of shaker. Add other ingredients, **SHAKE** with ice and fine strain into chilled glass.

7	fresh	**Raspberries**
2	shot(s)	**Ketel One vodka**
1/2	shot(s)	**Chambord black raspberry liqueur**
1/4	shot(s)	**Double (heavy) cream**
1/4	shot(s)	**Milk**
1/8	shot(s)	**Sugar syrup (2 sugar to 1 water)**

Origin: Created in 1997 by Giovanni Burdi at Match EC1, London, England.
Comment: A pink, fruity and creamy concoction.

MINT JULEP

This is the ultimate Deep South cocktail, famously served at the Kentucky Derby. The name derives from the Arabic word 'julab', meaning rosewater, and the first known written reference dates back to 1787.

When making a Mint Julep it is important to only bruise the mint as crushing the leaves releases the bitter, inner juices. Also be sure to discard the stems, which are also bitter.

It is imperative that the drink is served ice cold. Cocktail etiquette dictates that the shaker containing the mint and other ingredients should be placed in a refrigerator with the serving glass for at least two hours prior to adding ice, shaking and serving.

Variations on the Mint Julep include substituting the bourbon for rye whiskey, rum, gin, brandy, calvados or applejack brandy. Another variation calls for half a shot of aged rum to be floated on top of the bourbon-based julep.

MISSIONARY'S DOWNFALL

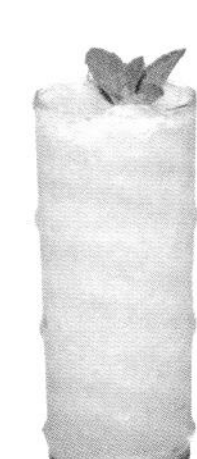

Glass: Collins
Garnish: Mint sprig
Method: Lightly **MUDDLE** mint (just to bruise) in base of shaker. Add other ingredients, **SHAKE** with ice and strain into glass filled with crushed ice.

- 12 fresh **Mint leaves**
- 2 shot(s) **Light white rum**
- ½ shot(s) **Teichenné Peach Schnapps Liqueur**
- 1½ shot(s) **Freshly squeezed lime juice**
- ½ shot(s) **Sugar syrup (2 sugar to 1 water)**
- 2 shot(s) **Freshly squeezed pineapple juice**

Origin: Created in the 1930s by Don The Beachcomber at his restaurant in Hollywood, California, USA.
Comment: Superbly balanced and refreshing rum, lime, mint and a hint of peach.

MISSISSIPPI PUNCH

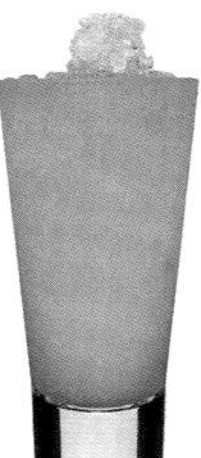

Glass: Collins
Garnish: Lemon slice
Method: **SHAKE** all ingredients with ice and strain into glass filled with crushed ice.

- 1½ shot(s) **Buffalo Trace bourbon whiskey**
- ¾ shot(s) **Rémy Martin cognac**
- ¾ shot(s) **Freshly squeezed lemon juice**
- 1 shot(s) **Sugar syrup (2 sugar to 1 water)**
- 2 shot(s) **Chilled mineral water**

Comment: Balanced and refreshing.

MISSISSIPPI SCHNAPPER

Glass: Martini
Garnish: Orange zest twist
Method: **SHAKE** all ingredients with ice and fine strain into chilled glass.

- 2 shot(s) **Jack Daniel's Tennessee whiskey**
- ¾ shot(s) **Teichenné Peach Schnapps Liqueur**
- ½ shot(s) **Cointreau triple sec**
- ¼ shot(s) **Freshly squeezed lime juice**
- ¼ shot(s) **Sugar syrup (2 sugar to 1 water)**

Origin: Created in 1999 by Dan Cottle at Velvet, Manchester, England.
Comment: Orange predominates with peach sweetness balanced by whiskey and lime.

MISTER STU

Glass: Collins
Garnish: Pineapple wedge on rim
Method: **SHAKE** all ingredients with ice and strain into ice-filled glass. Serve with straws.

- 2 shot(s) **Partida tequila**
- ½ shot(s) **Luxardo Amaretto di Saschira liqueur**
- ½ shot(s) **Malibu coconut rum liqueur**
- 1½ shot(s) **Pressed pineapple juice**
- 1½ shot(s) **Freshly squeezed orange juice**

Comment: There's a touch of the disco about this foamy drink, but it is still complex and interesting.

MITCH MARTINI [UPDATED #7]

Glass: Martini
Garnish: Lemon zest twist
Method: **SHAKE** all ingredients with ice and fine strain into chilled glass.

- 2 shot(s) **Zubrówka bison vodka**
- ¼ shot(s) **Teichenné Peach Schnapps Liqueur**
- 1 shot(s) **Pressed apple juice**
- ¼ shot(s) **Passion fruit syrup**

Origin: Created in 1997 by Giovanni Burdi at Match EC1, London, England.
Comment: One of London's contemporary classics. Far from a proper Martini, this is fruity and sweet, but not overly so.

MOCHA MARTINI

Glass: Martini
Garnish: Dust with cocoa powder
Method: **SHAKE** first four ingredients with ice and fine strain into chilled glass. **FLOAT** cream in centre of drink.

- 1½ shot(s) **Buffalo Trace bourbon whiskey**
- 1 shot(s) **Cold espresso coffee**
- ½ shot(s) **Irish cream liqueur**
- ½ shot(s) **Giffard brown crème de cacao**
- ½ shot(s) **Double (heavy) cream**

Comment: Made with great espresso, this drink is a superb, richly flavoured balance of sweet and bitter.

'LET'S GET OUT OF THESE WET CLOTHES AND INTO A DRY MARTINI.'
HOLLYWOOD PRESS AGENT

MODERNISTA

Glass: Martini
Garnish: Lemon zest twist
Method: **SHAKE** all ingredients with ice and fine strain into chilled glass.

- 2 shot(s) **Plymouth gin**
- ½ shot(s) **Goslings Black Seal rum**
- ¼ shot(s) **Pernod anis**
- 1 shot(s) **Carlshamns Swedish Torr Flaggpunsch**
- ¼ shot(s) **Freshly squeezed lemon juice**
- 1 dash **Fee Brothers orange bitters**

Origin: Adapted from a drink created by Ted Haigh (AKA Dr. Cocktail) and derived from the 'Modern Cocktail'. See Ted's book, 'Vintage Spirits & Forgotten Cocktails'.
Comment: A massive flavour hit to awaken your taste buds.

MOCKTAILS

A mocktail is a cocktail that does not contain any alcoholic ingredient. These are also sometimes referred to as 'Virgin Cocktails'.

Mocktails enable those who wish to avoid alcohol, such as drivers, pregnant or breast-feeding women and those on the wagon, to join their friends in a cocktail or two.

The following drinks contain no alcohol:

Apple Virgin Mojito
Banana Smoothie
Bloody Shame
Bora Bora Brew
Florida Cocktail
Gentle Breeze
Hobson's Choice
Honey Limeaid
Judy
Lime Blush
Limeade
Mint Limeade
Not So Cosmo
November Seabreeze
Piña Colada Virgin
Pineapple Smoothie
Pink Lemonade
Planter's Punchless
Pussyfoot
Real Lemonade
Roy Rogers
Saint Clements
Shirley Temple
Sorrelade
Sun Kissed Virgin

These contain so little alcohol that they are virtually non-alcoholic:

Cinderella
Fantasia
Honey Blossom
Lemon Lime & Bitters
St Kitts

MOJITO 

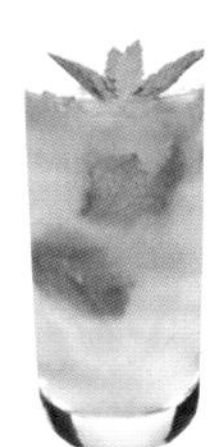

Glass: Collins
Garnish: Mint sprig
Method: Lightly **MUDDLE** mint (just to bruise) in base of glass. Add rum, lime juice and sugar. Half fill glass with crushed ice and **CHURN** (stir) with bar spoon. Fill glass with more crushed ice and **CHURN** some more. **TOP** with soda, stir and serve with straws.

12 fresh **Mint leaves**
2 shot(s) **Light white rum**
3/4 shot(s) **Freshly squeezed lime juice**
1/4 shot(s) **Sugar syrup (2 sugar to 1 water)**
Top up with **Soda water (club soda)**

Variant: Add a dash or two of Angostura aromatic bitters.
Comment: When well made, this Cuban cousin of the Mint Julep is one of the world's greatest and most refreshing cocktails.

'IF YOU DRINK, DON'T DIAL.'
PHONE OPERATOR, 1950S

MOJITO DE CASA

Glass: Collins
Garnish: Mint sprig
Method: Lightly **MUDDLE** mint (just to bruise) in base of glass. Add tequila, lime juice and sugar. Half fill glass with crushed ice and **CHURN** (stir) with bar spoon. Fill glass with more crushed ice and **CHURN** some more. **TOP** with soda, stir and serve with straws.

12 fresh **Mint leaves**
2 shot(s) **Partida tequila**
3/4 shot(s) **Freshly squeezed lime juice**
1/2 shot(s) **Sugar syrup (2 sugar to 1 water)**
Top up with **Soda water (club soda)**

Origin: Created at Mercadito, New York City, USA.
Comment: A tequila based Mojito.

MOJITO PARISIEN [NEW #7]

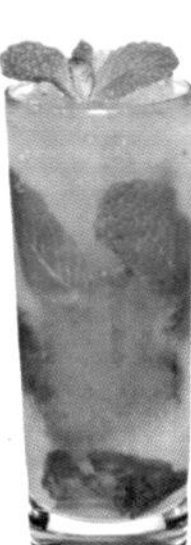

Glass: Collins
Garnish: Mint sprig
Method: Lightly **MUDDLE** mint (just to bruise) in base of glass. Add other ingredients, half fill glass with crushed ice and **CHURN** (stir) with bar spoon. Fill glass to brim with more crushed ice and churn some more. Serve with straws.

12 fresh **Mint leaves**
2 shot(s) **Light white rum**
1 1/2 shot(s) **St-Germain elderflower liqueur**
1 shot(s) **Freshly squeezed lime juice**

Origin: Recipe in 2006 by yours truly.
Comment: Those with a sweet tooth may want to add a dash of sugar syrup to taste.

MOLOTOV COCKTAIL

Glass: Martini
Garnish: Lemon zest
Method: SHAKE all ingredients with ice and fine strain into chilled glass.

1 1/2 shot(s) **Lime flavoured vodka**
1 1/4 shot(s) **Parfait Amour liqueur**
1/2 shot(s) **Freshly squeezed lemon juice**
1/2 shot(s) **Opal Nera black sambuca**

Origin: I created this drink after a visit to the Rajamäki distillery in Finland. At the start of the Second World War the plant was used to produce Molotov cocktails, inflammatory bombs with which the Finns put hundreds of Soviet tanks out of action.
Comment: The ingredients represent the four liquids used in the weapon. Vodka, stands for alcohol, parfait amour shares the purple hue of paraffin, lemon juice represents gasoline and black sambuca replaces tar.

LA MOMIE

Glass: Shot
Method: POUR pastis into chilled glass and top with chilled water.

1/2 shot(s) **Ricard pastis**
Top up with **Chilled water**

Origin: Pronounced 'Mom-Ee', this shot is very popular in the South of France.
Comment: A bite-sized aniseed tipple.

MOMISETTE

Glass: Collins (10oz max)
Method: POUR pastis and almond syrup into glass. Serve with bottle of sparkling water so the customer can dilute to their own taste. (I recommend five shots.) Lastly, add ice to fill glass.

1 shot(s) **Ricard pastis**
1/4 shot(s) **Almond (orgeat) syrup**
Top up with **Sparkling mineral water**

Origin: A traditional French drink, the name of which literally translates as 'tiny mummy'.
Comment: Complex balance of anis, almond and liquorice.

MOMO SPECIAL 

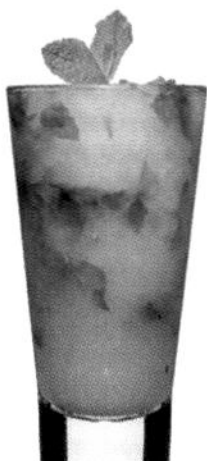

Glass: Collins
Garnish: Mint sprig
Method: Lightly **MUDDLE** mint (just to bruise) in base of shaker. Add next three ingredients, **SHAKE** with ice and strain into ice-filled glass. **TOP** with soda, lightly stir and serve with straws.

12 fresh **Mint leaves**
2 shot(s) **Ketel One vodka**
1/2 shot(s) **Freshly squeezed lime juice**
1/2 shot(s) **Sugar syrup (2 sugar to 1 water)**
Top up with **Soda water (club soda)**

Origin: Created in 1998 by Simon Mainoo at Momo, London, England.
Comment: Enrich the minty flavour by macerating the mint in the vodka some hours before making.

MOJITO

Between the wars, and especially during Prohibition, Cuba had a thriving international bar culture. In fact, when Prohibition was announced, numerous companies outfitted ferries for the overnight booze cruise to the island. At the heart of this bar culture were Cuba's bartenders, many of them trained at the Association Cantineros Cuba - the legendary Havana bar school.

A classic, long blend of rum, lime and mint, the Mojito was probably invented after Americans introduced the locals to the Mint Julep. Bodeguita del Medio is usually credited with the first Mojito and this is apparently where Hemingway went for his.

In January 2003 the Mojito had something of a boost when the newly released Bond film, Die Another Day, saw James visit Cuba and order a Mojito in preference to his more usual Vodka Martini.

MOJITO VARIATIONS

Apple Mojito
Apple Virgin Mojito
Bajan Mojito
Bajito
French Mojito
Ginger Mojito
Rude Mojito
Luxury Mojito
Milky Mojito
Mojito
Mojito de Casa
Momo Special
Orange Mojito
Pineapple Mojito
Strawberry & Balsamic Mojito

MONA LISA

Glass: Collins
Garnish: Orange slice
Method: SHAKE first three ingredients with ice and strain into ice-filled glass. **TOP** with tonic water.

1	shot(s)	**Green Chartreuse liqueur**
3	shot(s)	**Freshly squeezed orange juice**
2	dashes	**Angostura aromatic bitters**
Top up with		**Tonic water**

Comment: Chartreuse fans will appreciate this drink, which is also an approachable way for novices to acquire a taste for the green stuff.

MONARCH MARTINI [UPDATED #7]

Glass: Martini
Garnish: Lemon zest twist
Method: Lightly **MUDDLE** mint (just to bruise) in base of shaker. Add other ingredients, **SHAKE** with ice and fine strain into chilled glass.

7	fresh	**Mint leaves**
2	shot(s)	**Plymouth gin**
1/2	shot(s)	**St-Germain elderflower liqueur**
1/2	shot(s)	**Freshly squeezed lemon juice**
1/4	shot(s)	**Sugar syrup (2 sugar to 1 water)**
2	dashes	**Fee Brothers peach bitters**

Origin: Adapted from a drink created in 2003 by Douglas Ankrah at Townhouse, London, England.
Comment: Wonderfully floral and minty – worthy of a right royal drinker.

MONKEY GLAND #1

Glass: Martini
Garnish: Orange zest twist
Method: SHAKE all ingredients with ice and fine strain into chilled glass.

2	shot(s)	**Plymouth gin**
1/4	shot(s)	**La Fée Parisienne (68%) absinthe**
1 1/2	shot(s)	**Freshly squeezed orange juice**
1/4	shot(s)	**Pomegranate (grenadine) syrup**

Origin: Created in the 1920s by Harry MacElhone at his Harry's New York Bar in Paris. The Monkey Gland takes its name from the work of Dr Serge Voronoff, who attempted to delay the ageing process by transplanting monkey testicles.
Comment: Approach with caution. Due diligence reveals a dangerous base of gin and absinthe.

MONKEY GLAND #2

Glass: Old-fashioned
Garnish: Orange slice
Method: SHAKE all ingredients with ice and strain into ice-filled glass.

2	shot(s)	**Plymouth gin**
1 1/4	shot(s)	**Freshly squeezed orange juice**
1/2	shot(s)	**Bénédictine D.O.M. liqueur**
1/4	shot(s)	**Pomegranate (grenadine) syrup**

Comment: A somewhat off-putting name for a very palatable cocktail.

MONKEY SHINE

Glass: Martini
Garnish: Cinnamon rim
Method: SHAKE all ingredients with ice and fine strain into chilled glass.

2	shot(s)	**Golden rum**
1	shot(s)	**Malibu coconut rum liqueur**
1	shot(s)	**Pressed pineapple juice**

Origin: An adaptation of a drink discovered in 2003 at the Bellagio Resort & Casino, Las Vegas.
Comment: The sweet, tropical fruitiness of this drink is set off by the spicy rim.

MONKEY WRENCH

Glass: Collins
Method: POUR rum into ice-filled glass. Top with grapefruit juice, stir and serve with straws.

2	shot(s)	**Golden rum**
Top up with		**Squeezed pink grapefruit juice**

Comment: Simple but pleasant.

'I DO NOT LIVE IN THE WORLD OF SOBRIETY.'
OLIVER REED

MONK'S CANDY BAR

Glass: Martini
Garnish: Sprinkle with nutmeg
Method: SHAKE all ingredients with ice and fine strain into chilled glass.

1	shot(s)	**Frangelico hazelnut liqueur**
1/2	shot(s)	**Teichenné butterscotch Schnapps**
1/2	shot(s)	**Kahlúa coffee liqueur**
1	shot(s)	**Double (heavy) cream**
1	shot(s)	**Milk**

Comment: Creamy and sweet, with hazelnut, butterscotch and coffee.

MONK'S HABIT

Glass: Collins
Garnish: Orange slice
Method: SHAKE all ingredients with ice and strain into ice-filled glass.

1 1/2	shot(s)	**Light white rum**
1/2	shot(s)	**Cointreau triple sec**
1	shot(s)	**Frangelico hazelnut liqueur**
3	shot(s)	**Pressed pineapple juice**
1/4	shot(s)	**Pomegranate (grenadine) syrup**

Comment: Fruit and nut laced with rum. Slightly sweet.

MONTE CARLO

Glass: Collins
Garnish: Maraschino cherry
Method: POUR first three ingredients into empty glass. **ADD** soda water to half fill glass. Fill glass with ice and then top up with more soda. (This avoids 'shocking' the anis with the ice.) Serve with straws.

1	shot(s)	**Pernod anis**
1/2	shot(s)	**Luxardo maraschino liqueur**
3/4	shot(s)	**Freshly squeezed lime juice**
Top up with		**Soda water (club soda)**

Origin: An adaptation of a Martini style drink created in 2002 by Alex Turner, London, England.
Comment: A long, fragrant, almost floral summer cooler with lots of aniseed.

MONTE CARLO IMPERIAL

Glass: Martini
Garnish: Mint leaf
Method: SHAKE first three ingredients with ice and fine strain into chilled glass. **TOP** with champagne.

1 1/2	shot(s)	**Plymouth gin**
1/2	shot(s)	**Freshly squeezed lemon juice**
1/2	shot(s)	**Giffard white crème de Menthe Pastille**
Top up with		**Brut champagne**

Origin: Adapted from a recipe in Harry Craddock's 1930 Savoy Cocktail Book.
Comment: A classic, minty digestif.

MONTEGO BAY

Glass: Old-fashioned
Garnish: Lime wedge
Method: SHAKE all ingredients with ice and strain into ice-filled glass.

1 1/2	shot(s)	**Martinique agricole rum (50% alc./vol.)**
1/2	shot(s)	**Freshly squeezed lime juice**
1/2	shot(s)	**Cointreau triple sec**
1/4	shot(s)	**Sugar syrup (2 sugar to 1 water)**
2	dashes	**Angostura aromatic bitters**

Origin: Adapted from a recipe in the 1947-72 Trader Vic's Bartender's Guide by Victor Bergeron.
Comment: The name suggests Jamaica but the recipe requires agricole rum. This pungent style of rum is not Jamaican.

MONZA

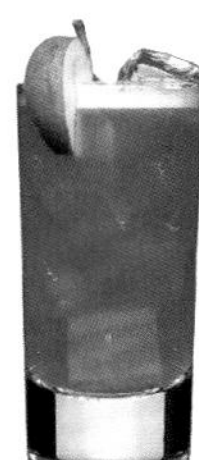

Glass: Collins
Garnish: Slice of apple
Method: Cut passion fruit in half and scoop flesh into shaker. Add other ingredients, **SHAKE** with ice and strain into ice-filled glass.

1	fresh	**Passion fruit**
2	shot(s)	**Ketel One vodka**
2	shot(s)	**Campari**
2	shot(s)	**Pressed apple juice**
1/4	shot(s)	**Sugar syrup (2 sugar to 1 water)**

Origin: A classic cocktail promoted by Campari and named after the Italian Grand Prix circuit.
Comment: If you like Campari you'll love this.

MOOD INDIGO [NEW #7]

Glass: Martini
Garnish: Violet blossom or mint sprig
Method: SHAKE all ingredients with ice and fine strain into chilled glass.

1 1/2	shot(s)	**Plymouth gin**
1/2	shot(s)	**Rémy Martin cognac**
1/2	shot(s)	**Benoit Serres violet liqueur**
1/2	fresh	**Egg white**
1/8	shot(s)	**Sugar syrup (2 sugar to 1 water)**
1/2	shot(s)	**Chilled mineral water** (omit if wet ice)

Origin: Named after the jazz standard that was a hit for Nat King Cole.
Comment: Smooth, delicate and floral: the gin and brandy add just enough bite.

MOONRAKER

Glass: Martini
Garnish: Maraschino cherry
Method: SHAKE all ingredients with ice and fine strain into chilled glass.

1 1/2	shot(s)	**Rémy Martin cognac**
1 1/2	shot(s)	**Dubonnet red**
3/4	shot(s)	**Teichenné Peach Schnapps Liqueur**
1/4	shot(s)	**Pernod anis**

Origin: Adapted from a recipe in the 1947-72 Trader Vic's Bartender's Guide by Victor Bergeron.
Comment: A diverse range of flavours come together surprisingly well.

MOON RIVER

Glass: Martini
Garnish: Mint leaf
Method: SHAKE all ingredients with ice and fine strain into chilled glass.

1 1/2	shot(s)	**Plymouth gin**
1/2	shot(s)	**Giffard apricot brandy du Roussillon**
1/2	shot(s)	**Cointreau triple sec**
1/4	shot(s)	**Galliano liqueur**
1/2	shot(s)	**Freshly squeezed lemon juice**
1/2	shot(s)	**Chilled mineral water** (omit if wet ice)

Origin: Adapted from a drink discovered in 2005 at Bar Opiume, Singapore.
Comment: There's a hint of aniseed in this fruity, sweet and sour drink.

MOONLIGHT MARTINI

Glass: Martini
Garnish: Lemon zest twist
Method: SHAKE all ingredients with ice and fine strain into chilled glass.

1 1/2	shot(s)	**Plymouth gin**
1/4	shot(s)	**Kirsch eau de vie**
1	shot(s)	**Sauvignon Blanc wine**
1 1/4	shot(s)	**Squeezed pink grapefruit juice**

Origin: Adapted from a recipe in Harry Craddock's 1930 Savoy Cocktail Book.
Comment: Craddock describes this as "a very dry cocktail". It is, but pleasantly so.

MOSCOW MULE

This classic combination was born in 1941. John G. Martin had acquired the rights to Smirnoff vodka for Heublein, a small Connecticut based liquor and food distributor. Jack Morgan, the owner of Hollywood's famous Cock'n'Bull Saloon, was trying to launch his own brand of ginger beer. The two men met at New York City's Chatham Bar and hit on the idea of mixing Martin's vodka with Morgan's ginger beer and adding a dash of lime to create a new cocktail, the Moscow Mule.

To help promote the drink, and hence their respective products, Morgan had the idea of marketing the Moscow Mule using specially engraved mugs. The five ounce mugs were embossed with a kicking mule and made at a copper factory a friend of his had recently inherited. The promotion helped turn Smirnoff into a major brand.

MOONSHINE MARTINI

Glass: Martini
Garnish: Maraschino cherry
Method: **SHAKE** all ingredients with ice and fine strain into chilled glass.

- 1½ shot(s) **Plymouth gin**
- 1 shot(s) **Dry vermouth**
- ½ shot(s) **Luxardo maraschino liqueur**
- ⅛ shot(s) **La Fée Parisienne (68%) absinthe**

Origin: Adapted from a recipe in the 1930 Savoy Cocktail Book by Harry Craddock.
Comment: A wet Martini with balanced hints of maraschino and absinthe.

MORAVIAN COCKTAIL

Glass: Old-fashioned
Garnish: Orange slice & cherry on stick (sail)
Method: **SHAKE** all ingredients with ice and strain into ice-filled glass.

- ¾ shot(s) **Slivovitz plum brandy**
- ¾ shot(s) **Becherovka Czech liqueur**
- 1½ shot(s) **Sweet vermouth**

Origin: Discovered in 2005 at Be Bop Bar, Prague, Czech Republic.
Comment: The hardcore, Czech answer to the Italian Negroni.

MORNING GLORY

Glass: Old-fashioned
Garnish: Lemon zest twist
Method: **SHAKE** all ingredients with ice and strain into ice-filled glass.

- 1 shot(s) **Rémy Martin cognac**
- ¾ shot(s) **Grand Marnier liqueur**
- ⅛ shot(s) **La Fée Parisienne (68%) absinthe**
- ½ shot(s) **Freshly squeezed lemon juice**
- ¼ shot(s) **Sugar syrup (2 sugar to 1 water)**
- 2 dashes **Angostura aromatic bitters**
- ½ shot(s) **Chilled mineral water** (omit if wet ice)

Origin: My interpretation of a classic.
Comment: Sophisticated and complex – one for sipping.

MORNING GLORY FIZZ

Glass: Old-fashioned
Garnish: Lime wheel
Method: **SHAKE** first six ingredients with ice and strain into ice-filled glass. **TOP** with soda water from a siphon.

- 1 shot(s) **Scotch whisky**
- ¼ shot(s) **La Fée Parisienne (68%) absinthe**
- ¾ shot(s) **Freshly squeezed lime juice**
- ¾ shot(s) **Freshly squeezed lemon juice**
- ¼ shot(s) **Sugar syrup (2 sugar to 1 water)**
- ½ fresh **Egg white**
- Top up with **Soda water from a siphon**

Comment: Considered a morning after pick-me-up but is great at any time.

MOSCOW LASSI

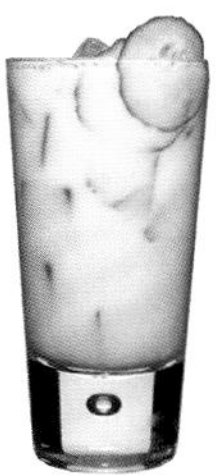

Glass: Collins
Garnish: Cucumber slices
Method: **MUDDLE** cucumber in base of shaker. Add other ingredients. **SHAKE** with ice and fine strain into ice-filled glass.

- 2 inches **Chopped & peeled cucumber**
- 1 shot(s) **Sweetened mango purée**
- 1½ shot(s) **Ketel One vodka**
- 2 shot(s) **Pressed apple juice**
- 3 spoon(s) **Natural yoghurt**
- ¼ shot(s) **Sugar syrup (2 sugar to 1 water)**

Origin: Created in 2001 by Jamie Stephenson at Gaucho Grill, Manchester, England.
Comment: One to serve with your Indian takeaway.

MOSCOW MULE [UPDATED]

Glass: Collins (or copper mug)
Garnish: Lime wedge & mint sprig
Method: **SHAKE** first four ingredients with ice and strain into ice-filled glass. **TOP** with ginger beer and stir.

- 2 shot(s) **Ketel One vodka**
- ½ shot(s) **Freshly squeezed lime juice**
- ¼ shot(s) **Sugar syrup (2 sugar to 1 water)**
- 3 dashes **Angostura aromatic bitters**
- Top up with **Ginger beer**

Origin: My take on the drink created in 1941 by John G. Martin and Jack Morgan.
Comment: A long, vodka based drink with spice provided by ginger beer and Angostura.

MOTHER RUM [NEW #7]

Glass: Old-fashioned
Garnish: Cinnamon stick
Method: **STIR** all ingredients with ice and strain into ice-filled glass.

- 2 shot(s) **Aged rum**
- ¼ shot(s) **Giffard white crème de cacao**
- ¼ shot(s) **Maple syrup**

Origin: Created in 2006 by Milo Rodriguez at Crazy Bear, London, England.
Comment: To quote Milo, this drink "is warm and comforting, just like the drinks my mother made."

MOTOX

Glass: Martini
Garnish: Coriander leaf
Method: **MUDDLE** ginger and coriander in base of shaker. Add other ingredients, **SHAKE** with ice and fine strain into chilled glass.

- 1 slice **Root ginger (thumbnail sized)**
- 10 fresh **Coriander leaves**
- 1½ shot(s) **Ketel One Citroen vodka**
- ½ shot(s) **Luxardo limoncello liqueur**
- 1 shot(s) **Pressed pineapple juice**
- 1 shot(s) **Pressed apple juice**

Origin: Adapted from a drink discovered in 2005 at Mo Bar, Landmark Mandarin Oriental Hotel, Hong Kong.
Comment: Each sip is fruity, lemon fresh and followed by a hot ginger hit.

MOUNTAIN

Glass: Martini
Garnish: Maraschino cherry
Method: SHAKE all ingredients with ice and fine strain into chilled glass.

2	shot(s)	**Buffalo Trace bourbon whiskey**
3/4	shot(s)	**Dry vermouth**
3/4	shot(s)	**Sweet vermouth**
1/2	fresh	**Egg white**

Comment: A perfect Manhattan smoothed by egg white.

MOUNTAIN SIPPER

Glass: Old-fashioned
Garnish: Orange zest twist
Method: SHAKE all ingredients with ice and strain into ice-filled glass.

2	shot(s)	**Jack Daniel's Tennessee whiskey**
1	shot(s)	**Cointreau triple sec**
1	shot(s)	**Ocean Spray cranberry juice**
1	shot(s)	**Freshly squeezed grapefruit juice**
1/8	shot(s)	**Sugar syrup (2 sugar to 1 water)**

Comment: Fruity citrus flavours balance the richness of the whiskey.

M

MRS ROBINSON #1

Glass: Old-fashioned
Garnish: Three raspberries
Method: MUDDLE raspberries in base of shaker. Add next four ingredients, **SHAKE** with ice and strain into ice-filled glass. **TOP** with soda, lightly stir and serve with straws.

8	fresh	**Raspberries**
2	shot(s)	**Buffalo Trace bourbon whiskey**
1	shot(s)	**Giffard crème de framboise**
1/4	shot(s)	**Freshly squeezed lemon juice**
1/4	shot(s)	**Sugar syrup (2 sugar to 1 water)**
Top up with		**Soda water (club soda)**

Origin: Created in 2000 by Max Warner at Long Bar, Sanderson, London, England.
Comment: Rich raspberry fruit laced with bourbon.

MRS. ROBINSON #2

Glass: Martini
Garnish: Quarter orange slice on rim
Method: SHAKE all ingredients with ice and fine strain into chilled glass.

2 1/2	shot(s)	**Ketel One vodka**
1	shot(s)	**Freshly squeezed orange juice**
1/2	shot(s)	**Galliano liqueur**

Origin: Discovered in 2006 on Kyle Branch's Cocktail Hotel blog. (www.cocktailhotel.blogspot.com).
Comment: A short Harvey Wallbanger.

MUCKY BOTTOM

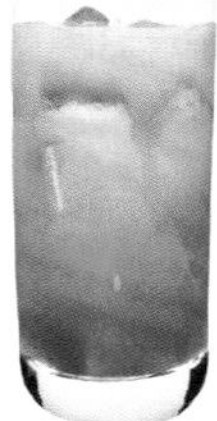

Glass: Collins
Method: SHAKE first three ingredients with ice and strain into ice-filled glass. **POUR** coffee liqueur around top of drink - this will fall to the base of the glass and create the mucky bottom.

2	shot(s)	**Malibu coconut rum liqueur**
1	shot(s)	**Pernod anis**
3	shot(s)	**Freshly squeezed grapefruit juice**
3/4	shot(s)	**Kahlúa coffee liqueur**

Origin: Created in 2003 by yours truly. (Formerly named Red Haze.)
Comment: Four very strong and distinctive flavours somehow tone each other down.

MUDDY WATER

Glass: Old-fashioned
Garnish: Float 3 coffee beans
Method: SHAKE all ingredients with ice and strain into ice-filled glass.

1	shot(s)	**Ketel One vodka**
1	shot(s)	**Kahlúa coffee liqueur**
1	shot(s)	**Irish cream liqueur**

Comment: Coffee and whiskey cream with added vodka.

MUDSLIDE

Glass: Hurricane
Garnish: Crumbled Cadbury's Flake bar
Method: BLEND all ingredients with two 12oz scoops of crushed ice and serve with straws.

1 1/2	shot(s)	**Irish cream liqueur**
1 1/2	shot(s)	**Kahlúa coffee liqueur**
1 1/2	shot(s)	**Ketel One vodka**
3	scoops	**Vanilla ice cream**

Comment: A simply scrumptious dessert drink with whiskey cream and coffee.

MUJER VERDE

Glass: Martini
Garnish: Lime zest twist
Method: SHAKE all ingredients with ice and fine strain into chilled glass.

1	shot(s)	**Plymouth gin**
1/2	shot(s)	**Green Chartreuse liqueur**
1/2	shot(s)	**Yellow Chartreuse liqueur**
1/2	shot(s)	**Freshly squeezed lime juice**
1/4	shot(s)	**Sugar syrup (2 sugar to 1 water)**
3/4	shot(s)	**Chilled mineral water** (omit if wet ice)

Origin: Discovered in 2006 at Absinthe, San Francisco, where 'D Mexican' resurrected this drink from his hometown of Guadalajara.
Comment: The name means 'Green Lady'... and she packs a Chartreuse punch.

MULATA DAIQUIRI

Glass: Martini
Garnish: Lime wedge on rim
Method: SHAKE all ingredients with ice and fine strain into chilled glass.

- 2 shot(s) **Aged rum**
- 1/2 shot(s) **Giffard brown crème de cacao**
- 1/2 shot(s) **Freshly squeezed lime juice**
- 1/4 shot(s) **Sugar syrup (2 sugar to 1 water)**

Comment: A classic Daiquiri with aged rum and a hint of chocolate.

MULE'S HIND LEG

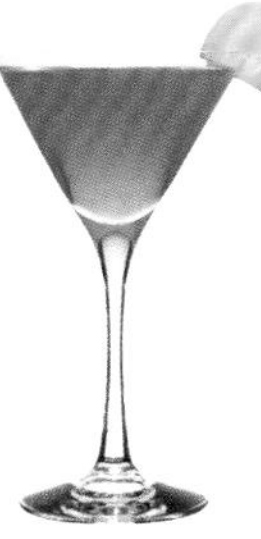

Glass: Martini
Garnish: Apricot slice on rim
Method: SHAKE all ingredients with ice and fine strain into chilled glass.

- 1 shot(s) **Plymouth gin**
- 1 shot(s) **Bénédictine D.O.M. liqueur**
- 1 shot(s) **Boulard Grand Solage Calvados**
- 1/4 shot(s) **Maple syrup**
- 3/4 shot(s) **Giffard apricot brandy du Roussillon**
- 1/2 shot(s) **Chilled mineral water** (omit if wet ice)

Origin: My version of a classic 1920s recipe.
Comment: Apricot and maple syrup dominate this medium sweet drink.

'A MAN SHOULDN'T FOOL WITH BOOZE UNTIL HE'S FIFTY; THEN HE'S A DAMN FOOL IF HE DOESN'T.'
WILLIAM FAULKNER

MULLED WINE

Glass: Toddy
Garnish: Cinnamon stick
Method: MUDDLE cloves in base of mixing glass. Add rest of ingredients apart from boiling water, **STIR** and fine strain into warmed glass. **TOP** with boiling water and **STIR**.

- 5 dried **Cloves**
- 1 pinch **Freshly grated nutmeg**
- 1 pinch **Ground cinnamon**
- 1 1/2 shot(s) **Warre's Otima Tawny Port**
- 1 1/2 shot(s) **Red wine**
- 1/4 shot(s) **Grand Marnier liqueur**
- 1/2 shot(s) **Freshly squeezed lemon juice**
- Top up with **Boiling water**

Variant: Better if several servings are made and the ingredients warmed in a saucepan.
Comment: Warming, soothing and potent.

MYRTLE MARTINI

Glass: Martini
Garnish: Sugar rim
Method: SHAKE all ingredients with ice and fine strain into chilled glass.

- 2 shot(s) **Ketel One vodka**
- 1/2 shot(s) **Giffard crème de myrtille**
- 2 shot(s) **Pressed apple juice**
- 1/4 shot(s) **Sugar syrup (2 sugar to 1 water)**
- 1/4 shot(s) **Freshly squeezed lime juice**

Origin: Created in 2003 at Cheyne Walk Brasserie & Salon, London, England.
Comment: A fruity concoction to remember should you find yourself with a bottle of crème de myrtille.

MYSTIQUE

Glass: Old-fashioned
Garnish: Orange zest twist & cherry
Method: SHAKE all ingredients with ice and strain into ice-filled glass.

- 1/2 shot(s) **Scotch whisky**
- 3/4 shot(s) **Drambuie liqueur**
- 1/2 shot(s) **Teichenné Peach Schnapps Liqueur**
- 1/4 shot(s) **Luxardo maraschino liqueur**
- 3 dashes **Fee Brothers orange bitters**

Origin: Created by Greg Pearson at Mystique, Manchester, England in 1999. Joint winner of the Manchester Food & Drink Festival cocktail competition.
Comment: Honeyed, peachy, orange Scotch.

MYSTIQUE MARTINI

Glass: Martini
Garnish: Raspberries on stick
Method: STIR all ingredients with ice and fine strain into chilled glass.

- 2 shot(s) **Scotch whisky**
- 1 shot(s) **Tuaca Italian liqueur**
- 3/4 shot(s) **Chambord black raspberry liqueur**

Origin: Created in 2002 by Tim Halilaj, Albania.
Comment: Rust coloured and fruit charged.

NACIONAL DAIQUIRI #1

Glass: Martini
Garnish: Maraschino cherry
Method: SHAKE all ingredients with ice and fine strain into chilled glass.

- 2 shot(s) **Light white rum**
- 3/4 shot(s) **Giffard apricot brandy du Roussillon**
- 1/2 shot(s) **Freshly squeezed lime juice**
- 3/4 shot(s) **Chilled mineral water** (omit if wet ice)

Origin: An old classic named after the Hotel Nacional, Havana, Cuba, where it was created.
Comment: A sophisticated complex apricot Daiquiri.

NACIONAL DAIQUIRI #2

Glass: Martini
Garnish: Maraschino cherry
Method: **SHAKE** all ingredients with ice and fine strain into chilled glass.

2	shot(s)	**Light white rum**
1/2	shot(s)	**Giffard apricot brandy du Roussillon**
1 1/2	shot(s)	**Pressed pineapple juice**
1/2	shot(s)	**Freshly squeezed lime juice**

Comment: An apricot Daiquiri with extra interest courtesy of pineapple.

NANTUCKET

Glass: Collins
Garnish: Lime wedge
Method: **SHAKE** all ingredients with ice and strain into ice-filled glass.

2	shot(s)	**Light white rum**
3	shot(s)	**Ocean Spray cranberry juice**
2	shot(s)	**Freshly squeezed golden grapefruit juice**

Origin: Popularised by the Cheers bar chain, this is named after the beautiful island off Cape Cod.
Comment: Essentially a Seabreeze with rum in place of vodka.

N

NAPOLEON MARTINI

Glass: Martini
Garnish: Lemon peel twist
Method: **SHAKE** all ingredients with ice and fine strain into chilled glass.

2	shot(s)	**Plymouth gin**
1/4	shot(s)	**Cointreau triple sec**
1/2	shot(s)	**Dubonnet Red**
1/4	shot(s)	**Fernet Branca**
1/2	shot(s)	**Chilled mineral water** (omit if wet ice)

Origin: Adapted from a recipe in Harry Craddock's 1930 Savoy Cocktail Book.
Comment: A beautifully balanced, very approachable, rust coloured Martini.

NARANJA DAIQUIRI

Glass: Martini
Garnish: Orange slice on rim
Method: **SHAKE** all ingredients with ice and fine strain into chilled glass.

1 3/4	shot(s)	**Light white rum**
3/4	shot(s)	**Grand Marnier liqueur**
1	shot(s)	**Freshly squeezed orange juice**
1/2	shot(s)	**Freshly squeezed lime juice**
1/8	shot(s)	**Sugar syrup (2 sugar to 1 water)**

Comment: The Latino version of an orange Daiquiri.

NATHALIA [NEW #7]

Glass: Old-fashioned
Garnish: Orange zest twist
Method: **STIR** all ingredients with ice and strain into ice-filled glass.

2	shot(s)	**Rémy Martin cognac**
3/4	shot(s)	**Yellow Chartreuse liqueur**
3/4	shot(s)	**Giffard crème de banane du Brésil**
1	shot(s)	**Fee Brothers orange bitters**

Origin: Adapted from a drink discovered in 2006 at English Bar, Regina Hotel, Paris, France.
Comment: Herbal bananas and cognac. Be warned, the subtle sweetness conceals its strength.

NATURAL DAIQUIRI

Glass: Martini
Garnish: Lime wedge
Method: **SHAKE** all ingredients with ice and fine strain into chilled glass.

2	shot(s)	**Light white rum (or aged rum)**
1/2	shot(s)	**Freshly squeezed lime juice**
1/4	shot(s)	**Sugar syrup (2 sugar to 1 water)**
1/2	shot(s)	**Chilled mineral water** (omit if wet ice)

Variant: Flavoured syrups may be substituted for sugar syrup. Alternatively you can use flavoured rum (see Vanilla Daiquiri) or add fresh fruit and/or fruit juice and/or fruit liqueur (see Melon Daiquiri etc.).
Origin: Created in 1896 by Jennings Cox, an American engineer who was working at a mine near Santiago, Cuba.
Comment: A deliciously simple, clean, refreshing sour drink.

NAUTILUS

Glass: Collins (or Nautilus seashell)
Garnish: Mint sprig
Method: **SHAKE** all ingredients with ice and strain into ice-filled glass. Serve with straws.

2	shot(s)	**Partida tequila**
2	shot(s)	**Ocean Spray cranberry juice**
1	shot(s)	**Freshly squeezed lime juice**
1/2	shot(s)	**Sugar syrup (2 sugar to 1 water)**

Origin: Adapted from a drink created by Victor Bergeron (Trader Vic).
Comment: Basically a Margarita lengthened with cranberry juice.

NAVIGATOR

Glass: Martini
Garnish: Lemon zest twist
Method: **SHAKE** all ingredients with ice and fine strain into chilled glass.

2	shot(s)	**Plymouth gin**
1	shot(s)	**Luxardo limoncello liqueur**
1	shot(s)	**Squeezed pink grapefruit juice**

Origin: Created in 2005 by Jamie Terrell, London, England.
Comment: This fruity, grapefruit-led drink is pleasantly bitter and sour.

NAVY GROG

Glass: Old-fashioned
Garnish: Lemon wedge
Method: STIR honey with rum in base of shaker to dissolve honey. Add next three ingredients, **SHAKE** with ice and strain into ice-filled glass.

3	spoons	**Runny honey**
$1^1/2$	shot(s)	**Pusser's Navy rum**
$^1/4$	shot(s)	**Freshly squeezed lime juice**
$2^1/2$	shot(s)	**Chilled mineral water**
2	dashes	**Angostura aromatic bitters**

Variant: Also great served hot. Top with boiling water and garnish with a cinnamon stick.
Comment: An extremely drinkable, honeyed cocktail.

NEAL'S BARBADOS COSMOPOLITAN [NEW #7]

Glass: Martini
Garnish: Orange zest twist
Method: SHAKE all ingredients with ice and fine strain into chilled glass.

$1^1/4$	shot(s)	**Golden rum**
$^3/4$	shot(s)	**Cointreau triple sec**
$^1/2$	shot(s)	**Freshly squeezed lime juice**
$1^1/2$	shot(s)	**Ocean Spray cranberry juice**

Origin: Discovered in 2006 at Bix, San Francisco, USA.
Comment: Your standard Cosmo made more complex by a slug of warm Caribbean spirit.

NEGRONI

Glass: Old-fashioned
Garnish: Orange zest twist
Method: STIR all ingredients with ice and strain into ice-filled glass.

1	shot(s)	**Plymouth gin**
1	shot(s)	**Campari**
1	shot(s)	**Sweet vermouth**

Variant: Serve in a Collins glass topped with soda water (club soda).
Origin: This drink takes its name from Count Camillo Negroni. In the mid-1920s, while drinking at the Casoni Bar in Florence, Italy, he is said to have asked for an Americano 'with a bit more kick'.
Comment: Bitter and dry, but very tasty.

NEGUS (HOT)

Glass: Toddy
Garnish: Dust with freshly ground nutmeg
Method: Place bar spoon in warmed glass. **POUR** all ingredients into glass and **STIR**.

3	shot(s)	**Warre's Otima Tawny Port**
1	shot(s)	**Freshly squeezed lemon juice**
$^1/2$	shot(s)	**Sugar syrup (2 sugar to 1 water)**
Top up with		**Boiling water**

Variant: Bishop
Origin: Colonel Francis Negus was the MP for Ipswich from 1717 to 1732. He created this diluted version of the original Bishop.
Comment: A tangy, citrussy hot drink.

NEVADA DAIQUIRI

Garnish: Lime wedge on rim
Method: SHAKE all ingredients with ice and fine strain into chilled glass.

2	shot(s)	**Pusser's Navy rum**
1	shot(s)	**Freshly squeezed grapefruit juice**
$^1/2$	shot(s)	**Freshly squeezed lime juice**
$^1/2$	shot(s)	**Sugar syrup (2 sugar to 1 water)**

Comment: A pungent Daiquiri with the intense flavour of Navy rum.

NEW ORLEANS MULE

Glass: Collins
Garnish: Lime wedge
Method: SHAKE first four ingredients with ice and fine strain into ice-filled glass. **TOP** with ginger beer.

2	shot(s)	**Buffalo Trace bourbon whiskey**
1	shot(s)	**Kahlúa coffee liqueur**
1	shot(s)	**Pressed pineapple juice**
$^1/2$	shot(s)	**Freshly squeezed lime juice**
Top up with		**Ginger beer**

Comment: A spicy, full-flavoured taste of the South.

NEW ORLEANS PUNCH

Glass: Collins
Garnish: Lemon slice
Method: SHAKE all ingredients with ice and strain into glass filled with crushed ice. Serve with straws.

$1^1/2$	shot(s)	**Buffalo Trace bourbon whiskey**
$^3/4$	shot(s)	**Aged rum**
$1^1/2$	shot(s)	**Chambord black raspberry liqueur**
$^3/4$	shot(s)	**Freshly squeezed lemon juice**
3	shot(s)	**Cold black camomile tea**

Comment: Raspberry is the predominant flavour in this long drink.

NEW PORT CODEBREAKER

Glass: Collins
Method: SHAKE all ingredients with ice and strain into ice-filled glass.

1	shot(s)	**Partida tequila**
1	shot(s)	**Pusser's Navy rum**
$^1/2$	shot(s)	**Bols advocaat liqueur**
$^1/2$	shot(s)	**Coco López cream of coconut**
4	shot(s)	**Freshly squeezed orange juice**

Origin: Adapted from a cocktail discovered in 1999 at Porter's Bar, Covent Garden, London.
Comment: This straw yellow drink is a most unusual mix of ingredients.

NEW YEAR'S ABSOLUTION

Glass: Old-fashioned
Garnish: Mint sprig
Method: STIR honey with absinthe in base of shaker until honey dissolves. Add apple juice, **SHAKE** with ice and strain into ice-filled glass. **TOP** with ginger ale and stir.

2	spoons	**Runny honey**
1	shot(s)	**La Fée Parisienne (68%) absinthe**
1	shot(s)	**Pressed apple juice**
Top up with		**Ginger ale**

Comment: The green fairy, tamed with honey and spiced with ginger.

NEW YORKER 

Glass: Martini
Garnish: Orange zest twist
Method: SHAKE all ingredients with ice and fine strain into chilled glass.

2	shot(s)	**Buffalo Trace bourbon whiskey**
1	shot(s)	**Claret (red wine)**
1/2	shot(s)	**Freshly squeezed lemon juice**
1/2	shot(s)	**Sugar syrup (2 sugar to 1 water)**

Comment: Sweet 'n' sour whiskey and wine.

NEW PORT CODEBREAKER

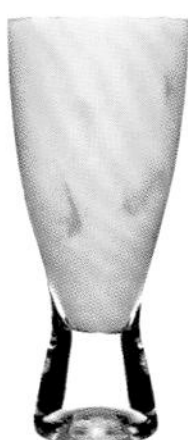

Glass: Collins
Method: SHAKE all ingredients with ice and strain into ice-filled glass.

1	shot(s)	**Partida tequila**
1	shot(s)	**Pusser's Navy rum**
1/2	shot(s)	**Bols advocaat liqueur**
1/2	shot(s)	**Coco López cream of coconut**
4	shot(s)	**Freshly squeezed orange juice**

Origin: Adapted from a cocktail discovered in 1999 at Porter's Bar, Covent Garden, London.
Comment: This straw yellow drink is a most unusual mix of ingredients.

NIAGARA FALLS

Glass: Flute
Garnish: Physalis
Method: SHAKE first four ingredients with ice and strain into chilled glass. **TOP** with ginger ale and lightly stir.

1	shot(s)	**Ketel One vodka**
1	shot(s)	**Grand Marnier liqueur**
1/2	shot(s)	**Freshly squeezed lemon juice**
1/4	shot(s)	**Sugar syrup (2 sugar to 1 water)**
Top up with		**Ginger ale**

Comment: Ginger ale and orange complement each other, fortified by vodka.

NICE PEAR-TINI

Glass: Martini
Garnish: Pear slice on rim
Method: SHAKE all ingredients with ice and fine strain into chilled glass.

1	shot(s)	**Rémy Martin cognac**
1/2	shot(s)	**Pear & cognac liqueur**
1/2	shot(s)	**Poire William eau de vie**
2	shot(s)	**Freshly extracted pear juice**
1/4	shot(s)	**Sugar syrup (2 sugar to 1 water)**

Origin: Created in 2002 by yours truly.
Comment: Spirited, rich and fruity.

NICKY FINN

Glass: Martini
Garnish: Lemon zest twist
Method: SHAKE all ingredients with ice and fine strain into chilled glass.

1	shot(s)	**Rémy Martin cognac**
1	shot(s)	**Cointreau triple sec**
1	shot(s)	**Freshly squeezed lemon juice**
1/4	shot(s)	**Pernod anis**

Origin: Adapted from a recipe in 'Cocktail: The Drinks Bible for the 21st Century' by Paul Harrington and Laura Moorhead.
Comment: Basically a Sidecar spiked with an aniseedy dash of Pernod.

NICKY'S FIZZ

Glass: Collins
Garnish: Orange slice
Method: SHAKE first two ingredients with ice and strain into ice-filled glass. **TOP** with soda, lightly stir and serve with straws.

2	shot(s)	**Plymouth gin**
2	shot(s)	**Freshly squeezed grapefruit juice**
Top up with		**Soda water (from siphon)**

Comment: A dry, refreshing, long drink.

NIGHT & DAY

Glass: Flute
Garnish: Orange zest twist
Method: POUR ingredients into chilled glass.

1/2	shot(s)	**Campari**
1/2	shot(s)	**Grand Marnier liqueur**
Top up with		**Brut champagne**

Comment: Dry, aromatic, orange champagne.

NIGHTMARE MARTINI

Glass: Martini
Garnish: Maraschino cherry
Method: SHAKE all ingredients with ice and fine strain into chilled glass.

1	shot(s)	**Plymouth gin**
1	shot(s)	**Dubonnet Red**
$^1/_2$	shot(s)	**Cherry (brandy) liqueur**
2	shot(s)	**Freshly squeezed orange juice**

Comment: Pleasant enough, with hints of cherry. Hardly a nightmare.

NINE-20-SEVEN

Glass: Flute
Method: POUR ingredients into chilled glass and lightly stir.

$^1/_4$	shot(s)	**Vanilla infused Ketel One vodka**
$^1/_4$	shot(s)	**Cuarenta Y Tres (Licor 43)**
Top up with		**Brut champagne**

Origin: Created in 2002 by Damian Caldwell at Home Bar, London, England. Damian was lost for a name until a customer asked the time.
Comment: Champagne with a hint of vanilla.

NO. 10 LEMONADE

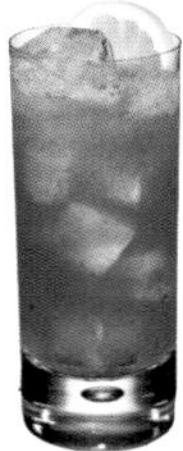

Glass: Collins
Garnish: Lemon slice
Method: MUDDLE blueberries in base of shaker. Add next three ingredients, **SHAKE** with ice and fine strain into ice filled glass. **TOP** with soda, lightly stir and serve with straws.

12	fresh	**Blueberries**
2	shot(s)	**Light white rum**
$1^1/_2$	shot(s)	**Freshly squeezed lemon juice**
$^3/_4$	shot(s)	**Sugar syrup (2 sugar to 1 water)**
Top up with		**Soda water (club soda)**

Origin: Adapted from a drink discovered in 2006 at Double Seven, New York City, USA.
Comment: Basically a long blueberry Daiquiri.

NOBLE EUROPE

Glass: Old-fashioned
Garnish: Orange slice in glass
Method: SHAKE all ingredients with ice and strain into glass filled with crushed ice.

$1^1/_2$	shot(s)	**Tokaji Hungarian wine**
1	shot(s)	**Ketel One vodka**
1	shot(s)	**Freshly squeezed orange juice**
1	dash	**Vanilla essence**

Origin: Created in 2002 by Dan Spink at Browns, St Martin's Lane, London, England.
Variant: Also great served 'up' in a Martini glass.
Comment: A delicious cocktail that harnesses the rich, sweet flavours of Tokaji and delivers them very approachably.

NOME

Glass: Martini
Garnish: Mint leaf
Method: STIR all ingredients with ice and strain into chilled glass.

$1^1/_2$	shot(s)	**Plymouth gin**
1	shot(s)	**Yellow Chartreuse liqueur**
$1^1/_2$	shot(s)	**Tio Pepe Fino sherry**

AKA: Alaska Martini
Origin: A classic cocktail whose origin is unknown.
Comment: This dyslexic gnome is dry and interesting.

NOON

Glass: Martini
Garnish: Orange zest twist
Method: SHAKE all ingredients with ice and strain into chilled glass.

$1^1/_2$	shot(s)	**Plymouth gin**
$^3/_4$	shot(s)	**Dry vermouth**
$^3/_4$	shot(s)	**Sweet vermouth**
$^3/_4$	shot(s)	**Freshly squeezed orange juice**
2	dashes	**Angostura aromatic bitters**
$^1/_2$	fresh	**Egg white**

Comment: This classic cocktail is smooth and aromatic.

NORTHERN LIGHTS

Glass: Martini
Garnish: Star anise
Method: SHAKE all ingredients with ice and fine strain into chilled glass.

$1^1/_2$	shot(s)	**Zubrówka bison vodka**
$^3/_4$	shot(s)	**Apple schnapps liqueur**
1	shot(s)	**Pressed apple juice**
$^1/_2$	shot(s)	**Freshly squeezed lime juice**
$^1/_2$	shot(s)	**Pernod anis**
$^1/_2$	shot(s)	**Sugar syrup (2 sugar to 1 water)**

Origin: Created in 2003 by Stewart Hudson at MJU Bar, Millennium Hotel, London, England.
Comment: Wonderfully refreshing: apple and anis served up on a grassy vodka base.

NORTH POLE MARTINI

Glass: Martini
Method: SHAKE first four ingredients with ice and fine strain into chilled glass. **FLOAT** cream over drink.

2	shot(s)	**Plymouth gin**
1	shot(s)	**Luxardo maraschino liqueur**
$^1/_2$	shot(s)	**Freshly squeezed lemon juice**
$^1/_2$	fresh	**Egg white**
Float		**Double (heavy) cream**

Origin: Adapted from a recipe in the 1947-72 Trader Vic's Bartender's Guide by Victor Bergeron.
Comment: An Aviation smoothed by egg white and cream.

NOT SO COSMO (MOCKTAIL)

Glass: Martini
Garnish: Orange zest twist
Method: SHAKE all ingredients with ice and fine strain into chilled glass.

1 shot(s) **Freshly squeezed orange juice**
1 shot(s) **Ocean Spray cranberry juice**
1 shot(s) **Freshly squeezed lime juice**
1 shot(s) **Freshly squeezed lemon juice**

Origin: Discovered in 2003 at Claridge's Bar, London, England.
Comment: This non-alcoholic cocktail may look like a Cosmo but it doesn't taste like one.

NOVEMBER SEABREEZE (MOCKTAIL)

Glass: Collins
Garnish: Lime wedge
Method: SHAKE first three ingredients with ice and strain into ice-filled glass. **TOP** with soda, gently stir and serve with straws.

2 shot(s) **Ocean Spray cranberry juice**
2 shot(s) **Pressed apple juice**
1 shot(s) **Freshly squeezed lime juice**
Top up with **Soda water (club soda)**

Comment: A superbly refreshing fruity drink, whatever the time of year.

NUCLEAR DAIQUIRI [NEW #7]

Glass: Martini
Garnish: Lime wedge on rim
Method: SHAKE all ingredients with ice and fine strain into chilled glass.

1 shot(s) **Wray & Nephew overproof rum**
3/4 shot(s) **Green Chartreuse liqueur**
1 shot(s) **Freshly squeezed lime juice**
1/4 shot(s) **Velvet Falernum**
1/2 shot(s) **Chilled mineral water** (omit if wet ice)

Origin: Created in 2005 by Gregor de Gruyther at LAB bar, London, England.
Comment: A great way to inflict mutually assured destruction, although there will be fallout the morning after.

NUTCRACKER SWEET

Glass: Martini
Garnish: Dust with cocoa powder
Method: SHAKE all ingredients with ice and fine strain into chilled glass.

2 shot(s) **Ketel One vodka**
1 shot(s) **Giffard white crème de cacao**
3/4 shot(s) **Luxardo Amaretto di Saschira liqueur**

Comment: After dinner, fortified almond and chocolate.

NUTS & BERRIES

Glass: Martini
Garnish: Float raspberry and almond flake
Method: STIR all ingredients with ice and strain into chilled glass.

1 shot(s) **Raspberry flavoured vodka**
1 shot(s) **Almond flavoured vodka**
1/4 shot(s) **Frangelico hazelnut liqueur**
1/4 shot(s) **Chambord black raspberry liqueur**
1 shot(s) **7-Up**

Origin: Created in 2004 by yours truly.
Comment: The inclusion of a carbonate (7-Up) may annoy some classical bartenders but it adds flavour, sweetness and dilution.

NUTTY BERRY'TINI

Glass: Martini
Garnish: Float mint leaf
Method: SHAKE all ingredients with ice and fine strain into chilled glass.

2 shot(s) **Cranberry flavoured vodka**
1/2 shot(s) **Cherry (brandy) liqueur**
1/2 shot(s) **Frangelico hazelnut liqueur**
1/4 shot(s) **Luxardo maraschino liqueur**
1 shot(s) **Ocean Spray cranberry juice**
1/2 shot(s) **Freshly squeezed lime juice**

Origin: Created by yours truly in 2003.
Comment: Cranberry vodka and juice, sweetened with cherry liqueur, dried with lime juice and flavoured with hazelnut.

NUTTY NASHVILLE

Glass: Martini
Garnish: Lemon zest twist
Method: STIR honey with bourbon in base of shaker to dissolve honey. Add other ingredients, **SHAKE** with ice and fine strain into chilled glass.

2 spoon(s) **Runny honey**
2 shot(s) **Buffalo Trace bourbon whiskey**
1 shot(s) **Frangelico hazelnut liqueur**
1 shot(s) **Krupnik honey liqueur**

Origin: Created in 2001 by Jason Fendick at Rockwell, Trafalgar Hotel, London, England.
Comment: Bourbon and hazelnut smoothed and rounded by honey.

NUTTY RUSSIAN

Glass: Old-fashioned
Method: SHAKE all ingredients with ice and strain into ice-filled glass.

1 1/2 shot(s) **Ketel One vodka**
3/4 shot(s) **Frangelico hazelnut liqueur**
3/4 shot(s) **Kahlúa coffee liqueur**

Comment: A Black Russian with hazelnut liqueur.

NUTTY SUMMER

Glass: Martini
Garnish: Drop three dashes of Angostura aromatic bitters onto surface of drink and stir around with a cocktail stick - essential to both the look and flavour.
Method: SHAKE all ingredients with ice and fine strain into chilled glass.

1½	shot(s)	**Bols advocaat liqueur**
¾	shot(s)	**Luxardo Amaretto di Saschira liqueur**
¾	shot(s)	**Malibu coconut rum liqueur**
¾	shot(s)	**Pressed pineapple juice**
½	shot(s)	**Double (heavy) cream**

Origin: Created in 2001 by Daniel Spink at Hush Up, London, England.
Comment: This subtle, dessert style cocktail is packed with flavour. A superb after dinner tipple for summer.

OATMEAL COOKIE

Glass: Shot
Method: SHAKE all ingredients with ice and fine strain into chilled glass.

½	shot(s)	**Teichenné butterscotch Schnapps**
¼	shot(s)	**Cinnamon schnapps liqueur**
¾	shot(s)	**Irish cream liqueur**

Comment: A well balanced, creamy shot with hints of butterscotch and cinnamon.

OÁZA

Glass: Old-fashioned
Garnish: Lime wedge
Method: SHAKE all ingredients with ice and strain into ice-filled glass.

2	shot(s)	**Becherovka**
¾	shot(s)	**Freshly squeezed lime juice**
¼	shot(s)	**Sugar syrup (2 sugar to 1 water)**

Origin: A popular drink in the Czech Republic where Becherovka, a herbal liquor, is the national drink.
Comment: Herbal and bittersweet. Not for everyone.

OBITUARY [NEW #7]

Glass: Martini
Garnish: Olive on stick
Method: STIR all ingredients with ice and strain into chilled glass.

2	shot(s)	**Plymouth gin**
⅛	shot(s)	**La Fée Parisienne (68%) absinthe**
¼	shot(s)	**Dry vermouth**

Comment: Way to go! A Dry Martini with a dash of the green fairy.

ODDBALL MANHATTAN DRY

Glass: Martini
Garnish: Two maraschino cherries
Method: STIR all ingredients with ice and strain into chilled glass.

2½	shot(s)	**Buffalo Trace bourbon whiskey**
1	shot(s)	**Dry vermouth**
½	shot(s)	**Yellow Chartreuse liqueur**
3	dashes	**Angostura aromatic bitters**

Comment: Not as oddball as it sounds, the Chartreuse combines harmoniously.

O'HENRY

Glass: Collins
Garnish: Lemon slice
Method: SHAKE first two ingredients with ice and strain into ice-filled glass. **TOP** with ginger ale, lightly stir and serve with straws.

2	shot(s)	**Buffalo Trace bourbon whiskey**
1	shot(s)	**Bénédictine D.O.M. liqueur**
Top up with		**Ginger ale**

Origin: Discovered in 2006 at Brandy Library, New York City, USA.
Comment: Herbal whiskey and ginger.

OH GOSH!

Glass: Martini
Garnish: Lemon zest twist
Method: SHAKE all ingredients with ice and fine strain into chilled glass.

1½	shot(s)	**Light white rum**
1	shot(s)	**Cointreau triple sec**
½	shot(s)	**Freshly squeezed lime juice**
¼	shot(s)	**Sugar syrup (2 sugar to 1 water)**
½	shot(s)	**Chilled mineral water** (omit if wet ice)

Origin: Created by Tony Conigliaro in 2001 at Isola, London, England. A customer requested a Daiquiri with a difference – when this was served he took one sip and exclaimed "Oh gosh!".
Comment: A very subtle orange twist on the classic Daiquiri.

OIL SLICK

Glass: Shot
Method: Refrigerate ingredients then **LAYER** in chilled glass by carefully pouring in the following order.

¾	shot(s)	**Opal Nera black sambuca**
¾	shot(s)	**Irish cream liqueur**

Comment: Whiskey cream and liquorice.

OLD FASHIONED

As with the Martini, the glass this cocktail is served in has taken the name of the drink. Supposedly the cocktail was created at the Pendennis Club in Louisville, Kentucky, for a Kentucky Colonel (and bourbon distiller) named James E. Pepper. As the drink predates the club, this cannot be true, but Pepper seems to have promoted it heavily to help market his product.

In the US orange segments and sometimes even a maraschino cherry are regularly muddled in this drink: the practice probably originated during Prohibition as a means of disguising rough spirits. As Crosby Gaige wrote in 1944, "Serious-minded persons omit fruit salad from Old Fashioneds."

OLD FASHIONED #1 (CLASSIC VERSION)

Glass: Old-fashioned
Garnish: Orange (or lemon) twist
Method: STIR one shot of bourbon with two ice cubes in a glass. Add sugar syrup and Angostura and two more ice cubes. Stir some more and add another two ice cubes and the rest of the bourbon. Stir lots more and add more ice.

2 1/2 shot(s) **Buffalo Trace bourbon whiskey**
1/2 shot(s) **Sugar syrup (2 sugar to 1 water)**
3 dashes **Angostura aromatic bitters**

Origin: This drink may well have been promoted by the 19th century distiller James E. Pepper.
Comment: The melting and stirring in of ice cubes is essential to the dilution and taste of this classic.

OLD FASHIONED #2 (US VERSION)

Glass: Old-fashioned
Garnish: Orange zest twist & maraschino cherry
Method: MUDDLE orange and cherries in base of shaker. Add other ingredients, **SHAKE** with ice and fine strain into ice-filled glass.

2 whole **Maraschino cherries**
1 fresh **Orange slice (cut into eight segments)**
2 shot(s) **Buffalo Trace bourbon whiskey**
1/8 shot(s) **Maraschino syrup (from the cherry jar)**
2 dashes **Angostura aromatic bitters**

Comment: This drink is often mixed in the glass in which it is to be served. Shaking better incorporates the flavours produced by muddling and fine straining removes the orange peel and cherry skin.

OLD FASHIONED CADDY

Glass: Old-fashioned
Garnish: Orange slice & cherry on stick (sail)
Method: SHAKE all ingredients with ice and strain into ice-filled glass.

2 shot(s) **Scotch whisky**
1/2 shot(s) **Cherry (brandy) liqueur**
1/2 shot(s) **Sweet vermouth**
2 dashes **Angostura aromatic bitters**

Origin: Created in 2005 by Wayne Collins, London, England.
Comment: Rich, red and packed with flavour.

OLD FLAME [NEW #7]

Glass: Martini
Garnish: Flamed orange peel
Method: SHAKE all ingredients with ice and fine strain into chilled glass.

1 shot(s) **Plymouth gin**
1/2 shot(s) **Cointreau triple sec**
1/2 shot(s) **Sweet vermouth**
1/4 shot(s) **Campari**
1 1/2 shot(s) **Freshly squeezed orange juice**

Origin: Created by Dale DeGroff, New York, USA.
Comment: Bittersweet, orchard fresh orange charged with gin.

OLD PAL [UPDATED #7]

Glass: Old-fashioned
Garnish: Orange slice
Method: STIR all ingredients with ice and strain into ice-filled glass.

1 1/4 shot(s) **Canadian whiskey**
1 1/4 shot(s) **Dry vermouth**
1 1/4 shot(s) **Campari**

Origin: Adapted from Harry Craddock's 1930 'The Savoy Cocktail Book'.
Comment: A dry, bitter sipper for the more hardened palate.

OLE

Glass: Martini
Garnish: Orange wheel on rim
Method: SHAKE all ingredients with ice and fine strain into chilled glass.

2 shot(s) **Rémy Martin cognac**
3/4 shot(s) **Cuarenta Y Tres (Licor 43) liqueur**
1 1/2 shot(s) **Freshly squeezed orange juice**

Comment: Vanilla, orange and brandy combine well.

OLYMPIC

Glass: Martini
Garnish: Orange zest twist
Method: SHAKE all ingredients with ice and fine strain into chilled glass.

1 1/4 shot(s) **Rémy Martin cognac**
1 1/4 shot(s) **Grand Marnier liqueur**
1 1/4 shot(s) **Freshly squeezed orange juice**

Origin: Adapted from a recipe in Harry Craddock's 1930 Savoy Cocktail Book.
Comment: The perfect balance of cognac and orange juice. One to celebrate the 2012 Games perhaps.

ONION RING MARTINI

Glass: Martini
Garnish: Onion ring
Method: MUDDLE onion in base of shaker. Add other ingredients, **SHAKE** with ice and fine strain into chilled glass.

2 ring(s) **Fresh red onion**
1 shot(s) **Sake**
2 shot(s) **Plymouth gin**
3 dashes **Fee Brothers orange bitters**
1/8 shot(s) **Sugar syrup (2 sugar to 1 water)**

Origin: Reputed to have been created at the Bamboo Bar, Bangkok, Thailand.
Comment: Certainly one of the most obscure Martini variations – drinkable, but leaves you with onion breath.

OPAL

Glass: Martini
Garnish: Orange zest twist
Method: SHAKE all ingredients with ice and fine strain into chilled glass.

2	shot(s)	**Plymouth gin**
1/2	shot(s)	**Cointreau triple sec**
1 1/4	shot(s)	**Freshly squeezed orange juice**
1/4	shot(s)	**Sugar syrup (2 sugar to 1 water)**
1/8	shot(s)	**Orange flower water (optional)**

Origin: Adapted from the 1920s recipe.
Comment: Fresh, fragrant flavours of orange zest and gin.

OPAL CAFÉ

Glass: Shot
Method: SHAKE first two ingredients with ice and fine strain into chilled glass. **FLOAT** thin layer of cream over drink.

1/2	shot(s)	**Opal Nera black sambuca**
1/2	shot(s)	**Cold espresso coffee**
Float		**Double (heavy) cream**

Comment: A great liquorice and coffee drink to sip or shoot.

OPENING SHOT

Glass: Shot
Method: SHAKE all ingredients with ice and fine strain into chilled glass.

1	shot(s)	**Buffalo Trace bourbon whiskey**
1/2	shot(s)	**Sweet vermouth**
1/8	shot(s)	**Pomegranate (grenadine) syrup**

Variant: Double the quantities and strain into a Martini glass and you have the 1920s classic I based this drink on.
Comment: Basically a miserly Sweet Manhattan.

OPERA

Glass: Martini
Garnish: Orange zest twist
Method: SHAKE all ingredients with ice and fine strain into chilled glass.

2	shot(s)	**Plymouth gin**
2	shot(s)	**Dubonnet Red**
1/4	shot(s)	**Luxardo maraschino liqueur**
3	dashes	**Fee Brothers orange bitters**

Origin: Adapted from the classic 1920s cocktail.
Comment: Dubonnet smoothes the gin while maraschino adds floral notes.

ORANG-A-TANG

Glass: Sling
Garnish: Orange slice on rim
Method: SHAKE first five ingredients with ice and strain into ice-filled glass. **FLOAT** layer of rum over drink.

1 1/2	shot(s)	**Ketel One vodka**
3/4	shot(s)	**Cointreau triple sec**
2	shot(s)	**Freshly squeezed orange juice**
1/2	shot(s)	**Freshly squeezed lime juice**
1/4	shot(s)	**Pomegranate (grenadine) syrup**
1/2	shot(s)	**Wood's 100 old navy rum**

Comment: Orange predominates in this long, tangy, tropical cooler.

ORANGE BLOOM MARTINI

Glass: Martini
Garnish: Maraschino cherry
Method: SHAKE all ingredients with ice and fine strain into chilled glass.

2	shot(s)	**Plymouth gin**
1	shot(s)	**Cointreau triple sec**
1	shot(s)	**Sweet vermouth**

Origin: Adapted from a recipe in the 1930s edition of the Savoy Cocktail Book by Harry Craddock.
Comment: Strong, fruity zesty orange laced with gin.

ORANGE BLOSSOM

Glass: Old-fashioned
Garnish: Orange zest twist
Method: SHAKE all ingredients with ice and strain into ice-filled glass.

1 1/2	shot(s)	**Plymouth gin**
1/2	shot(s)	**Cointreau triple sec**
1 1/2	shot(s)	**Freshly squeezed orange juice**
1/2	shot(s)	**Freshly squeezed lime juice**
1/8	shot(s)	**Pomegranate (grenadine) syrup**

Variant: Served long in a Collins glass this becomes a Harvester.
Comment: Gin sweetened with liqueur and grenadine, and soured with lime.

ORANGE BRÛLÉE

Glass: Martini
Garnish: Dust with cocoa powder
Method: SHAKE first three ingredients with ice and fine strain into chilled glass. **FLOAT** thin layer of cream over drink and turn glass to spread evenly.

1 1/2	shot(s)	**Luxardo Amaretto di Saschira liqueur**
1 1/2	shot(s)	**Grand Marnier liqueur**
3/4	shot(s)	**Rémy Martin cognac**
1/4	shot(s)	**Double (heavy) cream**

Origin: Created in 2005 by Xavier Laigle at Bar Le Forum, Paris, France.
Comment: A great looking, beautifully balanced after-dinner drink.

O

ORANGE CUSTARD MARTINI

Glass: Martini
Garnish: Orange zest twist
Method: SHAKE all ingredients with ice and fine strain into chilled glass.

2	shot(s)	**Bols advocaat liqueur**
1	shot(s)	**Tuaca Italian liqueur**
1/2	shot(s)	**Grand Marnier liqueur**
1/4	shot(s)	**Vanilla syrup**

Origin: I created this drink in 2002 after rediscovering advocaat on a trip to Amsterdam.
Comment: A smooth, creamy orangey dessert cocktail

ORANGE DAIQUIRI #1

Glass: Old-fashioned
Garnish: Orange zest twist
Method: SHAKE all ingredients with ice and fine strain into ice-filled glass.

2	shot(s)	**Aged rum**
3/4	shot(s)	**Freshly squeezed orange juice**
1/2	shot(s)	**Freshly squeezed lime juice**
1/4	shot(s)	**Sugar syrup (2 sugar to 1 water)**

AKA: Bolo
Origin: My take on a popular drink.
Comment: Far more serious than it looks. Sweet and sour in harmony.

ORANGE DAIQUIRI #2

Glass: Martini
Garnish: Orange zest twist
Method: SHAKE all ingredients with ice and fine strain into chilled glass.

2	shot(s)	**Clément Créole Shrubb liqueur**
1/2	shot(s)	**Freshly squeezed lime juice**
3/4	shot(s)	**Chilled mineral water** (omit if wet ice)

Variant: Derby Daiquiri
Origin: I conceived this drink in 1998, after visiting the company which was then importing Créole Shrubb. I took a bottle to London's Met Bar and Ben Reed made me my first Orange Daiquiri.
Comment: Créole Shrubb is an unusual liqueur made by infusing orange peel in casks of mature Martinique rum.

ORANGE MARTINI

Glass: Martini
Garnish: Orange zest twist
Method: SHAKE all ingredients with ice and fine strain into chilled glass.

2	shot(s)	**Plymouth gin**
1	shot(s)	**Freshly squeezed orange juice**
1/2	shot(s)	**Sweet vermouth**
1/4	shot(s)	**Sugar syrup (2 sugar to 1 water)**
3	dashes	**Fee Brothers orange bitters**

Origin: Adapted from the Orange Cocktail and Orange Martini Cocktail in the 1930s edition of the Savoy Cocktail Book by Harry Craddock.
Comment: A sophisticated, complex balance of orange and gin.

ORANGE MOJITO

Glass: Collins
Garnish: Mint sprig
Method: Lightly **MUDDLE** mint (just to bruise) in base of glass. Add other ingredients and half fill glass with crushed ice. **CHURN** (stir) with bar spoon. Fill with more crushed ice and churn some more. **TOP** with soda, stir and serve with straws.

8	fresh	**Mint leaves**
1 1/2	shot(s)	**Orange zest infused Ketel One vodka**
1/2	shot(s)	**Mandarine Napoléon liqueur**
1/2	shot(s)	**Light white rum**
1	shot(s)	**Freshly squeezed lime juice**
1/2	shot(s)	**Sugar syrup (2 sugar to 1 water)**
Top up with		**Soda water (club soda)**

Origin: Created in 2001 by Jamie MacDonald while working in Sydney, Australia.
Comment: Mint and orange combine to make a wonderfully fresh drink.

ABSTAINER: A WEAK PERSON WHO YIELDS TO THE TEMPTATION OF DENYING HIMSELF A PLEASURE.

ORANJINIHA

Glass: Collins
Garnish: Orange slice in glass
Method: SHAKE all ingredients with ice and strain into glass filled with crushed ice.

2	shot(s)	**Orange zest infused Ketel One vodka**
3	shot(s)	**Freshly squeezed orange juice**
1	shot(s)	**Freshly squeezed lemon juice**
1	shot(s)	**Sugar syrup (2 sugar to 1 water)**

Origin: Created in 2002 by Alex Kammerling, London, England.
Comment: A tall, richly flavoured orange drink.

ORCHARD BREEZE [UPDATED #7]

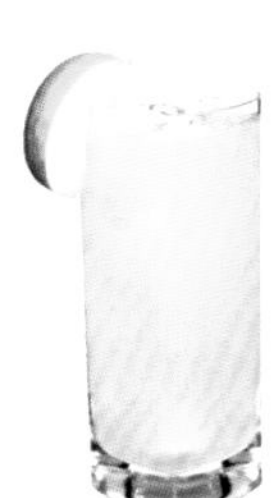

Glass: Collins
Garnish: Apple slice on rim
Method: SHAKE all ingredients with ice and strain into ice-filled glass.

2	shot(s)	**Ketel One vodka**
1	shot(s)	**St-Germain elderflower liqueur**
1	shot(s)	**Sauvignon Blanc wine**
2	shot(s)	**Pressed apple juice**
1/4	shot(s)	**Freshly squeezed lime juice**

Origin: Adapted from a drink created in 2002 by Wayne Collins, London, England.
Comment: A refreshing, summery combination of white wine, apple, lime and elderflower laced with vodka.

ORIENTAL GRAPE MARTINI

Glass: Martini
Garnish: Grapes on stick
Method: MUDDLE grapes in base of shaker. Add other ingredients, **SHAKE** with ice and fine strain into chilled glass.

12 fresh **Seedless white grapes**
1 1/2 shot(s) **Ketel One vodka**
1 1/2 shot(s) **Sake**
1/4 shot(s) **Sugar syrup (2 sugar to 1 water)**

Variants: Double Grape Martini, Grape Martini, Grapple.
Origin: Created by yours truly in 2004.
Comment: Sake adds some oriental intrigue to what would otherwise be a plain old Grape Martini.

ORIENTAL TART

Glass: Martini
Garnish: Peeled lychee in drink
Method: SHAKE all ingredients with ice and fine strain into chilled glass.

1 1/2 shot(s) **Plymouth gin**
1 shot(s) **Soho lychee liqueur**
2 shot(s) **Freshly squeezed golden grapefruit juice**

Origin: Created in 2004 by yours truly.
Comment: A sour, tart, fruity Martini with more than a hint of lychee.

OSMO

Glass: Martini
Garnish: Orange zest twist
Method: SHAKE all ingredients with ice and fine strain into chilled glass.

2 shot(s) **Sake**
1/2 shot(s) **Cointreau triple sec**
1/4 shot(s) **Freshly squeezed lime juice**
1 1/2 shot(s) **Ocean Spray cranberry juice**
1/8 shot(s) **Sugar syrup (2 sugar to 1 water)**

Origin: Adapted from a drink discovered in 2005 at Mo Bar, Landmark Mandarin Oriental Hotel, Hong Kong, China.
Comment: A sake based Cosmopolitan.

OUZI

Glass: Shot
Method: SHAKE all ingredients with ice and fine strain into chilled glass.

3/4 shot(s) **Ketel One vodka**
1/2 shot(s) **Ouzo**
1/4 shot(s) **Sugar syrup (2 sugar to 1 water)**
1/4 shot(s) **Freshly squeezed lemon juice**

Comment: A lemon and liquorice shooter.

PADOVANI [NEW #7]

Glass: Old-fashioned
Garnish: Lemon zest twist
Method: SHAKE all ingredients with ice and strain into ice-filled glass.

2 shot(s) **Scotch whisky**
2 shot(s) **St-Germain elderflower liqueur**

Origin: Created in 2006 and named after a fellow whisky fan, Xavier Padovani.
Comment: The peaty Scotch combines wonderfully with the floral, delicate elderflower liqueur.

PAGO PAGO

Glass: Martini
Garnish: Lime wedge on rim
Method: SHAKE all ingredients with ice and fine strain into chilled glass.

2 shot(s) **Golden rum**
1/4 shot(s) **Green Chartreuse liqueur**
1/2 shot(s) **Giffard white crème de cacao**
1/2 shot(s) **Freshly squeezed lime juice**
1/8 shot(s) **Sugar syrup (2 sugar to 1 water)**
1/2 shot(s) **Chilled mineral water** (omit if wet ice)

Comment: A Daiquiri with a liqueur twist.

PAINKILLER

Glass: Collins
Garnish: Pineapple wedge & cherry
Method: SHAKE all ingredients with ice and strain into ice-filled glass.

2 shot(s) **Pusser's Navy rum**
2 shot(s) **Pressed pineapple juice**
1 shot(s) **Freshly squeezed orange juice**
1 shot(s) **Coco López cream of coconut**

Origin: From the Soggy Dollar Bar on the island of Jost Van Dyke in the British Virgin Islands. The bar's name is logical, as most of the clientele are sailors and there is no dock. Hence they have to swim ashore, often paying for drinks with wet dollars.
Comment: Full-flavoured and fruity.

PAISLEY MARTINI

Glass: Martini
Garnish: Lemon zest twist
Method: STIR all ingredients with ice and strain into chilled glass.

2 1/2 shot(s) **Plymouth gin**
1/2 shot(s) **Dry vermouth**
1/4 shot(s) **Scotch whisky**

Comment: A dry Martini for those with a penchant for Scotch.

PALE RIDER

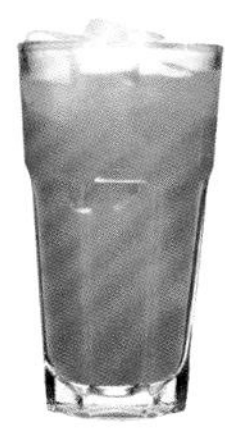

Glass: Collins
Garnish: Lime wedge
Method: SHAKE all ingredients with ice and strain into ice-filled glass.

2	shot(s)	**Raspberry flavoured vodka**
½	shot(s)	**Teichenné Peach Schnapps Liqueur**
2	shot(s)	**Ocean Spray cranberry juice**
1	shot(s)	**Pressed pineapple juice**
1	shot(s)	**Freshly squeezed lime juice**
½	shot(s)	**Sugar syrup (2 sugar to 1 water)**

Origin: Created in 1997 by Wayne Collins at Navajo Joe, London, England.
Comment: Sweet and fruity.

PALERMO

Glass: Martini
Garnish: Vanilla pod
Method: SHAKE all ingredients with ice and fine strain into chilled glass.

1½	shot(s)	**Vanilla infused light white rum**
1	shot(s)	**Sauvignon Blanc wine**
1¼	shot(s)	**Pressed pineapple juice**
¼	shot(s)	**Sugar syrup (2 sugar to 1 water)**

Origin: Adapted from a cocktail discovered in 2001 at Hotel du Vin, Bristol, England.
Comment: This smooth cocktail beautifully combines vanilla rum with tart wine and the sweetness of the pineapple juice.

PALL MALL MARTINI

Glass: Martini
Garnish: Orange zest twist
Method: SHAKE all ingredients with ice and fine strain into chilled glass.

1	shot(s)	**Plymouth gin**
1	shot(s)	**Dry vermouth**
1	shot(s)	**Sweet vermouth**
¼	shot(s)	**Giffard white crème de cacao**
1	dashes	**Fee Brothers orange bitters**

Comment: A classic Martini served 'perfect' with the tiniest hint of chocolate.

PALM BEACH

Glass: Martini
Garnish: Maraschino cherry
Method: SHAKE all ingredients with ice and fine strain into chilled glass.

2½	shot(s)	**Plymouth gin**
½	shot(s)	**Sweet vermouth**
1	shot(s)	**Squeezed pink grapefruit juice**

Origin: A classic from the 1940s.
Comment: Dry, aromatic and packs one hell of a punch.

PALM SPRINGS

Glass: Collins
Garnish: Apple slice & mint sprig
Method: SHAKE all ingredients with ice and strain into glass filled with crushed ice.

4	fresh	**Mint leaves**
1	shot(s)	**Passoã passion fruit liqueur**
1	shot(s)	**Golden rum**
¼	shot(s)	**Freshly squeezed lime juice**
1	shot(s)	**Pressed apple juice**
2	shot(s)	**Ocean Spray cranberry juice**

Comment: Sweet and aromatic.

'NOW FOR DRINKS, NOW FOR SOME DANCING WITH A GOOD BEAT.'
HORACE

PALMA VIOLET MARTINI

Glass: Martini
Garnish: Parma Violet sweets
Method: SHAKE all ingredients with ice and fine strain into chilled glass.

1½	shot(s)	**Ketel One vodka**
¼	shot(s)	**Teichenné Peach Schnapps Liqueur**
½	shot(s)	**Freshly squeezed lemon juice**
1	shot(s)	**Benoit Serres violet liqueur**
¼	shot(s)	**Sugar syrup (2 sugar to 1 water)**
1	dash	**Fee Brothers orange bitters**
½	shot(s)	**Chilled mineral water** (omit if wet ice)

Origin: Created in 2001 by Jamie Terrell at LAB, London, England.
Comment: A subtly floral drink with a delicate colour.

PALOMA

Glass: Collins
Garnish: Lime wedge & salt rim
Method: SHAKE first four ingredients with ice and strain into ice-filled glass. **TOP** with soda, lightly stir and serve with straws.

2	shot(s)	**Partida tequila**
3	shot(s)	**Squeezed pink grapefruit juice**
½	shot(s)	**Freshly squeezed lime juice**
¼	shot(s)	**Agave syrup (from health food shop)**
Top up with		**Soda water (club soda)**

Origin: The name is Spanish for 'dove' and the cocktail is well-known in Mexico.
Comment: A long, fruity, Margarita.

PANACHÉE [NEW #7]

Glass: Collins (10oz/290ml max)
Method: POUR first two ingredients into glass. SERVE iced water separately in a small jug (known in France as a 'broc') so the customer can dilute to their own taste (I recommend four-and-a-half shots). Lastly, add ice to glass.

1 shot(s) **La Fée Parisienne (68%) absinthe**
1 shot(s) **Anisette liqueur**
Top up with **Chilled mineral water**

Origin: This is one of the earliest known absinthe mixtures. Today if you order a 'panachée' at a French café, you will receive beer with lemonade (shandy).
Comment: Anisette sweetens the absinthe and adds a refreshing burst of herbal aniseed.

'COCKTAIL MUSIC IS ACCEPTED AS AUDIBLE WALLPAPER.'
ALISTAIR COOKE

PANCHO VILLA

Glass: Martini (saucer)
Garnish: Pineapple wedge on rim
Method: SHAKE all ingredients with ice and fine strain into chilled glass.

1 shot(s) **Light white rum**
1 shot(s) **Plymouth gin**
1 shot(s) **Giffard apricot brandy du Roussillon**
1/4 shot(s) **Cherry (brandy) liqueur**
1/4 shot(s) **Pressed pineapple juice**
1/2 shot(s) **Chilled mineral water** (omit if wet ice)

Origin: Adapted from a recipe in the 1947-72 Trader Vic's Bartender's Guide by Victor Bergeron.
Comment: To quote Victor Bergeron, "This'll tuck you away neatly – and pick you up and throw you right on the floor".

PAPPY HONEYSUCKLE

Glass: Martini
Garnish: Physalis fruit
Method: STIR honey with whiskey in base of shaker to dissolve honey. Add other ingredients, **SHAKE** with ice and fine strain into chilled glass.

1 1/2 shot(s) **Black Bush Irish whiskey**
2 spoons **Runny honey**
1 1/4 shot(s) **Sauvignon Blanc wine**
1 1/2 shot(s) **Pressed apple juice**
1/4 shot(s) **Passion fruit syrup**
1/4 shot(s) **Freshly squeezed lemon juice**

Origin: Created in 2002 by Shelim Islam at the GE Club, London, England.
Comment: Fresh and fruity with honeyed sweetness.

PARADISE #1

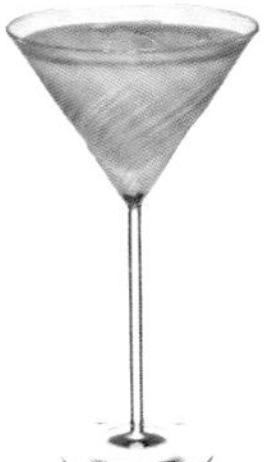

Glass: Martini
Garnish: Orange zest twist
Method: SHAKE all ingredients with ice and fine strain into chilled glass.

2 shot(s) **Plymouth gin**
1 shot(s) **Giffard apricot brandy du Roussillon**
1 shot(s) **Freshly squeezed orange juice**
1/4 shot(s) **Freshly squeezed lemon juice**

Origin: Proportioned according to a recipe in the 1930 edition of the Savoy Cocktail Book by Harry Craddock.
Comment: Orange predominates in this strong complex cocktail.

PARADISE #2

Glass: Martini
Garnish: Orange zest twist
Method: SHAKE all ingredients with ice and fine strain into chilled glass.

2 shot(s) **Plymouth gin**
3/4 shot(s) **Giffard apricot brandy du Roussillon**
1 3/4 shot(s) **Freshly squeezed orange juice**
3 dashes **Fee Brothers orange bitters (optional)**

Origin: This 1920s recipe has recently been revitalised by Dale DeGroff.
Comment: When well made, this wonderfully fruity cocktail beautifully harnesses and balances its ingredients.

PARADISE #3

Glass: Martini
Garnish: Orange zest twist
Method: Cut passion fruit in half and scoop flesh into shaker. Add other ingredients, **SHAKE** with ice and fine strain into chilled glass.

1 fresh **Passion fruit**
2 shot(s) **Plymouth gin**
3/4 shot(s) **Giffard apricot brandy du Roussillon**
3/4 shot(s) **Freshly squeezed orange juice**

Comment: Thick, almost syrupy. Rich and fruity.

PARIS SOUR

Glass: Old-fashioned
Garnish: Lemon zest twist
Method: SHAKE all ingredients with ice and strain into ice-filled glass.

2 shot(s) **Buffalo Trace bourbon whiskey**
1 1/4 shot(s) **Dubonnet Red**
1/4 shot(s) **Sugar syrup (2 sugar to 1 water)**
1/2 shot(s) **Freshly squeezed lemon juice**
1/2 fresh **Egg white**

Origin: Created in 2005 by Mark at Match Bar, London, England.
Comment: A wonderfully accommodating whiskey sour – it's easy to make and a pleasure to drink.

PARISIAN MARTINI #1

Glass: Martini
Garnish: Lemon peel twist
Method: SHAKE all ingredients with ice and fine strain into chilled glass.

$1^1/_4$	shot(s)	**Plymouth gin**
$1^1/_4$	shot(s)	**Giffard crème de cassis**
$1^1/_4$	shot(s)	**Dry vermouth**

Origin: A drink created in the 1920s to promote crème de cassis. This recipe is adapted from one in Harry Craddock's Savoy Cocktail Book.
Comment: Full-on rich cassis is barely tempered by gin and dry vermouth.

PARISIAN MARTINI #2 [NEW #7]

Glass: Martini
Garnish: Lime zest twist
Method: SHAKE all ingredients with ice and fine strain into chilled glass.

2	shot(s)	**Ketel One vodka**
1	shot(s)	**St-Germain elderflower liqueur**
$^1/_4$	shot(s)	**Dry vermouth**

AKA: Can Can
Origin: Created in 2006 by yours truly.
Comment: Floral, yet dry and aromatic. The character of the vodka shines through.

ST. GERMAIN SIDECAR [NEW #7]

Glass: Martini
Garnish: Lemon zest twist
Method: SHAKE all ingredients with ice and fine strain into chilled glass.

$1^1/_2$	shot(s)	**Rémy Martin cognac**
$1^1/_2$	shot(s)	**St-Germain elderflower liqueur**
1	shot(s)	**Freshly squeezed lemon juice**

Origin: Created in 2006 by yours truly.
Comment: An elderflower flavoured Sidecar named after the fashionable Left Bank area of Paris.

PARISIAN SPRING PUNCH

Glass: Collins
Garnish: Lemon zest knot
Method: SHAKE first four ingredients with ice and strain into ice-filled glass. **TOP** with champagne and serve with straws.

1	shot(s)	**Boulard Grand Solage Calvados**
$^1/_2$	shot(s)	**Dry vermouth**
$^1/_4$	shot(s)	**Freshly squeezed lemon juice**
$^1/_4$	shot(s)	**Sugar syrup (2 sugar to 1 water)**
Top up with		**Brut champagne**

Comment: Dry apple and champagne – like upmarket cider.

PARK AVENUE

Glass: Martini
Garnish: Maraschino cherry
Method: SHAKE all ingredients with ice and fine strain into chilled glass.

2	shot(s)	**Plymouth gin**
$^1/_2$	shot(s)	**Grand Marnier liqueur**
$^1/_2$	shot(s)	**Sweet vermouth**
1	shot(s)	**Pressed pineapple juice**

Origin: A classic from the 1940s.
Comment: Very fruity and well-balanced rather than dry or sweet.

PARK LANE

Glass: Martini
Garnish: Orange zest twist
Method: SHAKE all ingredients with ice and strain into chilled glass.

2	shot(s)	**Plymouth gin**
$^3/_4$	shot(s)	**Giffard apricot brandy du Roussillon**
$^3/_4$	shot(s)	**Freshly squeezed orange juice**
$^1/_8$	shot(s)	**Pomegranate (grenadine) syrup**
$^1/_2$	fresh	**Egg white**

Comment: This smooth, frothy concoction hides a mean kick.

PARLAY PUNCH

Glass: Collins
Garnish: Lime wedge
Method: SHAKE all ingredients with ice and strain into ice-filled glass.

$1^1/_2$	shot(s)	**Buffalo Trace bourbon whiskey**
1	shot(s)	**Southern Comfort liqueur**
1	shot(s)	**Pressed pineapple juice**
1	shot(s)	**Ocean Spray cranberry juice**
$^1/_2$	shot(s)	**Freshly squeezed orange juice**
$^1/_2$	shot(s)	**Freshly squeezed lime juice**

Origin: Adapted from a recipe discovered at Vortex Bar, Atlanta, USA.
Comment: Too many of these tangy punches and you'll be parlaying till dawn.

PARMA NEGRONI

Glass: Collins
Garnish: Orange slice
Method: SHAKE first five ingredients with ice and strain into ice-filled glass. **TOP** with tonic water, lightly stir and serve with straws.

1	shot(s)	**Plymouth gin**
1	shot(s)	**Campari**
1	shot(s)	**Squeezed pink grapefruit juice**
2	dashes	**Angostura aromatic bitters**
$^1/_2$	shot(s)	**Sugar syrup (2 sugar to 1 water)**
Top up with		**Tonic water**

Origin: Discovered in 2005 at Club 97, Hong Kong, China.
Comment: Negroni drinkers will love this fruity adaptation.

PASS-ON-THAT

Glass: Collins
Garnish: Crown with passion fruit half
Method: Cut passion fruit in half and scoop flesh into shaker. Add other ingredients, **SHAKE** with ice and fine strain into ice-filled glass.

1	fresh	**Passion fruit**
1	shot(s)	**Ketel One vodka**
1	shot(s)	**Passoã passion fruit liqueur**
3	shot(s)	**Ocean Spray cranberry juice**

Comment: Full-on passion fruit and berries.

PASSBOUR COOLER

Glass: Collins
Garnish: Orange slice in glass
Method: **SHAKE** all ingredients with ice and strain into ice-filled glass.

1 1/2	shot(s)	**Buffalo Trace bourbon whiskey**
3/4	shot(s)	**Passoã passion fruit liqueur**
3/4	shot(s)	**Cherry (brandy) liqueur**
3	shot(s)	**Ocean Spray cranberry juice**

Comment: Cherry and bourbon with passion fruit.

PASSION FRUIT CAIPIRINHA

Glass: Old-fashioned
Method: **MUDDLE** lime wedges in the base of sturdy glass (being careful not to break the glass). Cut the passion fruit in half and scoop out the flesh into the glass. **POUR** cachaça and sugar syrup into glass, add crushed ice and **CHURN** (stir) with barspoon. Serve with straws.

1	fresh	**Passion fruit**
3/4	fresh	**Lime cut into wedges**
2	shot(s)	**Leblon cachaça**
3/4	shot(s)	**Sugar syrup (2 sugar to 1 water)**

Comment: A tasty fruit Caipirinha. You may end up sipping this from the glass as the passion fruit pips tend to clog straws.

PASSION FRUIT COLLINS

Glass: Collins
Garnish: Lemon slice
Method: Cut passion fruit in half and scoop out flesh into shaker. Add next three ingredients, **SHAKE** with ice and fine strain into ice-filled glass. **TOP** with soda, stir and serve with straws.

2	fresh	**Passion fruit**
2	shot(s)	**Plymouth gin**
1 1/2	shot(s)	**Freshly squeezed lemon juice**
1/2	shot(s)	**Passion fruit syrup**
Top up with		**Soda water (club soda)**

Origin: Formula by yours truly in 2004.
Comment: This fruity adaptation of the classic Collins may be a tad sharp for some: if so, add a dash more sugar.

PASSION FRUIT DAIQUIRI

Glass: Martini
Garnish: Lime wedge on rim
Method: Cut passion fruit in half and scoop out flesh into shaker. Add other ingredients, **SHAKE** with ice and fine strain into chilled glass.

2	fresh	**Passion fruit**
2	shot(s)	**Light white rum**
1/2	shot(s)	**Freshly squeezed lime juice**
1/2	shot(s)	**Sugar syrup (2 sugar to 1 water)**

Origin: Formula by yours truly in 2004.
Comment: The rum character comes through in this fruity cocktail.

PASSION FRUIT MARGARITA

Glass: Coupette
Garnish: Salt & lime wedge rim
Method: Cut passion fruit in half and scoop out flesh into shaker. Add other ingredients, **SHAKE** with ice and fine strain into chilled glass.

1	fresh	**Passion fruit**
2	shot(s)	**Partida tequila**
1	shot(s)	**Cointreau triple sec**
1	shot(s)	**Freshly squeezed lime juice**
1/4	shot(s)	**Passion fruit syrup**

Origin: Formula by yours truly in 2004.
Comment: The flavour of tequila is very evident in this fruity adaptation.

PASSION FRUIT MARTINI #1

Glass: Martini
Garnish: Physalis (cape gooseberry)
Method: Cut passion fruit in half and scoop out flesh into shaker. Add other ingredients, **SHAKE** with ice and fine strain into chilled glass.

1	fresh	**Passion fruit**
2	shot(s)	**Ketel One vodka**
1/2	shot(s)	**Sugar syrup (2 sugar to 1 water)**

Origin: Formula by yours truly in 2004.
Comment: A simple but tasty cocktail that wonderfully harnesses the flavour of passion fruit.

PASSION FRUIT MARTINI #2

Glass: Martini
Garnish: Star fruit on rim
Method: Cut passion fruit in half and scoop out flesh into shaker. Add other ingredients, **SHAKE** with ice and fine strain into chilled glass.

2	fresh	**Passion fruit**
2	shot(s)	**Ketel One vodka**
1/2	shot(s)	**Passion fruit syrup**

Origin: Formula by yours truly in 2004.
Comment: Not for Martini purists, but a fruity, easy drinking concoction for everyone else.

PASSION FRUIT MARTINI #3

Glass: Martini
Garnish: Float passion fruit half
Method: Cut passion fruit in half and scoop out flesh into shaker. Add other ingredients, **SHAKE** with ice and fine strain into chilled glass.

2	fresh	**Passion fruit**
2	shot(s)	**Plymouth gin**
1/2	shot(s)	**Cointreau triple sec**
1/4	shot(s)	**Freshly squeezed lemon juice**
1/2	shot(s)	**Passion fruit syrup**
1/2	fresh	**Egg white**

Origin: Formula by yours truly in 2004.
Comment: Full-on passion fruit with gin and citrus hints.

PASSION KILLER

Glass: Shot
Method: Refrigerate ingredients then **LAYER** in chilled glass by carefully pouring in the following order.

1/2	shot(s)	**Midori melon liqueur**
1/2	shot(s)	**Passoã passion fruit liqueur**
1/2	shot(s)	**Partida tequila**

Comment: Tropical fruit and tequila.

PASSION PUNCH

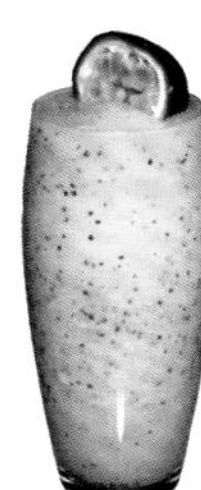

Glass: Collins (or individual scorpion bowl)
Garnish: Half passion fruit
Method: Cut passion fruit in half and scoop flesh into blender. Add other ingredients and **BLEND** with 12oz scoop crushed ice. Serve with straws.

1	fresh	**Passion fruit**
2	shot(s)	**Plymouth gin**
1/4	shot(s)	**Rémy Martin cognac**
3/4	shot(s)	**Freshly squeezed lime juice**
3/4	shot(s)	**Sugar syrup (2 sugar to 1 water)**
2	dashes	**Angostura aromatic bitters**

Origin: Adapted from a recipe in the 1947-72 Trader Vic's Bartender's Guide by Victor Bergeron.
Comment: To quote the Trader, "A robust libation with the opulence of 'down under'."

PASSIONATE RUM PUNCH

Glass: Collins
Garnish: Passion fruit quarter
Method: Cut passion fruit in half and scoop out flesh into shaker. Add other ingredients, **SHAKE** with ice and fine strain into glass filled with crushed ice.

3	fresh	**Passion fruit**
2 1/4	shot(s)	**Wray & Nephew overproof rum**
3/4	shot(s)	**Freshly squeezed lime juice**
1	shot(s)	**Sugar syrup (2 sugar to 1 water)**
1/2	shot(s)	**Passion fruit syrup**

Origin: Formula by yours truly in 2004.
Comment: Rum and fruit combine brilliantly in this tropical punch style drink.

PASSOVER

Glass: Collins
Garnish: Orange slice
Method: **SHAKE** all ingredients with ice and strain into ice-filled glass.

2	shot(s)	**Ketel One vodka**
1	shot(s)	**Passoã passion fruit liqueur**
3	shot(s)	**Squeezed pink grapefruit juice**

Comment: Tropical and sweet.

PAVLOVA SHOT

Glass: Shot
Method: Refrigerate ingredients then **LAYER** in chilled glass by carefully pouring in the following order.

3/4	shot(s)	**Chambord black raspberry liqueur**
3/4	shot(s)	**Ketel One vodka**

Comment: Pleasant, sweet shot.

PEACH DAIQUIRI

Glass: Martini
Garnish: Peach wedge on rim
Method: **SHAKE** all ingredients with ice and fine strain into chilled glass.

2	shot(s)	**Light white rum**
1	shot(s)	**Teichenné Peach Schnapps Liqueur**
1/2	shot(s)	**Freshly squeezed lime juice**
1/2	shot(s)	**Chilled mineral water** (omit if wet ice)

Origin: My take on the Cuban Daiquiri de Melocoton.
Comment: A classic Daiquiri with a hint of peach liqueur.

PEACH MELBA MARTINI

Glass: Martini
Garnish: Float flaked almonds
Method: **SHAKE** all ingredients with ice and fine strain into chilled glass.

1 1/2	shot(s)	**Vanilla infused Ketel One vodka**
3/4	shot(s)	**Teichenné Peach Schnapps Liqueur**
3/4	shot(s)	**Chambord black raspberry liqueur**
1	shot(s)	**Double (heavy) cream**
1	shot(s)	**Milk**

Origin: Melba is a name given to various dishes dedicated to Dame Nellie Melba, the 19th century Australian opera singer. Peach Melba was created in 1892 by the world famous chef Georges-Auguste Escoffier, who was the business partner of César Ritz.
Comment: Not quite Peach Melba dessert, but rich and tasty all the same.

PEANUT BUTTER & JELLY SHOT

Glass: Shot
Method: SHAKE all ingredients with ice and fine strain into chilled glass.

1/2	shot(s)	**Chambord black raspberry liqueur**
1/2	shot(s)	**Frangelico hazelnut liqueur**
1/2	shot(s)	**Irish cream liqueur**

Comment: Does indeed taste a little like peanut butter and jelly (jam in the UK).

PEAR DROP

Glass: Shot
Method: SHAKE all ingredients with ice and fine strain into chilled glass.

1/2	shot(s)	**Ketel One Citroen vodka**
1/2	shot(s)	**Soho lychee liqueur**
1/2	shot(s)	**Pear & cognac liqueur**

Comment: Sweet, sticky and strong.

PEAR & CARDAMOM SIDECAR

Glass: Martini
Garnish: Pear slice on rim
Method: MUDDLE cardamom in base of shaker. Add other ingredients, **SHAKE** with ice and fine strain into chilled glass.

2	pods	**Green cardamom**
1	shot(s)	**Rémy Martin cognac**
3/4	shot(s)	**Cointreau triple sec**
3/4	shot(s)	**Pear & cognac liqueur**
3/4	shot(s)	**Freshly squeezed lemon juice**
1/8	shot(s)	**Sugar syrup (2 sugar to 1 water)**
1/2	shot(s)	**Chilled mineral water** (omit if wet ice)

Origin: Adapted from a drink created in 2002 by Jason Scott at Oloroso, Edinburgh, Scotland.
Comment: A wonderful meld of aromatic ingredients.

PEAR DROP MARTINI

Glass: Martini
Garnish: Pear drop sweet in drink
Method: SHAKE all ingredients with ice and fine strain into chilled glass.

1 1/4	shot(s)	**Pear & cognac liqueur**
1	shot(s)	**Luxardo limoncello liqueur**
1	shot(s)	**Poire William eau de vie**
1	shot(s)	**Freshly extracted pear juice**

Origin: Created in 2002 by yours truly.
Comment: Not as sticky as the sweet it takes its name from but full-on tangy pear.

PEAR & ELDERFLOWER COCKTAIL

Glass: Martini
Garnish: Pear slice on rim
Method: SHAKE all ingredients with ice and fine strain into chilled glass.

1 1/2	shot(s)	**Ketel One vodka**
3/4	shot(s)	**St-Germain elderflower liqueur**
1 1/2	shot(s)	**Freshly extracted pear juice**

Origin: Adapted from a drink created in 2001 by Angelo Vieira at St. Martins, London, England.
Comment: Pear and elderflower are a match made in St Martin's Lane.

PEAR MARTINI [NEW #7]

Glass: Martini
Garnish: Pear wedge on rim
Method: SHAKE all ingredients with ice and fine strain into chilled glass.

1 1/2	shot(s)	**Pear flavoured vodka**
1 1/2	shot(s)	**St-Germain elderflower liqueur**
1/8	shot	**Dry vermouth**

Comment: Aromatic pear vodka and floral elderflower liqueur are a match made in heaven. Vermouth adds complexity.

PEAR & VANILLA RICKEY

Glass: Collins
Garnish: Lime wedge
Method: SHAKE first three ingredients with ice and strain into ice-filled glass. **TOP** with 7-Up, lightly stir and serve with straws.

1	shot(s)	**Vanilla infused Ketel One vodka**
1	shot(s)	**Pear & cognac liqueur**
1	shot(s)	**Freshly squeezed lime juice**
Top up with		**7-Up**

Comment: Vanilla and pear create a creamy mouthful cut by lime juice.

PEAR SHAPED #1 (DELUXE VERSION)

Glass: Martini
Garnish: Pear slice on rim
Method: Cut passion fruit in half and scoop out flesh into base of shaker. Add other ingredients, **SHAKE** with ice and fine strain into chilled glass.

1	fresh	**Passion fruit**
1 1/2	shot(s)	**Scotch whisky**
1	shot(s)	**Pear & cognac liqueur**
1	shot(s)	**Freshly extracted pear juice**
1	shot(s)	**Pressed apple juice**
1/4	shot(s)	**Freshly squeezed lime juice**

Comment: Wonderful balance of flavours but pear predominates with a dry yet floral finish.

PEAR SHAPED #2 (POPULAR VERSION)

Glass: Collins
Glass: Pear wedge on rim
Method: SHAKE all ingredients with ice and strain into ice-filled glass.

2	shot(s)	**Scotch whisky**
1	shot(s)	**Pear & cognac liqueur**
3	shot(s)	**Pressed apple juice**
1/2	shot(s)	**Freshly squeezed lime juice**
1/4	shot(s)	**Sonoma vanilla bean sugar syrup**

Origin: Adapted from a drink created in 2003 by Jamie Terrell at Dick's Bar, Atlantic, London, England.
Comment: Scotch, pear and apple combine wonderfully in this medium-sweet long drink.

PEAR TREE COCKTAIL [NEW #7]

Glass: Martini
Garnish: Pear wedge on rim
Method: SHAKE first two ingredients with ice and fine strain into chilled glass. **TOP** with champagne.

1 1/2	shot(s)	**Pear flavoured vodka**
1 1/2	shot(s)	**St-Germain elderflower liqueur**
Top up with		**Brut champagne**

Comment: Aromatic pear vodka and elderflower liqueur paired with biscuity champagne.

PEDRO COLLINS

Glass: Collins
Garnish: Orange slice & cherry on stick (sail)
Method: SHAKE first three ingredients with ice and strain into ice-filled glass. **TOP** with soda, lightly stir and serve with straws.

2	shot(s)	**Light white rum**
1	shot(s)	**Freshly squeezed lime juice**
1/2	shot(s)	**Sugar syrup (2 sugar to 1 water)**
Top up with		**Soda water (club soda)**

Comment: This rum based Tom Collins is basically a long Daiquiri with soda.

PEGGY MARTINI

Glass: Martini
Garnish: Orange zest twist
Method: SHAKE all ingredients with ice and fine strain into chilled glass.

2	shot(s)	**Plymouth gin**
1	shot(s)	**Dry vermouth**
1/4	shot(s)	**La Fée Parisienne (68%) absinthe**
1/4	shot(s)	**Dubonnet Red**
1/2	shot(s)	**Chilled mineral water** (omit if wet ice)

Origin: Adapted from a recipe in the 1930s edition of the Savoy Cocktail Book by Harry Craddock.
Comment: Very dry and aromatic. Sadly this will appeal to few palates.

PEGU CLUB #1

Glass: Martini
Garnish: Lime wedge on rim
Method: SHAKE all ingredients with ice and fine strain into chilled glass.

2	shot(s)	**Plymouth gin**
1	shot(s)	**Cointreau triple sec**
1/2	shot(s)	**Freshly squeezed lime juice**
1/4	shot(s)	**Sugar syrup (2 sugar to 1 water)**
1	dash	**Angostura aromatic bitters**
1	dash	**Fee Brothers orange bitters**
1/2	shot(s)	**Chilled mineral water** (omit if wet ice)

Origin: Created in the 1920s at the Pegu Club, an expat gentlemen's club in British colonial Rangoon, Burma.
The recipe was first published in Harry MacElhone's 1927 'Barflies and Cocktails'. In his seminal 1930 Savoy Cocktail Book, Harry Craddock notes of this drink, "The favourite cocktail of the Pegu Club, Burma, and one that has travelled, and is asked for, round the world."
Comment: I've added a dash of sugar to the original recipe to reduce the tartness of this gin based Margarita-like concoction.

PEGU CLUB #2 [NEW #7]

Glass: Martini
Garnish: Orange zest twist
Method: SHAKE all ingredients with ice and fine strain into chilled glass.

2	shot(s)	**Plymouth gin**
1	shot(s)	**Grand Marnier liqueur**
1/2	shot(s)	**Freshly squeezed lime juice**
1	dash	**Angostura aromatic bitters**
1	dash	**Fee Brothers orange bitters**
1/2	shot(s)	**Chilled mineral water** (omit if wet ice)

Comment: This version of the Burmese classic is richer in orange.

PENDENNIS COCKTAIL

Glass: Martini
Garnish: Maraschino cherry
Method: SHAKE all ingredients with ice and fine strain into chilled glass.

2	shot(s)	**Plymouth gin**
1	shot(s)	**Giffard apricot brandy du Roussillon**
1/2	shot(s)	**Freshly squeezed lime juice**
1	dash	**Peychaud's aromatic bitters**
3/4	shot(s)	**Chilled mineral water** (omit if wet ice)

Origin: This classic is named after the Pendennis Club in Louisville, Kentucky, which is popularly supposed to be the birthplace of the Old-Fashioned.
Comment: Tangy, subtle, sweet and sour.

PEPPER & VANILLA'TINI

Glass: Martini
Garnish: Strip yellow pepper
Method: **SHAKE** all ingredients with ice and fine strain into chilled glass.

1	shot(s)	**Vanilla-infused Ketel One vodka**
3/4	shot(s)	**Pepper vodka**
1	shot(s)	**Cuarenta Y Tres (Licor 43) liqueur**
3/4	shot(s)	**Tuaca liqueur**
1	shot(s)	**Freshly extracted yellow bell pepper juice**

Origin: Created in 2002 by yours truly.
Comment: Vanilla and pepper seem to complement each other in a sweet and sour kind of way.

BESSIE BRADDOCK: 'WINSTON, YOU'RE DRUNK.' WINSTON CHURCHILL: 'BESSIE, YOU'RE UGLY. BUT TOMORROW I SHALL BE SOBER.'

PEPPERED MARY

Glass: Collins
Garnish: Peppered rim & cherry tomato
Method: **SHAKE** all ingredients with ice and fine strain into chilled glass.

2	shot(s)	**Pepper vodka**
2	shot(s)	**Freshly extracted yellow bell pepper juice**
2	shot(s)	**Pressed tomato juice**
1/2	shot(s)	**Freshly squeezed lemon juice**
7	drops	**Tabasco hot pepper sauce**
1	spoon	**Lea & Perrins Worcestershire sauce**

Origin: Created in 2003 by yours truly.
Comment: Hot and sweet pepper spice this Bloody Mary.

PEPPERMINT VANILLA DAIQUIRI [NEW #7]

Glass: Old-fashioned
Garnish: Mint sprig
Method: **SHAKE** all ingredients with ice and strain into glass filled with crushed ice.

2	shot(s)	**Light white rum**
1/4	shot(s)	**Galliano liqueur**
1/4	shot(s)	**Giffard white crème de Menthe Pastille**
1/2	shot(s)	**Freshly squeezed lime juice**
1/8	shot(s)	**Sugar syrup (2 sugar to 1 water)**

Origin: Discovered in 2005 at Bellini, Auckland, New Zealand.
Comment: An intriguing combination for folk who want their Daiquiris served 'fresh'.

PERFECT ALIBI

Glass: Collins
Garnish: Mint leaf & lime squeeze
Method: **MUDDLE** ginger in base of shaker. Add other ingredients, **SHAKE** with ice and fine strain into ice-filled glass.

2	fresh	**Thumb-nail sized slices root ginger**
1/2	shot(s)	**Sugar syrup (2 sugar to 1 water)**
1 1/2	shot(s)	**Krupnik honey liqueur**
1/2	shot(s)	**Bärenjäger honey liqueur**
3	shot(s)	**Cold black jasmine tea (fairly weak)**

Origin: Created in 2001 by Douglas Ankrah for Akbar, London, England.
Comment: A very unusual and pleasant mix of flavours.

PERFECT JOHN

Glass: Martini
Garnish: Orange zest twist
Method: **SHAKE** all ingredients with ice and fine strain into chilled glass.

1	shot(s)	**Ketel One vodka**
3/4	shot(s)	**Cointreau triple sec**
1 1/2	shot(s)	**Freshly squeezed orange juice**
1/4	shot(s)	**Galliano liqueur**

Comment: A straight-up Harvey Wallbanger with Cointreau.

PERFECT LADY [NEW #7]

Glass: Martini
Garnish: Lemon zest twist
Method: **SHAKE** all ingredients with ice and fine strain into chilled glass.

2	shot(s)	**Plymouth gin**
1/4	shot(s)	**Teichenné Peach Schnapps Liqueur**
1/2	shot(s)	**Freshly squeezed lemon juice**
1	fresh	**Egg white**
1/8	shot(s)	**Sugar syrup (2 sugar to 1 water)**

Origin: I first discovered this vintage cocktail at Lonsdale, London, England, in 2006.
Comment: This twist on a White Lady uses peach liqueur in place of triple sec to make a lighter, more fruity blend.

PERFECT MARTINI

Glass: Martini
Garnish: Orange zest twist
Method: **SHAKE** all ingredients with ice and fine strain into chilled glass.

1 1/4	shot(s)	**Plymouth gin**
1 1/4	shot(s)	**Dry vermouth**
1 1/4	shot(s)	**Sweet vermouth**
1	dash	**Fee Brothers orange bitters (optional)**

Variant: Merry-Go-Round Martini
Origin: Adapted from a recipe in the 1930 edition of the Savoy Cocktail Book by Harry Craddock.
Comment: The high proportion of vermouth makes this Martini almost sherry-like.

P

PERIODISTA DAIQUIRI

Glass: Martini
Garnish: Lime wedge
Method: SHAKE all ingredients with ice and fine strain into chilled glass.

1½	shot(s)	**Light white rum**
½	shot(s)	**Freshly squeezed lime juice**
½	shot(s)	**Grand Marnier liqueur**
½	shot(s)	**Giffard apricot brandy du Roussillon**
½	shot(s)	**Chilled mineral water** (omit if wet ice)

Comment: Basically an orange and apricot Daiquiri.

PERISCOPE [NEW #7]

Glass: Martini
Garnish: Grapefruit zest twist
Method: SHAKE all ingredients with ice and fine strain into chilled glass.

1½	shot(s)	**Plymouth gin**
1	shot(s)	**St-Germain elderflower liqueur**
⅛	shot(s)	**Freshly squeezed lemon juice**
⅛	shot(s)	**Freshly squeezed lime juice**
½	fresh	**Egg white**

Variant: Serve in an ice-filled Collins glass and top with soda.
Origin: Created by Matt Gee at Milk & Honey, New York City, USA.
Comment: Fabulously light, almost creamy, and very refreshing.

'MR EDITOR. I LEAVE WHEN THE PUB CLOSES.'
WINSTON CHURCHILL

PERNELLE [NEW #7]

Glass: Collins
Garnish: Lemon zest twist & icing sugar dusted rosemary sprig
Method: SHAKE first four ingredients with ice and strain into glass filled with crushed ice. **TOP** with soda and serve with straws.

1	shot(s)	**Ketel One vodka**
1	shot(s)	**St-Germain elderflower liqueur**
1	shot(s)	**Pear liqueur**
1	shot(s)	**Freshly squeezed lemon juice**
Top up with		**Soda water (club soda)**

Origin: Created in 2007 by Colin Asare-Appiah, London, England, for U'Luvka vodka, this is named after the wife of the 14th century alchemist Nicolas Flamel, who supported him in his search for the Philosopher's Stone.
Comment: This long clear drink has a grassy, alpine aroma and a fresh pine finish.

PERNOD & BLACK MARTINI

Glass: Martini
Garnish: Blackberries
Method: MUDDLE blackberries in base of shaker. Add other ingredients, **SHAKE** with ice and fine strain into chilled glass.

7	fresh	**Blackberries**
½	shot(s)	**Pernod anis**
1½	shot(s)	**Ketel One vodka**
½	shot(s)	**Giffard mûre (blackberry)**
1	shot(s)	**Freshly squeezed lime juice**
⅛	shot(s)	**Sonoma vanilla bean sugar syrup**
¾	shot(s)	**Chilled mineral water** (omit if wet ice)

Origin: Created in 2003 by yours truly.
Comment: Pernod enhances the rich, tart flavours of blackberry.

PERROQUET

Glass: Collins (10oz / 290ml max)
Method: POUR pastis and mint syrup into glass. Serve iced water separately in a small jug (known in France as a 'broc') so the customer can dilute to their own taste (I recommend five shots). Lastly, add ice to fill glass.

1	shot(s)	**Ricard pastis**
¼	shot(s)	**Green mint (menthe) syrup**
Top up with		**Chilled mineral water**

Origin: Very popular throughout France, this drink is named after the parrot due to the bird's brightly coloured plumage.
Comment: The traditional French café drink with a hint of sweet mint.

PERRY-TINI

Glass: Martini
Garnish: Pear slice on rim
Method: SHAKE first three ingredients with ice and fine strain into chilled glass. **TOP** with champagne.

1	shot(s)	**Poire William eau de vie**
1	shot(s)	**Pear & cognac liqueur**
2	shot(s)	**Freshly extracted pear juice**
Top up with		**Brut champagne**

Origin: Created in 2002 by yours truly.
Comment: Pear with a hint of sparkle.

PERUVIAN ELDER SOUR [NEW #7]

Glass: Martini
Garnish: Lime wedge on rim
Method: SHAKE all ingredients with ice and fine strain into chilled glass.

2	shot(s)	**Barsol Quebranta pisco**
1	shot(s)	**St-Germain elderflower liqueur**
½	shot(s)	**Freshly squeezed lime juice**

Origin: Drinks writer Gary Regan created this in 2006 in New York, USA.
Comment: This tasty sour combines the aromatics of pisco and elderflower in an intriguing variation on the Margarita. Consider smoothing with fresh egg white.

PETER PAN COCKTAIL #1 [NEW #7]

Glass: Martini
Garnish: Orange zest twist
Method: SHAKE all ingredients with ice and fine strain into chilled glass.

1 shot(s) **Plymouth gin**
1 shot(s) **Dry vermouth**
1 shot(s) **Freshly squeezed orange juice**
3 dashes **Fee Brothers peach bitters**

Variant: Substitute Angostura aromatic bitters for peach bitters.
Origin: Adapted from a recipe in the 1930 edition of the Savoy Cocktail Book by Harry Craddock. The original recipe called for equal parts, including the bitters – surely a mistake.
Comment: Smoother, lighter and easier than most classic cocktails – perhaps a little too much so.

PETER PAN COCKTAIL #2 [NEW #7]

Glass: Martini
Garnish: Orange zest twist
Method: SHAKE all ingredients with ice and fine strain into chilled glass.

2 shot(s) **Plymouth gin**
1 shot(s) **Dry vermouth**
1 shot(s) **Freshly squeezed orange juice**
3 dashes **Fee Brother's peach bitters**

Origin: Adapted from a recipe in the 1930 edition of the Savoy Cocktail Book by Harry Craddock.
Comment: Orange predominates in this complex cocktail.

PETO MARTINI

Glass: Martini
Garnish: Orange zest twist
Method: SHAKE all ingredients with ice and fine strain into chilled glass.

2 shot(s) **Plymouth gin**
1 shot(s) **Dry vermouth**
1 shot(s) **Sweet vermouth**
1/4 shot(s) **Freshly squeezed orange juice**
1/8 shot(s) **Luxardo maraschino liqueur**

Origin: Adapted from a recipe in the 1930 edition of the Savoy Cocktail Book by Harry Craddock.
Comment: A wonderfully aromatic classic Martini served 'perfect' with a hint of orange juice and maraschino.

PHARMACEUTICAL STIMULANT

Glass: Old-fashioned
Garnish: Float three coffee beans
Method: SHAKE all ingredients with ice and strain into ice-filled glass.

2 shot(s) **Ketel One vodka**
1/2 shot(s) **Kahlúa coffee liqueur**
2 shot(s) **Cold espresso coffee**
1/4 shot(s) **Sugar syrup (2 sugar to 1 water)**

Origin: Created in 1998 by Dick Bradsell at The Pharmacy, London, England.
Comment: A real wake-up call and the drink that led to many an Espresso Martini.

PICADOR [NEW #7]

Glass: Martini
Garnish: Lime zest twist
Method: SHAKE all ingredients with ice and fine strain into chilled glass.

2 shot(s) **Partida tequila**
1 shot(s) **Freshly squeezed lime juice**
1 shot(s) **Cointreau triple sec**

Origin: Yes, you're right! This drink is exactly the same as a classically proportioned Margarita. But… it was published in W. J. Tarling's 1937 'Café Royal Cocktail Book', 16 years before the first known written reference to a Margarita. Was the British recipe copied? Or did the Margarita independently evolve?
Comment: The name might be more masculine but it still tastes exactly like a classic Margarita.

PICCA

Glass: Martini
Garnish: Maraschino cherry
Method: SHAKE all ingredients with ice and fine strain into chilled glass.

1 1/2 shot(s) **Scotch whisky**
1 shot(s) **Galliano liqueur**
1 shot(s) **Sweet vermouth**
3/4 shot(s) **Chilled mineral water** (omit if wet ice)

Comment: Bittersweet whisky.

PICCADILLY MARTINI

Glass: Martini
Garnish: Lemon zest twist
Method: SHAKE all ingredients with ice and fine strain into chilled glass.

2 shot(s) **Plymouth gin**
1 shot(s) **Dry vermouth**
1/8 shot(s) **La Fée Parisienne (68%) absinthe**
1/8 shot(s) **Pomegranate (grenadine) syrup**

Origin: Adapted from a recipe in Harry Craddock's 1930 Savoy Cocktail Book.
Comment: A classic Martini tempered by a hint of pomegranate and absinthe.

PICHUNCHO MARTINI

Glass: Martini
Garnish: Orange zest twist
Method: SHAKE all ingredients with ice and fine strain into a chilled glass.

2 1/4 shot(s) **Pisco**
1 1/2 shot(s) **Sweet vermouth**
1/4 shot(s) **Sugar syrup (2 sugar to 1 water)**

Origin: Based on a traditional Chilean drink: pisco and vermouth served on the rocks.
Comment: This drink craves the best pisco and the best sweet vermouth. Find those and measure carefully and it's sublime.

PIMM'S CUP

This quintessential English summer tipple is usually accredited to James Pimm, who in 1823-4 began trading as a shellfish-monger in London's Lombard Street. He later moved to nearby number 3 Poultry, also in the City of London, where he established Pimm's Oyster Warehouse. It is here, in 1840, that he is said to have first served this drink.

Others dispute this, maintaining that James Pimm only unwittingly lent his name to the drink. They say the true credit lies with his successor, Samuel Morey, who is recorded as having taken out a retail liquor licence in 1860. This would appear to be when the oyster bar first offered its customers spirits. Many establishments of the day mixed house spirits to serve with liqueurs and juices as 'cups', in reference to the tankards in which they were sold. Naturally the 'cup' made at Pimm's Oyster Bar was named after the establishment which retained the goodwill of its founder. Pimm's restaurant became very popular and changed hands a couple more times. Eventually Horatio David Davies, a wine merchant and owner of cafes in London bought the business. He became Sir Horatio, a Member of Parliament and between 1897-1898, Lord Mayor of London. He formed Pimm's into a private company in 1906, which was controlled by family trusts for another 57 years after his death.

The precise date that the drink Pimm's was first sold outside restaurants and bars controlled by the Pimm's company is unknown. However, it is certain that the original product, No.1, was based on gin and flavoured with numerous botanicals including quinine. A second Pimm's product based on Scotch (Pimm's No.2 Cup) was launched and a third (Pimm's No.3 Cup) was based on brandy. Pimm's became popular in Britain in the 1920s and took off internationally after the Second World War. Other versions were then introduced: Pimm's No.4 based on rum, Pimm's No.6 on vodka and Pimm's No.7 on rye whiskey.

PIERRE COLLINS

Glass: Collins
Garnish: Orange slice & cherry on stick (sail)
Method: SHAKE first three ingredients with ice and strain into ice-filled glass. **TOP** with soda, lightly stir and serve with straws.

- 2 shot(s) **Rémy Martin cognac**
- 1 shot(s) **Freshly squeezed lemon juice**
- ½ shot(s) **Sugar syrup (2 sugar to 1 water)**
- Top up with **Soda water (club soda)**

Comment: A Tom Collins made with cognac. The cognac's character shines through.

PILGRIM COCKTAIL

Glass: Martini
Garnish: Dust with grated nutmeg
Method: SHAKE all ingredients with ice and fine strain into chilled glass.

- 1½ shot(s) **Golden rum**
- ½ shot(s) **Grand Marnier liqueur**
- 1 shot(s) **Freshly squeezed orange juice**
- ¾ shot(s) **Freshly squeezed lime juice**
- ¼ shot(s) **World's End Pimento Dram liqueur**
- 3 dashes **Angostura aromatic bitters**

Variant: Can also be served hot by simmering ingredients gently in a saucepan.
Comment: Whether you serve this hot or cold, it's a delicately spiced drink to warm the cockles.

PIMM'S COCKTAIL

Glass: Martini
Garnish: Lemon & orange zest twist
Method: SHAKE first four ingredients with ice and strain into chilled glass. **TOP** with champagne.

- 2 shot(s) **Pimm's No.1 Cup**
- ½ shot(s) **Plymouth gin**
- ¼ shot(s) **Freshly squeezed lemon juice**
- ¼ shot(s) **Sugar syrup (2 sugar to 1 water)**
- Top up with **Brut champagne**

Comment: Luxuriate in this quintessentially English tipple.

PIMM'S CUP (OR CLASSIC)

Glass: Collins
Garnish: Mint sprig
Method: POUR Pimm's into glass half filled with ice. Add fruit and fill glass with more ice. Top with 7-Up (or ginger ale), lightly stir and serve with straws.

- 2 shot(s) **Pimm's No. 1 Cup**
- 1 slice **Lemon**
- 1 slice **Orange**
- 2 slices **Cucumber**
- 1 sliced **Strawberry**
- Top up with **7-Up (or ginger ale)**

Origin: Usually credited to James Pimm in 1840 but more likely to have been first made by Samuel Morey in the 1860s.
Comment: You've not properly experienced an English summer until you've drunk one of these whilst sheltering from the rain.

PIMM'S ROYALE

Glass: Flute
Garnish: Berries on stick with cucumber peel
Method: POUR Pimm's into chilled glass and **TOP** with champagne.

- 1 shot(s) **Pimm's No.1 Cup**
- Top up with **Brut champagne**

Comment: Dry, subtle and refreshing.

PIÑA COLADA #1

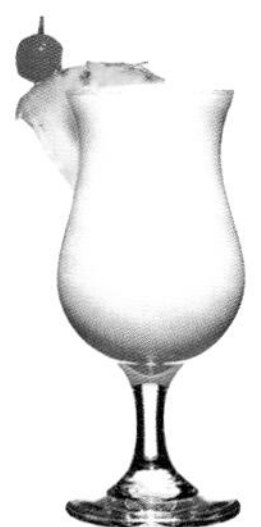

Glass: Hurricane (or hollowed out pineapple)
Garnish: Pineapple wedge & cherry
Method: BLEND all ingredients with one 12oz scoop crushed ice and serve with straws.

- 2 shot(s) **Golden rum**
- 3 shot(s) **Pressed pineapple juice**
- 2 shot(s) **Coco López cream of coconut**
- ½ shot(s) **Double (heavy) cream**

Variant: Made with dark rums.
Comment: A wonderful creamy, fruity concoction that's not half as sticky as the world would have you believe. Too much ice will detract from the creaminess and kill the drink.

PIÑA COLADA #2 (CUBAN STYLE) [NEW #7]

Glass: Collins
Garnish: Lime wedge on rim
Method: SHAKE all ingredients with ice and strain into ice-filled glass.

- 1½ shot(s) **Aged rum**
- 4 shot(s) **Pressed pineapple juice**
- ¼ shot(s) **Freshly squeezed lime juice**
- ¼ shot(s) **Sugar syrup (2 sugar to 1 water)**

Origin: Touted by some as the original Piña Colada from Cuba.
Comment: This Colada has no coconut, but it is smooth, balanced and rather tasty.

PIÑA COLADA VIRGIN (MOCKTAIL)

Glass: Hurricane
Garnish: Pineapple wedge & cherry on rim
Method: BLEND all ingredients with 18oz of crushed ice and serve with straws.

- 6 shot(s) **Pressed pineapple juice**
- ¾ shot(s) **Double (heavy) cream**
- ¾ shot(s) **Milk**
- 2 shot(s) **Coco López cream of coconut**

AKA: Snow White
Comment: A Piña Colada with its guts ripped out.

PIÑA COLADA

Three Puerto Rican bartenders contest the ownership of this drink. Ramón Marrero Pérez claims to have first made it at the Caribe Hilton hotel's Beachcomber Bar in San Juan on 15th August 1954 using the then newly available Coco López cream of coconut. Ricardo Garcia, who also worked at the Caribe, says that it was he who invented the drink. But Ramón Portas Mingot says he created it in 1963 at the Barrachina Bar in Old San Juan.

It is, however, commonly accepted that the Piña Colada was adapted from an existing creation at the Caribe Hilton Hotel, which has since promoted itself as the home of the drink and today credits Ramón Marrero Pérez with its invention. The Caribe was the first luxury hotel in San Juan and became a popular destination for the rich and famous who helped spread word of the drink.

The name 'Piña Colada' literally means 'strained pineapple', a reference to the freshly pressed and strained pineapple juice used in the drink's preparation. Another essential ingredient, 'cream of coconut', is a canned, non-alcoholic, thick, syrup-like blend of coconut juice, sugar, emulsifier, cellulose, thickeners, citric acid and salt.

The original brand, Coco López, was created in the early 1950s by Don Ramón López-Irizarry after receiving a development grant from the Puerto Rican government. Cream of coconut had previously been made but López-Irizarry mechanised the labour intensive process. The brand was launched in 1954 and is an essential part of the Piña Colada that has lasted through the decades.

PIÑA MARTINI

Glass: Martini
Garnish: Pineapple wedge on rim
Method: **SHAKE** all ingredients with ice and fine strain into chilled glass.

- 2 shot(s) **Ketel One vodka**
- 1 3/4 shot(s) **Pressed pineapple juice**
- 1/4 shot(s) **Freshly squeezed lime juice**
- 1/8 shot(s) **Sugar syrup (2 sugar to 1 water)**

Origin: Created in 2005 by yours truly.
Comment: Rich pineapple but not too sweet.

PINEAPPLE & SAGE MARGARITA

Glass: Coupette
Garnish: Pineapple wedge on rim
Method: Lightly **MUDDLE** sage in base of shaker. Add other ingredients, **SHAKE** with ice and fine strain into chilled glass.

- 5 fresh **Sage leaves**
- 2 shot(s) **Partida tequila**
- 1 shot(s) **Pressed pineapple juice**
- 1/2 shot(s) **Freshly squeezed lime juice**
- 1/4 shot(s) **Agave syrup (from health food store)**

Origin: Adapted from a drink created in 2005 at Green & Red Bar, London, England.
Comment: Herbal tequila and sweet pineapple in harmony.

PINEAPPLE & CARDAMOM DAIQUIRI

Glass: Martini
Garnish: Pineapple wedge on rim
Method: **MUDDLE** cardamom in base of shaker. Add other ingredients, **SHAKE** with ice and fine strain into chilled glass.

- 4 pods **Green cardamom**
- 2 shot(s) **Light white rum**
- 1 3/4 shot(s) **Pressed pineapple juice**
- 1/4 shot(s) **Freshly squeezed lime juice**
- 1/4 shot(s) **Sugar syrup (2 sugar to 1 water)**

Origin: Adapted from Henry Besant's Pineapple & Cardamom Martini.
Comment: One of the tastiest Daiquiris I've tried.

PINEAPPLE BLOSSOM 

Glass: Martini
Garnish: Pineapple wedge on rim
Method: **SHAKE** all ingredients with ice and fine strain into chilled glass.

- 2 shot(s) **Scotch whisky**
- 1 shot(s) **Pressed pineapple juice**
- 1/2 shot(s) **Freshly squeezed lemon juice**
- 1/2 shot(s) **Sugar syrup (2 sugar to 1 water)**

Origin: My interpretation of a classic.
Comment: Richly flavoured but drier than you might expect.

PINEAPPLE & CARDAMOM MARTINI

Glass: Martini
Garnish: Pineapple wedge on rim
Method: **MUDDLE** cardamom in base of shaker. Add other ingredients, **SHAKE** with ice and fine strain into chilled glass.

- 4 pods **Green cardamom**
- 2 shot(s) **Ketel One vodka**
- 2 shot(s) **Pressed pineapple juice**
- 1/4 shot(s) **Sugar syrup (2 sugar to 1 water)**

Origin: Created in 2002 by Henry Besant at Lonsdale Bar, London, England.
Comment: This is about as good as it gets: a spectacular pairing of fruit and spice.

PINEAPPLE DAIQUIRI #1 (ON-THE-ROCKS)

Glass: Old-fashioned
Garnish: Pineapple wedge & cherry
Method: **SHAKE** all ingredients with ice and fine strain into ice-filled glass.

- 2 shot(s) **Light white rum**
- 1 shot(s) **Pressed pineapple juice**
- 1/2 shot(s) **Freshly squeezed lime juice**
- 1/4 shot(s) **Sugar syrup (2 sugar to 1 water)**

Origin: Formula by yours truly.
Comment: Rum and pineapple are just meant to go together.

PINEAPPLE & GINGER MARTINI

Glass: Martini
Garnish: Pineapple wedge on rim
Method: **MUDDLE** ginger in base of shaker. Add other ingredients, **SHAKE** with ice and fine strain into chilled glass.

- 2 slices **Fresh root ginger (thumbnail sized)**
- 2 shot(s) **Ketel One vodka**
- 2 shot(s) **Pressed pineapple juice**
- 1/8 shot(s) **Sugar syrup (2 sugar to 1 water)**

Comment: Smooth, rich pineapple flavour with hints of vodka and ginger.

PINEAPPLE DAIQUIRI #2 (FROZEN)

Glass: Martini (Large)
Garnish: Pineapple wedge & cherry
Method: **BLEND** all ingredients with two 12oz scoops crushed ice and serve with straws.

- 2 shot(s) **Light white rum**
- 1 1/2 shot(s) **Pressed pineapple juice**
- 1/2 shot(s) **Freshly squeezed lime juice**
- 3/4 shot(s) **Sugar syrup (2 sugar to 1 water)**

Origin: Formula by yours truly.
Comment: Fluffy but very tasty.

PINEAPPLE FIZZ

Glass: Collins
Garnish: Lime wedge & cherry
Method: SHAKE first four ingredients with ice and strain into ice-filled glass. **TOP** with soda, lightly stir and serve with straws.

- 2 shot(s) **Golden rum**
- 1 1/2 shot(s) **Pressed pineapple juice**
- 1 shot(s) **Freshly squeezed lime juice**
- 1/2 shot(s) **Sugar syrup (2 sugar to 1 water)**
- Top up with **Soda water (club soda)**

Comment: A Pineapple Daiquiri lengthened with soda. Surprisingly tasty and refreshing.

PINEAPPLE MARGARITA

Glass: Coupette
Garnish: Pineapple wedge on rim
Method: SHAKE all ingredients with ice and fine strain into chilled glass.

- 2 shot(s) **Partida tequila**
- 3/4 shot(s) **Cointreau triple sec**
- 1 1/2 shot(s) **Pressed pineapple juice**

Variant: Add half a shot of pineapple syrup, blend with 12oz scoop of crushed ice and serve frozen.
Comment: A Tequila Margarita with a pineapple fruit kick.

PINEAPPLE MOJITO

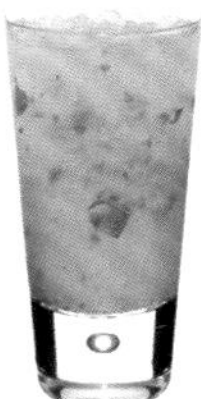

Glass: Collins
Method: Lightly **MUDDLE** mint (just to bruise) in glass. **POUR** other ingredients into glass and half fill with crushed ice. **CHURN** (stir) with barspoon. Fill glass with more crushed ice, churn and serve with straws.

- 12 fresh **Mint leaves**
- 2 shot(s) **Light white rum**
- 3/4 shot(s) **Cuarenta Y Tres (Licor 43) liqueur**
- 2 shot(s) **Pressed pineapple juice**
- 1 shot(s) **Freshly squeezed lime juice**

Origin: Discovered in 2003 at Apartment 195, London, England.
Comment: A fruity, vanilla-ed twist on the classic Mojito.

PINEAPPLE SMOOTHIE (MOCKTAIL)

Glass: Collins
Garnish: Pineapple wedge
Method: BLEND all ingredients with 12oz scoop crushed ice. Serve with straws.

- 2 tblspoon **Natural yoghurt**
- 2 tblspoon **Runny honey**
- 4 shot(s) **Pressed pineapple juice**

Comment: Fluffy in every sense of the word.

PINI

Glass: Martini
Garnish: Maraschino cherry
Method: SHAKE all ingredients with ice and fine strain into chilled glass.

- 2 shot(s) **Pisco**
- 1/2 shot(s) **Rémy Martin cognac**
- 1/4 shot(s) **Giffard white crème de cacao**
- 1/4 shot(s) **Sugar syrup (2 sugar to 1 water)**
- 1/2 shot(s) **Chilled mineral water** (omit if wet ice)

Comment: Use a great pisco and you'll have a wonderfully complex drink.

PINK CLOUD

Glass: Martini
Method: SHAKE all ingredients with ice and fine strain into chilled glass.

- 1 shot(s) **Luxardo Amaretto di Saschira liqueur**
- 1 shot(s) **Pomegranate (grenadine) syrup**
- 1 shot(s) **Giffard white crème de cacao**
- 3/4 shot(s) **Evaporated milk (sweetened)**

Origin: Adapted from a recipe in the 1947-72 Trader Vic's Bartender's Guide by Victor Bergeron.
Comment: To make this sweet after dinner drink I've used amaretto and pomegranate syrup in place of crème de noyaux. This almond flavoured liqueur made from apricot and peach stones is not currently available in the UK. US readers should use 2 shots of crème de noyaux in place of the first two ingredients.

PINK DAIQUIRI

Glass: Martini
Garnish: Lime wedge on rim
Method: SHAKE all ingredients with ice and fine strain into chilled glass.

- 2 shot(s) **Light white rum**
- 1/2 shot(s) **Freshly squeezed lime juice**
- 1/2 shot(s) **Pomegranate (grenadine) syrup**
- 1/4 shot(s) **Luxardo maraschino liqueur**
- 3 dashes **Angostura aromatic bitters**
- 1/2 shot(s) **Chilled mineral water** (omit if wet ice)

AKA: Daiquiri No.5
Origin: A classic from the 1930s.
Comment: The quality of pomegranate syrup will make or break this delicate Daiquiri.

PINK FLAMINGO

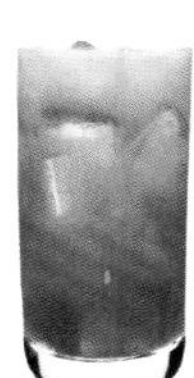

Glass: Collins
Garnish: Apple wheel
Method: SHAKE all ingredients with ice and fine strain into chilled glass.

- 2 shot(s) **Orange zest infused Ketel One vodka**
- 1 shot(s) **Sour apple liqueur**
- 1/2 shot(s) **Freshly squeezed lime juice**
- 1 shot(s) **Ocean Spray cranberry juice**

Origin: Created in 2002 by Wayne Collins for Maxxium UK.
Comment: Soapy and citrus flavoured – but in a nice way.

PINK GIN #1 (TRADITIONAL) [UPDATED]

Glass: Martini
Garnish: Lemon zest twist
Method: RINSE chilled glass with Angostura bitters. **POUR** gin and water into rinsed glass and stir.

- 2 dashes **Angostura aromatic bitters**
- 2 shot(s) **Plymouth gin (from freezer)**
- 2 shot(s) **Chilled mineral water**

Origin: Gin was a favourite of the Royal Navy – along with rum, which was served as a daily ration right up until the 70s. It was often mixed with healthy ingredients to make them more palatable. Pink gin was originally used against stomach upsets, as Angostura aromatic bitters were considered medicinal.
Comment: A traditionally made Pink Gin without ice.

PINK GIN #2 (MODERN)

Glass: Martini
Garnish: Lemon zest twist
Method: STIR all ingredients with ice and strain into chilled glass.

- 2 shot(s) **Plymouth gin**
- 2 shot(s) **Chilled mineral water (reduce if wet ice)**
- 1 dash **Angostura aromatic bitters**

Comment: Normally I'd advocate liberal use of Angostura bitters but this refined and subtle drink benefits from frugality.

PINK GIN & TONIC

Glass: Collins
Garnish: Lime slice
Method: POUR gin and Angostura bitters into ice-filled glass, top with tonic, lightly stir and serve with straws.

- 2 shot(s) **Plymouth gin**
- 4 dashes **Angostura aromatic bitters**
- Top up with **Tonic water**

Comment: Basically a G&T with an extra pep of flavour from Angostura, this has a wider appeal than the original Pink Gin.

PINK GRAPEFRUIT MARGARITA

Glass: Coupette
Garnish: Lime wedge on rim
Method: SHAKE all ingredients with ice and fine strain into chilled glass.

- 2 shot(s) **Partida tequila**
- 1 shot(s) **Squeezed pink grapefruit juice**
- $\frac{1}{2}$ shot(s) **Freshly squeezed lime juice**
- $\frac{1}{4}$ shot(s) **Sugar syrup (2 sugar to 1 water)**

Comment: Delivers exactly what the name promises.

PINK HOUND

Glass: Martini
Garnish: Lemon zest twist
Method: SHAKE all ingredients with ice and fine strain into chilled glass.

- 2 shot(s) **Plymouth gin**
- $1\frac{3}{4}$ shot(s) **Squeezed pink grapefruit juice**
- $\frac{1}{4}$ shot(s) **Sugar syrup (2 sugar to 1 water)**

Comment: A flavoursome balance of sweet and sour.

PINK LADY

Glass: Martini
Garnish: Lemon zest twist
Method: SHAKE all ingredients with ice and fine strain into chilled glass.

- 2 shot(s) **Plymouth gin**
- $\frac{1}{2}$ shot(s) **Freshly squeezed lemon juice**
- $\frac{1}{2}$ shot(s) **Pomegranate (grenadine) syrup**
- $\frac{1}{2}$ fresh **Egg white (optional)**

Variant: With the addition of half a shot apple brandy.
Origin: A classic cocktail named after a successful 1912 stage play.
Comment: Despite the colour, this is sharp and alcoholic.

PINK LEMONADE (MOCKTAIL)

Glass: Collins
Garnish: Lemon slice
Method: SHAKE first three ingredients with ice and strain into ice-filled glass. **TOP** with soda and serve with straws.

- 2 shot(s) **Freshly squeezed lemon juice**
- $\frac{1}{2}$ shot(s) **Pomegranate (grenadine) syrup**
- $\frac{1}{4}$ shot(s) **Sugar syrup (2 sugar to 1 water)**
- Top up with **Soda water (club soda)**

Origin: Discovered in 2004 in New York City.
Comment: A tall, pink, tangy, alcohol free cocktail.

PINK PALACE

Glass: Martini
Garnish: Lemon twist
Method: SHAKE all ingredients with ice and fine strain into chilled glass.

- 2 shot(s) **Plymouth gin**
- $\frac{1}{2}$ shot(s) **Grand Marnier liqueur**
- $\frac{1}{2}$ shot(s) **Freshly squeezed lemon juice**
- $\frac{1}{4}$ shot(s) **Pomegranate (grenadine) syrup**

Origin: The signature drink at The Polo Lounge, Beverly Hills Hotel, Los Angeles, USA. The hotel, which is lovingly termed the 'Pink Palace', inspired The Eagles' Hotel California and graces the album cover.
Comment: A great drink but rarely done justice at the Polo Lounge.

PINK SIN MARTINI

Glass: Martini
Garnish: Dust with cinnamon powder
Method: SHAKE all ingredients with ice and fine strain into chilled glass.

$1^1/_2$	shot(s)	**Ketel One vodka**
1	shot(s)	**Giffard white crème de cacao**
$^3/_4$	shot(s)	**Goldschläger cinnamon schnapps liqueur**
1	shot(s)	**Ocean Spray cranberry juice**

Comment: This looks a little like a Cosmo but delivers sweet cinnamon and chocolate.

PINK SQUIRREL [NEW #7]

Glass: Martini
Garnish: Mint leaf
Method: SHAKE all ingredients with ice and fine strain into chilled glass.

1	shot(s)	**Crème de noyaux liqueur**
1	shot(s)	**White crème de cacao**
$^1/_2$	shot(s)	**Double (heavy) cream**
$^1/_2$	shot(s)	**Milk**

Origin: Adapted from Victor Bergeron's 'Trader Vic's Bartender's Guide' (1972 revised edition).
Comment: Crème de noyaux, a pink almond liqueur, is now very hard to obtain: if in doubt, substitute with $^3/_4$ amaretto $^1/_4$ grenadine.

PINK TUTU

Glass: Old-fashioned
Garnish: Orange slice
Method: SHAKE all ingredients with ice and strain into ice-filled glass.

1	shot(s)	**Teichenné Peach Schnapps Liqueur**
$^1/_2$	shot(s)	**Ketel One vodka**
$^1/_2$	shot(s)	**Campari**
2	shot(s)	**Freshly squeezed grapefruit juice**
$^1/_4$	shot(s)	**Sugar syrup (2 sugar to 1 water)**

Origin: Created in 1999 by Dominique of Café Rouge, Leeds, England.
Comment: A cocktail that's both bitter and sweet.

PINKY PINCHER

Glass: Old-fashioned
Garnish: Mint sprig, orange & lemon slice
Method: SHAKE all ingredients with ice and strain into ice-filled glass.

2	shot(s)	**Buffalo Trace bourbon whiskey**
1	shot(s)	**Freshly squeezed orange juice**
1	shot(s)	**Freshly squeezed lemon juice**
$^1/_4$	shot(s)	**Orgeat (almond) sugar syrup**
$^1/_4$	shot(s)	**Sugar syrup (2 sugar to 1 water)**

Origin: Adapted from a drink created by Victor Bergeron (Trader Vic).
Comment: Fruity, sweetened bourbon.

PINO PEPE

Glass: Sling (or pineapple shell)
Garnish: Mint sprig
Method: BLEND all ingredients with 12oz scoop crushed ice. Pour into glass (or pineapple shell) and serve with straws. If using a pineapple shell, serve with ice cubes.

1	shot(s)	**Light white rum**
1	shot(s)	**Ketel One vodka**
$^1/_2$	shot(s)	**Cointreau /triple sec**
2	shot(s)	**Pressed pineapple juice**
$^1/_2$	shot(s)	**Freshly squeezed lime juice**
$^1/_4$	shot(s)	**Freshly squeezed lemon juice**
$^1/_2$	shot(s)	**Sugar syrup (2 sugar to 1 water)**

Origin: Adapted from a recipe in the 1947-72 Trader Vic's Bartender's Guide by Victor Bergeron.
Comment: To quote Trader Vic, "Lethal but smooth – pineapple at its best".

RUSSIANS CONSUME THE EQUIVALENT OF MORE THAN FOUR BILLION BOTTLES OF VODKA A YEAR.

PIRATE DAIQUIRI

Glass: Martini
Garnish: Lime wedge on rim
Method: SHAKE all ingredients with ice and fine strain into chilled glass.

$^3/_4$	shot(s)	**Wray & Nephew overproof rum**
$^3/_4$	shot(s)	**Pusser's Navy rum**
$^1/_2$	shot(s)	**Cinnamon schnapps liqueur**
$^1/_2$	shot(s)	**Freshly squeezed lime juice**
$^1/_4$	shot(s)	**Pomegranate (grenadine) syrup**
$^3/_4$	shot(s)	**Chilled mineral water** (omit if wet ice)

Origin: Created in 2004 by yours truly.
Comment: Why the name? Well, the rums are hard and nautical, the lime protects against scurvy, the liqueur contains gold and the syrup is red as blood.

PISCO COLLINS

Glass: Collins
Garnish: Orange slice & cherry on stick (sail)
Method: SHAKE first three ingredients with ice and strain into ice-filled glass. **TOP** with soda, lightly stir and serve with straws.

2	shot(s)	**Pisco**
1	shot(s)	**Freshly squeezed lime juice**
$^1/_2$	shot(s)	**Sugar syrup (2 sugar to 1 water)**
Top up with		**Soda water (club soda)**

Comment: The most aromatic and flavoursome of the Collins family.

PISCO PUNCH

The creation of the Pisco Punch is usually credited to Professor Jerry Burns of San Francisco's Bank Exchange. However, its origin could lie in the late 1800s, when the drink was served aboard steamships stopping in Chile en route to San Francisco. The following story of the Pisco Punch and the Bank Exchange comes from the 1973 edition of the California Historical Quarterly and Robert O'Brien's book, 'This Was San Francisco'.

The Bank Exchange was a ballroom that opened in 1854 and survived the earthquake and fire of 1906. Its popularity never waned and only Prohibition brought about its demise. Much of the Bank Exchange's notoriety was due to the Pisco Punch, so much so that the establishment gained the nickname 'Pisco John's' after one of its original owners.

The recipe was handed down from owner to owner in absolute secrecy. Duncan Nichol, the Scottish immigrant who owned the bar from the late 1870s until it closed, inherited it from the previous owners, Orrin Dorman and John Torrence, and is thought to have carried it to his grave.

PISCO NARANJA

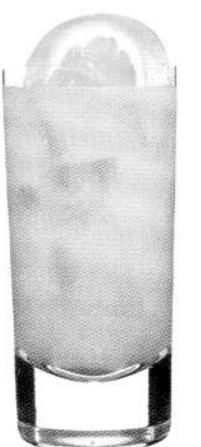

Glass: Collins
Garnish: Orange slice
Method: **SHAKE** all ingredients with ice and strain into ice-filled glass.

2	shot(s)	**Pisco**
3	shot(s)	**Freshly squeezed orange juice**
1	shot(s)	**Grand Marnier liqueur**

Origin: I based this recipe on the traditional Chilean combination of pisco and orange juice.
Comment: Aromatic brandy and orange juice pepped up and sweetened with a slug of orange liqueur.

PISCO PUNCH #1 (DIFFORD'S FORMULA)

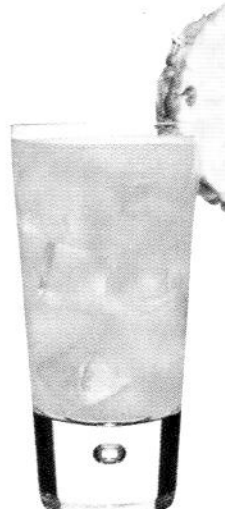

Glass: Collins
Garnish: Pineapple wedge on rim
Method: **MUDDLE** cloves in base of shaker. Add other ingredients except for champagne, **SHAKE** with ice and strain into ice-filled glass. **TOP** with champagne.

4	dried	**Cloves**
2¼	shot(s)	**Pisco**
1¾	shot(s)	**Pressed pineapple juice**
¼	shot(s)	**Freshly squeezed orange juice**
½	shot(s)	**Freshly squeezed lemon juice**
½	shot(s)	**Sugar syrup (2 sugar to 1 water)**
Top up with		**Brut champagne**

Origin: Created in 2003 by yours truly.
Variant: This recipe is improved by using the marinade prescribed in Alfredo Micheli's Pisco Punch in place of sugar syrup. If using the marinade drop one of the marinated pineapple wedges and cloves into the drink as the garnish.
Comment: A tangy, balanced combination of rich flavours. The quality of pisco used is crucial to the success of a Pisco Punch

PISCO PUNCH #2 (ALFREDO MICHELI'S FORMULA)

Glass: Goblet
Garnish: Pineapple wedge on rim
Method: **MUDDLE** orange and pineapple in base of shaker. Add pisco and pineapple marinade, **SHAKE** with ice and fine strain into ice-filled glass. **TOP** with no more than 2 shots of soda water.

2	fresh	**Orange slices**
3		**Marinaded pineapple wedges**
2	shot(s)	**Pisco**
¾	shot(s)	**Pineapple marinade**
Top up with		**Soda water (club soda)**

Recipe for marinade: Core and remove the rind from one ripe pineapple. Cut the pineapple into rings and then into wedges and place in a deep container. Add 30 cloves and one litre of sugar syrup and marinate for 24 hours.
Origin: Alfredo Micheli (who went by the nickname Mike) was employed at the Bank Exchange and spied on Duncan Nichol to learn how to make this legendary drink. After he believed he'd learnt the secret he left to start serving at a newly opened competitor to the Bank Exchange, Paoli's on Montgomery Street.
Comment: This subtly flavoured drink is justifiably legendary.

PISCO PUNCH #3 (LANES' FORMULA) [UPDATED]

Glass: Collins
Garnish: Pineapple wedge on rim
Method: SHAKE first four ingredients with ice and strain into glass filled with crushed ice. **TOP** with soda, lightly stir and serve with straws.

2½	shot(s)	**Pisco**
½	shot(s)	**Freshly squeezed lemon juice**
1	shot(s)	**Pressed pineapple juice**
½	shot(s)	**Sugar syrup (2 sugar to 1 water)**
Top up with		**Soda water (club soda)**

Origin: This recipe is said to herald from John Lanes, manager of the famous Bank Exchange when it closed in 1919.
Comment: Pisco's character comes through the fruit in this long, refreshing classic.

PISCO SOUR (DIFFORD'S VERSION) [UPDATED #7]

Glass: Old-fashioned
Garnish: Three drops of Angostura bitters
Method: SHAKE all ingredients with ice and fine strain into chilled glass.

2½	shot(s)	**Pisco**
1	shot(s)	**Freshly squeezed lime juice**
½	shot(s)	**Sugar syrup (2 sugar to 1 water)**
½	fresh	**Egg white**
1	dash	**Orange flower water**

Origin: My adaptation of the Chilean and Peruvian classic.
Comment: Traditionally this drink is blended with crushed ice, but I prefer it served straight-up. Be sure to drink it quickly while it's cold.

'THIS IS DISGRACEFUL... I AM AS DRUNK AS A LORD – BUT IT DOESN'T MATTER, BECAUSE I AM A LORD!'
BERTRAND RUSSELL

PISCO PUNCH #4 (PROSSER'S FORMULA)

Glass: Martini
Garnish: Grapes on rim
Method: MUDDLE grapes in base of shaker. Add other ingredients, **SHAKE** with ice and fine strain into chilled glass.

20	fresh	**Seedless white grapes**
2½	shot(s)	**Pisco**
1	shot(s)	**Pressed pineapple juice**
⅛	shot(s)	**La Fée Parisienne (68%) absinthe**

Origin: Jack Koeppler, the bartender at the Buena Vista Café in San Francisco who's also famous for being the first bartender in America to serve Irish Coffee, was given this recipe by the son of its creator, a fellow San Franciscan by the name of Mr Prosser. I've adapted this recipe from his, which originally comprised: 2 shots white grape juice, 2 shots pisco, 1 spoon pineapple juice and 1 spoon absinthe.
Comment: An aromatic take on the Pisco Punch.

PISCO SOUR (TRADITIONAL RECIPE)

Glass: Goblet
Garnish: Three drops of Angostura bitters
Method: BLEND all ingredients with 12oz scoop crushed ice and serve with straws.

2	shot(s)	**Pisco**
1	shot(s)	**Freshly squeezed lime juice**
1	shot(s)	**Sugar syrup (2 sugar to 1 water)**
½	fresh	**Egg white**

Variant: Dust with cinnamon powder.
Origin: Believed to have first been created in the 1920s, the Pisco Sour has since become the national drink of both Chile and Peru.
Comment: One of the few really brilliant blended drinks.

PISCOLA

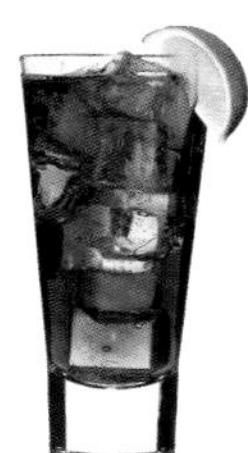

Glass: Collins
Garnish: Lime wedge
Method: POUR pisco and bitters into ice-filled glass, top with cola, stir and serve with straws.

2½	shot(s)	**Pisco**
3	dashes	**Angostura aromatic bitters**
Top up with		**Cola**

Origin: A popular long drink in its native Chile.
Comment: A 'brandy' and cola with a hint of angostura. Try it and see why the Chileans enjoy it.

PLANTATION PUNCH

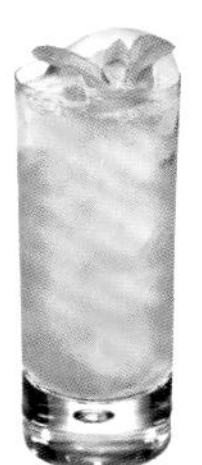

Glass: Collins
Garnish: Orange slice & mint sprig
Method: SHAKE first five ingredients with ice and strain into ice-filled glass. **TOP** with soda.

1½	shot(s)	**Southern Comfort liqueur**
1	shot(s)	**Light white rum**
¾	shot(s)	**Freshly squeezed lemon juice**
¼	shot(s)	**Sugar syrup (2 sugar to 1 water)**
2	dashes	**Angostura aromatic bitters**
Top up with		**Soda water (club soda)**

Comment: Southern Comfort drives this tropical punch.

DRINKS ARE GRADED AS FOLLOWS:

● DISGUSTING ●◐ PRETTY AWFUL ●● BEST AVOIDED ●●◐ DISAPPOINTING ●●● ACCEPTABLE ●●●◐ GOOD ●●●● RECOMMENDED ●●●●◐ HIGHLY RECOMMENDED ●●●●● OUTSTANDING / EXCEPTIONAL

PLANTER'S PUNCH

Glass: Collins
Garnish: Orange slice & mint sprig
Method: **SHAKE** all ingredients with ice and strain into ice-filled glass.

1½	shot(s)	**Myers's Planters' Punch rum**
1	shot(s)	**Freshly squeezed lime juice**
½	shot(s)	**Sugar syrup (2 sugar to 1 water)**
2	shot(s)	**Chilled mineral water**
3	dashes	**Angostura aromatic bitters**

Origin: Invented in the late 19th century by the founder of Myers's rum, Fred L. Myers. The recipe on the back of each bottle is known as the 'Old Plantation formula' and uses the classic rum punch proportions of 1 sour (lime), 2 sweet (sugar), 3 strong (rum) and 4 weak (water). Rather than this or the American formula (1 sweet, 2 sour, 3 weak and 4 strong), I've followed David A. Embury's recommendation of 1 sweet, 2 sour, 3 strong and 4 weak.
Comment: A twangy punch which harnesses the rich flavours of Myers's rum.

PLANTER'S PUNCHLESS (MOCKTAIL)

Glass: Collins
Garnish: Lime wedge
Method: **SHAKE** first three ingredients with ice and strain into ice-filled glass. **TOP** with 7-Up, lightly stir and serve with straws.

2	shot(s)	**Pressed apple juice**
¾	shot(s)	**Freshly squeezed lime juice**
¼	shot(s)	**Pomegranate (grenadine) syrup**
Top up with		**7-Up**

Comment: A pleasant, if uninspiring, driver's option.

PLANTEUR

Glass: Collins
Garnish: Orange slice
Method: **SHAKE** all ingredients with ice and strain into ice-filled glass.

2	shot(s)	**Martinique blanc agricole rum (50% alc./vol.)**
3½	shot(s)	**Freshly squeezed orange juice**
¼	shot(s)	**Pomegranate (grenadine) syrup**

Comment: Handle with extreme care.

PLATINUM BLONDE

Glass: Martini
Garnish: Freshly grated nutmeg
Method: **SHAKE** all ingredients with ice and fine strain into chilled glass.

1½	shot(s)	**Aged rum**
1½	shot(s)	**Grand Marnier liqueur**
½	shot(s)	**Double (heavy) cream**
½	shot(s)	**Milk**

Comment: An after dinner sipper.

PLAYA DEL MAR

Glass: Martini
Garnish: Pineapple wedge on rim
Method: **SHAKE** all ingredients with ice and fine strain into chilled glass.

1	shot(s)	**Partida tequila**
½	shot(s)	**Cointreau triple sec**
1	shot(s)	**Ocean Spray cranberry juice**
¾	shot(s)	**Pressed pineapple juice**
½	shot(s)	**Freshly squeezed lime juice**
¼	shot(s)	**Sugar syrup (2 sugar to 1 water)**

Origin: This cocktail was created in 1997 by Wayne Collins at Navajo Joe, London, England. The name translates as 'Beach of the Sea'.
Comment: A fruity complex taste with a hint of tequila.

PLAYMATE MARTINI

Glass: Martini
Garnish: Orange zest twist
Method: **SHAKE** all ingredients with ice and fine strain into chilled glass.

1	shot(s)	**Rémy Martin cognac**
1	shot(s)	**Grand Marnier liqueur**
1	shot(s)	**Giffard apricot brandy du Roussillon**
1	shot(s)	**Freshly squeezed orange juice**
½	fresh	**Egg white**
3	dashes	**Angostura aromatic bitters**

Comment: Smooth and easy drinking.

PLUM COCKTAIL

Glass: Martini
Garnish: Plum quarter on rim
Method: Cut plum into quarters, remove stone and peel. **MUDDLE** plum in base of shaker. Add other ingredients, **SHAKE** with ice and fine strain into chilled glass.

1	fresh	**Plum (stoned and peeled)**
2	shot(s)	**Zuta Osa Slivovitz plum brandy**
¼	shot(s)	**Dry vermouth**
¼	shot(s)	**Sugar syrup (2 sugar to 1 water)**

Origin: Formula by yours truly in 2004.
Comment: The slivovitz adds woody, brandied notes to the plum.

PLUM DAIQUIRI

Glass: Martini
Garnish: Lime wedge on rim
Method: Cut plum into quarters, remove stone and peel. **MUDDLE** plum pieces in base of shaker. Add other ingredients, **SHAKE** with ice and fine strain into chilled glass.

1	fresh	**Plum (stoned and peeled)**
2	shot(s)	**Light white rum**
½	shot(s)	**Freshly squeezed lime juice**
½	shot(s)	**Sugar syrup (2 sugar to 1 water)**

Origin: Formula by yours truly in 2004.
Comment: Depending on the ripeness of the plums, you may need to adjust the quantity of sugar.

PLUM MARTINI

Glass: Martini
Garnish: Plum quarter on rim (unpeeled)
Method: Cut plum into quarters, remove stone and peel. **MUDDLE** plum pieces in base of shaker. Add other ingredients, **SHAKE** with ice and fine strain into chilled glass.

1	fresh	**Plum (stoned and peeled)**
2	shot(s)	**Ketel One vodka**
3/4	shot(s)	**Dry vermouth**
1/2	shot(s)	**Sugar syrup (2 sugar to 1 water)**

Origin: Formula by yours truly in 2004.
Variant: Substitute vanilla sugar syrup for plain sugar syrup.
Comment: Fortified plum juice in a Martini glass.

PLUM PUDDING MARTINI

Glass: Martini
Garnish: Grate fresh nutmeg over drink
Method: Cut plum into quarters, remove stone and peel. **MUDDLE** plum pieces in base of shaker. Add other ingredients, **SHAKE** with ice and fine strain into chilled glass.

1	fresh	**Plum (stoned, peeled & chopped)**
1	shot(s)	**Raspberry flavoured vodka**
1	shot(s)	**Vanilla infused Ketel One vodka**
1/2	shot(s)	**Luxardo Amaretto di Saschira liqueur**
1/8	shot(s)	**Cinnamon schnapps liqueur**

Origin: Created in 2004 by yours truly.
Comment: Spicy and fruity.

PLUM SOUR

Glass: Old-fashioned
Garnish: Orange zest twist
Method: **MUDDLE** plum in base of shaker. Add other ingredients, **SHAKE** with ice and fine strain into ice-filled glass.

1	fresh	**Plum (peeled stoned and chopped)**
2	shot(s)	**Ketel One vodka**
1	shot(s)	**Freshly squeezed lemon juice**
1/2	shot(s)	**Sugar syrup (2 sugar to 1 water)**
1/2	fresh	**Egg white**

Comment: Soft, ripe plums are key to this fruity sour.

POET'S DREAM

Glass: Martini
Garnish: Squeezed lemon zest twist
Method: **STIR** all ingredients with ice and strain into chilled glass.

1	shot(s)	**Plymouth gin**
1	shot(s)	**Bénédictine D.O.M. liqueur**
1	shot(s)	**Dry vermouth**
3/4	shot(s)	**Chilled mineral water** (omit if wet ice)

Origin: Adapted from a recipe in the 1949 edition of Esquire's Handbook for Hosts.
Comment: Subtle, honeyed and herbal.

POGO STICK

Glass: Martini (large)
Garnish: Mint sprig
Method: **BLEND** all ingredients with 12oz scoop crushed ice. Serve with straws.

2	shot(s)	**Plymouth gin**
1/2	shot(s)	**Pressed pineapple juice**
1/2	shot(s)	**Squeezed pink grapefruit juice**
1/2	shot(s)	**Freshly squeezed lime juice**
1/2	shot(s)	**Sugar syrup (2 sugar to 1 water)**

Origin: Adapted from a recipe in the 1947-72 Trader Vic's Bartender's Guide by Victor Bergeron.
Comment: To quote Trader Vic, "A refreshing blend of gin with pineapple and grapefruit juice… a real romper".

POINSETTIA

Glass: Flute
Garnish: Quarter slice of orange on rim
Method: **POUR** first two ingredients into chilled glass. **TOP** with champagne.

1/2	shot(s)	**Cointreau triple sec**
1	shot(s)	**Ocean Spray cranberry juice**
Top up with		**Brut champagne**

Comment: Fruity champagne.

POLISH MARTINI

Glass: Martini
Garnish: Lemon zest twist
Method: **SHAKE** all ingredients with ice and fine strain into chilled glass.

1	shot(s)	**Ketel One vodka**
1	shot(s)	**Zubrówka bison vodka**
3/4	shot(s)	**Krupnik honey liqueur**
1 1/2	shot(s)	**Pressed apple juice**

Origin: Created by Dick Bradsell, for his (Polish) father-in-law, Victor Sarge.
Comment: A round, smooth and very tasty alternatini.

POLLY'S SPECIAL

Glass: Martini
Garnish: Grapefruit wedge on rim
Method: **SHAKE** all ingredients with ice and fine strain into chilled glass.

1 3/4	shot(s)	**Scotch whisky**
1	shot(s)	**Freshly squeezed grapefruit juice**
1	shot(s)	**Grand Marnier liqueur**
1/4	shot(s)	**Sugar syrup (2 sugar to 1 water)**

Origin: I adapted this recipe from a 1947 edition of Trader Vic's Bartender's Guide.
Comment: Sweet, sour, flavoursome and balanced – for grown-ups who like the taste of alcohol.

POMEGRANATE BELLINI

Glass: Flute
Method: Cut pomegranate in half and juice using a citrus juicer. **SHAKE** first three ingredients with ice and fine strain into chilled glass. **TOP** with sparkling wine.

1	shot(s)	**Freshly squeezed pomegranate juice**
1/2	shot(s)	**Cuarenta Y Tres (Licor 43) liqueur**
1/8	shot(s)	**Freshly squeezed lemon juice**
Top up with		**Prosecco sparkling wine**

Origin: Created in 2005 by yours truly.
Comment: This red drink is drier and more adult than it looks.

POMEGRANATE MARGARITA

Glass: Coupette
Garnish: Lime wedge on rim
Method: Cut pomegranate in half and juice using a citrus juicer. **SHAKE** all ingredients with ice and fine strain into chilled glass.

2	shot(s)	**Partida tequila**
1	shot(s)	**Freshly squeezed pomegranate juice**
1/2	shot(s)	**Freshly squeezed lime juice**
1/4	shot(s)	**Pomegranate (grenadine) syrup**

Origin: Recipe by yours truly in 2006.
Comment: Pomegranate and tequila combine harmoniously in this Margarita.

POMEGRANATE MARTINI

Glass: Martini
Garnish: Orange zest twist
Method: Cut pomegranate in half and juice using a citrus juicer. **SHAKE** all ingredients with ice and fine strain into chilled glass.

2	shot(s)	**Ketel One vodka**
1 1/2	shot(s)	**Freshly squeezed pomegranate juice**
1/2	shot(s)	**Pomegranate (grenadine) syrup**

Origin: Adapted from a drink discovered in 2005 at Lotus Bar, Sydney, Australia.
Comment: This drink was originally based on gin but I find that juniper and pomegranate clash.

POMME ET SUREAU [NEW #7]

Glass: Collins
Garnish: Apple wedge
Method: **POUR** first two ingredients into ice-filled glass. Top with soda.

1	shot(s)	**Boulard Grand Solage Calvados**
2	shot(s)	**St-Germain elderflower liqueur**
Top up with		**Soda water**

Origin: Created in 2006 by yours truly. The name means 'Apple & Elderflower' in French.
Comment: Light, long and refreshing apple and elderflower.

POMPANSKI MARTINI

Glass: Martini
Garnish: Orange zest twist
Method: **SHAKE** all ingredients with ice and fine strain into chilled glass.

1 3/4	shot(s)	**Ketel One vodka**
1/2	shot(s)	**Cointreau triple sec**
1 1/2	shot(s)	**Freshly squeezed grapefruit juice**
1/4	shot(s)	**Sugar syrup (2 sugar to 1 water)**
1	spoon	**Dry vermouth**

Comment: Dry and zesty with the sharp freshness of grapefruit and a hint of orange.

PONCE DE LEON

Glass: Flute
Method: **SHAKE** first four ingredients with ice and fine strain into chilled glass. **TOP** with champagne.

1/2	shot(s)	**Golden rum**
1/2	shot(s)	**Rémy Martin cognac**
1/2	shot(s)	**Cointreau /triple sec**
1/2	shot(s)	**Squeezed pink grapefruit juice**
Top up with		**Brut champagne**

Origin: A long lost classic.
Comment: A well-balanced champagne cocktail.

PONCHA

Glass: Collins
Garnish: Orange wedge
Method: **STIR** honey with aguardiente in base of shaker to dissolve honey. Add other ingredients, **SHAKE** with ice and strain into ice filled glass.

2	spoons	**Runny honey**
2 1/2	shot(s)	**Aguardiente (Torres Aqua d'Or)**
1	shot(s)	**Freshly squeezed lemon juice**
1/4	shot(s)	**Sugar syrup (2 sugar to 1 water)**
1 1/2	shot(s)	**Freshly squeezed orange juice**
1 1/2	shot(s)	**Freshly squeezed grapefruit juice**

Origin: My adaptation of a tradtitional drink from the island of Madeira.
Comment: This citrus refresher is reputedly an excellent cold remedy.

PONCHE DE ALGARROBINA

Glass: Goblet
Garnish: Dust with cinnamon
Method: **BLEND** all ingredients with 12oz scoop crushed ice. Serve with straws.

2	shot(s)	**Pisco**
1	fresh	**Egg yolk**
1	shot(s)	**Condensed milk**
1	spoon	**Algarrobo extract** (or malt extract from healthfood shops)

Tip: It pays to add the condensed milk and Algarrobo (or malt extract) after starting the blender.
Origin: A traditional Peruvian drink I discovered at Tito's Restaurant, London, England. Algarrobo is extracted from the fruits of the tree of the same name. It is a sticky honey-like liquid which I find tastes a little like malt extract.
Comment: A creamy frozen drink with real character.

PONTBERRY MARTINI

Glass: Martini
Garnish: Blackberries
Method: SHAKE all ingredients with ice and fine strain into chilled glass.

1½	shot(s)	**Ketel One vodka**
½	shot(s)	**Giffard mûre (blackberry)**
2	shot(s)	**Ocean Spray cranberry juice**

Origin: Created by Dick Bradsell in the late 90s for the opening of Agent Provocateur in Pont Street, London, England.
Comment: A light, fruity, easy drinking cocktail.

POOH'TINI

Glass: Martini
Garnish: Lemon zest twist
Method: STIR honey with vodka in base of shaker to dissolve honey. Add other ingredients, **SHAKE** with ice and fine strain into chilled glass.

2	spoon(s)	**Runny honey**
2	shot(s)	**Zubrówka bison grass vodka**
½	shot(s)	**Krupnik honey liqueur**
1½	shot(s)	**Cold black camomile tea**

Origin: Adapted from a drink discovered in 1999 at Lot 61, New York City.
Comment: Grassy honey with a spicy, slightly tannic, camomile finish.

PORT & MELON MARTINI

Glass: Martini
Garnish: Melon wedge on rim
Method: Cut melon into eight segments and deseed. Cut cubes of flesh from skin of one segment and **MUDDLE** in base of shaker. Add other ingredients, **SHAKE** with ice and fine strain into chilled glass.

⅛	fresh	**Cantaloupe / Galia melon**
1½	shot(s)	**Ketel One vodka**
1½	shot(s)	**Dry white port (e.g. Dow's Fine White)**
1	pinch	**Ground ginger**

Origin: Created in 2004 by yours truly.
Comment: The classic seventies starter served as a Martini.

PORT & STARBOARD

Glass: Shot
Method: Refrigerate ingredients then **LAYER** in chilled glass by carefully pouring in the following order.

½	shot(s)	**Pomegranate (grenadine) syrup**
½	shot(s)	**Giffard white crème de Menthe Pastille**

Origin: Named after and inspired by the red and green running lights which respectively mark the 'Port' (left-hand) and 'Starboard' (right-hand) sides of a ship. The red light is called the Port side because port wine is red. The original name for the opposite side was Larboard, but over the years it was corrupted to Starboard.
Comment: Easy to layer but hard to drink. Very sweet.

PORT LIGHT

Glass: Martini
Garnish: Passion fruit half
Method: STIR honey with bourbon in base of shaker to dissolve honey. Cut passion fruit in half and scoop flesh into shaker. Add other ingredients, **SHAKE** with ice and fine strain into chilled glass.

2	spoons	**Runny honey**
2	shot(s)	**Buffalo Trace bourbon whiskey**
1	fresh	**Passion fruit**
1	shot(s)	**Freshly squeezed lemon juice**
½	shot(s)	**Pomegranate (grenadine) syrup**
½	fresh	**Egg white**

Origin: Adapted from a drink created by Victor Bergeron (Trader Vic).
Comment: Strong and very fruity. Too many will put your lights out.

PORT WINE COCKTAIL

Glass: Martini
Garnish: Orange zest twist
Method: STIR all ingredients with ice and strain into chilled glass.

3	shot(s)	**Warre's Otima Tawny Port**
1	shot(s)	**Rémy Martin cognac**

Origin: A classic from the early 1900s.
Comment: Port and brandy served straight-up and dressed up.

'I LIKE GIN. YOU CAN SEE THROUGH IT. BEER IS LIKE A FISH-POND... I CAN DRINK TWENTY GLASSES IN THE COURSE OF A DAY, EASY.' VICTORIAN TAILOR QUOTED BY

POTTED PARROT

Glass: Sling
Garnish: Parrot on stick & mint sprig
Method: SHAKE all ingredients with ice and strain into glass filled with crushed ice.

2	shot(s)	**Light white rum**
½	shot(s)	**Cointreau triple sec**
2	shot(s)	**Freshly squeezed orange juice**
1	shot(s)	**Freshly squeezed lemon juice**
¼	shot(s)	**Almond (orgeat) sugar syrup**
¼	shot(s)	**Sugar syrup (2 sugar to 1 water)**

Origin: Adapted from a recipe in the 1947-72 Trader Vic's Bartender's Guide by Victor Bergeron. Popular in Trader Vic's restaurants.
Comment: Tangy orange, not too sweet.

POUSSE-CAFÉ [UPDATED #7]

Glass: Shot
Method: Refrigerate ingredients then **LAYER** in chilled glass by carefully pouring in the following order.

1/4	shot(s)	**Pomegranate (grenadine) syrup**
1/4	shot(s)	**Kahlúa coffee liqueur**
1/4	shot(s)	**Giffard green crème de menthe**
1/4	shot(s)	**Cointreau triple sec**
1/4	shot(s)	**Buffalo Trace bourbon whiskey**
1/4	shot(s)	**Wray & Nephew white overproof rum**

Origin: A pousse-café is now a term for any multi-layered cocktail. (See 'Layer' in the 'Bartending Basics' chapter at the beginning of this guide.) The term originally seems to have been a general term for a mixture of liqueurs and/or spirits served after dinner, and most probably originated in France.
Comment: More a test of patience and a steady hand than a drink.

PRADO [NEW #7]

Glass: Martini
Garnish: Lime wedge on rim
Method: **SHAKE** all ingredients with ice and fine strain into chilled glass.

2	shot(s)	**Partida tequila**
1	shot(s)	**Freshly squeezed lime juice**
1/2	shot(s)	**Luxardo maraschino liqueur**
1/2	shot(s)	**Egg white**

Comment: Rather like a cross between an Aviation and a Margarita.

PRAIRIE OYSTER

Glass: Coupette
Method: Taking care not to break the egg yolk, **PLACE** it in the centre hollow of the glass. **SHAKE** the rest of the ingredients with ice and strain over egg. Instruct drinker to down in one.

1	raw	**Egg yolk**
1	shot(s)	**Rémy Martin cognac**
1/4	shot(s)	**Worcestershire sauce**
1/4	shot(s)	**Tomato juice**
5	drops	**Tabasco**
2	pinches	**Pepper**
2	pinches	**Salt**
1/2	spoon	**Malt vinegar**

Origin: Thought to have been created in Germany in the 1870s. Jeeves makes something similar for Bertie Wooster in a P.G. Wodehouse tale.
Comment: Like many supposed hangover cures, this works on the kill or... basis. It tastes better than it looks.

PRESIDENT

Glass: Martini
Garnish: Orange zest twist
Method: **SHAKE** all ingredients with ice and fine strain into chilled glass.

2	shot(s)	**Light white rum**
1	shot(s)	**Freshly squeezed orange juice**
1/4	shot(s)	**Freshly squeezed lemon juice**
1/4	shot(s)	**Pomegranate (grenadine) syrup**
1/2	shot(s)	**Chilled mineral water** (omit if wet ice)

Origin: Adapted from a recipe in Harry Craddock's 1930 Savoy Cocktail Book.
Comment: A delicately fruity orange Daiquiri.

PRESIDENT VINCENT [NEW #7]

Glass: Martini
Garnish: Lime zest twist
Method: **SHAKE** all ingredients with ice and fine strain into chilled glass.

2	shot(s)	**Light white rum**
1/2	shot(s)	**Dry vermouth**
1/2	shot(s)	**Freshly squeezed lime juice**
1/4	shot(s)	**Sugar syrup (2 sugar to 1 water)**

Origin: Probably 1930s.
Comment: A dry, spicy take on the Daiquiri.

PRESIDENTE [UPDATED #7]

Glass: Martini
Garnish: Orange zest twist
Method: **SHAKE** all ingredients with ice and fine strain into chilled glass.

1 1/2	shot(s)	**Light white rum**
3/4	shot(s)	**Cointreau triple sec**
3/4	shot(s)	**Dry vermouth**
1/8	shot(s)	**Pomegranate (grenadine) syrup**
1/2	shot(s)	**Chilled mineral water** (omit if wet ice)

Variant: El Presidente #3
Origin: This classic was created during the 1920s in Vista Alegre, Havana, Cuba. The name refers to Mario García Menocal, who was president of Cuba from 1912 to 1920.
Comment: A lightly flavoured classic cocktail.

PRICKLY PEAR MULE

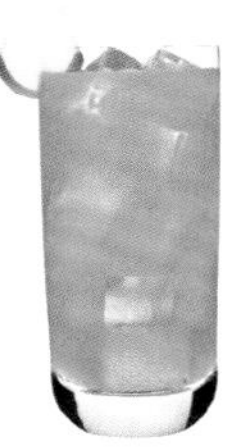

Glass: Collins
Garnish: Pear slice on rim
Method: **SHAKE** first five ingredients with ice and strain into ice-filled glass. **TOP** with ginger beer.

1 1/4	shot(s)	**Pear & cognac liqueur**
1 1/4	shot(s)	**Poire William eau de vie**
3	shot(s)	**Freshly extracted pear juice**
1/4	shot(s)	**Freshly squeezed lemon juice**
2	dashes	**Angostura aromatic bitters**
Top up with		**Jamaican ginger beer**

Origin: Created in 2002 by yours truly.
Tip: Fill the glass with ice and go easy on the ginger beer which can predominate and overpower the pear.
Comment: Subtle pear with ginger spice.

PRINCE CHARLIE

Glass: Martini
Garnish: Lemon zest twist
Method: SHAKE all ingredients with ice and fine strain into chilled glass.

1	shot(s)	**Rémy Martin cognac**
1	shot(s)	**Drambuie liqueur**
1	shot(s)	**Freshly squeezed lemon juice**
3/4	shot(s)	**Chilled mineral water** (omit if wet ice)

Origin: A long lost classic.
Comment: Cognac and honey with sweet and sourness in harmony.

PRINCE OF WALES

Glass: Flute
Garnish: Lemon peel twist
Method: Rub sugar cube with lemon peel, coat with bitters and drop into glass. **POUR** cognac and liqueur over soaked cube and top with champagne.

1	cube	**Brown sugar**
2	dashes	**Angostura aromatic bitters**
1/2	shot(s)	**Rémy Martin cognac**
1/2	shot(s)	**Grand Marnier liqueur**
Top up with		**Brut champagne**

Comment: More interesting than a classic Champagne Cocktail.

PRINCESS MARINA

Glass: Martini
Garnish: Orange zest twist
Method: SHAKE all ingredients with ice and fine strain into chilled glass.

1	shot(s)	**Plymouth gin**
1/2	shot(s)	**Boulard Grand Solage Calvados**
1/2	shot(s)	**Dubonnet Red**
1/2	shot(s)	**Cointreau triple sec**
1/2	shot(s)	**Carlshamns Swedish Torr Flaggpunsch**
3/4	shot(s)	**Chilled mineral water** (omit if wet ice)

Origin: Created in the late 1920s/early 1930s and named after Princess Marina, the late mother of The Duke of Kent, Prince Michael of Kent and Princess Alexandra.
Comment: Delicate yet loaded with alcohol and flavour.

PRINCESS MARY

Glass: Martini
Garnish: Dust with cocoa powder
Method: SHAKE all ingredients with ice and fine strain into chilled glass.

1 1/2	shot(s)	**Plymouth gin**
1	shot(s)	**Giffard white crème de cacao**
3/4	shot(s)	**Double (heavy) cream**
3/4	shot(s)	**Milk**

Origin: Created in 1922 by Harry MacElhone to celebrate H.R.H. Princess Mary's marriage. The original recipe featured equal parts of all four ingredients.
Comment: Slightly sweet, very creamy - drink after dinner.

PRINCESS MARY'S PRIDE

Glass: Martini
Garnish: Orange zest twist
Method: SHAKE all ingredients with ice and fine strain into chilled glass.

2	shot(s)	**Boulard Grand Solage Calvados**
1	shot(s)	**Dubonnet Red**
1	shot(s)	**Dry vermouth**

Origin: Created by Harry Craddock on 28th February 1922 to mark the wedding celebrations of H.R.H. Princess Mary. Recipe from 1930's Savoy Cocktail Book.
Comment: Apple brandy to the fore, followed by aromatised wine.

PRINCESS PRIDE

Glass: Martini
Garnish: Orange zest twist
Method: SHAKE all ingredients with ice and fine strain into chilled glass.

2	shot(s)	**Boulard Grand Solage Calvados**
1	shot(s)	**Dubonnet Red**
1	shot(s)	**Sweet vermouth**

Origin: Adapted from a recipe in the 1947-72 Trader Vic's Bartender's Guide by Victor Bergeron.
Comment: Vic's improved version of the drink above.

PRINCETON [UPDATED]

Glass: Martini
Garnish: Lemon zest twist
Method: STIR all ingredients with ice and strain into chilled glass.

2	shot(s)	**Plymouth gin**
1	shot(s)	**Warre's Otima Tawny Port**
1/4	shot(s)	**Sugar syrup (2 sugar to 1 water)**
2	dashes	**Fee Brothers orange bitters**

Origin: An old classic originally made with sweet 'Old Tom' gin and without the sugar syrup.
Comment: Overproof wine with a herbal orange garnish.

PRINCETON MARTINI

Glass: Martini
Garnish: Lime zest twist
Method: SHAKE all ingredients with ice and fine strain into chilled glass.

2	shot(s)	**Plymouth gin**
1/2	shot(s)	**Dry vermouth**
1/4	shot(s)	**Rose's lime cordial**
1/2	shot(s)	**Chilled mineral water** (omit if wet ice)

Comment: The Dry Martini meets the Gimlet. They should meet more often.

PRUNE FACE

Glass: Old-fashioned
Garnish: Orange zest twist
Method: POUR bourbon into glass with four ice cubes and **STIR** until ice has at least half melted. Add other ingredients and additional ice and stir some more.

2	shot(s)	**Buffalo Trace bourbon whiskey**
3/4	shot(s)	**Vieille de prune eau de vie**
1/4	shot(s)	**Mandarine Napoléon liqueur**
1/4	shot(s)	**Sugar syrup (2 sugar to 1 water)**

Origin: Created in 2002 by Daniel Warner at Zander, London, England and named after my friend's nickname for his stepmother.
Comment: Why muddle cherries into your Old Fashioned when you can add a hint of prune?

'I GAVE HER A DRINK. SHE WAS A GAL WHO'D TAKE A DRINK IF SHE HAD TO KNOCK ME DOWN TO GET THE BOTTLE.'

PRUNEAUX

Glass: Martini
Garnish: Prunes on stick
Method: SHAKE all ingredients with ice and fine strain into chilled glass.

1 1/2	shot(s)	**Plymouth gin**
1	shot(s)	**Amontillado sherry**
1/2	shot(s)	**Pedro Ximenez sherry**
3/4	shot(s)	**Freshly squeezed orange juice**
3/4	shot(s)	**Syrup from tinned prunes**

Origin: Adapted from a recipe in Harry Craddock's 1930 Savoy Cocktail Book.
Comment: Sherried prunes further fortified by gin.

P.S. I LOVE YOU

Glass: Martini
Garnish: Crumbled Cadbury's Flake bar
Method: SHAKE all ingredients with ice and fine strain into chilled glass.

1 1/4	shot(s)	**Irish cream liqueur**
1 1/4	shot(s)	**Luxardo Amaretto di Saschira liqueur**
3/4	shot(s)	**Golden rum**
3/4	shot(s)	**Kahlúa coffee liqueur**
1	shot(s)	**Double (heavy) cream**

Comment: P.S. You'll love this creamy flavoursome drink.

PUCCINI

Glass: Flute
Garnish: Mandarin (tangerine) segment
Method: MUDDLE segments in base of shaker. Add liqueur, **SHAKE** with ice and fine strain into chilled glass. **TOP** with Prosecco and lightly stir.

8	segments	**Fresh mandarin (tangerine/clementine/satsuma)**
3/4	shot(s)	**Mandarine Napoléon liqueur**
Top up with		**Prosecco sparkling wine**

Origin: Named after the composer of Madame Butterfly, this cocktail is popular in Venice and other areas of northern Italy. It is often made without mandarin liqueur.
Comment: The use of mandarin (tangerine) instead of orange makes the Puccini slightly sharper than the similar Mimosa.

PULP FICTION

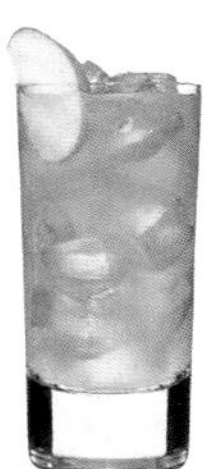

Glass: Collins
Method: SHAKE all ingredients with ice and strain into ice filled glass. **TOP** with 7-Up.

2	shot(s)	**Pressed apple juice**
2	shot(s)	**Rémy Martin cognac**
1	shot(s)	**Apple schnapps liqueur**
Top up with		**7-Up**

Origin: Discovered in 2001 at Teatro, London.
Comment: Originally made with apple pulp, this drink has a zingy apple taste.

THE PURITAN [NEW #7]

Glass: Martini
Garnish: Orange zest twst
Method: STIR all ingredients with ice and strain into chilled glass.

1 3/4	shot(s)	**Plymouth gin**
1/2	shot(s)	**Dry vermouth**
1/4	shot(s)	**Yellow Chartreuse liqueur**
1	dash	**Fee Brothers orange bitters**
1/2	shot(s)	**Chilled mineral water** (omit if wet ice)

Origin: An often overlooked classic which is thought to have originated at the end of the nineteenth century.
Comment: Vermouth enhances the aromatics; Chartreuse and orange bitters add a hint of sweetness and complexity; gin underpins the whole.

PURPLE COSMO

Glass: Martini
Garnish: Orange zest twist
Method: STIR all ingredients with ice and strain into chilled glass.

2	shot(s)	**Ketel One Citroen vodka**
3/4	shot(s)	**Parfait Amour liqueur**
1 1/2	shot(s)	**Ocean spray white cranberry**
1/4	shot(s)	**Freshly squeezed lime juice**

Variant: Blue Cosmo
Comment: If shaken this becomes more of a grey Cosmo. The flavour and colour make for an interesting twist.

PUNCH

Long before the Martini, the V-shaped glass and the cocktail shaker, the drink of choice at society gatherings was punch and the punch bowl was the centre of activity at every party.
Punch had existed in India for centuries before colonialists brought it back to Europe some time in the latter half of the 1600s. The name derives from the Hindi word for five, 'panch', and refers to the five key ingredients: alcohol, citrus, sugar, water and spices.

In India, it was made with arrack (the Arabic word for liquor and a local spirit distilled from palm sap or sugar cane). Back in Britain it was common for punches to be spiced with nutmeg or tea.

The classic proportions of a punch follow a mnemonic, 'one of sour, two of sweet, three of strong and four of weak.' It refers to lime juice, sugar, rum and water: the fifth element, spice, was added to taste. To fill a Collins glass I translate it as follows - all shaken with ice, strained and served over crushed ice.

1 sour =	3/4 shot(s)	**Freshly squeezed lemon or lime juice**
2 sweet =	1 1/2 shot(s)	Sugar syrup (2 sugar to 1 water) **(sweet)**
3 strong =	2 1/4 shot(s)	**Spirit (preferably overproof)**
4 weak =	3 shot(s)	**Chilled mineral water (or fruit juice)**
5 spice =	3 dashes	**Angostura aromatic bitters**

The basic punch principle of balancing sweet and sour with spirit and dilution remains key to making a good cocktail to this day. Indeed, the essential punch ingredients - spirit, citrus, sugar and water - lie at the centre of most modern day cocktails including the Daiquiri, Sour, Margarita, Caipirinha and Sidecar. Today's hip bartenders are now also reintroducing the fifth punch ingredient by muddling or macerating herbs and spices in their cocktails.

Two traditional punches remain on today's cocktail lists, the 'Rum Punch' and the 'Hot Whisky Punch', now better known as the 'Hot Toddy'. Also bear in mind that the Gin Punch probably led to the creation of the Collins.

PURPLE FLIRT #1

Glass: Martini
Garnish: Orange zest twist
Method: SHAKE all ingredients with ice and fine strain into chilled glass.

1½	shot(s)	**Ketel One vodka**
¾	shot(s)	**Opal Nera black sambuca**
2	shot(s)	**Ocean Spray cranberry juice**

Comment: This purple drink is surprisingly balanced with subtle hints of liquorice.

PURPLE FLIRT #2

Glass: Old-fashioned
Garnish: Orange slice & cherry (sail)
Method: SHAKE all ingredients with ice and strain into ice-filled glass.

1	shot(s)	**Goslings Black Seal rum**
¼	shot(s)	**Bols Blue curaçao liqueur**
1	shot(s)	**Pressed pineapple juice**
½	shot(s)	**Freshly squeezed lemon juice**
¼	shot(s)	**Pomegranate (grenadine) syrup**
½	fresh	**Egg white**

Comment: This popular drink is more brown than purple. It tastes OK, anyway.

PURPLE HAZE

Glass: Shot
Method: SHAKE first three ingredients with ice and strain into glass. **POUR** liqueur down the inside of the glass. This will fall to the bottom and form the purple haze.

1½	shot(s)	**Ketel One vodka**
½	shot(s)	**Freshly squeezed lime juice**
¼	shot(s)	**Sugar syrup (2 sugar to 1 water)**
⅛	shot(s)	**Chambord black raspberry liqueur**

Comment: A sweet and sour shot with a sweet, berry base.

PURPLE HOOTER

Glass: Collins
Garnish: Lime wedge
Method: SHAKE first three ingredients with ice and strain into ice-filled glass. **TOP** with soda.

2	shot(s)	**Ketel One vodka**
1	shot(s)	**Chambord black raspberry liqueur**
1	shot(s)	**Freshly squeezed lime juice**
Top up with		**Soda water (club soda)**

Comment: Tangy, fruity, long and refreshing.

PURPLE PEAR MARTINI

Glass: Martini
Garnish: Pear slice on rim
Method: SHAKE all ingredients with ice and fine strain into chilled glass.

2	shot(s)	**Poire William eau de vie**
2	shot(s)	**Benoit Serres liqueur de violette**
½	shot(s)	**Sugar syrup (2 sugar to 1 water)**

Origin: Created in 2002 by yours truly.
Comment: This floral drink suits its name.

PURPLE TURTLE

Glass: Shot
Method: SHAKE all ingredients with ice and fine strain into chilled glass.

½	shot(s)	**Partida tequila**
½	shot(s)	**Bols Blue curaçao liqueur**
½	shot(s)	**Plymouth sloe gin**

Comment: This aquamarine shooter goes down a treat.

PUSSYFOOT (MOCKTAIL)

Glass: Collins
Garnish: Orange slice
Method: MUDDLE mint in base of shaker. Add other ingredients, **SHAKE** with ice and fine strain into ice-filled glass.

7	fresh	**Mint leaves**
4	shot(s)	**Freshly squeezed orange juice**
½	shot(s)	**Freshly squeezed lemon juice**
½	shot(s)	**Freshly squeezed lime juice**
½	shot(s)	**Pomegranate (grenadine) syrup**
1	fresh	**Egg yolk**

Origin: Created in 1920 by Robert Vermeire at the Embassy Club, London, England. This non-alcoholic cocktail is named after 'Pussyfoot' (William E.) Johnson who was an ardent supporter of Prohibition.
Comment: Probably the best non-alcoholic cocktail ever.

QUARTER DECK

Glass: Martini
Garnish: Orange zest twist
Method: SHAKE all ingredients with ice and fine strain into chilled glass.

2	shot(s)	**Light white rum**
1	shot(s)	**Pedro Ximenez sherry**
¼	shot(s)	**Freshly squeezed lemon juice**
¾	shot(s)	**Chilled mineral water** (omit if wet ice)

Origin: Long lost classic.
Comment: Hints of prune, toffee and maple syrup. Very complex.

QUARTERBACK

Glass: Martini
Garnish: Orange zest twist
Method: SHAKE all ingredients with ice and fine strain into chilled glass.

1	shot(s)	**Yellow Chartreuse liqueur**
1	shot(s)	**Cointreau triple sec**
1	shot(s)	**Double (heavy) cream**
1	shot(s)	**Milk**

Comment: This white, creamy drink has a flavoursome bite.

QUEBEC

Glass: Martini
Garnish: Orange zest twist
Method: STIR all ingredients with ice and strain into chilled glass.

2	shot(s)	**Canadian whisky (or bourbon whiskey)**
2	shot(s)	**Dubonnet Red**
2	dashes	**Fee Brothers orange bitters**

Origin: Created in 2004 at Victoria Bar, Berlin, Germany.
Comment: Canadian whisky with French accents of aromatised wine – très Quebecois.

QUEEN MARTINI

Glass: Martini
Garnish: Maraschino cherry
Method: SHAKE all ingredients with ice and fine strain into chilled glass.

1½	shot(s)	**Plymouth gin**
½	shot(s)	**Dry vermouth**
½	shot(s)	**Sweet vermouth**
½	shot(s)	**Freshly squeezed orange juice**
½	shot(s)	**Pressed pineapple juice**

Comment: A 'perfectly' fruity Martini that's fit for a...

QUEEN'S PARK SWIZZLE [NEW #7]

Glass: Collins
Garnish: Lime wedge & mint sprig
Method: Lightly **MUDDLE** mint (just to bruise) in base of glass, add other ingredients and half fill glass with crushed ice. **SWIZZLE** with a swizzle stick or **CHURN** (stir) with a bar spoon. Fill glass with more crushed ice and repeat. Serve with straws.

7	fresh	**Mint leaves**
2	shot(s)	**Aged rum**
¾	shot(s)	**Freshly squeezed lime juice**
½	shot(s)	**Sugar syrup (2 sugar to 1 water)**
3	dashes	**Angostura aromatic bitters**

Origin: Created at the Queen's Park Hotel, Port of Spain, Trinidad.
Comment: This close relation to the Mojito is drier, more complex and less minty than its sibling.

QUELLE VIE

Glass: Martini
Garnish: Orange zest twist
Method: STIR all ingredients with ice and fine strain into chilled glass.

2	shot(s)	**Rémy Martin cognac**
½	shot(s)	**Kummel**
¾	shot(s)	**Chilled mineral water** (omit if wet ice)

Origin: Adapted from a recipe in the 1930 Savoy Cocktail Book by Harry Craddock.
Comment: In Craddock's words, "Brandy gives you courage and Kummel makes you cautious, thus giving you a perfect mixture of bravery and caution, with the bravery predominating."

'IT SHRINKS MY LIVER, DOESN'T IT? IT PICKLES MY KIDNEYS. YEAH. BUT WHAT DOES IT DO TO MY MIND? IT TOSSES THE SANDBAGS OVERBOARD SO THE BALLOON CAN SOAR. SUDDENLY, I'M ABOVE THE ORDINARY. I'M COMPETENT, SUPREMELY COMPETENT. I'M WALKING A TIGHTROPE OVER NIAGARA FALLS. I'M ONE OF THE GREAT ONES.'

QUINCE SOUR

Glass: Old-fashioned
Garnish: Lemon slice & cherry (sail)
Method: STIR quince jam with vodka in base of shaker to dissolve jam. Add other ingredients, **SHAKE** with ice and fine strain into ice-filled glass.

3	spoons	**Quince jam /membrillo Spanish quince paste**
2	shot(s)	**Ketel One vodka**
1	shot(s)	**Freshly squeezed lemon juice**
½	fresh	**Egg white**

Comment: The sweet quince both flavours and balances this sour.

RAGING BULL

Glass: Shot
Method: Refrigerate ingredients then **LAYER** in chilled glass by carefully pouring in the following order.

1/2	shot(s)	**Kahlúa coffee liqueur**
1/2	shot(s)	**Luxardo Sambuca dei Cesari**
1/2	shot(s)	**Partida tequila**

Comment: Coffee and sambuca make a great combination, as do coffee and tequila.

RAMOS GIN FIZZ [UPDATED #7]

Glass: Small Collins (8oz)
Method: Vigorously **SHAKE** first nine ingredients with ice until bored and strain into chilled (empty) glass. **TOP** with soda water from siphon.

2	shot(s)	**Plymouth gin**
3/4	shot(s)	**Milk**
3/4	shot(s)	**Double (heavy) cream**
1/2	shot(s)	**Freshly squeezed lemon juice**
1/2	shot(s)	**Freshly squeezed lime juice**
1/2	shot(s)	**Sugar syrup (2 sugar to 1 water)**
1/8	shot(s)	**Orange flower water**
3	drops	**Vanilla extract (optional)**
1	fresh	**Egg white**
Top up with		**Soda water from siphon**

Origin: This was the secret recipe of Henry C. Ramos, who opened his Imperial Cabinet Bar in New Orleans in 1888. At the onset of Prohibition his brother, Charles Henry Ramos, published it in a full-page advertisement, and since 1935 the Roosevelt (now named the Fairmont) Hotel, New Orleans, has held the trademark on the name Ramos Gin Fizz.
Comment: One of the great classic cocktails. A perfect balance of sweet and sour is enhanced by an incredibly smooth, even fluffy mouth feel.

RANDY

Glass: Old-fashioned
Garnish: Orange zest twist
Method: **STIR** all ingredients with ice and strain into ice-filled glass.

1 1/2	shot(s)	**Rémy Martin cognac**
1 1/2	shot(s)	**Tawny port**
1/2	shot(s)	**Grand Marnier liqueur**
1/4	shot(s)	**Vanilla sugar syrup**

Origin: Created in 2003 by yours truly.
Comment: Named after the rhyming slang for port and brandy, its base ingredients. Love interest comes courtesy of orange and vanilla.

RASPBERRY CAIPIRINHA

Glass: Old-fashioned
Method: **MUDDLE** lime and raspberries in base of glass. Add other ingredients and fill glass with crushed ice. **CHURN** drink with barspoon and serve with short straws.

3/4	fresh	**Lime cut into wedges**
8	fresh	**Raspberries**
2	shot(s)	**Leblon cachaça**
3/4	shot(s)	**Sugar syrup (2 sugar to 1 water)**

Variants: Substitute other berries and fruits for raspberries. Add raspberry liqueur in place of sugar. Use rum in place of cachaça to make a Raspberry Caipirissima.
Comment: A fruity twist on the popular Caipirinha.

RASPBERRY COLLINS

Glass: Collins
Garnish: Three raspberries & lemon slice
Method: **MUDDLE** raspberries in base of shaker. Add next five ingredients, **SHAKE** with ice and strain into ice-filled glass. **TOP** with soda, lightly stir and serve with straws.

10	fresh	**Raspberries**
2	shot(s)	**Plymouth gin**
1 1/2	shot(s)	**Freshly squeezed lemon juice**
1/2	shot(s)	**Giffard crème de framboise**
1/2	shot(s)	**Sugar syrup (2 sugar to 1 water)**
3	dashes	**Fee Brothers orange bitters (optional)**
Top up with		**Soda water (club soda)**

Variant: Raspberry Debonnaire
Origin: Created in 1999 by Cairbry Hill, London, England.
Comment: This fruity drink is the most popular modern adaptation of the classic Collins.

RASPBERRY COSMO

Glass: Martini
Garnish: Raspberries on stick
Method: **SHAKE** all ingredients with ice and fine strain into chilled glass.

1 1/2	shot(s)	**Ketel One Citroen vodka**
3/4	shot(s)	**Giffard crème de framboise bitters**
1	shot(s)	**Ocean Spray cranberry juice**
1/2	shot(s)	**Freshly squeezed lime juice**

Origin: Formula by yours truly in 2006.
Comment: Your classic Cosmo but with raspberry liqueur replacing orange liqueur.

HOW TO MAKE SUGAR SYRUP

To make your own sugar syrup, gradually pour TWO cups of granulated sugar into a saucepan containing ONE cup of hot water. Stir as you pour and carry on stirring and simmering until the sugar is dissolved. Do not let the water even come close to boiling and only simmer for as long as it takes to dissolve the sugar. Allow syrup to cool and pour into an empty bottle. Ideally, you should finely strain your syrup into the bottle to remove any undissolved crystals which could otherwise encourage crystallisation. If kept in a refrigerator this mixture will last for a couple of months.

RASPBERRY DEBONNAIRE

Glass: Collins
Garnish: Three raspberries & lemon slice
Method: MUDDLE raspberries in base of shaker. Add next five ingredients, **SHAKE** with ice and fine strain into ice-filled glass. **TOP** with soda, lightly stir and serve with straws.

10	fresh	**Raspberries**
2	shot(s)	**Ketel One vodka**
1½	shot(s)	**Freshly squeezed lemon juice**
½	shot(s)	**Giffard crème de framboise**
½	shot(s)	**Sugar syrup (2 sugar to 1 water)**
3	dashes	**Fee Brothers orange bitters (optional)**
Top up with		**Soda water (club soda)**

Variant: Raspberry Collins
Comment: If based on gin rather than vodka this would be a Raspberry Collins.

RASPBERRY LYNCHBURG

Glass: Collins
Garnish: Raspberries on drink
Method: SHAKE first three ingredients with ice and strain into ice-filled glass. **TOP** with 7-Up and **DRIZZLE** liqueur around surface of drink. It will fall through the drink, leaving coloured threads.

2	shot(s)	**Jack Daniel's Tennessee whiskey**
¾	shot(s)	**Freshly squeezed lime juice**
¼	shot(s)	**Sugar syrup (2 sugar to 1 water)**
Top up with		**7-Up**
½	shot(s)	**Chambord black raspberry liqueur**

Origin: Created in 1992 by Wayne Collins at Roadhouse, London, England.
Comment: This variation on a Lynchburg Lemonade has a sweet and sour flavour laced with whiskey.

RASPBERRY MARGARITA

Glass: Coupette
Garnish: Lime wedge on rim
Method: MUDDLE raspberries in base of shaker. Add other ingredients, **SHAKE** with ice and fine strain into chilled glass.

7	fresh	**Raspberries**
2	shot(s)	**Partida tequila**
1	shot(s)	**Cointreau triple sec**
1	shot(s)	**Freshly squeezed lime juice**
1/8	shot(s)	**Sugar syrup (2 sugar to 1 water)**

Comment: Just as it says – a raspberry flavoured Margarita.

RASPBERRY MARTINI #1

Glass: Martini
Garnish: Three raspberries on stick
Method: MUDDLE raspberries in base of shaker. Add other ingredients, **SHAKE** with ice and fine strain into chilled glass.

10	fresh	**Raspberries**
2½	shot(s)	**Ketel One vodka**
½	shot(s)	**Sugar syrup (2 sugar to 1 water)**

Comment: The simplest of raspberry Martinis but still tastes good.

RASPBERRY MARTINI #2

Glass: Martini
Garnish: Three raspberries on stick
Method: MUDDLE raspberries in base of shaker. Add other ingredients, **SHAKE** with ice and fine strain into chilled glass.

7	fresh	**Raspberries**
2	shot(s)	**Plymouth gin**
1	shot(s)	**Giffard crème de framboise**
2	dashes	**Fee Brothers orange bitters (optional)**

Origin: Created in 1997 by Dick Bradsell, London, England.
Comment: Great raspberry flavour integrated with gin.

RASPBERRY MOCHA'TINI

Glass: Martini
Garnish: Three raspberries on stick
Method: SHAKE all ingredients with ice and fine strain into chilled glass.

1½	shot(s)	**Raspberry flavoured vodka**
¾	shot(s)	**Giffard brown crème de cacao**
¾	shot(s)	**Giffard crème de framboise**
1	shot(s)	**Cold espresso coffee**

Origin: Discovered in 2002 at Lot 61, New York City, USA.
Comment: Sweet chocolate and raspberry tempered by dry coffee and vodka.

RASPBERRY MULE

Glass: Collins
Garnish: Lime wedge
Method: MUDDLE raspberries in base of shaker. Add next three ingredients, **SHAKE** with ice and fine strain into ice-filled glass. **TOP** with ginger beer, lightly stir and serve with straws.

12	fresh	**Raspberries**
2	shot(s)	**Ketel One vodka**
1	shot(s)	**Freshly squeezed lime juice**
½	shot(s)	**Sugar syrup (2 sugar to 1 water)**
Top up with		**Ginger beer**

Comment: The fruity alternative to a Moscow Mule.

RASPBERRY SAKE'TINI

Glass: Martini
Garnish: Three raspberries.
Method: SHAKE all ingredients with ice and fine strain into chilled glass.

1½	shot(s)	**Raspberry flavoured vodka**
1½	shot(s)	**Sake**
½	shot(s)	**Chambord black raspberry liqueur**
½	shot(s)	**Pressed pineapple juice**

Comment: Fruity with wafts of sake – reminiscent of a French Martini.

RASPBERRY WATKINS

Glass: Sling
Garnish: Three raspberries
Method: **SHAKE** first four ingredients with ice and strain into ice-filled glass. **TOP** with soda, lightly stir and serve with straws.

2 shot(s) **Ketel One vodka**
1/2 shot(s) **Chambord black raspberry liqueur**
1/2 shot(s) **Freshly squeezed lime juice**
1/4 shot(s) **Pomegranate (grenadine) syrup**
Top up with **Soda water (club soda)**

Comment: A light, long, fizzy and refreshing drink.

RASPUTIN

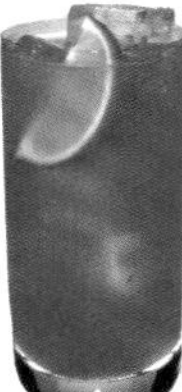

Glass: Collins
Garnish: Lime wedge
Method: **SHAKE** all ingredients with ice and strain into ice-filled glass.

2 shot(s) **Raspberry flavoured vodka**
2 1/2 shot(s) **Ocean Spray cranberry juice**
1 1/2 shot(s) **Freshly squeezed grapefruit juice**

Comment: This fruity adaptation of an Arizona Breeze is raspberry rich.

RAT PACK MANHATTAN

Glass: Martini
Garnish: Orange zest twist & maraschino cherry
Method: Chill glass, add Grand Marnier, swirl to coat and then **DISCARD. STIR** other ingredients with ice and strain into liqueur coated glass.

1/2 shot(s) **Grand Marnier liqueur**
1 1/2 shot(s) **Buffalo Trace bourbon whiskey**
3/4 shot(s) **Sweet vermouth**
3/4 shot(s) **Dry vermouth**
3 dashes **Angostura aromatic bitters**

Origin: Created in 2000 by Wayne Collins at High Holborn, London, England. Originally Wayne used different whiskies to represent each of the Rat Pack crooners. The wash of Grand Marnier was for Sammy Davis, the wild card of the bunch.
Comment: A twist on the classic Manhattan.

RATTLESNAKE

Glass: Martini
Garnish: Lemon zest twist
Method: **SHAKE** all ingredients with ice and fine strain into chilled glass.

2 shot(s) **Buffalo Trace bourbon whiskey**
1/4 shot(s) **Freshly squeezed lemon juice**
1/4 shot(s) **Sugar syrup (2 sugar to 1 water))**
1/8 shot(s) **La Fée Parisienne (68%) absinthe**
1/2 fresh **Egg white**
1/2 shot(s) **Chilled mineral water** (omit if wet ice)

Origin: Adapted from a recipe purloined from a 1930 edition of The Savoy Cocktail Book by Harry Craddock.
Comment: To quote Craddock, "So called because it will either cure rattlesnake bite, or kill rattlesnakes, or make you see them."

RATTLESNAKE SHOT

Glass: Shot
Method: Refrigerate ingredients then **LAYER** in chilled glass by carefully pouring in the following order.

1/2 shot(s) **Kahlúa coffee liqueur**
1/2 shot(s) **Giffard white crème de cacao**
1/2 shot(s) **Irish cream liqueur**

Comment: Tastes rather like a strong cappuccino.

RAY GUN

Glass: Flute
Garnish: Orange zest twist
Method: **POUR** Chartreuse and blue curaçao into chilled glass. Top with champagne.

1/2 shot(s) **Green Chartreuse liqueur**
3/4 shot(s) **Bols Blue curaçao liqueur**
Top up with **Brut champagne**

Comment: Not for the faint-hearted.

RAY'S HARD LEMONADE

Glass: Collins
Garnish: Mint sprig
Method: Lightly **MUDDLE** (just to bruise) mint in base of shaker. Add next four ingredients, **SHAKE** with ice and fine strain into ice-filled glass. **TOP** with soda, lightly stir and serve with straws.

7 fresh **Mint leaves**
2 shot(s) **Ketel One vodka**
1 shot(s) **Freshly squeezed lemon juice**
2 shot(s) **Freshly squeezed lime juice**
1 1/2 shot(s) **Sugar syrup (2 sugar to 1 water)**
Top up with **Soda water (club soda)**

Variant: Hard Lemonade
Origin: Discovered in 2004 at Spring Street Natural Restaurant, New York City, USA.
Comment: Alcoholic lemonade with mint? A vodka variation on the Mojito? However you describe it, it works.

RAZZITINI

Glass: Martini
Garnish: Lemon twist / raspberries on stick
Method: **SHAKE** first two ingredients with ice and fine strain into chilled glass. **TOP** with 7-Up.

2 1/2 shot(s) **Ketel One Citroen vodka**
3/4 shot(s) **Chambord black raspberry liqueur**
Top up with **7-Up**

Origin: Discovered in 2003 at Paramount Hotel, New York City, USA.
Comment: This citrus and raspberry Martini is a tad on the sweet side.

RAZZMATAZZ

Glass: Martini
Garnish: Float mint sprig
Method: STIR honey with vodka until honey is dissolved. Add other ingredients, **SHAKE** with ice and fine strain into chilled glass.

3	spoons	**Runny honey**
1 1/2	shot(s)	**Raspberry flavoured vodka**
1/2	shot(s)	**Cointreau triple sec**
1	shot(s)	**Pressed apple juice**
1/4	shot(s)	**Freshly squeezed lime juice**
6	fresh	**Mint leaves (torn)**

Origin: Created by Wayne Collins, London, England.
Comment: Fruity with plenty of razzmatazz.

RAZZZZZBERRY MARTINI

Glass: Martini
Garnish: Three raspberries on stick
Method: SHAKE all ingredients with ice and fine strain into chilled glass.

2	shot(s)	**Vanilla infused Ketel One vodka**
1/2	shot(s)	**Chambord black raspberry liqueur**
2	shot(s)	**Ocean Spray cranberry juice**

Comment: Raspberry and vanilla with characteristic dry cranberry fruit.

REAL LEMONADE (MOCKTAIL)

Glass: Collins
Garnish: Lemon wheel in glass
Method: POUR ingredients into ice-filled glass and lightly **STIR**. Serve with straws.

2	shot(s)	**Freshly squeezed lemon juice**
1	shot(s)	**Sugar syrup (2 sugar to 1 water)**
Top up with		**Soda water (club soda)**

Comment: The classic English summertime refresher.

REDBACK

Glass: Shot
Garnish: Maraschino cherry on rim
Method: POUR sambuca into glass, then pour advocaat down the side of the glass.

1	shot(s)	**Opal Nera black sambuca**
1/2	shot(s)	**Bols advocaat liqueur**

Comment: An impressive looking shot.

● DISGUSTING ●◐ PRETTY AWFUL ●● BEST AVOIDED
●●◐ DISAPPOINTING ●●● ACCEPTABLE ●●●◐ GOOD
●●●● RECOMMENDED ●●●●◐ HIGHLY RECOMMENDED
●●●●● OUTSTANDING / EXCEPTIONAL

RED ANGEL

Glass: Martini
Garnish: Orange zest twist
Method: SHAKE all ingredients with ice and fine strain into chilled glass.

2	shot(s)	**Shiraz red wine**
1	shot(s)	**Grand Marnier liqueur**
1/4	shot(s)	**Luxardo maraschino liqueur**
3/4	shot(s)	**Chilled mineral water** (omit if wet ice)

Origin: Created in 2001 by Tony Conigliaro at Isola, Knightsbridge, London, England.
Comment: A subtly flavoured cocktail with a dry, almost tannic edge.

RED APPLE

Glass: Martini
Garnish: Maraschino cherry
Method: SHAKE all ingredients with ice and fine strain into chilled glass.

1 1/2	shot(s)	**Buffalo Trace bourbon whiskey**
1/2	shot(s)	**Sour apple liqueur**
2	shot(s)	**Ocean Spray cranberry juice**

Variant: Sour Apple Martini
Comment: As Apple Martinis go, this one is rather good.

THE RED ARMY

Glass: Old-fashioned
Garnish: Two raspberries
Method: MUDDLE raspberries in base of shaker. Add other ingredients, **SHAKE** with ice and fine strain into a glass filled with crushed ice.

12	fresh	**Raspberries**
2	shot(s)	**Raspberry flavoured vodka**
1	shot(s)	**Freshly squeezed lime juice**
1/2	shot(s)	**Sugar syrup (2 sugar to 1 water)**
1/2	shot(s)	**Cointreau triple sec**
1/2	shot(s)	**Giffard crème de framboise**

Origin: Created in 2002 by Alex Kammerling, London, England.
Comment: Rather red and rather fruity.

RED BREAST

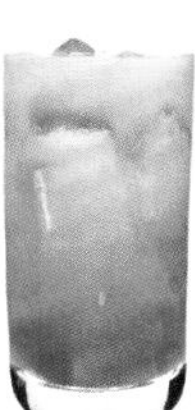

Glass: Collins
Garnish: Raspberry
Method: POUR first three ingredients into ice-filled glass and lightly stir. **DRIZZLE** raspberry liqueur over surface of drink.

2	shot(s)	**Scotch whisky**
1/2	shot(s)	**Freshly squeezed lime juice**
Top up with		**Ginger beer**
1/2	shot(s)	**Giffard crème de framboise**

Origin: Created in 2004 by Wayne Collins, England.
Comment: Long and a tad pink but packs a tasty punch.

RED HOOKER

Glass: Martini
Garnish: Peach slice on rim
Method: **SHAKE** all ingredients with ice and fine strain into chilled glass.

1	shot(s)	**White peach puree (sweetened)**
2	shot(s)	**Partida tequila**
3/4	shot(s)	**Giffard crème de framboise**
3/4	shot(s)	**Freshly squeezed lemon juice**

Comment: An appropriately named red, fruity drink with more than a hint of tequila.

RED LION #1 (MODERN FORMULA)

Glass: Martini
Garnish: Orange slice on rim
Method: **SHAKE** all ingredients with ice and fine strain into chilled glass.

1 1/4	shot(s)	**Plymouth gin**
1 1/4	shot(s)	**Grand Marnier liqueur**
1	shot(s)	**Freshly squeezed orange juice**
1	shot(s)	**Freshly squeezed lemon juice**
1/8	shot(s)	**Pomegranate (grenadine) syrup**

Origin: This classic drink is said to have been created for the Chicago World Fair in 1933. However, it won the British Empire Cocktail Competition that year and was more likely created by W J Tarling for Booth's gin and named after the brand's Red Lion Distillery in London.
Comment: The colour of a summer's twilight with a rich tangy orange flavour.

RED LION #2 (EMBURY'S FORMULA)

Glass: Martini
Garnish: Orange slice on rim
Method: **SHAKE** all ingredients with ice and fine strain into chilled glass.

2	shot(s)	**Plymouth gin**
1/4	shot(s)	**Grand Marnier liqueur**
1/2	shot(s)	**Freshly squeezed lime juice**
1/4	shot(s)	**Pomegranate (grenadine) syrup**
3/4	shot(s)	**Chilled mineral water** (reduce if wet ice)

Origin: Recipe adapted from one originally published in The Fine Art of Mixing Drinks by David Embury.
Comment: Embury is a Daiquiri fan and this is reminiscent of a Daiquiri in both style and proportions.

RED MARAUDER

Glass: Martini
Garnish: Raspberries on stick
Method: **SHAKE** all ingredients with ice and fine strain into chilled glass.

2	shot(s)	**Rémy Martin cognac**
1 1/2	shot(s)	**Ocean Spray cranberry juice**
1/2	shot(s)	**Chambord black raspberry liqueur**
1/4	shot(s)	**Freshly squeezed lime juice**

Origin: Originally created for Martell, long term sponsors of the Grand National, this is named after the horse that won in 2001.
Comment: Slightly sweet and fruity with a hint of raspberry and cognac's distinctive flavour.

RED MELON'TINI

Glass: Martini
Garnish: Watermelon wedge on rim
Method: Cut watermelon into 16 segments, chop the flesh from one segment into cubes and **MUDDLE** in base of shaker. Add other ingredients, **SHAKE** with ice and fine strain into chilled glass.

1/16	fresh	**Watermelon (diced)**
2	shot(s)	**Pepper flavoured vodka**
1/4	shot(s)	**Sugar syrup (2 sugar to 1 water)**
4	grinds	**Black pepper**

Origin: Discovered in 2002 at the Fifth Floor Bar, London, England.
Comment: Watermelon pepped up with vodka and the subtlest peppery finish.

RED NECK MARTINI

Glass: Martini
Garnish: Orange zest twist
Method: **SHAKE** all ingredients with ice and fine strain into chilled glass.

2	shot(s)	**Scotch whisky**
1	shot(s)	**Dubonnet Red**
1	shot(s)	**Cherry (brandy) liqueur**

Origin: Created by Sylvain Solignac in 2002 at Circus Bar, London, England.
Comment: Nicely balanced, aromatic and not too sweet – the flavour of the Scotch shines through.

RED OR DEAD

Glass: Collins
Garnish: Lime wedge
Method: **SHAKE** all ingredients with ice and strain into ice-filled glass.

1 1/2	shot(s)	**Southern Comfort liqueur**
3/4	shot(s)	**Campari**
3/4	shot(s)	**Freshly squeezed lime juice**
3	shot(s)	**Ocean Spray cranberry juice**

Comment: This long, ruby drink balances sweetness, sourness and bitterness.

RED ROVER

Glass: Old-fashioned
Garnish: Orange slice in glass
Method: **SHAKE** all ingredients with ice and strain into ice-filled glass.

3	shot(s)	**Red wine**
1	shot(s)	**Pusser's Navy rum**
1/2	shot(s)	**Chambord black raspberry liqueur**

Comment: Carpet-scaring red with the body of red wine but the palate of a cocktail.

RED RUM MARTINI

Glass: Martini
Garnish: Redcurrants draped over rim
Method: **MUDDLE** redcurrants in base of shaker. Add other ingredients, **SHAKE** with ice and fine strain into chilled glass.

24	fresh	**Redcurrants**
2	shot(s)	**Aged rum**
1/2	shot(s)	**Plymouth sloe gin liqueur**
1/2	shot(s)	**Freshly squeezed lemon juice**
1/2	shot(s)	**Vanilla sugar syrup**

Origin: Created by Jason Scott in 2002 at Oloroso, Edinburgh, Scotland. This cocktail, which is red and contains rum, is named after 'Red Rum', the only horse in history to win the Grand National three times (on his other two attempts he came second). He became a British hero, made an appearance on the BBC Sports Personality of the Year show and paraded right up until his death at the age of 30 in 1995.
Comment: A beautifully fruity, adult balance of bittersweet flavours.

RED SNAPPER

Glass: Collins
Garnish: Rim the glass with black pepper and celery salt, add cherry tomato on a stick
Method: **SHAKE** all ingredients with ice and strain into ice-filled glass. Serve with straws.

2	shot(s)	**Plymouth gin**
4	shot(s)	**Pressed tomato juice**
1/2	shot(s)	**Freshly squeezed lemon juice**
7	drops	**Tabasco pepper sauce**
4	dashes	**Lea & Perrins Worcestershire sauce**
1/2	shot(s)	**Tawny port**
2	pinch	**Celery salt**
2	grinds	**Black pepper**

Variant: Bloody Mary
Origin: A gin-based Bloody Mary, derived from Fernand Petiot's original.
Comment: Looks like a Bloody Mary but features gin's aromatic botanicals.

REEF JUICE

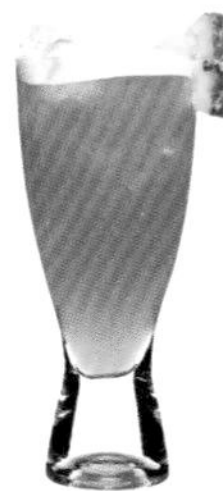

Glass: Collins
Garnish: Split pineapple wedge
Method: **SHAKE** all ingredients with ice and strain into ice-filled glass.

1 1/2	shot(s)	**Pusser's Navy rum**
1/2	shot(s)	**Ketel One vodka**
1	shot(s)	**Giffard crème de banane du Brésil**
1/2	shot(s)	**Freshly squeezed lime juice**
2 1/2	shot(s)	**Pressed pineapple juice**
1/2	shot(s)	**Pomegranate (grenadine) syrup**

Origin: Charles Tobias, proprietor of Pusser's, created this drink at the Beach Bar in Fort Lauderdale, Florida. It was a favourite of a friend who crashed his boat on the reef.
Comment: Tangy, fruity and dangerously moreish.

RED SNAPPER

Today, the term Red Snapper means a Bloody Mary made with gin instead of vodka. But the first known recipes, from the 1940s, describe a 50-50 blend of vodka and tomato juice, with spices, just like an early Bloody Mary: one book even states that the Red Snapper is identical to the Bloody Mary.

Cocktail lore states that the Bloody Mary was officially renamed the Red Snapper at the St. Regis Hotel, at some point after the fabulously wealthy Vincent Astor bought it in 1935. Fernand Petiot, who most likely created the original drink (see 'Bloody Mary'), was working there, but Astor apparently found the title too crude for his clientele and insisted the drink be renamed. Customers, of course, continued to order Bloody Marys, but the Red Snapper found a drink of its own in due course.

REGGAE RUM PUNCH

Glass: Collins
Garnish: Pineapple & cherry on rim
Method: SHAKE all ingredients with ice and strain into a glass filled with crushed ice.

1¾	shot(s)	**Wray & Nephew overproof rum**
½	shot(s)	**Giffard crème de fraise de bois**
¾	shot(s)	**Freshly squeezed lime juice**
¾	shot(s)	**Pomegranate (grenadine) syrup**
¾	shot(s)	**Pressed pineapple juice**
1½	shot(s)	**Freshly squeezed orange juice**

Origin: The most popular punch in Jamaica, where it is sold under different names with slightly varying ingredients. It always contains orange, pineapple and, most importantly, overproof rum.
Comment: Jamaicans have a sweet tooth and love their rum. This drink combines sweetness, strength and a generous amount of fruit.

REMEMBER THE MAINE

Glass: Old-fashioned
Garnish: Lemon peel twist
Method: POUR absinthe into ice-filled glass, top up with water and set to one side. Separately, **POUR** other ingredients into an ice-filled mixing glass and **STIR** well. **DISCARD** absinthe, water and ice from serving glass. Finally strain contents of mixing glass into the absinthe rinsed glass.

1	shot(s)	**La Fée Parisienne (68%) absinthe**
Top up with		**Chilled mineral water**
2	shot(s)	**Buffalo Trace bourbon whiskey**
¾	shot(s)	**Cherry (brandy) liqueur**
¾	shot(s)	**Sweet vermouth**

Origin: Adapted from a recipe created by Charles H. Baker Jr. in "memory of a night in Havana during the Unpleasantnesses of 1933" and named after the press slogan which allegedly provoked the 1898 Spanish-American War.
Comment: A twist on the Sazerac.

REMSEN COOLER

Glass: Collins
Garnish: Whole lemon peel
Method: POUR ingredients into ice-filled glass and serve with straws.

2½	shot(s)	**Scotch whisky**
Top up with		**Soda (fom siphon)**

Origin: Adapted from a recipe purloined from David Embury's classic book, The Fine Art of Mixing Drinks, and so named because it was originally made with the now defunct Remsen Scotch whisky. Embury claims this is "the original cooler".
Comment: Scotch and soda for the sophisticate.

RESOLUTE

Glass: Martini
Garnish: Lemon zest twist
Method: SHAKE all ingredients with ice and fine strain into chilled glass.

2	shot(s)	**Plymouth gin**
1	shot(s)	**Giffard apricot brandy du Roussillon**
½	shot(s)	**Freshly squeezed lemon juice**
¾	shot(s)	**Chilled mineral water** (omit if wet ice)

Origin: Adapted from a recipe purloined from a 1930 edition of The Savoy Cocktail Book by Harry Craddock.
Comment: Simple but tasty. All three flavours work in harmony.

RHETT BUTLER

Glass: Old-fashioned
Garnish: Lime wedge
Method: SHAKE all ingredients with ice and fine strain into ice-filled glass.

1	shot(s)	**Grand Marnier liqueur**
1	shot(s)	**Southern Comfort liqueur**
2	shot(s)	**Ocean Spray cranberry juice**
1	shot(s)	**Freshly squeezed lime juice**

Comment: A simple and well-balanced classic drink.

RHUBARB & CUSTARD MARTINI

Glass: Martini
Garnish: Grate fresh nutmeg over drink
Method: SHAKE all ingredients with ice and fine strain into chilled glass.

1¼	shot(s)	**Plymouth gin**
1¼	shot(s)	**Bols advocaat liqueur**
1¼	shot(s)	**Syrup from tinned rhubarb**

Origin: I created this drink in 2002. Rhubarb and Custard is a great British dessert and was a cult children's TV cartoon in the 1970s. It featured a naughty pink cat called Custard and a dog named Rhubarb who, like many British men, spent a lot of time in his garden shed.
Comment: As sharp, sweet, creamy and flavourful as the dessert it imitates.

RHUBARB & HONEY BELLINI

Glass: Flute
Garnish: Orange zest string
Method: SHAKE rhubarb syrup and honey liqueur with ice and fine strain into chilled glass. **TOP** with Prosecco and gently stir.

1¼	shot(s)	**Syrup from tinned rhubarb**
1¼	shot(s)	**Krupnik honey liqueur**
Top up with		**Prosecco sparkling wine**

Origin: A simplified adaptation of a drink created in 2003 by Tony Conigliaro at London's Shumi.
Comment: This implausible combination works surprisingly well.

RHUBARB & LEMONGRASS MARTINI

Glass: Martini
Garnish: Stick of lemongrass in drink
Method: MUDDLE lemongrass in base of shaker. Add other ingredients, **SHAKE** with ice and fine strain into chilled glass.

4	inches	**Fresh lemongrass (chopped)**
2	shot(s)	**Plymouth gin**
2	shot(s)	**Syrup from tinned rhubarb**
1/8	shot(s)	**Sugar syrup (2 sugar to 1 water)**

Origin: I based this drink on one I discovered in 2003 at Zuma, London, England.
Comment: Fragrant exotic lemon flavours combine with, well, rhubarb to make a surprisingly refreshing long drink.

FOR MORE INFORMATION SEE OUR INGREDIENTS APPENDIX ON PAGE 374

RIBALAIGUA DAIQUIRI #3

Glass: Martini
Garnish: Mint leaf
Method: SHAKE all ingredients with ice and fine strain into chilled glass.

2	shot(s)	**Light white rum**
1/2	shot(s)	**Luxardo maraschino liqueur**
1	shot(s)	**Squeezed pink grapefruit juice**
1/2	shot(s)	**Chilled mineral water** (omit if wet ice)

Variant: With gin in place of rum this becomes Seventh Heaven No. 2.
Origin: Named for Constantino Ribalaigua, who introduced Hemingway to the Daiquiri at El Floridita, Havana, Cuba.
Comment: This unusual Daiquiri leads with sweet maraschino and finishes with sour grapefruit.

RICKEY (GIN RICKEY)

Glass: Collins (small 8oz)
Garnish: Immerse length of lime peel in drink.
Method: SHAKE first three ingredients with ice and strain into ice-filled glass. **TOP** with soda.

2	shot(s)	**Plymouth gin**
1/2	shot(s)	**Freshly squeezed lime juice**
1/4	shot(s)	**Sugar syrup (2 sugar to 1 water)**
Top up with		**Soda water**

Origin: Believed to have been created at the Shoemaker's restaurant in Washington, circa 1900, and named after Colonel Joe Rickey.
Comment: Clean, sharp and refreshing.

RICKEYS

The Rickey is believed to have been created at the Shoemaker's restaurant in Washington, circa 1900, and named after Colonel Joe Rickey, for whom it was invented.

Many confuse the Rickey and the Collins. For the record, a Rickey is made with lime juice and a Collins with lemon juice. A Rickey is also usually served in a shorter glass than a Collins but this difference is secondary.

The best-known Rickey is the Gin Rickey but these drinks can be based on any liquor and the Vodka Rickey is also popular. Liqueurs also work brilliantly: try substituting apricot brandy for the base spirit to make an Apricot Rickey. (You will need to adjust the amount of sugar in the recipe according to the sweetness of the liqueur.)

THE RITZ COCKTAIL

Glass: Martini
Garnish: Orange zest twist
Method: **STIR** first four ingredients with ice and strain into chilled glass. **TOP** with a splash of champagne.

1	shot(s)	**Rémy Martin cognac**
$^1/_2$	shot(s)	**Cointreau triple sec**
$^1/_4$	shot(s)	**Luxardo maraschino liqueur**
$^1/_4$	shot(s)	**Freshly squeezed lemon juice**
Top up with		**Brut champagne**

Origin: Created in the mid-1980s by Dale DeGroff at Aurora, New York City, USA.
Comment: This combination of spirit, liqueurs, fruit and champagne tastes like alcoholic lemon tea.

ROA AÉ

Glass: Collins
Garnish: Pineapple wedge on rim
Method: **SHAKE** all ingredients with ice and strain into ice-filled glass.

$1^1/_2$	shot(s)	**Light white rum**
$^1/_2$	shot(s)	**Giffard apricot brandy du Roussillon**
$^1/_2$	shot(s)	**Grand Marnier liqueur**
$^1/_2$	shot(s)	**Pear & cognac liqueur**
3	shot(s)	**Pressed pineapple juice**
$^3/_4$	shot(s)	**Freshly squeezed lime juice**

Origin: Discovered in 2003 at Booly Mardy's, Glasgow, Scotland. Cocktail aficionados will be familiar with the Tahitian phrase 'Mai Tai – Roa Aé', or 'out of this world – the best', which gave the Mai Tai its name. This cocktail means simply 'the best'.
Comment: Not quite the best, but this long, fruity thirst-quencher isn't half bad.

RIVIERA BREEZE

Glass: Old-fashioned
Garnish: Orange slice in glass
Method: **POUR** pastis and orange juice into glass and then fill with ice. **TOP** with ginger ale and stir.

$1^1/_2$	shot(s)	**Ricard pastis**
2	shot(s)	**Freshly squeezed orange juice**
Top up with		**Ginger ale**

Origin: Created in 2003 by Roo Buckley at Café Lebowitz, New York City, USA.
Comment: An aniseed-rich summertime cooler.

THE ROADRUNNER

Glass: Martini
Garnish: Lemon zest twist
Method: **SHAKE** all ingredients with ice and fine strain into chilled glass.

2	shot(s)	**Vanilla infused Partida tequila**
$^3/_4$	shot(s)	**Freshly squeezed lemon juice**
$^1/_2$	shot(s)	**Maple syrup**
2	dashes	**Angostura aromatic bitters**
$^1/_2$	fresh	**Egg white**

Origin: Discovered in 2005 at The Cuckoo Club, London, England.
Comment: Citrus and tequila with a hint of maple and vanilla, smoothed with egg white.

'I RATHER LIKE MY REPUTATION, ACTUALLY, THAT OF A SPOILED GENIUS FROM THE WELSH GUTTER, A DRUNK, A WOMANIZER; IT'S RATHER AN ATTRACTIVE IMAGE.'

R

RIZZO [NEW #7]

Glass: Martini
Garnish: Float thin apple slice
Method: **SHAKE** all ingredients with ice and fine strain into chilled glass.

1	shot(s)	**Boulard Grand Solage Calvados**
1	shot(s)	**Plymouth gin**
$^3/_4$	shot(s)	**Squeezed pink grapefruit juice**
$^1/_2$	shot(s)	**Freshly squeezed lime juice**
$^1/_4$	shot(s)	**Passion fruit syrup**
$^1/_4$	shot(s)	**Pomegranate (grenadine) syrup**

Origin: Created in 2006 by Gregor de Gruyther at Ronnie Scott's, London, England, and named for Betty Rizzo, the leader of the Pink Ladies in the film Grease.
Comment: The tangy, sharp grapefruit reveals hints of apple spirit smoothed by grenadine.

ROB ROY #1

Glass: Martini
Garnish: Cherry & lemon zest twist (discard twist)
Method: **STIR** all ingredients with ice and strain into chilled glass.

2	shot(s)	**Scotch whisky**
1	shot(s)	**Sweet vermouth**
2	dashes	**Angostura aromatic bitters**
$^1/_8$	shot(s)	**Maraschino syrup (optional)**

Variant: 'Highland', made with orange bitters in place of Angostura.
Origin: Created in 1894 at New York's Waldorf-Astoria Hotel (the Empire State Building occupies the site today), and named after a Broadway show playing at the time.
Comment: A Sweet Manhattan made with Scotch in place of bourbon. The dry, peaty whisky and bitters ensure it's not too sweet.

ROB ROY #2

Glass: Martini
Garnish: Cherry & orange zest twist (discard twist)
Method: STIR all ingredients with ice and strain into chilled glass.

2	shot(s)	**Scotch whisky**
1	shot(s)	**Sweet vermouth**
2	dashes	**Peychaud's aromatic bitters**
1/2	shot(s)	**Chilled mineral water** (omit if wet ice)

Origin: This variation on the classic Rob Roy is recommended by author David Embury in his influential Fine Art of Mixing Drinks.
Comment: The Scotch answer to the Manhattan with added complexity courtesy of Peychaud's aromatic bitters.

THE ROFFIGNAC [UPDATED #7]

Glass: Collins
Garnish: Lime wedge
Method: SHAKE first two ingredients with ice and strain into ice-filled glass. **TOP** with soda, lightly stir and serve with straws.

2	shot(s)	**Rémy Martin cognac**
1	shot(s)	**Giffard crème de framboise**
Top up with		**Soda water (club soda)**

Origin: This classic cocktail is named after Count Louis Philippe Joseph de Roffignac, Mayor of New Orleans 1820-1828. Roffignac is noted for introducing street lights to the city and laying cobblestones on the roads in the French Quarter.
Comment: This bright red, fruity drink is simple but moreish.

ROBIN HOOD #1

Glass: Martini
Garnish: Apple wedge on rim
Method: SHAKE all ingredients with ice and fine strain into chilled glass.

1 3/4	shot(s)	**Light white rum**
1 1/4	shot(s)	**Apple schnapps liqueur**
3/4	shot(s)	**Rose's lime cordial**
1/2	shot(s)	**Freshly squeezed lime juice**

Origin: Adapted from a drink created in 2002 by Tony Conigliaro at Lonsdale House, London, England.
Comment: American readers might consider this an Apple Martini based on rum.

ROGER

Glass: Martini
Garnish: Peach slice on rim
Method: SHAKE all ingredients with ice and fine strain into chilled glass.

2	shot(s)	**Ketel One vodka**
2	shot(s)	**White peach purée**
1/2	shot(s)	**Freshly squeezed lemon juice**
1/4	shot(s)	**Sugar syrup (2 sugar to 1 water)**

Origin: A popular drink in Venice, where it is made using the peach purée mix prepared for Bellinis.
Comment: Thick and very fruity – one for a summer's afternoon.

ROC-A-COE

Glass: Martini
Garnish: Maraschino cherry
Method: STIR all ingredients with ice and strain into chilled glass.

1 1/2	shot(s)	**Plymouth gin**
2	shot(s)	**Amontillado sherry**
1/8	shot(s)	**Sugar syrup (2 sugar to 1 water)**
1/2	shot(s)	**Chilled mineral water** (omit if wet ice)

Origin: Adapted from a recipe purloined from a 1930 edition of The Savoy Cocktail Book by Harry Craddock.
Comment: Aromatic and balanced.

ROMAN PUNCH

Glass: Collins
Garnish: Lemon slice
Method: SHAKE all ingredients with ice and strain into glass filled with crushed ice. Serve with straws.

1 1/2	shot(s)	**Bénédictine D.O.M. liqueur**
3/4	shot(s)	**Freshly squeezed lemon juice**
1 1/2	shot(s)	**Rémy Martin cognac**
3/4	shot(s)	**Wray & Nephew overproof rum**
2	shot(s)	**Chilled mineral water**

Comment: Spirited and refreshing with herbal notes.

ROCKY MOUNTAIN ROOTBEER

Glass: Collins
Garnish: Lime wedge
Method: POUR vodka and liqueur into ice-filled glass, top up with cola and lightly stir.

2	shot(s)	**Ketel One vodka**
3/4	shot(s)	**Galliano liqueur**
Top up with		**Cola**

Comment: Does indeed taste reminiscent of alcoholic root beer.

LA ROSA MARGARITA

Glass: Coupette
Garnish: Lime wedge on rim
Method: SHAKE all ingredients with ice and fine strain ino chilled glass.

2	shot(s)	**Partida tequila**
3/4	shot(s)	**Blackberry (mûre) liqueur**
1	shot(s)	**Cold hibiscus tea (strong brewed)**
1/2	shot(s)	**Freshly squeezed lime juice**

Comment: A fruity yet dry crimson-coloured Margarita.

ROSARITA MARGARITA

Glass: Coupette
Garnish: Lime wedge & optional salted rim
Method: SHAKE all ingredients with ice and fine strain into chilled glass.

1 1/2	shot(s)	**Partida tequila**
3/4	shot(s)	**Grand Marnier liqueur**
1/2	shot(s)	**Ocean Spray cranberry juice**
1/2	shot(s)	**Rose's lime cordial**
3/4	shot(s)	**Freshly squeezed lime juice**
1/2	shot(s)	**Sugar syrup (2 sugar to 1 water)**

Origin: Created in 1999 by Robert Plotkin and Raymon Flores of BarMedia, USA.
Comment: This peachy coloured Margarita is well balanced and flavoursome.

THE ROSE #1 (ORIGINAL)

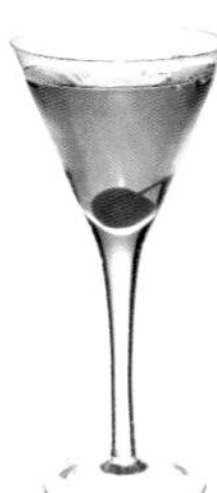

Glass: Martini
Garnish: Maraschino cherry
Method: STIR all ingredients with ice and fine strain into chilled glass.

2	shot(s)	**Dry vermouth**
1	shot(s)	**Kirsch eau de vie**
1/2	shot(s)	**Raspberry (or pomegranate) syrup**

Origin: Created in 1920 by Johnny Milta at the Chatham Hotel, Paris. This recipe is adapted from one in The Fine Art of Mixing Drinks by David Embury.
Comment: This salmon pink drink is wonderfully aromatic.

THE ROSE #2

Glass: Martini
Garnish: Maraschino cherry
Method: STIR all ingredients with ice and fine strain into chilled glass.

2	shot(s)	**Plymouth gin**
1	shot(s)	**Cherry (brandy) liqueur**
1	shot(s)	**Dry vermouth**

Origin: Adapted from a recipe in Harry Craddock's 1930 Savoy Cocktail Book.
Comment: Cherry and gin dried with vermouth.

THE ROSE #3

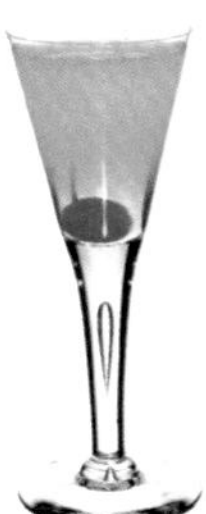

Glass: Martini
Garnish: Maraschino cherry
Method: SHAKE all ingredients with ice and fine strain into chilled glass.

1 1/2	shot(s)	**Kirsch eau de vie**
1 1/2	shot(s)	**Dry vermouth**
1/2	shot(s)	**Pomegranate (grenadine) syrup**

Origin: Adapted from a recipe in Harry Craddock's 1930 Savoy Cocktail Book.
Comment: Delicate, aromatic cherry – not too sweet.

ROSE PETALINI

Glass: Martini
Garnish: Float red rose petal
Method: STIR all ingredients with ice and strain into chilled glass.

1 1/2	shot(s)	**Rose vodka**
1 1/2	shot(s)	**Plymouth gin**
1	shot(s)	**Lychee syrup (from tinned lychees)**
3	dashes	**Peychaud's aromatic bitters**

Origin: Discovered in 2005 at Rain, Amsterdam, The Netherlands.
Comment: Peychaud's bitters give this fragrant cocktail a delicate pink hue.

ROSEHIP MARTINI [NEW #7]

Glass: Martini
Garnish: Orange zest twist
Method: SHAKE all ingredients with ice and fine strain into chilled glass.

2	shot(s)	**Ketel One vodka**
1	shot(s)	**St-Germain elderflower liqueur**
1/2	shot(s)	**Dry vermouth**
1/8	shot(s)	**Rosewater**

Origin: Created in 2006 by yours truly.
Comment: Dry, yet not bone dry, aromatic and floral.

ROSELYN MARTINI

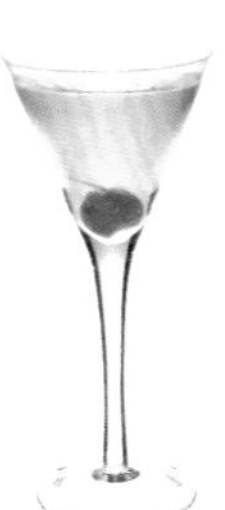

Glass: Martini
Garnish: Maraschino cherry
Method: SHAKE all ingredients with ice and fine strain into chilled glass.

2	shot(s)	**Plymouth gin**
1	shot(s)	**Dry vermouth**
1/4	shot(s)	**Pomegranate (grenadine) syrup**

Origin: Adapted from a recipe in Harry Craddock's 1930 Savoy Cocktail Book.
Comment: Subtle and beautifully balanced. A wet Martini made 'easy' by a dash of pomegranate syrup.

ROSITA

Glass: Old-fashioned
Garnish: Orange zest twist
Method: STIR all ingredients with ice and strain into ice-filled glass.

2	shot(s)	**Partida tequila**
3/4	shot(s)	**Campari**
3/4	shot(s)	**Dry vermouth**
3/4	shot(s)	**Sweet vermouth**
2	dashes	**Angostura aromatic bitters**

Comment: A bittersweet, tequila based, Negroni-like drink.

ROSSINI

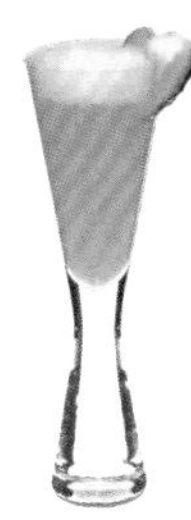

Glass: Flute
Garnish: Strawberry on rim
Method: MUDDLE strawberries in base of shaker. Add strawberry liqueur, **SHAKE** with ice and fine strain into chilled glass. **TOP** with Prosecco and gently stir.

4	fresh	**Strawberries**
3/4	shot(s)	**Giffard crème de fraise de bois**
Top up with		**Prosecco sparkling wine**

Origin: Named for the 19th century opera composer, this is one of the most popular Bellini variants in Venice.
Comment: Strawberries seem to complement Prosecco even better than white peaches.

ROSY MARTINI

Glass: Martini
Garnish: Orange zest twist
Method: STIR all ingredients with ice and strain into chilled glass.

2	shot(s)	**Ketel One Citroen vodka**
3/4	shot(s)	**Cointreau triple sec**
3/4	shot(s)	**Dubonnet Red**

Comment: An aptly named drink with hints of spice, citrus peel, honey and mulled wine.

ROULETTE

Glass: Martini
Garnish: Orange zest twist
Method: SHAKE all ingredients with ice and fine strain into chilled glass.

1 1/2	shot(s)	**Boulard Grand Solage Calvados**
3/4	shot(s)	**Light white rum**
3/4	shot(s)	**Carlshamns Swedish Torr Flaggpunsch**
1/2	shot(s)	**Chilled mineral water** (omit if wet ice)

Origin: Adapted from a recipe in Harry Craddock's 1930 Savoy Cocktail Book.
Comment: Balanced apple and spice.

ROUSING CHARLIE [UPDATED #7]

Glass: Martini
Garnish: Lychee from tin in drink
Method: STIR all ingredients with ice and strain into chilled glass.

3/4	shot(s)	**Pisco**
3/4	shot(s)	**St-Germain elderflower liqueur**
3/4	shot(s)	**Tio Pepe fino sherry**
3/4	shot(s)	**Sake**
1/2	shot(s)	**Lychee syrup from tinned fruit**

Origin: Adapted from a drink I created in 2002 and named after Charlie Rouse, a very lovely sherry lover.
Comment: Subtle with an interesting salty edge, this tastes almost like a wine.

ROY ROGERS (MOCKTAIL)

Glass: Collins
Garnish: Lime wedge
Method: POUR grenadine and cola into ice-filled glass and stir. Serve with straws.

1/4	shot(s)	**Pomegranate (grenadine) syrup**
Top up with		**Cola**

Comment: I wouldn't bother.

ROYAL BERMUDA YACHT CLUB DAIQUIRI

Glass: Martini
Garnish: Lime wedge on rim
Method: SHAKE all ingredients with ice and fine strain into chilled glass.

2 1/2	shot(s)	**Golden rum**
3/4	shot(s)	**Freshly squeezed lime juice**
1/2	shot(s)	**Velvet Falernum liqueur**
1/4	shot(s)	**Cointreau triple sec**

Origin: Created at the eponymous club, established in Bermuda in 1844 and largely frequented by British Army officers.
This recipe is adapted from one in Trader Vic's Bartender's Guide.
Comment: A full-flavoured, tangy Daiquiri.

ROYAL COSMOPOLITAN

Glass: Martini
Garnish: Orange zest twist
Method: SHAKE first four ingredients with ice and fine strain into chilled glass. **TOP** with champagne.

1	shot(s)	**Ketel One Citroen vodka**
1/2	shot(s)	**Cointreau triple sec**
1	shot(s)	**Ocean Spray cranberry juice**
1/4	shot(s)	**Freshly squeezed lime juice**
Top up with		**Brut champagne**

Origin: Created in 2003 by Wayne Collins, London, UK.
Comment: The classic Cosmopolitan with a layer of fizz on top adding a biscuity complexity. Sex And The City meets Ab Fab.

R

ROYAL MOJITO

Glass: Collins
Garnish: Mint sprig
Method: Lightly **MUDDLE** mint (just to bruise) in base of glass. Add rum, lime juice and sugar. Half fill glass with crushed ice and **CHURN** (stir) with bar spoon. Fill glass with more crushed ice and **CHURN** some more. **TOP** with champagne, lightly stir and serve with straws.

12	fresh	**Mint leaves**
2	shot(s)	**Light white rum**
3/4	shot(s)	**Freshly squeezed lime juice**
1/4	shot(s)	**Sugar syrup (2 sugar to 1 water)**
Top up with		**Brut champagne**

AKA: Luxury Mojito
Comment: A Mojito topped with champagne instead of soda water. There's posh!

ROYAL SMILE

Glass: Martini
Garnish: Lemon zest twist
Method: SHAKE all ingredients with ice and fine strain into chilled glass.

1	shot(s)	**Plymouth gin**
1	shot(s)	**Boulard Grand Solage Calvados**
1/2	shot(s)	**Freshly squeezed lemon juice**
1/4	shot(s)	**Pomegranate (grenadine) syrup**
1/2	shot(s)	**Chilled mineral water** (omit if wet ice)

Origin: Purloined from David Embury's classic book, The Fine Art of Mixing Drinks.
Comment: This balanced sweet and sour could put a smile on anyone's face. Unless one is not amused!

ROYAL VELVET MARGARITA

Glass: Coupette (or fresh pineapple shell)
Garnish: Lime wedge
Method: SHAKE all ingredients with ice and fine strain into chilled glass.

2	shot(s)	**Partida tequila**
1/2	shot(s)	**Chambord black raspberry liqueur**
1/2	shot(s)	**Luxardo Amaretto di Saschira liqueur**
1	shot(s)	**Freshly squeezed lime juice**

Origin: Discovered in 2005 at Velvet Margarita Cantina, Los Angeles, USA.
Comment: An almond and berry flavoured Margarita.

R U BOBBY MOORE?

Glass: Martini
Garnish: Apple wedge on rim
Method: STIR honey with Scotch and vodka in base of shaker until honey dissolves. Add other ingredients, **SHAKE** with ice and fine strain into chilled glass.

3	spoons	**Runny honey**
1	shot(s)	**Scotch whisky**
1	shot(s)	**Zubrówka bison vodka**
3/4	shot(s)	**Sauvignon Blanc wine**
1	shot(s)	**Pressed apple juice**

Origin: Created in 2002 by yours truly and named after the rhyming slang for 'are you bloody sure?' Bobby Moore was the 60s England football captain and West Ham United defender who regrettably died young in 1993. My dictionary of rhyming slang claims 'Bobby Moore' means 'door' – well, not in East London it doesn't.
Comment: It's common to pair both Scotch and zubrówka with apple, but combining all three together with wine and honey really works.

R

RUBY MARTINI #1

Glass: Martini
Garnish: Lemon slice on rim
Method: SHAKE all ingredients with ice and fine strain into chilled glass.

1 1/2	shot(s)	**Ketel One Citroen vodka**
1	shot(s)	**Cointreau triple sec**
1	shot(s)	**Squeezed pink grapefruit juice**
1/4	shot(s)	**Sugar syrup (2 sugar to 1 water)**

Origin: Several appearances in episodes of the hit US TV series, Sex And The City, helped this drink become fashionable in 2002, particularly in New York City. It is thought to have originated at the Wave restaurant in Chicago's W Hotel.
Comment: A sour, citrus-led variation on the Cosmopolitan.

RUBY MARTINI #2

Glass: Martini
Garnish: Raspberry & lemon twist
Method: SHAKE all ingredients with ice and fine strain into chilled glass.

1 1/2	shot(s)	**Rémy Martin cognac**
1/2	shot(s)	**Cointreau triple sec**
1/2	shot(s)	**Giffard crème de framboise**
1/2	shot(s)	**Sweet vermouth**

Origin: Created by Wayne Collins, London, England.
Comment: Fruity and slightly sweet.

RUDE COSMOPOLITAN

Glass: Martini
Garnish: Orange zest twist
Method: SHAKE all ingredients with ice and fine strain into chilled glass.

1	shot(s)	**Partida tequila**
1	shot(s)	**Cointreau triple sec**
1 1/2	shot(s)	**Ocean Spray cranberry juice**
1/2	shot(s)	**Freshly squeezed lime juice**
2	dashes	**Fee Brothers orange bitters (optional)**

AKA: Mexico City
Comment: Don't let the pink appearance of this Cosmopolitan (made with tequila in place of vodka) fool you into thinking it's a fluffy cocktail. It's both serious and superb.

'THE SECRET TO A LONG LIFE IS TO STAY BUSY, GET PLENTY OF EXERCISE AND DON'T DRINK TOO MUCH. THEN AGAIN, DON'T DRINK TOO LITTLE.'

RUDE GINGER COSMOPOLITAN

Glass: Martini
Garnish: Orange zest twist
Method: MUDDLE ginger in base of shaker. Add other ingredients, **SHAKE** with ice and fine strain into chilled glass.

2	slices	**Fresh root ginger (thumbnail sized)**
1½	shot(s)	**Partida tequila**
1	shot(s)	**Cointreau triple sec**
1	shot(s)	**Ocean Spray cranberry juice**
½	shot(s)	**Freshly squeezed lime juice**
¼	shot(s)	**Rose's lime cordial**

Origin: Created in 2003 by Jeremy Adderley at Halo, Edinburgh, Scotland.
Comment: To quote Halo's list, "Looks like a Cosmo, goes like a Mexican!"

'IF YOU DRINK, DON'T DRIVE. DON'T EVEN PUTT.'

RUM & RAISIN ALEXANDRA

Glass: Martini
Garnish: Three red grapes on stick
Method: MUDDLE grapes in base of shaker. Add other ingredients, **SHAKE** with ice and fine strain into chilled glass.

7	fresh	**Red seedless grapes**
1½	shot(s)	**Aged rum**
½	shot(s)	**Giffard crème de cassis**
½	shot(s)	**Double (heavy) cream**
½	shot(s)	**Milk**
¼	shot(s)	**Sugar syrup (2 sugar to 1 water)**

Origin: Created in 2003 by Ian Morgan, England.
Comment: Forgo the ice cream and try this creamy, quaffable, alcoholic dessert.

RUM PUNCH

Glass: Collins
Garnish: Orange slice & cherry (sail)
Method: SHAKE all ingredients with ice and strain into glass filled with crushed ice.

¾	shot(s)	**Freshly squeezed lime juice**
1½	shot(s)	**Sugar syrup (2 sugar to 1 water)**
2¼	shot(s)	**Wray & Nephew overproof rum**
3	shot(s)	**Chilled mineral water**
3	dashes	**Angostura aromatic bitters**

Comment: The classic proportions of this drink (followed above) are 'one of sour, two of sweet, three of strong and four of weak' – referring to lime juice, sugar syrup, rum and water respectively. In Jamaica, the spiritual home of the Rum Punch, they like their rum overproof (more than 57% alc./vol.) and serving over crushed ice dilutes and tames this very strong drink.

RUM PUNCH-UP

Glass: Martini
Garnish: Lime wedge on rim
Method: SHAKE all ingredients with ice and fine strain into chilled glass.

1½	shot(s)	**Wray & Nephew overproof rum**
½	shot(s)	**Freshly squeezed lime juice**
½	shot(s)	**Sugar syrup (2 sugar to 1 water)**
1	shot(s)	**Chilled mineral water** (reduce if wet ice)
2	dashes	**Angostura aromatic bitters**

Origin: Adapted from a drink discovered in 2006 at Albannach, London, England.
Comment: Exactly what the name promises – a rum punch served straight-up, Daiquiri style.

RUMBA

Glass: Old-fashioned
Garnish: Lime wedge
Method: SHAKE all ingredients with ice and strain into glass filled with crushed ice. Serve with straws.

¾	shot(s)	**Wray & Nephew overproof rum**
1	shot(s)	**Plymouth gin**
1	shot(s)	**Freshly squeezed lime juice**
½	shot(s)	**Pomegranate (grenadine) syrup**
¼	shot(s)	**Sugar syrup (2 sugar to 1 water)**
½	shot(s)	**Chilled mineral water** (omit if wet ice)

Origin: Recipe adapted from David Embury's classic book, The Fine Art of Mixing Drinks.
Comment: To quote Embury, "Whoever thought up this snootful of liquid dynamite certainly liked his liquor hard!"

RUM RUNNER

Glass: Hurricane
Garnish: Pineapple wedge & cherry
Method: SHAKE all ingredients with ice and strain into glass filled with crushed ice.

1½	shot(s)	**Pusser's Navy rum**
½	shot(s)	**Giffard mûre (blackberry) liqueur**
1	shot(s)	**Giffard crème de banane du Brésil**
1	shot(s)	**Freshly squeezed lime juice**
2	shot(s)	**Pressed pineapple juice**
½	shot(s)	**Pomegranate (grenadine) syrup**

Comment: Fruity, sharp and rounded.

RUM SOUR

Glass: Old-fashioned
Garnish: Orange zest twist
Method: SHAKE all ingredients with ice and strain into ice-filled glass.

2	shot(s)	**Aged rum**
1	shot(s)	**Freshly squeezed orange juice**
1	shot(s)	**Freshly squeezed lime juice**
½	shot(s)	**Sugar syrup (2 sugar to 1 water)**
½	fresh	**Egg white**

Comment: Smooth and sour – well balanced.

RUSSIAN

Glass: Martini
Garnish: Orange zest twist
Method: SHAKE all ingredients with ice and fine strain into chilled glass.

$1\frac{1}{2}$	shot(s)	**Plymouth gin**
1	shot(s)	**Ketel One vodka**
1	shot(s)	**Giffard white crème de cacao**

Origin: Adapted from a recipe in Harry Craddock's 1930 Savoy Cocktail Book.
Comment: Gin and vodka with a sweet hint of chocolate.

RUSSIAN BRIDE

Glass: Martini
Garnish: Dust with cocoa powder
Method: SHAKE all ingredients with ice and fine strain into chilled glass.

2	shot(s)	**Vanilla infused Ketel One vodka**
$\frac{3}{4}$	shot(s)	**Kahlúa coffee liqueur**
$\frac{1}{4}$	shot(s)	**Giffard white crème de cacao**
$\frac{1}{2}$	shot(s)	**Double (heavy) cream**
$\frac{1}{2}$	shot(s)	**Milk**

Origin: Created in 2002 by Miranda Dickson, A.K.A. the Vodka Princess, for the UK's Revolution bar chain, where some 500,000 are sold each year.
Comment: A little on the sweet side for some but vanilla, coffee and chocolate smoothed with cream is a tasty combination.

RUSSIAN QUALUUDE SHOT

Glass: Shot
Method: Refrigerate ingredients then **LAYER** in chilled glass by carefully pouring in the following order.

$\frac{1}{2}$	shot(s)	**Galliano liqueur**
$\frac{1}{2}$	shot(s)	**Green Chartreuse liqueur**
$\frac{1}{2}$	shot(s)	**Ketel One vodka**

Comment: An explosive herb and peppermint shot.

RUSSIAN SPRING PUNCH

Glass: Sling
Garnish: Lemon slice & berries
Method: SHAKE first four ingredients with ice and strain into glass filled with crushed ice. **TOP** with champagne, lightly stir and serve with straws.

1	shot(s)	**Ketel One vodka**
$\frac{1}{4}$	shot(s)	**Giffard crème de cassis**
1	shot(s)	**Freshly squeezed lemon juice**
$\frac{1}{4}$	shot(s)	**Sugar syrup (2 sugar to 1 water)**
Top up with		**Champagne**

Origin: My version of a drink created in the 1990s by Dick Bradsell, London, England.
Comment: Well balanced, complex and refreshing.

RUSTY NAIL

Glass: Old-fashioned
Garnish: Lemon zest twist
Method: STIR ingredients with ice and strain into ice-filled glass.

2	shot(s)	**Scotch whisky**
$\frac{3}{4}$	shot(s)	**Drambuie liqueur**

Origin: Created in 1942 at a Hawaiian bar for the artist Theodore Anderson.
Comment: The liqueur smoothes and wonderfully combines with the Scotch.

SAGE MARGARITA

Glass: Coupette
Garnish: Float sage leaf
Method: Lightly **MUDDLE** (just to bruise) sage in base of shaker. Add other ingredients, **SHAKE** with ice and fine strain into chilled glass.

3	fresh	**Sage leaves**
2	shot(s)	**Partida tequila**
1	shot(s)	**Cointreau triple sec**
1	shot(s)	**Freshly squeezed lime juice**
$\frac{1}{8}$	shot(s)	**Sugar syrup (2 sugar to 1 water)**

Comment: Exactly as promised – a sage flavoured Margarita.

SAGE MARTINI

Glass: Martini
Garnish: Float sage leaf
Method: Lightly **MUDDLE** (just to bruise) sage in base of shaker. Add other ingredients, **SHAKE** with ice and fine strain into chilled glass.

3	fresh	**Sage leaves**
$1\frac{1}{2}$	shot(s)	**Ketel One vodka**
$1\frac{1}{2}$	shot(s)	**Dry vermouth**
$\frac{3}{4}$	shot(s)	**Pressed apple juice**

Comment: Delicate sage and a hint of apple, dried with vermouth and fortified with vodka.

SAIGON COOLER

Glass: Collins
Garnish: Three raspberries
Method: MUDDLE raspberries in base of shaker. Add other ingredients, **SHAKE** with ice and fine strain into ice-filled glass.

7	fresh	**Raspberries**
2	shot(s)	**Plymouth gin**
$\frac{1}{2}$	shot(s)	**Chambord black raspberry liqueur**
3	shot(s)	**Ocean Spray cranberry juice**
$\frac{3}{4}$	shot(s)	**Freshly squeezed lime juice**

Origin: Created at Bam-Bou, London, England.
Comment: Well balanced sweet 'n' sour with a rich fruity flavour.

SAIGON SLING

Glass: Sling
Garnish: Pineapple wedge & cherry on rim
Method: SHAKE first seven ingredients with ice and strain into ice-filled glass. **TOP** with ginger ale.

$1\frac{1}{2}$	shot(s)	**Plymouth gin**
$\frac{3}{4}$	shot(s)	**Ginger & lemongrass cordial**
$\frac{1}{2}$	shot(s)	**Krupnik honey liqueur**
$\frac{3}{4}$	shot(s)	**Freshly squeezed lime juice**
1	shot(s)	**Pressed pineapple juice**
$\frac{1}{4}$	shot(s)	**Passoã passion fruit liqueur**
2	dashes	**Peychaud's aromatic bitters**
Top up with		**Ginger ale**

Origin: Created in 2001 by Rodolphe Manor for a London bartending competition.
Comment: A fusion of unusual flavours.

THE ST-GERMAIN [NEW #7]

Glass: Collins (12oz)
Garnish: Lime slice
Method: POUR wine and then elderflower liqueur into ice-filled glass. Top with soda (or champagne), lightly stir and serve with straws.

2	shot(s)	**Sauvignon Blanc wine**
$1\frac{1}{2}$	shot(s)	**St-Germain elderflower liqueur**
Top up with		**Soda water (or champagne)**

Variant: Also try 2 shots champagne, $1\frac{1}{2}$ shots St-Germain topped with soda.
Origin: Created in 2006 by yours truly, this is the signature drink of St-Germain elderflower liqueur.
Comment: A long, easy drinking summer cooler.

SAILOR'S COMFORT

Glass: Old-fashioned
Garnish: Lime wedge
Method: SHAKE first four ingredients with ice and strain into ice-filled glass. **TOP** with soda, lightly stir and serve with straws.

1	shot(s)	**Plymouth sloe gin liqueur**
1	shot(s)	**Southern Comfort liqueur**
1	shot(s)	**Rose's lime cordial**
3	dashes	**Angostura aromatic bitters**
Top up with		**Soda water (club soda)**

Origin: Discovered in 2002 at Lightship Ten, London.
Comment: Lime, peach and hints of berry make a light, easy drink.

ST KITTS (MOCKTAIL)

Glass: Collins
Garnish: Lime wedge
Method: SHAKE first three ingredients with ice and strain into ice-filled glass. **TOP** with ginger ale, lightly stir and serve with straws.

3	shot(s)	**Pineapple juice**
$\frac{1}{2}$	shot(s)	**Freshly squeezed lime juice**
$\frac{1}{4}$	shot(s)	**Pomegranate (grenadine) syrup**
Top up with		**Ginger ale**

Variant: Add 3 dashes Angostura aromatic bitters. This adds a tiny amount of alcohol but greatly improves the drink.
Comment: Rust coloured and refreshing.

'BY TWO-THIRTY THE NEXT AFTERNOON I WAS INSTALLED AT THE BAR OF LA FLORIDITA, GRATEFUL FOR THE COOL QUIET OF THE PLACE AND THE MAJESTIC FROZEN DAIQUIRI IN MY HAND.'
ERNEST HEMINGWAY

SAINT CLEMENTS (MOCKTAIL)

Glass: Collins
Garnish: Lime wedge
Method: POUR ingredients into ice-filled glass, lightly stir and serve with straws.

3	shot(s)	**Freshly squeezed orange juice**
Top up with		**Bitter lemon**

Comment: Only slightly more interesting than orange juice.

ST. PATRICK'S DAY

Glass: Old-fashioned
Garnish: Mint sprig/shamrock
Method: STIR all ingredients with ice and strain into ice-filled glass.

2	shot(s)	**Irish whiskey**
1	shot(s)	**Green Chartreuse liqueur**
1	shot(s)	**Green crème de menthe**
1	dash	**Angostura aromatic bitters.**

Origin: Created in 2006 by your truly.
Comment: Minty, herbal whiskey – a helluva craic.

SAKE'POLITAN

Glass: Martini
Garnish: Orange zest twist
Method: SHAKE all ingredients with ice and fine strain into chilled glass.

2¼	shot(s)	**Sake**
¾	shot(s)	**Cointreau triple sec**
¾	shot(s)	**Ocean Spray cranberry juice**
¼	shot(s)	**Freshly squeezed lime juice**
2	dashes	**Fee Brothers orange bitters (optional)**

Comment: A Cosmo with more than a hint of sake.

SAKE-TINI #1

Glass: Martini
Garnish: Three thin slices of cucumber
Method: STIR all ingredients with ice and strain into chilled glass.

1	shot(s)	**Plymouth gin**
2½	shot(s)	**Sake**
½	shot(s)	**Grand Marnier liqueur**

Comment: Sake and a hint of orange liqueur add the perfect aromatic edge to this Martini-style drink.

SAKE-TINI #2

Glass: Martini
Garnish: Orange zest twist
Method: SHAKE all ingredients with ice and fine strain into chilled glass.

1½	shot(s)	**Ketel One vodka**
1	shot(s)	**Plum wine**
½	shot(s)	**Sake**
1	shot(s)	**Ocean Spray cranberry juice**

Origin: Discovered in 2005 at Nobu Berkeley, London, England.
Comment: Salmon-coloured, light and fragrant with plum wine and sake to the fore.

S

SAKINI

Glass: Martini
Garnish: Olives on stick
Method: STIR all ingredients with ice and strain into chilled glass.

1	shot(s)	**Sake**
2½	shot(s)	**Ketel One vodka**

Comment: Very dry. The sake creates an almost wine-like delicacy.

SALFLOWER SOUR [NEW #7]

Glass: Martini
Garnish: Orange zest twist (discarded)
Method: SHAKE all ingredients with ice and fine strain into chilled glass.

2	shot(s)	**St-Germain elderflower liqueur**
¾	shot(s)	**Freshly squeezed orange juice**
¾	shot(s)	**Freshly squeezed lime juice**
1	dash	**Fee Brothers orange bitters**
½	fresh	**Egg white**

Origin: Created on 12th April 2007 by Salvatore Calabrese at Fifty, London, England.
Comment: Classic sweet and sour enhanced by floral notes.

SALTECCA

Glass: Martini
Garnish: Lemon zest twist
Method: STIR all ingredients with ice and fine strain into chilled glass.

2	shot(s)	**Partida tequila**
½	shot(s)	**Fino sherry**
1/8	shot(s)	**Brine from jar of salted capers**
1/8	shot(s)	**Sugar syrup (2 sugar to 1 water)**
½	shot(s)	**Chilled mineral water** (omit if wet ice)

Comment: Reminiscent of salted water after boiling vegetables but you've got to try these things.

SALTY DOG

Glass: Martini
Garnish: Salt rim
Method: SHAKE all ingredients with ice and fine strain into chilled glass.

2	shot(s)	**Ketel One vodka**
2¼	shot(s)	**Freshly squeezed grapefruit juice**
1/8	shot(s)	**Luxardo maraschino liqueur (optional)**

Origin: Created in the 1960s.
Comment: For a more interesting drink, try basing this classic on gin rather than vodka.

SALTY LYCHEE MARTINI

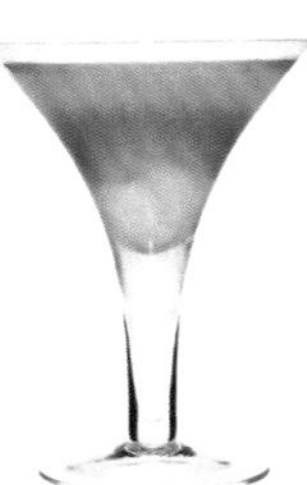

Glass: Martini
Garnish: Lychee from tin
Method: STIR all ingredients with ice and strain into chilled glass.

2	shot(s)	**Fino sherry**
1	shot(s)	**Lanique rose petal liqueur**
1	shot(s)	**Lychee syrup from tinned fruit**

Origin: I created this drink in 2002 after trying Dick Bradsell's Lychee & Rose Petal Martini (also in this guide).
Comment: Light pink in colour and subtle in flavour with the salty tang of Fino sherry.

SAN FRANCISCO

Glass: Collins
Garnish: Pineapple wedge on rim
Method: SHAKE all ingredients with ice and strain into ice-filled glass.

2 shot(s)	**Ketel One vodka**
1/2 shot(s)	**Cointreau triple sec**
1/2 shot(s)	**Giffard crème de banane du Brésil**
1 1/2 shot(s)	**Freshly squeezed orange juice**
1 1/2 shot(s)	**Pressed pineapple juice**
1/4 shot(s)	**Pomegranate (grenadine) syrup**

Comment: Long, fruity, slightly sweet and laced with vodka.

SANDSTORM

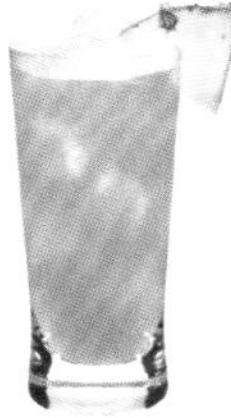

Glass: Collins
Garnish: Pineapple wedge on rim
Method: SHAKE all ingredients with ice and strain into ice-filled glass.

1 1/2 shot(s)	**Plymouth gin**
1 shot(s)	**Grand Marnier liqueur**
1/2 shot(s)	**Vanilla schnapps liqueur**
1 1/2 shot(s)	**Freshly squeezed grapefruit juice**
1 1/2 shot(s)	**Pressed pineapple juice**
1/4 shot(s)	**Sugar syrup (2 sugar to 1 water)**
1/4 shot(s)	**Freshly squeezed lime juice**
1/4 shot(s)	**Rose's lime cordial**

Origin: Created in 2003 by James Cunningham at Zinc, Glasgow, Scotland, and named for its cloudy yellow colour.
Comment: A long, fruity drink featuring well-balanced sweet and sourness.

SANDY GAFF

Glass: Boston
Method: POUR ale into glass, top with ginger ale and lightly stir.

2/3rds fill	**Dark beer**
Top up with	**Ginger ale**

AKA: Shandy Gaff
Origin: Adapted from a recipe purloined from David Embury's classic book, The Fine Art of Mixing Drinks.
Comment: Better than your average lager shandy.

LA SANG

Glass: Collins
Garnish: Chopped fruit
Method: SHAKE all ingredients with ice and strain into ice-filled glass.

2 shot(s)	**Rémy Martin cognac**
2 shot(s)	**Red wine**
2 shot(s)	**Freshly squeezed orange juice**
1/4 shot(s)	**Sugar syrup (2 sugar to 1 water)**

Origin: French for 'blood', this cocktail is a twist on the classic Spanish Sangria, which also means 'blood'.
Comment: The tannin in the wine balances the fruit and sweetness nicely.

SANGAREE

Glass: Collins
Garnish: Dust grated nutmeg
Method: SHAKE all ingredients with ice and strain into ice-filled glass.

1 shot(s)	**Rémy Martin cognac**
2 shot(s)	**Red wine**
1/2 shot(s)	**Grand Marnier liqueur**
1 shot(s)	**Freshly squeezed orange juice**
1/4 shot(s)	**Freshly squeezed lemon juice**
1/4 shot(s)	**Sugar syrup (2 sugar to 1 water)**
1 shot(s)	**Chilled mineral water** (reduce if wet ice)

Origin: This version of the Sangria was popular in 19th century America.
Comment: Basically red wine and orange liqueur, diluted with water, lemon juice and sugar.

SANGRIA

Glass: Collins
Garnish: Chopped fruit
Method: SHAKE all ingredients with ice and strain into ice-filled glass.

1 shot(s)	**Rémy Martin cognac**
2 shot(s)	**Shiraz red wine**
1/2 shot(s)	**Grand Marnier liqueur**
2 shot(s)	**Freshly squeezed orange juice**

Comment: This party classic from Spain suits serving in jugs or punch bowls.

SANGRIA MARTINI

Glass: Martini
Garnish: Quarter orange slice
Method: SHAKE all ingredients with ice and fine strain into chilled glass.

1 shot(s)	**Red wine**
3/4 shot(s)	**Freshly squeezed orange juice**
1 1/2 shot(s)	**Rémy Martin cognac**
1/2 shot(s)	**Apple schnapps liqueur**
1/2 shot(s)	**Giffard crème de framboise**

Origin: Created in 2003 by Angelo Vieira at Light Bar, St. Martins Hotel, London, England.
Comment: Brandy based and fruit laced – just like its namesake.

SANGRITA [UPDATED #7]

Glass: Shot
Method: **SHAKE** all ingredients with ice and fine strain into shot glass. Serve with a shot of tequila. The drinker can either down the tequila and chase it with sangrita or sip the two drinks alternately.

1/2	shot(s)	**Tomato juice**
1/2	shot(s)	**Pomegranate juice**
1/4	shot(s)	**Freshly squeezed orange juice**
1/2	shot(s)	**Freshly squeezed lime juice**
1/8	shot(s)	**Pomegranate (grenadine) syrup**
2	drops	**Tabasco**
2	dashes	**Worcestershire sauce**
1	pinch	**Salt**
1	grind	**Black pepper**

Origin: The name means 'little blood' in Spanish and the drink is served with tequila in practically every bar in Mexico.
Comment: In Mexico the quality of the homemade Sangrita can make or break a bar. This recipe is spicy and slightly sweet and perfect for chasing tequila.

SANTIAGO

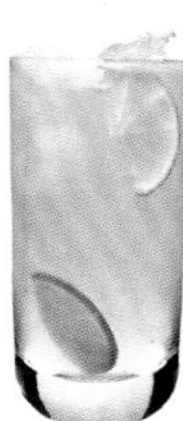

Glass: Collins
Garnish: Lime slices
Method: **SHAKE** first five ingredients with ice and strain into ice-filled glass. **TOP** with 7-Up, lightly stir and serve with straws.

1	shot(s)	**Light white rum**
1	shot(s)	**Spiced rum**
1/2	shot(s)	**Freshly squeezed lime juice**
1/2	shot(s)	**Freshly squeezed orange juice**
3	dashes	**Angostura aromatic bitters**
Top up with		**7-Up**

Comment: Light, refreshing and slightly spicy.

SANTIAGO DAIQUIRI

Glass: Martini
Garnish: Maraschino cherry
Method: **SHAKE** all ingredients with ice and fine strain into chilled glass.

2	shot(s)	**Light white rum**
1	shot(s)	**Freshly squeezed lemon juice**
1/2	shot(s)	**Pomegranate (grenadine) syrup**
1/2	shot(s)	**Chilled mineral water** (omit if wet ice)

Origin: Adapted from a recipe in Harry Craddock's 1930 Savoy Cocktail Book. Made with Bacardi rum this becomes the Bacardi Cocktail.
Comment: This Daiquiri is particularly delicate in its balance between sweet and sour.

SATSUMA MARTINI

Glass: Martini
Garnish: Orange zest twist
Method: **SHAKE** all ingredients with ice and fine strain into chilled glass.

1 1/2	shot(s)	**Orange zest infused Ketel One vodka**
3/4	shot(s)	**Grand Marnier liqueur**
2	shot(s)	**Pressed apple juice**
2	dashes	**Fee Brothers orange bitters**

Origin: Discovered in 2002 at the Fifth Floor Bar, London, England.
Comment: Tastes like its namesake – hard to believe it's almost half apple.

SATAN'S WHISKERS (STRAIGHT)

Glass: Martini
Garnish: Orange zest twist
Method: **SHAKE** all ingredients with ice and fine strain into chilled glass.

1	shot(s)	**Plymouth gin**
1	shot(s)	**Dry vermouth**
1	shot(s)	**Sweet vermouth**
1/2	shot(s)	**Grand Marnier liqueur**
1	shot(s)	**Freshly squeezed orange juice**
1	dash	**Fee Brothers orange bitters (optional)**

Variant: 'Curled' use triple sec in place of Grand Marnier.
Origin: Adapted from a recipe in Harry Craddock's 1930 Savoy Cocktail Book.
Comment: A variation on the Bronx. Perfectly balanced tangy orange.

SATURN MARTINI

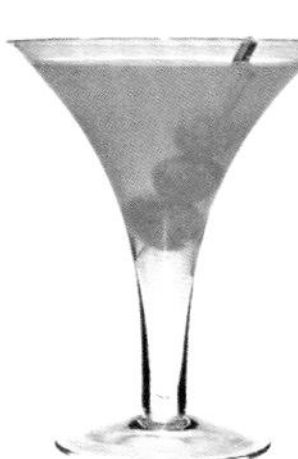

Glass: Martini
Garnish: Grapes on stick
Method: **MUDDLE** grapes in base of shaker. **STIR** honey with vodka and grapes to dissolve honey. Add wine, **SHAKE** with ice and fine strain into chilled glass.

7	fresh	**Seedless white grapes**
1 1/2	shot(s)	**Ketel One Citroen vodka**
2	shot(s)	**Runny honey**
1 1/2	shot(s)	**Sauvignon Blanc wine**

Origin: Created in 2001 by Tony Conigliaro at Isola, Knightsbridge, London, England.
Comment: Delicate, beautifully balanced and subtly flavoured.

SAÚCO MARGARITA [NEW #7]

Glass: Coupette
Garnish: Lime wedge & optional salt rim
Method: **SHAKE** all ingredients with ice and fine strain into chilled glass.

1 1/2	shot(s)	**Partida tequila**
1 1/2	shot(s)	**St-Germain elderflower liqueur**
3/4	shot(s)	**Freshly squeezed lime juice**

Origin: Created in 2006 by yours truly and named after 'flor saúco', which is Spanish for elderflower.
Comment: The floral notes of St-Germain combine wonderfully with the herbaceous tequila and citrusy lime.

SAZERAC

The rounded, distinctive flavour of this classic New Orleans cocktail is reliant on one essential ingredient: Peychaud's aromatic bitters.

Antoine Amedee Peychaud's father was forced to flee the island of San Domingo, where his family owned a coffee plantation, after the slaves rebelled. He arrived in New Orleans as a refugee in 1795.

His son became a pharmacist and bought his own Drug and Apothecary Store at what was then No. 123 Royal Street in 1834. There he created an 'American Aromatic Bitter Cordial' and marketed it as a medicinal tonic. Such potions were fashionable and there were many similar products.

Antoine also served his bitters mixed with brandy and other liquors. (It is often falsely claimed that the word 'cocktail' originated with Antoine, from a measure known as a 'coquetier' he used to prepare drinks. But it is undisputed that the term appeared in print in an upstate New York newspaper in 1806, when Antoine was only a child.)

Antoine Peychaud advertised his bitters in local newspapers and many New Orleans bars served drinks prepared with them. One such bar was the Sazerac Coffee House at 13 Exchange Alley, owned by John B. Schiller, who was also the local agent for a French cognac company called Sazerac-du-Forge et Fils of Limoges. It was here, in 1858, that a bartender called Leon Lamothe is thought to have created the Sazerac, probably using Peychaud's aromatic bitters, Sazerac cognac and sugar.

A decade or so later, one Thomas H Handy took over the coffee house and Antoine Peychaud fell upon hard times and sold his pharmacy store, along with the formula and brand name of his bitters. A combination of the phylloxera aphid (which devastated French vineyards) and the American Civil War made cognac hard to obtain and Handy was forced to change the recipe of the bar's now established house cocktail. He still used the all-important Peychaud's bitters but substituted Maryland Club rye whiskey, retaining a dash of cognac and adding a splash of the newly fashionable absinthe.

The Sazerac was further adapted in 1912 when absinthe was banned in the US and Herbsaint from Louisiana was substituted. Today the name Sazerac is owned by the Sazerac Company, who license it to the Sazerac Bar at the Fairmont Hotel.

SAVANNAH

Glass: Martini
Garnish: Orange zest twist
Method: SHAKE all ingredients with ice and fine strain into chilled glass.

$2\frac{1}{2}$	shot(s)	**Plymouth gin**
$\frac{3}{4}$	shot(s)	**Freshly squeezed orange juice**
$\frac{1}{2}$	shot(s)	**Giffard white crème de cacao**
$\frac{1}{2}$	fresh	**Egg white**

Origin: Adapted from a recipe in the 1949 edition of Esquire's Handbook for Hosts.
Comment: Gin and orange with a hint of chocolate – smoothed by egg white.

SCANDINAVIAN POP

Glass: Collins
Garnish: Lime wedge
Method: SHAKE first three ingredients with ice and strain into ice-filled glass. **TOP** up with ginger ale.

2	shot(s)	**Raspberry flavoured vodka**
2	shot(s)	**Ocean Spray cranberry juice**
$\frac{1}{2}$	shot(s)	**Freshly squeezed lime juice**
Top up with		**Ginger ale**

Origin: Created by Wayne Collins, London, England.
Comment: Berry fruit with a spicy splash of ginger.

SIR, IF YOU WERE MY HUSBAND, I WOULD POISON YOUR DRINK.
LADY ASTOR TO WINSTON CHURCHILL

MADAM, IF YOU WERE MY WIFE, I WOULD DRINK IT. HIS REPLY.

SAVOY SPECIAL #1

Glass: Martini
Garnish: Orange zest twist
Method: SHAKE all ingredients with ice and fine strain into chilled glass.

2	shot(s)	**Plymouth gin**
1	shot(s)	**Dry vermouth**
$\frac{1}{4}$	shot(s)	**Pomegranate (grenadine) syrup**
1/8	shot(s)	**La Fée Parisienne (68%) absinthe**
$\frac{1}{2}$	shot(s)	**Chilled mineral water** (omit if wet ice)

Origin: Adapted from a recipe in Harry Craddock's 1930 Savoy Cocktail Book.
Comment: Wonderfully dry and aromatic.

SCARLETT O'HARA

Glass: Martini
Garnish: Cranberries or lime wedge
Method: SHAKE all ingredients with ice and fine strain into chilled glass.

2	shot(s)	**Southern Comfort liqueur**
1	shot(s)	**Ocean Spray cranberry juice**
1	shot(s)	**Freshly squeezed lime juice**

Origin: Created in 1939 and named after the heroine of Gone With The Wind, the Scarlett O'Hara is said to have put Southern Comfort on the proverbial drink map.
Comment: The tang of lime and the dryness of cranberry balance the apricot sweetness of Southern Comfort.

S

SAZERAC

Glass: Old-fashioned
Garnish: Lemon zest twist
Method: POUR absinthe into ice-filled glass, top with water and leave to stand. Separately **SHAKE** bourbon, cognac, sugar and bitters with ice. **DISCARD** contents of glass (absinthe, water and ice) and **STRAIN** contents of shaker into absinthe-coated glass.

	In glass	
$\frac{3}{4}$	shot(s)	**La Fée Parisienne (68%) absinthe**
Top up with		**Chilled mineral water**
	In shaker	
1	shot(s)	**Buffalo Trace bourbon whiskey**
1	shot(s)	**Rémy Martin cognac**
$\frac{1}{2}$	shot(s)	**Sugar syrup (2 sugar to 1 water)**
3	dashes	**Angostura aromatic bitters**
3	dashes	**Peychaud's bitters**

Comment: Don't be concerned about chucking expensive absinthe down the drain - its flavour will be very evident in the finished drink. Classically this drink is stirred but it is much better shaken.

SCOFFLAW

Glass: Martini
Garnish: Lemon zest twist
Method: SHAKE all ingredients with ice and fine strain into chilled glass.

$1\frac{1}{2}$	shot(s)	**Buffalo Trace bourbon whiskey**
$1\frac{1}{2}$	shot(s)	**Dry vermouth**
$\frac{1}{2}$	shot(s)	**Freshly squeezed lemon juice**
$\frac{1}{4}$	shot(s)	**Pomegranate (grenadine) syrup**
1	dash	**Fee Brothers orange bitters**

Origin: During the height of Prohibition The Boston Herald ran a competition asking readers to coin a new word for "a lawless drinker of illegally made or illegally obtained liquor". Out of 25,000 entries, 'Scofflaw' was chosen and on 15th January 1924 the $200 prize was shared between the two people who had submitted the word. This cocktail was created by Jock at Harry's American Bar, Paris, to celebrate the new term.
Comment: This rust-coloured drink is made or broken by the quality of pomegranate syrup used.

SCORCHED EARTH [NEW #7]

Glass: Martini
Garnish: Lemon zest twist
Method: STIR all ingredients with ice and fine strain into chilled glass.

1 1/2	shot(s)	**Rémy Martin cognac**
1/2	shot(s)	**Sweet vermouth**
1/2	shot(s)	**Cynar**

Origin: Adapted from a recipe created in 2006 by Nicholas Hearin, at Restaurant Eugene in Atlanta, USA, and first published by Gary Regan.
Comment: Dry, very aromatic and bordering on bitter. Interesting but not to everybody's taste.

SCORPION

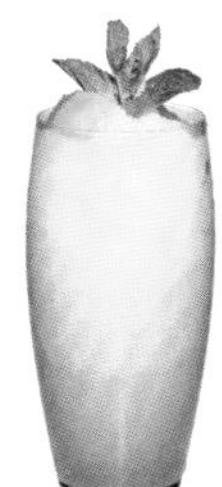

Glass: Collins
Garnish: Gardenia or orange slice & mint
Method: BLEND all ingredients with 12oz crushed ice and serve with straws.

1 1/2	shot(s)	**Light white rum**
3/4	shot(s)	**Rémy Martin cognac**
2	shot(s)	**Freshly squeezed orange juice**
1	shot(s)	**Freshly squeezed lemon juice**
1/2	shot(s)	**Almond (orgeat) sugar syrup**

Variant: With pisco in place of cognac.
Origin: Adapted from a recipe purloined from Trader Vic's Bartender's Guide.
Comment: Well balanced, refreshing spirit and orange. Not sweet.

SCOTCH BOUNTY MARTINI

Glass: Martini
Garnish: Orange zest twist
Method: SHAKE all ingredients with ice and fine strain into chilled glass.

1 1/2	shot(s)	**Scotch whisky**
1/2	shot(s)	**Giffard white crème de cacao**
1/2	shot(s)	**Malibu coconut rum liqueur**
1 1/2	shot(s)	**Freshly squeezed orange juice**
1/8	shot(s)	**Pomegranate (grenadine) syrup**

Comment: A medium-sweet combination of Scotch, coconut and orange.

SCOTCH MILK PUNCH

Glass: Martini
Garnish: Grate nutmeg over drink
Method: SHAKE all ingredients with ice and fine strain into chilled glass.

2	shot(s)	**Scotch whisky**
1/2	shot(s)	**Sugar syrup (2 sugar to 1 water)**
3/4	shot(s)	**Double (heavy) cream**
3/4	shot(s)	**Milk**

Comment: A creamy, malty affair.

SCOTCH NEGRONI

Glass: Old-fashioned
Garnish: Orange slice
Method: STIR all ingredients with ice and strain into ice-filled glass.

1	shot(s)	**Scotch whisky**
1	shot(s)	**Sweet vermouth**
1	shot(s)	**Campari**

Comment: Dry, slightly smoky – for palates that appreciate bitterness.

THE SCOTT

Glass: Martini
Garnish: Lemon zest twist
Method: STIR all ingredients with ice and strain into chilled glass.

2	shot(s)	**Scotch whisky**
1	shot(s)	**Dry vermouth**
1/2	shot(s)	**Drambuie liqueur**

Origin: Discovered in 2006 at The Clift Hotel, San Francisco, USA.
Comment: This golden drink is dry and sophisticated, yet honeyed and approachable.

SCREAMING BANANA BANSHEE

Glass: Hurricane
Garnish: Banana chunk on rim
Method: BLEND all ingredients with 12oz scoop of crushed ice and serve with straws.

2	shot(s)	**Ketel One vodka**
1	shot(s)	**Giffard crème de banane du Brésil**
1	shot(s)	**Giffard white crème de cacao**
1 1/2	shot(s)	**Double (heavy) cream**
1 1/2	shot(s)	**Milk**
1/2	fresh	**Peeled banana**

Origin: Without the vodka this is a plain 'Banana Banshee'.
Comment: An alcoholic milkshake – not too sweet.

SCREAMING ORGASM [NEW #7]

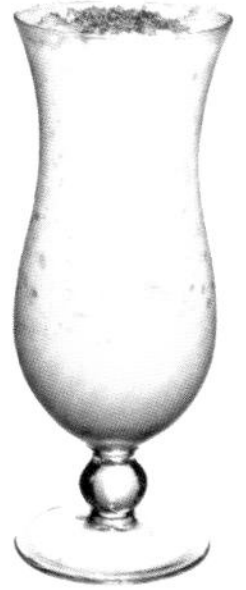

Glass: Hurricane
Garnish: Sprinkle with grated chocolate
Method: SHAKE all ingredients with ice and strain into glass filled with crushed ice.

1 1/4	shot(s)	**Ketel One vodka**
1 1/4	shot(s)	**Kahlúa coffee liqueur**
1 1/4	shot(s)	**Luxardo Amaretto di Saschira liqueur**
1 1/4	shot(s)	**Irish cream liqueur**
1 1/4	shot(s)	**Double (heavy) cream**
1 1/4	shot(s)	**Milk**

Origin: A dodgy drink from the 1980s.
Comment: Probably as fattening as it is alcoholic, this is a huge, creamy dessert in a glass.

SCREWDRIVER

Glass: Collins
Garnish: Orange slice
Method: POUR vodka into ice-filled glass and top with orange juice. Lightly stir and serve with straws.

2	shot(s)	**Ketel One vodka**
Top up with		**Freshly squeezed orange juice**

Origin: This cocktail first appeared in the 1950s in the Middle East. Parched US engineers working in the desert supposedly added orange juice to their vodka and stirred it with the nearest thing to hand, usually a screwdriver.
Comment: The temperature at which this drink is served and the freshness of the orange juice makes or breaks it.

SEABREEZE #1 (SIMPLE)

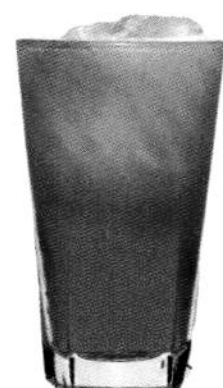

Glass: Collins
Garnish: Lime slice
Method: SHAKE all ingredients with ice and strain into ice-filled glass.

2	shot(s)	**Ketel One vodka**
3	shot(s)	**Ocean Spray cranberry juice**
$1^1/_2$	shot(s)	**Freshly squeezed grapefruit juice**

Origin: Thought to have originated in the early 1990s in New York City.
Comment: Few bartenders bother to shake this simple drink, instead simply pouring and stirring in the glass.

SEABREEZE #2 (LAYERED)

Glass: Collins
Garnish: Lime wedge
Method: POUR cranberry juice into ice-filled glass. **SHAKE** other ingredients with ice and carefully strain into glass to **LAYER** over the cranberry juice.

3	shot(s)	**Ocean Spray cranberry juice**
2	shot(s)	**Ketel One vodka**
$1^1/_2$	shot(s)	**Squeezed pink grapefruit juice**
$^1/_2$	shot(s)	**Freshly squeezed lime juice**

Comment: This layered version requires mixing with straws prior to drinking.

SEELBACH

Glass: Flute
Garnish: Orange zest twist
Method: POUR first four ingredients into chilled glass. Top with champagne.

$^3/_4$	shot(s)	**Buffalo Trace bourbon whiskey**
$^1/_2$	shot(s)	**Cointreau triple sec**
1	dash	**Angostura aromatic bitters**
1	dash	**Peychaud's aromatic bitters**
Top up with		**Brut champagne**

Origin: Created in 1917 and named after its place of origin, the Seelbach Hotel, Lousiville, Kentucky, USA.
Comment: This champagne cocktail is fortified with bourbon and orange liqueur.

SENSATION

Glass: Martini
Garnish: Maraschino cherry
Method: Lightly **MUDDLE** mint (just to bruise) in base of shaker. Add other ingredients, **SHAKE** with ice and fine strain into chilled glass.

12	fresh	**Mint leaves**
2	shot(s)	**Plymouth gin**
$^3/_4$	shot(s)	**Freshly squeezed lemon juice**
$^3/_4$	shot(s)	**Luxardo maraschino liqueur**
1/8	shot(s)	**Sugar syrup (2 sugar to 1 water)**
$^1/_2$	shot(s)	**Chilled mineral water** (omit if wet ice)

Origin: Adapted from a recipe in Harry Craddock's 1930 Savoy Cocktail Book.
Comment: Fresh, fragrant and balanced.

SERENDIPITY #1

Glass: Collins
Garnish: Slice of lemon
Method: MUDDLE blackberries in base of shaker. Add other ingredients, **SHAKE** with ice and strain into glass filled with crushed ice.

6	fresh	**Blackberries**
1	shot(s)	**Plymouth gin**
$^1/_2$	shot(s)	**Vanilla schnapps liqueur**
$^1/_2$	shot(s)	**Giffard crème de cassis**
3	shot(s)	**Ocean Spray cranberry juice**
$^1/_4$	shot(s)	**Freshly squeezed lemon juice**
$^1/_4$	shot(s)	**Sugar syrup (2 sugar to 1 water)**

Origin: Created in 2002 by Jamie Stephenson, Manchester, England.
Comment: Long, red, fruity, vanilla.

THE PIANO HAS BEEN DRINKING, NOT ME, NOT ME.
TOM WAITS

SERENDIPITY #2 [NEW #7]

Glass: Old-fashioned
Garnish: Mint sprig
Method: Lightly muddle mint (just to bruise) in base of shaker. Add calvados and apple juice, **SHAKE** with ice and strain into ice-filled glass. **TOP** with champagne.

7	fresh	**Mint leaves**
$1^1/_2$	shot(s)	**Boulard Grand Solage Calvados**
3	shot(s)	**Pressed apple juice**
Top up with		**Brut champagne**

Origin: My adaptation of one of Colin Field's drinks. He created it on 31 December 1994 in the Hemingway Bar of the Paris Ritz for Jean-Louis Constanza: upon tasting it, Jean-Louis exclaimed, "Serendipity".
Comment: Spirity, minty apple invigorated by a splash of champagne.

SETTLE PETAL

Glass: Martini
Garnish: Float rose petal
Method: STIR all ingredients with ice and strain into chilled glass.

2	shot(s)	**Plymouth gin**
1	shot(s)	**Cucumber flavoured vodka**
1/2	shot(s)	**Rosewater**
1/2	shot(s)	**Vanilla syrup**

Origin: Created in 2003 by Andy Fitzmorris at Eclipse, Notting Hill, London, England.
Comment: An aptly named floral Martini.

SEVENTH HEAVEN #2

Glass: Martini
Garnish: Mint leaf
Method: SHAKE all ingredients with ice and fine strain into chilled glass.

2 1/4	shot(s)	**Plymouth gin**
3/4	shot(s)	**Luxardo maraschino liqueur**
1 1/2	shot(s)	**Squeezed pink grapefruit juice**

Origin: Adapted from the Seventh Heaven No. 2 recipe in Harry Craddock's 1930 Savoy Cocktail Book.
Comment: Drink this and you'll be there.

THE 75 [UPDATED #7]

Glass: Martini
Garnish: Float star anise
Method: SHAKE all ingredients with ice and fine strain into chilled glass.

2	shot(s)	**Boulard Grand Solage Calvados**
1	shot(s)	**Plymouth gin**
1/4	shot(s)	**La Fée Parisienne (68%) absinthe**
1/4	shot(s)	**Pomegranate (grenadine) syrup**
1/2	shot(s)	**Chilled mineral water** (omit if wet ice)

Origin: Like the French 75, this was named after the celebrated 75, a French 75mm field gun developed during the 1890s and used by the French army during the First World War and beyond. The gun was unusually lethal due to its fast rate of fire.
Comment: Hardened palates will appreciate this fantastically dry, aromatic and complex cocktail.

SEX ON THE BEACH #1

Glass: Collins
Garnish: Orange slice & cherry (sail)
Method: SHAKE all ingredients with ice and strain into ice-filled glass.

2	shot(s)	**Ketel One vodka**
1/2	shot(s)	**Chambord black raspberry liqueur**
1/2	shot(s)	**Teichenné butterscotch Schnapps**
1 1/2	shot(s)	**Freshly squeezed orange juice**
1 1/2	shot(s)	**Ocean Spray cranberry juice**

Variant: With melon liqueur in place of peach schnapps.
Origin: An infamous cocktail during the 1980s.
Comment: Sweet fruit laced with vodka.

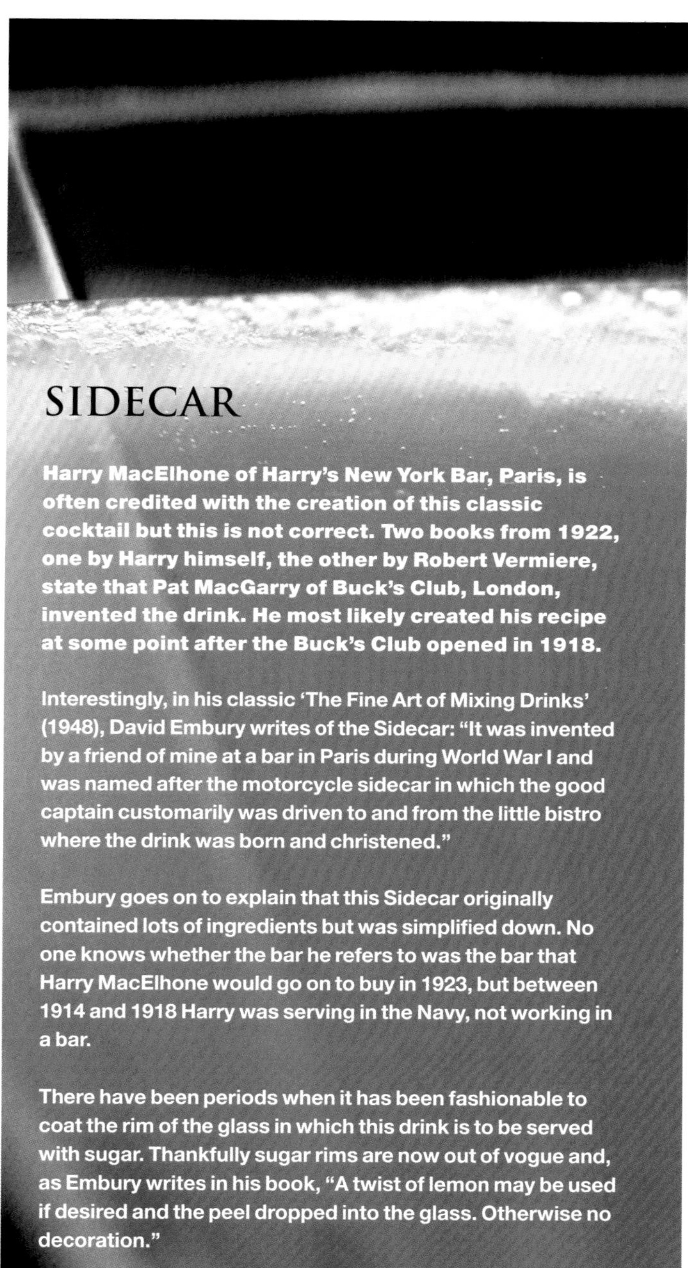

SIDECAR

Harry MacElhone of Harry's New York Bar, Paris, is often credited with the creation of this classic cocktail but this is not correct. Two books from 1922, one by Harry himself, the other by Robert Vermiere, state that Pat MacGarry of Buck's Club, London, invented the drink. He most likely created his recipe at some point after the Buck's Club opened in 1918.

Interestingly, in his classic 'The Fine Art of Mixing Drinks' (1948), David Embury writes of the Sidecar: "It was invented by a friend of mine at a bar in Paris during World War I and was named after the motorcycle sidecar in which the good captain customarily was driven to and from the little bistro where the drink was born and christened."

Embury goes on to explain that this Sidecar originally contained lots of ingredients but was simplified down. No one knows whether the bar he refers to was the bar that Harry MacElhone would go on to buy in 1923, but between 1914 and 1918 Harry was serving in the Navy, not working in a bar.

There have been periods when it has been fashionable to coat the rim of the glass in which this drink is to be served with sugar. Thankfully sugar rims are now out of vogue and, as Embury writes in his book, "A twist of lemon may be used if desired and the peel dropped into the glass. Otherwise no decoration."

Sidecar Variations

St-Germain Sidecar
Sidecar #1
Sidecar #2
Sidecar #3
Sidecarriage
Sidecar Named Desire

SINGAPORE SLING

This drink was created some time between 1911 and 1915 by Chinese-born Ngiam Tong Boon at the Long Bar in Raffles Hotel, Singapore.

Raffles Hotel is named after the colonial founder of Singapore, Sir Stamford Raffles, and was the Near East's expat central. As Charles H. Baker Jr. wrote in his 1946 Gentleman's Companion, "Just looking around the terrace porch we've seen Frank Buck, the Sultan of Johor, Aimee Semple McPherson, Somerset Maugham, Dick Halliburton, Doug Fairbanks, Bob Ripley, Ruth Elder and Walker Camp – not that this is any wonder". It still sticks out of modern-day Singapore like a vast, colonial Christmas cake.

Although there is little controversy as to who created the Singapore Sling, where he created it and (roughly) when, there is huge debate over the original name and ingredients. Singapore and the locality was colonially known as the 'Straits Settlements' and it seems certain that Boon's drink was similarly named the 'Straits Sling'. The name appears to have changed some time between 1922 and 1930.

Not even the Raffles Hotel itself is sure of the original recipe and visiting the present day Long Bar in search of enlightenment is hopless. Sadly, the Singapore Slings served there are made from a powdered pre-mix, which is also available in the gift shop below.

While contemporary sources are clear that it was cherry brandy that distinguishes the Singapore Sling from another kind of sling, a great debate rages over the type of cherry brandy used. Was it a cherry 'brandy' liqueur or actually a cherry eau de vie? Did fruit juice feature in the original recipe at all? We shall probably never know, so I've listed several versions which are generally accepted to pass for a Singapore Sling today. Please also see the entry for 'Straits Sling'.

SEX ON THE BEACH #2

Glass: Old-fashioned
Garnish: Orange slice & cherry (sail)
Method: SHAKE all ingredients with ice and strain into ice-filled glass.

2	shot(s)	**Ketel One vodka**
$\frac{1}{2}$	shot(s)	**Chambord black raspberry liqueur**
$\frac{1}{2}$	shot(s)	**Midori melon liqueur**
$1\frac{1}{2}$	shot(s)	**Pressed pineapple juice**

Comment: Sweeter than most.

SEX ON THE BEACH #3

Glass: Shot
Method: Refrigerate ingredients then **LAYER** in chilled glass by carefully pouring in the following order.

$\frac{1}{2}$	shot(s)	**Chambord black raspberry liqueur**
$\frac{1}{2}$	shot(s)	**Midori melon liqueur**
$\frac{1}{2}$	shot(s)	**Freshly squeezed lime juice**
$\frac{1}{2}$	shot(s)	**Pressed pineapple juice**

Comment: A sweet and sour shot, combining raspberry, melon, lime and pineapple.

SGROPPINO

Glass: Flute
Garnish: Lemon zest twist
Method: BLEND all ingredients without additional ice and serve in chilled glass.

$\frac{1}{2}$	shot(s)	**Ketel One vodka**
$\frac{1}{4}$	shot(s)	**Double (heavy) cream**
$1\frac{1}{2}$	shot(s)	**Prosecco sparkling wine**
2	scoop(s)	**Lemon sorbet (see recipe under L)**

AKA: Sorbetto
Origin: Pronounced 'scroe-pee-noe', this hybrid of cocktail and dessert is often served after meals in Venice. The name comes from a vernacular word meaning 'untie', a reference to the belief that it relaxes your stomach after a hearty meal.
Comment: Smooth and all too easy to quaff. A great dessert.

SHADY GROVE COOLER

Glass: Collins
Garnish: Lime wedge on rim
Method: SHAKE first three ingredients with ice and strain into ice-filled glass. **TOP** with ginger ale, lightly stir and serve with straws.

2	shot(s)	**Plymouth gin**
1	shot(s)	**Freshly squeezed lime juice**
$\frac{1}{2}$	shot(s)	**Sugar syrup (2 sugar to 1 water)**
Top up with		**Ginger ale**

Comment: Long and refreshing with lime freshness and a hint of ginger.

SHAKERATO

Glass: Martini
Garnish: Lemon zest twist
Method: SHAKE all ingredients with ice and fine strain into chilled glass.

$1^1/2$	shot(s)	**Campari**
$^1/4$	shot(s)	**Freshly squeezed lemon juice**
$^1/4$	shot(s)	**Sugar syrup (2 sugar to 1 water)**
$1^1/2$	shot(s)	**Chilled mineral water**

Comment: Campari lovers only need apply.

SHAMROCK #1

Glass: Martini
Garnish: Twist of orange (discarded)
Method: STIR all ingredients with ice and strain into chilled glass.

$2^1/2$	shot(s)	**Buffalo Trace bourbon whiskey**
1	shot(s)	**Sweet vermouth**
$^1/4$	shot(s)	**Green crème de menthe**
2	dashes	**Angostura aromatic bitters**

Origin: Purloined from David Embury's classic book, The Fine Art of Mixing Drinks.
Comment: Basically a Sweet Manhattan with a dash of green crème de menthe.

SHAMROCK #2

Glass: Martini
Garnish: Mint leaf
Method: SHAKE all ingredients with ice and fine strain into chilled glass.

$1^1/2$	shot(s)	**Irish whiskey**
$1^1/2$	shot(s)	**Dry vermouth**
$^1/2$	shot(s)	**Green Chartreuse liqueur**
$^1/2$	shot(s)	**Giffard green crème de menthe**
$^1/2$	shot(s)	**Chilled mineral water** (omit if wet ice)

Origin: Adapted from a recipe in Harry Craddock's 1930 Savoy Cocktail Book.
Comment: A great drink for St. Patrick's Day.

SHAMROCK EXPRESS

Glass: Old-fashioned
Method: SHAKE all ingredients with ice and strain into ice-filled glass.

$1^1/2$	shot(s)	**Cold espresso coffee**
$^3/4$	shot(s)	**Teichenné butterscotch Schnapps**
1	shot(s)	**Ketel One vodka**
1	shot(s)	**Irish cream liqueur**
$^1/4$	shot(s)	**Sugar syrup (2 sugar to 1 water)**

Origin: Created in 1999 by Greg Pearson at Mystique, Manchester, England.
Comment: Creamy coffee with the sweetness of butterscotch.

SHARK BITE

Glass: Hurricane
Method: BLEND first three ingredients with 18oz scoop crushed ice and pour into glass. **POUR** grenadine around edge of the drink. Do not stir before serving.

2	shot(s)	**Pusser's Navy rum**
3	shot(s)	**Freshly squeezed orange juice**
$^1/2$	shot(s)	**Freshly squeezed lime juice**
$^3/4$	shot(s)	**Pomegranate (grenadine) syrup**

Comment: Strong rum and orange juice. A tad sweet but easy to drink.

SHIRLEY TEMPLE (MOCKTAIL)

Glass: Collins
Garnish: Maraschino cherry & lemon slice
Method: POUR ingredients into ice-filled glass, lightly stir and serve with straws.

$^1/4$	shot(s)	**Pomegranate (grenadine) syrup**
$^1/4$	shot(s)	**Freshly squeezed lemon juice**
Top up with		**Ginger ale**

Comment: I've added a splash of lemon juice to the usual recipe. It's still not that exciting.

SHOWBIZ

Glass: Martini
Garnish: Blackcurrants on stick
Method: SHAKE all ingredients with ice and fine strain into chilled glass.

$1^3/4$	shot(s)	**Ketel One vodka**
1	shot(s)	**Giffard crème de cassis**
$1^3/4$	shot(s)	**Freshly squeezed grapefruit juice**

Comment: Sweet cassis soured with grapefruit and fortified with vodka.

SICILIAN NEGRONI

Glass: Old-fashioned
Garnish: Orange slice
Method: SHAKE all ingredients with ice and strain into ice-filled glass.

$1^1/2$	shot(s)	**Plymouth gin**
$1^1/2$	shot(s)	**Campari**
$1^1/2$	shot(s)	**Blood orange juice**

Origin: Discovered in 2006 at The Last Supper Club, San Francisco, USA.
Comment: Blood orange juice replaces sweet vermouth in this fruity Negroni.

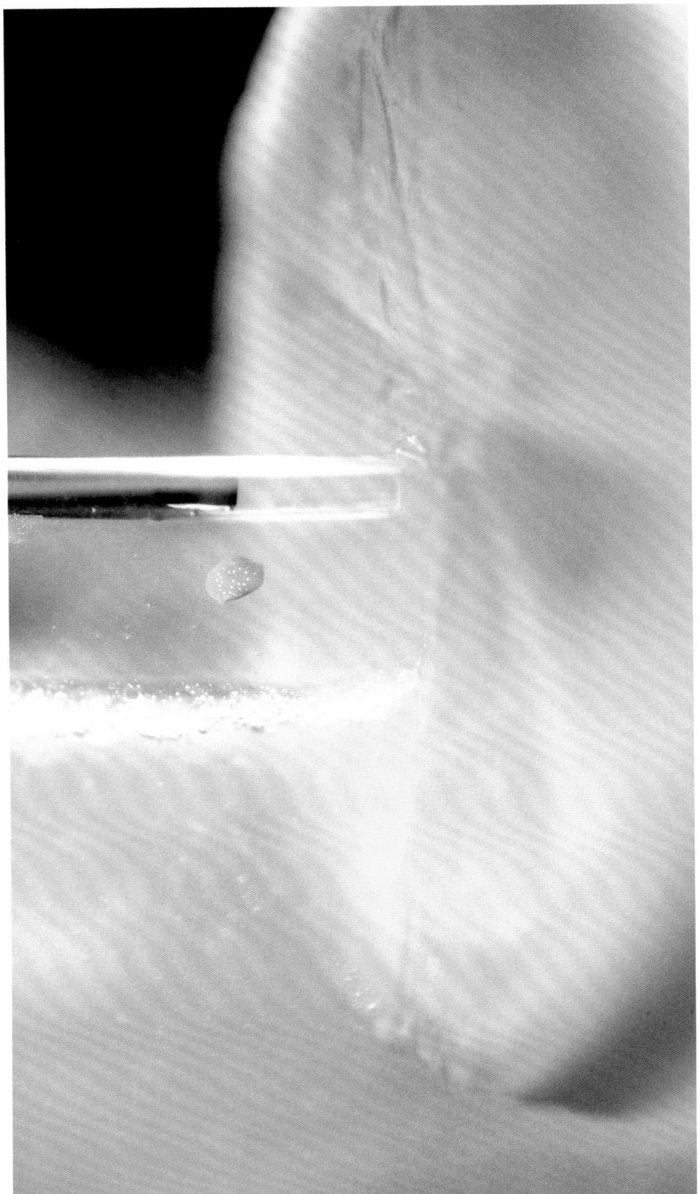

SIDECAR #1 (EQUAL PARTS CLASSIC FORMULA)

Glass: Martini
Garnish: Lemon zest twist
Method: **SHAKE** all ingredients with ice and fine strain into chilled glass.

1 1/4	shot(s)	**Rémy Martin cognac**
1 1/4	shot(s)	**Cointreau triple sec**
1 1/4	shot(s)	**Freshly squeezed lemon juice**

Variant: Apple Cart
Comment: Dry and tart but beautifully balanced and refined.

TIME IS NEVER WASTED WHEN YOU'RE WASTED ALL THE TIME.
CATHERINE ZANDONELLA

SIDECAR #2 (DIFFORD'S FORMULA) 

Glass: Martini
Garnish: Lemon zest twist
Method: **SHAKE** all ingredients with ice and fine strain into chilled glass.

1 1/2	shot(s)	**Rémy Martin cognac**
1	shot(s)	**Cointreau triple sec**
1	shot(s)	**Freshly squeezed lemon juice**
1/2	shot(s)	**Chilled mineral water** (omit if wet ice)

Origin: My take on the classic.
Comment: This formula helps the cognac rise above the liqueur and lemon juice.

SIDECAR #3 (EMBURY'S FORMULA) 

Glass: Martini
Garnish: Lemon zest twist
Method: **SHAKE** all ingredients with ice and fine strain into chilled glass.

2	shot(s)	**Rémy Martin cognac**
1/2	shot(s)	**Freshly squeezed lemon juice**
1/2	shot(s)	**Cointreau triple sec**
1/2	shot(s)	**Chilled mineral water** (omit if wet ice)

Origin: In The Fine Art of Mixing Drinks, David Embury writes of the 'equal parts' Sidecar, "This is the most perfect example of a magnificent drink gone wrong". He argues that "Essentially the Sidecar is nothing but a Daiquiri with brandy in the place of rum and Cointreau in the place of sugar syrup" and so the Daiquiri formula should be followed as above.
Comment: A Sidecar for those with a dry palate.

SLINGS

The word 'Sling' comes from the German 'schlingen', meaning 'to swallow', and Slings based on a spirit mixed with sugar and water were popularly drunk in the late 1800s.

Slings are similar to Toddies and like Toddies can be served hot. (Toddies, however, are never served cold.) The main difference between a Toddy and a Sling is that Slings are not flavoured by the addition of spices. Also, Toddies tend to be made with plain water, while Slings are charged with water, soda water or ginger ale.

The earliest known definition of 'cocktail' describes it as a bittered sling.

SIDECAR NAMED DESIRE

Glass: Martini
Garnish: Lemon zest twist
Method: SHAKE all ingredients with ice and fine strain into chilled glass.

2	shot(s)	**Boulard Grand Solage Calvados**
1	shot(s)	**Apple schnapps liqueur**
1	shot(s)	**Freshly squeezed lemon juice**

Comment: Take a classic Sidecar and add some love interest – apple!

SIDECARRIAGE [NEW #7]

Glass: Martini
Garnish: Lemon zest twist
Method: SHAKE all ingredients with ice and fine strain into chilled glass.

1½	shot(s)	**Boulard Grand Solage Calvados**
1½	shot(s)	**St-Germain elderflower liqueur**
1	shot(s)	**Freshly squeezed lemon juice**

Origin: Created in 2006 by yours truly.
Comment: Hints of cider come through in this calvados based Sidecar with an elderflower twist.

SIDEKICK

Glass: Martini
Garnish: Quarter orange slice on rim
Method: SHAKE all ingredients with ice and fine strain into chilled glass.

2	shot(s)	**Pear & cognac liqueur**
¾	shot(s)	**Cointreau triple sec**
1	shot(s)	**Freshly squeezed orange juice**
½	shot(s)	**Freshly squeezed lime juice**

Origin: Adapted from a drink discovered in 2003 at Temple Bar, New York City.
Comment: Rich pear and orange with a stabilising hint of sour lime.

SILENT THIRD

Glass: Martini
Garnish: Lemon zest twist
Method: SHAKE all ingredients with ice and fine strain into chilled glass.

2	shot(s)	**Scotch whisky**
½	shot(s)	**Cointreau triple sec**
¾	shot(s)	**Freshly squeezed lemon juice**
¾	shot(s)	**Chilled mineral water**

Comment: A sour, sharp whisky drink.

SILK PANTIES [NEW #7]

Glass: Martini
Garnish: Peach wedge on rim
Method: SHAKE all ingredients with ice and fine strain into chilled glass.

2	shot(s)	**Ketel One vodka**
1	shot(s)	**Teichenné Peach Schnapps Liqueur**
2	dashes	**Fee Brothers peach bitters (optional)**

Origin: Created sometime in the 1980s.
Comment: This drink may be sweet but despite the silly name it is more serious than you might expect.

SILK STOCKINGS

Glass: Martini
Garnish: Cinnamon dust
Method: SHAKE all ingredients with ice and fine strain into chilled glass.

2	shot(s)	**Partida tequila**
¾	shot(s)	**Giffard white crème de cacao**
¾	shot(s)	**Pomegranate (grenadine) syrup**
½	shot(s)	**Double (heavy) cream**
½	shot(s)	**Milk**

Comment: Smoothed and sweetened tequila with a hint of chocolate and fruit.

SILVER BULLET MARTINI [UPDATED #7]

Glass: Martini
Garnish: Lemon zest twist
Method: SHAKE all ingredients with ice and fine strain into chilled glass.

2	shot(s)	**Plymouth gin**
1	shot(s)	**Kümmel liqueur**
1	shot(s)	**Freshly squeezed lemon juice**
¼	shot(s)	**Sugar syrup (2 sugar to 1water)**

AKA: Retreat from Moscow
Variant: A modern variation is to substitute sambuca for kümmel.
Origin: Thought to have been created in the 1920s.
Comment: Caraway and fennel flavour this unusual, sweet and sour drink.

FOR MORE INFORMATION SEE OUR INGREDIENTS APPENDIX ON PAGE 374

SILVER FIZZ 

Glass: Collins (8oz max)
Garnish: Lemon slice
Method: **SHAKE** first four ingredients with ice and strain into chilled glass (no ice). **TOP** with soda from siphon.

2	shot(s)	**Spirit (gin, whiskey, vodka, brandy)**
1	shot(s)	**Freshly squeezed lemon or lime juice**
1/2	shot(s)	**Sugar syrup (2 sugar to 1 water)**
1/2	fresh	**Egg white (optional)**
Top up with		**Soda water (from siphon)**

Origin: A mid-19th century classic.
Variant: Omit the egg white and this is a mere Fizz.
Comment: I prefer my Fizzes with the addition of egg white. Why not also try a Derby Fizz, which combines liqueur and spirits?

JOHN GORRIE PATENTED THE WORLD'S FIRST ICE-MAKING MACHINE IN 1851. HE DIED PENNILESS FOUR YEARS LATER.

SILVER MARTINI

Glass: Martini
Garnish: Maraschino cherry
Method: **SHAKE** all ingredients with ice and fine strain into chilled glass.

1 1/2	shot(s)	**Plymouth gin**
1 1/2	shot(s)	**Dry vermouth**
1/4	shot(s)	**Luxardo maraschino liqueur**
2	dashes	**Fee Brothers orange bitters**

Origin: Adapted from a recipe in Harry Craddock's 1930 Savoy Cocktail Book.
Comment: Dry and aromatic – for serious imbibers only.

SINGAPORE SLING #1 (BAKER'S FORMULA)

Glass: Collins (10oz max)
Garnish: Lemon slice & cherry (sail)
Method: **SHAKE** first three ingredients with ice and strain into ice-filled glass. **TOP** with soda, lightly stir and serve with straws.

1 1/2	shot(s)	**Plymouth gin**
3/4	shot(s)	**Bénédictine D.O.M. liqueur**
3/4	shot(s)	**Cherry (brandy) liqueur**
Top up with		**Soda water (club soda)**

Variant: Straits Sling
Origin: Adapted from a recipe by Charles H. Baker Jr. and published in his 1946 Gentleman's Companion. He originally called for Old Tom gin.
Comment: Lacks the citrus of other Singapore Slings but dilution cuts and so balances the sweetness of the liqueurs.

SINGAPORE SLING #2

Glass: Sling
Garnish: Lemon slice & cherry (sail)
Method: **SHAKE** first six ingredients with ice and strain into ice-filled glass. **TOP** with soda, lightly stir and serve with straws.

2	shot(s)	**Plymouth gin**
1/2	shot(s)	**Bénédictine D.O.M. liqueur**
1/2	shot(s)	**Cherry (brandy) liqueur**
1	shot(s)	**Freshly squeezed lemon juice**
2	dashes	**Fee Brothers orange bitters**
2	dashes	**Angostura aromatic bitters**
Top up with		**Soda water (club soda)**

Comment: On the sour side of dry, this is decidedly more complex than most Singapore Sling recipes.

SINGAPORE SLING #3

Glass: Sling
Garnish: Orange slice & cherry (sail)
Method: **SHAKE** first eight ingredients with ice and strain into ice-filled glass. **TOP** with soda, lightly stir and serve with straws.

2	shot(s)	**Plymouth gin**
1/2	shot(s)	**Cherry (brandy) liqueur**
1/4	shot(s)	**Bénédictine D.O.M. liqueur**
1/4	shot(s)	**Cointreau triple sec**
1 1/2	shot(s)	**Pressed pineapple juice**
1/2	shot(s)	**Freshly squeezed lime juice**
1/4	shot(s)	**Pomegranate (grenadine) syrup**
2	dashes	**Angostura aromatic bitters**
Top up with		**Soda water (club soda)**

Comment: Foaming, tangy and very fruity.

SIR CHARLES PUNCH

Glass: Old-fashioned
Garnish: Orange zest twist
Method: **STIR** all ingredients with ice and strain into ice-filled glass.

1	shot(s)	**Tawny port**
1/2	shot(s)	**Rémy Martin cognac**
1/2	shot(s)	**Grand Marnier liqueur**
1/8	shot(s)	**Sugar syrup (2 sugar to 1 water)**

Origin: Adapted from a recipe in the 1949 edition of Esquire's Handbook for Hosts, which suggests serving it at Christmas.
Comment: Short but full of personality - like Kyle Minogue.

SIR THOMAS

Glass: Martini
Garnish: Maraschino cherry
Method: **STIR** all ingredients with ice and strain into chilled glass.

2	shot(s)	**Buffalo Trace bourbon whiskey**
1/2	shot(s)	**Cointreau triple sec**
1/2	shot(s)	**Cherry (brandy) liqueur**
1/2	shot(s)	**Sweet vermouth**

Origin: Created in 2005 by Tom Ward, England.
Comment: Akin to a fruit laced Sweet Manhattan.

SKI BREEZE

Glass: Collins
Garnish: Apple slice
Method: POUR ingredients into ice-filled glass, lightly stir and serve with straws.

2	shot(s)	**Raspberry flavoured vodka**
3	shot(s)	**Pressed apple juice**
3	shot(s)	**Ginger ale**

Comment: A meld of apple and berries with hint of ginger.

SLEEPING BISON-TINI

Glass: Martini
Garnish: Pear slice on rim
Method: SHAKE all ingredients with ice and fine strain into chilled glass.

1½	shot(s)	**Zubrówka bison vodka**
¼	shot(s)	**Giffard apricot brandy du Roussillon**
¼	shot(s)	**Pear & cognac liqueur**
1	shot(s)	**Freshly extracted pear juice**
1	shot(s)	**Pressed apple juice**
1	shot(s)	**Strong cold camomile tea**

Comment: A light cocktail featuring a melange of subtle flavours.

'THE CONDITION OF ALIENATION, OF BEING ASLEEP, OF BEING UNCONSCIOUS, OF BEING OUT OF ONE'S MIND, IS THE CONDITION OF THE NORMAL MAN.'

SLEEPY HOLLOW

Glass: Old-fashioned
Garnish: Lemon slice
Method: Lightly **MUDDLE** mint in base of shaker (just to bruise). Add other ingredients, **SHAKE** with ice and fine strain into glass filled with crushed ice. Serve with straws.

10	fresh	**Mint leaves**
2	shot(s)	**Plymouth gin**
½	shot(s)	**Giffard apricot brandy du Roussillon**
1	shot(s)	**Freshly squeezed lemon juice**
½	shot(s)	**Sugar syrup (2 sugar to 1 water)**

Origin: An adaption of a drink created in the early 1930s and named after Washington Irving's novel and its enchanted valley with ghosts, goblins and headless horseman.
Comment: Hints of lemon and mint with gin and apricot fruit. Very refreshing.

SLING

Glass: Sling
Garnish: Lemon slice
Method: SHAKE first three ingredients with ice and strain into ice-filled glass. Top up with soda or ginger ale.

2	shot(s)	**Liquor (gin, rum, scotch, whisky etc.)**
½	shot(s)	**Freshly squeezed lemon juice**
¼	shot(s)	**Sugar syrup (2 sugar to 1 water)**
Top with		**Soda or ginger ale**

Origin: 'Sling' comes from the German word 'schlingen', meaning 'to swallow' and is a style of drink which was popular from the late 1700s.
Comment: Sugar balances the citrus juice, the spirit fortifies and the carbonate lengthens.

SLIPPERY NIPPLE

Glass: Shot
Method: LAYER in glass by carefully pouring ingredients in the following order.

¼	shot(s)	**Pomegranate (grenadine) syrup**
¾	shot(s)	**Luxardo Sambuca dei Cesari**
¾	shot(s)	**Irish cream liqueur**

Comment: The infamous red, clear and brown shot. Very sweet.

SLOE GIN FIZZ

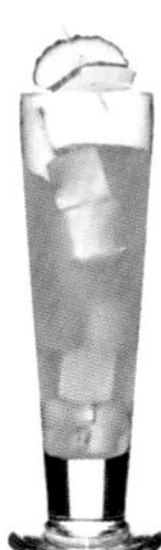

Glass: Sling
Garnish: Lemon slice or cucumber slice
Method: SHAKE first five ingredients with ice and strain into ice-filled glass. **TOP** with soda, stir and serve with straws.

1	shot(s)	**Plymouth gin**
1½	shot(s)	**Plymouth sloe gin liqueur**
1	shot(s)	**Freshly squeezed lime juice**
¼	shot(s)	**Sugar syrup (2 sugar to 1 water)**
½	fresh	**Egg white**
Top up with		**Soda water (club soda)**

Comment: A sour gin fizz with dark, rich sloe gin.

SLOE MOTION

Glass: Flute
Garnish: Lemon zest
Method: POUR liqueur into chilled glass and top with champagne.

¾	shot(s)	**Plymouth sloe gin liqueur**
Top up with		**Brut champagne**

Comment: Sloe gin proves to be an excellent complement to champagne.

SLOE TEQUILA

Glass: Old-fashioned
Garnish: Lime wedge
Method: SHAKE all ingredients with ice and strain into ice-filled glass.

1	shot(s)	**Plymouth sloe gin liqueur**
1	shot(s)	**Partida tequila**
1	shot(s)	**Rose's lime cordial**

Comment: Berry fruit and tequila with a surprisingly tart, bitter finish.

SLOPPY JOE

Glass: Martini
Garnish: Lime wedge
Method: SHAKE all ingredients with ice and fine strain into chilled glass.

1	shot(s)	**Light white rum**
1	shot(s)	**Dry vermouth**
1/4	shot(s)	**Cointreau triple sec**
1	shot(s)	**Freshly squeezed lime juice**
1/2	shot(s)	**Sugar syrup (2 sugar to 1 water)**
1/4	shot(s)	**Pomegranate (grenadine) syrup**

Comment: Nicely balanced sweet and sourness.

SLOW SCREW

Glass: Collins
Garnish: Orange slice
Method: SHAKE all ingredients with ice and strain into ice-filled glass.

1	shot(s)	**Plymouth sloe gin liqueur**
1	shot(s)	**Ketel One vodka**
4	shot(s)	**Freshly squeezed orange juice**

Comment: A Screwdriver with sloe gin.

SLOW COMFORTABLE SCREW

Glass: Collins
Garnish: Half orange slice
Method: SHAKE all ingredients with ice and strain into ice-filled glass.

1	shot(s)	**Ketel One vodka**
1	shot(s)	**Plymouth sloe gin liqueur**
1	shot(s)	**Southern Comfort liqueur**
3	shot(s)	**Freshly squeezed orange juice**

Comment: A Screwdriver with sloe gin and Southern Comfort. Fruity and fairly sweet.

SLOW COMFORTABLE SCREW AGAINST THE WALL

Glass: Collins
Method: SHAKE first four ingredients with ice and strain into ice-filled glass. Lastly **FLOAT** Galliano.

1	shot(s)	**Ketel One vodka**
1	shot(s)	**Plymouth sloe gin liqueur**
1	shot(s)	**Southern Comfort liqueur**
3	shot(s)	**Freshly squeezed orange juice**
1/2	shot(s)	**Galliano liqueur**

Comment: Galliano adds the wall (as in Harvey Wallbanger) and some herbal peppermint to this Slow Comfortable Screw.

SMARTINI

Glass: Martini
Garnish: Three Smarties in drink
Method: SHAKE all ingredients with ice and fine strain into chilled glass.

2	shot(s)	**Ketel One Citroen vodka**
1	shot(s)	**Giffard white crème de cacao**
1/4	shot(s)	**Sugar syrup (2 sugar to 1 water)**
3/4	shot(s)	**Chilled mineral water** (omit if wet ice)
3	dashes	**Fee Brothers orange bitters**

Comment: Citrus with a crispy chocolate edge. A sweetie.

SMOKY APPLE MARTINI

Glass: Martini
Garnish: Maraschino cherry
Method: SHAKE all ingredients with ice and fine strain into chilled glass.

2 1/2	shot(s)	**Scotch whisky**
1	shot(s)	**Sour apple liqueur**
1/2	shot(s)	**Rose's lime cordial**

Comment: Scotch adds some peaty character to this twist on the Sour Apple Martini.

SMOKY MARTINI #1

Glass: Martini
Garnish: Lemon zest twist
Method: STIR all ingredients with ice and strain into chilled glass.

2 1/2	shot(s)	**Plymouth gin**
1/2	shot(s)	**Dry vermouth**
1/4	shot(s)	**Scotch whisky**

Variant: Substitute vodka for gin.
Comment: A pleasant variation on the classic Dry Martini.

SMOKY MARTINI #2

Glass: Martini
Garnish: Orange zest twist
Method: STIR all ingredients with ice and strain into chilled glass.

2	shot(s)	**Plymouth gin**
1	shot(s)	**Plymouth sloe gin liqueur**
$^1/_4$	shot(s)	**Dry vermouth**
2	dashes	**Fee Brothers orange bitters**

Origin: Created in 1997 by Giovanni Burdi at Match EC1, London, England.
Comment: The basic Martini formula (gin plus vermouth) is enhanced with sloe gin and the traditional orange bitters variation, delivering a distinctive 'smoky' character.

SMOOTH & CREAMY'TINI

Glass: Martini
Garnish: Dust with grated nutmeg
Method: SHAKE all ingredients with ice and fine strain into chilled glass.

$1^1/_2$	shot(s)	**Golden rum**
1	shot(s)	**Malibu coconut rum liqueur**
$^1/_4$	shot(s)	**Giffard crème de banane du Brésil**
$^3/_4$	shot(s)	**Double (heavy) cream**
$^3/_4$	shot(s)	**Milk**

Comment: Creamy and moreish.

SNAKEBITE

Glass: Collins
Method: POUR lager into glass and top with cider.

Half fill with	**Lager**
Top up with	**Cider**

Variant: Add a dash of blackcurrant cordial to make a 'Snakebite & Black'.
Comment: The students' special.

SNOOD MURDEKIN

Glass: Shot
Method: SHAKE first three ingredients with ice and strain into chilled glass. **FLOAT** cream over drink.

$^1/_2$	shot(s)	**Ketel One vodka**
$^1/_2$	shot(s)	**Chambord black raspberry liqueur**
$^1/_2$	shot(s)	**Kahlúa coffee liqueur**
$^1/_4$	shot(s)	**Double (heavy) cream**

Origin: Created in the late 90s by Dick Bradsell at Detroit, London, England, for Karin Wiklund, and named for the sad, flute-playing Moomin Troll.
Comment: Moreish combination of coffee and raspberries topped by cream.

SOURS

Sours are aptly named drinks. Their flavour comes from either lemon or lime juice, which is balanced with sugar. Sours can be based on practically any spirit but the bourbon based Whiskey Sour is by far the most popular. Many (including myself) believe this drink is only properly made when smoothed with a little egg white.

Sours are served either straight-up in a Sour glass (rather like a small flute) or on the rocks in an old-fashioned glass. They are traditionally garnished with a cherry and an orange slice, or sometimes a lemon slice.

SNOOPY

Glass: Old-fashioned
Garnish: Orange zest twist
Method: SHAKE all ingredients with ice and fine strain into ice-filled glass.

1	shot(s)	**Galliano liqueur**
1½	shot(s)	**Buffalo Trace bourbon whiskey**
½	shot(s)	**Campari**
¾	shot(s)	**Grand Marnier liqueur**
¼	shot(s)	**Freshly squeezed lemon juice**

Comment: Tangy fruit with a balancing hint of citrus and bitterness.

SNOW FALL MARTINI

Glass: Martini
Garnish: Vanilla pod
Method: MUDDLE vanilla pod in base of shaker. Add other ingredients, **SHAKE** with ice and fine strain into chilled glass.

¼	pod	**Vanilla**
2	shot(s)	**Vanilla infused Ketel One vodka**
1¼	shot(s)	**Double (heavy) cream**
1¼	shot(s)	**Milk**
¼	shot(s)	**Sugar syrup (2 sugar to 1 water)**

Origin: Discovered in 2002 at Lot 61, New York City.
Comment: An alcoholic version of a vanilla milkshake.

SNOW ON EARTH

Glass: Shot
Method: SHAKE first three ingredients with ice and strain into chilled glass. Carefully **FLOAT** cream on drink.

½	shot(s)	**Kahlúa coffee liqueur**
½	shot(s)	**Chambord black raspberry liqueur**
½	shot(s)	**Krupnik honey liqueur**
½	shot(s)	**Double (heavy) cream**

Comment: A sweet, flavoursome shot.

SNOW WHITE DAIQUIRI

Glass: Martini
Garnish: Pineapple wedge on rim
Method: SHAKE all ingredients with ice and fine strain into chilled glass.

2	shot(s)	**Light white rum**
½	shot(s)	**Pressed pineapple juice**
½	shot(s)	**Freshly squeezed lime juice**
¼	shot(s)	**Sugar syrup (2 sugar to 1 water)**
½	fresh	**Egg white**

Origin: My adaptation of a classic cocktail.
Comment: The pineapple and albumen ensure that this delightful Daiquiri has an appropriately white frothy head.

SNOWBALL

Glass: Collins
Garnish: Lime slice on rim
Method: SHAKE first three ingredients with ice and strain into ice-filled glass. **TOP** with 7-Up, lightly stir and serve with straws.

2	shot(s)	**Warninks advocaat liqueur**
1	shot(s)	**Tio Pepe fino sherry**
¾	shot(s)	**Rose's lime cordial**
Top up with		**7-Up**

Origin: This is thought to have originated in Britain in the late 1940s or early 1950s, reaching its peak of popularity in the 1970s.
Comment: The classic light, fluffy concoction. Try it, you may like it.

SNYDER MARTINI

Glass: Martini
Garnish: Orange zest twist
Method: SHAKE all ingredients with ice and fine strain into chilled glass.

2	shot(s)	**Plymouth gin**
1	shot(s)	**Dry vermouth**
¼	shot(s)	**Grand Marnier liqueur**

Origin: Adapted from a recipe in Harry Craddock's 1930 Savoy Cocktail Book.
Comment: Dry, hardcore and yet mellow.

SOCIALITE

Glass: Old-fashioned
Method: SHAKE all ingredients with ice and strain into glass filled with crushed ice.

1	shot(s)	**Freshly squeezed lemon juice**
½	shot(s)	**Vanilla sugar syrup**
1	shot(s)	**Grand Marnier liqueur**
1	shot(s)	**Vanilla infused Ketel One vodka**
1	shot(s)	**Luxardo limoncello liqueur**

Origin: Discovered in 2001 at Lab Bar, London, England.
Comment: Rich citrus with lashings of vanilla.

SODDEN GRAPE MARTINI

Glass: Martini
Garnish: Three grapes on stick
Method: MUDDLE grapes in base of shaker. Add other ingredients, **SHAKE** with ice and fine strain into chilled glass.

7	fresh	**Seedless white grapes**
2	shot(s)	**Zubrówka bison vodka**
¾	shot(s)	**Icewine**

Origin: Created by yours truly in 2004.
Comment: A 'sod' is a piece of turf. Here 'sodden' refers to the bison grass, the flavour of which combines well with the grapes and icewine.

SOLENT SUNSET

Glass: Collins
Garnish: Pineapple wedge & cherry on rim
Method: SHAKE all ingredients with ice and fine strain into ice-filled glass.

2	shot(s)	**Pusser's Navy rum**
3/4	shot(s)	**Freshly squeezed lime juice**
3	shot(s)	**Pressed pineapple juice**
1/4	shot(s)	**Pomegranate (grenadine) syrup**

Comment: A Naval style tropical rum punch for those occasional hot sunny days on the Solent (the stretch of sea which separates the Isle of Wight from mainland Britain).

I DON'T HAVE A DRINKING PROBLEM EXCEPT WHEN I CAN'T GET A DRINK.
TOM WAITS

SOPHISTICATED SAVAGE

Glass: Old-fashioned
Garnish: Lime wedge
Method: SHAKE all ingredients with ice and strain into ice-filled glass.

2	shot(s)	**Tuaca liqueur**
1	shot(s)	**Leblon cachaça**
1/2	shot(s)	**Freshly squeezed lime juice**
1/2	fresh	**Egg white**

Origin: Created by: Poul Jensen, Brighton, England.
Comment: A sour drink with a horse's kick leading into a smooth subtle finish.

SORRELADE (MOCKTAIL)

Glass: Collins
Garnish: Lime wedge
Method: (This is a bulk recipe.) **SOAK** dried sorrel in water with ginger, ground cloves and honey for 12 hours. Bring this mixture to the **BOIL** then leave to cool and **SOAK** for a further 12 hours **STRAIN** and then keep refrigerated.

70g dried	**Sorrel (hibiscus flowers)**
1.25 litres	**Mineral water**
30g fresh	**Root ginger (sliced)**
1/2 spoon	**Ground cloves**
3 spoons	**Runny honey**

Origin: Jamaican sorrel, also known by its scientific name 'Hibiscus Sabdariffa', is a plant propagated for its red petals. In Jamaica these are used to make this refreshing drink. (Jamaican sorrel is not related to the English garden herb of the same name.)
Comment: Sorrelade looks a little like cranberry juice and like cranberry juice has a bittersweet, slightly spicy taste.

SORREL RUM PUNCH

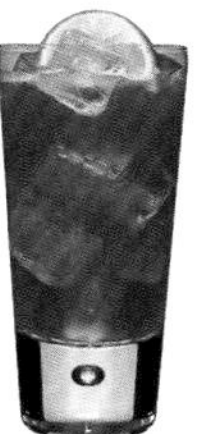

Glass: Collins
Garnish: Lime wedge
Method: SHAKE all ingredients with ice and strain into glass filled with crushed glass. Serve with straws.

2 1/4	shot(s)	**Wray & Nephew overproof rum**
3	shot(s)	**Sorrelade (see recipe above)**
3/4	shot(s)	**Freshly squeezed lime juice**
1 1/2	shot(s)	**Sugar syrup (2 sugar to 1 water)**

Origin: A classic Jamaican punch using the classic proportions of 'one of sour, two of sweet, three of strong and four of weak'.
Comment: This drink harnesses the flavour of sorrelade and combines it with the traditional strength and bittersweetness of rum punch. Jamaica in a glass.

S0-SO MARTINI

Glass: Martini
Garnish: Float wafer thin apple slice
Method: SHAKE all ingredients with ice and fine strain into chilled glass.

1 1/2	shot(s)	**Plymouth gin**
1 1/2	shot(s)	**Dry vermouth**
3/4	shot(s)	**Boulard Grand Solage Calvados**
1/2	shot(s)	**Pomegranate (grenadine) syrup**

Origin: Adapted from a recipe in Harry Craddock's 1930 Savoy Cocktail Book.
Comment: This beautifully balanced, appley drink is so much more than so-so.

SOUR

Glass: Old-fashioned
Garnish: Cherry & lemon slice sail
Method: SHAKE all ingredients with ice and strain into ice-filled glass

2	shot(s)	**Spirit (whiskey, gin, rum or brandy etc.)**
3/4	shot(s)	**Freshly squeezed lemon juice**
1	shot(s)	**Sugar syrup (2 sugar to 1 water)**
1/2	fresh	**Egg white**
3	dashes	**Angostura aromatic bitters**

Comment: This recipe follows the classic sour proportions: three quarter part of the sour ingredient (lemon juice), one part of the sweet ingredient (sugar syrup) and two parts of the strong ingredient (spirit) - 3:4:8. I prefer mine sourer with one part lemon juice and half a part sugar (4:2:8) and that's the formula I've tended to use in other sour drinks in this guide.

SOME FAMOUS FORMER BARTENDERS: SANDRA BULLOCK, BRUCE WILLIS, TOM ARNOLD, BILL COSBY, KRIS KRISTOFFERSON & CHEVY CHASE.

SOUR APPLE MARTINI #1 (POPULAR US VERSION)

Glass: Martini
Garnish: Cherry in glass
Method: SHAKE all ingredients with ice and fine strain into chilled glass.

2	shot(s)	**Ketel One vodka**
$1\frac{1}{2}$	shot(s)	**Sour apple liqueur**
$\frac{1}{4}$	shot(s)	**Rose's lime cordial**

Variant: Some bars add sour mix in place of Rose's, others add a dash of fresh lime and sugar.
Comment: A hugely popular drink across North America.

SOUTH CHINA BREEZE

Glass: Collins
Garnish: Orange slice
Method: SHAKE all ingredients with ice and strain into ice-filled glass.

2	shot(s)	**Orange zest infused Ketel One vodka**
3	shot(s)	**Freshly squeezed grapefruit juice**
$1\frac{1}{2}$	shot(s)	**Lychee syrup from tinned fruit**
3	dashes	**Angostura aromatic bitters**

Comment: Orange and grapefruit with an oriental influence by way of lychee.

SOUR APPLE MARTINI #2 (DELUXE US VERSION)

Glass: Martini
Garnish: Float wafer thin apple slice
Method: SHAKE all ingredients with ice and fine strain into chilled glass.

2	shot(s)	**Ketel One vodka**
1	shot(s)	**Sour apple liqueur**
$\frac{1}{2}$	shot(s)	**Freshly squeezed lime juice**
$\frac{1}{4}$	shot(s)	**Sugar syrup (2 sugar to 1 water)**
$\frac{1}{2}$	fresh	**Egg white**

Comment: A sophisticated version of the contemporary classic.

SOUTH OF THE BORDER

Glass: Martini
Garnish: Three coffee beans
Method: SHAKE all ingredients with ice and fine strain into chilled glass.

2	shot(s)	**Partida tequila**
1	shot(s)	**Kahlúa coffee liqueur**
$\frac{3}{4}$	shot(s)	**Freshly squeezed lime juice**
$\frac{1}{2}$	fresh	**Egg white**

Comment: A strange mix of lime and coffee.

SOURPUSS MARTINI

Glass: Martini
Garnish: Physalis (Cape gooseberry) on rim
Method: SHAKE all ingredients with ice and fine strain into chilled glass.

1	shot(s)	**Ketel One Citroen vodka**
$\frac{1}{2}$	shot(s)	**Midori melon liqueur**
$\frac{1}{2}$	shot(s)	**Sour apple liqueur**
2	shot(s)	**Pressed apple juice**

Origin: Created in 2001 by Colin 'Big Col' Crowden at Time, Leicester, England.
Comment: A lime-green, flavoursome cocktail that balances sweet and sour.

SOUTH PACIFIC

Glass: Martini
Garnish: Pineapple wedge on rim
Method: Cut passion fruit in half and scoop flesh into shaker. Add other ingredients, **SHAKE** with ice and fine strain into chilled glass.

1	fresh	**Passion fruit**
1	shot(s)	**Soho lychee liqueur**
1	shot(s)	**Ketel One Citroen vodka**
1	shot(s)	**Pressed pineapple juice**
$\frac{1}{2}$	shot(s)	**Freshly squeezed lime juice**

Origin: Adapted from a recipe created by Wayne Collins, London, England.

SOUTH BEACH

Glass: Martini
Garnish: Orange zest twist
Method: SHAKE all ingredients with ice and fine strain into chilled glass.

1	shot(s)	**Campari**
1	shot(s)	**Luxardo Amaretto di Saschira liqueur**
$2\frac{1}{2}$	shot(s)	**Freshly squeezed orange juice**
$\frac{1}{4}$	shot(s)	**Sugar syrup (2 sugar to 1 water)**

Origin: Created in 1992 by Dale DeGroff, New York City, USA.
Comment: An unusual, bittersweet combination with a strong orange and almond flavour.

SOUTH PACIFIC BREEZE

Glass: Collins
Garnish: Pineapple wedge on rim
Method: POUR gin and Galliano into ice-filled glass. **TOP** with 7-Up to just below the rim. **DRIZZLE** blue curaçao around top of drink (it will sink leaving strings of blue). Serve with straws.

$1\frac{1}{2}$	shot(s)	**Plymouth gin**
$\frac{3}{4}$	shot(s)	**Galliano liqueur**
Top up with		**7-Up**
$\frac{3}{4}$	shot(s)	**Bols Blue curaçao liqueur**

Comment: Quite sweet but flavoursome – looks great.

SOUTHERN CIDER

Glass: Martini
Garnish: Lime wedge
Method: SHAKE all ingredients with ice and fine strain into chilled glass.

2	shot(s)	**Southern Comfort liqueur**
1	shot(s)	**Freshly squeezed lime juice**
1½	shot(s)	**Ocean Spray cranberry juice**

Origin: Discovered at Opryland Hotel, Nashville, USA.
Comment: Strangely, this cocktail does have a cidery taste.

SOUTHERN PEACH

Glass: Collins
Garnish: Lime wedge
Method: SHAKE all ingredients with ice and strain into ice-filled glass. Serve with straws.

1	shot(s)	**Southern Comfort liqueur**
1	shot(s)	**Teichenné Peach Schnapps Liqueur**
3	shot(s)	**Ocean Spray cranberry juice**
1	shot(s)	**Freshly squeezed lime juice**

Comment: Fruity and slightly sweet but far from offensive.

SOUTHERN MANHATTAN

Glass: Martini
Garnish: Orange zest twist
Method: STIR all ingredients with ice and strain into chilled glass.

2	shot(s)	**Buffalo Trace bourbon whiskey**
1	shot(s)	**Southern Comfort liqueur**
1	shot(s)	**Sweet vermouth**
3	dashes	**Peychaud's aromatic bitters**

Origin: Created in by yours truly in August 2005 for Tales of the Cocktail, New Orleans, USA.
Comment: A Manhattan with Southern Comfort and Peychaud's adding a hint of southern flavour.

AN INTELLIGENT MAN IS SOMETIMES FORCED TO BE DRUNK TO SPEND TIME WITH HIS FOOLS.
FOR WHOM THE BELL TOLLS, ERNEST HEMMINGWAY

SOUTHERN MINT COBBLER

Glass: Old-fashioned
Garnish: Mint sprig
Method: Lightly **MUDDLE** mint (just to bruise) in base of shaker. Add other ingredients, **SHAKE** with ice and fine strain into glass filled with crushed ice. Serve with straws.

7	fresh	**Mint leaves**
2	shot(s)	**Southern Comfort liqueur**
1	shot(s)	**White peach puree (sweetened)**
½	shot(s)	**Freshly squeezed lemon juice**

Comment: Very fruity and very easy to drink.

SOUTHERN PUNCH

Glass: Collins
Garnish: Pineapple wedge on rim
Method: SHAKE all ingredients with ice and strain into ice-filled glass.

1½	shot(s)	**Southern Comfort liqueur**
½	shot(s)	**Jack Daniel's Tennessee whiskey**
2	shot(s)	**Pressed pineapple juice**
1	shot(s)	**Freshly squeezed lemon juice**
½	shot(s)	**Sugar syrup (2 sugar to 1 water)**
½	shot(s)	**Pomegranate (grenadine) syrup**

Comment: Tropical flavours with the warmth of the liquor trailed by a fresh lemon finish.

SOUTHERN MULE

Glass: Collins
Garnish: Lime wedge
Method: SHAKE first three ingredients with ice and strain into ice-filled glass. **TOP** with ginger beer, lightly stir and serve with straws.

2	shot(s)	**Southern Comfort liqueur**
½	shot(s)	**Freshly squeezed lime juice**
3	dashes	**Angostura aromatic bitters**
Top up with		**ginger beer**

Comment: Tangy, fruity and spiced with ginger.

SOUTHERN TEA-KNEE

Glass: Martini
Garnish: Apricot slice on rim
Method: SHAKE all ingredients with ice and fine strain into chilled glass.

1	shot(s)	**Southern Comfort liqueur**
½	shot(s)	**Plymouth gin**
½	shot(s)	**Giffard apricot brandy du Roussillon**
½	shot(s)	**Giffard crème de banane du Brésil**
2	shot(s)	**Strong cold Earl Grey tea**

Origin: Created by yours truly in 2002.
Comment: Sweet fruity flavours balanced by tannic bitterness in the tea.

SOUTHSIDE ROYALE

Glass: Martini
Garnish: Mint leaf
Method: Lightly **MUDDLE** (just to bruise) mint in base of shaker. Add next three ingredients, **SHAKE** with ice and fine strain into chilled glass. **TOP** with a splash of champagne.

7	fresh	**Mint leaves**
2	shot(s)	**Plymouth gin**
1	shot(s)	**Freshly squeezed lemon juice**
1/2	shot(s)	**Sugar syrup (2 sugar to 1 water)**
Top up with		**Brut champagne**

Variant: Topped with soda (from a siphon, please) in place of champagne this becomes a mere 'Southside'.
Origin: Created during Prohibition, either at a New York City speakeasy called Jack & Charlie's, or at Manhattan's Stork Club, or by Chicago's Southside gang to make their bootleg liquor more palatable.
Comment: A White Lady with fresh mint and champagne.

SOYER AU CHAMPAGNE

Glass: Martini (Parfait glass)
Method: **PLACE** scoop of ice cream in base of glass. **SHAKE** next three ingredients with ice and strain over ice cream. **TOP** with champagne and serve while foaming with straws that the drinker should use to mix.

1	scoop	**Vanilla ice cream**
1/2	shot(s)	**Rémy Martin cognac**
1/2	shot(s)	**Luxardo maraschino liqueur**
1/2	shot(s)	**Grand Marnier liqueur**
Top up with		**Brut champagne**

Origin: Adapted from a recipe in the 1949 edition of Esquire's Handbook For Hosts. Apparently this was "one of the most popular drinks at Christmas in the continental cafés".
Comment: A unique dessert of a drink.

SPARKLING PERRY

Glass: Flute
Garnish: Pear slice on rim
Method: **SHAKE** first three ingredients with ice and fine strain into chilled glass. **TOP** with champagne and lightly stir.

3/4	shot(s)	**Poire William eau de vie**
3/4	shot(s)	**Pear & cognac liqueur**
1	shot(s)	**Freshly extracted pear juice**
Top up with		**Brut champagne**

Origin: Created in December 2002 by yours truly.
Comment: Reminiscent of perry (pear cider).

SPENCER COCKTAIL

Glass: Martini
Garnish: Orange zest twist (discarded) & maraschino cherry
Method: **SHAKE** all ingredients with ice and fine strain into chilled glass.

2	shot(s)	**Plymouth gin**
1	shot(s)	**Giffard apricot brandy du Roussillon**
1/4	shot(s)	**Freshly squeezed orange juice**
1	dash	**Angostura aromatic bitters**

Origin: Adapted from a recipe in Harry Craddock's 1930 Savoy Cocktail Book.
Comment: To quote Craddock, "Very mellifluous: has a fine and rapid action: for morning work."

SPEYSIDE MARTINI

Glass: Martini
Garnish: Lemon zest twist
Method: **MUDDLE** grapes in base of shaker. Add other ingredients, **SHAKE** with ice and fine strain into chilled glass.

7	fresh	**Seedless white grapes**
2	shot(s)	**Scotch whisky**
3/4	shot(s)	**Giffard apricot brandy du Roussillon**
3/4	shot(s)	**Freshly squeezed grapefruit juice**

Origin: Discovered in 2004 at Indigo Yard, Edinburgh, Scotland.
Comment: Scotch, grape juice, apricot liqueur and grapefruit may seem an unlikely combo but they get on well together.

SPICED APPLE DAIQUIRI

Glass: Martini
Garnish: Apple wedge on rim
Method: **SHAKE** all ingredients with ice and fine strain into chilled glass.

2	shot(s)	**Light white rum**
1/2	shot(s)	**Apple schnapps liqueur**
1/4	shot(s)	**Cinnamon schnapps liqueur**
1/2	shot(s)	**Freshly squeezed lime juice**
3/4	shot(s)	**Pressed apple juice**

Origin: Created in 1999 by yours truly.
Comment: Sour apple and cinnamon laced with rum.

SPICED CRANBERRY MARTINI

Glass: Martini
Garnish: Cranberry juice & cinnamon rim
Method: **MUDDLE** cloves in base of shaker. Add other ingredients, **SHAKE** with ice and fine strain into chilled glass.

7	dried	**Cloves**
1	shot(s)	**Cranberry flavoured vodka**
1	shot(s)	**Pusser's Navy rum**
2	shot(s)	**Ocean Spray cranberry juice**
1/2	shot(s)	**Sugar syrup (2 sugar to 1 water)**

Origin: Created in 2003 by yours truly.
Comment: The cloves and the colour add a festive note to this notional Martini.

SPICED PEAR

Glass: Old-fashioned
Garnish: Pear slice
Method: SHAKE all ingredients with ice and strain into ice-filled glass.

1	shot(s)	**Pear & cognac liqueur**
1	shot(s)	**Spiced rum**
1	shot(s)	**Freshly extracted pear juice**
1/2	shot(s)	**Freshly squeezed lime juice**
1/2	shot(s)	**Sugar syrup (2 sugar to 1 water)**

Origin: Created in 2002 by James Stewart, Edinburgh, Scotland.
Comment: Just as it says on the tin – spiced pear.

SPICY FINN

Glass: Martini
Garnish: Blueberry or raspberry on rim
Method: MUDDLE ginger in base of shaker. Add other ingredients, **SHAKE** with ice and fine strain into chilled glass.

3	slices	**Root ginger (thumb nail sized)**
2	shot(s)	**Cranberry flavoured vodka**
1/2	shot(s)	**Campari**
1/2	shot(s)	**Sugar syrup (2 sugar to 1 water)**
1	shot(s)	**Chilled mineral water** (reduce if wet ice)

Origin: Created by Michael Mahe at Hush, London.
Comment: Cranberry vodka, Campari and ginger with a dash of gomme to sweeten things up.

SPICY VEGGY

Glass: Martini
Garnish: Chunk of carrot on rim
Method: MUDDLE coriander seeds in base of shaker. Add other ingredients, **SHAKE** with ice and fine strain into chilled glass.

2	dozen	**Coriander seeds**
2	shot(s)	**Plymouth gin**
2	shot(s)	**Freshly extracted carrot juice**
1/4	shot(s)	**Sugar syrup (2 sugar to 1 water)**
1	pinch	**Black pepper**
1	pinch	**Salt**

Origin: Created in 2002 by yours truly.
Comment: Reminiscent of alcoholic carrot and coriander soup.

SPIKED APPLE CIDER (HOT)

Glass: Toddy
Garnish: Cinnamon dust
Method: MUDDLE cloves in base of shaker. Add cognac and apple juice, **SHAKE** without ice and fine strain into glass. **WARM** in microwave then **FLOAT** double cream over drink.

2	dried	**Cloves**
2	shot(s)	**Rémy Martin cognac**
3	shot(s)	**Pressed apple juice**
Float		**Double (heavy) cream**

Origin: Adapted from a drink discovered in 2006 at Double Seven, New York City, USA.
Comment: Warming and lightly spiced under a creamy head.

SPORRAN BREEZE

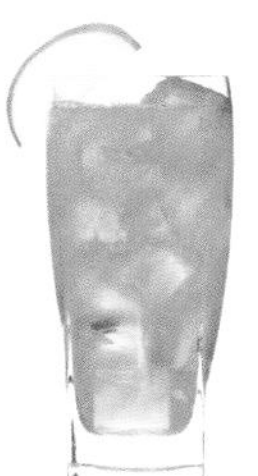

Glass: Collins
Garnish: Apple slice on rim
Method: SHAKE all ingredients with ice and strain into ice-filled glass. Serve with straws.

2	shot(s)	**Scotch whisky**
1/2	shot(s)	**Passion fruit syrup**
4	shot(s)	**Pressed apple juice**

Origin: Phillip Jeffrey created this drink for me in 2002 at the GE Club, London, England. I take credit (if any's due) for the name.
Comment: As with all simple drinks, the quality and flavour of the three ingredients used greatly affects the end product – choose wisely and you'll have a deliciously fresh blend of malty fruit.

SPRITZ AL BITTER

Glass: Old-fashioned
Garnish: Orange zest twist
Method: POUR ingredients into ice-filled glass and lightly stir.

1 1/2	shot(s)	**Campari**
1 1/2	shot(s)	**White wine**
Top up with		**Soda water (club soda)**

Origin: The origins of this Venetian speciality date back to the end of the 19th century when the Austrians ruled the city.
Comment: Basically a Spritzer with a generous splash of Campari – dry and very refreshing.

SPRITZER

Glass: Goblet
Garnish: Lemon zest twist
Method: POUR ingredients into chilled glass and lightly stir. No ice!

3	shot(s)	**Chilled dry white wine**
Top up with		**Soda water (club soda)**

Comment: The ultimate 'girlie' drink. To avoid ridicule when diluting a glass of white wine try adding a couple of ice cubes instead.

SPUTNIK

Glass: Martini
Garnish: Orange zest twist
Method: SHAKE all ingredients with ice and fine strain into chilled glass.

1	shot(s)	**Ketel One vodka**
1	shot(s)	**Teichenné Peach Schnapps Liqueur**
1 1/2	shot(s)	**Freshly squeezed orange juice**
1	shot(s)	**Double (heavy) cream**

Comment: Blasts of fruit cut through this soft creamy drink.

SPUTNIK #2

Glass: Old-fashioned
Garnish: Orange slice
Method: **SHAKE** all ingredients with ice and strain into ice-filled glass.

1	shot(s)	**Light white rum**
1	shot(s)	**Rémy Martin cognac**
2	shot(s)	**Freshly squeezed orange juice**
1/2	shot(s)	**Sugar syrup (2 sugar to 1 water)**

Origin: A cocktail served in underground clubs all over the former Eastern Bloc. It was originally made with cheap Cuban rum, Georgian brandy and tinned orange juice.
Comment: Orange, cognac and rum meld well.

SQUASHED FROG

Glass: Shot
Method: Refrigerate ingredients then **LAYER** in chilled glass by carefully pouring in the following order.

1/2	shot(s)	**Pomegranate (grenadine) syrup**
1/2	shot(s)	**Midori melon liqueur**
1/2	shot(s)	**Bols advocaat liqueur**

Comment: Very sweet. However, the taste is not as offensive as the name might suggest.

STAIRS MARTINI

Glass: Martini
Garnish: Pear slice on rim
Method: **SHAKE** all ingredients with ice and fine strain into chilled glass.

2	shot(s)	**Ketel One vodka**
1	shot(s)	**Freshly extracted pear juice**
1	shot(s)	**Pressed apple juice**
1/4	shot(s)	**Freshly squeezed lemon juice**
1/4	shot(s)	**Sugar syrup (2 sugar to 1 water)**
2	dashes	**Fee Brothers orange bitters**

Origin: Created in 2000 by Ian Baldwin at the GE Club, London, England.
Comment: In London's cockney rhyming slang 'apples and pears' means stairs. So this tasty cocktail is appropriately named.

STANLEY COCKTAIL

Glass: Martini
Garnish: Lemon zest twist
Method: **SHAKE** all ingredients with ice and fine strain into chilled glass.

1 1/2	shot(s)	**Plymouth gin**
1 1/2	shot(s)	**Light white rum**
1/2	shot(s)	**Freshly squeezed lemon juice**
1/2	shot(s)	**Pomegranate (grenadine) syrup**

Origin: Adapted from a recipe in Harry Craddock's 1930 Savoy Cocktail Book.
Comment: Salmon pink and reminiscent of a Daiquiri with a splash of gin.

THE STAR #1

Glass: Martini
Garnish: Olive on stick
Method: **STIR** all ingredients with ice and fine strain into chilled glass.

1 1/2	shot(s)	**Boulard Grand Solage Calvados**
1 1/2	shot(s)	**Sweet vermouth**
1	dash	**Angostura aromatic bitters**

Variant: T.N.T. Special - with the addition of a dash of sugar.
Origin: Recipe from Harry Craddock's 1930 Savoy Cocktail Book. Created in the 1870s by a bartender at the legendary Manhattan Club, which once stood at the north corner of 34th Street and 5th Avenue, New York City.
Comment: Like many old classics, this drink needs dilution so stir until you're bored and thirsty.

STARS & STRIPES SHOT

Glass: Shot
Method: Refrigerate ingredients then **LAYER** in chilled glass by carefully pouring in the following order.

1/2	shot(s)	**Giffard crème de cassis**
1/2	shot(s)	**Luxardo maraschino liqueur**
1/2	shot(s)	**Green Chartreuse liqueur**

Origin: Adapted from a recipe in Harry Craddock's 1930 Savoy Cocktail Book.
Comment: The taste is too sweet and the colours aren't quite right. A shame.

S. TEA G. [NEW #7]

Glass: Collins
Garnish: Lemon slice
Method: **SHAKE** first three ingredients with ice and strain into ice-filled glass. **TOP** with tonic water.

1 1/2	shot(s)	**Plymouth gin**
1 1/2	shot(s)	**St-Germain elderflower liqueur**
1	shot(s)	**Cold English Breakfast tea**
Top up with		**Tonic water**

Origin: Created in 2006 by yours truly.
Comment: Floral, long and refreshing.

STEALTH

Glass: Shot
Method: Refrigerate ingredients then **LAYER** in chilled glass by carefully pouring in the following order.

1/2	shot(s)	**Kahlúa coffee liqueur**
1/2	shot(s)	**Tuaca Italian liqueur**
1/2	shot(s)	**Irish cream liqueur**

Origin: Created by Poul Jensen, at St. James', Brighton, England. Another of the B-52 family of drinks, but named after Stealth bombers instead.
Comment: Reminiscent of a vanilla cappuccino.

STEEL BOTTOM

Glass: Collins
Method: POUR ingredients into glass, lightly stir and serve with straws.

1	shot(s)	**Wray & Nephew overproof rum**
Top up with		**Red Stripe beer**

Origin: A very popular drink in Jamaica.
Comment: For those who like their beer turbo charged.

STEEP FLIGHT

Glass: Collins
Garnish: Apple or pear slice
Method: SHAKE all ingredients with ice and fine strain into ice-filled glass.

1	shot(s)	**Boulard Grand Solage Calvados**
1	shot(s)	**Pear flavoured vodka**
1	shot(s)	**Pear & cognac liqueur**
3	shot(s)	**Pressed apple juice**

Origin: Created in 2005 by yours truly. Awarded a Gold in Long Drink category at the Drinks International Bartender's Challenge on 31st May 2006.
Comment: 'Apples and pears' is the cockney rhyming slang for stairs, hence the flavours in this particular flight.

THE STIG [NEW #7]

Glass: Martini
Garnish: Float wafer thin apple slice
Method: SHAKE all ingredients with ice and fine strain into chilled glass.

1	shot(s)	**Boulard Grand Solage Calvados**
1	shot(s)	**St-Germain elderflower liqueur**
1	shot(s)	**Sauvignon Blanc wine**

Origin: Created in 2006 by yours truly. I named it partly for our in-house abbreviation for St-Germain and partly after 'The Stig', the mysterious racing driver on the 'Top Gear' TV series.
Comment: Easy to make yet complex to savour, with hints of apple and elderflower.

STILETTO

Glass: Collins
Garnish: Lime wedge
Method: SHAKE all ingredients with ice and strain into ice-filled glass.

2	shot(s)	**Buffalo Trace bourbon whiskey**
1	shot(s)	**Luxardo Amaretto di Saschira liqueur**
2½	shot(s)	**Ocean Spray cranberry juice**
½	shot(s)	**Freshly squeezed lime juice**
¼	shot(s)	**Sugar syrup (2 sugar to 1 water)**

Comment: Long and fruity with a hint of bourbon and almond.

STINGER

Glass: Old-fashioned
Garnish: Mint sprig
Method: SHAKE all ingredients with ice and strain into glass filled with crushed ice. Serve with straws.

2	shot(s)	**Rémy Martin cognac**
¾	shot(s)	**Giffard White crème de menthe**

Origin: In the classic film 'High Society', Bing Crosby explains to Grace Kelly how the Stinger gained its name: "It's a Stinger. It removes the sting."
Comment: A refreshing, peppermint and cognac digestif.

STONE & GRAVEL

Glass: Old-fashioned
Method: POUR ingredients into glass filled with crushed ice and stir.

1	shot(s)	**Wray & Nephew overproof rum**
3	shot(s)	**Stone's green ginger wine**

Origin: A popular drink in Jamaica.
Comment: Simple, strong and surprisingly good.

STORK CLUB

Glass: Martini
Garnish: Orange zest twist
Method: SHAKE all ingredients with ice and fine strain into chilled glass.

1	shot(s)	**Plymouth gin**
1	shot(s)	**Cointreau triple sec**
1	shot(s)	**Freshly squeezed orange juice**
½	shot(s)	**Freshly squeezed lime juice**
2	dashes	**Fee Brothers orange bitters (optional)**

Comment: Orange and gin with a souring splash of lime juice.

STRAITS SLING

Glass: Sling
Garnish: Orange slice & cherry (sail)
Method: SHAKE first six ingredients with ice and strain into ice-filled glass. **TOP** with soda, lightly stir and serve with straws.

2	shot(s)	**Plymouth gin**
½	shot(s)	**Bénédictine D.O.M. liqueur**
½	shot(s)	**Kirsch eau de vie**
1	shot(s)	**Freshly squeezed lemon juice**
2	dashes	**Fee Brothers orange bitters**
2	dashes	**Angostura aromatic bitters**
Top up with		**Soda water (club soda)**

Origin: Thought to be the original name of the Singapore Sling. Conjecture, partly based on a reference to 'Kirsch' in Embury's Fine Art of Mixing Drinks, has it that the drink was originally based on cherry eau de vie and not the cherry liqueur used in most Singapore Sling recipes today.
Comment: Dry cherry and gin come to the fore in this long, refreshing drink.

STRASBERI SLING

Glass: Sling
Garnish: Mint sprig
Method: SHAKE all ingredients with ice and strain into ice-filled glass.

$1\frac{1}{2}$	shot(s)	**Raspberry flavoured vodka**
1	shot(s)	**Pimm's No. 1 Cup**
$\frac{1}{2}$	shot(s)	**Sugar syrup (2 sugar to 1 water)**
1	shot(s)	**Freshly squeezed lime juice**
3	shot(s)	**Pressed apple juice**

Origin: Created in 2002 by Alex Kammerling, London, England.
Comment: Raspberry and apple combine beautifully in this refreshing drink with its clean citrus tang.

'YOU'RE NOT DRUNK IF YOU CAN LIE ON THE FLOOR WITHOUT HOLDING ON.'
DEAN MARTIN

STRAWBERRY & BALSAMIC MOJITO

Glass: Collins
Garnish: Strawberry & lime wedge
Method: MUDDLE strawberries in base of shaker. Add next five ingredients, **SHAKE** with ice and fine strain into chilled glass. **TOP** with soda.

7	fresh	**Strawberries**
2	shot(s)	**Light white rum**
$\frac{3}{4}$	shot(s)	**Freshly squeezed lime juice**
$\frac{1}{4}$	shot(s)	**White balsamic vinegar**
$\frac{1}{2}$	shot(s)	**Sugar syrup (2 sugar to 1 water)**
12	fresh	**Mint leaves (torn)**
Top up with		**Soda water**

Origin: Adapted from a drink created in 2005 by Simon Warneford at Blanch House, Brighton, England.
Comment: A fruity twist on the classic Mojito.

STRAWBERRY BLONDE MARTINI

Glass: Martini
Garnish: Float basil leaf
Method: MUDDLE basil in mixing glass. Add other ingredients, **STIR** with ice and fine strain into chilled glass.

4	fresh	**Basil leaves**
$2\frac{1}{2}$	shot(s)	**Raspberry flavoured vodka**
$\frac{1}{2}$	shot(s)	**Dry vermouth**
$\frac{1}{2}$	shot(s)	**Giffard crème de fraise de bois**
1/8	shot(s)	**Sugar syrup (2 sugar to 1 water)**

Origin: Adapted from a recipe discovered in 2003 at Oxo Tower Bar, London, England.
Comment: Berry vodka dominates with hints of strawberry and basil.

STRAWBERRY COSMO

Glass: Martini
Garnish: Strawberry on rim
Method: SHAKE all ingredients with ice and fine strain into chilled glass.

2	shot(s)	**Ketel One Citroen vodka**
$\frac{3}{4}$	shot(s)	**Giffard crème de fraise de bois**
$1\frac{1}{4}$	shot(s)	**Ocean Spray cranberry juice**
$\frac{1}{2}$	shot(s)	**Freshly squeezed lime juice**

Origin: Formula by yours truly in 2004.
Comment: Strawberry liqueur replaces the usual orange liqueur in this contemporary classic.

STRAWBERRY DAIQUIRI

Glass: Martini
Garnish: Strawberry on rim
Method: MUDDLE strawberries in base of shaker. Add other ingredients, **SHAKE** with ice and fine strain into chilled glass.

7	fresh	**Hulled strawberries**
2	shot(s)	**Light white rum**
$\frac{1}{2}$	shot(s)	**Freshly squeezed lime juice**
$\frac{1}{4}$	shot(s)	**Sugar syrup (2 sugar to 1 water)**

Origin: A popular drink in Cuba where it is known as a Daiquiri de Fresa.
Comment: Makes strawberries and cream appear very dull.

THE STRAWBERRY ÉCLAIR

Glass: Shot
Method: SHAKE all ingredients with ice and fine strain into chilled glass.

$\frac{1}{2}$	shot(s)	**Frangelico hazelnut liqueur**
$\frac{1}{2}$	shot(s)	**Giffard crème de fraise de bois**
$\frac{1}{4}$	shot(s)	**Freshly squeezed lime juice**

Origin: This drink heralds from Australia where it is a popular shot.
Comment: Far from sophisticated (some would say like Australia) but very appropriately named..

STRAWBERRY FROZEN DAIQUIRI

Glass: Martini
Garnish: Split strawberry
Method: BLEND all ingredients with 6oz scoop of crushed ice.

2	shot(s)	**Light white rum**
$\frac{3}{4}$	shot(s)	**Freshly squeezed lime juice**
$\frac{1}{2}$	shot(s)	**Sugar syrup (2 sugar to 1 water)**
5	fresh	**Hulled strawberries (chopped)**

Comment: A delicious twist on a classic – Strawberry Mivvi for grown-ups.

STRAWBERRY MARGARITA 

Glass: Martini
Garnish: Strawberry on rim
Method: **MUDDLE** strawberries in base of shaker. Add other ingredients, **SHAKE** with ice and fine strain into chilled glass.

5	fresh	**Hulled strawberries**
2	shot(s)	**Partida tequila**
1	shot(s)	**Freshly squeezed lime juice**
3/4	shot(s)	**Sugar syrup (2 sugar to 1 water)**

Origin: Formula by yours truly in 2004.
Comment: Fresh strawberries combine well with tequila in this fruit margarita.

STRAWBERRY MARTINI 

Glass: Martini
Garnish: Strawberry on rim
Method: **MUDDLE** strawberries in base of shaker. Add other ingredients, **SHAKE** with ice and fine strain into chilled glass.

5	fresh	**Hulled strawberries (chopped)**
2 1/2	shot(s)	**Ketel One vodka**
1/2	shot(s)	**Sugar syrup (2 sugar to 1 water)**
2	grinds	**Black pepper**

Origin: Created by yours truly in 2004.
Comment: Rich strawberries fortified with vodka and a hint of pepper spice.

STRAWBERRY 'N' BALSAMIC MARTINI

Glass: Martini
Garnish: Strawberry on rim
Method: **MUDDLE** strawberries in base of shaker. Add other ingredients, **SHAKE** with ice and fine strain into chilled glass.

5	fresh	**Hulled strawberries (chopped)**
2 1/2	shot(s)	**Ketel One vodka**
1/8	shot(s)	**Balsamic vinegar**
1/2	shot(s)	**Sugar syrup (2 sugar to 1 water)**

Origin: My version of a drink that became popular in London in 2002 and I believe originated in Che.
Comment: The balsamic adds a little extra interest to the fortified strawberries.

STRUDEL MARTINI

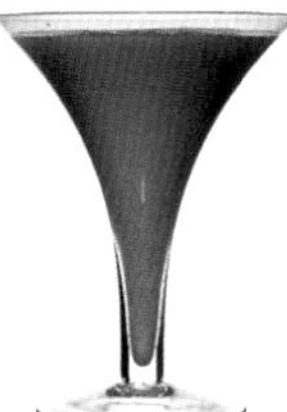

Glass: Martini
Garnish: Dust with cinnamon powder
Method: **SHAKE** all ingredients with ice and fine strain into chilled glass.

1 1/2	shot(s)	**Ketel One vodka**
1/2	shot(s)	**Pedro Ximénez sherry**
3/4	shot(s)	**Pressed apple juice**
1/2	shot(s)	**Double (heavy) cream**
1/2	shot(s)	**Milk**

Origin: Created in 2002 by Jason Borthwick, Tiles, Edinburgh, Scotland.
Comment: Still think sherry is just for Granny?

SWIZZLE

Swizzles originated in the Caribbean. They are sour style drinks that, distinctively, must be churned with a swizzle stick.

Originally a twig with a few forked branches, today swizzle sticks are usually made of metal or plastic and have several blades or fingers attached to the base at right angles to the shaft. To use one, simply immerse the blades in the drink, hold the shaft between the palms of both hands and rotate the stick rapidly by sliding your hands back and forth against it. If you do not have a bona fide swizzle stick, use a barspoon in the same manner.

Swizzles can be served as short drinks or lengthened with mineral water.

STUPID CUPID

Glass: Martini
Garnish: Lemon zest twist
Method: **SHAKE** all ingredients with ice and fine strain into chilled glass.

2	shot(s)	**Ketel One Citroen vodka**
1/2	shot(s)	**Plymouth sloe gin liqueur**
1	shot(s)	**Freshly squeezed lime juice**
1/2	shot(s)	**Sugar syrup (2 sugar to 1 water)**

Comment: Citrussy with subtle sloe gin.

SUBURBAN

Glass: Old-fashioned
Garnish: Orange zest twist
Method: **STIR** all ingredients with ice and strain into ice-filled glass.

1 1/2	shot(s)	**Buffalo Trace bourbon whiskey**
3/4	shot(s)	**Aged rum**
3/4	shot(s)	**Tawny port**
1	dash	**Fee Brothers orange bitters**
1	dash	**Angostura aromatic bitters**

Origin: Created at New York's old Waldorf-Astoria Hotel (the Empire State Building occupies the site today) for James R Keene, a racehorse owner whose steeds ran in the Suburban Handicap at Brooklyn's Sheepshead Bay track.
Comment: An interesting alternative to an Old-fashioned.

SUITABLY FRANK

Glass: Shot
Method: Refrigerate ingredients then **LAYER** in chilled glass by carefully pouring in the following order.

1/2	shot(s)	**Cuarenta Y Tres (Licor 43) liqueur**
1/2	shot(s)	**Cherry (brandy) liqueur**
1/2	shot(s)	**Ketel One vodka**

Comment: Frankly – it's a good shot.

S

SUMMER BREEZE [UPDATED #7]

Glass: Collins
Garnish: Apple slice
Method: **SHAKE** all ingredients with ice and strain into ice-filled glass.

2	shot(s)	**Ketel One vodka**
1	shot(s)	**St-Germain elderflower liqueur**
2	shot(s)	**Pressed apple juice**
1	shot(s)	**Ocean Spray cranberry juice**

Origin: Adapted from a drink created in 1998 by Dick Bradsell, London, England.
Comment: Cranberry, apple and elderflower fortified with vodka.

SUMMER ROSE MARTINI

Glass: Martini
Garnish: Red rose petal (edible)
Method: **STIR** first three ingredients with ice and strain into chilled glass. **POUR** grenadine into the centre of the drink. This should sink and settle to form a red layer in the base of the glass.

1 1/2	shot(s)	**Ketel One vodka**
3/4	shot(s)	**Giffard white crème de cacao**
1/2	shot(s)	**Soho lychee liqueur**
1/2	shot(s)	**Pomegranate (grenadine) syrup**

Origin: Created in 2003 by Davide Lovison at Isola Bar, London, England.
Comment: This red and white layered drink could have been named War of the Roses. Unless you've a sweet tooth don't mix the factions – sip from the chocolate and lychee top and stop when you hit red.

SUMMER TIME MARTINI

Glass: Martini
Garnish: Kumquat
Method: **SHAKE** all ingredients with ice and fine strain into chilled glass.

1 1/2	shot(s)	**Plymouth gin**
1	shot(s)	**Grand Marnier liqueur**
1 1/2	shot(s)	**Freshly squeezed orange juice**
1/4	shot(s)	**Pomegranate (grenadine) syrup**

Comment: Smooth, gin laced fruit for a summer's day.

SUMO IN A SIDECAR

Glass: Martini
Garnish: Orange zest twist
Method: **SHAKE** all ingredients with ice and fine strain into chilled glass.

2 1/2	shot(s)	**Sake**
1	shot(s)	**Giffard apricot brandy du Roussillon**
1/2	shot(s)	**Freshly squeezed lemon juice**

Comment: Hints of sake but retains the Sidecar style.

SUN KISSED VIRGIN (MOCKTAIL)

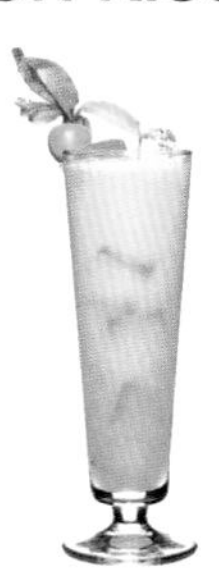

Glass: Sling
Garnish: Physalis (cape gooseberry) on rim
Method: **SHAKE** all ingredients with ice and strain into ice-filled glass.

2	shot(s)	**Freshly squeezed orange juice**
2	shot(s)	**Pressed pineapple juice**
1	shot(s)	**Freshly squeezed lime juice**
1/2	shot(s)	**Almond (orgeat) sugar syrup**

Comment: Golden, slightly sweet and very fruity – just like a Sun Kissed Virgin should be. Sorry.

THE SUN SALUTATION

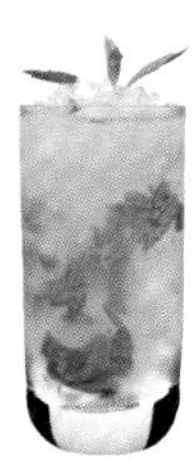

Glass: Collins
Garnish: Berries & mint sprig
Method: MUDDLE mint in base of shaker. Add next three ingredients, **SHAKE** with ice and fine strain into ice-filled glass. **TOP** with soda.

10	fresh	**Mint leaves**
1	shot(s)	**Ketel One vodka**
$1^1/_2$	shot(s)	**Soho lychee liqueur**
$^3/_4$	shot(s)	**Freshly squeezed lemon juice**
Top up with		**Soda (club soda)**

Origin: Adapted from a recipe by David Nepove, Enrico's Bar & Restaurant, San Francisco.
Comment: Mint with a hint of lychee – long and refreshing.

SUNDOWNER #1

Glass: Martini
Garnish: Orange zest twist
Method: SHAKE all ingredients with ice and fine strain into chilled glass.

2	shot(s)	**Rémy Martin cognac**
$^1/_2$	shot(s)	**Grand Marnier liqueur**
$^1/_2$	shot(s)	**Freshly squeezed orange juice**
$^1/_4$	shot(s)	**Freshly squeezed lemon juice**
$^3/_4$	shot(s)	**Chilled mineral water** (omit if wet ice)

Variant: Red Lion
Origin: This cocktail is popular in South Africa where it is made with locally produced brandy and a local orange liqueur called Van der Hum.
Comment: Cognac and orange served 'up'.

SUNDOWNER #2

Glass: Old-fashioned
Garnish: Mint sprig
Method: SHAKE all ingredients with ice and strain into ice-filled glass.

$1^1/_2$	shot(s)	**Southern Comfort liqueur**
$^3/_4$	shot(s)	**Grand Marnier liqueur**
2	shot(s)	**Sauvignon Blanc wine**

Origin: Adapted from a cocktail created in 2002 by Gary Regis at Bed Bar, London, England.
Comment: Subtle meld of summer and citrus flavours.

SUNNY BREEZE

Glass: Collins
Garnish: Half orange slice
Method: SHAKE all ingredients with ice and strain into glass filled with crushed ice.

$1^1/_2$	shot(s)	**Pernod anis**
$^1/_2$	shot(s)	**Cointreau triple sec**
$^1/_2$	shot(s)	**Grand Marnier liqueur**
3	shot(s)	**Squeezed pink grapefruit juice**

Origin: Created in 2003 by yours truly.
Comment: A suitably named refreshing long drink with an adult dry edge and kick.

SUNSHINE COCKTAIL #1

Glass: Martini
Garnish: Pineapple wedge on rim
Method: SHAKE all ingredients with ice and fine strain into chilled glass.

$1^1/_2$	shot(s)	**Light white rum**
$1^1/_2$	shot(s)	**Dry vermouth**
$1^1/_2$	shot(s)	**Pressed pineapple juice**
1/8	shot(s)	**Pomegranate (grenadine) syrup**

Origin: Adapted from a recipe in my 1949 copy of Esquire's Handbook For Hosts.
Comment: Light, fruity and a tad on the sweet side, but could well brighten your day.

SUNSHINE COCKTAIL #2

Glass: Martini
Garnish: Lemon zest twist
Method: SHAKE all ingredients with ice and fine strain into chilled glass.

$1^1/_2$	shot(s)	**Light white rum**
$1^1/_2$	shot(s)	**Dry vermouth**
$^1/_4$	shot(s)	**Giffard crème de cassis**
$^1/_4$	shot(s)	**Freshly squeezed lemon juice**

Origin: Adapted from a recipe in Harry Craddock's 1930 Savoy Cocktail Book.
Comment: More a sunset but fruity, flavoursome and well-balanced all the same.

SUNSTROKE

Glass: Martini
Garnish: Orange zest twist (round to make sun)
Method: SHAKE all ingredients with ice and fine strain into chilled glass.

1	shot(s)	**Ketel One vodka**
1	shot(s)	**Cointreau triple sec**
2	shot(s)	**Squeezed pink grapefruit juice**

Comment: Fruity but balanced. One to sip in the shade.

SUPERMINTY-CHOCOLATINI

Glass: Martini
Garnish: Chocolate powder rim
Method: SHAKE all ingredients with ice and fine strain into chilled glass.

2	shot(s)	**Ketel One vodka**
1	shot(s)	**Giffard white crème de cacao**
1	shot(s)	**Giffard White crème de menthe**

Comment: Obvious but nicely flavoured.

SURFER ON A.C.D.

Glass: Shot
Method: SHAKE first two ingredients with ice and fine strain into chilled glass. **FLOAT** Jägermeister.

1/2 shot(s) **Malibu coconut rum liqueur**
3/4 shot(s) **Pressed pineapple juice**
1/4 shot(s) **Jägermeister liqueur**

Comment: The spirity herbal topping counters the sweet coconut and pineapple base.

THE SUZY WONG MARTINI

Glass: Martini
Garnish: Orange zest twist
Method: MUDDLE basil in base of shaker. Add other ingredients, **SHAKE** with ice and fine strain into chilled glass.

7 fresh **Basil leaves**
2 shot(s) **Orange zest infused Ketel One vodka**
1/2 shot(s) **Grand Marnier liqueur**
1 shot(s) **Freshly squeezed orange juice**
1/2 shot(s) **Freshly squeezed lime juice**
1/4 shot(s) **Sugar syrup (2 sugar to 1 water)**

Origin: Discovered in 2005 at Suzy Wong, Amsterdam, The Netherlands.
Comment: Fresh tasting orange with a hint of basil.

SWAMP WATER

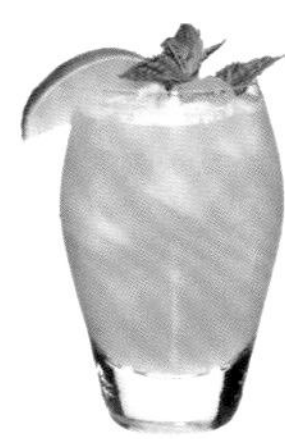

Glass: Collins
Garnish: Lime wedge & mint leaf
Method: SHAKE all ingredients with ice and strain into ice-filled glass.

1 1/2 shot(s) **Green Chartreuse liqueur**
4 shot(s) **Pressed pineapple juice**
1/2 shot(s) **Freshly squeezed lime juice**

Comment: Long and refreshing - the herbal taste of Chartreuse combined with the fruitiness of pineapple.

SWEDISH BLUE MARTINI

Glass: Martini
Garnish: Orange peel twist
Method: SHAKE all ingredients with ice and fine strain into chilled glass.

2 shot(s) **Ketel One vodka**
1/2 shot(s) **Bols Blue curaçao liqueur**
1/2 shot(s) **Teichenné Peach Schnapps Liqueur**
1/4 shot(s) **Freshly squeezed lime juice**
1/4 shot(s) **Sugar syrup (2 sugar to 1 water)**
2 dashes **Fee Brothers orange bitters**
1/2 shot(s) **Chilled mineral water** (omit if wet ice)

Origin: Created in 1999 by Timothy Schofield at Teatro, London, England.
Comment: A fruity, blue concoction laced with vodka. Slightly sweet.

SWEET LOUISE

Glass: Martini
Garnish: Blackberry
Method: Cut passion fruit in half and scoop out flesh into shaker. Add other ingredients, **SHAKE** with ice and fine strain into chilled glass.

1 fresh **Passion fruit**
1 shot(s) **Raspberry flavoured vodka**
1/2 shot(s) **Chambord black raspberry liqueur**
1/2 shot(s) **Luxardo Amaretto di Saschira liqueur**
3/4 shot(s) **Freshly squeezed lime juice.**
1/4 shot(s) **Pomegranate (grenadine) syrup**

Origin: Created in 2000 at Monte's Club, London, England
Comment: Lots of contrasting flavours but she's a sweet girl.

SWEET SCIENCE

Glass: Martini
Garnish: Orange zest twist
Method: SHAKE all ingredients with ice and fine strain into chilled glass.

2 shot(s) **Scotch whisky**
3/4 shot(s) **Drambuie liqueur**
1 1/2 shot(s) **Freshly squeezed orange juice**

Origin: Created by Charles Schumann, Munich, Germany.
Comment: Herbal Scotch and orange.

SWEET TART

Glass: Sling
Garnish: Sugar rim & redcurrants
Method: SHAKE first four ingredients with ice and strain into ice-filled glass. **TOP** with 7-Up.

2 shot(s) **Ketel One vodka**
3/4 shot(s) **Chambord black raspberry liqueur**
3/4 shot(s) **Luxardo Amaretto di Saschira liqueur**
1 shot(s) **Freshly squeezed lime juice**
Top up with **7-Up**

Comment: As the name suggests, a fruity combination of sweet and sour.

SWIZZLE

Glass: Old-fashioned
Garnish: Fruit or mint sprigs
Method: POUR ingredients into glass filled with crushed ice. **SWIZZLE** with a swizzle stick and serve with straws.

2 shot(s) **Liquor (rum, brandy, gin or whiskey etc.)**
1/2 shot(s) **Fresh lemon or lime juice**
1/2 shot(s) **Sugar syrup (2 sugar to 1 water)**

Variants: With rum try orgeat syrup or Velvet Falernum in place of the sugar syrup. With whiskey try Chartreuse.
Origin: Adapted from a recipe purloined from David Embury's classic book, The Fine Art of Mixing Drinks.
Comment: Match the appropriate citrus juice and sweetener to your spirit and you'll have a superb drink.

TAILOR MADE

Glass: Martini
Garnish: Grapefruit zest twist
Method: STIR honey with bourbon in base of shaker to dissolve honey. Add other ingredients, **SHAKE** with ice and fine strain into chilled glass.

1	spoon	**Runny honey**
$1\frac{1}{2}$	shot(s)	**Buffalo Trace bourbon whiskey**
$\frac{1}{4}$	shot(s)	**Velvet Falernum liqueur**
1	shot(s)	**Squeezed pink grapefruit juice**
1	shot(s)	**Ocean Spray cranberry juice**

Origin: Created by Dale DeGroff, New York City, USA.
Comment: Light, balanced fruit and bourbon.

TAINTED CHERRY

Glass: Martini
Garnish: Maraschino cherry
Method: SHAKE all ingredients with ice and fine strain into chilled glass.

$1\frac{3}{4}$	shot(s)	**Ketel One vodka**
$\frac{3}{4}$	shot(s)	**Cherry (brandy) liqueur**
$1\frac{3}{4}$	shot(s)	**Freshly squeezed orange juice**

Comment: Orange and cherry combine to produce a flavour rather like amaretto.

TANGO MARTINI #1

Glass: Martini
Garnish: Orange zest twist
Method: SHAKE all ingredients with ice and fine strain into chilled glass.

$1\frac{1}{2}$	shot(s)	**Plymouth gin**
$\frac{1}{2}$	shot(s)	**Sweet vermouth**
$\frac{1}{2}$	shot(s)	**Dry vermouth**
$\frac{1}{2}$	shot(s)	**Cointreau triple sec**
1	shot(s)	**Freshly squeezed orange juice**

Origin: Adapted from a recipe in Harry Craddock's 1930 Savoy Cocktail Book.
Comment: Balanced and complex with hints of gin and orange.

TANGO MARTINI #2

Glass: Martini
Garnish: Orange zest twist
Method: SHAKE all ingredients with ice and fine strain into chilled glass.

$1\frac{3}{4}$	shot(s)	**Plymouth gin**
$\frac{3}{4}$	shot(s)	**Passoã passion fruit liqueur**
2	shot(s)	**Freshly squeezed grapefruit juice**
$\frac{1}{4}$	shot(s)	**Sugar syrup (2 sugar to 1 water)**

Origin: Adapted from a drink discovered in 2003 at the Bellagio, Las Vegas, USA.
Comment: Floral and balanced.

TEQUILA SLAMMER

Originally topped with ginger ale and not champagne, this infamous libation is thought to have started out as a Hell's Angel drink – it needs no ice and can be carried in a bike bag.

The simplest slammer is a lick of salt, a shot of tequila and then a bite of lemon (or lime). A Bermuda Slammer involves straight tequila, salt, a slice of lemon and a partner: one has to lick the salt off the other one's neck and bite the lemon (held between their partner's teeth) before downing a shot of tequila.

To quote Victor Bergeron (Trader Vic), "You know, this rigmarole with a pinch of salt and lemon juice and tequila - in whatever order - was originally for a purpose: It's hot in Mexico. People dehydrate themselves. And they need more salt. Here, it's not so hot, and we don't need salt in the same way. So you can drink tequila straight right out of the bottle, if you want to."

TANTRIS SIDECAR

Glass: Martini
Garnish: Lemon zest twist
Method: SHAKE all ingredients with ice and fine strain into chilled glass.

1½	shot(s)	**Boulard Grand Solage Calvados**
¼	shot(s)	**Cointreau triple sec**
½	shot(s)	**Green Chartreuse liqueur**
¼	shot(s)	**Freshly squeezed lemon juice**
2	shot(s)	**Pressed pineapple juice**

Origin: Adapted from a drink created by Audrey Saunders at Bemelmans Bar at The Carlyle Hotel, New York City, USA.
Comment: A Sidecar with extra interest courtesy of Chartreuse, pineapple and Calvados.

TARRABERRY'TINI

Glass: Martini
Garnish: Tarragon sprig
Method: MUDDLE tarragon in base of shaker. Add other ingredients, **SHAKE** with ice and fine strain into chilled glass.

2	sprigs	**Fresh tarragon**
1½	shot(s)	**Cranberry flavoured vodka**
¼	shot(s)	**Pernod anis**
2	shot(s)	**Ocean Spray cranberry juice**
¼	shot(s)	**Freshly squeezed lemon juice**

Origin: Created in 2003 by yours truly.
Comment: Cranberry with subtle hints of tarragon and lemon.

TARTE AUX POMMES

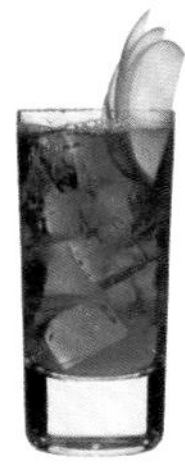

Glass: Collins
Garnish: Apple chevron
Method: SHAKE all ingredients with ice and strain into ice-filled glass.

1	shot(s)	**Boulard Grand Solage Calvados**
½	shot(s)	**Giffard crème de cassis**
¼	shot(s)	**Cinnamon schnapps liqueur**
4	shot(s)	**Ocean Spray cranberry juice**
3	dashes	**Angostura aromatic bitters**

Origin: Created in 2001 by Jamie Stephenson at The Lock, Manchester, England.
Comment: Rich in flavour and well balanced.

TARTE TATIN MARTINI

Glass: Martini
Garnish: Cinnamon dust
Method: SHAKE first three ingredients with ice and strain into chilled glass. **SHAKE** cream with ice and carefully pour so as to **LAYER** over drink.

2	shot(s)	**Vanilla infused Ketel One vodka**
¾	shot(s)	**Apple schnapps liqueur**
¾	shot(s)	**Cartron caramel liqueur**
2	shot(s)	**Double (heavy) cream**

Origin: Created in 2003 by yours truly. The name means a tart of caramelised apples cooked under a pastry lid, a dish created by the Tatin sisters.
Comment: A creamy top hides a vanilla, apple and caramel combo.

TARTINI

Glass: Martini
Garnish: Raspberry
Method: MUDDLE raspberries in base of shaker. Add other ingredients, **SHAKE** with ice and fine strain into chilled glass.

12	fresh	**Raspberries**
2	shot(s)	**Raspberry flavoured vodka**
½	shot(s)	**Chambord black raspberry liqueur**
1½	shot(s)	**Ocean Spray cranberry juice**

Origin: Adapted from a cocktail I found at Soho Grand, New York City, USA.
Comment: Rich raspberry flavour, well balanced with bite.

TATANKA

Glass: Old-fashioned
Garnish: Apple slice
Method: SHAKE all ingredients with ice and strain into ice-filled glass.

2	shot(s)	**Zubrówka bison vodka**
2½	shot(s)	**Pressed apple juice**

Origin: This Polish drink takes its name from the film 'Dances with Wolves' (1990). Tatanka is a Native American word for buffalo and refers to the bison grass flavoured vodka the cocktail is based on.
Comment: The taste of this excellent drink (which is equally good served straight-up) is a little reminiscent of Earl Grey tea.

TATANKA ROYALE

Glass: Flute
Garnish: Apple slice
Method: SHAKE first two ingredients with ice and fine strain into chilled glass. **TOP** with champagne.

1	shot(s)	**Zubrówka bison vodka**
1	shot(s)	**Pressed apple juice**
Top up with		**Brut champagne**

Origin: Discovered in 2004 at Indigo Yard, Edinburgh, Scotland.
Comment: Champagne with a subtle, grassy hint of apple.

TAWNY-TINI

Glass: Martini
Garnish: Orange zest twist
Method: SHAKE all ingredients with ice and fine strain into chilled glass.

2	shot(s)	**Ketel One vodka**
2	shot(s)	**Tawny port**
¼	shot(s)	**Maple syrup**

Comment: Dry yet rich. Port combines wonderfully with the maple syrup and is further fortified by the grainy vodka.

TEDDY BEAR'TINI

Glass: Martini
Garnish: Pear slice
Method: **SHAKE** all ingredients with ice and fine strain into chilled glass.

1½	shot(s)	**Pear & cognac liqueur**
¾	shot(s)	**Apple schnapps liqueur**
1½	shot(s)	**Pressed apple juice**
1	pinch	**Ground cinnamon**

Origin: Created in 2002 at The Borough, Edinburgh, Scotland. Originally named after a well-known cockney duo but renamed after the rhyming slang for pear.
Comment: Beautifully balanced apple and pear with a hint of cinnamon spice.

TENNESSEE BERRY MULE

Glass: Collins
Garnish: Three raspberries
Method: **MUDDLE** raspberries in base of shaker. Add next four ingredients, **SHAKE** with ice and strain into ice-filled glass. **TOP** with ginger beer, lightly stir and serve with straws.

8	fresh	**Raspberries**
1½	shot(s)	**Jack Daniel's Tennessee whiskey**
1	shot(s)	**Luxardo Amaretto di Saschira liqueur**
1½	shot(s)	**Ocean Spray cranberry juice**
½	shot(s)	**Freshly squeezed lime juice**
Top up with		**Ginger beer**

Origin: Adapted in 2003 from a recipe Alex Kammerling created for TGI Friday's UK. Named partly for the ingredients and partly as a reference to Jack Daniel's proprietor (and nephew),
Lemuel Motlow, who took up mule trading during Prohibition.
Comment: A berry rich cocktail laced with whiskey, flavoured with amaretto and topped with ginger beer.

TENNESSEE ICED TEA

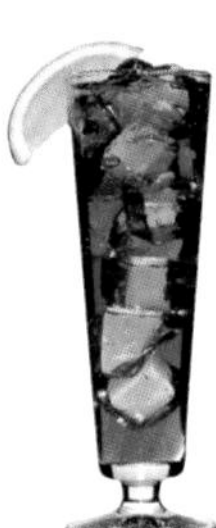

Glass: Sling
Garnish: Lemon wedge on rim
Method: **SHAKE** first six ingredients with ice and strain into ice-filled glass. **TOP** with cola and serve with straws.

1	shot(s)	**Jack Daniel's Tennessee whiskey**
½	shot(s)	**Light white rum**
½	shot(s)	**Ketel One vodka**
½	shot(s)	**Cointreau triple sec**
¾	shot(s)	**Freshly squeezed lemon juice**
¼	shot(s)	**Sugar syrup (2 sugar to 1 water)**
Top up with		**Cola**

Comment: JD and cola with extra interest courtesy of several other spirits and lemon juice.

TENNESSEE RUSH

Glass: Collins
Garnish: Lime wedge
Method: **SHAKE** all ingredients with ice and strain into ice-filled glass.

2	shot(s)	**Jack Daniel's Tennessee whiskey**
1	shot(s)	**Mandarine Napoléon liqueur**
2½	shot(s)	**Ocean Spray cranberry juice**
½	shot(s)	**Freshly squeezed lime juice**

Comment: This ruby red cocktail is long, fruity, refreshing and not too sweet.

TEQUILA FIZZ

Glass: Sling
Garnish: Orange zest twist
Method: **SHAKE** first four ingredients with ice and strain into ice-filled glass. **TOP** with 7-Up.

2	shot(s)	**Partida tequila**
1	shot(s)	**Freshly squeezed orange juice**
1	shot(s)	**Freshly squeezed lime juice**
½	shot(s)	**Sugar syrup (2 sugar to 1 water)**
Top up with		**7-Up/lemonade**

Comment: Refreshing with lingering lime.

TEQUILA MOCKINGBIRD [UPDATED #7]

Glass: Martini
Garnish: Mint leaf
Method: **SHAKE** all ingredients with ice and fine strain into chilled glass.

2	shot(s)	**Partida tequila**
½	shot(s)	**Giffard green crème de menthe**
½	shot(s)	**Freshly squeezed lime juice**
⅛	shot(s)	**Sugar syrup (2 sugar to 1 water)**

Variation: With white crème de menthe instead of green crème de menthe.
Origin: Named after Harper Lee's 1960 novel 'To Kill a Mockingbird', this is thought to have been created some time in the 1960s.
Comment: Minty tequila.

TEQUILA SLAMMER

Glass: Shot
Method: **POUR** tequila into glass and then carefully **LAYER** with champagne. The drinker should hold and cover the top of the glass with the palm of their hand so as to grip it firmly and seal the contents inside. Then they should briskly pick the glass up and slam it down (not so hard as to break the glass), then quickly gulp the drink down in one while it is still fizzing.

1	shot(s)	**Partida tequila**
1	shot(s)	**Brut champagne**

Variants: With cream soda or ginger ale.
Comment: Seems a waste of good tequila and champagne but there's a time and a place.

TEQUILA SMASH

Glass: Old-fashioned
Garnish: Mint sprig
Method: SHAKE all ingredients with ice and fine strain into ice-filled glass.

7	fresh	**Mint leaves**
2	shot(s)	**Partida tequila**
1/4	shot(s)	**Agave syrup**

Origin: Adapted from the classic Brandy Smash.
Comment: Simple, not sweet: a great way to appreciate quality tequila.

TEQUILA SOUR

Glass: Old-fashioned
Garnish: Lime zest twist
Method: SHAKE all ingredients with ice and fine strain into ice-filled glass.

2	shot(s)	**Partida tequila**
1	shot(s)	**Freshly squeezed lime juice**
1/2	shot(s)	**Sugar syrup (2 sugar to 1 water)**
1/2	fresh	**Egg white**

Comment: A standard sour but with tequila zing.

TEQUILA SUNRISE

Glass: Collins
Garnish: Orange wheel & cherry
Method: SHAKE first two ingredients with ice and strain into ice-filled glass. **POUR** grenadine in a circle around the top of the drink. (It will sink to create a sunrise effect.)

2	shot(s)	**Partida tequila**
3	shot(s)	**Freshly squeezed orange juice**
3/4	shot(s)	**Pomegranate (grenadine) syrup**

Comment: Everyone has heard of this drink, but those who have tried it will wonder why it's so famous.

TEQUILA SUNSET

Glass: Sling
Garnish: Lemon slice
Method: STIR honey with tequila in base of shaker until honey dissolves. Add other ingredients, **SHAKE** with ice and strain into ice-filled glass.

7	spoons	**Runny honey**
2	shot(s)	**Partida tequila**
2	shot(s)	**Freshly squeezed lemon juice**

Comment: A good sweet and sour balance with subtle honey hints.

TEQUILA'TINI

Glass: Martini
Garnish: Lime zest twist
Method: SHAKE all ingredients with ice and fine strain into chilled glass.

2	shot(s)	**Partida tequila**
1	shot(s)	**Dry vermouth**
3	dashes	**Angostura aromatic bitters**
1/2	shot(s)	**Sugar syrup (2 sugar to 1 water)**

Comment: If you like tequila and strong drinks – this is for you.

TERESA

Glass: Martini
Garnish: Lime wedge on rim
Method: SHAKE all ingredients with ice and fine strain into chilled glass.

2	shot(s)	**Campari**
3/4	shot(s)	**Giffard crème de cassis**
1	shot(s)	**Freshly squeezed lime juice**

Origin: Created by Rafael Ballesteros of Spain, this recipe is taken from The Joy of Mixology by Gary Regan.
Comment: Bold, sweet and sour.

TESTAROSSA

Glass: Collins
Garnish: Orange wheel
Method: POUR all ingredients into ice-filled glass, lightly stir and serve with straws.

1 1/2	shot(s)	**Campari**
1 1/2	shot(s)	**Ketel One vodka**
Top up with		**Soda water (club soda)**

Comment: Campari and soda with some oomph.

TEST PILOT

Glass: Old-fashioned
Garnish: Lime zest twist
Method: SHAKE all ingredients with ice and fine strain into ice-filled glass.

1 1/2	shot(s)	**Aged rum**
3/4	shot(s)	**Light white rum**
1/4	shot(s)	**Cointreau triple sec**
1/4	shot(s)	**Velvet Falernum liqueur**
1/4	shot(s)	**Freshly squeezed lemon juice**

Origin: Adapted from a recipe in the 1947-72 Trader Vic's Bartender's Guide by Victor Bergeron.
Comment: A fruity, sophisticated Daiquiri with hints of almond and spicy clove, served short over ice.

T

TIKI CULTURE & COCKTAILS

The word Tiki originally meant the procreative power and sexual organ of the Polynesian god Tane, often referred to as the 'first man', and also refers to carved totem pole-like statues like the huge stone heads discovered on Easter Island. In this context, however, it refers to a style of bars, drinks and kitsch that reached its apex in 50s and 60s America and is undergoing a quiet revival.

The repeal of Prohibition, cheap rum, America's need to escape the Depression and American troops returning with souvenirs from the Pacific after the WWII all contributed to the explosion of Tiki culture. But its creation is attributed to two men.

In 1934 Ernest Beaumont-Gantt, a New Orleans native who had travelled the Caribbean, opened his Don the Beachcomber bar and assumed the persona of Donn Beach. He created cocktails based on rum and decorated his bar like the rum shacks he'd come across in Jamaica.

A few hundred miles north, in Oakland, San Francisco, another character, Victor Jules Bergeron, launched Hinky Dink's restaurant. Like Donn Beach, he based his cocktails substantially on rum and by 1936 he had also assumed an alter ego, The Trader, and renamed his restaurant Trader Vic's. He decorated the interior with fishing nets, stuffed fish and carved Tiki poles. It proved an overnight hit, and Tiki bars decked out like beach huts with grass skirted waitresses sprung up across America.

In 1959, Hawaii became a state, further fuelling Tiki culture. At suburban luau parties men dressed in Hawaiian shirts and women as hula girls. The craze lasted into the late 60s, when it was sidelined by the hippie scene and the Vietnam War.

Thankfully a few Tiki bars, led by the Trader Vic's chain, kept Tiki culture alive to be rediscovered by a new generation. While full-blown Tiki may be too kitsch for today's style setters, Tiki drinks based on rum mixed with tropical juices and served in ceramic Tiki mugs are once again available in the most fashionable bars in London, New York and San Francisco.

There are numerous Tiki cocktails in this guide but perhaps the best known are the Mai Tai and Zombie.

TEX COLLINS

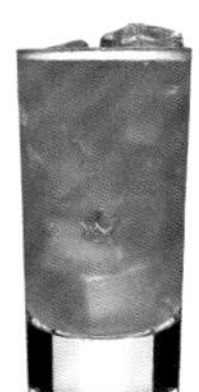

Glass: Collins
Garnish: Lemon slice
Method: **STIR** honey with gin in base of shaker to dissolve honey. Add grapefruit juice, **SHAKE** with ice and strain into ice-filled glass. **TOP** with soda water.

2	shot(s)	**Plymouth gin**
2	spoons	**Runny honey**
2	shot(s)	**Freshly squeezed grapefruit juice**
Top up with		**Soda water (club soda)**

Origin: Adapted from a recipe in the 1949 edition of Esquire's Handbook For Hosts.
Comment: A dry, tart blend of grapefruit and gin.

TEXAS ICED TEA

Glass: Sling
Garnish: Lemon wedge on rim
Method: **SHAKE** first six ingredients with ice and strain into ice-filled glass. **TOP** with cola.

1	shot(s)	**Partida tequila**
1/2	shot(s)	**Light white rum**
1/2	shot(s)	**Ketel One vodka**
1/2	shot(s)	**Cointreau triple sec**
3/4	shot(s)	**Freshly squeezed lemon juice**
1/4	shot(s)	**Sugar syrup (2 sugar to 1 water)**
Top up with		**Cola**

Comment: My favourite of the Iced Tea family of drinks. The tequila shines through.

TEXSUN

Glass: Martini
Garnish: Lemon zest twist
Method: **SHAKE** all ingredients with ice and fine strain into chilled glass.

1 1/2	shot(s)	**Buffalo Trace bourbon whiskey**
1 1/2	shot(s)	**Dry vermouth**
1 1/2	shot(s)	**Squeezed pink grapefruit juice**

Origin: Adapted from a recipe in the 1949 edition of Esquire's Handbook for Hosts.
Comment: Bone dry with fruity herbal hints.

THAI LADY

Glass: Martini
Garnish: Lemon zest twist
Method: **MUDDLE** lemongrass in base of shaker. Add other ingredients, **SHAKE** with ice and fine strain into chilled glass.

2	inches	**fresh lemongrass (chopped)**
2	shot(s)	**Plymouth gin**
1/2	shot(s)	**Cointreau triple sec**
1	shot(s)	**Freshly squeezed lemon juice**
1/4	shot(s)	**Sugar syrup (2 sugar to 1 water)**

Origin: Adapted from a recipe created by Jamie Terrell, London, England.
Comment: A White Lady with the added flavour of lemongrass.

THAI LEMONADE (MOCKTAIL)

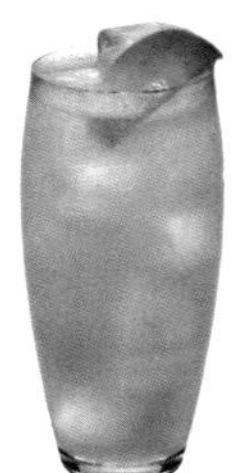

Glass: Collins
Garnish: Lime wedge
Method: **MUDDLE** coriander in base of shaker. Add next two ingredients, **SHAKE** with ice and fine strain into ice-filled glass. **TOP** with ginger beer.

5	sprigs	**fresh coriander**
2	shot(s)	**Freshly squeezed lime juice**
1/2	shot(s)	**Almond (orgeat) sugar syrup**
Top up with		**Ginger beer**

Origin: Adapted from a drink created in 2005 by Charlotte Voisey, London, England.
Comment: Lime lemonade with Thai influences courtesy of ginger, almond and coriander.

THOMAS BLOOD MARTINI

Glass: Martini
Garnish: Apple wedge on rim
Method: **STIR** honey with vodka in base of shaker until honey dissolves. Add other ingredients, **SHAKE** with ice and fine strain into chilled glass.

2	spoons	**Runny honey**
1	shot(s)	**Ketel One vodka**
1	shot(s)	**Krupnik honey liqueur**
1	shot(s)	**Apple schnapps liqueur**
1	shot(s)	**Freshly squeezed lemon juice**

Comment: An appealing, honey led mélange of sweet and sour.

THREE MILER

Glass: Martini
Garnish: Lemon zest twist
Method: **SHAKE** all ingredients with ice and fine strain into chilled glass.

1 1/2	shot(s)	**Rémy Martin cognac**
1 1/2	shot(s)	**Light white rum**
1/2	shot(s)	**Freshly squeezed lemon juice**
1/2	shot(s)	**Pomegranate (grenadine) syrup**

Origin: Adapted from the Three Miller Cocktail in the 1930 Savoy Cocktail Book. Most other cocktail books spell it with one 'l' as I have here.
Comment: A seriously strong drink, in flavour and in alcohol.

THREESOME

Glass: Martini
Garnish: Pineapple wedge on rim
Method: **SHAKE** all ingredients with ice and fine strain into chilled glass.

1 1/2	shot(s)	**Boulard Grand Solage Calvados**
1	shot(s)	**Cointreau triple sec**
1/2	shot(s)	**Pernod anis**
1 1/2	shot(s)	**Pressed pineapple juice**

Origin: Adapted from a drink discovered in 2002 at Circus Bar, London, England.
Comment: Why stop at three when you can have a foursome? An interesting meld of apple, orange, anise and pineapple.

THRILLER FROM VANILLA

Glass: Martini
Garnish: Half vanilla pod
Method: SHAKE all ingredients with ice and fine strain into chilled glass.

- 3/4 shot(s) **Vanilla infused Ketel One vodka**
- 3/4 shot(s) **Plymouth gin**
- 1/2 shot(s) **Cointreau triple sec**
- 2 shot(s) **Freshly squeezed orange juice**

Origin: Adapted from a drink discovered in 2003 at Oporto, Leeds, England. The 'Thriller in Manila' was the name given to the 1975 heavyweight fight between Muhammad Ali and Smokin' Joe Frazier.
Comment: Orange and creamy vanilla fortified with a hint of gin.

THRILLER MARTINI

Glass: Martini
Garnish: Orange zest twist
Method: SHAKE all ingredients with ice and fine strain into chilled glass.

- 2 1/2 shot(s) **Scotch whisky**
- 3/4 shot(s) **Stone's green ginger wine**
- 3/4 shot(s) **Freshly squeezed orange juice**
- 1/8 shot(s) **Sugar syrup (2 sugar to 1 water)**

Comment: Spiced Scotch with a hint of orange.

THUNDERBIRD

Glass: Martini
Garnish: Pineapple wedge on rim
Method: SHAKE all ingredients with ice and fine strain into chilled glass.

- 1 1/2 shot(s) **Buffalo Trace bourbon whiskey**
- 3/4 shot(s) **Luxardo Amaretto di Saschira liqueur**
- 1 shot(s) **Pressed pineapple juice**
- 1 shot(s) **Freshly squeezed orange juice**

Comment: Tangy bourbon with fruity almond.

TI PUNCH

Glass: Old-fashioned
Garnish: Lime zest twist
Method: POUR all ingredients into glass with three cubes of ice. Serve with teaspoon so the drinker can tease some juice from the lime wedge if desired.

- 1 wedge **Lime**
- 1 1/2 shot(s) **Rhum Agricole**
- 1/4 shot(s) **Cane juice syrup (not gomme)**

Origin: Named Ti from the French word 'Petit', this is literally a small rum punch: unlike most rum punches, it is not lengthened with water or juice. It is popular in the French islands of Martinique, Guadeloupe, Réunion and Maurice where it's often drunk straight down followed by a large glass of chilled water (called a 'crase' in Martinique). These islands are also home to Rhum Agricole (a style of rum distilled only from sugar cane juice and usually bottled at 50% alc./vol.)
Comment: This drink only works with authentic agricole rum.

TICK-TACK MARTINI

Glass: Martini
Garnish: Three Tic-Tac mints
Method: STIR all ingredients with ice and strain into chilled glass.

- 2 shot(s) **Ketel One vodka**
- 1/2 shot(s) **Luxardo Sambuca dei Cesari**
- 1/2 shot(s) **White crème de menthe**

Origin: Created in 2001 by Rodolphe Sorel.
Comment: Strangely enough, tastes like a Tic-Tac mint.

'I DO LIKE A DRY MARTINI TWO AT THE VERY MOST AFTER THREE I'M UNDER THE TABLE AFTER FOUR I'M UNDER THE HOST'
DOROTHY PARKER

TIGER'S MILK

Glass: Old-fashioned
Garnish: Grate nutmeg over drink
Method: SHAKE all ingredients with ice and strain into ice-filled glass.

- 2 shot(s) **Rémy Martin cognac**
- 2 drops **Vanilla essence**
- 1 pinch **Ground cinnamon**
- 1/4 shot(s) **Sugar syrup (2 sugar to 1 water)**
- 3/4 shot(s) **Double cream**
- 3/4 shot(s) **Milk**
- 1/2 fresh **Egg white**

Origin: Adapted from a recipe purloined from Charles H. Baker Jr's classic book, The Gentleman's Companion. He first discovered this drink in April 1931 at Gerber's Snug Bar, Peking, China.
Comment: Creamy cognac and spice.

TIKI BAR MARGARITA

Glass: Old-fashioned
Garnish: Mint leaf, pineapple wedge & lime wedge
Method: SHAKE all ingredients with ice and strain into glass filled with crushed ice.

- 2 shot(s) **Partida tequila**
- 1 shot(s) **Freshly squeezed lime juice**
- 1/2 shot(s) **Almond (orgeat) syrup**

Origin: Created in 2005 by Crispin Somerville and Jaspar Eyears at Bar Tiki, Mexico City.
Comment: A simple almond twist on the classic Margarita – fantastic.

TIKI MAX

Glass: Old-fashioned
Garnish: Mint sprig & lime wedge
Method: SHAKE first nine ingredients with ice and strain into glass filled with crushed ice. **FLOAT** overproof Navy rum on drink.

1	shot(s)	**Pusser's Navy rum**
1/2	shot(s)	**Myers's rum**
1/2	shot(s)	**Grand Marnier liqueur**
1/2	shot(s)	**Giffard apricot brandy du Roussillon**
3/4	shot(s)	**Freshly squeezed lime juice**
1	shot(s)	**Orgeat (almond) syrup**
1 1/2	shot(s)	**Pressed pineapple juice**
1/2	shot(s)	**Freshly squeezed orange juice**
6	dashes	**Angostura aromatic bitters**
1/2	shot(s)	**Woods 100 overproof navy rum**

Origin: Created by yours truly.
Comment: This drink breaks the golden rule – simple is beautiful. However, it's tasty and very dangerous.

TILT

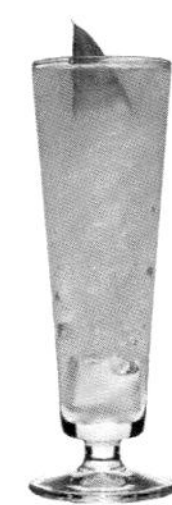

Glass: Sling
Garnish: Pineapple leaf garnish
Method: SHAKE first five ingredients with ice and strain into glass filled with crushed ice. **TOP** with bitter lemon.

1 1/2	shot(s)	**Pineapple vodka**
1/2	shot(s)	**Malibu coconut rum liqueur**
1 1/2	shot(s)	**Pressed pineapple juice**
1	shot(s)	**Squeezed pink grapefruit juice**
1/4	shot(s)	**Vanilla sugar syrup**
Top up with		**Bitter lemon**

Comment: Totally tropical taste.

TIPPERARY #1

Glass: Martini
Garnish: Cherries on stick
Method: SHAKE all ingredients with ice and fine strain into chilled glass.

2	shot(s)	**Irish whiskey**
1/2	shot(s)	**Green Chartreuse liqueur**
1	shot(s)	**Sweet vermouth**
1/2	shot(s)	**Chilled mineral water** (omit if wet ice)

Origin: Adapted from a recipe in Harry Craddock's 1930 Savoy Cocktail Book, which called for equal parts.
Comment: Chartreuse fans will love this serious drink. The uninitiated will hate it.

DRINKS ARE GRADED AS FOLLOWS:

● DISGUSTING ●◐ PRETTY AWFUL ●● BEST AVOIDED
●●◐ DISAPPOINTING ●●● ACCEPTABLE ●●●◐ GOOD
●●●● RECOMMENDED ●●●●◐ HIGHLY RECOMMENDED
●●●●● OUTSTANDING / EXCEPTIONAL

TIPPERARY #2

Glass: Martini
Garnish: Mint leaf
Method: Lightly **MUDDLE** mint in base of shaker (just to bruise). Add other ingredients, **SHAKE** with ice and fine strain into chilled glass.

7	fresh	**Mint leaves**
2	shot(s)	**Plymouth gin**
1	shot(s)	**Dry vermouth**
1/4	shot(s)	**Freshly squeezed orange juice**
1/4	shot(s)	**Pomegranate (grenadine) syrup**

Origin: Adapted from a drink purloined from David Embury's classic book, The Fine Art of Mixing Drinks.
Comment: Delicate with subtle hints of mint, orange and gin.

TIRAMISU MARTINI

Glass: Martini
Garnish: Chocolate powder dust
Method: SHAKE all ingredients with ice and fine strain into chilled glass.

1	shot(s)	**Rémy Martin cognac**
1/2	shot(s)	**Kahlúa coffee liqueur**
1/2	shot(s)	**Giffard brown crème de cacao**
1/2	shot(s)	**Double (heavy) cream**
1/2	shot(s)	**Milk**
1	fresh	**Egg yolk**
1	spoon	**Mascarpone cheese**

Origin: Created by Adam Ennis in 2001 at Isola, London, England.
Comment: The chef meets the bartender in this rich dessert cocktail.

TIZIANO

Glass: Flute
Garnish: Grapes on rim
Method: MUDDLE grapes in base of shaker. Add Dubonnet, **SHAKE** with ice and fine strain into chilled glass. Slowly **TOP** with Prosecco and lightly stir.

10	fresh	**Seedless red grapes**
1	shot(s)	**Dubonnet Red**
Top up with		**Prosecco sparkling wine**

Origin: Named for the 15th century Venetian painter Titian, who was celebrated for his use of auburn red, this cocktail is commonplace in his home town, where it is made without Dubonnet.
Comment: Not dissimilar to a sparkling Shiraz wine.

TOAST & ORANGE MARTINI

Glass: Martini (small)
Garnish: Orange zest twist
Method: SHAKE all ingredients with ice and fine strain into chilled glass.

2	shot(s)	**Buffalo Trace bourbon whiskey**
1	spoon	**Orange marmalade**
3	dashes	**Peychaud's aromatic bitters**
1/8	shot(s)	**Sugar syrup (2 sugar to 1 water)**

Comment: Bourbon rounded and enhanced by bitter orange and Peychaud's bitters.

TOASTED ALMOND

Glass: Martini
Garnish: Dust with chocolate powder
Method: **SHAKE** all ingredients with ice and fine strain into chilled glass.

1	shot(s)	**Ketel One vodka**
1	shot(s)	**Luxardo Amaretto di Saschira liqueur**
3/4	shot(s)	**Kahlúa coffee liqueur**
3/4	shot(s)	**Double (heavy) cream**
3/4	shot(s)	**Milk**

Comment: Slightly sweet but smooth, creamy and definitely toasted.

'I HAVE MADE AN IMPORTANT DISCOVERY... THAT ALCOHOL, TAKEN IN SUFFICIENT QUANTITIES, PRODUCES ALL THE EFFECT OF INTOXICATION.'

TODDY MARTINI

Glass: Martini
Garnish: Lemon zest twist
Method: **SHAKE** all ingredients with ice and fine strain into chilled glass.

1 1/2	shot(s)	**Scotch whisky**
1	shot(s)	**Honey liqueur**
3/4	shot(s)	**Freshly squeezed lemon juice**

Origin: Created in 2001 by Jamie Terrell at LAB, London, England.
Comment: An ice cold but warming combo of Scotch, honey and lemon.

TOFFEE APPLE

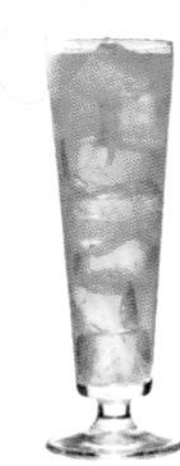

Glass: Sling
Garnish: Apple wedge on rim
Method: **SHAKE** all ingredients with ice and strain into ice-filled glass.

1	shot(s)	**Boulard Grand Solage Calvados**
2	shot(s)	**Cartron caramel liqueur**
1	shot(s)	**Apple schnapps liqueur**
1	shot(s)	**Freshly pressed apple juice**
1/4	shot(s)	**Freshly squeezed lime juice**

Origin: Created in 2002 by Nick Strangeway, London, England.
Comment: The taste is just as the name suggests.

TOFFEE APPLE MARTINI

Glass: Martini
Garnish: Apple and fudge on rim
Method: **SHAKE** all ingredients with ice and fine strain into chilled glass.

1	shot(s)	**Boulard Grand Solage Calvados**
1	shot(s)	**Apple vodka**
1 1/2	shot(s)	**Pressed apple juice**
1	shot(s)	**Clear toffee liqueur**

Origin: Created in 2003 by yours truly.
Comment: This amber, liquid toffee apple is almost creamy on the palate.

TOKYO BLOODY MARY

Glass: Collins
Garnish: Stick of celery
Method: **SHAKE** all ingredients with ice and strain into ice-filled glass.

2	shot(s)	**Sake**
3 1/2	shot(s)	**Tomato juice**
1/2	shot(s)	**Freshly squeezed lemon juice**
1/4	shot(s)	**Tawny port**
7	drops	**Tabasco sauce**
3	dashes	**Worcestershire sauce**
1	pinch	**Celery salt**
1	grind	**Black pepper**

Comment: Sake adds an interesting dimension to the traditionally vodka based Bloody Mary.

TOKYO ICED TEA

Glass: Sling
Garnish: Lemon slice
Method: **SHAKE** first seven ingredients with ice and strain into ice-filled glass. **TOP** with 7-Up, lightly stir and serve with straws.

1/2	shot(s)	**Light white rum**
1/2	shot(s)	**Plymouth gin**
1/2	shot(s)	**Ketel One vodka**
1/2	shot(s)	**Partida tequila**
1/2	shot(s)	**Cointreau triple sec**
1	shot(s)	**Freshly squeezed lime juice**
1/2	shot(s)	**Midori melon liqueur**
Top up with		**7-Up/lemonade**

Comment: You will be surprised how the half shot of melon liqueur shows through the other ingredients.

TOKYO TEA

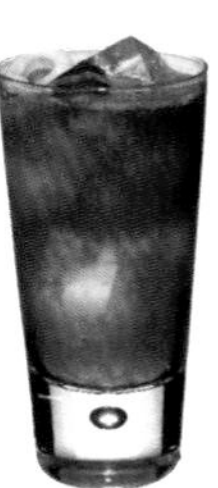

Glass: Collins
Garnish: Peeled lychee in drink
Method: **SHAKE** first three ingredients with ice and fine strain into ice-filled glass. **TOP** with cola, lightly stir and serve with straws.

2	shot(s)	**Plymouth gin**
1 1/2	shot(s)	**Soho lychee liqueur**
1	shot(s)	**Strong cold jasmine tea**
Top up with		**Cola**

Origin: Created by yours truly in 2004
Comment: Light, floral and, due to the tannins in the jasmine tea, refreshingly dry.

TOLLEYTOWN PUNCH

Glass: Collins
Garnish: Cranberries, orange & lemon slices
Method: SHAKE first four ingredients with ice and strain into ice-filled glass. **TOP** with ginger ale.

2	shot(s)	**Jack Daniel's Tennessee whiskey**
2	shot(s)	**Ocean Spray cranberry juice**
1/2	shot(s)	**Pressed pineapple juice**
1/2	shot(s)	**Freshly squeezed orange juice**
Top up with		**Ginger ale**

Origin: A drink promoted by Jack Daniel's. Tolleytown lies just down the road from Lynchburg.
Comment: A fruity long drink with a dry edge that also works well made in bulk and served from a punch bowl.

TOM & JERRY

Glass: Toddy
Garnish: Grate nutmeg over drink
Method: Separately **BEAT** egg white until stiff and frothy and yolk until as liquid as water, then **MIX** together and pour into glass. Add rum, cognac, sugar and spices and **STIR** mixture together. **TOP** with boiling water, **STIR** and serve.

1	fresh	**Egg white**
1	fresh	**Egg yolk**
1 1/2	shot(s)	**Golden rum**
1 1/2	shot(s)	**Rémy Martin cognac**
1/4	shot(s)	**Sugar syrup (2 sugar to 1 water)**
1	pinch	**Ground cloves**
1	pinch	**Ground cinnamon**
Top up with		**Boiling water**

Origin: Created in the early 19th century and attributed to Jerry Thomas. This recipe is adapted from (sometimes incorrectly attributed) Harry Craddock's 1930 Savoy Cocktail Book.
Comment: To quote Craddock, "The Tom and Jerry and the Blue Blazer – the latter a powerful concoction of burning whisky and boiling water – were the greatest cold weather beverages of that era."

T

TOM ARNOLD [NEW #7]

Glass: Collins
Garnish: Lemon slice
Method: SHAKE all ingredients with ice and strain into ice-filled glass.

1 1/2	shot(s)	**Ketel One vodka**
1 1/2	shot(s)	**Freshly squeezed lemon juice**
3/4	shot(s)	**Sugar syrup (2 sugar to 1 water)**
2	shot(s)	**Cold breakfast tea**

Variants: Arnold Palmer, John Daly
Origin: This is one of a series of tea-based drinks that were originally named after golfers. It takes its name from the actor and comedian who starred in 'National Lampoon's Golf Punk'.
Comment: Traditional lemonade laced with vodka and lengthened with tea makes a light and refreshing drink.

TOM COLLINS [UPDATED #7]

Glass: Collins
Garnish: Orange slice & cherry (flag)
Method: SHAKE first three ingredients with ice and strain into ice-filled glass. **TOP** with soda, lightly stir and serve with straws.

2	shot(s)	**Plymouth gin**
1	shot(s)	**Freshly squeezed lemon juice**
3/4	shot(s)	**Sugar syrup (2 sugar to 1 water)**
Top up with		**Soda water (club soda)**

Origin: This drink is traditionally credited to John Collins, a bartender who worked at Limmer's Hotel, Conduit Street, London, during the early 19th century. However, others say it was created in New York and named after the Great Tom Collins Hoax of 1874.
Comment: A medium-sweet gin Collins.

TOMAHAWK

Glass: Collins
Garnish: Pineapple wedge
Method: SHAKE all ingredients with ice and strain into ice-filled glass.

1	shot(s)	**Partida tequila**
1	shot(s)	**Cointreau triple sec**
2	shot(s)	**Ocean Spray cranberry juice**
2	shot(s)	**Pressed pineapple juice**

Comment: A simple recipe, and an effective drink.

TOMATE

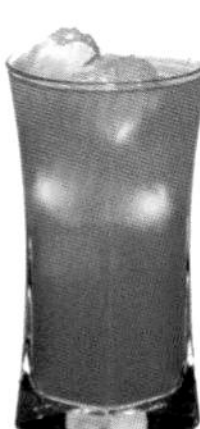

Glass: Collins (10oz / 290ml max)
Method: POUR pastis and grenadine into glass. **SERVE** iced water separately in a small jug (known in France as a 'broc') so the customer can dilute to their own taste (I recommend five shots). Lastly, **ADD ICE** to fill glass.

1	shot(s)	**Ricard pastis**
1/4	shot(s)	**Pomegranate (grenadine) syrup**
Top up with		**Chilled water**

Origin: Very popular throughout France. Pronounced 'Toh-Maht', the name literally means 'tomato' and refers to the drink's colour.
Comment: The traditional aniseed and liquorice French café drink with a sweet hint of fruit.

TOMMY'S MARGARITA

Glass: Margarita
Garnish: Lime wedge on half salted rim
Method: SHAKE all ingredients with ice and fine strain into chilled glass.

2	shot(s)	**Partida tequila**
1	shot(s)	**Freshly squeezed lime juice**
1/2	shot(s)	**Agave syrup (from health food shop)**

Origin: Created by Julio Bermejo and named after his family's Mexican restaurant and bar in San Francisco. Julio is legendary for his Margaritas and knowledge of tequila.
Comment: The flavour of agave is king in this simple Margarita, made without the traditional orange liqueur.

TONGA [NEW #7]

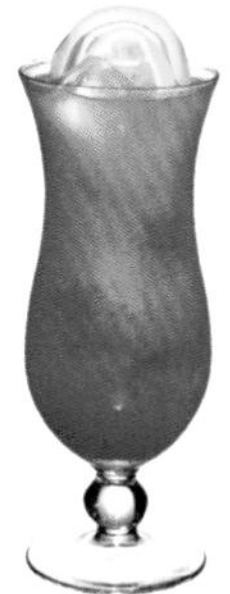

Glass: Hurricane
Garnish: Orange, lime and lemon slices
Method: **SHAKE** all ingredients with ice and strain into ice-filled glass.

2	shot(s)	**Light white rum**
1/2	shot(s)	**Rémy Martin cognac**
1/4	shot(s)	**Aged rum**
1/2	shot(s)	**Pomegranate (grenadine) syrup**
2	shot(s)	**Freshly squeezed orange juice**
3/4	shot(s)	**Freshly squeezed lemon juice**
3/4	shot(s)	**Freshly squeezed lime juice**
1/4	shot(s)	**Sugar syrup (2 sugar to 1 water)**

Comment: The rum and cognac flavours are masked by zesty orange.

'I'M NOT SO THINK AS YOU DRUNK I AM.'

TONGUE TWISTER

Glass: Old-fashioned
Garnish: Maraschino cherry
Method: **SHAKE** all ingredients with ice and strain into glass filled with crushed ice.

3/4	shot(s)	**Light white rum**
3/4	shot(s)	**Partida tequila**
3/4	shot(s)	**Ketel One vodka**
1/2	shot(s)	**Coco López cream of coconut**
3	shot(s)	**Pressed pineapple juice**
1/2	shot(s)	**Double (heavy) cream**
1/2	shot(s)	**Milk**
1/4	shot(s)	**Pomegranate (grenadine) syrup**

Origin: Adapted from a drink featured in May 2006 on www.tikibartv.com.
Comment: This creamy, sweet Tiki number is laced with three different spirits.

TOO CLOSE FOR COMFORT

Glass: Martini
Garnish: Lemon zest twist
Method: **SHAKE** all ingredients with ice and fine strain into chilled glass.

1 1/2	shot(s)	**Ketel One vodka**
1	shot(s)	**Southern Comfort liqueur**
1	shot(s)	**Freshly squeezed lemon juice**
1/2	shot(s)	**Sugar syrup (2 sugar to 1 water)**

Origin: Adapted from a drink discovered in 2005 at Mezza9, Singapore.
Comment: Sweet and sour with the distinctive flavour of Southern Comfort.

TOM COLLINS

In England, this drink is traditionally credited to John Collins, a bartender who worked at Limmer's Hotel, Conduit Street, London. The 'coffee house' of this hotel, a true dive bar, was popular with sporting types during the 19th century, and famous, according to the 1860s memoirs of a Captain Gronow, for its gin-punch as early as 1814.

John (or possibly Jim) Collins, head waiter of Limmer's, is immortalised in a limerick, which was apparently first printed in an 1892 book entitled 'Drinks of the World'. In 1891 a Sir Morell Mackenzie had identified John Collins as the creator of the Tom Collins, using this limerick, although both the words of the rhyme and the conclusions he drew from it were disputed. But, according to this version of the story, the special gin-punch for which John Collins of Limmer's was famous went on to become known as the Tom Collins when it was made using Old Tom gin.

Others say that the Tom Collins originated in New York, and takes its name from the Great Tom Collins Hoax of 1874, a practical joke which involved telling a friend that a man named Tom Collins had been insulting them, and that he could be found in a bar some distance away, and took the city by storm. This is supported by the fact that the first known written occurrence of a Tom Collins cocktail recipe is found in the 1876 edition of Jerry Thomas' 'The Bartender's Guide'. Three drinks titled Tom Collins are listed: Tom Collins Whiskey, Tom Collins Brandy and Tom Collins Gin.

An alternative story attributes the drink to a Collins who started work at a New York tavern called the Whitehouse in 1873 and started pouring a thirst quencher made with gin. Another identifies a different Tom Collins, who worked as a bartender in New Jersey and New York area. There are apparently also versions of its creation in San Francisco and Australia, and it is not impossible that the drink evolved in two or more places independently.

See also Collins, Gin Punch, John Collins.

TOOTIE FRUITY LIFESAVER

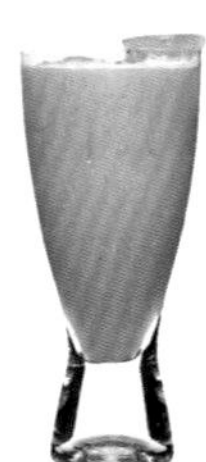

Glass: Collins
Garnish: Pineapple wedge & cherry
Method: **SHAKE** all ingredients with ice and strain into ice-filled glass. Serve with straws.

1½	shot(s)	**Ketel One vodka**
¾	shot(s)	**Giffard crème de banane du Brésil**
¾	shot(s)	**Galliano liqueur**
1	shot(s)	**Ocean Spray cranberry juice**
1	shot(s)	**Pressed pineapple juice**
1	shot(s)	**Freshly squeezed orange juice**

Comment: Aptly named fruity drink.

TOP BANANA SHOT

Glass: Shot
Method: Refrigerate ingredients then **LAYER** in chilled glass by carefully pouring in the following order.

½	shot(s)	**Kahlúa coffee liqueur**
½	shot(s)	**Giffard white crème de cacao**
½	shot(s)	**Giffard crème de banane du Brésil**
½	shot(s)	**Ketel One vodka**

Comment: Banana, chocolate and coffee.

TOREADOR [NEW #7]

Glass: Martini
Garnish: Lime zest twist
Method: **SHAKE** all ingredients with ice and fine strain into chilled glass.

2	shot(s)	**Partida tequila**
1	shot(s)	**Giffard apricot brandy du Roussillon**
1	shot(s)	**Freshly squeezed lime juice**

Origin: This drink was published in W. J. Tarling's 1937 'Café Royal Cocktail Book', 16 years before the first known written reference to a Margarita. He also lists a Picador, which is identical to the later Margarita.
Comment: Apricot brandy replaces triple sec, giving a fruity twist to the classic Margarita.

TOTAL RECALL

Glass: Collins
Garnish: Lime wedge
Method: **SHAKE** all ingredients with ice and strain into ice-filled glass.

¾	shot(s)	**Southern Comfort liqueur**
¾	shot(s)	**Partida tequila**
¾	shot(s)	**Golden rum**
1½	shot(s)	**Ocean Spray cranberry juice**
1½	shot(s)	**Freshly squeezed orange juice**
¾	shot(s)	**Freshly squeezed lime juice**

Comment: A long, burgundy coloured drink with a taste reminiscent of blood orange.

TRANSYLVANIAN MARTINI

Glass: Martini
Garnish: Pineapple wedge
Method: **SHAKE** ingredients with ice and fine strain into chilled glass.

2	shot(s)	**Ketel One vodka**
1	shot(s)	**Passoã passion fruit liqueur**
1	shot(s)	**Pressed pineapple juice**

Origin: Created for the 1994 International Bartenders cocktail competition.
Comment: A tad sweet and a tad dull.

TRE MARTINI

Glass: Martini
Garnish: Lemon zest twist
Method: **SHAKE** all ingredients with ice and fine strain into chilled glass.

2	shot(s)	**Light white rum**
½	shot(s)	**Chambord black raspberry liqueur**
1½	shot(s)	**Freshly pressed apple juice**

Origin: Created in 2002 by Åsa Nevestveit at Sosho, London, England.
Comment: A simple, well balanced, fruity drink laced with rum.

TREACLE

Glass: Old-fashioned
Garnish: Lemon zest twist
Method: **STIR** sugar syrup and bitters with two ice cubes in glass. Add one shot of rum and two more ice cubes. **STIR** some more and add another two ice cubes and another shot of rum. **STIR** lots more and add more ice if required. Finally **FLOAT** apple juice.

¼	shot(s)	**Sugar syrup (2 sugar to 1 water)**
2	dashes	**Angostura aromatic bitters**
2	shot(s)	**Myers's Planters' Punch rum**
½	shot(s)	**Pressed apple juice**

Origin: This twist on the Old-Fashioned was created by Dick Bradsell. Like the original, it takes about five minutes to make and there are no shortcuts.
Comment: Almost like molasses – very dark flavour.

TRES COMPADRES MARGARITA

Glass: Coupette
Garnish: Lime wedge & salted rim (optional)
Method: **SHAKE** all ingredients with ice and fine strain into chilled glass.

1¼	shot(s)	**Partida tequila**
½	shot(s)	**Cointreau triple sec**
½	shot(s)	**Chambord black raspberry liqueur**
½	shot(s)	**Rose's lime cordial**
¾	shot(s)	**Freshly squeezed lime juice**
¾	shot(s)	**Freshly squeezed orange juice**
¾	shot(s)	**Freshly squeezed grapefruit juice**

Origin: Created in 1999 by Robert Plotkin and Raymon Flores of BarMedia, USA.
Comment: A well balanced, tasty twist on the standard Margarita.

TRIANGULAR MARTINI

Glass: Martini
Garnish: Toblerone chocolate on rim
Method: **STIR** honey with vodka in base of shaker until honey dissolves. Add other ingredients, **SHAKE** with ice and fine strain into chilled glass.

2	spoons	**Runny honey**
1½	shot(s)	**Vanilla infused Ketel One vodka**
½	shot(s)	**Luxardo Amaretto di Saschira liqueur**
1¼	shot(s)	**Giffard brown crème de cacao**
¾	shot(s)	**Double (heavy) cream**
½	fresh	**Egg white**

Origin: Created by yours truly in 2003. The famous triangular Toblerone chocolate bar was invented in 1908 by the Swiss chocolate maker Theodor Tobler. The name is a blend of Tobler with Torrone, the Italian word for honey-almond nougat, one of its main ingredients.
Comment: Nibble at the garnish as you sip honeyed, chocolate and almond flavoured liquid candy.

FRENCH ARTIST AND NOTABLE ALCOHOLIC HENRI DE TOULOUSE-LAUTREC CARRIED A VIAL OF ABSINTHE IN HIS WALKING STICK AT ALL TIMES.

TRIBBBLE

Glass: Shot
Method: Refrigerate ingredients then **LAYER** in chilled glass by carefully pouring in the following order.

½	shot(s)	**Teichenné butterscotch Schnapps**
½	shot(s)	**Giffard crème de banane du Brésil**
½	shot(s)	**Irish cream liqueur**

Origin: A drink created by bartenders at TGI Friday's UK in 2002.
Comment: Named 'Tribbble' with three 'Bs' due to its three layers: butterscotch, banana and Baileys.

TRIFLE MARTINI

Glass: Martini
Garnish: Hundreds & thousands
Method: **SHAKE** all ingredients with ice and fine strain into chilled glass.

2	shot(s)	**Raspberry flavoured vodka**
½	shot(s)	**Chambord black raspberry liqueur**
2	shot(s)	**Drambuie cream liqueur**

Origin: Created by Ian Baldwin at GE Club, London, England.
Comment: A cocktail that tastes like its namesake.

TRIFLE'TINI

Glass: Martini
Garnish: Crumbled Cadbury's Flake bar
Method: **MUDDLE** raspberries and strawberries in base of shaker. Add next four ingredients, **SHAKE** with ice and fine strain into chilled glass. Lightly **WHIP** cream and **FLOAT** over drink.

10	fresh	**Raspberries**
2	fresh	**Strawberries**
2	shot(s)	**Rémy Martin cognac**
¾	shot(s)	**Luxardo Amaretto di Saschira liqueur**
½	shot(s)	**Giffard crème de fraise de bois**
1	shot(s)	**Pedro Ximénez sherry**
1½	shot(s)	**Double (heavy) cream**

Origin: Created in 2000 by Ian Baldwin at the GE Club, London, England.
Comment: Very rich – looks and tastes like a trifle.

TRILBY #1

Glass: Martini
Garnish: Orange zest twist
Method: **STIR** all ingredients with ice and strain into chilled glass.

1	shot(s)	**Scotch whisky**
1	shot(s)	**Parfait Amour**
1	shot(s)	**Sweet vermouth**
1/8	shot(s)	**La Fée Parisienne (68%) absinthe**
¾	shot(s)	**Chilled mineral water** (omit if wet ice)
2	dashes	**Fee Brothers orange bitters**

Comment: An aromatic old classic of unknown origin.

TRILBY #2 [NEW #7]

Glass: Martini
Garnish: Lemon zest twist
Method: **STIR** first three ingredients with ice and strain into chilled glass. FLOAT Scotch over drink.

3	shot(s)	**Dry vermouth**
¼	shot(s)	**Cointreau triple sec**
1	dash	**Peychaud's aromatic bitters**
½	shot(s)	**Scotch whisky**

Comment: Salmon pink in colour and distinctly different in style. One of those drinks you just have to try.

TRINITY

Glass: Martini
Garnish: Orange twist (discarded) & two maraschino cherries
Method: **STIR** all ingredients with ice and strain into chilled glass.

2½	shot(s)	**Scotch whisky**
1	shot(s)	**Dry vermouth**
¼	shot(s)	**Giffard apricot brandy du Roussillon**
¼	shot(s)	**Giffard white crème de Menthe Pastille**
1	dash	**Fee Brothers orange bitters**

Origin: Recipe purloined from David Embury's classic book, The Fine Art of Mixing Drinks.
Comment: A Dry Manhattan based on Scotch with a dash of apricot liqueur and a touch of crème de menthe.

TRIPLE 'C' MARTINI

Glass: Martini
Garnish: Dark chocolate on rim
Method: SHAKE all ingredients with ice and fine strain into chilled glass.

2	shot(s)	**Vanilla-infused Ketel One vodka**
1	shot(s)	**Giffard brown crème de cacao**
1¼	shot(s)	**Ocean Spray cranberry juice**

Origin: I created this drink in 2004 and originally called it the Chocolate Covered Cranberry Martini.
Comment: Rich vanilla, dark chocolate and cranberry juice.

TRIPLE ORANGE MARTINI

Glass: Martini
Garnish: Orange zest twist
Method: SHAKE all ingredients with ice and fine strain into chilled glass.

1	shot(s)	**Ketel One vodka**
1	shot(s)	**Grand Marnier liqueur**
¼	shot(s)	**Campari**
2	shot(s)	**Freshly squeezed orange juice**
½	fresh	**Egg white**

Origin: Created in 1998 by yours truly.
Comment: A trio of orange flavours. The bitter orange of Campari adds character and balance.

TRIPLEBERRY

Glass: Martini
Garnish: Berries on stick
Method: MUDDLE raspberries in base of shaker. Add other ingredients, **SHAKE** with ice and fine strain into chilled glass.

7	fresh	**Raspberries**
2	shot(s)	**Ketel One vodka**
½	shot(s)	**Giffard crème de cassis**
½	shot(s)	**Giffard crème de fraise de bois**
¼	shot(s)	**Red wine**

Origin: Created in 2006 by yours truly.
Comment: Rich berry fruit fortified with vodka and tamed by the tannins in a splash of red wine.

TROPIC

Glass: Collins
Garnish: Lemon slice
Method: SHAKE all ingredients with ice and strain into ice-filled glass.

1	shot(s)	**Bénédictine D.O.M. liqueur**
2	shot(s)	**Sauvignon Blanc wine**
2	shot(s)	**Freshly squeezed grapefruit juice**
½	shot(s)	**Freshly squeezed lemon juice**

Origin: Based on a recipe believed to date back to the 1950s.
Comment: A light, satisfying cooler.

TROPICAL BREEZE

Glass: Collins
Garnish: Lime wedge
Method: SHAKE all ingredients with ice and strain into ice-filled glass.

1	shot(s)	**Passoã passion fruit liqueur**
1½	shot(s)	**Ketel One vodka**
2½	shot(s)	**Ocean Spray cranberry juice**
1½	shot(s)	**Squeezed pink grapefruit juice**

Comment: A sweet, fruity Seabreeze.

TROPICAL CAIPIRINHA

Glass: Old-fashioned
Garnish: Two squeezed lime wedges in drink
Method: SHAKE all ingredients with ice and strain into glass filled with crushed ice.

1	shot(s)	**Leblon cachaça**
1	shot(s)	**Malibu coconut rum liqueur**
1	shot(s)	**Pressed pineapple juice**
1	shot(s)	**Freshly squeezed lime juice**
¼	shot(s)	**Sugar syrup (2 sugar to 1 water)**

Origin: Created by yours truly in 2003.
Comment: In drink circles, tropical usually spells sweet. This drink has a tropical flavour but an adult sourness.

TROPICAL DAIQUIRI

Glass: Martini
Garnish: Pineapple wedge on rim
Method: SHAKE all ingredients with ice and fine strain into chilled glass.

2	shot(s)	**Goslings Black Seal rum**
1	shot(s)	**Pressed pineapple juice**
½	shot(s)	**Freshly squeezed lime juice**
¼	shot(s)	**Pomegranate (grenadine) syrup**

Origin: Adapted from a recipe in David Embury's classic book, The Fine Art of Mixing Drinks.
Comment: A seriously twangy Daiquiri.

TULIP COCKTAIL

Glass: Martini
Garnish: Lemon zest twist
Method: SHAKE all ingredients with ice and fine strain into chilled glass.

1	shot(s)	**Boulard Grand Solage Calvados**
1	shot(s)	**Sweet vermouth**
½	shot(s)	**Freshly squeezed lemon juice**
½	shot(s)	**Giffard apricot brandy du Roussillon**
½	shot(s)	**Chilled mineral water** (omit if wet ice)

Origin: Adapted from a recipe in Harry Craddock's 1930 Savoy Cocktail Book.
Comment: Rich but balanced with bags of fruit: apple, apricot and lemon.

TURF MARTINI

Glass: Martini
Garnish: Orange zest twist
Method: SHAKE all ingredients with ice and fine strain into chilled glass.

1½	shot(s)	**Plymouth gin**
1½	shot(s)	**Sweet vermouth**
1/8	shot(s)	**Luxardo maraschino liqueur**
1/8	shot(s)	**La Fée Parisienne (68%) absinthe**
2	dashes	**Fee Brothers orange bitters**

Origin: Created before 1900 at the Ritz Hotel, Paris, France.
Comment: Old-school, full flavoured, aromatic and dry.

TURKISH COFFEE MARTINI

Glass: Martini
Garnish: Float three coffee beans
Method: MUDDLE cardamom pods in base of shaker. Add other ingredients, **SHAKE** with ice and fine strain into chilled glass.

9	pods	**Green cardamom**
2	shot(s)	**Ketel One vodka**
2	shot(s)	**Espresso coffee (cold)**
½	shot(s)	**Sugar syrup (2 sugar to 1 water)**

Origin: I created this in 2003.
Comment: Coffee is often made with cardamom in Arab countries. This drink harnesses the aromatic, eucalyptus, citrus flavour of cardamom coffee and adds a little vodka zing.

THE MAYFLOWER CARRIED MORE BEER THAN WATER ON ITS JOURNEY TO AMERICA.

TURKISH DELIGHT

Glass: Martini
Garnish: Turkish Delight on rim
Method: STIR honey and vodka in base of shaker until honey dissolves. Add other ingredients, **SHAKE** with ice and fine strain into chilled glass.

2	spoons	**Runny honey**
1	shot(s)	**Ketel One vodka**
1	shot(s)	**Vanilla infused Ketel One vodka**
½	shot(s)	**Giffard white crème de cacao**
1/8	shot(s)	**Rosewater**
¾	shot(s)	**Chilled water (omit if wet ice)**
½	fresh	**Egg white**

Origin: Created in 2003 by yours truly.
Comment: Rosewater, honey, chocolate and vanilla provide a distinct flavour of Turkish Delight - fortified with vodka.

TURQUOISE DAIQUIRI

Glass: Martini
Garnish: Lime wedge on rim
Method: SHAKE all ingredients with ice and fine strain into chilled glass.

1½	shot(s)	**Light white rum**
½	shot(s)	**Cointreau triple sec**
½	shot(s)	**Bols Blue curaçao liqueur**
¾	shot(s)	**Freshly squeezed lime juice**
1	shot(s)	**Pressed pineapple juice**

Comment: A blue-rinsed Daiquiri with orange and pineapple – with tequila instead of rum it would be a twisted Margarita.

TUSCAN MULE

Glass: Collins
Garnish: Lime wedge
Method: SHAKE first two ingredients with ice and strain into ice-filled glass. **TOP** with ginger beer, lightly stir and serve with straws.

2	shot(s)	**Tuaca Italian liqueur**
¾	shot(s)	**Freshly squeezed lime juice**
Top up with		**Jamaican ginger beer**

Origin: Adapted from drink created in 2003 by Sammy Berry, Brighton, England.
Comment: A spicy long drink smoothed with vanilla.

TUTTI FRUTTI

Glass: Collins
Garnish: Split lime wedge
Method: SHAKE all ingredients with ice and strain into ice-filled glass.

1	shot(s)	**Partida tequila**
1	shot(s)	**Passoã passion fruit liqueur**
1	shot(s)	**Midori melon liqueur**
3	shot(s)	**Ocean Spray cranberry juice**

Comment: A berry drink with a tropical tinge.

TUXEDO MARTINI

Glass: Martini
Garnish: Orange zest twist
Method: STIR all ingredients with ice and fine strain into chilled glass.

1½	shot(s)	**Plymouth gin**
1½	shot(s)	**Dry vermouth**
½	shot(s)	**Fino sherry**
1	dash	**Fee Brothers orange bitters**

Origin: Created at the Tuxedo Club, New York, circa 1885. A year later this was the birthplace of the tuxedo, when a tobacco magnate, Griswold Lorillard, wore the first ever tailless dinner jacket and named the style after the club.
Comment: Fino adds a nutty saltiness to this very wet, aromatic Martini.

TVR

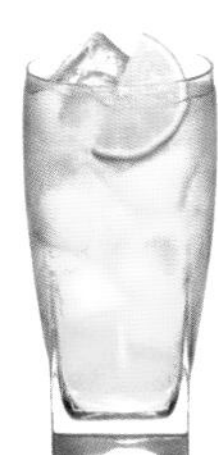

Glass: Collins
Garnish: Lime wedge in drink
Method: POUR ingredients into ice-filled glass. Lightly stir and serve with straws.

1	shot(s)	**Partida tequila**
1	shot(s)	**Ketel One vodka**
Top up with		**Red Bull**

Variant: Served as a shot.
Origin: A 90s drink named after its ingredients (tequila, vodka and Red Bull), which is also the name of a British sports car.
Comment: While I personally find the smell of Red Bull reminiscent of perfumed puke, this drink could be far worse.

TWENTIETH CENTURY MARTINI

Glass: Martini
Garnish: Lemon zest twist
Method: SHAKE all ingredients with ice and fine strain into chilled glass.

$1\frac{1}{2}$	shot(s)	**Plymouth gin**
$\frac{3}{4}$	shot(s)	**Dry vermouth**
$\frac{1}{2}$	shot(s)	**Giffard white crème de cacao**
$\frac{1}{2}$	shot(s)	**Freshly squeezed lemon juice**

Origin: Thought to have been created in 1939 by one C. A. Tuck and named after the express train that travelled between New York City and Chicago.
Comment: Chocolate and lemon juice. 21st century tastes have moved on.

TWINKLE [UPDATED #7]

Glass: Martini
Garnish: Lemon zest twist
Method: SHAKE first two ingredients with ice and fine strain into chilled glass. **TOP** with prosecco (or champagne).

3	shot(s)	**Ketel One vodka**
$\frac{3}{4}$	shot(s)	**St-Germain elderflower liqueur**
Top up with		**Prosecco (or brut champagne)**

Origin: Adapted from a drink created in 2002 by Tony Conigliaro at Lonsdale House, London, England.
Comment: It's hard to believe this floral, dry, golden beauty contains three shots of vodka – until you've had a few.

TWISTED SOBRIETY

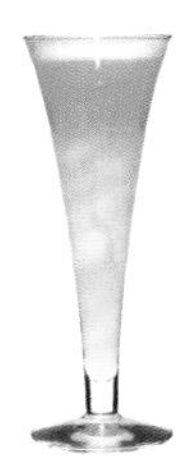

Glass: Flute
Method: SHAKE first two ingredients with ice and fine strain into chilled glass. **TOP** with champagne.

1	shot(s)	**Rémy Martin cognac**
1	shot(s)	**Poire William liqueur**
Top up with		**Brut champagne**

Comment: Fortified champagne with a hint of pear.

TWO 'T' FRUITY MARTINI

Glass: Martini
Garnish: Tooty Frooties
Method: SHAKE all ingredients with ice and fine strain into chilled glass.

$2\frac{1}{2}$	shot(s)	**Ketel One vodka**
$\frac{3}{4}$	shot(s)	**Passion fruit syrup**
3	dashes	**Fee Brothers orange bitters**

Origin: Created in 2002 at Hush, London, England.
Comment: Simple is beautiful – this drink is both. The rawness of vodka is balanced with sweet passion fruit and hints of orange bitterness.

TYPHOON

Glass: Old-fashioned
Method: STIR all ingredients with ice and strain into ice-filled glass.

$1\frac{3}{4}$	shot(s)	**Plymouth gin**
$\frac{1}{2}$	shot(s)	**Luxardo Sambuca dei Cesari**
$\frac{1}{2}$	shot(s)	**Rose's lime cordial**

Comment: Great if you love sambuca.

'MAYBE A NATION THAT CONSUMES AS MUCH BOOZE AND DOPE AS WE DO AND HAS OUR KIND OF DIVORCE STATISTICS SHOULD PIPE DOWN ABOUT "CHARACTER ISSUES."'

P. J. O'ROURKE

UGURUNDU

Glass: Shot
Method: Lightly **MUDDLE** mint in base of shaker (just to bruise). Add other ingredients, **SHAKE** with ice and fine strain into chilled glass.

3	fresh	**Mint leaves**
$\frac{1}{2}$	shot(s)	**Cranberry flavoured vodka**
$\frac{1}{2}$	shot(s)	**Rose's lime cordial**

Origin: Created in 2004 by Peter Kubista at Bugsy's Bar, Prague, Czech Republic.
Comment: Fresh tasting and all too easy to knock back.

UMBONGO

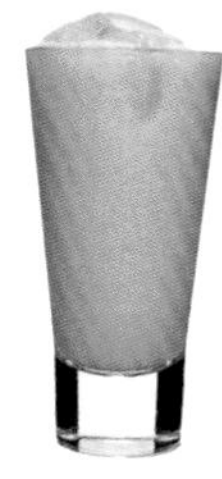

Glass: Collins
Garnish: Orange slice in glass
Method: Cut passion fruit in half and scoop out flesh into shaker. Add next three ingredients, **SHAKE** with ice and fine strain into ice-filled glass. **TOP** with ginger ale.

1	fresh	**Passion fruit**
1	shot(s)	**Passoã passion fruit liqueur**
1	shot(s)	**Ketel One vodka**
1	shot(s)	**Freshly squeezed orange juice**
Top up with		**Ginger ale**

Comment: Pleasant, light and medium sweet tropical style drink.

UNCLE VANYA

Glass: Martini
Garnish: Lime wedge on rim
Method: SHAKE all ingredients with ice and fine strain into chilled glass.

1¾	shot(s)	**Ketel One vodka**
1	shot(s)	**Giffard mûre (blackberry) liqueur**
1	shot(s)	**Freshly squeezed lime juice**
½	shot(s)	**Sugar syrup (2 sugar to 1 water)**
½	fresh	**Egg white**

Origin: Named after Anton Chekhov's greatest play – a cheery tale of envy and despair. A popular drink in Britain's TGI Friday's bars, its origins are unknown.
Comment: Simple but great – smooth, sweet 'n' sour blackberry, although possibly a tad on the sweet side for some.

UNION CLUB

Glass: Martini
Garnish: Orange zest twist
Method: SHAKE all ingredients with ice and fine strain into chilled glass.

2	shot(s)	**Buffalo Trace bourbon whiskey**
¼	shot(s)	**Cointreau triple sec**
½	shot(s)	**Freshly squeezed lime juice**
1/8	shot(s)	**Orgeat sugar syrup**
1/8	shot(s)	**Pomegranate (grenadine) syrup**
½	fresh	**Egg white**

Origin: Adapted from a recipe purloined from David Embury's classic book, The Fine Art of Mixing Drinks.
Comment: Balanced sweet and sour with bourbon to the fore.

UNIVERSAL SHOT

Glass: Shot
Method: Refrigerate ingredients then **LAYER** in chilled glass by carefully pouring in the following order.

½	shot(s)	**Midori melon liqueur**
½	shot(s)	**Squeezed pink grapefruit juice**
½	shot(s)	**Ketel One vodka**

Comment: Sweet melon liqueur toned down by grapefruit and fortified by vodka.

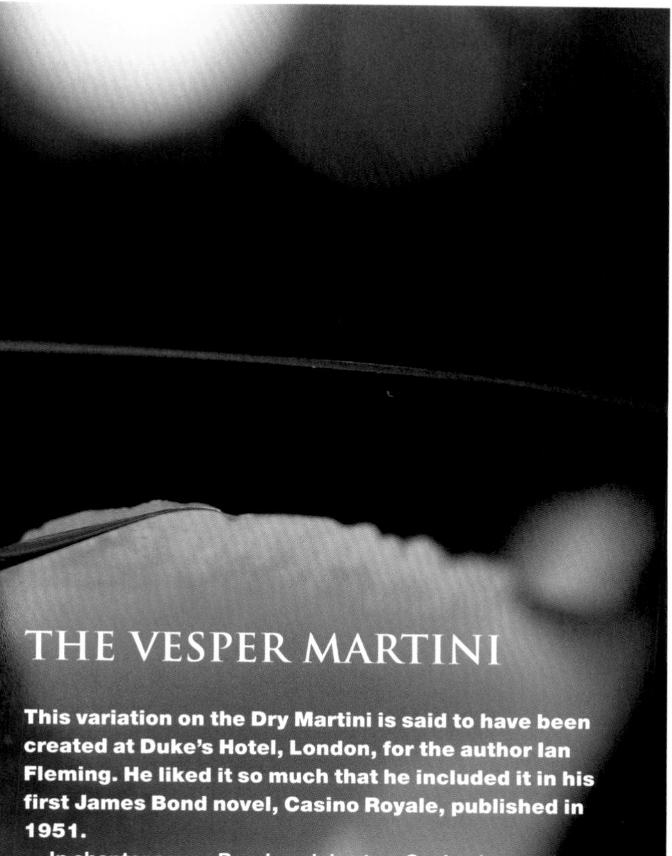

THE VESPER MARTINI

This variation on the Dry Martini is said to have been created at Duke's Hotel, London, for the author Ian Fleming. He liked it so much that he included it in his first James Bond novel, Casino Royale, published in 1951.

In chapter seven Bond explains to a Casino bartender exactly how to make and serve the drink: "In a deep champagne goblet. Three measures of Gordon's, one of vodka, half a measure of Kina Lillet [now called Lillet Blanc]. Shake it very well until it's ice-cold, then add a large slice of lemon peel."

When made, 007 compliments the bartender, but tells him it would be better made with a grain-based vodka. He also explains his Martini to Felix Leiter, the CIA man, saying, "This drink's my own invention. I'm going to patent it when I can think of a good name."

In chapter eight, Bond meets the beautiful agent Vesper Lynd. She explains why her parents named her Vesper and Bond asks if she'd mind if he called his favourite Martini after her. Like so many of Bond's love interests Vesper turns out to be a double agent and the book closes with his words, "The bitch is dead now."

Many bartenders advocate that a Martini should be stirred and not shaken, some citing the ridiculous argument that shaking will "bruise the gin". If you like your Martinis shaken (as I do) then avoid the possible look of distaste from your server and order a Vesper. This Martini is always shaken, an action that aerates the drink, and makes it colder and more dilute than simply stirring. It also gives the drink a slightly clouded appearance and can leave small shards of ice on the surface of the drink. This is easily prevented by the use of a fine strainer when pouring.

UPSIDE-DOWN RASPBERRY CHEESECAKE

Glass: Martini
Garnish: Sprinkle crunched Graham Cracker or digestive biscuits
Method: First layer: **MUDDLE** raspberries in base of shaker. Add Chambord, **SHAKE** with ice and fine strain into centre of glass. Second layer: Grate lemon zest into shaker. Add rest of ingredients, **SHAKE** all ingredients with ice and strain into glass over spoon so as to **LAYER** over raspberry base.

4	fresh	**Raspberries**
1/2	shot(s)	**Chambord black raspberry liqueur**

NEXT LAYER

1/2	fresh	**Lemon zest (grated)**
2	shot(s)	**Vanilla infused Ketel One vodka**
1/2	shot(s)	**Vanilla liqueur**
1/2	shot(s)	**Sugar syrup (2 sugar to 1 water)**
5	spoons	**Mascarpone cheese**
1	shot(s)	**Double (heavy) cream**

Origin: I created this in 2003 after adapting Wayne Collins' original cheesecake recipe.
Comment: Surprisingly, the biscuity top continues to float as you sip the vanilla cream layer right down to the point when you hit the raspberry topping – sorry, base.

URBAN HOLISTIC

Glass: Martini
Garnish: Lemon zest twist
Method: SHAKE first two ingredients with ice and fine strain into chilled glass. **TOP** with ginger ale.

2	shot(s)	**Sake**
1	shot(s)	**Dry vermouth**
Top up with		**Ginger ale**

Origin: Adapted from a drink discovered in 2005 at Mo Bar, Landmark Mandarin Oriental Hotel, Hong Kong, China.
Comment: East meets west in this dry refreshing cocktail.

URBAN OASIS

Glass: Martini
Garnish: Orange zest twist
Method: SHAKE all ingredients with ice and fine strain into chilled glass.

1 1/2	shot(s)	**Orange zest infused Ketel One vodka**
1/2	shot(s)	**Raspberry flavoured vodka**
1/4	shot(s)	**Chambord black raspberry liqueur**
2	shot(s)	**Pressed pineapple juice**

Origin: Discovered in 2003 at Paramount Hotel, New York City, USA.
Comment: Alcoholic orange sherbet – how bad is that?

U.S. MARTINI

Glass: Martini
Garnish: Vanilla pod
Method: SHAKE all ingredients with ice and fine strain into chilled glass.

1 1/2	shot(s)	**Vanilla infused Rémy Martin cognac**
1 1/4	shot(s)	**Sauvignon Blanc wine**
1 1/2	shot(s)	**Pressed pineapple juice**
1/4	shot(s)	**Sugar syrup (2 sugar to 1 water)**

Origin: Adapted from the Palermo cocktail discovered in 2001 at Hotel du Vin, Bristol, England. I created this drink in 2003 and named it after the grape varieties Ugni and Sauvignon. Ugni Blanc is the most common grape in Cognac, and Sauvignon Blanc is the grape used in the wine.
Comment: A relatively dry cocktail where the vanilla combines beautifully with the cognac and the acidity of the wine balances the sweetness of the pineapple juice.

UTTERLY BUTTERLY

Glass: Collins
Garnish: Apple wedge
Method: STIR peanut butter with vodka in base of shaker. Add other ingredients, **SHAKE** with ice and fine strain into ice-filled glass.

1	spoon	**Smooth peanut butter**
2	shot(s)	**Ketel One vodka**
1/4	shot(s)	**Cinnamon schnapps liqueur**
1/2	shot(s)	**Malibu coconut rum liqueur**
1 1/2	shot(s)	**Pressed apple juice**
1 1/2	shot(s)	**Pressed pineapple juice**
3/4	shot(s)	**Freshly squeezed lime juice**

Comment: Yup, your eyes are not deceiving you and nor will your taste buds – it's made with peanut butter. Refreshingly different.

VACATION

Glass: Martini
Garnish: Pineapple wedge or orange slice on rim
Method: This drink can be finished with your choice of three different coloured and flavoured liqueurs. **SHAKE** first five ingredients with ice and fine strain into chilled glass. Then **POUR** your favoured final ingredient into the centre of the drink. It should sink.

2	shot(s)	**Vanilla infused Ketel One vodka**
1/2	shot(s)	**Malibu coconut rum liqueur**
1/2	shot(s)	**Freshly squeezed lime juice**
1	shot(s)	**Pressed pineapple juice**
1/4	fresh	**Egg white**
1/4	shot(s)	**Chambord (red) or Midori (green) or Blue curaçao liqueur (blue)**

Origin: My adaptation (in 2003) of the signature drink at the Merc Bar, New York City, USA.
Comment: A great looking, fairly sweet cocktail with hints of vanilla, coconut and pineapple.

U

VALENCIA

Glass: Flute
Garnish: Orange zest twist
Method: POUR first three ingredients into chilled glass. **TOP** with champagne.

1/2	shot(s)	**Giffard apricot brandy du Roussillon**
1/4	shot(s)	**Freshly squeezed orange juice**
4	dashes	**Fee Brothers orange bitters (optional)**
Top up with		**Brut champagne**

Variant: Also served as a Martini with gin in place of champagne.
Origin: Adapted from the Valencia Cocktail No. 2 in The Savoy Cocktail Book.
Comment: Floral and fruity – makes Bucks Fizz look a tad sad.

VALENTINO [NEW #7]

Glass: Martini
Garnish: Lemon zest twist
Method: STIR all ingredients with ice and strain into a chilled glass.

2	shot(s)	**Plymouth gin**
1/2	shot(s)	**Campari**
1	shot(s)	**Sweet vermouth**

Comment: A variation on the Negroni. More gin and less Campari, make for an unusual bittersweet Martini.

VALKYRIE

Glass: Old-fashioned
Garnish: Lemon zest twist
Method: SHAKE all ingredients with ice and strain into glass filled with crushed ice. Serve with straws.

2	shot(s)	**Vanilla infused Ketel One vodka**
1/2	shot(s)	**Freshly squeezed lemon juice**
1/2	shot(s)	**Vanilla sugar syrup**

Origin: Created in 2003 by yours truly. The name comes from Norse mythology and literally translates as 'chooser of the slain'.
Comment: This sipping drink has a rich vanilla, sweet 'n' sour flavour.

VAMPIRO

Glass: Old-fashioned
Garnish: Lime wedge
Method: SHAKE all ingredients with ice and strain into ice-filled glass.

2	shot(s)	**Partida tequila**
1	shot(s)	**Pressed tomato juice**
1	shot(s)	**Freshly squeezed orange juice**
1/2	shot(s)	**Freshly squeezed lime juice**
1/2	shot(s)	**Pomegranate (grenadine) syrup**
7	drops	**Hot pepper sauce**
1	pinch	**Celery salt**
1	pinch	**Freshly ground black pepper**

Origin: The national drink of Mexico where it's often made with pomegranate juice in place of tomato juice and without the grenadine.
Comment: Something of a supercharged Bloody Mary with tequila and a hint of sweet grenadine.

VANCOUVER [NEW #7]

Glass: Martini
Garnish: Lemon zest twist
Method: STIR all ingredients with ice and fine strain into chilled glass.

1 1/2	shot(s)	**Plymouth gin**
3/4	shot(s)	**Sweet vermouth**
1/4	shot(s)	**Bénédictine D.O.M. liqueur**
1	dash	**Fee Brothers orange bitters**

Comment: A herbal medium dry Martini.

VANDERBILT

Glass: Martini
Garnish: Lemon zest twist
Method: SHAKE all ingredients with ice and fine strain into chilled glass.

2 1/4	shot(s)	**Rémy Martin cognac**
3/4	shot(s)	**Cherry (brandy) liqueur**
1/8	shot(s)	**Sugar syrup (2 sugar to 1 water)**
2	dashes	**Angostura aromatic bitters**

Origin: Adapted from a recipe in Harry Craddock's 1930 Savoy Cocktail Book.
Comment: Tangy, rich cherry and hints of vanilla fortified with brandy.

VANILLA & GRAPEFRUIT DAIQUIRI

Glass: Martini
Garnish: Grapefruit zest twist (discarded) & vanilla pod
Method: SHAKE all ingredients with ice and fine strain into chilled glass.

2 1/2	shot(s)	**Vanilla infused light white rum**
1/2	shot(s)	**Freshly squeezed lime juice**
1/2	shot(s)	**Sonoma vanilla bean sugar syrup**
1	shot(s)	**Squeezed pink grapefruit juice**

Origin: Created in 2003 by yours truly.
Comment: Reminiscent of a Hemingway Special, this flavoursome, vanilla laced Daiquiri has a wonderfully tangy bittersweet finish.

VANILLA & RASPBERRY MARTINI

Glass: Martini
Garnish: Raspberries on stick
Method: MUDDLE raspberries in base of shaker. Add other ingredients, **SHAKE** with ice and fine strain into chilled glass.

12	fresh	**Raspberries**
2	shot(s)	**Vanilia infused Ketel One vodka**
1/4	shot(s)	**Red wine**
1/4	shot(s)	**Sugar syrup (2 sugar to 1 water)**
1/2	shot(s)	**Chilled mineral water** (omit if wet ice)

Origin: Created in 2006 by yours truly.
Comment: Exactly that – vanilla and raspberry.

VANILLA DAIQUIRI

Glass: Martini
Garnish: Lime wedge on rim
Method: **SHAKE** all ingredients with ice and fine strain into chilled glass.

2	shot(s)	**Vanilla infused light white rum**
1/2	shot(s)	**Freshly squeezed lime juice**
1/4	shot(s)	**Sugar syrup (2 sugar to 1 water)**
3/4	shot(s)	**Chilled mineral water** (omit if wet ice)

Comment: The classic 'Natural Daiquiri' with a hint of vanilla.

VANILLA VODKA SOUR

Glass: Flute
Garnish: Lemon & orange zest twists
Method: **SHAKE** all ingredients with ice and fine strain into chilled glass.

2	shot(s)	**Vanilla infused Ketel One vodka**
3/4	shot(s)	**Cuarenta Y Tres (Licor 43) liqueur**
3/4	shot(s)	**Freshly squeezed lemon juice**
1/2	fresh	**Egg white**

Comment: A Vodka Sour with a blast of spicy vanilla.

VANILLA LAIKA

Glass: Collins
Garnish: Berries
Method: **SHAKE** all ingredients with ice and strain into glass filled with crushed ice.

1 1/2	shot(s)	**Vanilla infused Ketel One vodka**
3/4	shot(s)	**Giffard mûre (blackberry) liqueur**
1/4	shot(s)	**Freshly squeezed lemon juice**
3/4	shot(s)	**Sugar syrup (2 sugar to 1 water)**
4	shot(s)	**Pressed apple juice**

Origin: Created by Jake Burger in 2002 at Townhouse, Leeds, England. Laika was a Russian dog and the first canine in space.
Comment: Vanilla berry fruit in a tall, refreshing drink.

VANILLA'TINI

Glass: Martini
Garnish: Half vanilla pod
Method: **STIR** all ingredients with ice and strain into chilled glass.

2 1/2	shot(s)	**Vanilla infused Ketel One vodka**
1/2	shot(s)	**Frangelico hazelnut liqueur**
1 1/2	shot(s)	**7-Up/lemonade**

Origin: Discovered in 2003 at Paramount Hotel, New York City.
Comment: Vanilla, hazelnut and a hint of creamy citrus.

VANILLA MARGARITA

Glass: Old-fashioned
Garnish: Lime wedge
Method: **SHAKE** all ingredients with ice and fine strain into ice filled chilled glass.

2	shot(s)	**Vanilla infused Partida tequila**
1	shot(s)	**Freshly squeezed lemon juice**
1	shot(s)	**Cointreau triple sec**

Origin: I first discovered this drink in 1998 at Café Pacifico, London, England.
Comment: A classic Margarita with a hint of vanilla.

VANITINI

Glass: Martini
Garnish: Pineapple wedge on rim
Method: **SHAKE** all ingredients with ice and fine strain into chilled glass.

2	shot(s)	**Vanilla infused Ketel One vodka**
2	shot(s)	**Sauvignon Blanc wine**
3/4	shot(s)	**Sour pineapple liqueur**
1/4	shot(s)	**Giffard mûre (blackberry) liqueur**

Comment: Vanilla and pineapple dried by the acidity of the wine, and sweetened and flavoured by blackberry liqueur.

VANILLA SENSATION

Glass: Martini
Garnish: Float wafer thin apple slice
Method: **SHAKE** all ingredients with ice and fine strain into chilled glass.

2	shot(s)	**Vanilla infused Ketel One vodka**
1	shot(s)	**Sour apple liqueur**
1/2	shot(s)	**Dry vermouth**

Origin: Created in 2003 but by whom is unknown.
Comment: A pleasing vanilla twist on an Apple Martini.

VANTE MARTINI

Glass: Martini
Garnish: Orange zest twist
Method: **MUDDLE** cardamom in base of shaker. Add other ingredients, **SHAKE** with ice and fine strain into chilled glass.

4	pods	**Cardamom**
1 1/2	shot(s)	**Vanilla infused Ketel One vodka**
1 1/2	shot(s)	**Sauvignon Blanc wine**
1	shot(s)	**Cuarenta Y Tres (Licor 43) liqueur**
1/4	shot(s)	**Pressed pineapple juice**

Origin: Created in 2003 by yours truly.
Comment: Bold, aromatic and complex flavours.

VAVAVOOM [UPDATED #7]

Glass: Flute
Method: POUR ingredients into chilled glass and lightly stir.

1/2	shot(s)	**Freshly squeezed lemon juice**
1/2	shot(s)	**Cointreau triple sec**
1/4	shot(s)	**Sugar syrup (2 sugar to 1 water)**
Top up with		**Brut champagne**

Origin: Adapted from a drink created in 2002 by Yannick Miseriaux at The Fifth Floor Bar, London, England, and named after the Renault television advertisements.
Comment: The ingredients do indeed give champagne vavavoom.

VELVET FOG

Glass: Martini
Garnish: Orange peel twist (discarded) & freshly grated nutmeg
Method: SHAKE all ingredients with ice and fine strain into chilled glass.

1 1/2	shot(s)	**Ketel One vodka**
1 1/4	shot(s)	**Freshly squeezed lime juice**
3/4	shot(s)	**Velvet Falernum liqueur**
3/4	shot(s)	**Freshly squeezed orange juice**
2	dashes	**Angostura aromatic bitters**

Origin: Created by Dale DeGroff, New York City, USA.
Comment: Tangy, fresh and bittersweet.

VELVET HAMMER

Glass: Martini
Garnish: Grate nutmeg over drink
Method: SHAKE all ingredients with ice and fine strain into chilled glass.

1	shot(s)	**Ketel One vodka**
3/4	shot(s)	**Cointreau triple sec**
3/4	shot(s)	**Giffard white crème de cacao**
3/4	shot(s)	**Double (heavy) cream**
3/4	shot(s)	**Milk**
1/4	shot(s)	**Pomegranate (grenadine) syrup**

Variant: With apricot brandy and coffee liqueur in place of cacao and grenadine.
Comment: Lots of velvet with a little bit of hammer courtesy of a shot of vodka.

VENETO

Glass: Martini
Garnish: Lemon zest twist
Method: SHAKE all ingredients with ice and fine strain into chilled glass.

2	shot(s)	**Rémy Martin cognac**
1/2	shot(s)	**Luxardo Sambuca dei Cesari**
1/2	shot(s)	**Freshly squeezed lemon juice**
1/8	shot(s)	**Sugar syrup (2 sugar to 1 water)**
1/2	shot(s)	**Egg white**

Comment: A serious, Stinger-like drink.

VENUS IN FURS

Glass: Collins
Garnish: Berries & lemon wheel in glass
Method: SHAKE all ingredients with ice and strain into ice-filled glass.

1	shot(s)	**Raspberry flavoured vodka**
1	shot(s)	**Ketel One Citroen vodka**
3 1/2	shot(s)	**Pressed apple juice**
3	dashes	**Angostura aromatic bitters**

Origin: A cocktail which emerged in London's bars early in 2002.
Comment: Juicy flavours with a hint of spice make for a refreshing, quaffable drink.

VENUS MARTINI

Glass: Martini
Garnish: Raspberry in drink
Method: MUDDLE raspberries in base of shaker. Add other ingredients, **SHAKE** with ice and fine strain into chilled glass.

7	fresh	**Raspberries**
2	shot(s)	**Plymouth gin**
1	shot(s)	**Cointreau triple sec**
1/4	shot(s)	**Sugar syrup (2 sugar to 1 water)**
3	dashes	**Peychaud's aromatic bitters (optional)**

Comment: Raspberry with hints of bitter orange and gin – surprisingly dry.

VERDANT

Glass: Martini
Garnish: Float mint leaf
Method: SHAKE all ingredients with ice and fine strain into chilled glass.

2	shot(s)	**Zubrówka bison vodka**
1/8	shot(s)	**Green Chartreuse liqueur**
2	shot(s)	**Pressed apple juice**
1/2	shot(s)	**Freshly squeezed lime juice**

Origin: I created this drink in 2003 and named it after the hue of its ingredients.
Comment: A herbal apple pie of a drink.

VERDI MARTINI

Glass: Martini
Garnish: Pineapple wedge on rim
Method: SHAKE all ingredients with ice and fine strain into chilled glass.

1 3/4	shot(s)	**Raspberry flavoured vodka**
1/2	shot(s)	**Midori melon liqueur**
1/2	shot(s)	**Teichenné Peach Schnapps Liqueur**
1	shot(s)	**Pressed pineapple juice**
1	shot(s)	**Pressed apple juice**
1/4	shot(s)	**Freshly squeezed lime juice**

Origin: Adapted from a drink discovered in 2002 at the Fifth Floor Bar, London, England.
Comment: A melange of fruits combine in a gluggable short drink.

VERT'ICAL BREEZE

Glass: Collins
Garnish: Lemon wedge
Method: SHAKE all ingredients with ice and strain into ice-filled glass.

- 1 shot(s) **La Fée Parisienne (68%) absinthe**
- 2½ shot(s) **Ocean Spray cranberry juice**
- 2½ shot(s) **Freshly squeezed grapefruit juice**

Comment: For those who don't speak French, 'vert' means green – the colour of absinthe. Vertical suggests takeoff – try it and see.

THE VESPER MARTINI

Glass: Martini
Garnish: Lemon zest twist
Method: SHAKE all ingredients with ice and fine strain into chilled glass.

- 3 shot(s) **Plymouth gin**
- 1 shot(s) **Ketel One vodka**
- ½ shot(s) **Dry vermouth**

Origin: 007's original 'shaken not stirred' Martini as chronicled in the first James Bond novel, Casino Royale.
Comment: Enough alcohol to drop a rhino – licensed to kill.

VIAGRA FALLS

Glass: Martini
Garnish: Orange zest twist
Method: SHAKE all ingredients with ice and fine strain into chilled glass.

- ¾ shot(s) **La Fée Parisienne (68%) absinthe**
- 1½ shot(s) **Sour apple liqueur**
- 1¾ shot(s) **Chilled mineral water**
- 2 dashes **Fee Brothers orange bitters**

Origin: Created by Jack Leuwens, London, England.
Comment: Aniseed and apple – sure to get your pecker up.

VICTORIAN LEMONADE [NEW #7]

Glass: Collins
Garnish: Lemon slice
Method: Lightly MUDDLE mint (just to bruise) in base of shaker. Add other ingredients, **SHAKE** with ice and fine strain into ice-filled glass.

- 12 fresh **Mint leaves**
- 1½ shot(s) **Plymouth gin**
- 1 shot(s) **Freshly squeezed lemon juice**
- ¾ shot(s) **Sugar syrup (2 sugar to 1 water)**
- 2½ shot(s) **Chilled mineral water**

Comment: Gin laced, mint flavoured, traditional lemonade.

VIEUX CARRÉ COCKTAIL [UPDATED #7]

Glass: Old-fashioned
Garnish: Lemon zest twist
Method: STIR all ingredients with ice and strain into ice-filled glass.

- 1 shot(s) **Buffalo Trace bourbon whiskey**
- 1 shot(s) **Rémy Martin cognac**
- 1 shot(s) **Sweet vermouth**
- ¼ shot(s) **Bénédictine D.O.M. liqueur**
- 1 dashes **Peychaud's aromatic bitters**
- 1 dashes **Angostura aromatic bitters**

Origin: Created in 1938 by Walter Bergeron, the head bartender at what is now the Carousel bar at the Monteleone Hotel, New Orleans, USA. Pronounced 'Voo-Ka-Ray', the name is French for the city's French Quarter and literally translates as 'old square'.
Comment: Rather like an ultra-smooth and complex Sweet Manhattan served on the rocks.

VIOLET AFFINITY

Glass: Martini
Garnish: Lemon zest twist
Method: STIR all ingredients with ice and strain into chilled glass.

- 2 shot(s) **Benoit Serres liqueur de violette**
- 1 shot(s) **Sweet vermouth**
- 1 shot(s) **Dry vermouth**

Origin: An adaptation of the classic Affinity.
Comment: Amazingly delicate and complex for such a simple drink.

VODKA COLLINS

Glass: Collins
Garnish: Orange slice & cherry on stick (sail)
Method: SHAKE first three ingredients with ice and strain into ice-filled glass. **TOP** with soda, lightly stir and serve with straws.

- 2 shot(s) **Ketel One vodka**
- 1 shot(s) **Freshly squeezed lemon juice**
- ½ shot(s) **Sugar syrup (2 sugar to 1 water)**
- Top up with **Soda water (club soda)**

AKA: Joe Collins
Comment: A Tom Collins with vodka – a refreshing balance of sweet and sour.

VODKA ESPRESSO

Glass: Old-fashioned
Garnish: Three coffee beans
Method: SHAKE all ingredients with ice and strain into ice-filled glass.

- 2 shot(s) **Ketel One vodka**
- 1½ shot(s) **Cold espresso coffee**
- ½ shot(s) **Kahlúa coffee liqueur**
- ¼ shot(s) **Sugar syrup (2 sugar to 1 water)**

Origin: Created in 1983 by Dick Bradsell at the Soho Brasserie, London, England.
Comment: Vodka and coffee combine in this tasty wake up call.

VODKA GIMLET

Glass: Martini
Garnish: Lime wedge or cherry
Method: STIR all ingredients with ice and strain into chilled glass.

2 1/2 shot(s) **Ketel One vodka**
1 1/4 shot(s) **Rose's lime cordial**

Variants: Shaken. The original Gimlet is based on gin.
Comment: Sweetened lime fortified with vodka.

VODKA SOUR

Glass: Old-fashioned
Garnish: Lemon wheel & cherry on stick (sail)
Method: SHAKE all ingredients with ice and strain into ice-filled glass.

2 shot(s) **Ketel One vodka**
1 shot(s) **Freshly squeezed lemon juice**
1/2 shot(s) **Sugar syrup (2 sugar to 1 water)**
3 dashes **Angostura aromatic bitters**
1/2 fresh **Egg white**

Comment: A great vodka based drink balancing sweet and sour.

VODKATINI [UPDATED #7]

Glass: Martini
Garnish: Lemon zest twist / olives
Method: SHAKE all ingredients with ice and fine strain into chilled glass.

2 1/2 shot(s) **Ketel One vodka**
1/4 shot(s) **Dry vermouth**

Variant: Stir rather than shake.
Comment: Temperature is key to the enjoyment of this modern classic. Consume while icy cold.

VOLGA BOATMAN

Glass: Martini
Garnish: Orange zest twist
Method: SHAKE all ingredients with ice and fine strain into chilled glass.

1 1/2 shot(s) **Ketel One vodka**
3/4 shot(s) **Kirsch eau de vie**
1 1/2 shot(s) **Freshly squeezed orange juice**

Origin: Recipe adapted from David Embury's classic Fine Art of Mixing Drinks. Named after the epic (and somewhat camp) Cecil B. De Mille movie, which took its name from a Russian folksong hymning the Volga, Europe's longest river.
Comment: A Screwdriver served straight-up with a twist of cherry.

VOODOO

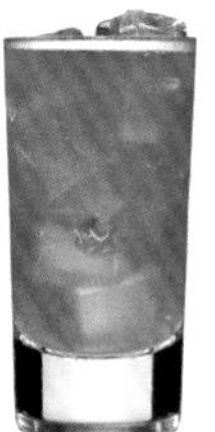

Glass: Collins
Garnish: Dust with cinnamon sprinkled through flame
Method: SHAKE all ingredients with ice and strain into ice-filled glass.

2 shot(s) **Aged rum**
3/4 shot(s) **Sweet vermouth**
2 1/2 shot(s) **Pressed apple juice**
1/2 shot(s) **Freshly squeezed lime juice**
1/4 shot(s) **Sugar syrup (2 sugar to 1 water)**

Origin: Created in 2002 by Alex Kammerling, London, England.
Comment: The rich flavour of the aged rum marries well with apple and lime juice.

VOWEL COCKTAIL

Glass: Martini
Garnish: Orange zest twist
Method: SHAKE all ingredients with ice and fine strain into chilled glass.

1 1/4 shot(s) **Scotch whisky**
1 shot(s) **Kümmel liqueur**
1 shot(s) **Sweet vermouth**
3/4 shot(s) **Freshly squeezed orange juice**
2 dashes **Angostura aromatic bitters**

Origin: Adapted from a recipe in Vintage Spirits & Forgotten Cocktails by Ted Haigh (AKA Dr. Cocktail).
Comment: Caraway from the Kümmel subtly dominates this aromatic drink.

WAGON WHEEL

Glass: Old-fashioned
Garnish: Lemon slice in drink
Method: SHAKE all ingredients with ice and fine strain into glass filled with crushed ice.

1 1/2 shot(s) **Southern Comfort liqueur**
1 1/2 shot(s) **Rémy Martin cognac**
3/4 shot(s) **Freshly squeezed lemon juice**
1/4 shot(s) **Pomegranate (grenadine) syrup**

Origin: Adapted from a recipe purloined from David Embury's Fine Art of Mixing Drinks.
Comment: This classic cocktail will be best appreciated by lovers of Southern Comfort.

WAH-WAH [NEW #7]

Glass: Martini
Garnish: Orange zest twist
Method: SHAKE all ingredients with ice and fine strain into chilled glass.

1 1/2 shot(s) **Pisco**
1 shot(s) **St-Germain elderflower liqueur**
3/4 shot(s) **Aperol**
3/4 shot(s) **Freshly squeezed grapefruit juice**
1 dash **Angostura aromatic bitters**

Origin: Created in 2007 at Range, San Francisco, USA.
Comment: Bittersweet and complex with hints of elderflower and grapefruit.

WALNUT MARTINI

Glass: Martini
Garnish: Float walnut half
Method: **STIR** all ingredients with ice and strain into chilled glass.

2	shot(s)	**Ketel One vodka**
3/4	shot(s)	**Tuaca Italian liqueur**
3/4	shot(s)	**Toschi Nocello walnut liqueur**
3/4	shot(s)	**Dry vermouth**

Origin: Created in 2005 by yours truly.
Comment: Nutty but nice.

WALTZING MATILDA

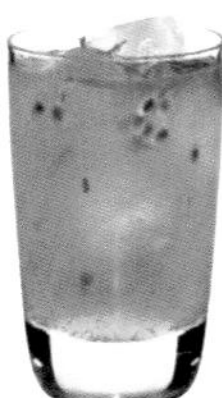

Glass: Collins
Garnish: Half orange slice
Method: Cut passion fruit in half and scoop out flesh into shaker. Add next three ingredients, **SHAKE** with ice and fine strain into ice-filled glass. **TOP** with ginger ale.

1	fresh	**Passion fruit**
1	shot(s)	**Plymouth gin**
2	shot(s)	**Sauvignon Blanc wine**
1/8	shot(s)	**Grand Marnier liqueur**
Top up with		**Ginger ale**

Origin: Adapted from a recipe from David Embury's classic book, The Fine Art of Mixing Drinks.
Comment: Passion fruit, gin, wine and ginger ale all combine well in this refreshing drink.

WANTON ABANDON

Glass: Martini
Garnish: Strawberry on rim
Method: **MUDDLE** strawberries in base of shaker. Add next three ingredients, **SHAKE** with ice and fine strain into chilled glass. **TOP** with champagne.

5	fresh	**Strawberries**
2	shot(s)	**Ketel One vodka**
3/4	shot(s)	**Freshly squeezed lemon juice**
1/2	shot(s)	**Sugar syrup (2 sugar to 1 water)**
Top up with		**Brut champagne**

Comment: A crowd pleaser – looks great and its fruity, balanced flavour will offend few.

WARD EIGHT

Glass: Martini
Garnish: Orange slice & cherry
Method: **SHAKE** all ingredients with ice and fine strain into chilled glass.

2 1/4	shot(s)	**Buffalo Trace bourbon whiskey**
3/4	shot(s)	**Freshly squeezed lemon juice**
3/4	shot(s)	**Freshly squeezed orange juice**
1/4	shot(s)	**Pomegranate (grenadine) syrup**
1/2	shot(s)	**Chilled mineral water** (omit if wet ice)

Origin: Ward Eight was a voting district of Boston and famed for its political corruption. This drink was first served by Tom Hussion in November 1898 at Boston's Locke-Ober Café, in honour of Martin Lomasney, who owned the café and was running for election in Ward Eight.
Comment: This is a spirited, sweet and sour combination – like most politicians.

WARSAW

Glass: Martini
Garnish: Orange zest twist
Method: **STIR** all ingredients with ice and strain into chilled glass.

2	shot(s)	**Ketel One vodka**
1/2	shot(s)	**Polska Wisniówka cherry liqueur**
1/4	shot(s)	**Cointreau triple sec**
2	dashes	**Angostura aromatic bitters**
3/4	shot(s)	**Chilled mineral water** (omit if wet ice)

Comment: Subtle cherry notes with orange.

WARSAW COOLER

Glass: Collins
Garnish: Mint sprig & orange zest
Method: **STIR** honey with vodka in base of shaker until honey dissolves. Add other ingredients, **SHAKE** with ice and strain into ice-filled glass.

2	spoons	**Runny honey**
1 1/2	shot(s)	**Zubrówka bison vodka**
1/2	shot(s)	**Spiced rum**
1/4	shot(s)	**Cointreau triple sec**
1/2	shot(s)	**Sugar syrup (2 sugar to 1 water)**
3/4	shot(s)	**Freshly squeezed lemon juice**
2	shot(s)	**Pressed apple juice**

Origin: Created in 2002 by Morgan Watson of Apartment, Belfast, Northern Ireland.
Comment: Orange, honey, apple and spice laced with Polish bison grass vodka.

WASABI MARTINI

Glass: Martini
Garnish: Float strips of yaki nori seaweed.
Method: Squeeze a pea-sized quantity of wasabi paste onto a barspoon and **STIR** with vodka until wasabi dissolves. Add other ingredients, **SHAKE** with ice and fine strain into chilled glass.

2	shot(s)	**Ketel One vodka**
1	pea	**Wasabi paste**
3/4	shot(s)	**Freshly squeezed lemon juice**
1/2	shot(s)	**Sugar syrup (2 sugar to 1 water)**

Origin: Created in 2004 by Philippe Guidi at Morton's, London, England.
Comment: Wonderfully balanced with spicy heat and a zesty finish.

WASH HOUSE [NEW #7]

Glass: Martini
Garnish: Fresh thyme sprig
Method: Lightly **MUDDLE** basil (just to bruise) in base of shaker. Add other ingredients, **SHAKE** with ice and fine strain into chilled glass.

4	fresh	**Basil leaves**
2	shot(s)	**Ketel One vodka**
1/2	shot(s)	**Freshly squeezed lime juice**
1/2	shot(s)	**Sugar syrup (2 sugar to 1 water)**
1/2	shot(s)	**Chilled mineral water** (omit if wet ice)

Origin: Adapted from a recipe by Neyah White at Nopa, San Francisco, USA. The building that now houses Nopa was once a laundry, hence the name.
Comment: Delicately herbal – simple but refreshing.

WASHINGTON APPLE

Glass: Collins
Garnish: Apple slice
Method: SHAKE first four ingredients with ice and fine strain into ice-filled glass. **DRIZZLE** grenadine over drink. Serve with straws.

2	shot(s)	**Ketel One vodka**
3	shot(s)	**Pressed apple juice**
1/4	shot(s)	**Freshly squeezed lime juice**
1/2	shot(s)	**Sour apple liqueur**
1/4	shot(s)	**Pomegranate (grenadine) syrup**

Origin: Created by Wayne Collins, London, England.
Comment: A long version of the once ubiquitous Sour Apple Martini.

WATERMELON & BASIL MARTINI

Glass: Martini
Garnish: Watermelon wedge on rim
Method: Cut watermelon into 16 segments, chop the flesh from one segment into cubes and **MUDDLE** in base of shaker. Add other ingredients, **SHAKE** with ice and fine strain into chilled glass.

1/16	fresh	**Watermelon (diced)**
7	fresh	**Basil leaves (torn)**
2	shot(s)	**Plymouth gin**
1/2	shot(s)	**Sugar syrup (2 sugar to 1 water)**

Comment: Refreshing watermelon with interesting herbal hints from the basil and gin.

WATERMELON & BASIL SMASH

Glass: Collins
Garnish: Watermelon wedge on rim
Method: Cut watermelon into 16 segments, chop the flesh from one segment into cubes and **MUDDLE** in base of shaker. Add next three ingredients, **SHAKE** with ice and fine strain into ice-filled glass. **TOP** with ginger ale.

1/16	fresh	**Watermelon (diced)**
8	fresh	**Torn basil leaves**
2	shot(s)	**Partida tequila**
3/4	shot(s)	**Luxardo limoncello liqueur**
Top up with		**Ginger ale**

Comment: Sweet and sour, long and refreshing with subtle hints of basil, ginger and tequila amongst the fruit.

WATERMELON COSMO

Glass: Martini (large)
Garnish: Watermelon wedge on rim
Method: Cut watermelon into 16 segments, chop the flesh from one segment into cubes and **MUDDLE** in base of shaker. Add other ingredients, **SHAKE** with ice and fine strain into chilled glass.

1/16	fresh	**Watermelon (diced)**
2	shot(s)	**Ketel One Citroen vodka**
3/4	shot(s)	**Freshly squeezed lime juice**
3/4	shot(s)	**Ocean Spray cranberry juice**
1/2	shot(s)	**Midori melon liqueur**
1/8	shot(s)	**Rose's lime cordial**
2	dashes	**Fee Brothers orange bitters**

Origin: Created in 2003 by Eric Fossard at Cecconi's, London, England.
Comment: Looks like a standard Cosmo but tastes just as the name suggests.

WATERMELON MAN [UPDATED #7]

Glass: Collins
Garnish: Lime wedge
Method: SHAKE first five ingredients with ice and strain into ice-filled glass. **TOP** with soda and serve with straws.

2	shot(s)	**Ketel One vodka**
1	shot(s)	**Watermelon liqueur**
1	shot(s)	**Freshly squeezed lime juice**
1/2	shot(s)	**Freshly squeezed orange juice**
1	shot(s)	**Pomegranate (grenadine) syrup**
Top up with		**Soda water (club soda)**

Origin: Named after the Herbie Hancock track and popularised by a club night promoter called Cookie in Berlin during the mid-1990s. He started serving this cocktail at his club nights and now practically every bar in Berlin offers it. Try the original at his Cookie Club.
Comment: Sweet and far from sophisticated, but better than the fodder peddled at most clubs.

WATERMELON MARTINI

Glass: Martini
Garnish: Watermelon wedge on rim
Method: Cut watermelon into 16 segments, chop the flesh from one segment into cubes and **MUDDLE** in base of shaker. Add other ingredients, **SHAKE** with ice and fine strain into chilled glass.

1/16	fresh	**Watermelon (diced)**
2	shot(s)	**Ketel One vodka**
1/2	shot(s)	**Sugar syrup (2 sugar to 1 water)**

Comment: So fruity, you can almost convince yourself this is a health drink!

WEBSTER MARTINI

Glass: Martini
Garnish: Lime zest twist
Method: SHAKE all ingredients with ice and fine strain into chilled glass.

2	shot(s)	**Plymouth gin**
1	shot(s)	**Dry vermouth**
1/2	shot(s)	**Giffard apricot brandy du Roussillon**
1/2	shot(s)	**Freshly squeezed lime juice**

Origin: Adapted from a recipe in Harry Craddock's 1930 Savoy Cocktail Book. Craddock writes of this drink, "A favourite cocktail at the bar of the S.S. Mauretania."
Comment: Balanced rather than sweet. The old-school Dry Martini meets the contemporary fruit driven Martini.

WEEPING JESUS

Glass: Old-fashioned
Method: SHAKE first three ingredients with ice and strain into glass filled with crushed ice. **TOP** with 7-Up.

1	shot(s)	**La Fée Parisienne (68%) absinthe**
1	shot(s)	**Teichenné Peach Schnapps Liqueur**
1	shot(s)	**Pomegranate (grenadine) syrup**
Top up with		**7-Up/lemonade**

Origin: Created in 2002 by Andy Jones at Yates's, London, England.
Comment: This bright red cocktail makes the strong aniseed flavours of absinthe approachable.

THE WENTWORTH

Glass: Martini
Garnish: Orange zest twist
Method: SHAKE all ingredients with ice and fine strain into chilled glass.

1 1/4 shot(s) **Buffalo Trace bourbon whiskey**
1 1/4 shot(s) **Dubonnet Red**
1 1/4 shot(s) **Ocean Spray cranberry juice**

Origin: Created in 2003 by Sharon Cooper at the Harvest Restaurant, Pomfret, Connecticut, USA.
Comment: Bourbon adds backbone to this fruity drink.

WET MARTINI

Glass: Martini
Garnish: Olive or twist?
Method: STIR all ingredients with ice and strain into chilled glass.

3 shot(s) **Plymouth gin**
1 1/2 shot(s) **Dry vermouth**

Origin: A generous measure of vermouth to two of gin, hence the name 'Wet' Martini.
Comment: Reputed to be a favourite of HRH Prince Charles.

THE WET SPOT

Glass: Martini
Garnish: Lemon zest twist
Method: SHAKE all ingredients with ice and fine strain into chilled glass.

1 1/2 shot(s) **Plymouth gin**
1/2 shot(s) **Giffard apricot brandy du Roussillon**
1 shot(s) **St-Germain elderflower liqueur**
1 shot(s) **Pressed apple juice**
3/4 shot(s) **Freshly squeezed lemon juice**

Origin: Adapted from a drink created by Willy Shine and Aisha Sharpe at Bed Bar, New York City, USA.
Comment: Sharp but fresh tasting and moreish.

WHAT THE HELL

Glass: Martini
Garnish: Lime wedge on rim
Method: SHAKE all ingredients with ice and fine strain into chilled glass.

2 shot(s) **Plymouth gin**
1 shot(s) **Giffard apricot brandy du Roussillon**
3/4 shot(s) **Dry vermouth**
1/4 shot(s) **Freshly squeezed lime juice**
1/8 shot(s) **Sugar syrup (2 sugar to 1 water)**

Comment: Gin and dry apricots.

WHIP ME & BEAT ME

Glass: Shot
Method: SHAKE all ingredients with ice and fine strain into chilled glass.

1/2 shot(s) **La Fée Parisienne (68%) absinthe**
1/2 shot(s) **Malibu coconut rum liqueur**
1/2 shot(s) **Double (heavy) cream**
1/2 shot(s) **Milk**

Comment: A creamy, coconut, absinthe laden shotn.

WHISKEY COBBLER

Glass: Goblet
Garnish: Lemon slice & mint sprig
Method: SHAKE all ingredients with ice and strain into glass filled with crushed ice.

2 shot(s) **Scotch whisky**
1/2 shot(s) **Rémy Martin cognac**
1/2 shot(s) **Grand Marnier liqueur**

Comment: A hardcore yet sophisticated drink.

WHISKEY COLLINS

Glass: Collins
Garnish: Orange slice & cherry (sail)
Method: SHAKE first four ingredients with ice and strain into ice-filled glass. **TOP** with soda water, lightly stir and serve with straws.

2 shot(s) **Buffalo Trace bourbon whiskey**
3/4 shot(s) **Freshly squeezed lemon juice**
1/2 shot(s) **Sugar syrup (2 sugar to 1 water)**
3 dashes **Angostura aromatic bitters**
Top up with **Soda water (club soda)**

Comment: A whiskey based twist on the classic Tom Collins.

WHISKEY DAISY

Glass: Martini
Garnish: Lemon zest twist
Method: SHAKE all ingredients with ice and fine strain into chilled glass.

1 3/4 shot(s) **Buffalo Trace bourbon whiskey**
3/4 shot(s) **Freshly squeezed lemon juice**
1/2 shot(s) **Cointreau triple sec**
1/4 shot(s) **Pomegranate (grenadine) syrup**

Comment: This venerable, bourbon led classic has a strong citrus flavour.

WHISKEY SOUR #1 (CLASSIC FORMULA)

Glass: Old-fashioned
Garnish: Lemon slice & cherry (sail)
Method: SHAKE all ingredients with ice and strain into ice-filled glass.

2 shot(s) **Buffalo Trace bourbon whiskey**
3/4 shot(s) **Freshly squeezed lemon juice**
1 shot(s) **Sugar syrup (2 sugar to 1 water)**
3 dashes **Angostura aromatic bitters**
1/2 fresh **Egg white**

Origin: This recipe follows the classic sour proportions (3:4:8): three quarter part of the sour ingredient (lemon juice), one part of the sweet ingredient (sugar syrup) and two parts of the strong ingredient (whiskey).
Comment: I find the classic formulation more sweet than sour and prefer the 4:2:8 ratio below.

WHISKEY SOUR #2 (DIFFORD'S FORMULA)

Glass: Old-fashioned
Garnish: Lemon slice & cherry (sail)
Method: SHAKE all ingredients with ice and strain into ice-filled glass.

2	shot(s)	**Buffalo Trace bourbon whiskey**
1	shot(s)	**Freshly squeezed lemon juice**
1/2	shot(s)	**Sugar syrup (2 sugar to 1 water)**
3	dashes	**Angostura aromatic bitters**
1/2	fresh	**Egg white**

Origin: My 4:2:8 sour formula.
Comment: Smooth with a hint of citrus sourness and an invigorating blast of whiskey.

WHISKEY SQUIRT

Glass: Collins
Garnish: Peach slice
Method: SHAKE first three ingredients with ice and strain into ice-filled glass. **TOP** with soda from a siphon. Serve with straws.

2	shot(s)	**Peach puree (sweetened)**
2	shot(s)	**Buffalo Trace bourbon whiskey**
1/4	shot(s)	**Grand Marnier liqueur**
Top up with		**Soda (from siphon)**

Origin: Adapted from a recipe purloined from David Embury's classic book, The Fine Art of Mixing Drinks.
Comment: Peach combines wonderfully with bourbon and this drink benefits from that marriage.

WHISKY FIZZ

Glass: Collins
Garnish: Lemon slice
Method: SHAKE first three ingredients with ice and strain into ice-filled glass. **TOP** with soda, lightly stir and serve with straws.

2	shot(s)	**Scotch whisky**
1	shot(s)	**Freshly squeezed lemon juice**
1/2	shot(s)	**Sugar syrup (2 sugar to 1 water)**
Top up with		**Soda from siphon**

Comment: The character of the whisky shines through this refreshing, balanced, sweet and sour drink.

WHISKY MAC

Glass: Old-fashioned
Method: POUR ingredients into ice-filled glass and lightly stir.

2	shot(s)	**Scotch whisky**
1	shot(s)	**Stone's green ginger wine**

Comment: Ginger wine smoothes and spices Scotch.

WHITE COSMO

Glass: Martini
Garnish: Orange zest twist
Method: SHAKE all ingredients with ice and fine strain into chilled glass.

1	shot(s)	**Ketel One Citroen vodka**
1	shot(s)	**Cointreau triple sec**
1 1/2	shot(s)	**White cranberry & grape juice**
1/2	shot(s)	**Freshly squeezed lime juice**

AKA: Cosmo Blanco
Origin: Emerged during 2002 in New York City.
Comment: Just what it says on the tin.

WHITE ELEPHANT

Glass: Martini
Garnish: Dust with cocoa powder
Method: SHAKE all ingredients with ice and fine strain into chilled glass.

1 3/4	shot(s)	**Ketel One vodka**
3/4	shot(s)	**Giffard white crème de cacao**
3/4	shot(s)	**Double (heavy) cream**
3/4	shot(s)	**Milk**

AKA: White Beach
Comment: Smooth and creamy with a hint of chocolate.

WHITE GIN FIZZ

Glass: Collins
Garnish: Lemon wedge in drink
Method: SHAKE first four ingredients with ice and strain into ice-filled glass. **TOP** with soda from a siphon.

2	shot(s)	**Plymouth gin**
1	shot(s)	**Freshly squeezed lemon juice**
1/4	shot(s)	**Sugar syrup (2 sugar to 1 water)**
2	scoops	**Lemon sorbet (see recipe under 'L')**
Top up with		**Soda water (from siphon)**

Origin: Created in 2003 by Tony Conigliaro at Shumi, London, England.
Comment: Almost creamy in consistency, this gin fizz reminds me of the Sgroppino found in Venice.

WHITE KNIGHT

Glass: Martini
Garnish: Grated nutmeg
Method: SHAKE all ingredients with ice and fine strain into chilled glass.

3/4	shot(s)	**Scotch whisky**
3/4	shot(s)	**Kahlúa coffee liqueur**
3/4	shot(s)	**Drambuie liqueur**
3/4	shot(s)	**Double (heavy) cream**
3/4	shot(s)	**Milk**

Comment: This creamy after-dinner drink features Scotch and honey with a hint of coffee. Not too sweet.

WHITE LADY

Glass: Martini
Garnish: Lemon zest twist
Method: SHAKE all ingredients with ice and fine strain into chilled glass.

2	shot(s)	**Plymouth gin**
3/4	shot(s)	**Cointreau triple sec**
3/4	shot(s)	**Freshly squeezed lemon juice**
1	fresh	**Egg white**

Origin: In 1919 Harry MacElhone, while working at Ciro's Club, London, England, created his first White Lady with 2 shots triple sec, 1 shot white crème de menthe and 1 shot lemon juice. In 1923, he created the White Lady above at his own Harry's New York Bar in Paris, France.
Comment: A simple but lovely classic drink with a sour finish

WHITE LION

Glass: Martini
Garnish: Lime wedge on rim
Method: SHAKE all ingredients with ice and fine strain into chilled glass.

2	shot(s)	**Light white rum**
1/4	shot(s)	**Cointreau triple sec**
1/2	shot(s)	**Freshly squeezed lime juice**
1/4	shot(s)	**Pomegranate (grenadine) syrup**

Origin: Adapted from a recipe purloined from David Embury's classic book, The Fine Art of Mixing Drinks.
Comment: This fruity Daiquiri is superb when made with quality pomegranate syrup and rum.

WHITE RUSSIAN

Glass: Old-fashioned
Garnish: Dust with grated nutmeg
Method: SHAKE all ingredients with ice and strain into ice-filled glass.

2	shot(s)	**Ketel One vodka**
1	shot(s)	**Kahlúa coffee liqueur**
3/4	shot(s)	**Double (heavy) cream**
3/4	shot(s)	**Milk**

Variant: Shake and strain vodka and coffee liqueur, then float cream.
Comment: A Black Russian smoothed with cream.

WHITE SANGRIA

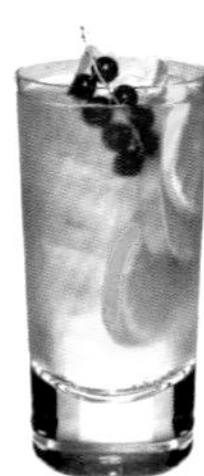

Glass: Old-fashioned
Garnish: Fruit slices
Method: SHAKE first three ingredients with ice and strain into ice-filled glass. **TOP** with 7-Up.

1	shot(s)	**Grand Marnier liqueur**
2	shot(s)	**Sauvignon Blanc wine**
1	shot(s)	**Ocean Spray white cranberry**
Top up with		**7-Up**

Comment: A twist on the traditional Spanish and Portugese punch.

WHITE SATIN

Glass: Martini
Garnish: Cocoa dust
Method: SHAKE all ingredients with ice and fine strain into chilled glass.

1 1/2	shot(s)	**Galliano liqueur**
1	shot(s)	**Kahlúa coffee liqueur**
3/4	shot(s)	**Double (heavy) cream**
3/4	shot(s)	**Milk**

Comment: Smoother than a cashmere codpiece!

WHITE STINGER

Glass: Old-fashioned
Method: SHAKE all ingredients with ice and strain into ice-filled glass.

2	shot(s)	**Ketel One vodka**
1/2	shot(s)	**White crème de menthe**
1/2	shot(s)	**Giffard white crème de cacao**

Comment: Liquid After Eights.

WIBBLE

Glass: Martini
Garnish: Lemon zest twist
Method: SHAKE all ingredients with ice and fine strain into chilled glass.

1	shot(s)	**Plymouth gin**
1	shot(s)	**Plymouth sloe gin liqueur**
1	shot(s)	**Freshly squeezed grapefruit juice**
1/4	shot(s)	**Freshly squeezed lemon juice**
1/8	shot(s)	**Sugar syrup (2 sugar to 1 water)**
1/8	shot(s)	**Giffard mûre (blackberry) liqueur**

Origin: Created in 1999 by Dick Bradsell at The Player, London, England, for Nick Blacknell, a conspicuous lover of gin.
Comment: As Dick once said to me, "It may make you wobble, but it won't make you fall down." Complex and balanced.

WIDOW'S KISS

Glass: Martini
Garnish: Mint leaf
Method: SHAKE all ingredients with ice and fine strain into chilled glass.

1 1/2	shot(s)	**Boulard Grand Solage Calvados**
3/4	shot(s)	**Bénédictine D.O.M. liqueur**
3/4	shot(s)	**Yellow Chartreuse liqueur**
3/4	shot(s)	**Chilled water (omit if ice wet)**
2	dashes	**Angostura aromatic bitters**

Origin: Created before 1895 by George Kappeler at New York City's Holland House. This classic was originally made with green Chartreuse but is better with yellow.
Comment: Fantastically herbal with hints of apple, mint and eucalyptus.

WILD HONEY [UPDATED #7]

Glass: Martini
Garnish: Grate nutmeg over drink
Method: SHAKE all ingredients with ice and fine strain into chilled glass.

- 1 shot(s) **Scotch whisky**
- 1/2 shot(s) **Vanilla infused Ketel One vodka**
- 3/4 shot(s) **Drambuie liqueur**
- 1/2 shot(s) **Galliano liqueur**
- 1/2 shot(s) **Double (heavy) cream**
- 1/2 shot(s) **Milk**

Origin: Created in 2001 by James Price at Bar Red, London, England.
Comment: A serious yet creamy after dinner cocktail with whisky and honey.

WILD PROMENADE MARTINI

Glass: Martini
Garnish: Float 3 raspberries
Method: MUDDLE cucumber and raspberries in base of shaker. Add other ingredients, **SHAKE** with ice and fine strain into ice-filled glass.

- 2 inch **Chopped cucumber**
- 5 fresh **Raspberries**
- 1 1/2 shot(s) **Ketel One vodka**
- 1/2 shot(s) **Raspberry flavoured vodka**
- 1/2 shot(s) **Giffard crème de framboise**
- 1/4 shot(s) **Sugar syrup (2 sugar to 1 water)**

Origin: Created in 2002 by Mehdi Otmann at The Player, London, England.
Comment: Rich raspberry with green hints of cucumber.

WILTON MARTINI

Glass: Martini
Garnish: Float cinnamon dusted apple slice
Method: SHAKE all ingredients with ice and fine strain into chilled glass.

- 1 shot(s) **Ketel One vodka**
- 1 shot(s) **Boulard Grand Solage Calvados**
- 1/2 shot(s) **Apple schnapps liqueur**
- 1/8 shot(s) **Cinnamon schnapps liqueur**
- 1 1/2 shot(s) **Pressed apple juice**

Origin: An adaptation (2003) of the signature cocktail at The Blue Bar, London, England.
Comment: Refined cinnamon and apple.

WIMBLEDON MARTINI

Glass: Martini
Garnish: Strawberry on rim
Method: MUDDLE strawberries in base of shaker. Add other ingredients, **SHAKE** with ice and fine strain into chilled glass.

- 6 fresh **Hulled strawberries**
- 1 1/2 shot(s) **Light white rum**
- 1 1/2 shot(s) **Giffard crème de fraise de bois**
- 1/4 shot(s) **Sugar syrup (2 sugar to 1 water)**
- 1/2 shot(s) **Double (heavy) cream**
- 1/2 shot(s) **Milk**

Comment: Takes some getting through the strainer, but when you do it's simply strawberries and cream.

THE WINDSOR ROSE

Glass: Martini
Garnish: Float rose petal
Method: SHAKE all ingredients with ice and fine strain into chilled glass.

- 1 shot(s) **Orange zest infused Ketel One vodka**
- 1 shot(s) **Cointreau triple sec**
- 1 1/2 shot(s) **Ocean Spray cranberry juice**
- 1/2 shot(s) **Freshly squeezed lime juice**
- 1/8 shot(s) **Rosewater**

Origin: Discovered in 2005 at The Polo Club Lounge, New Orleans, USA.
Comment: An range vodka and rosewater Cosmo.

WINDY MILLER

Glass: Collins
Garnish: Thin slices of lemon
Method: SHAKE first three ingredients with ice and strain into glass filled with crushed ice. **TOP** with 7-Up.

- 1 shot(s) **Ketel One Citroen vodka**
- 1 shot(s) **Mandarine Napoléon liqueur**
- 1/2 shot(s) **La Fée Parisienne (68%) absinthe**
- Top up with **7-Up**

Origin: Discovered in 2000 at Teatro, London, England.
Comment: British readers over 40 may remember the children's TV series Trumpton, Chigley and Camberwick Green. If you do, then sing between sips, 'Pugh, Pugh, Barney McGrew, Cuthbert, Dibble and Grubb.'

WINE COOLER

Glass: Collins
Method: POUR first four ingredients into ice-filled glass. **TOP** with 7-Up, lightly stir and serve with straws.

- 4 shot(s) **Sauvignon Blanc wine**
- 1/2 shot(s) **Ketel One Citroen vodka**
- 1/2 shot(s) **Freshly squeezed lemon juice**
- 1/2 shot(s) **Freshly squeezed orange juice**
- Top up with **7-Up/lemonade**

Comment: Like a citrussy white wine Spritzer.

WINK

Glass: Old-fashioned
Garnish: Wink as you serve
Method: POUR absinthe into ice-filled glass. **TOP** with chilled water and leave to stand. Separately **SHAKE** other ingredients with ice. **DISCARD** contents of glass and strain contents of shaker into empty (absinthe washed) glass.

- 1/2 shot(s) **La Fée Parisienne (68%) absinthe**
- 2 shot(s) **Plymouth gin**
- 1/2 shot(s) **Sugar syrup (2 sugar to 1 water)**
- 1/4 shot(s) **Cointreau triple sec**
- 2 dashes **Peychaud's aromatic bitters**
- 1/2 shot(s) **Chilled mineral water** (omit if wet ice)

Origin: Created in 2002 by Tony Conigliaro at Lonsdale House, London, England.
Comment: A pink rinsed drink with a wonderfully aromatic flavour.

WINTER MARTINI

Glass: Martini
Garnish: Lemon zest twist
Method: **STIR** all ingredients with ice and strain into chilled glass.

2	shot(s)	**Rémy Martin cognac**
1/2	shot(s)	**Sour apple liqueur**
1/2	shot(s)	**Dry vermouth**
1/8	shot(s)	**Sugar syrup (2 sugar to 1 water)**

Comment: Reminiscent of an Apple Cart (a Calvados Sidecar), this is simple, balanced and tastes great.

WISECRACK FIZZ [NEW #7]

Glass: Collins
Garnish: Lemon zest twist
Method: **SHAKE** first four ingredients with ice and strain into an ice-filled glass. **TOP** with soda and serve with straws.

1 1/2	shot(s)	**Pisco**
1	shot(s)	**St-Germain elderflower liqueur**
1	shot(s)	**Freshly squeezed grapefruit juice**
1/2	shot(s)	**Freshly squeezed lemon juice**
Top up with		**Soda water (club soda)**

Origin: Created in 2007 by Matt Gee at Milk & Honey, New York City, USA.
Comment: Light, balanced and refreshing. The pisco character shines through.

WONKY MARTINI

Glass: Martini
Garnish: Orange zest twist
Method: **STIR** all ingredients with ice and strain into chilled glass.

1 1/2	shot(s)	**Vanilla infused Ketel One vodka**
1 1/2	shot(s)	**Tuaca Italian liqueur**
1 1/2	shot(s)	**Sweet vermouth**
2	dashes	**Fee Brothers orange bitters**

Origin: Created in 2003 by yours truly.
Comment: A sweet, wet Vodkatini invigorated with orange and vanilla.

WOODLAND PUNCH

Glass: Collins
Garnish: Lime wedge
Method: **SHAKE** first four ingredients with ice and strain into ice-filled glass. **TOP** with soda, lightly stir and serve with straws.

2	shot(s)	**Southern Comfort liqueur**
1/4	shot(s)	**Cherry (brandy) liqueur**
1/2	shot(s)	**Freshly squeezed lime juice**
2	shot(s)	**Pressed pineapple juice**
Top up with		**Soda water**

Origin: Adapted from a drink created in 1997 by Foster Creppel. This is the signature drink at his Woodland Plantation, the great house on the west bank of the Mississippi that features on every bottle of Southern Comfort.
Comment: Tart, tangy and refreshing.

WOO WOO

Glass: Old-fashioned
Garnish: Split lime wedge
Method: **SHAKE** all ingredients with ice and strain into ice-filled glass.

2	shot(s)	**Ketel One vodka**
1	shot(s)	**Teichenné Peach Schnapps Liqueur**
3	shot(s)	**Ocean Spray cranberry juice**

Comment: Fruity, dry cranberry laced with vodka and peach. Not nearly as bad as its reputation but still lost in the eighties.

YACHT CLUB

Glass: Martini
Garnish: Lemon zest twist
Method: **STIR** all ingredients with ice and strain into chilled glass.

2	shot(s)	**Golden rum**
1	shot(s)	**Sweet vermouth**
1/4	shot(s)	**Giffard apricot brandy du Roussillon**

Origin: Adapted from a recipe purloined from David Embury's classic book, The Fine Art of Mixing Drinks.
Comment: Rich and slightly sweet with hints of apricot fruit.

YELLOW BELLY MARTINI

Glass: Martini
Garnish: Lemon zest twist
Method: **SHAKE** all ingredients with ice and fine strain into chilled glass.

1	shot(s)	**Ketel One Citroen vodka**
1	shot(s)	**Freshly squeezed lemon juice**
1	shot(s)	**Luxardo limoncello liqueur**
1/8	shot(s)	**Sugar syrup (2 sugar to 1 water)**
1/2	shot(s)	**Chilled mineral water** (omit if wet ice)

Comment: Lemon, lemon, lemon. Nice, though...

YELLOW BIRD [UPDATED #7]

Glass: Martini
Garnish: Banana slice on rim
Method: **SHAKE** all ingredients with ice and fine strain into chilled glass.

1 1/2	shot(s)	**Golden rum**
1/2	shot(s)	**Giffard crème de banane du Brésil**
1/4	shot(s)	**Giffard apricot brandy du Roussillon**
1 1/2	shot(s)	**Pressed pineapple juice**
1/4	shot(s)	**Freshly squeezed lime juice**
1/4	shot(s)	**Galliano liqueur**

Comment: A sweet and sour cocktail with four different fruits, rum and a splash of Galliano.

YELLOW FEVER MARTINI

Glass: Martini
Garnish: Pineapple wedge on rim
Method: SHAKE all ingredients with ice and fine strain into chilled glass.

2½	shot(s)	**Ketel One vodka**
½	shot(s)	**Galliano liqueur**
1½	shot(s)	**Pressed pineapple juice**
½	shot(s)	**Freshly squeezed lime juice**
1/8	shot(s)	**Sugar syrup (2 sugar to 1 water)**

Comment: Fortified pineapple with a subtle hint of cooling peppermint.

YELLOW PARROT

Glass: Martini
Garnish: Orange zest twist
Method: SHAKE all ingredients with ice and fine strain into chilled glass.

¼	shot(s)	**La Fée Parisienne (68%) absinthe**
1	shot(s)	**Yellow Chartreuse liqueur**
1	shot(s)	**Giffard apricot brandy du Roussillon**
1	shot(s)	**Chilled mineral water** (reduce if wet ice)

Origin: Some say this was created in 1935 by Albert Coleman at The Stork Club, New York City, but the drink featured in Harry Craddock's Savoy Cocktail Book five years before that.
Comment: The aniseed of the absinthe combines well with the other ingredients. A bit of a sweety but a strong old bird.

YULE LUVIT

Glass: Shot
Garnish: Grate nutmeg over drink
Method: Refrigerate ingredients then **LAYER** in chilled glass by carefully pouring in the following order.

¾	shot(s)	**Hazelnut liqueur**
¾	shot(s)	**Buffalo Trace bourbon whiskey**

Comment: Actually, you'll find it strongly nutty and sweet.

YUM

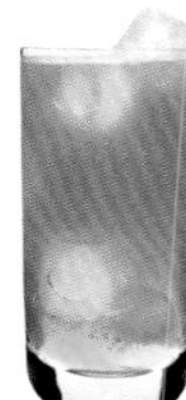

Glass: Collins
Garnish: Lemon wedge
Method: SHAKE all ingredients with ice and strain into ice-filled glass.

1½	shot(s)	**Mandarine Napoléon liqueur**
½	shot(s)	**Teichenné Peach Schnapps Liqueur**
¼	shot(s)	**Chambord black raspberry liqueur**
1	shot(s)	**Freshly squeezed lemon juice**
3	shot(s)	**Pressed apple juice**

Comment: If you like sweet, fruity 'disco drinks' then this is indeed yummy.

Z MARTINI

Glass: Martini
Garnish: Hand stuffed blue cheese olives
Method: STIR all ingredients with ice and strain into chilled glass.

2½	shot(s)	**Ketel One vodka**
1¼	shot(s)	**Dry white port (e.g. Dow's Fine White)**

Origin: Discovered in 2004 at Les Zygomates, Boston, USA.
Comment: Grainy vodka with dry, wine-like notes. Top marks for the garnish alone.

ZABAGLIONE MARTINI

Glass: Martini
Method: Separately **BEAT** egg white until stiff and frothy and yolk until this is as liquid as water, then pour into shaker. Add other ingredients, **SHAKE** with ice and fine strain into chilled glass.

1	fresh	**Egg yolk**
1	fresh	**Egg white**
1½	shot(s)	**Bols advocaat liqueur**
½	shot(s)	**Rémy Martin cognac**
1	shot(s)	**Marsala**
¾	shot(s)	**Freshly squeezed lemon juice**

Origin: I created this drink in 2003 after the classic Italian dessert, which incidentally derives its name from the Neapolitan dialect word 'zapillare', meaning 'to foam'.
Comment: Like the dessert, this is sweet and rich with flavours of egg and fortified wine.

ZAKUSKI MARTINI

Glass: Martini
Garnish: Lemon zest & cucumber peel
Method: MUDDLE cucumber in base of shaker. Add other ingredients, **SHAKE** with ice and fine strain into chilled glass.

1	inch	**Peeled cucumber (chopped)**
2	shot(s)	**Ketel One Citroen vodka**
½	shot(s)	**Cointreau triple sec**
½	shot(s)	**Freshly squeezed lemon juice**
¼	shot(s)	**Sugar syrup (2 sugar to 1 water)**

Origin: Created in 2002 by Alex Kammerling, London, England.
Comment: Appropriately named after the Russian snack.

THE ZAMBOANGA 'ZEINIE' COCKTAIL

Glass: Martini
Garnish: Lime zest twist (discarded) & cherry
Method: SHAKE all ingredients with ice and fine strain into chilled glass.

2	shot(s)	**Rémy Martin cognac**
1	shot(s)	**Pressed pineapple juice**
½	shot(s)	**Freshly squeezed lime juice**
¼	shot(s)	**Maraschino syrup (from cherries)**
2	dashes	**Angostura aromatic bitters**

Origin: Adapted from a recipe in Charles H. Baker Jr's classic book, The Gentleman's Companion. He describes this as "another palate twister from the land where the Monkeys Have No Tails. This drink found its way down through the islands to Mindanao from Manila. . .".
Comment: Reminiscent of a tropical Sidecar.

ZANZIBAR

Glass: Old-fashioned
Garnish: Lime zest twist
Method: SHAKE all ingredients with ice and strain into glass filled with crushed ice.

2	shot(s)	**Goslings Black Seal rum**
1/4	shot(s)	**Giffard apricot brandy du Roussillon**
1/4	shot(s)	**Grand Marnier liqueur**
1/2	shot(s)	**Freshly squeezed orange juice**
1/2	shot(s)	**Freshly squeezed lime juice**
1/8	shot(s)	**Almond (orgeat) syrup**

Origin: Discovered in 2005 at Zanzi Bar, Prague, Czech Republic.
Comment: Tangy rum and citrus with fruit and hints of almond.

ZAZA [UPDATED #7]

Glass: Martini
Garnish: Orange zest twist
Method: SHAKE all ingredients with ice and fine strain into chilled glass.

2	shot(s)	**Plymouth gin**
2	shot(s)	**Dubonnet Red (French made)**

AKA: Dubonnet Cocktail
Variant: Substitute sloe gin or fino sherry for gin.
Origin: I've adapted this from a recipe in Harry Craddock's 1930 'Savoy Cocktail Book'. It is named after a French play which was a hit around the verge of the 20th century and was followed by opera and film versions.
Comment: Zaza is a diminutive of Isabelle. But there's nothing diminutive about this simple, yet fantastic drink.

ZELDA MARTINI

Glass: Martini
Garnish: Mint sprig
Method: Lightly **MUDDLE** mint (just to bruise) in base of shaker. Add other ingredients, **SHAKE** with ice and fine strain into chilled glass.

5	fresh	**Mint leaves**
2	shot(s)	**Zubrówka bison vodka**
1	shot(s)	**Freshly squeezed lime juice**
3/4	shot(s)	**Almond (orgeat) syrup**
1/2	shot(s)	**Chilled mineral water** (omit if wet ice)

Origin: Created in May 2002 by Phillip Jeffrey at the GE Club, London, England. He made it for a friend called Zelda – and the name really wouldn't have worked if she'd been called Tracy.
Comment: Bison grass vodka combines brilliantly with mint and almond.

ZESTY

Glass: Old-fashioned
Garnish: Lime zest twist
Method: SHAKE all ingredients with ice and strain into glass filled with crushed ice.

2	shot(s)	**Frangelico hazelnut liqueur**
1/2	shot(s)	**Freshly squeezed lime juice**

Comment: Citrus fresh with a nutty touch.

ZEUS MARTINI

Glass: Martini
Garnish: Float three coffee beans
Method: POUR Fernet Branca into frozen glass, swirl round and **DISCARD. MUDDLE** raisins with cognac in base of shaker. Add other ingredients, **SHAKE** with ice and fine strain into chilled glass.

1	shot(s)	**Fernet Branca**
25	dried	**Raisins**
2	shot(s)	**Rémy Martin cognac**
1/4	shot(s)	**Maple syrup**
1/8	shot(s)	**Kahlúa coffee liqueur**
1	shot(s)	**Chilled mineral water** (reduce if wet ice)

Origin: Adapted from Dr Zeus, a cocktail created by Adam Ennis in 2001 at Isola, London, England.
Comment: Rich, pungent and not sweet.

ZHIVAGO MARTINI

Glass: Martini
Garnish: Float wafer thin apple slice
Method: SHAKE all ingredients with ice and fine strain into chilled glass.

1 1/2	shot(s)	**Vanilla infused Ketel One vodka**
1/2	shot(s)	**Buffalo Trace bourbon whiskey**
1/2	shot(s)	**Sour apple liqueur**
1	shot(s)	**Freshly squeezed lime juice**
3/4	shot(s)	**Sugar syrup (2 sugar to 1 water)**

Origin: Created in by Alex Kammerling, London.
Comment: Perfectly balanced sweet and sour – sweet apple, vanilla and bourbon balanced by lime juice..

ZINGY GINGER MARTINI

Glass: Martini
Garnish: Lemon zest twist
Method: SHAKE all ingredients with ice and fine strain into chilled glass.

2 1/2	shot(s)	**Ketel One Citroen vodka**
1/2	shot(s)	**Freshly squeezed lemon juice**
1/2	shot(s)	**Ginger cordial**
1/2	shot(s)	**Chilled mineral water** (omit if wet ice)

Origin: Created in 2001 by Reece Clark at Hush Up, London, England.
Comment: It sure is both zingy and gingery..

ZOMBIE #1 (INTOXICA! RECIPE)

Glass: Hurricane
Garnish: Mint sprig
Method: STIR brown sugar with lemon juice in base of shaker until it dissolves. Add other ingredients, **SHAKE** with ice and strain into ice-filled glass.

1	spoon	**Brown sugar**
1	shot(s)	**Freshly squeezed lemon juice**
1	shot(s)	**Light white rum**
1	shot(s)	**Golden rum**
1	shot(s)	**Demerara 151° overproof rum**
1	shot(s)	**Pressed pineapple juice**
1	shot(s)	**Freshly squeezed lime juice**
1	shot(s)	**Passion fruit syrup**
1	dash	**Angostura aromatic bitters**

Origin: The above recipe for Don the Beachcomber's classic cocktail is based on one published in Intoxica! by Jeff Berry.**Comment:** Plenty of flavour and alcohol with tangy rum and fruit.

W

ZOMBIE #2 (VIC'S FORMULA)

Glass: Collins (14oz)
Garnish: Mint sprig
Method: **BLEND** all ingredients with one 12oz scoop crushed ice. Serve with straws.

3/4	shot(s)	**Light white rum**
3/4	shot(s)	**Aged Jamaican rum**
1/2	shot(s)	**Grand Marnier liqueur**
1 1/2	shot(s)	**Freshly squeezed orange juice**
2 1/2	shot(s)	**Pressed pineapple juice**
1	shot(s)	**Freshly squeezed lemon juice**
1/2	shot(s)	**Freshly squeezed lime juice**
1/4	shot(s)	**Pomegranate (grenadine) syrup**

Origin: Adapted from a recipe in the 1947-72 Trader Vic's Bartender's Guide by Victor Bergeron.
Comment: More fruit than alcohol but tangy not sweet.

ZOMBIE #3 (MODERN FORMULA)

Glass: Hurricane
Garnish: Pineapple wedge
Method: **SHAKE** first nine ingredients with ice and strain into glass filled with crushed ice. **FLOAT** rum.

3/4	shot(s)	**Light white rum**
3/4	shot(s)	**Pusser's Navy rum**
3/4	shot(s)	**Golden rum**
1/2	shot(s)	**Giffard apricot brandy du Roussillon**
1/2	shot(s)	**Grand Marnier liqueur**
2 1/2	shot(s)	**Freshly squeezed orange juice**
2 1/2	shot(s)	**Pressed pineapple juice**
1	shot(s)	**Freshly squeezed lime juice**
1/2	shot(s)	**Pomegranate (grenadine) syrup**
1/2	shot(s)	**Wray & Nephew overproof rum**

Comment: A heady mix of four different rums with pineapple, orange, lime and grenadine.

ZOOM 

Glass: Martini
Garnish: Dust with cocoa powder
Method: **SHAKE** all ingredients with ice and fine strain into chilled glass.

2 1/2	shot(s)	**Rémy Martin cognac**
3	spoons	**Runny honey**
1/2	shot(s)	**Double (heavy) cream**
1/2	shot(s)	**Milk**

Variant: Base on other spirits or add a dash of cacao.
Comment: Cognac is smoothed with honey and softened with milk and cream in this classic cocktail.

ZUB-WAY

Glass: Collins
Garnish: Three raspberries
Method: Chop watermelon and **MUDDLE** in base of shaker with raspberries. Add other ingredients, **SHAKE** with ice and fine strain into ice-filled glass.

1/16	fresh	**Watermelon (diced)**
2 1/2	shot(s)	**Zubrówka bison vodka**
1/2	shot(s)	**Sugar syrup (2 sugar to 1 water)**

Origin: Created in 1999 by Jamie Terrell, London.
Comment: Few ingredients, but loads of flavour.

ZOMBIE

This cocktail is thought to have been created in 1934 by Don the Beachcomber at his Beachcomber restaurant in Hollywood.

However, Charles H Baker claimed that a man named Christopher Clark invented a Zombie cocktail in 1935 after returning from Haiti. Joseph Lanza claimed that a Zombie cocktail debuted at the 1939 World's Fair in Flushing, New York. And a Zombie with an overproof rum float seems to have appeared in Patrick Duffy's bar manual of 1934.

But whatever the truth of the matter, the recipes here derive from Don the Beachcomber's Zombie, a drink that David Embury describes as the "grandfather of all pixies, and great-uncle to the gremlins". Trader Vic, with Beach the founding father of Tiki drinks, wrote of this drink on his menus, "a real dirty stinker".

DON'S ORIGINAL ZOMBIE FORMULA

Glass: 14 oz
Garnish: Pineapple wedge, orange slice, cherry & mint sprig
Method: BLEND all ingredients with crushed ice and pour into a glass with three or four ice cubes.

1 1/4	shot(s)	Puerto Rican Ramirez Royal rum
1	shot(s)	Demerara 151° overproof rum
1	shot(s)	Cuban Palau 30 year old rum
1	shot(s)	Jamaican 32 year old rum
1	shot(s)	Myers's Planter's Punch rum
3/4	shot(s)	Maraschino liqueur
1/2	shot(s)	Velvet Falernum liqueur
1/2	shot(s)	Freshly squeezed grapefruit juice
3/4	shot(s)	Freshly squeezed lime juice
1/2	shot(s)	Sugar syrup (2 sugar to 1 water)
2	dashes	Pernod anis
2	dashes	Angostura aromatic bitters
3	dashes	Grenadine syrup

Origin: The above recipe is from a book called Hawai'i: Tropical Rum Drinks & Cuisine by Don The Beachcomber, written by Arnold Bitner & Phoebe Beach (Don's widow).

INGREDIENTS INDEX

ABSINTHE

See 'La Fée Parisienne (68%) Absinthe'

ADVOCAAT LIQUEUR

See 'Bols Advocaat Liqueur'

AGAVE SYRUP

Agave syrup (also called agave nectar) is a sweetener which can be used in place of sugar and honey, and pairs particularly well with tequila, the spirit from its parent plant. It is as much as two-thirds sweeter than sugar but is less viscous than honey.

Agave syrup is commercially produced in Jalisco, Mexico, from several species of agave, in a roughly similar way to maple syrup. Juices are tapped from the core of the agave, the piña, and filtered, then heated, to turn carbohydrates into sugars. Agave syrup reportedly has a much lower glycemic index than sugar.

Almond Old Fashioned ●●●●◐
Chihuahua Margarita ●●●◐○
Estes ●●●●○
Estilo Viejo ●●●●◐
Paloma ●●●●◐
Pineapple & Sage Margarita ●●●●◐
Tequila Smash ●●●●◐
Tommy's Margarita ●●●●●

ALMOND (ORGEAT) SUGAR SYRUP

0% **alc./vol.** (0°proof)
This is a sweet syrup traditionally made from almonds, sugar and rose water or orange flower water. It is nown in French as 'orgeat sirop' (pronounced 'Ohr-Zhat'), and many older recipes will call for simply 'Orgeat'.

Army & Navy ●●●●○
Blue Bird ●●●○○
Cameron's Kick ●●●●○
Cool Orchard ●●●●○
Cosmopolitan Delight ●●●●◐
Daiquiri De Luxe ●●●●○
Dead Man's Mule ●●●◐○
Fog Cutter #1 ●●●●○
Green Eyes ●●●◐○
Japanese Cocktail ●●●●○
Kiwi Crush ●●●●○
Lemon Butter Cookie ●●●●○
Mai Tai #3 ●●●●● (Difford's Formula)
Marama Rum Punch ●●●●○
Mauresque ●●●○○
Menehune Juice ●●●●○
Momisette ●●●●○
Pinky Pincher ●●●●○
Potted Parrot ●●●◐○
Scorpion ●●●●○
Sun Kissed Virgin ●●●○○ (Mocktail)
Thai Lemonade ●●●◐○ (Mocktail)
Tiki Bar Margarita ●●●●◐
Tiki Max ●●●●○
Union Club ●●●●○
Zanzibar ●●●◐○
Zelda Martini ●●●●○

AMARETTO LIQUEUR

See 'Luxardo Amaretto di Saschira Liqueur'

AMONTILLADO

See 'Sherry – Amontillado'

ANGOSTURA AROMATIC BITTERS

44.7% **alc./vol.**

(89.4°proof)
www.angostura.com
Producer: Angostura Ltd, Laventille, Port of Spain, Trinidad, West Indies.

These famous bitters were first made in 1824 by the German Surgeon-General of a military hospital in the town of Angostura, Venezuela, to help treat stomach disorders and indigestion. In 1875, due to unrest in Venezuela, production was moved to Trinidad. It was here that the laid-back Caribbean attitude affected Angostura's packaging.
One day a new batch of labels was ordered and a simple mistake led to them being too big for the bottles. The error was spotted in time but everyone thought somebody else would deal with the problem. No one did, so they simply stuck the labels on the bottles, intending to fix the next batch. No one quite got round to it and the oversized label became a trademark of the brand.
One of the smallest bottles on any bar, Angostura is packed with flavour: Turkish coffee, jasmine, dried mint, fruit poached with cloves and cinnamon, cherry, orange and lemon zest. A dash adds that indefinable something which brings cocktails to life.

Abbey Martini ●●●◐○
Absinthe Cocktail #2 ●●●◐○
Adam & Eve ●●●●○
Affinity ●●●◐○
The Alamagoozlum Cocktail ●●●●◐
Alfonso ●●●◐○
Alfonso Martini ●●●●○
Amaretto Sour ●●●◐○
Americana ●●●○○
Ante ●●●●○
Apple Brandy Sour ●●●●◐
Apple Virgin Mojito (Mocktail) ●●●●○
Apricot Martini ●●●○○
Aunt Agatha ●●●◐○
Bahama Mama ●●●●○
Banana Cow ●●●○○
Barbara West ●●●◐○
Barnum ●●●●○ (Was Right)
Biarritz ●●●◐○
Bitter Elder ●●●◐○
Black Feather ●●●●○
Blackthorn Irish ●●●◐○
Blade Runner ●●●●○
Boomerang ●●●●○
Bourbon Smash ●●●◐○
Brandy Crusta ●●●●◐
Brandy Sour ●●●●◐
Brooklyn #1 ●●●●○
Brubaker Old-Fashioned ●●●●○
Buena Vida ●●●●◐
Call Me Old-Fashioned ●●●●◐
Caribbean PiÀa Colada ●●●◐○
Causeway ●●●◐○
Champagne Cocktail ●●●○○
Champagne Daisy ●●●○○
Chihuahua Magarita ●●●◐○
Cinderella (Mocktail) ●●◐○○
Club Cocktail #3 ●●●●○
The Comet ●●●●◐
Concealed Weapon ●●●○○
Coronation ●●●○○
Covadonga ●●●○○
Cranberry Delicious ●●●○○ (Mocktail)
Daiquiri No. 5 ●●●●○
Dandy Cocktail ●●●●◐
De La Louisiane #1 ●●●●○
Delmonico ●●●●○
Delmonico Special ●●●◐○
DNA #2 ●●●○○
Double Vision ●●●○○
The Dubonnet Cocktail ●●●●○
East India #1 ●●●●◐
East India #2 ●●●●○
El Burro ●●●●○
El Presidente #2 ●●●◐○
Elderflower Manhattan ●●●●◐
Elysian ●●●●○
Embassy Cocktail ●●●○○
Esquire #1 ●●●●○
Estilo Viejo ●●●●◐
Fancy Brandy ●●●◐○
Fancy Free ●●●●◐
Fantasia ●●●◐○ (Mocktail)
Fine & Dandy ●●●◐○
Flying Scotsman ●●●●○
Flying Tigre Coctel ●●●●○
Four W Daiquiri ●●●●○
French Mule ●●●●○
Gin Cocktail ●●●●○
Gin Gin Mule ●●●●○
Gin Punch ●●●●◐
Gin Sour ●●●●◐
Glenn's Bride ●●●●◐
Golden Dawn ●●●◐○
Golf Cocktail ●●●●○
Grand Passion ●●●○○
Grand Sazerac ●●●●○
Grape Delight ●●●●○
Grappa Manhattan ●●●●○
Green Fairy ●●●●○
Green Swizzle ●●●●○
Grog ●●●●○
Hazelnut Alexander ●●●●○
Hearst Martini ●●●●○
Hoa Sua ●●●●○
Honey Blossom ●●●○○ (Mocktail)
Honey Vodka Sour ●●●●○
Horse's Neck With a Kick ●●●○○
Hurricane #3 ●●●○○
I'll Take Manhattan ●●●●○
Imperial Martini ●●●○○
Incognito ●●●◐○
Income Tax Cocktail ●●●●○
Jack-In-The-Box ●●●●○
Jack Punch ●●●●○
Japanese Cocktail ●●●●○
Jerez ●●●●○
Jockey Club ●●●●○
The Journalist ●●●●○
Julep ●●●●●
The Juxtaposition ●●●●○
Kentucky Dream ●●●●○
Kool Hand Luke ●●●●○
Lemon Lime & Bitters ●●●◐○
Limey ●●●◐○
Liquorice Whiskey Sour ●●●●◐
Lolita Margarita ●●●●◐
Luxury Cocktail ●●●◐○
Luxury Mojito ●●●●○
Mai Tai #2 ●●●●○
Manhattan Dry ●●●●◐
Manhattan Perfect ●●●●●
Manhattan Sweet ●●●●●
Manhattan Island ●●●●○
Maple Old-Fashioned ●●●●○
Marama Rum Punch ●●●●○
Martini Special ●●●●◐
Medicinal Solution ●●●◐○
Merry Widow #1 ●●●◐○
Metropole ●●●◐○
Mexican 55 ●●●●○
Mexican Manhattan ●●●●○
Mint Julep ●●●●●
Mona Lisa ●●●●○
Montego Bay ●●●◐○
Morning Glory ●●●●○
Moscow Mule ●●●●○
Navy Grog ●●●●○
Noon ●●●●○
Oddball Manhattan Dry ●●●●○
Old Fashioned #1 ●●●●● (Classic Version)
Old Fashioned Caddy ●●●●○
Parma Negroni ●●●●○
Passion Punch ●●●◐○
Pegu Club ●●●●○
Pilgrim Cocktail ●●●●○
Pink Daiquiri ●●●●○
Pink Gin #1 ●●●●○ (Traditional)
Pink Gin #2 ●●●●○ (Modern)
Pink Gin & Tonic ●●●●○
Piscola ●●●◐○
Plantation Punch ●●●◐○
Planter's Punch ●●●●○
Playmate Martini ●●●●◐
Prickly Pear Mule ●●●●○
Prince Of Wales ●●●◐○
Queen's Park Swizzle ●●●●○
Rat Pack Manhattan ●●●●○
The Roadrunner ●●●●○
Rob Roy #1 ●●●●○
Rosita ●●●●○
Rum Punch ●●●●●
Rum Punch-Up ●●●●◐
Sailor's Comfort ●●●○○
St. Patrick's Day ●●●●○
St. Germain Sidecar ●●●●◐
Santiago ●●●○○
Sazerac ●●●●●
Seelbach ●●●○○
Shamrock #1 ●●●○○
Singapore Sling #2 ●●●●○
Singapore Sling #3 ●●●◐○
Sour ●●●◐○
South China Breeze ●●●●○
Southern Mule ●●●◐○
Spencer Cocktail ●●●●○
The Star #1 ●●●●○
Straits Sling ●●●●○
Suburban ●●●●○
Tarte Aux Pommes ●●●●○
Tequila'tini ●●●◐○
Tiki Max ●●●●○
Treacle ●●●●◐
Vanderbilt ●●●●◐
Velvet Fog ●●●●◐
Venus in Furs ●●●◐○
Vieux Carré Cocktail ●●●●◐
Vodka Sour ●●●●○
Vowel Cocktail ●●●●◐
Warsaw ●●●◐○
Whiskey Collins ●●●●◐
Whiskey Sour #1 (Classic Formula) ●●●●○
Whiskey Sour #2 (Difford's Formula) ●●●●●
Widow's Kiss ●●●●●
The Zamboanga 'Zeinie' Cocktail ●●●●○
Zombie #1 ●●●●○ (Intoxica! Recipe)

ANIS

See 'Pernod Anis'

ANISETTE LIQUEUR

This sweet, aniseed-flavoured liqueur often includes coriander and various other herbs. It is popular throughout the Mediterranean - in France, Spain and North Africa.

Absinthe Cocktail #2 ●●●◐○
Absinthe Frappé ●●●●○
Absinthe Italiano Cocktail ●●●○○
Absinthe Special Cocktial ●●●○○
Dream Cocktail ●●●●○
Fontainebleau Special ●●●◐○
Panachée ●●●○○

APPLEJACK BRANDY

See 'Calvados'

APPLE JUICE

The best way to use apples in cocktails is as a juice. You can make your own in a standard electric juice extractor. There's no need to peel or core apples, as the skin and core contain over half the fruit's nutrients. Simply remove the stalks and chop the fruit into small enough chunks to fit through the feeder. Choose a flavoursome variety like Bramley over more bland types like Washington Red or Golden Delicious.
Unchecked, the juice will quickly oxidise and discolour but a splash of lime juice helps prevent this without too much effect on the flavour. You'll find that crisper apples yield clearer juice. Most supermarkets carry at least one quality pressed apple juice and the best of these cloudy juices make DIY juicing unnecessary. Avoid the packaged 'pure', clear apple juices as these tend to be overly sweet and artificial tasting.

Achilles Heel ●●●●○
Alan's Apple Breeze ●●●◐○
Almond Martini #1 ●●●●○
Amber ●●●●◐
American Pie Martini ●●●●○
Aphrodisiac ●●●○○
Apple & Blackberry Pie ●●●◐○
Apple & Elderflower Martini ●●●●○ (Fresh Fruit)
Apple Breeze ●●●●○
Apple Buck ●●●●○
Apple Crumble Martini #1 ●●●◐○
Apple Crumble Martini #2 ●●●●○
Apple Daiquiri ●●●●○
Apple Mac ●●●●○
Apple Martini #1 ●●●●○ (simple version)
Apple Martini #2 ●●●●○
Apple of One's Eye ●●●◐○
Apple Pie Martini ●●●●○
Appleissimo ●●●●○
Apple Strudel #1 ●●●○○
Apple Strudel #2 ●●●●◐
Apple Virgin Mojito (Mocktail) ●●●●○
Applesinth ●●●●○
Applily Married ●●●●◐
Apricot Sour ●●●●○
Artlantic ●●●○○
Auntie's Hot Xmas Punch ●●●●○
Autumn Martini ●●●●○
Azure Martini ●●●●○
Banana Smoothie ●●●●◐ [Mocktail]
Bee Sting ●●●●○
Beetle Jeuse ●●●●○
Bitter Elder ●●●◐○
Black Bison Martini ●●●●◐
Black Bison Martini #2 ●●●●◐
Bossa Nova #1 ●●●●○
Canandian Apple ●●●●○ (Mocktail)
Chimayo ●●●●○
Chin Chin ●●●●○
Cider Apple Cooler ●●●●○
Cider Apple Martini ●●●●○
Congo Blue ●●●◐○
Coolman Martini ●●●●◐
Cranapple Breeze ●●●◐○
Crimea ●●●○○
Cucumber & Mint Martini ●●●●○
Cyder Press ●●●●○
Double Vision ●●●○○
Dutch Courage ●●●●○
Eastern Martini ●●●●◐
Eden ●●●●◐
El Torado ●●●●◐
Elder & Wiser ●●●●○
English Garden ●●●●○
Epiphany ●●●◐○
Escalator Martini ●●●●●
Extradition ●●●●○
French Monkey ●●●◐○
Frisky Bison ●●●●◐
Fuego Manzana No. 2 ●●●●○
Galvanised Nail ●●●◐○
GE Blonde ●●●●◐
Gin Garden ●●●●○
Ginger & Lemongrass Martini ●●●●○
Ginger Cosmos ●●●◐○
Ginger Martini ●●●●○
Gingerbread Martini ●●●●○
Giuseppe's Habit ●●●●○
Gold Member ●●●●○
Golden Dragon ●●●◐○
Grand Passion ●●●○○
Granny's ●●●●○
Grape Delight ●●●●○
Grapple Martini ●●●●○
Green Apple & Cucumber Martini ●●●●○
Green Destiny ●●●◐○
Green Tea Martini #1 ●●●●○
Gusto ●●●●○
Hakkantini ●●●●○
Havanatheone ●●●●●
Hawaiian Cosmopolitan ●●●●○
Highland Sling ●●●●○
Hobson's Choice ●●◐○○ (Mocktail)
Honey Apple Martini ●●●●○
The Honeysuckle Orchard ●●●●○
I B Damm'd ●●●●◐
Icewine Martini ●●●●○
Ignorance Is Bliss ●●●◐○
Jade Garden ●●●●○
Ja-Mora ●●●●○
Jules Delight ●●●●○
Jumbled Fruit Julep ●●●◐○
Katrina Cocktail ●●●○○
Kentucky Dream ●●●●○
Kentucky Mac ●●●◐○
Kentucky Muffin ●●●●○
Kentucky Pear ●●●●◐
Kiwi Crush ●●●●○
Krakow Tea ●●●●○
Kurrent Affair ●●●○○
The Last Straw ●●●●○
Lemon Butter Cookie ●●●●○
Lighter Breeze ●●●◐○
Long Flight of Stairs ●●●●◐
Love Junk ●●●◐○
Madroska ●●●○○
Mandarintini ●●●○○
Mango Rum Cooler ●●●◐○
Maple Pomme ●●●●○
The Mayflower Martini ●●●◐○
Mint Lineade ●●●●◐ (Mocktail)
Mitch Martini ●●●●○
Monza ●●●◐○
Moscow Lassi ●●●○○
Motox ●●●●○
Myrtle Martini ●●●◐○
New Year's Absolution ●●●◐○
Northern Lights ●●●●○
November Seabreeze ●●●◐○ (Mocktail)
Orchard Breeze ●●●●○
Palm Springs ●●●◐○
Pappy Honeysuckle ●●●●◐
Pear Shaped #1 ●●●●◐ (Deluxe Version)
Pear Shaped #2 ●●●●○ (Popular Version)
Planter's Punchless ●●●○○ (Mocktail)
Polish Martini ●●●●●
Pulp Fiction ●●●●○
Razzmatazz ●●●○○
R U Bobby Moore? ●●●●◐
Sage Martini ●●●●○
Satsuma Martini ●●●◐○
Serendipity #2 ●●●●○
Ski Breeze ●●●○○
Sleeping Bison-tini ●●●●○
Sourpuss Martini ●●●●○
Spiced Apple Daiquiri ●●●●○
Spiked Apple Cider (Hot) ●●●●○
Sporran Breeze ●●●●◐
Stairs Martini ●●●●●
Steep Flight ●●●●●
Strasberi Sling ●●●◐○
Strudel Martini ●●●●◐
Summer Breeze ●●●◐○
Tatanka ●●●●◐
Tatanka Royale ●●●●○
Teddy Bear'tini ●●●●○
Toffee Apple ●●●●○
Toffee Apple Martini ●●●●○
Tre Martini ●●●●○
Treacle ●●●●◐
Utterly Butterly ●●●◐○
Vanilla Laika ●●●◐○
Venus in Furs ●●●◐○
Verdant Martini ●●●●○
Verdi Martini ●●●●○
Voodoo ●●●●○
Warsaw Cooler ●●●●◐
Washington Apple ●●●●◐
The Wet Spot ●●●●○
Wilton Martini ●●●●○
Yum ●●●○○

APPLE SCHNAPPS LIQUEUR

The term schnapps traditionally suggests a clear strong spirit. However, over the last decade or so the term has come to refer to sweet liqueurs of only 20-24% alc./vol., which bear no resemblance to the strong, dry, almost vodka-style schnapps from which they take their name. I call such drinks 'schnapps liqueurs' to avoid confusion, which would certainly spoil a drink.

Amber ●●●●◐
American Pie Martini ●●●●○
Apple & Cranberry Pie ●●●◐○
Apple & Custard Cocktail ●●●◐○
Apple Manhattan #1 ●●●●○
Apple Manhattan #2 ●●●●○
Apple Martini #2 ●●●●○
Apple Mojito ●●●●○
Appleissimo ●●●●○
Apple Spritz ●●●●○
Apple Strudel #1 ●●●○○
Apple Strudel #2 ●●●●◐
Applesinth ●●●●○
Big Apple Martini ●●●◐○
Black Bison Martini ●●●●◐
Black Bison Martini #2 ●●●●◐
Cider Apple Cooler ●●●●○
Cider Apple Martini ●●●●○
Frisky Bison ●●●●◐
Fruit Pastel ●●●◐○
Fuego Manzana No. 2 ●●●●○
Gold Member ●●●●○
Granny's ●●●●○
Jean Marc ●●●●○
Northern Lights ●●●●○
Pulp Fiction ●●●●○
Robin Hood #1 ●●●●○
Sangria Martini ●●●●○
Sidecar Named Desire ●●●●○
Spiced Apple Daiquiri ●●●●○
Tarte Tatin Martini ●●●●○
Teddy Bear'tini ●●●●○
Thomas Blood Martini ●●●◐○
Toffee Apple ●●●●○
Wilton Martini ●●●●○

APRICOT BRANDY LIQUEUR

See 'Giffard Abricot Brandy du Roussillon'

BANANA

The fruit of a perennial herb that looks like a tree, bananas come in a range of hues from purple to yellow, although we are most familiar with the yellow kind. These are transported green and ripened prior to sale in dedicated ripening warehouses, and should not be stored in refrigerators as exposure to low temperatures turns the fruit black. They bring a distinctively sweet, smooth tropical flavour to drinks but suffer from association with disco drinks.

Avalanche ●●●○○
Banana Batida ●●●◐○
Banana Colada ●●●●○
Banana Cow ●●●○○
Banana Daiquiri ●●●◐○
Banana Smoothie ●●●●◐ [Mocktail]
Banoffee Martini ●●●●○
Beach Blonde ●●●●○
Dirty Banana ●●●●○
Funky Monkey ●●●●○
Hummingbird ●●●○○
Screaming Banana Banshee ●●●◐○

BASIL LEAVES

This aromatic herb has a strong lemon and jasmine flavour. There are hundreds of different basil varieties, each with subtly different colour and flavour profiles.

Bajito ●●●●◐
Basil & Honey Daiquiri ●●●●●
Basil & Lime Gimlet ●●●●◐
Basil Beauty ●●●●○
Basil Bramble Sling ●●●●○
Basil Grande ●●●●○
Basil Mary ●●●●○
Basilian ●●●◐○
Basilico ●●●◐○
Byzantine ●●●●○
Gin Atomic ●●●◐○
Ginger Cosmos ●●●◐○
Milly Martini ●●●●○
Strawberry Blonde Martini ●●●◐○
The Suzy Wong Martini ●●●◐○
Washhouse ●●●●○
Watermelon & Basil Martini ●●●●○
Watermelon & Basil Smash ●●●●○

BECHEROVKA (CARLSBAD BECHER) CZECH LIQUEUR

The national liqueur of the Czech Republic is a memorable bitter herbal drink.

Be-ton ●●●◐○
Bohemian Iced Tea ●●●●◐
Moravian Cocktail ●●●○○
Oáza ●●●◐○

BEER (DARK & LIGHT)

This popular beverage does not greatly feature in the world of cocktails. At least, not yet! Suggestions to simon@diffordsguide.com, please.

Black & Tan ●●●◐○
Boilermaker ●●●◐○
Depth Charge ●●○○○
Flaming Dr Pepper ●●○○○
Michelada ●●●○○
Sandy Gaff ●●●◐○
Snakebite ●●●○○
Steel Bottom ●●●○○

BÉNÉDICTINE D.O.M. LIQUEUR

Apricot Martini ●●●○○
B2C2 ●●●◐○
B & B ●●●●○
BBC ●●●◐○
Bobby Burns ●●●●○
Brainstorm ●●●●◐
Brass Rail ●●●●○
Brighton Punch ●●●●◐
Caprice ●●●●○
Chas ●●●●○
The Cold Winter Warmer Sour ●●●●○
Collection Martini ●●●○○
De La Louisiane #1 ●●●●○
De La Louisiane #2 ●●●●○
English Channel ●●●●◐
Froupe Cocktail ●●●●○
Gypsy Queen ●●●●○
Honeymoon ●●●●○
Honolulu Cocktail No. 2 ●●●◐○
The Horseshoe Sling ●●●●○
Irresistible ●●●○○
Jubilant ●●●●◐
Jungle Fire Sling ●●●○○
Maxim's Coffee ●●●●○ (Hot)
Merry Widow #1 ●●●◐○
Monkey Gland #2 ●●●●○
Mule's Hind Leg ●●●●◐
O'Henry ●●●◐○
Poet's Dream ●●●●◐
Roman Punch ●●●●○
Singapore Sling #1 ●●●◐○ (Baker's formula)
Singapore Sling #2 ●●●●○
Singapore Sling #3 ●●●◐○
Straits Sling ●●●●○
Tropic ●●●●◐
Vancouver ●●●◐○
Vieux Carré Cocktail ●●●●◐
Widow's Kiss ●●●●●

BENOIT SERRES VIOLET LIQUEUR

25% **alc./vol.** (50°proof)
www.benoit-serres.com
Producer: Benoit Serres, Toulouse, France

This vivid purple, sweet liqueur looks like methylated spirits and is flavoured by the infusion of violet roots and leaves. It offers a lightly perfumed violet flavour and subtle hints of dark chocolate, espresso and lemon zest.

The Atty Cocktail ●●●●○
Aviation #2 ●●●●◐ (Classic Formula)
Blue Moon ●●●●○
Bramblette ●●●◐○
Brazen Martini ●●●●○
Flower Power Martini ●●●●◐
Mood Indigo ●●●●○
Palma Violet Martini ●●●◐○
Purple Pear Martini ●●●●○
Violet Affinity ●●●●◐

BILBERRIES

See 'Giffard Crème de Myrtilles Liqueur'

BLACKBERRIES

See 'Raspberries & Blackberries'

BLACKBERRY (CRÈME DE MÛRE) LIQUEUR

See 'Giffard Crème de Mûre Liqueur'

BLACKCURRANTS

The fruit of a native northern European shrub that is now widely cultivated in France, Germany, the Netherlands and Belgium. In the French Côte d'Or blackcurrants are heavily used in the production of cassis liqueur.

Brazilian Berry ●●●●○

BLUEBERRIES

Blueberry pie is as much an American icon as the Stars and Stripes. This bushy shrub, which is virtually identical to the bilberry, is native to the States and many different types grow there – not all of them blue. The lowbush blueberry, which is called the 'bleuet' in Quebec, tends to be smaller and sweeter than other varieties and is often marketed as 'wild blueberry'. The larger, highbush blueberry is the variety most cultivated in the US.
These soft berries are best muddled in the base of your shaker or glass. Recipes in this guide specify the number required for each drink. Alternatively, you can make a purée. Just stick them in the blender and add a touch of sugar syrup. Fresh blueberries should not be stored in the refrigerator.

Black 'N' Blue Caipirovska ●●●●○
Blue Wave ●●●○○
Blueberry Daiquiri ●●●◐○
Blueberry Martini #1 ●●●◐○
Blueberry Martini #2 ●●●◐○
Forbidden Fruits ●●●●○
Kentucky Muffin ●●●●○
No. 10 Lemonade ●●●●◐

BLUEBERRY LIQUEUR

See 'Giffard Crème de Myrtille Liqueur'

BOKMA GENEVER

38% **alc./vol.** (76°proof)
www.bokma.com
Producer: Lucas Bols, Amsterdam, The Netherlands

This famous Dutch genever was first created by the Bokma family in 1826 in the Frisian capital of Leeuwarden. 'Bok' means a male goat, hence the goat emblem on the crest. Bokma's unique square bottle was designed in 1894 so predates other famous quadrilaterals such as Cointreau.
Also known as geneva, hollands and jenever, genever is a juniper-flavoured spirit from Holland, Belgium and northern France. The juniper flavouring means that genever is technically a gin, and it was the forerunner of the London gin styles which dominate today's market.
But genever is a very distinctive style of juniper spirit. Unlike most gins, it is a blend of two very different spirits – botanical-infused neutral spirit and malt-wine, a kind of unaged whiskey. Due to this, it retains more of the flavour of some of its base ingredients - rye, malted barley and maize - than most common gin styles, which are based on neutral spirit alone.
There are three basic styles of genever - 'oude' (literally, 'old'), 'jonge' ('young') and 'korenwijn' ('corn wine'). They differ in their use of botanicals and the percentage of malt-wine contained.
Jonge genever is so named because it is a modern, young style. It was first developed in the 1950s in response to consumer demand for a lighter flavoured, more mixable genever. Jonge genevers contain a lower percentage of malt-wine than either oude or korenwijn styles.
Oude genevers, despite the name, are not aged. They are so called because they are traditional, old-style genevers, as opposed to the more modern jonge genevers. They must contain at least 15% malt-wine and often feature more botanicals than jonge styles.

The third category of genever is 'korenwijn' (corn wine), which Bols spell 'corenwyn'. Confusingly, unlike oude genevers, korenwijn styles are cask aged. By law they must contain at least 51% malt-wine.
Bokma make exellent jonge and oude genevers and we recommend Bols Extra Oude Corenwyn. Recipes calling for genever in this guide state which style of genever best suits that particular cocktail.

The Alamagoozlum Cocktail ●●●●◐
Amsterdam Cocktail ●●●●○
Collins ●●●●○
Flying Dutchman Martini ●●●●○
I B Damm'd ●●●●◐
Jenever Sour ●●●●○
Medicinal Solution ●●●◐○

BOLS ADVOCAAT LIQUEUR

20% **alc./vol.** (40°proof)
www.bols.com
Producer: Lucas Bols, Amsterdam, The Netherlands

This Dutch liqueur is made from brandy, egg yolks and sugar. It is derived from an alcoholic drink that Dutch colonists in South Africa made from the yellowish pulp of the abacate fruit. In Holland, egg yolks took the place of the abacate fruit and the name, already evolved into avocado by Portuguese colonists in Brazil, became Advocaat in Dutch.
Bols Advocaat is an entirely natural product, made only using brandy, egg yolks, sugar and vanilla without any preservatives or artificial thickeners. It has has a luscious custardy consistency, with subtle flavours of creamy vanilla, cocoa powder and a hint of cooked egg yolk.

Ambrosia'tini Ambrosia Cocktail ●●●◐○
Apple & Custard Cocktail ●●●◐○
Beach Blonde ●●●●○
Bessie & Jessie ●●●◐○
Canary Flip ●●●●◐
Casablanca ●●●○○ #2
Crème Anglaise Martini ●●●●○
Custard Tart ●●●●○
Dutch Breakfast Martini ●●●●○
Dutch Courage ●●●●○
Egg Custard Martini ●●●◐○
Fluffy Duck ●●●◐○
Granny's Martini ●●●◐○
Jaded Lady ●●●◐○
New Port Codebreaker ●●●◐○
Nutty Summer ●●●●◐
Orange Custard Martini ●●●◐○
Redback ●●●○○
Rhubarb & Custard Martini ●●●●○
Snowball ●●●◐○
Squashed Frog ●●●○○
Zabaglione Martini ●●●◐○

BOLS BLUE CURAÇAO LIQUEUR

21% **alc./vol.** (42°proof)
www.bols.com
Producer: Lucas Bols, Amsterdam, The Netherlands

This vivid blue curaçao liqueur is probably the best known of the Bols range. The company was founded in Amsterdam in 1575 by a Dutchman called Lucas Bols Prevented from distilling within the city walls due to the fire risk, Lucas distilled from a wooden shed outside Amsterdam. Today Bols is one of the largest liqueur producers in the world.
Bols Blue is distilled from a blend of predominantly natural products from around the world – herbs, sweet red oranges, the characteristically flavourful bitter Curaçao oranges and the rare Kinnow oranges. This gives Bols Blue a fresh, yet complex orange scent and taste. Bols Blue is frequently used by bartenders due to its distinctive colour and refreshing taste, which features orange zest with a hint of spice.

Alexander's Big Brother ●●●○○
Artlantic ●●●○○
Baby Blue Martini ●●●◐○
Bazooka Joe ●●◐○○
Bikini Martini ●●●●○
Black Mussel ●●●○○.5
Blue Angel ●●◐○○
Blue Bird ●●●○○
Blue Champagne ●●●○○
Blue Cosmo ●●●◐○
Blue Hawaiian ●●●○○
Blue Heaven ●●◐○○
Blue Kamikaze ●●●◐○
Blue Lady ●●●○○
Blue Lagoon ●●●○○
Blue Margarita ●●●◐○
Blue Monday ●●●◐○
Blue Passion ●●●●○
Blue Riband ●●●○○
Blue Star ●●●○○
Blue Velvet Margarita ●●●●○
Blue Wave ●●●○○
Catus Jack ●●●◐○
China Blue ●●●◐○
China Blue Martini ●●●●○
Fourth Of July Cocktail ●●●○○
Green Eyes ●●●◐○
Ink Martini #1 ●●●◐○
Ink Martini #2 ●●●●○
Jaded Lady ●●●◐○
Liminal Shot ●●●○○
Liquorice All Sort ●●●◐○
Lotus Martini ●●●●○
Purple Flirt #2 ●●●○○
Purple Turtle ●●●◐○
Ray Gun ●●●○○
Swedish Blue Martini ●●●◐○
Turquoise Daiquiri ●●●◐○

BOULARD GRAND SOLAGE CALVADOS

40% **alc./vol.** (80°proof)
www.calvados-boulard.com
Producer: Calvados Boulard S.A., Fecamp, France.

Calvados is a French brandy made from apples, although some styles also contain pears. The name is an appellation contrôlée, meaning that Calvados can only be produced in defined areas of north-west France.
Like Cognac and Armagnac, the Calvados-making district is divided into smaller areas. Pays d'Auge, the area around the villages of Orne and Eure, is generally considered to produce the best Calvados and by law all AOC Pays d'Auge Calvados must be double-distilled in pot stills.
Boulard Grand Solage is a Pays d'Auge Calvados produced by traditional methods and aged from three to five years. The house of Boulard was founded in 1825 by Pierre-August Boulard, and is still owned by his fifth generation descendant Vincent. 120 different varieties of apple are used in Boulard's production: their own orchards contribute 20% of the total, while a network of 500 local growers supply the remainder. Boulard produce all their own cider at their cider plant, and double distill it in their eight copper pot stills before ageing in seasoned oak casks.

A.J. ●●●●○
Ambrosia ●●●●○
Angel Face ●●●●◐
Ante ●●●●○
Apple & Custard Cocktail ●●●◐○
Apple & Spice ●●●○○
Apple Blossom Cocktail ●●●●◐
Apple Brandy Sour ●●●●◐
Apple Buck ●●●●○
Apple Cart ●●●●○
Apple Sunrise ●●●○○
Aunt Emily ●●●●○
Avenue ●●●◐○
Bentley ●●●●○
Bolero ●●●◐○
Calvados Cocktail ●●●●◐
Castro ●●●◐○
Cider Apple Cooler ●●●●○
Cider Apple Martini ●●●●○
Corpse Reviver No. 1 #1 ●●●◐○
Cyder Press ●●●●○
Deauville #1 ●●●●○
Deauville #2 ●●●◐○
Dempsey ●●●◐○
Depth Bomb ●●●◐○
Diki-Diki ●●●●◐
Elysian ●●●●○
Empire Cocktail ●●●○○
Fallen Leaves ●●●●○
Feather Dusta Crusta ●●●●○
Fiesta ●●●●○
First Of July ●●●●○
Golden Dawn ●●●◐○
Harvard Cooler ●●●●◐
Honeymoon ●●●●○
Jack Collins ●●●●◐
Jack Maple ●●●◐○
Jack Rose ●●●●○
Jack-In-The-Box ●●●●○
Jean Gabin ●●●●○
Jersey Sour ●●●●●
Julep ●●●●●
Long Flight of Stairs ●●●●◐
Mule's Hind Leg ●●●●◐
Parisian Spring Punch ●●●●○
Pomme et Sureau ●●●●◐
Princess Marina ●●●●○
Princess Mary's Pride ●●●○○
Princess Pride ●●●◐○
Rizzo ●●●●○
Roulette ●●●●○
Royal Smile ●●●●○

Serendipity #2
Sidecar Named Desire
Sidecarriage
So-So Martini
Steep Flight
Tantris Sidecar
Tarte Aux Pommes
The 75
The Delicious Sour
The Last Straw
The Star #1
The Stig
Threesome
Toffee Apple
Toffee Apple Martini
Tulip Cocktail
Widow's Kiss
Wilton Martini

BOURBON

See 'Buffalo Trace'

BUFFALO TRACE

45% **alc./vol.(90 proof)**
www.buffalotrace.com
Producer: Buffalo Trace Distillery, Kentucky USA

For thousands of years wild buffalo carved their way across the wilderness of America, leaving huge paths in their wake. Early pioneers used these paths, or traces as they were later known, on their adventure westward to discover new lands. The largest of these traces, the Great Buffalo Trace, is situated north of the Kentucky River and it is here, where the trace crossed the river, that a settlement was established and distillation commenced in 1787. In 1857 a modern distillery was built on the site, the first to incorporate steam power and today, on this same site, stands Buffalo Trace Distillery, a family owned business producing over 25 different American whiskeys.

Buffalo Trace Kentucky Straight Bourbon Whiskey, the flagship whiskey of the distillery is made in batches of just 20-25 barrels using Indiana corn, rye and malted barley. It is laid down to age for 9-11 years, slowly maturing and developing the characteristics of a superb bourbon.

Jim Murray describes Buffalo Trace as 'one of the world's great whiskeys'. It has a light palate with well-integrated flavours including vanilla, ginger, clove, chocolate, espresso coffee, mint, aniseed and honey.

Adam & Eve
Algonquin
American Pie Martini
Americana
Apple Manhattan #1
Apple Manhattan #2
Apricot Sour
Avenue
Barbary Coast Highball
Bensonhurst
Blinker
Boilermaker
Boomerang
Borderline
Boston Flip
Boulevard
Bourbon Blush
Bourbon Cookie
Bourbon Crusta
Bourbon Milk Punch
Bourbon Smash
Bourbonella
Brighton Punch
Brooklyn #1
Brooklyn #2
Caramel Manhattan
Cassanova
Chas
Chocolate Sazerac
Colonel Collins
Colonel T
Commodore #2
Cruel Intention
The Currier
Daisy Duke
Dandy Cocktail
De La Louisiane #1
De La Louisiane #2
De La Louisiane #3
Delmarva Cocktail No. 1
Delmarva Cocktail No. 2
Derby Fizz
Devil's Manhattan
Difford's Old-Fashioned
Dixie Dew
Doughnut Martini
Egg Custard Martini
Elder & Wiser
Elder Fashioned
Elderflower Manhattan
Embassy Royal
Epiphany
Esquire #1
Fancy Free
Fizz
Flaming Henry
Flamingo #1
Flip
Fourth Of July Cocktail
Fruit Sour
Gingerbread Martini
Glenn's Bride
Golden Nail
Grand Sazerac
Great Mughal Martini
Horse's Neck With a Kick
I'll Take Manhattan
Irish Manhattan
Jambouree
Julep
Julep Martini
Kentucky Colonel
Kentucky Dream
Kentucky Jewel
Kentucky Mac
Kentucky Muffin
Kentucky Pear
Kentucky Tea
King Cole Cocktail
Klondike
Little Italy
Lucky Lindy
Man-Bour-Tini
Manhattan Dry
Manhattan Perfect
Manhattan Sweet
Maple Old-Fashioned
Maple Leaf
Marquee
Met Manhattan
Millionaire
Mint Julep
Mississippi Punch
Mocha Martini
Mountain
Mrs Robinson #1
New Orleans Mule
New Orleans Punch
New Yorker
Nutty Nashville
Oddball Manhattan Dry
O'Henry
Old Fashioned #1 (Classic Version)
Old Fashioned #2 (US Version)
Opening Shot
Paris Sour
Parlay Punch
Passbour Cooler
Pinky Pincher
Port Light
Pousse-café
Prune Face
Rat Pack Manhattan
Rattlesnake
Red Apple
Remember The Maine
Sazerac
Scofflaw
Seelbach
Shamrock #1
Silver Fizz
Sir Thomas
Sling
Snoopy
Sour
Southern Manhattan
Stiletto
Suburban
Swizzle
Tailor Made
Texsun
Thunderbird
Toast & Orange Martini
Union Club
Vieux Carré Cocktail
Ward Eight
The Wentworth
Whiskey Collins
Whiskey Daisy
Whiskey Sour #1 (Classic)
Whiskey Sour #2 (Difford's)
Whiskey Squirt
Yule Luvit
Zhivago Martini

BUTTERSCOTCH SCHNAPPS LIQUEUR

See 'Teichenné Butterscotch Schnapps Liqueur'

CACAO DARK (CRÈME DE) LIQUEUR

See 'Giffard Brown Crème de Cacao liqueur'

CACAO WHITE (CRÈME DE) LIQUEUR

See 'Giffard White Crème de Cacao Liqueur'

CACHAÇA

See 'Leblon cachaça'

CALVADOS

See 'Boulard Grand Solage Calvados'

CHAMBORD LIQUEUR

Achilles Heel
Arnaud Martini
Basil Grande
Berry Nice
Black Cherry Martini
Black Forest Gateau Martini
Camomile & Blackfruit Breeze
Cascade Martini
Cham 69 #2
Cham 69=#1
Cham Cham
Chimayo
Concealed Weapon
Country Breeze
Creamy Bee
Crimson Blush
Crown Stag
Dirty Sanchez
Dorothy Parker
Eclipse
Encantado
Estes
Finitaly
First Of July
Flirtini #1
French Bison-tini
French Daiquiri
French Kiss #2
French Martini
French Mojito
Fresca
Fruit & Nut Chocolate Martini
Fruits Of The Forest
Gin Berry
Honey Berry Sour
Hot Tub
Icy Pink Lemonade
Jam Roll
Ja-Mora
Juliette
Katrina Cocktail
Kentucky Jewel
Loved Up
Lush
Marquee
Miss Martini
Mystique Martini
New Orleans Punch
Nuts & Berries
Pavlova Shot
Peach Melba Martini
Peanut Butter & Jelly Shot
Purple Haze
Purple Hooter
Raspberry Lynchburg
Raspberry Sake'tini
Raspberry Watkins
Razzitini
Razzzzzberry Martini
Red Marauder
Red Rover
Royal Velvet Margarita
Saigon Cooler
Sex On The Beach #1
Sex On The Beach #2
Sex On The Beach #3
Snood Murdekin
Snow On Earth
Sweet Louise
Sweet Tart
Tartini
Tre Martini
Tres Compadres Margarita
Trifle Martini
Urban Oasis
Yum

CAMPARI

25% **alc./vol.(90 proof)**
www.campari.com
Producer: Campari SpA, Milan, Italy.

Renowned for its distinctive, bitter-sweet taste and vivid red colour, Campari was created between 1860 and 1867 by Gaspare Campari in the cellars of his Caffè Campari coffee shop in Milan. It is made from a secret recipe of 68 herbs, plants, fruit and spices which remains unchanged to this day.

Campari may be enjoyed at whatever time of day and a few fundamentals should always be followed for it to be appreciated at its fullest:
Campari must always be served chilled to enhance its balanced taste.
The bottle must be kept from direct sunlight and heat, ideally in a refrigerator.
When adding a garnish to a drink containing Campari, always use a slice of orange, as lemon impairs the true flavour.
When serving Campari with a mixer such as tonic, soda or grapefruit juice, mix 50/50.

Americano
Bellissimo
Bitterest Pill
Bloodhound
Cardinale
Copper Illusion
Covadonga
Cumbersome
CVO Firevault
Diamond Dog
Diana's Bitter
Dolce-Amaro

Dolce Havana ●●●●○
Garibaldi ●●●○○
Hakkantini ●●●●○
Ignorance Is Bliss ●●●◐○
Inga From Sweden ●●●●○
Italian Job #1 ●●●◐○
Jasmine ●●●○○
Jungle Bird ●●●●○
Lucien Gaudin ●●●●○
Mambo ●●●◐○
Mandarintini ●●●○○
Milano ●●●●◐
Monza ●●●◐○
Negroni ●●●●◐
Night & Day ●●●◐○
Old Flame ●●●●○
Old Pal ●●●◐○
Parma Negroni ●●●●○
Pink Tutu ●●●◐○
Red Or Dead ●●●○○
Rosita ●●●●○
Scotch Negroni ●●●●○
Shakerato ●●●◐○
Sicilian Negroni ●●●●○
Snoopy ●●●●○
South Beach ●●●●○
Spicy Finn ●●●●○
Spritz al Bitter ●●●◐○
Teresa ●●●○○
Testarossa ●●●◐○
Triple Orange Martini ●●●●○
Valentino Martini ●●●●○

CARAMEL LIQUEUR

Derived from the Latin 'canna mella' for sugar cane, caramel means melted sugar that has been browned by heating. Tiny amounts of caramel have long been used to colour spirits and liqueurs but caramel flavoured liqueurs are a relatively recent phenomenon.

Caramel Manhattan ●●●●◐
Crème Brûlée Martini ●●●●○
Tarte Tatin Martini ●●●●○
Toffee Apple ●●●●○

CHAMPAGNE

The vineyards of the Champagne region are the most northerly in France, lying north-east of Paris, on either side of the River Marne. Most of the champagne houses are based in one of two towns: Epernay and Reims. Champagne, surprisingly, is made predominantly from black grapes. The three grape varieties used are Pinot Noir (the red grape of Burgundy), Pinot Meunier (a fruitier relative of Pinot Noir) and Chardonnay. Pinot Meunier is the most commonly used of these three varieties with Chardonnay, the only white grape, accounting for less than 30% of vines in the Champagne region. Pinot Meunier buds late and ripens early so can be relied upon to ripen throughout the Champagne region, which probably explains its domination.

Absolutely Fabulous ●●●●○
Air Mail ●●●●◐
Alfonso ●●●◐○
Ambrosia ●●●●○
Americana ●●●○○
Anita's Attitude Adjuster ●●●○○
Apple Spritz ●●●●○
Atomic Cocktail ●●●○○
Autumn Punch ●●●●◐
B2C2 ●●●◐○
Baltic Spring Punch ●●●●○
Beverly Hills Iced Tea ●●●◐○
Black Magic ●●●●○
Black Mussel ●●●○○.5
Black Velvet ●●●◐○
Bling! Bling! ●●●●◐
Blue Champagne ●●●○○
Breakfast At Terrell's ●●●●○
Buck's Fizz ●●●○○
Carol Channing ●●●○○
Cham 69 #2 ●●●◐○
Cham Cham ●●●◐○
Champagne Cocktail ●●●○○
Champagne Cup ●●●◐○
Champagne Daisy ●●●○○
Chin Chin ●●●●○
Colonel's Big Opu ●●●◐○
Cordless Screwdriver ●●●○○
D'Artagnan ●●●◐○
Death In The Afternoon ●●●○○
Diamond Fizz ●●●●○
Dorothy Parker ●●●◐○
Earl Grey Fizz ●●●●○
Elderflower Pisco Punch ●●●●◐
Elle For Leather ●●●●◐
Flirtini #2 ●●●●○
French 75 ●●●◐○
French 76 ●●●●○
French 77 ●●●●○
French Daisy ●●●◐○
French Pear ●●●●◐
French Spring Punch ●●●●○
Fresca Nova ●●●◐○
Fru Fru ●●●◐○
Gloria ●●●◐○
Gold Rush Slammer ●●●○○
Golden Screw ●●●◐○
Grand Mimosa ●●●◐○
Grape Escape ●●●●◐
Greenbelt ●●●◐○
Guillotine ●●●●○
Happy New Year ●●●○○
Hemingway ●●●○○
Henry VIII ●●●◐○
The Horseshoe Sling ●●●●○
Hot Tub ●●●●○
Jacuzzi ●●●◐○
Ja-Mora ●●●●○
Jayne Mansfield ●●●●○
Kir Royale ●●●◐○
Limeosa ●●●◐○
Lush ●●●◐○
Luxury Mojito ●●●●○
Martini Royale ●●●◐○
Mimosa ●●●◐○
Monte Carlo Imperial ●●●○○
Night & Day ●●●◐○
Nine-20-Seven ●●●●○
Parisian Spring Punch ●●●●○
Perry-tini ●●●●○
Pimm's Cocktail ●●●●◐
Pimm's Royal ●●◐○○
Pisco Punch #1 ●●●●◐ (Difford's Formula)
Poinsettia ●●●◐○
Prince Of Wales ●●●◐○
Ray Gun ●●●○○
The Ritz Cocktail ●●●●○
Royal Cosmopolitan ●●●●○
Royal Mojito ●●●●●
Russian Spring Punch ●●●●◐
Seelbach ●●●○○
Serendipity #2 ●●●●○
Sloe Martini ●●●◐○
Southside Royal ●●●●○
Soyer Au Champagne ●●●◐○
Sparkling Perry ●●●●○
Tatanka Royale ●●●●○
Tequila Slammer ●●●○○
Twinkle ●●●●◐
Twisted Sobriety ●●●●○
Valencia ●●●●○
Vavavoom ●●●●○
Wanton Abandon ●●●●○

CHARTREUSE GREEN

Angel's Share #2 ●●●●◐
Aphrodisiac ●●●○○
Beetle Jeuse ●●●●○
Bijou ●●●●◐
The Broadmoor ●●●●◐
Champagne Daisy ●●●○○
Daiquiri Elixir No. 1 ●●●●●
Elixir ●●●●○
Emerald Martini ●●●●○
Episcopal ●●●●◐
Every-Body's Irish Cocktail ●●●○○
Flaming Ferrari ●●○○○
Gator Bite ●●●◐○
Golden Retriever ●●●●◐
Green Fly ●●●◐○
Gypsy ●●●●○
Head Shot ●●◐○○
Hong Kong Fuey ●●●○○
Jean Marc ●●●●○
Jewel Cocktail ●●●○○
The Last Word ●●●●◐
Martini Thyme ●●●●○
Mary Queen of Scots ●●●●◐
Mary Rose #1 ●●●●○
Medicinal Solution ●●●◐○
Mona Lisa ●●●●○
Mujer Verde ●●●●○
Nuclear Daiquiri ●●●●○
Pago Pago ●●●◐○
Ray Gun ●●●○○
Russian Qualuude Shot ●●●○○
St. Patrick's Day ●●●●○
Shamrock #2 ●●●●○
Stars & Stripes Shot ●●◐○○
Swamp Water ●●●●○
Tantris Sidecar ●●●●○
Tipperary #1 ●●●●◐
Verdant Martini ●●●●○

CHARTREUSE YELLOW

The Alamagoozlum Cocktail ●●●●◐
Alaska Martini ●●●●○
Alaska Martini ●●●●○
Ambrosia'tini Ambrosia Cocktail ●●●◐○
Barnacle Bill ●●●○○
Brandy Crusta ●●●●◐
Brandy Fix ●●●●◐
Champagne Daisy ●●●○○
Cheeky Monkey ●●●●○
Club Cocktail #2 ●●●●○
Daisy Cutter Martini ●●●●◐
Episcopal ●●●●◐
Gin Daisy ●●●●○
Golden Slipper ●●●◐○
Lemony ●●●●○
Mujer Verde ●●●●○
Nathalia ●●●◐○
Nome ●●●●○
Oddball Manhattan Dry ●●●●○
The Puritan ●●●●●
Quarterback ●●●●○
Widow's Kiss ●●●●●
Yellow Parrot ●●●●○

CHERRY (BRANDY) LIQUEUR

See 'Marnier Cherry Liqueur'

CINNAMON SCHNAPPS LIQUEUR

Cinnamon is obtained from the bark of several tropical trees. Sri Lanka and China are the largest producers. Cinnamon liqueurs have a warm, sweet, spicy flavour.

Apple Pie Martini ●●●●○
Apple Strudel #1 ●●●○○
Azure Martini ●●●●○
Butterfly's Kiss ●●●◐○
Carrot Cake ●●●◐○
Cinnamon Daiquiri ●●●◐○
Creamy Bee ●●●●○
Dead Man's Mule ●●●◐○
Fireball ●●○○○
Gold Member ●●●●○
Gold Rush Slammer ●●●○○
Granny's ●●●●○
Oatmeal Cookie ●●●◐○
Pink Sin Martini ●●●○○
Pirate Daiquiri ●●●●○
Plum Pudding Martini ●●●◐○
Spiced Apple Daiquiri ●●●●○
Tarte Aux Pommes ●●●●○
Utterly Butterly ●●●◐○
Wilton Martini ●●●●○

COCONUT RUM LIQUEUR

Coconut rums are mostly made in the Caribbean but are also found in France and Spain. They are made by blending rectified white rum with coconut extracts and tend to be presented in opaque white bottles.

Alien Secretion ●●●◐○
Atomic Dog ●●●○○
Bahama Mama ●●●●○
Bahamas Daiquiri ●●●●◐
Black & White Daiquiri ●●●●◐
Black Widow ●●●○○
Caribbean Cruise ●●●◐○
Caribbean Punch ●●●●○
Chill-Out Martini ●●●○○
Coco Cabana ●●●◐○
Coconut Daiquiri ●●●●○
Coconut Water ●●●●○
Georgetown Punch ●●●●○
Goombay Smash ●●●●◐
Hawaiian ●●●○○
Island Breeze ●●●◐○
Jelly Belly Beany ●●●●○
June Bug ●●●◐○
Key Lime Pie #1 ●●●●○
Key West Cooler ●●●○○
Melon Collie Martini ●●●●○
Meloncholy Martini ●●●●○
Mister Stu ●●●◐○
Monkey Shine ●●●●○
Mucky Bottom ●●●◐○
Nutty Summer ●●●●◐
Scotch Bounty Martini ●●●◐○
Smooth & Creamy'tini ●●●●○
Surfer on A.C.D. ●●●◐○
Tilt ●●●●○
Tropical Caipirinha ●●●●◐
Utterly Butterly ●●●◐○
Vacation ●●●◐○
Whip Me & Beat Me ●●●○○

COFFEE (ESPRESSO)

Coffee beans are the dried and roasted seed of a cherry which grows on a bush in the tropics. There are two main species of coffee plant: Coffea Arabica and Coffea Canephora. These are commonly known as Arabica and Robusta. Arabica is relatively low in caffeine, more delicate and requires more intensive cultivation. Robusta is higher in caffeine, more tolerant of climate and parasites, and can be grown fairly cheaply. Robusta beans tend to be woody and bitter while Arabica beans have well-rounded, subtle flavours. Most of the recipes in this guide which use coffee call for espresso and, as with other ingredients, the quality of this will greatly affect the finished drink. I strongly recommend using an Arabica coffee brewed in an espresso machine or a moka pot.

Black Martini ●●●●◐
Brazilian Coffee ●●●◐○
Coffee Batida ●●●○○
Cola de Mono ●●●●◐
Cuppa Joe ●●●●○
Espresso Daiquiri ●●●●◐
Espresso Martini ●●●●○
Grappacino ●●●◐○
Hot Shot ●●●○○
Insomniac ●●●●◐
Irish Coffee Martini ●●●●◐
Irish Espresso'tini ●●●●◐
Irish Frappé ●●●◐○
I.V.F. Martini ●●●◐○
Jalisco Espresso ●●●●◐
Jolt'ini ●●●●○
Lazarus ●●●●◐
Lotus Espresso ●●●●◐
Mocha Martini ●●●●◐
Opal Café ●●●●○
Pharmaceutical Stimulant ●●●●○
Raspberry Mocha'tini ●●●●○
Shamrock Express ●●●◐○
Turkish Coffee Martini ●●●●○
Vodka Espresso ●●●●◐

COFFEE LIQUEUR

Coffee flavoured liqueurs are made by infusing coffee beans in alcohol or by infusing beans in hot water and then blending with alcohol. Look for brands made using Arabica coffee beans.

Adios
After Six Shot
Afterburner
Aggravation
Alexander The Great
Alexandra
Alice From Dallas
All Fall Down
Apache
Attitude Adjuster
Avalanche Shot
B5200
B-52 Shot
B-53 Shot
B-54 Shot
B-55 Shot
B-52 Frozen
Baby Guinness
Bahamas Daiquiri
Bartender's Root Beer
Beam-me-up Scotty
Beam-me-up Scotty Shot
Black Irish
Black Russian
Blow Job
Blushin' Russian
Brazilian Monk
Bulldog
Bumble Bee
Buona Sera Shot
Burnt Toasted Almond
Café Toddy
California Root Beer
Carrot Cake
Cassanova
Chocolarita
Chocolate Biscuit
Coffee & Vanilla Daiquiri
Cola de Mono
Colorado Bulldog
Crème de Café
Dirty Banana
Dr Zeus
Dreamsicle
F-16 Shot
Fat Sailor
FBI
Flutter
Fourth Of July Cocktail
Heavens Above
Hummingbird
Iguana
Insomniac
International Incident
Irish Chocolate Oranj'tini
I.V.F. Martini
Jolt'ini
Katrina Cocktail
K.G.B.
Lazarus
Lonely Bull
Long Beach Iced Tea
Lotus Espresso
Mad Monk Milkshake
Mayan
Mayan Whore
Midnight Over Tennessee
Monk's Candy Bar
Muddy Water
Mudslide
Mucky Bottom
New Orleans Mule
Nutty Russian
Pharmaceutical Stimulant
Pousse-café
P.S. I Love You
Raging Bull
Rattlesnake Shot
Russian Bride
Screaming Orgasm
Snood Murdekin
Snow On Earth
South Of The Border
Stealth
Tiramisu Martini
Toasted Almond
Top Banana Shot
Vodka Espresso
White Knight
White Russian
White Satin
Zeus Martini

COGNAC

See 'Remy Martin Cognac'.

COINTREAU LIQUEUR

40% **alc./vol.** (80ºproof)
www.cointreau.com
Producer: Rémy Cointreau, Angers, France

The distilling firm of Cointreau was started in 1849 by two brothers, Adolphe and Edouard-Jean Cointreau, who were confectioners in Angers. The liqueur we know today was created by Edouard Cointreau, the son of Edouard-Jean, and first marketed in the 1870s. Cointreau should not be confused with other liqueurs labelled 'triple sec'. This term is a confusing one as it means 'triple dry' and they tend to be very sweet, but like them Cointreau is made from the peels of bitter and sweet oranges.
A versatile cocktail ingredient, Cointreau can also be served straight over ice, or mixed with fruit juices, tonic or lemonade.
The mainstay of many classic recipes, Cointreau has a luscious, ripe taste featuring bitter orange, zesty, citrus hints, a splash of orange juice and a hint of spice.

Acapulco Daiquiri
Agent Orange
Alexander's Big Brother
Algeria
Allegrottini
Ambrosia
Amsterdam Cocktail
Anita's Attitude Adjuster
Ante
Apple Cart
Apple Manhattan #2
Attitude Adjuster
B2C2
Balalaika
Bamboo
Beach Iced Tea
Beachcomber
Beha Flor 4.5
Between the Sheets #1 (Classic Formula)
Between the Sheets #2 (Difford's Formula)
Beverly Hills Iced Tea
The Big Easy
Bitter Sweet Symphony
Black Feather
Blue Champagne
Blue Monday
Blue Riband
Blue Velvet Margarita
Bombay No. 2
Boston Tea Party
Bourbon Crusta
Bourbonella
Brandy Crusta
Brazilian Cosmopolitan
Breakfast Martini
Cable Car
Call Me Old-Fashioned
Canaries
Cappercaille
Casablanca #1
Celtic Margarita
Charles Daiquiri
Chas
Chelsea Sidecar
Cherry Blossom
China Martini
Citrus Martini
Claridge Cocktail
Colonel's Big Opu
Coolman Martini
Copper Illusion
Corpse Reviver #2
Cosmopolitan #1 (simple version)
Cosmopolitan #2 (complex version)
Cosmopolitan #3 (popular version)
Cosmopolitan #4 (1934 recipe)
Cranapple Breeze
Crossbow
Crux
Cuban Special
Daiquiri No. 2
Damn-The-Weather
Dandy Cocktail
De La Louisiane #3
Deauville #1
Deauville #2
Detropolitan
Dixie Dew
Dolce Havana
Dorothy Parker
Dream Cocktail
Dreamsicle
Dry Oranage Martini
Dyevitchka
East India House
El Presidente #3
El Presidente #4
Elegante Margarita
Embassy Cocktail
F. Willy Shot
Fair & Warmer Cocktail
Fancy Brandy
Fine & Dandy
Flirtini #2
Floridita Margarita
Fluffy Duck
Flying Dutchman Martini
Frank Sullivan Cocktail
The Frankenjack Cocktail
French Sherbet
Frozen Margarita
Fruit Sour
Fu Manchu Daiquiri
Gator Bite
Gin Cocktail
Gin Fixed
Giuseppe's Habit
Glass Tower
Gloom Chaser Cocktail #1
Gold
Golden Dream
Golden Fizz #2
Golden Wave
Goombay Smash
Grateful Dead
Gun Club Punch No. 1
Hawaiian
Honula-Honula Cocktail
The Hypnotic Margarita
Iced Tea
Illusion
Italian Margarita
Jackie O's Rose
Jade Daiquiri
Jaffa Martini
James Joyce
Jasmine
Jean Lafitte Cocktail
Jodi May
John Daly
The Journalist
Jungle Juice
Kamikaze
Kentucky Colonel
Kentucky Jewel
Kentucky Tea
Key Lime Pie #1
Koi Yellow
L.A. Iced Tea
Lago Cosmo
Lemon Drop
Lemon Drop Martini
Lemongrass Cosmo
Leninade
Limelite
Limey Cosmo
Long Island Iced Tea
Long Island Spiced Tea
Loved Up
Lucien Gaudin
Lynchburg Lemonade
Mai Tai #2
Mai Tai #3 (Difford's Formula)
Maiden's Blush
Maiden's Prayer
Mainbrace
Major Bailey #2
Magic Bus
Malcolm Lowry
Mambo
Mango Margarita #1 (Served 'Up')
Mango Margarita #2 (Frozen)
Marama Rum Punch
Margarita #1 (Straight-up)
Margarita #2 (On the Rocks)
Margarita #3 (Frozen)
Margarita #4 (Salt Foam Float)
Marmarita
Martinez
Mat The Rat
Matador
Menehune Juice
Metropolitan
Millionaire
Mississippi Schnapper
Monk's Habit
Montego Bay
Moon River
Mountain Slipper
Napoleon Martini
Navy Grog
Nicky Finn
Old Flame
Opal
Orang-A-Tang
Orange Bloom Martini
Orange Blossom
Osmo
Passion Fruit Margarita
Passion Fruit Martini #3
Pear & Cardamom Sidecar
Pegu Club
Perfect John
Picador [NEW # 7]
Pineapple Margarita
Pino Pepe
Playa Del Mar
Poinsettia
Pompanski Martini
Ponce de Leon
Potted Parrot
Pousse-café
Presidente
Princess Marina
Quarterback
Raspberry Margarita
Razzmatazz
The Red Army
The Ritz Cocktail
Rosy Martini
Royal Bermuda Yacht Club Daiquiri
Royal Cosmopolitan
Ruby Martini #1
Ruby Martini #2
Rude Cosmopolitan
Rude Ginger Cosmopolitan
Sage Margarita
Sake'politan
San Francisco
Seelbach
Sidecar #1 (Equal parts classic formula)
Sidecar #2 (Difford's formula)
Sidecar #3 (Embury's formula)
Sidekick
Silent Third
Sir Thomas
Sloppy Joe
Stork Club
Sunny Breeze
Sunstroke
Tango Martini #1
Tantris Sidecar
Tennessee Iced Tea
Test Pilot
Texas Iced Tea
Thai Lady
Threesome
Thriller From Vanilla
Tokyo Iced Tea
Tomahawk
Tres Compadres Margarita
Trilby #2

Turquoise Daiquiri
Union Club
Vanilla Margarita
Vavavoom
Velvet Hammer
Venus Martini
Warsaw
Warsaw Cooler
Whiskey Daisy
White Cosmo
White Lady
White Lion
The Windsor Rose
Wink
Zakuski Martini

CRANBERRY JUICE

See 'Ocean Spray cranberry juice' and 'Ocean Spray White Cranberry & Grape Drink'

CREAM (DOUBLE/HEAVY)

I've specified 'double' or 'heavy' cream in preference to lighter creams. In many recipes this is diluted with an equal measure of milk – a combination known in the trade as 'Half & Half'. You'll find these ingredients separately in this guide.

Absinthe Suisesse
Ace
Aggravation
Alessandro
Alexander
Alexander The Great
Alexander's Big Brother
Alexander's Sister .5
Alexandra
Apple & Blackberry Pie
Apple & Cranberry Pie
Apple & Spice
Apple Strudel #1
Atholl Brose
Avalanche
Baltimore Egg Nog
Bananas & Cream
Banoffee Martini
Banashee
Barbara
Barbary Coast Highball
Barbary Coast Martini
Barnamint
Barranquilla Green Jade
Bazooka
BBC
Bees Knees #1
Bird of Paradise
Black Forest Gateau Martini
Black Widow
Blue Angel
Blush Martini
Blushin' Russian
Bourbon Cookie
Bourbon Milk Punch
Brandy Alexander
Brandy Flip
Brandy Milk Punch
Brazilian Coffee
Breakfast At Terrell's
Bubblegum Shot
Bulldog
Bullfrog
Burnt Toasted Almond
Buzzard's Breath
Café Toddy
Casablanca #2
Cassanova
Chatham Hotel Special
Cherry Alexander
Cicada Cocktail
Coco Cabana
Colorado Bulldog
Creamiscle
Creamy Creamsicle
Cream Cake
Crème Brûlée Martini
Crème de Café
Dirty Banana
Don Juan
Donna's Creamy'tini
Dreamsicle
Egg Nog #1 (Cold)
Egg Nog #2 (Hot)
The Estribo
Fifth Avenue Shot
Flip
Flying Grasshopper
Fourth Of July Cocktail
French Kiss #2
Fresca Nova
Friar Tuck
Frida's Brow
Fruit & Nut Chocolate Martini
Funky Monkey
Give Me A Dime
Golden Cardillac
Golden Dream
Grasshopper
Hair Of The Dog
Hazelnut Alexander
Hot Shot
Insomniac
Irish Alexander
Irish Coffee Martini
I.V.F. Martini
Key Lime Pie #1
Lemon Meringue Pie'tini
Lola
Lonely Bull
Mad Monk Milkshake
Melon Collie Martini
Meloncholy Martini
Mexican Coffee (Hot)
Mexicano (Hot)
Midnight Over Tennessee
Milk & Honey
Milk Punch
Miss Martini
Mocha Martini
Monk's Candy Bar
North Pole Martini
Nutty Summer
Opal Café
Orange Brûlée
Peach Melba Martini
Piña Colada #1
Piña Colada Virgin (Mocktail)
Pink Squirrel
Platinum Blonde
Princess Mary
P.S. I Love You
Quarterback
Ramos Gin Fizz
Rum & Raisin Alexandra
Russian Bride
Scotch Milk Punch
Screaming Banana Banshee
Screaming Orgasm
Sgroppino
Silk Stockings
Smooth & Creamy'tini
Snood Murdekin
Snow Fall Martini
Snow On Earth
Spiked Apple Cider (Hot)
Sputnik
Strudel Martini
Tarte Tatin Martini
Tiger's Milk
Tiramisu Martini
Toasted Almond
Tongue Twister
Triangular Martini
Trifle'tini
Upside-Down Raspberry Cheesecake
Velvet Hammer
Whip Me & Beat Me
White Elephant
White Knight
White Russian
White Satin
Wild Honey
Wimbledon Martini
Zoom

CREAM OF COCONUT

This is a non-alcoholic, sticky blend of coconut juice, sugar, emulsifier, cellulose, thickeners, citric acid and salt. Fortunately it tastes better than it sounds and is an essential ingredient of a good Piña Colada. One 15oz/425ml can will make approximately 25 drinks. Once opened the contents should be transferred to a suitable container and stored in a refrigerator. This may thicken the product, so gentle warming may be required prior to use. Coconut milk is very different and cannot be used as a substitute.

Bahia
Banana Colada
Batida de Coco
Blue Hawaiian
Buzzard's Breath
Caribbean PiÂa Colada
Coco Naut
Funky Monkey
Hawaiian
Hummingbird
New Port Codebreaker
Painkiller
Piña Colada #1
Piña Colada Virgin (Mocktail)
Tongue Twister

CRÈME DE BANANE(S) LIQUEUR

See 'Giffard Crème de Banane du Brésil Liqueur'

CRÈME DE CACAO LIQUEUR

See 'Giffard Brown Crème de Cacao Liqueur' and 'Giffard White Crème de Cacao Liqueur'

CRÈME DE CASSIS LIQUEUR

See 'Giffard Crème de Cassis Liqueur'

CRÈME DE FRAISE LIQUEUR

See 'Giffard Crème de Fraise des Bois Liqueur'

CRÈME DE FRAMBOISE LIQUEUR

See 'Giffard Crème de Framboise Liqueur'

CRÈME DE MENTHE LIQUEUR

See 'Giffard Green Crème de Menthe Liqueur' or 'Giffard White Crème de Menthe Pastille Liqueur'

CRÈME DE MÛRE LIQUEUR

See 'Giffard Crème de Mûre Liqueur'

CRÈME DE MYRTILLE LIQUEUR

See 'Giffard Crème de Myrtille Liqueur'

CRÈME DE VIOLETTE LIQUEUR

See 'Benoit Serres Violet Liqueur'

CUARENTA Y TRES (LICOR 43) LIQUEUR

Ambrosia'tini Ambrosia Cocktial
Angel's Share #1
Bloomsbury Martini
Crème Brûlée Martini
Don Juan
Doughnut Martini
Golden Retriever
Hornitos Lau
Jack Punch
Key Lime Pie #1
Lemon Meringue Pie'tini
Nine-20-Seven
Ole
Pineapple Mojito
Pomegranate Bellini
Suitably Frank
Vanilla Vodka Sour
Vante Martini

CUCUMBER

The fruit of a climbing plant originating from the foothills of the Himalayas, cucumbers should be used as fresh as possible, so look for firm, unwrinkled fruit. The skin can be quite bitter so cucumber is best peeled before use in cocktails. Either muddle in the base of your shaker or juice using an extractor.

Basilian
Cucumber Martini
Cucumber & Mint Martini
Cucumber Sake-Tini
Cumbersome
Gin Garden
Green Apple & Cucumber Martini
Green Destiny
Moscow Lassi
Wild Promenade Martini
Zakuski Martini

DRAMBUIE LIQUEUR

Atholl Brose
Bonnie Prince Charles
Causeway
Dean's Gate Martini
Embassy Royal
Galvanised Nail
Golden Shot
Heather Julep
Jack Frost
The MacKinnon
Mary Queen of Scots
Mystique
Prince Charlie
Rusty Nail
The Scott
Sweet Science
Trifle Martini
White Knight
Wild Honey

DUBONNET RED

This French wine based aperitif blends Roussillon wines from five different grape varietals with an infusion of herbs and spices including bitter bark and quinine. It is aged for three to four years in oak vats.
Many years ago the American rights to the Dubonnet Red brand were sold. The Dubonnet available in the US is now made from California wine that has been fortified with grape brandy. It is quite different from the French made product and is available in red and white styles.

Alfonso
Ante
Aviator
Bartender's Martini
Bentley
Blackthorn Cocktail

Crux ●●●●○
Dandy Cocktail ●●●●◐
De La Louisiane #3 ●●●●○
Dolores ●●●●○
The Dubonnet Cocktail ●●●●○
Fly Like A Butterfly ●●●●○
Merry Widow #2 ●●●◐○
Moonraker ●●●●○
Napoleon Martini ●●●●◐
Nightmare Martini ●●●○○
Opera ●●●●○
Paris Sour ●●●●○
Peggy Martini ●●●○○
Princess Marina ●●●●○
Princess Mary's Pride ●●●○○
Princess Pride ●●●◐○
Quebec ●●●●○
Red Neck Martini ●●●●○
Rosy Martini ●●●●○
Tiziano ●●●◐○
The Wentworth ●●●●○
Za-Za ●●●●○

EGGS

Raw eggs can be hazardous to health so you may decide it is safer to use commercially produced pasteurised egg white, particularly if you are infirm or pregnant (but then you probably shouldn't be drinking cocktails anyway).
Many cocktails only taste their best when made with fresh eggs. I'm sure I've suffered more upset stomachs from drinking too much alcohol than I have as a result of bad eggs. That said, it's worth taking steps to reduce the risk of Salmonella poisoning and therefore I recommend you store small, free range eggs in a refrigerator and use them well before the sell-by-date. Don't consume raw eggs if:

1. You are uncertain about their freshness.
2. There is a crack or flaw in the shell.
3. They don't wobble when rolled across a flat surface.
4. The egg white is watery instead of gel-like.
5. The egg yolk is not convex and firm.
6. The egg yolk bursts easily.
7. They smell foul.

Absinthe Sour ●●●◐○
Absinthe Suisesse ●●●○○
Acapulco Daiquiri ●●●●○
Ace ●●●◐○
The Alamagoozlum Cocktail ●●●●◐
Amaretto Sour ●●●◐○
Apple Brandy Sour ●●●●◐
Apricot Lady Sour ●●●◐○
Autumn Martini ●●●●○
Baltimore Egg Nog ●●●○○
Barranquilla Green Jade ●●●○○
Behemoth ●●●●○
Biarritz ●●●◐○
Blue Lady ●●●○○
Blue Moon ●●●◐○
Bolero Sour ●●●●●
Bosom Caresser ●●●●○
Boston Flip ●●●●○
Brandy Flip ●●●●◐
Brandy Sour ●●●●◐
Brass Rail ●●●●○
Cable Car ●●●●◐
Casablanca ●●●●○ #1
Champagne Daisy ●●●○○
Clover Leaf Cocktail #1 ●●●●○ (Classic Formula)
Clover Leaf Cocktail #2 ●●●◐○ (Modern Formula)
The Cold Winter Warmer Sour ●●●●○
Commodore #1 ●●●●○
Concealed Weapon ●●●○○
Crème Brûlée Martini ●●●●○
The Delicious Sour ●●●●○
Delores ●●●◐○
Derby Fizz ●●●●○
Dino Sour ●●●●◐
Earl Grey Mar-tea-ni ●●●●◐
Easter Martini ●●●●◐
Egg Nog #1 ●●●○○ (Cold)
Egg Nog #2 ●●●●○ (Hot)
Elder Sour ●●●●◐
Fizz ●●●●○
Flamingo #1 ●●●◐○
Flip ●●●●◐
Fosbury Flip ●●●●◐
Froth Blower Cocktail ●●●●◐
Fruit Sour ●●●●○
Fruits Of The Forest ●●●○○
Gin Sour ●●●●◐
Gloom Lifter ●●●●○
Gold Medallion ●●●◐○
Golden Fizz #1 ●●●◐○
Golden Girl ●●●●○
Golden Slipper ●●●◐○
Grand Passion ●●●○○
Grande Champagne Cosmo ●●●●○
Grapparita ●●●◐○
Green Fairy ●●●●○
Green Horn ●●●◐○
Honey Berry Sour ●●●●○
Honey Blossom ●●●○○ (Mocktail)
Honey Vodka Sour ●●●●○
Honeymoon ●●●●○
Hoopla ●●●●○
In-Seine ●●●●●
Jaffa Martini ●●●◐○
Jean Lafitte Cocktail ●●◐○○
Jenever Sour ●●●●○
Jersey Sour ●●●●●
Jubilant ●●●●◐
Lemon Sorbet ●●●●○
Lime Sour ●●●●○
Liquorice Whiskey Sour ●●●●◐
Mandarine Sour ●●●◐○
Margarita #4 (Salt Foam Float) ●●●◐○
Milano Sour ●●●●○
The Million Dollar Cocktail ●●●●◐
Millionaire ●●●●○
Mood Indigo ●●●●○
Morning Glory Fizz ●●●●○
Mountain ●●●◐○
Noon ●●●●○
North Pole Martini ●●●●○
Paris Sour ●●●●○
Park Lane ●●●●◐
Perfect Lady ●●●●○
Periscope ●●●●●
Pink Lady ●●●●◐
Pisco Sour ●●●●◐ (Traditional Recipe)
Pisco Sour ●●●●● (Difford's Version)
Playmate Martini ●●●●◐
Plum Sour ●●●●○
Ponche de Algarrobina ●●●◐○
Port Light ●●●◐○
Prado ●●●◐○
Prairie Oyster ●●●◐○
Purple Flirt #2 ●●●○○
Pussyfoot ●●●●◐ (Mocktail)
Quince Sour ●●●●○
Ramos Gin Fizz ●●●●●
Rattlesnake ●●●◐○
The Roadrunner ●●●●○
Rum Sour ●●●●○
Salflower Sour ●●●●○
Savannah ●●●◐○
Silver Fizz ●●●●○
Sloe Gin Fizz ●●●◐○
Snow White Daiquiri ●●●●○
Sophisticated Savage ●●●◐○
Sour ●●●◐○
Sour Apple Martini #2 ●●●●◐ (Deluxe US version)
South Of The Border ●●●○○
Tequila Sour ●●●●◐
Tiger's Milk ●●●◐○
Tiramisu Martini ●●●●○
Tom & Jerry ●●●○○
Triangular Martini ●●●●○
Triple Orange Martini ●●●●○
Turkish Delight ●●●●○
Uncle Vanya ●●●●○
Union Club ●●●●○
Vacation ●●●◐○
Vanilla Vodka Sour ●●●●○
Veneto ●●●◐○
Vodka Sour ●●●●○
Whiskey Sour #1 (Classic Formula) ●●●●○
Whiskey Sour #2 (Difford's Formula) ●●●●●
White Lady ●●●●○
Zabaglione Martini ●●●◐○

ELDERFLOWER LIQUEUR

See 'St-Germain Elderflower Liqueur'

LA FÉE PARISIENNE (68%) ABSINTHE

68% **alc./vol.** (136°proof)
www.eabsinthe.com
Producer: Produced under licence in Paris, France.

La Fée is made in Paris to a 19th century recipe containing wormwood (Artemisia absinthium) and flavoured with anise, hyssop and other aromatic herbs. It was launched in 2000 by George Rowley, the man responsible for importing the first absinthe into the UK since before the Second World War, and the originator of absinthe's renaissance.
This was the first traditional absinthe to be commercially produced in France since it was banned in 1914-15. A mark of La Fée's authenticity is its endorsement by Marie-Claude Delahaye, founder and curator of the Absinthe Museum in Auvers-sur-Oise, France. As should be the case in a traditional French absinthe, La Fée turns cloudy with the addition of water. The bottle is as distinctive as its contents, with its label dominated by an illustration of an eye.
La Fée has the flavour profile of a traditional French absinthe. It has clean, fresh and rounded aniseed flavours and well-balanced liquorice, mint, lemon, angelica, and rootier notes.
La Fée also produce a Bohemian absinth made in the Czech Republic (note the missing 'e'). This has a bluer tinge to its green colour and a more subtle aniseed flavour than its French counterpart. It is not usual for Czech absinth to turn cloudy when water is added. Unless specified, recipes in this guide call for La Fée Parisienne (68%) absinthe.

Absinthe Cocktail #1 ●●●◐○
Absinthe Cocktail #2 ●●●◐○
Absinthe Drip Cocktail #2 (Czech method) ●●●○○
Absinthe Drip Cocktail #1 (French method) ●●●○○
Absinthe Frappé ●●●●○
Absinthe Italiano Cocktail ●●●○○
Absinthe Special Cocktial ●●●○○
Absinthe Suisesse ●●●○○
Absinthe Without Leave ●●◐○○
Applesinth ●●●●○
The Atty Cocktail ●●●●○
B-55 Shot ●●●○○
Bombay No. 2 ●●●●◐
Chocolate Sazerac ●●●●○
Colonial Rot ●●●○○
Concealed Weapon ●●●○○
Corpse Reviver #2 ●●●●○
De La Louisiane #2 ●●●●○
Dead Man's Mule ●●●◐○
Death In The Afternoon ●●●○○
Glad Eye Cocktail ●●●○○
Gloom Chaser Cocktail #2 ●●●◐○
Grand Sazerac ●●●●○
Green Fairy ●●●●○
Green Hornet ●●●●○
Hammer Of The Gods ●●◐○○
Henry VIII ●●●◐○
In-Seine ●●●●●
I.V.F. Martini ●●●◐○
Jean Lafitte Cocktail ●●◐○○
Katrina Cocktail ●●●○○
Knockout Martini ●●●●○
L'Amour en Fuite ●●●●○
Linstead ●●●●◐
London Cocktail ●●●○○
Martini Special ●●●●◐
Mauresque ●●●○○
Maurice Martini ●●●◐○
Merry Widow #1 ●●●◐○
Monkey Gland #1 ●●●●○
Moonshine Martini ●●●●◐
Morning Glory ●●●●○
Morning Glory Fizz ●●●●○
New Year's Absolution ●●●◐○
Obituary ●●●●○
Panachée ●●●○○
Peggy Martini ●●●○○
Piccadilly Martini ●●●●◐
Pisco Punch #4 ●●●●● (Prosser's Formula)
Rattlesnake ●●●◐○
Remember The Maine ●●●●◐
Savoy Special #1 ●●●●○
Sazerac ●●●●●
The 75 ●●●●◐
Trilby #1 ●●●●○
Turf Martini ●●●●○
Vert'ical Breeze ●●●●○
Viagra Falls ●●●◐○
Weeping Jesus ●●●◐○
Whip Me & Beat Me ●●●○○
Windy Miller ●●●●○
Wink ●●●●○
Yellow Parrot ●●●●○

FERNET BRANCA

Dr Zeus ●●●●◐
Hanky-Panky Martini ●●●●○
King Cole Cocktail ●●●●○
Napoleon Martini ●●●●◐
Zeus Martini ●●●●◐

FINO

See 'Sherry – Fino'

FRANGELICO HAZELNUT LIQUEUR

24% **alc./vol.** (48°proof)
www.frangelico.com
Producer: Barbero 1981 S.p.A. (Cantrell & Cochrane), Canale D'Alba, Italy

Frangelico is a hazelnut flavoured liqueur produced in the Piedmont region of Northern Italy. Its origins are said to date back some 300 years to Christian monks living in the local hills. Their knowledge and understanding of nature was the inspiration for Frangelico, which is made using wild hazelnuts collected in the area. These are toasted, combined with cocoa, vanilla, herbs and spices, then aged in oak casks to add character and depth of flavour.
Frangelico is named after a monk named Fra Angelico who lived as a hermit in the Piedmont hills during the 17th century. It is instantly recognisable by its eye-catching monk-shaped bottle and rope tie.
Frangelico has a rich and balanced flavour, now essential to many popular cocktails. The taste is complex. As well as the obvious hazelnut, it includes cheesecake base, butter and hints of espresso, citrus and vanilla.

Bellissimo ●●●○○
The Bistro Sidecar ●●●●○
Black Nuts ●●◐○○
Brazilian Monk ●●●◐○
Butterfly's Kiss ●●●◐○
Cherry & Hazelnut Daiquiri ●●●●○
Choc & Nut Martini ●●●◐○
Creamy Bee ●●●●○
Cuppa Joe ●●●●○
DC Martini ●●●●○
Envy ●●●●○
Fosbury Flip ●●●●◐
Friar Tuck ●●●◐○
Fruit & Nut Chocolate Martini ●●●●○
Fruit & Nut Martini ●●●●○
Ginger Nut ●●●◐○
Giuseppe's Habit ●●●●○
Golden Mac ●●●◐○

Hazel'ito
Hazelnut Alexander
Hazelnut Martini
Insomniac
International Incident
Italian Sun
Jam Roll
Knicker Dropper Glory
Mad Monk Milkshake
Monk's Candy Bar
Monk's Habit
Nuts & Berries
Nutty Berry'tini
Nutty Nashville
Nutty Russian
Peanut Butter & Jelly Shot
The Strawberry Éclair
Vanilla'tini
Yule Luvit
Zesty

GALLIANO LIQUEUR

30% **alc./vol.** (60°proof)
www.galliano.com
Producer: Lucas Bols, Amsterdam, The Netherlands

Galliano is a vibrant, golden, vanilla flavoured liqueur from Italy, easily recognised by its tall, fluted bottle, inspired by Roman columns. Invented in 1896, Galliano is made from over 30 ingredients including star anise, lavender, ginger and vanilla. A noted cocktail ingredient, Galliano's signature drink is the Harvey Wallbanger. Apparently, Harvey was a surfer at Manhattan Beach, California, and his favourite drink was a Screwdriver with added Galliano. One day in the late 60s, while celebrating winning a surfing competition, he staggered from bar to bar banging his surfboard on the walls and so the cocktail was born.
The versatility of Galliano ensures that it can be enjoyed in cocktails and as a long drink. It also works particularly well as a hot shot with coffee and cream. The lovely smell of Galliano is reminiscent of a pack of Tic-Tac sweets, while its smooth vanilla taste is complimented by peppermint and spiced with cinnamon, ginger, nutmeg and citrus.

Adam & Eve
Atlantic Breeze
Bartender's Root Beer
Bossa Nova #1
Bossa Nova #2
Bourbon Milk Punch
California Root Beer
Caribbean Punch
Casablanca #2
Dutch Breakfast Martini
Flaming Ferrari
Fourth Of July Cocktail
Freddy Fudpucker
Fruit Salad
Giuseppe's Habit
Golden Cadillac
Golden Dream
Harvey Wallbanger
Highland Sling
Hot Shot
Hurricane #3
Jumping Jack Flash
K.G.B.
Kiss of Death
Maxim's Coffee (Hot)
Milano Sour
Moon River
Mrs Robinson #2
Peppermint Vanilla Daiquiri
Perfect John
Picca
Rocky Mountain Rootbeer
Russian Qualuude Shot
Slow Comfortable Screw Against the Wall

Snoopy
South Pacific Breeze
Tootie Fruity Lifesaver
White Satin
Wild Honey
Yellow Bird
Yellow Fever Martini

GENEVER

See 'Bokma Genever'

GIFFARD APRICOT BRANDY DU ROUSSILLON

25% **alc./vol.** (50°proof)
www.giffard.com
Producer: Giffard & Cie, Angers, France

Apricot Brandy is sometimes also known as 'apry'. It is a liqueur produced by infusing apricots in selected cognacs and flavouring the infusion with various herbs to bring out the best flavour and aroma of the apricots. This amber coloured liqueur is one of Giffard's most popular liqueurs.
With an aroma of juicy apricots, this distinctively flavoured liqueur is suited to use in a variety of different cocktails. The light clean taste features apricot with a hint of brandy and almond.

Alan's Apple Breeze
Algeria
Angel Face
Apricot Fizz
Apricot Lady Sour
Apricot Mango Martini
Apricot Martini
Apricot Sour
Aquarius
Aunt Emily
Banana Boomer
Barnum (Was Right)
Bermuda Rose Cocktail
Bingo
Bitter Sweet Symphony
Bossa Nova #1
Bossa Nova #2
Boston
Cappercaille
Charlie Chaplin
Claridge Cocktail
Colonel T
Columbus Daiquiri
Cruel Intention
Cuban Cocktail No. 3 #2
DNA #1
DNA #2
Dulchin
Eastern Promise
Empire Cocktail
Fairbanks Cocktail No. 1
Fifth Avenue Shot
The Flirt
Fosbury Flip
The Frankenjack Cocktail
Fruit Tree Daiquiri
Golden Dawn
Golden Screw
Golden Slipper
Highland Sling
Hop Toad #1
Hop Toad #2
Hop Toad #3
Incognito
Indian Rose
Intimate Martini
Katinka
Kentucky Dream
Leave It To Me Martini
Lutkins Special Martini
Mambo

Mayfair Cocktail
The Mayflower Martini
Millionaire's Daiquiri
Moon River
Mule's Hind Leg
Nacional Daiquiri #1
Nacional Daiquiri #2
Pancho Villa
Paradise #1
Paradise #2
Paradise #3
Park Lane
Pendennis Cocktail
Periodista Daiquiri
Playmate Martini
Resolute
Roa Aé
Sleeping Bison-tini
Sleepy Hollow
Southern Tea-Knee
Spencer Cocktail
Speyside Martini
Sumo in a Sidecar
Tiki Max
Toreador
Trinity
Tulip Cocktail
Valencia
Webster Martini
The Wet Spot
What The Hell
Yacht Club
Yellow Bird
Yellow Parrot
Zanzibar
Zombie #3 (Modern formula)

GIFFARD BROWN CRÈME DE CACAO LIQUEUR

25% **alc./vol.** (50°proof)
www.giffard.com
Producer: Giffard & Cie, Angers, France

The finest roasted cacao beans are used to prepare Giffard Brown Crème de Cacao, combined with carefully selected herbs to enhance their flavour. Please note that 'brown crème de cacao' liqueurs are sometimes alternatively named 'dark crème de cacao'.
Giffard Brown Crème de Cacao is perfect for adding a rich chocolate flavour to any cocktail. Choose between the lighter, more delicately flavoured white or this rich, dark version.

Apple Strudel #1
Barbary Coast Highball
Black Martini
Brandy Alexander
Brazilian Monk
Café Toddy
Chatham Hotel Special
Chocolarita
Chocolate Biscuit
Chocolate Puff
Chocolate Sidecar
Death By Chocolate
DiVino's
Donna's Creamy'tini
Fifth Avenue Shot
Friar Tuck
Funky Monkey
Hazelnut Alexander
Heavens Above
Honey Wall
Jaffa Martini
Melon Collie Martini
Midnight Over Tennessee
Mocha Martini
Mulata Daiquiri
Raspberry Mocha'tini
Tiramisu Martini
Triangular Martini
Triple 'C' Martini

GIFFARD CRÈME DE BANANE DU BRESIL LIQUEUR

25% **alc./vol.** (50°proof)
www.giffard.com
Producer: Giffard & Cie, Angers, France

The French term 'crème de' indicates that one particular flavour predominates in the liqueur - it does not imply that the liqueur contains cream. Many fruit liqueurs are described as 'crème de' followed by the name of a fruit. This refers to the liqueur's quality, as in the phrase 'crème de la crème'. Therefore crème de bananes is a banana flavoured liqueur.
To create Giffard Banane du Brésil Liqueur the finest Brazilian bananas are slowly macerated in neutral spirit. Essence of banana is added for an intense aroma and strengthened by a touch of Cognac.

Avalanche
Banana Batida
Banana Boomer
Banana Colada
Banana Daiquiri
Bananas & Cream
Banoffee Martini
Banashee
Bazooka
Bazooka Joe
Beam-me-up Scotty
Beam-me-up Scotty Shot
Beha Flor 4.5
Blow Job
Canaries
Caribbean Breeze
Chiclet Daiquiri
Dirty Banana
Flamingo #1
Fruit Salad
Funky Monkey
Gold
Golden Bird
Gulf Coast Sex on the Beach
Hummingbird
Jumping Jack Flash
June Bug
Landslide
Luxury Cocktail
Mellow Martini
Nathalia
Reef Juice
Rum Runner
San Francisco
Screaming Banana Banshee
Smooth & Creamy'tini
Southern Tea-Knee
Tootie Fruity Lifesaver
Top Banana Shot
Tribbble
Yellow Bird

GIFFARD CRÈME DE FRAMBOISE LIQUEUR

18% **alc./vol.** (36°proof)
www.giffard.com
Producer: Giffard & Cie, Angers, France

The French refer to raspberry liqueurs as 'crème de framboise'. This comes from the French word for raspberry 'framboise' and 'crème' as in the French phrase 'crème de la crème'. It means that the liqueur expresses the essential flavour of raspberries, not that it

contains raspberries and cream.

Giffard Crème de Framboise is made by macerating fresh raspberries in neutral alcohol which gives this liqueur an intense, rich, raspberry flavour.

Carol Channing
Finn Rouge
Raspberry Collins
Raspberry Cosmo
Raspberry Debonair
Raspberry Martini #2
Raspberry Mocha'tini
The Red Army
Red Breast
Red Hooker
The Roffignac
Ruby Martini #2
Sangria Martini
Wild Promenade Martini

GIFFARD CRÈME DE MÛRES LIQUEUR

16% **alc./vol.** (32°proof)
www.giffard.com
Producer: Giffard & Cie, Angers, France

The French refer to blackberry liqueurs as 'crème de mûre'. This comes from the French word for blackberry 'mûre' and 'crème', meaning 'cream' or 'essence'.

Giffard Crème de Mûres is made by macerating fresh blackberries. Hence its intense, rich blackberry flavour.

Basil Bramble Sling
Black & White Daiquiri
Bramble
Collection Martini
Congo Blue
Epiphany
Especial Day
Godfrey
Hedgerow Sling
The Legend
Pernod & Black Martini
Pontberry Martini
La Rosa Margarita
Rum Runner
Uncle Vanya
Vanilla Laika
Vanitini
Wibble

GIFFARD CRÈME DE MYRTILLE LIQUEUR

16% **alc./vol.** (32°proof)
www.giffard.com
Producer: Giffard & Cie, Angers, France

The French refer to blueberry liqueurs as 'crème de myrtille'. This comes from the French word for blueberry 'myrtille' and 'crème' a term often used of high quality French liqueurs. Giffard Crème de Myrtille draws its potent blueberry flavour from the rich essence of bilberries, the European blueberry, which is extracted by slow maceration.

American Pie Martini
Blueberry Martini #1
Myrtle Martini

GIFFARD CRÈME DE CASSIS NOIR DE BOURGOGNE LIQUEUR

20% **alc./vol.** (40°proof)
www.giffard.com
Producer: Giffard & Cie, Angers, France

Crème de cassis is a blackcurrant liqueur which originated in France and can be made by infusion and/or maceration: it never contains cream. The original recipe for a crème de cassis is thought to have been formulated by Denis Lagoute in 1841 in the French Dijon region. Many of the best examples are still produced in this region.

EEC law states that crème de cassis must contain a minimum of 400g of sugar per litre and have a minimum alcoholic strength of 15%. Unfortunately no minimum is set for the fruit content, although the best brands will contain as much as 600g of blackcurrants per litre. Giffard Crème de Cassis Noir de Bourgogne owes its fruity taste and deep hue to its high fruit content.

Apple Sunrise
Arnaud Martini
Ballet Russe
Black Forest Gateau Martini
Black Jack Cocktail
Black Mussel .5
Blimey
Bolshoi Punch
Brazilian Berry
Cardinal Punch
Casino
Chimayo
Country Breeze
Detropolitan
Diable Rouge
El Diablo
Epestone Daiquiri
The Estribo
French Daisy
Gina
Guillotine
Kir
Kir Martini
Kir Royale
Liquorice Shot
Lychee & Blackcurrant Martini
Macka
Martini Royale
Mexican Martini
Parisian Martini #1
Rum & Raisin Alexandra
Russian Spring Punch
Serendipity #1
Showbiz
Stars & Stripes Shot
Sunshine Cocktail #2
Tarte Aux Pommes
Teresa
Tripleberry

GIFFARD CRÈME DE FRAISE DES BOIS LIQUEUR

18% **alc./vol.** (36°proof)
www.giffard.com
Producer: Giffard & Cie, Angers, France

'Fraise' is French for strawberry and Giffard Crème de Fraise des Bois is a strawberry liqueur made by infusion and maceration. 'Fraises des bois' refers to the tiny wild strawberries from which this liqueur is produced.

This liqueur has a rich ripe strawberry flavour with light hints of citrus fruit. It is great served chilled, in a cocktail, over strawberries or in a fruit salad.

Black Forest Gateau Martini
Black Widow
Bourbon Blush
Exotic Passion
French Spring Punch
Fru Fru
Jayne Mansfield
Reggae Rum Punch
Rossini
Strawberry Blonde Martini
Strawberry Cosmo
The Strawberry Éclair
Trifle'tini
Tripleberry
Wimbledon Martini

GIFFARD GREEN CRÈME DE MENTHE LIQUEUR

21% **alc./vol.** (48°proof)
www.giffard.com
Producer: Giffard & Cie, Angers, France

Giffard Green Crème de Menthe is a classic, green coloured liqueur flavoured with peppermint - extracted, of course, from fresh mint leaves. The mint oils are distilled, to deliver a high quality and very refreshing mint flavour, which has stood the test of time as a digestive liqueur.

After Eight
Alexander's Sister .5
Barnamint
Barranquilla Green Jade
Bullfrog
Caruso Martini
Every-Body's Irish Cocktail
Flying Grasshopper
Grasshopper
Green Dragon
Green Fizz
Green Fly
Green Swizzle
Green Tea Martini #1
Irish Flag
Jade Daiquiri
Midnight Over Tennessee
Mint Martini
Port & Starboard
Pousse-café
St. Patrick's Day
Shamrock #1
Shamrock #2
Tequila Mockingbird

GIFFARD WHITE CRÈME DE CACAO LIQUEUR

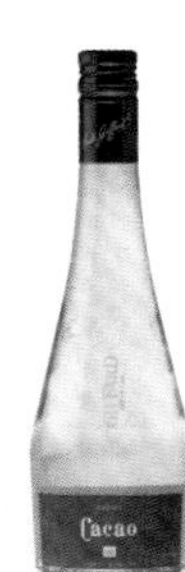

25% **alc./vol.** (50°proof)
www.giffard.com
Producer: Giffard & Cie, Angers, France

A number of recipes require the chocolate flavour of crème de cacao yet not the dark brown colour. In order to preserve the taste but eliminate the colour, Giffard extract the flavour of the finest roasted cacao beans by means of distillation instead of percolation. This process also gives Giffard White Crème de Cacao a lighter flavour than Giffard Brown Crème de Cacao. Giffard cacao adds a rich chocolate flavour to any cocktail. Choose between this lighter, more delicately flavoured white or the rich, dark version.

Ace of Clubs Daiquiri
After Eight
Alexander
Alexander The Great
All White Frappé
Apple Strudel #1
Avalanche
Avalanche Shot
Banashee
Barbara
Barbary Coast Martini
Behemoth
Bird of Paradise
Brandy Alexander
Butterscotch Martini
Cherry Alexander
Choc & Nut Martini
Chocolate & Cranberry Martini
Chocolate Martini
Chocolate Mint Martini
Chocolate Sazerac
Commodore #2
Crossbow
DC Martini
Delmarva Cocktail No. 2
Delores
Easter Martini
El Floridita Daiquiri No. 2
Flying Grasshopper
French Kiss #2
Frida's Brow
Fruit & Nut Chocolate Martini
Give Me A Dime
Golden Cardillac
Grasshopper
Hazelnut Martini
Kretchma
Lemon Chiffon Pie
Lola
Mother Rum
Nutcracker Sweet
Pago Pago
Pall Mall Martini
Pini
Pink Cloud
Pink Sin Martini
Pink Squirrel
Princess Mary
Rattlesnake Shot
Russian
Russian Bride
Savannah
Scotch Bounty Martini
Screaming Banana Banshee
Silk Stockings
Smartini
Summer Rose Martini
Superminty-Chocolatini
Top Banana Shot
Turkish Delight
Twentieth Century Martini
Velvet Hammer
White Elephant
White Stinger

GIFFARD WHITE CRÈME DE MENTHE PASTILLE LIQUEUR

24% **alc./vol.** (48°proof)
www.giffard.com
Producer: Giffard & Cie, Angers, France

This iconic liqueur has a matter-of-fact origin. More than a century ago, Emile Giffard was a dispensing chemist in Angers. As he was working late one night a patron from the hotel next door arrived on his doorstep complaining of indigestion. She asked if Emile could concoct a drink from mint tablets, so he ground the tablets into a fine powder, to which he added some spirit.

The mixture cured the lady's indigestion and left Emile with a great idea. He set about formulating a liqueur and imported peppermint leaves from England, which he used to distil a clear liqueur he called 'Menthe Pastille'. He began to market the liqueur, which proved an instant success, leading him to establish his own distillery. Menthe Pastille is still made to the original recipe at a distillery run by Emile's great grandson.

This aromatic liqueur is great served over crushed ice as a digestif or blended in a range of cocktails.

After Six Shot ●●◐○○
Afterburner ●●●◐○
All White Frappé ●●●◐○
Amercian Beauty #1 ●●●●◐
American Beauty #2 ●●●●○
Chiclet Daiquiri ●●●◐○
Chocolate Mint Martini ●●●●○
Delmarva Cocktail No. 1 ●●●●◐
Dixie Dew ●●●●◐
Fu Manchu Daiquiri ●●●●○
Glad Eye Cocktail ●●●○○
Irish Charlie ●●●○○
Knockout Martini ●●●●○
Miami Daiquiri ●●●●○
Mint Cocktail ●●●●◐
Mint Fizz ●●●◐○
Monte Carlo Imperial ●●●○○
Peppermint Vanilla Daiquiri ●●●○○
Stinger ●●●●○
Superminty-Chocolatini ●●●◐○
Ti Punch ●●●●○
Trinity ●●●○○
White Stinger ●●●◐○

GIN

See 'Plymouth Gin'

GINGER (ROOT - FRESH)

Ginger is an edible rhizome that is commonly used as a spice in cooking. Although often referred to as a root, it is in fact the horizontal, subterranean stem of the plant which is used in cooking.

Recipes in this guide call for fresh root ginger. Clean the stem by cutting away the outer skin and slice into thin, thumbnail-sized pieces. Muddle a number of these in the base of your shaker as specified in the recipe.

Various brands of liqueurs flavoured with root ginger are available, we particularly recommend 'Giffard Ginger of the Indies'.

Amber ●●●●◐
Aphrodisiac ●●●○○
Asian Ginger Martini ●●●●○
Asian Mary ●●●●○
Caipiginger ●●●◐○
Chinese Whisper Martini ●●●●○
Cool Orchard ●●●●○
Deep South ●●●○○
Easy Tiger ●●●●○
Gin Gin Mule ●●●●○
Ginger & Lemongrass Martini ●●●●○
Gin-Ger & Tonic ●●●●○
Ginger Cosmos ●●●◐○
Ginger Martini ●●●●○
Ginger Punch ●●●◐○
Gin-Ger Tom ●●●●○
Golden Mac ●●●◐○
Jean Marc ●●●●○
Kentucky Mac ●●●◐○
Motox ●●●●○
Perfect Alibi ●●●●○
Pineapple & Ginger Martini ●●●●○
Port of Melon Martini ●●●●◐
Rude Ginger Cosmopolitan ●●●●○
Sorrelade ●●●◐○ (Mocktail)
Spicy Finn ●●●●○

GINGER ALE

Make this non-alcoholic drink by adding ginger essence, colouring and sweeteners to aerated water. It is not as powerful in flavour as ginger beer.

Apple Buck ●●●●○
Basilian ●●●◐○
Bee Sting ●●●●○
The Big Easy ●●●●○
Bora Bora Brew (Mocktail) ●●●○○
Brandy Buck ●●●◐○
The Buck ●●●◐○
Causeway ●●●◐○
Cranapple Breeze ●●●◐○
Drowned Out ●●●◐○
Enchanted ●●●◐○
Fog Horn ●●●◐○
Ginger Mojito ●●●●○
Ginger Punch ●●●◐○
Horse's Neck With a Kick ●●●○○
Kentucky Tea ●●●◐○
Limey Mule ●●●●○
Loch Almond ●●●●○
Maple Pomme ●●●●○
New Year's Absolution ●●●◐○
Niagara Falls ●●●◐○
O'Henry ●●●◐○
Riviera Breeze ●●●◐○
Saigon Sling ●●●◐○
St Kitts ●●●●○ (Mocktail)
Sandy Gaff ●●●◐○
Scandinavian Pop ●●●○○
Shady Grove Cooler ●●●◐○
Shirley Temple ●●●○○ (Mocktail)
Ski Breeze ●●●○○
Sling ●●●●○
Tequila Slammer ●●●○○
Tolleytown Punch ●●●◐○
Umbongo ●●●○○
Urban Holistic ●●●◐○
Waltzing Matilda ●●●●○
Watermelon & Basil Smash ●●●●○

GINGER BEER

This fizzy drink is flavoured with ginger and sometimes contains small quantities of alcohol. Buy a quality brand or brew your own as follows:
Combine 2oz/56 grams of peeled and crushed root ginger, 2 lemons sliced into thick rings, 1 teaspoon of cream of tartar, 1lb/450 grams sugar and 1 gallon/4 litres water in a large stainless steel saucepan and bring to the boil. Stir and leave to cool to blood temperature. Stir in 1oz/28 grams of yeast and leave to ferment for 24 hours. Skim off the yeast from the surface and fine strain the liquid into four sterilised 1 litre plastic bottles with screw caps. (Leave at least 2 inches/5cm of air at the top of each bottle and ensure all utensils are scrupulously clean.). Place bottles upright and release excess pressure after 12 hours. Check again after another 12 hours. Once the bottles feel firm and under pressure, place them in the refrigerator and consume their contents within three days.

Apple of One's Eye ●●●◐○
Berry Nice ●●●◐○
Bomber ●●●●○
Dark 'N' Stormy ●●●●○
Dead Man's Mule ●●●◐○
Desert Cooler ●●●◐○
El Diablo ●●●◐○
Dirty Sanchez ●●●●○
El Burro ●●●●○
Emperor's Memoirs ●●●●○
Forbidden Fruits ●●●●○
French Mule ●●●●○
Gin Gin Mule ●●●●○
Ginger Nut ●●●◐○
Jamaican Mule ●●●◐○
Mandarine Songbird ●●●○○
Mexican Mule ●●●●◐
New Orleans Mule ●●●◐○
Prickly Pear Mule ●●●●○
Raspberry Mule ●●●●○
Red Breast ●●●◐○
Southern Mule ●●●◐○
Tennessee Berry Mule ●●●●○
Thai Lemonade ●●●◐○ (Mocktail)
Tuscan Mule ●●●◐○

GINGER LIQUEUR

Various brands of liqueurs flavoured with root ginger are available, for example King's Ginger Liqueur.

China Beach ●●●●○
Collar & Cuff ●●●●○
Ginger Cosmo ●●●●○
Ginger Margarita ●●●●○
Gingertini ●●●●○

GRAND MARNIER LIQUEUR

40% **alc./vol.** (80?proof)
www.grand-marnier.com
Producer: Marnier-Lapostolle (Société des Produits), Paris, France.

Grand Marnier is one of the best known and most widely sold premium liqueurs in the world. With a cognac base, its unique flavour and aroma come from the maceration and distillation of tropical orange peels.
Founded in 1827 by Jean Baptiste Lapostolle, Grand Marnier is still a family-run business and continues to use traditional production methods and the original Grand Marnier recipe. But despite its heritage credentials, Grand Marnier is an essential cocktail ingredient in today's leading style bars.
Grand Marnier is silky rich with a zesty, juicy flavour. It has a good underlying bite of bitter orange and hints of marmalade with cognac richness at the edges, making it the perfect cocktail partner.
Grand Marnier also produce two special cuvées or blends, 'Grand Marnier Cuvée du Centenaire', created in 1927 by Louis-Alexandre Marnier-Lapostolle to celebrate the 100th anniversary of the company's foundation; and 'Grand Marnier Cuvée du Cent Cinquantenaire', an exceptional Grand Marnier created in 1977 by the Chairman of the company, Jacques Marnier-Lapostolle, to celebrate the company's 150th anniversary. Some cocktails in this guide which call for Grand Marnier may benefit from the extra complexity provided by these exceptional cuvées. I've marked these drinks with an '*' in the list below and after Grand Marnier in the recipe.

Agent Orange ●●●●○
The Alamagoozlum Cocktail ●●●●◐
Alfonso Martini ●●●●○
Alice From Dallas ●●●◐○
Alice In Wonderland ●●●○○
Attitude Adjuster ●●●○○
B-52 Shot ●●●◐○
B-52 Frozen ●●●◐○
B.J. Shot
Bartender's Martini ●●●●○
Basil Grande ●●●●○
Basilian ●●●◐○
Biarritz ●●●◐○
Bingo ●●●○○
Black Magic ●●●●○
Blow Job ●●●◐○
Blueberry Tea ●●●●○
Bosom Caresser ●●●●○
Boulevard ●●●●○
Brandy Buck ●●●◐○
Bull's Blood ●●●◐○
Cactus Banger ●●●●○
Café Toddy ●●●◐○
Californian Martini ●●●●○
Caravan ●●●○○
Champagne Cup ●●●◐○
Charente Çollins ●●●●○
Chas ●●●●○
Claret Cobbler ●●●●○
Classic Cocktail ●●●●●
Clockwork Orange ●●●○○
The Comet ●●●●◐
Cosmopolitan Delight ●●●●◐
Creamiscle ●●●○○
D'Artagnan ●●●◐○
Derby Fizz ●●●●○
Dorian Gray ●●●◐○
Dramatic Martini ●●●◐○
Dubliner ●●●●○
Dulchin ●●●●◐
East India #1 ●●●●◐
East India #2 ●●●●○
English Channel ●●●●◐
Esquire #1 ●●●●○
Fancy Drink ●●●◐○
57 T-Bird Shot ●●●●○
Flaming Ferrari ●●○○○
French Tear #1 ●●●●○
Fresca Nova ●●●◐○
Gloom Chaser Cocktail #1 ●●●●○
Godfrey ●●●●○
Golden Bird ●●●◐○
Grand Cosmopolitan ●●●●◐
Grand Mimosa ●●●◐○
Grand Sazerac ●●●●○
Grand Sidecar ●●●●○
Grande Champagne Cosmo ●●●●○
Hakkantini ●●●●○
Hot Red Blooded Frenchman ●●●●○
Irish Chocolate Oranj'tini ●●●◐○
Irish Flag ●●●○○
Irish Manhattan ●●●●○
Jambouree ●●●●○
Knickerbocker Special ●●●●○
Larchmont ●●●●◐
Leap Year Martini ●●●○○
Mandarintini ●●●○○
Marny Cocktail ●●●●◐
Met Manhattan ●●●●○
Mexico City ●●●●◐
Mexicano ●●●●◐ (Hot)
Million Dollar Margarita ●●●●◐
Mimosa ●●●◐○
Morning Glory ●●●●○
Mulled Wine ●●●●○
Naranja Daiquiri ●●●●○
Niagara Falls ●●●◐○
Night & Day ●●●◐○
Olympic ●●●●◐
Orange Brûlée ●●●●●
Orange Custard Martini ●●●◐○
Park Avenue ●●●●○
Pegu Club ●●●●○
Periodista Daiquiri ●●●●○
Pilgrim Cocktail ●●●●○
Pink Palace ●●●●◐
Pisco Naranja ●●●◐○
Platinum Blonde ●●●◐○
Playmate Martini ●●●●◐
Polly's Special ●●●●○
Prince Of Wales ●●●◐○
Randy ●●●●○
Rat Pack Manhattan ●●●●○
Redback ●●●○○
Red Lion #1 ●●●●◐ (Modern Formula)
Red Lion #2 ●●●●◐ (Embury's Formula)
Rhett Butler ●●●●○
Roa Aé ●●●◐○
Rosarita Margarita ●●●●○
Sake-tini #1 ●●●●○
Sandstorm ●●●●○
Sangaree ●●●●○
Sangria ●●●◐○
Satsuma Martini ●●●◐○
Satan's Whiskers (Straight) ●●●●◐
Satan's Whiskers ●●●◐○
Sir Charles Punch ●●●●○
Snoopy ●●●●○
Snyder Martini ●●●●○
Socialite ●●●◐○
Soyer Au Champagne ●●●◐○
Summer Time Martini ●●●◐○
Sundowner #1 ●●●●○
Sundowner #2 ●●●●○
Sunny Breeze ●●●◐○
The Suzy Wong Martini ●●●◐○
Tiki Max ●●●●○
Triple Orange Martini ●●●●○
Waltzing Matilda ●●●●○
Whiskey Cobbler ●●●○○
Whiskey Squirt ●●●●○
White Sangria ●●●◐○
Zanzibar ●●●◐○
Zombie #2 ●●●◐○ (Vic's formula)
Zombie #3 ●●●●○ (Modern formula)

GRAPEFRUIT JUICE

This citrus fruit may take its unusual name from the way the unripe fruit hangs in green clusters from the tree like bunches of grapes. Or maybe some early botanist just got confused.
As a rule of thumb,the darker the flesh, the sweeter the juice and the more antioxidants and vitamins. But even the sweetest of grapefruits are wonderfully sharp and tart.
I must confess that I tend to use packaged 'freshly squeezed' grapefruit juice from the supermarket. However, this is a relatively easy fruit to juice yourself using a citrus press or an electric spinning juicer. Simply cut in half and juice away, taking care to avoid the pith, which can make the juice bitter. As with other citrus fruits, avoid storing in the refrigerator immediately prior to use as cold fruit yield less juice.

A.J. ●●●●○
Acapulco ●●●◐○
Arizona Breeze ●●●●○
Baby Blue Martini ●●●◐○
Bald Eagle Martini ●●●●◐
Bitter Sweet Symphony ●●●◐○
Blinker ●●●●○
Bloodhound ●●●◐○
Buena Vida ●●●●◐
Chihuahua Magarita ●●●◐○
China Blue ●●●◐○
China Blue Martini ●●●●○
Crimson Blush ●●●●○
Daiquiri No. 3 ●●●●○
Diki-Diki ●●●●◐
Durango ●●●◐○
El Floridita Daiquiri No. 1 ●●●●○
Exotic Passion ●●●◐○
Fancy Drink ●●●◐○
Feather Dusta Crusta ●●●●○
First Of July ●●●●○
Florida Cocktail ●●●○○ (Mocktail)
Florida Daiquiri ●●●●◐
Floridita Margarita ●●●●○
Four W Daiquiri ●●●●○
Fresca ●●●◐○
Fru Fru ●●●◐○
Fruit Tree Daiquiri ●●●●○
Gentle Breeze ●●●○○ (Mocktail)
Golden Fizz #2 ●●●●○
Grape Martini ●●●●○
Grapefruit Julep ●●●●◐
Greyhound ●●●○○
Hemingway Special Daiquiri ●●●●◐
Hemingway Martini ●●●●○
Island Breeze ●●●◐○
Italian Job #1 ●●●◐○
Judy ●●●◐○ (Mocktail)
LCB Martini ●●●●○
Light Breeze ●●●◐○
Lima Sour ●●●◐○
Lime Blush (Mocktail) ●●●○○
M.G.F. ●●●●○
Mai Tai #2 ●●●●○
Mainbrace ●●●●○
Mesa Fresca ●●●●○
Monkey Wrench ●●●◐○
Moonlight Martini ●●●●○
Mountain Slipper ●●●◐○
Mucky Bottom ●●●◐○
Nantucket ●●●◐○
Navigator ●●●●○
Nevada Daiquiri ●●●●○
Nicky's Fizz ●●●◐○
Oriental Tart ●●●●○
Palm Beach ●●●◐○
Paloma ●●●●◐
Parma Negroni ●●●●○
Passover ●●●○○
Pink Grapefruit Magarita ●●●●○
Pink Hound ●●●●○
Pink Tutu ●●●◐○
Pogo Stick ●●●●○
Polly's Special ●●●●○
Pompanski Martini ●●●●○
Ponce de Leon ●●●●○
Poncha ●●●●○
Rasputin ●●●○○
Ribalaigua Daiquiri #3 ●●●●○
Rizzo ●●●●○
Ruby Martini #1 ●●●●○
Salty Dog ●●●●○
Sandstorm ●●●●○
Seabreeze #1 (Simple) ●●●◐○
Seabreeze #2 ●●●◐○ (Layered)
Seventh Heaven #2 ●●●●◐
Showbiz ●●●●○
South China Breeze ●●●●○
Speyside Martini ●●●●○
Sunny Breeze ●●●◐○
Sunstroke ●●●●○
Tailor Made ●●●●○
Tango Martini #2 ●●●●○
Tex Collins ●●●◐○
Texsun ●●●◐○
The Hive ●●●●○
Tilt ●●●●○
Tres Compadres Margarita ●●●●◐
Tropic ●●●●◐
Tropical Breeze ●●●○○
Universal Shot ●●●○○
Vanilla & Grapefruit Daiquiri ●●●●◐
Vert'ical Breeze ●●●●○
Wah-Wah ●●●●○
Wibble ●●●●◐
Wisecrack Fizz ●●●●◐

GRAPES (RED & WHITE)

Oddly, many of the grapes which are classically used for winemaking are not particularly good to eat. Only a few, like Gamay, Tokay, Zinfandel and Muscat, are used for both purposes.
The main commercially available table grapes are Concord, which gives a purple juice which is used for concentrates and jellies, Emperor, which is red and thick-skinned, and Thompson Seedless, which is green and sweet. Seedless grapes are easiest to use in cocktails and produce a fresh juice with a delicate, subtle flavour which is very different from the syrupy stuff in cartons.
The best way to extract juice is to muddle the required number of grapes in the base of your shaker. Recipes in this guide call for 'seedless red grapes' or 'seedless white grapes'. Obviously, if you've opted for a grape that has seeds you'll need to remove them yourself before you muddle the grapes. Crushing the seeds releases bitter flavours which can spoil a drink.

Black Magic ●●●●○
Caipiruva ●●●●○
The Comet ●●●●◐
Double Grape Martini ●●●●◐
Enchanted ●●●◐○
Grape Delight ●●●●○
Grape Effect ●●●●○
Grape Escape ●●●●◐
Grape Martini ●●●●○
Grapple Martini ●●●●○
Greenbelt ●●●◐○
Gusto ●●●●○
Jalisco ●●●●○
Marie Rose #2 ●●●●○
Oriental Grape Martini ●●●●◐
Pisco Punch #4 ●●●●● (Prosser's Formula)
Rum & Raisin Alexandra ●●●●○
Saturn Martini ●●●●◐
Sodden Grape Martini ●●●●○
Speyside Martini ●●●●○
Tiziano ●●●◐○

GRAPPA

Grappa is a brandy distilled from pomace (pressed grape skins left after extracting their juice for wine production).According to the European Union, it must be distilled in Italy from Italian pomace and have an alcoholic strength of not less than 37.5%. (As with American 'Champagne', this legislation has not stopped production of US 'Grappa'.)

Grappa Manhattan ●●●●○
Grappacino ●●●◐○
Grapparita ●●●◐○

GREEN BANANA LIQUEUR

See 'Pisang Ambon Green Banana Liqueur'

GRENADINE

See 'Pomegranate (Grenadine) Syrup'

GUINNESS STOUT

A dry stout beer based upon London's original porter style and brewed at Arthur Guinness' St. James's Gate Brewery in Dublin, Ireland.

Black & Tan ●●●◐○
Black Beard ●●●○○
Black Jack Shot ●●●○○
Black Velvet ●●●◐○

HALF AND HALF

This blend of 50% milk and 50% cream is relatively unknown in the UK. I've listed milk and cream as separate ingredients in both the American and the British versions of this guide.

HONEY (RUNNY)

Many bartenders dilute honey with equal parts of warm water to make it easier to mix. I prefer to use good quality runny honey (preferably orange blossom) and dissolve it by stirring it into the cocktail's base spirit prior to adding the other ingredients. This may be a tad time consuming but it avoids unnecessary dilution. Decant your honey into a squeezy plastic bottle with a fine nozzle for easy dispensing.

Aged Honey Daiquiri ●●●●●
Air Mail ●●●●◐
Applily Married ●●●●◐
Atholl Brose ●●●●○
Banana Smoothie ●●●●◐ [Mocktail]
Basil & Honey Daiquiri ●●●●●
Bebbo ●●●●◐
Bee Sting ●●●●○
Bee's Knees ●●●●○ #1
Bee's Knees ●●●●◐ #2
Bee's Knees ●●●●◐ #3
Bishop ●●●●○
Blue Blazer ●●●○○
Canchanchara ●●●◐○
Cappercaille ●●●●○
Chin Chin ●●●●○
Cold Comfort ●●●●○
The Cold Winter Warmer Sour ●●●●○
Collar & Cuff ●●●●○
Dowa ●●●●○
Easy Tiger ●●●●○
Ginger & Lemongrass Martini ●●●●○
Ginger Punch ●●●◐○
Golden Fizz #2 ●●●●○
Golden Mac ●●●◐○
Grapefruit Julep ●●●●◐
Grog ●●●●○
Hair Of The Dog ●●●●○
Havanatheone ●●●●●
The Hive ●●●●○
Honey & Marmalade Dram'tini ●●●●◐
Honey Bee ●●●●○
Honey Daiquiri ●●●●◐
Honey Limeaid ●●●●○ (Mocktail)
Honeysuckle Daiquiri ●●●●●
The Honeysuckle Orchard ●●●●○
Hot Buttered Rum ●●●●○
Hot Grog ●●●●○
Hot Toddy #1 ●●●●◐
Hot Toddy #2 ●●●●◐
The Juxtaposition ●●●●○
Lemon Beat ●●●●○
Lolita Margarita ●●●●◐
Lucky Lily Margarita ●●●●◐
Lucky Lindy ●●●◐○
Maria Theresa Margarita ●●●●○
Milk & Honey ●●●●◐
Mint & Honey Daiquiri ●●●●◐
Navy Grog ●●●●○
New Year's Absolution ●●●◐○
Nutty Nashville ●●●●○
Pappy Honeysuckle ●●●●◐
Pineapple Smoothie ●●●◐○ (Mocktail)
Poncha ●●●●○
Pooh'tini ●●●●◐
Port Light ●●●◐○
Razzmatazz ●●●○○
R U Bobby Moore? ●●●●◐
Saturn Martini ●●●●◐
Sorrelade ●●●◐○ (Mocktail)
Tailor Made ●●●●○
Tequila Sunset ●●●●○
Tex Collins ●●●◐○
Thomas Blood Martini ●●●◐○
Triangular Martini ●●●●○
Turkish Delight ●●●●○
Warsaw Cooler ●●●●◐
Zoom ●●●●◐

HONEY LIQUEUR

There are many varieties of honey liqueur but the Polish brands claim the oldest heritage. Traditional Polish vodka-based honey liqueurs are thought to have originated in the 16th century. Besides the cocktails below, these liqueurs are worth enjoying neat and slightly warmed in a balloon glass – at London's Baltic they warm the bottle in a baby's bottle warmer.

Bohemian Iced Tea ●●●●◐
Chinese Cosmopolitan ●●●●○
Creamy Bee ●●●●○
Grassy Finnish ●●●●○
Heaven Scent ●●●◐○
The Hive ●●●●○
Honey Apple Martini ●●●●○
Honey Berry Sour ●●●●○
Honey Vodka Sour ●●●●○
Lemon Butter Cookie ●●●●○
Limited Liability ●●●●◐
Limousine ●●●●○
Nutty Nashville ●●●●○
Perfect Alibi ●●●●○
Polish Martini ●●●●●
Pooh'tini ●●●●◐
Rhubarb & Honey Bellini ●●●●○
Saigon Sling ●●●◐○
Snow On Earth ●●●○○
Thomas Blood Martini ●●●◐○
Toddy Martini ●●●◐○

ICE CREAM (VANILLA)

Vanilla ice cream may not be exciting, but it is safe and almost universally liked. There are few people who can honestly say they hate the stuff, making it the obvious choice for the freezer. Splash out on a decent brand. You'll taste the difference.

Barnamint ●●●○○
Black Irish ●●●○○
Brazilian Monk ●●●◐○
FBI ●●●●○
Lemon Chiffon Pie ●●●●○
Mudslide ●●●●○
Soyer Au Champagne ●●●◐○

ICEWINE

A type of sweet dessert wine produced from grapes which have not been harvested until frosts have caused them to freeze while still on the vine. This causes water within the grapes to freeze while sugars and other dissolved solids do not. Thus the wine made from these grapes has a very concentrated, usually very sweet flavour.

Ice Maiden Martini
Ice 'T' Knee
Ice White Cosmo
Iced Sake Martini
Icewine Martini
Sodden Grape Martini

INFUSIONS

Some recipes call for an infused spirit, such as vanilla-infused rum. You make this by putting three split vanilla pods in a bottle of rum and leaving it to stand for a fortnight. Warming and turning the bottle frequently can speed the infusion.
Other herbs, spices and even fruits can be infused in a similar manner in vodka, gin, rum, whiskey and tequila. Whatever spirit you decide to use, pick a brand that is at least 40% alcohol by volume.
Be aware that when the level of spirit in a bottle drops below the flavouring, the alcohol loses its preservative effect and the flavouring can start to rot. Also be careful not to load the spirit with too much flavour or leave it to infuse for too long. Sample the infusion every couple of days to ensure the taste is not becoming overpowering.

IRISH CREAM LIQUEUR

In November 1974 R&A Bailey perfected the technique of combining Irish whiskey, cocoa and fresh cream without souring the cream. Sales grew quickly and it is now the world's best selling liqueur. There are, however, many equally good alternatives.

A.B.C.
Absinthe Without Leave
After Six Shot
Apache
B5200
B-52 Shot
B-53 Shot
B-54 Shot
B-55 Shot
B-52 Frozen
B.J. Shot
Baby Guinness
Bananas & Cream
Barnamint
Bazooka Joe
Beam-me-up Scotty
Beam-me-up Scotty Shot
Bit-O-Honey
Black Dream
Black Irish
Bumble Bee
Burnt Toasted Almond
Butterscotch Delight
Carrot Cake
Chill-Out Martini
Creamy Bee
Cream Cake
Death By Chocolate
Dramatic Martini
E.T.
F-16 Shot
FBI
Flaming Henry
Fruit & Nut Chocolate Martini
Golden Shot
La Grand Feu
Grey Mouse
International Incident
Irish Alexander
Irish Charlie
Irish Chocolate Oranj'tini
Irish Espresso'tini
Irish Flag
Irish Frappé
Irish Latte
Jam Roll
Landslide
Lemon Meringue Martini
Mad Monk Milkshake
Mocha Martini
Muddy Water
Mudslide

Oatmeal Cookie
Oil Slick
Peanut Butter & Jelly Shot
P.S. I Love You
Rattlesnake Shot
Screaming Orgasm
Shamrock Express
Slippery Nipple
Stealth
Tribbble

JÄGERMEISTER

35% **alc./vol.** (70°proof)
www.jager.com
Producer: Mast-Jägermeister Ag, Wolfenbüttel, Germany.

This German bitter-sweet liqueur is made from 56 varieties of herbs, fruits and spices, macerated in spirit for up to six weeks and then matured in oak before blending.
Pronounced 'Yey-Ger-My-Stir', the name means 'master of the hunt'. The logo has a deer with a cross between its antlers, recalling a vision in the life of St Hubert, the patron saint of hunters. Serve mixed with tonic, lemonade or cola, or alternatively drink straight and frozen, as a shooter or a chaser.

Assisted Suicide
Crown Stag
Surfer on A.C.D.

JENEVER

See 'Bokma Genever'

KETEL ONE VODKA

40% **alc./vol.** (80°proof)
www. KetelOne.com
Producer: Nolet Distillery, Schiedam, the Netherlands.

Ketel One is the creation of one of Holland's oldest distilling dynasties, the Nolet family of Schiedam, who have beenmaking spirits since Johannes Nolet started his business in 1691.
The Dutch refer to their pot stills as 'ketels', thus this vodka is named after the Nolets' original coal-fired pot still number one, still used today in the production of Ketel One. After distillation, this small batch distilled spirit is then slowly filtered through charcoal to ensure its purity. Ten generations after Joannes, Carolus Nolet now runs the company with the help of his two sons, Carl and Bob. They introduced Ketel One to the US in 1991 and the UK in 1999. Both markets have seen phenomenal growth. Ketel One's balanced and clean palate with its classic wheat character makes beautifully smooth Martinis without neutralising the quality of the base spirit.

Absolutely Fabulous
After Eight
Agent Orange
Alabama Slammer #1
Alexander The Great
Alien Secretion
Almond Martini #1
Almond Martini #2
Anis'tini

Anita's Attitude Adjuster
Apple & Blackberry Pie
Apple & Cranberry Pie
Apple & Elderflower Martini (Fresh Fruit)
Apple & Melon Martini
Apple Martini #1 (simple version)
Apple Martini #2
Applily Married
Apricot Cosmo
Asian Ginger Martini
Atomic Cocktail
Awol
B-53 Shot
Baby Woo Woo
Balalaika
Bali Trader
Ballet Russe
Banana Boomer
Barbara
Basil Grande
Basilico
Bay Breeze
Beach Iced Tea
Bellini-Tini
Berry Nice
Beverly Hills Iced Tea
Big Apple Martini
Bingo
Bitter Sweet Symphony
Bitterest Pill
Black Cherry Martini
Black Forest Gateau Martini
Black Irish
Black 'N' Blue Caipirovska
Black Russian
Blimey
Bling! Bling!
Bloodhound
Blood Orange
Bloody Caesar
Bloody Mary (Modern Receipe)
Blue Champagne
Blue Kamikaze
Blue Lagoon
Blueberry Martini #1
Blueberry Martini #2
Blush Martini
Blushin' Russian
Boston Tea Party
Brazen Martini
Bullfrog
Burnt Toasted Almond
Caipirovska
California Root Beer
Californian Martini
Cape Codder
Casablanca #2
Cascade Martini
Cassini
Celery Martini
Cham 69=#1
Cham 69 #2
Cherrute
China Beach
Choc & Nut Martini
Chocolate Martini
Chocolate Mint Martini
Cobbled Raspberry Martini
Coconut Water
Collection Martini
Colorado Bulldog
Cranberry & Mint Martini
Cranberry Sauce
Crown Stag
Cucumber Martini
Cucumber & Mint Martini
Cucumber Sake-Tini
Cuppa Joe
Daisy Cutter Martini
Death By Chocolate
Depth Charge
Detox
Detroit Martini
Detropolitan
Diable Rouge
DiVino's
Double Grape Martini
Dowa
Dry Ice Martini
Dyevitchka
Eastern Martini
Egg Custard Martini
Elderflower Cosmo
Elderflower Martini #2
Envy

Espresso Martini
Esquire #2
E.T.
Evita
Exotic Passion
F. Willy Shot
FBI
57 T-Bird Shot
Fizz
Flip
Flirtini #1
Flirtini #2
Flying Grasshopper
Fourth Of July Cocktail
French 76
French Apple Martini
French Kiss #1
French Kiss #2
French Leave
French Martini
Fruit Salad
Ginger Martini
Grape Martini
Grapefruit Julep
Grapple Martini
Grateful Dead
Green Hornet
Greyhound
Gypsy Queen
Hard Lemonade
Harvey Wallbanger
Haydenistic
Hazelnut Martini
The Hive
Hong Kong Fuey
Hot Passion
Hot Tub
Ice 'T' Knee
Ice White Cosmo
Iced Sake Martini
Icewine Martini
Icy Pink Lemonade
Iguana
Iguana Wana
Illusion
Ink Martini #2
Insomniac
International Incident
Intimate Martini
Italian Surfer With A Russian Attitude
Jade Garden
Ja-Mora
Japanese Pear
Jasmine & Elderflower Martini
Jules Delight
Jungle Juice
Katinka
Key West Cooler
Killer Punch
Kir Martini
Kiwi Bellini
Kiwi Collins
Kiwi Martini (Simple)
Koolaid
Kretchma
L.A. Iced Tea
Lazarus
LCB Martini
The Legend
Lemon Butter Cookie
Lemon Drop
Lemon Martini
Lemongrad
Life (Love In The Future Ecstasy)
Limoncello Martini
Liquorice Shot
Long Beach Iced Tea
Long Island Iced Tea
Long Island Spiced Tea
Lotus Espresso
Love Junk
Lush
Lychee Martini
Madras
Madroska
Mae West Martini
Mambo
Mandarito
Martini Royale
Melon Ball
Melon Martini #1
Melon Martini #2 (Fresh Fruit)
Meloncholy Martini
Mellow Martini

Merry Widow #2
Milano
Mint Martini
Miss Martini
Momo Special
Monza
Moscow Lassi
Moscow Mule
Mrs Robinson #2
Muddy Water
Mudslide
Myrtle Martini
Niagara Falls
Noble Europe
Nutcracker Sweet
Nutty Russian
Orang-A-Tang
Orchard Breeze
Oriental Grape Martini
Ouzi
Palma Violet Martini
Parisian Martini #2
Pass-on-that
Passion Fruit Martini #1
Passion Fruit Martini #2
Passover
Pavlova Shot
Pear & Elderflower Cocktail
Perfect John
Pernelle
Pernod & Black Martini
Pharmaceutical Stimulant
Piña Martini
Pineapple & Cardamom Martini
Pineapple & Ginger Martini
Pink Sin Martini
Pink Tutu
Pino Pepe
Plum Martini
Plum Sour
Polish Martini
Pompanski Martini
Pontberry Martini
Port of Melon Martini
Purple Flirt #1
Purple Haze
Purple Hooter
Quince Sour
Raspberry Debonair
Raspberry Martini #1
Raspberry Mule
Raspberry Watkins
Ray's Hard Lemonade
Reef Juice
Rocky Mountain Rootbeer
Roger
Rose-hip Martini
Russian
Russian Qualuude Shot
Russian Spring Punch
Sage Martini
Sake-tini #2
Sakini
Salty Dog
San Francisco
Screaming Banana Banshee
Screaming Orgasm
Screwdriver
Seabreeze #1 (Simple)
Seabreeze #2 (Layered)
Sex On The Beach #1
Sex On The Beach #2
Sgroppino
Shamrock Express
Showbiz
Silk Panties
Silver Fizz
Slow Screw
Slow Comfortable Screw
Slow Comfortable Screw Against the Wall
Snood Murdekin
Sour Apple Martini #1 (Popular US version)
Sour Apple Martini #2 (Deluxe US version)
Sputnik
Stairs Martini
Strawberry Martini
Strawberry 'N' Balsamic Martini
Strudel Martini
Suitably Frank
Summer Breeze
Summer Rose Martini
The Sun Salutation

Sunstroke
Superminty-Chocolatini
Swedish Blue Martini
Sweet Tart
Tainted Cherry
Tawny-Tini
Tennessee Iced Tea
Testarossa
Texas Iced Tea
Thomas Blood Martini
Ti Punch
Toasted Almond
Tokyo Iced Tea
Tom Arnold
Tongue Twister
Too Close For Comfort
Tootie Fruity Lifesaver
Top Banana Shot
Transylvanian Martini
Triple Orange Martini
Tripleberry
Tropical Breeze
Turkish Coffee Martini
Turkish Delight
TVR
Twinkle
Two 'T' Fruity Martini
Umbongo
Uncle Vanya
Universal Shot
Utterly Butterly
Velvet Fog
Velvet Hammer
The Vesper Martini
Vodka Collins
Vodka Espresso
Vodka Gimlet
Vodka Sour
Vodkantini
Volga Boatman
Walnut Martini
Wanton Abandon
Warsaw
Wasabi Martini
Washhouse
Washington Apple
Watermelon Man
Watermelon Martini
White Elephant
White Russian
White Stinger
Wild Promenade Martini
Wilton Martini
Woo Woo
Yellow Fever Martini
Z Martini

KETEL ONE CITROEN VODKA

40% **alc./vol.** (80°proof)
www. KetelOne.com
Producer: Nolet Distillery, Schiedam, the Netherlands.

Having already created what they and many top bartenders consider the perfect vodka for Martinis, the Nolet family wanted to create a flavoured vodka of equal excellence for making the ultimate Cosmopolitan. The family spent more than two years researching and evaluating different blending and infusion methods, before arriving at the costly but effective process of hand-crafting in small batches and infusing with natural citrus flavour until the perfect balance is reached.
Ketel One Citroen combines the smooth qualities of the original Ketel One Vodka with the refreshing natural essence of citrus fruit. To ensure continuity in the quality of Ketel One Citroen, a member of the Nolet family personally samples each batch produced prior to release.
There are few other citrus-flavoured vodkas with the rich, natural lemon peel oil flavours found in Ketel One Citroen. These combine with a clean grain character to make this vodka an ideal base for Cosmopolitans and other contemporary cocktails.

Allegrottini
Asian Mary
Basil Beauty
Blue Cosmo
Blue Fin
Blue Monday
Bohemian Iced Tea
Brass Monkey
Camomile & Blackfruit Breeze
Cheeky Monkey
Cherry Martini
Chinese Whisper Martini
Citrus Caipirovska
Citrus Martini
The Cold Winter Warmer Sour
Collection Martini
Colonial Rot
Cosmopolitan #1 (simple version)
Cosmopolitan #2 (complex version)
Cosmopolitan #3 (popular version)
Cranapple Breeze
Crimson Blush
Dorothy Parker
Double Vision
Elderflower Collins #2
Fresca
Fruit Pastel
Ginger Cosmo
Ginger Nut
Grand Cosmopolitan
Green Eyes
Hawaiian Cosmopolitan
Henry VIII
Ignorance Is Bliss
John Daly
Key Lime Pie #3
Kiwi Crush
Kurrent Affair
Lemon Curd Martini
Lemon Drop Martini
Lemon Meringue Martini
Lemongrad
Lemongrass Cosmo
Leninade
M.G.F.
Mango Martini
Motox
Pear Drop
Purple Cosmo
Raspberry Cosmo
Razzitini
Rosy Martini
Royal Cosmopolitan
Ruby Martini #1
Saturn Martini
Smartini
Sourpuss Martini
South Pacific
Strawberry Cosmo
Stupid Cupid
Venus in Furs
Watermelon Cosmo
White Cosmo
Windy Miller
Wine Cooler
Yellow Belly Martini
Zakuski Martini
Zingy Ginger Martini

KETEL ONE ORANGE INFUSED VODKA

To make your own orange infused vodka:
1. Scrub two large oranges to clean and remove any wax coating.
2. Peeel the zest from oranges using a knife or potato peeler. Be careful not to cut into white pith: alternatively trim off white pith from peel.
3. Feed orange zest into an empty and clean Ketel One Vodka bottle.
4. Fill bottle containing orange zest with Ketel One Vodka using a funnel to help pour from new bottle.
5. Replace cap securely and shake.
6. Leave to infuse for at least a week, turning daily.

Blood Orange
Chill-Out Martini
Cordless Screwdriver
Creamiscle
Creamy Creamsicle
CVO Firevault
Eden
Hemingway Martini

KETEL ONE VANILLA INFUSED VODKA

The pods of a tropical vine which belongs to the orchid family, vanilla has long been a prized flavouring. Once the pods are harvested, they undergo months of curing to develop and refine their distinctive flavour. To make your own vanilla infused vodka simply take two quality vanilla pods (roughly 6in/15cm long) and split them lengthwise with a sharp knife on a cutting board. Place them in a newly opened bottle of Ketel One Vodka and leave it to infuse for a fortnight, turning occasionally.

Aphrodisiac
Apple Strudel #2
Banoffee Martini
Bon Bon
Butterfly's Kiss
Cherry Alexander
Chocolate & Cranberry Martini
Crème Anglaise Martini
Crème Brûlée Martini
Easter Martini
Egg Custard Martini
Fruit & Nut Martini
Heaven Scent
Hunk Martini
Irish Espresso'tini
Jolt'ini
Karamel Sutra Martini
Key Lime
Key Lime Pie #2
Nine-20-Seven
Palermo
Peach Melba Martini
Pear & Vanilla Rickey
Pepper & Vanilla'tini
Plum Pudding Martini
Razzzzzberry Martini
Russian Bride
Snow Fall Martini
Socialite
Tarte Tatin Martini
Thriller From Vanilla
Triangular Martini
Triple 'C' Martini
Turkish Delight
Upside-Down Raspberry Cheesecake
Vacation
Valkyrie
Vanilla & Grapefruit Daiquiri
Vanilla Laika
Vanilla Sensation
Vanilla Vodka Sour
Vanilla'tini
Vanitini
Vante Martini
Wild Honey
Wonky Martini
Zhivago Martini

KIRSCHWASSER EAU DE VIE

'Kirsch' is German for cherry, and kirsch is a clear, cherry-flavoured spirit made from cherry kernels, traditionally produced in the area where France, Germany and Switzerland meet. Kirschwasser indicates a spirit distilled from fermented fruit ('wasser' means 'water' in German). This German product is drier and stronger than French kirsch, which is distilled at a lower point to retain more of the fruit flavour.

Black Jack Cocktail
Blackthorn Cocktail

Cherry Blossom ●●●◐○
Moonlight Martini ●●●●○
The Rose #1 (original) ●●●●◐
The Rose #3 ●●●●◐
Straits Sling ●●●●○
Volga Boatman ●●●◐○

KIWI FRUIT

The kiwi is also known as the Chinese gooseberry. Seeds from China's Yangtze valley reached New Zealand in the early 20th century, and were cultivated commercially 40 years later. It was rebranded as a kiwi fruit, partly for reasons of Cold War politics and partly because its brown, furry exterior resembles New Zealand's national bird. Despite the fruit's name, New Zealand no longer enjoys an export monopoly, but remains the largest producer.

Preparation: The kiwi fruit is best muddled. Simply slice the fruit in half, scoop out the juicy flesh and muddle.

Green Destiny ●●●◐○
Kee-Wee Martini ●●●●○
Kiwi Batida ●●●○○
Kiwi Bellini ●●●●○
Kiwi Collins ●●●●○
Kiwi Crush ●●●●○
Kiwi Martini ●●●●○ (Simple)

KÜMMEL LIQUEUR

This clear liqueur is distilled from grain or potatoes and flavoured with caraway seeds, fennel, orris and other herbs.

The Currier ●●●●○
Green Dragon ●●●◐○
Quelle Vie ●●●◐○
Silver Bullet Martini ●●●●○
Vowel Cocktail ●●●●◐

LEBLON CACHAÇA

40% **alc./vol.**
www.leblonspirit.com
Producer: Leblon, Minas Gerais, Brazil

Pronounced 'Ka-Shah-Sa', cachaça is the spirit of Brazil. As it is based on sugar cane, it is very similar to rum. However, most rums are produced from molasses, a by-product of sugar refining, but cachaça is distilled from fermented sugar cane juice.

Leblon is an ultra-premium cachaça inspired by its namesake and place of origin, Leblon Beach in Rio de Janeiro, Brazil.

While relaxing at a beach bar in Leblon, Roberto Stoll Nogueira dreamt of producing a world class Brazilian cachaça. Insisting on the very best, Roberto called upon a team of Brazilian and international specialists to lend their expertise to producing this unique cachaça.

Leblon is made from fresh cane juice obtained within three hours of harvesting by pressing only the middle and best part of the sugar cane. This fresh sugar juice is fermented through a strictly controlled process and then carefully distilled through an alambic distillation process to fully harness the flavour. The cachaça is then lightly aged in French XO cognac barrels for approximately 3 months to form a perfectly blended, fresh and smooth super premium white spirit.

Abaci Batida ●●●●○
Azure Martini ●●●●○
Banana Batida ●●●◐○
Basilian ●●●◐○
Batida de Coco ●●●○○
Beha Flor 4.5
Berry Caipirinha ●●●●○
Brazilian Berry ●●●●○
Brazilian Coffee ●●●◐○
Brazilian Cosmopolitan ●●●◐○
Buzzard's Breath ●●●◐○
Cachaça Daiquiri ●●●◐○
Caipiginger ●●●◐○
Caipirinha ●●●●◐ (Classic Serve)
Caipirinha ●●●●◐ (Difford's Style)
Caipiruva ●●●●○
Carneval Batida ●●●●○
Coffee Batida ●●●○○
Fresa Batida ●●●◐○
Kiwi Batida ●●●○○
Lemon Beat ●●●●○
Mango Batida ●●●●○
Maracuja Batida ●●●●○
Milho Verde Batida ●●●◐○
Passion Fruit Caipirinha ●●●●○
Raspberry Caipirinha ●●●●○
Sophisticated Savage ●●●◐○
Tropical Caipirinha ●●●●◐

LEMONADE, 7-UP OR SPRITE

Cham 69=#1 ●●●◐○
Colonial Rot ●●●○○
Fantasia ●●●◐○ (Mocktail)
Fresca ●●●◐○
Frisky Lemonade ●●●◐○
Glass Tower ●●●○○
Golden Fizz #2 ●●●●○
Hong Kong Fuey ●●●○○
Lemon Lime & Bitters ●●●◐○
Limelite ●●●○○
Liquorice All Sort ●●●◐○
Lucky Lindy ●●●◐○
Lynchburg Lemonade ●●●●○
Marama Rum Punch ●●●●○
Mat The Rat ●●●◐○
Mint Lineade ●●●◐○ (Mocktail)
Nuts & Berries ●●●●○
Pear & Vanilla Rickey ●●●◐○
Planter's Punchless ●●●○○ (Mocktail)
Pulp Fiction ●●●●○
Raspberry Lynchburg ●●●◐○
Razzitini ●●●◐○
Santiago ●●●○○
Snowball ●●●●○
South Pacific Breeze ●●●◐○
Sweet Tart ●●●◐○
Tequila Fizz ●●●●○
Tokyo Iced Tea ●●●◐○
Vanilla'tini ●●●◐○
Weeping Jesus ●●●◐○
White Sangria ●●●◐○
Windy Miller ●●●◐○
Wine Cooler ●●●◐○

LEMONCELLO

See 'Luxardo Limoncello Liqueur'

LEMONS & LIMES

Originally from India or Malaysia, lemons are available throughout the year and in many different varieties, distinguishable by their shape, size and thickness of skin.
The smaller and more fragrant lime is closely related to the lemon. It is cultivated in tropical countries and is widely used in Caribbean and Brazilian cuisine.

Both these citrus fruits are bartender staples and their juice is used to balance sweetness and add depth to a bewildering range of cocktails. Lemon and lime juice will curdle cream and cream liqueurs but will happily mix with most other spirits and liqueurs. Limes generally pair well with rum while lemons are preferable in drinks based on whiskey or brandy.
Limes and lemons last longer if stored in the refrigerator, although you'll get more juice out of them if you let them warm up to room temperature then roll the fruit on a surface under the palm of your hand before you cut them. Save hard fruits for garnishing: soft fruits have more juice and flavour.
To juice, simply cut in half widthways and juice using a press, squeezer or spinning juicer, taking care not to grind the pith. Ideally you should juice your lemons and limes immediately prior to use as the juice will oxidise after a couple of hours.
I'd guess that, along with sugar syrup, these fruits are the most frequently used ingredients in this guide. Hence I've not even tried to index them.

LIME CORDIAL

Lauchlan Rose started importing lime juice from the West Indies to England in the 1860s, when ships were compelled to carry lime or lemon juice to prevent scurvy. In 1867 he devised a method for preserving juice without alcohol and so created lime cordial, the world's first concentrated fruit drink. Thankfully all the drinks in this guide that call for his invention are alcoholic.

Acapulco Daiquiri ccccd
Blue Heaven ccedd
Caribbean Breeze ccccd
Castro ccced
Acapulco Daiquiri ●●●●○
Basil & Lime Gimlet ●●●●◐
Blue Heaven ●●◐○○
Caribbean Breeze ●●●●○
Castro ●●●◐○
Cosmopolitan #2 ●●●●● (complex version)
The Currier ●●●●○
Daiquiri De Luxe ●●●●○
Dean's Gate Martini ●●●◐○
Diamond Dog ●●●◐○
Dulchin ●●●●◐
Elegante Margarita ●●●●◐
F. Willy Shot ●●●◐○
Fat Sailor ●●●●○
Floridita Margarita ●●●●○
Fog Horn ●●●◐○
Gimlet #1 ●●●●○
Gimlet #2 ●●●●◐ (Schumann's recipe)
Green Hornet ●●●◐○
Hong Kong Fuey ●●●○○
Honolulu Juicer ●●●◐○
Hurricane #1 ●●●●○
Judy ●●●◐○ (Mocktail)
Key Lime ●●●●○
Key Lime Pie #2 ●●●●○
Key Lime Pie #3 ●●●●○
Lime Blush (Mocktail) ●●●○○
Limey ●●●◐○
Limey Cosmo ●●●●○
Limnology ●●●◐○
Luxury Cocktail ●●●◐○
Lychee & Blackcurrant Martini ●●●●○
Metropolitan ●●●●○
Mexican Surfer ●●●●○
Princeton Martini ●●●●○
Robin Hood #1 ●●●●○
Rosarita Margarita ●●●●○
Rude Ginger Cosmopolitan ●●●●○
Sailor's Comfort ●●●○○
Sandstorm ●●●●○
Sloe Tequila ●●●◐○
Smoky Apple Martini ●●●◐○
Snowball ●●●◐○
Sour Apple Martini #1 ●●●●○ (Popular US version)
Tres Compadres Margarita ●●●●◐
Typhoon ●●●○○
Ugurundu ●●●◐○
Vodka Gimlet ●●●●○
Watermelon Cosmo ●●●◐○

LITCHI LIQUEUR

See 'Soho Lychee Liqueur'

LUXARDO AMARETTO DI SASCHIRA LIQUEUR

28% **alc./vol.** (56°proof)
Producer: Girolamo Luxardo SpA., Torreglia, Padova, Italy.

This delicate liqueur is an Italian classic, packed with the unique flavour of sweet almond. The Luxardo family have been distilling fine liqueurs in the Veneto region of Italy for six generations. They make their amaretto with the pure paste of the finest almonds, from Avola in southern Sicily, and age it for eight months in larch vats to impart its distinctive, well-rounded taste. Their very contemporary amaretto has a palate of almond and marzipan, making it a vital tool in any mixologist's flavour armoury.

A.B.C. ●●●◐○
57 T-Bird Shot ●●●●○
Alabama Slammer #2 ●●●○○
Almond Martini #2 ●●●●○
Almond Old Fashioned ●●●●◐
Amaretto Sour ●●●◐○
Artlantic ●●●○○
Atholl Brose ●●●●○
Avalanche ●●●○○
B-54 Shot ●●●○○
Bananas & Cream ●●●●○
Bella Donna Daiquiri ●●●●◐
Bird of Paradise ●●●●◐
Blue Heaven ●●◐○○
Blueberry Tea ●●●●○
Blush Martini ●●●◐○
Blushin' Russian ●●●●○
Brake Tag ●●●◐○
Brooklyn #2 ●●●●○
Bubblegum Shot ●●●○○
Buona Sera Shot ●●●◐○
Burnt Toasted Almond ●●●○○
Canteen Martini ●●●◐○
Caribbean Punch ●●●●○
Cham 69 #2 ●●●◐○
Cham 69=#1 ●●●◐○
Chas ●●●●○
Cicada Cocktail ●●●◐○
Cranberry Cooler ●●●○○
Cream Cake ●●●◐○
Creamy Creamsicle ●●●◐○
Cruel Intention ●●●●○
Damson In Distress ●●●●○
Dingo ●●●○○
Disaronno Originale Amaretto
Dolce-Amaro ●●●◐○
Donna's Creamy'tini ●●●◐○
Downhill Racer ●●●●○
Durango ●●●◐○
F. Willy Shot ●●●◐○
Flaming Dr Pepper ●●○○○
Flaming Henry ●●●◐○
Godfather ●●●◐○
Grappacino ●●●◐○
Hawaiian Cocktail ●●●●○
International Incident ●●●●○
Italian Job #2 ●●●●○
Italian Margarita ●●●◐○
Italian Surfer With A Russian Attitude ●●●○○
Jockey Club ●●●●○
Kamaniwanalaya ●●●◐○
Killer Punch ●●●◐○
Koolaid ●●●●○
Landslide ●●●○○
Loch Almond ●●●●○
Mae West Martini ●●●●○
Mister Stu ●●●◐○
Nutcracker Sweet ●●●◐○
Nutty Summer ●●●●◐
Orange Brûlée ●●●●●
P.S. I Love You ●●●●○
Pink Cloud ●●●○○
Plum Pudding Martini ●●●◐○
Royal Velvet Margarita ●●●◐○
Screaming Orgasm ●●◐○○

South Beach ●●●●○
Stiletto ●●●◐○
Sweet Louise ●●●○○
Sweet Tart ●●●◐○
Tennessee Berry Mule ●●●●○
The GTO Cocktail ●●●◐○
Thunderbird ●●●●○
Toasted Almond ●●●●○
Triangular Martini ●●●●○
Trifle'tini ●●●◐○

LUXARDO LIMONCELLO LIQUEUR

27% **alc./vol.** (54° proof)
Producer: Girolamo Luxardo SpA., Torreglia, Padova, Italy.

Despite its vibrant yellow-green hue, this is an extremely traditional Italian liqueur – and, since the 90s, one of Italy's most popular. For generations, families have macerated lemon zest in spirit and sugar, encapsulating the mixologist's favourite combination of sour citrus, sweet and spirit: the formula at the heart of the Daiquiri, the Caipirinha and many more.
Luxardo Limoncello delivers a rich sweet lemon flavour in a blast of sour citrus, lemon zest and candied citrus, which somehow remains pure and balanced. It is increasingly popular among bartenders seeking new ways of delivering that vital citrus tang.

Basilico ●●●◐○
Bellissimo ●●●○○
Bon Bon ●●●○○
Clementine ●●●○○
Grapparita ●●●◐○
Italian Sun ●●●●○
Lemon Meringue Pie'tini ●●●●○
Lemon Sorbet ●●●●○
Lemony ●●●●○
Limoncello Martini ●●●◐○
Motox ●●●●○
Navigator ●●●●○
Pear Drop Martini ●●●●○
Socialite ●●●◐○
Watermelon & Basil Smash ●●●●○
Yellow Belly Martini ●●●●○

LUXARDO MARASCHINO ORIGINALE LIQUEUR

32% **alc./vol.** (64°proof)
www.luxardo.it
Producer: Girolamo Luxardo SpA., Torreglia, Padova, Italy.

Until well into the 20th century, the bitter Marasca cherry grew only on the Dalmatian coast. When Girolamo Luxardo's wife began making a liqueur from the local cherries, Zara, Dalmatia was part of Italy.
So popular did her maraschino become that in 1821 Girolamo founded a distillery to mass-produce it. The business prospered until the disruption of the Second World War, after which the family moved production to Italy and Dalmatia became part of Croatia.
Today the Luxardos base their liqueur on cherries from their own 200 acre orchard and age it for two years in white Finnish ashwood vats. The silky palate features hints of dark chocolate, vanilla and marmalade alongside subtle cherry notes, with an elegant white chocolate and cherry finish, making it essential to a range of classic and modern cocktails.

Absinthe Italiano Cocktail ●●●○○
Aviation #1 ●●●●◐ (Simple Formula)
Aviation #2 ●●●●◐ (Classic Formula)
Beachcomber ●●●●○
Bensonhurst ●●●●◐
Boomerang ●●●●○
Bourbon Crusta ●●●●◐
Brandy Crusta ●●●●◐
Brooklyn #1 ●●●●○
Casablanca ●●●●○ #1
Casino ●●●●○
Cherry & Hazelnut Daiquiri ●●●●○
Classic Cocktail ●●●●●
Coronation ●●●○○
Coronation Cocktail No. 1 ●●●●◐
Cuban Cocktail No. 2 #1 ●●●◐○
Daiquiri No. 3 ●●●●○
Daiquiri No. 5 ●●●●○
Diplomat ●●●●●
Donegal ●●●●○
East India #1 ●●●●◐
The Elder Aviator ●●●●◐
Elderflower Collins #2 ●●●●○
Fancy Free ●●●●◐
Feather Dusta Crusta ●●●●○
Florida Daiquiri ●●●●◐
El Floridita Daiquiri No. 1 ●●●●○
Greta Garbo ●●●●○
The Harlem ●●●●○
Havana Special ●●●●○
Hemingway Special Daiquiri ●●●●◐
Honolulu Cocktail No. 2 ●●●◐○
Imperial Martini ●●●○○
The Last Word ●●●●◐
Lima Sour ●●●◐○
Lux Daiquiri ●●●●○
Manhattan Island ●●●●○
Mary Pickford ●●●●●
Monte Carlo ●●●◐○
Moonshine Martini ●●●●◐
Mystique ●●●◐○
North Pole Martini ●●●●○
Nutty Berry'tini ●●●◐○
Opera ●●●●○
Peto Martini ●●●●◐
Pink Daiquiri ●●●●○
Prado ●●●◐○
Redback ●●●○○
Ribalaigua Daiquiri #3 ●●●●○
The Ritz Cocktail ●●●●○
Salty Dog ●●●●○
Sensation ●●●●○
Seventh Heaven #2 ●●●●◐
Silver Martini ●●●◐○
Soyer Au Champagne ●●●◐○
Stars & Stripes Shot ●●◐○○
Turf Martini ●●●●○

LUXARDO SAMBUCA DEI CESARI

38% alc. /vol. (76°proof)
www.luxardo.it
Producer: Girolamo Luxardo SpA., Torreglia, Padova, Italy.

Luxardo Sambuca is made from a traditional aniseed base and elderberries macerated in alcohol to give a rich flavour. The essential oils of the star anise are extracted by steam distilling. Its traditional after-dinner serve is in a shot glass and sipped in the classic Italian way with three coffee beans floating - con la mosca. Carefully ignite the surface and extinguish the flame. Its popularity as a layered shot style of cocktail called "shotails" is fast increasing. Try it layered with a cream liqueur.
Today, Sambuca is considered by many as the national liqueur of Italy. The anise plant was appreciated in ancient times for its therapeutic properties. Originating from China, it became widespread through the centuries along the Mediterranean coast. Its name derives from the Arab word Zammut (anise). The word zammù still exists in the Sicilian dialect, meaning an anise drink diluted with water.

All White Frappé ●●●◐○
Anis'tini ●●●●○
Bumble Bee ●●●◐○
Crème de Café ●●●◐○
Flatliner 1.●●●●●
Glass Tower ●●●○○
Kiss of Death ●●◐○○
Liquorice Shot ●●●◐○
Raging Bull ●●●◐○
Slippery Nipple ●●○○○
Ti Punch ●●●●○
Typhoon ●●●○○
Veneto ●●●◐○

LYCHEE LIQUEUR

See 'Soho Lychee Liqueur'

MADEIRA

Madeira is a fortified wine from the semi-tropical island of the same name in the Atlantic, 600km off the coast of Morocco. Until the opening of the Suez Canal, Madeira enjoyed a strategic position on the Atlantic shipping lanes and during the 17th and 18th centuries ships sailing from Britain carried the island's wine as ballast. The wine was slowly warmed during the voyage through the tropics, creating a mellow, baked flavour. This unusual, richly flavoured wine became popular. So the ships' journeys were replicated on the island using a heating process called 'estufagem'.
There are four predominant styles of Madeira available: Sercial (dry), Verdelho (medium dry and traditionally referred to as 'Rainwater'), Bual (medium sweet) and Malmsey (sweet).

Baltimore Egg Nog ●●●○○
Bosom Caresser ●●●●○
Boston Flip ●●●●○
Cassanova ●●●●○

MANDARINE NAPOLÉON LIQUEUR

38% **alc./vol.** (76°proof)
www.mandarine-napoleon.com
Producer: Fourcroy S.A., Rue Steyls 119, B1020 Brussels, Belgium.

Emperor Napoléon Bonaparte's physician, Antoine-Francois de Fourcroy, created a special liqueur for the Emperor based on aged cognacs and exotic mandarin oranges. Mandarins, often known as tangerines, had been introduced into Europe from China in the 18th century and grew particularly well in Corsica, Bonaparte's birthplace.
Mandarine Napoléon was first commercially distilled in 1892, using the finest aged French cognacs and mandarin peels from the Mediterranean area blended with an infusion of herbs and spices. The distillate is aged for at least three years, until it acquires the rich mellow flavour which makes Mandarine Napoléon one of the great classic liqueurs of the world.
Mandarine Napoléon is brilliantly suited to cocktail mixing and distinctly different from other orange liqueurs on bartenders' shelves. Its luscious zesty tangerine flavour with a herbal backnote gives a sophisticated twist to a Cosmopolitan but is also superb on its own, long over ice with a splash of tonic.

Breakfast At Terrell's ●●●●○
Clementine ●●●○○
Donegal ●●●●○
Italian Job #1 ●●●◐○
Jacktini ●●●◐○
Lola ●●●◐○
Man-Bour-Tini ●●●●○
Mandarine Collins ●●●○○
Mandarine Sidecar ●●●●○
Mandarine Songbird ●●●○○
Mandarine Sour ●●●◐○
Mandarito ●●●●○
Orange Mojito ●●●●○
Prune Face ●●●●○
Puccini ●●●◐○
Tennessee Rush ●●●◐○
Windy Miller ●●●●○
Yum ●●●○○

MAPLE SYRUP

The boiled-down sap of the North American sugar maple, authentic maple syrup has a complex sweetness appreciated all over the world. Please be wary of synthetic imitations, which are nowhere near as good as the real thing.
Maple syrups are graded and categorised according to their colour and flavour, but names vary according to the different states in the US and Canada. I favour a medium amber or light amber top grade syrup.
Maple syrup should be stored in the refrigerator and consumed within 28 days of opening. To use in a cocktail, simply pour into a thimble measure and follow the recipe.

Banoffee Martini ●●●●○
Borderline ●●●◐○
Bourbon Blush ●●●●◐
Bull's Milk ●●●◐○
Canandian Apple ●●●●○ (Mocktail)
Che's Revolution ●●●●◐
Elysian ●●●●○
Four W Daiquiri ●●●●○
Jack Maple ●●●◐○
Jean Gabin ●●●●○
Lotus Espresso ●●●●◐
Louisiana Trade ●●●◐○
Maple Old-Fashioned ●●●●○
Maple Leaf ●●●●○
Maple Pomme ●●●●○
Mother Rum ●●●●◐
Mule's Hind Leg ●●●●◐
The Roadrunner ●●●●○
Tawny-Tini ●●●●○
Zeus Martini ●●●●◐

MARASCHINO LIQUEUR

See 'Luxardo Maraschino Originale Liqueur'

Maraschino Syrup
The sweet liquid from a jar of maraschino cherries.
Champagne Cup ●●●◐○
Cherry Blossom ●●●◐○
Cherry Daiquiri ●●●●○
Club Cocktail #3 ●●●●○
Daiquiri No. 1 #3 ●●●●● (Difford's Lux Formula)
Dragon Blossom ●●●○○
Fruit Tree Daiquiri ●●●●○
Grappa Manhattan ●●●●○
Hemingway Martini ●●●●○
Lux Daiquiri ●●●●○
Manhattan Sweet ●●●●●
Metropole ●●●◐○
Old Fashioned #2 ●●●●◐ (US Version)
Rob Roy #1 ●●●●○
The Zamboanga 'Zeinie' Cocktail ●●●●○

MARNIER CHERRY LIQUEUR

24% **alc./vol.** (48°proof)
www.grand-marnier.com
Producer: Marnier-Lapostolle (Société des Produits), Paris, France

This superb cherry liqueur from the Grand Marnier stable is made to an original recipe created by Jean-Baptiste Lapostolle when he founded his distillery in 1827.
Marnier Cherry is still made at Neauphle-le-Château where morello cherries are crushed and macerated in brandy. This is then strained and the pulp and crushed stones removed to be distilled to produce an aromatic marc. The result of the maceration and this marc are then mixed and blended with sugar syrup. The blend is then aged in vats for several months to acquire its balance and roundness before being filtered and bottled.
Marnier Cherry has a velvety palate with rich morello cherries, blackcurrant, raspberry and warming brandy. Notes of bitter almond from the crushed cherry stones are very evident with subtle vanilla and chocolate extending the palate.

Banana Boomer ●●●●○
Blood & Sand #2 (Difford's Formula) ●●●●◐
Canaries ●●●○○
Cherrute ●●●●○
Cherry Alexander ●●●●○
Cherry Blossom ●●●◐○
Cherry Daiquiri ●●●●○
Cherry Mash Sour ●●●◐○
Cherry Martini ●●●●○
Delores ●●●◐○
Desert Cooler ●●●◐○
Donna's Creamy'tini ●●●◐○
Florida Sling ●●●○○
Fog Cutter #2 ●●●●○
Gin Sling ●●●●○
The Horseshoe Sling ●●●●○
I'll Take Manhattan ●●●●○
Jungle Fire Sling ●●●○○
Nightmare Martini ●●●○○
Nutty Berry'tini ●●●◐○
Old Fashioned Caddy ●●●●○
Pancho Villa ●●●●○
Passbour Cooler ●●●○○
Red Neck Martini ●●●●○
Remember The Maine ●●●●◐
The Rose #2 ●●●◐○
Singapore Sling #1 ●●●◐○ (Baker's formula)
Singapore Sling #2 ●●●●○
Singapore Sling #3 ●●●◐○
Sir Thomas ●●●●○
Suitably Frank ●●●◐○
Tainted Cherry ●●●○○
Vanderbilt ●●●●◐
Woodland Punch ●●●○○

MIDORI GREEN MELON LIQUEUR

20% **alc./vol.** (40°proof)
www.midori-world.com
Producer: Suntory Limited, Japan.

Midori is flavoured with extracts of honeydew melons and can rightly claim to be the original melon liqueur. Its vibrant green colour, light melon taste and great versatility has ensured its demand in bars worldwide since its launch in 1978 at New York's Studio 54 nightclub.
The name is Japanese for 'green' and 'Midori' is owned by Suntory, Japan's leading producer and distributor of alcoholic beverages. Midori is one of the most noted modern day cocktail ingredients due to its vibrant colour and flavour.

Alien Secretion ●●●◐○
Apache ●●●○○
Apple & Melon Martini ●●●◐○
Atomic Dog ●●●○○
Awol ●●●●○
Black Japan ●●◐○○
Bubblegum Shot ●●●○○
Coco Cabana ●●●◐○
Congo Blue ●●●◐○
Cool Martini ●●●◐○
Envy ●●●●○
E.T. ●●●●○
Evita ●●●◐○
Grateful Dead ●●●◐○
Green Fly ●●●◐○
Green Horn ●●●◐○
Gulf Coast Sex on the Beach ●●●●○
Hong Kong Fuey ●●●○○
Illusion ●●●●○
Japanese Slipper ●●●●○
June Bug ●●●◐○
Killer Punch ●●●◐○
Koolaid ●●●●○
L.A. Iced Tea ●●●◐○
Love Junk ●●●◐○
Mae West Martini ●●●●○
Melon Ball ●●●○○
Melon Collie Martini ●●●●○
Melon Daiquiri #1 ●●●●○ ('Up')
Melon Daiquiri #2 ●●●◐○ (Frozen)
Melon Margarita #1 ●●●●○ ('Up')
Melon Margarita #2 ●●●◐○ (Frozen)
Melon Martini #1 ●●●○○
Meloncholy Martini ●●●●○
Passion Killer ●●●○○
Sex On The Beach #2 ●●●○○
Sex On The Beach #3 ●●◐○○
Sourpuss Martini ●●●●○
Squashed Frog ●●●○○
Tokyo Iced Tea ●●●◐○
Tutti Fruitti ●●●○○
Universal Shot ●●●○○
Verdi Martini ●●●●○
Watermelon Cosmo ●●●◐○

MINT LEAVES

This perennial herb grows in most temperate parts of the world. The varieties which non-botanists call 'mint' belong to the genus mentha. Mentha species include apple mint, curly mint, pennyroyal, peppermint, pineapple mint, spearmint and water or bog mint.
Spearmint, or garden mint, is the most common kind and you may well find it growing in your garden. Peppermint is the second most common kind. Its leaves produce a pungent oil which is used to flavour confectionery, desserts and liqueurs such as crème de menthe.
The main visible difference between peppermint and spearmint is in the leaves. Spearmint leaves have a crinkly surface and seem to grow straight out of the plant's main stem, while peppermint leaves have a smoother surface and individual stems. Which type of mint you choose to use in drinks is largely a matter of personal taste: some recommend mentha nemorosa for Mojitos.
Growing your own mint, be it spearmint, peppermint or otherwise is easy – but be sure to keep it in a container or it will overrun your garden. Either buy a plant or place a sprig in a glass of water. When it roots, pot it in a large, shallow tub with drainage holes. Place bricks under the tub to prevent the roots from growing through the holes.

Aku Aku ●●●●◐
Apple Mojito ●●●●○
Apple Virgin Mojito (Mocktail) ●●●●○
Bajan Mojito ●●●◐○
Bajito ●●●●◐
Beetle Jeuse ●●●●○
Bourbon Smash ●●●◐○
Brandy Smash ●●●●○
Charente Collins ●●●●○
Che's Revolution ●●●●◐
Clover Leaf Cocktail #2 ●●●◐○ (Modern)
Colonial Rot ●●●○○
Cowboy Martini ●●●◐○
Cranberry Delicious ●●●○○ (Mocktail)
Cranberry & Mint Martini ●●●◐○
Cucumber & Mint Martini ●●●●○
Detroit Martini ●●●●○
Elderflower Jojito ●●●●◐
Elixir ●●●●○
French Mojito ●●●●◐
Frisky Bison ●●●●◐
Gin Genie ●●●●○
Ginger Mojito ●●●●○
Grape Escape ●●●●◐
Grapefruit Julep ●●●●◐
Havanatheone ●●●●●
Hazel'ito ●●●●○
Heather Julep ●●●●◐
Hornitos Lau ●●●●○
Jean Marc ●●●●○
Julep ●●●●●
Julep Martini ●●●●◐
Jumbled Fruit Julep ●●●◐○
Kentucky Mac ●●●◐○
Krakow Tea ●●●●○
Life (Love In The Future Ecstasy) ●●●◐○
Lotus Martini ●●●●○
Luxury Mojito ●●●●○
Mai Tai #2 ●●●●○
Major Bailey #1 ●●●●◐
Mandarito ●●●●○
Marama Rum Punch ●●●●○
Milky Mojito ●●●◐○
Mint & Honey Daiquiri ●●●●◐
Mint Cocktail ●●●●◐
Mint Collins ●●●●○
Mint Daiquiri ●●●●●
Mint Fizz ●●●◐○
Mint Julep ●●●●●
Mint Lineade ●●●●◐ (Mocktail)
Mint Martini ●●●●○
Missionary's Downfall ●●●●●
Mojito ●●●●●
Mojito de Casa ●●●●○
Mojito Parisien ●●●●◐
Momo Special ●●●●○
Monarch Martini ●●●●○
Orange Mojito ●●●●○
Palm Springs ●●●◐○
Pineapple Mojito ●●●●◐
Pussyfoot ●●●●◐ (Mocktail)
Queen's Park Swizzle ●●●●○
Ray's Hard Lemonade ●●●●○
Razzmatazz ●●●○○
Royal Mojito ●●●●●
Sensation ●●●●○
Serendipity #2 ●●●●○
Sleepy Hollow ●●●●○
Southern Mint Cobbler ●●●●○
Southside Royal ●●●●○
Strawberry & Balsamic Mojito ●●●●○
The Sun Salutation ●●●●○
Tequila Smash ●●●●◐
Tipperary #2 ●●●●◐
Ugurundu ●●●●○
Victorian Lemonade ●●●◐○
Zelda Martini ●●●●○

OCEAN SPRAY CRANBERRY JUICE DRINK - RED

0% **alc./vol.** (0°proof)
www.oceanspray.com
Producer: Ocean Spray Cranberries, Inc., Lakeville-Middleboro, Massachusetts, USA

Cranberries are native to North America and are grown in rich acid peat bogs. The fields are flooded during harvesting when large machines, fondly known as egg beaters, release the berries from the vines. Air pockets in the fruit allow them to bob to the surface to create a stunning crimson carpet. You can tell when a cranberry is good enough to eat because it bounces – all part of its quality test.
Cranberries are rich in unique antioxidants which help protect you inside and are best known as a natural remedy for a number of infections. Some brands of cranberry only contain a tiny proportion of cranberry concentrate and consequently taste weak and sometimes far too sweet. Ocean Spray Cranberry Classic and Cranberry Select contain a high proportion of natural cranberry juice, providing the authentic taste of the fruit. Ocean Spray is an agricultural co-operative, formed in 1930 by just three cranberry growers and now has more than 650 growers.

Absolutely Fabulous ●●●●○
Alan's Apple Breeze ●●●◐○
American Pie Martini ●●●●○
Apple & Cranberry Pie ●●●◐○
Apple Breeze ●●●●○
Apple Pie Martini ●●●●○
Appleissimo ●●●●○
Apricot Cosmo ●●●●◐
Aquarius ●●●◐○
Arizona Breeze ●●●●○
Baby Woo Woo ●●●○○
Bald Eagle Martini ●●●●◐
Basil Grande ●●●●○
Bay Breeze ●●●◐○
Beach Iced Tea ●●●◐○
Between Decks ●●●◐○
Blood Orange ●●●●○
Blush Martini ●●●◐○
Bourbon Smash ●●●◐○
Brake Tag ●●●◐○
Brazilian Cosmopolitan ●●●◐○
C C Kazi ●●●●○
Cape Codder ●●●◐○
Caribbean Breeze ●●●●○
Cascade Martini ●●●●○
Casino ●●●●○
China Beach ●●●●○
Chinese Cosmopolitan ●●●●○
Chocolate & Cranberry Martini ●●●◐○
Cool Martini ●●●◐○
Cosmopolitan #1 ●●●●◐ (simple version)
Cosmopolitan #2 ●●●●● (complex version)
Cosmopolitan #3 ●●●●◐ (popular version)
Cranapple Breeze ●●●◐○
Cranberry Cooler ●●●○○
Cranberry Delicious ●●●○○ (Mocktail)
Cranberry & Mint Martini ●●●◐○
Cranberry Sauce ●●●◐○
Detox ●●●○○
Detropolitan ●●●●○
Dorian Gray ●●●◐○
Dragon Blossom ●●●○○
Eclipse ●●●●◐
Estes ●●●●○
Finn Rouge ●●●◐○
Finnberry Martini ●●●●○
The Flirt ●●●◐○
Floridita Margarita ●●●●○
Fruit & Nut Martini ●●●●○
Gentle Breeze ●●●○○ (Mocktail)
Georgetown Punch ●●●●○
Gin Berry ●●●◐○
Ginger Cosmo ●●●●○
Grand Cosmopolitan ●●●●◐
Grande Champagne Cosmo ●●●●○
Gulf Coast Sex on the Beach ●●●●○
Hawaiian Seabreeze ●●●◐○
Highland Sling ●●●●○
Hot Passion ●●●○○
Illicit Affair ●●●◐○
Inga From Sweden ●●●●○
Ink Martini #1 ●●●◐○
Ink Martini #2 ●●●●○
Island Breeze ●●●◐○
Italian Job #2 ●●●●○
Italian Surfer With A Russian Attitude ●●●○○
Jamaican Sunset ●●●●○
Jodi May ●●●◐○
Juliette ●●●○○
Jungle Juice ●●●◐○
Kentucky Jewel ●●●●○
Key West Cooler ●●●○○
Killer Punch ●●●◐○
Koolaid ●●●●○
Lemongrass Cosmo ●●●●◐
Light Breeze ●●●◐○
Lighter Breeze ●●●◐○
Lime Blush (Mocktail) ●●●○○
Limey Cosmo ●●●●○
Long Beach Iced Tea ●●●◐○
Madras ●●●◐○

Madroska
Mae West Martini
Magic Bus
Maria Theresa Margarita
Marquee
Metropolitan
Mexico City
Mountain Slipper
Nantucket
Nautilus .5
Navy Grog
Not So Cosmo (Mocktail)
November Seabreeze (Mocktail)
Nutty Berry'tini
Osmo
Pale Rider
Palm Springs
Parlay Punch
Pass-on-that
Passbour Cooler
Pink Flamingo
Pink Sin Martini
Playa Del Mar
Poinsettia
Pontberry Martini
Purple Flirt #1
Raspberry Cosmo
Rasputin
Razzzzzberry Martini
Red Apple
Red Marauder
Red Or Dead
Rhett Butler
Rosarita Margarita
Royal Cosmopolitan
Rude Cosmopolitan
Rude Ginger Cosmopolitan
Saigon Cooler
Sake'politan
Sake-tini #2
Scandinavian Pop
Scarlett O'Hara
Seabreeze #1 (Simple)
Seabreeze #2 (Layered)
Serendipity #1
Sex On The Beach #1
Southern Cider
Southern Peach
Spiced Cranberry Martini
Stiletto
Strawberry Cosmo
Summer Breeze
Tailor Made
Tarraberry'tini
Tarte Aux Pommes
Tartini
Tennessee Berry Mule
Tennessee Rush
Tolleytown Punch
Tomahawk
Tootie Fruity Lifesaver
Total Recall
Triple 'C' Martini
Tropical Breeze
Tutti Fruitti
Vert'ical Breeze
Watermelon Cosmo
The Wentworth
The Windsor Rose
Woo Woo

OCEAN SPRAY WHITE CRANBERRY JUICE

0% **alc./vol.** (0°proof)
www.oceanspray.com
Producer: Ocean Spray Cranberries, Inc., Lakeville-Middleboro, Massachusetts, USA

Ocean Spray White cranberry juice drinks are made with natural white cranberries which are harvested in late summer before they fully develop: the red are harvested in the autumn. This early harvesting not only affects the colour, but means the berries' flavour is milder and less tart than the more familiar red cranberry juice.

Blue Cosmo
Blue Fin
Ice White Cosmo
Purple Cosmo
White Cosmo
White Sangria

OPAL NERA BLACK SAMBUCA

40% **alc./vol.** (80°proof)
www.opalnera.com
Producer: Fratelli Francoli S.p.A., Ghemme, Corso Romagnano, Italy.

In 1989 Alessandro Francoli was on honeymoon in America, when he took time out to present his company's traditional Italian grappas and sambucas to a potential buyer. He noticed the interest the buyer showed in a coffee sambuca, and this dark liqueur set Alessandro thinking. He experimented with different flavours and created Opal Nera, a black coloured sambuca with a hint of lemon. Opal Nera's seductive and unmistakable colour comes from elderberries, a key ingredient in all sambucas: Francoli macerate their purple-black skins.
Opal Nera Black Sambuca is a favourite with many bartenders due to its colour and flavour, which includes aniseed, soft black liquorice, light elderberry spice and lemon zest.

Alessandro
Black Dream
Black Jack Shot
Black Nuts
Black Widow
Flaming Ferrari
Grey Mouse
Head Shot
Liquorice All Sort
Liquorice Martini
Molotov Cocktail
Oil Slick
Opal Café
Purple Flirt #1
Redback

ORANGE BITTERS

Sadly, this key cocktail ingredient is hard to find in modern liquor stores. There are a number of brands that profess to be 'orange bitters' but many hardly taste of orange and are more like sweet liqueurs than bitters. Search the internet for suitable brands or make your own. See drinkboy.com/LiquorCabinet/Flavorings/OrangeBitters.htm

Absinthe Special Cocktial
Adonis
Alaska Martini
Almond Old Fashioned
Amsterdam Cocktail
Apricot Cosmo
The Argyll [#6.1]
Bamboo
Banana Bliss
Bijou
Blackthorn English
Blue Monday
Boulevard
Bourbon Crusta
Bradford
Brass Rail
The Broadmoor
Californian Martini
Call Me Old-Fashioned
Caprice
Casino
Causeway
Chancellor
Cheeky Monkey
Citrus Martini
Club Cocktail #1
Colonel's Big Opu
Commodore #2
Coronation Cocktail No. 1
Cosmopolitan #2 (complex version)
Cowboy Martini
Cuban Cocktail No. 2 #1
Cuban Cocktail No. 3 #2
Diplomat
DNA #1
Dr Zeus
Dry Martini #1 (Traditional)
Dry Oranage Martini
Dubliner
East India House
East Indian
Elder Fashioned
Elder Sour
Fancy Free
Flying Dutchman Martini
Golden Cardillac
Grand Cosmopolitan
Harvard
Hearst Martini
Hoffman House Martini
Intimate Martini
Jack Maple
Jaded Lady
Jaffa Martini
Jalisco
Jelly Belly Beany
Jewel Cocktail
Jockey Club
The Legend
Lemon Sorbet
Leninade
London Calling
London Cocktail
Mac Orange
Marguerite Martini
Marny Cocktail
Martinez
Merry Widow #2
Met Manhattan
Milly Martini
Modernista
Mystique
Nathalia
Onion Ring Martini
Opera
Orange Martini
Pall Mall Martini
Palma Violet Martini
Paradise #2
Pegu Club
Perfect Martini
Princeton
The Puritan
Quebec
Raspberry Collins
Raspberry Debonair
Rude Cosmopolitan
Sake'politan
Salflower Sour
Satsuma Martini
Satan's Whiskers (Straight)
Satan's Whiskers
Scofflaw
Silver Martini
Singapore Sling #2
Smartini
Smoky Martini #2
Stairs Martini
Stork Club
Straits Sling
Suburban
Swedish Blue Martini
Trilby #1
Trinity
Turf Martini
Tuxedo Martini
Two 'T' Fruity Martini
Valencia
Vancouver
Viagra Falls
Watermelon Cosmo
Wonky Martini

ORANGE JUICE

The orange is now so commonly available in our shops and markets that it's hard to believe it was once an exotic and expensive luxury. Although native to China, its name originates from 'naranga' in the old Indian language of Sanskrit.
There are many different types of orange but the best ones for bartending purposes are Washington Navels, which are in season from the end of October. These have a firm, rough skin perfect for cutting twists from and are juicy and slightly sour.
Simply cut in half and juice with a hand press. If using an electric spinning citrus juicer take care not to grind the pith.

Abbey Martini
Agent Orange
Air Mail
Alabama Slammer #1
Alabama Slammer #2
Allegrottini
Amercian Beauty #1
American Beauty #2
Amsterdam Cocktail
Apple Sunrise
Apricot Fizz
Apricot Martini
April Shower
Aunt Agatha
Aunt Emily
Bahama Mama
Banana Boomer
Beach Blonde
Bebbo
Bee's Knees #1
Bee's Knees #2
Bermuda Cocktail
Bermuda Rum Swizzle
Between Decks
The Big Easy
Bishop
The Bistro Sidecar
Blood & Sand #2 (Difford's Formula)
Blood Orange
Blue Star
Bolero Sour
Boston Tea Party
Brake Tag
Breakfast At Terrell's
Bronx
Buck's Fizz
Bull's Blood
Cactus Banger
Catus Jack
Call Me Old-Fashioned
Canaries
Carneval Batida
Casablanca #2
Castro
Cheeky Monkey
Chill-Out Martini
Cinderella (Mocktail)
Clockwork Orange
Covadonga
Cranberry Cooler
Creamy Creamsicle
Cuban Master
Cumbersome
CVO Firevault
Daiquiri No. 2
Damn-The-Weather
D'Artagnan
Deep South
Derby Daiquiri
Desert Cooler
Diamond Dog
Dingo
Dolce Havana
Don Juan
Dorian Gray
Dreamsicle
Embassy Royal
Esquire #1
Evita
Fat Tire
Flamingo #1
Florida Cocktail (Mocktail)
Fluffy Duck
Fly Like A Butterfly
Fog Cutter #1
Fort Lauderdale

Fosbury Flip ●●●●◐
Fourth Of July Cocktail ●●●○○
Freddy Fudpucker ●●●◐○
French Kiss #1 ●●●○○
French Leave ●●●○○
French Sherbet ●●●◐○
Fresca Nova ●●●◐○
Fruit & Nut Martini ●●●●○
Fruit Salad ●●●○○
Fruits Of The Forest ●●●○○
Fuzzy Navel ●●◐○○
Garibaldi ●●●○○
Gin & Sin ●●●◐○
Gold Medallion ●●●◐○
Golden Bird ●●●◐○
Golden Cardillac ●●●◐○
Golden Dawn ●●●◐○
Golden Dream ●●●●○
Golden Screw ●●●◐○
Grand Mimosa ●●●◐○
Green Eyes ●●●◐○
Gypsy Queen ●●●●○
Happy New Year ●●●○○
Harvey Wallbanger ●●●◐○
Hawaiian ●●●○○
Hawaiian Cocktail ●●●●○
Hobson's Choice ●●◐○○ (Mocktail)
Honey & Marmalade Dram'tini ●●●●◐
Honeysuckle Daiquiri ●●●●●
Honolulu Cocktail No. 1 ●●●◐○
Hot Red Blooded Frenchman ●●●●○
Honula-Honula Cocktail ●●●○○
Hurricane #1 ●●●●○
Hurricane #2 ●●●○○
Hurricane #3 ●●●○○
Iced Tea ●●●◐○
Iguana Wana ●●●○○
Illicit Affair ●●●◐○
Income Tax Cocktail ●●●●○
Jack Frost ●●●◐○
Jacuzzi ●●●◐○
Jaded Lady ●●●◐○
Jaffa Martini ●●●◐○
Jamaican Sunset ●●●●○
Jambalaya ●●●◐○
Ja-Mora ●●●●○
Jodi May ●●●◐○
Jubilant ●●●●◐
Jumping Jack Flash ●●●●○
Jungle Juice ●●●◐○
Jupiter Martini ●●●◐○
Key West Cooler ●●●○○
Klondike ●●●◐○
Knickerbocker Special ●●●●○
Koolaid ●●●●○
Lago Cosmo ●●●◐○
Limeosa ●●●◐○
Lola ●●●◐○
Loved Up ●●●◐○
Lutkins Special Martini ●●●◐○
Mac Orange ●●●◐○
Madroska ●●●○○
Maiden's Prayer ●●●◐○
Magic Bus ●●●◐○
Mambo ●●●◐○
Mandarine Songbird ●●●○○
Mat The Rat ●●●◐○
Maurice Martini ●●●◐○
Mayfair Cocktail ●●●●○
Melon Ball ●●●○○
Mexican Melon Ball ●●●◐○
Mimosa ●●●◐○
Mister Stu ●●●◐○
Mona Lisa ●●●●○
Monkey Gland #1 ●●●●○
Monkey Gland #2 ●●●●○
Mrs Robinson #2 ●●●◐○
Naranja Daiquiri ●●●●○
New Port Codebreaker ●●●◐○
Nightmare Martini ●●●○○
Noble Europe ●●●●◐
Noon ●●●●○
Not So Cosmo ●●●◐○ (Mocktail)
Old Flame ●●●●○
Ole ●●●◐○
Olympic ●●●●◐
Opal ●●●●◐
Orang-A-Tang ●●●●○
Orange Blossom ●●●◐○
Orange Daiquiri #1 ●●●●◐
Orange Martini ●●●●○
Oranjiniha ●●●●○
Painkiller ●●●●○
Paradise #1 ●●●◐○
Paradise #2 ●●●●◐
Paradise #3 ●●●◐○
Park Lane ●●●●◐
Parlay Punch ●●●○○
Perfect John ●●●●○
Peter Pan Cocktail ●●●○○
Peter Pan Martini ●●●●○
Peto Martini ●●●●◐
Pilgrim Cocktail ●●●●○
Pinky Pincher ●●●●○
Pisco Punch #1 ●●●●◐ (Difford's Formula)
Pisco Naranja ●●●◐○
Planteur ●●●●○
Playmate Martini ●●●●◐
Poncha ●●●●○
Potted Parrot ●●●◐○
President ●●●●○
Pruneaux ●●●●○
Pussyfoot ●●●●◐ (Mocktail)
Red Lion #1 ●●●●◐ (Modern Formula)
Reggae Rum Punch ●●●●◐
Riviera Breeze ●●●◐○
Rum Sour ●●●●○
Saint Clements ●●●○○ (Mocktail)
Salflower Sour ●●●●○
San Francisco ●●●◐○
La Sang ●●●●○
Sangaree ●●●●○
Sangria ●●●◐○
Sangria Martini ●●●●○
Sangrita ●●●●○
Santiago ●●●○○
Satan's Whiskers (Straight) ●●●●◐
Satan's Whiskers ●●●◐○
Savannah ●●●◐○
Scorpion ●●●●○
Scotch Bounty Martini ●●●◐○
Screwdriver ●●●◐○
Sex On The Beach #1 ●●◐○○
Shark Bite ●●●◐○
Sidekick ●●●●○
Slow Screw ●●●○○
Slow Comfortable Screw ●●●◐○
Slow Comfortable Screw Against the Wall ●●●◐○
South Beach ●●●●○
Spencer Cocktail ●●●●○
Sputnik ●●●◐○
Sputnik #2 ●●●●○
Stork Club ●●●●○
Summer Time Martini ●●●◐○
Sun Kissed Virgin ●●●○○ (Mocktail)
Sundowner #1 ●●●●○
The Suzy Wong Martini ●●●◐○
Sweet Science ●●●◐○
Tainted Cherry ●●●◐○
Tango Martini #1 ●●●●○
Tequila Fizz ●●●●○
Tequila Sunrise ●●●◐○
Thriller Martini ●●●●○
Thriller From Vanilla ●●●●○
Thunderbird ●●●●○
Tiki Max ●●●●○
Tipperary #2 ●●●●◐
Tolleytown Punch ●●●◐○
Tonga ●●●◐○
Tootie Fruity Lifesaver ●●●○○
Total Recall ●●●◐○
Tres Compadres Margarita ●●●●◐
Triple Orange Martini ●●●●○
Umbongo ●●●○○
Valencia ●●●●○
Vampiro ●●●●○
Velvet Fog ●●●●◐
Volga Boatman ●●●◐○
Vowel Cocktail ●●●●◐
Ward Eight ●●●●○
Watermelon Man ●●●○○
Wine Cooler ●●●◐○
Zanzibar ●●●◐○
Zombie #2 ●●●◐○ (Vic's formula)
Zombie #3 ●●●●○ (Modern formula)

OUZO 12

38% alc. /vol. (76°proof)
www.ouzo12.com
Producer: ???? Name & address ?????

The first bottled Ouzo and still the world's best selling brand. Ouzo 12 was first produced by the Kaloyannis brothers in 1880 and its name comes from one of the first batches produced. It was the blend in cask number twelve that the brothers agreed would be their house style. Ouzo 12 is made by double distilling grape alcohol with anise, cardamom, cinnamon, coriander and nutmeg.

PARFAIT AMOUR LIQUEUR

A French, lilac coloured curaçao liqueur flavoured with rose petals, vanilla pods and almonds. The name means 'perfect love'.

Barnacle Bill ●●●○○
Blue Angel ●●●○○
Brazen Martini ●●●●○
Barnacle Bill ●●●○○
Blue Angel ●●◐○○
Eden Martini ●●●◐○
English Rose ●●●●○
Esquire #2 ●●●◐○
Fruit Pastel ●●●◐○
Joan Bennett ●●●○○
Jungle Fire Sling ●●●○○
Jupiter Martini ●●●◐○
Lavender Martini ●●●●○
Molotov Cocktail ●●●◐○
Purple Cosmo ●●●●◐
Trilby #1 ●●●●○

PARTIDA TEQUILA

40% **alc./vol.** (80°proof)
www.partidatequila.com
Producer: Familia Partida, S.A. DE C.V., Amatitan, Jalisco, Mexico. NOM 1454

Partida is a super-premium tequila (called by noted spirits expert F. Paul Pacult 'the finest tequila money can buy') made from estate-grown, 100% blue agave grown on the Partida family estate, just outside the village of Amatitán. The agave are harvested at seven to ten years old to ensure full development of the natural sugars in the plant, so the tequila is naturally sweet with delicious agave flavour.

Stainless steel ovens are used to bake the agave piñas (hearts), avoiding the smoky flavour associated with old-fashioned, soot-lined brick ovens. The cooked piñas are crushed to release the juice which is fermented, then double distilled in stainless steel pot stills.

Partida is aged in one-pass Jack Daniels American oak barrels. The empty casks are hot-washed twice with distilled water so only a little of the 'toast' and Jack Daniel's character is left to subtly influence the tequila, which is bottled without any additives such as glycerine, colourings or caramel unlike many other tequilas.

Acapulco ●●●◐○
Adios ●●●◐○
Alice From Dallas ●●●◐○
Alice In Wonderland ●●●○○
All Fall Down ●●●◐○
Almond Old Fashioned ●●●●◐
Anita's Attitude Adjuster ●●●○○
Armillita Chico ●●●◐○
Bald Eagle Martini ●●●●◐
Batanga ●●●●○
Beach Iced Tea ●●●◐○
Bee Sting ●●●●○
Bird of Paradise ●●●●◐
Bloody Maria ●●●●○
Blue Margarita ●●●◐○
Blue Velvet Margarita ●●●●○
Boston Tea Party ●●●○○
Buena Vida ●●●●◐
Burning Bush Shot ●●○○○
C C Kazi ●●●●○
Cactus Banger ●●●●○
Catus Jack ●●●◐○
Chihuahua Margarita ●●●◐○
Chimayo ●●●●○
Chocolarita ●●●●○
Cool Martini ●●●◐○
Crouching Tiger ●●●○○
El Diablo ●●●◐○
Dirty Sanchez ●●●●○
Durango ●●●◐○
Easy Tiger ●●●●○
El Burro ●●●●○
El Torado ●●●●◐
Elegante Margarita ●●●●◐
Encantado ●●●●○
Estes ●●●●○
Estilo Viejo ●●●●◐
The Estribo ●●●◐○
Flatliner 1.●●●●●
The Flirt ●●●◐○
Floridita Margarita ●●●●○
Flutter ●●●●◐
Freddy Fudpucker ●●●◐○
Frida's Brow ●●●●○
Frozen Margarita ●●●●○
Fuego Manzana No. 2 ●●●●○
Ginger Margarita ●●●●○
Gloria ●●●◐○
Gold Rush Slammer ●●●○○
Golden Dragon ●●●◐○
Grand Margarita ●●●●●
Gusto ●●●●○
Hong Kong Fuey ●●●○○
Hornitos Lau ●●●●○
The Horseshoe Sling ●●●●○
The Hypnotic Margarita ●●●●○
Iguana ●●●◐○
Italian Margarita ●●●◐○
Jalisco ●●●●○
Jalisco Espresso ●●●●◐
Jambalaya ●●●◐○
Japanese Slipper ●●●●○
Jose Collins ●●●●○
Kamikaze ●●●●○
Katrina Cocktail ●●●○○
Lavender Margarita ●●●●●
Lolita Margarita ●●●●◐
Lonely Bull ●●●◐○
Long Beach Iced Tea ●●●◐○
Long Island Iced Tea ●●●◐○
Long Island Spiced Tea ●●●◐○
Loved Up ●●●◐○
Lucky Lily Margarita ●●●●◐
Magic Bus ●●●◐○
Malcolm Lowry ●●●●○
Mango Margarita #1 (Served 'Up') ●●●●○
Mango Margarita #2 (Frozen) ●●●●○
Margarita #1 (Straight-up) ●●●●◐
Margarita #2 (On the Rocks) ●●●●◐
Margarita #3 (Frozen) ●●●●○
Maria Theresa Margarita ●●●●○
Marmarita ●●●●○
Matador ●●●●○
Mayan ●●●◐○
Mayan Whore ●●●●○
Melon Margarita #1 ●●●●○ (Served 'Up')
Melon Margarita #2 ●●●◐○ (Served Frozen)
Mesa Fresca ●●●●○
Mexican ●●●●○
Mexican 55 ●●●●○
Mexican Coffee ●●●◐○ (Hot)
Mexican Manhattan ●●●●○
Mexican Martini ●●●◐○
Mexican Melon Ball ●●●◐○
Mexican Mule ●●●●◐
Mexican Surfer ●●●●○
Mexican Tea ●●●●◐ (Hot)

Mexico City ●●●●◐
Mexicano ●●●●◐ (Hot)
Million Dollar Margarita ●●●●◐
Mister Stu ●●●◐○
Mojito de Casa ●●●●○
Nautilus ●●●●○.5
New Port Codebreaker ●●●◐○
Paloma ●●●●◐
Passion Fruit Margarita ●●●●○
Passion Killer ●●●○○
Picador ●●●●● [NEW # 7]
Pineapple & Sage Margarita ●●●●◐
Pineapple Margarita ●●●●○
Pink Grapefruit Magarita ●●●●○
Playa Del Mar ●●●●○
Pomegranate Margarita ●●●●◐
Prado ●●●◐○
Purple Turtle ●●●◐○
Raging Bull ●●●◐○
Raspberry Margarita ●●●●○
Red Hooker ●●●◐○
La Rosa Margarita ●●●●○
Rosarita Margarita ●●●●○
Rosita ●●●●○
Royal Velvet Margarita ●●●◐○
Rude Cosmopolitan ●●●●◐
Rude Ginger Cosmopolitan ●●●●○
Sage Margarita ●●●●○
Saltecca ●●●○○
Saúco Margarita ●●●●◐
Silk Stockings ●●●◐○
Sloe Tequila ●●●◐○
South Of The Border ●●●○○
Strawberry Margarita ●●●●○
Tequila Fizz ●●●●○
Tequila Mockingbird ●●●○○
Tequila Slammer ●●●○○
Tequila Smash ●●●●◐
Tequila Sour ●●●●◐
Tequila Sunrise ●●●◐○
Tequila Sunset ●●●●○
Tequila'tini ●●●◐○
Texas Iced Tea ●●●◐○
Tiki Bar Margarita ●●●●◐
Tokyo Iced Tea ●●●◐○
Tomahawk ●●●◐○
Tommy's Margarita ●●●●●
Tongue Twister ●●●○○
Toreador ●●●●○
Total Recall ●●●◐○
Tres Compadres Margarita ●●●●◐
Tutti Fruitti ●●●○○
TVR ●●●○○
Vampiro ●●●●○
Watermelon & Basil Smash ●●●●○

PASSION FRUIT

The fruit of the passion flower (Passiflora), a climbing plant which is native to South America but grown around the world, is an ugly, spherical outgrowth about the size of a hen's egg.

Known in Spanish as 'granadilla' ('little pomegranate'), the passion fruit has a thick, leathery, yellowish-green or brownish-red skin, which is smooth and shiny when unripe and pockmarked, almost wrinkly when ripe. The inside yields intensely flavoured, slightly acidic, yellow flesh with small, edible, crunchy black seeds. Select heavy fruits as the light ones tend to be dried out and lacking in juice.

Preparation: Cut the fruit in half with a sharp knife and scoop the flesh out of the shell into your shaker (or simply push flesh out by squeezing the fruit half between your fingers). If you are making a blended drink it is advisable to pass the flesh through a sieve to strain out the seeds before combining it with other ingredients. However, this isn't necessary with shaken drinks, as the seeds should be removed when the drink is fine strained into the glass.

Autumn Punch ●●●●◐
Avenue ●●●◐○
Bajan Mojito ●●●◐○
Bajan Passion ●●●●○
Basil Beauty ●●●●○
Grand Passion ●●●○○
Hurricane #2 ●●●○○
Maracuja Batida ●●●●○
Mitch Martini ●●●●○
Monza ●●●◐○
Paradise #3 ●●●◐○
Pass-on-that ●●●○○
Passion Fruit Caipirinha ●●●●○
Passion Fruit Collins ●●●●○
Passion Fruit Daiquiri ●●●●○
Passion Fruit Margarita ●●●●○
Passion Fruit Martini #1 ●●●●○
Passion Fruit Martini #2 ●●●●○
Passion Fruit Martini #3 ●●●●○
Passion Punch ●●●◐○
Passionate Rum Punch ●●●●○
Pear Shaped #1 ●●●●◐ (Deluxe Version)
Port Light ●●●◐○
South Pacific ●●●◐○
Sporran Breeze ●●●●◐
Umbongo ●●●○○
Waltzing Matilda ●●●●○

PASSION FRUIT SUGAR SYRUP

Passion fruit syrup is sugar syrup flavoured with passion fruit juice. Make your own or buy commercially available products such as Monin or Giffard brands.

Autumn Martini ●●●●○
Autumn Punch ●●●●◐
Beetle Jeuse ●●●●○
Bitterest Pill ●●●◐○
Bourbon Cookie ●●●●○
Byzantine ●●●●○
Extradition ●●●●○
Feather Dusta Crusta ●●●●○
Gauguin ●●●○○
Golden Dragon ●●●◐○
Grape Martini ●●●●○
Great Mughal Martini ●●●●○
Hurricane #1 ●●●●○
Hurricane #2 ●●●○○
Hurricane #3 ●●●○○
Ignorance Is Bliss ●●●◐○
Jumbled Fruit Julep ●●●◐○
Pappy Honeysuckle ●●●●◐
Passion Fruit Collins ●●●●○
Passion Fruit Margarita ●●●●○
Passion Fruit Martini #2 ●●●●○
Passion Fruit Martini #3 ●●●●○
Passionate Rum Punch ●●●●○
Rizzo ●●●●○
Two 'T' Fruity Martini ●●●●○
Zombie #1 ●●●●○ (Intoxica! Recipe)

PASTIS

See 'Ricard Pastis'

PEACH PURÉE (WHITE)

Fruit purees are made from fresh white peaches which have been chopped up and liquidised. When making your own puree add roughly five to ten percent sugar syrup depending on the fruit's ripeness. Alternatively buy commercially available products such as Funkin.

Kentucky Colonel ●●●◐○
Red Hooker ●●●◐○
Roger ●●●◐○
Southern Mint Cobbler ●●●●○
Whiskey Squirt ●●●●○

PEACH SCHNAPPS LIQUEUR

See 'Teichenné Peach Schnapps Liqueur'

PEAR JUICE

Unless otherwise stated, pear in this guide means the Western varieties. Conference is widely available and works well in cocktails. Pears will ripen after they are picked, but spoil quickly, so care is needed in storage.

The best way to extract the flavour of a pear is to use an electric juice extractor. Surprisingly, you'll find that beautifully ripe fruits yield little and much of that is in the form of slush. Instead, look for pears which are on their way to ripeness but still have a good crunch. Remove the stalk but don't worry about peeling or removing the core. Cut the fruit into chunks small enough to push into the juicer. If you hate cleaning an electric juice extractor then use a blender or food processor.

Asian Pear Martini ●●●●○
Autumn Punch ●●●●◐
Kentucky Pear ●●●●◐
Nice Pear-tini ●●●●◐
Pear & Elderflower Cocktail ●●●◐○
Pear Drop Martini ●●●●○
Pear Shaped #1 ●●●●◐ (Deluxe Version)
Perry-tini ●●●●○
Prickly Pear Mule ●●●●○
Sleeping Bison-tini ●●●●○
Sparkling Perry ●●●●○
Spiced Pear ●●●●◐
Stairs Martini ●●●●●

PERNOD ANIS

40% **alc./vol.** (80°proof)
www.pernod.net
Producer: Pernod Enterprise, France

Pernod's story starts in 1789 when Dr Pierre Ordinaire first prescribed his pain relieving and reviving 'absinthe elixir' in Switzerland. Ten years later, Major Dubied bought the formula and set up an absinthe factory in Couvet, Switzerland, with his son-in-law, Henri-Louis Pernod. In 1805, Henri-Louis Pernod established Pernod Fils in Pontarlier, France, and created an authentic absinthe.

Pernod quickly gained fame as THE absinthe of Parisian café society. But a prohibitionist movement and massive press campaign blamed absinthe abuse as the cause of insanity, tuberculosis and even murder. On 7th January 1915, absinthe was banned and Pernod Fils was forced to close. But by 1920, anise liquors were legalised again, albeit in a more sober form, and in its new guise Pernod remained as popular as ever.

Today it contains 14 herbs, including star anise, fennel, mint and coriander, and is best served long with cranberry juice, apple juice or bitter lemon, diluted five to one.

Anis'tini ●●●●○
Appleissimo ●●●●○
Asylum Cocktail ●●●○○
Barnacle Bill ●●●○○
Blackthorn Irish ●●●◐○
Doctor Funk ●●●◐○
Drowned Out ●●●◐○
French Kiss #1 ●●●○○
French Leave ●●●○○
Greta Garbo ●●●●○
Hemingway ●●●○○
Light Breeze ●●●◐○
Lighter Breeze ●●●◐○
London Fog ●●●○○
Milky Mojito ●●●◐○
Modernista ●●●●○
Monte Carlo ●●●◐○
Moonraker ●●●●○
Mucky Bottom ●●●◐○
Nicky Finn ●●●●○
Northern Lights ●●●●○
Pernod & Black Martini ●●●●○
Sunny Breeze ●●●◐○
Tarraberry'tini ●●●●○
Threesome ●●●◐○

PEYCHAUD'S AROMATIC BITTERS

Adelaide Swizzle ●●●●○
Algonquin ●●●●○
Auntie's Hot Xmas Punch ●●●●○
Behemoth ●●●●○
Bentley ●●●●○
Bloomsbury Martini ●●●●○
Bourbonella ●●●●○
Brake Tag ●●●◐○
Caramel Manhattan ●●●●◐
Chocolate Sazerac ●●●●○
Concealed Weapon ●●●○○
De La Louisiane #2 ●●●●○
De La Louisiane #3 ●●●●○
Devil's Manhattan ●●●●○
Elysian ●●●●○
Especial Day ●●●●◐
Feather Dusta Crusta ●●●●○
Free Town ●●●●○
Gansevoort Fizz ●●●◐○
Golden Nail ●●●●○
Grand Sazerac ●●●●○
Jack Rose ●●●●○
Jean Lafitte Cocktail ●●◐○○
Lychee & Rose Petel Martini ●●●●○
Pendennis Cocktail ●●●●○
Rob Roy #2 ●●●●◐
Rose Petalini ●●●●○
Saigon Sling ●●●◐○
Sazerac ●●●●●
Seelbach ●●●○○
Southern Manhattan ●●●●○
Toast & Orange Martini ●●●●○
Trilby #2 ●●●●○
Venus Martini ●●●●○
Vieux Carré Cocktail ●●●●◐
Wink ●●●●○

PIMM'S NO. 1 CUP

Luxury Cocktail ●●●◐○
Pimm's Cocktail ●●●●◐
Pimm's Royal ●●◐○○
Strasberi Sling ●●●◐○

PINEAPPLE JUICE

Pineapples are widely grown in the West Indies, Africa and Asia. There are many varieties which vary significantly in both size and flavour, but most are ripe when the skin is brown. These tropical fruits tend to deteriorate at temperatures below 7°C (45°F) so are best left out of the refrigerator.

Pineapple is one of the most satisfying fruits to juice due to the quantity of liquid it yields. Chop the crown and bottom, then slice the skin, without worrying too much about the little brown dimples that remain. Finally slice the fruit along its length around the hard central core, and chop into pieces small enough to fit into your juice extractor. The base is the sweetest part of a pineapple, so if you are only juicing half be sure to divide the fruit lengthways.

For convenience I still often end up buying cartons of 'pressed pineapple juice' from the supermarket chill cabinet. As with all such juices, look for those labelled 'not from concentrate'. When buying supermarket own brand pineapple juice, read the label carefully.

Abaci Batida ●●●●○
Aku Aku ●●●●◐
Algonquin ●●●●○
Alien Secretion ●●●◐○
Atlantic Breeze ●●●○○
Atomic Dog ●●●○○
Aunt Agatha ●●●◐○
Awol ●●●●○
Baby Blue Martini ●●●◐○
Bahama Mama ●●●●○
Bahamas Daiquiri ●●●●◐
Bahia ●●●◐○
Bali Trader ●●●◐○
Banana Boomer ●●●●○

Banana Colada
Basil Beauty
Bay Breeze
Bermuda Rum Swizzle
Blade Runner
Blue Hawaiian
Blue Heaven
Blue Wave
Blueberry Daiquiri
Bora Bora Brew (Mocktail)
Bossa Nova #2
Brandy Crusta
Brandy Fix
Brighton Punch
Buena Vida
Buzzard's Breath
Byzantine
Catus Jack
Canaries
Cappercaille
Caramel Manhattan
Caribbean Breeze
Caribbean Cruise
Caribbean PiÀa Colada
Caribbean Punch
Caribe Daiquiri
Che's Revolution
Cinderella (Mocktail)
Coco Cabana
Colonel T
Cool Orchard
Cox's Daiquiri
Cruel Intention
Cuban Master
Cuban Special
CVO Firevault
Diable Rouge
Downhill Racer
Dyevitchka
East India #2
East India House
El Presidente No. 1 (Daiquiri) #1
Elderflower Cosmo
Elderflower Pisco Punch
Especial Day
The Estribo
Exotic Passion
Fat Tire
Flamingo #2
Flirtini #1
Flirtini #2
The Flo Ziegfeld
Florida Sling
Flutter
French Bison-tini
French Martini
French Tear #1
Full Circle
Georgetown Punch
Gin Fixed
Ginger Cosmos
Golden Bird
Golden Girl
Golden Wave
Goombay Smash
Green Horn
The GTO Cocktail
Gulf Coast Sex on the Beach
Gun Club Punch No. 1
The Harlem
Havana Special
Hawaiian
Hawaiian Cocktail
Hawaiian Martini
Hawaiian Seabreeze
Heavens Above
Honey Blossom (Mocktail)
Honolulu
Honolulu Cocktail No. 1
Honolulu Juicer
The Horseshoe Sling
Hot Tub
Hunk Martini
Hurricane #1
Hurricane #2
Hurricane #3
Illusion
Italian Surfer With A Russian Attitude
Jack-In-The-Box
Jack Punch
Joan Bennett
Judy (Mocktail)
Juliette
Jumping Jack Flash

June Bug
Jungle Bird
Jungle Juice
The Juxtaposition
Kamaniwanalaya
Kava
Key Lime Pie #2
Key Lime Pie #3
Knickerbocker Special
Linstead
Lucky Lily Margarita
Major Bailey #2
Mary Pickford
Matador
Mayan
Mayan Whore
Meloncholy Martini
Mellow Martini
Mexican
Mexican Martini
Mexican Surfer
Miami Beach
The Million Dollar Cocktail
Milly Martini
Missionary's Downfall
Mister Stu
Monkey Shine
Monk's Habit
Motox
Nacional Daiquiri #2
New Orleans Mule
Nutty Summer
Painkiller
Pale Rider
Palermo
Pancho Villa
Park Avenue
Parlay Punch
Piña Martini
Piña Colada #1
Piña Colada #2 (Cuban Style)
Piña Colada Virgin (Mocktail)
Pineapple & Cardamom Daiquiri
Pineapple & Cardamom Martini
Pineapple & Ginger Martini
Pineapple & Sage Margarita
Pineapple Blossom
Pineapple Daiquiri # 1 (On-the-rocks)
Pineapple Daiquiri #2 (Frozen)
Pineapple Fizz
Pineapple Margarita
Pineapple Mojito
Pineapple Smoothie (Mocktail)
Pino Pepe
Pisco Punch #1 (Difford's Formula)
Pisco Punch #3 (Lanes' Formula)
Pisco Punch #4 (Prosser's Formula)
Playa Del Mar
Pogo Stick
Purple Flirt #2
Raspberry Sake'tini
Reef Juice
Reggae Rum Punch
Roa Aé
Rum Runner
Saigon Sling
St Kitts (Mocktail)
San Francisco
Sandstorm
Sex On The Beach #2
Sex On The Beach #3
Singapore Sling #3
Snow White Daiquiri
Solent Sunset
South Pacific
Southern Punch
Sun Kissed Virgin (Mocktail)
Sunshine Cocktail #1
Surfer on A.C.D.
Swamp Water
Tantris Sidecar
Threesome
Thunderbird
Tiki Max
Tilt
Tolleytown Punch
Tomahawk
Tongue Twister
Tootie Fruity Lifesaver
Transylvanian Martini
Tropical Caipirinha
Tropical Daiquiri
Turquoise Daiquiri
Urban Oasis

U.S. Martini
Utterly Butterly
Vacation
Vante Martini
Verdi Martini
Woodland Punch
Yellow Bird
Yellow Fever Martini
The Zamboanga 'Zeinie' Cocktail
Zombie #1 (Intoxica! Recipe)
Zombie #2 (Vic's formula)
Zombie #3 (Modern formula)

PISANG AMBON GREEN BANANA LIQUEUR

Absinthe Without Leave
Bali Trader
Golden Dragon
Green Hornet
Green Tea Martini #1

PISCO

A type of brandy and the national drink of both Chile and Peru, pisco probably takes its name from the port of Pisco in Peru.
The best pisco is made from the fermented juice of the Muscat grape, which grows in the Ica region of southwestern Peru and in Chile's Elqui Valley. There are many varieties of Muscat. The Quebranta grape is favoured in Peru where it is usually blended with one or two other varietals such as Italia, Moscatel, Albilla, Negra, Mollar and Torontel. In Chile Common Black, Mollar, Pink Muscat, Torontel, Pedro Jimenez and Muscat of Alexandria are all used.

Algeria
Cola de Mono
Dulchin
Elderflower Pisco Punch
Extradition
Greenbelt
Lima Sour
Peruvian Elder Sour
Pichuncho Martini
Pini
Pisco Collins
Pisco Punch #1 (Difford's Formula)
Pisco Punch #2 (Alfredo Micheli's)
Pisco Punch #3 (Lanes' Formula)
Pisco Punch #4 (Prosser's)
Pisco Naranja
Pisco Sour (Traditional Recipe)
Pisco Sour (Difford's Version)
Piscola
Ponche de Algarrobina
Rousing Charlie
Wah-Wah
Wisecrack Fizz

PLUMS

Plums originated in Asia but were introduced to Western Europe by the Crusaders. They can be yellow, green, red or purple. Dried plums, or prunes, were used in a great deal of English cuisine before the raisin began to replace them in the seventeenth century. British plums are in season from July to September but imported varieties are available all year round.

Ideally plums should be left until ripe, but not overripe, when they turn soft and wrinkled. The matt, whitish 'bloom' on the fruit's surface is easily rubbed off: the lack of this can be a sign of over-handling.

Preparation: When plums are ripe they are best muddled. Cut the fruit into quarters, remove the stone and peel each segment. Muddle the skinned flesh in the base of your shaker.
Unripe plums are best quartered, stoned and put through an electric juice extractor. The skin adds colour.

Plum Cocktail
Plum Daiquiri
Plum Martini
Plum Pudding Martini
Plum Sour

PLYMOUTH GIN

41.2% **alc./vol.**

(82.4°proof)
www.plymouthgin.com
Producer: V&S Plymouth Ltd, Black Friars Distillery, Plymouth, England

Since 1793, Plymouth Gin has been hand-crafted in England's oldest working distillery – Black Friars in Plymouth. It is still bottled at the unique strength of 41.2% alc./vol., and is based on a recipe that is over 200 years old. Plymouth Gin, which can only be produced in Plymouth, differs from London gins due to the use of only sweet botanicals combined with soft Dartmoor water. The result is a wonderfully aromatic and smooth gin with fresh juniper lemony bite with deeper, earthy notes.

Abbey Martini
Absinthe Special Cocktial
Ace
Adios Amigos Cocktail
Alaska Martini
Alaska Martini
Alessandro
Alexander
Alexander's Big Brother
Alexander's Sister
Alfonso Martini
Angel Face
Anita's Attitude Adjuster
Apple & Elderflower Collins
Apricot Mango Martini
Apricot Martini
Arizona Breeze
Army & Navy
Arnaud Martini
Asylum Cocktail
Attitude Adjuster
The Atty Cocktail
Aunt Emily
Aviation #1 (Simple Formula)
Aviation #2 (Classic Formula)
Aviator
Baby Blue Martini
Barbara West
Barbary Coast Highball
Barbary Coast Martini
Barnum (Was Right)
Barranquilla Green Jade
Bartender's Martini
Basil & Lime Gimlet
Basil Bramble Sling
Beach Iced Tea
Bebbo
Bee's Knees #2
Bee's Knees #3
Bermuda Cocktail
Bermuda Rose Cocktail
Between Decks
Beverly Hills Iced Tea
Bijou
Bikini Martini
Bitter Elder
Black Bison Martini
Black Bison Martini #2
Black Jack Cocktail
Blackthorn Cocktail
Blackthorn English
Bloomsbury Martini
Blue Bird
Blue Lady
Blue Lagoon
Blue Moon
Blue Riband
Blue Star
Blue Wave
Boston

Boston Tea Party ●●●○○
Bradford ●●●●○
Bramble ●●●●◐
Bramblette ●●●◐○
Breakfast Martini ●●●●●
Bronx ●●●●○
The Buck ●●●◐○
Byzantine ●●●●○
Caprice ●●●●○
Cardinale ●●●●○
Caruso Martini ●●●○○
Casino ●●●●○
Chelsea Sidecar ●●●●◐
China Martini ●●●◐○
Claridge Cocktail ●●●●○
Clover Leaf Cocktail #1 ●●●●○ (Classic Formula)
Clover Leaf Cocktail #2 ●●●◐○ (Modern Formula)
Club Cocktail #2 ●●●●○
Colonel's Big Opu ●●●◐○
Copper Illusion ●●●●○
Corpse Reviver #2 ●●●●○
Cosmopolitan #4 ●●●●○ (1934 recipe)
Country Breeze ●●●◐○
Cowboy Martini ●●●◐○
Crimea ●●●○○
Crossbow ●●●○○
Cumbersome ●●●●○
Curdish Martini ●●●●○
Damn-The-Weather ●●●◐○
Delmonico Special ●●●◐○
Dempsey ●●●◐○
Desert Cooler ●●●◐○
Diamond Fizz ●●●●○
Diana's Bitter ●●●○○
Dickens' Martini ●●●●◐
Dirty Martini ●●●◐○
DNA #1 ●●●◐○
DNA #2 ●●●○○
Dry Martini #1 (Traditional) ●●●●●
Dry Martini #2 (Naked) ●●●●○
Dry Oranage Martini ●●●●◐
The Dubonnet Cocktail ●●●●○
Ductch Breakfast Martini ●●●●○
Dutch Courage ●●●●○
Earl Grey Mar-tea-ni ●●●●◐
Eden Martini ●●●◐○
The Elder Aviator ●●●●◐
Elderflower Collins #1 ●●●●◐
Elk Martini ●●●◐○
Emperor's Memoirs ●●●●○
Empire Cocktail ●●●○○
English Breakfast Martini ●●●●◐
English Garden ●●●●○
English Martini ●●●●◐
English Rose ●●●●○
Fairbanks Cocktail No. 1 ●●●○○
Fifty-Fifty Martini ●●●●○
Fine & Dandy ●●●◐○
Fizz ●●●●○
Flip ●●●●◐
The Flo Ziegfeld ●●●◐○
Floral Martini ●●●●○
Florida Sling ●●●○○
Flower Power Martini ●●●●◐
Fluffy Duck ●●●◐○
Flying Tigre Coctel ●●●●○
Fog Cutter #1 ●●●●○
Fog Cutter #2 ●●●●○
Fog Horn ●●●◐○
Forbidden Fruits ●●●●○
The Frankenjack Cocktail ●●●◐○
Franklin Martini ●●●●●
French 75 ●●●◐○
French Sherbet ●●●◐○
Froth Blower Cocktail ●●●●◐
Full Circle ●●●●○
G & Tea ●●●●○
Geisha Martini ●●●●○
Gibson ●●●●◐
Gimlet #1 ●●●●○
Gimlet #2 ●●●●◐ (Schumann's recipe)
Gin & It ●●●●○
Gin & Sin 3.5/
Gin & Tonic ●●●●●
Gin Atomic ●●●◐○
Gin Berry ●●●◐○
Gin Cocktail ●●●●○
Gin Daisy ●●●●○
Gin Fix ●●●●○
Gin Fixed ●●●●○
Gin Fizz ●●●●○
Gin Gin Mule ●●●●○
Gin Punch ●●●●◐
Gin Sling ●●●●○
Gin Sour ●●●●◐
Gina ●●●◐○
Ginger & Lemongrass Martini ●●●●○
Gin-Ger & Tonic ●●●●○
Ginger Cosmos ●●●◐○
Gin-Ger Tom ●●●●○
Gingertini ●●●●○
Gloom Chaser Cocktail #2 ●●●◐○
Golden Dawn ●●●◐○
Golden Fizz #1 ●●●◐○
Golden Fizz #2 ●●●●○
Golf Cocktail ●●●●○
Granny's Martini ●●●◐○
Grape Delight ●●●●○
Grateful Dead ●●●◐○
Green Dragon ●●●◐○
Green Fizz ●●●○○
Green Tea Martini #2 ●●●●○
Gypsy ●●●●○
Gypsy Martini ●●●●○
Hanky-Panky Martini ●●●●○
The Harlem ●●●●○
Hawaiian Martini ●●●●○
Hearst Martini ●●●●○
Hoffman House Martini ●●●●○
Hong Kong Fuey ●●●○○
Honolulu Cocktail No. 1 ●●●◐○
Honolulu Cocktail No. 2 ●●●◐○
Honula-Honula Cocktail ●●●○○
Huapala Cocktail ●●●●○
Ice Maiden Martini ●●●●○
Ice Tea Martini ●●●●○
Imperial Martini ●●●○○
Income Tax Cocktail ●●●●○
Indian Rose ●●●●○
Ink Martini #1 ●●●◐○
Jack Dempsey ●●●◐○
Jacuzzi ●●●◐○
Jaded Lady ●●●◐○
Jasmine ●●●○○
Jewel Cocktail ●●●○○
Jockey Club ●●●●○
John Collins ●●●●○
The Journalist ●●●●○
Jubilant ●●●●◐
Julep ●●●●●
Jupiter Martini ●●●◐○
Kee-Wee Martini ●●●●○
Knickerbocker Martini ●●●◐○
Knockout Martini ●●●●○
L.A. Iced Tea ●●●◐○
L'Amour en Fuite ●●●●○
The Last Word ●●●●◐
Leap Year Martini ●●●○○
Leave It To Me Martini ●●●●○
Left Bank ●●●●◐
Lemony ●●●●○
Liquorice Martini ●●●◐○
Livingstone ●●●●○
London Calling ●●●◐○
London Cocktail ●●●○○
London Fog ●●●○○
Long Beach Iced Tea ●●●◐○
Long Island Iced Tea ●●●◐○
Long Island Spiced Tea ●●●◐○
Lotus Martini ●●●●○
Loud Speaker Martini ●●●◐○
Lucien Gaudin ●●●●○
Lutkins Special Martini ●●●◐○
Luxury Cocktail ●●●◐○
Lychee & Blackcurrant Martini ●●●●○
Lychee & Rose Petel Martini ●●●●○
Lychee & Sake Martini ●●●●○
Lychee Rickey ●●●◐○
Macka ●●●◐○
Maiden's Blush ●●●●◐
Maiden's Prayer ●●●◐○
Mainbrace ●●●●○
Major Bailey #1 ●●●●◐
Mandarine Collins ●●●○○
Mango Collins ●●●●○
Marguerite Martini ●●●●○
Marmalade Cocktail ●●●●◐
Marny Cocktail ●●●●◐
Martinez ●●●●●
Martini Special ●●●●◐
Martini Thyme ●●●●○
Mary Rose #1 ●●●●○
Marie Rose #2 ●●●●○
Maurice Martini ●●●◐○
Mayfair Cocktail ●●●●○
The Mayflower Martini ●●●◐○
M.C. Martini ●●●●●
Medium Martini ●●●●◐
Merry Widow #1 ●●●◐○
Merry-Go-Round Martini ●●●●○
Miami Beach ●●●●○
Milano Sour ●●●●○
The Million Dollar Cocktail ●●●●◐
Milly Martini ●●●●○
Mint Cocktail ●●●●◐
Mint Collins ●●●●○
Modernista ●●●●○
Monarch Martini ●●●●○
Monkey Gland #2 ●●●●○
Monte Carlo Imperial ●●●○○
Mood Indigo ●●●●○
Moon River ●●●◐○
Moonlight Martini ●●●●○
Moonshine Martini ●●●●◐
Mujer Verde ●●●●○
Mule's Hind Leg ●●●●◐
Napoleon Martini ●●●●◐
Navigator ●●●●○
Negroni ●●●●◐
Nicky's Fizz ●●●◐○
Nightmare Martini ●●●○○
Nome ●●●●○
Noon ●●●●○
North Pole Martini ●●●●○
Obituary ●●●●○
Old Flame ●●●●○
Onion Ring Martini ●●●○○
Opal ●●●●◐
Opera ●●●●○
Orange Bloom Martini ●●●●◐
Orange Blossom ●●●◐○
Orange Martini ●●●●○
Oriental Tart ●●●●○
Paisley Martini ●●●●○
Pall Mall Martini ●●●●○
Palm Beach ●●●◐○
Pancho Villa ●●●●○
Paradise #1 ●●●◐○
Paradise #2 ●●●●◐
Paradise #3 ●●●◐○
Parisian Martini #1 ●●●●○
Park Avenue ●●●●○
Park Lane ●●●●○
Parma Negroni ●●●●○
Passion Fruit Collins ●●●●○
Passion Fruit Martini #3 ●●●●○
Passion Punch ●●●◐○
Peggy Martini ●●●○○
Pegu Club ●●●●○
Pendennis Cocktail ●●●●○
Perfect Lady ●●●●○
Perfect Martini ●●●◐○
Periscope ●●●●●
Peter Pan Cocktail ●●●○○
Peter Pan Martini ●●●●○
Peto Martini ●●●●◐
Piccadilly Martini ●●●●◐
Pimm's Cocktail ●●●●◐
Pink Gin #1 ●●●●○ (Traditional)
Pink Gin #2 ●●●●○ (Modern)
Pink Gin & Tonic ●●●●○
Pink Hound ●●●●○
Pink Lady ●●●●◐
Pink Palace ●●●●◐
Poet's Dream ●●●●◐
Pogo Stick ●●●●○
Princess Marina ●●●●○
Princess Mary ●●●◐○
Princeton ●●●●○
Princeton Martini ●●●●○
Pruneaux ●●●●○
The Puritan ●●●●●
Queen Martini ●●●●○
Ramos Gin Fizz ●●●●●
Raspberry Collins ●●●●○
Raspberry Martini #2 ●●●●○
Red Lion #1 ●●●●◐ (Modern Formula)
Red Lion #2 ●●●●◐ (Embury's Formula)
Red Snapper ●●●●○
Resolute ●●●●○
Rhubarb & Custard Martini ●●●●○
Rhubarb & Lemongrass Martini ●●●●○
Rickey (Gin Rickey) ●●●●○
Rizzo ●●●●○
Roe-A-Coe ●●●◐○
The Rose #2 ●●●◐○
Rose Petalini ●●●●○
Roselyn Martini ●●●●◐
Royal Smile ●●●●○
Rumba ●●●●○
Russian ●●●◐○
Saigon Cooler ●●●◐○
Saigon Sling ●●●◐○
Sake-tini #1 ●●●●○
Sandstorm ●●●●○
Satan's Whiskers (Straight) ●●●●◐
Satan's Whiskers ●●●◐○
Savannah ●●●◐○
Savoy Special #1 ●●●●○
Sensation ●●●●○
Serendipity #1 ●●●●○
Settle Petal ●●●●○
Seventh Heaven #2 ●●●●◐
The 75 ●●●●◐
Shady Grove Cooler ●●●◐○
Sicilian Negroni ●●●●○
Silver Bullet Martini ●●●●○
Silver Fizz ●●●●○
Silver Martini ●●●◐○
Singapore Sling #1 ●●●◐○ (Baker's formula)
Singapore Sling #2 ●●●●○
Singapore Sling #3 ●●●◐○
Sleepy Hollow ●●●●○
Sling ●●●●○
Sloe Gin Fizz ●●●◐○
Smoky Martini #1 ●●●●○
Smoky Martini #2 ●●●○○
Snyder Martini ●●●●○
So-So Martini ●●●●●
Sour ●●●◐○
South Pacific Breeze ●●●◐○
Southern Tea-Knee ●●●●◐
Southside Royal ●●●●○
Spencer Cocktail ●●●●○
Spicy Veggy ●●●◐○
Stanley Cocktail ●●●●○
S Tea G ●●●◐○
Stork Club ●●●●○
Straits Sling ●●●●○
Swizzle ●●●●◐
Tango Martini #1 ●●●●○
Tango Martini #2 ●●●●○
Tex Collins ●●●◐○
Thai Lady ●●●●○
Thriller From Vanilla ●●●●○
Tipperary #2 ●●●●◐
Tokyo Iced Tea ●●●◐○
Tokyo Tea ●●●●○
Tom Collins ●●●●○
Turf Martini ●●●●○
Tuxedo Martini ●●●●◐
Twentieth Century Martini ●●●◐○
Typhoon ●●●○○
Valentino Martini ●●●●○
Vancouver ●●●◐○
Venus Martini ●●●●○
The Vesper Martini ●●●●●
Victorian Lemonade ●●●◐○
Waltzing Matilda ●●●●○
Watermelon & Basil Martini ●●●●○
Webster Martini ●●●◐○
Wet Martini ●●●●◐
The Wet Spot ●●●●○
What The Hell ●●●●○
White Gin Fizz ●●●◐○
White Lady ●●●●○
Wibble ●●●●◐
Wink ●●●●○
Za-Za ●●●●○

PLYMOUTH SLOE GIN LIQUEUR

26% **alc./vol.** (52°proof)
www.plymouthgin.com
Producer: Coates & Co Ltd, Plymouth.

The making of fruit liqueurs is a long tradition in the British countryside and Plymouth Gin stays true to a unique 1883 recipe. The sloe berries are slowly and gently steeped in high strength Plymouth Gin, soft Dartmoor water and a further secret ingredient. It is an unhurried process and the drink is bottled only when the Head Distiller decides the perfect flavour has been reached. The result is an entirely natural product with no added flavouring or colouring.

This richly flavoured liqueur is initially dry but opens with smooth, sweet, lightly jammy, juicy cherry and raspberry notes alongside a complimentary mixture of figs, cloves, set honey and stewed fruits. The finish has strong almond notes.

Alabama Slammer #2 ●●●◐○
Blackthorn English ●●●●○
Charlie Chaplin ●●●○○
Alabama Slammer #2 ●●●○○
Blackthorn English ●●●●○
Charlie Chaplin ●●●◐○
Gin Genie ●●●●○
Grape Delight ●●●●○
Hedgerow Sling ●●●◐○
London Calling ●●●◐○
Millionaire's Daiquiri ●●●◐○
Purple Turtle ●●●◐○
Red Rum Martini ●●●●◐
Sailor's Comfort ●●●○○
Sloe Gin Fizz ●●●◐○
Sloe Martini ●●●◐○
Sloe Tequila ●●●◐○
Slow Screw ●●●○○
Slow Comfortable Screw ●●●◐○
Slow Comfortable Screw Against the Wall ●●●◐○
Smoky Martini #2 ●●●○○
Stupid Cupid ●●●○○
Summer Time Martini ●●●◐○
Wibble ●●●●◐

POIRE WILLIAM EAU-DE-VIE

Eau-de-vie means 'water of life' and is the French term for brandies made from a fruit other than grapes. Produced in France, Germany, Yugoslavia and Scandinavia, these 'fruit brandies' are clear and colourless and generally sold at 40 - 45% alc. /vol.
Piore William is a particular variety of pear favoured by distillers for making eau-de-vie.

Asian Pear Martini ●●●●○
Escalator Martini ●●●●●
Guillotine ●●●◐○
Japanese Pear ●●●●○
Nice Pear-tini ●●●●◐
Pear Drop Martini ●●●●○
Perry-tini ●●●●○
Prickly Pear Mule ●●●●○
Purple Pear Martini ●●●●○
Sparkling Perry ●●●●○
Twisted Sobriety ●●●●○

POMEGRANATE (GRENADINE) SYRUP

Originally grenadine was syrup flavoured with pomegranate. Sadly, most of today's commercially available grenadine syrups are flavoured with red berries and cherry juice. They may be blood red but they don't taste of pomegranate. Hunt out one of the few genuine commercially made pomegranate syrups or make your own.
1. Simple: Gradually pour and stir two cups of granulated sugar into a saucepan containing one cup of pomegrate juice and gently warm until the sugar is dissolved (do not let the juice even simmer!). Consider adding half a split vanilla pod for extra flavour. Allow syrup to cool and fine strain into an empty bottle. If kept in a refrigerator this mixture will last for a week or so (please be aware of the use-by date of your pomegranate juice).
2. Messy: Separate the seed cells from the outer membranes and skin of eight pomegranates. Simmer these in a saucepan with 25ml/1oz of sugar syrup and ? of a vanilla pod for each pomegranate for at least an hour. Allow to cool, strain through a cheesecloth-layered sieve and store in a refrigerator.

Ace ●●●◐○
Alabama Slammer #1 ●●●○○
Amercian Beauty #1 ●●●●◐
American Beauty #2 ●●●●○
Apricot Martini ●●●○○
Armillita Chico ●●●●○
Asylum Cocktail ●●●○○
Aunt Emily ●●●●○
Avenue ●●●◐○
Bacardi Cocktail ●●●●◐
Bermuda Cocktail ●●●●○
Bermuda Rose Cocktail ●●●●○
Blinker ●●●●○
Bora Bora Brew (Mocktail) ●●●○○
Bosom Caresser ●●●●○
Boston ●●●◐○
Bourbonella ●●●●○
Caribbean Cruise ●●●◐○
Caribbean Punch ●●●●○
Champagne Daisy ●●●○○
Cinderella (Mocktail) ●●◐○○
Clipper Cocktail ●●●◐○
Clover Leaf Cocktail #1 ●●●●○ (Classic Formula)
Clover Leaf Cocktail #2 ●●●◐○ (Modern Formula)
Commodore #1 ●●●●○
Commodore #2 ●●●○○
Cosmopolitan #4 ●●●●○ (1934 recipe)
Covadonga ●●●○○
Cranberry & Mint Martini ●●●◐○
The Crow Cocktail ●●●○○
Cuban Cocktail No. 2 #1 ●●●◐○
Daiquiri No. 5 ●●●●○
Daisy Duke ●●●◐○
Dempsey ●●●◐○
Depth Bomb ●●●◐○
Dingo ●●●○○
Doctor Funk ●●●◐○
Dulchin ●●●●◐
East India #1 ●●●●◐
El Presidente No. 1 (Daiquiri) #1 ●●●●◐
El Presidente #3 ●●●○○
English Rose ●●●●○
Fairbanks Cocktail No. 1 ●●●○○
Feather Dusta Crusta ●●●●○
La Feuille Morte ●●●◐○
Fiesta ●●●●○
Flaming Ferrari ●●○○○
Flamingo #2 ●●●◐○
Florida Sling ●●●○○
El Floridita Daiquiri No. 2 ●●●◐○
Flying Tigre Coctel ●●●●○
Fosbury Flip ●●●●◐
Fourth Of July Cocktail ●●●○○
French Kiss #1 ●●●○○
Frida's Brow ●●●●○
Froth Blower Cocktail ●●●●◐
Fruit Salad ●●●○○
Gin & Sin ●●●◐○
Gin Daisy ●●●●○
Gloom Chaser Cocktail #1 ●●●●○
Gloom Chaser Cocktail #2 ●●●◐○
Gloom Lifter ●●●●○
Grapefruit Julep ●●●●◐
Gun Club Punch No. 1 ●●●●◐
Hobson's Choice ●●◐○○ (Mocktail)
Honolulu ●●●◐○
Huapala Cocktail ●●●●○
Hurricane #2 ●●●○○
Jack Frost ●●●◐○
Jack Rose ●●●●○
Jambalaya ●●●◐○
Kava ●●●●○
Kretchma ●●●◐○
Leave It To Me Martini ●●●●○
Lime Blush (Mocktail) ●●●○○
Liminal Shot ●●●○○
Lotus Martini ●●●●○
Maiden's Blush ●●●●◐
Mary Pickford ●●●●●
Mexican ●●●●○
The Million Dollar Cocktail ●●●●◐
Millionaire ●●●●○
Millionaire's Daiquiri ●●●◐○
Monkey Gland #1 ●●●●○
Monkey Gland #2 ●●●●○
Monk's Habit ●●●○○
Opening Shot ●●●◐○
Orang-A-Tang ●●●●○
Orange Blossom ●●●◐○
Park Lane ●●●●◐
Piccadilly Martini ●●●●◐
Pink Cloud ●●●○○
Pink Daiquiri ●●●●○
Pink Lady ●●●●◐
Pink Lemonade ●●●●○ (Mocktail)
Pink Palace ●●●●◐
Pirate Daiquiri ●●●●○
Planter's Punchless ●●●○○ (Mocktail)
Planteur ●●●●○
Pomegranate Margarita ●●●●◐
Port & Starboard ●●◐○○
Port Light ●●●◐○
Pousse-café ●●◐○○
President ●●●●○
Presidente ●●●●○
Purple Flirt #2 ●●●○○
Pussyfoot ●●●●◐ (Mocktail)
Raspberry Watkins ●●●○○
Red Lion #1 ●●●●◐ (Modern Formula)
Red Lion #2 ●●●●◐ (Embury's Formula)
Reef Juice ●●●●○
Reggae Rum Punch ●●●●◐
Rizzo ●●●●○
The Rose #1 (original) ●●●●◐
The Rose #3 ●●●●◐
Roselyn Martini ●●●●◐
Roy Rogers ●●◐○○ (Mocktail)
Royal Smile ●●●●○
Rumba ●●●●○
Rum Runner ●●●●○
St Kitts ●●●●○ (Mocktail)
San Francisco ●●●◐○
Sangrita ●●●●○
Santiago Daiquiri ●●●●●
Savoy Special #1 ●●●●○
Scofflaw ●●●●○
Scotch Bounty Martini ●●●◐○
The 75 ●●●●◐
Shark Bite ●●●◐○
Shirley Temple ●●●○○ (Mocktail)
Silk Stockings ●●●◐○
Singapore Sling #3 ●●●◐○
Slippery Nipple ●●◐○○
Sloppy Joe ●●●●○
Solent Sunset ●●●●○
So-So Martini ●●●●●
Southern Punch ●●●◐○
Squashed Frog ●●●○○
Stanley Cocktail ●●●●○
Summer Rose Martini ●●●●○
Summer Time Martini ●●●◐○
Sunshine Cocktail #1 ●●●●◐
Sweet Louise ●●●○○
Tequila Sunrise ●●●◐○
Three Miler ●●●●○
Tipperary #2 ●●●●◐
Tomate ●●●○○
Tonga ●●●●○
Tongue Twister ●●●○○
Tropical Daiquiri ●●●●◐
Union Club ●●●●○
Vampiro ●●●●○
Wagon Wheel ●●●○○
Ward Eight ●●●●○
Washington Apple ●●●●◐
Watermelon Man ●●●○○
Weeping Jesus ●●●◐○
Whiskey Daisy ●●●◐○
White Lion ●●●●○
Zombie #2 ●●●◐○ (Vic's formula)
Zombie #3 ●●●●○ (Modern formula)

PORT (PORTO)

Port, or to give it its full name 'vinho do porto', is a Portuguese wine from the area known as the Upper Douro which starts 45 miles from the coast at the town of Oporto and stretches east to the Spanish border. The young wine is fortified with grape brandy, which stops fermentation before it is complete by raising the alcoholic strength beyond that at which the fermenting yeasts can survive. This produces wines with residual sugars, giving port its inherently sweet style.

American Beauty #2 ●●●●○
Angel's Share #2 ●●●●◐
Basil Mary ●●●●○
Bishop ●●●●○
Bloody Joseph ●●●◐○
Bloody Maria ●●●●○
Bloody Mary (Modern Receipe) ●●●●◐
Chancellor ●●●●○
Chatham Hotel Special ●●●●○
Chocolate Sidecar ●●●●○
Club Cocktail #1 ●●●●○
Devil's Cocktail ●●●◐○
Free Town ●●●●○
Golden Girl ●●●●○
Happy New Year ●●●○○
Havanna Cobbler ●●●●○
Mulled Wine ●●●●○
Negus ●●●●○ (Hot)
Port (Tawny)
Port & Melon Martini ●●●●◐
Port Wine Cocktail ●●●◐○
Princeton ●●●●○
Randy ●●●●○
Red Snapper ●●●●○
Sir Charles Punch ●●●●○
Suburban ●●●●○
Tawny-Tini ●●●●○
Tokyo Bloody Mary ●●●●○
Z Martini ●●●●●

PROSECCO SPARKLING WINE

Prosecco is a wine produced around the towns of Conegliano and Valdobbiadene in the Italian province of Treviso. It can be still, semi-sparkling or sparkling, dry, off-dry or sweet. The style called for in this guide, and the preferred style for export, is dry and sparkling. 'Frizzante' means 'semi-sparkling' and 'spumante' means 'sparkling'.
The better wines from hillside vineyards are labelled 'Prosecco di Conegliano-Valdobbiadene'. The best are 'Prosecco Superiore di Cartizze' from the great hill of Cartizze in the Valdobbiadene sub-region.

Bellini #1 (original) ●●●●○
Bellini #2 (Difford's Formula) ●●●●○
Hot Tub ●●●●○
Kiwi Bellini ●●●●○
Pomegranate Bellini ●●●◐○
Puccini ●●●◐○
Rhubarb & Honey Bellini ●●●●○
Rossini ●●●●○
Sgroppino ●●●●◐
Tiziano ●●●◐○
Twinkle ●●●●◐

PUREES

Fruit purees are made from fresh fruit which has been chopped up and liquidised. When making your own puree add roughly 5-10% sugar syrup depending on the fruit's ripeness. Commercial purees contain differing amounts of sugar and so you may have to adjust the balance of your drink.

PUSSER'S NAVY RUM

47.75% **alc./vol.**

(95.5°proof)
www.pussers.com
Producer: Pusser's Rum Limited, Tortola, British Virgin Islands.

The name 'Pusser' is slang in the Royal Navy for purser, the officer with responsibility for the issue of rum on board ship. For more than 300 years the British Navy issued a daily 'tot' of Pusser's rum, with a double issue before battle. This tradition, which started in Jamaica in 1665, was finally broken on 31st July 1970, a day now known as 'Black Tot Day'.
In 1979 the Admiralty approved the re-blending of Pusser's rum to the original specifications by Charles Tobias in the British Virgin Islands. A significant donation from the sale of each bottle accrues to the benefit of The Royal Navy Sailor's Fund, a naval charity established to compensate sailors for their lost tot.
In our opinion, this is the best Navy rum, delivering a rich medley of flavours: molasses, treacle, vanilla, cinnamon, nutmeg, sticky toffee pudding, espresso and creamy tiramisu with subtle hints of oak.

Alexandra ●●●◐○
All Fall Down ●●●◐○
Aunt Agatha ●●●◐○
Bahama Mama ●●●●○
Baltimore Egg Nog ●●●○○
Bee's Knees ●●●●○ #1
Boston Tea Party ●●●○○
Caribbean Breeze ●●●●○
Charles Daiquiri ●●●●◐
Dark Daiquiri ●●●●◐
Fat Sailor ●●●●○
Flaming Ferrari ●●○○○
Grog ●●●●○
Gun Club Punch No. 1 ●●●●◐
Hot Grog ●●●●○
Hurricane #1 ●●●●○
Kamaniwanalaya ●●●◐○
Navy Grog ●●●●○
Nevada Daiquiri ●●●●○
Painkiller ●●●●○
Pirate Daiquiri ●●●●○
Red Rover ●●●●○
Reef Juice ●●●●○
Rum Runner ●●●●○
Shark Bite ●●●◐○
Solent Sunset ●●●●○
Spiced Cranberry Martini ●●●●○
Tiki Max ●●●●○
Zombie #3 ●●●●○ (Modern formula)

RASPBERRIES & BLACKBERRIES

Both these berries grow on brambly bushes and are related to the rose. Both can be cultivated in a wide range of colours, from white or yellow to orange, pink or purple, as well as the more common red and black, and that's before we get to their family tree. The loganberry is a cross between a blackberry and a raspberry and is named after its Californian creator, James H Logan. Other later hybrids of the two fruits include the tayberry (named after the Scottish river) and the boysenberry (named after its creator). The juice of both raspberries and blackberries is intense and a little goes a long way. This is just as well because there's precious little juice in each berry and you'll find putting them through an electric juicer a complete waste of time. Instead, either blend them into a puree or (as I do) muddle the fruits in the base of your shaker or in the glass. Recipes in this guide state how many fruits you should muddle for each drink.

Apple & Blackberry Pie ●●●◐○
Berry Caipirinha ●●●●○
Berry Nice ●●●◐○
Black & White Daiquiri ●●●●◐
Black 'N' Blue Caipirovska ●●●●○
Blimey ●●●◐○
Bling! Bling! ●●●●◐
Blood Orange ●●●●○
Bourbon Smash ●●●◐○
Brazilian Berry ●●●●○
Cascade Martini ●●●●○
Clover Leaf Cocktail #2 ●●●◐○ (Modern Formula)
Cobbled Raspberry Martini ●●●●○
Eclipse ●●●●◐
Especial Day ●●●●◐
Estes ●●●●○
Finn Rouge ●●●◐○
First Of July ●●●●○
Forbidden Fruits ●●●●○
Miss Martini ●●●◐○
Mrs Robinson #1 ●●●●○
Pernod & Black Martini ●●●●○
Raspberry Caipirinha ●●●●○
Raspberry Collins ●●●●○
Raspberry Debonair ●●●◐○
Raspberry Margarita ●●●●○
Raspberry Martini #1 ●●●●○
Raspberry Martini #2 ●●●●○
Raspberry Mule ●●●●○
The Red Army ●●●◐○
Saigon Cooler ●●●◐○

Serendipity #1 ●●●●○
Tartini ●●●●○
Tennessee Berry Mule ●●●●○

Trifle'tini ●●●◐○
Tripleberry ●●●●○
Vanilla & Raspberry Martini ●●●●○
Venus Martini ●●●●○
Wild Promenade Martini ●●●●○

RASPBERRY (CRÈME DE FRAMBOISE) LIQUEUR

See 'Giffard Crème de Framboise Liqueur'

REMY MARTIN V.S.O.P COGNAC

40% **alc./vol.** (80°proof)
www.remy.com
Producer: Rémy Martin & Co SA, Cognac, France

When Rémy Martin founded his company in 1724 he was already an experienced producer of cognac and he set out to make the Cognacs that carried his name amongst the finest. This tradition is still pursued at Rémy Martin with all the company's blends being made exclusively from Fine Champagne Cognacs using grapes only from the two premiers crus, Grande and Petite Champagne. The wine is double distilled on the lees in small stills and aged in small oak casks from the nearby Limousin forest.

Rémy Martin V.S.O.P. is a blend of 45% Petite Champagne and 55% Grande Champagne is also the world's best selling V.S.O.P.

Rémy Martin V.S.O.P. is an ideal cognac to use in cocktails due to its rich, ripe, fruit and vanilla with tasting notes including fruitcake and stewed fruit.

A.B.C. ●●●◐○
Adios Amigos Cocktail ●●●◐○
Ambrosia ●●●●○
Ambrosia'tini Ambrosia Cocktial ●●●◐○
Ambrosia'tini Ambrosia Cocktial ●●●◐○
American Beauty #1 ●●●●◐
American Beauty #2 ●●●●○
Angel's Share #2 ●●●●◐
Apple of One's Eye ●●●◐○
April Shower ●●●●○
Atomic Cocktail ●●●○○
Auntie's Hot Xmas Punch ●●●●○
B2C2 ●●●◐○
B & B ●●●●○
Baltimore Egg Nog ●●●○○
Banana Bliss ●●●◐○
BBC ●●●◐○
Between the Sheets ●●●◐○ #1 (Classic Formula)
Between the Sheets ●●●●◐ #2 (Difford's Formula)
Biarritz ●●●◐○
The Bistro Sidecar ●●●●○
Black Feather ●●●●○
Blue Angel ●●◐○○
Bolero Sour ●●●●●
Bombay No. 2 ●●●●◐
Bonnie Prince Charles ●●●●○
Bosom Caresser ●●●●○
Brandy Alexander ●●●●○
Brandy Blazer ●●●◐○
Brandy Buck ●●●◐○
Brandy Crusta ●●●●◐
Brandy Fix ●●●●◐
Brandy Fizz ●●●●○
Brandy Flip ●●●●◐
Brandy Milk Punch ●●●◐○
Brandy Smash ●●●●○
Brandy Sour ●●●●◐
Brighton Punch ●●●●◐
Bull's Blood ●●●◐○
Bull's Milk ●●●◐○
Call Me Old-Fashioned ●●●●◐
Carrol Cocktail ●●●◐○
Champagne Cocktail ●●●○○
Champagne Cup ●●●◐○
Champus-Elysées ●●●●◐
Chatham Hotel Special ●●●●○
Chocolate Biscuit ●●●◐○
Chocolate Sidecar ●●●●○
Claret Cobbler ●●●●○
Classic Cocktail ●●●●●
Clockwork Orange ●●●○○
The Comet ●●●●◐
Corpse Reviver No. 1 #1 ●●●◐○
Cosmopolitan Delight ●●●●◐
Crux ●●●●○
Cuban Cocktail No. 3 #2 ●●●●○
Cuban Master ●●●○○
Deauville #1 ●●●●○
Deauville #2 ●●●◐○
Delmonico ●●●●○
Delmonico Special ●●●◐○
Delores ●●●◐○
Depth Bomb ●●●◐○
Don Juan ●●●◐○
Dr Zeus ●●●●◐
Dream Cocktail ●●●●○
East India #1 ●●●●◐
East India #2 ●●●●○
East India House ●●●●○
Egg Nog #1 ●●●○○ (Cold)
Egg Nog #2 ●●●●○ (Hot)
Embassy Cocktail ●●●○○
Encantado ●●●●○
Enchanted ●●●◐○
Fallen Leaves ●●●●○
Fancy Brandy ●●●◐○
Fish House Punch #1 ●●●●○
Fish House Punch #2 ●●●●○
Fizz ●●●●○
Flip ●●●●◐
Fog Cutter #1 ●●●●○
Fog Cutter #2 ●●●●○
Fontainebleau Special ●●●◐○
Frank Sullivan Cocktail ●●●○○
French Daisy ●●●◐○
French Mule ●●●●○
French Spring Punch ●●●●○
Froupe Cocktail ●●●●○
Gloom Lifter ●●●●○
Godfrey ●●●●○
Gold Medallion ●●●◐○
Golden Screw ●●●◐○
La Grand Feu ●●●○○
Grande Champagne Cosmo ●●●●○
Grape Escape ●●●●◐
Happy New Year ●●●○○
Harvard ●●●◐○
Hazelnut Alexander ●●●●○
Hoopla ●●●●○
Hot Rum Punch ●●●◐○
Hot Toddy #3 ●●●◐○
Hulk ●●◐○○
Iced Tea ●●●◐○
In-Seine ●●●●●
Incognito ●●●◐○
Irish Alexander ●●●◐○
Japanese Cocktail ●●●●○
Julep ●●●●●
Juliette ●●●○○
Jungle Fire Sling ●●●○○
K.G.B. ●●◐○○
Lazarus ●●●●◐
Loud Speaker Martini ●●●◐○
Mandarine Sidecar ●●●●○
Manhattan Island ●●●●○
Maxim's Coffee ●●●●○ (Hot)
Metropole ●●●◐○
Milk Punch ●●●●○
Mississippi Punch ●●●●○
Mood Indigo ●●●●○
Moonraker ●●●●○
Morning Glory ●●●●○
Nathalia ●●●◐○
Nice Pear-tini ●●●●◐
Nicky Finn ●●●●○
Ole ●●●◐○
Olympic ●●●●◐
Orange Brûlée ●●●●●
Parisian Sidecar ●●●●◐
Passion Punch ●●●◐○
Pear & Cardamom Sidecar ●●●●◐
Pierre Collins ●●●●○
Pini ●●●●◐
Playmate Martini ●●●●◐
Ponce de Leon ●●●●○
Port Wine Cocktail ●●●◐○
Prairie Oyster ●●●◐○
Prince Charlie ●●●●○
Prince Of Wales ●●●◐○
Pulp Fiction ●●●●○
Quelle Vie ●●●◐○
Randy ●●●●○
Red Marauder ●●●●◐
The Ritz Cocktail ●●●●○
The Roffignac ●●●●○
Roman Punch ●●●●○
Ruby Martini #2 ●●●◐○
St. Germain Sidecar ●●●●◐
La Sang ●●●●○
Sangaree ●●●●○
Sangria ●●●◐○
Sangria Martini ●●●●○
Sazerac ●●●●●
Scorched Earth ●●●◐○
Scorpion ●●●●○
Sidecar #1 ●●●●◐ (Equal parts classic formula)
Sidecar #2 ●●●●● (Difford's formula)
Sidecar #3 ●●●◐○ (Embury's formula)
Silver Fizz ●●●●○
Sir Charles Punch ●●●●○
Sour ●●●◐○
Soyer Au Champagne ●●●◐○
Spiked Apple Cider (Hot) ●●●●○
Sputnik #2 ●●●●○
Stinger ●●●●○
Sundowner #1 ●●●●○
Swizzle ●●●●◐
Three Miler ●●●●○
Tiger's Milk ●●●◐○
Tiramisu Martini ●●●●○
Tom & Jerry ●●●○○
Tonga ●●●◐○
Trifle'tini ●●●◐○
Twisted Sobriety ●●●●○
Vanderbilt ●●●●◐
Veneto ●●●◐○
Vieux Carré Cocktail ●●●●◐
Wagon Wheel ●●●○○
Whiskey Cobbler ●●●○○
Winter Martini ●●●●◐
Zabaglione Martini ●●●◐○
The Zamboanga 'Zeinie' Cocktail ●●●●○
Zeus Martini ●●●●◐
Zoom ●●●●◐

RICARD PASTIS

45% **alc./vol.** (90°proof)
Producer: Pernod (Group Pernod Ricard), Créteil, France.

A French classic, this liquorice based spirit is Europe's number one selling spirit brand and the third biggest brand worldwide. Created by Paul Ricard in Marseille in 1932, it is now produced in Bessan, Southern France. The unique flavour of this pastis derives from liquorice root, green anise, fennel and seven different aromatic herbs from Provence.
It is anethole, made from fennel and green anise, which produces Ricard's most distinctive effect: it turns milky on contact with water or ice.
Traditionally served over ice diluted with five parts of water, Ricard adds a rich aniseed flavour and distinctive cloudy appearance to a number of classic and modern cocktails. Besides the predominant aniseed, its dry palate features fennel, soft liquorice and a delicious minty lemon freshness.

Canarie ●●●◐○
Dempsey ●●●◐○
La Feuille Morte ●●●◐○
Liquorice Whiskey Sour ●●●●◐
La Momje ●●●○○
Momisette ●●●●○
Perroquet ●●●○○
Riviera Breeze ●●●◐○
Tomate ●●●○○

RUM

Rum is a spirit made from sugar cane or its by-products. The recipes in this guide call for a number of styles of rum, as explained below.

RUM - AGED (AÑEJO)

Like other distillates, rum is clear when it condenses after distillation. The fact that ageing in oak barrels improved the raw rum was discovered when ships carried rum on the long passage to Europe: it arrived darker in colour and with an enhanced flavour. Today, rum is aged in barrels from France or the United States which have previously been used to age cognac, bourbon or whiskey. They may be charred or scraped clean to remove any previous charring before receiving the rum: the treatment of the barrels is reflected in the character they impart to the finished rum.

Aged Honey Daiquiri ●●●●●
Bahama Mama ●●●●○
Bolero Sour ●●●●●
Brass Rail ●●●●○
Castro ●●●◐○
Cool Orchard ●●●●○
Daiquiri No. 1 #1 ●●●●● (Classic Formula)
Daiquiri No. 1 #2 ●●●●● (Modern Formula)
Daiquiri No. 1 #3 ●●●●● (Difford's Lux Formula)
Daiquiri Elixir No. 1 ●●●●●
Daiquiri On The Rocks ●●●●●
Dark Daiquiri ●●●●◐
Difford's Daiquiri ●●●●●
Dirty Banana ●●●●○
Doctor ●●●●◐
Dolores ●●●●○
Downhill Racer ●●●●○
East India House ●●●●○
Fat Tire ●●●●○
Flamingo #2 ●●●◐○
Fosbury Flip ●●●●◐
Gansevoort Fizz ●●●◐○
Golden Girl ●●●●○
Grape Martini ●●●●○
Green Horn ●●●◐○
Honey Wall ●●●●○
Hop Toad #2 ●●●●○
Jean Lafitte Cocktail ●●◐○○
Luxury Mojito ●●●●○
Mai Tai #3 ●●●●● (Difford's Formula)
Mother Rum ●●●●◐
Mulata Daiquiri ●●●●◐
Nathalia ●●●◐○
New Orleans Punch ●●●◐○
Orange Daiquiri #1 ●●●●◐
Piña Colada #2 ●●●●○ (Cuban Style)
Platinum Blonde ●●●◐○
Queen's Park Swizzle ●●●●○
Red Rum Martini ●●●●◐
Rum & Raisin Alexandra ●●●●○
Rum Sour ●●●●○
Suburban ●●●●○
Test Pilot ●●●●○
Tonga ●●●◐○
Voodoo ●●●●○
Georgetown Punch ●●●●○
Honolulu Juicer ●●●◐○
Hurricane #2 ●●●○○
Hurricane #3 ●●●○○
Iced Tea ●●●◐○
Jean Gabin ●●●●○
Jungle Bird ●●●●○
Milk Punch ●●●●○
Modernista ●●●●○
Purple Flirt #2 ●●●○○
Tropical Daiquiri ●●●●◐
Zanzibar ●●●◐○

RUM - BERMUDAN DARK

A few recipes in this guide require the use of Bermudan rum, a distinctive dark blend. The best know brand is Goslings Black Seal.

Bella Donna Daiquiri ●●●●○
Bermuda Rum Swizzle ●●●◐○
Bull's Milk ●●●◐○
Bella Donna Daiquiri ●●●●◐
Bermuda Rum Swizzle ●●●◐○
Blade Runner ●●●●○
Bull's Milk ●●●◐○
Dark 'N' Stormy ●●●●○
Dino Sour ●●●●◐
Doctor Funk ●●●◐○

RUM - GOLDEN

An amber coloured rum aged in wood and often coloured with caramel.

Abacaxi Ricaço ●●●●○
Acapulco ●●●◐○
Ace of Clubs Daiquiri ●●●●◐
Air Mail ●●●●◐
Bajan Daiquiri ●●●●○
Bajan Mojito ●●●◐○
Bajan Passion ●●●●○
Banana Colada ●●●●○
Bossa Nova #1 ●●●●○
Bossa Nova #2 ●●●◐○
Butterscotch Martini ●●●●○
Chocolate Puff ●●●●○
Club Cocktail #3 ●●●●○
Columbus Daiquiri ●●●●○
Commodore #1 ●●●●○
Crème de Café ●●●◐○
Cuban Cocktail No. 3 #2 ●●●●○
Fat Sailor ●●●●○
Fish House Punch #1 ●●●●○
Four W Daiquiri ●●●●○
Funky Monkey ●●●●○
Ginger Punch ●●●◐○
Hawaiian Eye ●●●◐○
Heavens Above ●●●◐○
Hot Buttered Rum ●●●●○
Hot Rum Punch ●●●◐○
Kava ●●●●○
Lola ●●●◐○
The MacKinnon ●●●●○
Monkey Shine ●●●●○
Monkey Wrench ●●●◐○
Neal's Caribbean Cosmo ●●●●○
Pago Pago ●●●◐○
Palm Springs ●●●◐○
Pilgrim Cocktail ●●●●○
Piña Colada #1 ●●●●◐
Pineapple Fizz ●●●●●
Ponce de Leon ●●●●○
P.S. I Love You ●●●●○
Royal Bermuda Yacht Club Daiquiri ●●●●○
Smooth & Creamy'tini ●●●●○
Tom & Jerry ●●●○○
Total Recall ●●●◐○
Yacht Club ●●●◐○
Yellow Bird ●●●○○
Zombie #1 ●●●●○ (Intoxica! Recipe)
Zombie #3 ●●●●○ (Modern formula)

RUM - LIGHT/WHITE

Rum is termed 'light' or 'heavy', depending on the purity to which it was distilled. Essentially, the flavour of any spirit comes from 'congeners' – products of fermentation which are not ethyl alcohol. When alcohol is concentrated during distillation, the levels of congeners are reduced. The fewer congeners, the lighter the rum. The more congeners, the heavier.
The fermentation process also affects whether a rum is light or heavy. A longer, slower fermentation will result in a heavier rum.
The odour, texture and taste of light rums are more subtle and refined than those of heavy rums, which have a heavy, syrupy flavour to match their dark colour.

Light rums tend to originate from countries originally colonised by the Spanish, such as Cuba, the Dominican Republic, Puerto Rico and Venezuela.

Acapulco Daiquiri ●●●●○
Adelaide Swizzle ●●●●○
Adios Amigos Cocktail ●●●◐○
Aku Aku ●●●●◐
Alan's Apple Breeze ●●●◐○
Anita's Attitude Adjuster ●●●○○
Apple Daiquiri ●●●●○
Apple Mojito ●●●●○
Apricot Lady Sour ●●●◐○
Atlantic Breeze ●●●○○
Atomic Dog ●●●○○
Bacardi Cocktail ●●●●◐
Bahia ●●●◐○
Bajito ●●●●◐
Banana Cow ●●●○○
Banana Daiquiri ●●●◐○
Basil & Honey Daiquiri ●●●●●
Beach Iced Tea ●●●◐○
Beachcomber ●●●●○
Bee's Knees ●●●●○ #1
Between the Sheets ●●●●○ #1 (Classic Formula)
Between the Sheets ●●●●◐ #2 (Difford's Formula)
Black & White Daiquiri ●●●●◐
Black Martini ●●●●◐
Blade Runner ●●●●○
Blue Hawaiian ●●●○○
Blue Heaven ●●◐○○
Blue Passion ●●●●○
Blue Wave ●●●○○
Blueberry Daiquiri ●●●◐○
Bolero ●●●◐○
Bomber ●●●●○
Brass Monkey ●●●◐○
The Buck ●●●◐○
Bulldog ●●●◐○
Bull's Blood ●●●◐○
Butterscotch Daiquiri ●●●◐○
Caipirissima ●●●●○
Canaries ●●●○○
Canchanchara ●●●◐○
Canteen Martini ●●●◐○
Caribbean Cruise ●●●◐○
Caribbean PiÀa Colada ●●●◐○
Caribe Daiquiri ●●●●○
Casablanca ●●●●○ #1
Charles Daiquiri ●●●●◐
Cherry & Hazelnut Daiquiri ●●●●○
Che's Revolution ●●●●◐
Chiclet Daiquiri ●●●◐○
Cinnamon Daiquiri ●●●◐○
Clipper Cocktail ●●●◐○
Coconut Daiquiri ●●●●○
Cuba Libre ●●●◐○
Cuba Pintada ●●●●○
Cuban Cocktail No. 2 #1 ●●●◐○
Cuban Island ●●●◐○
Cuban Master ●●●○○
Cuban Special ●●●○○
Cubanita ●●●●○
Custard Tart ●●●●○
Daiquiri No. 1 #1 ●●●●● (Classic Formula)
Daiquiri No. 1 #2 ●●●●● (Modern Formula)
Daiquiri No. 1 #3 ●●●●● (Difford's Lux Formula)
Daiquiri No. 2 ●●●◐○
Daiquiri No. 3 ●●●●○
Daiquiri No. 5 ●●●●○
Daiquiri Elixir No. 1 ●●●●●
Daiquiri De Luxe ●●●●○
Daiquiri On The Rocks ●●●●●
Dean's Gate Martini ●●●◐○
Derby Daiquiri ●●●●◐
Derby Fizz ●●●●○
Dingo ●●●○○
Dino Sour ●●●●◐
Dolce Havana ●●●●○
Dorian Gray ●●●◐○
Doughnut Martini ●●●◐○
El Presidente No. 1 (Daiquiri) #1 ●●●●◐
El Presidente #2 ●●●◐○
El Presidente #3 ●●●○○
El Presidente #4 ●●●●○
Elderflower Daiquiri ●●●●○
Elderflower Jojito ●●●●◐
Embassy Cocktail ●●●◐○
Epestone Daiquiri ●●●●○
Especial Day ●●●●◐
Espresso Daiquiri ●●●●◐
F-16 Shot ●●●○○
F. Willy Shot ●●●◐○
Fair & Warmer Cocktail ●●●○○
Fancy Drink ●●●◐○
Fiesta ●●●●○
Fish House Punch #2 ●●●●○
Florida Daiquiri ●●●●◐
El Floridita Daiquiri No. 1 ●●●●○
El Floridita Daiquiri No. 2 ●●●◐○
Flying Tigre Coctel ●●●●○
Fog Cutter #1 ●●●●○
Fog Cutter #2 ●●●●○
Fort Lauderdale ●●●○○
Free Town ●●●●○
French Daiquiri ●●●●○
French Mojito ●●●●◐
Frozen Daiquiri ●●●●○
Fruit Tree Daiquiri ●●●●○
Fu Manchu Daiquiri ●●●●○
Gauguin ●●●○○
Georgetown Punch ●●●●○
Ginger Mojito ●●●●○
Glass Tower ●●●○○
Golden Bird ●●●◐○
Golden Retriever ●●●●◐
Golden Wave ●●●○○
Grand Passion ●●●○○
Granny's ●●●●○
Grape Effect ●●●●○
Grateful Dead ●●●◐○
Green Swizzle ●●●●○
Greta Garbo ●●●●○
Gulf Coast Sex on the Beach ●●●●○
Gun Club Punch No. 1 ●●●●◐
Havanna Cobbler ●●●●○
Havana Special ●●●●○
Havanatheone ●●●●●
Hawaiian ●●●○○
Hawaiian Cocktail ●●●●○
Hawaiian Eye ●●●◐○
Hazel'ito ●●●●◐
Hemingway Special Daiquiri ●●●●◐
Hoa Sua ●●●●○
Honey Bee ●●●●○
Honey Daiquiri ●●●●◐
Honeysuckle Daiquiri ●●●●●
Hong Kong Fuey ●●●○○
Honolulu ●●●◐○
Hop Toad #1 ●●●●○
Huapala Cocktail ●●●●○
Hummingbird ●●●○○
Hurricane #1 ●●●●○
Hurricane #2 ●●●○○
Hurricane #3 ●●●○○
Irresistible ●●◐○○
Jack Dempsey ●●●◐○
Jackie O's Rose ●●●●○
Jade Daiquiri ●●●◐○
Jayne Mansfield ●●●●○
Jelly Belly Beany ●●●●○
Joan Bennett ●●●○○
Julep ●●●●●
Jungle Juice ●●●◐○
Kamaniwanalaya ●●●◐○
Kava ●●●●○
Knickerbocker Special ●●●●○
L.A. Iced Tea ●●●◐○
Larchmont ●●●●◐
Lemon Chiffon Pie ●●●●○
Long Beach Iced Tea ●●●◐○
Long Island Iced Tea ●●●◐○
Lux Daiquiri ●●●●○
Mai Tai #2 ●●●●○
Major Bailey #2 ●●●●◐
Mango Daiquiri ●●●●○
Mango Rum Cooler ●●●◐○
Mary Pickford ●●●●●
Melon Collie Martini ●●●●○
Melon Daiquiri #1 ●●●●○ (Served 'Up')
Melon Daiquiri #2 ●●●◐○ (Served Frozen)
Menehune Juice ●●●●○
Miami Daiquiri ●●●●○
Millionaire's Daiquiri ●●●◐○
Mint & Honey Daiquiri ●●●●◐
Mint Daiquiri ●●●●●
Missionary's Downfall ●●●●●
Mojito ●●●●●
Mojito Parisien ●●●●◐
Monk's Habit ●●●○○
Nacional Daiquiri #1 ●●●●◐
Nacional Daiquiri #2 ●●●●◐
Nantucket ●●●◐○
Naranja Daiquiri ●●●●○
Naranja Daiquiri ●●●●●
No. 10 Lemonade ●●●●◐
Orange Mojito ●●●●○
Pancho Villa ●●●●○
Passion Fruit Daiquiri ●●●●○

Peach Daiquiri
Pedro Collins
Peppermint Vanilla Daiquiri
Periodista Daiquiri
Pineapple & Cardamom Daiquiri
Pineapple Daiquiri # 1 (On-the-rocks)
Pineapple Daiquiri #2 (Frozen)
Pineapple Mojito
Pink Daiquiri
Pino Pepe
Plantation Punch
Plum Daiquiri
Potted Parrot
President
President Vincent
Presidente
Quarter Deck
Ribalaigua Daiquiri #3
Roa Aé
Robin Hood #1
Roulette
Royal Mojito
Santiago
Santiago Daiquiri
Scorpion
Sling
Sloppy Joe
Snow White Daiquiri
Sour
Spiced Apple Daiquiri
Sputnik #2
Stanley Cocktail
Strawberry & Balsamic Mojito
Strawberry Daiquiri
Strawberry Frozen Daiquiri
Sunshine Cocktail #1
Sunshine Cocktail #2
Swizzle
Tennessee Iced Tea
Test Pilot
Texas Iced Tea
Three Miler
Tokyo Iced Tea
Tonga
Tongue Twister
Tre Martini
Turquoise Daiquiri
White Lion
Wimbledon Martini
Zombie #1 (Intoxica! Recipe)
Zombie #2 (Vic's formula)
Zombie #3 (Modern formula)

RUM - NAVY

See 'Pusser's Navy Rum'

RUM – OVERPROOF WHITE RUM

See 'Wray & Nephew Overproof Rum'

The Alamagoozlum Cocktail
Beach Blonde
Malcolm Lowry
Pousse-café

RUM - SPICED

Spiced rums are continuously distilled light rums flavoured with spices including ginger, cinnamon, clove and vanilla.

Artlantic
Black Beard
Bomber
Cable Car
French Tear #1
Jamaican Mule
Long Island Spiced Tea
Mat The Rat
Santiago
Spiced Pear
Warsaw Cooler

RUM - VANILLA INFUSED

The pods of a tropical plant which belongs to the orchid family, vanilla has long been a prized flavouring. In this guide, recipes utilise its magic by infusing it in a spirit, most often rum or vodka. Simply take two quality vanilla pods (roughly 6in/15cm long) and split them lengthwise with a sharp knife. Place them in the bottle of spirit you want to flavour and leave it to infuse for a fortnight, turning occasionally.

Buona Sera Shot
Cherry Daiquiri
Coffee & Vanilla Daiquiri
Coquetail Au Vanilla
Cox's Daiquiri
DC Martini
Vanilla Daiquiri

SAKE

Sometimes described as a rice wine, sometimes as a rice beer, sake shares qualities of both. It is fermented from specially developed rice and water by brewmasters ('toji'). But, although sake is brewed like a beer, it is served like a wine and, like a wine, can either be dry or sweet, heavy or light. But it is slightly more alcoholic than wine, and much more boozy than beer, at 14-18% alc./vol..

Sake (pronounced Sar-Keh – heavy on the K!) is native to Japan (and parts of China). The basic outline of production has changed little since the 11th century, but complex and fragrant sake has only been generally available since the 1970s.

Asian Ginger Martini
Asian Pear Martini
Bloody Maru
Cucumber Sake-Tini
Hoa Sua
Iced Sake Martini
Japanese Pear
Lychee & Sake Martini
Onion Ring Martini
Oriental Grape Martini
Osmo
Raspberry Sake'tini
Rousing Charlie
Sake'politan
Sake-tini #1
Sake-tini #2
Sakini
Sumo in a Sidecar
Tokyo Bloody Mary
Urban Holistic

SAMBUCA BLACK

See 'Opal Nera Black Sambuca'

SAMBUCA WHITE

See 'Luxardo Sambuca dei Cesari'

SCOTCH

See 'Whisky – Scotch'

SHERRY

A fortified wine produced around the region of Jerez, Spain, the area from which both the style of wine and the English word 'sherry' originate. See below for styles of sherry used in this guide.

SHERRY – AMONTILLADO

An Amontillado sherry begins as a Fino, a pale, dry sherry produced under a layer of a kind of yeast known as 'flor'. Once the flor dies, increasing the oxidisation and changing the flavour of the wine, the sherry becomes an Amontillado. There are two distinct Amontillado styles. One is naturally dry, while the other is sweetened. Recipes in this guide which call for Amontillado sherry require the better quality, dry style.

Atomic Cocktail
Barbara West
Fog Cutter #1
Pruneaux
Roe-A-Coe

SHERRY – FINO

Pronounced 'Fee-No' this pale, dry style of sherry is best drunk young. It is produced under a layer of a kind of yeast known as 'flor' which protects the wine from oxidation.

Adonis
Alaska Martini
Bamboo
Bartender's Martini
Club Cocktail #1
Coronation
Coronation Cocktail No. 1
Dolores
East Indian
Granny's Martini
Hot Rum Punch
Jerez
Nome
Rousing Charlie
Saltecca
Salty Lychee Martini
Snowball
Tuxedo Martini

SHERRY - PEDRO XIMENEZ

This superbly rich dessert sherry is made from sun-dried Pedro Ximénez grapes.

Auntie's Hot Xmas Punch
Fruit & Nut Martini
Jerez
Pruneaux
Quarter Deck
Strudel Martini
Trifle'tini

SLOE GIN LIQUEUR

See 'Plymouth Sloe Gin Liqueur'

SOHO LYCHEE LIQUEUR

24% **alc./vol.** (48°proof)
Producer: Pernod (Group Pernod Ricard), Créteil, France.

Native to South China, the lychee's distinctive floral, fragrant flavour has a luscious delicacy which is distinctly Asian. Revered for over two thousand years as a symbol of love and romance, in part for its flavour and in part for its similarity to the heart, lychee is making waves around the world. Pernod Ricard distils this clear liqueur in France, from Asian lychees. It has a distinct smoothness and a light, fresh taste of rich lychee and raspberry, alongside a touch of citrus and raspberry jam.

China Blue
China Blue Martini
China Martini
Chinese Cosmopolitan
Chinese Whisper Martini
Crouching Tiger
Dragon Blossom
Enchanted
Lychee & Sake Martini
Lychee Mac
Lychee Martini
Lychee Rickey
Mellow Martini
Oriental Tart
Pear Drop
South Pacific
Summer Rose Martini
The Sun Salutation
Tokyo Tea

SOUR APPLE SCHNAPPS LIQUEUR

In the following recipes, a standard apple schnapps liqueur will not work: a sour version is required e.g. Sour Apple Pucker Schnapps or Sourz Apple.

Apple & Melon Martini
Apple Buck

Big Apple Martini
Curdish Martini
Green Apple & Cucumber Martini
Pink Flamingo
Red Apple
Smoky Apple Martini
Sour Apple Martini #1 (Popular)
Sour Apple Martini #2 (Deluxe)
Sourpuss Martini
Vanilla Sensation
Viagra Falls
Washington Apple
Winter Martini
Zhivago Martini

SOUR MIX

Sour mix is a term for a blend of lemon or lime juice mixed with sugar syrup. Commercial pre-mixed sour mix is available in a dried crystal or powdered form, often with the addition of pasteurised egg white. Margarita mix is a similar pre-mix, but with the addition of orange flavours. I strongly advocate the use of freshly squeezed juice and sugar syrup and in this guide they appear as separate ingredients.

SOUTHERN COMFORT

Alabama Slammer #1
Alabama Slammer #2
The Argyll
Avalanche Shot
Bazooka
The Big Easy
Brake Tag
Canteen Martini
Devil's Manhattan
Golden Nail
Hawaiian Cocktail
Honolulu Juicer
Kentucky Colonel
Louisiana Trade
Parlay Punch
Plantation Punch
Red Or Dead
Rhett Butler
Sailor's Comfort
Scarlett O'Hara
Slow Comfortable Screw
Slow Comfortable Screw Against the Wall
Southern Cider

Southern Manhattan ●●●●○
Southern Mint Cobbler ●●●●○
Southern Mule ●●●◐○
Southern Peach ●●●○○
Southern Punch ●●●◐○
Southern Tea-Knee ●●●●◐
Sundowner #2 ●●●●○
Too Close For Comfort ●●●◐○
Total Recall ●●●◐○
Wagon Wheel ●●●○○
Woodland Punch ●●●○○

ST-GERMAIN LIQUEUR

20% **alc./vol.** (40°proof)
www.stgermain.fr
Producer: Maison St-Germain, Saint Germain, Paris, France

St-Germain is the world's first elderflower liqueur and unlike other elderflower products which tend to be made from freeze dried and frozen blossoms, St-Germain is produced only using freshly picked flowers.

The fresh elderflowers used to make St-Germain are harvested from the foothills of the French Alps, in Haute Savoie, where elder trees grow abundantly. The elder shrubs (sambucus nigra) flower for a few weeks in late spring but are only at their ripest for about a week. A group of local French farmers harvest the flowers by hand, as has long been the tradition in this region of France. Incredibly, several of the farmers ride blossom layden bicycles between the elder trees which grow along side rural country roads. Once picked, speed is of the essence in order to capture the blossoms' fragrance and flavour as the flowers dull and fade.
The elderflowers are macerated in eau-de-vie made from a blend of Chardonnay and Gamay grapes. The elderflower infused spirit is then blended with just enough Caribbean cane sugar to enhance the natural flavours. With just 180 grams of sugar per litre (18%), St-Germain has a lot less sugar than many other liqueurs. It mixes well with all white fruits, particularly apple, pear and white grapes. The acidity of white wine also superbly balances St-Germain and the grassy, gooseberry notes of Sauvignon Blanc work particularly well with the delicate floral notes of the liqueur.

Apple & Elderflower Collins ●●●●○
Apple & Elderflower Martini ●●●●○
Bitter Elder ●●●◐○
Charente Collins ●●●●○
Cyder Press ●●●●○
Daisy Cutter Martini ●●●●◐
Eden ●●●●◐
Elder & Wiser ●●●●○
Elder Fashioned ●●●●○
Elder Sour ●●●●◐
Elderflower Collins #1 ●●●●◐
Elderflower Cosmo ●●●●◐
Elderflower Daiquiri ●●●●○
Elderflower Jojito ●●●●◐
Elderflower Manhattan ●●●●◐
Elderflower Martini #1 ●●●●○
Elderflower Martini #2 ●●●●◐
Elderflower Pisco Punch ●●●●◐
English Breakfast Martini ●●●●◐
English Garden ●●●●○
English Martini ●●●●◐
Floral Martini ●●●●○
Flower Power Martini ●●●●◐
French 77 ●●●●○
French Apple Martini ●●●●○
French Daisy ●●●◐○
French Monkey ●●●◐○
French Pear ●●●●◐
Fruits Of The Forest ●●●○○
G & Tea ●●●●○
Galvanised Nail ●●●◐○
Gin Atomic ●●●◐○
Gin Garden ●●●●○
Glenn's Bride ●●●●◐
Grape Effect ●●●●○
Greenbelt ●●●◐○
Gypsy ●●●●○
Haydenistic ●●●●○
I B Damm'd ●●●●◐
In-Seine ●●●●●
Jade Garden ●●●●○
Jasmine & Elderflower Martini ●●●●○
L'Amour en Fuite ●●●●○
Left Bank ●●●●◐
Lemongrad ●●●◐○
Marie Rose #2 ●●●●○
Mojito Parisien ●●●●◐
Monarch Martini ●●●●○
Orchard Breeze ●●●●○
Padovani ●●●●○
Parisian Martini #2 ●●●●◐
Parisian Sidecar ●●●●◐
Pear & Elderflower Cocktail ●●●◐○
Pear Martini ●●●●◐
Periscope ●●●●●
Pernelle ●●●●◐
Peruvian Elder Sour ●●●●◐
Pomme et Sureau ●●●●◐
Rose-hip Martini ●●●●●
Rousing Charlie ●●●◐○
S Tea G ●●●◐○
Salflower Sour ●●●●○
Saúco Margarita ●●●●◐
Sidecarriage ●●●●○
St. Germain Sidecar ●●●●◐
Summer Breeze ●●●◐○
The Elder Aviator ●●●●◐
The Last Straw ●●●●○
The Mayflower Martini ●●●◐○
The St. Germain ●●●●◐
The Stig ●●●●●
Twinkle ●●●●◐
Wah-Wah ●●●●○
Wisecrack Fizz ●●●●◐

STONE'S ORIGINAL GREEN GINGER WINE

Apple Mac ●●●●○
Ginger Martini ●●●●○
Gingerbread Martini ●●●●○
Havanna Cobbler ●●●●○
Kentucky Mac ●●●◐○
Lychee Mac ●●●◐○
Mac Orange ●●●◐○

Stone & Gravel ●●●◐○
Thriller Martini ●●●●○
Whisky Mac ●●●◐○

STRAWBERRIES

Like the raspberry and the blackberry, the strawberry is a member of the rose family, indigenous to both Old and New Worlds. Wild strawberries are small and fine-flavoured, with an intensely musky scent: sadly they are also expensive. Most strawberries for the last few centuries have been a hybrid of old world and new.

Strawberries are delicate and do not keep much longer than 48 hours in the refrigerator. Opt for smaller, darker berries, and wash them briefly in warm water.

Preparation: You can do pretty much what you like with strawberries: stick them through the electric juicer, puree them or muddle them. I muddle mine, probably because I hate cleaning the blender, let alone the juicer. Recipes in this guide state how many average size berries should be muddled for each drink.

Basil Grande ●●●●○
Bourbon Blush ●●●●◐
Extradition ●●●●○
Forbidden Fruits ●●●●○
Fresa Batida ●●●●○
Inga From Sweden ●●●●○
Jayne Mansfield ●●●●○
Jules Delight ●●●●○
Jumbled Fruit Julep ●●●◐○
Rossini ●●●●○
Strawberry & Balsamic Mojito ●●●●○
Strawberry Daiquiri ●●●●○
Strawberry Frozen Daiquiri ●●●◐○
Strawberry Margarita ●●●●○
Strawberry Martini ●●●●○
Strawberry 'N' Balsamic Martini ●●●●◐
Trifle'tini ●●●◐○
Wanton Abandon ●●●●○
Wimbledon Martini ●●●●○

STRAWBERRY (CRÈME DE FRAISE) LIQUEUR

See 'Giffard Crème de Fraise de Bois'

SUGAR SYRUP

Many cocktails benefit from sweetening but granulated sugar does not dissolve easily in cold drinks. Hence pre-dissolved sugar syrup (also known as 'simple syrup') is used. Commercially made 'gomme sirop' (gum syrup) is sugar syrup with the addition of gum arabic, the crystallised sap of the acacia tree, which adds mouth-feel and smoothness to some drinks, but not all.
Make your own sugar syrup by gradually pouring and stirring two cups of granulated sugar into a saucepan containing one cup of hot water and simmer until the sugar is dissolved. Do not let the water even come close to boiling and only simmer for as long as it takes to dissolve the sugar. Allow syrup to cool and pour into an empty bottle. Ideally, you should finely strain your syrup into the bottle to remove any undissolved crystals which could otherwise encourage crystallisation. If kept in a refrigerator this mixture will last for a couple of months.
A wide range of flavoured sugar syrups are commercially available. Orgeat (almond), passion fruit and vanilla are among the most popular. See also 'Pomegranate (Grenadine) Syrup'.

SWEDISH PUNCH

Swedish Punch is a style of liqueur based on Batavia arrack from the island of Java (now part of Indonesia). This is made from fermented rice and distilled in a pot still, then aged in local hardwood. The arrack is sweetened and flavoured with cardamom, nutmeg and cinnamon to make this distinctive liqueur which is best served mixed with rum. Brands to look for include Carlshamns Flaggpunsch and Facile.

Corpse Reviver #2 ●●●●○
Diki-Diki ●●●●◐
Doctor ●●●●◐
Modernista ●●●●○
Princess Marina ●●●●○
Roulette ●●●●○

TEICHENNÉ BUTTERSCOTCH SCHNAPPS LIQUEUR

20% **alc./vol.** (40°proof)
www.teichenne.com
Producer: Teichenné S.A., Tarragona, Spain.

A family owned distiller and liqueur producer, the Teichenné firm was founded in 1956 when Juan Teichenné Senaux launched his distillery in the small town of L'Arboç (40 miles south of Barcelona). Born in France, Teichenné moved to Spain as part of the French wine industry's search for new production sources. In those early days, production was very small, concentrating on 'handmade' brandies and liqueurs for sale locally in the Penedès Region. Expansion did not start until the 70s, when Joan Teichenné Canals took over the business after his father's death. In the 80s Teichenné led the Spanish boom in liqueur schnapps. These fruit liqueurs also opened doors to international markets which have grown significantly ever since.
Teichenné butterscotch schnapps has a rich butterscotch and fudge flavour with a hint of cinnamon, baked apple and nutmeg.

Apple Crumble Martini #1 ●●●◐○
Banoffee Martini ●●●●○
Bit-O-Honey ●●●○○
Bon Bon ●●●○○
Bourbon Cookie ●●●●○
Butterscotch Daiquiri ●●●◐○
Butterscotch Delight ●●●◐○
Butterscotch Martini ●●●●○
Doughnut Martini ●●●◐○
Gingerbread Martini ●●●●○
Give Me A Dime ●●●●○
Gold Member ●●●●○
Golden Mac ●●●◐○
Met Manhattan ●●●●○
Monk's Candy Bar ●●●○○
Oatmeal Cookie ●●●◐○
Shamrock Express ●●●◐○
Tribbble ●●●●○

TEICHENNÉ PEACH SCHNAPPS LIQUEUR

20% **alc./vol.** (40°proof)
www.teichenne.com
Producer: Teichenné S.A., Tarragona, Spain.

In the eighties, when schnapps were just beginning to emerge as a new category of liqueur, Juan Teichenné led the way. Teichenné Peach Schnapps was one of the Spanish producer's original flavours. It was quickly picked up by the world's bartenders and became a key ingredient in many contemporary cocktails.
While Teichenné have since developed their schnapps range to include a plethora of excellent new flavours, Teichenné Peach Schnapps remains one of the bestselling, illustrating its quality and mixability. The rich nose of ripe peach skin and peach kernel enhances the soft, succulent flavour which lightens on the palate.

Achilles Heel ●●●●○
Aku Aku ●●●●◐
Apple Spritz ●●●●○
Baby Woo Woo ●●●○○
Bellini #2 (Difford's Formula) ●●●●○
Bellini-Tini ●●●●○
Bermuda Cocktail ●●●●○
Bikini Martini ●●●●○
Bohemian Iced Tea ●●●●◐
Cream Cake ●●●◐○
Custard Tart ●●●●○
The Delicious Sour ●●●●○
Detox ●●●○○
Encantado ●●●●○
Envy ●●●●○
Fish House Punch #1 ●●●●○
Fish House Punch #2 ●●●●○
Fuzzy Navel ●●◐○○
Glass Tower ●●●◐○
I B Damm'd ●●●●◐
Iguana Wana ●●●○○
Ink Martini #1 ●●●◐○
Jacuzzi ●●●◐○
Jambalaya ●●●◐○
Jelly Belly Beany ●●●●○

Jerez ●●●●○
Love Junk ●●●◐○
Missionary's Downfall ●●●●●
Mississippi Schnapper ●●●◐○
Mitch Martini ●●●●○
Moonraker ●●●●○
Mystique ●●●◐○
Pale Rider ●●●○○
Palma Violet Martini ●●●◐○
Peach Daiquiri ●●●●○
Peach Melba Martini ●●●◐○
Perfect Lady ●●●●○
Pink Tutu ●●●◐○
Sex On The Beach #1 ●●◐○○
Silk Panties ●●●○○
Southern Peach ●●●○○
Sputnik ●●●◐○
Swedish Blue Martini ●●●◐○
Verdi Martini ●●●●○
Weeping Jesus ●●●◐○
Woo Woo ●●●◐○
Yum ●●●○○

TEQUILA

See 'Partida Tequila'

TOMATO JUICE

Originally from Peru, the tomato was imported into Spain in the 16th century. Although technically a fruit, its sharp, fresh, slightly salty qualities have associated it with a range of savoury cocktails for over 80 years. Buy a quality, chilled, freshly pressed juice or make your own. Avoid sweet, packaged juices made from concentrate.

Basil Mary ●●●●○
Bloody Joseph ●●●◐○
Bloody Maria ●●●●○
Bloody Mary (1930's recipe) ●●◐○○
Bloody Mary (Modern Receipe) ●●●●◐
Bloody Shame ●●●◐○ (Mocktail)
Cubanita ●●●●○
Peppered Mary ●●●●○
Prairie Oyster ●●●◐○
Red Snapper ●●●●○
Sangrita ●●●●○
Tokyo Bloody Mary ●●●●○
Vampiro ●●●●○

TRIPLE SEC

An orange-flavoured liqueur often used in cocktails. Cointreau makes a good substitute.

TUACA LIQUEUR

Apple Crumble Martini #2 ●●●●○
The Bistro Sidecar ●●●●○
Dramatic Martini ●●●◐○
Hammer Of The Gods ●●◐○○
Honey Wall ●●●●○
Irish Manhattan ●●●●○
Italian Job #2 ●●●●○
I.V.F. Martini ●●●◐○
Karamel Sutra Martini ●●●○○
Mystique Martini ●●●●○
Orange Custard Martini ●●●◐○
Sophisticated Savage ●●●◐○
Stealth ●●●◐○
Tuscan Mule ●●●◐○
Walnut Martini ●●●●○
Wonky Martini ●●●●◐

VANILLA (SCHNAPPS) LIQUEUR

The term schnapps traditionally suggests a clear, strong spirit. However, in recent years the term has come to refer to sweet liqueurs of only 20-24% alc./vol., bearing no resemblance to the strong dry schnapps from which they take their name. I've added the term 'liqueur' in this guide to help make the type of vanilla schnapps called for more obvious.

Blush Martini ●●●◐○
Cool Orchard ●●●●○
Doughnut Martini ●●●◐○
Elle For Leather ●●●●◐
La Grand Feu ●●●○○
Hemingway Martini ●●●●○
Kentucky Dream ●●●●○
Key Lime Pie #3 ●●●●○
Sandstorm ●●●●○
Serendipity #1 ●●●●○
Upside-Down Raspberry Cheesecake ●●●●○

VANILLA SUGAR SYRUP

Buy it commercially or make your own to inject a little vanilla flavour into your cocktails.

Bajan Passion ●●●●○
Buena Vida ●●●●◐
Cascade Martini ●●●●○
Honey Blossom ●●●○○ (Mocktail)
Irish Manhattan ●●●●○
Orange Custard Martini ●●●◐○
Randy ●●●●○
Red Rum Martini ●●●●◐
Settle Petal ●●●●○
Socialite ●●●◐○
Tilt ●●●●○
Valkyrie ●●●◐○

VELVET FALERNUM LIQUEUR

A flavoursome non-alcoholic syrup and liqueur developed by John D. Taylor of Bridgetown, Barbados in 1890. Based on sugar cane, its flavour comes from an infusion of lime and 'botanicals' including almonds and cloves.

Adelaide Swizzle ●●●●○
Bajan Daiquiri ●●●●○
Bermuda Rum Swizzle ●●●◐○
Caribe Daiquiri ●●●●○
Coquetail Au Vanilla ●●●●◐
Golden Wave ●●●○○
Hawaiian Eye ●●●◐○
Haydenistic ●●●●○
Nuclear Daiquiri ●●●●○
Mai Tai #2 ●●●●○
Royal Bermuda Yacht Club Daiquiri ●●●●○
Tailor Made ●●●●○
Test Pilot ●●●●○
Velvet Fog ●●●●◐

VERMOUTH DRY

Vermouth as we know it today was invented during the 18th century in the ancient Kingdom of Savoy, which is now divided between north-west Italy and parts of southern and eastern France. At that time the region had an abundance of grapes and produced only very ordinary wines. As a result, enterprising types fortified wine, added herbs and spices, and created vermouth.

Adios Amigos Cocktail ●●●◐○
Affinity ●●●◐○
Alfonso Martini ●●●●○
Algonquin ●●●●○
Allegrottini ●●●◐○
Almond Martini #2 ●●●●○
American Beauty #1 ●●●●◐
American Beauty #2 ●●●●○
Apple Strudel #2 ●●●●◐
Arnaud Martini ●●●●○
The Atty Cocktail ●●●●○
Aviator ●●●●○
Bamboo ●●●●◐
Bartender's Martini ●●●●○
Bensonhurst ●●●●◐
Black Bison Martini ●●●●◐
Black Bison Martini #2 ●●●●◐
Black Feather ●●●●○
Blackthorn Irish ●●●◐○
Bloomsbury Martini ●●●●○
Blue Monday ●●●◐○
Blue Star ●●●○○
Bombay No. 2 ●●●●◐
Boomerang ●●●●○
Boston Tea Party ●●●○○
Boulevard ●●●●○
Bourbonella ●●●●○
Bradford ●●●●○
Brainstorm ●●●●◐
Bronx ●●●●○
Brooklyn #1 ●●●●○
Brooklyn #2 ●●●●○
Cajun Martini ●●●○○
Californian Martini ●●●●○
Caprice ●●●●○
Cardinale ●●●●○
Caruso Martini ●●●○○
Chancellor ●●●●◐
Cherry Martini ●●●●○
China Martini ●●●◐○
Chocolate & Cranberry Martini ●●●◐○
Chocolate Martini ●●●●○
Chocolate Mint Martini ●●●●○
Claridge Cocktail ●●●●○
Clipper Cocktail ●●●◐○
Club Cocktail #3 ●●●●○
Coronation ●●●○○
Coronation Cocktail No. 1 ●●●●◐
Cuban Island ●●●◐○
Daisy Cutter Martini ●●●●◐
Delmarva Cocktail No. 1 ●●●●◐
Delmarva Cocktail No. 2 ●●●●◐
Delmonico ●●●●○
Delmonico Special ●●●◐○
Devil's Cocktail ●●●◐○
Diamond Dog ●●●◐○
Dickens' Martini ●●●●◐
Diplomat ●●●●●
Dirty Martini ●●●◐○
Donegal ●●●●○
Dry Ice Martini ●●●●◐
Dry Martini #1 (Traditional) ●●●●●
Dry Martini #2 (Naked) ●●●●○
Dry Oranage Martini ●●●●◐
East Indian ●●●●◐
El Presidente #2 ●●●◐○
El Presidente #3 ●●●○○
El Presidente #4 ●●●●○
El Torado ●●●●◐
Elderflower Manhattan ●●●●◐
Elderflower Martini #1 ●●●●○
Elderflower Martini #2 ●●●●◐
Elk Martini ●●●◐○
Elysian ●●●●○
English Rose ●●●●○
Fairbanks Cocktail No. 1 ●●●○○
Fallen Leaves ●●●●○
Fiesta ●●●●○
Fifty-Fifty Martini ●●●●○
Floral Martini ●●●●○
Flower Power Martini ●●●●◐
Fly Like A Butterfly ●●●●○
Fontainebleau Special ●●●◐○
Frank Sullivan Cocktail ●●●○○
The Frankenjack Cocktail ●●●◐○
Franklin Martini ●●●●●
French Apple Martini ●●●●○
Frisky Lemonade ●●●◐○
Gibson ●●●●◐
Ginger & Lemongrass Martini ●●●●○
Gingertini ●●●●○
Gloom Chaser Cocktail #2 ●●●◐○
Golf Cocktail ●●●●○
Green Tea Martini #2 ●●●●○
Harvard ●●●◐○
Hawaiian Martini ●●●●○
Hemingway Martini ●●●●○
Hoffman House Martini ●●●●○
Hoopla ●●●●○
Ice Tea Martini ●●●●○
Imperial Martini ●●●○○
Incognito ●●●◐○
Income Tax Cocktail ●●●●○
Intimate Martini ●●●●○
Jasmine & Elderflower Martini ●●●●○
The Journalist ●●●●○
Jupiter Martini ●●●◐○
Knickerbocker Martini ●●●◐○
Knockout Martini ●●●●○
L'Amour en Fuite ●●●●○
Lavender Martini ●●●●○
Lemon Martini ●●●●◐
Livingstone ●●●●○
Lucien Gaudin ●●●●○
Lutkins Special Martini ●●●◐○
Lychee Martini ●●●●○
Macka ●●●◐○
Manhattan Dry ●●●●◐
Manhattan Perfect ●●●●●
Marguerite Martini ●●●●○
Maurice Martini ●●●◐○
Medium Martini ●●●●◐
Merry Widow #1 ●●●◐○
Merry Widow #2 ●●●◐○
Metropole ●●●◐○
Merry-Go-Round Martini ●●●●○
Mint Martini ●●●●○
Moonshine Martini ●●●●◐
Mountain ●●●◐○
Noon ●●●●○
Obituary ●●●●○
Oddball Manhattan Dry ●●●●○
Old Pal ●●●◐○
Paisley Martini ●●●●○
Pall Mall Martini ●●●●○
Parisian Martini #1 ●●●●○
Parisian Martini #2 ●●●●◐
Parisian Spring Punch ●●●●○
Pear Martini ●●●●◐
Peggy Martini ●●●○○
Perfect Martini ●●●◐○
Peter Pan Cocktail ●●●○○
Peter Pan Martini ●●●●○
Peto Martini ●●●●◐
Piccadilly Martini ●●●●◐
Plum Cocktail ●●●◐○
Plum Martini ●●●●○
Poet's Dream ●●●●◐
Pompanski Martini ●●●●○
President Vincent ●●●◐○
Presidente ●●●●○
Princess Mary's Pride ●●●○○
Princeton Martini ●●●●○
The Puritan ●●●●●
Rat Pack Manhattan ●●●●○
The Rose #1 (original) ●●●●◐
The Rose #2 ●●●◐○
The Rose #3 ●●●●◐
Rose-hip Martini ●●●●●
Roselyn Martini ●●●●◐
Rosita ●●●●○
Sage Martini ●●●●○
Satan's Whiskers (Straight) ●●●●◐
Satan's Whiskers ●●●◐○
Savoy Special #1 ●●●●○
Scofflaw ●●●●○
The Scott ●●●●○
Shamrock #2 ●●●●○
Silver Martini ●●●◐○
Sloppy Joe ●●●●○
Smoky Martini #1 ●●●●○
Smoky Martini #2 ●●●○○
Snyder Martini ●●●●○
So-So Martini ●●●●●
Strawberry Blonde Martini ●●●◐○
Sunshine Cocktail #1 ●●●●◐
Sunshine Cocktail #2 ●●●●○
Tango Martini #1 ●●●●○
Tequila'tini ●●●◐○
Texsun ●●●◐○
Tipperary #2 ●●●●◐
Trilby #2 ●●●●○
Trinity ●●●○○
Tuxedo Martini ●●●●◐
Twentieth Century Martini ●●●◐○
Urban Holistic ●●●◐○
Vanilla Sensation ●●●●○
The Vesper Martini ●●●●●
Violet Affinity ●●●●◐
Vodkantini ●●●●◐
Walnut Martini ●●●●○
Webster Martini ●●●◐○
Wet Martini ●●●●◐
What The Hell ●●●●○
Winter Martini ●●●●◐

VERMOUTH (SWEET)

Popular belief has it that Italian vermouth was originally sweet and produced from red wine, while French vermouth was typically dry and white. Hence, many old cocktail books refer to 'French' for dry vermouth and 'Italian' where sweet vermouth is called for. The truth is that the division between the styles of the two countries was never that defined and producers in both countries now make both sweet (rosso) and dry styles. Although red vermouth was initially based on red wine, now virtually all is made from white wine with caramel blended in to give an amber colour.

Abbey Martini ●●●◐○
Adonis ●●●●○
Affinity ●●●◐○
Alfonso Martini ●●●●○
Americano ●●●●○
Apple Blossom Cocktail ●●●●◐
Apple Manhattan #1 ●●●●○
Apple Manhattan #2 ●●●●○
The Argyll ●●●○○ [#6.1]
Aviator ●●●●○
Behemoth ●●●●○
Bijou ●●●●◐
Blackthorn English ●●●●○
Blood & Sand #2 (Difford's Formula) ●●●●◐
Bobby Burns ●●●●○
Bolero ●●●◐○
Bombay No. 2 ●●●●◐
Boomerang ●●●●○
Bronx ●●●●○
Brooklyn #1 ●●●●○
Caramel Manhattan ●●●●◐
Carrol Cocktail ●●●◐○
Club Cocktail #2 ●●●●○
Club Cocktail #3 ●●●●○
Corpse Reviver No. 1 #1 ●●●◐○
Covadonga ●●●○○
Damn-The-Weather ●●●◐○
De La Louisiane #2 ●●●●○
Delmonico ●●●●○
Devil's Manhattan ●●●●○
Diplomat ●●●●●
Elysian ●●●●○
Embassy Royal ●●●◐○
Especial Day ●●●●◐
Fair & Warmer Cocktail ●●●○○
Fallen Leaves ●●●●○
Finitaly ●●●●○
El Floridita Daiquiri No. 2 ●●●◐○
Fly Like A Butterfly ●●●●○
Flying Scotsman ●●●●○
Fort Lauderdale ●●●○○
Froupe Cocktail ●●●●○
Gin & It ●●●●○
Grappa Manhattan ●●●●○
Hanky-Panky Martini ●●●●○
Harvard ●●●◐○
Hawaiian Martini ●●●●○
Hearst Martini ●●●●○
I'll Take Manhattan ●●●●○
Income Tax Cocktail ●●●●○
James Joyce ●●●●○
Jewel Cocktail ●●●○○
The Journalist ●●●●○
Knickerbocker Martini ●●●◐○
Leap Year Martini ●●●○○
Leave It To Me Martini ●●●●○
Little Italy ●●●◐○
London Calling ●●●◐○
Loud Speaker Martini ●●●◐○
Luxury Cocktail ●●●◐○
Macka ●●●◐○
Manhattan Perfect ●●●●●
Manhattan Sweet ●●●●●
Manhattan Island ●●●●○
Martinez ●●●●●
Martini Special ●●●●◐
Maurice Martini ●●●◐○
Medium Martini ●●●●◐
Merry-Go-Round Martini ●●●●○
Mexican Manhattan ●●●●○
Milano ●●●●◐
The Million Dollar Cocktail ●●●●◐
Moravian Cocktail ●●●○○
Mountain ●●●◐○
Negroni ●●●●◐
Noon ●●●●○
Old Fashioned Caddy ●●●●○
Old Flame ●●●●○
Opening Shot ●●●◐○
Orange Bloom Martini ●●●●◐
Orange Martini ●●●●○
Pall Mall Martini ●●●●○
Palm Beach ●●●◐○
Park Avenue ●●●●○
Perfect Martini ●●●◐○
Peto Martini ●●●●◐
Picca ●●●●○
Pichuncho Martini ●●●●◐
Princess Pride ●●●◐○
Rat Pack Manhattan ●●●●○
Remember The Maine ●●●●◐
Rob Roy #1 ●●●●○
Rob Roy #2 ●●●●◐
Rosita ●●●●○
Ruby Martini #2 ●●●◐○
Satan's Whiskers (Straight) ●●●●◐
Satan's Whiskers ●●●◐○
Scorched Earth ●●●◐○
Scotch Negroni ●●●●○
Shamrock #1 ●●●◐○
Sir Thomas ●●●●○
Southern Manhattan ●●●●○
The Star #1 ●●●●○
Tango Martini #1 ●●●●○
Tipperary #1 ●●●●◐
Trilby #1 ●●●●○
Tulip Cocktail ●●●●○
Turf Martini ●●●●○
Valentino Martini ●●●●○
Vancouver ●●●◐○
Vieux Carré Cocktail ●●●●◐
Violet Affinity ●●●●◐
Voodoo ●●●●○
Vowel Cocktail ●●●●◐
Wonky Martini ●●●●◐
Yacht Club ●●●◐○

VIOLET LIQUEUR

See 'Benoit Serres Violet Liqueur'

VODKA – ALMOND FLAVOURED

Nuts & Berries ●●●●○

VODKA – APPLE FLAVOURED

French Apple Martini ●●●●○
Toffee Apple Martini ●●●●○

VODKA – BISON GRASS FLAVOURED

See 'Zubrówka vodka'

VODKA – CITRUS FLAVOURED

See 'Ketel One Citroen'

VODKA - CRANBERRY FLAVOURED

Finitaly ●●●●○
Finnberry Martini ●●●●○
The Juxtaposition ●●●●○
Lago Cosmo ●●●◐○
Nutty Berry'tini ●●●◐○
Spiced Cranberry Martini ●●●●○
Spicy Finn ●●●●○
Tarraberry'tini ●●●●○
Ugurundu ●●●◐○

VODKA - CUCUMBER FLAVOURED

Green Apple & Cucumber Martini ●●●●○
Settle Petal ●●●●○

VODKA - LIME VODKA

Emerald Martini ●●●●○
Frisky Lemonade ●●●◐○
Grassy Finnish ●●●●○
Key Lime ●●●●○
Lime Breeze ●●●◐○
Lime Sour ●●●●○
Limelite ●●●○○
Limeosa ●●●◐○
Limerick ●●●●○
Limey ●●●◐○
Limey Cosmo ●●●●○
Limey Mule ●●●●○
Liminal Shot ●●●○○
Limited Liability ●●●●◐
Limnology ●●●◐○
Limousine ●●●●○
Molotov Cocktail ●●●◐○

VODKA - MANGO FLAVOURED

Hawaiian Seabreeze ●●●◐○
Jumbled Fruit Julep ●●●◐○

VODKA – ORANGE FLAVOURED

See 'Ketel One Orange Infused Vodka'

VODKA – PEAR FLAVOURED

French Pear ●●●●◐
Long Flight of Stairs ●●●●◐
Pear Martini ●●●●◐
Steep Flight ●●●●●

VODKA - PEPPER INFUSED/FLAVOURED

Basil Mary ●●●●○
Cajun Martini ●●●○○
Henry VIII ●●●◐○
Pepper & Vanilla'tini ●●●●◐
Peppered Mary ●●●●○
Red Melon'tini ●●●◐○

VODKA - UNFLAVOURED GRAIN

See 'Ketel One Vodka'

VODKA – ROSE PETAL

Dragon Blossom ●●●○○
Lychee & Rose Petal Martini ●●●●○
Rose Petalini ●●●●○

VODKA - VANILLA FLAVOURED

See 'Ketel One Vanilla Infused Vodka'

WATERMELON

Botanically unrelated to other melons, the watermelon is native to Africa. It was eaten in Egypt well before 2000 BC and was taken to the US by slave traders in the early 17th century.

The juice is more refreshing than flavoursome, with a faint sweetness; the seeds, usually discarded, are nonetheless edible.

Preparation: Watermelons are best muddled in cocktails. Cut chunks of flesh from a segment, taking care to avoid the rind, and muddle in a shaker. Be sure to strain the drink to exclude the seeds.

Red Melon'tini ●●●◐○
Watermelon & Basil Martini ●●●●○
Watermelon & Basil Smash ●●●●○
Watermelon Cosmo ●●●◐○
Watermelon Martini ●●●●○
Zub-Way ●●●●○

WHISKEY - BOURBON

See 'Buffalo Trace'

WHISKY – CANADIAN

John Molson, though better known for brewing, is credited with first introducing whisky to Canada in 1799. His lead was followed by Scottish emigrants who found their new home had plentiful and cheap grain. Whisky production started at Kingston, on Lake Ontario, and spread as farming developed. However, barley was not common, so they reduced the amount of barley and added corn, wheat and rye instead.

In 1875, government regulation specified that Canadian whisky must be made from cereal grains in Canada, using continuous distillation. The rules also state that Canadian whisky must be aged a minimum of 3 years and a maximum of 18 years in charred oak barrels.

Captain Collins ●●●◐○
Old Pal ●●●◐○
Quebec ●●●●○

WHISKEY - IRISH

Due to the domination of Irish Distillers, the producers' group now owned by Pernod-Ricard, as a rule Irish whiskey is triple-distilled and not peated and hence light and smooth. (The independent Cooley Distillery produces some notable exceptions to these rules.)

Blackthorn Irish ●●●◐○
Cameron's Kick ●●●●○
Causeway ●●●◐○
Donegal ●●●●○
Dubliner ●●●●○
Every-Body's Irish Cocktail ●●●○○
Gloom Lifter ●●●●○
Irish Coffee ●●●●◐
Irish Coffee Martini ●●●●◐
James Joyce ●●●●○
Pappy Honeysuckle ●●●●◐
St. Patrick's Day ●●●●○
Shamrock #2 ●●●●○
Tipperary #1 ●●●●◐

WHISKY - SCOTCH

For whisky to be called 'Scotch whisky' it must be a) made in Scotland and b) aged in oak casks for a minimum of three years. Malt whisky – based on malted barley - was the original Scottish whisky and is at the core of all decent Scotch. But, although it has recently become extremely popular, the majority of pot still malt whisky is sold in blends (which include non-malt whiskies), not as single malt whiskies (which do not).
Blended Scotch whisky, or 'Scotch' for short, is the world's most popular whisky and accounts for well over 85% of all Scottish whisky.
A standard blended whisky will probably contain 15-40% malt and have no age statement (though every whisky in it will have been aged at least three years). Some blends describe themselves as 'deluxe' - this is a reference to the percentage of malt whisky in the blend and the average age of the whisky. A deluxe brand will usually contain more than 45% pot-still malt and will show an age statement of 12 years or more.

Affinity ●●●◐○
Aggravation ●●●●○
Apple Crumble Martini #1 ●●●◐○
Apple Mac ●●●●○
Apple Strudel #2 ●●●●◐
Aquarius ●●●◐○
Atholl Brose ●●●●◐
Barbary Coast Martini ●●●●○
Bessie & Jessie ●●●◐○
Blood & Sand #2 (Difford's Formula) ●●●●◐
Bloody Joseph ●●●◐○
Blue Blazer ●●●○○
Bobby Burns ●●●●○
Boston Tea Party ●●●○○
The Broadmoor ●●●●◐
Brubaker Old-Fashioned ●●●●○
The Buck ●●●◐○
Cameron's Kick ●●●●○ [DAN – previously called Cameron'tini]
Cappercaille ●●●●○
Celtic Margarita ●●●●◐
Chancellor ●●●●◐
Chin Chin ●●●●○
Collar & Cuff ●●●●○
The Crow Cocktail ●●●○○
Elle For Leather ●●●●◐
Flying Scotsman ●●●●○
French Monkey ●●●◐○
Galvanised Nail ●●●◐○
GE Blonde ●●●●◐
GE Blonde ●●●●◐
Godfather ●●●◐○
Gold ●●●○○
Golden Mac ●●●◐○
Golden Shot ●●●○○
Hair Of The Dog ●●●●○
Heather Julep ●●●●◐
Highland Sling ●●●●○
Honey & Marmalade Dram'tini ●●●●◐
Hot Toddy #1 ●●●●◐
Hot Toddy #2 ●●●●◐
Linstead ●●●●◐
Liquorice Whiskey Sour ●●●●◐
Loch Almond ●●●●○
Lychee Mac ●●●◐○
Mac Orange ●●●◐○
Maple Pomme ●●●●○
Mary Queen of Scots ●●●●◐
Milk & Honey ●●●●◐
Morning Glory Fizz ●●●●○
Mystique ●●●◐○
Mystique Martini ●●●●○
Old Fashioned Caddy ●●●●○
Paisley Martini ●●●●○
Pear Shaped #1 ●●●●◐ (Deluxe Version)
Pear Shaped #2 ●●●●○ (Popular Version)
Picca ●●●●○
Pineapple Blossom ●●●●○
Polly's Special ●●●●○
Red Breast ●●●◐○
Red Neck Martini ●●●●○
Remsen Cooler ●●●●○
Rob Roy #1 ●●●●○
Rob Roy #2 ●●●●◐
R U Bobby Moore? ●●●●◐
Rusty Nail ●●●●○
Scotch Bounty Martini ●●●◐○
Scotch Milk Punch ●●●◐○
Scotch Negroni ●●●●○
The Scott ●●●●○
Silent Third ●●●◐○
Sling ●●●●○
Smoky Apple Martini ●●●◐○
Smoky Martini #1 ●●●●○
Sour ●●●◐○
Speyside Martini ●●●●○
Sporran Breeze ●●●●◐
Sweet Science ●●●◐○
Swizzle ●●●●◐
Thriller Martini ●●●●○
Toddy Martini ●●●◐○
Trilby #1 ●●●●○
Trinity ●●●○○
Vowel Cocktail ●●●●◐
Whiskey Cobbler ●●●○○
Whisky Fizz ●●●●○
Whisky Mac ●●●◐○
White Knight ●●●◐○
Wild Honey ●●●◐○

WHISKEY - TENNESSEE

The main difference between bourbon and Tennessee whiskey lies in the Lincoln County Process, a form of charcoal filtration. In the 1820s someone (possibly Alfred Eaton) started filtering whiskey through maple charcoal. Tennessee whiskeys are now filtered through 10-12 feet of maple charcoal before they are bottled, removing impurities and giving a 'sooty' sweetness to the finished spirit.
A Tennessee whiskey must be made from at least 51% of one particular grain. This could be rye or wheat, but most often, as with bourbon, corn is the favoured base.

Bee Sting ●●●●○
Black Jack Shot ●●●○○
Cherry Mash Sour ●●●◐○
Cicada Cocktail ●●●◐○
Dingo ●●●○○
Eclipse ●●●●◐
The GTO Cocktail ●●●◐○
Hot Buttered Jack ●●●●○
Jack Frost ●●●◐○
Jack Punch ●●●●○
Jacktini ●●●◐○
Jodi May ●●●◐○
Jumping Jack Flash ●●●●○
Lynchburg Lemonade ●●●●○
Midnight Over Tennessee ●●●●◐
Mississippi Schnapper ●●●◐○
Mountain Slipper ●●●◐○
Raspberry Lynchburg ●●●◐○
Southern Punch ●●●◐○
Tennessee Berry Mule ●●●●○
Tennessee Iced Tea ●●●●○
Tennessee Rush ●●●◐○
Tolleytown Punch ●●●◐○

WINE – RED

The acidity in table wine can balance a cocktail in a similar way to citrus juice. Avoid heavily oaked wines.

Amercian Beauty #1 ●●●●◐
Caravan ●●●○○
Cardinal Punch ●●●◐○
Claret Cobbler ●●●●○
Cobbled Raspberry Martini ●●●●○
Cosmopolitan Delight ●●●●◐
Hot Red Blooded Frenchman ●●●●○
Italian Job #2 ●●●●○
Mulled Wine ●●●●○
New Yorker ●●●●○
Red Rover ●●●●○
Redback ●●●○○
La Sang ●●●●○
Sangaree ●●●●○
Sangria ●●●◐○
Sangria Martini ●●●●○
Tripleberry ●●●●○
Vanilla & Raspberry Martini ●●●●○

WINE - WHITE

The acidity in table wine can balance a cocktail in a similar way to citrus juice. The grassy notes in Sauvignon Blanc make this grape varietal particularly suitable for cocktail use.

Aphrodisiac ●●●○○
Blueberry Martini #2 ●●●◐○
Brazilian Berry ●●●●○
Canary Flip ●●●●◐
Coronation ●●●○○
Double Grape Martini ●●●●◐
GE Blonde ●●●●◐
Grapple Martini ●●●●○
Ice Maiden Martini ●●●●○
Italian Sun ●●●●○
Jerez ●●●●○
Kir ●●●◐○
Kir Martini ●●●◐○
LCB Martini ●●●●○
Left Bank ●●●●◐
M.C. Martini ●●●●●
Mint Cocktail ●●●●◐
Mint Martini ●●●●○
Moonlight Martini ●●●●○
Orchard Breeze ●●●●○
Palermo ●●●●◐
Pappy Honeysuckle ●●●●◐
R U Bobby Moore? ●●●●◐
Saturn Martini ●●●●◐
Spritz al Bitter ●●●◐○
Spritzer ●●●○○
Sundowner #2 ●●●●○
The St. Germain ●●●●◐
The Stig ●●●●●
Tropic ●●●●◐
U.S. Martini ●●●●●
Vanitini ●●●◐○
Vante Martini ●●●●◐
Waltzing Matilda ●●●●○
White Sangria ●●●◐○
Wine Cooler ●●●◐○

WRAY & NEPHEW OVERPROOF RUM

63% **alc./vol.** (126°proof)
www.rum.co.uk
Producer: J. Wray & Nephew Ltd, Kingston, Jamaica.

Wray & Nephew is the world's top selling high strength rum. Any spirit equal to or over 57% alc./vol. is termed 'overproof'. This unaged white rum is one such example. Made by J Wray & Nephew, the oldest distilling company in Jamaica, this brand is an intrinsic part of Jamaica's culture, heritage and tradition, and a staple in every Jamaican household. It is used as part of medicine, ritual and everyday living, and accounts for over 90% of all rum consumed on the island.
This iconic brand has a wonderful, fruity natural aroma with a rich molasses top note and hints of pineapple, banana, orange and coconut. Although strong, when used correctly its complex bouquet and unique flavour characteristics make it an excellent base for cocktails and a must in punches.

Afterburner ●●●◐○
Assisted Suicide ●●●◐○
Awol ●●●●○
Coco Naut ●●◐○○
Cold Comfort ●●●●○
Jamaican Sunset ●●●●○
Mango Punch ●●●●○
Marama Rum Punch ●●●●○
Nuclear Daiquiri ●●●●○
Passionate Rum Punch ●●●●○
Pirate Daiquiri ●●●●○
Reggae Rum Punch ●●●●◐
Rum Punch ●●●●●
Rum Punch-Up ●●●●◐
Rumba ●●●●○
Sorrel Rum Punch ●●●●◐
Steel Bottom ●●●○○
Stone & Gravel ●●●◐○
Zombie #3 ●●●●○ (Modern formula)

ZEN GREEN TEA LIQUEUR

Geisha Martini ●●●●○
Green Tea Martini #2 ●●●●○
Life (Love In The Future Ecstasy) ●●●◐

ZUBRÓWKA BISON VODKA

40% **alc./vol.** (80°proof)
Producer: Polmos Bialystok, Bialystok, Poland.

Pronounced 'Zhu-bruff-ka', this Polish vodka is flavoured with Hierochloe Odorata grass, a blade of which is immersed in each bottle, giving the vodka a translucent greenish colour and a subtle flavour. The area where this grass grows in the Bialowieza Forest is the habitat of wild Polish bison – so, although the bison don't eat this variety of grass, the vodka has the nickname 'Bison vodka'. The Hierochloe Odorata grass is harvested by hand in early summer when its flavour is best, then dried, cut to size and bound in bunches for delivery to the Bialystok distillery. The vodka is forced through the grass to absorb its aromatic flavour rather as espresso coffee machines force water through coffee.
The palate is herby and grassy with flavours of citrus, vanilla, lavender, tobacco, cold jasmine tea and caffè latte, plus hints of dry chocolate/vanilla. This subtle and delicately flavoured vodka is extremely mixable.

Achilles Heel ●●●●○
Amber ●●●●◐
Apple Breeze ●●●●○
Apple Pie Martini ●●●●○
Autumn Martini ●●●●○
Autumn Punch ●●●●◐
Beetle Jeuse ●●●●○
Congo Blue ●●●◐○
Coolman Martini ●●●●◐
Cucumber Martini ●●●●◐
Earl Grey Fizz ●●●●○
Elderflower Martini #1 ●●●●○
Elderflower Martini #2 ●●●●◐
Escalator Martini ●●●●●
French Bison-tini ●●●●○
Frisky Bison ●●●●◐
Fruits Of The Forest ●●●○○
Green Destiny ●●●◐○
Green Tea Martini #1 ●●●●○
Honey Apple Martini ●●●●○
The Honeysuckle Orchard ●●●●○
Krakow Tea ●●●●○
Lemon Butter Cookie ●●●●○
Mitch Martini ●●●●○
Northern Lights ●●●●○
Pooh'tini ●●●●◐
R U Bobby Moore? ●●●●◐
Sleeping Bison-tini ●●●●○
Sodden Grape Martini ●●●●○
Tatanka ●●●●◐
Tatanka Royale ●●●●○
Verdant Martini ●●●●○
Warsaw Cooler ●●●●◐
Zelda Martini ●●●●○
Zub-Way ●●●●○

GREAT COCKTAIL BARS OF THE WORLD

THESE ARE A FEW OF MY FAVOURITE BARS IN SOME OF THE GREATEST CITIES IN THE WORLD. AS ALWAYS, IT IS BASED ON PERSONAL CHOICE, BUT A TRULY GREAT BAR GOES BEYOND THE LATEST TRENDS. IF YOU'D LIKE TO KNOW MORE ABOUT GREAT BARS AROUND THE WORLD, REGISTER YOUR EMAIL ADDRESS AT **diffordsguide.com** AND SIGN UP FOR OUR NEW ONLINE MAGAZINE **digital.diffordsguide.**

AMSTERDAM, NETHERLANDS

HARRY'S BAR

285 Spuistraat, Amsterdam, 1012 VR, The Netherlands
Tel: +31 (0)20 624 4384, **www.**harrysbar.nl
Type: Tourist hot spot & cocktail bar

ATLANTA, USA

HALO LOUNGE

817 West Peachtree Street NW (entrance on 6th St), Midtown, Atlanta, GA 30308, USA
Tel: +1 404 962 7333, **www.**halolounge.com
Type: Lounge bar-styled club

AUCKLAND, NEW ZEALAND

COCO CLUB

3 Fort Lane, Central, Auckland, New Zealand
Tel: +64 (0)9 309 3848, **www.**thecococlub.co.nz
Type: Hidden lounge bar

CROW BAR

26 Wyndham Street, Central, Auckland, New Zealand
Tel: +64 (0)9 366 0398 www.http://crowbar.co.nz
Type: Booth-lined basement bar

SUITE BAR

2 Hobson Street (corner Wolfe St), Auckland, New Zealand
Tel: +64 (0)9 307 7030, **www.**suitebar.co.nz
Type: Cocktail lounge bar

BARCELONA, SPAIN

BOADAS COCKTAIL BAR

1 Tallers (@ Rambla), Barcelona, Catalunya, 08001, Spain
Tel: +34 93 318 8826
Type: Legendary vintage cocktail bar

DRY MARTINI

162-166 Carrer Aribau, Barcelona, Catalunya, 08036, Spain
Tel: +34 93 217 5072, **www.**drymartinibcn.com
Type: Classic Martini led lounge bar

GIMLET BAR

24 Carrer Rec (btwn Passeig del Born & Carrer del Sabateret), Downtown, Barcelona, Catalunya, 08003, Spain **Tel:** +34 93 310 1027 **Type:** Cocktail bar

GIMLET

46 Carrer Santaló (btwn Maria Cubi & Laforia), Barcelona, Catalunya, 08021, Spain
Tel: +34 93 201 5306, **www.**gimletbcn.com
Type: Cocktail lounge & café bar

IDEAL COCKTAIL BAR

89 Carrer Aribau (@ Carrer de Mallorca), Barcelona, Catalunya, 08036, Spain
Tel: +34 93 453 1028
Type: Old-school cocktail bar

TIRSA COCKTAIL BAR

174 Carrer Rafael de Campalans, L'Hospitalet, Barcelona, 08903, Spain
Tel: +34 93 431 2302
Type: Suburban, neighbourhood cocktail bar

BERLIN, GERMANY

DIE HAIFISCH BAR

25 Arndtstrasse (btwn Nostitz & Friesen), Kreuzberg, West Berlin, 10965, Germany
Tel: +49 (0)30 691 1352
Type: Cocktail lounge & sushi bar

GREEN DOOR

50 Winterfeldstrasse, Schoeneberg, Berlin, 10781, Germany
Tel: +49 (0)30 215 2515, **www.**greendoor.de
Type: Lounge bar

BAR AM LÜTZOWPLATZ

7 Lützowplatz, Tiergarten, West Berlin, Germany
Tel: +49 (0)30 262 6807, **www.**baramluetzowplatz.com
Type: DJ & cocktail lounge bar

REINGOLD

11 Novalisstrasse, Mitte, East Berlin, 10115, Germany
Tel: +49 (0)30 2838 7676, **www.**reingold.de
Type: DJ & cocktail lounge bar

VICTORIA BAR

102 Potsdamer Strasse (btwn Lützowstrasse & Pohlstrasse), Tiegarten, West Berlin, 10785, Germany
Tel: +49 (0)30 2575 9977, **www.**victoriabar.de
Type: Contemporary lounge bar

BELFAST, NORTHE N IRELAND

THE MERCHANT HOTEL BAR

The Merchant Hotel, 35-9 Waring Street, Belfast, Northern Ireland **Tel:** +44 (0)28 9023 4888, **www.**themerchanthotel.com **Type:** Hotel lounge bar

Gimlet - Barcelona

Tirsa Cocktail Bar - Barcelona

Dragonfly - Edinburgh

Hawksmoor - London

Coco - Auckland

Dry Martini - Barcelona

Gimlet - Barcelona

Lotus - Sydney

Crow Bar - Auckland

BOSTON & CAMBRIDGE, USA

B-SIDE LOUNGE

92 Hampshire Street (@ Windsor St), Cambridge, Massachusetts, MA 02139, USA
Tel: +1 617 354 0766, **www.**bsidelounge.com
Type: Eccentric lounge bar

CUCHI CUCHI

795 Main Street (@ Windsor St), Cambridge, Massachusetts, MA 02139, USA
Tel: +1 617 864 2929, **www.**cuchicuchi.cc
Type: Theatrical lounge bar

EASTERN STANDARD KITCHEN & DRINKS

Hotel Commonwealth, 528 Commonwealth Avenue, Back Bay, Boston, Massachusetts, MA 02215, USA
Tel: +1 617 532 9100, **www.**eastern standardboston.com **Type:** Bistro on steroids

EXCELSIOR

272 Boylston Street, Boston, Massachusetts, MA 02116, USA
Tel: +1 617 426 7878, **www.**excelsiorrestaurant.com **Type:** Sharp suits of Boston hang out here

NO. 9 PARK

9 Park Street (btwn Beacon & Tremont Sts), Beacon Hill, Boston, Massachusetts, MA 02108, USA
Tel: +1 617 742 9991, **www.**no9park.com
Type: Modern European restaurant bar

OM LOUNGE

92 Winthrop Street (corner JFK St), Harvard Square, Cambridge, Massachusetts, MA 02138, USA
Tel: +1 617 576 2800, **www.**omrestaurant.com
Type: Asian fusion restaurant bar

RADIUS

8 High Street (@ Summer St), Financial District, Boston, Massachusetts, MA 02110, USA
Tel: +1 617 426 1234, **www.**radiusrestaurant.com
Type: Upscale restaurant bar

TROQUET

140 Boylston Street (btwn South Charles & Tremont Sts), Back Bay, Boston, Massachusetts, MA 02116, USA
Tel: +1 617 695 9463, **www.**troquetboston.com
Type: Food and wine boutique

BRIGHTON, ENGLAND

BLANCH HOUSE

17 Atlingworth Street, Kemptown, Brighton, East Sussex, BN2 1PL, England
Tel: +44 (0)1273 603 504, **www.**blanchhouse.co.uk
Type: Charming contemporary guest house bar

THE HANBURY CLUB

83 St. Georges Road, Kemp Town, Brighton, East Sussex, BN2 1EF, England
Tel: +44 (0)1273 605 789, **www.**thehanburyclub.com
Type: Members' club

KOBA

135 Western Road (@ Preston St), Brighton, East Sussex, BN1 2LA, England
Tel: +44 (0)1273 270 059, **www.**kobauk.com
Type: Members' club

PINTXO PEOPLE

95-99 Western Road, Brighton, BN1 2LB
Tel: +44 (0)1273 732 323, **www.**pintxopeople.co.uk"
www.pintxopeople.co.uk
Type: Tapas restaurant and cocktail bar

EDINBURGH, SCOTLAND

DRAGONFLY

52 West Port, Edinburgh, EH1 2LD, Scotland
Tel: +44 (0)131 228 4543, **www.**dragonflycocktailbar.com
Type: DJ & cocktail lounge bar

HALO

3 Melville Place, Edinburgh, EH3 7PR, Scotland
Tel: +44 (0)131 539 8500, **www.**halobar.co.uk
Type: Bijou local's lounge bar

FORTH FLOOR

Harvey Nichols, St. Andrew Square, New Town, Edinburgh, Midlothian, EH2 2AD, Scotland
Tel: +44 (0)131 524 8350, **www.**harveynichols.com
Type: Department store bar & restaurant

OLOROSO

33 Castle Street, New Town, Edinburgh, Midlothian, EH2 3DN, England **Tel:** +44 (0)131 226 7614, **www.**oloroso.co.uk
Type: Restaurant bar with a view

TIGERLILY

125 George Street, New Town, Edinburgh, EH2 4JN, Scotland
Tel: +44 (0)131 225 5005, **www.**tigerlilyedinburgh.co.uk
Type: Hotel restaurant & lounge bar

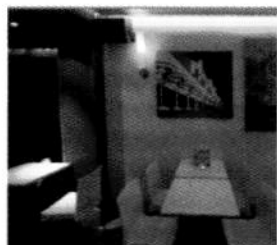

TONIC

34a North Castle Street, New Town, Edinburgh, Midlothian, EH2 3BN, Scotland
Tel: +44 (0)131 225 6431
Type: Bartender owned cocktail bar

VILLAGER

49-50 George IV Bridge, Edinburgh, Midlothian, EH1 1EJ, Scotland**Tel:** +44 (0)131 226 2781, HYPERLINK "http://**www.**villager-e.com" **www.**villager-e.com
Type: Contemporary lounge bar

Boutique - Leeds

GLASGOW, SCOTLAND

SALTY DOG
2nd Floor Terrace, Princes Square (off Buchanan St), Glasgow, G1 3JN, Scotland
Tel: + 44 (0)141 221 7800, **www.**salty-dog.info
Type: Shopping mall café bar

HELSINKI, FINLAND

KÄMP BAR & LIBRARY
Hotel Kämp, 29 Pohjoiseplanadi, Helsinki, 00100, Finland
Tel: +358 (0)9 576 111, **www.**hotelkamp.fi
Type: Luxury hotel cocktail bar

AMERICAN BAR
Ground Floor, Hotel Torni, 26 Yrjönkatu, Helsinki, 00100, Finland
Tel: +358 (0)20 1234 604, **www.**sokoshotels.fi
Type: Hotel lounge bar

HONG KONG, CHINA

AQUA SPIRIT
29th & 30th Floors, One Peking Road, Tsim Sha Tsui (Kowloon side), Hong Kong, China
Tel: +852 852 3427 2288, **www.**aqua.com.hk
Type: Über-glam bar & restaurant

DROP BAR
Basement, On Lok Mansion, 39-43 Hollywood Road, (entrance off Cochrine St), Hong Kong, China
Tel: +852 2543 8856
Type: DJ-owned, music led club

FEATHER BOA
38 Staunton Street, Soho, Central, Hong Kong, China
Tel: +852 2857 2586
Type: Renaissance-styled lounge

FINDS
2nd Floor, LKF Tower, 33 Wyndham Street, Lan Kwai Fong, Central, Hong Kong, China
Tel: +852 2522 9318, **www.**finds.com.hk
Type: Snow white restaurant & bar

LAS VEGAS, USA

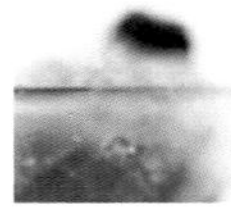

NORA'S CUISINE
6020 West Flamingo Road (@ Red Rock St.), Spring Valley, Las Vegas, Nevada, NV 89103, USA
Tel: +1 702 873 8990, **www.**norascuisine.com
Type: Italian family restaurant & bar

PARASOL DOWN
Ground Floor, Wynn Las Vegas, 3131 Las Vegas Boulevard South, North Strip, Las Vegas, NV 89109, USA
Tel: +1 702 770 7000, **www.**wynnlasvegas.com
Type: Lakeside bar with lightshow

SENSI
Bellagio Via Foire Promenade, 3600 Las Vegas Boulevard South, Las Vegas, Nevada, NV 89109, USA
Tel: +1 877 234 6358, **www.**bellagio.com
Type: Zen-like restaurant & bar

TABÚ ULTRA LOUNGE
Ground Floor, MGM Grand Hotel, 3799 Las Vegas Boulevard, Las Vegas, Nevada, NV 89109, USA
Tel: +1 702 891 7129, **www.**mgmgrand.com
Type: Glamorous casino club

LEEDS, ENGLAND

BOUTIQUE
11-13 Hirst Yard, Off Call Lane, Leeds, West Yorkshire, LS1 6NJ, England
Tel: +44 (0)113 245 6595, **www.**boutique-leeds.co.uk
Type: Split-level lounge

JAKE'S BAR & GRILL
27 Call Lane, Leeds, West Yorkshire, LS1 7BT, England
Tel: +44 (0)113 243 1110, **www.**jakes-bar.co.uk
Type: Bar for real drinkers

MOJO
18 Merrion Street, Leeds, West Yorkshire, LS1 6PQ, England
Tel: +44 (0)113 244 6387, **www.**mojobar.co.uk
Type: Rock & roll bar

SKIPPY'S
Upstairs at Trio Bar and Grill, 44 North Lane, Headingley, Leeds, LS6 3HU, England
Tel: +44 (0)113 203 6090, **www.**arcinspirations.com
Type: Intimate lounge bar

LONDON, ENGLAND

AKBAR
The Red Fort, 77 Dean Street, Soho, London, W1D 3SH, England
Tel: +44 (0)20 7437 2525, **www.**redfort.co.uk/akbar
Type: Indian restaurant bar

ALL STAR LANES
Victoria House, Bloomsbury Place (off Southampton Row), Holborn, London, WC1 4DA, England
Tel: +44 (0)20 7025 2676, **www.**allstarlanes.co.uk
Type: Retro bowling alley, bar & restaurant

Jake's Bar & Grill - Leeds

Koba - Brighton

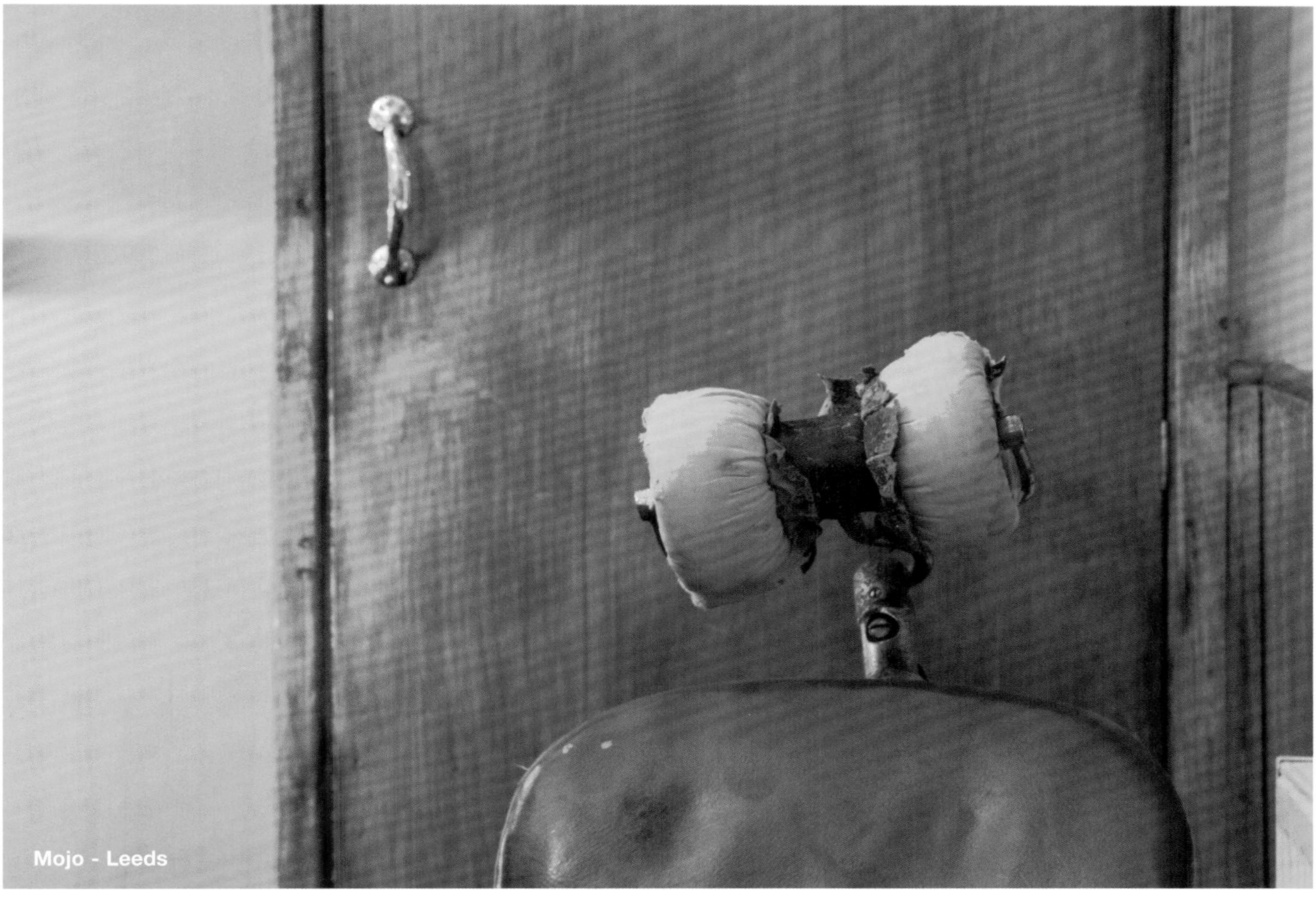

Mojo - Leeds

THE AMERICAN BAR
The Stafford Hotel, St James's Place, St James's, London SW1A 1NJ, England
Tel: +44 (0)20 4493 0111, **www.**thestaffordhotel.co.uk
Type: Classic 'American' hotel bar

ARTESIAN
Langham Hotel, 1C Portland Place, Regent Street, London, W1B 1JA, England
Tel: +44 (0)20 7636 1000, **www.**artesian-bar.co.uk
Type: Lavish hotel lounge bar

AURORA BAR
Great Eastern Hotel, Liverpool Street, London, EC2M 7QN, England **Tel:** +44 (0)20 7618 7000, **www.**aurora-restaurant.co.uk
Type: Hotel's deluxe restaurant bar

B@1
85 Battersea Rise (nr Northcote Rd), Battersea, London, SW11 1HW, England
Tel: +44 (0)20 7978 6595, **www.**beatone.co.uk
Type: Downbeat & fun cocktail bar

BALTIC
74 Blackfriars Road (@ The Cut), Waterloo, London, SE1 8HA, England
Tel: +44 (0)20 7928 1111, **www.**balticrestaurant.co.uk
Type: Polish restaurant & bar

BLUE BAR
The Berkeley Hotel, Wilton Place (@ Knightsbridge), Knightsbridge, London, SW1X 7RL, England
Tel: +44 (0)20 7201 1680, **www.**the-berkeley.co.uk
Type: Bijou & plush lounge bar

CAFÉ PACIFICO
5 Langley St, Covent Garden, London, WC2H 9JA, England
Tel: +44 (0)20 7379 7728, **www.**cafepacifico-laperla.com
Type: London's original Mexican bar & restaurant

COBDEN CLUB
170 Kensal Road, Notting Hill, London, W10 5BN, England
Tel: +44 (0)20 8960 4222, **www.**thecobden.co.uk
Type: Member's den

CLARIDGE'S BAR
Claridges's Hotel, 55 Brook Street (corner of Davies St.), Mayfair, London, W1A 2JQ, England
Tel: +44 (0)20 7629 8860, **www.**savoygroup.com
Type: Lounge for the Mayfair set

COCOON
65 Regent Street (entrance on Air Street), London, W1B 4EA, England **Tel:** +44 (0)20 7494 7600, **www.**cocoon-restaurants.com
Type: Asian-influenced bar & restaurant

CRAZY BEAR BAR
Basement, 26-28 Whitfield Street, Fitzrovia, London, W1T 2RG, England
Tel: +44 (0)20 7631 0088, **www.**crazybeargroup.co.uk
Type: Lounge & visual treat

CRAZY HOMIES
127 Westbourne Park Road, Notting Hill, London, W2 5QL, England **Tel:** +44 (0)20 7727 6771, **www.**crazyhomieslondon.co.uk
Type: Quaint, kitsch tequila bar & Mexican restaurant

DETROIT
35 Earlham Street, Covent Garden, London, WC2 9LD, England
Tel: +44 (0)20 7240 2662, **www.**detroit-bar.com
Type: Esoteric warren of a club

THE DORCHESTER BAR
53 Park Lane, Mayfair, London, W1A 2HJ, England
Tel: +44 (0)20 7629 8888, **www.**thedorchester.com
Type: Blingy, modern but majestic hotel lounge

DUKE'S BAR
Dukes Hotel, St James's Place, London SW1 1NY, England
Tel: +44 (0)20 7491 4840, **www.**dukeshotel.com
Type: Martini-centric cocktail lounge

DUSK BAR, KITCHEN & LOUNGE
339 Battersea Park Road, London, SW11 4LS, England
Tel: +44 (0)20 7622 2112, **www.**duskbar.co.uk
Type: Locals lounge & party venue

THE FIFTH FLOOR BAR
5th Floor, Harvey Nichols, 109-125 Knightsbridge, London, SW1X 7RJ, England
Tel: +44 (0)20 7201 8771, **www.**harveynichols.com
Type: Lounge for style conscious shoppers

FLORIDITA
Mezzo Basement, 100 Wardour Street, Soho, London, W1F 0TN, England
Tel: +44 (0)20 7314 4000, **www.**floriditalondon.com
Type: Cuban themed bar & restaurant

GREEN & RED BAR & CANTINA
51 Bethnal Green Road, Shoreditch, London, E1 6LA, England
Tel: +44 (0)20 7749 9670, **www.**green red.co.uk **Type:** London's foremost tequila bar

GROUCHO CLUB
45 Dean Street (@ Old Compton Street) Soho, London, W1D 4QB, England
Tel: + 44 (0)20 7439 4685, **www.**thegrouchoclub.com
Type: Celebrity members' club

HAKKASAN
8 Hanway Place, Fitzrovia, London, W1T 9HD, England
Tel: +44 (0)20 7927 7000, **www.**hakkasan.com
Type: Pan Asian restaurant & bar

HAWKSMOOR
157 Commercial Street, Spitalfields, London, E1 6BJ, England
Tel: +44 (0)20 7247 7392, **www.**thehawksmoor.com
Type: Superb steakhouse & cocktail bar

Baltic - London

THE HIDE BAR
39-45 Bermondsey Street (corner of Crucifix Lane), Bermondsey, London, SE1 3XF, England
Tel: +44 (0)20 7403 6655, **www.**thehidebar.com
Type: Discerning drinker's lounge bar

HUSH
8 Lancashire Court (off Brook Street), Mayfair, London, W1S 1EY, England
Tel: +44 (0)20 7659 1500, **www.**hush.co.uk
Type: Plush lounge for flush types

THE KINGLY CLUB
4 Kingly Court, Soho, London, W1B 5PW, England
Tel: +44 (0)20 7287 9100, **www.**kinglyclub.co.uk
Type: Subterranean, tunnel-like club

KOSMOPOL
138 Fulham Road, Chelsea, London, SW10 9PY, England
Tel: +44 (0)20 7373 6368, **www.**kosmopol.co.uk
Type: Swedish influenced lounge

LAB
12 Old Compton Street (Charing Cross Rd end), Soho, London, W1V 5PG, England
Tel: +44 (0)20 7437 7820, **www.**lab-bar.com
Type: 70s retro bartenders' hang-out

LIBRARY BAR
Lanesborough Hotel, Hyde Park Corner, Mayfair, London, SW1X 7TA, England
Tel: +44 (0)20 7259 5599, **www.**lanesborough.com
Type: Classic mahogany panelled hotel bar

LIGHT BAR
St. Martins Lane Hotel, 45 St. Martin's Lane, Covent Garden, London WC2N 4HX, England
Tel: +44 (0)20 7300 5599, **www.**morgans hotelgroup.com **Type:** Guest list only hotel lounge

LONSDALE
44-48 Lonsdale Road, Notting Hill, London, W11 2DE, England
Tel: +44 (0)20 7727 4080
Type: Where beautiful people drink balanced cocktails

LOST SOCIETY
697 Wandsworth Road, Clapham, London, SW8 3JF, England
Tel: +44 (0)20 7652 6526, **www.**lostsociety.co.uk
Type: Cocktail lounge & party bar

LOUNGELOVER
1 Whitby Street (off Club Row), Shoreditch, London, E2
Tel: +44 (0)20 7012 1234, **www.**loungelover.co.uk
Type: Kleptomaniac's cocktail lounge

MATCH EC1
45-47 Clerkenwell Road, Clerkenwell, London, EC1M 5RS, England
Tel: +44 (0)20 7250 4002, **www.**matchbar.com
Type: First of a respected group of lounges

MATCHBAR
37-38 Margaret Street (nr Oxford Circus), London, W1G 0JF, England
Tel: +44 (0)20 7499 3443, **www.**matchbar.com
Type: Centrally located cocktail lounge

MAHIKI
1 Dover St, Mayfair, London, W1S 4LD, England
Tel: +44 (0)20 7493 9529. **www.**mahiki.com
Type: Wonderfully kitsch Tiki bar

MAZE
10-13 Grosvenor Square, Mayfair, London, W1K 6JP, England
Tel: +44 (0)20 7107 0000, **www.**gordonramsay.com
Type: Ramsay owned restaurant & bar

THE MET BAR
18-19 Old Park Lane, Mayfair, London, W1K 1LB, England
Tel: +44 (0)20 7447 4757, **www.**metropolitan.co.uk
Type: Loungy club and former paparazzi camp

MILK & HONEY
61 Poland Street, Soho, London, W1F 7NU, England
Tel: 07000 655 469, **www.**mlkhny.com
Type: 30s styled speakeasy

MINT LEAF
Suffolk Place (off Haymarket), Trafalgar Square, London, SW1Y 4HX, England **Tel:** +44 (0)20 7930 9020, **www.**mintleafrestaurant.com
Type: Subterranean Indian restaurant & cocktail bar

MONTGOMERY PLACE
31 Kensington Park Road, Notting Hill, London, W11 2EU, England **Tel:** +44 (0)20 7792 3921, **www.**montgomeryplace.co.uk
Type: Tiny but serious cocktail lounge

OXO TOWER
8th Floor, Oxo Tower Wharf, Barge House Street, London, SE1 9PH, England
Tel: +44 (0)20 7803 3888, **www.**oxotower.co.uk
Type: Curvaceous padded island cocktail bar with view

RIVOLI BAR
Ritz Hotel, 150 Piccadilly, London, W1J 9BR, England
Tel: +44 (0)20 7493 8181, **www.**theritzhotel.co.uk
Type: Graceful & opulent Art Deco hotel bar

RONNIE'S BAR
47 Frith Street, Soho, London, W1D 4HT, England
Tel: +44 (0)20 7439 0747, **www.**ronniescotts.co.uk
Type: Plush lounge over famous jazz club

THE ROYAL EXCHANGE GRAND CAFÉ & BAR
The Royal Exchange, Threadneedle Street, Bank, London, EC3V 3LR, England **Tel:** +44 (0)20 7618 2480, **www.**conran.com
Type: Covered courtyard bar with twin lounges

Crazy Bear Bar - London

The Dorchester Bar - London

Cocoon - London

Hakkasan - London

SALVATORE
Ground Floor, Fifty, 50 St James' Street, London, SW1A 1JT, England
Tel: +44 (0)8704 155 050, **www.**fiftylondon.com
Type: Cocktail lounge at London's most opulent casino

SANDERSON HOTEL BARS
Long Bar & Purple Bar, 50 Berners Street, Fitzrovia, London, W1P 3AD, England **Tel:** +44 (0)20 7300 1400, **www.**sandersonhotel.com **Type:** Where finance & fashion clientele check each other out

SHOCHU LOUNGE
Roka, 37 Charlotte Street, Fitzrovia, London, W1T 1RR, England
Tel: +44 (0)20 7580 6464
Type: Shochu meets molecular mixology

SOSHO
2a Tabernacle Street, Shoreditch, London, EC2A 4LU, England
Tel: + 44 (0)20 7920 0701, **www.**matchbar.com
Type: Trendy Shoreditch club & cocktail lounge

TRADER VIC'S
The Hilton Hotel (basement), 22 Park Lane, Mayfair, London, W1Y 4BE, England
Tel: +44 (0)20 7208 4113, **www.**tradervics.com
Type: Classic Tiki with class

TRAILER HAPPINESS
Basement, 177 Portobello Road (@ Elgin Crescent), Notting Hill, London, W11 2DY, England
Tel: +44 (0)20 7727 2700, **www.**trailerh.com
Type: Lightly Tiki, heavily fun

VILLAGE EAST
171-173 Bermondsey Street, Bermondsey, London, SE1 3UW, England
Tel: +44 (0)20 7357 6082, **www.**villageeast.co.uk
Type: Contemporary, unpretentious gastro bar

ZANDER
Bank Restaurant, 45 Buckingham Gate (opp. Vandon St), Westminster, London, SW1E 6BS, England
Tel: +44 (0)20 7379 9797, **www.**bankrestaurants.com
Type: Lanky (long & narrow) cocktail lounge

LOS ANGELES, USA

THE CLUB BAR
The Peninsula Hotel, 9882 Little Santa Monica Boulevard, Beverly Hills, California, CA 90212, USA
Tel: +1 310 551 2888,
Type: Old-school hotel bar

FAT FISH LOUNGE
616 N Robertson Boulevard (btwn Santa Monica & Melrose), West Hollywood, Los Angeles, California, CA 90069, USA **Tel:** +1 310 659 3882, **www.**fatfishla.com
Type: Cocktail lounge behind Euro-Asian restaurant

BAR MARMONT
8171 West Sunset Boulevard (@Crescent Heights Blvd), West Hollywood, Los Angeles, California, CA 90046, USA
Tel: +1 323 650 0575, **www.**chateaumarmont.com
Type: - The Bar of the legendary Chateau

THE PENTHOUSE
18th floor, Huntley Hotel, 1111 Second Street, Santa Monica, CA 90403, USA
Tel: +1 310 394 5454, **www.**thehuntleyhotel.com
Type: Lounge with beautiful view of LA and Malibu

PROVIDENCE
5955 Melrose Avenue, Los Angeles, California, CA 90038, USA
Tel: +1 323 460 4170, **www.**providenceLA.com
Type: Restaurant with small bar serving amazing cocktails

SEVEN GRAND
2nd Floor, 515 W Seventh Street (@Grand Av.), Down Town, Los Angeles, CA 90014, USA
Tel: +1 (213) 614 0737, **www.**sevengrand.la
Type: Whiskey bar with pool tables and great cocktails

TIKI-TI
4427 West Sunset Boulevard (btwn Virtgil Pl & N Hoover St), Silverlake, Los Angeles, CA 90027, USA
Tel: +1 323 669 9381, **www.**tiki-ti.com
Type: Tiny, family-owned Tiki shack

TRADER VIC'S
Beverly Hilton Hotel, 9876 Wilshire Boulevard, Beverly Hills, CA 90210, USA
Tel: +1 310 274 7777, **www.**tradervics.com
Type: The oldest of the legendary Tiki chain

MANCHESTER, ENGLAND

CLOUD 23
23rd Floor, Hilton Manchester, Beetham Tower, 303 Deansgate, Manchester, Lancashire, M3 4LQ, England
Tel: +44 (0)161 870 1600, **www.**hilton.co.uk /manchester **Type:** Lofty & glamorous hotel cocktail bar

HARVEY NICHOLS 2ND FLOOR BAR
Harvey Nichols Store, Exchange Square, 21 New Cathedral Street, Manchester, Lancashire, M1 1AD, England **Tel:** +44 (0)161 828 8898, **www.**harveynichols.com
Type: Stylish cocktail bar in a department store

OBSIDIAN BAR & RESTAURANT
Arora International Hotel, 18-24 Princess Street, Manchester, Lancashire, M1 4LY, England
Tel: +44 (0)161 238 4348
Type: Taste of New York to Mancunian's lounge bar

PANACEA
14 John Dalton Street, Manchester, Lancashire, M2 6JR, England **Tel:** +44 (0)161 839 9999, **www.**panaceamanchester.co.uk
Type: Glam cocktail bar & restaurant

Ronnie's Bar - London

ROOM

81 King Street, Manchester, Lancashire, M2 4ST, England
Tel: *+44 (0)161 839 2005*
Type: *Grand yet 'Liberal' Cocktail bar and restaurant*

SOCIO-REHAB

100-102 High Street, Northern Quarter, Manchester, Lancashire, M1 1HP, England
Tel: *+44 (0)161 832 4529,* **www.***sociorehab.com*
Type: *Cosy and intimate neighbourhood cocktail bar*

MELBOURNE, AUSTRALIA

COOKIE

1st Floor, 252 Swanston Street, Swanston, Melbourne, Victoria, 3000, Australia **Tel:** *+61 (0)3 9663 7660,* **www.***cookie.melbourneaustralia.com.au*
Type: *Bar and restaurant offering immense choice*

CROFT INSTITUTE

21-25 Croft Alley, Melbourne, Victoria, 3000, Australia
Tel: *+61 (0)3 9671 4399,* **www.***thecroftinstitute.com.au*
Type: *Chemistry lab hidden at end of alley*

DER RAUM

438 Church Street (btwn Swan St & Bridge Rd), Richmond, Melbourne, Victoria, 3121, Australia
Tel: *61+ (0)3 9428 0055,* **www.***derraum.com.au*
Type: *Cocktail lounge with bungee bottles*

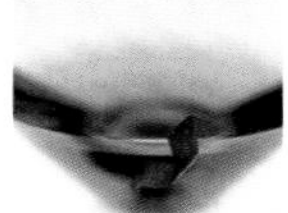

GINGER

272 Brunswick Street, Fitzroy, Melbourne, Victoria, 3065, Australia
Tel: *+61 (0)3 9419 8058*
Type: *Arty cocktail lounge*

GIN PALACE

190 Little Collins Street (Entrance 10 Russell place), Melbourne, Victoria, Australia
Tel: *+61 (0)3 9654 0522*
Type: *Hidden speakeasy-style lounge*

MANCHURIA

First Floor, 7 Waratah Place, Melbourne, Victoria, 3000, Australia
Tel: *(03) 9663 1997*
Type: *Plush, Oriental influenced lounge*

MINK

Prince of Wales Hotel, 2b Acland Street, St Kilda, Melbourne, 3182, Australia
Tel: *+61 3 9536 1199,* **www.***theprince.com.au*
Type: *Post communist Russian bar*

MEXICO CITY, MEXICO

CAFEINA

73 Nuevo Leon, Condesa, Mexico City, 06140, Mexico
Tel: *+52 55 5212 0090*
Type: *DJ led lounge*

BAR TIKI

227 Querétaro, Colonia Roma, Mexico City, Mexico
Tel: *+52 55 5584 2668,* **www.***tiki.com.mx*
Type: *Tiki bar*

THE W LIVING ROOM

W Hotel, 252 Campos Eliseos Chapulaapec, Polanco, Mexico City, 11560, Mexico
Tel: *+52 55 9138 1800,* **www.***whotels.com*
Type: *Chilled lobby lounge bar*

MIAMI, USA

THE RALEIGH LOBBY BAR

Raleigh Hotel, 1775 Collins Avenue (@ 22nd St), South Beach, Miami Beach, Florida, FL 33139, USA
Tel: *+1 305 534 6300,* **www.***raleighhotel.com*
Type: *Wood panelled 1940s lobby bar*

MILAN, ITALY

GOLD BAR

Pizza Risorgimento, Milan, 20129, Italy
Tel: *+39 (0)2 757 7771,* **www.***dolcegabbanagold.it*
Type: *Cocktail lounge bar*

MARTINI BAR

Dolce & Gabbana Menswear Boutique, 15 Corso Venezia, Fashion District, Milan, Lombardy, 20121, Italy
Tel: *+39 (0)2 7601 1154*
Type: *Slick cocktail lounge in menswear store*

NASHVILLE, USA

THE BOUND'RY RESTAURANT

911 Twentieth Avenue South, Nashville, Tennessee, TN 37212, USA
Tel: *+1 615 321 3043,* **www.***pansouth.net*
Type: *Neighbourhood bar, lounge & restaurant*

NEW ORLEANS, USA

ARNAUD'S FRENCH 75 BAR

813 Bienville Street (nr Bourbon St), French Quarter, New Orleans, Louisiana, LA 70112, USA
Tel: *+1 504 523 5433,* **www.***arnauds.com*
Type: *Classic, old-school lounge bar*

CAROUSEL PIANO BAR & LOUNGE

Hotel Monteleone, 214 Royal Street, New Orleans, LA 70130, USA **Tel:** *+1 504 523 3341,* **www.***hotelmonteleone.com*
Type: *Spinning, fairground themed hotel lobby bar*

LIBRARY LOUNGE

Ritz Carlton Hotel, 921 Canal Street, New Orleans, LA 70112, USA
Tel: *+1 504 524 1331,* **www.***ritzcarlton.com*
Type: *Classic hotel bar with legendary Mint Juleps*

THE SWIZZLE STICK BAR

Café Adelaide, Loews Hotel, 300 Poydras Street, Warehouse District, New Orleans, Louisiana, LA 70130, USA **Tel:** *+1 504 595 3305,* **www.***cafeadelaide.com*
Type: *Lounge & home of The Adelaide Swizzle*

NEW YORK, USA

ANGEL'S SHARE

8 Stuyvesant Street (@ 9th St & Third Ave), East Village, Manhattan, New York City, NY 10003, USA
Tel: *+1 212 777 5415*
Type: *Eastern-influenced speakeasy*

B FLAT (BB)

277 Church (btwn Franklin & White), Tribeca, Manhattan, New York City, NY 10013, USA
Tel: *+1 212 219 2970*
Type: *Jazz led, refined cocktail lounge*

BLUE OWL

196 Second Avenue (btwn 12th & 13th Sts), East Village, Manhattan, New York City, NY 10003, USA
Tel: *+1 212 505 2583,* **www.***blueowlnyc.com*
Type: *Speakeasy-style cocktail lounge*

BRANDY LIBRARY

25 North Moore Street (@ Varick St), Tribeca, Manhattan, New York, NY 10013, USA
Tel: *+1 212 226 5545,* **www.***brandylibrary.com*
Type: *A veritable booze library*

DEATH & CO

433 East 6th Street, Manhattan, New York, NY 10009, USA
Tel: *+1 212 388 0882,* **www.***deathandcompany.com*
Type: *Speakeasy-style cocktail lounge*

EAST SIDE COMPANY BAR

49 Essex Street (btwn Grand & Hester Sts), Lower East Side, Manhattan, New York City, NY 10002, USA
Tel: *+1 212 614 7408*
Type: *Speakeasy-style cocktail lounge*

EMPLOYEES ONLY

510 Hudson Street, Tribeca, Manhattan, New York, NY 10014, USA
Tel: *+1 212 242 3021,* **www.***employeesonlynyc.com*
Type: *Art deco-styled cocktail lounge*

FLATIRON LOUNGE

37 West 19th Street (btwn 5th & 6th Aves), Flatiron District, New York City, NY 10011, USA
Tel: *+1 212 727 7741,* **www.***flatironlounge.com*
Type: *Art deco-styled cocktail lounge*

GOLDBAR

389 Broome Street, Soho, Manhattan, New York City, NY 10013, USA
Tel: *+1 212 274 1568,* **www.***goldbarnewyork.com*
Type: *Blingy lounge bar & club*

LEXINGTON BAR & BOOKS

1020 Lexington Avenue (@ 73rd St), Upper East Side, Manhattan, New York City, NY 10021, USA
Tel: *+1 212 717 3902,* **www.***barandbooks.net*
Type: *Cigar and whiskey lounge bar*

LITTLE BRANCH

22 Seventh Avenue South (btwn Clarkson & Leroy Sts), Greenwich Village, Manhattan, New York City, NY 10014, USA
Tel: *+1 212 929 4360*
Type: *Speakeasy-style cocktail lounge*

MILK & HONEY

134 Eldridge Street (just south of Delancey), Lower East Side, New York City, NY 10002, USA
Tel: *withheld*
Type: *Legendary speakeasy-style cocktail lounge*

PDT

113 St. Marks Place (btwn Ave A & 1st Ave), Manhattan, New York City, USA
Tel: *+1 212 614 0386,* **www.***pdtnyc.com*
Type: *Prohibition-style cocktail lounge*

PEGU CLUB

77 West Houston Street (btwn Laguardia Pl & Wooster St), New York City, NY 10012, USA
Tel: *+1 212 473 7348,* **www.***peguclub.com*
Type: *Colonial cocktail lounge in New York*

RAYUELA

165 Allen Street (btwn Stanton & Rivington Sts), Lower East Side, Manhattan, New York City, NY 10002, USA
Tel: *+1 212 253 8840,* **www.***rayuelanyc.com*
Type: *South American restaurant & bar*

TEMPLE BAR

332 Lafayette Street (btwn Bleecker & Houston Sts), Soho, New York City, NY 10012, USA
Tel: *+1 212 925 4242,* **www.***templebarnyc.com*
Type: *Classy little Martini lounge*

WD-50

50 Clinton Street (btwn Stanton & Rivington Sts), Lower East Side, Manhattan, New York City, NY 10002, USA
Tel: *+1 212 477 2900,* **www.***wd-50.com*
Type: *Restaurant bar and home to 'Juice'*

Village East - London

Mahiki - London

Ronnie's Bar - London

Lonsdale - London

Obsidian Bar & Restaurant - Manchester

Jake's Bar & Grill - Leeds

Obsidian Bar & Restaurant - Manchester

Café Pacifico - London

Green & Red Bar & Cantina - London

Cloud 23 - Manchester

PARIS, FRANCE

APICIUS

20 Rue d'Artois (btwn Rue de Berri & Rue Paul Baudry), Paris, 75008, France
Tel: +33 (0)1 4380 1966, **www.**relaischateaux.com
Type: Lounge bar & restaurant

BAR LE FORUM

4 Boulevard Malesherbes (@ Pl de la Madeleine), Paris, 75008, France
Tel: +33 (0)1 4265 3786, **www.**bar-le-forum.com
Type: Old-school cocktail lounge

HARRY'S NEW YORK BAR

5 Rue Daunou (btwn Ave de l'Opéra & Rue de la Paix), Paris, 75002, France
Tel: +33 (0)1 4261 7114, **www.**harrys-bar.fr
Type: American cocktail saloon in Paris

BAR HEMINGWAY

Ritz Hotel, 15 Place Vendôme, Paris, 75001, France
Tel: +33 (0)1 4316 3030, **www.**ritzparis.com
Type: El Papa's pequeño cocktail lounge

LE BAR MONTAIGNE

Hotel Plaza Athénée, 25 Avenue Montaigne (btwn Rue du Boccador & Rue Clement Marot), Paris, 75008, France
Type: Über bling hotel lounge bar

PORTLAND, USA

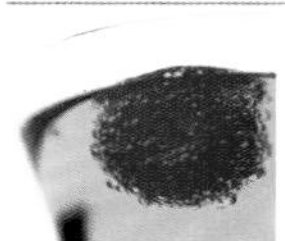

THE BRAZEN BEAN

The Brazen Bean, 2075 NW Glisan St, Portland, OR 97209, USA
Tel: +1 503 2[illegible]0636,
Type: Upscale cocktail lounge

PRAGUE, CZECH REPUBLIC

ALCOHOL BAR

6 Du‰ni, Prague 1, Czech Republic
Tel: +420 241 430 762, **www.**alcoholbar.cz
Type: Lounge bar & club

BUGSY'S

10 Pafiîïská, Staré Mûsto, Prague 1, 110 00, Czech Republic
Tel: +420 224 810 287, **www.**bugsysbar.cz
Type: The original Prague lounge bar

TRETTER'S BAR

3 V Kolkovnû, Prague 1, 110 00, Czech Republic
Tel: +420 224 811 165, **www.**tretters.cz
Type: 1930s Parisian-style cocktail lounge bar

T˝NSKÁ BAR & BOOKS

19 T˝nská, Prague 1, Czech Republic
Tel: +420 224 808 250, **www.**barandbooks.net
Type: Cocktail lounge bar

SAN FRANCISCO, USA

ABSINTHE BRASSERIE & BAR

398 Hayes Street (@ Gough), Hayes Valley District, San Francisco, California, CA 94102, USA
Tel: +1 415 551 1590, **www.**absinthe.com
Type: French bistro with great drinks

THE ALEMBIC

1725 Haight Street (btwn Cole & Shrader Sts), San Francisco, California, CA 94117, USA
Tel: +1 415 666 0822, **www.**alembicbar.com
Type: Old school/new school bar

BIX

56 Gold Street (off Montgomery btwn Pacific & Jackson Sts), Financial District, San Francisco, California, CA 94133, USA **Tel:** +1 415 433 6300, **www.**bixrestaurant.com **Type:** Classic jazzy supper club

BOURBON & BRANCH

501 Jones Street (@ O'Farrell Street), San Francisco, California, CA 94102, USA **Tel:** Register on website for number, **www.**bourbonandbranch.com
Type: Speakeasy-style lounge bar

CANTINA

580 Sutter Street (@ Mason St.), San Francisco, California, CA, 94102, USA
Tel: +1 415 398 0195, **www.**cantinasf.com
Type: Art bar & cocktail lounge

FORBIDDEN ISLAND TIKI LOUNGE

1304 Lincoln Avenue (@ Sherman), Alameda, California, CA 94501, USA **Tel:** +1 510 749 0332, **www.**forbiddenislandalameda.com **Type:** Tiki cocktail lounge & rum emporia

NOPA

560 Divisadero Street (corner of Hayes St), San Francisco, California, CA 94117, USA
Tel: +1 415 864 8643, **www.**nopasf.com
Type: Mediterranean influenced restaurant & bar

RANGE

842 Valencia St (btwn 19th 20th), San Francisco, California, CA 94110, USA
Tel: +1 415 282 8283, **www.**rangesf.com
Type: Neighbourhood restaurant & bar

THE SLANTED DOOR LOUNGE

1 Ferry Building #3, San Francisco, California, CA 94111, USA
Tel: +1 415 861 8032, **www.**slanteddoor.com
Type: Modern Vietnamese restaurant & bar

Apicius - Paris

TOMMY'S
5929 Geary Boulevard (btwn 24th & 23rd Aves), Outer Richmond, San Francisco, California, CA 94121, USA
Tel: +1 415 387 4747, **www.**tommystequila.com
Type: Authentic Mexican restaurant & tequila bastion

VIC'S
9 Anchor Drive (off Powell St), Emeryville, California, CA 94608, USA
Tel: +1 510 653 3400, **www.**tradervics.com
Type: Flagship Tiki lounge & restaurant

TRES AGAVES
130 Townsend Street (@ Second St), SoMa, San Francisco, California, CA 94107, USA
Tel: +1 415 227 0500, **www.**tresagaves.com
Type: Mexican kitchen & tequila lounge

SEATTLE, USA

VESSEL
1312 5th Ave, Seattle, Washington, WA 98101, USA
Tel: +1 206 652 5222, **www.**vesselseattle.com
Type: Cocktail lounge bar

ZIG ZAG CAFÉ
1501 Western Ave (#202), Seattle, Washington, WA 98101, USA
Tel: +1 206 625 1146, **www.**zigzagcafe.net
Type: Unpretentious cocktail bar

SYDNEY, AUSTRALIA

JIMMY LIKS
188 Victoria Street, Potts Point, Sydney, NSW 2011, Australia
Tel: +61 (0)2 8354 1400, **www.**jimmyliks.com
Type: Asian-influenced lounge & restaurant

LOTUS BAR
22 Challis Avenue Potts Point, Sydney, Australia
Tel: +61 (0)2 9326 9000, **www.**merivale.com
Type: Retro-elegant cocktail bar

WATER BAR
Blue Sydney Hotel, The Wharf at Woolloomooloo, Sydney, NSW 2011, Australia
Tel: +61 (0)2 9331 9000
Type: Lounge in aircraft hanger-style hotel lobby

ZETA BAR
Hilton Hotel, Level 4, 488 George Street, Sydney, NSW 2000, Australia
Tel: +61 (0)2 9265 6070, **www.**zetabar.com.au
Type: Contemporary hotel bar

VENICE, ITALY

TIEPOLO BAR
The Westin Europa & Regina Hotel, San Marco 2159, Venice 30124, Italy
Tel: +39 (0)41 240 0001, **www.**westin.com
Type: Five-star luxury hotel lounge

WASHINGTON DC, USA

DEGREES
The Ritz-Carlton Georgetown, 3100 South Street Northwest, Washington, District of Columbia, DC 20007, USA
Tel: +1 202 912 4100, **www.**ritzcarlton.com
Type: Stylish hotel lobby bar

WARSAW, POLAND

THE KURT SCHELLER BAR
Rialto Hotel, 73 ul. Wilcza, Warsaw, 00-6, 70, Poland
Tel: +48 (0)22 58 48 784, **www.**hotelrialto.com.pl
Type: Art deco-styled hotel with restaurant & lounge bar

CAFÉ BAR
12 ul. Mazowiecka, Warsaw, 00-048, Poland
Tel: +48 (0)22 828 4219, **www.**paparazzi.com.pl
Type: Café bar

PORTO PRAGA
23 ul. Okrzei, Praga, Warsaw, 03-715, Poland
Tel: +48 (0)22 698 50 01, **www.**portopraga.pl
Type: Bar, restaurant & club

SENSE
19 Nowy Âwiat (@ Al. Jerozolimshie), Warsaw, 00-929, Poland
Tel: +48 (0)22 826 6570, **www.**sensecafe.com
Type: Pan-Asian gastro bar

DIGITAL.DIFFORDSGUIDE

FOR MORE ON GREAT BARS IN THE WORLD'S GREATEST CITIES REGISTER YOUR EMAIL ADDRESS AT DIFFORDSGUIDE.COM AND I'LL EMAIL YOU REGULAR LINKS TO DIGITAL.DIFFORDSGUIDE WHERE I POST REVIEWS OF CITIES AS I VISIT THEM.

Tommy's - San Francisco

Jimmy Liks - Sydney

Zeta Bar - Sydney

Zeta Bar - Sydney